Brief Contents

Detailed Contents

READINGS   238

Section V Pretrial Proceedings   295

Foreword

You hold in your hands a book that we think is a different approach. It is billed as a "text/reader." What that means is we have attempted to take the two most commonly used types of books, the textbook and the reader, and blend them in a way that will appeal to both students and faculty.

Our experience as teachers and scholars has been that textbooks for the core classes in criminal justice (or any other social science discipline) leave many students and professors cold. The textbooks are huge, crammed with photographs, charts, highlighted material, and all sorts of pedagogical devices intended to increase student interest. Too often, though, these books end up creating a sort of sensory overload for students and suffer from a focus on "bells and whistles" such as fancy graphics at the expense of coverage of the most current research on the subject.

Readers, on the other hand, are typically composed of recent and classic research articles on the subject. They generally suffer, however, from an absence of meaningful explanatory material. Articles are simply lined up and presented to the students, with little or no context or explanation. Students, particularly undergraduate students, are often confused and overwhelmed.

This text/reader represents our attempt to take the best of both the textbook and reader approaches. This book is composed of research articles on courts. This text/reader is intended to serve either as a supplement to a core undergraduate textbook or as a stand-alone text. The book includes previously published articles and textual material introducing these articles and providing some structure and context for the selected readings.

The book is divided into nine sections that track the typical content and structure of a textbook on the subject. Each section has an introduction that explains and provides context for the readings that follow. The readings are a selection of the best recent research that has appeared in academic journals as well as some classic readings, where appropriate. The articles are edited as necessary to make them accessible to students. This variety of research and perspectives will provide the student with a grasp of the development of research as well as an understanding of the current status of research in the subject area. This approach gives the student the opportunity to learn the basics (in the introduction to each section) and to read some of the most interesting research on the subject.

In Section I, there is an explanation of the organization and content of the book, which provides a context for the articles that follow. This introductory chapter provides a framework for the text and articles that follow and introduces relevant themes, issues, and concepts. This will assist the student in understanding the articles.

Each section includes a summary of the material covered and discussion questions. These summaries and discussion questions should facilitate student thought and class discussion of the material.

It is our belief that this method of presenting the material is more interesting for both students and faculty. We acknowledge that this approach may be viewed by some as more challenging than the traditional textbook. To that we say, Yes! It is! But we believe that if we raise the bar, our students will rise to the challenge. Research shows that students and faculty often find textbooks boring. It is our belief that many criminal justice instructors welcome the opportunity to teach without having to rely on a "standard" textbook that covers only the most basic information and that lacks both depth of coverage and an attention to current research. This book provides an alternative for instructors who want to get more out of the basic criminal justice courses and curriculum than one can get from a basic textbook that is aimed at the lowest common denominator and filled with flashy, but often useless, features that merely serve to drive up the cost of the textbook.

We also believe students will find this approach more interesting. They are given the opportunity to read current, cutting-edge research on the subject, while also being provided with background and context for this research. In addition to including the most topical and relevant research, we have included a short text, "How to Read a Research Article," in Section II. The purpose of this text is to provide students with an overview of the components of a research article. It also walks them through the process of reading a research article, lessening their trepidation and increasing their ability to comprehend the material presented therein. Many students will be unfamiliar with reading and deciphering research articles; we hope this feature will help them to do so. In addition, we provide a student study site on the Internet. This site has additional research articles, study questions, practice quizzes, and other pedagogical material that will assist the student to learn the material. We chose to put these pedagogical tools on a companion study site rather than in the text to allow instructors to focus on the material, while still giving student the opportunity to learn more.

We hope that this unconventional approach will be more interesting to students and faculty alike and thus make learning and teaching more fun. Criminal justice is a fascinating subject, and the topic deserves to be presented in an interesting manner. We hope you will agree.

—Craig Hemmens

Preface

 ## Why This Book?

There are a number of excellent courts textbooks and readers available to students and professors, so why this one? The reason is that stand-alone textbooks and readers (often assigned as an expensive addition to a textbook) have a pedagogical fault that we seek to rectify with the present book. Textbooks focus on providing a broad overview of the subject and lack depth, while readers often feature in-depth articles about a single topic with little or no text to unify the readings and little in the way of pedagogy. This book provides more in the way of text and pedagogy and uses recent research-based articles to help students understand courts. This book is unique in that it is a hybrid text/reader offering the best of both worlds. It includes a collection of articles on courts that have previously appeared in a number of leading criminal justice/criminology journals along with original textual material that serves to explain and synthesize the readings. We have selected some of the best recent research and literature reviews and assembled them in this text/reader for an undergraduate or graduate courts class.

Journal articles have been selected based primarily on how they add to and complement the textual material and how interesting we perceive them to be for students. In our opinion, these articles are the best contemporary work on the issues they address. However, journal articles are written for professional audiences, not for students, and thus often contain quantitative material students are not expected to understand. Mindful of this, the articles contained in this text/reader have been edited and abridged to make them as student-friendly as possible. We have done this without doing injustice to the core points raised by the authors or detracting from the authors' key findings and conclusions. Those wishing to read these articles (and others) in their entirety are able to do so by accessing the Sage website provided for users of this book.

This book can serve as a supplemental reader or the primary text for an undergraduate course in courts or as the primary text for a graduate course. In a graduate course in courts, it would serve as both an introduction to the extant literature and a sourcebook for additional reading, as well as a springboard for enhanced class discussion. When used as a supplement to an undergraduate course, this book can provide greater depth than the standard textbook. It is important to note that the readings and the introductory textual material in this book provide a comprehensive survey of the current state of scientific literature in virtually all areas of courts and provide a history of how we got to this point in each topic area.

 ## Structure of the Book

The structure of this book mirrors that found in standard textbooks on courts and case processing. We begin with an overview of the structure and organization of courts and then proceed to a more detailed discussion of the actors in the criminal court system: the prosecutor, the defense attorney, the judge, and the jury. The next three sections focus on the decision-making process, including pretrial proceedings, plea bargaining, and sentencing, and the final two sections focus on the appellate process and specialized courts.

1. Introduction: Courts and Case Processing. The book begins with an introduction to courts and case processing. We first explain why it is important to study courts and the decisions that court actors make as they process criminal cases. We then provide an overview of the historical development of the court system, with a focus on the federal courts, and we discuss the structure and organization of federal and state courts today. This is followed by an introduction to each of the courtroom actors and the roles they play and by a discussion of the path that the typical criminal case follows as it is processed through the court system. We end the introduction with an examination of the "realities" of decision making in criminal courts. We discuss the wedding cake metaphor and the concept of the courtroom workgroup and explain how each can help us understand the work that courts do and the outcomes they produce.

2. Historical and Contemporary Perspectives on Courts. The second section of the book discusses the origins of the modern court system, which can be traced back hundreds of years to early Roman law and to English common law. We also explain how the traditional view of courts, in which courts and court actors simply apply the law, is inadequate; because laws are vague and ambiguous, courts also make law. We then discuss two competing views of the criminal justice system—the crime control model and the due process model—and explain how these models can be used to examine and analyze the criminal court system. We end the section with a discussion of the juvenile court and of the changes that have occurred in the processing of youths charged with serious crimes.

3. Prosecutors and Defense Attorneys. Our focus in this section is on prosecutors and defense attorneys and the roles they play in the criminal justice system. We discuss the inadequacies of the traditional adversarial model, and we explain that criminal case processing is characterized more by cooperation and consensus than by conflict. Our discussion of prosecuting attorneys focuses on their highly discretionary and largely invisible charging decisions and the factors that affect these decisions. We also discuss legal and practical constraints on prosecutorial discretion and explore the relatively recent phenomenon of community prosecution. Our discussion of defense attorneys includes an examination of the right to counsel and of Supreme Court decisions interpreting that right, as well as an examination of research comparing the effectiveness of private attorneys and public defenders.

4. Judges and Jurors. This section of the book examines judges and jurors. We explain that the judge plays an important, but limited, role in the criminal process; the power of judges is constrained by rules that require them to be fair and unbiased, by procedures to disqualify or remove them if they are not impartial, and by appellate court rulings on questions of law and procedure. We also discuss the methods of selecting judges, the effects of recruiting more women and racial minorities to the bench, and the consequences of using nonlawyer judges. Our discussion of jurors focuses on the jury selection process, with an emphasis on the issue of racial discrimination in the selection of jurors. We also examine the role of jury consultants, the factors that jurors take into consideration during deliberations, and the practice of jury nullification.

5. Pretrial Proceedings. This section covers the various stages in the pretrial process, from arrest through arraignment and jury selection. Particular attention is paid to the role of discretion at this stage of the process. It is here that many cases are disposed of, either by plea or dismissal. Reasons for these case outcomes are discussed. Attention is also paid to the role of the prosecutor and the various factors that may influence the charging decision.

6. Plea Bargaining and Trial Dynamics. Media depictions of trials notwithstanding, the typical criminal case is settled by guilty plea and not by trial. In this section, we therefore focus on plea bargaining and its role in case processing. We begin with a discussion of the history and current status of plea bargaining in the United States. We also present the arguments for and against plea bargaining and discuss attempts to restrict or ban plea bargaining in several jurisdictions. We then cover a diverse range of court-related topics, including the courtroom workgroup, courtroom legal culture, and media influence in criminal trials.

7. Sentencing. This section of the book is devoted to an examination of judges' sentencing decisions. We discuss the goals of sentencing, focusing on retributive and utilitarian justifications for punishment. We also examine the judge's options at sentencing and summarize the results of research analyzing the factors that judges take into account as they attempt to fashion sentences that fit offenders and their crimes.

8. Beyond Conviction and Sentencing. The final section of the book examines the postconviction process, with a focus on criminal appeals and habeas corpus proceedings. We discuss the rules that guide the appellate process, and we explain how the writ of habeas corpus has evolved over time. We end the section with a discussion of executive clemency.

9. Specialized Courts and Other Trends in Adjudication. Our focus in this section is on specialized, or problem-solving, courts. We explain that these courts—drug courts, domestic violence courts, homeless courts, teen courts, and reentry courts—take a broader and more comprehensive approach to delinquency and criminality; they also attempt to address the underlying social and economic factors that contributed to the defendant's involvement in crime. We summarize the results of research designed to measure the efficacy of these courts, and we explain how they often incorporate the principles of therapeutic jurisprudence and restorative justice.

Acknowledgments

We would first of all like to thank executive editor Jerry Westby. Jerry's faith in and commitment to the project helped make this book a reality. We also would like to thank Jerry's developmental editors, Denise Simon, Eve Oettinger, and Erim Sarbuland, who helped shepherd the book through the review process and whose gentle prodding ensured that deadlines would be met. Our copy editor, Diana Breti, made sure that there were no errant commas, misspelled words, or missing references and also smoothed out our occasionally tangled prose. Our production editor, Catherine Chilton, prepared the manuscript for publication and ensured that the transition from manuscript to book would be seamless. We also would like to express our gratitude to Erin Conley, who wrote the "How to Read a Research Article" guide for students. Thank you one and all.

We are also very grateful to the reviewers who took the time to review early drafts of our work and who provided us with helpful suggestions for improving both the introductory material and the edited readings. Their comments undoubtedly made the book better than it otherwise would have been. Heartfelt thanks to the following experts: Mario V. Cano, Arizona State University; Neal S. McNabb, Buena Vista University; Richard D. Hartley, University of Texas at San Antonio; Stephanie Mizrahi, California State University, Sacramento; P. Ann Dirks-Linhorst, Southern Illinois University Edwardsville; Elvira M. White, Fayetteville State University; Kimberly D. Hassell, University of Wisconsin–Milwaukee; Stanley S. Jacobs, Villanova University; Jacinta Gau, California State University at San Bernardino; Emmanuel Onyeozili, University of Maryland East Shore; and Gad Bensinger, Loyola University, Chicago.

Cassia Spohn dedicates this book to her children, Josh and Jessica.

*Craig Hemmens dedicates this book, all the books in this series, and everything of value
that he has ever done to his father, George Hemmens, who showed him the way;
James Marquart and Rolando Del Carmen, who taught him how; and
Mary and Emily, for giving him something he loves even more than his work.*

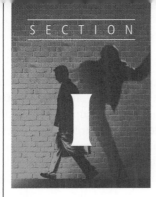

SECTION

I

Introduction
Courts and Case Processing

Section Highlights

- Why Study Courts?
- The Structure and Jurisdiction of U.S. Courts
- Courtroom Actors
- Court Process
- Decision Making
- Overview of the Book

 ## Why Study Courts?

A glance at the headlines of any major U.S. newspaper reveals that crime is a pressing national concern. Stories about crime, especially violent crime, figure prominently, as do the crime-fighting strategies proposed by legislators, county attorneys, and other government officials. Decisions by prosecutors and judges—particularly in high-profile cases involving heinous crimes or well-known victims or defendants—also get front-page billing, along with appellate court decisions that strike down or affirm criminal convictions and Supreme Court decisions that affect the operation of the criminal court system. Clearly, the editors of these newspapers believe that the public has a voracious appetite for news about crime and the handling of crime by our nation's courts.

This degree of media attention to courts and case outcomes is not really surprising. Every day, in cities throughout the United States, court officials make decisions that affect the lives of ordinary Americans

1

and determine how private businesses and governmental institutions will operate. Some of these decisions—such as a judge's ruling that a woman ticketed for speeding must pay a small fine—are relatively trivial and have little impact on persons other than the defendant. Other decisions—for example, a prosecutor's decision to seek the death penalty or a jury's decision to acquit a defendant charged with a serious crime—are weightier and have greater impact. Decisions of appellate courts, and especially those handed down by the United States Supreme Court, have even more far-reaching impact. Consider, for example, the Supreme Court's 1963 decision that all persons charged with felonies in state courts have the right to an attorney or its decision in 2005 that U.S. District Court judges are not required to follow the federal sentencing guidelines. Both of these decisions changed the way courts operate and had important implications for criminal defendants.

That courts make decisions that touch the lives of citizens is one reason why it is important to understand how they are structured and how they operate. Another reason is that the courts in this country are dynamic entities that continue to evolve. Many court systems are undergoing a transformation. Problem-solving and other specialized courts, such as drug courts and domestic violence courts, are proliferating, and jurisdictions are experimenting with alternatives to the traditional sanctions of probation, jail, and prison. Punitive sentencing reforms promulgated during the war on crime fought during the past three decades are being reexamined, as are crime-control measures that made it easier to process juvenile offenders in adult court and that required mandatory minimum prison sentences for offenders addicted to drugs. Courts also are dealing with issues such as gender and racial/ethnic bias, the prevalence of plea bargaining, and the competence of attorneys representing indigent defendants. These are important issues that animate public discussions of crime and crime control and help explain why "what the courts do (and don't do) and how they do it (but rarely why) occupies center stage in the nation's continuing focus on crime" (Neubauer, 2005, p. 17).

This introductory chapter assumes that readers have little familiarity with the courts in this country, the actors who work in them, and the process by which criminal prosecutions unfold. We cover basic court structure, the various courtroom actors, and the court process in some detail. After that, we look at the relationships between, for instance, prosecutors and defense attorneys, and we also cover several of the informal mechanisms of justice (e.g., plea bargaining) that routinely play out in the halls of our nation's courts. The last section of this chapter provides an overview of the seven major sections of this book.

Some Definitions

The term *court* often conjures up an image of a majestic building (see photo) in which black-robed judges serve as neutral referees in an adversarial battle waged between the state and the defense. There are, however, many different types of courts, and not all of them fit this idealized image of what courts are and what they do. According to the Federal Judicial Center (n.d.), a court "is an institution that the government sets up to settle disputes through a

▲ **Photo 1.1**   The United States Supreme Court in Washington, DC

legal process" (p. 1). The disputes that courts hear and settle include criminal matters, civil matters, and, for some courts, appeals from lower courts.

Throughout this book, we use the term *adjudication*, which describes what courts do—they settle disputes through a legal process. More specifically, adjudication means to hear and settle a case by judicial procedure. This implies a formal decision by a duly recognized court of law. Adjudication encompasses a judge's (or a panel of judges') decision at any stage of the criminal or civil process, from the pretrial process through the trial and appellate proceedings.

Another important term is *jurisdiction,* which refers to the persons over whom a court has power and the subject matter about which a court can make a legally binding decision. If we say that a court has jurisdiction in a particular type of case, we mean that the court has the power to hear the case (or motion) and issue a ruling. A court's jurisdiction can be defined in a variety of ways: in terms of geography, in terms of subject matter, in terms of the persons or parties entitled to bring cases before the court, and in terms of the functions or responsibilities of the court. *Geographical jurisdiction* refers to the courts' entitlement to hear and decide disputes arising within specified political boundaries: a city, a county, a state, a group of states, or the nation. The jurisdiction of a state court never extends beyond the state's boundaries; a court in California, therefore, does not have jurisdiction to try a person accused of committing a crime in Arizona or any other state. *Subject matter jurisdiction* refers to the types of cases the court is entitled to hear. Whereas some courts (primarily those in thinly populated rural areas) have jurisdiction over all types of criminal and civil matters, others have jurisdiction over only certain types of criminal (e.g., felonies, misdemeanors, cases involving drug offenses or domestic violence) or civil matters (e.g., cases involving specified amounts of money, domestic relations cases, probate cases). A court's jurisdiction also might be based on the persons or parties who can be brought before the court or who can bring suits in court. Juvenile courts, for example, have jurisdiction over those who were under a certain age at the time the crime was committed, and the federal courts have jurisdiction over cases involving residents of two different states (see "Supreme Court Decides Who Owns Ellis Island," below). Finally, courts can have original jurisdiction or appellate jurisdiction, or both. *Original jurisdiction* refers to the court's power to try a case and issue a ruling; *appellate jurisdiction,* on the other hand, refers to the court's authority to review decisions made by a lower court. Some courts have both original and appellate jurisdiction. The United States Supreme Court, for example, is primarily an appellate court but has original jurisdiction in disputes between states and in certain other types of cases.

SUPREME COURT DECIDES WHO OWNS ELLIS ISLAND: NEW YORK OR NEW JERSEY?

In 1998, the United States Supreme Court, exercising its original jurisdiction in cases involving two states, settled a dispute between New York and New Jersey over which state owned 24.5 acres of land that had been added to Ellis Island, the historic immigration site. After arguments from both states, the Court held that New Jersey had sovereign jurisdiction over the filled portions of the island, leaving New York with jurisdiction over the original 3-acre area of the island.

The Structure and Jurisdiction of U.S. Courts

It is somewhat misleading to talk about "the court system" in the United States. In reality, we have a **dual court system** composed of 50 separate state court systems, which differ from one another on a number of important dimensions, and the federal court system. This makes our judicial system more complex than the systems found in other countries, most of which do not have complete sets of trial and appellate courts at both the state and federal levels. Rather, countries such as Germany and Austria have a single federal court, similar to our United States Supreme Court.

In the sections that follow, we discuss the structure and jurisdiction of courts in the United States. We begin with the historical development of the federal court system, followed by a discussion of the federal courts and then the state courts.

A Brief Historical Overview[1]

Article III of the U.S. Constitution provides that "the judicial power of the United States shall be vested in one supreme court, and in such inferior courts as the Congress may from time to time ordain and establish." The provision giving Congress the power to establish inferior courts represented a compromise between states' rights advocates (later called the Anti-Federalists), who argued that state courts should hear all cases in the first instance and that the federal supreme court should only hear appeals from the state courts, and advocates for a strong national government (the Nationalists, later known as the Federalists), who wanted a complete set of trial and appellate courts that would hear cases involving the national government or citizens from different states. By establishing only the Supreme Court but giving Congress the power to establish other federal courts, the framers of the Constitution in essence postponed debate on this contentious issue.

The debate was not postponed for long, however. When the first Congress convened in 1789, the first Senate bill introduced was the **Judiciary Act of 1789**, which created a federal judicial system composed of the Supreme Court; 3 circuit courts, each made up of two Supreme Court justices and a district court judge; and 13 district courts. Although the creation of a system of lower federal courts was a significant victory for the Federalists, passage of the Act represented a compromise between the Federalists and the Anti-Federalists on a number of issues. For example, the Act placed significant limitations on federal trial court jurisdiction, due to the Anti-Federalists' concerns about an overbearing judiciary. Also, the Act stipulated that the boundaries of the federal district and circuit courts were to be drawn along state lines. This structure was not achieved by accident; it reflected the Anti-Federalists' desire to see the federal courts "connected" in some sense to the political culture of each state. Finally, the Act required federal district judges to be residents of their districts—that is, each judge was required to be a resident of the state in which the district court was located.

Enactment of the Judiciary Act did not end the debate over the structure and jurisdiction of the federal court system. The Federalists were successful in convincing Congress to enact the Judiciary Act of 1801, which added permanent circuit court judges and expanded the jurisdiction of the federal courts. The Act was repealed the following year, however, when the Anti-Federalists took control of Congress. The federal judicial system reverted to the previous structure and remained relatively unchanged until the late 1800s, when Congress passed a number of laws expanding the jurisdiction of the federal courts and adding new circuit court judges. Congress responded to concerns about the increasing caseload of the U.S. Supreme

---

[1]Much of the discussion presented in this section draws from Wheeler and Harrison (1994).

Court by enacting the **Court of Appeals Act of 1891**, which created the circuit courts of appeal, a new layer of intermediate appellate courts that would hear appeals from the district courts, and gave the Supreme Court more discretion in deciding which cases to hear. The issue of discretionary appeal to the Supreme Court was also addressed in the Judges Bill, passed by Congress in 1925. This bill gave the district courts original jurisdiction to try cases involving federal questions, with the right of one appeal to the circuit courts. As a result of the passage of this bill, most cases can no longer be appealed as a matter of right to the Supreme Court.

Although Congress has continued to tinker with the structure and operation of the federal judiciary—creating, for example, U.S. magistrate judges in 1968 and ordering the U.S. Sentencing Commission to develop sentencing guidelines in 1984—the basic structure and jurisdiction of the federal court system has not changed much since 1925.

The history of each state court system is beyond the scope of this book. However, it is important to note that state courts emerged more or less independently of the federal courts, even though the state and federal court structure look quite similar. State courts differ from the federal courts, though, in the sense that they handle most disputes, especially criminal cases. This is not just because, for instance, most crimes are defined in state statutes. Having most matters adjudicated at the local level once again is owing to the framers' concerns that the federal judiciary (and, indeed, the federal government) would become too powerful. Perhaps more important, though the history of the federal court system captures our attention, there is a lengthier history behind current state court structures. That is because even before the writing of the Constitution in 1787, the colonies, as sovereign entities, already had their own constitutions—and their own court structures. This is the reason that state court structures do not necessarily mirror the federal court structure.

Federal Courts[2]

The federal courts have much more limited jurisdiction than do the state courts, especially with regard to criminal matters (see Figure 1.1, which illustrates the structure of the federal court system). Federal courts only hear cases in which the United States is a party, cases involving violations of the U.S. Constitution or a law passed by Congress, cases involving citizens of different states, and some special types of cases such as bankruptcy cases and patent cases. In some cases, such as those involving citizens of different states, the federal courts have exclusive jurisdiction; these types of cases cannot be handled in a state court. In other cases—for example, criminal cases involving cross-border drug-trafficking offenses—both the state and the federal courts have jurisdiction, and the case can be tried in either type of court. Generally, however, if a criminal case involves a violation of a federal law, it will be tried in federal court. This means that when someone violates one or more provisions of the United States Code, he or she will be prosecuted in federal court. For example, an individual who is arrested for failure to pay federal income taxes will be tried in federal court, as will an individual who is arrested for embezzling money from a national bank.

The U.S. District Courts. There are 94 U.S. District Courts, which are the trial courts of the federal judicial system. This includes 89 district courts spread throughout the 50 states and one each in Puerto Rico, the Virgin Islands, the District of Columbia, Guam, and the Northern Mariana Islands. Each state has at least one district court, and due to the Judiciary Act of 1789, no district court's jurisdiction can extend across

---

[2]A comprehensive introduction to the federal judicial system may be found in Administrative Office of the United States Courts (n.d.).

Figure 1.1   The Structure of the Federal Court System

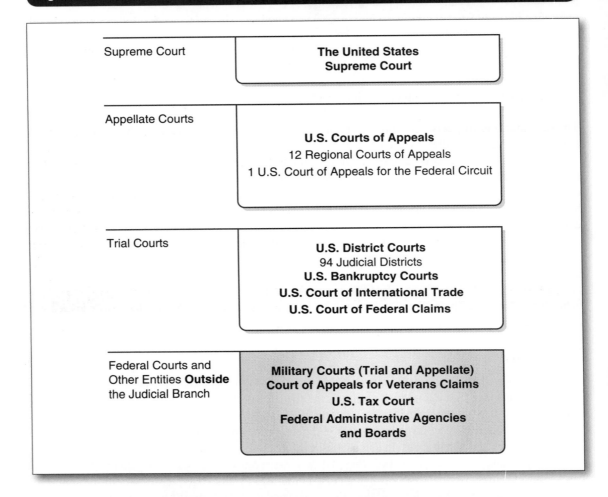

state lines. Small states typically have only one district court, but larger states often have several. California and Texas, for example, each have four district courts.

The U.S. Congress created 680 positions for district court judges; 667 of these are permanent, and the rest are temporary. Several of the district courts (i.e., Vermont, Western District of Wisconsin, Northern District of Iowa, North Dakota and Idaho) have only two authorized judgeships; other courts (i.e., Southern District of New York, Eastern District of Pennsylvania, Northern District of Illinois, and Central District of California) have 20 or more. Each district court also has a number of magistrate judges who assist the district court judges in both civil and criminal cases. According to the Administrative Office of the United States Courts, there are 429 full-time magistrate judges and 76 part-time magistrate judges.

Most of the cases heard in federal courts are civil cases rather than criminal cases. In fiscal year 2010, for example, 282,895 civil cases, but only 78,428 criminal cases, were filed in the U.S. District Courts

(Administrative Office of the United States Courts, 2010). Another criminal matter that district courts deal with is petitions for habeas corpus relief. Prisoners who are incarcerated enjoy the constitutional right to petition the federal courts (usually district courts) to review the constitutionality of their confinement. In 2010, the district courts responded to more than 51,000 such petitions.

As shown in Figure 1.1, there are a number of specialized trial courts in the federal system. They include the U.S. Bankruptcy Courts, the U.S. Court of International Trade, and the U.S. Federal Claims Court. There also are courts that are outside the judicial branch of government: military courts, the Court of Appeals for Veterans Claims, and the U.S. Tax Court.

The U.S. Courts of Appeals. The next layer of the federal court system includes the U.S. Courts of Appeals, which, as their name implies, handle appeals of decisions handed down by the U.S. District Courts in the circuit. There are 13 courts of appeals, including one for the federal circuit and one for the District of Columbia (see Figure 1.2). These courts were originally called circuit courts of appeals but were renamed, and now the circuit is specified in each individual court name (e.g., United States Court of Appeals for the Second Circuit). Both criminal and civil matters can be heard by the courts of appeals, and these appellate courts also hear their share of habeas corpus petitions. In 2010, 43,737 appeals from U.S. District Courts were filed in the courts of appeals; two thirds of these cases involved civil matters and one third involved

Figure 1.2 Map of the U.S. Courts of Appeals

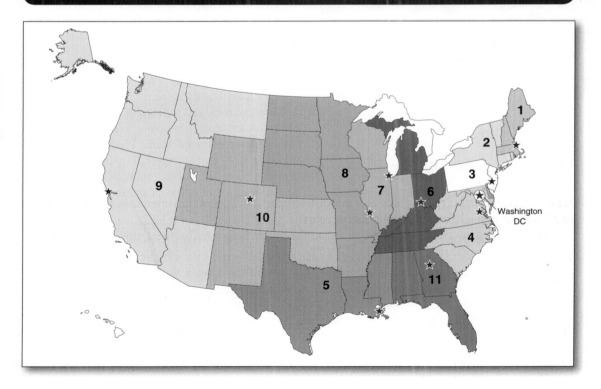

criminal matters (Administrative Office of the United States Courts, 2010). There are 179 judges assigned to the courts of appeals. The Ninth Circuit, which includes California, Arizona, and five other western states, is staffed by 28 judges. In contrast, the First Circuit, which is made up of Maine, Massachusetts, New Hampshire, and Puerto Rico, is staffed by only six judges.

In deciding cases, the courts of appeals typically use panels made up of three judges from the circuit; the panel may include visiting judges from the district courts that fall within the court of appeal's jurisdiction. After reading written arguments and listening to oral arguments, the panel of judges discusses the case and votes whether to affirm or reverse the lower court ruling. In criminal cases in which offenders convicted in federal court are appealing their sentences for drug trafficking, for example, the judges would decide whether to uphold or strike down each offender's sentence imposed by the district court judge. Occasionally, the judges in the circuit may decide to sit **en banc**; this means that all of the judges will hear the case, which will be decided by a majority vote.

▲ **Photo 1.2** The Justices of the United States Supreme Court, 2011

The U.S. Supreme Court. Not all matters are resolved at the level of the courts of appeals. Sometimes decisions of those courts are appealed to the U.S. Supreme Court, the highest court in the country (and often called simply "the Court"). The Supreme Court consists of one chief justice and eight associate justices (see photo).

There is, with only very few exceptions, no right to appeal to the U.S. Supreme Court. The Supreme Court selects the cases it will hear from the many it is asked to review each year. In a typical year, the Court is asked to review approximately 7,000 cases but agrees to hear fewer than 100. Cases reach the Supreme Court through the **writ of certiorari,** which is an order to the lower court to send the records in the case forward for review. In deciding whether to issue the writ, the justices follow the **rule of four:** The case will be heard and the writ issued if four of the nine justices agree to hear the appeal. It is important to point out that the Supreme Court's refusal to hear a case does not mean that the Supreme Court agrees with the lower court's decision; rather, the Court's refusal means only that, for whatever reasons, the Court does not want to hear the case at the time of the review.

Whereas appeals to the federal courts of appeals come only from the U.S. district courts, the Supreme Court hears appeals from both U.S. courts of appeals and state supreme courts. The decisions of state supreme courts, however, will be reviewed by the Supreme Court only if they involve a substantial federal question. An example of a criminal appeal from a state supreme court that the Court might agree to hear would be a case in which the defendant claimed that his or her constitutional rights were violated—the defendant was denied a fair trial or speedy trial, the jury was selected in a racially discriminatory manner, or the defendant did not receive adequate representation by his or her defense attorney. In fact, many of the landmark Supreme Court cases in the area of criminal procedure are cases that were appealed from state supreme courts.

It is important to emphasize that most disputed criminal and civil matters never come to the attention of the U.S. Supreme Court. As a result, there may be contradictory decisions from one state to the next, from one federal district to the next, or from one federal circuit to the next. For example, the Court of Appeals for the Ninth Circuit may decide that a certain type of search is unconstitutional, but the Court of Appeals for the Fifth Circuit might decide otherwise. Only the Supreme Court can resolve the dispute, but again, only if it decides to hear a case involving this issue. That said, if there are conflicting decisions among the courts of appeals on an important legal question, the Supreme Court often agrees to hear a case and settle the conflict.

State Courts

Most criminal and civil cases are heard in state courts, not federal courts. Each year, more than 100 million cases are processed in the state and federal courts; 98% of these cases are handled in the state courts. In 2008, the state court caseload included 57.5 million traffic cases, 21.3 million criminal cases, 19.4 million civil cases, 5.7 million domestic relations cases, and 2.1 million juvenile cases (LaFountain, Schauffler, Strickland, Bromage, Gibson, & Mason, 2010, p. 19).

Discussion of state courts is complicated because all states have not adopted one model. In fact, there are significant variations from one state to the next. Some states, such as Illinois and Florida, have unified court systems, with a uniform three- or four-tier court structure for the entire state. Other states, such as New York and Texas, have more complicated systems, with multiple layers of courts that often have overlapping jurisdiction. In the states without unified court systems, there may even be variations in court structure from one county to the next.

The first level of state trial courts is the trial courts of limited jurisdiction, which are charged with trying traffic offenses and other infractions, minor criminal offenses, and civil cases involving small amounts of money. Known as county courts, city courts, municipal courts, or justice of the peace courts, these are the courts that process the millions of Americans cited each year for traffic offenses or arrested each year for misdemeanors, such as disturbing the peace, shoplifting, and driving under the influence of alcohol or drugs. These courts also may be responsible for the preliminary stages of felony cases: initial appearances and bail decisions, appointment of counsel for indigent defendants, and preliminary hearings.

State courts of limited jurisdiction are quite common. By one author's count, there are about 13,500 such courts in the United States, and they are staffed by nearly 20,000 judicial officers (Neubauer, 2005). Six states (California, Illinois, Iowa, Minnesota, Missouri, and South Dakota) and the District of Columbia have no trial courts of limited jurisdiction; other states (e.g., Texas and New York) have more than 2,500 of these lower courts. A unique feature of limited jurisdiction courts is that they are often not part of the state court system. Most of them are controlled by the local governing authority—typically a county—that established them and funds them.

The next courts in the state court hierarchy are the courts of general jurisdiction. These are the major trial courts of the state court system. Known variously as circuit courts, district courts, superior courts, supreme courts (New York only), and court of common pleas (Pennsylvania only), these courts hear all civil and criminal matters not specifically delegated to the lower courts. There are roughly 2,000 general jurisdiction courts throughout the 50 states, and they are staffed by more than 11,000 judges (Rottman, Flango, Cantrell, Hansen, & LaFountain, 2000). In 2008, the state courts of general jurisdiction and the unified courts (which handle both minor and major cases) processed 14.1 million traffic cases, 8.7 million civil cases, 6.6 million criminal cases, 4.1 million domestic relations cases, and 1.4 million juvenile cases (National Center for State Courts, 2010, p. 20).

At the next level of the state court system are the appellate courts. A century ago, the state court system included only a single appellate court: the state court of last resort. As the number of cases appealed from the trial courts increased and threatened to overwhelm the state courts of last resort, states created intermediate courts of appeals. Today, these courts—which go by such names as appeals courts, appellate courts, appellate divisions, and courts of appeals—are found in 39 states. Larger states often have several such courts, and they may divide them into civil and criminal divisions.

Finally, state supreme courts are the highest courts—or the courts of last resort—in each state. As is the case with other courts in the state court system, the names of these courts vary from state to state: Supreme Court (43 states); Court of Appeals (2 states and the District of Columbia); Supreme Judicial Court (2 states); Court of Criminal/Civil Appeals (2 states); and Supreme Court of Appeals (one state). Texas and Oklahoma have two courts of last resort, one for criminal appeals and one for civil appeals. The number of judges also varies, from a low of three to a high of nine.

The state appellate courts—like the federal courts of appeals—hear civil and criminal appeals from the lower courts within their jurisdiction. Defendants who have been convicted and sentenced in one of the state trial courts (or in a federal district court) have the right to appeal to one higher court and to have the appeal heard by that court; this right of appeal is designed to ensure that the law was applied and interpreted correctly and that proper procedures were followed at every stage in the process. Appellate courts do not decide matters of fact, such as whether a person convicted of a crime is actually guilty. Appellate courts review the record from the trial court; they do not hear new testimony from the persons involved in the case and they do not consider new evidence. Issues commonly raised on appeal include defects in the procedures used to select the jury, ineffective assistance of counsel, failure to exclude evidence that was obtained improperly, and coerced confessions or guilty pleas.

Appellate courts have both mandatory and discretionary jurisdiction. *Mandatory jurisdiction* means that the court must hear all properly filed appeals; *discretionary jurisdiction* means that the court can decide which cases it wants to hear. Intermediate appellate courts and supreme courts in states without an intermediate appellate court primarily handle mandatory appeals. State supreme courts in states with an intermediate appellate court, on the other hand, hear most cases under their discretionary jurisdiction. The National Center for State Courts compared the mandatory and discretionary caseloads of 22 states with both intermediate appellate courts and supreme courts. In 2004, 72% of the cases heard by the intermediate appellate courts in these states were mandatory appeals; in contrast, 86% of the cases heard by the supreme courts were discretionary appeals (National Center for State Courts, 2006, p. 75).

Other Courts

Both the federal and state court systems include a number of specialized courts, such as juvenile courts, military tribunals, and specialized or problem-solving courts. We discuss these types of courts in subsequent sections and in section introductions throughout the text. We also provide reprinted articles that deal with developments in these areas.

 # Courtroom Actors

Courtroom actors are the "regulars" who appear in a typical trial or other proceedings. Often referred to as "the courtroom workgroup" (Eisenstein & Jacob, 1977) or the courthouse "community" (Eisenstein, Flemming, & Nardulli, 1988), these are the individuals who work together day after day to process the civil and criminal cases that come before the court. The primary actors in a criminal case are, of course, the prosecutor, the defense attorney, the judge, the jury (in a small percentage of cases), and the defendant. Other actors include victims and witnesses, the bailiff, and other support staff.

In the sections that follow, we provide a brief introduction to the key players in the court system. Because the focus of this book is the criminal court system, we emphasize the roles they play in processing criminal cases.

Prosecutors

Prosecutors are representatives of the executive branch of government. They are found in both federal and state courts, and their primary responsibility is to bring criminal charges against individuals who are accused of a crime and to represent the government's interest in court.

In the federal court system, prosecution of criminal cases is the responsibility of the U.S. Department of Justice, which is headed by the U.S. Attorney General. The attorneys who prosecute cases in the federal courts are called the U.S. attorneys. There are 93 U.S. attorneys, one for each of the district courts, with the exception of Guam and the Northern Mariana Islands, which share one attorney. These attorneys are appointed by the president to four-year terms, with the advice and consent of the U.S. Senate; they serve at the pleasure of the president. The 93 U.S. attorneys are assisted by more than 4,000 assistant U.S. attorneys. Another federal official who exercises prosecutorial functions is the U.S. Solicitor General, who is the third-ranking official in the Department of Justice. The Solicitor General represents the interests of the executive branch in cases that appear before the U.S. Supreme Court.

Three types of prosecutors are found in the state court system. At the top of the hierarchy is the state attorney general, who is the state's chief legal officer. The attorney general represents the state in court when state laws and practices are challenged but plays a very limited role in criminal trials and does not supervise the activities of local prosecutors. The attorneys who prosecute criminal cases are found at the local level. The chief prosecutor, who in all but five states and the District of Columbia is elected, and his or her deputies charge and prosecute those accused of crime at the local, typically the county, level. Known variously as county attorneys, district attorneys, prosecuting attorneys, and state's attorneys, these attorneys are mandated to prosecute "all known criminal cases." They also give legal advice to county officials. Finally, city attorneys sometimes engage in prosecutorial functions. This is especially true of large cities where, in addition to representing city interests, city attorneys prosecute misdemeanor offenses and handle the preliminary stages of felony cases in the trial courts of limited jurisdiction.

At the state level, the organization of the prosecutor's office and the procedures used to assign cases to assistant prosecutors vary from one jurisdiction to another (Abadinsky, 1988). Some jurisdictions assign assistant prosecutors to cases based on the attorney's expertise and skill; others assign attorneys to courtrooms, either permanently or for a specified period of time. In many large urban jurisdictions, assistant prosecutors are assigned to courtrooms, and cases are prosecuted horizontally: Different prosecutors handle the case at each stage in the process. In other jurisdictions, cases are prosecuted vertically: Each case is assigned to an assistant prosecutor (typically after the decision to charge has been made by the felony review unit), who stays with the case until final disposition.

A number of large jurisdictions combine horizontal and vertical prosecution. Routine cases are prosecuted horizontally, whereas targeted cases (e.g., homicides, sex offenses, white-collar crimes, cases involving career criminals) are prosecuted vertically. Typically, the targeted cases are assigned to specialized units within the prosecutor's office. In some jurisdictions, the prosecutors assigned to the unit handle cases from arrest through disposition; in other jurisdictions, the decision to charge is made by the felony review unit, and cases are assigned to the specialized unit after screening. Figure 1.3 presents the organization chart for the Maricopa County (Arizona) County Attorney's Office.

Prosecutors in the state and federal courts enjoy a significant amount of unchecked discretionary power. The prosecutor decides who will be charged, what charge will be filed, who will be offered a plea

Figure 1.3   Organizational Structure of the Maricopa County (Arizona) Attorney's Office

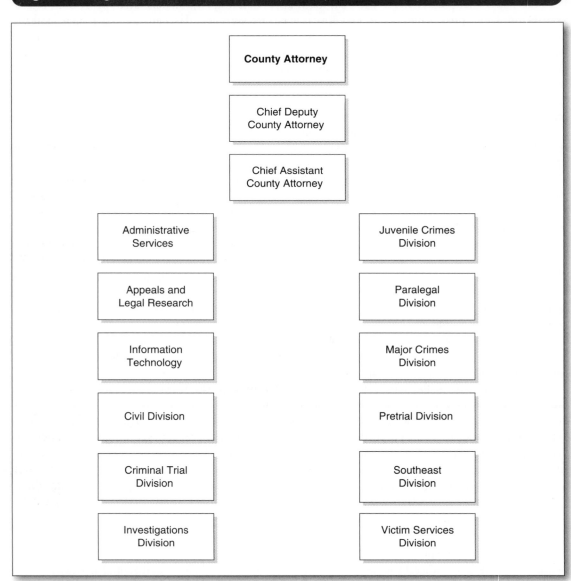

bargain, and the type of bargain that will be offered. The prosecutor presents to the judge or jury evidence designed to prove that the defendant is guilty beyond a reasonable doubt and argues for the defendant's conviction. The prosecutor also may make a recommendation to the judge regarding bail and often will recommend the sentence the offender should receive. In the federal court system, the prosecutor (i.e., U.S. attorney) can affect the sentence an offender receives by filing a motion for a downward departure from the federal sentencing guidelines as a result of the defendant's "substantial assistance" in the prosecution and conviction of other offenders. If the defendant appeals his or her conviction, the prosecutor appears before the appellate court to argue that the conviction should not be overturned.

The power that prosecutors exercise has become an object of considerable scrutiny by both higher courts and the academic community. Appellate courts, and especially the Supreme Court, have placed a number of constraints on the exercise of prosecutorial discretion. We examine some of these decisions—and their impact—in a later section that deals with prosecutors in more detail. In addition, researchers have conducted a number of studies on the factors that affect prosecutors' charging and plea bargaining decisions. We look at some of this research as well.

Defense Attorneys

The Sixth Amendment to the U.S. Constitution states, "In all criminal prosecutions, the accused shall enjoy the right to have the assistance of counsel for his defense." Historically, this meant simply that a defendant who had the means to hire an attorney could bring the attorney along to defend him or her. This clearly was of no help to defendants who were too poor to hire their own attorneys. Recognizing this, the United States Supreme Court handed down a series of decisions requiring the appointment of counsel for indigent defendants.

Arguably, the most important of the Court's decisions regarding right to counsel was its 1963 decision in *Gideon v. Wainwright*. Noting that "lawyers in criminal courts are necessities, not luxuries," the Court ruled that all indigent criminal defendants charged with felonies are entitled to lawyers to assist them in their defense. In subsequent decisions, the Court expanded this right, ruling that no person could be imprisoned for any offense unless he or she was represented by counsel (*Argersinger v. Hamlin*, 1972) and that the right to counsel applies to all "critical stages" of the criminal justice process.[3]

The Court's decisions had a significant impact on state criminal justice systems, which had to devise ways to represent large numbers of poor defendants at trial and other critical stages in the criminal process. Today, states use either the public defender system, an assigned counsel system, a contract system, or some combination of the three types of systems. **Public defenders**, like prosecuting attorneys, are salaried government employees; they are hired by the state (or by a county within a state) to represent indigent defendants. Public defender systems are most likely to be found in large urban jurisdictions with high caseloads. In jurisdictions that use an assigned counsel system, judges assign private defense attorneys to represent indigent defendants on a case-by-case basis. Traditionally, members of local bar associations volunteered for this service, which they provided pro bono, but today most jurisdictions reimburse attorneys for representing indigent defendants. Under the contract model, jurisdictions enter into contracts with individual private attorneys or law firms; they agree to provide legal services to indigent defendants for a fixed sum.

---

[3]A defendant is entitled to counsel at every stage "where substantial rights of the accused may be affected" that require the "guiding hand of counsel" (*Mempa v. Rhay*, 1967). These critical stages include arraignment, preliminary hearing, entry of a plea, trial, sentencing, and the first appeal.

All of the systems used to assign attorneys to indigent defendants have come under criticism. Much of the harshest criticism is directed—some would say unfairly (Wice, 1985)—at the public defender system. Public defenders are government employees who are charged with representing indigent defendants. These attorneys tend to have large caseloads, and they are not always paid as well as either privately retained attorneys or prosecuting attorneys, so questions have arisen as to their ability to adequately defend their clients (Weitzer, 1996, p. 313). Similar concerns have been voiced about the assigned counsel system. Critics charge that these systems, and especially those that rely on lawyers who volunteer for indigent defense, do not necessarily result in the appointment of lawyers with the skills or the experience to defend those charged with crimes. The contract system has been criticized because of the concern that the contracts go to the lowest bidder and not necessarily to the most experienced attorneys.[4]

Defense attorneys, whether hired by the defendant or appointed by the state, provide a number of services. They represent their clients at various (although not necessarily all) stages of the criminal process, sometimes even before criminal charges have been filed. They also participate in plea bargaining with prosecutors, defend the accused at trial, and otherwise act as their clients' advocates whenever the need arises. And just as prosecutors face certain constraints in their day-to-day activities, so do defense attorneys. For example, it is not sufficient to provide representation to an indigent criminal defendant; the defense attorney must be effective. In Section III, we examine the meaning of effective assistance of counsel, and we review the results of research comparing the effectiveness of privately retained versus government-provided defense attorneys.

No discussion of defense attorneys would be complete without some attention to ethical considerations. The stereotypical view—which is shaped by television, movies, and the mass media—is that defense attorneys seek to exploit legal loopholes with no other concern than gaining an acquittal for their clients. Questions regarding defense attorneys' character are also raised, especially when they decide to represent unsavory individuals. According to one observer, "a lawyer who defends notoriously unpopular clients becomes identified in the public's mind, and not infrequently in the mind of his own profession, with his client" (Kaplan, 1973, as quoted in Neubauer, 2002). Defense attorneys who behave inappropriately or unethically run the risk of disbarment. To say, however, that incompetent defense attorneys are routinely disbarred is incorrect; this rarely happens. All defense attorneys must abide by professional standards of conduct, two of which are reprinted in Figure 1.4.

Judges

The stereotypical view of the role played by a criminal court **judge** is that the judge presides over trials and imposes sentences. But judges make important decisions at all stages of the criminal process. They issue search warrants that enable police officers to search for contraband or evidence. After an arrest is made, judges decide whether bail is required and, if so, how much it should be, whether there is sufficient evidence to hold the defendant for trial, and whether pretrial motions filed by the prosecutor or the defense attorney should be granted or not. During the trial, judges play an important role in jury selection, in that they decide whether jurors can be excused for cause (i.e., because of bias or prejudice toward one side or the other or because the juror has already made up his or her mind about the defendant's guilt). They also are responsible for maintaining order in the courtroom and for deciding whether to

---

[4]In *Smith v. State* (1984), the Arizona Supreme Court invalidated a contract system for this very reason.

Figure 1.4 American Bar Association's Model Rules of Professional Conduct (2002)

Client-Lawyer Relationship

Rule 1.1: Competence

A lawyer shall provide competent representation to a client. Competent representation requires the legal knowledge, skill, thoroughness and preparation reasonably necessary for the representation.

Rule 1.2: Scope of Representation and Allocation of Authority Between Client and Lawyer

(a) Subject to paragraphs (c) and (d), a lawyer shall abide by a client's decisions concerning the objectives of representation and . . . shall consult with the client as to the means by which they are to be pursued. . . . A lawyer shall abide by a client's decision whether to settle a matter. In a criminal case, the lawyer shall abide by the client's decision, after consultation with the lawyer, as to a plea to be entered, whether to waive jury trial and whether the client will testify.

(b) A lawyer's representation of a client, including representation by appointment, does not constitute an endorsement of the client's political, economic, social or moral views or activities.

(c) A lawyer may limit the scope of the representation if the limitation is reasonable under the circumstances and the client gives informed consent.

(d) A lawyer shall not counsel a client to engage, or assist a client, in conduct that the lawyer knows is criminal or fraudulent, but a lawyer may discuss the legal consequences of any proposed course of conduct with a client and may counsel or assist a client to make a good faith effort to determine the validity, scope, meaning or application of the law.

sustain or overrule objections to questions asked or evidence introduced. In bench trials—cases tried by the judge alone, without a jury—judges determine whether the prosecutor has proven the defendant's guilt beyond a reasonable doubt. If the defendant pleads guilty or is found guilty at trial, the judge determines the sentence.

Different procedures are used to select federal and state judges. Federal judges, including the justices of the Supreme Court, are appointed by the president, confirmed by the United States Senate, and serve life terms with "good behavior." (The magistrate judges who assist the U.S. District Court judges are appointed by the district court judges for terms of either eight years, for full-time judges, or four years, for part-time judges). Senate confirmation hearings for lower federal court judges tend to be routine and rarely generate much controversy, but confirmation hearings for Supreme Court judges are often contentious and highly publicized. President George H. W. Bush's 1991 nomination of Clarence Thomas, who was African American but did not support affirmative action, was highly controversial and was opposed by groups such as the NAACP, the Urban League, and the National Organization of Women. More recently, President George W. Bush's 2005 nomination of Samuel Alito, a staunchly conservative judge who was sitting on the United States Court of Appeals for the Third Circuit, was opposed by the American Civil

Liberties Union and by a number of prochoice groups, and President Barack Obama's 2010 nomination of Elena Kagan was opposed by all but five Senate Republicans. Thomas was approved by a narrow majority of senators (52 to 48), Alito's nomination was confirmed by a vote of 58 to 42, and Kagan won her seat by a vote of 63 to 37.

Federal judges may be removed from the bench only if Congress determines, through a process known as impeachment, that they are guilty of "treason, bribery, or other high crimes and misdemeanors." Removal of federal judges, however, is rare; only 16 judges have been impeached (meaning that formal allegations were filed in the U.S. House of Representatives), and only 8 of the 16 were convicted by the Senate and removed from office. (Three other judges who were the subjects of investigations resigned before impeachment proceedings could begin.) The most recent judge to be impeached was U.S. District Judge G. Thomas Porteous, who was removed from office in December of 2010. Porteous was convicted of accepting cash and favors from attorneys and bail bondsmen who appeared in his courtroom.

In contrast to federal judges, who, as noted earlier, are nominated by the president and confirmed by the Senate, most state court judges (87%) are elected (or face election after being initially appointed; Rottman, Bromage, Zose, & Thompson, 2006, p. 1). Elections can be either partisan (the nominee's political party affiliation is listed on the ballot) or nonpartisan (no party affiliation is listed). In some states, judges first run in a partisan election and then stand for retention in subsequent elections; this means that the judge runs uncontested and the voters decide whether he or she should be retained in office. Other methods of selecting judges include appointment by the governor or the state legislator and the merit selection system. Judges selected under the **merit system**, also known as the Missouri Bar Plan, are nominated by a judicial nominating commission that includes lawyers and laypersons. The governor appoints one of the persons suggested by the nominating commission, and the judge stands for retention in subsequent elections. Most states use a single method to select all appellate and general jurisdiction court judges; other states use different selection methods for trial and appellate court judges. California, for example, uses appointment followed by retention elections for appellate judges and nonpartisan elections for trial judges (Rottman et al., 2006, p. 1).

When state court judges must face the electorate, questions of politics invariably arise. Many legal scholars believe that judges should not run partisan campaigns or discuss their positions on issues that may come before them. They argue that judges, who are expected to be neutral and detached, should not announce their positions or indicate how they would vote on issues such as abortion or the death penalty. Some judges, however, run highly politicized campaigns. In 1994, for example, Stephen W. Mansfield campaigned for the Texas Court of Appeals "on promises of the death penalty for killers . . . and sanctions for attorneys who file 'frivolous appeals, especially in death penalty cases'" (Bright & Keenan, 1995, p. 762). Many states have canons of judicial conduct that prohibit judges from announcing their views on disputed legal or political issues. However, in 2002, the United States Supreme Court ruled that these restrictions violate the freedom of speech protections of the First Amendment (*Republican Party of Minnesota v. White*, 2002).

We examine judges and the politics of judicial selection in more detail in Section IV. We consider constraints on judges, particularly their need to remain neutral and detached, and we discuss alternatives to traditional judicial positions, such as having nonlawyers act as judges.

Jurors

Jurors clearly play an important role in the criminal process; they decide whether those charged with crimes are guilty and, in some jurisdictions, what the sentence should be if the defendant is convicted. But whereas prosecutors, defense attorneys, and judges are staples of the criminal process, juries are not. That is because most criminal cases are settled by a guilty plea rather than a jury trial. In 2002, for example, 95% of convictions obtained in felony cases tried in states courts in the 75 largest counties in the United States were obtained through a guilty plea (Bureau of Justice Statistics, n.d. a). Similarly, 96% of all convicted defendants in U.S. District Courts in 2004 pled guilty or no contest (Bureau of Justice Statistics, n.d. b).

The Sixth Amendment provides that the "accused shall enjoy the right to a speedy and public trial, by an impartial jury," but this right has been restricted by the Supreme Court. First, there is no Sixth Amendment constitutional right to a jury trial in noncriminal proceedings. Second, in *Baldwin v. New York* (1970), the Court argued that the "disadvantages, onerous though they may be," of denying a jury trial for petty crimes are "outweighed by the benefits that result from speedy and inexpensive nonjury adjudication" (p. 73). Specifically, the Court decided that a defendant has a right to a trial by jury only when the penalty he or she faces consists of more than six months' incarceration.

The Supreme Court also has had to interpret the Sixth Amendment's requirement that the defendant be tried by an "impartial jury." In doing so, the Court has ruled that the jury pool must be a random cross-section of the community This means that the **jury pool**—that is, the list of names from which actual jurors will be chosen—should represent all the groups in the community and that no group, such as African Americans or women, should be intentionally excluded. This requirement, however, does not apply to the composition of the actual jury in a particular case. As Supreme Court Justice Murphy stated in 1946, the Sixth Amendment does not mean

> that every jury must contain representatives of all the economic, social, religious, racial, political and geographical groups of the community; frequently such complete representation would be impossible. But it does mean that prospective jurors shall be selected by court officials without systematic and intentional exclusion of any of these groups. (*Thiel v. Southern Pacific Co.*, 1946)

The process of selecting a jury begins with the selection of the jury pool (sometimes referred to as the **venire**). The method of selecting names for the jury pool varies, but many states use voter registration lists and drivers' license lists. Some states even use telephone directory lists or lists of utility customers. Other states rely on jury commissioners, who are appointed by judges and who compile the jury pool. Each state determines who is eligible for jury duty. All states have minimum qualifications (i.e., the individual must be at least 19 years old, a United States citizen, and a resident of the jurisdiction where the case will be heard), and many disqualify persons who are illiterate, physically or mentally ill, or who have been convicted of a felony. Until recently, most states also gave automatic exemptions to persons, such as doctors, teachers, and police officers, whose jobs were deemed so important that they couldn't be released from them for jury duty; most of these exemptions have been eliminated.

Once the jury pool is formed, people are selected from the list for jury service. Individuals selected from the jury pool for a particular case are usually called the **jury panel**. Members of the jury panel are called into court, and, in a process known as **voir dire** (which is Old French for "to speak the truth"), they are asked a series of questions by the judge or the lawyers. They are asked about their background, their familiarity with the case, whether they are friends or acquaintances of any of the parties to the case, and their attitudes about certain issues that may arise during the trial. These questions are, at least in theory, designed to determine whether the potential jurors are unbiased and can decide the case fairly and impartially. As we explain in more detail later, potential jurors can be excused—or challenged—by either the prosecutor or the defense attorney. Both sides have an unlimited number of challenges for cause; these challenges, which require the judge's approval, are used to excuse jurors who cannot be fair and impartial. In addition, each side has a limited number of peremptory challenges, which can be used to excuse potential jurors without giving any reason. The peremptory challenge has been criticized on a number of grounds, the most important of which concerns allegations that prosecutors use them to remove African Americans and Hispanics from juries trying racial minorities.

We return to the topic of jury selection in Section IV. We also consider the practice of using professional jury consultants, who are individuals hired to assist either the prosecution or the defense during the voir dire process, with the goal of selecting jurors who are sympathetic to their views. We examine research exploring the factors that affect jury decision making, and we discuss the controversy surrounding the practice of jury nullification.

Other Actors

A number of other actors are familiar faces in America's courts. They can be placed into two categories: professionals and nonprofessionals. The first professional is the bailiff. This person is usually an armed peace officer (often a sheriff's deputy) whose job is to maintain order in the courtroom and transport incarcerated defendants to and from court proceedings. At the federal level, bailiffs are U.S. Marshals.

Court administrators also work closely with the courts. These individuals are responsible for facilitating the smooth flow of cases. They maintain the court records, schedule cases for hearings and for trial, and manage court personnel. Court administrators tend to work behind the scenes, but two professionals whose jobs are closely related to court administration are highly visible in court. One is the court reporter, whose job is to record the court proceedings and to produce a transcript of the trial. The other is the court clerk, who maintains the records of all cases. He or she also prepares the jury pool, issues summonses for jury duty, and subpoenas witnesses to testify at trial.

The last "professional" courtroom actor is the expert witness. These individuals are professionals insofar as they must possess certain qualifications or credentials. More often than not, experts are relied on to introduce scientific and other complicated forms of evidence. The hope is that they can take a complicated matter, such as a DNA test, and explain it in simple terms for the jury. Unfortunately, though, expert witnesses hired by the prosecution and the defense often give conflicting testimony, which can increase juror confusion.

As for nonprofessionals, jurors fit into this category, but so do lay witnesses. Lay witnesses are the individuals who are called to testify for either the prosecution or the defense. What makes them different from expert witnesses is that they are not allowed to offer opinions. Only expert witnesses can do this. Even so, lay witnesses perform valuable functions. Their job is to shed light on the facts surrounding the alleged crime. A witness may have been present at the crime scene and may well have been a victim. Lay witnesses also may be called to vouch for the character of the defendant.

Court Process

Earlier in this chapter, we pointed out that it is impossible to perfectly describe the court structure in this country due to the many variations from one state to the next. The same can be said of the court process. It differs considerably from one place to the next. Likewise, it differs depending on the level of government: State procedure differs in a number of important ways from federal procedure. Finally, the court process varies depending on the type of offense charged. Whereas serious charges are often adjudicated with formal adversarial trials, minor offenses are more likely to produce guilty pleas and typically are disposed of quickly and efficiently. What we present, therefore, is a generic overview of the typical court process in the state court system.

Pretrial Proceedings

Before the court process gets underway, someone must be arrested (or must turn himself or herself in to law enforcement). The arrestee is booked at the arresting officer's station. Booking consists of filling out paperwork that records who is arrested, the time of the alleged offense, the facts involved, and so on. Fingerprints and photographs are taken. Then the arrestee might be placed in a holding cell and allowed to contact family or an attorney (or both). Many arrestees are promptly released, especially if the offense in question is minor and there is no concern that he or she won't show up for court proceedings.

In most urban jurisdictions, the prosecutor reviews the arrest report and other available evidence and decides whether to file formal criminal charges and, if so, what the charges should be. In making this decision, the prosecutor exercises wide discretion. Moreover, a decision to reject the case is not subject to review and cannot be challenged by the victim or other criminal justice officials. If the prosecutor decides to file charges, he or she proceeds using one of a number of different types of charging documents. In cases involving misdemeanors, this is likely to be a criminal complaint, which lays out the facts in the case and is signed by the arresting officer or the complainant or victim. If the charge is a felony and the state does not use the grand jury, the prosecutor files an information, which is similar to a criminal complaint, in that it describes the facts of the case and lists the charge or charges the accused is facing. In states that proceed using indictment by grand jury, the information is the initial charging document presented to the grand jury.

If a suspect is arrested, booked, and placed in confinement, he or she is later brought before a lower court judge for an initial appearance. The initial appearance, which is usually held within a few hours or, at most, a few days of arrest, serves to advise the accused why he or she is being detained and to explain his or her rights. The judge reads the charges filed against the accused and explains the penalties for each charge. The judge also informs the accused of the right to a trial by jury and the right to counsel, including the right to have an attorney appointed if the accused is indigent. Individuals charged with misdemeanors enter a plea at this stage in the process. If the accused pleads guilty, the judge either imposes a sentence immediately (typically, a fine, probation, or a jail term) or sets a date for sentencing; if the accused enters a not guilty plea, the judge sets a date for trial. Felony accused, on the other hand, do not enter a plea at the initial appearance; judges in courts of limited jurisdiction are not authorized to accept pleas in felony cases. The judge informs the accused of the right to a preliminary hearing, explains the purpose of the preliminary hearing, and sets a date for the hearing.

Decisions regarding bail may be made at the initial appearance or at a bail hearing that is scheduled soon after the initial appearance. The judge must decide whether to release the accused on bail and, if so, the type and amount of bail to impose. When a judge concludes that an accused poses a significant risk of flight or of harm to others, bail is not granted. But if the accused's failure to appear at trial is not a concern and he or she is not seen as dangerous, the accused may either be released on his or her own recognizance (i.e., without paying bail) or be required to pay monetary bail. Interestingly, there is no constitutional right to bail. The Eighth Amendment only provides that "excessive bail shall not be required." This means that bail should be an amount that is not unreasonable but that will guarantee the defendant's appearance at trial. In many jurisdictions, judges follow bail schedules, except in cases of serious or unusual offenses.

The next step in the proceedings involves a determination that there is probable cause to hold the accused for trial—that is, a determination that there is sufficient evidence to support the charges filed against the accused. In about half the states, this is accomplished by a **preliminary hearing** in which a lower court judge assesses the evidence presented by the prosecutor and decides whether there is enough evidence to merit a trial. According to one Supreme Court decision, the purpose of the preliminary hearing is to prevent "hasty, malicious, improvident, and oppressive prosecutions" and to ensure that "there are substantial grounds upon which a prosecution may be based" (*Thies v. State*, 1922, p. 103). In the federal system and the rest of the states, the probable cause determination is made by the grand jury on the basis of evidence presented by the prosecutor. If the grand jury believes that there is sufficient evidence to hold the defendant for trial, the jurors return an indictment (also called a true bill); if the grand jury does not believe that the evidence is adequate, the jurors return a no bill.

After the judge at the preliminary hearing or the grand jury decides that there is sufficient evidence to proceed with the case, the defendant is arraigned. The purpose of arraignment is to formally notify the defendant of the charge or charges and to ask the defendant to enter a plea. The defendant enters one of three pleas at this stage: guilty, not guilty, or nolo contendere. The first two are self-explanatory. A plea of *nolo contendere* means "I do not desire to contest the action." This plea resembles a guilty plea but is different in one important respect: It cannot be used against the defendant in any later civil litigation arising from the acts that gave rise to the initial criminal charge. Also, a plea of nolo contendere means that the defendant does not admit to the crime. A guilty plea, by contrast, requires that the defendant admit and explain (known as allocution) what happened.

The last significant step leading up to trial, or adjudication, is discovery and suppression. **Discovery** is the process by which both parties to the case learn of the evidence the opposing side will use at trial. Rule 16 of the Federal Rules of Evidence provides, for example, that the defendant may, on request, discover from the prosecution

> any written statements or transcriptions of oral statements made by the defendant that are in the prosecution's possession; (2) the defendant's prior criminal record; and (3) documents, photographs, tangible items, results from physical and mental evaluations, as well as other forms of real evidence considered material to the prosecution's case. (Legal Information Institute, Cornell Law School, 2007)

There is considerable variation among the states in the types of information that are discoverable by the defense and the prosecution. In some states, only the defendant's statements and physical evidence need be disclosed to the defense; in other states, there is a presumption that the prosecutor, with only narrow exceptions, will disclose most of the evidence against the defendant. According to the Supreme Court's decision in *Brady v. Maryland* (1970), prosecutors are not allowed to conceal exculpatory evidence, which is evidence tending to show that the defendant is innocent. Some states also require reciprocal discovery; that is, the defense is required to turn over certain types of evidence to the prosecutor. Generally, the defense is required to notify the prosecutor if the defendant is going to enter an insanity plea or use an alibi defense; in the latter situation, the defense may have to provide a list of witnesses who will support the alibi defense so that the state can be prepared to cross-examine them.

Evidence that the prosecution hopes to present must have been secured within the limits of the Constitution. According to the **exclusionary rule**, evidence that is wrongfully obtained, such as through an unconstitutional search, is not admissible at trial. This rule stems from *Weeks v. United States* (1914), in which the Supreme Court held that papers seized following a search that was in violation of the Fourth Amendment should have been returned rather than used in a criminal trial against the petitioner. Then, in *Mapp v. Ohio* (1961), the Supreme Court made the rule binding on the states through the due process clause of the Fourteenth Amendment (in contrast, *Weeks* was only binding on the federal courts). The Court offered the following reasoning for the exclusionary rule:

> The criminal goes free, if he must, but it is the law that sets him free. Nothing can destroy a government more quickly than its failure to observe its own law, or worse, its disregard of the charter of its own existence. (*Elkins v. United States*, 364 U.S. 206, 1960, p. 222)

The exclusionary rule is highly controversial. Opponents claim that it prevents the prosecution from using reliable and valid evidence and ensures that at least some guilty persons go free as a result of legal "technicalities." Supporters counter that the rule is needed to deter police misconduct and protect citizens against unreasonable searches and seizures.

The Supreme Court created several exceptions to the exclusionary rule. For instance, good faith mistakes do not necessarily result in the exclusion of evidence. An example of this would be a situation in which the judge issuing a search warrant made a minor, technical error but the police officer executing the warrant thought that it was valid (i.e., he acted in good faith); in all likelihood, the evidence discovered would not be suppressed. Likewise, if the evidence is turned over to authorities by an independent source not connected with the police, it is likely to be admitted. Another exception to the exclusionary rule is the inevitable discovery doctrine.[5] It holds that evidence obtained as a result of an unlawful search or seizure is admissible in court if it can be established that normal police investigation would have inevitably led to the discovery of the evidence.

Plea Bargaining

Most criminal cases do not go on to the next stage—trial and adjudication. As noted earlier, more than 90% of defendants charged with felonies in state and federal courts plead guilty. Many, but not all, of these guilty pleas result from **plea bargaining** between prosecutors and defense attorneys. This happens in two ways. One is by charge bargaining, in which the prosecutor offers to reduce the severity of the charges or the number of counts in exchange for a guilty plea. For example, the prosecutor might agree to reduce the charge from first-degree sexual assault to second-degree sexual assault or from robbery to attempted robbery. If the defendant is facing multiple counts of burglary, the prosecutor might agree to drop all but one of the counts. The second type of plea bargaining is sentence bargaining, in which the prosecutor agrees to recommend leniency at the sentencing stage.

Plea bargaining is both necessary and controversial. It is necessary because there are not enough resources for every offender to be tried by a jury. Perhaps more important, in most criminal cases, the evidence of the defendant's guilt is overwhelming, and, thus, a trial would be nearly pointless. Consequently, trials tend to be more common in cases involving relatively serious crimes or when the facts are clearly in dispute. At the same time, plea bargaining has been criticized for undercutting the constitutional protections afforded those charged with crime, including the right to a trial by jury. Critics also charge that the prevalence of plea bargaining may pressure innocent defendants to plead guilty or, conversely, may allow the guilty to escape punishment for crimes they did commit.

---

[5]The inevitable discovery doctrine was established in *Nix v. Williams* 467 U.S. 431 (1984).

Trial and Adjudication

After the defendant is arraigned and enters a plea of not guilty, the trial takes place. Trials can be either jury trials or bench trials. In a **bench trial,** the judge presiding over the case decides whether the defendant is to be held accountable for the crime in question. Criminal trials usually proceed in either three (bench trials) or four (jury trials) stages. If the defendant is to be tried by a jury, the first step is the selection of the jurors to try the case. After the members of the jury have been sworn in, the prosecution and defense present their opening statements. This is when both sides lay out the arguments they will make. Each side then puts on its case and calls witnesses as needed. Witnesses are first questioned by the party calling them (e.g., prosecution witnesses are questioned first by the prosecutor). This is known as direct examination. Then each witness is questioned by the opposing side, a process known as cross-examination. Sometimes there is even redirect and recross-examination, if circumstances warrant. After the prosecution and defense present their cases, they make their closing arguments. This is when both parties summarize their arguments and attempt to convince the judge or jury to decide in their favor.

During the course of a criminal trial, both the prosecutor and defense attorney must follow elaborate rules of evidence. Such rules govern everything from the questioning of witnesses to the presentation of evidence. Even the results of scientific tests (e.g., DNA) must conform to rules of evidence:

> Evidence law is intended to ensure that jurors hear or see only the information that is both relevant and competent. Relevant evidence is evidence that pertains to the matter at hand that has some bearing on the trial. For example, evidence about a defendant's feelings about the murder victim might be useful in explaining why the defendant killed (or did not kill) the victim. Competent evidence is evidence that is in a form the jury is permitted to hear or see. For example, hearsay evidence is sometimes deemed incompetent because it lacks reliability. (Worrall & Hemmens, 2005, p. 24)

It is important to note that the rules of evidence are not the same as trial procedure. The order of events at a criminal trial is quite distinct from the types and forms of evidence introduced at a criminal trial—and the rules for doing so.

Once the trial is over, the judge or jury begins deliberations. Jury deliberations can proceed quickly or be drawn out, depending on the nature of the case and how convincing the defense and prosecution arguments were. Jury voting requirements vary by state and by the nature of the offense. Juries also vary in size.[6] All federal criminal cases use a 12-person jury, and federal statutes require unanimity in criminal cases tried in federal court. The situation is more complicated in the state courts. The Supreme Court has held that the Sixth Amendment does not require juries in criminal cases to be the traditional size of 12 persons. Juries cannot, however, consist of fewer than six persons (*Williams v. Florida*, 1970). Many states use smaller juries for misdemeanor cases, but only a few allow juries of fewer than 12 members for felony trials. The Supreme Court also held that guilty verdicts from 6-person juries must be unanimous, but those from 12-person juries need not be (9 votes is constitutionally permissible; *Apodaca v. Oregon*, 1972). All states except Louisiana and Oregon require unanimous verdicts in felony cases, and only Oregon permits a nonunanimous verdict in misdemeanor cases.

---

[6]For a discussion of jury size and unanimity requirements in state courts, see Bureau of Justice Statistics (2006b, Table 42).

Sentencing and Appeals

After a guilty verdict has been returned or a defendant has entered a guilty or nolo contendere plea, sentencing takes place. Sentencing usually takes place at a separate, post-trial hearing. There are several types of sentences that can be handed down. Among the most common, especially in misdemeanor cases, are fines and probation. A straight probation sentence does not entail confinement in jail or prison. Rather, the judge imposes a set of conditions agreed to by the offender, who is then released into the community. The court retains control over the offender while he or she is on probation; if the conditions of probation are violated, the judge can modify the conditions or revoke probation and sentence the offender to jail or prison.

Offenders convicted of misdemeanors or felonies also can be sentenced to jail or prison. Although there are some exceptions, offenders sentenced to jail typically serve up to 12 months. Offenders sentenced to prison can serve sentences that range from one or two years to life in prison, with or without the possibility of parole. In 2006, 73% of all felons convicted in state courts in large urban jurisdictions were sentenced to a period of confinement—40% to state prisons and 33% to local jails. The average jail sentence was 6 months and the average prison sentence was 49 months (Bureau of Justice Statistics, 2010). Among offenders convicted in federal courts in the 2006 fiscal year, 88.6% were sentenced to prison, and the average prison sentence was 51.8 months (United States Sentencing Commission, 2007, Tables 12 and 13). For some offenses, a prison sentence is not simply an option; rather, it is required. All jurisdictions in the United States now have laws that prescribe mandatory terms of incarceration for selected crimes—especially crimes involving the use of a deadly weapon and serious drug offenses—or for offenders convicted under repeat or habitual offender statutes.

Assuming an offender is convicted, and further assuming that he or she is sent to prison, an appeal may be filed. Appeals come in two varieties: automatic (also known as appeals of right) and discretionary. Automatic appeals are granted to the defendant by law. Nearly every criminal conviction carries with it the right to make one of these automatic appeals; the court to which the case is appealed must hear the case and make a ruling. Discretionary appeals can be filed on countless occasions, but it is up to the reviewing court to decide whether it wants to hear the appeal. Insofar as there are fewer appellate courts than there are trial courts, far fewer discretionary appeals are heard than are filed. When appeals are not heard, and when defendants have exhausted all appellate remedies, the U.S. Constitution (see U.S. Const., Art. I Section 9, clause 2) extends defendants the right to habeas corpus. Habeas corpus—which literally means "you have the body"—gives prisoners a means of challenging the constitutionality of their confinement.

The habeas corpus process begins when the offender petitions the U.S. Supreme Court or one of the federal district courts and asks the court to issue a **writ of habeas corpus**. Then, if the court decides to issue the writ, the petitioner is brought before the court so the constitutionality of his or her confinement can be reviewed. Of importance to note, the Constitution permits prisoners to petition the federal courts for habeas review, but that does not guarantee a hearing. Also, habeas corpus has been significantly restricted in this country, thanks in large part to the Antiterrorism and Effective Death Penalty Act (AEDPA) of 1996, which was passed after the Oklahoma City bombing of 1995. The AEDPA limits the time period in which the inmate can file an appeal to either six months or one year, depending on whether the inmate was represented by counsel for postconviction proceedings (a time limit of six months) or not (a time limit of one year). The AEDPA also restricts successive habeas corpus petitions. It states that a "claim presented in a second or successive habeas corpus application shall be dismissed" (28 U.S.C.A. Section 2244[b][1]).

Decision Making

It is one thing to examine basic court structure and procedure and to learn the roles of various courtroom actors. It is quite another to examine the reality of decision making in the criminal court system. As research conducted by social scientists and legal scholars clearly reveals, the operation of the system does not always comport with the idealized image of courts as arenas where the adversarial process plays out and where justice is blind.

The Equal Protection Clause of the Fourteenth Amendment to the Constitution states that "no state shall . . . deny to any person within its jurisdiction the equal protection of the laws." Furthermore, the Fifth and Fourteenth Amendments provide that "no person shall be . . . deprived of life, liberty, or property, without due process of law." Applied to the criminal court system, these provisions mean that similarly situated offenders should be treated the same and that all offenders should be processed similarly, regardless of the nature of the offense of which they are accused or for which they have been convicted. This suggests that every person accused of a crime gets his or her day in court and benefits—no matter who he or she is or what he or she did—from the same adversarial criminal process. In reality, the system works very differently. Neither cases nor offenders are treated equally. Sometimes this is intentional and justifiable, as when jury trials are available to some types of defendants but not to others or when the type of prosecution (vertical or horizontal) depends on the type of case being adjudicated. Other times, differential treatment of offenders and cases is unintentional (or at least less intentional) and not justifiable, as when the severity of the sentence depends on whether the offender is a man or a woman or whether the victim is white or African American. Either way, it is clear that the criminal court system does not always operate according to the "law on the books."

The Wedding Cake

A simple viewing of the evening news or reading of the local paper makes it clear that not all offenders and not all crimes are treated equally. Consider what happens when a celebrity or other high-profile offender is arrested for a serious crime. There is a lengthy jury selection process, a drawn-out trial, and extensive (and expensive) work by the attorneys on both sides. For example, when O. J. Simpson, the actor and former professional football player, was accused of killing his wife, Nicole Brown Simpson, and Ronald Goldman, the preliminary hearing lasted six days, jury selection took more than two months, and the trial itself went on for more than a year. At the opposite extreme are the millions of cases involving unknown suspects who commit minor crimes. For these cases, the system operates more like a factory "where defendants are processed like so many sausages" (Downie, 1971, p. 33). The routine case is disposed of quickly and expeditiously in an effort to make room for the next case on the assembly line. In short, the seriousness of the offense—and the person allegedly responsible—can do a great deal to shape the way a case will be handled.

In their book *The Roots of Justice*, Lawrence Friedman and Robert Percival (1981) adopted a **wedding cake metaphor** to describe the variations in the treatment of criminal offenders and their cases. They argued that there is no criminal justice "system." Rather, there are several systems layered on top of one another that function simultaneously. The big bottom layer of the wedding cake, in their view, is composed of the vast majority of criminal cases: the misdemeanors. In the middle, smaller layer, are the routine felony cases. The top layer consists of a much smaller number of especially serious crimes and crimes committed by highly visible people. Shortly after *The Roots of Justice* was published, Gottfredson and Gottfredson published *Decision Making in Criminal Justice* (1988), in which they argued that the middle layer of the wedding cake actually consists of two layers of felonies. In their view, serious crimes committed by repeat offenders and crimes against strangers fall into one layer, and other felonies fall into another.

The point of the wedding cake metaphor is not simply to illustrate that there are far more misdemeanors and not-so-serious felonies than there are celebrated cases. It also illustrates the treatment of such cases. Because there are so many misdemeanors relative to other types of crime, it is in the interest of the criminal justice system to dispose of these cases quickly and efficiently. Likewise, most felony cases are disposed of administratively and, in the words of Friedman and Percival (1981), with a "profound sense of routine" (p. 312). In contrast, the highly publicized and celebrated cases that make up the top layer of the wedding cake are handled in a way that resembles more closely the adversarial ideal.

The Courtroom Workgroup

The popular view of the criminal court system is that of an adversarial system in which the prosecutor and the defense battle it out before an impartial jury, with the judge sitting as a neutral arbitrator to ensure that each side follows the established rules. This "traditional legal metaphor" also holds that "Courts, judges and attorneys provide the setting and the personnel who simply apply the law to specific circumstances (cases) that arise" (Eisenstein et al., 1988, p. 5). This idealized version of what goes on in criminal court does not reflect the reality of the decision-making process. As Eisenstein and his colleagues noted, the traditional legal metaphor is a "poor tool to employ in trying to understand courts" (p. 7).

A more realistic view of the criminal court system is that it is a system in which the members of the **courtroom workgroup** or the courthouse community cooperate to process cases as expeditiously as possible. According to this view, judges, prosecutors, and defense attorneys work together, day after day, to move cases through the court system quickly and efficiently. Walker (2001) described the realities of the courtroom workgroup in this way:

> Working together every day, members of the courtroom work group reach a general consensus about how different kinds of cases should be handled. This involves shared understanding about how much cases are "worth." There are "heavy" cases (that is, serious violent crimes) and "garbage" cases (relatively minor theft). This valuation allows them to move cases along quickly. Conflict between prosecution and defense is the exception rather than the rule. Although in theory we have an *adversarial* process, in which truth is to be determined through conflict between prosecution and defense, the reality is that an *administrative* system is in effect, with a high degree of consensus and cooperation. (p. 53)

As Walker (2001) noted, the system is characterized by consensus and cooperation rather than conflict. This ensures that there will be a measure of predictability about outcomes as each case is shepherded through the system. If one asked a judge, a prosecutor, and a defense attorney from the same courthouse to predict what would happen to a defendant with a particular criminal history and who allegedly committed a particular offense, all of them would generally agree about the outcome of the case. There would be consensus about whether the case would result in a plea bargain or a trial and about the appropriate sentence. The point is that there is a degree of predictability to the criminal court process. There *has to be*. If the outcome of every case were totally unpredictable—if prosecutors, defense attorneys, and judges could not work together to process the heavy caseloads found in most large jurisdictions—the wheels of justice would grind to a halt.

Summary

This introduction to the criminal court system has provided a basic overview of the structure and organization of federal and state courts and the processing of criminal cases. There are many issues that we are unable to cover in this chapter and others that we introduced only briefly. For example, we did not describe sentencing policies and practices or plea bargaining in any detail, and we did not discuss the emergence of problem-solving courts, therapeutic jurisprudence, and restorative justice. Similarly, we did not examine such things as habeas corpus reform, jury decision making, or victim participation in the criminal process. These and other topics are discussed in subsequent sections of the book.

Overview of the Book

Our purpose in writing this book is to provide an alternative to the typical introductory criminal courts textbook. This book is an alternative in the sense that it covers all of the relevant subject matter in the section introductions but also includes carefully selected readings that highlight the issues with which court researchers are currently grappling. Each section introduction is followed by a set of edited readings; some of the technical material has been removed, as have most of the explanatory footnotes. This book, in other words, is a hybrid; it combines the best features of a courts textbook and a courts reader into a single resource.

This book is organized into nine sections, including this introductory section, which provides an overview of the types of courts and examines their day-to-day operation. The second section discusses the emergence of the modern court system and focuses on the role of the courts in the criminal justice system. The third section discusses the roles played by prosecutors and defense attorneys, and in Section IV the focus shifts to judges and jurors. Sections V and VI build on the discussion of the decision-making process presented in this chapter and examine issues such as charging, plea bargaining, jury selection, the operation of the courtroom workgroup, and local legal culture. Section VII covers important sentencing issues, including factors that affect sentencing and the relative effectiveness of certain sentencing strategies. Section VIII takes readers beyond sentencing and conviction by looking at both appellate and habeas corpus issues. Finally, Section IX looks at specialized courts, particularly drug courts and domestic violence courts. It also includes recent studies on therapeutic jurisprudence and restorative justice practices.

KEY TERMS

Adjudication	Judiciary Act of 1789	Public defenders
Bench trial	Jurisdiction	Rule of four
Court of Appeals Act of 1891	Jury panel	Venire
Courtroom workgroup	Jury pool	Voir dire
Discovery	Magistrate judges	Wedding cake metaphor
Dual court system	Merit system	Writ of certiorari
En banc	Plea bargaining	Writ of habeas corpus
Exclusionary rule	Preliminary hearing	
Judge	Prosecutors	

DISCUSSION QUESTIONS

1. Consider the court of last resort (i.e., supreme court or superior court) in your state. What types of jurisdiction does this court have?

2. How does the structure of the federal court system reflect debate over the power of the federal government vis-à-vis the power of the states?

3. What types of cases do the federal courts (trial and appellate) hear? What determines whether a criminal case will be tried in state or federal court?

4. Defense attorneys who lose in court often say, "We are going to take this case all the way to the U.S. Supreme Court." Is this a realistic option? Why or why not?

5. Why is it difficult to describe the structure of the state court system?

6. Who are the members of the courtroom workgroup? What role does each member play in the criminal court system?

7. What is the difference between horizontal and vertical prosecution? What types of cases would be most likely to be prosecuted vertically?

8. How has the Supreme Court expanded the defendant's right to counsel in a criminal case?

9. How can judges be removed from office? Are these procedures an effective check on judicial behavior? Why or why not?

10. Tom Smith has been arrested for armed robbery, a felony offense. Outline the steps his case will follow as it proceeds through the state court system. Where on the "criminal justice wedding cake" would you find his case?

WEB RESOURCES

Federal Courts and What They Do: http://www.fjc.gov/public/pdf.nsf/lookup/FCtsWhat.pdf/$file/FCtsWhat.pdf

Federal Judicial Center: http://www.fjc.gov

Statistics on Criminal Cases Filed & Outcomes—Sourcebook of Criminal Justice Statistics Online: http://www.albany.edu/sourcebook

United States Sentencing Commission: http://www.ussc.gov

National Center for State Courts: http://www.ncsconline.org

Administrative Office of the U.S. Courts: http://www.uscourts.gov

SECTION

II

Historical and Contemporary Perspectives on Courts

⊠ Conflict: The Wellspring of the Modern Court

The emergence of formal courts closely paralleled the emergence of formal legal systems. Both arose out of a need for conflict resolution. In early preindustrial societies, conflicts were often settled by the parties involved or resolved by someone in a position of leadership, such as a tribal leader. As early societies grew and became more complex, conflict became more frequent, more complicated, and less easily resolved using informal methods of settling disputes. Legal codes and courts for enforcing them were developed to resolve the conflicts that inevitably arise in civilized societies. Conflict, in other words, is the wellspring of the modern court system (Shapiro, 1981).

Western legal traditions, including their mechanisms for conflict resolution, can be traced to the **Code of Hammurabi**, the first known written legal code. Dating back to 1760 BCE in ancient Mesopotamia, the code delineated crimes and their punishments and also enumerated settlements for common disputes.

Early Roman law also shaped the first formal legal systems, including those that emerged in western Europe. The Norman conquest of 1066, which brought feudal law to the British Isles, led to the establishment of new forms of government, including courts of law. Officials, who might be seen as analogous to modern judges, cooperated with the king to settle disputes and to decide whether residents of the realm were guilty of offenses against the state. In making these decisions, they applied the "common custom of the realm rather than the parochial traditions of a particular shire or village" (Murphy, Pritchett, Epstein, & Knight, 2006, p. 6). Thus was born English **common law**.

By the time of Henry II (1154–1189), a body of law had been developed, and decisions of the courts were written down and circulated. This resulted in a more unified system of law, one that ensured a measure of predictability from one court to the next. This common law system was well developed in England by the 13th century and was eventually transplanted, in a similar form, to the American colonies. To this day, our criminal justice system's common law origins are apparent, particularly in the courts.

Why Government Courts?

When people speak of "courts" today, they are usually referring to government-sanctioned, government-run courts. Historically, however, there have been other types of courts. In the Middle Ages, **ecclesiastical courts**, which were found in many parts of Europe and were also called **Courts Christian**, exercised jurisdiction over religious matters and sometimes other matters as well (Jason, 1997). These courts dealt with matters of canon law, or the religious laws put forth by the dominant church, most notably the Roman Catholic Church. In 1072, however, King William I of England initiated a writ that changed the legal landscape of the time. He said that "God's business was to be separated from Caesar's, with the appropriate renders being made in different courts" (Jason, 1997). Legal scholars claim that this writ eventually dealt a blow to the authority of the ecclesiastical courts.

Although the kings' authority in feudal England was considered absolute, it was limited by the fact that the kings depended on those beneath them, the lords, for food, and soldiers—and money. Accordingly, the lords (and lesser lords) of the manor settled their own disputes. So-called manor courts were created for this purpose. They were heavily decentralized courts that settled various legal matters and disputes without the king's involvement. As the Church began to lose authority over matters that it had once adjudicated, and as feudal systems of government were replaced with democratic forms, ecclesiastical and manor courts gave way to more centralized, government-run courts. Thus, the emergence of the courts one sees today closely parallels the emergence of democratic governance itself (Shapiro, 1981, p. 71).

Not all methods of settling disputes that exist today involve government-run courts. Methods of informal dispute resolution, such as mediation and arbitration, are common, especially in civil matters. **Mediation** involves bringing a neutral third party and the parties to a dispute together to resolve the matter. A couple seeking a divorce, for example, might use mediation to work out a child custody agreement, or two neighbors might mediate a disagreement over a tree owned by one neighbor that is encroaching on the property of the other neighbor. The mediator works with the parties to the dispute to reach a mutually agreeable solution, but the mediator does not have any authority to render a decision. In contrast, **binding arbitration** requires that the parties to the dispute agree to abide by the neutral party's decision, which cannot be appealed. Arbitration is, in essence, a privately conducted trial. Many contract disputes between businesses and consumers must be settled using binding arbitration. Most real estate contracts, for instance, require the buyer and seller to pursue arbitration before litigation. However, neither mediation nor arbitration can be used to dispose of criminal matters.

⬚ How Courts Make Law

It is often said that our political system is a government of laws, not men. This means that individuals in our system are governed by laws and not by the whims of those in power; it also means that the law applies to everyone—even to those in power—and that no one is above the law. Related to this is the notion that the law is "a set of rules transcending time, geography, and the circumstances surrounding specific cases" (Eisenstein et al., 1988, p. 5). According to this line of reasoning, judges simply apply the law in a rigid and mechanistic way to the specific cases that arise. Stated another way, judges "find" the applicable law and apply it to the case at hand.

The problem with this traditional view of law and the role of courts is that much of "the law" is broad and ambiguous. Thus, the judges, who are charged with enforcing the law, must first interpret it. They must decide what the law means and whether it is applicable in the given situation. Consider, for instance, a legislatively enacted statute that prohibits disturbing the peace, which is defined as "willfully disrupting the peace and security of the community." This statute, which does not define *willful* or offer examples of conduct that would "disrupt the peace and security," obviously leaves room for interpretation. Constitutional provisions, which are another source of law, have similar limitations. Take, for instance, the Fourth Amendment to the U.S. Constitution. It protects against unreasonable searches and seizures, but it does not define *unreasonable*. Because of these inherent ambiguities in criminal statutes, in state and federal constitutions, and in other sources of law, judges are called on to interpret the law.

Stare Decisis and Precedent

When interpreting the law and deciding whether it is applicable in a given situation, judges typically follow the principle of *stare decisis*, a Latin term that means "let the decision stand." If the law is ambiguous and the same issue has come up before, it makes sense to look to past decisions—that is, to **precedent**—to see how the matter has been resolved previously. In other words, when deciding whether searches are unreasonable under the Fourth Amendment, it makes sense for judges to examine past decisions regarding the issue. *Stare decisis* is thus the judicial practice of looking to the past for pertinent decisions and deferring to them. As Benjamin Cardozo (2005), who was a Supreme Court justice from 1932 to 1939, put it, the first thing a judge does

> is to compare the case before him with the precedents, whether stored in his mind or hidden in books . . . in a system so highly developed as our own, precedents have so covered the ground that they fix the point of departure from which the labor of the judge begins. (p. 32)

Although the concepts of precedent and *stare decisis* are fundamental to understanding the way courts, especially appellate courts, work today, they provide a somewhat misleading explanation of the work courts do. For example, precedent is binding only on those courts within the jurisdiction of the court issuing the opinion. Decisions of the U.S. Supreme Court are binding on all courts, but decisions handed down by lower federal courts and by state supreme courts are binding only on the courts within their jurisdiction. Moreover, when judges look to the past and can find no guiding precedent among the cases decided by other courts in their jurisdiction, they must decide the case according to their interpretation of legal principles. Quoting once again former Supreme Court Justice Benjamin Cardozo (2005), "It is when . . . there is no decisive precedent that the serious business of the judge begins. He must then fashion Law for the litigants before him" (p. 32).

There also are situations in which judges do not follow precedent, either because they believe that the facts in the case at hand distinguish it from cases decided previously or because they believe that the precedent, though once valid, should be overruled. In the first instance, the judge rules that facts in the case being decided are sufficiently different from those found in previous cases that the legal principles announced in these cases do not apply. In *Gideon v. Wainwright* (1963), for example, the United States Supreme Court ruled that Clarence Gideon, an indigent defendant who was charged with a felony in a Florida state court, should have been provided with an attorney to assist him with his defense. According to the Court, "In our adversary system of criminal justice, any person haled into court, who is too poor to hire a lawyer, cannot be assured a fair trial unless counsel is provided for him." Sixteen years later, however, the Court ruled in the case of *Scott v. Illinois* (1979) that an indigent defendant who was sentenced only to pay a fine was not entitled to an attorney. The Court's earlier ruling that the right to a fair trial required the appointment of counsel for "*any person* haled into court" notwithstanding, in this case the Court stated that the Constitution required only "that no indigent defendant be sentenced to a term of imprisonment unless the state has afforded him the right to assistance of appointed counsel in his defense." What distinguished the two cases, in other words, was the fact that Gideon was sentenced to prison, whereas Scott was not.

Occasionally, judges decide that the precedent is no longer valid and should not be followed. Judges can handle this in two ways. They can simply ignore the earlier case and decide the case at hand as if there were no binding precedent, or they can overrule the earlier case. Often the process of overruling a precedent is gradual. The court increasingly finds more circumstances that distinguish new cases from the earlier case, until it becomes obvious that the precedent has outlived its usefulness. Former Supreme Court Justice William O. Douglas (1974) argued that this gradual erosion of precedent "breeds uncertainty" because "years of litigation may be needed to rid the law of mischievous decisions which should have fallen with the first of the series to be overruled" (p. 404).

According to Justice Douglas, then, it makes more sense for the court to overrule the outdated precedent as soon as it is clear that it has to go. The Supreme Court has done so on a number of occasions. In *Taylor v. Louisiana* (1975), for example, the Supreme Court considered a Louisiana law that gave women a blanket exemption from jury service; women who wanted to serve were required to ask that their names be placed on the lists from which jurors were chosen. The result was that few women volunteered, and most defendants, including Billy Taylor, were tried by all-male juries. In *Taylor*, which was decided in 1975, the Supreme Court struck down the Louisiana law and overruled a 1961 decision, *Hoyt v. Florida* (1961), upholding a nearly identical Florida law. In the *Hoyt* case, the Court ruled that women "are the center of home and family life" and therefore should be allowed to decide for themselves whether jury service was an unreasonable burden. According to the Court's decision in the *Hoyt* case, it is not "constitutionally impermissible for a State, acting in pursuit of the general welfare, to conclude that a woman should be relieved from the civic duty of jury service unless she herself determines that such service is consistent with her own special responsibilities." Fourteen years later, the Court changed its mind, ruling that "if it was ever the case that women were unqualified to sit on juries or were so situated that none of them should be required to perform jury service, that time has long since passed." Clearly, the Court's interpretation of the requirement that the jury pool must be drawn from a random cross-section of the population, as well as its view of the role of women, had changed. (See Table 2.1 for examples of other instances in which the Supreme Court overruled its own decisions.)

That statutes and constitutional provisions are ambiguous and that judges cannot always look to precedent for guidance in specific cases, then, means that judges are frequently called on to make law. Judges, in other words, do not simply "find the law." As the *Hoyt* (1961) and *Taylor* (1975) cases reveal, when interpreting the law judges often must choose between competing social, economic, and political values.

Table 2.1 Examples of Supreme Court Decisions Overruled by Subsequent Decisions

Original Cases	Overruling Subsequent Cases
Plessy v. Ferguson (1896) Upheld the constitutionality of racial segregation in public accommodations (i.e., railroad cars) under the "separate but equal" doctrine.	*Brown v. Board of Education* (1954) Struck down a Kansas law that established racially segregated public schools and stated that the doctrine of separate but equal has no place in education: "separate educational facilities are inherently unequal."
Bowers v. Hardwick (1986) Upheld the constitutionality of a Georgia sodomy law; the right to privacy found in the Fourteenth Amendment does not extend to this type of sexual conduct.	*Lawrence v. Texas* (2003) Struck down a Texas sodomy law; held that intimate consensual sexual conduct was protected by the Fourteenth Amendment.
Booth v. Maryland (1987) Eighth Amendment bars the use of victim-impact statements during penalty phase of a capital case; information provided in them is not relevant to the blameworthiness of the defendant. *South Carolina v. Gathers* (1989) Eighth Amendment precludes prosecutors from introducing evidence of the victim's character during the penalty phase of a capital case.	*Payne v. Tennessee* (1991) The Eighth Amendment does not bar the admission of victim-impact evidence or prosecutorial argument regarding the victim's character during the penalty phase of a capital trial: "a State may legitimately conclude that evidence about the victim and about the impact of the murder on the victim's family is relevant to the jury's decision as to whether or not the death penalty should be imposed."
Arkansas v. Sanders (1979) A police search of personal luggage taken from a lawfully detained vehicle requires a warrant under the Fourth Amendment.	*California v. Acevedo* (1991) Police may open a container in a vehicle without a warrant if they have probable cause to believe that it holds contraband or evidence.

The Role of the Courts in Criminal Justice

It is misleading to view criminal courts as institutions isolated from the rest of the criminal justice system. Courts, which clearly are integral to the administration of justice, are but one part of the larger criminal justice system. However, there are two important and unique roles the courts play in the criminal justice system. The first, and most common, is adjudication of criminal offenses. The second is **oversight**.

Adjudication

The primary role played by the courts is to adjudicate criminal offenses—to process defendants who have been arrested by the police and formally charged with criminal offenses. Prosecutors decide who should be charged and then, provided a plea agreement does not circumvent trial, the defendant is brought to court. The state presents its case, and so does the defense. The judge decides matters of law and the judge or jury decides whether the defendant should be held accountable for the crime in question. If the defendant is convicted, the judge also imposes a sentence.

Both law enforcement and corrections officials play supporting roles in the adjudication of criminal offenses. The police determine who will be brought to court, and corrections officials make postsentencing decisions that affect offenders' punishment. However, "the *official* labeling of someone as a convicted criminal, and the determination of legitimate punishment can be done only by a court" (Eisenstein et al., 1988, p. 9). This adjudication function is most prevalent in limited and general jurisdiction courts at the state level and in U.S. District Courts at the federal level. Moreover, adjudication is *the* most common court function. That is because there are many more trial courts than appellate courts and many more criminal defendants that must be processed than appeals that are filed.

Oversight

Courts, particularly the appellate courts, provide oversight, not just over the lower courts but over the criminal justice system in general. First, when cases are appealed to a higher level, the appellate court decides whether proper procedure was followed at the lower level. The appellate court may be asked to decide whether the procedures used to select the jury were appropriate, whether the defendant was denied effective assistance of counsel, or whether the trial court judge should have moved the case to another jurisdiction because of prejudicial pretrial publicity. The appellate decision may come months, or even years, after the trial that led to the appeal, but the very ability of the appellate court to influence what can happen or should have happened at the lower level is the essence of oversight.

Appellate courts also oversee the actions of other criminal justice officials. They decide whether the behavior of police, prosecutors, defense attorneys, and corrections officials comports with or violates laws and constitutional provisions. Consider, for instance, the Supreme Court's landmark 1985 decision in *Tennessee v. Garner*. The Court ruled that police officers cannot use deadly force to apprehend unarmed fleeing felons unless use of deadly force is necessary to prevent the suspect's escape *and* "the officer has probable cause to believe that the suspect poses a significant threat of death or serious physical injury to the officer or others." The Court held that the Tennessee statute that permitted officers to use "all the necessary means to effect the arrest" of a fleeing suspect was unconstitutional. Because of the Supreme Court's far-reaching jurisdiction, its decision had implications for police officers across the nation. That the appellate courts—and particularly the Supreme Court—can tell criminal justice officials how to behave (so as to protect people's constitutional rights) is an important element of their oversight function.

⬚ Striking a Difficult Balance

Every matter of controversy in criminal justice has at its core two—at least two—competing sets of ideas. With regard to courts, every decision a judge makes, either at the trial or appellate level, tends to pit two contradictory sets of values against each other. Consider a criminal trial. The prosecutor presents a case that represents the interests of the state, one that is designed to prove that the defendant is guilty and should be held accountable for the crime with which he or she is charged. In contrast, the defense attorney presents a case in the interest of his or her client. The defense attorney attempts to raise doubt about the defendant's guilt and insists that the legal procedures designed to protect the defendant's rights be followed. The competing sets of values that each of these actors brings to the table—and that are found at all other stages of the criminal justice process as well—have been described by Herbert Packer (1968) as the crime control and due process perspectives.

Packer's (1968) models of the criminal process are just that—models, and not depictions of reality. He saw the models as polarities—as the two ends of a continuum along which the actual operation of the criminal justice system falls. He also cautioned against depicting one model as the way things work and the other as the way things ought to work. In his words, the two models "represent an attempt to abstract two separate value systems that compete for priority in the operation of the criminal process" (p. 153). The value systems that "compete for priority" are regulating criminal conduct and preventing crime, which the crime control model views as the most important function of the criminal process, and protecting the rights of individuals, which the due process model emphasizes.

In the sections that follow, we describe the crime control and due process models in detail, focusing on their differences. These differences are summarized in Table 2.2.

Table 2.2   Packer's Crime Control and Due Process Models

Issue	Crime Control Model	Due Process Model
View of criminal justice system	Assembly line	Obstacle course
Goal of criminal justice system	Controlling crime	Protecting rights of defendants
Values emphasized	Efficiency, speed, and finality	Reliability
Process of adjudication	Informal screening by police and prosecutor	Formal, adversarial procedures
Focus	Factual guilt	Legal guilt

The Crime Control Model

As its name suggests, the **crime control model** (Packer, 1968, pp. 158–163) views the suppression of criminal conduct—that is, controlling crime—as the most important function of the criminal justice system. The primary function of the system is to control crime by apprehending, convicting, and punishing those who violate the law. Failure to control crime, according to this perspective, leads to a breakdown in public order. If citizens believe that laws are not being enforced, they will have fewer incentives to obey the law, which will lead to an increase in crime and to a greater risk of victimization among law-abiding citizens. As Packer noted, failure to control crime eventually leads "to the disappearance of an important condition of human freedom" (p. 158).

According to the crime control model, *efficiency* is the key to the effective operation of the criminal process. A high proportion of offenders whose offenses become known must be apprehended, tried, convicted, and sentenced. Moreover, this must be accomplished in a system where the crime rate is high and resources for dealing with crime are limited. Thus, the model emphasizes *speed*, which depends on informality and uniformity, and *finality*, which means that there should be few opportunities for challenging outcomes. The requirement of informality means that cases should be screened by police and prosecutors to determine the facts and to separate the probably innocent from the probably guilty; judicial fact finding, which is more time-consuming and thus less efficient, should be the exception rather than the norm. *Uniformity* means that officials should follow routine procedures in most cases. As Packer (1968) put it, "The process must not be cluttered up with ceremonious rituals that do not advance the progress of the case" (p. 159).

The metaphor that Packer (1968) used to describe the operation of the criminal process under the crime control model is that of an assembly line:

> an assembly-line conveyor belt down which moves an endless stream of cases, never stopping, carrying the cases to workers . . . who perform on each case as it comes by the same small but essential operation that brings it one step closer to being a finished product . . . a closed file. (p. 159)

As this suggests, the goal is to move cases through the justice process as swiftly as possible. Suspects who are "probably innocent" are screened out early in the process by police and prosecutors; those who are "probably guilty" are moved quickly and perfunctorily through the remaining stages in the process and are convicted, usually by a plea of guilty, as expeditiously as possible. Thus, the system achieves the goal of controlling crime by separating the innocent from the guilty early in the process, by extracting early guilty pleas from those who are not screened out by police and prosecutors, and by avoiding trials.

A key to the operation of the crime control model is the **presumption of guilt**, which rests on a belief in the reliability of the screening process operated by police and prosecutors. That is, defendants who are not screened out early in the process by police and prosecutors are probably guilty and therefore can be passed quickly through the remaining stages in the process. It is important to point out that the presumption of guilt, which is descriptive and factual, is not the opposite of the presumption of innocence, which is normative and legal. The presumption of guilt is simply a prediction of outcome: Those not screened out early in the process are probably guilty and more than likely will plead guilty or be found guilty at trial. The **presumption of innocence**, on the other hand, means that until the defendant has been adjudicated guilty, he is "to be treated, for reasons that have nothing whatever to do with the probable outcome of the case, as if his guilt is an open question" (Packer, 1968, p. 161).

In summary, the crime control model views the apprehension and conviction of criminals as the most important function of the criminal justice system. It characterizes the criminal process as an assembly line that moves cases forward in a uniform and predictable way. The model places great faith in the reliability of fact finding by police and prosecutors. It suggests that the process is operating with maximum efficiency if cases involving the probably innocent are screened out early by police and prosecutors and if the rest of the cases, which involve defendants who are presumed to be guilty, are disposed of as quickly as possible, preferably with guilty pleas.

The Due Process Model

Whereas the crime control model views the criminal process as an assembly line, the **due process model** sees the process as an obstacle course. Each stage in the process, according to Packer (1968, pp. 163–172), is designed not to move cases forward as expeditiously as possible but rather to throw up hurdles to carrying the case from one stage to the next. There are other differences as well. Where the crime control model stresses efficiency, the due process model stresses reliability and minimization of the potential for mistakes. And where the crime control model places great faith in the ability of police and prosecutors to separate the probably innocent from the probably guilty, the due process model contends that informal, nonadjudicatory fact finding carries with it a strong likelihood of error.

It is important to point out that the values underlying the due process model are not the opposite of those found in the crime control model. Like the crime control model, the due process model acknowledges the importance of controlling crime. However, the due process model rejects the premise that screening of cases by police and prosecutors is reliable. More to the point, the due process model stresses the likelihood of error in these informal screening processes. According to Packer (1968):

> People are notoriously poor observers of disturbing events … confessions and admissions by persons in police custody may be induced by physical or psychological coercion so that the police end up hearing what the suspect thinks they want to hear rather than the truth; witnesses may be animated by a bias or interest that no one would trouble to discover except one specially charged with protecting the interests of the accused (as the police are not). (p. 163)

Because of the strong possibility of mistakes in the early stages of the process, the due process model calls for fact-finding procedures that are formal, adjudicative, and adversarial. The case against the accused, in other words, should be "publicly heard by an impartial tribunal" and "evaluated only after the accused has had a full opportunity to discredit the case against him" (Packer, 1968, p. 164). The model also rejects the notion of finality; rather, there should constant scrutiny of outcomes to ensure that mistakes have not been made.

There also are sharp differences between the two models in the degree to which mistakes can be tolerated. That is, there are differences in the weight given to reliability (a strong probability that factual guilt has been accurately determined) and efficiency (expeditious handling of the large number of cases that the system takes in). The crime control model is willing to sacrifice some reliability in pursuit of efficiency. It tolerates mistakes up to the level at which they interfere with the goal of preventing crime; if too many guilty people go free or if there is a general view that the system is not reliable, crime might increase rather than decrease. The due process model rejects this view, arguing that mistakes must be prevented and eliminated. To the extent that efficiency requires shortcuts that reduce the reliability of outcomes, efficiency must be sacrificed.

To ensure a high degree of reliability in the process, the due process model requires that both factual guilt and legal guilt be proved. **Factual guilt** simply means that the evidence shows that there is a high probability that the defendant committed the crime of which he or she is accused. **Legal guilt**, on the other hand, refers to the process by which determinations of guilt are made. Defendants are not to be deemed guilty unless all of the mandated procedures and rules designed to protect the rights of the accused have been followed. A defendant charged with an assault that was witnessed by a number of bystanders who are willing to testify against the defendant may well be factually guilty of assault. His legal guilt at the time of charging, on the other hand, is an open question. If the determination of factual guilt is not made in a procedurally correct way, the defendant is not legally guilty and cannot be held accountable for the crime with which he or she is charged.

The due process model, then, resembles an obstacle course in which cases must navigate hurdles set up to ensure that determinations of guilt are reliable. The key to the model is formal, adjudicative, and adversarial fact-finding procedures with constant scrutiny of outcomes to ensure that mistakes have not been made. Defendants are presumed to be innocent until proven guilty, legally as well as factually.

The Ongoing Battle

In an ideal world, judges and other criminal justice officials balance due process and crime control ideals. They strive for efficiency, while at the same time insisting on reliability. In the real world, this is probably not possible; many decisions tip in one direction or another. High caseloads, limited resources, and concerns about protecting the community may lead to shortcuts that threaten reliability or to decisions that chip away at the procedural regulations that protect the rights of criminal defendants. Similarly, concerns about restraining the power of criminal justice officials may lead to decisions that make it more difficult for those enforcing the criminal process to apprehend and convict those who commit crimes.

A good example of an issue where use of the crime control and due process models leads to different conclusions is plea bargaining. According to the crime control model, the criminal process is operating most efficiently when defendants who are not screened out by police and prosecutors plead guilty at the earliest possible moment. The criminal process breaks down if too many defendants insist on taking their cases to trial. The crime control model thus sees nothing wrong with allowing prosecutors to reduce charges or drop counts in exchange for guilty pleas or permitting judges to make it clear to defendants that those who plead guilty will be treated more leniently than those who insist on a trial. Although plea bargaining may result in guilty pleas by those who are innocent, this type of mistake is likely to be rare because those who have survived the screening process are in all probability guilty. Disposing of a large portion of cases as quickly as possible via guilty pleas is, according to this model, the only feasible means of achieving the goal of crime control.

It is no surprise that use of the due process model leads to a different conclusion. According to this model, guilty pleas, which effectively preclude any oversight of the early, informal stages of the process, should be discouraged. The due process model values reliability and contends that mistakes are likely early in the process; because of this, guilty pleas that occur soon after the prosecutor makes a decision to charge have a high probability of producing unreliable factual determinations of guilt. In addition, the model does not allow prosecutors or judges to promise defendants leniency in return for a guilty plea. Defendants, no matter how overwhelming the evidence, have the right to have the charges against them tried using the procedures required by law; they should not be coerced to enter a guilty plea or punished for exercising their constitutionally protected rights. Moreover, before accepting a guilty plea, the judge adjudicating the case should be required to both establish the defendant's factual guilt and ensure that the process that brought the defendant into court has been free of mistakes. According to the due process model, it is only by following these rules that reliability of outcomes can be guaranteed and mistakes minimized.

The Juvenile Court

Our discussion of courts thus far has been largely limited to criminal courts that adjudicate adult offenders. We have not paid much attention to juvenile offenders or the courts they come before. Juvenile courts, at least historically, have departed significantly in both their composition and operation from adult courts. Indeed, the whole juvenile justice system, which is focused on the rehabilitation of young offenders, looks quite different from the adult system, which is more concerned about punishment.

The original guiding principle of the juvenile justice system was ***parens patriae***,[1] a medieval doctrine that permitted the state to take away the rights of the natural parent and to act as the parent or guardian of a child if his or her welfare were at risk. Juvenile courts, then, were charged with "taking over" when parents could not control their children's behavior. As Peter Greenwood (2002) put it, "the new court represented one aspect of a broad progressive movement to accommodate urban institutions to an increasingly industrial-immigrant population, and to incorporate recent discoveries in the behavioral, social, and medical sciences into the rearing of children" (p. 81).

---

[1] A Latin phrase meaning "father of the country," it refers to the government's right and obligation to act on behalf of a child (or a person who is mentally ill).

The philosophy of the juvenile justice system, including the juvenile court, rests on the notion that young offenders have a good chance of being rehabilitated and therefore should be treated differently than adult offenders. The juvenile justice system reflects this thinking in a number of ways. First, there are differences in the procedures used to process adult and juvenile offenders. The juvenile justice system is more discretionary and less formal than the adult system. Juvenile court judges often wear street clothes instead of traditional black robes, and during court proceedings they may engage youthful offenders in conversations designed to shed light on the forces that motivated their crimes. In an effort to protect the privacy of juveniles, juvenile court proceedings are less likely than adult proceedings to be open to the public. Following adjudication, the overwhelming majority of youth offenders are placed on probation (Stahl, 2003). Those who are placed in confinement are sent to juvenile detention facilities that often have less ominous names than adult prisons (e.g., "youth camps"), consistent with the spirit of rehabilitation. At the same time, though, juveniles have historically enjoyed fewer constitutional protections than adults.

The increase in juvenile crime during the 1980s and early 1990s, coupled with highly publicized cases of very young children accused of murder and other violent crimes, prompted a number of states to alter procedures for handling certain types of juvenile offenders. In 1995, for example, Illinois lowered the age of admission to prison from 13 to 10 years. This change was enacted after two boys, ages 10 and 11 years old, dropped a 5-year-old boy out of a 14th-floor window of a Chicago public housing development. In 1996, a juvenile court judge ordered that both boys, who were then 12 and 13 years old, be sent to a high-security juvenile penitentiary; her decision made the 12-year-old the nation's youngest inmate at a high-security prison ("Chicago Boy," 1996).

Other states responded to the increase in serious juvenile crime by either lowering the age when children can be transferred from juvenile court to (adult) criminal court or expanding the list of offenses for which juveniles can be waived to criminal court (or both). A report by the United States General Accounting Office (1995, p. 2) indicated that between 1978 and 1995, 44 states passed new laws regarding the **waiver of juveniles to adult court**; in 24 of these states, the new laws increased the population of juveniles that potentially could be sent to criminal court. California, for example, changed the age at which juveniles could be waived to criminal court from 16 to 14 years (for specified offenses); Missouri reduced the age at which children could be certified to stand trial as adults from 14 to 12 years.

By 2004, there were 15 states with mandatory waiver in cases that met certain age, offense, or other criteria, and 15 states with a rebuttable presumption in favor of waiver in certain kinds of cases. Currently, all but four states give juvenile court judges the power to waive jurisdiction over juvenile cases that meet certain criteria—generally, a minimum age, a specified type or level of offense, or a sufficiently serious record of prior delinquency (National Center for Juvenile Justice, 2004b). Fifteen states have direct file waiver provisions, which allow the prosecutor to file certain types of juvenile cases directly in criminal court.

A report by the National Center for Juvenile Justice (2004a, p. 34) noted that the number of delinquency cases waived to criminal court increased by 70% from 1985 to 1994 but declined by 54% between 1994 and 2000. (The report attributed the decline in the number of cases waived to criminal court in part to statutory changes that excluded certain cases from juvenile court or allowed prosecutors to file serious cases directly in criminal court.) During most of this time period, the waiver rate was highest for person offenses; from 1989 to 1992, the rate was higher for drug offenses than for person offenses. Not surprisingly, cases involving older youth were more likely than those involving youths 15 and younger to be waived, and cases involving males were substantially more likely than those involving females to be waived (National Center for Juvenile Justice, 2004a, p. 36).

Decisions to transfer juveniles to adult criminal courts are important because of the sentencing consequences of being convicted in criminal, rather than juvenile, court. Although there is some evidence that transferred youth are treated more leniently in criminal court than they would have been in juvenile court (Office of Juvenile Justice and Delinquency Prevention, 1982)—in large part because they appear in criminal court at a younger age and with shorter criminal histories than other offenders—most studies reveal just the opposite. One study, for example, compared juvenile and criminal court outcomes for 15- and 16-year-old felony offenders in New York (where they were excluded from juvenile court) and New Jersey (where they were not; Fagan, 1991). The results of the study revealed that youth processed in criminal courts were twice as likely as those processed in juvenile courts to be incarcerated.

The juvenile court clearly plays an important role in the criminal justice system. Judges in these courts, which operate according to the doctrine of *parens patriae*, focus more on the juvenile offender's potential for rehabilitation than on his or her need for punishment. Increases in serious juvenile crime during the 1980s and 1990s, however, led many jurisdictions to implement more punitive options, including waiver to adult court, for youthful offenders. These changes, in turn, have led a number of scholars to raise questions about the future of the juvenile court.

 ## Summary: Historical and Contemporary Perspectives on Courts

The origins of the American criminal court system can be traced back hundreds of years to early Roman law and to English common law. Courts developed to resolve conflict and settle disputes, to provide oversight of other governmental agencies and officials, and to ensure a measure of predictability in the law. This is not to say, however, that courts—and the judges who serve them—simply apply the law in a mechanistic way to cases and conflicts that arise. The law is ambiguous and dynamic, which means that judges are called on to interpret the law. This lends a degree of unpredictability to the law. Although most judges adhere to the principle of *stare decisis* most of the time, precedents are overruled and laws and procedures are changed. The work of the courts is also affected by tension between the belief that courts should control crime by efficiently and expeditiously processing those who violate the law and the expectation that courts will ensure that the rights of criminal defendants are protected. As we discuss in more detail in Sections III and IV, these complexities, coupled with the discretion inherent in the criminal justice system, complicate the fact-finding process.

KEY TERMS

Binding arbitration	Ecclesiastical courts	Precedent
Code of Hammurabi	Factual guilt	Presumption of guilt
Common law	Legal guilt	Presumption of innocence
Courts Christian	Mediation	*Stare decisis*
Crime control model	Oversight	Waiver of juveniles to adult court
Due process model	*Parens patriae*	

DISCUSSION QUESTIONS

1. In what sense is conflict the "wellspring of the modern court"? Why did conflict among citizens lead to the development of the institutions we call courts?

2. Why is it important that judges generally follow the principle of *stare decisis*? Why is it important that they have the option of discarding precedent?

3. What are the essential differences between the crime control model and the due process model?

4. How would advocates of the due process and crime control models evaluate the exclusionary rule, which precludes the admission of evidence gained by illegal means?

5. How does the role of the juvenile court differ from that of the adult court?

WEB RESOURCES

Cornell University Law School, Supreme Court Collection: http://www.law.cornell.edu/supct/index.html

Federal Judicial Center: http://www.fjc.gov

National Center for State Courts: http://www.nscsonline.org/

National Center for Juvenile Justice: http://www/ncjj.org/

How to Read a Research Article

As you travel through your criminal justice/criminology studies, you will soon learn that some of the best-known or emerging explanations of crime and criminal behavior come from research articles in academic journals. This book includes research articles throughout its sections, but you may be asking yourself, "How do I read a research article?" We hope to answer this question with a quick summary of the key elements of a research article, followed by the questions you should be answering as you read through the assigned sections.

Every research article published in a social science journal contains the following elements: (1) introduction, (2) literature review, (3) methodology, (4) results, and (5) discussion/conclusion.

In the introduction, you will find an overview of the purpose of the research. Within the introduction, you will also find the hypothesis or hypotheses. A hypothesis is most easily defined as an educated statement or guess. In most hypotheses, you will find that the format usually followed is "if X, Y will occur." For example, a simple hypothesis may be "If the price of gas increases, more people will ride bikes." This is a testable statement that the researcher wants to address in his or her study. Usually, authors state the hypothesis directly, but not always. Therefore, you must be aware of what the author is actually testing in the research project. If you are unable to find the hypothesis, ask yourself what is being tested or manipulated and what results are expected.

The next section of the research article is the literature review. At times the literature review is separated from the text in its own section, and at other times it can be found in the introduction. In any case, the literature review is an examination of what other researchers have already produced in terms of the research question or hypothesis. For example, returning to the hypothesis on the relationship between gas prices and bike riding, the author may find that five researchers conducted studies on the increase of gas prices. In the literature review, the author will discuss their findings and then discuss what his or her study will add to the existing research. The literature review may also be used as a platform of support for the hypothesis. For example, one researcher may have already determined that an increase in gas causes more people to roller-blade to work. The author can use this study as evidence to support the hypothesis that increased gas prices will lead to more bike riding.

The methods used in the research design are found in the next section of the research article. In the methodology section, you will find the following: who or what was studied, how many subjects were studied, the research tool (e.g., interview, survey, observation), how long the subjects were studied, and how the data were collected and analyzed. The methods section is usually very concise, with every step of the research project recorded. This is important because a major goal of the researcher is reliability—or, if the research is done repeatedly in the same way, will the results be the same?

The results section is an analysis of the researcher's findings. If the researcher conducted a quantitative study (using numbers or statistics to explain the research), you will find statistical tables and analyses that explain whether or not the researcher's hypothesis is supported. If the researcher conducted a qualitative study (nonnumerical research for the purpose of theory construction), the results will usually be displayed as a theoretical analysis or interpretation of the research question.

The research article concludes with a discussion and summary of the study. In the discussion, you will find that the hypothesis is usually restated and perhaps a short discussion of the rationale for the hypothesis is provided. You will also find a brief overview of the methodology and results. Finally, the section ends with a discussion of the implications of the research and what future research is still needed.

Now that you know the key elements of a research article, let us examine a sample article from your text.

The Process Is the Punishment: Handling Cases in a Lower Criminal Court

1. What is the thesis or main idea in this article?

   - The thesis or main idea may be found in the abstract of this article, which is the italicized writing prior to the introduction to the piece. In the abstract, the main idea is simply stated as "Malcolm Feeley's study of the Court of Common Pleas, New Haven, Connecticut, shows that the punishment given out by the judge is not the only cost imposed by the criminal justice system." In other words, this article is based on a study of the lower criminal court and examines the ways in which case processing in the lower criminal court imposes punishment on the accused.

2. What is the hypothesis?

   - The hypothesis is found in the paragraph prior to the section titled "Introduction." Feeley states in the first sentence of this piece, "This article develops the argument that in the lower criminal courts the process itself is the punishment." Feeley then restates the hypothesis in other sections of the article (e.g., the end of the introduction and the beginning of the conclusion) to emphasize to the reader his main argument.

3. Is there prior literature related to the hypothesis?

   - Feeley does not offer any prior literature related to the hypothesis. The notes of this piece include some literature related to the argument, but Feeley does not offer this material in the body of this article. Because this article is an excerpt from Feeley's book, it would be safe to assume that the literature review is found in another chapter of the book.

4. What methods are used to support the hypothesis?

   - Although Feeley does not outwardly discuss his methodology, it may be inferred that Feeley is using a methodology known as secondary data analysis. In other words, Feeley developed support for his hypothesis by examining records from the lower criminal courts of New Haven, Connecticut. Feeley investigated data regarding length of time in pretrial custody, the process and costs of pretrial release, the role of attorneys, the costs of continuances, the effects of failing to appear, and pretrial diversion. The analysis is derived from data generated by court agencies (e.g., New Haven Pretrial Services Council), police personnel, attorneys, and judges. Feeley also used informal discussions, rather than interviews, to generate data to support his hypothesis.

5. Is this a qualitative study, a quantitative study, or a mixed methods study?

    - To determine whether or not a study is qualitative or quantitative, you must look at the results. Is Feeley using numbers to support his hypothesis (quantitative) or is he developing a non-numerical theoretical argument (qualitative)? Although Feeley cautions the reader that the figures in this piece are estimates and should not be read at face value, he still uses these numbers to demonstrate the costs of the lower court, thereby categorizing this study as quantitative in nature. In some cases, the researcher uses both qualitative and quantitative data.

6. What are the results and how does the author present the results?

    - The results are displayed in numerical tables. The tables illustrate release and detention rates, as well as length of time in pretrial detention. The results are then restated in the conclusion of this piece. In the first paragraph, Feeley concludes: "The real punishment for many people is the pretrial process itself; that is why criminally accused invoke so few of the adversarial options available to them." Earlier in the same paragraph, Feeley supports this claim by emphasizing that his results are drawn from "tangible, direct, and immediate penalties extracted from those accused of minor criminal offenses."

7. Do you believe that the author provided a persuasive argument? Why or why not?

    - This answer is ultimately up to the reader, but looking at this article, we think it is safe to assume that the readers will agree that Feeley offered a persuasive argument. Let us return to his major premise: "In the lower courts, the process itself is the primary punishment." Feeley supports this proposition with a review of existing data derived from court offices, police officers, and attorneys, concluding that the costs and processes of the lower court are punishments often overlooked by criminal justice scholars and professionals.

8. What does the article add to your knowledge of the subject?

    - This research assumes a level of groundbreaking knowledge, as Feeley states in the conclusion, "The costs of lower court . . . are not those factors which have received the greatest attention from legal scholars, social scientists, or indeed court officials." Feeley states that the processes of the lower court lead to harsh treatment of defendants and time loss for victims, and the expected functions are not performed. Thus, the processes of the lower court that have traditionally been deemed as committed and prompt are actually forms of punishment virtually unaddressed in the criminal justice system.

9. What are the implications for criminal justice policy that can be derived from this article?

    - One policy that Feeley recommends in the conclusion of the article is implementing alternatives to the lower court processes (e.g., rehabilitation). Of course, the alternatives to the lower court come with their own shortcomings, yet Feeley emphasizes that this alternative should not be overlooked. Another policy Feeley touches on is community-based courts, which would more likely respond to the problems found within the lower courts. Finally, Feeley discusses the possibility of police court magistrates "meting out immediate kadi-like justice without reliance on defense counsel—but also without the need for bail, repeated court appearances, and the like." All of these recommendations are implications for criminal justice policy that can be derived from this article.

10. Who is the intended audience of this article?

- As you read the article, ask yourself, to whom is the author speaking? After you read this article, you will see that Feeley is writing for not only students but also professors, criminologists, judicial officials, and criminal justice personnel. The target audience may most easily be identified if you ask yourself, "Who will benefit from reading this article?"

Now that we have discussed the elements of a research article, it is your turn to continue through your text, reading the various articles and answering the same questions. You may find that some articles are easier to follow than others, but do not be dissuaded. Remember that each article follows the same format: introduction, literature review, methods, results, and discussion. If you have any problems, refer to this introduction for guidance.

READING

Malcolm Feeley's 1992 book, *The Process Is the Punishment: Handling Cases in a Lower Criminal Court*, is a classic study of the lower criminal courts that process the millions of defendants cited for traffic offenses and charged with minor crimes each year. Feeley studied adjudication patterns in the Court of Common Pleas in New Haven, Connecticut, a court with jurisdiction over minor offenses. He concluded that these offenses were adjudicated quickly and informally. He found, for instance, that defendants in the 1,600 cases he observed had the right to counsel, but not one insisted on an attorney. He further found that very few cases took more than a minute to dispose of; most were handled in mere seconds. More important, Feeley developed the argument that the *process* for the adjudication of misdemeanors is a more relevant punishment than the ultimate sentence handed down at the end of the trial. Specifically, he argued that the pretrial process imposes a series of "price tags" on the accused. These include the costs of paying bail, hiring an attorney, and losing work wages to attend court hearings.

Feeley's work is important because it takes us to the bottom of the criminal justice wedding cake. It gives us a window into the operation of one criminal court, but one that is surely a microcosm of misdemeanor courts more generally. His study shows us that criminal trials are not what they are portrayed to be on television and in movies. Most crimes are minor ones, and most of them are dealt with swiftly and perfunctorily. To do otherwise would take a significant financial toll on a criminal justice system with many cases and limited resources.

The Process Is the Punishment

Handling Cases in a Lower Criminal Court

Malcolm M. Feeley

This article develops the argument that in the lower criminal courts the process itself is the primary punishment. I identify the costs involved in the pretrial process and examine the ways they affect the organization, as well as the way a defendant will proceed on his journey through the court. This examination should help explain why lower courts do not fit their popular image, and why cases are processed so quickly in the Court of Common Pleas, New Haven, Connecticut.

Introduction

The first set of factors I examine deals with the consequences of pretrial detention and the problems of securing pretrial release. The second explores the costs of securing an attorney. There are obvious financial outlays involved in retaining a private attorney, but there are also hidden costs associated with obtaining free counsel. A third set of factors deals with the problem of continuances. While delay often benefits the defendant, its importance for the defendant is often exaggerated, and it is crucial to distinguish defendant-induced delay from continuances which are arranged for the convenience of the court.

By themselves these costs may appear to be minor or even trivial in a process formally structured to focus on the crucial questions of adjudication and sentencing. However, in the aggregate, and in comparison with the actual consequences of adjudication and sentencing, they often loom large in the eyes of the criminally accused, and emerge as central concerns in getting through the criminal justice system.

These pretrial costs account for a number of puzzling phenomena: why so many people waive their right to free appointed counsel; why so many people do not show up for court at all; and why people choose the available adversarial options so infrequently. Furthermore, pretrial costs are part of the reason why pretrial diversion programs designed to *benefit* defendants and provide alternatives to standard adjudication do not receive a more enthusiastic response. The accused often perceive these programs as cumbersome processes which simply increase their contact with the system.

The relative importance of the pretrial process hinges on one important set of considerations. Students of the criminal courts often overlook what many criminologists and students of social class do not, that the fear of arrest and conviction does not loom as large in the eyes of many people brought into court as it does in the eyes of middle-class researchers. While I did not systematically interview a sample of defendants, I had informal and often extended discussions with dozens of defendants who were waiting for their cases to be called, and I watched still more discuss their cases with attorneys and prosecutors. While there were obvious and numerous exceptions, I was nevertheless struck by the frequent lack of concern about the stigma of conviction and by the more practical and far more immediate concerns

about what the sentence would be and how quickly they could get out of court.

There are several reasons for this. First, many arrestees already have criminal records, so that whatever stigma does attach to a conviction is already eroded, if not destroyed.[1] Second, many arrestees, particularly young ones, are part of a subculture which spurns conventional values and for which arrest and conviction may even function as a celebratory ritual, reinforcing their own values and identity. In fact, they may even perceive it as part of the process of coming of age.[2] Third, lower-class people tend to be more *present*-oriented than middle-class people, and for obvious reasons.[3] Many defendants are faced with an immediate concern for returning to work or their children, and these concerns often take precedence over the desire to avoid the *remote* consequences that a (or another) conviction might bring. This *relative* lack of concern about conviction is reinforced by the type of employment opportunities available to lower-class defendants. If an employee is reliable, it may make little difference whether or not he pleads guilty to a minor charge emerging from a "Saturday night escapade." Indeed, an employer is not likely to find out about the incident unless his employee has to arrange to miss work in order to appear in court.

If the stigma of the criminal sanction is not viewed as a significant sanction, the concrete costs of the pretrial process take on great significance. When this occurs, the process itself becomes the punishment.

 ## Pretrial Release: An Overview

A quick reading of the relevant Connecticut statutes, case law, and administrative directives conveys the impression that the state has an unswerving commitment to prompt pretrial release. There is an elaborate multi-layered system for decision and review, there are a variety of pretrial release alternatives, and assurance of appearance at trial is the sole criterion for establishing release conditions.

The police are empowered to make the initial release decision and can either release a suspect at the site of the arrest or take him to the central booking facility. Once the suspect is booked, police retain the power to establish release conditions, and they may release suspects on a written promise to appear (PTA) or on bond, which they set. If they do not release the arrestee, at this point, the police are then required to notify a bail commissioner who in turn is supposed to "promptly conduct [an] interview and investigation as he deems necessary to reach an independent decision." If after this the accused is still not released, then the bail commissioner "shall set forth his reasons . . . in writing."[4] The accused has a third opportunity to seek release at arraignment and all subsequent appearances, at which time he can request the judge to consider a bond reduction or release on PTA.

This liberal release policy is reflected in practice as well. Table 2.3 indicates that 89 percent of those arrested were released prior to the disposition of their cases, and that 52 percent of them were released on nonfinancial conditions, by police field citation or PTA. Thirty-seven percent were released on bond, and only 11 percent were detained until disposition. Although the proportion of arrestees released pending trial is typically regarded as the most important measure of a jurisdiction's "liberality," it is far from a complete picture. Two additional questions must be answered. First, at what point in the process do people secure release? To identify as "released" only those who were free at the time their cases were disposed of is to overlook those who were held in detention for a while before eventually securing release.

Table 2.3   Release and Detention Rates

Condition Immediately Prior to Disposition	N	%
Released on Citation	244	16
Released on PTA	565	36
Released on Bond	567	37
(Subtotal released)	(1376)	(89)
Detained	166	11
Total	1542	100

And if a person is released on bail, at what price was freedom purchased?

Length of Time in Pretrial Custody

Table 2.4 provides a breakdown of the length of time defendants in my sample were in custody before being released. Seventeen percent were released almost immediately on police citations. A much larger group—44 percent—was released within three hours after being taken to the "lockup," and a third group was released within a period of thirteen to twenty-four hours after arrest. Many of the people in this group were released in court the morning after their arrest, at which time they were able to secure reductions in the amount of bond or contact a bondsman or family member to post bond; some pleaded guilty and were discharged from custody. However, 6 percent of the sample remained in pretrial custody for a period of two days or longer, and a small number were held three weeks or more.

Other arrestees secure delayed release because the lockup facility becomes overcrowded. On Saturday evenings police may "weed out" the lockup by granting PTA's to Friday evening's arrestees in order to make

Table 2.4   Length of Time in Pretrial Detention

Length of time	N	%
none	244	17
0–3 hours	624	43
4–7 hours	82	6
8–12 hours	92	6
13–24 hours	308	21
2 days	31	2
3 days	10	1
4–7 days	12	1
8–20 days	18	1
over 20 days	17	1
Total	1438	99*

* Rounding error.

room for new arrivals. Women are housed in a separate facility in another location and are generally more likely to be released earlier on lower bond.

Pretrial Release: Process

The Role of the Police

Although most students of the pretrial process focus on judicial bail setting at arraignment, their observations may often miss the mark, since in many jurisdictions—including New Haven—the bulk of the pretrial release decisions is made by other people before the accused is ever presented in court. In New Haven it is not the judge or the bail commissioner who dominates the release process, but rather the police. They are responsible not only for arresting and charging suspects, but also for releasing them before a trial. A number of observers have commented that Connecticut in general, and New Haven in particular, has liberal policies on pretrial release. They attribute these to the multi-layered system of decision and review, and the existence of bail commissioners. But in fact one cannot attribute these practices directly to this elaborate system. In fact, they probably have more to do with the intuitive judgments of the initial decision makers, the police.

Unless a suspect is released on a field citation at the site of an arrest, the arresting officer takes him to the central booking facility. After the booking, the officer is required by departmental order to complete a detailed bail interview form which seeks information about the arrestee's ties to the community and other factors on which the release decision is to be based. The form also provides a space for reasons if the arrestee should not be released. Rarely is there anything that might be characterized as an "interview." Only occasionally is the bail interview form completed in detail, and whatever information it does record is likely to have been filled in *after* a release decision has already been made. While different officers have different practices, most of them require little more than the accused's name, address, and the charges being pressed before making a decision to release on PTA or a small bond.

If the charges are more serious, or if the arrestee has a prior record of arrests or failure to appear (and well over 50 percent do), then the officer may insist on a bond. In setting its amount, he often consults a "bail schedule." This document, prepared by the Judicial Department and adopted by a resolution of all Circuit Court judges in 1967, specifies a monetary amount for each type of charge, and provides for "discounts," depending upon the accused's ties to the community.

Although officers setting the conditions of release must complete a section of the bail interview form which calls for a statement of reasons if an arrestee is not released immediately, this section is rarely filled out. In my review of over 100 bail interview forms for people who were *not* immediately released, only a handful—15 or so—had this section completed. Only occasionally did they specify that the arrestee was a "poor risk" because he had no local address, or because he had a record of failures to appear. Most of the reasons related instead to the police officer's perception of the arrestee's condition, which was often characterized as "abusive," "threatening," or "wants to return to the incident," reasons which encouraged them to favor immediate situational justice or specific deterrence.

These officers are often in a dilemma. They are agents of the community, expected to enforce the law and make arrests. But then they must immediately turn around and release those very people whom they have just apprehended and arrested. It is not surprising that the tensions produced by these conflicting roles place a strain in the formal rules these people are charged with applying, and that they have taken advantage of the lax enforcement of the law to pursue their own conceptions of rough justice. Occasionally they use this detention power arbitrarily to administer their own system of punishment. Often they fear that an arrestee will return to a fight if he is released, so that they purposefully set bail beyond the arrestee's means in order to detain him until they think he has calmed down. The statutes on release make no provision for this latter concern, and the police can pursue it only by ignoring the literal letter of the law. But in bending the law in this "reasonable" direction, the door is opened for justifications to bend it for other, less benign reasons. Police may impose situational sanctions on arrestees whom they think deserve to "sit in jail for a time" because the courts will just "let them out."

Securing an Attorney

A person accused of a criminal offense must decide whether or not to obtain an attorney. This seemingly simple choice in fact involves a complex set of decisions: whether or not to get a lawyer; and who to get, a public defender or a private attorney; if a private attorney, then which one? The decision is confusing and costly in terms of both time and money.

Private Counsel

Unless an arrestee has had prior experience with a particular lawyer and has been satisfied, he is confused about what to do, whom to call, if anyone, how much it will cost him, and whether the amount is reasonable. He is overly suspicious and afraid of being taken advantage of. Some arrestees will call in an attorney with whose name he or his friends are familiar. Others may turn to other inmates or their captors—the police—for advice, or perhaps to a bondsman. Still others, fearful of the expense, decide to do without representation.

If the arrestee telephones an attorney from the lockup, the attorney is likely to ask him a few questions about the charges, then ask to speak to the police officer in charge or contact a bail commissioner in an effort to get bond lowered to an amount the arrestee can make. After this he may contact a bondsman. If the arrestee secures his release before arraignment, the case is scheduled for a week or two later, and in the interim the attorney will arrange an appointment with his caller. If the arrestee is not released, the attorney will try to meet his prospective client just before arraignment in order to argue for bail reduction and afterward hold a brief conference to discuss financial terms and the case.

It is important that an attorney assess his would-be client's ability to pay early on; once he has begun to represent a defendant, he is bound by the canon of ethics to continue representation until disposition. While it is possible to withdraw later from a case, it can be awkward and embarrassing. Most attorneys can relate instances of being "taken" by clients, and the result is a rather hardnosed approach to fees, even among the more liberal "client-oriented" attorneys who are frequently young, not well-established, and in particular need of the income.

Fees and billing practices vary widely from attorney to attorney and from case to case. Most private attorneys expect an initial retainer based on their own assessment of the "worth of the case." As one private attorney observed:

> I want to get enough at the outset, so that if I don't get any more out of the case, I won't get burned. This amount varies. For instance, I told a guy it would cost a minimum of five hundred to take his case—it was a messy child-molesting thing—and perhaps more, but that I wanted five hundred dollars to begin with. He later called and said he could come up with three hundred, and I said I would take it. So now, even if he can't pay, I won't get burned too badly. . . . I suppose as I pick up business, I'll have to get tougher on this, but now I need the business and will take the chances. On a routine breach [of peace] or disorderly [conduct], I might very well take fifty dollars.

Although most attorneys bill clients based on the amount of time they spend—or say they spend—on a case (and all things being equal, they feel that the type of charge provides a rough indication of this), they also adjust this amount according to their assessment of their client's ability to pay. Some attorneys are critical of such billing practices, but those who use them claim that they allow the better-off to subsidize the less fortunate.

Some attorneys have experimented with a flat fee for a case, which in one small firm is $300 for a case in the lower court and $1,000 for a case in the upper court. But this means that those people whose cases are disposed of quickly after only one or two court appearances pay an extremely high per hour or per appearance cost, while those whose cases require considerable research, investigation, court appearances, or trial get a real bargain.

Public Defenders

In order to obtain a public defender, a person must be poor. There are rather rigid guidelines for eligibility, but they are not strictly adhered to, and in fact most arrestees who apply for a PD routinely obtain one. There are several reasons for this. Perhaps most important is the prevailing belief among prosecutors, public defenders, and most judges that the formal guidelines are overly restrictive, and that by denying a person *free* counsel they are in effect denying him *any* counsel. As a consequence they may overlook an income ceiling or an obvious undervaluing of personal assets. Although some judges occasionally suggest it, few in fact seriously expect an applicant to sell his five-year-old automobile in order to raise an attorney's fee.

A second reason is the drive for administrative efficiency. The application form requires detailed information about the applicant's financial condition, and to verify all of it would require more effort than the PD is willing to extend in most cases. The PD's staff finds it far easier to take the partial information at face value and recommend assignment of a PD knowing that errors will be made. They justified this by arguing that it might permit a few more people to have a PD than deserve one, but at least it does not exclude those who do. In addition, PDs are reluctant to question or challenge ambiguous or inconsistent answers about income and assets, feeling that to do so would create an atmosphere of suspicion and hostility, and undercut their ability to gain the full confidence of their clients.

But it can still be difficult to obtain an attorney. In court, the prosecutor's first question to an unrepresented defendant is: "Do you want to get your own attorney, apply for a public defender, or get your case over with today?" The very way the question is phrased encourages people *not* to seek counsel, and suggests preferential treatment if they plead guilty immediately.

If someone asks for a PD, then he is shunted off for an interview to determine his eligibility, and the interview itself can become a humiliating experience.

In light of the consistently lenient sentences and the casual way in which so many cases linger on, it is understandable why many defendants do not obtain attorneys—public or private—at all, and when they do, why so many of them desire little more than a quick and perfunctory meeting with their attorneys.

Continuances

Although defendants usually want to get their cases over with as quickly as possible, they are not always successful. The court has its own pace, which is often at odds with the defendant's self-interest. Defense attorneys and prosecutors usually turn (or return) their attentions to a case on the morning it is scheduled on the calendar, and if they are not able to resolve any differences before the calendar call, they will agree to a (or another) continuance. Problems which impede the resolution of a case can vary considerably, and a great many continuations stem from confusion and carelessness. A defense attorney may have overcommitted himself on that day, or in a more difficult case be unwilling to spend a few additional moments to track down a full-time prosecutor. Occasionally a defendant may appear in court only to find that his case is not on the calendar. Or the defense attorney may forget to show up. A court-ordered report such as a laboratory report on drugs may not have been completed, or a defendant's file may simply be lost. Whatever the reasons for delay, it may be two or three hours after the defendant has first taken his seat in the gallery before he is informed that his case will be continued. Rarely is this decision made in consultation with him or even with an appreciation of the problems it might involve for him. Unable to comprehend the details of court operations, most defendants are overwhelmed by the details of the processes. Rarely can they distinguish reasonable from unreasonable, careful from careless decisions, and they are left with generalized discontent and haunting suspicions.

But delay is not always the result of bumbling, and it is often a highly effective defense strategy. As one attorney observed:

> We can make life difficult for the prosecutors by filing a lot of motions. . . . So when I push a legalistic line I am not expecting to have a complicated legal discourse; rather it's part of my ammunition to secure my objectives. They know I'm serious and that I'll spend a lot of time to pursue it. I'll wear them down that way.

Motions may be filed one at a time, so that a case may be strung out over a long period. Strategic delay can also be secured by pleading not guilty and asking for a trial by jury. This request automatically provides a several-week (and at times a several-month) continuance, during which period the complainant may calm down or restitution can be arranged.

Because delay can be and often is an effective defense strategy, it can also be used successfully by a defense attorney to justify his own carelessness or actions performed for the sake of convenience. While public defenders may use it to cope with a pressing caseload, private attorneys may use it to boost their own fees or insure payment. In any case, all but the most knowledgeable of defendants will be unable to identify the *real* reasons for delay.

Failure to Appear

The Causes of Nonappearance

For many arrestees the central question is not how to maneuver to reduce the chances of conviction, a harsh sentence, or the number of court appearances, but whether to show up in court at all. This consideration is not restricted to a small handful of "absconders" or would-be absconders; it concerns large numbers of arrestees. Roughly one-third of those in my sample missed one or more of their scheduled court appearances, and a substantial number (one person in five) never did return to court even after they received repeated letters of warning. While a number of these people had their cases terminated by a court action which called for a "bond forfeiture with no further action," about one in every eight or nine cases was never formally resolved by the court in any way, and are filed as outstanding, closed only if and when the accused is arrested on other unrelated charges. Most of those who fail to appear (FTA) are charged with minor misdemeanors, but the problem is by no means restricted to them. A third of the FTAs were charged with the most serious class of misdemeanors, and fully 20 percent of them were charged with felonies. Both in terms of absolute numbers and the seriousness of the charges, failures to appear present a serious and continuing problem for the court.

Like other efforts, mine to identify predictors of appearance/nonappearance focused on characteristics of *individual* defendants. Yet the discussion above suggests that the label FTA itself is problematic because it depends in part on whether a bondsman is present in court to secure a continuance and whether a prosecutor is willing to make accommodations for those who step out of the courtroom momentarily. Furthermore, by focusing on the *personal* characteristics of the defendant we overlook the importance of *organizational features* in the court which may encourage nonappearance. People without attorneys may *show up* in court with the same frequency as those with attorneys, but because their cases are not called until late in the day some of them give up and go home, either because they are bored and irritated or because they think a recess is an adjournment. My observations of the court lead me to believe that nonappearance is more likely to be accounted for in terms of how well defendants understand the operations of the court (for example, are they in the correct courtroom?), how much respect they have for the court, how seriously they take the proceedings, how aware they are of their scheduled court appearances, and what they believe the consequences will be if they fail to appear. In other words, the *interaction between the court organization and the accused* is likely to provide the best explanation for appearance or nonappearance.

Pretrial Diversion

One way for an accused person to reduce the charges of conviction and postconviction penalty is to make an advance effort to "rehabilitate" himself. There are a variety of ways in which the accused can demonstrate this effort to the court. . . . One way is the Pretrial Diversion Program sponsored by the New Haven Pretrial Services Counsel. Representatives of this program approach new arrestees who meet its initial eligibility criteria, and offer them an opportunity to participate in its in-house group counseling program or to take advantage of its job placement services. If those who are accepted faithfully participate in these activities for a period of ninety days, then the program will recommend to the prosecutor that the charges be nolled.

Despite the seeming benefits which flow from this program, very few of the eligible arrestees take advantage of it. Estimates constructed from my sample indicated that over three-quarters of all arrestees met the program's *initial* eligibility requirements, but of the 800 eligibles for whom data were available, only 19, or 2.3 percent of them, actually participated in the diversion program. Officials of the diversion program attempt to account for these low numbers by pointing to the prosecutor's discretion to veto prospective participants who are otherwise eligible and interested. While these factors certainly limit the program's size, there is another much more important reason for its limited effectiveness: arrestees consider participation in the program itself a penalty that is much more severe than the one they think they will receive if they do *not* participate.

One evaluation of the program attempted to estimate what might have happened to the program's participants if they had not been "diverted." Identifying a control group and tracing its path through the court, the researchers found that one-fifth to one-third of the "control group" obtained nolles or dismissals; most of them pleaded guilty and received a small fine of $10 to $20. *None* of them went to jail. In short, they concluded tentatively, those people who are eligible but decline to enter the diversion program are not likely to be treated harshly by the court.

In contrast, people who do participate in the program must agree to participate in regularly scheduled meetings for a three month period with no definite assurances that their cases will be nolled afterward. It is not surprising, then, that so many people pass up the diversion program.

Conclusion: The Aggregated Effects of the Pretrial Process

The figures on pretrial costs presented in the preceding discussion are rough estimates and should not be interpreted as facts. Because they suggest comparisons between groups and costs which are themselves quite different, they must also be interpreted with caution. Still, these figures point to the inescapable conclusion that the costs of lower court—the tangible, direct, and immediate penalties extracted from those accused of minor criminal offenses—are not those factors which have received the greater attention from legal scholars, social scientists, or indeed court officials. Liberal legal theory directs attention to formal outcomes, to the conditions giving rise to the application of the criminal sanction at adjudication and sentence. Much social science research has followed this lead, searching for the causes of sanctioning at these stages. But this emphasis produces a distorted vision of the process and the sanctions it dispenses. The real punishment for many people is the pretrial process itself; that is why criminally accused invoke so few of the adversarial options available to them.

This inverted system of justice dramatizes the dilemma of lower courts. Expanded procedures designed to improve the criminal process are not invoked because they might be counterproductive. Efforts to slow the process down and make it truly deliberative might lead to still harsher treatment of defendants and still more time loss for complainants and victims. Devices designed to control official discretion do not perform their expected functions (the failure to litigate bail is a clear case in point). And whereas rapid and perfunctory practices foster error and caprice, they do reduce pretrial costs and in the aggregate may render rough justice.

In light of the pretrial costs and the actual penalties meted out in the lower court, one is tempted to scoff at the formal theory which so ineffectively governs official behavior in the lower court and to dismiss it as unworkable and overly elegant—as proceduralism run amok—for the types of petty problems presented to the court. Would not simple summary justice with a minimum of procedures provide a more appropriate and workable set of standards? Perhaps the police court magistrate meting out immediate kadi-like justice without reliance on defense counsel—but also without the need for bail, repeated court appearances, and the like—might be more satisfactory. Or perhaps community-based courts might be more adept at ferreting out the underlying causes of conflict and providing ameliorating responses.

In a great many cases these alternatives might work more effectively; yet the impulse for formality, even with its manifest shortcomings, cannot be so quickly dismissed. While lower courts sentence very few people to terms in jail, in theory almost all of those appearing before them face a slim possibility of incarceration. While creating a record of petty criminal offenses may not significantly affect the future of most people who find themselves before the bench, it can have a long-lasting and unpredictable impact on some. Citizenship can be placed in jeopardy, careers destroyed, aspirations dampened, delinquent propensities reinforced. Such problems may be few in number, but they do occur. And it is impossible to tell in advance which cases may precipitate these more serious consequences, since the specific impact of a record may not make itself felt until much later in life.

As long as conviction for petty criminal offenses carries the possibility of a jail sentence or of jeopardizing one's future, the ideal of a formal, adversarial process will remain strong and attractive even to those who acknowledge that the process itself is the punishment for most people. However, there may be some alternatives which both facilitate the rapid handling of petty cases and protect the interests of the accused.

Notes

1. Over half the arrestees in my sample had a record of prior arrests by the New Haven police, and a large proportion of them had records of conviction. These figures are probably drastically low, however, since local authorities do not systematically obtain records from other jurisdictions, either within or outside the state.

2. Discussions of arrest and conviction frequently assume that arrestees have a great fear of the stigma of a conviction and will go to great lengths to avoid being formally labeled as criminals. But my observations are consistent with the findings of many criminologists who have studied juvenile delinquency and concluded that the disproportionate rate of criminal conduct by young lower-class males stems from a subculture which promotes such activity as a social mechanism for becoming a male adult. Rather than being a brand of inferiority for many lower- and working-class youths, arrest and conviction often reinforce the values of their subculture and can even enhance their status among their peers. This has been noted time and again in the literature on juvenile courts, but altogether overlooked and ignored in "adult" courts. See Walter B. Miller, "Lower Class Culture as a Generating Milieu of Gang Delinquency," *Journal of Social Issues* 14 (1958): 5–19; and Albert K. Cohen, *Delinquent Boys: The Culture of the Gang* (New York: Free Press, 1955). Also see Edwin H. Sutherland and Donald Cressey, *Principles of Criminology*, 7th ed. (Philadelphia: J. B. Lippincott, 1966), pp. 183–199; and Richard Quinney, *The Social Reality of Crime* (Boston: Little Brown, 1970), pp. 207–276.

3. See Edward Banfield, *The Unheavenly City* (Boston: Little Brown, 1971), pp. 45–56; and Edward Banfield and James Q. Wilson, "Public Regardingness as a Value Premise in Voting Behavior," *American Political Science Review* 58 (1964): 876–887.

4. Connecticut General Statute 54–63 (C) (A).

DISCUSSION QUESTIONS

1. Feeley noted that "the fear of arrest and conviction does not loom as large in the eyes of many people brought into court as it does in the eyes of middle-class researchers." What explains this?

2. What are the "costs" of the pretrial process?

3. What role do the police play in the pretrial release process? In what sense do the police pursue "their own conceptions of rough justice"?

4. Why do so few defendants charged with minor offenses obtain an attorney?

5. What are the "organizational features of courts" that encourage nonappearance for court hearings?

6. Why do so few defendants take advantage of pretrial diversion?

7. Explain why "the process is the punishment" in courts that adjudicate minor offenses. Would this also be the case in courts that adjudicate serious felonies? Why or why not?

READING

Some scholars argue that the upsurge in serious crime by juveniles, coupled with recent trends toward trying young offenders as adults, raises questions about the future of the juvenile court. Some have gone so far as to argue that the juvenile court, and even the juvenile justice system, should be abandoned altogether. This is the issue that Barry Feld, one of the foremost experts on the juvenile court, explores in the article "The Honest Politician's Guide to Juvenile Justice in the Twenty-First Century." Feld argues that the juvenile court has been transformed "from a social welfare agency into a deficient criminal court." He cites a number of substantive and procedural deficiencies of juvenile courts today and calls for the abolition of the juvenile court. He argues that the juvenile court should be replaced with an integrated criminal justice system that views the youth of the offender as a mitigating circumstance and that provides a "youth discount" at sentencing.

The Honest Politician's Guide to Juvenile Justice in the Twenty-First Century

Barry C. Feld

The public and politicians perceive a significant and frightening increase in youth crime and violence. Concerns about the inability of juvenile courts to rehabilitate chronic and violent young offenders while simultaneously protecting public safety accompany the growing fear of youth crime. Sensational media depictions of young criminals as a different breed of super-predators further heighten public anxiety. A desire to get tough, fueled in part by frustration with the intractability of crime, provides political

SOURCE: Originally published in 1994 in *Annals, AAPSS,* Vol. 564, pp. 10–27.

impetus to crack down and transfer some young offenders to criminal courts for prosecution as adults and to strengthen the sanctioning powers of juvenile courts for the remaining delinquents.

Within the past three decades, judicial decisions, legislative amendments, and administrative changes have transformed the juvenile court from a nominally rehabilitative social welfare agency into a scaled down, second-class criminal court for young offenders that provides them with neither therapy nor justice (Feld 1993a, 1997). This transformation occurred because of the migration of African Americans from the rural South to the urban North that began three-quarters of a century ago, the macrostructural transformation of American cities and the economy over the past quarter of a century, and the current linkages in the popular and political culture between race and serious youth crime (Feld 1998). Two competing cultural and legal conceptions of young people have facilitated the transformation. On the one hand, legal culture views young people as innocent, vulnerable, fragile, and dependent children whom their parents and the state should protect and nurture. On the other hand, the legal culture perceives young people as vigorous, autonomous, and responsible almost adultlike people from whose criminal behavior the public needs protection.

The ambivalent and conflicted jurisprudence of youth enables policymakers selectively to manipulate the competing social constructs of innocence and responsibility to maximize the social control of young people. Over the past three decades, juvenile justice legal reforms have engaged in a process of criminological triage. At the soft end of juvenile courts' jurisdiction, reforms have shifted noncriminal status offenders out of the juvenile justice system into a hidden system of social control in the private sector mental health and chemical dependency industries. At the hard end of juvenile courts' jurisdiction, states transfer increasing numbers of youths into the criminal justice system for prosecution as adults. Juvenile court sentencing policies and practices escalate the punishments imposed on those delinquents who remain in an increasingly criminalized juvenile justice system.

In this article, I briefly describe the transformation of the juvenile court from a social welfare agency into a deficient criminal court. Second, I argue that juvenile courts' underlying idea is fundamentally flawed because in it the courts attempt to combine social welfare and penal social control in one agency. Because welfare and control functions embody inherent and irreconcilable contradictions, juvenile courts inevitably do both badly. If a state separates social welfare goals from criminal social control functions, then no need remains for a separate juvenile court. Rather, a state could try all offenders in one integrated criminal justice system. But children do not possess the same degree of criminal responsibility as adults. Adolescent developmental psychology, criminal law jurisprudence, and sentencing policy provide a rationale to formally recognize youthfulness as a mitigating factor when judges sentence younger offenders. A "youth discount" provides a sliding scale of criminal responsibility for younger offenders who have not quite learned to be responsible or developed fully their capacity for self-control. Combining enhanced procedural safeguards with formal mitigation of sentences provides youths with greater protections and justice than they currently receive in either the juvenile or criminal justice systems.

The Juvenile Court

The juvenile court is the byproduct of changes in two cultural ideas that accompanied modernization and industrialization a century ago: childhood and social control. Social structural changes associated with the shift from an agricultural to an urban industrial society, and the separation of work from the home, produced a new social construction of children as innocent, dependent, and vulnerable (Ainsworth 1991). Progressive child savers used the new imagery of childhood to advance a number of reform agendas: compulsory school attendance, child labor, and child welfare laws. A more modern, scientific conception of social control embraced positivist criminology and medical analogies to treat offenders rather than to punish them for their offenses. Positivism attempted to identify the antecedent variables that caused crime and deviance and challenged the classic formulation of crime as the product of blameworthy, free-will choices (Allen 1964, 1981). By attributing criminal behavior to external and deterministic forces, Progressive reformers reduced an actor's moral responsibility for crime and focused on efforts to reform rather than to punish the offender. The juvenile court combined the new conception of children with new strategies of social control to produce a judicial-welfare alternative to criminal justice, to remove children from the adult process, to enforce the newer conception of children's dependency, and to substitute the state as *parens patriae*. The juvenile court's rehabilitative ideal rested on several sets of assumptions about positive criminology, children's malleability, and the availability of effective intervention strategies to act in the child's best interests.

Procedure and substance intertwined in the juvenile court. Procedurally, juvenile courts used informal processes, conducted confidential hearings, and employed a euphemistic vocabulary to obscure and disguise the reality of coercive social control. Substantively, juvenile courts used indeterminate, non-proportional dispositions, emphasized treatment and supervision rather than punishment, and purportedly focused on offenders' future welfare rather than past offenses. Despite their benevolent rhetoric, however, the Progressive child savers who created the juvenile court deliberately designed it to discriminate, to Americanize immigrants and the poor, and to provide a coercive mechanism to distinguish between "our children" and "other people's children."

In their pursuit of the rehabilitative ideal, the Progressives situated the juvenile court on a number of cultural, legal, and criminological fault lines. They created several binary conceptions for the juvenile and criminal justice systems: either child or adult; either determinism or free will; either dependent or responsible; either treatment or punishment; either welfare or deserts; either procedural informality or formality; either discretion or the rule of law. The past three decades have witnessed a tectonic shift from the former to the latter of each of these pairs in response to

the structural and racial transformation of cities, the rise in serious youth crime, and the erosion of the rehabilitative assumptions of the juvenile court.

The Transformation of the Juvenile Court

During the 1960s, the Warren Court's civil rights decisions, criminal due process rulings, and "constitutional domestication" of the juvenile court responded to broader structural and demographic changes taking place in America, particularly those associated with race and youth crime (Feld 1999). In the decades prior to and after World War II, black migration from the rural South to the urban North increased minority concentrations in urban ghettos, made race a national rather than a regional issue, and provided the impetus for the civil rights movement (Lemann 1992). The 1960s also witnessed the baby boom increases in youth crime that continued until the late 1970s. During the 1960s, the rise in youth crime and urban racial disorders provoked cries for "law and order" and provided the initial political impetus to get tough. Republicans seized crime control and welfare as wedge issues with which to distinguish themselves from Democrats, and crime policies for the first time became a central issue in partisan politics (Beckett 1997). As a result of sound-bite politics, symbols and rhetoric have come to shape penal policies more than knowledge or substance has. Since the 1960s, politicians' fear of being labeled soft on crime has led to a constant ratcheting-up of punitiveness.

The Supreme Court's due process decision responded to the macro-structural and demographic changes and attempted to guarantee civil rights, to protect minority citizens, and to limit the authority of the state. *In re Gault* (387 U.S. 1 [1967]) began to transform the juvenile court into a very different institution from that which the Progressives contemplated. *In re Gault* demonstrated the linkage between procedure and substance in the juvenile court and engrafted some formal procedures at trial onto the individualized treatment schema (Feld 1984). Although the Court did not intend its decisions to alter juvenile courts' therapeutic mission, in the aftermath of *In re Gault*, judicial, legislative, and administrative changes have fostered a procedural and substantive convergence with criminal courts (Feld 1993a, 1997). *In re Gault* shifted the focus of delinquency hearings from real needs to proof of legal guilt and formalized the connection between criminal conduct and coercive intervention. Providing a modicum of procedural justice also legitimated greater punitiveness in juvenile courts. Thus *In re Gault's* procedural reforms provided the impetus for the substantive convergence between juvenile and criminal courts, so that today juvenile courts constitute a wholly owned subsidiary of the criminal justice system. It is a historical irony that race provided the initial impetus for the Supreme Court to expand procedural rights to protect minority youths' liberty interests, and now juvenile courts impose increasingly punitive sentences disproportionately on minority offenders. In *McKeiver v. Pennsylvania* (403 U.S. 528 [1971]), however, the Court denied to juveniles the constitutional right to jury trials in delinquency proceedings. *McKeiver* relied on the purported differences between juvenile courts' treatment and criminal courts' punishment to justify the procedural distinctions between the two systems.

Juvenile Courts' Procedural Deficiencies

Unfortunately, *In re Gault* constituted an incomplete procedural revolution, and a substantial gulf still remains between the law on the books and the law in action. States continue to manipulate the fluid concepts of children and adults, or treatment and punishment in order to maximize the social control of young people. On the one hand, states treat juveniles just like adults when formal equality results in practical inequality. For example, states use the adult standard of "knowing, intelligent, and voluntary under the totality of the circumstances" to gauge juveniles' waivers of rights (*Fare v. Michael C.*, 442 U.S. 707 [1979]; Feld 1984), even though juveniles lack the legal competence of adults. Research on juveniles' waivers of *Miranda* rights (Grisso 1980) and waivers of their right to counsel provide compelling evidence of the procedural deficiencies of the juvenile court (Feld 1989, 1993b). On the other hand, even as

juvenile courts have become more punitive, most states continue to deny juveniles access to jury trials or other rights guaranteed to adults (Feld 1988, 1995). Juvenile courts provide a procedural regime in which few adults charged with crimes and facing the prospect of confinement would consent to be tried.

Criminological Triage

Simultaneously, juvenile courts' increased procedural formality have provided the impetus to adopt substantive criminological triage policies. This process entails diverting status offenders out of the juvenile system at the soft end, waiving serious offenders for adult criminal prosecution at the hard end, and punishing more severely the residual, middle range of ordinary delinquent offenders.

At the soft end, judicial and legislative disillusionment with juvenile courts' responses to noncriminal youths have led to diversion, deinstitutionalization, and decriminalization reforms (Feld 1993a, 1998). Deinstitutionalization reduced access to secure facilities for noncriminal offenders and provided the impetus to transfer many white, female, and middle-class youths whom juvenile courts formerly handled as status offenders into the private sector system of mental health and chemical dependency treatment and confinement (Schwartz 1989).

At the hard end, states transfer more juveniles to criminal courts. As a result of recent get-tough laws, judges, prosecutors, and legislators waive increasing numbers of younger offenders to criminal courts for prosecution as adults. The rate of judicial waiver increased 68 percent between 1988 and 1992 (Snyder and Sickmund 1995). Prosecutors in Florida alone transfer more juveniles to criminal court than do all of the juvenile court judges in the country together (Bishop and Frazier 1991). In an effort to crack down on youth crime, legislators exclude various combinations of age and offenses from juvenile courts' jurisdiction and then further expand the lists of excluded offenses and reduce the age of criminal responsibility.

The get-tough juvenile justice policies of the early 1990s reflect macrostructural, economic, and racial demographic changes in cities during the 1970s and 1980s; the emergence of the black underclass; and the rise in gun violence and youth homicides (Massey and Denton 1993; Blumstein 1995). Between World War II and the early 1970s, semiskilled high school graduates could get well-paying jobs in the automobile, steel, and construction industries. Beginning in the 1970s, the transition from an industrial to an information and service economy reduced employment opportunities in the manufacturing sectors and produced a bifurcation of economic opportunities based on skills and education. During the post–World War II period, government highway, housing, and mortgage policies encouraged suburban expansion (Massey and Denton 1993). The migration of whites to the suburbs, the growth of information and service jobs in the suburbs, the bifurcation of the economy, and the deindustrialization of the urban core increased racial segregation and the concentration of poverty among blacks in the major cities (Wilson 1987, 1996). In the mid-1980s, the emergence of a structural underclass, the introduction of crack cocaine into the inner cities, and the proliferation of guns among youths produced a sharp escalation in black youth homicide rates (Blumstein 1995). The age-offense-race-specific increase in youth homicide provided further political impetus to get tough and to crack down on youth crime. In this context, because of differences in rates of offending by race, getting tough on violence meant targeting young black men. As a result of the connection in the public and political minds between race and youth crime, juveniles have become the symbolic Willie Horton of the 1990s (Beckett 1997).

These get-tough waiver policies reflect juvenile courts' broader jurisprudential changes from rehabilitation to retribution. The overarching themes of these legislative amendments include a shift from individualized justice to just deserts, from offender to offense, from "amenability to treatment" to public safety, and from immature delinquent to responsible criminal. State legislatures use offense criteria in waiver laws as dispositional guidelines either to structure and limit judicial discretion, to guide prosecutorial charging decisions, or automatically to exclude certain youths from juvenile court jurisdiction (Feld 1987, 1995; Torbet et al. 1996).

These trends in waiver policy also reflect a fundamental cultural and legal reconceptualization of youth from innocent and dependent to responsible and autonomous. Politicians' sound bites, like "adult crime/adult time," reflect typical criminal policies that provide no formal recognition of youthfulness as a mitigating factor in sentencing. Once youths make the transition to the adult system, criminal court judges sentence them as if they are adults, impose the same sentences, send them to the same prisons, and even inflict capital punishment on them for the crimes they committed as children (Feld 1998; *Stanford v. Kentucky*, 492 U.S. 361 [1989]).

State legislators adopt social control policies within a binary framework: either child or adult, either treatment or punishment, either juvenile court or criminal court. Unfortunately, jurisdictional bifurcation frustrates effective and rational social control and often results in a punishment gap when youths make the transition between the two systems. While violent young offenders receive dramatically more severe sentences as adults than they would have received as juveniles, chronic property offenders who constitute the bulk of youths judicially transferred actually get shorter sentences as adults than they would have obtained as delinquents had they remained within the juvenile system (Podkopacz and Feld 1995, 1996). Many of the recent changes in waiver laws represent an effort to improve the fit between waiver criteria and criminal court sentencing practices, to use juvenile prior records more extensively to enhance the sentences of young adult offenders, and to respond to career offenders and career criminality that begins in early adolescence but continues into adulthood (Feld 1998). Efforts to integrate juvenile and criminal court sentencing practices and records represent an effort to rationalize social control of serious and chronic offenders on both sides of the juvenile and criminal court line. The recent emergence of blended jurisdiction laws, intermediate sentencing options like extended jurisdiction prosecutions, and blended juvenile-criminal sentences provide examples of states' groping toward graduated, escalating sanctions for young offenders across the adolescent and criminal career developmental continuum (Feld 1995, 1998; Torbet et al. 1996).

Finally, the criminological triage process has resulted in increased punishment of those ordinary delinquents who remain within the jurisdiction of the juvenile justice system (Feld 1988; Sheffer 1995). Legislative preambles and court opinions explicitly endorse punishment as an appropriate component of juvenile sanctions. States' juvenile sentencing laws increasingly emphasize responsibility and accountability and provide for determinate and/or mandatory minimum sentences keyed to the seriousness of the offense (Sheffer 1995; Feld 1998; Torbet et al. 1996). These statutory provisions use principles of proportionality and determinacy to rationalize sentencing decisions, to increase the penal bite of juvenile sanctions, and to allow legislators symbolically to demonstrate their toughness.

Two general conclusions emerge clearly from empirical research evaluating juvenile court judges' sentencing practices. First, the "principle of offense"— present offense and prior record—accounts for most of the variance in juvenile court sentences that can be explained. Every methodologically rigorous study of juvenile court sentencing practices reports that judges focus primarily on the seriousness of the present offense and prior record when they sentence delinquents (Feld 1998). Second, after controlling for legal and offense variables, the individualized justice of juvenile courts produces racial disparities in the sentencing of minority offenders (Bishop and Frazier 1996). According to the juvenile court's treatment ideology, judges' discretionary decisions should disproportionally affect minority youths, because the Progressives intended judges to focus on youths' social circumstances rather than simply their offenses and designed them to discriminate between "our children" and "other people's children."

Evaluating juvenile correctional facilities for their effectiveness provides another indicator of the increased punitiveness of juvenile justice. Evaluations of juvenile correctional facilities in the decades following *In re Gault* reveal a continuing gap between the rhetoric of rehabilitation and the punitive reality (Feld 1977, 1981). Criminological research, judicial opinions, and investigative studies report staff beatings of inmates, the use of drugs for social control purposes, extensive reliance on solitary confinement, and a virtual absence of meaningful rehabilitative programs (Feld 1998; Parent et al. 1994). Despite rehabilitative rhetoric and a euphemistic vocabulary, the simple truth is that juvenile court judges increasingly consign disproportionately minority offenders to overcrowded custodial warehouses that constitute little more than youth prisons.

Evaluations of juvenile treatment programs provide little evidence that training schools, the most common form of institutional treatment for the largest numbers of serious and chronic delinquents, effectively treat youths or reduce their recidivism rates (Feld 1998). Despite these generally negative results, proponents of the traditional juvenile court continue their quest for the elusive rehabilitative grail and offer literature reviews, meta-analyses, or program descriptions that report that some interventions produce positive effects on selected clients under certain conditions. A recent comprehensive meta-analysis of 200 studies of interventions with serious juvenile offenders reported, "The average intervention effect for these studies was positive, statistically significant, and equivalent to a recidivism reduction of about 6 percentage points, for example, from 50% to 44%" (Lipsey and Wilson 1998, 330). Typically, positive treatment effects appear in small, experimental programs that provide an intensive and integrated response to the multitude of problems that delinquent youths present. Favorable results occur primarily under optimal conditions, for example, when mental health or other nonjuvenile correctional personnel provide services with high treatment integrity in well-established programs.

Even though some programs apparently are successful for some offenders under some circumstances and produce marginal improvements in the life chances of some juveniles, most states do not elect to provide these programs or services to delinquents generally. Rather, they confine most delinquents in euphemistically sanitized youth prisons with fewer procedural safeguards than adults enjoy. Thus, even if model programs can reduce recidivism rates, public officials appear unwilling to provide such treatment services when they face fiscal constraints, budget deficits, and competition from other, more politically potent interest groups. Organizational imperatives to achieve economies of scale mandate confining ever larger numbers of youths and thereby preclude the possibility of matching offenders with appropriate treatment programs.

The Inherent Contradictions of the Juvenile Court

Juvenile courts punish rather than treat young offenders and use a procedural regime under which no adult would consent to be tried. The fundamental shortcoming of the juvenile court's welfare idea reflects a failure of conception and not simply a century-long failure of implementation. The juvenile court's creators envisioned a social service agency in a judicial setting and attempted to fuse its welfare mission with the power of state coercion. Combining social welfare and penal social control functions in one agency ensures that juvenile courts do both badly. Providing for child welfare represents a societal responsibility rather than a judicial one. Juvenile courts lack control over the resources necessary to meet child welfare needs exactly because of the social class and racial characteristics of their clients and because of the public's fear of "other people's children." In practice, juvenile courts almost inevitably subordinate welfare concerns to crime control considerations.

If we formulated child welfare programs ab initio, would we choose a juvenile court as the most appropriate agency through which to deliver social services, and would we make criminality a condition precedent to the receipt of services? If we would not initially choose a court to deliver social services, then does the fact of a youth's criminality confer upon the court any special competency as a welfare agency? Many young people who do not commit crimes desperately need social services, and many youths who commit crimes do not require or will not respond to social services. In short, criminality represents an inaccurate and haphazard criterion upon which to allocate social services. Because our society denies adequate help and assistance to meet the social welfare needs of all young people, juvenile courts' treatment ideology serves primarily to legitimate judicial coercion of some youths because of their criminality.

The attempt to combine social welfare and criminal social control in one agency constitutes the fundamental flaw of the juvenile court. The juvenile court subordinates social welfare concerns to criminal social control functions because of its inherently penal focus. Legislatures do not define juvenile courts' jurisdiction on the basis of characteristics of children for which the children are not responsible and for which effective intervention could improve their lives. For example, juvenile court law does not define eligibility for welfare services or create an enforceable right or entitlement based upon young people's lack of access to quality education, lack of adequate housing or nutrition, unmet health needs, or impoverished families—none of which are their fault. In all of these instances, children bear the burdens of their parents' circumstances literally as innocent bystanders. Instead, states' juvenile codes define juvenile court jurisdiction based upon a youth's committing a crime, a prerequisite that detracts from a compassionate response. Unlike disadvantaged social conditions that are not their fault, criminal behavior represents the one characteristic for which adolescent offenders do bear at least partial responsibility. In short, juvenile courts define eligibility for services on the basis of the feature least likely to elicit sympathy and compassion, and they ignore the social structural conditions or personal circumstances more likely to evoke a greater desire to help. Juvenile courts' defining characteristic strengthens public antipathy to "other people's children" by emphasizing primarily that they are law violators. The recent criminological triage policies that stress punishment, accountability, and personal responsibility further reinforce juvenile courts' penal foundations and reduce the legitimacy of youths' claims to humanitarian assistance.

The Kid Is a Criminal, and the Criminal Is a Kid

States should uncouple social welfare from social control, try all offenders in one integrated criminal justice system, and make appropriate substantive and procedural modifications to accommodate the youthfulness of some defendants. Substantive justice requires a rationale to sentence younger offenders differently from and more leniently than older defendants, a formal recognition of youthfulness as a mitigating factor. Procedural justice requires providing youths with full procedural parity with adult defendants and additional safeguards to account for the disadvantage of youth in the justice system. These substantive and procedural modifications can avoid the worst of both worlds, provide youths with protections functionally equivalent to those accorded adults, and do justice in sentencing.

My proposal to abolish juvenile courts constitutes neither an unqualified endorsement of punishment nor a primitive throwback to earlier centuries' vision of children as miniature adults. Rather, it honestly acknowledges that juvenile courts currently engage in criminal social control, asserts that younger offenders in a criminal justice system deserve less severe penalties for their misdeeds than do more mature offenders simply because they are young, and addresses many problems created by trying to maintain dichotomous and contradictory criminal justice systems based on an arbitrary age classification of a youth as a child or as an adult (Feld 1997).

Formulating a sentencing policy when the kid is a criminal and the criminal is a kid entails two tasks. First, I will provide a rationale for sentencing younger offenders differently from and more leniently than adult offenders. Explicitly punishing younger offenders rests on the premise that adolescents possess sufficient moral reasoning, cognitive capacity, and volitional control to hold them partially responsible for their behavior, albeit not to the same degree as adults. Developmental psychological research, jurisprudence, and criminal sentencing policy provide the rationale for why young offenders deserve less severe consequences for their misdeeds than do older offenders and justify formal recognition of youthfulness as a mitigating factor. Second, I will propose a youth discount—shorter sentences for reduced responsibility—as a practical administrative mechanism to implement youthfulness as a mitigating factor in sentencing.

The idea of deserved punishment entails censure and condemnation for making blameworthy choices and imposes sanctions proportional to the seriousness of a crime (von Hirsch 1976, 1993). Two elements—harm and culpability—define the seriousness of a crime. A perpetrator's age has relatively little bearing on assessments of harm—the nature of the injury inflicted, risk created, or value taken. But evaluations of seriousness also entail the quality of the actor's choice to engage in the criminal conduct that produced the harm. Youthfulness is a very important factor with respect to the culpability of a criminal actor because it directly affects the quality of choices. Responsibility for choices hinges on cognitive and volitional competence. Youths differ socially, physically, and psychologically from adults: they have not yet fully internalized moral norms, developed sufficient empathic identification with others, acquired adequate moral comprehension, or had sufficient opportunity to develop the ability to restrain their actions. They possess neither the rationality (cognitive capacity) nor the self-control (volitional capacity) for their criminal responsibility to be equated fully with that of adults. In short, their immaturity affects the quality of their judgments in ways that are relevant to criminal sentencing policy. Ultimately, a youth sentencing policy should enable young offenders to survive the mistakes of adolescence with their life chances intact.

Adolescence as a Form of Reduced Culpability

Certain characteristic developmental differences distinguish the quality of decisions that young people make from the quality of decisions by adults, and justify a somewhat more protective stance when states sentence younger offenders. Psychosocial maturity, judgment, and temperance provide conceptual prisms through which to view adolescents' decision-making competencies and to assess the quality of their choices (Cauffman and Steinberg 1995; Steinberg and Cauffman 1996; Scott 1992; Scott and Grisso 1997). Adolescents and adults differ in the quality of judgment and self-control they exercise because of relative differences in breadth of experience, short-term versus long-term temporal perspectives, attitudes toward risk, impulsivity, and the importance they attach to peer influences. These developmentally unique attributes affect youths' degree of criminal responsibility. Young people are more impulsive, exercise less self-control, fail adequately to calculate long-term consequences, and engage in more risky behavior than do adults. Adolescents may estimate the magnitude or probability of risks, may use a shorter time frame, or may focus on opportunities for gains rather than possibilities of losses differently from adults (Furby and Beyth-Marom 1992). Young people may discount the negative value of future consequences because they have more difficulty than adults in integrating a future consequence into their more limited experiential baseline (Gardner and Herman 1990). Adolescents' judgments may differ from those of adults because of their disposition toward sensation seeking, impulsivity related to hormonal or physiological changes, and mood volatility (Steinberg and Cauffman 1996; Cauffman and Steinberg 1995). Adolescents respond to peer group influences more readily than do adults because of the crucial role that peer relationships play in identity formation (Scott 1992; Zimring 1981). Most adolescent crime occurs in a group context, and having delinquent friends precedes an adolescent's own criminal involvement (Elliott and Menard 1996). Group offending places normally law abiding youths at greater risk of involvement and reduces their ability publicly to withdraw. Because of the social context of adolescent crime, young people require time, experience, and opportunities to develop the capacity for autonomous judgments and to resist peer influence.

Developmental processes affect adolescents' quality of judgment and self-control, directly influence their degree of criminal responsibility and deserved punishment, and justify a different criminal sentencing policy. While young offenders possess sufficient understanding and culpability to hold them accountable for their acts, their crimes are less blameworthy than adults' because of reduced culpability and limited appreciation of consequences and also because their life circumstances understandably limit their capacity to learn to make fully responsible choices.

When youths offend, the families, schools, and communities that socialize them bear some responsibility for the failures of those socializing institutions. Human beings depend upon others to nurture them and to enable them to develop and exercise the moral capacity for constructive behavior. The capacity for self-control and self-direction is not simply a matter of moral luck or good fortune but a socially constructed developmental process that provides young people with the opportunity to develop a moral character. Community structures affect social conditions and the contexts within which adolescents grow and interact with peers. Unlike presumptively mobile adults, juveniles, because of their dependency, lack the means or ability to escape from their criminogenic environments.

Zimring (1982) describes the "semi-autonomy" of adolescence as a "learner's permit" that gives youths the opportunity to make choices and to learn to be responsible but without suffering fully the long-term consequences of their mistakes. The ability to make responsible choices is learned, and the dependent status of youth systematically deprives adolescents of chances to learn to be responsible. Young people's socially constructed life situation understandably limits their capacity to develop self-control, restricts their opportunities to learn and exercise responsibility, and supports a partial reduction of criminal responsibility. A youth sentencing policy would entail both shorter sentences and a higher offense-seriousness threshold before a state incarcerates youths than for older offenders.

Youth Discount

The binary distinctions between children and adults that provide the basis for states' legal age of majority and the jurisprudential foundation of the juvenile court ignore the reality that adolescents develop along a continuum, and create an unfortunate either-or forced choice in sentencing. By contrast, shorter sentences for reduced responsibility represent a more modest and readily attainable reason to treat young offenders differently from adults than the rehabilitative justifications advanced by Progressive child savers. Protecting young people from the full penal consequences of their poor decisions reflects a policy to preserve their life chances for the future, when they presumably will make more mature and responsible choices. Such a policy both holds young offenders accountable for their acts because they possess sufficient culpability and mitigates the severity of consequences because their choices entail less blame than those of adults.

Sentencing policy that integrates youthfulness, reduced culpability, and restricted opportunities to learn self-control with penal principles of proportionality would provide younger offenders with categorical fractional reductions of adult sentences. If adolescents as a class characteristically make poorer choices than adults, then sentencing policies should protect young people from the full penal consequences of their bad decisions. Because youthfulness constitutes a universal form of reduced culpability or diminished responsibility, states should treat it categorically as a mitigating factor, without regard to nuances of individual developmental differences. Youth development is a highly variable process, and chronological age is a crude, imprecise measure of criminal maturity and the opportunity to develop the capacity for self-control. Despite the variability of adolescence, however, a categorical youth discount that uses age as a conclusive proxy for reduced culpability and shorter sentences remains preferable to any individualized inquiry into the criminal responsibility of each young offender. Developmental psychology does not possess reliable clinical indicators of moral development that equate readily with criminal responsibility and accountability. For young criminal actors who are responsible, to some degree, clinical testimony to precisely tailor sanctions to culpability is not worth the burden or diversion of resources that the effort would entail. Because youthful mitigated criminal responsibility is a legal concept, there simply is no psychiatric analogue to which clinical testimony would correspond. Rather, a youth discount categorically recognizes that criminal choices by young people are to some degree qualitatively different from those of adults and constitute a form of partial responsibility without any additional clinical indicators.

This categorical approach would take the form of an explicit youth discount at sentencing, a sliding scale of criminal responsibility. A 14-year-old offender might receive, for example, 25–33 percent of the adult penalty; a 16-year-old defendant, 50–66 percent; and an 18-year-old adult, the full penalty, as currently occurs (Feld 1997). The deeper discounts for younger offenders correspond to the developmental continuum and their more limited opportunities to learn to be responsible and to exercise self-control. Because reduced culpability provides the rationale for youthful mitigation, younger adolescents bear less responsibility and deserve proportionally shorter sentences than older youths. With the passage of time, increased age, and more numerous opportunities to develop the capacity for self-control, social tolerance of criminal deviance and claims for youthful mitigation decline. Discounted sentences that preserve younger offenders' life chances require that the maximum sentences they receive remain very substantially lower than those imposed on adults. Capital sentences and draconian mandatory minimum sentences—for example, life without parole—have no place in sentencing presumptively less blameworthy adolescents. Because of the rapidity of adolescent development and the life-course-disruptive consequences of incarceration, the rationale for a youth discount also supports requiring a higher in/out threshold of offense seriousness and culpability as a prerequisite for imprisonment.

Only states whose criminal sentencing laws provide realistic, humane, and determinate sentences that enable a judge actually to determine real-time sentences can readily implement a proposal for explicit fractional reductions of youths' sentences. One can know the value of a youth discount only in a sentencing system in which courts know in advance the standard, or going rate, for adults. In many jurisdictions, implementing a youth discount would require significant modification of the current sentencing laws, including adoption of presumptive sentencing guidelines with strong upper limits on punishment severity, elimination of all mandatory minimum sentences, and introduction of some structured judicial discretion to mitigate penalties based on individual circumstances. Attempts to apply youth discounts idiosyncratically within the flawed indeterminate or mandatory-minimum sentencing regimes that currently prevail in many jurisdictions runs the risk of simply reproducing all of their existing inequalities and injustices.

 ## Virtues of an Integrated Criminal Justice System

A graduated age-culpability sentencing scheme in an integrated criminal justice system avoids the inconsistencies associated with the binary either-juvenile-or-adult drama currently played out in judicial waiver proceedings and in prosecutorial charging decisions, and it introduces proportionality to the sentences imposed on the many youths currently tried as adults. It also avoids the punishment gap when youths make the transition from one justice system to the other, and it ensures similar consequences for similarly situated offenders. Adolescence and criminal careers develop along a continuum; the current bifurcation between the two justice systems confounds efforts to respond consistently to young career offenders. A sliding scale of criminal sentences based on an offender's age as a proxy for culpability accomplishes simply and directly what the various blended-jurisdiction statutes attempt to achieve indirectly (Feld 1995). A formal policy of youthfulness as a mitigating factor avoids the undesirable forced choice between inflicting undeservedly harsh penalties on less culpable actors and doing nothing about the manifestly guilty.

An integrated justice system also allows for integrated record keeping and enables officials to identify and respond to career offenders more readily than the current jurisdictional bifurcation permits. Even adolescent career offenders deserve enhanced sentences based on an extensive record of prior offending. But an integrated justice system does not require integrated prisons. The question of how long differs from questions of where and what. States should maintain age-segregated youth correctional facilities both to protect younger offenders from adults and to protect geriatric prisoners from younger inmates. Virtually all young offenders will return to society, and the state should provide them with resources for self-improvement because of its basic responsibility to its citizens and its own self-interest. A sentencing and correctional policy must offer youths room to reform and provide opportunities and resources to facilitate young offenders' constructive use of their time.

Finally, affirming partial responsibility for youth constitutes a virtue. The idea of personal responsibility and accountability for behavior provides an important cultural counterweight to a popular culture that endorses the idea that everyone is a victim, that all behavior is determined, and that no one is responsible. The juvenile court elevated determinism over free will, characterized delinquents as victims rather than perpetrators, and subjected them to an indeterminate quasi-civil commitment process. The juvenile court's treatment ideology denied youths' personal responsibility, reduced offenders' duty to exercise self-control, and eroded their obligations to change. If there is any silver lining in the current cloud of get-tough policies, it is the affirmation of responsibility. A culture that values autonomous individuals must emphasize both freedom and responsibility. A criminal law that bases sentences on blameworthiness and responsibility must recognize the physical, psychological, and socially constructed differences between youths and adults. Affirming responsibility forces politicians to be honest when the kid is a criminal and the criminal is a kid. The real reason states bring young offenders to juvenile courts is not to deliver social services but because the offenders committed a crime. Once politicians recognize that simple truth, then justice can follow.

 ## References

Ainsworth, Janet E. 1991. Re-imagining Childhood and Re-constructing the Legal Order: The Case for Abolishing the Juvenile Court. *North Carolina Law Review* 69:1083–133.

Allen, Francis A. 1964. Legal Values and the Rehabilitative Ideal. In *The Borderland of the Criminal Law: Essays in Law and Criminology.* Chicago: University of Chicago Press.

_____. 1981. *Decline of the Rehabilitative Ideal.* New Haven, CT: Yale University Press.

Beckett, Katherine. 1997. *Making Crime Pay: Law and Order in Contemporary American Politics.* New York: Oxford University Press.

Bishop, Donna and Charles Frazier. 1991. Transfer of Juvenile to Criminal Court: A Case Study and Analysis of Prosecutorial Waiver. *Notre Dame Journal of Law, Ethics & Public Policy* 5:281–302.

_____. 1996. Race Effects in Juvenile Justice Decision-Making: Findings of a Statewide Analysis. *Journal of Criminal Law & Criminology* 86:392–413.

Blumstein, Alfred. 1995. Youth Violence, Guns, and the Illicit-Drug Industry. *Journal of Criminal Law & Criminology* 86:10–36.

Cauffman, Elizabeth and Laurence Steinberg. 1995. The Cognitive and Affective Influences on Adolescent Decision Making. *Temple Law Review* 68:1763–89.

Elliott, Delbert and Scott Menard. 1996. Delinquent Friends and Delinquent Behavior: Temporal and Developmental Patterns. In *Delinquency and Crime: Current Theories,* ed. J. David Hawkins. New York: Cambridge University Press.

Feld, Barry C. 1977. *Neutralizing Inmate Violence: Juvenile Offenders in Institutions.* Cambridge, MA: Ballinger.

_____. 1981. A Comparative Analysis of Organizational Structure and Inmate Subcultures in Institutions for Juvenile Offenders. *Crime & Delinquency* 27:336–63.

_____. 1984. Criminalizing Juvenile Justice: Rules of Procedure for Juvenile Court. *Minnesota Law Review* 69:141–276.

_____. 1987. Juvenile Court Meets the Principle of Offense: Legislative Changes in Juvenile Waiver Statutes. *Journal of Criminal Law & Criminology* 78:471–533.

_____. 1988. Juvenile Court Meets the Principle of Offense: Punishment, Treatment, and the Difference It Makes. *Boston University Law Review* 68:821–915.

_____. 1989. The Right to Counsel in Juvenile Court: An Empirical Study of When Lawyers Appear and the Difference They Make. *Journal of Criminal Law & Criminology* 79:1185–346.

_____. 1993a. Criminalizing the American Juvenile Court. In *Crime and Justice: A Review of Research,* ed. Michael Tonry. Vol. 17. Chicago: University of Chicago Press.

_____. 1993b. *Justice for Children: The Right to Counsel and the Juvenile Court.* Boston: Northeastern University Press.

_____. 1995. Violent Youth and Public Policy: A Case Study of Juvenile Justice Law Reform. *Minnesota Law Review* 79:965–1128.

_____. 1997. Abolish the Juvenile Court: Youthfulness, Criminal Responsibility, and Sentencing Policy. *Journal of Criminal Law & Criminology* 88:68–136.

_____. 1998. Juvenile and Criminal Justice Systems' Responses to Youth Violence. *Crime and Justice: A Review of Research* 24:189–261.

_____. 1999. *Bad Kids: Race and the Transformation of the Juvenile Court.* New York: Oxford University Press.

Furby, Lita and Ruth Beyth-Marom. 1992. Risk Taking in Adolescence: A Decision-Making Perspective. *Developmental Review* 12:1–44.

Gardner, William and Janna Herman. 1990: Adolescents' AIDS Risk Taking: A Rational Choice Perspective. In *Adolescents and the AIDS Epidemic,* ed. William Gardner, Susan G. Millstein, and Bruce Leroy Cox. San Francisco: Jossey-Bass.

Grisso, Thomas. 1980. Juveniles' Capacities to Waive *Miranda* Rights: An Empirical Analysis. *California Law Review* 68:1134–66.

Lemann, Nicholas. 1992. *The Promised Land: The Great Black Migration and How It Changed America.* New York: Vintage Books.

Lipsey, Mark W. and David B. Wilson. 1998. Effective Intervention for Serious Juvenile Offenders. In *Serious and Violent Juvenile Offenders: Risk Factors and Successful Interventions,* ed. Rolf Loeber and David P. Farrington. Thousand Oaks, CA: Sage.

Massey, Douglas and Nancy Denton. 1993. *American Apartheid: Segregation and the Making of the Underclass.* Cambridge, MA: Harvard University Press.

Parent, Dale G., Valerie Lieter, Stephen Kennedy, Lisa Livens, Daniel Wentworth, and Sarah Wilcox. 1994. *Conditions of Confinement: Juvenile Detention and Corrections Facilities.* Washington, DC: Department of Justice, Office of Juvenile Justice and Delinquency Prevention.

Podkopacz, Marcy Rasmussen and Barry C. Feld. 1995. Judicial Waiver Policy and Practice: Persistence, Seriousness and Race. *Law & Inequality: A Journal of Theory and Practice* 14:73–178.

_____. 1996. The End of the Line: An Empirical Study of Judicial Waiver. *Journal of Criminal Law & Criminology* 86:449–92.

Schwartz, Ira M. 1989. *Injustice for Juveniles: Rethinking the Best Interests of the Child.* Lexington, MA: Lexington Books.

Scott, Elizabeth S. 1992. Judgment and Reasoning in Adolescent Decision Making. *Villanova Law Review* 37:1607–69.

Scott, Elizabeth S. and Thomas Grisso. 1997. The Evolution of Adolescence: A Developmental Perspective on Juvenile Justice Reform. *Journal of Criminal Law & Criminology* 88:137–89.

Sheffer, Julianne P. 1995. Serious and Habitual Juvenile Offender Statutes: Reconciling Punishment and Rehabilitation Within the Juvenile Justice System. *Vanderbilt Law Review* 48:479–512.

Snyder, Howard and Melissa Sickmund. 1995. *Juvenile Offenders and Victims: A National Report.* Washington, DC: Department of Justice, Office of Juvenile Justice and Delinquency Prevention, National Center for Juvenile Justice.

Steinberg, Laurence and Elizabeth Cauffman. 1996. Maturity of Judgment in Adolescence: Psychosocial Factors in Adolescent Decision Making. *Law and Human Behavior* 20:249–72.

Torbet, Patricia, Richard Gable, Hunter Hurst IV, Imogene Montgomery, Linda Szymanski, and Douglas Thomas. 1996. *State Responses to Serious and Violent Juvenile Crime: Research Report.* Washington, DC: Department of Justice, Office of Juvenile

Justice and Delinquency Prevention, National Center for Juvenile Justice.

von Hirsch, Andrew. 1976. *Doing Justice*. New York: Hill & Wang.

_____. 1993. *Censure and Blame*. New York: Oxford University Press.

Wilson, William Julius. 1987. *The Truly Disadvantaged*. Chicago: University of Chicago Press.

_____. 1996. *When Work Disappears: The World of the New Urban Poor.* New York: Knopf.

Zimring, Franklin. 1981. Kids, Groups and Crime: Some Implications of a Well-Known Secret. *Journal of Criminal Law & Criminology* 72:867–902.

_____. 1982. *The Changing Legal World of Adolescence.* New York: Free Press.

DISCUSSION QUESTIONS

1. Feld argues that "two competing cultural and legal conceptions of youth" have facilitated the transformation of the juvenile court from a social welfare agency focused on rehabilitation into a "second-class criminal court." What are these two competing conceptions?

2. What forces led to the development of the juvenile court?

3. How did the Supreme Court decision *In re Gault* affect the juvenile court? Why did Feld argue that this case "constituted an incomplete procedural revolution"?

4. How did the "tough on crime" attitudes and policies of the 1980s and 1990s affect the juvenile court and the treatment of youthful offenders?

5. According to Feld, what is the "fundamental flaw of the juvenile court"?

6. Why does Feld advocate abolishing juvenile courts? What would he substitute for them?

7. Do you agree or disagree with Feld's proposal for a "youth discount" at sentencing?

8. How would policymakers respond to Feld's proposal for an integrated criminal justice system? What types of officials would support it? Who might oppose it?

READING

The United States Supreme Court is the highest court in the land. Although it is primarily an appellate court, it exercises original jurisdiction over certain offenses. Decisions handed down by the Supreme Court have had an important effect on the daily operations of the criminal justice system. Through scores of appeals emanating from the lower courts, the Supreme Court has handed down a wide array of decisions that affect police officers, court officials, corrections officials, and defendants. These decisions dictate such things as how juries are to be selected, trials conducted, and sentences imposed. Clearly, the Supreme Court plays an important role in the criminal process.

The stereotypical image of judges is that they are neutral and detached arbiters of legal matters. In reality, though, courts, including the Supreme Court, can be highly politicized institutions. In choosing nominees for the Court, presidents consider not only the candidate's experience and qualifications but also his or her party affiliation, political ideology, and policy preferences. Republican presidents tend to appoint Republican judges, who are ideologically conservative, and Democratic presidents tend to appoint Democratic judges, who have more liberal views. The choices that presidents make when filling vacancies on the Supreme Court, therefore, have the potential to affect the ideological makeup of the Court and thus the decisions handed down by the court. (Presidents, however, are not always satisfied with the judges they appoint. President Eisenhower, for example, appointed two justices—Earl Warren and William Brennan—whom he thought were conservative but who turned out to be extremely liberal. When asked whether he had made any mistakes as president, Eisenhower replied, "Yes, two, and they are both sitting on the Supreme Court" [Baum, 1985, p. 41].) Scholars have given much attention to the ideological leanings of the Supreme Court, which often depend not only on the conservative/liberal ratio of judges but also on the ideological stance of the chief justice.

One such examination is Christopher Smith's study, "The Rehnquist Court and Criminal Justice: An Empirical Assessment." Smith's study reveals how, under the leadership of (now deceased) Chief Justice Rehnquist, the Supreme Court handed down many decisions that favored criminal justice officials rather than individuals accused of crimes. Many have called the "Rehnquist Court" a conservative Court because of this tendency to side with law enforcement officials and other criminal justice professionals. Smith's study also provides a glimpse of the power and influence the Supreme Court can exert over the operation of the criminal justice system. Not unlike Feeley's article on the lower criminal courts, Smith's study illustrates how the Supreme Court *does* operate rather than how it *should* operate.

The Rehnquist Court and Criminal Justice

An Empirical Assessment

Christopher E. Smith

When scholars articulate conclusions about institutions, processes, and social phenomena, they inevitably summarize and generalize. Generalizations, if produced thoughtfully and supported by evidence, can reflect accurate insights. Yet generalizations, especially those concerning human behavior and complex social phenomena, by their very nature diminish or omit inconsistencies, cross-currents, and complexities that would provide a more complete picture of developments. Thus, there are risks that the often-repeated generalizations about the subjects of scholarly study will obscure details that are essential for comprehensive understanding of trends and consequences.

When the U.S. Supreme Court is the subject of study, it is especially important to analyze trends in the context of other developments. The Court plays a central role in shaping law and public policy affecting criminal justice. During William Rehnquist's tenure as Chief Justice, the Court has gained a reputation as a consistent supporter of expanded discretionary authority

SOURCE: Smith, Christopher E. (2003, May). The Rehnquist Court and Criminal Justice: An Empirical Assessment. *Journal of Contemporary Criminal Justice, 19*(2), 161–181.

for state legislatures, prosecutors, police officers, and corrections officials. In part, these generalizations flow from the Rehnquist Court's sharp contrast with the rights-expanding performance of the Warren Court era (Cox, 1968). As a result, the actions of the Rehnquist Court tend to be summarized as being conservative and advancing a diminution of constitutional rights for criminal suspects, defendants, and convicted offenders. For example, in the words of John C. Domino in his book *Civil Rights and Liberties: Toward the 21st Century* (1994),

> By rethinking established modes of constitutional adjudication and by returning to constitutional literalism, the Rehnquist Court has tipped the scales in favor of states' rights, community interests, law and order, and majority rule, bringing us nearly full circle to the judicial philosophy of the pre-Warren era. (p. 285)

Despite the consistency of certain trends, the Rehnquist Court is not a monolithic entity that inevitably acts in a predictable fashion. The human beings who comprise the Court form shifting and sometimes surprising internal majorities whose decisions expand governmental authority in many instances yet impose limits on police and prosecutors in other circumstances. One way to gain a more nuanced and complete understanding of the Rehnquist Court's cases affecting criminal justice is to empirically examine the decision making of the Court and its justices. Empirical data about judicial decision making do not adequately describe and provide a basis for analyzing all important aspects of the Supreme Court's performance and consequences, especially with respect to doctrinal developments and policy impacts. However, empirical data can provide systematically developed, comprehensive "snapshots" of the decisions by the Court and its justices. The use of such data can help to alleviate the limiting effects of generalizations based on perceived trends affecting specific doctrinal issues. This article uses empirical data about the Supreme Court to look beyond the Rehnquist Court's trends and reputation and thereby identify less recognized underlying characteristics and developments.

 # Method

For several decades, scholars in political science have analyzed court decisions through quantitative techniques (e.g., Segal, 1986). The use of these techniques requires that cases be classified and coded. As a result, several large databases of court decisions have been developed that provide scholars with categories of information about each court decision. The analysis of Supreme Court trends in this article is based on case classifications that emulate those in the Supreme Court Judicial Data Base. The Supreme Court Judicial Data Base provides information about legal issues and each justice's vote for all U.S. Supreme Court decisions since 1953 (Spaeth, 2001).

Cases were individually coded for the purposes of this article rather than relying on the Supreme Court Judicial Data Base. The coding for the Supreme Court Judicial Data Base is described as follows:

> Although the criteria for the identification of issues are hard to articulate, the focus here is on the subject matter of the controversy rather than its legal basis.... The objective is to categorize the case from a public policy standpoint. (Spaeth, 2001, p. 70)

In contrast with the public policy emphasis of the coding for the Supreme Court Judicial Data Base, this article focused on the legal basis for the Supreme Court's decisions. For example, in the Supreme Court Judicial Data Base, Fourth Amendment cases are classified under the categories search and seizure; search and seizure, vehicles; and search and seizure, Crime Control Act. In addition, Fourth Amendment cases may also be found with alternative classifications such as civil rights, juveniles, in which they may be mixed with other kinds of cases. Cases concerning juveniles cover such Fourth Amendment matters as drug testing within schools or school locker searches as well as other legal issues affecting juveniles' rights. Thus, for the purposes of this article, the author classified individual cases based on the legal issues involved in the cases rather than seek to find, for example, where all of the Fourth Amendment cases might be located in various categories within the Supreme Court Judicial Data Base.

All of the Supreme Court's decisions from the 1995 term through the 2000 term were examined to determine which ones are related to criminal justice. This study broadly defines criminal justice-related cases. In addition to cases concerning statutory interpretations of substantive criminal law and constitutional interpretations affecting criminal defendants' rights, the study includes decisions concerning civil rights litigation that affects officials in the criminal justice system. These cases concerning civil litigation were included because civil rights lawsuits against police and corrections officials significantly influence the development of policies, practices, and training in the criminal justice system (Smith & Hurst, 1997). This study excludes immigration cases, such as those concerning the deportation of individuals with criminal records.

The time period for study was selected to examine the Rehnquist Court during its era of most stable composition. The same nine justices have been on the Court since the appointment of Justice Stephen Breyer in 1994. Thus, this study is able to examine an actual court with consistent composition rather than a changing institutional entity that bears the name "Rehnquist Court" merely because of the tradition of labeling Supreme Court eras according to the identity of the chief justice. The time period for this study begins with the 1995 term rather than with the arrival of Justice Breyer in 1994 to avoid the risk that Breyer's initial performance might have been distorted by the "freshman effect," a much-debated hypothesis concerning new justices' initial inconsistency and lack of confidence in participating in the Court's group decision-making process during the first term of service (e.g., Heck & Hall, 1981; Melone, 1990; Snyder, 1958).

Each criminal justice–related case was classified according to the legal issue raised in the case. If there was more than one issue in a case, the case was classified according to the issue that received the most attention in the Court's opinions or the issue that caused the greatest division among the justices. There were no multiple-issue cases in which the issue that caused the

greatest division was not also the issue that received the most extensive attention in the opinions. In an effort to maintain consistency, the classifications were checked against the case syllabi provided on Cornell University's Web site for Supreme Court decisions (see http://www.law.cornell.edu) as well as against yearly postterm coding for all Supreme Court civil rights and liberties cases done by a team of three professors in preparation of annual supplements for a Supreme Court textbook (e.g., Hensley, Smith, & Baugh, 1998).

The outcome of each case was classified as "liberal" or "conservative," as is commonly done in empirical studies of judicial decisions. The definitions of liberal and conservative are modeled on the classifications in the Supreme Court Judicial Data Base in which "liberal decisions in the area of civil liberties are pro-person accused or convicted of a crime, pro-civil liberties or civil rights claimant, pro-indigent, pro-Native American, and anti-government in due process and privacy" (Segal & Spaeth, 1989, p. 104). By contrast, conservative decisions in criminal justice cases favor the government's interests in prosecuting and punishing offenders over recognition or expansion of rights for individuals. The votes of each justice were similarly classified according to these definitions.

 ## The Supreme Court's Criminal Justice Docket

Cases concerning criminal justice comprise a substantial portion of the Supreme Court's docket. Indeed, if the Supreme Court's cases were divided among categories defined by the titles of law courses taught at universities, criminal law and criminal procedure would have few rivals for their claim to a lion's share of the Court's attention. The contemporary predominance of criminal justice cases on the Supreme Court's docket is consistent with the importance of such cases as a central focus of the Court's attention since the 1960s (O'Brien, 1990). As indicated in Table 2.5, during the period of the Supreme Court's 1995 term through its 2000 term, an era in which the Court produced full written opinions after oral arguments in only 74 to 85 cases each year (e.g., Coyle, 2000; Greenhouse, 1996), the Court decided between 22 and 35 criminal justice cases each year. The table includes constitutional law decisions, such as those defining individuals' rights in the criminal justice system, and statutory interpretation decisions concerning such issues as substantive criminal law and sentencing guidelines.

Table 2.5 highlights two striking but infrequently acknowledged characteristics of the Supreme Court's decision making and impact on criminal justice. First, although most scholarly analyses of the Supreme Court's impact on criminal justice focus on constitutional law decisions affecting individuals' rights and the scope of officials' discretionary authority, most of the Supreme Court's decisions concerning criminal justice do not address constitutional issues. During a 6-year period, the Supreme Court devoted more attention to cases concerning sentencing guidelines, habeas corpus procedures, and federal substantive criminal law than to cases defining the constitutional rights of suspects, defendants, and convicted offenders. Unlike constitutional decisions about searches and seizures that affect thousands of encounters between citizens and police every day throughout the country, these nonconstitutional cases typically concern relatively narrow issues of statutory interpretation that affect only limited numbers of federal criminal prosecutions. Even the Court's primary nonconstitutional issue of broad potential applicability, habeas corpus procedures, actually affects only a limited number of cases because of the relatively small number of incarcerated

offenders who file such petitions in the federal courts (Hanson & Daley, 1995).

Second, the relatively small number of constitutional decisions affecting criminal justice, typically only a dozen per year in recent terms, highlights the need to avoid exaggerating the highest court's importance in shaping case outcomes when constitutional rights are at issue. Although the Court has made many important decisions concerning individuals' rights and its decisions provide guidance for decision making by other courts, the Supreme Court examines and settles only the tiniest fraction of constitutional claims that arise annually in criminal justice cases. State supreme courts, state intermediate appellate courts, and federal courts of appeals throughout the country each determine the outcomes in many more cases affecting individuals' rights in the criminal justice *system* than does the U.S. Supreme Court (Maguire & Pastore, 2001). Despite its image as the ultimate institutional guardian of constitutional rights, the contemporary Court decides very few such cases. In reality, the protection of constitutional rights in criminal justice rests most heavily on the knowledge, ethics, and professionalism of police officers and others who make discretionary decisions about the investigation and prosecution of crimes. State courts and lower federal courts provide a potential check on officials' improper decisions, but the U.S. Supreme Court is seldom involved in evaluating the propriety of decisions in the justice system. There is no doubt that Supreme Court justices aspire to select for decision those criminal justice issues that will have broad applicability. However, the small numbers of

Table 2.5 Annual Number of Constitutional and Nonconstitutional Criminal Justice Cases Decided by the U.S. Supreme Court From the 1995 Term Through the 2000 Term

Term	1995	1996	1997	1998	1999	2000	Overall Total
Constitutional	10	13	12	12	20	11	78
Statutory and other	12	17	23	10	11	14	87
Annual total	22	30	35	22	31	25	165

constitutional issues they choose to examine annually as well as the percentage of the justices' decisions that endorse and expand officials' actions at the expense of individuals' claims of right (see Table 2.8) effectively limit the Supreme Court's practical role and impact as the protector of rights in criminal justice.

Table 2.6 shows the nature and frequency of criminal justice issues addressed by the Rehnquist Court during six terms. Among constitutional cases, issues arose most frequently concerning the Fourth Amendment. The predominance of search and seizure cases is not surprising in light of the many technical details affecting the legal rules on this subject. There is no single rule or principle that defines rights and limits

of official authority under the Fourth Amendment. Instead, the Court typically defines search and seizure guidelines by balancing governmental investigatory interests against individuals' privacy interests in specific situations. A variety of issues arise with great regularity because of the frequency with which police officers conduct stops and searches in diverse contexts and unique factual circumstances.

Among nonconstitutional issues, the significant attention given to habeas corpus procedures reflects the effort by the Rehnquist Court majority to limit opportunities for convicted offenders to mount collateral attacks on their convictions within the federal courts (Yackle, 1994). In addition, the Court has

Table 2.6   Issues in the U.S. Supreme Court's Criminal Justice Cases From the 1995 Term Through the 2000 Term

Constitutional Issues	78 (47.3%)	Statutory and Other Issues	87 (52.2%)
Fourth Amendment	20	Habeas corpus procedures	25
Due process	11	Federal criminal statutes	21
Sixth Amendment right to counsel	6	Civil rights litigation	13
Capital jury instructions	6	Federal sentencing statute and guidelines	11
Fifth Amendment self-incrimination	5	Federal rules of criminal procedure	5
Fifth Amendment double jeopardy	4	Appellate review standards	3
Ex post facto clause	4	Interstate detainers/extradition	2
Sixth Amendment confrontation clause	3	Forfeiture procedures	2
Equal protection		Federal rules of evidence	1
First Amendment	3	Federal prison regulations	1
Sixth Amendment fair trial	3	Lawyer-client privilege	1
Separation of powers	2	Tribal court jurisdiction	1
Sixth Amendment trial by jury	2	Other federal statute	1
Sixth Amendment compulsory process	1		
Eighth Amendment excessive fines	1		
Habeas corpus suspension	1		
Prisoners' access to courts	1		
Appointments clause	1		
Federalism	1		
Fourteenth Amendment right to practice law	1		
Privacy	1		

interpreted a recent statute (Anti-Terrorism and Effective Death Penalty Act) that places congressional limitations on habeas corpus.

The Court's attention devoted to the interpretation of federal criminal statutes is a predictable consequence of two ongoing developments affecting the criminal justice system. First, Congress has acted with increasing frequency to "federalize" crimes by enacting new statutes defining offenses and punishments (Gest, 2001). Because there are more federal crimes than in the past, the Supreme Court should expect more numerous requests to clarify the meaning of the statutes that define those crimes. Second, the expansion of federal law enforcement agencies and their activities inevitably produces more investigations, prosecutorial decisions, and new factual circumstances for which the meaning and applicability of criminal laws may be disputed.

In Table 2.7, the major categories of criminal justice cases are divided according to Supreme Court term to discern any evidence of patterns or changes of attention to specific issues.

If one hypothesized that the Supreme Court justices harbor specific agendas concerning areas of law and policy they seek to shape with their decisions (Baum, 1989), then patterns of issues accepted for hearing and decision might reveal preferences and priorities. Although there are specific reasons, as previously discussed, for the Fourth Amendment, habeas corpus, and federal criminal law to comprise important segments of the Court's docket, there is little indication that annual figures on cases concerning these issues can be attributed to anything other than unpredictable patterns of particular cases brought to the Court each year and the justices' inclinations to tackle specific cases. Cases concerning habeas corpus, federal crimes, and search and seizure have been accepted for hearing each year, sometimes with more cases than in the past but with no clear trajectory. By contrast, the Court's increased attention to right to counsel and capital jury instructions in recent terms may reflect the emergence of these issues due to increased public attention and political controversies surrounding the death penalty (e.g., Wilgoren, 2002). The highly publicized problems with erroneous convictions and inadequate representation of capital defendants may have drawn the Court's attention to these issues that did not previously secure a regular place on the docket.

Table 2.7 Number of Case Decisions for Major Issue Areas From the 1995 Term Through the 2000 Term

Issue	Term						
	1995	1996	1997	1998	1999	2000	Total
Habeas corpus procedures	3[a]	4	7	2	4	5	25
Federal criminal statute	1	3	6	5	4	2	21
Fourth Amendment	1	4	2	5	3	5	20
Civil rights litigation	0	4	5	2	0	2	13
Federal sentencing law	4	2	3	0	2	0	11
Due process	3	3	0	2	2	1	11
Sixth Amendment right to counsel	0	0	0	0	4	2	6
Capital jury instructions	0	0	2	1	1	2	6

a. The Supreme Court also decided a fourth habeas corpus-related case in the 1995 term. Unlike the nonconstitutional procedural issues in other habeas corpus cases, this case concerned the application of the Habeas Corpus Suspension Clause to and the constitutionality of the habeas corpus provisions of the Anti-Terrorism and Effective Death Penalty Act (*Felker v. Turpin*, 1996).

Empirical Measures of Supreme Court Decision Making in Criminal Justice

In deciding criminal justice cases, the Rehnquist Court has been characterized as "moving to the Right" (Lock, 1999, p. 90). This characterization stems from the generally accepted observation that the Court's majority is composed of conservatives who have "been active in narrowing or overturning many Warren and Burger Court precedents that were favorable to the rights" of individuals in the criminal justice system (Fliter, 2001, p. 183). None of the contemporary justices had the experience of representing criminal defendants in their prejudicial careers as attorneys (Fortunato, 1999). The only justice whose work as an attorney included advocacy for constitutional rights, Ruth Bader Ginsburg, focused on the applicability of the Equal Protection Clause to gender discrimination cases (Cole, 1984). The other justices' prejudicial careers gave them legal experience in government, representing corporate interests, or both (e.g., *The Supreme Court at Work,* 1990). The majority of Warren Court members had personal experiences that gave them an empathic understanding of the risk that suspects and defendants could experience maltreatment at the hands of abusive law enforcement officials (Smith, 1990). By contrast, most of the Rehnquist Court justices' contacts with criminal justice came through experiences as lawyers on the staffs of county prosecutors, state attorney generals, or the U.S.

Justice Department (i.e., Sandra Day O'Connor, William Rehnquist, Antonin Scalia, Clarence Thomas, David Souter). Moreover, most of the Rehnquist Court justices were selected by Republican presidents who emphasized "law and order" crime control policies and sought to identify judicial appointees who would reflect those views. Because the Supreme Court's decisions are driven by the values and policy preferences of its members (Baum, 1989), one would expect the contemporary Supreme Court to generally favor the maintenance of justice officials' discretionary authority over the expansion of constitutional rights for criminal suspects, defendants, and convicted offenders.

Table 2.8 portrays the Supreme Court's pattern of decision making from the 1995 term through the 2000 term. In the table, the labels *liberal* and *conservative* are used as a convenient shorthand to describe the outcomes supported by individual justices and the Court majority. Such labels are commonly used in empirical studies of the Supreme Court, and their use enhances scholars' ability to make systematic comparisons of different Court terms and eras.

Despite the Rehnquist Court's reputation for conservatism in criminal justice cases, 37% of its decisions supported individuals' claims. Moreover, nearly half of these liberal decisions (28 of 61) were unanimous. In addition, the justices demonstrated a complete consensus on conservative outcomes in an additional 35 cases. Despite the strong differences of opinion among justices that are evident in many cases, the justices were in

Table 2.8 Case Distribution by Vote and Liberal-Conservative Outcomes in U.S. Supreme Court Criminal Justice Decisions From the 1995 Term Through the 2000 Term

Vote	Liberal	Conservative	Total
9–0	28	35	63
8–1	4	13	17
7–2	9	15	24
6–3	7	13	20
5–4	13	28	41
Total	61 (37%)	104 (63%)	165

complete agreement in 38% of criminal justice cases (63 of 165). The data on unanimous liberal decisions indicate that the Rehnquist Court justices, including the conservatives, regularly encounter cases in which they share a consensus about the need to protect constitutional rights and to fulfill the legislative intent underlying federal statutes. The justices' consensus in such cases leads to the imposition of limitations on criminal justices officials' asserted authority. Previous studies highlight the risk that a Supreme Court's ideological reputation will obscure the reality of its production of ideologically mixed outcomes during any given era (Smith & Hensley, 1993). As indicated by Table 2.8, the conservative Rehnquist Court's regular support for liberal outcomes in criminal justice cases is consistent with these studies.

The dominance of the conservative majority is evident in the split decisions produced by the Court. Whenever there is disagreement among the justices, those who prefer conservative outcomes prevail in nearly 70% of nonunanimous cases. Attorneys who bring criminal defendants' cases to the Supreme Court undoubtedly recognize that the justices support the government more frequently than they support individuals' claims. However, the Court endorses individuals' claims with sufficient regularity that attorneys ought to believe that it is worth "taking a shot" for many issues that have not been firmly and decisively defined in prior precedents.

In deciding criminal justice cases, individual justices differ from each other in their tendency to support individuals' claims. Table 2.9 shows each justice's support for liberal and conservative outcomes in criminal justice cases during six terms. For comparative purposes, the table also displays the percentages for justices serving on the Warren Court in 1968 (Smith, 1997a). Data for the Warren Court were drawn from the Supreme Court Judicial Data Base, whereas the Rehnquist Court data were classified and calculated by the author.

The percentages displayed in the table are generally consistent with conventional wisdom about the Rehnquist Court justices' values and reputations, although some

Table 2.9   Individual Rehnquist Court Justices' Liberal-Conservative Voting Percentages in U.S. Supreme Court Criminal Justice Decisions From the 1995 Term Through the 2000 Term Compared With 1968 Warren Court Justices' Lifetime Percentages for Criminal Justice Cases

Rehnquist Court			Warren Court		
Justice	Liberal	Conservative	Justice	Liberal	Conservative
Rehnquist	26.1% (43)	73.9% (122)	White	33%	67%
Thomas	27.9%(46)	72.1% (119)	Harlan	38%	62%
Scalia	30.9% (51)	69.1% (114)	Stewart	45%	55%
O'Connor	31.5% (52)	68.5% (113)	Black	70%	30%
Kennedy	34.5% (57)	65.5% (108)	Warren	74%	26%
Breyer[a]	54.9% (90)	45.1% (74)	Brennan	76%	24%
Souter	57.6% (95)	42.4% (70)	Marshall	80%	20%
Ginsburg	60% (99)	40% (66)	Fortas	83%	17%
Stevens	69.7% (115)	30.3% (50)	Douglas	89%	11%

a. Justice Breyer participated in only 24 of the 25 criminal justice cases during the 2000–2001 term. Thus, his total number of decisions is one fewer than that of his colleagues. He recused himself from participating in *United States v. Oakland Cannabis Buyers' Cooperative* (2001), presumably because his brother is a federal judge who made a decision in the case in the lower courts.

observers might have guessed that the ordering of the justices would be slightly different. The listing of percentages for the individual Rehnquist Court justices shows how much the Supreme Court has changed since the 1960s when they are compared with the percentages for Warren Court justices. As indicated by Table 2.9, six Warren Court justices (Black, Warren, Brennan, Marshall, Fortas, and Douglas) were as or more liberal than the most liberal Rehnquist Court justice (Stevens) with respect to their patterns of decisions for criminal justice cases. Conversely, five Rehnquist Court justices (Rehnquist, Thomas, Scalia, O'Connor, and Kennedy) are as or more conservative than the most conservative Warren Court justice (White).

Consistent with their reputations, Chief Justice Rehnquist and Justices Thomas and Scalia are the justices least likely to support individuals' claims. Among the Court's four most liberal justices, there is a notable 20% gap between the most conservative liberal (Breyer) and the most liberal conservative (Kennedy). This gap would seem to justify descriptions of the Court as split between two distinctive wings for criminal justice cases. It is also apparent that Justice Stevens is notably more consistent than are his colleagues in supporting liberal outcomes because there is a 10% gap between him and the next most liberal justice (Ginsburg), who is tightly bunched (i.e., within 5%) with the other two liberals (Breyer and Souter).

It is not surprising that the dividing line between the Court's two wings defines the outcomes for most of the Court's most closely contested cases. As indicated in Table 2.10, the losing liberal minority coalition in 5-to-4 conservative decisions was composed of the Court's four most liberal justices in 23 of 28 decisions.

The most surprising aspect of the Rehnquist Court percentages in Table 2.9 may be the evidence that Justices O'Connor and Kennedy are nearly as conservative as Justice Scalia in criminal justice cases. Although O'Connor and Kennedy are regarded as two dependable members of the dominant five-member conservative majority, they are often described as the Court's "centrists" who periodically abandon their conservative colleagues to enable the four most liberal justices to gain a five-member majority in specific cases (Greenhouse, 1992). Despite this reputation for relative moderation in criminal justice cases, they were no more likely than Justices Scalia and Thomas to join five-member majorities to create liberal outcomes in criminal justice cases during the time period examined. As demonstrated in Table 2.11, which depicts the majority coalitions in the Court's thirteen 5-to-4 liberal decisions, the tandem of Scalia and Thomas abandoned their conservative colleagues to help the liberal justices form a razor-thin majority just as frequently (i.e., 4 times) as O'Connor and Kennedy acted individually to achieve the same results. In fact, Clarence Thomas, one of the Court's most conservative justices, was actually the individual justice who helped the liberals form majorities in the largest number of closely divided decisions (5) because he acted on his own in

Table 2.10   Dissenting Coalitions and Frequency of Their Existence in the Rehnquist Court's 5-to-4 Conservative Decisions From the 1995 Term Through the 2000 Term

Dissenting Coalition	Frequency
Stevens, Souter, Breyer, and Ginsburg	23
Stevens, Souter, Breyer, and O'Connor	1
Stevens, Souter, Breyer, and Kennedy	1
Stevens, Breyer, Ginsburg, and O'Connor	1
Souter, Ginsburg, Rehnquist, and Scalia	1
Stevens, Breyer, Scalia, and Thomas	1

Table 2.11 Majority Coalitions in the Supreme Court's 5-to-4 Liberal Decisions From the 1995 Term Through the 2000 Term With the Conservative Coalition Members Highlighted

Case	Justices in Majority Coalition
1995 term	There were no 5-to-4 liberal decisions
1996 term	
Richardson v. McKnight (1997)	**O'Connor,** Breyer, Souter, Stevens, Ginsburg
Lindh v. Murphy (1997)	**O'Connor,** Breyer, Souter, Stevens, Ginsburg
Old Chief v. United States (1997)	**Kennedy,** Breyer, Souter, Stevens, Ginsburg
1997 term	
Hohn v. United States (1998)	**Kennedy,** Breyer, Souter, Stevens, Ginsburg
Crawford-El v. Britton (1998)	**Kennedy,** Breyer, Souter, Stevens, Ginsburg
Gray v. Maryland (1998)	**O'Connor,** Breyer, Souter, Stevens, Ginsburg
United States v. Bajakajian (1998)	**Thomas,** Breyer, Souter, Stevens, Ginsburg
1998 term	
Mitchell v. United States (1999)	**Kennedy,** Breyer, Souter, Stevens, Ginsburg
Jones v. United States (1999)	**Thomas, Scalia,** Souter, Stevens, Ginsburg
1999 term	
Apprendi v. New Jersey (2000)	**Thomas,** Scalia, Souter, Stevens, Ginsburg
Carmell v. Texas (2000)	**Thomas, Scalia,** Souter, Stevens, Breyer
Stenberg v. Carhart (2000)	**O'Connor,** Breyer, Souter, Stevens, Ginsburg
2000 term	
Kyllo v. United States (2001)	**Thomas, Scalia,** Souter, Breyer, Ginsburg

one case in addition to the four cases in which he acted in concert with Scalia. These examples provide evidence that specific legal issues can draw justices away from their usual ideological allies because these issues strike a chord with the justices' individualistic, or perhaps idiosyncratic, analysis or philosophy concerning specific principles of statutory and constitutional interpretation.

Table 2.12 shows an analysis of interagreement between individual justices on the Supreme Court. Such interagreement tables are used to detect the existence of voting blocs on the high court (e.g., Johnson & Smith, 1992). In empirical studies of the Supreme Court, voting blocs are determined according to the Sprague criterion. The Sprague criterion is calculated by subtracting the average agreement score for the entire Court from 100.

Table 2.12 Interagreement Percentages for Paired Justices in U.S. Supreme Court Criminal Justice Decisions From the 1995 Term Through the 2000 Term

	Thomas	Scalia	Rehnquist	O'Connor	Kennedy	Souter	Breyer	Ginsburg	Stevens
Thomas		92.1	86.1	80.6	80.0	64.2	63.4	58.2	50.9
Scalia			85.5	78.2	75.2	63.6	59.1	58.2	49.1
Rehnquist				87.3	84.2	64.8	64.6	62.4	52.7
O'Connor					84.8	70.9	72.6	68.5	57.6
Kennedy						70.9	72.0	67.3	62.4
Souter							85.4	89.1	80.0
Breyer								86.0	81.1
Ginsburg									81.8
Court mean		72.0							
Sprague criterion		86.0							
Voting blocs									
Thomas, Scalia, and Rehnquist				87.9					
Souter, Breyer, and Ginsburg				86.8					

The resulting number is divided by two and added to the Court average to establish the threshold level for defining a bloc. A bloc exists when the average of individual agreement scores for a set of justices exceeds the threshold established by the Sprague criterion calculation (Sprague, 1968). During the six terms examined in this study, there were two strong voting blocs in criminal justice cases, one conservative and one liberal. Chief Justice Rehnquist and Justices Scalia and Thomas formed the conservative bloc, in part because Scalia and Thomas agreed with each other at the highest rate of any pair of justices (92.1%). Justices Breyer, Ginsburg, and Souter formed a connected liberal threesome. If these blocs are characterized in light of the percentages evident for Warren Court justices in Table 2.9, one could say that the Rehnquist-Thomas-Scalia bloc is strongly

conservative because it is composed of the three most conservative justices of the two eras examined. By contrast, the Breyer-Ginsburg-Souter voting bloc is only moderately liberal when compared with both Justice Stevens and the six Warren Court justices who supported individuals' claims in criminal justice cases with much greater frequency.

 Explaining the Liberalism of the Rehnquist Court

Empirical data on the Supreme Court's decision making during six terms confirm the validity of the Rehnquist Court majority's conservative reputation for generally deciding in favor of the government in criminal justice cases. Five justices each favor the government's position in two-thirds or more of all criminal justice cases. Simultaneously, however, the data show that simple generalizations about the Court's conservatism may obscure recognition of the Rehnquist Court's regular support for individuals' claims, albeit in a minority of criminal justice cases. Moreover, because five justices are consistently conservative, a liberal outcome can only be produced when one or more of the conservative justices join liberal colleagues in support of individuals' arguments about rights and legal protections. The conservative justices' willingness to support individuals' claims in selected cases is most evident in the 28 unanimous decisions favoring liberal outcomes, but it is also apparent in the other liberal decisions constituting nearly 40% of the Court's total criminal justice cases.

Whenever the Rehnquist Court decides a criminal justice case in favor of the government's position, few commentators are surprised because the dominance of the Court's five consistent conservatives casts such results as virtually expected outcomes. The Rehnquist Court's conservatism is both anticipated and explainable, largely because of the political history underlying the selection of justices by Republican presidents as well as the justices' well-established track records of decision making in criminal justice cases. The members of the Rehnquist Court's conservative majority have served on the high court for periods ranging from 11 years (Thomas) to 30 years (Rehnquist), and they have all been consistently conservative in criminal justice cases throughout their Supreme Court careers (Hensley, Smith, & Baugh, 1997). Although the nature, basis, and consequences of the Rehnquist Court's conservative decisions deserve careful analysis, their regular production does not require special analysis to be predictable, explained, and understood. By contrast, the Rehnquist Court's liberal decisions present a puzzling question. When and why does a Supreme Court dominated by a solid majority of consistent conservatives decide criminal justice cases in favor of suspects, defendants, and convicted offenders?

Although the foregoing question is intriguing on its face, the analysis of the question requires a major caveat. The Court's decisions in favor of individuals' claims do not necessarily establish new constitutional protections in the mold of the Warren Court's innovative jurisprudence. The Rehnquist Court's liberal outcomes often merely reaffirm an established precedent or provide a procedural protection for a convicted offender whose ultimate fate, a significant period of incarceration, will not change as a result of the Court's decision. Despite the possibility that the Rehnquist Court's liberal decisions may have a relatively modest impact on the lives of people drawn into the criminal justice system, the fact that a Supreme Court dominated by conservatives regularly makes such decisions is a matter worthy of examination.

Because the Supreme Court's decisions are produced by shifting majority coalitions of varying sizes, no single causal factor can explain all of the Court's liberal decisions. Obviously, unanimous liberal decisions are generated by different contexts and decision-making processes than those that lead to 5-to-4 decisions in which a single conservative justice abandons his or her usual allies to produce an outcome favoring individuals' claims. Moreover, it is difficult for analysts to claim to have discovered definitive, verifiable explanations for the decision-making behavior of individual Supreme Court justices or the Court as a whole (Clayton, 1999). Scholars focus on a variety of factors that influence judicial decision making, including justices' individual values and judicial philosophies as well as strategic behavior and institutional processes (Baum, 1997). The strength and importance of these factors may vary depending on the historical moment in which a particular legal issue arises. As a result, no single explanation can account for all of the Court's liberal criminal justice decisions. Thus, distinct causal factors may be associated with particular categories of cases or specific legal issues.

Of the Court's 61 liberal decisions during the terms analyzed in the foregoing data, 34 concerned nonconstitutional issues, primarily statutory interpretation. In these cases, it may be easier for justices to reach consensus if they have a shared understanding that their job is to ensure that statutes' underlying legislative intent is fulfilled. For example, the Court's unanimous decision in *Pennsylvania Department of Corrections v. Yeskey* (1998) declared that prisoners are entitled to file actions against state prisons under the Americans With Disabilities Act. In light of the fact that the Rehnquist Court has consistently declined to expand rights for convicted offenders (Fliter, 2001) and has actually diminished previously established rights (e.g., *O'Lone v. Estate of Shabazz, 1987*; *Wilson v. Seiter,* 1991), it would be very surprising if the *Yeskey* decision embodied a consensus about the need to give prisoners additional protections. Instead, the decision is best understood by recognizing that liberal and conservative justices will follow legislative intent without regard to their ideological preferences about the outcome (Scalia, 1997), albeit not necessarily in every single statutory interpretation case.

Another source of liberal outcomes can be individual conservative justices' reactions to specific legal issues that cause them to abandon their usual allies. This can occur when the Court is presented with new issues about which the conservative majority lacks informative precedents or prior opportunities to examine and discuss the implications. For example, Justice Thomas's decision to join his liberal colleagues and provide the decisive fifth vote for identifying a violation of the Eighth Amendment's Excessive Fines Clause (*United States v. Bajakajian,* 1998) was apparently based on his individualistic reaction to this issue on first impression. Such outcomes can also be produced when cases raise new aspects of previously decided issues for which individual conservative justices have already indicated reluctance to join their usual allies. This appears to be the case in Justice O'Connor's decision to join the liberals in striking down a Nebraska statute that sought to criminalize so-called partial birth abortions (*Stenberg v. Carhart,* 2000). Justice O'Connor's vote in the case appears to be consistent with her position in previous decisions that upheld the constitutional right to make choices about abortion (e.g., *Planned Parenthood v. Casey,* 1992).

Liberal decisions can also be produced when conservative justices feel compelled to define limits on justice system officials' authority when those officials take actions that test previously defined boundaries. Because of the Rehnquist Court's reputation for conservatism and its consistent record of generally endorsing expanded governmental powers in criminal justice, police officers, prosecutors, corrections officials, and lower court judges may feel encouraged to push and test the limitations created by prior precedents. Their observations and experiences may indicate to them that the Rehnquist Court is likely to eliminate, diminish, or create exceptions to rights-enforcing rules established in prior Supreme Court decisions (e.g., *Payne v. Tennessee,* 1991; *Wilson v. Seiter,* 1991). In reality, as indicated by the Court's recent record of favoring individuals in nearly 40% of criminal justice decisions, including 28 unanimous liberal decisions in recent terms, all of the justices believe individuals are entitled to some measure of constitutional and statutory protection in the criminal justice system. Because the dominant conservative majority may be perceived as supporting the diminution of rights, the Court can expect to find itself periodically called on to reinforce the message that there are, in fact, limits to officials' authority. For example, in *Florida v. J.L.* (2000), a unanimous Court reiterated the requirement that police officers use reliable information to form the necessary reasonable suspicion for a "stop and frisk" under the doctrine of *Terry v. Ohio* (1968). Similarly, in *Bond v. United States* (2000), a seven-member majority, including consistent conservatives Rehnquist, Thomas, O'Connor, and Kennedy, declared that a border patrol officer violated reasonable expectations of privacy under the Fourth Amendment by randomly squeezing and manipulating soft-sided luggage on an interstate bus. In *Knowles v. Iowa* (1998), a unanimous Court declared that police officers cannot automatically search automobiles in conjunction with the issuance of a traffic citation, even if such searches are authorized by state statute. These decisions serve to protect rights by reaffirming the existence of limits on officials' authority. As a result, they serve as barriers against encroachment through experimental exercises of police investigative powers.

Analysts have raised questions about why the conservative-dominated Rehnquist Court has not reversed the major iconic precedents of the Warren Court era (Alexander, 1990). For example, the Rehnquist Court has declined to overturn *Mapp v. Ohio* (1961) and *Miranda v. Arizona* (1966), despite opportunities to do so. It may be the case that decisions in the Burger and Rehnquist Court eras that weakened or created exceptions to such precedents have made the liberal principles' impacts largely symbolic and thereby dissipated clashes between Warren Court doctrines and the values of Rehnquist Court conservatives (Smith, 1997b). The conservative justices may also recognize that police officers' strategic adaptations to the Warren Court's decisions have permitted law enforcement officials to secure confessions and undertake searches with sufficient freedom to fulfill crime control objectives, thus obviating any perceived need to eliminate famous precedents (Leo, 1996). The foregoing reasons may very well have motivated several conservative justices to join their liberal colleagues in reiterating the Court's commitment to the constitutional requirement of *Miranda* warnings prior to custodial interrogations (*Dickerson v. United States,* 2000). They certainly provide an additional plausible basis for the production of liberal outcomes by a conservative-dominated Court.

 Conclusion

An empirical examination of the Rehnquist Court's criminal justice decisions during a 6-year period confirms the high court's reputation for generally supporting the government's position in opposition to constitutional rights claims by individual suspects, defendants, and convicted offenders. However, systematic analysis also reveals that the Court regularly supports individuals' claims and that a large segment of the Court's criminal justice docket is composed of nonconstitutional cases, especially statutory interpretation.

The voting patterns of individual justices indicate the existence of two distinct wings within the Rehnquist Court. One wing contains five justices who are as or more conservative than any justice on the 1968 Warren Court. By contrast, the Rehnquist Court's most liberal justice (Stevens) supports liberal outcomes in criminal justice cases less frequently than did six justices on the 1968 Warren Court. These data provide evidence of the nature and extent of change in the Court's composition since the 1960s era in which the justices were especially active in expanding constitutional rights and limiting the scope of justice system officials' authority.

Within the Rehnquist Court, two 3-member groups of justices vote together with such significant frequency that they qualify for classification as consistent voting blocs. One bloc contains the three most conservative justices (Rehnquist, Thomas, and Scalia), and the other contains the moderately liberal justices (Breyer, Ginsburg, and Souter). The existence of a conservative voting bloc on a Court with two additional individual justices who favor the government's position in two thirds or more of criminal justice cases helps to explain the source of the Court's reputation and record for rejecting most claims from individuals.

Close examination of the Court's 5-to-4 liberal decisions indicates that they are not consistently driven solely by occasional defections by the two conservative justices, Kennedy and O'Connor, who have reputations as moderate "swing" voters. In fact, the voting records of these justices in criminal justice cases are nearly as conservative as that of noted conservative spokesperson Justice Scalia. Moreover, the strongly conservative Justice Thomas more frequently defected from the conservative majority to produce liberal outcomes in close cases. Thus, individual justices' reactions to specific issues seem to play an important role in determining coalition shifts that produce decisions supporting individuals' claims. These individualistic reactions are not, however, the sole source of liberal outcomes because the Court produced more than two dozen liberal decisions that garnered complete support from all of the justices. As a result, examinations of the reasons for the production of liberal decisions by a conservative-dominated Court must also consider other potential causal factors, including consensual norms about statutory interpretation, the need to rein in criminal justice officials by reaffirming limits on authority, and the reiteration of symbolic principles.

References

Apprendi v. New Jersey, 530 U.S. 255 (2000).

Alexander, R. (1990). The *Mapp, Escobedo,* and *Miranda* decisions: Do they serve a liberal or conservative agenda? *Criminal Justice Policy Review, 4,* 39–52.

Baum, L. (1997). *The puzzle of judicial behavior.* Ann Arbor: University of Michigan Press.

Baum, L. (1989). *The Supreme Court* (3rd ed.). Washington, DC: Congressional Quarterly Press.

Bond v. United States, 529 U.S. 334 (2000).

Carmell v. Texas, 529 U.S. 513 (2000).

Clayton, C. (1999). Law, politics, and the Rehnquist Court: Structural influences on Supreme Court decision making. In H. Gillman & C. Clayton (Eds.), *The Supreme Court in American politics: New institutionalist interpretations* (pp. 151–177). Lawrence: University Press of Kansas.

Cole, D. (1984). Strategies of difference: Litigating for women's rights in a man's world. *Law & Inequality, 2,* 33–85.

Cox, A. (1968). *The Warren Court: Constitutional decision as an instrument of reform.* Cambridge, MA: Harvard University Press.

Coyle, M. (2000, August 7). A small, potent docket. *National Law Journal,* p. A1.

Crawford-El v. Britton, 523 U.S. 574 (1998).

Dickerson v. United States, 530 U.S. 428 (2000).

Domino, J. C. (1994). *Civil rights and liberties: Toward the 21st century.* New York: HarperCollins.

Felker v. Turpin, 518 U.S. 651 (1996).

Filter, J. (2001). *Prisoners' rights: The Supreme Court and evolving standards of decency.* Westport, CT: Greenwood.

Florida v. J. L., 529 U.S. 266 (2000).

Fortunato, S. (1999). The Supreme Court's experience gap. *Judicature, 82,* 251.

Gest, T. (2001). *Crime and politics: Big government's erratic campaign for law and order.* New York: Oxford University Press.

Gray v. Maryland, 523 U.S. 185 (1998).

Greenhouse, L. (1992, July 5). Moderates on Court defy predictions. *New York Times,* pp. E1–E2.

Greenhouse, L. (1996, July 3). In Supreme Court's decisions, a clear voice, and a murmur. *New York Times,* p. A20.

Hanson, R. A., & Daley, H. W. K. (1995). *Federal habeas corpus review: Challenging state court convictions.* Washington, DC: Bureau of Justice Statistics.

Heck, E., & Hall, M. (1981). Bloc voting and the freshman justice revisited. *Journal of Politics, 43,* 852–860.

Hensley, T. R., Smith, C. E., & Baugh, J. A. (1997). *The changing Supreme Court: Constitutional rights and liberties.* St. Paul, MN: West.

Hensley, T. R., Smith, C. E., & Baugh, J. A. (1998). *Supreme Court update: 1997.* Belmont, CA: Wadsworth.

Hohn v. United States, 524 U.S. 236 (1998).

Johnson, S. P., & Smith, C. E. (1992). Justice David Souter's first term on the Supreme Court: The impact of a new justice. *Judicature, 75,* 238–243.

Jones v. United States, 526 U.S. 227 (1999).

Knowles v. Iowa, 525 U.S. 113 (1998).

Kyllo v. United States, 533 U.S. 27 (2001).

Leo, R. (1996). *Miranda's revenge*: Police interrogation as a confidence game. *Law and Society Review, 30,* 259–288.

Lindh v. Murphy, 117 S.Ct. 2059 (1997).

Lock, S. (1999). *Crime, public opinion, and civil liberties.* New York: Praeger.

Maguire, K., & Pastore, A. L. 2001. *Sourcebook of criminal justice statistics 2000.* Available from http://www.albany.edu/sourcebook

Mapp v. Ohio, 367 U.S. 643 (1961).

Melone, A. (1990). Revisiting the freshman effect hypothesis: The first two terms of Justice Anthony Kennedy. *Judicature, 74,* 6–13.

Miranda v. Arizona, 384 U.S. 436 (1966).

Mitchell v. United States, 526 U.S. 314 (1999).

O'Brien, D. M. (1990). *This honorable court: The Supreme Court in American politics* (2nd ed.). New York: Norton.

Old Chief v. United States, 519 U.S. 172 (1997).

O'Lone v. Estate of Shabazz, 482 U.S. 342 (1987).

Payne v. Tennessee, 501 U.S. 808 (1991).

Pennsylvania Department of Corrections v. Yeskey, 524 U.S. 206 (1998).

Planned Parenthood v. Casey, 505 U.S. 833 (1992).

Richardson v. McKnight, 521 U.S. 399 (1997).

Scalia, A. (1997). *A matter of interpretation: Federal courts and the law.* Princeton, NJ: Princeton University Press.

Segal, J. (1986). Supreme Court justices as human decision makers: An individual-level analysis of search and seizure cases. *Journal of Politics, 48,* 938–955.

Segal, J., & Spaeth, H. (1989). Decisional trends on the Warren and Burger Courts: Results from the Supreme Court judicial data base project. *Judicature, 73,* 103–107.

Smith, C. E. (1990). Police professionalism and the rights of criminal defendants. *Criminal Law Bulletin, 26,* 155–166.

Smith, C. E. (1997a). *The Rehnquist Court and criminal punishment.* New York: Garland.

Smith, C. E. (1997b). Turning rights into symbols: The U.S. Supreme Court and criminal justice. *Criminal Justice Policy Review, 8,* 99–117.

Smith, C. E., & Hensley, T. R. (1993). Assessing the conservatism of the Rehnquist Court. *Judicature, 77,* 83–89.

Smith, C. E., & Hurst, J. (1997). The forms of judicial policy making: Civil liability and criminal justice policy. *The Justice System Journal, 19,* 341–354.

Snyder, E. (1958). The Supreme Court as a small group. *Social Forces, 36,* 232–238.

Spaeth, H. J. (2001). *United States Supreme Court judicial data base, 1953–2001.* Ann Arbor, MI: Inter-university Consortium for Political and Social Research.

Sprague, J. D. (1968). *Voting patterns of the United States Supreme Court.* Indianapolis, IN: Bobbs-Merrill.

Stenberg v. Carhart, 530 U.S. 914 (2000).

The Supreme Court at Work. (1990). Washington, DC: Congressional Quarterly Press.

Terry v. Ohio, 392 U.S. 1 (1968).

United States v. Bajakajian, 524 U.S. 321 (1998).

United States v. Oakland Cannabis Buyers' Cooperative, 532 U.S. 483 (2001).

Wilgoren, J. (2002, April 15). Illinois panel: Death sentence needs overhaul. *New York Times.* Available from http://www.nytimes.com

Wilson v. Seiter, 501 U.S. 294 (1991).

Yackle, L. (1994). *Reclaiming the federal courts.* Cambridge, MA: Harvard University Press.

DISCUSSION QUESTIONS

1. Smith contends that the Supreme Court plays an important role in shaping criminal justice policy. Discuss the role played by the Court in this arena.

2. Smith classified each Supreme Court decision as "liberal" or "conservative." Explain what these labels mean.

3. Discuss the types of criminal justice cases that were decided by the Court from 1995 through 2000 (see Tables 2.5–2.7).

4. Do the data support the claim that the Rehnquist Court, as a whole, was a conservative court (in terms of decisions regarding criminal justice issues)?

5. How do the nine Rehnquist Court judges compare with the judges on the Warren Court?

6. How does Smith answer the following question: "When and why does a Supreme Court dominated by a solid majority of consistent conservatives decide criminal justice cases in favor of suspects, defendants, and convicted offenders?"

READING

The two models of the criminal process outlined by Packer—the crime control model and the due process model—have different views about the reliability of the informal screening of criminal cases by police and prosecutors. The crime control model assumes that police and prosecutors generally make accurate decisions during the pretrial process and that defendants who are not screened out early can be presumed to be guilty and can be treated as such. In contrast, the due process model holds that the informal screening of cases by police and prosecutors is unreliable and that mistakes are likely; this model contends that a formal, adversarial process is needed to ensure reliability.

SOURCE: Ramsey, Robert J., & Frank, James. (2007). Wrongful conviction: Perceptions of criminal justice professionals regarding the frequency of wrongful conviction and the extent of system errors. *Crime & Delinquency, 53,* 436–470.

In this article, Ramsey and Frank use data from a survey of criminal justice officials to examine perceptions regarding the frequency of system errors. The results of their study reveal that the officials they surveyed— and especially defense attorneys—believe that wrongful convictions are not infrequent and that they can be attributed to a variety of system errors on the part of police, prosecutors, defense attorneys, and judges. The article concludes with a discussion of the ways in which high caseloads and limited resources can lead to wrongful convictions.

Wrongful Conviction

Perceptions of Criminal Justice Professionals Regarding the Frequency of Wrongful Conviction and the Extent of System Errors

Robert J. Ramsey and James Frank

The wrongful conviction of innocent defendants in the United States is a continuing concern among criminal justice professionals and policy makers. Attention to this problem has come from the highest levels of government. Former prosecutor and now U.S. Senator Patrick Leahy stated,

> These mistakes carry a high personal and social price. They undermine the public's confidence in our judicial system, they produce unbearable anguish for innocent people and their families and for the victims of these crimes, and they compromise public safety because for every wrongly convicted person, there is a real criminal who may still be roaming the streets. (Leahy, 2003)

In 2000, Illinois Governor George Ryan imposed a moratorium on the state's death penalty after stating

> We have now freed more people than we have put to death under our system—13 people have been exonerated and 12 have been put to death. There is a flaw in the system, without question, and it needs to be studied. (CNN, 2000)

Continuing concern about the possible execution of innocent individuals led to the Justice for All Act of 2004 that passed both chambers of the U.S. Congress and was signed into law on October 30, 2004. The act includes many key provisions that assist states that have the death penalty to create effective systems for the appointment and performance of qualified counsel, together with better training and monitoring for both the defense and prosecution, and also provides substantial funding to states for increased reliance on DNA testing in new criminal investigations.

Concern about wrongful conviction is not limited to those involved in the death penalty debate. In fact, approximately two thirds of exposed wrongful conviction cases involve noncapital crimes such as rape or assault where the death penalty is not applicable (Innocence Project, 2006). In recent years, numerous articles have appeared in the national media reporting cases of wrongfully convicted individuals who have served long prison terms for various noncapital cases before new evidence either proved their innocence or at least cast doubt on their guilt. As such, the problem of wrongful conviction should be viewed as one that affects defendants irrespective of the seriousness of the offense.

⬙ **Background**

The basic impulses for examining issues related to wrongful conviction are related to three primary concerns. First is the concern for individual justice. The belief that all law-abiding people should be free of oppression from the criminal justice system makes wrongful conviction especially repugnant to many U.S. citizens.

A second impulse that drives the research on wrongful conviction is that of public safety. When a wrongfully accused individual is convicted of a crime, that person is punished in place of the person who actually committed the offense. Therefore, for every suspect wrongfully convicted, there is a corresponding guilty individual who has not been brought to justice and who may be continuing to commit crimes in the community (see Justice Thurgood Marshall's dissent in *Manson v. Brathwaite,* 1977). Scheck, Neufeld, and Dwyer (2000) note. "All wrongfully convicted individuals take the lash of punishment for someone else's crime; that is the very definition of their predicament. Far too often, they are surrogates for serial criminals and killers" (p. 244).

Third, wrongful conviction is a concern to many people because it undermines public confidence in the criminal justice system. Every year, stories come from the media concerning individuals who have languished for years in prison or who have faced execution and are later found to have been wrongfully convicted. Stories of this nature can shake the faith of criminal justice professionals and the citizenry alike in the ability of the criminal justice system to identify criminals and achieve justice. Wrongful convictions, therefore, can damage the symbolic status of the criminal justice process—a process that symbolizes America's moral stance against crime and the desire to achieve justice (Liebman et al., 2002). This damage ultimately places a burden on the integrity, prestige, reputation, credibility, and effectiveness of the entire criminal justice process.

The pioneering research in wrongful conviction was conducted by Yale University law professor Edwin Borchard in 1932 when he documented 65 cases where innocent people were convicted. Borchard's book,

Convicting the Innocent, was a qualitative effort involving case studies of wrongfully convicted individuals. The book was written in response to a local district attorney who told Borchard that "innocent men are never convicted. . . . It is a physical impossibility" (Borchard, 1932, p. v). Borchard's work was followed by other qualitative and quantitative studies of the phenomenon of wrongful conviction.

The broad concept of *wrongful conviction* has received considerable attention from scholars during the past several decades. In 1987, Bedau and Radelet published a groundbreaking article examining the cases of 350 convicted defendants they determined were factually innocent. This article served as the catalyst for renewed interest in the plight of innocent yet convicted defendants (Drizin & Leo, 2003–2004). Since the mid-1980s, the development of DNA technology and its acceptance within the court community has allowed numerous defendants to conclusively prove their innocence. These cases proved newsworthy and attracted increased media attention showing that claims concerning the fallibility of court decisions were not solely the ranting of academics. Accumulating proof that wrongful convictions occur, and that they occur with a frequency that was not previously anticipated, has resulted in more resources being devoted to discovering cases involving factually innocent defendants and in increased academic interest in the extent and causes of wrongful convictions; in turn, system actors have become increasingly aware of the problems and dangers of convicting innocent defendants.

Studies following in the tradition of Borchard (1932) have examined a variety of issues associated with wrongful convictions. Many researchers have focused on providing a better overall picture of the phenomenon (Brandon & Davies, 1973; Carter & Beth, 1978; Christianson, 2004; Conners, Lundregan, Miller, & McEwen, 1996; Frank & Frank, 1957; Huff & Rattner, 1988; Huff, Rattner, & Sagarin, 1996; MacNamara, 1969; McCloskey, 1989; Radin, 1964; Ramsey, 2003; Scheck et al., 2000; C. Walker & Keir, 1999; S. Walker, 2006; Westervelt & Humphrey, 2002; Yant, 1991), whereas other studies have focused on addressing specific issues. For example, some researchers have focused on discussing and diagnosing cases of specific defendants who have been wrongfully convicted (Barlow, 1999; Cooper, Cooper, & Reese, 1995; Frisbie & Garrett, 1998; Hirsch, 2000; Humes, 1999; Linscott & Frame, 1994; Potter & Bost, 1997; Protess & Warden, 1998). Others have focused primarily on the issues concerning wrongful conviction and capital punishment (Bedau & Radelet, 1987, 1988; Cohen, 2003; Dieter, 1997; Fan, Keltner, & Wyatt, 2002; Gross, 1998; Liebman, Fagan, & West, 2000; Radelet & Bedau, 1998; Radelet, Bedau, & Putnam, 1992; McCloskey, 1996; Unnever & Cullen, 2005; Weinstock & Schwartz, 1998). Still other studies have focused on specific types of errors, such as eyewitness error (Wells & Olson, 2003), false confessions (Connery, 1996; Drizin & Leo, 2003–2004; Kassin, 1997; Leo & Ofshe, 1997–1998), police error (McMahon, 1995), prosecutor error (Gershman, 1999), ineffective counsel (Finer, 1973), and the impact of race (Harmon, 2004; Parker, Dewees, & Radelet, 2002; Young, 2004). Some researchers have sought to better understand and determine the nature and extent of wrongful convictions (Gross, Jacoby, Matheson, Montgomery, & Patel, 2005; Huff & Rattner, 1988; Huff et al., 1996; Huff, Rattner, & Sagarin, 1986; Poveda, 2001; Ramsey, 2003; Rattner, 1988).

 ## How Frequently Wrongful Conviction Occurs

Initially, the debate on wrongful conviction centered on whether the phenomenon actually occurred (see Radelet & Bedau, 1998). Revelations concerning wrongfully convicted defendants during the past several decades conclusively have shown that such does occur and now a seminal question concerns how frequently wrongful conviction occurs. Various studies have provided estimates of the frequency of wrongful conviction ranging from .5% to as high as 20% (Huff et al., 1986; McCloskey, 1989; Poveda, 2001). Considering the fact that the Justice Department reports that there are now in excess of 2,000,000 people behind bars (Bureau of Justice Statistics, 2004), these estimations suggest that between 10,000 and 400,000 wrongfully convicted individuals are incarcerated. Even if one accepts an error rate at the low end of the spectrum, say 1%, this translates into 20,000 individuals now incarcerated for crimes they did not commit.

Most of the information we have on the frequency of wrongful conviction has come from case studies. Developments in forensic DNA technology during the past 20 years can be credited for shedding some light on the frequency issue. The Innocence Project, an independent nonprofit legal clinic and resource center founded in 1992 at the Benjamin N. Cardozo School of Law, handles and keeps track of cases where post conviction DNA testing of evidence has yielded conclusive proof of innocence. As of January 5, 2006, the Innocence Project's Web site reported that new forensic tests conducted on old evidence (i.e., evidence that was gathered before the advent of modern DNA technology) had led to the identification, release, and exoneration of at least 172 wrongfully convicted individuals (Innocence Project, 2006).

Revelations of the incidence of wrongful conviction through the use of DNA technology have heightened the awareness of the problem of wrongful conviction and spawned new research into cases where convictions have been overturned for reasons other than the reanalysis of old evidence using DNA—usually wrongful convictions that in some way were influenced by, or are the result of, system breakdowns within the criminal justice process. Gross et al. (2005) found 183 cases of exonerations of defendants convicted of serious crimes since 1989 where evidence other than DNA was used to declare a defendant not guilty of a crime for which he or she had previously been convicted.[1] Liebman et al. (2000) determined that 7% of the defendants in their sample of cases reversed on appeal were found not guilty when they were retried for the initial capital conviction offense.

Although the identification of these cases of wrongful conviction demonstrates that a problem does exist, the actual extent of the problem remains unknown. Many researchers who have studied the phenomenon believe these revealed cases represent only the tip of the iceberg concerning the black hole of wrongful conviction (Gross et al., 2005; Huff et al., 1996; McCloskey, 1989; Poveda, 2001; Scheck et al., 2000). Radelet and

Bedau (1998, p. 117) addressed the frequency issue by discussing the likelihood that someone convicted of a capital offense is actually innocent. They contend that for each conviction, there is a perceived level of certainty (i.e., 95% certain) that the person is actually guilty. When this level of certainty is multiplied across all defendants in similar circumstances, the conviction error rate continues to increase—the larger the population the larger the odds of having innocent defendants on death row. Therefore, without providing an estimate of the frequency of these situations, they suggest the conviction of factually innocent people may be more likely than others have suggested.

The belief that the frequency of wrongful conviction is typically underestimated is primarily due to two reasons. First, cases of wrongful conviction are not typically exposed because of a properly working criminal justice system that has a tendency to correct its own errors. Instead, most cases are the result of some serendipitous circumstance wherein a wrongly convicted individual fortuitously happens to have his or her case investigated by an individual or organization that champions their case and commits the resources necessary to see that justice is done (Adams, Hoffer, & Hoffer, 1991; Protess & Warden, 1998; Scheck et al., 2000). Likely, many wrongfully convicted individuals who have not been so fortuitous remain incarcerated. As Bedau and Radelet (1987) contend, "the coincidences involved in exposing so many of the errors and the luck that is so often required suggest that only a fraction of the wrongly convicted are eventually able to clear their names" (p. 70). Gross et al. (2005) note that "a large number of false convictions in noncapital cases are never even discovered because nobody ever seriously investigates these cases" (p. 10). Another reason for believing that the revealed cases represent only a fraction of all wrongful convictions is because a large number of these revelations resulted from the use of modern forensic techniques where scientists were able to apply DNA technology to reanalyze old evidence—usually involving blood, hair, semen, or other body fluids—to determine that a convicted individual was innocent. Unfortunately, materials amenable to DNA analysis are available in only a small percentage of criminal cases (Gross et al., 2005; Scheck et al., 2000). It is therefore logical to assume that for every case of wrongful conviction uncovered using DNA technology, there are other cases involving incarcerated innocent individuals who will never be able to benefit from this new science.

 ## Why Wrongful Conviction Occurs

In addition to answering the question of how frequently wrongful convictions occur, researchers are ultimately interested in answering the question of why they occur. Leo and Ofshe (1997–1998) note that knowledge of the frequency of system errors is important but suggest that the more important question is "How can such errors be prevented?" (p. 492). Answering the why question(s) would allow for more focused efforts to reduce system errors and consequentially reduce the frequency of wrongful convictions.

Many writers have provided general comments concerning the potential causes of wrongful conviction. Liebman et al. (2000) state that the most common errors prompting reversals are incompetent defense attorneys and police and prosecutors who fail to suppress exculpatory evidence. Radelet and Bedau (1998) argue that innocent people are placed on death row because of "politically ambitious prosecutors, angry juries and incompetent defense counsel" (p.111). Gross et al. (2005) suggest that eyewitness identifications, perjury, and false confessions are the key causes of wrongful convictions. Drizin and Leo (2003–2004) claim that false confessions lead to erroneous convictions. Unfortunately, these general comments are not specific enough to allow for the development of effective remedies.

Major research projects conducted by the National Institute of Justice (Connors et al., 1996) and by the Innocence Project at the Benjamin N. Cardozo School of Law (Scheck et al., 2000) have analyzed cases of wrongful conviction to identify factors commonly associated with wrongful conviction. A primary focus of the present study is to identify and evaluate the perceptions of criminal justice professionals regarding many of the findings and conclusions of the Conners et al. (1996) and Scheck et al. (2000) studies.

It must be noted that although system errors may be a primary cause of wrongful convictions, it is possible that factually innocent defendants may be wrongfully convicted even when there is no system error (Frank & Frank, 1957). Because decisions are rendered by fallible human beings, it is entirely possible that innocent defendants may be found guilty, even when testimony and physical evidence is properly collected. The North Carolina case of Ronald Cotton is a prime example of a wrongful conviction that could have possibly occurred where system error did not occur. Mr. Cotton was mistakenly identified as a rapist by the victim and then spent more than 10 years in prison before DNA analysis of the rape kit excluded him and matched another individual who was already incarcerated for another crime (Simon, 2003; see also Innocence Project, 2006). As Supreme Court Justice Thurgood Marshall commented in *Furman v. Georgia* (1972), "No matter how careful courts are, the possibility of perjured testimony, mistaken honest testimony and human error remain all too real" (p. 79). In sum, innocent people will be convicted even when system actors properly do their jobs. All we can expect by improving the system of justice, therefore, is a reduction in—and not an eradication of—wrongful convictions.

The Present Study

This study replicates, in part, previous research conducted by Huff et al. (1986). Included in the Huff et al. study was an analysis of Rattner's (1983) survey of Ohio criminal justice professionals who investigated perceptions regarding the frequency of wrongful conviction and its associated causes. Rattner solicited the opinions of police, prosecutors, defense attorneys, and judges because he surmised that those professionals "closest to the trial process" were in an ideal position to provide insights regarding these issues (Huff et al., 1996, p. 55).

Twenty years have passed since the Rattner (1983) survey and many advancements have occurred in the area of forensic science (especially DNA testing) that have shed further light on the phenomenon of wrongful conviction. Anticipating that this new information might help to either clarify or dispute the opinions proffered by respondents to the Rattner survey, we conducted our own 2002 to 2003 survey of a similar group of Ohio criminal justice professionals—revisiting and expanding on many of the issues dealt with in the Rattner survey and the Huff et al. (1986) article.

This research, however, takes a narrower approach than was taken by Huff et al. (1986). Although Huff et al. addressed both perceptions of system errors (errors or misconduct by police, prosecutor, defense attorney, and judge) and nonsystem errors (e.g., eyewitnesses and expert testimony error, false accusations, false confessions, community pressure), the focus of this article is on the perceptions of criminal justice professionals concerning only system errors that have been determined by prior research to be associated with wrongful conviction. This narrower approach is taken because numerous research endeavors in the past 20 years suggest that it is system errors that often precipitate, exacerbate, and amplify nonsystem errors. For example, eyewitness error has been associated with inadequate police investigation and faulty identification procedures (Conners et al., 1996; Loftus, 2003; Wells & Olson, 2003); false confessions have been found to occur because of overzealousness on the part of police officials or prosecutors (Gross et al., 2005; Scheck et al., 2000); false accusations, especially those by jail-house snitches, have been encouraged and attenuated by overzealous police or prosecutorial actions or inadequate investigations (Huff et al., 1996; Scheck et al., 2000; see also *State of Oklahoma v. Ronald Keith Williamson and Dennis Leon Fritz*, 1991); and wrongful conviction because of forensic error has often occurred because of system errors associated with inadequate counsel, overzealous prosecution, and judicial error (Scheck et al., 2000). Also, community pressure to obtain a conviction for a particular crime has, at times, provoked all members of the criminal justice profession into system error actions (Huff et al., 1996). In sum, research suggests that a reduction in system error should ultimately lead to a reduction in nonsystem errors.

At the same time, we expand on the prior work of Huff et al. (1986). Whereas the Rattner (1983) survey asked respondents to simply rank order a list of possible system errors (from *most frequent* to *least frequent)*, the present study asks respondents to estimate (on a 9-point scale ranging from *never* to *always)* how often they believe specific system errors occur—errors that have been determined by recent research to be associated with wrongful conviction. Also, the Rattner survey only inquired into the perceived frequency of police, prosecutorial, and judicial error and did not address perceived error by defense attorneys,[2] unlike our study that adds the variable *defense attorney error* (DE) and examines and compares respondents' perceptions of the frequency of particular system errors committed by four groups of system actors (police, prosecutor, judges, and defense attorneys). Finally, we expand on the Huff et al. (1986) study by garnering the opinions of system actors on how wrongful conviction might he reduced—opinions often based on revelations due to modern DNA technology that was not available at the time of the Rattner survey. The following is a brief discussion of the types of system error that are addressed in this study.

Police Error (PE) and Misconduct

Police officers or detectives are often the first members of the criminal justice system to intervene in a criminal case and become involved at a very critical time—the beginning. The activities of the police at this juncture and how well they do their job can have dramatic implications for an innocent individual who has become a suspect. Prosecutors, when making a decision concerning whether to prosecute a case, rely heavily on the evidence presented to them by police officials. Evidence properly collected by police should be able to be properly reviewed by prosecutors. However, when police conduct sloppy investigations or manufacture evidence (e.g., the Rampart scandal[3]) or produce mistaken eyewitness identification because of biased identification techniques (e.g., misuse of show tips or conducting biased photo spreads or lineups), prosecutors may make decisions to use such evidence without full knowledge

of how it was acquired. Thus, once PE or misconduct contributes to a wrongful arrest, there is an increased likelihood that other criminal justice officials will add momentum to the mistake. Huff et al. (1996) call this phenomenon the ratification of error:

> The criminal justice system, starting with the police investigation of an alleged crime and culminating in the appellate courts, tends to ratify errors made at the lower levels of the system. The further the case progresses in the system, the less chance there is that the error will be discovered and corrected, unless it involves a basic issue of constitutional rights and due process. (p. 144)

For example, Leo and Ofshe (1997–1998) found that police-induced false confessions substantially bias jury evaluations of evidence and are perceived as dispositive of issues of guilt (see also Gross, 1996, 1998).

Extant research confirms that PE and misconduct are significant contributors to the wrongful conviction of the innocent (Conners et al., 1996; Gross et al., 2005; Huff et al., 1986, 1996; Leo & Ofshe, 1997–1998; McCloskey, 1989; Radelet et al., 1992; Scheck et al., 2000; Yant, 1991).[4]

Prosecutorial Error (PrE) and Misconduct

Prosecutorial error or misconduct is another factor associated with wrongful conviction (see *Buckley v. Fitzsimmons,* 1993; *Miller v. Pale,* 1967). The prosecutor is considered by many to be the most powerful individual within the criminal justice process (Gershman, 1999; Gottfredson & Gottfredson, 1988). Because of their position within the criminal justice process, prosecutors' errors or misconduct can result in devastating consequences to an innocent suspect (Huff et al., 1996; Leo & Ofshe, 1997–1998). Prosecutors, who enjoy significant immunity, have wide discretion regarding how many investigative resources to use, which cases to dismiss, and which cases to prosecute. By deciding to dismiss a case believed to be based on unreliable evidence (e.g., a false confession, misidentification) or where there exists trustworthy exculpatory evidence, prosecutors can correct errors of other system participants. On the other hand, when a prosecutor pursues a case based on bias, limited information, or less than reliable evidence, a wrongful conviction can occur.

Inadequacy of Counsel (DE)

Inadequacy of counsel refers to instances where innocent individuals are wrongfully convicted of a crime they did not commit because, in part, their defense lawyers were incompetent, lazy, ill-prepared, and underfunded. Huff and Rattner (1988) list inadequacy of counsel as an important factor in wrongful conviction. They found that inexperienced original defense counsel, often with inadequate investigative resources, did not adequately represent the interests of the suspect (see also Liebman et al., 2000, who found that the most common error in death penalty cases is "egregiously incompetent defense lawyering" [p. 5] that accounts for 37% of state postconviction reversals). Yant (1991) suggested that some defense attorneys—without fully investigating their clients' claims of innocence—too often use plea bargaining as a standard operating procedure to reduce their workload. He also criticized defense lawyers for seldom taking the time to properly challenge forensic evidence offered by the prosecution (see also Conners et al., 1996; Scheck et al., 2000). This may occur because the attorney is unable to conduct independent tests necessary to assess the conclusions of the state's forensic expert because of limited resources, time, or a lack of sufficient effort (Huff et al., 1996; Scheck et al., 2000).

Judicial Error (JE) and Bias

This category was not specifically included in the National Institute of Justice or Innocence Project's findings as being related to wrongful conviction. Other research, however, has concluded that JE and bias are associated with wrongful convictions (Huff et al., 1986; Rattner, 1983). As an integral part of the "courtroom work group" (S. Walker, 2006, p. 57), judges bear responsibility for permitting various types of misleading evidence to enter the courtroom. Wrongful convictions can occur because judges allow incompetent defense

attorneys, overzealous police and prosecutors, and questionable forensic evidence to permeate the courtroom. Sometimes, the biases of the judges themselves lead to trial errors that are not reversible but nevertheless influence decision making (Huff et al., 1996; Rattner, 1983). Scheck et al. (2000) note that the occurrences of wrongful conviction are attenuated when appellate judges issue only one-line judicial orders that do not specify the reasons for overturning a conviction. Huff et al. (1986) lists three major types of JE associated with wrongful conviction: JEs affected by bias, judicial neglect of duty, and technical errors in judicial decisions.

 # Data and Method

For these analyses, four groups of Ohio criminal justice professionals were surveyed: law enforcement (sheriffs and chiefs of police), prosecutors (chiefs and assistants), defense attorneys (private and public defenders), and judges (common pleas, appellate, and Supreme Court). Using a single large state, such as Ohio, serves to control for the effect of varying legal definitions while still allowing for a diversity of settings. Furthermore, Rattner (1983) conducted his survey in Ohio, and his findings therefore provide a baseline for comparison purposes.[5]

The perceptions of criminal justice professionals were chosen as a measure because there may be no better way to approach the question of prevalence than through perceptions (Huff et al., 1986). Because no research approach has yet been devised to exactly measure the extent of the problem, the perceptions elicited in the present study offer a best estimate of the phenomenon. The professionals surveyed are in a position to make such observations because they are exposed, on almost a daily basis, to the environment where wrongful convictions might occur. Because of their experience within the criminal justice system, their perceptions regarding the issues of this study may enable them to offer data close enough to objective truth to provide a reasonable baseline estimate of the frequency of system errors.

The research reported here is designed to provide insight into the perceptions of criminal justice professionals regarding the following four questions: (a) How frequently does wrongful felony conviction occur? (b) What is an acceptable level of wrongful convictions? (c) How frequently are the types of system errors, previously identified by research to be associated with wrongful conviction, committed by criminal justice professionals? and (d) Do groups of criminal justice professionals differ in their perceptions?

The survey was administered using a version of Dillman's (2000) tailored design method that uses a 5-step multiple mailing procedure to improve survey response rates.[6] Sample sizes were determined using Dillman's formula based on the amount of sampling error that can be tolerated, the population size from which the sample is to be drawn, how varied the population is with respect to the characteristics of interest, and the required confidence level. Sample sizes for the present survey were determined using

the formula to target a 95% confidence level, with a ±5% sampling error. An overall response rate of 53.2% was attained (see Table 2.13).

Sample

To examine these issues, a 53-item questionnaire was mailed to 1,500 Ohio criminal justice professionals. The sampling frame consisted of all 230 presiding common pleas court judges, 67 appellate court judges, and 7 Supreme Court judges; all 88 chief county prosecutors; and all 88 county sheriffs.[7] Also surveyed were 132 randomly selected assistant prosecutors, 400 randomly selected chiefs of police, 250 randomly selected county public defenders, and 238 randomly selected private defense attorneys. Table 2.14 contains demographic information on the sample.

Table 2.13 Survey Response Rates

Group	Surveys Mailed	Responses	Response Rate
Police	488	274	56.1
Sheriffs	88	62	70.4
Chiefs of police	400	212	53.0
Prosecutors	220	103	46.8
Chief prosecutors	88	62	70.4
Assistant prosecutors	132	41	31.1
Defense attorneys	488	235	48.2
Private	238	98	41.1
Public defenders	250	137	54.8
Judges	304	186	61.2
Common pleas	230	142	61.7
Appellate	67	41	61.2
Supreme	7	3	42.9
Total	1,500	798	53.2

Table 2.14   Group Comparisons: Demographic Variables

Variable	Police	Prosecutors	Attorneys	Judges	Total[a]
Age					
18 to 29	5	7	13	0	25
30 to 39	32	22	71	4	129
40 to 49	106	34	66	30	236
50 to 59	112	37	67	82	298
60 to 69	18	0	16	50	94
70 to 79	2	0	4	9	15
80 or older	0	0	0	0	0
Race					
White	272	98	219	167	756
Black	0	1	8	2	11
Hispanic	0	0	2	1	3
Asian	0	0	1	0	1
Other	1	1	3	1	6
Gender					
Male	271	86	194	148	699
Female	4	14	43	31	92
Jurisdiction					
Village	98	0	2	0	100
Township	28	2	1	2	33
City	82	2	29	2	115
County	61	92	112	123	388
State	1	0	20	32	53
Multiple	5	3	70	19	97

a. Not all respondents provided demographic data.

Measures

Wrongful conviction. For purposes of the survey, the term *wrongful conviction* is defined as people who have been convicted of a criminal offense but are in fact innocent. This definition of wrongful conviction appeared on the inside front cover of the survey instrument. Following in the tradition of Borchard (1932) and others (Bedau & Radelet, 1987; Gross, 1996, 1998;

Gross et al., 2005; Huff et al., 1986), our definition refers to convicted individuals who are factually innocent. This is in contrast to legal innocence, which includes persons who may or may not be factually guilty but were nevertheless improperly convicted because of a prejudicial legal error at trial (see Liebman et al., 2000).

Frequency of wrongful conviction. Three survey items addressed the issue of respondent's perceptions of the frequency of wrongful conviction. The first two items asked respondents to estimate what they perceive to be the percentage of wrongful felony conviction occurring in their own jurisdiction and then in the United States. The third survey item asked respondents what they believed to be an acceptable level of wrongful conviction. A 10-item scale was used (see list) with values ranging from "0%" to "more than 25%."

a. 0%

b. less than .5%

c. .5% to 1%

d. 1% to 3%

e. 4% to 5%

f. 6% to 10%

g. 11% to 15%

h. 16% to 20%

i. 21% to 25%

j. More than 25%

Specific types of system error or misconduct. As noted, extant research has identified specific types of police, prosecutorial, attorney, and judicial errors that are associated with wrongful conviction. In an effort to move beyond general perceptions of the frequency of this phenomenon, respondents were also queried about the extent to which each group of criminal justice actors engaged in the listed types of conduct.

Specifically, for each survey item, respondents were asked to indicate on a 9-item response scale ranging from *never* to *always* (hereafter called 9-item scale; see Figure 2.1) how often they believed the named group of criminal justice officials participated in the listed behavior.

Police error (PE) or misconduct. The following five types of PE have been identified as being associated with wrongful conviction (Conners et al., 1996; Drizin & Leo, 2003–2004; Gross, 1996; Gross et al., 2005; Huff et al., 1996; Leo & Ofshe, 1997–1998; McMahon, 1995; Radelet et al., 1992; Scheck et al., 2000):

> Inadequate police investigation
>
> Police coaching witnesses in pretrial identification procedures
>
> Police suppressing exculpatory evidence
>
> Police using false evidence
>
> Police using undue pressure to obtain a confession

All respondents were asked to use the 9-item scale to estimate how often police commit each of these types of error.

Prosecutorial error (PrE) or misconduct. Five prosecutorial errors have been found to be commonly associated with the incidence of wrongful conviction (Conners et al., 1996; Huff et al., 1996;

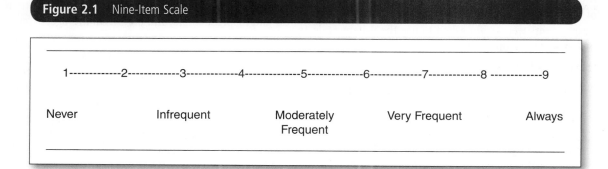

Figure 2.1 Nine-Item Scale

1------------2------------3------------4------------5------------6------------7------------8------------9

Never   Infrequent   Moderately   Very Frequent   Always
                                    Frequent

Humes, 1999; Liebman et al., 2000; Radelet et al., 1992; Scheck et al., 2000):

> Inadequate investigation of case by prosecutor
>
> Prosecutor suppressing exculpatory evidence
>
> Prosecutor using undue plea-bargaining pressure
>
> Prosecutor prompting witnesses
>
> Prosecutor knowingly using false testimony

This variable was also operationalized and measured using the 9-item scale.

Inadequacy of defense counsel (DE). Defense attorney error (DE) was operationalized and measured by asking respondents to indicate, on the same 9-item scale, how often they believe defense attorneys are involved in the following five types of defense error found to be associated with wrongful conviction (Conners et al., 1996; Finer, 1973; Huff et al., 1996; Gross et al., 2005; Liebman et al., 2000; Scheck et al., 2000):

> Inadequate investigation of case by defense attorney
>
> Defense attorney failing to file proper motions
>
> Defense attorney not adequately challenging forensic evidence
>
> Defense attorney not adequately challenging witnesses
>
> Defense attorney making unwarranted plea-bargain concessions

Judicial error (JE). Prior research suggests four types of JEs are associated with wrongful conviction. Respondents were again asked to use the 9-item scale to indicate how often they believe each of these four types of JE occur (Rattner, 1983):

> Judicial error concerning the admissibility of physical evidence
>
> Judicial error concerning the admissibility of eyewitness testimony

> Judicial error concerning the admissibility of expert testimony
>
> Error resulting from judicial bias

Statistical Analysis

The main emphasis of the statistical analysis was to examine the response rates of all participants regarding each of the study's research questions and to use statistical tests to measure variations in frequency of responses across groups of participants. Responses to questions concerning the frequency of wrongful conviction and the specific types of error were analyzed using a four-step process. First, the response frequencies were examined. Second, the overall mean score was calculated and then the mean score for each group. Third, analysis of variance was used to determine if differences in group means existed. Finally, if ANOVA indicated that differences existed among group means, post hoc Tukey range tests and pairwise multiple comparisons were used to determine which group means were significantly different from one another.

Findings

Frequency of Wrongful Felony Conviction

Respondents, as a group, perceive wrongful felony conviction to occur in their own jurisdictions between .5% and 1% of the time (Table 2.15). When responses across groups are compared, defense attorneys perceive higher rates of wrongful conviction in their jurisdictions than do judges, prosecutors, and police. On average, defense attorneys believe that in-jurisdiction wrongful conviction occurs in 1% to 3% of all felony cases. Judges perceive wrongful convictions to occur less often (.5% to 1%), whereas both prosecutors and police believe these phenomena only occur in less than .5% of all felony cases. Statistically significant differences ($p = .000$) in the mean scores among the four groups were determined by ANOVA. A post hoc Tukey honestly

Table 2.15 Percentages—Wrongful Conviction in Own Jurisdiction

Response	Police		Prosecutors		Defense Attorneys		Judges		All	
	%	n	%	n	%	n	%	n	%	n
1 = 0%	33.2	91	29.0	29	1.8	4	15.5	26	19.5	150
2 = less than .5%	43.4	119	49.0	49	2.2	5	31.0	52	29.3	225
3 = .5% to 1%	13.5	37	13.0	13	9.3	21	21.4	36	13.9	107
4 = 1% to 3%	6.2	17	6.0	6	26.5	60	19.0	32	15.0	115
5 = 4% to 5%	3.3	9	1.0	1	18.6	42	6.0	10	8.1	62
6 = 6% to 10%	0.4	1	2.0	2	17.3	39	5.4	9	6.6	51
7 = 11% to 15%	—	—	—	—	9.3	21	1.2	2	3.0	23
8 = 16% to 20%	—	—	—	—	7.1	16	0.6	1	2.2	17
9 = 21% to 25%	—	—	—	—	5.3	12	—	—	1.6	12
10 = more than 25%	—	—	—	—	2.7	6	—	—	0.8	6
TOTAL	100.0	274	100.0	100	100.0	226	100.0	168	100.0	768

significantly different (HSD) analysis indicates that group responses significantly differ from one another except those of prosecutors and police (in other words, differences were observed between defense attorneys and police and prosecutors and judges; also judges differed from defense attorneys and police from prosecutors, whereas the group responses of police and prosecutors did not differ).

When respondents were queried about the frequency of wrongful conviction across all jurisdictions of the United States (Table 2.16), three important findings are apparent. First, almost one fourth (24%) of all respondents believe that wrongful convictions occur between 1% and 3% of the time, and an additional 40.7% of the respondents believed they occur in more than 3% of all cases. Second, for each group of respondents, their estimate of the frequency of wrongful conviction in the United States is higher than their estimate of wrongful conviction in their own jurisdictions. Third, when group responses are compared, defense attorneys again report higher rates of wrongful conviction than do judges, prosecutors, and police.

ANOVA indicates statistically significant differences in the mean scores among the four groups. Analysis of the subgroups again reveals that the responses of defense attorneys differ significantly ($p = .000$) from those of the other three groups. In their own jurisdiction, however, judges' responses differ only from those of prosecutors ($p = .001$) and defense attorneys ($p = .000$). No significant differences are reported in the police perceptions when compared with those of prosecutors or judges.

Table 2.17 contains the response frequencies of respondents concerning their beliefs about what is an acceptable rate of wrongful conviction. Overall, slightly more than half of all respondents (51.4%) believe that only a rate of 0% is acceptable. Another one fourth of all respondents (26.6%) think that a rate of less than .5% is acceptable, and approximately one tenth of all respondents (11.5%) feel that a .5% to 1% rate is acceptable. Only 10% of all respondents chose an acceptable wrongful conviction rate of 1% or more. An ANOVA test revealed no significant differences in the mean scores among the four groups.

Table 2.16 Percentages—Wrongful Conviction in United States

Response	Police		Prosecutors		Defense Attorneys		Judges		All	
	%	n	%	n	%	n	%	n	%	n
1 = 0%	1.1	3	1.0	1	0.5	1	—	—	0.7	5
2 = less than .5%	21.3	57	30.2	29	1.9	4	17.0	26	15.8	116
3 = .5% to 1%	23.6	63	31.3	30	6.0	13	20.3	31	18.7	137
4 = 1% to 3%	29.6	79	24.0	23	14.4	31	28.1	43	24.0	176
5 = 4% to 5%	14.2	38	10.4	10	25.9	56	18.3	28	18.0	132
6 = 6% to 10%	5.2	14	1.0	1	19.4	42	10.5	16	10.0	73
7 = 11% to 15%	2.2	6	2.1	2	8.8	19	3.9	6	4.5	33
8 = 16% to 20%	2.2	6	—	—	13.0	28	1.3	2	4.9	36
9 = 21% to 25%	0.4	1	—	—	2.3	5	—	—	0.8	6
10 = more than 25%	—	—	—	—	7.9	17	0.7	1	2.5	18
TOTAL	100.0	267	100.0	96	100.0	216	100.0	153	100.0	732

Table 2.17 Percentages—Acceptable Level of Wrongful Conviction

Response	Police		Prosecutors		Defense Attorneys		Judges		All	
	%	n	%	n	%	n	%	n	%	n
1 = 0%	54.6	148	48.5	48	49.1	113	51.1	89	51.4	398
2 = less than .5%	24.7	67	29.3	29	27.0	62	27.6	48	26.6	206
3 = .5% to 1%	10.7	29	13.1	13	10.9	25	12.6	22	11.5	89
4 = 1% to 3%	6.3	17	8.1	8	8.3	19	6.3	11	7.1	55
5 = 4% to 5%	1.1	3	1.0	1	3.0	7	2.3	4	1.9	15
6 = 6% to 10%	1.5	4	—	—	1.7	4	—	—	1.0	8
7 = 11% to 15%	0.7	2	—	—	—	—	—	—	0.3	2
8 = 16% to 20%	0.4	1	—	—	—	—	—	—	0.1	1
9 = 21% to 25%	—	—	—	—	—	—	—	—	—	—
10 = more than 25%	—	—	—	—	—	—	—	—	—	—
TOTAL	100.0	271	100.0	99	100.0	230	100.0	174	100.0	774

Specific System Error or Misconduct

The next four tables present mean responses to questions regarding perceptions of the frequency of specific types of error or misconduct involving the police, prosecutors, defense attorneys, and judges. Also reported, for each group and each type of error, is an additive scale that was created in each instance from the responses to individual survey items displayed in the table (e.g., PE, PrE, DE, and JE). Mean scores are derived from the 9-item scale responses to the survey questions.

Police Error (PE)

Table 2.18 reports mean responses for the four groups of respondents on each of the five PE measures. For each of the items, defense attorney means were the highest of the four groups. Mean responses for judges were the second highest, followed by police and then prosecutors (except for the question on inadequate investigations where the order of police and prosecutors is reversed).

A reliability test (Cronbach's alpha) was conducted to determine if all five items measure the same concept of PE.[8] A Cronbach's alpha of .9179 suggests that the responses presented in Table 2.18 have enough intercorrelation to be combined as a single variable. As

such, an additive scale was produced and a single variable PE created. Mean response to the variable PE (3.24) indicates respondents believe this type of error to occur more than infrequent but less than moderately frequent.

When group responses are analyzed separately, defense attorneys think PE occurs more frequently than do judges, prosecutors, and police. Judges perceive PE to occur more frequently than do prosecutors and police but less frequently than defense attorneys. An ANOVA test of the variable PE indicates that there are statistically significant differences ($p = .000$) in the mean scores of the four groups. The results of the post hoc Tukey HSD test indicate that the opinions of both defense attorneys and judges differ significantly ($p = .000$) from the members of the other three groups, whereas the responses of police and prosecutors do not differ significantly from one another (although each does differ from those of defense attorneys and judges).

Prosecutorial Error (PrE)

Table 2.19 reports mean frequencies for each PrE item. The same pattern of responses that was observed for PE was evident with prosecutorial error. Specifically, the highest mean responses for each item were observed with defense attorneys followed by judges, police, and then prosecutors.

Table 2.18 Perceptions of Five Types of Police Error (Mean Responses)[a]

Type of Police Error	Police	Prosecutors	Defense Attorneys	Judges	All Respondents
Inadequate police investigation	3.57	3.93	5.90	4.63	4.55
Police using undue pressure to obtain a confession	2.79	2.68	6.23	3.66	4.01
Police coaching witnesses in pretrial I.D. procedures	2.87	2.48	5.65	3.44	3.78
Police suppressing exculpatory evidence	2.55	2.27	5.52	3.39	3.60
Police using false evidence	1.94	1.64	3.71	2.46	2.55
Mean scores	2.74	2.60	5.40	3.52	3.24

a. Survey question: Based on your knowledge and experience, estimate the frequency of each type of police error.

Table 2.19   Perceptions of Five Types of Prosecutorial Error (Mean Responses)[a]

Type of Prosecutorial Error	Police	Prosecutors	Defense Attorneys	Judges	All Respondents
Inadequate investigation of case by prosecutor	3.67	2.67	5.28	4.03	4.11
Prosecutor using undue plea-bargain pressure	3.94	2.20	5.65	3.57	4.15
Prosecutor prompting witnesses	3.27	2.22	5.83	3.73	4.01
Prosecutor suppressing exculpatory evidence	2.67	1.59	4.66	2.88	3.18
Prosecutor knowingly using false testimony	1.84	1.25	3.11	1.96	2.17
Mean scores	3.08	1.99	4.91	3.23	3.52

a. Survey question: Based on your knowledge and experience, estimate the frequency of each type of prosecutorial error.

Again, a reliability test was conducted to determine if all five items measure the same concept of PrE (Cronbach's alpha = .8998). An additive scale was created using all five survey items, and a single variable PrE was created. The mean response for all respondents for the variable PrE is 3.52. On the 9-item response scale, a rating of 3.52 translates as more than "infrequent" and "less than moderately frequent."

An ANOVA test of the variable PrE reveals statistically significant (p = .000) differences in mean scores of the four groups. The results of a post hoc Tukey HSD test indicate that prosecutors perceive a significantly (p = .000) different rate of their own error than do members of the other three groups. In contrast to perceptions of PE, prosecutor responses also differ significantly from the other three groups (p = .000), whereas judges and police responses perceptions do not differ from one another. When the group responses to the PrE scale are analyzed separately, the major differences in perceptions are best understood when the responses are broken down into *infrequent or less* and *more than infrequent* categories. Only 8.9% of defense attorneys perceive PrE to occur at the infrequent or less level. On the other hand, prosecutors and police selected responses of *infrequent or less* at a rate 8 times higher than defense attorneys and at a rate almost 6 times higher than judges. Conversely, 91.1% of defense attorneys perceive PrE to occur more than infrequent—almost double the

perception rate of judges and police, and 13 times higher than perceived by prosecutors.

Defense Attorney Error (DE)

Mean responses of all four groups of criminal justice professionals, individually and compositely, are reported in Table 2.20. Contrary to the findings reported in the prior two tables, there is no consistent pattern of response means across the four groups. Defense attorneys do have the highest means and prosecutors the lowest means. However, the means of judges and police are very similar.

The Cronbach's alpha (.8879) indicated that all five defense attorney questions measure the same concept of *DE*. An additive scale was produced using the five survey items, and a single variable DE was created. Overall, the mean response for DE is above the more than infrequent level and below the moderately frequent level (M = 4.29). There is consensus among prosecutors, police, and judges that DE occurs less than moderately frequently. Only defense attorneys believe their group's own error to be above the moderately frequent level.

An analysis of variance test reveals that significant differences (p = .05) exist in the mean scores of the four groups. The results of a post hoc Tukey HSD test indicate that defense attorneys perceive significantly (p = .000) different rates of their own group's

Table 2.20   Perceptions of Five Types of Defense Error (Mean Responses)[a]

Type of Defense Attorney Error	Police	Prosecutors	Defense Attorneys	Judges	All Respondents
Inadequate investigation of case by defense attorney	4.54	4.31	5.35	4.70	4.79
Defense attorney not adequately challenging forensic evidence	3.84	3.71	5.24	4.07	4.30
Defense attorney failing to file proper motions	4.02	3.87	4.69	4.02	4.21
Defense attorney making unwarranted plea-bargain concessions	4.30	3.12	4.59	3.85	4.14
Defense attorney not adequately challenging witnesses	3.68	3.43	4.61	3.96	3.99
Mean scores	4.08	3.69	4.90	4.12	4.29

a. Survey question: Based on your knowledge and experience, estimate the frequency of each type of defense attorney error.

error than do members of the other three groups, whereas prosecutors report significantly different rates of DE than do police $(p = .039)$ and judges $(p = .025)$. Police and judges' perceptions do not significantly differ.

Judicial Error (JE)

Table 2.21 displays the responses to the four JE items. Similar to the other reported responses, defense attorneys believe that each form of JE is more common than

do police, prosecutors, or judges. Furthermore, the difference in means of defense attorneys is quite substantial, whereas the means of the other three groups of criminal justice actors are quite similar. Still, prosecutor means are the lowest on each item, whereas response means of judges are the second lowest on two items. For the remaining two items, police means either are the same as judges or slightly lower.

A Cronbach's alpha of .8772 suggests that all four items can be combined as a single variable and as

Table 2.21   Perceptions of Four Types of Judicial Error (Mean Responses)[a]

Type of Judicial Error	Police	Prosecutors	Defense Attorneys	Judges	All Respondents
Error resulting from judicial bias	2.90	2.36	5.07	2.69	3.44
Error concerning admissibility of physical evidence	3.00	2.87	4.55	3.00	3.45
Error concerning admissibility of testimony	3.01	2.50	4.45	2.84	3.35
Error concerning admissibility of expert testimony	2.79	2.54	4.25	2.94	3.23
Mean scores	2.93	2.57	4.58	2.87	3.37

a. Survey question: Based on your knowledge and experience, estimate the frequency of each type of judicial error.

such an additive scale was produced. Overall, the mean response for the variable JE is above the infrequent level $(M = 3.37)$ and below the moderately frequent level. An ANOVA test of the variable JE reveals that significant differences exist in the group mean scores. Whereas defense attorneys perceive a significantly $(p = .000)$, different rate of error than do members of the other three groups, the perceptions of prosecutors, police, and judges do not differ significantly from one another.

⊠ Discussion

The frequency of wrongful convictions within the criminal justice system is unknown. The figure remains elusive because knowledge of cases where defendants are wrongfully convicted usually occurs only when defendants have resources that are sufficient to proffer evidence of some nature to persuade a court that they have been unjustly convicted or, when no financial resources are available, others with resources agree to become involved. Additionally, the "criminal justice system is not designed to scrutinize its own decisions for a range of factual errors once a decision is reached" (Bedau & Radelet, 1987, p. 70; see also Gross et al., 2005, p. 2). As such, it is likely that most incidences of wrongful conviction are not discovered. Also, although much has been learned in recent years about the system errors associated with wrongful conviction, little research has been conducted to determine the extent of these errors. The present study extends previous research by providing information on system actors' perceptions concerning both the frequency of wrongful convictions in general and also the frequency with which specific system errors associated with wrongful convictions occur in the processing of criminal cases. Several of the findings are especially worthy of further mention and discussion.

Regarding the perceived frequency of wrongful conviction in the United States, when the results of the current study are compared with the findings of the 1983 Rattner survey, estimations of the frequency of wrongful conviction appears to have increased among criminal justice professionals. For example, respondents to our survey perceive that wrongful convictions occur more frequently in the United States (between 1% and 3% of all felony cases) than did respondents to the Rattner survey (less than 1%). Also, it appears that the belief of some criminal justice professionals that wrongful convictions never occur is dissipating. Only 0.7% of our survey respondents believe that wrongful conviction never happens in the United States—significantly less than the 5.6% of respondents to the 1983 survey who believed this to be true.

When perceptions of in-jurisdiction frequency are compared, respondents to our survey estimated a rate between .5% and 1% of all felony cases[9]—similar to the Rattner (1983) survey respondents' estimations of less than 1%. However, when the actual responses are examined, differences in the perceptions of the respondents to the two surveys emerge. For example, in the earlier survey about one in three respondents (36.8%) believed that wrongful felony conviction never occurred in their own jurisdictions, whereas in our survey, this figure changed to about one in five (19.5%). Similarly, when the 1% to 5% categories are compared, only 6.5% of respondents to the 1983 survey selected this option compared to 23% of respondents to the present survey—an almost fourfold increase. Thus, although the average responses were similar, there appear to be differences in the individual responses.

These changes in aggregate-level responses likely result because of several reasons. First, as previously mentioned, DNA technology has provided conclusive proof in many instances that wrongfully convicted individuals were factually innocent. Second, media outlets have reported the activities of several prominent organizations that have tracked wrongful convictions in capital crimes throughout the United States (i.e., Innocence Project, Death Penalty Information Center, and the Center on Wrongful Convictions). Another likely factor is the publicity surrounding the blanket clemency and death penalty moratorium implemented by Governor George Ryan in Illinois. Ultimately, however, answers to whether these increases are because of factors associated with the revelations of modern DNA technology and the accompanying media attention and professional discussion remains an empirical question (Gross et al., 2005; Drizin & Leo, 2003–2004).

Findings regarding the perceived frequency of system errors associated with wrongful conviction are also informative. We did not expect the majority of our respondents to perceive that system errors never occur, but we did expect that criminal justice actors would believe that such error occurs infrequently or less. Whereas it is not uncommon for system actors to occasionally criticize the system's dysfunctions, it is uncommon for a majority of queried system actors to state that error occurs more than infrequently. This is exactly what our respondents indicated. Across all categories of system error—PE, PrE, DE, and JE—respondents in total believe that error occurs more than infrequently. It is worth noting that the two lowest estimates of error concerned corrupt action (i.e., police using false evidence, prosecutor knowingly using false evidence), possibly reflecting the likelihood that respondents are more likely to acknowledge issues concerning negligence and poor training than they are to acknowledge issues involving corruption.

Interestingly, when survey responses were grouped according to the respondent's role within the system (police, prosecutors, defense counsel, judges), defense attorneys perceived each measured system error to be significantly more likely to occur than each of the other group of respondents. At the same time, for 18 of 19 comparisons, prosecutors on average perceived system errors to be least likely or common, and their responses were often quite similar to those voiced by police chiefs. Judges, although often similar to police chiefs, most often voiced responses indicating the belief that these errors were more likely to result than did police, although they believed they were less likely to occur than did defense attorneys.

It is not surprising that prosecutors perceive the least error given their primary role in the criminal justice system; the prosecutor picks the cases to prosecute, selects the charge(s), recommends the bail amount, makes and approves plea-bargain agreements, and urges the judge to impose a particular sentence. Tied to this decision-making process is an organizational culture in many prosecutors' offices that promotes a win-at-any-cost instead of a doing-justice mentality (Huff et al., 1996). Prosecutors thus are susceptible to using a guilty-until-proven-innocent approach to prosecutions that contributes to perceptions that wrongful convictions are rare. In sum, because prosecutors hold more responsibility in the processing of wrongful convicted individuals than any other court actor, they are particularly situated to deny that wrongful convictions occur with any frequency.

On the other hand, we find that defense attorneys perceive more error than the other system actors. This may, in part, be because of the adversarial professional relationship they have with these actors. Often, defense attorneys find themselves trying to refute police testimony and counter prosecutorial motions and contesting judicial verdicts (Cole & Smith, 2005). Although defense attorneys, like prosecutors, are also involved in a case from arrest through verdict, they have relatively little influence on what cases are to be prosecuted, what bail will be set, or what sentence recommendations come from the prosecutor.

Police officials and judges generally occupied the midranges of the group means. In other words, these two groups generally perceive more error than prosecutors and less error than defense attorneys, although judges in most instances believed there was more error than did police officials. The more moderate estimations of police officials may be because of their relatively limited involvement in cases of wrongful conviction.

An encouraging finding of this study is when respondents were asked what they believed to be an acceptable level of wrongful conviction in the United States, we found that a gap exists between what the majority believes is an acceptable frequency (0%) and what the majority believes to be the actual frequency (1% to 3%). A foundation for reform is therefore in place. Also, irrespective of their role or their perceptions regarding the frequency of wrongful conviction and system errors, those who responded to the survey assert that reductions in the frequency of wrongful conviction and the rate of system error are not only preferable but also possible. It is often the case that individuals are readily prepared to critique and criticize the criminal justice process but are unprepared to provide proposed solutions. In this study, however, two thirds of the respondents offered quite insightful, and well-informed, written suggestions concerning how the frequency of wrongful conviction might be reduced. The fact that almost 500 of the 798 respondents answered the survey's open-ended question "In your opinion, what steps could be taken by criminal justice professionals to reduce the incidence of wrongful conviction?" indicates, we believe, that there exists a deep concern about this problem among criminal justice professionals. Many of the suggestions of these practitioners reflect those offered by prior research (for example, see Drizen & Leo, 2003–2004; Gross, 1996; Harmon, 2004; Huff et al., 1986) and should provide significant procedural implications and food for thought for policy makers. Reflecting the multifaceted and complex nature of wrongful conviction, respondent suggestions addressed a variety of issues. The following is a sample of some representative written comments provided by respondents.

System Overload

Members of all groups of criminal justice professionals agree that they and their colleagues are often overwhelmed by heavy caseloads, especially in large cities. More than 100 respondents provided comments concerning how the avalanche of cases in some jurisdiction may either cause, or contribute to, wrongful conviction. They suggest that often high caseloads lead to inadequate investigations, rushes to judgment, and forced confessions. One judge wrote,

> The tools are available to improve upon reducing the rate of wrongful conviction. However, the overwhelming volume of cases imposed upon the courts in certain jurisdictions within certain time spans without adequate investigation and preparation by law enforcement, prosecutors, defense counsel and the courts, will always impact upon a perfect system.

Leadership by professionals in their respective fields will affect the wrongful conviction rate.

A chief county prosecutor said, "The biggest problem I see is that all of us—at every step—have so darn many cases that it is sometimes very difficult to do the job you know needs to be done."

Police Practices

A major criticism of police practices involved the lack of thoroughness during investigations. One police official said, "Many experienced and inexperienced investigators form an opinion at the onset of their investigation and develop their fact base on their preconceived opinions. The facts need to speak for themselves."

Police identification procedures were also a topic of significant criticism. A defense attorney wrote, "The reliability of eyewitness testimony varies from reliable to unreliable depending on the time between crime and identification—and type of lineup used. There is a need for less suggestive I.D. procedures and less reliance on stranger I.D."

Other suggestions revolved around the need to videotape all police interrogations and confessions. A defense attorney noted,

> Supposed "confessions" are often summaries prepared by the police and signed by an undereducated, unsophisticated client who is assured of leniency for cooperating and giving a statement. In this day and age, all statements should be videotaped. In fact, arrest to booking should be videotaped. When police video or audio an interview, they frequently do a "run-through" ahead of time. What is not on the tape is the 3 hours of interviews where the accused is told he "will fry" if he doesn't confess or some other such nonsense.

A judge remarked, "Require the video-taping of a defendant from the moment police contact begins, not just 30 seconds of 'confession.'"

Prosecutorial Practices

Prosecutors also received their fair share of criticism. Many respondents were concerned about prosecutorial overzealousness and the withholding of exculpatory evidence.

One defense attorney stated, "Chief prosecutors should refrain from pushing their assistant 'to win at all costs' irregardless [sic] of justice," whereas a judge wrote, "Prosecutors need to be better prepared, less overindicting, and realize the abuses of their power and be held accountable."

Another typical comment came from a police official who stated, "Prosecuting attorneys are 'graded' on conviction rates. Young prosecutors appear pressured to get some type of conviction. Emphasis must be placed on the truth."

Defense Attorney Practices

Defense attorneys were often criticized for lack of preparedness. Widely noted, however, was the problem defense attorneys often have in acquiring the necessary resources to properly defend their client. Many respondents noted that rarely do defense attorneys have the necessary resources to offset the resources of the prosecution.

A prosecutor commented,

> Police officers do occasionally get sloppy and arrest the wrong person. It would be nice if we could make police more thorough and objective, but the reality is that our system relies on defense lawyers to make sure justice is done. Unfortunately it is rare for a lawyer to have the resources necessary to properly investigate and defend. In other words, sadly, justice requires money.

A public defender remarked, "The defense attorney does not have the support staff the prosecution has. The playing field is not balanced because the legwork must be done by the defense attorney him/herself."

Judicial Practices

Criticism of judges primarily revolved around personal bias, competency, and judicial pressure exerted on the plea-bargaining process. One defense attorney wrote,

> Most judges in my county are less than impartial in criminal cases. Individuals very often confess to a crime they did not commit because most judges will tell the defense attorney they will max your client's sentence if they go to trial and lose.

A police official commented. "Judges should be appointed based on skills, knowledge, experience, and abilities—not because of who they know or how popular they are."

Increased Professionalism and Training

Many respondents spoke of the need for increased professionalism and improved training across the criminal justice profession. Almost 100 respondents suggested that wrongful convictions might be reduced if more stringent selection and hiring standards were put in place. Another consistent suggestion was that more and better training should be provided (including ethical training) and that such training should not only occur when individuals are beginning their careers but also on a continuing basis. Finally, many respondents called for raising professional standards and stricter discipline for those who consistently make errors or are involved in professional misconduct. A police official wrote,

> Set minimum requirements of training and continuing legal education for criminal defense attorneys—particularly in death penalty cases nationwide. Also, a minimum requirement of continuing training hours (annually) for police officers in general, and detectives in particular, regarding identification procedures, forensic evidence collection, and securing statements, in addition to others.

Conclusions and Recommendations for Future Research

The scientific study of wrongful conviction has now been carried on for approximately 75 years. When reviewing the conclusions of the early researchers regarding the frequency and causes of wrongful conviction one cannot help but take note of how little their research has been contradicted by modern science; most of the conclusions of these early researchers appear to remain valid today. Each researcher has consistently pointed to the same criteria: Eyewitness error, faulty science, professional error and misconduct, false witnesses, rushes to judgment, and presumption of guilt are the factors most often mentioned. Twenty-first century science has, to date, only tended to confirm the hunches of the earlier researchers that wrongful conviction is basically a product of a complex mix of these factors. It is yet to be determined, however, if the laments and policy proposals of these writers—from Borchard in 1932, through Garner and Frank and Frank in the 1950s, Radin in the 1960s, and echoed by Huff et al., Bedau and Radelet, and McCloskey in the 1980s—have not significantly reduced the incidence of wrongful convictions or only served to cast some light on the problem. In many ways, we are still in the Dark Ages of understanding how to improve our system of justice in regards to separating the innocent from the guilty. We can take some comfort in the findings of this study—that those individuals who work in the criminal justice system are increasingly acknowledging that wrongful convictions and system errors occur at an unacceptable frequency.

Future research should continue to focus on determining what causes wrongful convictions. This study could only ask respondents to indicate their perceptions regarding errors that have been determined to be associated with the phenomenon of wrongful conviction because, to date, no direct causal relationships between the identified errors and wrongful convictions have been proven. Previous research appears to suggest that no single factor causes a wrongful conviction; in almost every proven case of wrongful conviction, numerous errors occurred in the processing of the accused. The challenge for the future research is to determine which errors, and which interactions, contribute to wrongful conviction. Finally, future research should be conducted to determine if the dynamics of wrongful conviction vary when large metropolitan jurisdictions are compared to smaller rural jurisdictions.

There is widespread recognition that, due to the human condition, the phenomenon of wrongful conviction is not likely to ever be totally eliminated. However, seeking to reduce the incidence of wrongful conviction is a noble task—given the misery that a wrongful conviction can impose on the wrongly convicted themselves, their families, the victims and their families, witnesses, jurors, and even those who work in the criminal justice system. Much work still needs to be done. We trust that this article has advanced the cause of justice.

 Notes

1. Not included in these findings are an additional 174 cases of mass exonerations involving defendants whose cases were set aside after investigations revealed that they had been framed by rogue police officers.

2. One question in the Rattner survey asked respondents to estimate the number of cases where additional investigation by a public defender aided in the exoneration of a wrongfully convicted individual.

3. Officials investigating the Los Angeles Police Department's Rampart Community Resources Against Street Hoodlums unit uncovered a tangled web linking officers with street gangs, drug dealing, and the gangster-rap underworld.

4. Conners, Lundregan, Miller, and McEwen's (1996) investigation and discussion of wrongful conviction note,

> This report does not discuss the issue of government misconduct because it is not particularized to the use of DNA technology. Beyond the limited instances noted in this report, enough examples of government misconduct in the criminal justice system exist in the popular media for government officials to be well aware of the problem. (p. 20)

5. State of Ohio criminal justice professionals were targeted for the Rattner survey because it was believed the use of a single large state, such as Ohio, served to control for the effect of varying legal definitions while still allowing for a diversity of settings. The present study targeted Ohio criminal justice professionals for the similar reasons. Ohio is the seventh largest state in terms of population (U.S. Bureau of Census. 2000) with slightly more than 11 million people. Ohio has law enforcement and court systems similar to most states (elected sheriffs, prosecutors and judges, and pressure to solve and close cases) and is likely to suffer from issues associated with the processing of defendants as they proceed through overburdened criminal justice systems. In other words, we know of no reasons why their perceptions should be unique. Also, at the time of the present survey Ohio was politically a swing state evenly split between Democrats and Republicans, which should increase the generalizability of the data as compared to less politically diverse states. We would welcome a national replication of the study.

6. The five mailings included (a) prenotice postcard, (b) initial mailing of survey with cover letter, (c) reminder or thank you post card, (d) second mailing of survey and cover letter, and (e) third mailing of survey and cover letter.

7. Ohio has 88 counties.

8. Cronbach's alpha was determined using SPSS. Cronbach's alpha can be written as a function of the number of survey items and the average intercorrelation among them. A reliability coefficient of .80 or higher is considered acceptable in most social science applications.

9. This estimate is lower than estimates by respondents for the frequency in the United States. It is believed the differences in these two estimates may result from estimations made by respondents from smaller jurisdictions, where smaller caseloads prevail and where rates of wrongful conviction may be lower than in larger jurisdictions where caseloads are heavier.

References

Adams, R. D., Hoffer, W., & Hoffer, M. (1991). *Adams v. Texas.* New York: St. Martin's.

Barlow, A. (1999). The wrong man. *The Atlantic Monthly, 284,* 66–91.

Bedau, H. A., & Radelet, M. L. (1987). Miscarriages of justice in potentially capital cases. *Stanford Law Review, 40,* 21–179.

Bedau, H. A., & Radelet, M. L. (1988). The myth of infallibility: A reply to Markman and Cassell. *Stanford Law Review, 41,* 161–170.

Borchard, E. M. (1932). *Convicting the innocent: Sixty-five actual errors of criminal justice.* Garden City, NY: Doubleday.

Brandon, R., & Davie, C. (1973). *Wrong imprisonment: Mistaken convictions and their consequences.* London: Allen & Unwin.

Buckley v. Fitzsimmons, 113 S.Ct. 2606 (1993).

Bureau of Justice Statistics. (2004). *Corrections statistics.* Retrieved on March 12, 2005, from http://www.ojp.usdoj.gov/bjs/correct.htm

Carter, L. H., & Beth, L. P. (1978). The rule of law in criminal justice: An innocent convicted. *Journal of Politics, 40,* 898–907.

Christianson, S. (2004). *Innocent: Inside wrongful conviction cases.* New York: New York University Press.

CNN. (2000, January 31). *Illinois suspends death penalty.* Retrieved on January 31, 2000, from CNN.com

Cohen, S. (2003). *The wrong men.* New York: Carroll and Graf.

Cole, G., & Smith. C. (2005). *The American system of criminal justice.* Belmont, CA: Wadsworth.

Connery, D. (Ed.). (1996). *Convicting the innocent: The story of a murder, a false confession and the struggle to free a "wrong man."* Cambridge. MA: Brookline.

Connors, E., Lundregan, T., Miller, N., & McEwen, T. (1996). *Convicted by juries, exonerated by science: Case studies in the use of DNA evidence to establish innocence after trial.* Alexandria, VA: National Institute of Justice.

Cooper, C., Cooper. S., & Reese, S. (1995). *Mockery of justice: True story of the Sam Shepard murder case.* Boston: Northeastern University Press.

Dieter, R. (1997). *Innocence and the death penalty: The increasing danger of executing the innocent. Death Penalty Information Center.* Retrieved on March 18, 2005, from http://www.deathpenaltyinfo.org/article.php?scid=45&did=292

Dillman, D. A. (2000). *Mail and internet surveys: A tailored design method.* New York: John Wiley.

Drizin, S. A., & Leo, R. A. (2003–2004). The problem of false confessions in the post-DNA world. *North Carolina Law Review, 82,* 891–1008.

Fan, D. P., Keltner, K. A., & Wyatt, R. O. (2002). A matter of guilt or innocence: How news reports affect support for the death penalty. *International Journal of Public Opinion Research, 14,* 439–451.

Finer, J. J. (1973). Ineffective assistance of counsel. *Cornell Law Review, 58,* 1077–1120.

Frank, J., & Frank, B. (1957). *Not guilty.* New York: Doubleday.

Frisbie, T., & Garrett, R. (1998). *Victims of justice.* New York: Avon.

Furman v. Georgia, 408 U.S. 238 (1972).

Gershman, B. (1999). *Prosecutorial misconduct.* Deerfield, IL: Clark Boardman Callaghan.

Gottfredson, M. R., & Gottfredson, D. M. (1988). *Decision making in criminal justice: Toward the rational exercise of discretion* (2nd ed.). New York: Plenum.

Gross, S. R. (1996). The risks of death: Why erroneous convictions are common in capital cases. *Buffalo Law Review, 44,* 469–500.

Gross, S. R. (1998). Lost lives: Miscarriages of justice in capital cases. *Law and Contemporary Problems, 61,* 125–152.

Gross, S. R., Jacoby, K., Matheson, D., Montgomery, N., & Patel, S. (2005). Exonerations in the United States: 1989 through 2003. *Journal of Criminal Law and Criminology, 95,* 523–560.

Harmon, T. R. (2004). Race for your life: An analysis of the role of race in erroneous capital convictions. *Criminal Justice Review, 29,* 76–96.

Hirsch, J. (2000). *The miraculous journey of Rubin Carter.* New York: Houghton Muffin.

Huff, R. C., & Rattner, A. (1988). Convicted but innocent: False positives and the criminal justice process. In J. E. Scott & T. Hirschi (Eds.), *Controversial issues in crime and justice* (pp. 53–82). Newbury Park, CA: Sage.

Huff, C. R., Rattner, A., & Sagarin, E. (1986). Guilty until proven innocent: Wrongful conviction and public policy. *Crime and Delinquency, 32,* 518–544.

Huff, C. R., Rattner, A., & Sagarin, E. (1996). *Convicted but innocent: Wrongful conviction and public policy.* London: Sage.

Humes, E. (1999). *Mean justice: A town's terror, a prosecutor's power, a betrayal of innocence.* New York: Simon & Schuster.

Innocence Project. (2006). *Innocence Project case profiles.* Retrieved on January 5, 2006, from http://www.innocenceproject.org

Justice for All Act, H.R. 5107 (2004).

Kassin, S. M. (1997). The psychology of confession evidence. *American Psychologist, 52,* 221.

Leahy, P. (2003). *Bipartisan, bicameral breakthrough reached on Death Penalty Bill reform.* Retrieved on October 1, 2003, from http://www .senate.gov/-leahy/pressy200310/100103.html

Leo, R. A., & Ofshe, R. J. (1997–1998). The consequences of false confessions: Deprivations of liberty and miscarriages of justice in the age of psychological interrogation. *Journal of Criminal Law and Criminology, 88,* 429–496.

Liebman, J., Fagan, J., & West, V. (2000). *A broken system: Error rates in capital cases. 1973–1995.* Retrieved on February 9, 2005, from http://justice.policy.net/proactive/newsroom/release.vtml?id-l8200

Liebman, J., Fagan, J., West, V., Gelman, A., Davies, A., & Kiss, A. (2002). *A broken system: Part II: Why there is so much error in capital cases and what can be done about it.* Retrieved on February 9, 2005, from http://justice.policy:.net/proactive/newsroon/release .vtml?id-2664l

Linscott, S., & Frame, R. L. (1994). *Maximum security.* Wheaton, IL: Crossway.

Loftus, E. F. (2003). Our changeable memories: Legal and practical implications. *Nature Reviews: Neuroscience, 4,* 231–234.

MacNamara, D. E. J. (1969). Convicting the innocent. *Crime and Delinquency, 15,* 57–61.

Manson v. Brathwaite, 432 U.S. 98 (1977).

McCloskey, J. (1989). Convicting the innocent. *Criminal Justice Ethics, 8,* 2–12.

McCloskey, J. (1996). The death penalty: A personal view. *Criminal Justice Ethics, 8,* 54–59.

McMahon, M. (1995). False confessions and police deception: The interrogation, incarceration, and release of an innocent veteran. *American Journal of Forensic Psychology, 5,* 5–43.

Miller v. Pate, 386 U.S. 1 (1967).

Parker, K., Dewees, M., & Radelet, M. (2002). Racial bias and the conviction of the innocent. In S. D. Westervelt & J. A. Humphrey (Eds.), *Wrongly convicted: Perspectives on failed justice* (pp. 114–131). Piscataway, NJ: Rutgers University Press.

Potter, J., & Bost, F. (1997). *Fatal justice: Reinvestigating the MacDonald murders.* New York: Norton.

Poveda, T. G. (2001). Estimating wrongful convictions. *Justice Quarterly, 18,* 6S9-70S.

Protess, D., & Warden, R. (1998). *A promise of justice: The eighteen-year fight to save four innocent men.* New York: Hyperion.

Radelet, M. L., & Bedau, H. A. (1998). The execution of the innocent. *Law and Contemporary Problems, 61,* 105–124.

Radelet, M. L., Bedau, H. A., & Putnam, C. E. (1992). *In spite of innocence: Erroneous convictions in capital cases.* Boston: Northeastern University Press.

Radin, E. D. (1964). *The innocents.* New York: William Morrow.

Ramsey, R. J. (2003). *False positives in the criminal justice process—An analysis of factors associated with wrongful conviction of the innocent.* Unpublished doctoral dissertation, University of Cincinnati.

Rattner, A. (1983). *When justice goes wrong: Convicting the innocent.* Unpublished doctoral dissertation. The Ohio State University, Columbus.

Rattner, A. (1988). Convicted but innocent: Wrongful conviction and the criminal justice system. *Law and Human Behavior, 12,* 283–293.

Scheck, B., Neufeld, P., & Dwyer, J. (2000). *Actual innocence: Five days to execution, and other dispatches from the wrongly convicted.* New York: Random House.

Simon, T. (2003). *The innocents.* New York: Umbrage.

State of Oklahoma v. Ronald Keith Williamson and Dennis Leon Fritz, CRF87-90 (1991).

Unnever, J. D., & Cullen, F. T. (2005). Executing the innocent and support for capital punishment: Implications for public policy. *Criminology & Public Policy, 4,* 3–37.

U.S. Bureau of Census. (2000). *U.S. Census Bureau State and county quick facts.* Washington, DC: Government Printing Office.

Walker, C., & Keir, S. (Eds.). (1999). *Miscarriages of justice: A review of justice in error.* London: Blackstone.

Walker, S. (2006). *Sense and nonsense about crime and drugs: A policy guide.* Pacific Grove, CA: Brooks/Cole.

Weinstock, D., & Schwartz, G. E. (1998). Executing the innocent: Preventing the ultimate injustice. *Criminal Law Bulletin, 31,* 328–347.

Wells, G. L., & Olson, E. (2003). Eyewitness identification. *Annual Review of Psychology, 54,* 277–295.

Westervelt, S. D., & Humphrey, J. A. (2002). *Wrongly convicted: Perspectives on failed justice.* Piscataway, NJ: Rutgers University Press.

Yant, M. (1991). *Presumed guilty: When innocent people are wrongly convicted.* Buffalo, NY: Prometheus.

Young, R. L. (2004). Guilty until proven innocent: Conviction orientation, racial attitudes, and support for capital punishment. *Deviant Behavior, 25,* 151–167.

DISCUSSION QUESTIONS

1. According to Ramsey and Frank, what "drives" research on wrongful convictions? That is, why is research on wrongful convictions important?

2. How common are wrongful convictions? Why do scholars believe that official data on wrongful conviction underestimate the true frequency of these miscarriages of justice?

3. The focus of the survey conducted by Ramsey and Frank was "system errors that have been determined by prior research to be associated with wrongful conviction." What are these "system errors" and how do they lead to wrongful conviction?

4. How did the authors define *wrongful conviction?*

5. According to the respondents, how frequently do wrongful convictions occur in their own jurisdictions? In jurisdictions throughout the United States? What is an acceptable rate of wrongful conviction, according to the respondents?

6. According to the authors, why are the estimates of the frequency of wrongful conviction found in this study higher than estimates found in previous research?

7. How did the perceptions of defense attorneys differ from those of law enforcement officials, prosecutors, and judges? What explains these differences?

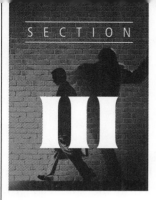

SECTION

III

Prosecutors and Defense Attorneys

The Adversarial System

The Anglo American system of criminal justice is an **adversarial system** (Kagan, 2001; Landsman, 1984). This system pits two parties—prosecution and defense—against each other in the pursuit of truth. It puts the burden of proof in a criminal case on the prosecutor, who must demonstrate beyond a reasonable doubt that the defendant committed the crime. The defense attorney's role is to argue for his or her client's innocence and to insist that the client's rights be protected at every stage in the process. The judge serves as a neutral arbitrator, largely to ensure that proper law and procedures are followed, and a jury made up of citizens determines issues of fact. Each side calls witnesses and questions them about their knowledge of the alleged crime. Each attorney has an opportunity to cross-examine the other attorney's witnesses; the goal is to cast doubt on the reliability of the witness's testimony by showing that the witness is biased or that the evidence presented is irrelevant. According to this somewhat idealized version of the adversarial process (see "Lawyers Seek Victory, Not Truth" in Box 3.1), then, the prosecutor and defense attorney fight it out in a process designed to ensure that truth will emerge.

BOX 3.1

Lawyers Seek Victory, Not Truth

What is the role of the lawyers in bringing the evidence before the trial court?...The lawyer considers it his duty to create a false impression, if he can, of any [adverse] witness who gives such testimony. If such a witness happens to be timid, frightened by the unfamiliarity of courtroom ways, the lawyer, in his cross-examination, plays on that weakness, in order to confuse the witness and make it appear that he is concealing significant facts....The lawyer seeks not only to discredit adverse witnesses but also to hide the defects of witnesses who testify favorably to his client. If, when interviewing such a witness before trial, the lawyer notes that the witness has mannerisms...that might discredit him, the lawyer teaches him how to cover up those traits when testifying....Lawyers freely boast of their success with these tactics....In short, the lawyer aims at victory, at winning in the fight, not at aiding the court to discover the facts. (Frank, 1949, pp. 82–85).

Contrast the adversarial system with the **inquisitorial system** found in most countries on the European continent. Inquisitorial systems are the opposite of adversarial systems in many respects. For one, the parties to the case provide all of the relevant evidence to the court, and the judge, not the attorneys for the state or the defense, calls and examines witnesses. As Goldberg and Hartman (1983) noted, "The European trial is considered more like an investigation than competition between two opposing sides. Underlying the theory of this system is faith in the fairness and good will of the judges" (p. 69). An example of an inquisitorial system is the legal system in France. There, a *juge d'instruction* (i.e., an investigating magistrate) engages in fact finding and investigation in cases of serious and complex crimes. The goal of the judge is to determine the truth—what actually happened—and therefore the judge looks for both exculpatory and incriminating evidence. If the judge determines that there is sufficient evidence against the defendant, the case is referred to court for trial.

The court to which the case is referred may be the Cour d'Assises, which relies on jurors, but not in the same way American criminal courts do. Instead, nine lay jurors sit with three professional judges, deliberate with them, and vote with them. Each vote carries equal weight, and a majority of eight is necessary to convict. This approach is limited to serious offenses, however, such as murder, rape, and armed robbery. Juries are thus the exception. But it is also possible for an adversarial system to avoid juries. The key to distinguishing between adversarial and inquisitorial systems, though, does not require a focus on juries. Simply put, adversarial systems pit the prosecution and defense against each other in the pursuit of truth. The attorneys in inquisitorial systems are much more passive, and judges take on a more prominent role in the pursuit of truth.

Prosecutors and Defense Attorneys: Mortal Enemies?

The idealized version of the adversarial system suggests that prosecutors and defense attorneys are mortal enemies. But are they? If one's impression of our legal system was based on the trials depicted on TV and in movies, then the answer would most certainly be yes. These fictional courtroom dramas depict prosecutors and defense attorneys battling it out in court, constantly undermining the other side's case and springing last-minute surprises on their opponents. This clearly is a distorted image of the reality of case processing in American criminal courts today. The typical criminal case is more likely to involve negotiation and cooperation than conflict.

Why is it, then, that prosecutors and defense attorneys are not always adversaries? One answer can be found in the concept of the courtroom workgroup. Prosecutors, defense attorneys, and judges are all part of a courtroom workgroup or courthouse community with common goals and agreed-upon procedures for achieving those goals. As one study noted, "Courts are not an occasional assemblage of strangers who resolve a particular conflict and then dissolve, never to work together again. Courts are permanent organizations" (Eisenstein & Jacob, 1977). Moreover, because most criminal defendants are represented by public defenders rather than private attorneys, the defense attorneys who appear most frequently in criminal courts are government employees who often have offices in the same building as the prosecutors. As a result, prosecutors and public defenders interact with one another frequently. This is exacerbated by the fact that in many large jurisdictions, prosecutors and public defenders are assigned to courtrooms, not to cases. All cases assigned to the judge are processed by the attorneys who are assigned to the judge's courtroom. This organizational structure obviously provides incentives for cooperation rather than conflict.

As a number of classic case studies of court systems reveal (Blumberg, 1970; Eisenstein & Jacob, 1977; Mather, 1979; Nardulli, Eisenstein, & Flemming, 1988), prosecutors and defense attorneys typically do not fight it out in court; rather, they cooperate with one another to process cases as effectively and expeditiously as possible. What this means in practice, of course, is that most cases result in negotiated guilty pleas, not contested trials. This helps explain why prosecutors and defense attorneys are not the mortal enemies that the media would have us believe they are. If the goal of the criminal court system is to settle as many cases as possible by guilty pleas, opportunities for disagreement will be limited. Although it is true that "prosecutors and defenders sometimes use the adversary tactics of poker and chess in an attempt to win concessions from each other," in practice, "most cases are disposed of in cooperative agreements reaching a consensus on facts and, therefore, on appropriate punishment" (Rossett & Cressy, 1976, p. 15). We return to this issue in Section VI when we discuss the dynamics of the plea bargaining process.

 ## Prosecutors

All of the decision makers in the American criminal justice system have a significant amount of discretionary power, but the one who stands apart from the rest is the prosecutor. The prosecutor decides who will be charged, what charge will be filed, who will be offered a plea bargain, and the type of bargain that will be offered. The prosecutor also may recommend the sentence the offender should receive. As Supreme Court Justice Jackson stated in 1940, "the prosecutor has more control over life, liberty, and reputation than any other person in America" (Davis, 1969, p. 190).

Although research on prosecutors and prosecutorial decision making is limited, there is an emerging body of research on the factors affecting **charging decisions**. Much of this research focuses on charging decisions in sexual assault, domestic violence, and death penalty cases. There also is some research, and a large body of case law, focusing on the constraints on prosecutorial decision making. We explore these issues in the sections that follow. We also discuss the development and implementation of community prosecution.

Prosecutors' Charging Decisions

None of the discretionary decisions made by the prosecutor is more critical than the initial decision to prosecute or not, which has been characterized as "the gateway to justice" (Kerstetter, 1990). Prosecutors have wide discretion at this largely invisible stage in the process; there are no legislative or judicial guidelines on charging, and a decision not to file charges ordinarily is immune from review. As the Supreme Court noted in *Bordenkircher v. Hayes* (1978),

> So long as the prosecutor has probable cause to believe that the accused committed an offense defined by statute, the decision whether or not to prosecute, and what charge to file or bring before a grand jury generally rests entirely in his discretion.

In most prosecutors' offices, there are no explicit criteria or concrete guidelines for prosecutors to use in deciding whether to charge or not. Although the American Bar Association (ABA, 1993) has promulgated standards on charging, the standards are relatively broad. For example, the ABA's standards state that "[a] prosecutor should not institute, or cause to be instituted . . . criminal charges when the prosecutor knows that the charges are not supported by probable cause" and that "[t]he prosecutor should not bring or seek charges greater in number or degree than can reasonably be supported with evidence at trial or than are necessary to fairly reflect the gravity of the offense." These provisions require prosecutors to dismiss the case if the evidence is not sufficient to support the charges and prohibit overcharging, but they provide little guidance regarding how the determination of probable cause or the decision regarding the number and type of charges is to be made.

There are a number of reasons why prosecutors might decide not to file charges against a suspect who has been arrested by the police. One reason might be that the prosecutor believes that the suspect is not guilty of the crime with which he or she is charged. The prosecutor is a representative of the government who is supposed to ensure that justice is done. If the evidence does not support the charges, the case against the suspect should not be pursued.

Another reason—in fact, a more likely reason—for charge dismissal is that the prosecutor believes that the suspect is guilty but doesn't believe a conviction is possible. Even though the prosecutor is supposed to see that justice is done, he or she is nonetheless concerned about the possibility of conviction. Because the prosecutor is evaluated—by other members of the courtroom workgroup and by the public—on his or her record of securing convictions, the prosecutor is sensitive to losing. Therefore, prosecutors evaluate the evidence and attempt to predict how the case will be viewed by the judge or jurors who will be asked to assess the suspect's guilt. If the prosecutor believes that the police investigation has not produced sufficient evidence to prove the case beyond a reasonable doubt, or that the victim or other essential witnesses either will refuse to cooperate as the case moves forward or will not be viewed as credible by the judge or jury, the prosecutor may decide to dismiss the case rather than risk losing at trial.

Some researchers assert that prosecutorial charging decisions are not simply a product of individuals exercising discretion but rather reflect departmental policies that dictate—or at least influence—how cases are evaluated. Joan Jacoby (1980), for example, argued that prosecutors' offices operate within one of four distinct types of prosecutorial policies: legal sufficiency, trial sufficiency, system efficiency, and defendant rehabilitation. Prosecutors operating under the **legal sufficiency policy** accept all cases in which the legal elements of the crime are present. Because prosecutors operating under this policy do not necessarily "screen out" cases where the evidence is weak, there is both a high proportion of cases that are accepted for prosecution and a large percentage of cases that are dismissed at preliminary hearings and trials. In contrast, prosecutors operating under a **trial sufficiency policy** evaluate cases in terms of their likelihood of conviction at trial; they file charges only if the odds of conviction at trial are good. Thus, this policy produces both a high rate of rejection at initial screening and a high conviction rate for the cases that are not screened out. The remaining two policies are less concerned with either legal sufficiency or convictability. The **system efficiency policy**, which emphasizes case screening as a way of decreasing office workload, is characterized by high levels of referrals to diversionary programs and by overcharging (for the purpose of enhancing the prosecutor's power in plea negotiations). **Defendant rehabilitation policy** is based on the notion that the majority of defendants—and particularly first offenders accused of nonviolent crimes—should not be processed through the criminal justice system; the focus of this policy is on early diversion of defendants and the use of noncriminal justice alternatives. According to Jacoby, then, the factors that motivate prosecutors to file or reject charges depend, to some extent, on formal and informal departmental policies.

Factors Affecting Prosecutors' Charging Decisions

Studies of the charging process demonstrate that prosecutors exercise their discretion and reject a significant percentage of cases at screening (Frazier & Haney, 1996; Spears & Spohn, 1997; Spohn, Beichner, & Davis-Frenzel, 2001; Spohn, Gruhl, & Welch, 1987; Spohn & Holleran, 2001). A classic study of the deterioration of felony arrests in New York City, for example, found that 43% of the cases were dismissed by the prosecutor (Vera Institute of Justice, 1977). A more recent study of charging decisions in sexual assault cases in three large urban jurisdictions found that the dismissal rate was 50.6% in Philadelphia, 42.5% in Kansas City, and 41.4% in Miami (Spohn & Holleran, 2001). Most studies of the charging process also conclude that prosecutors attempt to "avoid uncertainty" (Albonetti, 1986, 1987) by filing charges in cases where the odds of conviction are good and by rejecting charges in cases where conviction is unlikely. The results of these studies reveal that prosecutors' assessments of convictability are based primarily, but not exclusively, on legally relevant factors, such as the seriousness of the offense, the strength of evidence in the case, and the culpability of the defendant.

A second fairly consistent finding is that prosecutors' assessments of convictability, and thus their charging decisions, also reflect the influence of legally irrelevant characteristics of the suspect and victim. Some researchers suggest that prosecutors attempt to predict how the background, behavior, and motivation of the suspect and victim will be interpreted by other decision makers, especially jurors. Lisa Frohmann (1997), for example, contends that prosecutors' concerns about convictability create "a '**downstream orientation**' in prosecutorial decision making—that is, an anticipation and consideration of how others (i.e., jury and defense) will interpret and respond to a case" (p. 535). Other studies conclude that the race of the suspect (Spohn et al., 1987) or the racial composition of the suspect pair (Keil & Vito, 1989; LaFree, 1989; Paternoster, 1984; Radelet & Pierce, 1985; Sorensen & Wallace, 1996) affect the prosecutor's decision to charge, especially in sexual assault and homicide cases; charging is more likely if the defendant is nonwhite or if the defendant is black and the victim is white. Other research indicates that prosecutors are more likely to file charges against men (Spohn et al., 1987) and those who are unemployed (Schmidt & Steury, 1989).

Victim characteristics also play a role in the charging process. Stanko (1988), in fact, concluded that "the character and credibility of the victim is a key factor in determining prosecutorial strategies, one at least as important as 'objective' evidence about the crime or characteristics of the defendant" (p. 170). In assessing victim credibility, prosecutors rely on stereotypes about appropriate behavior (Frohmann, 1991);

they attribute credibility to victims "who fit society's stereotypes of who is credible: older, White, male, employed victims" (Stanko, 1988, p. 172). The relationship between the victim and the suspect also affects case processing; several studies conclude that prosecutors are less likely to file charges if the victim knew the offender (Albonetti, 1987; Hepperle, 1985). These studies suggest that a prior relationship with the offender may cause the prosecutor to question the truthfulness of the victim's story and may lead the victim to refuse to cooperate as the case moves forward (Vera Institute of Justice, 1977).

A number of other extralegal factors besides suspect and victim characteristics could also help explain prosecutors' charging decisions. Such factors may include limited resources, a lack of motivation on the part of the prosecutors' office, and, with respect to domestic violence, "the questionable wisdom of state intervention in family affairs" (Schmidt & Steury, 1989, p. 488). In fact, some researchers found that prosecutors pursue charges more aggressively when the case is brought to them by the police rather than by a crime victim or other concerned citizen (Ford & Burke, 1987). As one team of researchers put it, "citizen-invoked complaints of domestic violence stand a slim change of producing criminal charges because of their lower legal visibility and because, as critics claim, prosecutors view such cases as more appropriate for social service agencies" (Schmidt & Steury, 1989, p. 489).

The theoretical perspectives guiding research on prosecutorial decision making are not as well developed as those that guide research on judicial decision making. Researchers generally agree that prosecutors' charging decisions reflect, first and most important, their assessments of the likelihood of conviction. Spohn et al. (2001) elaborated on this, arguing that prosecutors' charging decisions, like judges' sentencing decisions, are guided by a set of "focal concerns" (Steffensmeier, Ulmer, & Kramer, 1998). According to the focal concerns perspective, judges' sentencing decisions reflect their assessment of the blameworthiness or culpability of the offender, their desire to protect the community by incapacitating dangerous offenders or deterring potential offenders, and their concerns about the practical consequences or social costs of sentencing decisions.

Spohn and her colleagues (2001) maintained that the focal concerns that guide prosecutors' charging decisions are similar, but not identical to, those that guide judges' sentencing decisions. Prosecutors, like judges, are motivated by the practical constraints on and consequences of decisions. They are more likely to file charges when the crime is serious, when it is clear that the victim has suffered real harm, and when the evidence against the suspect is strong. Prosecutors' concerns, however, are somewhat different from those of judges. Although both sets of officials are concerned about maintaining relationships with other members of the courtroom workgroup, prosecutors' concerns about the practical consequences of charging decisions focus on the likelihood of conviction rather than the social costs of punishment. In other words, prosecutors' "downstream orientation" (Frohmann, 1997) forces them to predict how the victim, the suspect, and the incident will be interpreted and evaluated by the judge and jurors. Steffensmeier et al. (1998, p. 767) and Hawkins (1981, p. 208) contended that because prosecutors' predictions are inherently uncertain, they develop a "perceptual shorthand" that incorporates stereotypes of real crimes and genuine victims. As a result, prosecutors consider not only the legally relevant indicators of case seriousness and offender culpability but also the background, character, and behavior of the victim; the relationship between the suspect and the victim; and the willingness of the victim to cooperate as the case moves forward.

In summary, the strength of evidence against the defendant plays a key role in prosecutors' charging decisions, but other legal and extralegal factors also influence the decision to file charges or not. Prosecutors, and particularly those operating under a trial sufficiency screening policy, are concerned about the likelihood of conviction. As a result, characteristics of the suspect and the victim inevitably come into play.

Constraints on Prosecutorial Discretion

As emphasized previously, prosecutors exercise very broad discretion in deciding whether to file formal charges against those who have been accused of crimes, and their decisions to charge (or not to charge) are rarely challenged. Those who object to a prosecutor's refusal to file charges can raise the issue with the prosecutor's supervisor or before a judge at a court hearing (see, e.g., *NAACP v. Levi*, 1976), but it is unlikely that the decision would be overturned. The Supreme Court, in fact, has argued that judges should not be allowed to overrule a prosecutor's failure to press charges. According to the Court, judicial oversight of charging decisions should be avoided because

> such factors as the strength of the case, the prosecution's general deterrence value, the Government's enforcement priorities, and the case's relationship to the Government's overall enforcement plan are not readily susceptible to the kind of analysis the courts are competent to make. (*Wayte v. United States*, 1985, p. 606)

This suggests that judges, and other criminal justice officials, should defer to the prosecutor's judgment that charges should not be filed.

At the same time, the Supreme Court has stated that the discretion of prosecutors, though broad, "is not unfettered" (*United States v. Batchelder*, 1979). The Court has ruled that the decision to prosecute may not be "deliberately based upon an unjustifiable standard such as race, religion, or other arbitrary classification" (*Bordenkircher v. Hayes*, 1978). Thus, prosecutors cannot single out racial minorities or men for prosecution or selectively prosecute only persons from certain religious groups. Similarly, a prosecutor cannot file charges vindictively or with revenge as a motive. Doing so violates the due process clause of the Fourteenth Amendment, which states that "no state shall deprive any person of life, liberty, or property, without due process of law." This was the decision reached in *Blackledge v. Perry* (1974), a case in which the defendant was convicted in a lower court for misdemeanor assault with a deadly weapon. After the defendant filed an appeal with the county superior court, the prosecutor obtained an indictment charging the offender with *felony* assault for the same conduct. The defendant pled guilty to this offense and was sentenced to five to seven years. The Supreme Court, stating that a "person convicted of an offense is entitled to pursue his statutory right to [appeal his conviction] without apprehension that the State will retaliate by substituting a more serious charge for the original one" (p. 32), overturned his conviction on the felony offense. The Court also stated that "vindictiveness against a defendant for having successfully attacked his first conviction must play no part in the sentence he receives after a new trial" (p. 33).

It needs to be emphasized that the Supreme Court's *Blackledge* (1974) decision is limited; it applies only after the charged individual exercises his or her legal right to appeal and the prosecutor "ups the ante" in response. If the prosecutor threatens the defendant with more serious charges during the *pretrial* phase— for example, the prosecutor threatens more serious charges if the defendant refuses to plead guilty—the Fourteenth Amendment will not be violated (*Bordenkircher v. Hayes*, 1978). There is nothing inherently wrong with such a practice because it is possible, for instance, that additional evidence could become available prior to trial, thus justifying a more serious charge. However, if the more serious charge is purely motivated by revenge, it will not be allowed (*United States v. Goodwin*, 1982).

Prosecutors also are expected to follow professional standards of conduct. The standards regarding charging are spelled out in the ABA's *Standards for Criminal Justice: The Prosecution Function*. Standard 3-3.9(b), for example, states that "the prosecutor is not obliged to present all charges which the evidence might support" and delineates the factors that the prosecutor "may properly consider in exercising his or her discretion." Included are such things as reasonable doubt that the accused is guilty, the harm caused by the offense, improper motives of a complainant or reluctance of the complainant to testify, and the cooperation of the accused in the apprehension or conviction of other offenders. Such standards help prosecutors decide which cases are worthy of prosecution, and they also help prosecutors decide which charges to pursue.

A recent, and highly publicized, example of a situation in which the prosecutor's decision to file charges was called into question is the 2006 case involving three members of the Duke University lacrosse team. In April of 2006, Durham County (North Carolina) District Attorney Mike Nifong filed first-degree forcible rape, first-degree sexual offense, and kidnapping charges against the players after a woman who had been hired as a stripper for a team party claimed that she had been repeatedly raped by the players. The charges were filed despite several changes in the complainant's story and the failure of DNA tests to connect any of the accused to the alleged sexual assault. In the weeks and months following the filing of charges, District Attorney Nifong gave dozens of interviews to local and national media. He stated repeatedly that he was "confident that a rape occurred" ("Duke Suspends Lacrosse Team," 2006) and he called the players "a bunch of hooligans" whose "daddies could buy them expensive lawyers" ("Duke Rape Suspects," 2006).

The case against the three Duke University students began to unravel during the summer and fall of 2006. In mid-December it was revealed that Nifong had withheld exculpatory DNA evidence (i.e., evidence that proved none of the three men accused of the assaults was involved) from defense lawyers, and on December 22, Nifong dropped the rape charges, but not the sexual offense and kidnapping charges. Six days later the North Carolina Bar Association filed ethics charges against Nifong, alleging that he had engaged in "conduct that involves dishonesty, fraud, deceit or misrepresentation, as well as conduct that is prejudicial to the administration of justice" ("Duke DA," 2007). In January of 2007, Nifong asked to be taken off the case, which was then turned over to North Carolina Attorney General Roy Cooper. After conducting his own investigation, Cooper dropped all of the remaining charges. Cooper stated that his office "believed these three individuals are innocent of these charges." He also alleged that the charges resulted from a "tragic rush to accuse and a failure to verify serious allegations" and showed "the enormous consequences of overreaching by a prosecutor" (Beard, 2007).

Nifong resigned from his position as Durham County District Attorney in June. Two days earlier, he was disbarred after a disciplinary hearing committee of the North Carolina Bar ruled that he had committed numerous violations of the state's rules of professional conduct. In August, Nifong was held in criminal contempt of court and sentenced to 1 day in jail for his actions in the case.

As this case illustrates, prosecutors have an ethical obligation to "do justice." Their charging decisions cannot be motivated by "personal or political advantages or disadvantages which might be involved" or by "a desire to enhance [their conviction records]" (ABA, 1993).

The Changing Role of the American Prosecutor: Community Prosecution

The traditional picture of prosecution is one of attorneys for the state dragging offenders into court and subjecting them to jury trials. The public—and many aspiring prosecutors—believe that trying murderers, rapists, and other serious criminals is the essence of what prosecutors do. As we explained, however, most cases are settled by guilty pleas rather than trials; as a result, prosecutors spend substantially more time negotiating pleas than trying cases. Moreover, in recent years, the structure and organization of prosecution has undergone a number of changes. These changes are similar to changes that have affected the police, most of which fall under the label of "community policing." Community policing represents a philosophical and programmatic shift in American police work from a more detached style to an interactive and customer-based strategy. Rather than simply reacting to calls for service, police officers engaged in community policing focus on addressing the crime-related problems that plague the community. Prosecutors are starting to engage in similar activities through community prosecution.

Community prosecution is intended to improve cooperation and collaboration between prosecutors and other individuals both inside and outside the criminal justice system. Collaborations are formed between prosecutors and other government officials, such as code enforcement officers, and between prosecutors and social service agencies, business leaders, and other community stakeholders. Barbara Boland (1996) offered this more comprehensive definition of community prosecution:

> More than anything else, community prosecution is an organizational response to the grassroots public safety demands of neighborhoods, as expressed in highly concrete terms by the people who live in them. They identify immediate, specific crime problems they want addressed and that the incident-based 911 system is ill-suited to handle. (p. 35)

Community prosecutors often target low-level offenses, such as quality of life crimes. Indeed, many city attorneys, whose jobs often require the prosecution of misdemeanors, claim that they have been doing community prosecution for years. Their observations are certainly correct, but what makes community prosecution different from the traditional prosecution of misdemeanors (i.e., taking offenders to court) is the two-way relationship between prosecutors and outsiders. This collaboration has been largely absent in the past.

Community prosecution, like much of community policing, is premised on Wilson and Kelling's (1982) **broken windows theory**, which suggests that low-level offenses should be prioritized in an effort to keep serious crime in check. The broken windows argument is so connected to community prosecution, in fact, that George Kelling has shifted some of his attention to this new approach to prosecution. He, along with Catherine Coles, contends that two factors were responsible for ushering in the new community prosecution era:

> First, prosecutors themselves were attempting to develop greater capacities for addressing specific crime problems having a grave impact on public safety and the quality of life.... Second, prosecutors met up with the newly developing movement identified widely today as "community justice," which placed pressure on criminal justice agencies to question their "professional" mode of operation, and increase their responsiveness and accountability to citizens. (Coles & Kelling, 1998, p. 5)

Not everyone agrees with the concept of community prosecution, just as community policing does not enjoy unanimous support. One reason it lacks support is because it is ill-defined. Prosecutors' offices have called a number of activities community prosecution, even though some rely on virtually no collaboration with community members or other government agencies. But even if community prosecution is an inappropriate label, it is nonetheless synonymous with a significant change in prosecution. It is a change that seeks to make prosecutors more proactive and problem oriented than reactive. To illustrate, here is one author's (Glazer, 1999) description of the traditional prosecutorial role:

> The traditional ... prosecutor likes to think of himself as the consummate carnivore: a learned lawyer, a compelling oral advocate, a relentless pursuer of the truth who fights crime by putting "bad guys" in jail. His allies in this fight are the ... investigative agencies. Those agencies identify trends in criminal behavior and "bring" the prosecutor the significant cases.

There is of course more to the new prosecution than collaboration with investigative agencies. The point is that prosecutors are starting to view their role in a new light. Like police, they are realizing that justice is not a solitary pursuit; involving other individuals and agencies is critical for successful crime prevention. But does it work? Unfortunately, because these changes are relatively new, there are no studies available that shed light on their relative effectiveness. One team of researchers (Worrall, 2006) found that aggressive prosecution of misdemeanors may reduce serious crime, but another study (Rainville & Nugent, 2002) showed that it is sometimes difficult for prosecutors to part with traditional practices.

Defense Attorneys

The Right to Counsel

The Sixth Amendment to the U.S. Constitution states, "In all criminal prosecutions, the accused shall enjoy the right to have the assistance of counsel for his defense." Historically, this meant simply that if the defendant had an attorney, the attorney could be brought along to defend the defendant. The problem, of course, was that this was of no help to the majority of defendants, who were too poor to hire their own attorneys. The U.S. Supreme Court, recognizing that defendants could not obtain fair trials without the assistance of counsel, began to interpret the Sixth Amendment to require the appointment of counsel for indigent defendants. The process began in 1932, when the Court ruled in *Powell v. Alabama* that states must provide attorneys for indigent defendants charged with capital crimes. The Court's decision in a 1938 case, *Johnson v. Zerbst*, required the appointment of counsel for all indigent defendants in federal criminal cases, but the requirement was not extended to the states until *Gideon v. Wainwright* was decided in 1963. In that 1963 decision, Justice Black's majority opinion stated:

> Reason and reflection require us to recognize that in our adversary system of criminal justice, any person haled into court, who is too poor to hire a lawyer, cannot be assured a fair trial unless counsel is provided for him. . . . The right of one charged with crime to counsel may not be deemed fundamental and essential to fair trials in some countries, but it is in ours.

In subsequent decisions, the Court ruled that "no person may be imprisoned, for any offense, whether classified as petty, misdemeanor, or felony, unless he was represented by counsel" (*Argersinger v. Hamlin*, 1972) and that the **right to counsel** is not limited to trial but applies to all "critical stages" in the criminal justice process.[1] As a result of these rulings, most defendants must be provided with counsel from arrest and interrogation through sentencing and the appellate process. The Supreme Court also has ruled that defendants are entitled to *effective* assistance of counsel (*Strickland v. Washington*, 1984).

At the time the *Gideon* (1963) decision was handed down, 13 states had no statewide requirement for appointment of counsel except in capital cases (Lewis, 1964). Other states relied on members of local bar associations to defend indigents, often on a pro bono basis. Following *Gideon*, it became obvious that other procedures would be required if all felony defendants were to be provided attorneys. States moved quickly to implement the constitutional requirement articulated in *Gideon*, either by establishing **public defender systems** or by appropriating money for court-appointed attorneys. The number of public defender systems grew rapidly. In 1951, there were only 7 public defender organizations in the United States; in 1964, there were 136, and by 1973, the total had risen to 573 (McIntyre, 1987).

---

[1]A defendant is entitled to counsel at every stage "where substantial rights of the accused may be affected" that require the "guiding hand of counsel" (*Mempa v. Rhay*, 1967). These critical stages include arraignment, preliminary hearing, entry of a plea, trial, sentencing, and the first appeal.

As noted in Section I, there are two other methods of providing indigent defense services: the **assigned counsel system**, in which attorneys are appointed on a case-by-case basis, and the **contract system**, in which private attorneys or law firms contract with the jurisdiction to represent indigent defendants. Some jurisdictions use a combination of methods. The public defender, for example, might represent all indigent defendants with the exception of those charged with drug offenses, whose cases would be assigned to the attorneys under contract with the jurisdiction. Alternatively, the public defender might represent all indigent defendants except those in cases with codefendants, who would be represented by private attorneys assigned by the judge. Indigent defendants tried in U.S. District Courts are represented by either the federal public defender or by Criminal Justice Act (CJA) panel attorneys. The CJA panel attorneys are private attorneys who are selected to be on a panel of qualified attorneys and who are assigned to represent federal defendants on a case-by-case basis. The federal public defender and the CJA panel attorneys in each district split the caseload according to a predetermined ratio; cases are randomly assigned to either the federal defender or the pool of CJA attorneys (Iyengar, 2006).

A national survey of indigent defense services in all U.S. prosecutorial districts found that 21% used a public defender program, 19% used an assigned counsel system, and 7% used a contract attorney system; the remaining districts (43%) reported that a combination of methods was used (Bureau of Justice Statistics, 2000, Table 5). A survey of inmates incarcerated in state and federal prisons in 1997 revealed that about 73% of the state inmates and 60% of the federal inmates had been represented by a public defenders or assigned counsel (Bureau of Justice Statistics, 2000).

Quality of Legal Representation: Do Indigent Defendants Get What They Pay For?

As a result of Supreme Court decisions expanding the right to counsel and the development of federal and state policies implementing those decisions, indigent defendants are no longer routinely denied legal representation at trial or at any of the other critical stages in the process. Questions have been raised, however, about the quality of legal representation provided to indigent defendants by public defenders (see Box 3.2 "Do You Get What You Pay For?"). A recent article in the *Harvard Law Review*, for example, claimed that

> Nearly four decades after *Gideon*, the states have largely, and often outrageously, failed to meet the Court's constitutional command. The widespread, lingering deficiencies in the quality of indigent counsel have led some to wonder whether this right, so fundamental to a fair and accurate adversarial criminal process, is unenforceable. ("Notes: Gideon's promise," 2000, p. 2062)

According to this author, the fact that most criminal defendants are indigent, coupled with the "low quality of indigent defense," raises fundamental questions about the "overall fairness of the criminal justice system" ("Notes: Gideon's promise," 2000, p. 2065). This was echoed by former U.S. Attorney General Janet Reno, who stated in 1999 that "if we do not adequately support criminal defense for poor Americans, people will think that you only get justice if you can afford to pay a lawyer" (National Symposium on Indigent Defense, 1999, p. 6).

There is evidence suggesting that defendants share this view. In fact, one of the most oft-quoted statements about public defenders is the answer given by an unidentified prisoner in a Connecticut jail to the question of whether he had a lawyer when he went to court. "No," he replied, "I had a public defender" (Casper, 1971, p. 1). Neubauer (2002) similarly noted that in prison "'PD' stands not for 'public defender' but for 'prison deliverer'" (p. 186). Some social scientists (see, e.g., Blumberg, 1967; Sudnow, 1965) echo this negative assessment, charging that public defenders, as part of the courtroom workgroup, are more concerned with securing guilty pleas as efficiently and as expeditiously as possible than with aggressively defending their clients. Weitzer (1996) noted,

> In many jurisdictions, public defenders and state-appointed attorneys are grossly underpaid, poorly trained, or simply lack the resources and time to prepare for a case—a pattern documented in cases ranging from the most minor to the most consequential, capital crimes. (p. 313)

Other social scientists disagree (Casper, 1978; Hartley, 2005; Levin, 1977; McIntyre, 1987; Oaks & Lehman, 1970; Silverstein, 1965; Wheeler & Wheeler, 1980). Citing studies showing that criminal defendants represented by public defenders do not fare worse than those represented by private attorneys, these researchers suggest that critics "have tended to underestimate the quality of defense provided by the public defender" (Skolnick, 1967, p. 67). Wice (1985), in fact, concluded that the public defender is able to establish a working relationship with prosecutors and judges "in which the exchange of favors, so necessary to greasing the squeaky wheel of justice, can directly benefit the indigent defendant." As part of the courtroom workgroup, in other words, public defenders are in a better position than private attorneys to negotiate favorable plea bargains and thus to mitigate punishment.

BOX 3.2

Do You Get What You Pay For?

Questions have been raised about the quality of legal services provided to indigent defendants. Consider the following examples:

> Capital defendant George McFarland's court-appointed lawyer, John Benn, slept through much of his 1992 trial. "His mouth kept falling open and his head lolled back on his shoulders...again. And again. And again," wrote a newspaper reporter. "It's boring," the lawyer told the judge. But the constitutional right to counsel was not violated, according to the trial judge, because "the Constitution doesn't say the lawyer has to be awake." The Texas Court of Criminal Appeals upheld McFarland's death sentence, and the U.S. Supreme Court denied review.

> In one California county, a three-attorney firm provided representation in more than 5,000 cases in one year under a fixed-fee contract. A single attorney was responsible for handling all misdemeanors—more than 3,500 per year, compared with the cap of 400 recommended under national standards. The firm filed no discovery motions, took only 12 cases to trial, and retained one part-time investigator for 10 hours per week. The contracting lawyer acknowledged that there is an "inherent conflict" in the fact that every dollar spent on an investigator or an expert means one less dollar in compensation for him, but stated that he regarded this as a "political reality" (National Symposium on Indigent Defense, 1999, p. 6).

A report by the Bureau of Justice Statistics (2000) revealed that case outcomes for state and federal defendants represented by public attorneys did not differ dramatically from those represented by private counsel. As shown in Table 3.1, there were only very slight differences in the conviction rates of defendants represented by public and private attorneys, but somewhat larger differences in the incarceration rates. At the federal level, 87.6% of the defendants represented by public attorneys were sentenced to prison, compared to 76.5% of the defendants with private attorneys. The authors of the report attributed this to the fact that public counsel represented a higher percentage of violent, drug, and public-order offenders, whereas private attorneys represented a higher percentage of white-collar defendants. Felony defendants in state courts also faced lower odds of incarceration if they were represented by private attorneys (53.9%) rather than public defenders (71.3%). In both state and federal court, on the other hand, defendants represented by private attorneys got longer sentences than those represented by public defenders. At the federal level, the mean sentences were 58 months (public attorneys) and 62 months (private attorneys); at the state level, they were 31.2 months (public attorneys) and 38.3 months (private attorneys).

Somewhat different results surfaced in a recent study comparing public defenders, court-appointed attorneys, and private attorneys in Denver, Colorado. The authors of this study examined the sentences

Table 3.1 Case Outcomes for Defendants Represented by Public and Private Attorneys in State and Federal Courts

	75 Largest U.S. Counties, 1996		U.S. District Courts, 1998	
Type of attorney				
Public defender/federal defender	68.3%		30.1%	
Assigned counsel/panel attorney	13.7%		36.3%	
Private attorney	17.6%		33.4%	
	Public Attorney	**Private Attorney**	**Public Attorney**	**Private Attorney**
Case disposition				
Guilty by plea	71.0%	72.8%	87.1%	84.6%
Guilty by trial	4.4%	4.3%	5.2%	6.4%
Case dismissed	23.0%	21.2%	6.7%	7.4%
Acquittal	1.3%	1.6%	1.0%	1.6
Sentence				
Incarcerated	71.3%	53.9%	87.6%	76.5%
Mean prison sentence	31.2 months	38.3 months	58 months	62 months

imposed on 3,777 defendants charged with felonies in 2002. Their measure of defense counsel effectiveness compared the maximum sentence each defendant faced (in years) to the actual sentence the defendant received (in years); acquittals, dismissals, and probation sentences were all coded as zero years of incarceration (Bureau of Justice Statistics, 2000, p. 234). Using this measure, they found that public defenders were "substantially less effective" than private attorneys; defendants represented by public defenders received sentences that averaged three years longer than those received by defendants represented by private attorneys and court-appointed attorneys. To explain this result, the authors looked more closely at the types of cases handled by private attorneys and public defenders. They concluded that public defenders are less effective "not because they are bad or overworked lawyers, but simply because they attract less winnable cases" (p. 246). That is, they found that "marginally indigent defendants"—defendants who were indigent based on the standards used by the court but who could conceivably scrape together the money to hire their own attorneys—were more likely to hire their own attorneys if the charges were serious and there was at least some chance of acquittal. As the authors noted, "assuming a sufficient number of marginally indigent defendants, public defenders will tend, on average, to get less serious and less winnable cases, which is exactly what our data shows" (p. 246).

Defendants' perceptions and anecdotal evidence notwithstanding, it thus appears that there are few differences in the case outcomes of indigent defendants represented by public defenders and private attorneys once crime seriousness and other legally relevant factors are taken into consideration.

Constraints on Defense Attorneys

Defense attorneys, like prosecutors, must abide by codes of ethics promulgated by the American Bar Association and by other organizations. One of the most important principles is that defendants must be afforded **effective assistance of counsel**. What, then, constitutes effective assistance of counsel? The Supreme Court has attempted to answer this question on a number of occasions. First, in *McMann v. Richardson* (1970), the Court held that counsel is effective when his or her legal advice is "within the range of competence demanded of attorneys in criminal cases" (p. 771). Because that definition was somewhat vague, in 1984 the Court created a new test in the case of *Strickland v. Washington*. The court ruled that to establish ineffectiveness, a defendant must prove the following:

- First, "that counsel's performance was deficient. This requires showing that counsel made errors so serious that counsel was not functioning as the 'counsel' guaranteed the defendant by the Sixth Amendment."
- Second, "that the deficient performance prejudiced the defense. This requires showing that counsel's errors were so serious as to deprive the defendant of a fair trial."

In *Strickland v. Washington* (1984), the Court also stated that to establish ineffectiveness, a "defendant must show that counsel's representation fell below an objective standard of reasonableness." To establish prejudice, the defendant "must show that there is a reasonable probability that, but for counsel's unprofessional errors, the result of the proceeding would have been different."

The Court revisited this issue in 2000, ruling in *Williams v. Taylor* that Terry Williams had been denied effective assistance of counsel. Williams was convicted of robbery and murder and sentenced to death after a Virginia jury concluded that he had a high probability of future dangerousness. At the sentencing hearing,

Williams's lawyer failed to introduce evidence that Williams was borderline mentally retarded and did not advance beyond sixth grade. He also failed to introduce the testimony of prison officials, who described Williams as among the inmates "least likely to act in a violent, dangerous, or provocative way." Instead, Williams's lawyer spent most of his time explaining that he realized it would be difficult for the jury to find a reason to spare Williams's life. His comments included the following:

> I will admit too that it is very difficult to ask you to show mercy to a man who maybe has not shown much mercy himself. . . . Admittedly, it is very difficult to . . . ask that you give this man mercy when he has shown so little of it himself. But I would ask that you would.

The Supreme Court ruled that Williams's right to effective assistance of counsel had been violated. According to the Court, "there was a reasonable probability that the result of the sentencing proceeding would have been different if competent counsel had presented and explained the significance of all the available evidence" (*Williams v. Taylor*, 2000).

Summary: Prosecutors and Defense Attorneys

The idealized adversarial model of the criminal courts suggests that prosecutors and defense attorneys are in constant battle with one another. In reality, criminal case processing is characterized more by cooperation and consensus than by conflict. This reflects, in large part, that trials are rare, and, thus, the opportunities for conflict are limited. It also can be attributed to both prosecutors and defense attorneys being part of a courtroom workgroup with common goals (i.e., efficient and expeditious case processing) and agreed-upon procedures for attaining those goals.

Researchers interested in the roles played by prosecutors and defense attorneys have focused on two questions: What factors influence charging decisions by prosecutors? Do defendants with private attorneys receive more effective representation than those represented by public defenders? Studies of prosecutors' charging decisions reveal that these highly discretionary and largely invisible decisions reflect a mix of (1) legally relevant measures of case seriousness and evidence strength and (2) legally irrelevant characteristics of the victim and suspect. Studies comparing public and private attorneys reveal that there are few differences in case outcomes. The edited readings that follow explore these, and other, issues in greater detail.

KEY TERMS

Adversarial system	Contract system	Legal sufficiency policy
Assigned counsel system	Defendant rehabilitation policy	Public defender system
Broken windows theory	Downstream orientation	Right to counsel
Charging decision	Effective assistance of counsel	System efficiency policy
Community prosecution	Inquisitorial system	Trial sufficiency policy

DISCUSSION QUESTIONS

1. How does the American adversarial system of criminal justice differ from the inquisitorial system found in most European countries?

2. How does the courtroom workgroup limit the adversarial nature of the criminal court system?

3. Why is the prosecutor often described as the most powerful person in the criminal justice system?

4. Mary Jones, a single mother of two who has no prior felony convictions and is a teacher at a local high school, has been arrested for credit card fraud. She used a credit card that did not belong to her to charge groceries at a local supermarket. Her case has been referred to the district attorney, who must decide whether to file charges or not. Explain why a prosecutor following the legal sufficiency policy might arrive at a different decision than one following the defendant rehabilitation policy.

5. What does empirical research reveal about the factors affecting prosecutors' charging decisions?

6. How do the "focal concerns" that guide prosecutors' charging decisions differ from the "focal concerns" that guide judges' sentencing decisions?

7. The U.S. Supreme Court has stated that the prosecutor's discretion, while broad, is not unfettered. What are the constraints on prosecutors' charging and plea bargaining decisions?

8. How does traditional prosecution differ from community prosecution?

9. What are the three systems of providing indigent defense services? In your opinion, which one is the best system? Why?

10. Based on the research reviewed in this section, how would you answer the question, "Do indigent defendants get what they pay for"?

11. Why is it difficult for a criminal defendant to prove that he or she had "ineffective assistance of counsel"?

WEB RESOURCES

American Bar Association: http://www.abanet.org

American Prosecutors' Research Institute: http://www.ndaa.org/apri/

Association of Federal Defense Attorneys: http://www.afda.org

Indigent Defense, Bureau of Justice Statistics: http://bjs.ojp.usdoj.gov/index.cfm?ty=tp&tid=28

National Association of Criminal Defense Lawyers: http://www.nacdl.org

National District Attorneys Association: http://www.ndaa.org/index.html

Prosecution Statistics, Bureau of Justice Statistics: http://bjs.ojp.usdoj.gov/index.cfm?ty=tp&tid=63

Prosecutors in State Courts, Bureau of Justice Statistics: http://bjs.ojp.usdoj.gov/index.cfm?ty=tp&tid=27

United States Department of Justice, Office of the Attorney General: http://www.usdoj.gov/ag/

U.S. Prosecuting Attorney Web Sites: http://www.prosecutor.info

READING

In this article, Heather Schoenfeld discusses the relationship between prosecutorial misconduct at trial and wrongful convictions. She proposes a comprehensive theory of prosecutorial misconduct that views prosecutors as agents of trust and that sees prosecutorial misconduct as violations of the norms of trust. Arguing that the public "trusts prosecutors to use their skills, knowledge, and power to prosecute people who break the law," the author suggests that "misconduct occurs when prosecutors positively evaluate motives and opportunities for misconduct in a way that neutralizes symbolic constraints against misconduct." She discusses the motivations that prosecutors have for engaging in misconduct and the opportunities for misconduct that arise at trial. She also explores the sanctions for prosecutorial misconduct, which she characterizes as underutilized and ineffective.

Violated Trust

Conceptualizing Prosecutorial Misconduct

Heather Schoenfeld

In the past 30 years, the prosecutor has become the most powerful position in the criminal justice system (Saltzburg & Capra, 2000). Unfortunately, this power has contributed to convictions of innocent defendants. Although the full extent of prosecutorial misconduct is unknown (Meares, 1995), recent studies suggest cause for concern. Prosecutorial misconduct was a factor in 45% of recent cases overturned because of DNA evidence (Scheck, Neufeld, & Dwyer, 2000, p. 361) and 24% of recently overturned death penalty cases (Warden, 2001). The Center for Public Integrity found that since 1970, appellate courts have reviewed 11,452 criminal cases where the defendant claimed the prosecutor acted improperly. In 20% of the cases, the court dismissed, reversed, or reduced the original sentence partly because of the misconduct (Weinberg, Gordon, & Williams, 2005).

The aforementioned reports and the recent media coverage of wrongdoing by prosecutors point to the need for systematic analyses of prosecutorial misconduct and its causes.[1] New empirical research on misconduct should be grounded in a comprehensive theory. However, existing theories of prosecutorial misconduct do not take into account the structure of the prosecutorial profession while specifying conditions under which prosecutorial misconduct is more likely. This article proposes an alternative more comprehensive theory— with the goal of generating testable hypotheses. The theory builds from the characterization of prosecutors as agents of trust and prosecutorial misconduct as violations of the norms of trust. Borrowing from theories of occupational crime to explain how the structure of the trust relationship creates motivation and opportunities for misconduct, the theory can explain why

SOURCE: Schoenfeld, H. (2005). Violated trust: Conceptualizing prosecutorial misconduct. *Journal of Contemporary Criminal Justice, 21*, 250–271.

some prosecutors, despite their mandate to seek justice, use improper and unethical tactics.

Prosecutorial misconduct can occur during any part of the criminal justice process, including presentation to the grand jury, charging decisions, discovery, plea negotiations, trial, and postconviction appeals. However, the following argument focuses on prosecutorial misconduct around criminal trials—either during pretrial discovery, trial, or posttrial appeals—because this type of misconduct is most implicated in wrongful conviction cases.[2] Because most convictions are obtained through a guilty plea, the scope of the argument is necessarily limited. However, because approximately one third of murder defendants' cases go to trial (Rainville & Reaves, 2003), including many high-profile cases, the potential incidence of prosecutorial misconduct presents a significant obstacle to the legitimacy and reliability of the current criminal justice system.

 ## Explanations for Prosecutorial Misconduct

Knowledge of prosecutorial conduct is derived mainly from journalistic accounts and legal scholarship, none of which adequately explains why some prosecutors engage in misconduct and others do not. Alternatively, social scientists have developed theories of legal decision making; however, these theories do not specifically address misbehavior.

Legal Accounts of Misconduct

Legal analysts usually rely on either a so-called tunnel vision or a conviction psychology explanation for prosecutorial misconduct. The first contends that prosecutors ultimately seek justice, and because most defendants are guilty, prosecutors feel compelled to sidestep problems that could sacrifice a guilty verdict (Jonakait, 1987). For example, some prosecutors feel justified allowing a witness to lie about his or her background because they believe this behavior serves the interest of so-called truth (Dershowitz, 2003). Tunnel vision, or the cognitive process of applying stereotypes

to cases, can also cause legal actors to discount conflicting information (Anderson, Lepper, & Ross, 1980) or neglect evidence that is contrary to their version of events (Martin, 2002; McCloskey, 1989). In this scenario, prosecutors' unwavering belief in the defendant's guilt is the prime cause of their misconduct.

Other accounts blame misconduct on prosecutors' "score-keeping mentality" or conviction psychology that compels them to win at all costs (Felkenes, 1975).[3] This mentality stems from institutional, professional, and political pressures to win convictions (Bresler, 1996; Fisher, 1988; Gershman, 2001). For example, district attorneys (DAs) feel pressure to convict because voters use convictions as a quantifiable measure of success when choosing a DA candidate (Gordon & Huber, 2002). Legal analysts argued that the desire to win convictions, coupled with limited sanctions for misconduct, can lead to misconduct (Meares, 1995).

Prosecutorial Decision Making

Sociologists' and criminologists' analyses of decision making by prosecutors, defense attorneys, and judges have primarily focused on plea bargaining (Albonetti, 1986; Emmelman, 1997; Sudnow, 1965) or sentencing (Albonetti, 1991; Maynard, 1982; Steffensmeier, Ulmer, & Kramer, 1998) as these activities constitute the core activity of most courts (Ulmer, 1997).[4] They posited that to make decisions under conditions of uncertainty, legal actors use socially constructed subjective definitions of "normal crimes" or "typical defendants" that act as "shorthand reference terms for [legal actors'] knowledge of the social structure and criminal events" (Sudnow, 1965, p. 275; see also Albonetti, 1986; Farrell & Holmes, 1991). These notions develop through the interaction and interdependency of prosecutors, defense attorneys, and judges who must work together to run an efficient system with limited financial or human capital (Eisenstein, Flemming, & Nardulli, 1988; Ulmer, 1997).

Professional identities and internal organizational culture also structure legal actors' decisions. In their comprehensive research of nine court communities in the late 1970s, Flemming, Nardulli, and Eisenstein (1992) identified three DA leadership styles. Insurgent DAs work aggressively to increase the power of their office, organize their offices hierarchically, employ lax charging standards but implement strict restrictions on plea bargaining in favor of tough punishment. Reformer DAs, also interested in increasing the power of their office, tend to focus more on office efficiency—requiring tight charging standards along with plea-bargaining restrictions. Finally, conservator DAs are satisfied with the status quo and allow their assistant district attorneys (ADAs) more discretion within a decentralized organization structure.

While neither of these literatures directly focuses on prosecutorial misconduct, they identify structural realities and individual-level cognitive factors that could contribute to misconduct. Legal scholarship, for example, points to the inherent contradictions within the profession and the external and internal systems of rewards and sanctions for misconduct. The decision-making literature points to cases that, falling outside of understood categories of crime and criminals, are less likely to be subject to plea bargaining and more likely to be subject to the adversarial process (Sudnow, 1965). It is often in the context of these so-called exceptional cases that the opportunity for misconduct arises (Farrell & Holmes, 1991).

 ## Prosecutors as Agents of Trust

Characterizing the Trust Relationship

The Supreme Court held in 1935 that prosecutors have a unique role in the legal system as the "representatives" of the "sovereignty." The opinion states

> The United States Attorney is the representative not of an ordinary party to a controversy, but of a sovereignty whose obligation to govern impartially is as compelling as its obligation to govern at all. . . . As such, he is in a peculiar and very definite sense the

servant of the law, the twofold aim of which is that guilt shall not escape or innocence suffer. He may prosecute with earnestness and vigor—indeed he should do so. But, while he may strike hard blows, he is not at liberty to strike foul ones. (*Berger v. United States*, 1935, p. 88)

Where the sovereignty derives its power from the people, prosecutors represent the public within the bounds of a trust relationship. In the sociology of trust, principals (in this case the public) transfer power and delegate resources to agents (prosecutors), so that the agents may perform specialized services or complex projects (Shapiro, 1990, p. 348). In the United States' judicial system, the public entrusts prosecutors to develop specialized skills and gain specialized knowledge through the powers bestowed on the role (such as the right to subpoena; Guerrieri, 2001). The public then trusts prosecutors to use their skills, knowledge, and power to prosecute people who break the law.

Trust relationships are inherently unbalanced for three reasons. First, agents hold monopolies of information from which their actions are based. Second, because of their status as repositories for delegated power and their rights to resources and discretion they have the power to control principals' well-being. Third, agents' role is ambivalent, creating conflict between an "acting for" role and self-interest (Shapiro, 1990, p. 348). To properly balance the trust relationship, both parties tacitly agree to the following norms of the trust: (a) both parties disclose fully and honestly, (b) agents put the interests of principals above their own, and (c) agents maintain role competence and duties of diligence and prudence (Shapiro, 1990). Agents who violate the trust relationship do so by violating the norms of trust—of disclosure, disinterestedness, and role competence.

Violations of the Norms of Trust

Prosecutors' acts of misconduct are essentially violations of the norms of trust and, therefore, stem from the nature of trust relationships. The courts have identified three categories of prosecutor misconduct during trial: personal remarks, remarks promoting bias, and improper conduct around the facts of the case. The Court's opinions about the first two types of misconduct clearly demonstrate how the trust relationship creates the violation.

> It is fair to say that the average jury, in a greater or less degree, *has confidence* [emphasis added] that . . . [obligations to serve justice] will be faithfully observed. Consequently, improper suggestions, insinuations and, especially, assertions of personal knowledge are apt to carry much weight against the accused when they should properly carry none. (*Berger v. United States*, 1935, p. 88)

Later, in *United States v. Young* (1985), the Court wrote that the "prosecutor's opinion carries with it the imprimatur of the Government and *may induce the jury to trust the Government's judgment* [emphasis added] rather than its own view of the evidence" (p. 18).

The third category of misconduct, improper conduct, includes knowingly presenting false testimony, letting false testimony stand without correction, making material misstatements of law or fact (or evidence),[5] and not disclosing evidence favorable to defendant (Hetherington, 2002). Each jurisdiction has its own rules of disclosure.[6] However, because of constitutional requirements for a fair trial, prosecutors must also disclose evidence that is "material either to guilt or punishment" or of "sufficient probative value" to create reasonable doubt as to guilt.[7] While the criteria for materiality and probative value can be ambiguous, the Court has increasingly ruled in the spirit of *United States v. Agurs* (1976) that the "prudent prosecutor will resolve doubtful questions in favor of disclosure" (p. 108). It is these violations of disclosure that are most often implicated in wrongful convictions (Innocence Project, 2001).

Role Duality in Trust Relationships

The problem of prosecutorial misconduct is intimately linked to the role of the prosecutor in the U.S. legal system as the repository for delegated power. As agents in trust relationships, prosecutors have a dual role—they are to be impartial representatives and vigorous advocates (Fisher, 1988). Recall the Supreme Court opinion, *Berger v. United States* (1935), which obliges prosecutors to "govern impartially" and "prosecute with earnestness and vigor." The American Bar Association (1993) also recognizes this duality calling the prosecutor an "administrator of justice, an advocate, and an officer of the court" (sec. 3-1.2). Prosecutors, similar to other agents of trust, can face a conflict between their acting-for role and their self-interest as a vigorous lawyer.

As an impartial judicial officer of the court, prosecutors seek truth, fairness, and the rights of the accused. As a zealous advocate, prosecutors seek convictions and penal severity (Fisher, 1988). Thus, the role of a prosecutor, as an agent of trust, necessitates constant discretion concerning when to act impartially and when to advocate.

The nature of the trust relationship with its monopoly on information, necessary discretion, and role conflict generates conditions that can lead to prosecutorial misconduct. A theory of prosecutorial misconduct should start from the premise that prosecutorial misconduct is a violation of delegated trust. In this sense, theoretical explanations for occupational crimes that violate the norms of trust are useful in generating a comprehensive theory of prosecutorial misconduct (Shapiro, 1990).[8] Although differential association theory (Akers, 1998) or social control theory (Hirschi, 1969) could be used to explain occupational crime, an integrated theory of occupational crime can better explain how structural factors interact with individual-level social-psychological variables to cause misconduct. Borrowing from integrated theories of occupational crime that focus on confluence of motivation, opportunity, and choice (Coleman, 1987; McKendall & Wagner, 1997), the following sections lay out a theory of prosecutorial misconduct that posits that misconduct occurs when prosecutors positively evaluate motives and opportunities for misconduct in a way that neutralizes symbolic constraints against misconduct.

Toward a Theory of Prosecutorial Misconduct

Prosecutorial Motivation

In his often-cited article synthesizing the research on white-collar crime, Coleman (1987) used a symbolic interactionist approach to define motivation as the "meaning that individuals attribute to a particular situation and to social reality . . . [which] structures their experience and makes certain courses of action seem appropriate while others are excluded or ignored" (p. 410). Socially created meanings or symbolic constructs (Blumer, 1969; Goffman, 1959) also allow individuals to anticipate the responses of others that, in turn, help them to define the situation. Prosecutors' motivation to engage in misconduct is structured by the meanings they attach to so-called success, their perceived expectations of their role as prosecutors, and the availability of neutralizations for misbehavior.

Defining Success

Coleman (1987) argued that motivation to engage in occupational crime originates in the "culture of competition" that stresses the value of personal gain, winning, and success as measures of people's intrinsic worth. Essentially, prosecutors want, as do most professionals, to be good at their job. As one prosecutor who had four cases reversed because of misconduct said "Nobody told us to cheat. Nobody told us to do wrong. It was to be smart, be tenacious . . . [be] the best prosecutors in the office" (Armstrong & Possley,1999c, p. 1).

It is how prosecutors understand the role of a so-called good prosecutor that motivates their behavior. However, because of the intrinsic nature of the trust relationship, prosecutors are likely to have role ambivalence. If, as suggested by many legal scholars, DAs use convictions as a criterion for raises and promotions, ADAs are likely to define success through convictions (Bresler, 1996; Ferguson-Gilbert, 2001; Fisher, 1988). Political ambitions and the political impetus to be "tough on crime" (Garland, 2001) may also cause

prosecutors to tend toward their advocate role (Fisher, 1988; Medwed, 2004). In addition, insurgent DAs could induce ADAs to emphasize punishment over fairness (Flemming et al., 1992). For example, one DA who was cited for misconduct in more than 20 felony trials stated, "It's my obligation as District Attorney to present the evidence in the light most favorable to the state . . . the people are entitled to have a D.A. who argues their position very vigorously" (Armstrong & Possley, 1999b, p. 13).

Neutralizations

The meaning that prosecutors attribute to situations not only motivates behavior, but also constrains it. For example, while prosecutors want to be good at their jobs and meet their supervisors' expectations, their actions are also constrained by their understanding that fabricating evidence is wrong. Consequently, when people behave against norms they must neutralize their symbolic constraints (Sykes & Matza, 1957). Common techniques to neutralize occupational crime include denial that the act causes harm to others, insistence that the laws violated are wrong or unfair, arguing that the position necessitated the illegal behavior, or taking the so-called everyone does it stance (for a review, see Coleman, 1987). These neutralizations allow people who behave illegally to construct their behavior as "right," thus becoming part of their motivational framework.

While there is no systematic data on prosecutors' neutralizations for their misbehavior, certain structural realities of the prosecutorial profession make various neutralizations available—increasing the likelihood that prosecutors could think they are doing the right thing despite their misconduct. First, because part of the prosecutor's role is to serve justice—an undefined concept—prosecutors can neutralize misconduct that ultimately ends in their idea of justice. Commenting on the indictment of three former prosecutors and four police officers for the framing of Rolando Cruz, who spent 12 years wrongfully incarcerated, Larry Marshall, a leading expert on wrongful convictions, stated, "There's a feeling that that is how it works, that it's legitimate to bend the truth sometimes when you are doing it with—'the greater good'—in mind" (as cited in Armstrong & Possley, 1999d, p. 1).

Second, prosecutorial behavior often walks a fine line between legitimate behavior and misconduct. For example, when selecting a jury prosecutors are not allowed to use race as a determining factor in peremptory challenges (*Batson v. Kentucky*, 1986). After the defense claimed that prosecutors deliberately eliminated African Americans from the jury in all three trials of the Ford Heights 4 in Illinois, who were later exonerated, the lead prosecutor stated "I wouldn't say it [race] was a totally irrelevant factor—but it certainly wasn't a determining factor" (Armstrong & Possley, 1999d, p. 1). Third, because the system (including prosecutors and defense attorneys) in practice assumes defendants' guilt, prosecutors could neutralize misconduct because they believe they are prosecuting guilty defendants (Sudnow, 1965; Ulmer, 1997). As one judge stated about a prosecutor whose office has repeatedly wrongly withheld evidence:

> From [the prosecutor's] perspective, bad guys are bad guys and whatever we need to do to put them away is OK. But the problem is, every now and then, it's not a bad guy. Every now and then, you've got the wrong guy. (Armstrong & Possley, 1999e, p. 1)

Fourth, prosecutors are held to different standards than defense attorneys who have "a special prerogative to engage in truth defeating tactics" (Fisher, 1988). Consequently, some legal scholars argue that prosecutors engage in misconduct because they find it difficult to understand why defense attorneys can behave in ways that are prohibited for prosecutors (Dershowitz, 2003). Prosecutors could potentially use this discrepancy as a neutralization technique.

Opportunity for Prosecutorial Misconduct

Motivation alone, however, does not lead to improper behavior. For improper behavior to take place, the actor must have opportunities to misbehave. Coleman (1987)

defined *opportunity* as "a potential course of action, made possible by a particular set of social conditions, which has been symbolically incorporated into an actor's repertoire of behavioral possibilities" (p. 424). According to research on occupational crime, certain structural realities provide more opportunities for misbehavior (McKendall & Wagner, 1997). Similarly, routine activity theory suggests that, given the motivation, certain situations will give rise to misconduct (Clarke & Felson, 1993; Cohen & Felson, 1979). In the case of prosecutorial misconduct, the nature of trust relationships shapes opportunities through the structure of professional standards, office organization, and informal and formal social control.

Professional Standards

In a trust relationship, principals must allow agents discretion within the norms of trust because principals do not have access to all pertinent information (Shapiro, 1990). Accordingly, prosecutors have discretion within the rules laid out by court decisions and are not subject to uniform standards (B. A. Green & Zacharias, 2004, p. 843). For example, although it is clear that prosecutors must disclose evidence that points to defendants' innocence, the law does not explicate guidelines that help prosecutors make the determination between exculpatory and nonexculpatory evidence. This type of ambiguity provides a central opportunity for misconduct. In fact, the Illinois Governor's Commission on Capital Punishment (2002) cited lack of standards for disclosure as one of the factors behind wrongful convictions in Illinois. The Commission recommended that the state Supreme Court adopt a rule defining exculpatory evidence to provide clear guidance to prosecutors (Governor's Commission on Capital Punishment, 2002).

Organizational Structure

The organizational characteristics of trust relationships can also lead to opportunities for deception. Although prosecutors' offices are not all organized in the same manner (Flemming et al., 1992), organizational theory suggests that similarly situated professional organizations will tend toward uniformity for reasons of efficiency (DiMaggio & Powell, 1983). For example, Flemming et al. (1992) found that DA office size affects organizational structure: Smaller offices can maintain looser structures, while large offices have to bureaucratize, with midsize offices variable. As such, the following are opportunities that develop from potential organizational impediments to informal social control. First, agent activities tend to be socially, organizationally, temporally, and geographically distant from their principals (Shapiro, 1990). In other words, agents' activities are not transparent to the intended beneficiaries. Likewise, the activities of prosecutors' offices are hidden from public purview, except in the case of trials. While the public holds prosecutors accountable through elections, the public does not scrutinize prosecutors' daily activities. Even when trials face heavy public scrutiny, as in the trials of the Oklahoma City bombers, prosecutors can fail to disclose evidence and present perjured testimony (Romano, 2003; Thomas, 2001).

Second, the organizational structure common to trust relationships includes hierarchy, specialization, and internal diversification—all of which mask illicit acts and block the flow of information, not only from outsiders but also from insiders as well (Shapiro, 1990). For example, ADAs in midsize to large offices are often responsible for certain types of cases or cases from certain geographical areas (Flemming et al., 1992). This segmentation could allow prosecutors to act in bad faith without internal checks (B. A. Green & Zacharias, 2004). Third, the outputs of trust relationships provide few red flags indicating violation. In other words, an outcome (or process) that involves misconduct may look exactly like a legitimate outcome or process (Shapiro, 1990). Consequently, misconduct can be concealed as discretionary decision making. Violations such as nondisclosure or allowing perjured testimony are very difficult to detect because the violations are based on the prosecutors' discretion and knowledge. Finally, trust services are typically carried out and recorded in documents that can be destroyed or easily falsified (Shapiro, 1990). Demonstrating

prosecutorial misconduct often requires, for example, uncovering documents that prove that evidence was not turned over or documents that show that the prosecutor made a deal with a witness.

Punishment Structure

In addition to the opportunities created by the organizational structure, trust relationships also bring about formal punishment structures that make misconduct a viable option. Punishment structures are particularly important because the attractiveness of misconduct is strongly influenced by perceptions of the certainty and severity of punishment (Nagin, 1998). Perceptions, although not always in line with reality, will necessarily be based on the actual structure and imposition of available sanctions (Keppler & Nagin, 1989). Shapiro (1990) argued that accountability and punishment are difficult within trust relationships because, one, agents can easily diffuse culpability for their misdeeds to others or to the nature of their position; and, two, enforcers are reluctant to destroy the organizational apparatus through individual sanctioning (see also Hagan & Parker, 1985). The trust relationship enjoyed by prosecutors similarly leads to an underused and ineffective system of sanctions including appellate review and reversal, professional or judicial sanctions, civil penalties, and criminal prosecution (Lawless, 2003; Meares, 1995).

Appellate review and reversal. The Supreme Court has held that if prosecutorial misconduct violates a defendant's right to due process, federal appeals courts must reverse the conviction unless the "error was harmless beyond reasonable doubt" (*Chapman v. California*, 1967). If harmless, appeals courts must ignore the error in the interest of the "prompt administration of justice" (*United States v. Hasting*, 1983). Circuit courts use a variety of factors to determine so-called harmless error, such as the severity of the misconduct, the curative measures taken by the trial court, whether the weight of the evidence made conviction certain absent the improper conduct, and the impact on the jury (Hetherington, 2002). In general, courts are reluctant to use reversal as a means to discipline prosecutors because of concern for finality and trial resources (Gershman, 1985).

Professional or judicial sanctions. State bar associations or disciplinary agencies can provide professional sanctions (such as censure, temporary suspension, or permanent disbarment) for prosecutors who engage in misconduct. However, bar associations, interested in upholding the credibility of the legal profession, infrequently sanction prosecutors for misconduct (Meares, 1995). The 1999 investigation by the *Chicago Tribune* found that of 381 convictions that were reversed on appeal because of misconduct, not one single prosecutor received a public sanction from the state disciplinary agency and only two were privately censured (Armstrong & Possley, 1999a, p. 1). Internal review offices are also often ineffective in sanctioning misconduct because of lack of will or resources (Abramowitz & Scher, 1998; Meares, 1995).

In addition, courts are unwilling to use judicial sanctions (such as contempt of court, fines, public reprimand, suspension and/or recommendation for a professional investigation) to punish prosecutors for misconduct. Rarely do courts identify the violating prosecutor by name, and when they do, the court writes an unpublished opinion (Ferguson-Gilbert, 2001).

Civil penalties. Prosecutors are granted wide immunity from civil suits, even if their conduct at trial is unlawful and malicious or causes direct harm to defendants. The courts hold that for prosecutors to fulfill their duties as advocates they must be free from the threat of litigation (*Imbler v. Pachtman*, 1976). Consequently, victims of wrongful convictions can rarely sue the individual prosecutors responsible for their convictions.

Criminal prosecution. Criminal sanctions for misconduct are practically nonexistent. In one rare case, a prosecutor who was convicted of fabricating evidence, withholding evidence, and knowingly introducing misleading and perjured testimony received a US $500 fine and an official censure from the court (Hessick, 2002). The criminal prosecution of prosecutors creates a conflict of interest because the state attorney's office is usually responsible for initiating criminal proceedings against prosecutors, yet doing so is tantamount to prosecuting one of their own—thereby bringing public scrutiny to the office as a whole. In addition, the individuals charged with investigating and indicting the prosecutor may be current or former coworkers of the accused.

Dynamics of Choice

The negligible likelihood of detection, punishment or official rebuke, coupled with ambiguous professional standards, creates opportunities for prosecutorial misconduct. However, despite the opportunities trust relationships provide for misconduct, many, if not most, agents adhere to the norms of trust. A rational choice framework suggests that, in general, agents make decisions to violate the norms of trust loosely based on the expectation that their choice will provide benefits with minimal risk (for a review, see Tallman & Gray, 1990). Alternatively, a framework of "bounded rationality" suggests that actors do not always maximize outcomes but choose the first alternative that is "good enough" (Simon, 1979). Either way, agents' evaluation of their options is influenced by the ethical context of the decision and moral considerations.

Ethical Environment

Theorists of occupational crime recognize that choice to engage in illegal activity on the job often depends on the ethical climate of the workplace (McKendall &Wagner, 1997). Coleman (1987) noted that members of professions such as medicine and law enforcement are expected to identify with their profession, support their colleagues, and work to advance their common interests. The more insular a work-related subculture, the easier it is for members of the subculture to "maintain a definition of certain criminal activities as acceptable or even required behavior, when they are clearly condemned by society as a whole" (Coleman, 1987, p. 423).

Prosecutors function within the subculture of law enforcement in their district and the occupational subculture of prosecutors in general. Some initial work on these subcultures suggests that law enforcement officers are isolated, insular, and defend each other to outsiders (Jackall, 1997). This behavior may be reinforced by conservator-style DA offices, where ADAs are chosen for their similar views (Flemming et al., 1992). The tendency to defend other prosecutors' actions is evidenced, in part, by a pattern among prosecutors to defend police officer testimony and resist postconviction claims of innocence in the face of new evidence highly suggestive of innocence (Liptak, 2003; Medwed, 2004; Possley & Mills, 2003). For example, in spite of the resignation of the ADA assigned to defend Rolando Cruz's conviction (because of her belief that Cruz was innocent), the Illinois Attorney General stated

> It is not for me to look at the record and make a ruling . . . a jury has found this individual guilty and given him the death penalty. It is my role to see to it that it is upheld. That's my job. (Frisbie & Garnett, 1998, p. 224)

Prosecutors also work within their immediate organizational subculture that can vary on the value placed on punishment and/or efficiency and inform office practices such as charging or plea bargaining (Flemming et al., 1992). As one former ADA commented about prosecutors who place a high value on punishment:

> They cannot make the distinction, in my opinion, between innocence and not guilty, and there is a distinction. An innocent man never committed the crime; a not guilty one cannot be proved without a reasonable doubt. They say he's either innocent or he's guilty. There is no middle ground. There's no not guilty. (Flemming et al., 1992, p. 42)

On the other hand, an organizational culture that places equal emphasis on punishment and efficiency reinforces prosecutors' "reasonableness" and concern with fairness (Flemming et al., 1992, p. 44). Finally, the culture of the so-called court community could either encourage or constrain misconduct (Eisenstein et al., 1988).

Moral Considerations

The values, attitudes, and beliefs that individuals bring to the workplace also play a role in "determining which of the definitions they learn on the job become part of their taken-for-granted reality . . . and which are rejected out of hand" (Coleman, 1987, p. 423). Consequently, even when the workplace defines motivations and opportunities for illegality as acceptable, individual actors have the capacity to reject them because of earlier socialization on acceptable behavior (McKendall & Wagner, 1997; Paternoster & Simpson, 1993). However, some actors bring attitudes to the workplace that make it easier for them to construe misbehavior as right. Prosecutors who engage in misconduct may exhibit orienting attitudes and beliefs that neutralize normative constraints on misconduct. For example, some prosecutors could have preconceived notions of the prototypical criminal because of media portrayals of young African-American men as criminals (Russell, 1998) and residential segregation by race (therefore limiting their exposure to people of color; Massey & Nancy, 1993). As suggested by analysts of prosecutorial decision making in routine situations (Albonetti, 1986; Farrell & Holmes, 1991; Sudnow, 1965), these preconceived notions then play out in criminal investigations (as, e.g., when police and prosecutors focus their investigations in minority communities), and decisions to prosecute (as when prosecutors feel justified in ignoring signs of innocence because the suspect fits the criminal profile; Lofquist, 2001). Conversely, those who become prosecutors without racial prejudices or with the goal of increasing social justice may be less likely to take advantage of opportunities for misconduct (see Smith, 2001, for a discussion of so-called well intentioned prosecutors).

 ## Conclusion: Studying Prosecutorial Misconduct

The report by the Center for Public Integrity concludes that prosecutors in all 2,341 jurisdictions in the United States "have stretched, bent or broken rules to win convictions" (Weinberg et al., 2005, p. 2). The theory of prosecutorial behavior presented here explains why misconduct is potentially widespread and why some prosecutors (or DA's offices) are more likely to engage in misconduct than others. The theory develops from the intrinsic nature of the trust relationship between prosecutors and the public that requires prosecutors to act for the public and adhere to the norms of trust—disclosure, disinterestedness, and role competence. However, prosecutors' trust relationship with the public is inherently conflictual as prosecutors strive to be successful in their roles.

Prosecutors' misbehavior depends on the confluence of motivation, opportunity and choice—thus emphasizing the structural realities of the occupation and the agency of prosecutors. Motivation to engage in misconduct is a result of prosecutors' definitions of success, which are influenced by the reward structure and the availability of techniques of neutralization. Opportunities for misconduct arise because of the organization of the prosecutorial role and weak informal and formal sanctions for prosecutors' behavior. Finally, prosecutors' decision to engage in misconduct, given the motivation and opportunity, depends on their evaluation of existing opportunities for rewards and risks, which is influenced by their workplace subculture and their values and beliefs.

Generating Hypotheses

Although the nature of the prosecutorial profession creates opportunities for misconduct through lack of informal and formal social control, variation in the organizational structure of prosecutors' offices allows for variation in the probability that prosecutors will decide to misbehave. Thus, it can be hypothesized that opportunities for misconduct will be more available if (a) the jurisdiction has no guidelines (or underemphasized guidelines) for prosecutorial decision making, (b) the organization of the DA's office is highly compartmentalized and provides little daily supervision of prosecutors, or (c) the DA's office lacks an effective internal (or external) review system. Individual prosecutors will also vary in how they define success and interpret their situation. Prosecutors are more likely to positively evaluate

opportunities to engage in misconduct if (d) they face a competitive reward structure or evaluations based on the number of convictions they win, (e) they feel political pressure to win convictions, or (f) they adopt available neutralizations for misbehavior. Finally, the context of prosecutors' evaluation of opportunities for misconduct will increase the likelihood of misconduct if (g) prosecutors' are firmly embedded in law enforcement culture, (h) the DA's office culture emphasizes punishment over fairness, and (i) prosecutors hold prejudices against minority group members.

Developing a Research Agenda

Testing these hypotheses will require multiple research projects with different foci. For example, to learn which organizational variables affect prosecutorial misconduct, researchers could survey a national sample of DA offices to gather information on hiring and promotion policies, size, internal organizational structure, existence of guidelines, office political affiliation, and presence of internal review system. Researchers could then test for correlations between these variables and the jurisdictions' number of cases appealed that include claims of misconduct during a specific time frame. Researchers could also use a comparative case study method to identify organizational factors in misconduct by selecting for variation on the dependant variable.

Ethnography or comparative ethnography of prosecutors' offices could uncover how prosecutors manage their dual role and whether they employ neutralizations if they subvert the law. Although it is difficult to generalize from a few cases, ethnographies can help refine theories of prosecutorial misbehavior, just as Sudnow's (1965) classic ethnography did 40 years ago. Only through systematic observation of the daily routine and narratives of prosecutors can researchers identify the meanings prosecutors attach to winning, succeeding, losing, and/or sanctions.

Finally, researchers could also replicate the self-report survey methods of occupational crime research to identify individual-level factors that contribute to misconduct. Survey questions could solicit information about why prosecutors chose their profession, their prejudices, values, ambitions, and their degree of embeddedness in law enforcement culture. Researchers could look for which of these factors correlate with prosecutors' own admission of various types of misbehavior. Self-report surveys could also provide a benchmark for future research.

Most studies of prosecutorial behavior were completed before the mid-1980s, yet prosecutors' circumstances have changed dramatically in the past 20 years. With the proliferation of sentencing guidelines, mandatory minimum sentences, and truth-in-sentencing legislation, prosecutors' decisions about who and what to charge have increasing consequences for defendants, their families, and crime victims (Zimring, Hawkins, & Kamin, 2001). Although DNA technology now provides the occasional ability to detect wrongful convictions because of misconduct, most defendants have little recourse if wrongfully convicted. Thus it is vitally important that research begin anew on this topic. The alternative is the continued conviction of innocent people through prosecutorial misconduct and the eventual undermining of the legal system though the loss of the public's trust.

Notes

1. See, for example, the following news stories. In October 2003 and April 2005, a federal district court judge in Boston released two mafia members because of federal prosecutors' "extraordinary misconduct" (Murphy, 2005). In January of 1999, the *Chicago Tribune* ran a 5-part series titled "Trial & Error: How Prosecutors Sacrifice Justice to Win." The *Tribune* investigation found that since 1963, 381 people have had their convictions for homicide overturned because of prosecutorial misconduct during trial. Sixty-seven of those defendants were sentenced to death (Armstrong & Possley, 1999e). The *Pittsburgh Post-Gazette* published a similar 10-part series in 1998 titled "Win at All Costs" that exposed systematic misconduct in the federal prosecutor's office.

2. In addition this argument focuses on wrongdoing designated by the courts as "misconduct" (such as personal remarks or remarks promoting bias, and improper conduct around the facts of the case). Even though this type of misconduct is often in contention, it differs from behavior that is deemed "unethical" by some, but not misconduct by the courts (see Smith, 2001). Thus the argument does not address practices of overcharging or undercharging (Alschuler, 1968; Brunk, 1979; Meares, 1995).

3. For a recent review of examples, see Ferguson-Gilbert, 2001, p. 291.

4. Feminist criminologists have been especially concerned with the decision making around domestic violence and sexual assault cases (Frohmann, 1991, 1997; Spears & Spohn, 1996; Spohn, Beichner, & Davis-Frenzel, 2001).

5. The Supreme Court has established that prosecutors' deliberate use of perjured testimony violates due process constitutionally guaranteed to defendants (*Mooney v. Holohan*, 1935). The Court later ruled that prosecutors' failure to correct testimony known to be false (*Alcota v. Texas*, 1957) and false testimony on witness credibility (*Napue v. Illinois*, 1959) also violates due process.

6. Rules of disclosure at a minimum require that prosecutors turn over to the defense statements made by the defendant, the defendant's prior record, documents, objects and reports to be used at trial, and expert witness testimony (see Federal Rule of Criminal Procedure, Rule 16[a]).

7. In *Brady v. Maryland* (1963) the Supreme Court held that a defendant's due process is violated when the prosecution suppresses evidence requested by the defense that is "material either to guilt or punishment" irrespective of the intentions of the prosecution (p. 87). This includes evidence that could impeach a government witness (*Giglio v. United States*, 1972). Later, the Court defined evidence as "material" if there is "reasonable probability" that the result of the proceeding would have been different if the evidence had been disclosed (*United States v. Bagley*, 1985, p. 82). When evidence is not specifically requested by the defense, prosecutors must disclose evidence of "sufficient probative value" to create reasonable doubt as to guilt (*United States v. Agurs*, 1976). In addition, prosecutors have "a duty to learn of any favorable evidence known to the others acting on the government's behalf in the case, including the police" (*Kyles v. Whitley*, 1995, p. 421). The *Brady* rule includes evidence relevant to sentencing proceedings (*Banks v. Dretke*, 2004) and evidence discovered postconviction if it "casts doubt upon the correctness of the conviction" (*Imbler v. Pachtman*, 1976, p. 427).

8. G. S. Green (1990) defined *occupational crime* as "any act punishable by law which is committed through opportunity created in the course of an occupation that is legal" (p. 12). Early conceptions of occupational crime hinged on the violation of delegated or implied trust (Sutherland, 1940).

References

Abramowitz, E., & Scher, P. (1998, January 6). The Hyde Amendment: Congress creates a toehold for curbing wrongful prosecution. *New York Law Journal*, 3.

Akers, R. L. (1998). *Social learning and social structure: A general theory of crime and deviance.* Boston: Northeastern University Press.

Albonetti, C. A. (1986). Criminality, prosecutorial screening, and uncertainty: Toward a theory of discretionary decision making in felony case proceedings. *Criminology, 24*(4), 623–643.

Albonetti, C. A. (1991). An integration of theories to explain judicial discretion. *Social Problems, 38*(2), 247–266.

Alcota v. Texas, 355 U.S. 28 (1957).

Alschuler, A. W. (1968). The prosecutor's role in plea bargaining. *University of Chicago Law Review, 36*, 50–96.

American Bar Association. (1993). The function of a prosecutor. In *Standards for criminal justice prosecution function and defense function standard* (3rd ed., pp. 3–115). Chicago: American Bar Association.

Anderson, C. A., Lepper, M. R., & Ross, L. (1980). Perseverance of social theories: The role of explanation in the persistence of discredited information. *Journal of Personality and Social Psychology, 39*, 1037–1049.

Armstrong, K., & Possley, M. (1999a, January 14). Break rules, be promoted, series: Trial and error, how prosecutors sacrifice justice to win, five in a five part series. *Chicago Tribune*, p. 1.

Armstrong, K., & Possley, M. (1999b, January 10). 'Cowboy Bob' ropes wins—but at considerable cost, Oklahoma County prosecutor has put 53 defendants on death row but records show he's broken many rules to do so. *Chicago Tribune*, p. 13.

Armstrong, K., & Possley, M. (1999c, January 11). The flip side of a fair trial, series: Trial and error, how prosecutors sacrifice justice to win, second in a five part series. *Chicago Tribune*, p. 1.

Armstrong, K., & Possley, M. (1999d, January 12). Prosecution on trial in DuPage, series: Trial and error, how prosecutors sacrifice justice to win, third in a five part series. *Chicago Tribune*, p. 1.

Armstrong, K., & Possley, M. (1999e, January 10). The verdict: Dishonor, series: Trial and error, how prosecutors sacrifice justice to win, first in a five part series. *Chicago Tribune*, p. 1.

Banks v. Dretke, 124 S.Ct. 1256 (2004).

Batson v. Kentucky, 476 U.S. 79 (1986).

Berger v. United States, 295 U.S. 78 (1935).

Blumer, H. (1969). *Symbolic interactionism: Perspective and method.* Englewood Cliffs, NJ: Prentice Hall.

Brady v. Maryland, 373 U.S. 83 (1963).

Bresler, K. (1996). "I never lost a trial": When prosecutors keep score of criminal convictions. *Georgetown Journal of Legal Ethics, 9*, 537–580.

Brunk, C. G. (1979). The problem of voluntariness and coercion in the negotiated plea. *Law and Society Review, 13*, 527–553.

Chapman v. California, 386 U.S. 18 (1967).

Clarke, R. V., & Felson, M. (Eds.). (1993). *Routine activity and rational choice* (Vol. 5). New Brunswick, NJ: Transaction Publishers.

Cohen, L. E., & Felson, M. (1979). Social change and crime rate trends: A routine activity approach. *American Sociological Review, 44*, 588–608.

Coleman, J. W. (1987). Toward an integrated theory of white-collar crime. *American Journal of Sociology, 93*(2), 406–439.

Dershowitz, A. (2003). Foreword. In J. F. J. Lawless (Ed.), *Prosecutorial misconduct* (3rd ed.). San Francisco: Matthew Bender & Co.

DiMaggio, P. J., & Powell, W. W. (1983). The iron cage revisited: Institutional isomorphism and collective rationality in organizational fields. *American Sociological Review, 48*, 147–160.

Eisenstein, J., Flemming, R., & Nardulli, P. (1988). *The contours of justice: Communities and their courts.* Boston: Little, Brown.

Emmelman, D. S. (1997). Gauging the strength of evidence prior to plea bargaining: The interpretive procedures of court-appointed defense attorneys. *Law and Social Inquiry, 22*(4), 927–955.

Farrell, R. A., & Holmes, M. D. (1991). The social and cognitive structure of legal decision-making. *Sociological Quarterly, 32*(4), 529–542.

Felkenes, G. (1975). The prosecutor: A look at reality. *Southwestern University Law Review, 7*, 98.

Ferguson-Gilbert, C. (2001). It is not whether you win or lose, it is how you play the game: Is win-loss scorekeeping mentality doing justice for prosecutors? *California Western Law Review, 38*, 283–309.

Fisher, S. Z. (1988). In search of the virtuous prosecutor: A conceptual framework. *American Journal of Criminal Law, 15*, 197–254.

Flemming, R., Nardulli, P., & Eisenstein, J. (1992). *The craft of justice: Work and politics in criminal court communities.* Philadelphia: University of Philadelphia Press.

Frisbie, T., & Garnett, R. (1998). *Victims of justice: The true story of two innocent men condemned to die and a prosecution out of control.* New York: Avon Books.

Frohmann, L. (1991). Discrediting victims' allegations of sexual assault: Prosecutorial accounts of case rejection. *Social Problems, 38*, 213–226.

Frohmann, L. (1997). Convictability and discordant locales: Reproducing race, class, and gender ideologies in prosecutorial decision making. *Law and Society Review, 31*(3), 531–555.

Garland, D. (2001). *Culture of control: Crime and social order in contemporary society.* Chicago: University of Chicago Press.

Gershman, B. (1985). The Burger Court and prosecutorial misconduct. *Criminal Law Bulletin, 21*(3), 217–226.

Gershman, B. (2001). The prosecutor's duty to truth. *Georgetown Journal of Legal Ethics, 14*, 309–354.

Giglio v. United States, 405 U.S. 150 (1972).

Goffman, E. (1959). *The presentation of self in everyday life.* Garden City, NY: Doubleday.

Gordon, S. C., & Huber, G. A. (2002). Citizen oversight and the electoral incentives of criminal prosecutors. *American Journal of Political Science, 46*(2), 334–351.

Governor's Commission on Capital Punishment. (2002). *Report of the Governor's Commission on Capital Punishment.* Chicago: State of Illinois.

Green, B. A., & Zacharias, F. C. (2004). Prosecutorial neutrality. *Wisconsin Law Review*, 837–904.

Green, G. S. (1990). *Occupational crime.* Chicago: Nelson-Hall.

Guerrieri, F. (2001, Winter). Law and order: Redefining the relationship between prosecutors and police. *Southern Illinois Law Journal, 25*, 353–388.

Hagan, J., & Parker, P. (1985). White-collar crime and punishment: The class structure and legal sanctioning of security violations. *American Sociological Review, 50,* 302–316.

Hessick, C. (2002). Prosecutorial subornation of perjury: Is the fair justice agency the solution we have been looking for? *South Dakota Law Review, 47,* 255–281.

Hetherington, A. M. (2002). Thirty-first annual review of criminal procedure: III. Trial: Prosecutorial misconduct. *Georgetown Law Journal, 90,* 1679–1689.

Hirschi, T. (1969). *Causes of delinquency.* Berkeley: University of California Press.

Imbler v. Pachtman, 424 U.S. 409 (1976).

Innocence Project. (2001). *Police and prosecutor misconduct.* Available at www.innocenceproject.org/causes/policemisconduct.php

Jackall, R. (1997). *Wild cowboys: Urban marauders and the forces of order.* Cambridge, MA: Harvard University Press.

Jonakait, R. N. (1987). The ethical prosecutor's misconduct. *Criminal Law Bulletin, 23,* 550.

Keppler, S., & Nagin, D. (1989). Tax compliance and perceptions of the risks of detection and criminal prosecution. *Law and Society Review, 23,* 209–240.

Kyles v. Whitley, 514 U.S. 419 (1995).

Lawless, J. F. J. (Ed.). (2003). *Prosecutorial misconduct* (3rd ed.). San Francisco: Matthew Bender & Co.

Liptak, A. (2003, August 29). Prosecutors fight DNA use for exoneration. *New York Times,* p. 1.

Lofquist, W. S. (2001). Whodunit? An examination of the production of wrongful convictions. In J. A. Humphrey & S. D. Westervelt (Eds.), *Wrongly convicted: Perspectives of failed justice* (pp. 174–198). New Brunswick, NJ: Rutgers University Press.

Martin, D. L. (2002). Lessons about justice from the "laboratory" of wrongful convictions: Tunnel vision, the construction of guilt and informer evidence. *University of Missouri at Kansas City Law Review, 70,* 847–864.

Massey, D. S., & Nancy, D. A. (1993). *American apartheid: Segregation and the making of the underclass.* Cambridge, MA: Harvard University Press.

Maynard, D. (1982). Defendant attributes in plea-bargaining: Notes on the modeling of sentencing decisions. *Social Problems, 29,* 345–360.

McCloskey, J. (1989). Convicting the innocent. *Criminal Justice Ethics, 8,* 2–70.

McKendall, M. A., & Wagner, J. A. (1997). Motive, opportunity, choice and corporate illegality. *Organizational Science, 8*(6), 624–647.

Meares, T. L. (1995). Rewards for good behavior: Influencing prosecutorial discretion and conduct with financial incentives. *Fordham Law Review, 64,* 851–921.

Medwed, D. S. (2004). The zeal deal: Prosecutorial resistance to post-conviction claims of innocence. *Boston University Law Review, 84,* 125–183.

Mooney v. Holohan, 294 U.S. 103 (1935).

Murphy, S. (2005, April 13). Judge throws out mobster's sentence. *Boston Globe,* p. A1.

Nagin, D. (1998). Criminal deterrence research at the outset of the twenty-first century. *Crime and Justice: A Review of the Research, 23*(1), 1–42.

Napue v. Illinois, 360 U.S. 499 (1959).

Paternoster, R., & Simpson, S. (1993). A rational choice theory of corporate crime. In R. V. Clarke & M. Felson (Eds.), *Routine activities and rational choice: Advances in criminological theory* (Vol. 5). New Brunswick, NJ: Transaction Publishers.

Possley, M., & Mills, S. (2003, April 19). State backs sentence despite DNA. *Chicago Tribune,* p. 12.

Rainville, G., & Reaves, B. A. (2003). *Felony defendants in large urban counties, 2000* (No. 202021). Washington, DC: Bureau of Justice Statistics.

Romano, L. (2003, May 1). McVeigh lawyers express ire over letter. *Washington Post,* p. A10.

Russell, K. K. (1998). *The color of crime: Racial hoaxes, White fear, Black protectionism, police harassment, and other macroaggressions.* New York: New York University Press.

Saltzburg, S. A., & Capra, D. J. (2000). *American criminal procedure* (6th ed.). St. Paul, MN: West Group.

Scheck, B., Neufeld, P., & Dwyer, J. (2000). *Actual innocence: When justice goes wrong and how to make it right.* New York: Signet.

Shapiro, S. (1990). Collaring the crime, not the criminal: Reconsidering the concept of white collar crime. *American Sociological Review, 55,* 346–365.

Simon, H. (1979). Rational decision making in business organizations. *American Economics Review, 69,* 493–513.

Smith, A. (2001). Can you be a good person and a good prosecutor? *Georgetown Journal of Legal Ethics, 14,* 355–400.

Spears, J. W., & Spohn, C. C. (1996). The genuine victim and prosecutors' charging decisions in sexual assault cases. *American Journal of Criminal Justice, 20*(2), 183–205.

Spohn, C., Beichner, D., & Davis-Frenzel, E. (2001). Prosecutorial justifications for sexual assault case rejection: Guarding the "gateway to justice." *Social Problems, 48*(2), 206–235.

Steffensmeier, D., Ulmer, J., & Kramer, J. (1998). The interaction of race, gender, and age in criminal sentencing: The punishment cost of being young, Black and male. *Criminology, 36*(4), 763–798.

Sudnow, D. (1965). Normal crimes: Sociological features of the penal code in a public defender office. *Social Problems, 12,* 255–275.

Sutherland, E. H. (1940). White-collar criminality. *American Sociological Review, 5,* 1–12.

Sykes, G. K., & Matza, D. (1957). Techniques of neutralization: A theory of delinquency. *American Sociological Review, 22,* 667–670.

Tallman, I., & Gray, L. N. (1990). Choices, decisions, and problem-solving. *Annual Review of Sociology, 16,* 405–433.

Thomas, J. (2001, September 6, 2001). Oklahoma prosecutor to seek death for bombing. *New York Times,* p. 14.

Ulmer, J. (1997). *Social worlds of sentencing: Court communities under sentencing guidelines.* Albany: State University of New York Press.

United States v. Agurs, 427 U.S. 97 (1976).

United States v. Bagley, 473 U.S. 667 (1985).

United States v. Hasting, 461 U.S. 499 (1983).

United States v. Young, 470 U.S. 1 (1985).

Warden, R. (2001). *An analysis of wrongful convictions since restoration of the death penalty following Furman v. Georgia.* Chicago: Center on Wrongful Convictions.

Weinberg, S., Gordon, N., & Williams, B. (2005). *Harmful error: Investigating America's local prosecutors.* Washington, DC: Center for Public Integrity.

Zimring, F., Hawkins, D., & Kamin, S. (2001). *Punishment and democracy: Three strikes and you're out in California.* Oxford, UK: Oxford University Press.

DISCUSSION QUESTIONS

1. Why does Schoenfeld focus on prosecutorial misconduct during pretrial discovery, trial, and posttrial appeals?

2. Summarize in your own words what the Supreme Court said about the role of the prosecutor in *Berger v. United States* (1935).

3. Explain how "violations of the trust relationship" create the three categories of misconduct that Schoenfeld discusses (personal remarks, remarks promoting bias, and improper conduct around the facts in the case).

4. Describe the "dual role" that the prosecutor plays and explain how this leads to misconduct.

5. Schoenfeld states that "prosecutors' motivation to engage in misconduct is structured by the meanings they attach to so-called success, their role as prosecutors, and the availability of neutralizations for misbehavior." Explain how each of these motivates prosecutors to engage in misconduct.

6. Discuss the sanctions for prosecutorial misconduct and explain why Schoenfeld characterizes them as "underused and ineffective."

7. You have been asked to submit a grant application to the National Science Foundation for a study of prosecutorial misconduct. Explain who you will study and how you will collect data on misconduct.

READING

This study focuses on prosecutors' charging decisions in sexual assault cases. Spohn, Beichner, and Davis-Frenzel analyze the reasons given by prosecutors for rejecting charges in sexual assault cases. They use qualitative data on sexual battery cases cleared by arrest in Miami, as well information gleaned from interviews with the prosecuting attorneys who handled these cases, to test assertions that prosecutors' concerns about obtaining convictions lead them to file charges only in cases of "real rape," where it is clear that the complainant is a "genuine victim." Although the results of their study confirm that prosecutors' charging decisions are motivated by stereotypes regarding this type of crime, they also found that a substantial number of cases were

SOURCE: Spohn, Cassia, Beichner, Dawn, & Davis-Frenzel, Erika. (2001). Prosecutorial justifications for sexual assault case rejection: Guarding the "gateway to justice." *Social Problems, 48*, 206–235. Reprinted with permission.

rejected because the victim failed to show up for an interview with the prosecutor, asked that the case not be prosecuted, or recanted her testimony. According to the authors of this study, the "prosecution of sexual assault cases remains problematic."

Prosecutorial Justifications for Sexual Assault Case Rejection

Guarding the "Gateway to Justice"

Cassia Spohn, Dawn Beichner, and Erika Davis-Frenzel

This study focuses explicitly on prosecutors' charging decisions in sexual assault cases. Estrich (1987) and others argue that the factors that influence decision making in sexual assault cases differ somewhat from the factors that affect decision making in other types of cases. More to the point, they suggest that case outcomes are affected by stereotypes about rape and rape victims, and that only "real rapes" will be taken seriously. Estrich (1987:28), for example, suggests that criminal justice officials differentiate between the "aggravated, jump-from-the-bushes stranger rapes and the simple cases of unarmed rape by friends, neighbors, and acquaintances."

Studies of sexual assault case processing decisions, including the decision to charge or not, support these assertions. These studies reveal that sexual assault case outcomes are affected by the victim's age, occupation, and education (McCahill, et al. 1979; Spears and Spohn 1997), by "risk-taking" behavior such as hitchhiking, drinking, or using drugs (Kalven and Zeisel 1966; LaFree 1981; McCahill, et al. 1979; Spears and Spohn 1997), and by the reputation or moral character of the victim (Kalven and Zeisel 1966; McCahill, et al. 1979; Reskin and Visher 1986; Spears and Spohn 1997). Sexual assault case outcomes also are affected by the relationship between the victim and the suspect. Stranger rapes are investigated more thoroughly (McCahill, et al. 1979) and are less likely to be unfounded by the police (Kerstetter 1990) or rejected by the prosecutor (Battelle Memorial Institute 1977; but see Spohn and Holleran 2001). A prior relationship similarly affects the decision to dismiss the charges rather than prosecute fully (Vera Institute of Justice 1981), the likelihood that the defendant will be convicted (Battelle Memorial Institute 1977), the odds of incarceration (McCahill, et al. 1979), and the length of the sentence (Kingsnorth, et al. 1999).

Evidence such as this has led to conclusions that the response of the criminal justice system to the crime of rape is predicated on stereotypes about rape and rape victims. LaFree (1989), for example, asserts that nontraditional women, or women who engage in some type of "risk-taking" behavior are less likely to be viewed as victims who are deserving of protection under the law. Frohmann (1991) similarly maintains that the victim's allegations will be discredited if they conflict with decision makers' "repertoire of knowledge" about the characteristics of sexual assault incidents and the behavior of sexual assault victims. The authors of a recent comprehensive review of research on the treatment of acquaintance rape in the criminal justice system (Bryden and Lengnick 1997:1326) reach a similar conclusion, noting that "the prosecution's heavy burden of proof has played an important role in the justice system's treatment of acquaintance rape cases, but so have public biases against *certain classes* of alleged rape victims" (emphasis added).

Prosecutorial Accounts of Case Rejections

The notion that decisions in rape cases are affected by the "typifications of rape held by processing agents" (LaFree 1989:241) plays a central role in the research conducted by Frohmann (1991, 1997). In contrast to the studies discussed above, most of which are statistical analyses of the factors associated with sexual assault case processing decisions, Frohmann's qualitative research used data gathered during observations of the case screening process and interviews with prosecutors to analyze prosecutorial explanations of and justifications for case rejection. According to Frohmann (1991:214), "Examining the justifications for decisions provides an understanding of how these decisions appear rational, necessary, and appropriate to decision-makers as they do the work of case screening."

Frohmann (1991) suggests that prosecutors' concerns about convictability lead them to question the credibility of the rape victim and the veracity of her story. She suggests that "prosecutors are actively looking for 'holes' or problems that will make the victim's version of 'what happened' unbelievable or not convincing beyond a reasonable doubt" (Frohmann 1991:214). This focus on victim credibility reflects prosecutors' orientation toward potential jurors. Thus, "the ability to construct a credible narrative for the jury and the jurors' ability to understand what happened from the victim's viewpoint are pivotal in prosecutors' assessment of case convictability" (Frohmann 1997:536).

Frohmann's observations and interviews led her to conclude that prosecutors use a variety of techniques to discredit victims' accounts of sexual assault and, thus, to justify case rejections. One technique, which Frohmann (1991) labels "discrepant accounts," involves using inconsistencies in the victim's story or incongruities between the victim's account and prosecutors' beliefs about "typical" rapes to justify case rejection. The victim's credibility, in other words, will be called into question if her story changes with each re-telling or is contradicted by the version told by the suspect or other witnesses. Her account also may be discredited if it conflicts with prosecutors' "repertoire of knowledge"

about the characteristics of sexual assault incidents and the behavior of sexual assault victims. These beliefs, which Frohmann (1991:217) refers to as "typifications of rape-relevant behavior," are further subdivided into the following categories:

(1) Typifications of rape scenarios: the victim's version of what happened is inconsistent with the prosecutor's beliefs about what *typically* happens in this type of sexual assault (e.g., the typical kidnapping-rape involves a variety of sexual acts and the victim states that the assault included only forced intercourse) or her behavior at the time of the assault raises questions about her character (e.g., the fact that she was walking alone late at night suggests that she is a prostitute);

(2) Typifications of post-incident interaction: the behavior of the victim of an acquaintance rape is incongruent with the behavior of the typical victim (e.g., she has consensual sexual intercourse with the suspect following the alleged incident);

(3) Typifications of rape reporting: the victim failed to make a prompt report and her reasons for late reporting are inconsistent with officially acknowledged and legitimate reasons (e.g., the victim did not report the crime for several days and there is no evidence that her failure to report was motivated by physical injury or psychological trauma);

(4) Typifications of victim's demeanor: the victim's facial expressions, mannerisms, and body language are inconsistent with those of a typical rape victim and/or suggest that the victim is not telling the truth.

As Frohmann (1991) notes, incongruities between the victim's version of the alleged assault and these official typifications can be used to discredit the victim's account and to justify case rejection.

A second technique used by prosecutors to discredit victims' allegations of sexual assault, according to Frohmann (1991), is to impute ulterior motives to the victim. Prosecutors use their knowledge about the victim's current circumstances, relationship with the suspect, and behavior at the time of the incident to question her assertion that the sexual activity was nonconsensual and/or to suggest that she had a reason to file a false complaint. Evidence that the victim was attempting to cover up non-marital sexual activity or illegal behavior or to explain away a pregnancy or sexually transmitted disease, in other words, can be used to justify case rejection or to bolster the argument for rejection based on "discrepant accounts."

In a later study, Frohmann (1997) identified an additional method—the "construction of discordant locales"—used by prosecutors to account for sexual assault case rejection. Frohmann argued that legal agents, including prosecutors, tend to ascribe the stereotypical features of a neighborhood to the victims, suspects, and jurors who live or pass through there. Because victims and suspects typically reside in racially mixed, lower-class neighborhoods that differ significantly from the white middle- and upper-class neighborhoods inhabited by potential jurors, the likelihood of conviction rests to some extent on potential jurors' ability to understand, interpret, and make sense of the behavior of the victim and suspect. Cultural differences in the places where victims and jurors live, in other words, "lead to misinterpretation by jurors of victims that would result in 'not guilty' verdicts if the cases were forwarded."

Although Frohmann's research on prosecutorial accounts of case rejections is widely cited, to our knowledge it has not been replicated. There are no other studies that focus explicitly on the reasons given by prosecutors to justify rejection of charges in sexual assault cases. In addition, Frohmann provides no information on the frequency with which prosecutors used discrepant accounts, ulterior motives, or discordant locales to justify case rejection. She notes that the various explanations often were used in conjunction with one another, but again provides no estimates of the frequency with which this occurred.

The purpose of this paper is to replicate and extend Frohmann's important work. Using data on cases cleared by arrest in Miami, we examine prosecutorial accounts of case rejection. We apply a modified version of Frohmann's typology to categorize cases based on the reason(s) given. We also describe and compare the characteristics of cases that fall into each category.

Research Design

We obtained data on all sexual battery cases ($N = 140$) involving victims over the age of 12 that were cleared by arrest in 1997 from the Sexual Crimes Bureau of the Miami-Dade (Miami, Florida) Police Department. Officials in the Sexual Crimes Bureau provided us with photocopies of the incident report, arrest affidavit, and closeout memorandum for each case. The incident report, which is the document prepared by the police officer who took the complaint, includes a description of the crime, statements made by victims and witnesses at the time the initial complaint was made, and a narrative description of the investigation conducted by the officer from the Sexual Crimes Bureau who was assigned to the case. The narrative of the investigation includes statements made by the victim, by witnesses, and by the suspect during the course of the investigation. The arrest affidavit contains information about the background characteristics of the defendant and the charges filed at arrest. The closeout memorandum, which was prepared by the state's attorney to whom the case was assigned, summarizes the disposition in the case. For cases in which charges were not filed by the state's attorney, the closeout memo also includes a statement of the reasons for case rejection.

We use the information included in the closeout memorandums to examine and categorize prosecutorial justifications for charge rejection. Although Frohmann (1997) argues that the official reason given to explain case rejection may not always be the "real" reason, the closeout memorandums in these cases generally included a detailed rationale for case rejection. There were very few cases, in other words, where the state's attorney indicated that the case was "no actioned" and then simply provided a cryptic reason, such as "victim refused to cooperate" or "insufficient evidence to prove allegations beyond a reasonable doubt." We contend that the detailed descriptions of the reasons for case rejection, coupled with the written case narratives, some of which were more than 100 pages long, provide sufficient information on which to base conclusions regarding the prevalence of various types of prosecutorial justifications for case rejection.

We supplement the information obtained from the case narratives and the closeout memorandums with information about the charging process obtained from interviews with prosecutors in the Dade County State's Attorney's Office. The principal investigator interviewed seven of the prosecutors whose names appeared on the closeout memos for the 1997 cases. Prosecutors were not asked about specific cases. Rather, the interviews, which were anonymous and confidential, focused on such things as the factors that generally influence decision-making in sexual assault cases, how attorneys evaluate victim credibility and the strength of evidence in the case, the types of cases that are most (and least) likely to be prosecuted successfully, and the reasons why victims would report a sexual assault and then decide not to cooperate. We use the attorneys' answers to these questions to illustrate and elaborate upon our findings regarding the justifications for charge rejection.

The Context of Case Screening in Dade County

Sexual battery cases are screened by one of three units in the Dade County State's Attorney's Office. The most serious cases (i.e., sexual batteries classified as 1st degree felonies) are handled by the Felony Division. This division, which is responsible for prosecution of all cases assigned to the Dade County Circuit Court, screens all 1st degree felonies. If charges are filed, the case is prosecuted vertically. The Sexual Battery Unit, technically, is responsible for screening and (vertical) prosecution of less serious (i.e., those classified as 2nd and 3rd degree felonies) sexual batteries. However, according to the Chief of the Felony Division of the Dade County State's Attorney's Office [information obtained during personal interview], the unit primarily handles cases

involving children, which tend to be more difficult to prosecute and, thus, more time consuming. Therefore, most arrests for sexual battery are screened by the Felony Screening Unit (FSU), which reviews and makes charging decisions for all 2nd and 3rd degree felonies. The FSU includes 22 assistant state attorneys, some of whom are assigned permanently and some of whom rotate through the unit. If charges are filed, the case is forwarded to the Felony Division for assignment to one of the circuit judges. The case is then prosecuted by one of the three attorneys assigned to that courtroom.

The prosecutor has a number of options at screening. She can reduce the charge to a misdemeanor, file different (i.e., more serious, less serious, or additional) charges than what is indicated on the arrest affidavit, or file charges identical to those on the arrest affidavit. She also can reject the charges, which in Dade County is reflected in a decision to "no action" the case. Finally, she can send the case back to the police department for further investigation; officially, the case is "no actioned," but it can be re-filed if additional evidence is obtained.

The standard used in screening cases in Dade County is a modified reasonable doubt standard. According to the Chief of the Felony Trial Division, "we will not file charges unless we believe in good faith that we can get a conviction." She also indicated that the office policy is "to file the highest (most serious) charge that we can in good faith file and to file all of the charges that we can legitimately file." She explained that this policy reflects a belief that it is better to start the plea bargaining process "from a position of strength rather than a position of weakness" and that filing less serious charges in the beginning leaves little room for bargaining at a later stage in the process. As a result, "we do a certain amount of charge bargaining to effectuate guilty pleas."

 Findings

Consistent with previous research, Dade County prosecutors rejected charges in more than one third of the sexual battery cases that resulted in an arrest during 1997. As shown in Table 3.2, which displays the final

Table 3.2 Disposition of Sexual Battery Cases in Miami, 1997

	%	N
Case Disposition		
Charges Rejected By Prosecutor	41.4	58
Charges Filed But Later Dismissed	11.4	16
Defendant Convicted by Plea or Trial	45.7	64
Defendant Not Convicted	1.4	2
Most Serious Charge at Arrest		
Armed Sexual Battery	12.1	17
Sexual Battery	52.1	73
Sexual Battery on a Minor	10.7	15
Other Sex Offense	24.3	34
Non-sex Offense	0.7	1
Most Serious Charge Filed by Prosecutor		
Armed Sexual Battery	6.4	9
Sexual Battery	18.6	26
Sexual Battery on a Minor	6.5	9
Other Sex Offense	19.3	27
Non-sex Offense	7.9	11
Not Charged	41.4	58

disposition for each case in the data file, 58 of the 140 cases (41.4%) were rejected by the prosecutor at the initial screening. Charges were filed and then later dismissed by the prosecutor in an additional 16 (11.4%) cases. The remaining 66 cases (47.1%) were fully prosecuted; of these, all but two resulted in a conviction, either by plea or at trial.

Prosecutorial Justifications for Charge Rejections

We used the following procedures to categorize the justifications for charge rejection. Each of the three researchers independently read and categorized the written reasons for case rejection provided in the closeout memorandums. In classifying the justifications, we used Frohmann's (1991) categories of "discrepant accounts" and "ulterior motives," plus three additional categories—the victim failed to appear for the pre-file interview or could not be located, the victim refused to cooperate in the investigation or asked that the case be dropped, and the victim recanted her testimony. Although our initial classifications were remarkably similar, there were several cases where we disagreed. We discussed these cases, re-read relevant portions of the case narratives, and resolved the discrepancies.

The types of reasons used to justify case rejection in these sexual battery cases are presented in

Table 3.3. Although we attempted to put each case into a single category, there were a number of cases in which prosecutors gave more than one type of reason. In one case, for example, the closeout memo stated in part:

> there are lots of reasonable doubts arising from the victim's story to R.T.C. (the rape treatment center), to the detective, and to me. Furthermore, there appears to be a motive for the victim to fabricate. . . . Victim clearly indicated that she has always disliked suspect, who was mother's live-in boyfriend.

Because the closeout memorandum mentioned both inconsistencies in the victim's story to the rape treatment center, the detective and the state's attorney, and the fact that the victim had a motive to fabricate the allegations, this case was included under discrepant accounts and ulterior motives. A few additional cases were similarly "double-categorized."

As shown in Table 3.3, most of the justifications for charge rejection did not involve either discrepant accounts or ulterior motives. Rather, 30 of these cases charges were rejected because the victim failed to appear for the pre-file interview or could not be located, because the victim was unwilling to cooperate and/or asked that charges be dropped, or because the victim recanted her testimony. Prosecutors used discrepant accounts to justify charge rejection in 24 cases; most of these involved inconsistencies in the victim's and suspect's accounts of the incident. In seven cases, the decision to reject the case was based on the victim's motive to lie or bias against the suspect. There also was one case (not included here) where the charges were dismissed because the suspect pled guilty in another case.

In the sections that follow, we describe the justifications included in each category in more detail. Using information provided in the case narratives, as well as the closeout memos, we also discuss the types of cases that fall into each category.

Table 3.3 Prosecutorial Justifications of Case Rejection

Type of Justification	Number of Cases[a]
Discrepant Accounts	
• Inconsistencies in victim's accounts or between victim's and suspect's accounts[a]	13
• Using typifications of rape relevant behavior	
○ Typifications of rape scenarios	4
○ Typifications of rape scenarios and inferences about the victim based on this	5
○ Typifications of rape reporting	2
Ulterior Motives	7
Other Reasons	
• Victim failed to appear or could not be located	15
• Victim would not cooperate or asked that case be dropped	10
• Victim recanted	5
Unable to Classify	4

a. Although 58 of the 140 cases were rejected at screening, the number of cases does not add up to 58 because some of the cases were placed in more than one category.

Case Rejection Based on Discrepant Accounts

As previously mentioned, a common justification for rejection of a sexual assault case is the detection of inconsistencies, either in the victim's recounting of events or between her statements and statements made by the suspect or witnesses. In one discrepant account case, the victim reported that the suspect, who was her former boyfriend, came to her residence in an attempt to reconcile their relationship. The victim stated that the suspect pushed his way into her apartment and refused to leave or to allow her to leave. He bound her arms behind her back with duct tape and sexually assaulted her. Following the assault, the suspect released the victim and apologized for his actions. He then began banging his head against the wall and later attempted to jump from an exterior stairwell. The victim stopped him from jumping, but during the struggle, the suspect fell down a flight of stairs. At this point, the victim telephoned police. The suspect was arrested and taken into police custody. Following review of the case, the ASA decided not to charge, using the following justification:

> The victim made *inconsistent statements* as to whether or not the defendant penetrated her. She told fire rescue that he didn't penetrate her and she told the uniformed officer that he did penetrate her. *Additionally, the allegation is that the defendant bound the victim prior to the rape.* The victim indicated during her pre-file conference that she has permitted the defendant to bind her and have sexual intercourse with her in the past. She indicated that the defendant has a video of this. *The defendant told the officers that this was consensual sex.* The duct tape used to bind the victim was kept in her home (in her bedroom closet). *Additionally, after the act, the victim calls 911 and doesn't report the rape.* She reports that the defendant might have injured himself because she saw him lying in the stairwell. Also *the victim declined to go to the rape treatment center on the day of rape so there is no*

DNA evidence. The victim also said that *a couple of days before the assault, she and the defendant had consensual sex although they had broken up.* For the foregoing reason, it is the undersigned's belief, along with the chief of the domestic crimes unit, that there is insufficient evidence to file the case.

In this justification, the prosecutor states that the victim gave different accounts of the assault to the fire rescue team, who responded to the 911 call regarding the suspect's injuries, and to the investigating police officer. Additionally, the prosecutor discredits the victim's allegation of rape based on her prior relationship with the suspect and based on the similarities between the alleged assault and prior consensual sexual relations between the victim and the suspect. Thus, the victim's consensual relationship with the suspect in the recent past and the suspect's claim that the act was consensual, coupled with the victim's late reporting and inconsistent statements, provides adequate justification for the prosecutor to refuse to file charges in the case.

Case Rejection Based on Typifications of Rape-Relevant Behavior

The next two cases illustrate prosecutorial case rejection based on incongruities between the victim's version of events and the prosecutor's knowledge of typical behavior in rape cases like this. As Frohmann (1991:217) notes, "In the routine handling of sexual assault cases, prosecutors develop a repertoire of knowledge about the features of these crimes." If the victim's account contradicts this "repertoire of knowledge," the prosecutor may conclude that the victim is not credible, and the case, as a result, not convictable.

The victim in the first case is a white, 17-year-old female, who made allegations of "date rape" against a black male teacher's aide at her high school. According to the victim's report to police, she went to the suspect's house to watch a movie. She stated that she and the suspect watched the movie while lying on his bed, during which time they engaged in consensual foreplay. Subsequently, the suspect tried to convince her to engage in sexual intercourse; when she refused, he attempted to force intercourse on her. The victim then demanded that the suspect take her home and he complied. The victim reported the incident nearly two weeks later by submitting an anonymous letter to the school principal. The prosecutorial rejection read:

> This case was no actioned because it is this ASA's opinion that the charge of sexual battery by physical force cannot be proven beyond a reasonable doubt because there were several facts that would prevent the state from *showing the defendant was on notice that his actions were against the victim's consent.* See note in file regarding these actions by the victim. *At no time during the alleged incident did the defendant threaten physical harm or prevent the victim from leaving the apartment.*

The note alluded to in the closeout memo lists a number of things the victim did that are inconsistent with the ASA's beliefs about a typical sexual assault:

- The victim admits to flirting with the defendant and finding him attractive.
- The victim allowed the defendant to remain in the room wearing nothing other than boxer shorts.
- The victim laid on the defendant's bed.
- Prior to the start of the movie, the victim asked the defendant for a hug.
- The victim allowed the defendant to touch her throughout the beginning of the movie. While she kept her hand on top of his to guide his hand, at no time did she remove his hand so that it wouldn't be touching her.
- The defendant was allowed to kiss the victim; the victim left to go to the bathroom, but then came back, sat on top of the defendant and continued to kiss him.
- In response to the defendant's questions about the color of her underwear, the victim showed him the top of her underwear.
- In response to his requests to remove her pants, the victim [said] that she "put up a little struggle, but it was very little."

- The victim allowed the defendant to kiss her breast.
- After the defendant first kissed the victim's vagina, the victim remained in the room, on the bed, partially undressed.
- Even after the defendant's first attempt at penetration, the victim remained in the room partially undressed and complied with his request to stand by the chair and his request to walk back again to the bed.
- The victim allowed the defendant to drive her home.
- *The victim did not immediately call the police and instead waited for a full disclosure until she was upset that the defendant had not been fired from the school.*

According to the extensive written justification presented above, the prosecutor believed that the sexual acts between the victim and the defendant were consensual; she notes that the victim allowed the suspect to engage in certain types of activities and made no attempt to flee when he demanded more. The language used by the prosecutor—"the victim *asked for* a hug," "the victim *allowed* the defendant to touch her . . . [and] kiss her," "the victim *remained* in the room . . . and *complied with* his request"—implies that the victim subtly encouraged, or at the very least did not object to, the defendant's behavior. The prosecutor's written justification also suggests that the victim's general behavior during and after the incident was inconsistent with the behavior of a typical rape victim. The prosecutor notes, for example, that the victim allowed the defendant to drive her home after the incident. All of these facts, considered together, led the prosecutor to conclude that she would not be able to prove that the sexual contact was non-consensual.

A second case that was rejected because it conflicted with the prosecutor's "repertoire of knowledge" about typical sexual assaults involved a 19-year-old black female who claimed that her ex-boyfriend, a 20-year-old black male, attempted to force her to engage in oral sex. The victim stated that she allowed the suspect to perform oral sex on her, but when he demanded fellatio in return, she refused. The suspect then choked the victim and attempted to put his penis inside her mouth. The suspect's attempts were interrupted by his mother, who heard the victim screaming. The written justification for case rejection indicated:

> In this case *the victim and defendant have a long history of breaking up and returning to an intimate relationship.* The victim reports that in this case, *she went to the defendant's home in the early morning hours* in response to his telephone call.... *She reports that he performed oral sex on her which she told detectives was consensual.* The victim said that the defendant then demanded something in return and attempted to force her to perform oral sex on him.... The defendant and his mother refused to give the detective a statement. *The victim was not seen at RTC and there was no sign of injury (nor was any reported) to the victim.* Without any corroborative evidence either in the form of witnesses or medical evidence, there is insufficient evidence to prove this case beyond a reasonable doubt.

The justification for the preceding case emphasizes the prior volatile relationship between the victim and the suspect. It also highlights two aspects of the victim's behavior that appear to be inconsistent with those of a typical victim in a non-consensual rape: (1) the victim went to the suspect's house early in the morning; and (2) the victim consented to some sexual acts, but refused to engage in others. Coupled with the lack of evidence that the victim suffered any type of injury, these facts apparently led the prosecutor to conclude that the victim's allegations were unfounded.

Case Rejection Based on Typifications of Rape Scenarios and Inferences About the Victim

The following case further illustrates the use of prosecutorial typifications of rape scenarios by incorporating inferences based on the victim's character and behavior at the time of the incident. In this case, the victim, a 31-year-old white female, stated that she went out drinking with her boyfriend, the suspect (her half-brother), and several other people. When the victim got home, she was extremely intoxicated and went directly to bed. A short time later, the suspect entered her bedroom, removed her clothing, and began engaging in sexual intercourse with her. The victim woke up and demanded that the suspect stop. The suspect then attempted to force the victim to engage in fellatio; when she resisted, he resumed having sexual intercourse with her. Due to her intoxication, the victim passed out during the incident. When she awoke, she reported the incident to the police. The prosecutor provided the following written justification:

> This case is being no actioned for the following reasons: 1) *the victim was very intoxicated on the night of the incident. She had consumed 2 beers, 2 long island iced teas, 2 glasses of wine, a large glass of vodka and coke, and medication for AIDS.* 2) She told me under oath that she has *no recollection of the events that took place in her bedroom* that evening. There is no way to prove an essential element of the crime, which is the victim's lack of consent. She told me *she's not sure whether she consented or not.* It is the undersigned's belief that this case cannot be proved beyond a reasonable doubt.

The reasons for not charging in this case clearly are related to the victim's behavior on the night of the alleged assault. The prosecutor notes not only that the victim had engaged in risky behavior by drinking to intoxication, but also that she was taking medication for a sexually transmitted disease. By referring to "medication for AIDS," which is irrelevant to the victim's intoxication, the prosecutor implies that the victim is sexually promiscuous. These inferences about the victim's character and behavior at the time of the incident, coupled with the fact that the victim cannot recall what happened and doesn't know whether she consented or not, provide sufficient justification to reject the case.

Case Rejection Based on Typifications of Rape Reporting

Included in prosecutors' "repertoire of knowledge" about rape case scenarios are beliefs about rape reporting. Prosecutors expect victims to report the incident to the police soon after it occurs. If the victim does not report the crime promptly, "her motives for reporting and the sincerity of her allegations are questioned if they fall outside the typification of officially recognizable/explainable reasons for late reporting" (Frohmann 1991:219). A late report, in other words, will lead the prosecutor to question the victim's credibility and the veracity of her story unless she can provide a legitimate explanation: she was emotionally traumatized by the incident; she was embarrassed or worried about the reaction of family and friends; or she was afraid of retaliation by the suspect.

Delay in reporting was a key factor in the rejection of a spousal sexual battery case. In this case, the victim, a white 38-year-old female, stated that her husband forced her to engage in vaginal intercourse against her will. The victim stated that after the assault, she remained in their bed and fell asleep. The victim stated that she did not attempt to make any noise or summon help because she did not want her guests to know what was happening. The victim did not contact the police immediately following the incident; in fact, she left the country and did not report the incident until she returned. The victim also stated that she had consensual sex with the suspect after the rape. The prosecutor provided the following justification for case rejection:

> *The victim reported the crime approximately six weeks after it occurred.* The victim did not respond to the rape treatment center or call the police the night of the crime. The victim left the country and called the police upon her return. There is no physical or corroborating evidence. *Given the lack of evidence and the time between the date of the incident and the date of the report the state has no choice but to no action this case.*

In this case, the victim's failure to make a prompt report raised questions in the mind of the prosecutor. Because the victim offered no explanation for the late report and because there are other elements of the case that appear to conflict with prosecutors' typifications of rape (the victim and suspect are married, the victim did not cry out or summon help at the time of the incident, and the victim and suspect engaged in consensual sexual relations following the incident), the prosecutor reports that she "has no choice" but to reject the case.

Case Rejection Based on Ulterior Motives

The final justification for case rejection discussed by Frohmann (1991) involves ulterior motives on the part of the victim. As Frohmann (1991:221) notes, "Ulterior motives rest on the assumption that a woman consented to sexual activity and for some reason needed to deny it afterwards." The prosecutors interviewed by Frohmann described a number of motives for filing a false complaint, including the victim's need to cover up illegal (i.e., drug abuse or prostitution) or otherwise deviant behaviors (i.e., premarital or extramarital sex). Frohmann suggested that prosecutors used their knowledge of the victim's current situation, as well as information regarding the relationship between the victim and suspect, to construct these notions of victim motive.

One of the ulterior motive cases included in our study involved a 13-year-old black female, who reported that her stepfather fondled her, digitally assaulted her as often as five times per week, and attempted to rape her. Although the felony review unit initially filed charges in this case, facts that came to light as the case moved toward trial caused the state's attorney to whom it was assigned to file a motion to dismiss the charges. The ASA filed the following justification for dismissing the charges prior to trial:

> The victim is the stepdaughter of the defendant. The victim disclosed to her school counselor that the defendant had sexually molested her starting in Kansas when she was eleven and continuing up until approximately one

week before she disclosed to him. *The victim, when initially interviewed by this ASA, was very credible as there was physical evidence of penetration. While preparing for trial, however, motives for the victim to fabricate became apparent. In addition, the victim repeatedly [said] that she had never been involved with anyone else and had never had a boyfriend. Sunday night before the trial was to begin, this ASA was contacted by defense counsel that he was adding two witnesses to the defense list. The first was [a sixteen year old male], who would testify that while visiting the defendant during the summer of 1997, he and the victim had consensual sex. The second was the victim's cousin by marriage, who would testify that she had overheard the victim threaten the defendant "that she would do to him what she had done to her grandfather."* On Monday morning, the victim was confronted by this ASA with these allegations. The victim admitted that she and the stepbrother had made out, petted, and that she had "hunched" with him, but had not had sex. The victim then became hysterical in the ASA's office and stated that she did not wish to go forward with the trial.

In this case, the prosecutorial justification for dismissal of charges was twofold: first, the willingness of the victim's cousin to testify that the victim had threatened that she would do to her stepfather "what she had done to her grandfather"; and second, the availability of a witness who could contradict the victim's statements about her sexual inexperience. Although the victim ultimately decided not to pursue the case, in the presence of this motive for the victim to fabricate, it is unlikely that the prosecutor would have proceeded with a trial.

The second case illustrates a different type of ulterior motive. The victim in this case was a white 46-year-old female who had been living with the suspect, a white 45-year-old male, for seven years. According to the victim's statements to police, the suspect held her in her

apartment for three days, during which time he forced her to submit to sexual intercourse four times. In addition to the sexual assaults over the three-day period, the victim filed a second report. In the second case, the victim advised that while she and the suspect were arguing, he became extremely angry, grabbed a knife, and threatened to kill her. At this point, she called the police and the suspect was arrested. The victim later helped the suspect make bond and let him back into the house. The prosecutor included the following facts in the close-out memo:

> Under oath, the victim recanted the events as she had reported them in both cases. *She says that she lied to the police because she was jealous and wanted [the suspect] to leave and didn't know any other way to get him out. The victim insisted that all of the sexual contact during the second incident was consensual and that she was always free to leave.* [A friend of the victim told me] that the victim said that she was going to say nothing happened and the friend told her that if she lied she could go to jail and she would not bond her out. The victim denies this conversation and insists . . . that her jealousy is the reason why she told the lies. *The victim and defendant have been living together for seven years with no children in common.* The victim is illiterate and depends on the defendant for financial support.

According to the prosecutor who reviewed this case, the victim stated that she fabricated the sexual assault because she was jealous and wanted the suspect to leave the house, but "didn't know any other way to get him out." Additional information presented in the written justification suggests that the prosecutor may have believed that the victim actually had ulterior motives for *recanting* her original testimony. The prosecutor notes that the victim's statement that she fabricated the sexual assault is inconsistent with the statements made by a witness in the case and also implies that she recanted her original statements to protect her relationship with and financial support by the suspect. In this case, in other words, the prosecutor suggests that the victim's statement that she fabricated the complaint because of ulterior motives was itself based on ulterior motives.

A Case Incorporating Multiple Justifications

A number of the closeout memos examined for this study provided multiple justifications for case rejection. One case, for example, involved the alleged sexual assault of a Hispanic woman by a Hispanic man with whom she was acquainted. The victim's report indicated that the suspect drove her to the local correctional center to visit her husband. Following the prison visit, the victim and suspect ate dinner at a restaurant, stopped and bought a bottle of rum from a liquor store, and went to the beach together. After spending several hours at the beach, the suspect drove the victim home. According to the victim, it was at this time that the defendant forced her to have sexual intercourse with him. The justification in this case read:

> This case was no actioned because it is the opinion of this ASA that the case cannot be proven beyond a reasonable doubt due to insufficient corroborating evidence. *The victim and defendant were with each other several hours prior to the offense. Despite saying that she did not drink much alcohol beyond a couple of sips, the victim is unable to account for several hours prior to the incident from her leaving the beach after 8:00 p.m. and returning around midnight (shortly before the alleged incident).* The victim also *gave the police a false name.* It was several days later when the victim finally admitted that she gave a false name because she was worried about confidentiality and the victim later admitted that her bigger concern for giving a false name was that she may have had a misdemeanor arrest warrant against her in her true name. *Furthermore, there is an inadequate explanation for the delayed reporting* and the

victim's husband is in ICDC for a misdemeanor battery against victim. According to the husband's and the landlord's statements, the husband had been calling all night and learned that the victim was out with the defendant. When the husband's telephone call woke the victim up, *the victim did not immediately report the alleged incident to the husband. The victim did not report the incident to the police until several hours after the alleged offense and a couple of hours after the husband's telephone call.*

The written justification provided by the prosecutor in this case highlights several reasons for case rejection: (1) the inconsistent statements made by the victim (she gave the police a false name and then lied about her reasons for doing so); (2) delay in reporting (she did not report the crime until two hours after she talked with her husband on the telephone); (3) ulterior motives (the husband was told that the victim was out with the suspect until midnight and the victim did not report the rape until after she talked with her husband); and (4) inferences about the victim (she spent most of the day with the suspect [a man to whom she is not married], cannot explain where she was or what she was doing from 8 p.m. to midnight, and is married to a man who is in jail for physically assaulting her). Reading between the lines, it appears that the prosecutor believed that the victim and the suspect engaged in consensual sexual intercourse and that the victim fabricated the sexual assault to cover this up and to account for her failure to answer her husband's phone calls until after midnight. In conjunction with the inconsistencies in the victim's statements and the lack of corroborating evidence, these assumptions led the prosecutor to reject the case.

Case Rejection Based on Lack of Victim Cooperation

The prosecutorial justifications for case rejection discussed thus far are consistent with Frohmann's (1991:224) assertion regarding the "centrality of victim discredibility." They confirm that prosecutors use a variety of techniques to discredit the victim's allegations and justify rejecting the case. However, as shown in Table 3.3, a substantial number of the written justifications in these cases focused on the *victim's lack of cooperation* and not on the *prosecutor's concerns* about the victim's character, reputation, or behavior at the time of the incident. There were 15 cases in which the victim failed to appear for the pre-file interview or could not be located to arrange an interview, 10 cases in which the victim would not cooperate or asked that the case be dropped, and five cases in which the victim formally recanted her testimony.

The written justifications in the 15 cases in which the victim failed to appear or could not be located describe repeated unsuccessful attempts to contact the victim. One case, for example, involved the alleged kidnapping and sexual assault of a 16-year-old black female by an 18-year-old black male. The victim claimed that the suspect, who was the boyfriend of one of her friends, offered to drive her to the grocery store. Instead, he drove her from Ft. Lauderdale to Miami; when she insisted that he take her home, he stopped the car, fondled and digitally penetrated her, and attempted to rape her. The prosecutor assigned to this case attempted to contact the victim and her girlfriend, both of whom resided in Broward County, a number of times; she also subpoenaed the victim and other witnesses to appear for a pre-file interview. The prosecutor's justification for rejecting the case stated:

> All witnesses *subpoenaed repeatedly*. All *failed to appear*. Victim in Broward [County]. Did locate, had investigations personally serve victim. *Victim still failed to appear.*

Another "failure to appear" case involved a 30-year-old Hispanic female who was an admitted crack addict. She reported that she smoked crack on the night of the alleged assault and stated that about 5:00 a.m. she approached the suspect, whom she knew from the neighborhood, and asked if she could borrow enough money for transportation home. She stated that she accompanied the suspect to the 1979 Chevrolet van where he was living and that he sexually assaulted her there. The suspect denied that the victim had been in his van that evening and stated that he did not sexually assault her. The prosecutor's closeout memo stated,

> Victim *failed to appear for pre-file conference twice*. Detectives *did not think she intended to pursue this case*. Personal service attempted. Subpoena served on her brother who said he does not know of victim's whereabouts, but if he sees her, he would deliver the subpoena.

The justifications provided in the "could not locate" cases were somewhat different. In several of these cases, the prosecutor attributed his/her difficulty in locating the victim either to the fact that the victim did not have a phone (or the phone had been disconnected) or was "a street person," "homeless," a "prostitute," or a "runaway." Typical of these justifications for case rejection are the following:

> Victim *is a runaway* with substance abuse and psychological problems. . . . *With no way to find victim,* state could not proceed with case.

> Victim and witness are *homeless prostitutes.* Unable to locate.

> Victim *can't be located.* Victim is a *street person.* She *failed to appear* for deposition twice. Detective *cannot locate* her. The witness who had permitted her to be on his property also *tried to locate her without any success.*

As these written justifications document, prosecutors often made aggressive attempts to locate the victims and witnesses in these cases. It is certainly possible that, had these victims been found, their allegations eventually would have been discredited by the prosecutor's use of one of the techniques Frohmann (1991) describes. However, the fact that they could not be located limited the prosecutor's options. Without a victim/witness, the prosecutor had no choice but to reject the case.

Prosecutors' options also were limited in those cases in which the victim would not cooperate, asked that the case be dropped, or recanted. Although prosecutors are not legally precluded from pursuing a case with a reluctant victim, their goal of "avoiding uncertainty" (Albonetti 1987) makes this unlikely. The closeout memos filed in several of these cases suggested that the prosecutor assigned to the case believed that the victim *had been* sexually assaulted. One case, for example, involved a woman who claimed that she had been sexually assaulted by her ex-boyfriend, who broke into her house in the middle of the night. The prosecutor, apparently convinced that the victim was telling the truth, made numerous attempts to secure her cooperation and even had the victim arrested and held in jail for four days for failure to cooperate. Eventually, however, the victim recanted her testimony. The prosecutor explained that the case was rejected

> because the *victim refused to assist in the prosecution* of this case. She *failed to appear* in my office after personal service on August 5, 1997 and August 12, 1997.... Thereafter, I had the court issue a writ of bodily attachment against her. She was arrested on 9/19/97 and held for 4 days. On 9/23/97, I took a sworn statement from her where *she recanted entirely.* Therefore, it is impossible to prosecute this case without her cooperation.

In several of the cases rejected because of the victim's lack of cooperation, the prosecutor's written justification implied that the assault may have been fabricated or that the sexual contact was consensual. In one case, for example, a 27-year-old woman claimed that she was sexually assaulted by her 21-year-old boyfriend at his parent's house (where they were living). She reported that they were "having problems in their relationship," and that on the night in question, she found him in his room with another woman. She stated that they got into an argument when he returned from driving the other woman home and that he grabbed her when she attempted to leave the bedroom. She also stated that during the course of the assault, he tore her

underwear, pulled her hair, punched her, and bit her on the breast. The suspect admitted that he and the victim engaged in sexual intercourse, but insisted that it was consensual; he also stated that they had engaged in "rough sex" in the past. The incident report indicated that the police officer investigating the crime repeatedly asked the victim to obtain the ripped underwear so that they could be examined for physical evidence, and attempted to contact the victim and the witnesses in the case without success. Three weeks later, the case was rejected by the prosecutor, who noted that the victim *"recanted, without explanation, her statements made orally and in writing* to the detective at the time the defendant was arrested." The prosecutor also stated that the victim acknowledged that the defendant *"could have believed that all of the acts he did during this incident were done with her consent."*

Other cases in the "victim would not cooperate/asked that charges be dropped" category involved teenage girls who admitted under questioning that the sexual contact was consensual. In some of these cases, the complaint was filed, not by the alleged victim, but by the victim's parents. The written justifications filed in these cases included the following:

> Victim is fourteen years old; defendant is nineteen years old. Both parties *engage in consensual sex.* Victim *does not want to prosecute.* Initially, victim's mother wants to prosecute, but acknowledges later on that she just *wanted to teach her daughter a lesson.*

> No actioned. 1) The victim was 15 years old having *consensual sexual intercourse* with the defendant who was 27 years old. 2) She *does not want the State to prosecute* this case. 3) She indicated that she loves the defendant.

As the closeout memos in these cases indicate, the victim's decision not to cooperate may be based on a number of different considerations. Regardless of the motivation, her lack of cooperation obviously makes it difficult, if not impossible, for the prosecutor to proceed with the case.

Case Rejection Based on Discordant Locales

We noted earlier that Frohmann (1997) identified an additional technique—the "construction of discordant locales"—that prosecutors use to account for sexual assault case rejection. According to Frohmann (1997:533), "When jurors, victims, and defendants are from discordant locales, prosecutors anticipate that jurors will misunderstand the victim's actions and misinterpret case facts and thus lower the probability of guilty verdicts at trial." Like Frohmann, who stated that evidence of prosecutors' use of discordant locales was provided in oral, rather than written accounts, we found no direct evidence of this justification in the written close-out memos. Although there were a number of references to victims who were "crack addicts," "homeless prostitutes," or "living on the streets," none of the attorneys explicitly stated that he/she believed that jurors would be unable to understand the victim's lifestyle or behavior at the time of the incident.

Prosecutors interviewed for this study indirectly referred to this issue in discussing the ways in which they evaluate victim credibility. Several attorneys, for example, stated that they asked themselves whether the victim's story "made sense." One attorney commented that he asked himself, "Can she explain to me—and later to the jury—why she behaved the way she did?" This attorney also noted that he was trying a case involving a woman from Finland who claimed that she was raped by a cab driver. He stated that

> there are a number of things about this case that jurors aren't going to like. She's white, but she goes to a bar with a cab driver (who is Haitian) to look for her boyfriend (who is black). She goes to a bar where everyone but her is black, she sits in the front seat of the cab, and she has a boyfriend who might be curious about where she was and what she was doing.

Although the attorney acknowledged that this would not be an "easy" case to try, he stated that he believed the victim and that his job would be "to convince the jury that she's telling the truth." In this case, in other words, the prosecutor used discordant locales not to justify case rejection, but to structure his case strategy.

Case Outcomes and Case Characteristics

The findings discussed thus far indicate that prosecutors use a variety of techniques to justify charge rejection. They also provide clues to the characteristics of the cases found in each category. However, the cases used to illustrate the various types of justifications were not randomly selected from all rejected cases; as a result, the characteristics of *these cases* may not accurately represent the types of cases in each category. To explore this issue, we used the quantitative data collected for this study to compare the victim, suspect, and case characteristics of sexual battery cases that were rejected or dismissed (all types of justifications) with the characteristics of cases that were fully prosecuted. We also compare the characteristics of cases that were rejected because of discrepant accounts or ulterior motives on the part of the victim with those that were rejected because the victim could not be located, refused to cooperate, or recanted.

The victim, suspect, and incident characteristics of rejected/dismissed and fully prosecuted cases are presented in Table 3.4. Although most of these variables are self-explanatory, several require elaboration. Our victim/suspect relationship variable includes four relationship types. We classified cases in which the suspect and victim were complete strangers or in which the victim had not met, and could not identify, the suspect as cases involving "strangers." We categorized cases in which the suspect and victim were relatives as cases involving "relatives." We classified cases in which the suspect and victim were friends or acquaintances, or the suspect was either an authority figure or the boyfriend of the victim's mother or another relative as cases involving "acquaintances." The final category "intimate partners"—includes cases in which the victim and the suspect were (or had been) dating, were currently living together, or were (or had been) married

Table 3.4   Case Outcomes and Case Characteristics for Sexual Battery Cases: Cases Rejected/Dismissed and Cases Prosecuted

| | Charges Rejected or Dismissed | | | | | | Case Fully Prosecuted | |
| | All Rejections and Dismissals | | Rejected: Victim Credibility or Motives[a] | | Rejected: Lack of Cooperation or Recanted[b] | | | |
	%	N	%	N	%	N	%	N
Victim Characteristics								
Race								
Black	58.1	43	43.5	10	61.3	19	47.0	31
White	31.1	23	43.5	10	25.8	8	45.5	30
Hispanic/Other	10.9	8	12.9	3	12.9	4	7.6	5
Age (mean)	22.4		25.6		23.3		21.1	
13 to 16 years old	37.0	27	27.3	6	25.8	8	43.9	29
Evidence of risk-taking behavior[c] (% yes)	33.8	25	39.1	9	32.3	10	21.2	14
Questions about moral character[d] (% yes)	50.0	37	43.5	10	51.6	16	30.3	20
Relationship to the suspect								
Stranger	20.5	15	0.0	0	25.8	8	4.5	3
Acquaintance	32.9	24	43.5	10	32.3	10	30.3	20
Relative	13.7	10	21.7	5	12.9	4	27.3	18
Intimate Partner	32.9	24	34.8	8	29.0	9	37.9	25
Prior sexual relationship w/suspect (% yes)	31.1	23	34.8	8	29.0	9	33.3	22
Suspect Characteristics								
Race								
Black	64.9	48	56.5	13	64.5	20	48.5	32
White	18.9	14	30.4	7	19.4	6	25.8	17
Hispanic/Other	16.2	12	13.0	3	16.1	5	25.8	17
Age (mean)	27.7		30.2		27.9		30.8	
Case and Incident Characteristics								
Most serious chg. at arrest = sexual battery	77.0	57	78.3	18	87.1	27	72.7	48
Offender used a gun or knife (% yes)	12.2	9	4.3	1	16.1	5	16.7	11
Victim injured (% yes)	24.3	18	26.1	6	25.8	8	34.8	23
Physical evidence available (% yes)	60.8	45	52.2	12	67.7	21	51.5	34

	Charges Rejected or Dismissed							
	All Rejections and Dismissals		Rejected: Victim Credibility or Motives[a]		Rejected: Lack of Cooperation or Recanted[b]		Case Fully Prosecuted	
	%	N	%	N	%	N	%	N
Witness to incident (% yes)	27.4	20	26.1	6	19.4	6	38.1	24
Incident reported within one hour (% yes)	25.0	18	26.1	6	22.6	7	27.7	18
Victim physically resisted suspect (% yes)	58.1	43	56.5	13	51.6	16	57.6	38
Suspect claims victim consented (% yes)	32.4	24	26.1	6	41.9	13	31.8	21
Suspect claims incident fabricated (% yes)	24.3	18	21.7	5	16.1	5	24.2	16
Location where assault occurred								
Victim's residence	51.4	38	69.6	16	51.6	16	45.5	30
Suspect's residence	17.6	13	13.0	3	19.4	6	18.2	12
Somewhere else	31.0	19	17.4	4	29.0	9	36.4	24
At least one aggravating circumstance[e]	35.1	26	34.8	8	38.7	12	43.9	29

a. In these cases the justification for rejecting or dismissing the charges was based on discrepant accounts or ulterior motives (see Table 3.3).

b. In these cases the justification for rejecting or dismissing the charges was either that the victim failed to appear or could not be located, the victim asked that the case be dropped, or the victim recanted (see Table 3.3).

c. This variable was coded 1 if the police report contained any reference to the following types of risk-taking behavior by the complainant: walking alone late at night; hitch-hiking; accompanying the offender to his residence; inviting the offender to complainant's residence; being in a bar alone; being in an area where drugs are known to be sold; alcohol use at the time of the incident; or drug use at the time of the incident.

d. This variable was coded 1 if the police report included any information about the complainant's prior sexual activities with someone other than the offender; pattern of alcohol use; pattern of drug use; work history in a disreputable situation (e.g., go-go dancer, massage parlor); criminal record; out of wedlock pregnancy or birth; or work as a prostitute.

e. One of the following aggravating circumstances was present: the victim and suspect were strangers, there were multiple offenders, the suspect used a gun or knife, or the victim suffered some type of collateral injury.

to each other. We labeled this category "intimate partners," rather than "partners," because most of the relationships involved prior consensual sexual intercourse; 43 of the 49 (87.8%) victims indicated that they had had a prior sexual relationship with the suspect.

Our measures of risk-taking behavior by the victim and the victim's moral character are summary measures that incorporate several types of risky behavior and moral character issues. Both of these items are intended to capture what LaFree (1989:50) refers to as "nontraditional" behavior or behavior that deviates from gender norms; they are behaviors that might be

perceived (by jurors and thus, by prosecutors) as risky or nontraditional. The risk-taking variable is coded 1 if the police file indicated that at the time of the assault, the victim was walking alone late at night, was hitch-hiking, was in a bar alone, was using alcohol or drugs, willingly accompanied the suspect to his residence, or invited the suspect to her residence. The moral character variable is coded 1 if the police file contained information about the victim's prior sexual activity with someone other than the suspect, out of wedlock pregnancy or birth, pattern of alcohol and/or drug abuse, prior criminal record, work as a prostitute, work as an exotic dancer or in a massage parlor, or history of running away from home. Measures of offense seriousness include whether the offender used a gun or knife during the assault (yes = 1; no = 0) and whether the victim suffered collateral injuries such as bruises, cuts, burns, or internal injuries (yes = 1; no = 0). The strength of evidence in the case is measured by the existence of a witness to the assault (yes = 1; no = 0) and the presence of physical evidence, such as semen, blood, clothing, bedding, or hair, that can corroborate the victim's testimony (yes = 1; no = 0).

Comparison of rejected and prosecuted cases. As shown in Table 3.4, there are important differences between cases that were rejected/dismissed and those that were fully prosecuted. Prosecutors rejected charges more often if the victim was a racial minority or if the suspect was black; they rejected charges less often if the victim was between 13 and 16 years old. Charge rejection also was more likely if the victim engaged in any risk-taking behavior at the time of the incident, or if the victim's moral character was called into question by evidence in the file. Somewhat surprisingly, cases involving strangers were substantially more likely than those involving other types of victim/suspect relationships to be rejected or dismissed.

The data presented in Table 3.4 also indicate that prosecutors were less likely to reject or dismiss the charges if the suspect used a gun or knife to commit the crime, if the victim was injured, if there was a witness who could corroborate the victim's testimony, or if the assault took place somewhere other than the victim's or the suspect's home or apartment. In contrast, prosecutors rejected charges *more often* if there was physical evidence to connect the suspect to the crime. Moreover, the odds of charge rejection or dismissal did not vary depending upon the promptness of the victim's report, whether the victim physically resisted the suspect, or whether the suspect claimed that the victim consented or fabricated the incident.

Comparison of cases rejected for different reasons. As noted above, we also compared the characteristics of cases that were rejected because of discrepant accounts

or ulterior motives on the part of the victim with those that were rejected because the victim could not be located, refused to cooperate, or recanted. Although the results of these comparisons must be interpreted with caution because of the relatively small number of cases in each category, there are some intriguing differences. We found, for example, that cases rejected because the victim could not be located or refused to cooperate were more likely than those rejected because of victim credibility or motive problems to involve questions about the victim's moral character. There was evidence of an out of wedlock pregnancy or birth in six of these cases, evidence that the victim had a prior sexual relationship with someone other than the suspect in four, evidence of a history of drug abuse in two, evidence suggesting that the victim was a prostitute in two, and evidence that the victim had repeatedly run away from home in two. Cases rejected because of discrepant accounts or ulterior motives on the part of the victim involved evidence of prior sexual relations with someone other than the suspect (3 cases), evidence of a history of drug or alcohol abuse (3 cases), evidence suggesting that the victim was a prostitute (3 cases) and evidence of an out of wedlock pregnancy or birth (2 cases). Evidence that the victim had engaged in risk-taking behavior was somewhat more common in cases rejected because of discrepant accounts or ulterior motives, but the types of risky behavior found in the two categories were very similar: either the victim invited the suspect to her home or apartment, accompanied him to his home or apartment, or used drugs and/or alcohol at the time of the incident.

There also were differences in the types of victim/suspect relationships found in the two categories of case rejection. Eight of the cases rejected because the victim failed to appear or refused to cooperate, but none of the cases rejected because of discrepant accounts or ulterior motives, involved a victim and suspect who were complete strangers. With only two exceptions, on the other hand, the case and incident characteristics of the two types of cases did not vary. The suspect was more likely to claim that the victim consented in cases rejected for lack of cooperation (41.9%) than in cases rejected because of discrepant accounts or ulterior motives

(26.1%). The other exception is that a larger percentage of the cases rejected for a lack of cooperation involved an assault that took place in the victim's home or apartment (69.6% versus 51.6%).

 Discussion

The purpose of this study was to replicate and extend Frohmann's (1991) research on prosecutorial accounts of case rejection. Using data on all sexual assaults cleared by arrest in Miami in 1997, we examined the decision to charge or not, focusing on the prosecutor's written justification for charge rejection. Consistent with previous research, we found that more than half of the sexual battery cases were rejected at screening, or filed and then later dismissed.

This finding confirms the importance of the decision to charge or not and suggests that the prosecutor does "control the doors to the courthouse" (Neubauer 1988:200). However, our findings regarding prosecutors' reasons for rejecting charges suggest that the explanation for the high rate of charge rejection is complex. Frohmann (1991, 1997) argues that the decision to reject charges in sexual assault cases is inextricably linked to prosecutors' "downstream concern with convictability," which is itself linked to stereotypes concerning real rapes, credible victims, and rape-relevant behavior. Although the findings of our study are consistent with her assertion that charging decisions primarily reflect the prosecutor's assessment of the likelihood of conviction, they also suggest that this assessment is based on factors other than typifications of rape and rape victims. In a substantial number of the cases examined for this study, the decision to reject charges could be traced to the victim's failure to appear for a pre-file interview, the victim's refusal to cooperate in the prosecution of the case, or the victim's admission that the charges were fabricated. In these types of cases, in other words, the odds of conviction were low (or nonexistent), not because the prosecutor believed that the facts in the case contradicted potential jurors' assumptions about rape and rape victims, but because the unavailability of a victim who was willing to testify made it impossible to proceed with the case.

When we compared the characteristics of cases that were rejected/dismissed to those of cases that were fully prosecuted, we found that the decision to prosecute reflected both legally relevant case characteristics (use of a weapon and injury to the victim) and characteristics of the victim. Prosecution was more likely if the victim and the suspect were non-strangers or if the victim was a young teenager; it was less likely if there were questions about the victim's moral character or behavior at the time of the incident. (This pattern of results was confirmed by a logistic regression analysis of the decision to charge or not.) Further analysis comparing the characteristics of cases rejected for different reasons revealed that evidence of risk-taking was somewhat more common in cases rejected because they didn't fit with prosecutors' typifications of rape cases and rape-relevant behavior or because it appeared that the victim had ulterior motives, while questions about the victim's moral character surfaced more often in cases rejected because the victim could not be located or refused to cooperate. We also found that cases rejected for lack of cooperation were more likely than those rejected for discrepant accounts or ulterior motives to involve a victim and suspect who were complete strangers, a suspect who claimed that the victim consented, and an assault that took place in the victim's residence.

A number of these findings merit comment. The results of our multivariate analysis of the decision to charge or not are consistent with previous research demonstrating that prosecutors attempt to avoid uncertainty by filing charges in cases where the likelihood of conviction is good and by rejecting charges when conviction seems unlikely. This is confirmed by the fact that all but two of the cases that were prosecuted resulted in a conviction. It also is confirmed by our findings regarding the predictors of charging decisions. As noted above, the odds of charging were greater in the more serious cases in which the victim was young, the suspect used a gun or knife, or the victim was injured. Our results also reveal, however, that there are "extralegal sources of uncertainty" (Albonetti 1987:311) and that one of the primary focal concerns of prosecutors in sexual battery cases is the credibility of the victim. In these cases, most of which involved victims and offenders who were non-strangers, prosecutors' anticipation of a consent defense and downstream orientation toward judges and juries apparently led them to scrutinize more carefully the character and behavior of the victim. Evidence that challenged the victim's credibility or fostered a belief that she was not entirely blameless increased uncertainty about the outcome of the case and thus reduced the odds of prosecution.

The comments of the state's attorneys interviewed for this study are consistent with these conclusions. When we asked prosecutors to identify the factors that influenced their decision to file charges in a sexual battery case, all of them mentioned the strength of evidence in the case and the credibility of the victim. A prosecutor who had been prosecuting rape cases in Dade County for more than eight years, in fact, stated that "the *key factor* is the credibility of the victim." As he noted,

> As long as I have sufficient belief in the victim's credibility, I can overcome almost everything else. The bottom line is whether the jury will believe the victim. Rape cases rarely involve witnesses and don't always involve physical evidence, so it all comes down to the victim and her credibility.

When asked to explain how they evaluated victim credibility, all of the respondents noted that inconsistencies between the victim's and suspect's account of the incident and inconsistent or contradictory statements by the victim would lead them to question her credibility. One prosecutor noted, for example, that she asked herself, "Is what the victim telling me plausible and consistent with everything else I know about this case? Is her story consistent with the evidence we have and with the statements of other witnesses?" Other respondents emphasized the victim's demeanor during the interview, as well as inconsistencies in the victim's and the suspect's version of the incident. One respondent explained that,

> You have to look at the victim, her demeanor and her behavior. You have to look closely at the allegations that have been made. If there is other evidence or testimony that conflicts with what she's saying—if, for example, the

suspect has an entirely different account of the encounter and there are witnesses who corroborate his story—then you have to determine what set of circumstances you accept and what you don't find credible.

These comments suggest that Dade County state's attorneys, like the prosecutors in Frohmann's study (1991:214), "are actively looking for 'holes' or problems that will make the victim's version of 'what happened' unbelievable or not convincing beyond a reasonable doubt."

When asked what the typical juror is looking for in a sexual battery case, each of the respondents acknowledged that jurors come into the courtroom with preconceived ideas about rape. According to one prosecutor, "jurors tend to be suspicious of cases involving people who know each other or victims who don't fit the stereotype of a rape victim." Another respondent explained that,

> People come into the jury box with the perceptions they get from TV. They expect the victim to be dragged off the street by a stranger and brutally assaulted. Then they get these convoluted stories that involve people who generally know each other and that don't jibe at all with their perceptions of rape. The process has to start with jury selection. You have to emphasize that crimes committed by family members, friends, and lovers are serious. If you can't get them to admit that, you have to try to get them off the jury.

A third prosecutor, who asserted that "the cases the jurors wrestle with . . . are the date-rape type of cases," noted that in these types of cases "jurors typically have questions about her behavior at the time of the incident—why did she agree to go back to his room after the date, why did she agree to watch pornographic movies with him, and so on." These statements confirm Frohmann's (1991) assertion that it is the prosecutors' orientation toward potential jurors that motivates them to scrutinize the victim's background and behavior and look for holes in her story.

Our findings concerning the effect of the victim/ suspect relationship are somewhat surprising. Not only were there very few cases involving strangers in the data file, which included all cases of sexual battery that resulted in an arrest in 1997, but cases involving strangers were *less likely* than those involving acquaintances, relatives, or intimate partners to be prosecuted. This clearly contradicts general assertions that crimes involving strangers are regarded as more serious than crimes involving non-strangers (Black 1976; Gottfredson and Gottfredson 1988), as well as more specific assertions that sexual assaults involving acquaintances are not regarded as "real rapes" (Estrich 1987) and that women victimized by these crimes are not regarded as "genuine victims." At least in this jurisdiction, prosecutors are not reluctant to proceed with cases involving friends, relatives, and intimate partners.

This conclusion is somewhat at odds with the comments made by the prosecutors we interviewed. When asked whether the relationship between the victim and suspect influenced the decision to charge or not, most respondents indicated that it did play a role. One prosecutor noted that "family relationships and interpersonal dynamics complicate a sexual battery case." He added that "it doesn't necessarily change the way you look at the evidence, but it probably will change the way the jury looks at the evidence." Other respondents explained that acquaintance cases are complicated by the possibility that the victim might have a motive to lie or to fabricate. As one attorney noted,

> We have to recognize that there are situations in which people make false allegations—a woman may be angry at her husband, who is having an affair, and may see this as a way to get back at him. Or, a woman may falsely claim that she was raped in order to cover up a premarital or extra-marital sexual relationship or to explain away a sexually transmitted disease or pregnancy. In these situations, you have to determine whether the victim is being truthful. You have to see if there are circumstances that allow you to conclude that the allegation is real.

The fact that a fairly substantial number of the stranger cases were rejected because the victim could not be located or refused to cooperate also is puzzling. Because it seemed unlikely that a woman attacked by a complete stranger would disappear or fail to show up for a pre-file interview or would refuse to cooperate or ask that the charges be dropped, we examined the characteristics of each of these eight cases in more detail. Four of these cases did not involve a suspect who used a weapon or collateral injury to the victim; in two of these cases, the victim did not make a prompt report, willingly went to the suspect's residence, and had a history of prior consensual sex with someone other than the suspect. In the other two cases, the victim reported the crime within one hour, but there was either evidence of risk-taking behavior or questions about her moral character. In the remaining four cases, the suspect did use a weapon or injure the victim. In one of these more aggravated cases, the victim made a prompt report and there was no moral character evidence or evidence that she had engaged in risky behavior; in this case, the victim indicated that she did not want to pursue the case and asked that the charges be dropped. In the other three cases, the victim either was walking alone late at night or was a prostitute. Although this suggests that all of these stranger cases, with one exception, had some type of evidentiary problem, the problems found in most of the cases do not appear to be so damaging that they would motivate the victim to disappear, request that the charges be dropped, or recant.

The comments of the prosecutors interviewed for this study provide some clues to victim motivation in these types of cases. According to one state's attorney, "When a woman has just been raped, she wants everyone's help. But once she knows what it is going to mean to proceed with the case through the criminal justice system, she may decide it's not worth it." Another attorney voiced a similar opinion, stating,

> Although we do our best to process cases in a timely fashion, I think that sometimes victims just get worn down by all of the delays. The victim is asked to tell her story over and over—to the police, to the prosecutor, at the

deposition—and if the case drags on too long, she loses interest or decides that it simply isn't worth it. I also think that we have to acknowledge that sometimes women get subtle or not-so-subtle messages from police and prosecutors that their veracity is being questioned or that the case is unlikely to lead to a conviction.

A third prosecutor focused more on the victim's fear of public exposure. He stated that

A sexual battery charge deals with probably the most intimate relationship between a man and a woman. I do believe that quite a number of people are petrified about having to describe the gory details of the violation to strangers. We're asking someone who has been violated and probably feels very humiliated to describe the attack in great detail to jurors who are complete strangers. I don't find it all that surprising that some women don't want to put themselves through that. In addition, there are situations involving prostitutes or drug addicts or homeless women who are reluctant to proceed with the case because they know that their lifestyle is a strike against them and they suspect that the jury won't believe them.

These comments suggest that the victim's reluctance to proceed with a case against a stranger who sexually assaulted her may be motivated both by her disillusionment with the criminal justice system and by her reluctance to have her private life made public.

Although the explanations presented above also could apply to cases in which the victim and suspect were non-strangers, the closeout memos and the comments of prosecutors suggested additional reasons why the victim in non-stranger cases might refuse to cooperate or recant. In a number of these cases, it was clear that the prosecutor believed the victim had been sexually assaulted and was reluctant to drop the charges; there were a number of cases where the victim was

subpoenaed to testify at the pre-file interview and one where the victim was arrested and held in jail for four days in an attempt to induce her to cooperate. The fact that the victims in these cases either failed or appear or refused to cooperate suggests that the victim believed prosecution was not in her best interest. This was confirmed by the prosecutors we interviewed. One noted for example, that "there are cases where the victim actually forgives the offender or is reconciled with the offender." She added that in cases in which the offender is a close relative or an intimate partner, "as time goes by she may come to believe that it wasn't that big a deal. There are a lot of the dynamics of domestic violence cases working in sexual assault cases involving intimates." Another stated that some of these cases involve

women who are attacked by men they know, perhaps even by men with whom they have an intimate relationship, and who reconcile with the offender and decide that they no longer want to prosecute. In those situations, there is not much to be gained by filing charges, since she won't show up and won't agree to testify if the case goes forward.

Several respondents emphasized that in these types of cases, they "take what the victim wants into account." One noted, however, that "society has an interest in the outcome of this case as well" and that "you can't always let the victim dictate what will happen." As he explained,

When I have a victim who comes in and tells me that she wants to leave his punishment up to God, which happens more than you would think, I'll say to her, "Fine, God can deal with him when he gets there, but we have to decide what to do about this now." I ask the victim what would satisfy her—what would make her think that justice had been done.

Considered together, the results of our analysis and the comments of the state's attorneys we interviewed suggest that the reluctance of victims to proceed with the case can be attributed to a combination of factors: a belief that prosecution of the suspect is not in her own interest; a belief that prosecution of the suspect is not worth either the time and effort required or the humiliation of testifying about her victimization; and a belief, either arrived at independently or communicated by police and prosecutors, that her character and behavior at the time of the incident make conviction unlikely. The victims in these cases, in other words, may have made a rational decision that pursuing the case would be too traumatic and/or would be a waste of time given the low odds of conviction.

Although we can only speculate, the acquaintance and intimate partner cases in which the victim disappeared, asked that the charges be dropped, or recanted also may reflect the fact that these victims were using "prosecution as a power resource" (Ford 1991:320). Like battered women, in other words, these victims of sexual violence may have brought charges in order to send a message that further violence will not be tolerated and to achieve, at least in the short-run, a satisfactory solution to their interpersonal problems. As Ford (1991:326) notes, "victims who are otherwise powerless in the face of violence seek to use prosecution for leverage in managing conjugal conflict or arranging favorable settlements." Because victims' names were redacted from the case materials we received, we were not able to question them about their reasons for recanting or asking that charges be dropped. Given what we know about the motivations of battered women, this would be an interesting avenue for future research.

 Conclusion

Our study confirms that prosecutors guarding the "gateway to justice" often use "assumptions about relationships, gender, and sexuality" (Frohmann 1991:224) in making the decision to accept or reject charges in sexual assault cases. Consistent with Frohmann's (1991) work, we found that Dade County State's attorneys used a variety of techniques to discredit the victim's allegations and thereby justify charge rejection.

We also found, however, that not all charge rejections reflected prosecutorial concerns about the victim's character, reputation, and behavior at the time of the incident. A substantial number of cases were rejected because the victim failed to appear for a pre-file interview, asked that the charges be dropped, or recanted her testimony. In these cases, in other words, prosecution was terminated, not because of the prosecutor's concerns about convictability, but because of the victim's unwillingness to go forward. Although it is possible that the victim's decision was motivated by signals from police and prosecutors that the odds of conviction were low, her decision also might have been based on either a rational calculation of the costs and benefits of pursuing the case or a belief that the problems that led her to seek charges had been resolved. Future research should examine this issue more closely and should attempt to determine why sexual assault victims decide not to pursue prosecution.

The results of our study also confirm that prosecutors' charging decisions, like judges' sentencing decisions, are guided by a set of "focal concerns" (Steffensmeier, et al. 1998). Because prosecutors are concerned about reducing uncertainty and securing convictions, they are more likely to file charges when the crime is serious, when it is clear that the victim has suffered real harm, and when the evidence against the suspect is strong. Our findings also suggest, however, that the focal concerns that structure prosecutors' charging decisions in sexual assault cases are somewhat different than those found in other types of cases. Because victim credibility plays a particularly important role in sexual assault cases, the perceptual shorthand that prosecutors develop to reduce uncertainty and assess convictability rests explicitly on stereotypes about rape, rape victims, and rape-relevant behavior. As Estrich (1987) and LaFree (1989) have noted, criminal justice officials, including prosecutors, use a set of victim characteristics to create an image, not of a *typical* rape victim, but of a *genuine* rape victim. Complainants whose backgrounds and behavior conform to this image will be taken more seriously and their allegations treated more seriously than complainants whose backgrounds and behavior are at odds with this image. The results of our study, which highlight the pivotal role of victim credibility and demonstrate that cases involving questions about the victim's moral character and behavior at the time of the incident are more likely to be rejected, indicate that prosecutors' focal concerns in sexual assault cases incorporate these stereotypes.

A final comment concerns the prosecution of sexual assault cases in the post-rape reform era. Beginning in the mid-1970s, most states, including Florida, adopted reforms designed to shift the focus in a rape case from the character and behavior of the victim to the behavior of the offender; the overall goal of these reforms was to encourage reporting and reduce case attrition (see Estrich 1987; Spohn and Horney 1992). The most common reforms included changes in the definition of rape, elimination of resistance and corroboration requirements, and enactment of rape shield laws designed to preclude the use of testimony concerning the victim's sexual history. As Spohn and Horney (1992) note, these reforms were designed primarily to increase the odds of successful prosecution in cases in which the victim and the suspect were acquainted and the suspect claimed that the victim consented. Although research evaluating the impact of the rape law reforms generally concludes that the statutory changes did not produce the widespread instrumental changes that reformers anticipated, there is evidence that the reforms did encourage arrest and prosecution in "borderline cases" in which the victim and the offender were non-strangers and the suspect did not use a weapon or seriously injure the victim. Our findings are consistent with this. Most of the cases included in this study were cases in which the victim and the offender were non-strangers. Moreover, cases involving acquaintances/relatives and intimate partners were more likely than those involving strangers to be prosecuted and there were no differences in the likelihood of charging between the two types of non-stranger cases.

Although these results are encouraging, the fact that over half of the sexual battery cases were not prosecuted, coupled with the fact that prosecutors questioned the victim's credibility in a substantial number of the cases that were rejected, suggests that the prosecution of sexual assault cases remains problematic. The rape law reforms notwithstanding, prosecutors continue to use a decision making calculus that incorporates stereotypes of real rape and legitimate victims.

References

Albonetti, Celesta. 1987. "Prosecutorial discretion: The effects of uncertainty." *Law and Society Review* 21:291–313.

Amir, Menachem. 1971. *Patterns in Forcible Rape.* Chicago: University of Chicago Press.

Battelle Memorial Institute Law and Justice Study Center. 1977. *Forcible Rape: A National Survey of the Response by Prosecutors.* National Institute on Law Enforcement and Criminal Justice. Washington, D.C.: U.S. Government Printing Office.

Black, Donald. 1976. *The Behavior of Law.* New York: Academic Press.

Bryden, David P. and Sonja Lengnick. 1997. "Rape in the criminal justice system." *Journal of Criminal Law and Criminology* 87:1194–1384.

Davis, Kenneth Culp. 1969. *Discretionary Justice: A Preliminary Inquiry.* Baton Rouge, LA: Louisiana State University Press.

Estrich, Susan. 1987. *Real Rape.* Cambridge, MA: Harvard University Press.

Ford, David A. 1991. "Prosecution as a victim power resource: A note on empowering women in violent conjugal relationships." *Law and Society Review* 25:313–334.

Frohmann, Lisa. 1991. "Discrediting victims' allegations of sexual assault: Prosecutorial accounts of case rejections." *Social Problems* 38:213–226.

Frohmann, Lisa. 1997. "Convictability and discordant locales: Reproducing race, class, and gender ideologies in prosecutorial decision-making." *Law and Society Review* 31:531–555.

Frazier, Patricia A. and Beth Haney. 1996. "Sexual assault cases in the legal system: Police, prosecutor, and victim perspectives." *Law and Human Behavior* 20:607–628.

Gottfredson, Michael R. and Don M. Gottfredson. 1988. *Decision-Making in Criminal Justice: Toward the Rational Exercise of Discretion.* 2nd. Edition. New York: Plenum.

Hawkins, Darnell. 1981. "Causal attribution and punishment for crime." *Deviant Behavior* 1:207–230.

Jacoby, Joan, L. Mellon, E. Ratledge, and Susan Turner. 1982. *Prosecutorial Decision-Making: A National Study.* Washington, D.C.: U.S. Department of Justice, National Institute of Justice.

Kalven, Harry and Hans Zeisel. 1966. *The American Jury.* Boston: Little, Brown and Company.

Kerstetter, Wayne. 1990. "Gateway to justice: Police and prosecutorial response to sexual assaults against women." *Criminology* 81:267–313.

Kingsnorth, Rodney, John Lopez, Jennifer Wentworth, and Debra Cummings. 1998. "Adult sexual assault: The role of racial/ethnic composition in prosecution and sentencing." *Journal of Criminal Justice* 26:359–371.

Kingsnorth, Rodney, Randall C. MacIntosh, and Jennifer Wentworth. 1999. "Sexual assault: The role of prior relationship and victim characteristics in case processing." *Justice Quarterly* 16:275–302.

LaFree, Gary D. 1980. "The effect of sexual stratification by race on official reactions to rape." *American Sociological Review* 45:842–854.

LaFree, Gary D. 1981. "Official reactions to social problems: Police decisions in sexual assault cases." *Social Problems* 28:582–594.

LaFree, Gary D. 1989. *Rape and Criminal Justice: The Social Construction of Sexual Assault.* Belmont, CA: Wadsworth.

Mather, Lynn. 1979. *Plea Bargaining or Trial?* Lexington, MA: Heath.

Matoesian, Gregory M. 1995. "Language, law, and society: Policy implications of the Kennedy Smith rape trial." *Law and Society Review* 29:669–701.

McCahill, Thomas W., Linda C. Meyer, and Arthur M. Fischman. 1979. *The Aftermath of Rape.* Lexington, MA: Lexington Books.

Miller, Frank. 1969. *Prosecution: The Decision to Charge a Suspect with a Crime.* Boston: Little, Brown and Company.

Myers, Martha. 1982. "Common law in action: The prosecution of felonies and misdemeanors." *Sociological Inquiry* 52:1–15.

Myers, Martha and John Hagan. 1979. "Private and public trouble: Prosecutors and the allocation of court resources." *Social Problems* 26:439–451.

Nagel, Ilene and John Hagan. 1983. "Gender and crime: Offense patterns and criminal court sanctions." In *Crime and Justice: An Annual Review of Research,* Vol. 4, Michael Tonry and Norval Morris, Eds. Chicago: University of Chicago Press.

Neubauer, David. 1988. *American's Courts and the Criminal Justice System.* Pacific Grove, CA: Brooks/Cole.

Neubauer, David. 1974. "After the arrest: The charging decision in Prairie City." *Law and Society Review* 8:475–517.

Paternoster, Raymond. 1984. "Prosecutorial discretion in requesting the death penalty: A case of victim-based racial discrimination." *Law and Society Review* 18:437–478.

Rauma, David. 1984. "Going for the gold: Prosecutorial decision-making in cases of wife assault." *Social Science Research* 13:321–351.

Reskin, Barbara and Christy Visher. 1986. "The impacts of evidence and extralegal factors in jurors' decisions." *Law and Society Review* 20:423–438.

Schmidt, Janell and Ellen Hochstedler Steury. 1989. "Prosecutorial discretion in filing charges in domestic violence cases." *Criminology* 27:487–510.

Simon, Lenore M. 1996. "Legal treatment of the victim-offender relationship in crimes of violence." *Journal of Interpersonal Violence* 11:94–106.

Spears, Jeffrey and Cassia Spohn. 1997. "Prosecutors' charging decisions in sexual assault cases." *Justice Quarterly* 14:501–524.

Spohn, Cassia, John Gruhl, and Susan Welch. 1987. "The impact of the ethnicity and gender of defendants on the decision to reject or dismiss felony charges." *Criminology* 25:175–191.

Spohn, Cassia and David Holleran. 2001. "Prosecuting sexual assault: A comparison of charging decisions in sexual assault cases involving strangers, acquaintances, and intimate partners." *Justice Quarterly* (in press).

Spohn, Cassia and Julie Horney. 1992. *Rape Law Reform: A Grassroots Revolution and Its Impact.* New York: Plenum Press.

Spohn, Cassia and Jeffrey Spears. 1996. "The effect of offender and victim characteristics on sexual assault case processing decisions." *Justice Quarterly* 13:649–679.

Stanko, Elizabeth. 1988. "The impact of victim assessment on prosecutor's screening decisions: The case of the New York County District Attorney's Office." In *Criminal Justice: Law and Politics,* George Cole, Ed. Pacific Grove, CA: Brooks/Cole Publishing Company.

Steffensmeier, Darrell, Jeffery Ulmer, and John Kramer. 1998. "The interaction of race, gender, and age in criminal sentencing: The punishment cost of being young, black, and male." *Criminology* 36:763–798.

Swiggert, Victoria Lynn and Ronald A. Farrell. 1976. *Murder, Inequality, and the Law.* Lexington, MA: D.C. Heath.

Vera Institute of Justice. 1981. *Felony Arrests: Their Prosecution and Disposition in New York City's Courts.* New York: Longman.

DISCUSSION QUESTIONS

1. Why might charging decisions in sexual assault cases differ from those in other types of cases?

2. According to Lisa Frohmann, what are the techniques that prosecutors use to discredit victims' accounts of sexual assault and, thus, to justify case rejection?

3. How does the research design and methodology of the Spohn et al. study differ from Frohmann's research?

4. Describe the case screening procedures used in Dade County. What standard do prosecutors there use in deciding whether to file charges or not?

5. Are Spohn et al.'s findings consistent with those of Frohmann? What was the main area of disagreement between the two studies?

6. What did the authors find when they compared the characteristics of cases that were rejected or dismissed to those cases that were fully prosecuted? How did the credibility of the victim affect the charging decision?

7. Spohn and her coauthors concluded that their findings "concerning the effect of the victim/suspect relationship are somewhat surprising." What did their research reveal about this and why were they surprised? How did they account for this unexpected finding?

8. What were the "focal concerns" that guided charging decisions in sexual assault cases in this jurisdiction?

READING

Research on the effect of race on the imposition of the death penalty reveals that both the race of the offender and the race of the victim play a role. Sorensen and Wallace focus on the effect of race on the prosecutor's decision to seek the death penalty. This study is unique in that it focuses on decisions made by a single prosecuting attorney in one jurisdiction, which the authors refer to as "Midwest County." The authors examine three separate charging decisions: the decision to charge the defendant with first-degree murder rather than a lesser degree of murder; the decision to file aggravating factors (and thus to serve notice to the defense that the prosecutor would seek the death penalty); and the decision to take the case to trial before a death-qualified jury. Consistent with previous research, the results of their analysis reveal that both the race of the offender and the race of the victim affected these decisions. The prosecutor was more likely to try the case as a capital crime if the offender was black and the victim was white.

Prosecutorial Discretion in Seeking Death

An Analysis of Racial Disparity in the Pretrial Stages of Case Processing in a Midwestern County

Jon Sorensen and Donald H. Wallace

In the 1987 case of *McCleskey v. Kemp*, the U.S. Supreme Court appeared to foreclose the possibility of challenging racial bias in capital sentencing by using statistically based claims of discrimination. In that case, the appellant presented evidence from the most extensive empirical study ever conducted on racial bias in the administration of capital punishment (see Baldus, Woodworth, and Pulaski 1990). Although the study showed that race influenced the sentencing decision even after controlling for 230 nonracial variables,

SOURCE: "Prosecutorial Discretion in Seeking Death: An Analysis of Racial Disparity in the Pretrial Stages of Case Processing in a Midwestern County," by Jon Sorensen and Donald H. Wallace in *Justice Quarterly*, vol. 16, pp. 559–577, 1999. Reprinted by permission of the publisher, Taylor & Francis Ltd., http://www .informaworld.com.

the Court held that the correlation between race and sentence did not rise to the level of constitutionally unacceptable risk in violation of the Eighth Amendment. Nor did the appellant meet his burden of proof under the equal protection clause of the Fourteenth Amendment, which, according to the majority, required a showing of "purposeful discrimination" against the appellant.

The debate surrounding systemic racial bias in the administration of capital punishment did not end with the *McCleskey* decision. Prompted by Justice Powell's admonition that such questions are more appropriately addressed by legislatures, Congress ordered the Government Accounting Office (GAO) to conduct a study of racial bias in the administration of capital punishment in conjunction with the Anti Drug Abuse Act of 1988. More commonly known as the "drug kingpin" statute, that act included a provision for the death penalty as punishment for murders related to drug trafficking. According to the GAO report, victim's race influenced the decision making in capital sentencing in 82 percent of the 28 empirical studies reviewed, this confirming the statistical findings presented to the Court in *McCleskey*.

Since that time, various members of Congress have proposed legislation that includes provisions for challenging capital convictions on the basis of racial bias in the court system using evidence similar to that employed in *McCleskey*. Various versions of a Racial Justice Act were introduced between 1988 and 1994 (Bedau 1997; also see Baldus et al. 1994). The proposed legislation would have empowered the federal courts to review capital cases for possible racial bias and to place the burden on the government to overcome a prima facie showing of racial bias (Bedau 1997). Although the resulting Omnibus Crime Control Bill passed the House in 1994, the House-Senate Conference Committees dropped that provision from the final version (Bedau 1997).

A report prepared for Congress in 1994 showed that 89 percent of the defendants selected by federal prosecutors for capital punishment under the drug kingpin statute were African American or Mexican American, whereas the majority of those charged under the general statute had been white (Subcommittee

1994). Despite overwhelming evidence of racial bias, the violent Crime Control Act of 1994 added numerous offenses to the list of capital crimes, bringing to nearly 60 the number of federal crimes eligible for capital punishment. Although the proposed racial justice provisions were not included in the final enactment, Attorney General Reno instituted a protocol whereby a hearing was required before U.S. attorneys would be authorized to seek the death penalty. The protocol allows defense attorneys to challenge a prosecution on the grounds of racial bias. This appears, however, to be an empty formality; almost immediately after its implementation, it was bypassed in the Oklahoma City bombing prosecution (Christianson 1996).

In view of the refusal of Congress and the U.S. Supreme Court to remedy obvious instances of racial discrimination in implementing capital punishment, the question of statistical analyses of racial bias might appear at first to be purely academic. After all, federal and state courts have interpreted *McCleskey* broadly, routinely refusing to grant hearings on claims of racial discrimination in applying the death penalty (Baldus et al. 1994). States initiating their own Racial Justice Acts have also enjoyed little success. Further, in response to *McCleskey*, the State of California abandoned a probe into the issue of racial bias and the death penalty (Cox 1987).

Some states, however, offer more protection and potential remedies for racial discrimination in imposing capital punishment than does the federal government. The New Jersey Supreme Court has held that the level of disparity found in *McCleskey* would be considered significant under the Equal Protection Clause of the New Jersey Constitution (*State v. Marshall* 1992). It also appears that states with a comparative proportionality review process, such as New Jersey and Florida, are more likely than states without such a process, if it is taken seriously, to discover unexplained differences among cases involving particular racial categories and to treat those differences as constitutionally suspect (see *Foster v State* 1992; *State v. Bey* 1994).

Despite *McCleskey* and the response of lower federal courts, there is still hope of remedy in federal court. The most immediate and most influential critics of the *McCleskey* decision were members of the U.S. Supreme Court. The 5–4 decision was fraught with internal inconsistencies. Justice Brennan, joined by other dissenting justices, argued that the Baldus study showed that race probably entered into the decision in cases involving defendants convicted of killing white victims; such a capricious pattern of sentencing would show an equal protection violation if not for the majority's "crippling burden of proof" (*McCleskey* 1987:337). Ironically, Justice Lewis Powell, a pioneer in reconciling the demands of consistent sentencing and individual fairness, head of a commission charged with finding ways to accelerate the federal postconviction process in death penalty cases, and author of the majority opinion in *McCleskey,* admitted that the inability to conduct executions expeditiously and in a nonarbitrary and noncapricious manner had since led him to reject the post-*Furman* jurisprudence with which he had been so intimately involved. Referring to the Supreme Court's post-*Furman* jurisprudence as "a failed experiment," Powell said he regretted his decision in *McCleskey* (Jeffries 1994:451–54).

It is shortsighted to perceive that all race-based challenges to capital punishment in the Supreme Court are foreclosed by *McCleskey*. In its ruling the Court realized that it had to distinguish some cases in which it had accepted statistics as proof of intent to discriminate so as to establish a prima facie case. The convincing point for the Court was the nature of the decision maker in these contexts, in contrast to the compositions of the numerous individual juries that had decided on the sentences in the Baldus et al. research.

> The decisions of a jury commission or of an employer over time are fairly attributable to the commission or the employer. Therefore, an unexplained statistical discrepancy can be said to indicate a consistent policy of the decision maker. The Baldus study seeks to deduce a state "policy" by studying the combined effects of the decisions of hundreds of juries that are unique in their composition. (*McCleskey v. Kemp* 1987:295, n. 15)

Although it imposes limitations, the *McCleskey* decision does not preclude a court from adopting the statistical examination of the results by a single decision maker. Thus the U.S. Supreme Court has yet to address the impact of a study of the decisions made by one prosecutor over a period of time. Individual juries decide on individual sentences; in contrast, a single prosecutor, over a span of time, decides, with a number of homicide cases, whether to file capital charges, to serve notice of aggravating circumstances, and to proceed to capital trial. A statistical examination of these decisions should not raise the concerns expressed in *McCleskey*. Such evidence should demonstrate a prima facie case of an equal protection violation, as it would in venire selection or Title VII cases. After reviewing the relevant literature, we examine the various decisions made by a single prosecutor in homicide cases to examine the extent, if any, of racial disparity in outcomes.

Prior Research

Studies of racial bias in implementing capital punishment typically are reviewed in chronological order, by jurisdiction studied, or by the stage of case processing analyzed. What follows here, however, is not meant to be an exhaustive review of the literature but a guide for constructing a sound empirical study. In developing this guide, we examine previous studies in terms of their strengths and weaknesses. In the report issued by the Government Accounting Office, the research designs and analyses of 28 previous studies were scrutinized. Three major limitations among the studies were identified: "(1) the threat of sample selection bias, (2) the problem of omitted variables, and (3) small sample sizes" (GAO 1990:3–4).

Sample selection bias occurs when cases chosen for analysis do not represent the universe of cases from which they are drawn, but have certain characteristics in common which make them dissimilar to the cases excluded from the analysis. Sample selection bias is most likely to result when the pool of cases is limited to those in which a decision was made overtly during the later stages of case processing, such as the sentencing decision in a pool of convicted first-degree murderers who have advanced to the penalty stage of a capital trial. When samples are limited in this manner, the effects of racial discrimination occurring at earlier decision points are not taken into consideration. Cases involving particular racial combinations of offenders and/or victims may be systematically included or excluded from the pool of convicted capital murder cases because of bias in the pretrial stages of case processing. At the same time, the sentencing decision may be found to lack racial bias, thus giving the appearance that the system of capital punishment in the jurisdiction studied is not influenced by race (Heilbrun, Foster, and Golden 1989; Klein and Rolph 1991).

If murders involving particular racial combinations (e.g., blacks who kill whites) are regularly selected for prosecution as capital murder even in the least aggravated cases, then during the sentencing phase, when legally relevant case criteria are taken into consideration, one should expect a lower death-sentencing rate among those cases than among cases involving other offender/victim racial combinations. A finding of no difference in the rates of death sentencing among racial combinations actually could indicate racial bias, masked by researchers' failure to consider decisions made earlier in the process.

Studies that include a broader pool of cases and earlier decision-making stages are not immune from sample selection bias if the decisions are analyzed consecutively. Most studies that have analyzed both pretrial and trial decisions have not found evidence of racial bias in sentencing (Nakell and Hardy 1987; Paternoster and Kazyaka 1988; Radelet and Pierce 1985; Sorensen and Marquart 1991; Vito and Keil 1988). To determine whether sentencing decisions are influenced indirectly by earlier decisions, one must factor into subsequent models the effects of race on pretrial decision making (Berk 1983; Keil and Vito 1990).

Another limitation of previous empirical studies identified by the GAO is that important variables are often omitted from consideration. Many variables related to the egregiousness of the offense and to the defendant's culpability may legitimately influence decision making in capital cases. Unless these factors are controlled in statistical models along with race, one cannot determine whether apparent racial disparities are warranted by legally relevant case characteristics. Only the residual racial disparity remaining after controlling for these characteristics may be presumed to result from racial bias.

Many post-*Furman* studies have compared the racial makeup of death row inmates with the racial proportions of those arrested for homicide, using information available in the *Supplemental Homicide Reports* (SHR) (Bowers and Pierce 1980; Ekland-Olson 1988; Gross and Mauro 1984; Kleck 1981; Radelet and Pierce 1985; Smith 1987; Zeisel 1981). These studies often find large discrepancies based on the victim's race or on the offender/victim racial combinations. The main problem with studies using the SHR is that they omit important variables, including most of those which determine death eligibility under various state statutes.

The last major limitation identified in the GAO report concerned small sample size. Studies that examine one jurisdiction during a limited period typically suffer from this limitation (Arkin 1980; Murphy 1984). The advantage of studying one jurisdiction is that data collection is easier and more comprehensive within one locale; thus it is easier to analyze pretrial decision making. Furthermore, with comprehensive data on one jurisdiction, legal challenges can target individual decision makers more readily. The main disadvantage is that the studies of one jurisdiction may begin with a reasonable number of homicide cases in the pool, but only a handful typically result in a death sentence. When such small numbers of cases result in death sentences, it is also difficult to determine whether any differences found to exist are statistically significant or the result of chance. Further, when the dependent variable of interest is divided in this manner, it is difficult to control simultaneously for the many necessary control variables in order to perform a rigorous statistical comparison.

In addition to limitations, the GAO set criteria for determining the quality of the studies reviewed. In the GAO report, a study was considered to be of high quality if it "was characterized by a sound design that analyzed homicide cases throughout the sentencing process; included legally relevant variables (aggravating and mitigating circumstances); and used statistical techniques to control for variables that corresponded with race and/or capital sentencing" (GAO 1990:3). According to these criteria, the study completed by Baldus and colleagues and offered as evidence in the *McCleskey* case is the highest-quality study ever conducted: It uses sophisticated statistical techniques to control for 230 nonracial variables in a broad pool of homicide cases in examining the effects of racial bias during various decision-making stages.

In agreement with the findings of the Baldus study, the GAO's synthesis revealed that the victim's race influenced the processing of capital cases. Whether the defendant's race influenced outcomes was uncertain, but many of the studies included in the GAO synthesis found that the racial combination involving black defendants and white victims was most likely to receive the death penalty. Among the studies included in the GAO report, statistical disparities based on the victim's race or the offender/victim racial combination were strongest in the presentencing stages of case processing.

 The Current Study

In the current study we take into account the strengths and weaknesses identified in previous studies in order to conduct a methodologically defensible analysis. To meet the criteria for a high-quality study and to avoid the shortcomings identified by the GAO, we analyze a pool of homicide cases from inception through the early pretrial stages. We include indicators of the statutory aggravating and mitigating circumstances in addition to other legally relevant variables found in previous studies to be most consistently related to decision making, and we employ appropriate multivariate statistical techniques to control for variables that correlate with race and decision making. Taking cues from court decisions, particularly the dicta in *McCleskey,* we limit the sample to decisions made by, or under the direction of, a single individual in a particular jurisdiction.

Pool of Cases

To determine the extent of racial disparity, if any, resulting during the current tenure of a prosecutor in one jurisdiction, here called "Midwest County," we examine all potential capital cases acted upon in the pretrial stages of processing after the prosecutor assumed official duties on January 1, 1991. This universe of cases, compiled from lists provided by the State Supreme Court and the Department of Corrections, includes Midwest County cases disposed of from 1991 through 1996.

The pool of cases to be used in the analysis, however, was limited to those in which the prosecutor could exercise complete discretion, at least theoretically, in seeking the death penalty. Some observers may suggest that the pool of cases should be limited to those resulting in first-degree murder convictions. Information contained in police reports and files kept by the Parole Board, however, suggested that nearly all of the cases eventually resulting in second-degree murder convictions, and even those resulting in convictions for voluntary manslaughter, could be considered death-eligible. In fact, the majority of defendants convicted of those lesser degrees of homicide were charged initially with first-degree murder. Further, it was impossible to conclude that any of the cases did not include some circumstance that could be construed as aggravating under the broad statutory criteria used in death sentencing (see Suni 1986:553). To exclude any of the cases, an arbitrary decision would have to be made. Because indicators of the statutory criteria are included in the code sheet, the analyses performed can control for the inevitability that at least some of the cases are less death-eligible than others. The final pool of cases examined in the following analyses includes 133 cases in which defendants were convicted of first-degree murder, second-degree murder, or voluntary manslaughter.

Data Collection

We collected data from official records of state agencies. The State Department of Corrections files kept by the Parole Board served as the primary source of information. These files typically included police reports, presentence investigations, intake summaries, and clinical reports. Together these documents contained a wealth of official information from which data could be collected. Trial judge reports maintained by the State Supreme Court were a strong secondary source of information, although somewhat more limited and less complete than the inmate files. Midwest County Court records were accessed to code the pretrial decisions made in each case. In some instances, Midwest County Coroner's records were consulted to fill in missing information concerning the victim. Through comparison of the sources the strengths of each data source were utilized, while verification held in check the weaknesses of each individual data source.

Measurement

Prosecutorial decision making. In one approach to measuring prosecutorial discretion, the dependent variable, the researcher examines each stage at which the prosecutor makes an identifiable decision to chart or continue a case on a death penalty course. The prosecutor makes three identifiable decisions during the pretrial stages of capital case processing: (1) the decision to charge first-degree murder, (2) the decision to file aggravating factors as notice to seek the death penalty, and (3) the decision to proceed to capital trial before a death-qualified jury. The initial decision to charge the defendant with first-degree murder rather than a lesser degree of murder is a result of the prosecutor's unhampered discretion, as is the decision to file aggravating circumstances in the case. Filing notice of aggravating circumstance, in essence, is the means of communicating to the court and the defense that the prosecutor intends to seek the death penalty. The final pretrial decision made by the prosecutor is whether to proceed to a capital trial—a first-degree murder trial with a death qualified jury and notice of aggravating factors filed.

Each stage of prosecutorial decision making can be treated as a binary dependent variable. In addition, the number of stages of prosecutorial decision making through which a case passes, when charted on a death-penalty course, serves as a summary measure of prosecutorial discretion. In this summary measure, a case

that is not charged as first-degree murder is coded 0; other cases are coded 1 through 3, corresponding to the stages of decision making described above. This measure translates into the number of unfavorable pretrial decisions made by the prosecutor in a particular case; "unfavorable" means decisions that would lead to imposing the death penalty.

Most of the previous studies examined each of the binary responses separately. By using a summary measure, however, we can examine simultaneously the incremental steps made during the pretrial stage of case processing so as to take full advantage of the ordered nature of the dependent variable. By doing so we ameliorate some of the problems associated with small samples and sequential analyses, such as a loss of explanatory power, the inability to control for numerous legally relevant variables, and the threat of sample selection bias.

Racial disparity. Racial disparity, the independent variable, is often defined broadly as significant differences in the treatment of blacks and whites. Racial disparity usually refers to the offender's race, but also may refer to disparity based on the victim's race or on the combination of offender's race. As we stated earlier, the review of post-*Furman* empirical studies by the GAO found a pattern of racial disparity in capital punishment, resulting mainly from decisions made by prosecutors during the pretrial stages of case processing. The racial combination found most likely to result in a capital murder charge and to proceed to capital trial was that of blacks who kill whites (BkW).

Another dimension of racial disparity is that cases involving blacks who kill blacks (BkB) may be marginalized. Because blacks are less likely than other racial groups to marshal the resources of the justice system, BkB cases may be less likely to result in capital murder charges and proceed to capital trials.

The coextensive laxity in processing black-on-black homicide and harshness in processing black-on-white homicides, if not taken into consideration, could mask racial differences in the treatment of black and white offenders, as may have occurred in previous studies. In this analysis, in line with previous research findings, we consider the race of offenders and victims simultaneously to determine their influence on prosecutorial decision making.

Unadjusted racial disparity is defined as the difference in the proportions of particular offender/victim racial categories that advance through various stages of pretrial case processing charted on a death-penalty course. To determine the unadjusted level of racial disparity, one can compare these proportions as they advance through each of the pretrial stages. Because we are concerned mainly with the possibility of disparate treatment of black offenders based on their victims' race, we compare the proportion of BkW and BkB cases advancing through each stage of case processing with the proportion of all other cases advancing through each stage. We calculate a ratio of proportions indicating how much more or less likely it is that a case involving BkW or BkB will advance through each stage, in comparison with all other cases.

Unwarranted racial disparity refers to the difference in treatment of particular racial groups that is not justified by the nature of the offenses committed by members of those groups. Legally relevant factors concerning the egregiousness of the offense and the offender's culpability can rightly be expected to influence prosecutorial discretion. Racial disparities are warranted insofar as racial groups differ in the seriousness of the crime and the defendants' culpability. Only the effects of race beyond legally relevant considerations may be considered unwarranted and hence discriminatory.

Case seriousness measures. To determine the extent of unwarranted racial disparity, if any, the analyses must include measures of case seriousness as control variables. The code sheet used to collect data includes indicators of all the statutory aggravating and mitigating circumstances. Because some of the statutory circumstances are broad and subjective, we used objective indicators to measure multiple dimensions of the statutory criteria. The indicators encompass most of the

measures of case seriousness and offender culpability used in previous studies of pretrial racial disparity (e.g., number of victims, defendant's criminal record); we also coded additional variables found to be significant predictors in prior studies (e.g., victim's age, relationship between offender and victim). We use these control variables to measure the level of seriousness of a case; thus we consider them legitimate predictors of pretrial decision making.

From these variables we created two types of measures. The first, an aggregate measure, simply sums the numbers of aggravating and mitigating factors present in each case. The second, a fact-specific measure, includes only the specific variables which are statistically significant predictors of prosecutorial decision making. In two separate equations using both of these measures, the influence of the legally relevant factors on prosecutorial decision making is considered simultaneously with the influence of race. Any warranted racial disparities in case processing are indicated by the coefficients of the legally relevant factors in these equations. Any disparities not attributable to legally relevant factors are indicated by the coefficients for BkW.

In other words, if blacks who kill whites pass through more stages of prosecutorial decision making because of the level of seriousness or the specific aggravating factors present in their cases, the coefficient for BkW will be 0. Yet, should these legally relevant considerations not account entirely for the harsher treatment, in the pretrial stages of case processing, of blacks who kill whites, the coefficient for BkW will differ significantly from 0. Any effect of race beyond that explained by the legally relevant variables is to be considered unwarranted and hence discriminatory.

⊠ Analysis and Findings

Unadjusted Racial Disparity

The first stage of this analysis involves bivariate comparisons of racial groups by pretrial decisions. Table 3.5 displays the probabilities that cases advance through

Table 3.5 Probability That Cases Will Progress Through Prosecutorial Decision-Making Stages, by Race of Defendant and Victim

Prosecutorial Decision-Making Stages	Defendant's Race/Victim's Race			Ratio of Probabilities Between Selected Racial Categories Versus Other	
	Black/Black	Black/White	White/White	Black/Black	Black/White
All Cases	(77)	(31)	(25)	(133)	(133)
First-Degree Murder Charge	.597 (46)	.871 (27)	.640 (16)	.78:1*	1.43:1**
Notice of Aggravating Factors	.143 (11)	.290 (9)	.160 (4)	.62:1	1.97:1*
Capital Trial	.078 (6)	.194 (6)	.120 (3)	.12:1	2.20:1*

*$p < .05$; **$p < .01$

successive stages of prosecutorial decision making, by race of defendants and victims. These probabilities show that disparities are based on the race of offenders in conjunction with the race of victims. For cases involving black offenders, the likelihood of advancing through the stages on a death-penalty course depends on the victim's race. Cases involving a black defendant and a white victim are the most likely to pass through each of the three stages.

The ratio of probabilities presented in the fourth column of Table 3.5 can be used to examine the likelihood that cases involving BkB will advance through pretrial decision-making stages, in comparison with all cases involving other racial combinations (BkW and WkW). The probabilities listed in the last column can be used to compare BkW with the other cases (BkB and WkW; five cases involving other racial combinations were dropped from the analysis).

Figures in the first row indicate that blacks who kill blacks are charged with first-degree murder at a ratio of .78:1. That is, BkB cases are only about three-quarters as likely to result in first-degree murder charges as are cases involving all other racial combinations. Figures for BkW indicate that blacks who kill whites are 143 percent, or nearly 1½ times, more likely to be charged with first-degree murder than offenders in the other racial categories. The ratios in the remaining rows suggest that

this initial disparity increases throughout the stages of processing. BkB are only about two-thirds as likely as other combinations to have notice of aggravating factors filed in their case, and only about one-tenth as likely to proceed to a capital trial. The ratios in these rows indicate that blacks who kill whites are more than twice as likely as all other cases both to be served with notice of aggravating factors and to proceed to capital trial. Although not presented in the table, cases involving BkW were over 4½ times more likely to result in death sentences than cases involving other racial combinations.

Unwarranted Racial Disparity

The probabilities presented in Table 3.5 are unadjusted race effects that do not include the influence of legally relevant case measures; hence the racial disparity presented is not purged of disparity warranted by the egregiousness of the offense and by the offender's culpability. As mentioned earlier, only disparities remaining after controlling for legally relevant factors may be considered unwarranted and consequently racially discriminatory.

Aggregate measure. Our analysis of using the aggregate measure revealed that the number of aggravating and mitigating factors is influential in pretrial decision making. As expected, the number of aggravating factors present in a case increases the likelihood that the case will advance through the pretrial decisions charted on a death-penalty course. Also as expected, the more mitigating factors present in a case, the less likely that a case will advance through these pretrial stages.

When the number of aggravating and mitigating factors is held constant, BkW increases the number of unfavorable decisions made by prosecutors. At the prosecutor's discretion, if two cases are equal in the number of aggravating and mitigating factors, one is significantly more likely than the other to be tracked on a death-penalty course during the pretrial stages of case processing if the offender is black and the victim is white. Other indicators of race could not be included in this model; however, in models estimated separately, we found that BkB, victim's race, and offender's race were not significant.

When we controlled for the level of case seriousness and offender culpability by considering the influence of specific legally relevant case features, unexplained racial disparities still were present. Although several other legally relevant factors helped to explain pretrial decision making, they did not eliminate the significance of race. In fact, the predicted probability that the prosecutor will advance a case to capital trial is 2½ times greater when a black kills a white than in all other racial combinations.

We estimated separate models with the same predictor variables, but included different racial indicators. In these models, the victim's race and BkB were significant, but not the offender's race. In the model estimated with the indicator BkB, the predicted probability that the prosecutor will advance a case to capital trial declines to about half as great when a black kills a black as in all other racial combinations. These analyses show that the influence of race on prosecutorial decision making may be masked unless the offender's and the victim's race are considered simultaneously. Blacks who killed whites were treated more harshly; blacks who killed blacks were treated more leniently.

 ## Conclusion

Given the findings presented here, we conclude that racial disparity exists in the pretrial stages of decision making for potential capital murder cases processed in Midwest County from 1991 through 1996. Further, the fact that this disparity still was statistically significant after controlling for legally relevant considerations suggests that the disparity is unwarranted and hence discriminatory. Homicide cases involving blacks who kill whites are more likely to result in first-degree murder charges, to be served with notice of aggravating circumstances, and to proceed to capital trials than are similar cases involving other offender-victim racial combinations. This pattern of racial discrimination, occurring during the pretrial stages of case processing in Midwest County, can be attributed to decisions made during the tenure of the current prosecuting attorney.

In the current study we have been able to isolate the discriminatory pattern in the pretrial decisions made by a particular actor in the criminal justice system. *McCleskey* is inapplicable because this study examined the decisions of only a single prosecutor. Such evidence of discriminatory decision making by individual actors in the criminal justice system cannot receive superficial treatment as easily as in previous studies, which showed the aggregate disparities of many decision makers.

Although the effects of these results should not be governed by *McCleskey's* demands of proof of discriminatory intent in making systemic challenges, they may lead to a further challenge to the statewide policy of capital punishment, of which this prosecutor is a part. Similar findings for other prosecutors in this state may suggest systemic defects. Such a piecemeal approach to a statewide challenge also may reveal equal protection violations in other counties. Yet other, less populous counties may reveal no statistically significant results because of an insufficiently large number of homicides for such a study. If these results are replicated in other populous jurisdictions in the state, however, such replication should meet the demands of *McCleskey* for a systematic challenge to prosecutorial decision making.

Though these findings may not challenge the state's death penalty policy, a statistically based claim of discrimination is well founded. Clearly, a prima facie case of intentional discrimination in this jurisdiction has been made. At the very least, the prosecutor should take up the burden of persuasion in an attempt to justify the apparent discrepancies.

 ## References

Arkin, S.D. 1980. "Discrimination and Arbitrariness in Capital Punishment: An Analysis of Post-*Furman* Murder Cases in Dade County, Florida, 1973–1976." *Stanford Law Review* 33:75–101.

Baldus, D.C.,G. Woodworth, and C. Pulaski. 1990. *Equal Justice and the Death Penalty*. Boston: Northeastern University Press.

———. 1994. "Reflections on the 'Inevitability' of Racial Discrimination in Capital Sentencing and the 'Impossibility' of Its Prevention, Detection, and Correction." *Washington and Lee Law Review* 51:359–430.

Bedau, H.A. 1997. *The Death Penalty in America: Current Controversies*. New York: Oxford University Press.

Berk, R.A.1983. "An Introduction to Sample Selection Bias in Sociological Data." *American Sociological Review* 48:386–98.

Bowers W.J. and G.L. Pierce. 1980. "Arbitrariness and Discrimination under Post-*Furman* Capital Statutes." *Crime and Delinquency* 26:563–635.

Christianson, S. 1996. "Corrections Law: Federal Death Penalty Protocol Safeguard or Window Dressing?" *Criminal Law Bulletin* 32:374–79.

Cox, G.D. 1987. "Calif. Death Penalty Probe Aborted." *National Law Journal*, November 16, p. 3.

Ekland-Olson, S. 1988. "Structured Discretion, Racial Bias, and the Death Penalty: The First Decade after *Furman* in Texas." *Social Science Quarterly* 69:853–73.

Government Accounting Office (GAO). 1990. *Death Penalty Sentencing: Research Indicates Pattern of Racial Disparities*. Washington, DC: USGAO.

Gross, S.R. and R. Mauro. 1984. "Patterns of Death: An Analysis of Racial Disparities in Capital Sentencing and Homicide Victimization." *Stanford Law Review* 37:27–153.

Heilbrun, A.B., Jr., A. Foster, and J. Golden. 1989. "The Death Sentence in Georgia, 1974–1987: Criminal Justice or Racial Injustice?" *Criminal Justice and Behavior* 16:139–54.

Jacoby, J.E. 1980. *The American Prosecutor: A Search for Identity*. Lexington, MA: Heath.

Jeffries, J.C. 1994. *Justice Lewis F. Powell, Jr.* New York: Scribner's.

Keil, T.J., and G.F. Vito. 1990. "Race and the Imposition of Death Penalty in Kentucky Murder Trials: An Analysis of Post-*Gregg* Outcomes." *Justice Quarterly* 7:189–207.

Kennedy, P. 1992. *A Guide to Econometrics*. 3rd ed. Cambridge, MA: MIT Press.

Kleck, G. 1981. "Racial Discrimination in Criminal Sentencing: A Critical Evaluation of the Evidence with Additional Evidence on the Death Penalty." *American Sociological Review* 46:783–805.

Klein, S.P. and J.E. Rolph. 1991. "Relationship of Offender and Victim Race to Death Penalty Sentences in California." *Jurimetrics* 32:33–48.

Maxfield, M.G. 1989. "Circumstances in Supplementary Homicide Reports: Variety and Validity." *Criminology* 27:671–95.

Murphy, E. 1984. "The Application of the Death Penalty in Cook County." *Illinois Bar Journal* 93:90–95.

Nakell, B. and K.A. Hardy. 1987. *The Arbitrariness of the Death Penalty*. Philadelphia: Temple University Press.

Paternoster, R. and A.M. Kazyaka. 1988. "Racial Considerations in Capital Punishment: The Failure of Evenhanded Justice." Pp. 113–48 in *Challenging Capital Punishment: Legal and Social Science Approaches*, edited by K.C. Haas and J.A. Inciardi. Beverly Hills: Sage.

Petersen, T. 1985. "A Comment on Presenting the Results from Logit and Probit Models." *American Sociological Review* 50:130–31.

Radelet, M.L. and G.L. Pierce. 1985. "Race and Prosecutorial Discretion in Homicide Cases." *Law and Society Review* 19:587–621.

Smith, M.D. 1987. "Patterns of Discrimination in Assessment of the Death Penalty: The Case of Louisiana." *Journal of Criminal Justice* 15:279–86.

Sorensen, J.R. and J.W. Marquart. 1991. "Prosecutorial and Jury Decision Making in Post-*Furman* Texas Capital Cases." *New York University Review of Law and Social Change* 18:743–76.

Subcommittee on Civil and Constitutional Rights. 1994. *Racial Disparity in Federal Death Penalty Prosecutions 1988–1994*. Washington, DC: Death Penalty Information Center.

Suni, E.Y. 1986. "Recent Developments in Missouri: The Death Penalty." *University of Missouri—Kansas City Law Review* 58:523–80.

Vito, G.F. and T.J. Keil. 1988. "Capital Sentencing in Kentucky: An Analysis of the Factors Influencing Decision Making in the Post-*Gregg* Period." *Journal of Criminal Law and Criminology* 79:483–503.

Zeisel, H. 1981. "Race Bias in the Administration of the Death Penalty: The Florida Experience." *Harvard Law Review* 95:456–68.

Cases Cited

Arlington Heights v. Metropolitan Housing Dev. Corp., 429 U.S. 252 (1977).

Batson v. Kentucky, 476 U.S. 79 (1986).

Bazemore v. Friday, 478 U.S. 385 (1986).

Dobbs v. Zant, 729 F.Supp. 1566 N.D.Ga. (1989).

Foster v. State 614 So.2d 455 Fla. (1992).

McCleskey v. Kemp, 481 U.S. 279 (1987).

State v. Bey, 645 A.2d 685 N.J. (1994).

State v. Marshall, 613 A.2d 1059 N.J. (1992).

DISCUSSION QUESTIONS

1. Why did *McClesky v. Kemp* "appear to foreclose the possibility of challenging racial bias in capital sentencing by using statistically based claims of discrimination"? Why do Sorensen and Wallace argue that, these considerations notwithstanding, "there is still hope of remedy in federal court"?

2. How does the Sorensen/Wallace study address the Supreme Court's concerns (expressed in *McCleskey*) about the validity of conclusions regarding racial discrimination in decisions made by "hundreds of juries that are unique in their composition"?

3. Sorensen and Wallace use a "summary measure" of prosecutorial decision making in capital cases. Describe this measure.

4. The independent variables of interest in this study are the race of the offender and the race of the victim. Why do the authors combine these two racial variables? Why is white offender/black victim not included in the analysis?

5. What do the results presented in Table 3.5 reveal about the effect of the racial combination of the victim/offender pair? Are blacks who kill whites treated more harshly at each of the three stages in the decision-making process?

6. What did the authors find when they controlled for the level of case seriousness and for other factors that affect outcomes in capital cases?

7. How would you interpret the results of this study? Was this prosecuting attorney making racially biased charging decisions in death penalty cases?

READING

This study explores the professional values and practices of small-town lawyers who represent criminal defendants. Worden uses data from a survey of lawyers in small towns in the state of Georgia to examine the dimensions of lawyers' attitudes toward criminal defense work. The results of her study revealed that lawyers varied in their views of the importance of due process and defendants' rights and in their attitudes toward capital punishment, the deterrent value of punishment, and defendants' potential for rehabilitation. She also found that these attitudes were affected to some extent by the respondent's age, but that other demographic and professional characteristics did not affect commitment to due process or the other dimensions. When she examined the amount of time that the respondent devoted to criminal defense work, Worden found that lawyers who expressed more support of due process, greater opposition to capital punishment, and greater skepticism of the deterrent value of punishment were more likely to spend a significant amount of their time doing criminal defense. Worden concludes by exploring the meaning of her findings given common perceptions of "the type of person relegated to criminal defense work."

SOURCE: Worden, A. P. (1998). Representing the accused: Professional values and professional choices of small-town lawyers. *Criminal Justice Review, 23,* 1–28.

Representing the Accused

Professional Values and Professional Choices of Small-Town Lawyers

Alissa Pollitz Worden

Current social science knowledge of the professional values of lawyers, particularly criminal defense lawyers, has emerged largely from qualitative studies that have documented considerable variation in the ways that attorneys view their work, their clients, and the rules and policies that constrain their practices. Between the two stereotypes of criminal lawyers encountered in popular culture and in early social science literature—the committed, adversarial idealists of Perry Mason vintage and the "con men" prowling urban courthouses for hapless clients in Blumberg's classic study (1967)—lies a diverse set of portraits that illustrate the complexity of lawyers' professional incentives and motivations (Flemming, 1986; Flemming, Nardulli, & Eisenstein, 1992; Heumann, 1981; Mather, 1974; McIntyre, 1987; Nardulli, 1986).

However, although they oversimplify the diversity of lawyers' orientations, these two stereotypes are of some value insofar as they highlight an interesting and seldom explored empirical question about lawyers' professional values and choices, particularly choices about specialization. The first stereotype, that of the idealistic, due-process-oriented, and client-centered advocate, implies a process of self-selection into criminal defense work, based on values, preferences, and empathy for the accused. The second, that of the jaded and professionally marginal practitioner who pursues criminal defendants for want of more lucrative and prestigious business, suggests that this sort of work is the last refuge of lawyers who cannot attract clients in other fields.[1] Although it is safe to say that neither image is accurate, we cannot say with much confidence which more closely approximates the truth: whether lawyers' choice to concentrate in criminal rather than civil practice is more strongly influenced by personal values or by lack of better opportunities.

This study attempts to contribute to a more complete understanding of small-town lawyers' attitudes about criminal defense work and their professional choices through both description and analysis of survey data from a sample of lawyers in private practice in communities of 30,000 or fewer residents. First, this study explores the dimensionality of lawyers' professional values and empirically derives measures of four attitudinal constructs regarding criminal defense work. Second, it examines the relationships between attorneys' social and professional backgrounds and these attitudinal dimensions. Third, it tests hypotheses about the influences of social background, professional experience, professional status, and professional values on specialization, measured as the proportion of practice devoted to criminal defense work, explicitly testing the strength of the associations between indicators of professional marginality on the one hand (and pro-defense orientations on the other) with degree of involvement in criminal defense practice. Finally, this study sheds some light, albeit indirectly, on the interplay between professional socialization and professional specialization by returning to an interesting and important question that has been raised but not conclusively answered by other researchers (Heinz & Laumann, 1982; Heumann, 1981): Do lawyers gravitate toward specializations that are compatible with their values and beliefs, or are their attitudes shaped by experiences in their chosen fields;

---

[1]The durability of this urban image is illustrated in Flemming, Nardulli, and Eisenstein's introductory discussion of criminal defense lawyers (1992, p. 3, footnote 4). These authors identify as "three seminal pieces" the work of Sudnow (1965), Blumberg (1967), and Skolnick (1967).

that is, do lawyers adopt specialties to suit their beliefs and interests, or do they adapt to the needs and interests of the clients who seek their counsel?

 ## The Professional Values of Lawyers

Most of what is known about lawyers' work and beliefs is based on three types of research. Efforts to compile data at the national level (Curran, 1986; Halliday, 1986) have revealed a great deal about the distribution of employment in the legal field, about the changing status of the traditional law firm, and about the evolving demographics of the profession. Analyses of data compiled from alumni surveys, most frequently administered by prestigious law schools, have provided information about the career paths, and the professional and financial success, of lawyers in different fields. Some of these studies have also yielded insight into the experiences of women and minorities competing in a predominantly white male profession (Chambers, 1989). However, these types of studies tell us little about how lawyers actually see and construct their practices. Richer, albeit more qualitative and anecdotal, information about lawyers' perceptions of their work has emerged from numerous case studies involving interviews and observation of lawyers and other court actors. These studies suggest that lawyers' perspectives are diverse and complex, that they may be influenced by personal and professional experiences, and that important career choices, including the decision to build criminal rather than exclusively civil practices, may be influenced by their perspectives on criminal justice issues as well as by professional opportunity and ability. Hence the literature offers a research agenda that calls for examination of the dimensions on which lawyers' professional attitudes vary, examination of the associations between personal and professional background and those attitudes, testing of hypotheses about the effects of social background, professional experience, and attitudes on the distribution of practice between criminal and civil law, and careful consideration of the implications of the findings of such analyses for our understanding of the socialization process.

Dimensionality and Disparity in Lawyers' Perspectives

One of the most important conclusions to be drawn from research on lawyers' beliefs and behavior is that their outlooks on criminal defense practice are neither uniform nor unidimensional. The disparity in outlooks (and behavior) along as fundamental a dimension as adversariness has been documented frequently. Many studies that have taken as their topic the practice of criminal law have focused intensively on public defender offices, reasonably enough inasmuch as in many cities public defenders handle almost all felony cases. Early studies were particularly concerned with describing the degree to which lawyers have or have not been coopted by the courts (Lichenstein, 1984; Schulhofer, 1988). Sudnow's classic study (1965) portrayed public defenders as more bureaucratic than adversarial, concerned with pigeonholing cases into prototypical categories in order to facilitate imposition of agreed-upon sentences. In contrast, at two different points in time Eisenstein and Jacob (1977) and McIntyre (1987) depicted the Chicago Public Defender's Office as imbued with an advocacy, if not adversarial, orientation toward dealings with clients and prosecutors. At an early point in the evolution of this literature, Mather (1974) noted that public defenders' professional orientations varied, prompting reconsideration of the stereotypes already in place (see also Skolnick, 1967). Eisenstein and Jacob (1977) further observed that the character of defense bars varied at the jurisdictional as well as the individual level, contrasting a pro-defendant and advocacy-oriented bar in Detroit with a conservative and cooperative circle of specialists in Baltimore.

Because most of these studies had as their primary objective the mapping of the plea bargaining process or the characterization of local legal cultures, they understandably attended less to the finer points of lawyers' attitudes than to more general assessments of their behavior in and out of court (see also Church, 1985).

Further, because they focused on criminal courts, they produced little in the way of comparisons between criminal defense specialists and other lawyers, or between lawyers who took on varying amounts of criminal defense work, and, importantly, they seldom addressed dimensions of lawyers' professional values other than commitment to the adversarial role and such dimensions as views on punishment, empathy with clients, and the implicit trade-off between due process protections and crime control. Recent research has attempted to address some of these issues more directly. The work of Eisenstein, Flemming, and Nardulli (1988) in nine middle-sized Midwestern communities entailed extensive interviews with lawyers who, notwithstanding their regular appearances in criminal court, maintained varying levels of involvement in other fields of law as well. From these scholars' analyses we find confirmation of the view that lawyers are concerned with their professional images and success but that such concerns do not necessarily entail trade-offs with the well-being of criminal clients (Flemming, 1986; Nardulli, 1986). These analyses also reveal fewer differences between "regulars" and "occasionals" than some have speculated may exist, and they offer suggestive evidence that lawyers' attitudes toward criminal clients may depend upon the nature of the professional relationship, i.e., whether the client has retained the lawyer or was assigned to him or her by the court (Flemming, 1986).

Other studies, notably Heumann's classic study of young lawyers' transition from law school to courthouse, reveal variation in commitment to adversarial ideals, acceptance of plea bargaining, and empathy with clients (Church, 1985; Heumann, 1981). Unsurprisingly, still other research reveals that lawyers, like other court actors, express varying beliefs about the utility of criminal sanctions and sentencing philosophies (e.g., Maynard, 1984). Such studies suggest not only that lawyers' attitudes are heterogeneous but also that they vary across related but separable dimensions, such as orientations toward clients, attitudes about adjudicative processes, and views on punishment.

The first objective of the present study is to untangle the dimensions of lawyers' attitudes toward criminal defense work, in an effort, first, to determine whether or not such attitudes constitute separable dimensions (or, alternatively, are so closely related that they constitute a single continuum) and, second, to construct measures of lawyers' attitudes toward criminal work as a prelude to modeling the correlates and consequences of attitudinal variation.

Lawyers' Attributes, Experience, and Attitudes

Because the dimensions of lawyers' attitudes toward work have not been mapped systematically, it is not surprising that little work has been done to assess the associations between attitudes and social and professional backgrounds. However, associations between attitudes and such characteristics as age, sex, ethnicity, and professional experiences are important for at least two reasons. First, associations between professional values and such attributes, if they exist, may carry implications for the collective orientation of the defense bar as it becomes more diverse. Second, because attributes such as sex and ethnicity may also be associated with specialization (for reasons having to do with employment opportunities; see Heinz & Laumann, 1982), for the purpose of examining the relationships between professional values and specialization in criminal defense work it is important to control for the possible influences of social and professional background.[2]

One of the few studies that explicitly examined attributes and attitudes was Heinz and Laumann's examination of the Chicago bar (1982). Heinz and Laumann observed, not surprisingly, that age was correlated with conservative stands on both civil libertarian and economic issues. Beyond this, very few systematic studies have reported information about professional values and personal characteristics, and our knowledge is based largely on case studies and qualitative research. Jack and Jack (1989), Menkel-Meadow

---

[2]For example, Heinz and Laumann (1982) and Levin (1977) have documented the barriers to prestigious firms and fields that are encountered by members of ethnic minorities, and Curran (1986) observed disparity in the positions held by male and female lawyers.

(1989), and others (Cain, 1988; DuBois, Dunlap, Gilligan, MacKinnon, & Menkel-Meadow, 1985) have hypothesized that gender is associated with beliefs about the optimal balance between individual freedom and rights, on the one hand, and meeting the needs of all parties to legal actions, on the other. Some of these writers have suggested that in the resolution of legal disputes women are less committed to protecting individual rights at all costs when those costs include damage and risks to others or stand in the way of a morally appropriate solution. At the same time, however, some scholars have expected to find among women stronger sympathy for the disadvantaged, a sympathy that might translate into stronger commitment to criminal defendants (Menkel-Meadow, 1989). In contrast to these theoretically based predictions, Epstein has claimed empirical support for the argument that male and female lawyers do not differ much in their professional orientations and that whatever differences do exist are greatly overshadowed by similarities (Epstein, 1988). Although the associations between race and ethnicity and attitudes have seldom been examined, there is some reason to believe that lawyers who are members of ethnic minorities are more sympathetic to society's underdogs (Heinz & Laumann, 1982; Levin, 1977).

The literature further suggests that certain professional experiences may be associated with beliefs about criminal defense work. Experience in a prosecutor's office, which is often believed to be a way station to private practice, may nevertheless render one more cynical about clients and about the adversarial process (Heumann, 1981). Professional status or marginality may also be associated with orientations toward criminal defense work, although not necessarily in a causal fashion. Portraits of urban defense "regulars"—predominantly solo practitioners operating financially marginal practices—reveal jaded individuals who are indifferent to the needs or fates of their clients (Blumberg, 1967; Casper, 1972). However,

it is by no means clear that professional marginality causes one to be less sympathetic to clients, or that indifference toward clients leads one into this often unremunerative work, or—as may be the case—that the popular stereotype is not in fact a misrepresentation of the views of criminal law specialists, at least outside a few urban areas.

The second objective of this study, therefore, is to examine the correlations between social and professional background characteristics and attitudes. Specifically, it is hypothesized that older lawyers hold less strongly pro-defendant views and that male lawyers exhibit stronger affinity than female lawyers for some (but not all) elements of criminal defense work.[3] The correlations between attitudes and indicators of professional success or marginality are examined in order to evaluate the stereotype of the indifferent marginal practitioner and as a prelude to examining the independent effects of professional marginality and pro-defendant attitudes on specialization in criminal defense work.

Experiences, Attitudes, and Specialization

The third issue addressed by this study, modeling the determinants of specialization in criminal defense work, has seldom been subject to analysis. The most significant study of specialization is again Heinz and Laumann's Chicago study (1982), whose data implicitly offered support for the notion that criminal defense practice is not so much a choice as a last resort for unsuccessful lawyers, insofar as it further confirmed what many had observed elsewhere: that criminal defense work was of low status not only in the community but within the bar itself. Heinz and Laumann attributed this not only to the economic perils of such work—criminal defendants are often unable or unwilling to pay legal bills, particularly following conviction—but also to more successful lawyers' perceptions that civil clients

---

[3]Unfortunately, the absence of data on attorney race precludes testing hypotheses about the influence of minority status on attitudes toward criminal justice and criminal defendants. This is a potentially important set of hypotheses in a state that has historically used the criminal justice system as a means of controlling black populations (Myers, 1993).

would be unenthusiastic about sharing their attorneys' talents and waiting rooms with accused criminals. This observation lends support to the notion that criminal defense work, as a less than altogether desirable vocation, might be avoided by most lawyers and sought only by those who failed in other fields of practice.

However, Heinz and Laumann's analysis also yielded some support for the hypothesis that values and beliefs shape choices about specialization, insofar as they found that attitudes were correlated with practice fields in predictable ways. Specifically, they observed that, compared with specialists in other fields, criminal defense lawyers held attitudes toward civil libertarianism and economic liberalism that were consistent with a sympathetic and advocacy-oriented role toward clients. In attempting to account for these associations, Heinz and Laumann offered several possible explanations. Observing stronger associations between specialization and attitudes in older cohorts of lawyers, they suggested that although attorneys may opt into and out of specializations based upon their personal and professional beliefs, resulting in attitudinally "purer" older cohorts of lawyers in a given field, it may also be the case that lawyers take on values that are compatible with the interests of the clients they must represent, thereby minimizing the dissonance between their personal values and their professional roles; hence an attorney who finds himself or herself engaged in personal injury or union work might begin to espouse more populist views over time, whereas one working in a corporate setting might become increasingly critical of regulation.[4]

In something of a contrast with Heinz and Laumann's speculations about the process of socialization, Heumann (1981) observed that lawyers entering criminal defense practice adapted to their roles by adopting the perspective of other courthouse actors, not their clients, modifying their original strong due process and adversarial orientations and in fact becoming more cynical (or perhaps more realistic) about the factual and legal innocence of their clients. Although Heumann's study did not directly compare criminal defense lawyers with other practitioners, it suggests that exposure to the realities of criminal court prompts lawyers to distance themselves from the adversarial and advocacy-focused orientation inculcated in law school and to cultivate instead pragmatic working relationships with other courthouse regulars, prosecutors and judges. Specifically, Heumann observed that within the first year or so of criminal practice young attorneys became less adversarial, less committed to due process ideals, and more cynical about defendants' claims. Furthermore, he observed that these changes resulted at least as much from the attorneys' growing belief in the inaccuracy of their law school idealizations of the job (and of clients) as from the purposeful attempts by more seasoned court actors to induce their conformity to local norms of plea bargaining and negotiation.

A somewhat different perspective on specialization is implied by Jack and Jack's study (1989), the findings of which suggest that, at least in the context of criminal defense practice, although attitudes may not lead lawyers into fields of practice that are compatible with their values, they may keep them out of those fields with which they are incompatible. Jack and Jack examined the tensions between lawyers' professional ethics, their loyalties to clients, and the ways in which they defined the lawyer's role in society in the context of competing definitions of morality. Drawing upon research that identified broad differences in the ways in which people define morality, particularly when trade-offs must be made between the rights of individuals and the protection of relationships within groups and communities (see Gilligan, 1982), these authors concluded that some lawyers confront difficult moral and ethical dilemmas when faced with real and hypothetical criminal cases.[5] To some extent, their findings suggest, the choice to

---

[4]These patterns only imprecisely reflect the experience of criminal defense specialists, however, because Heinz and Laumann grouped criminal defense, civil rights, and labor union attorneys together for some of their analyses.

[5]The hypotheticals that Jack and Jack used to examine moral dilemmas included a criminal case in which, as in "every lawyer's nightmare" (McIntyre, 1987), a lawyer's skillful use of tactics might result in the acquittal of a factually guilty and dangerous client. Some lawyers in that study found it impossible to reconcile their ethical commitment to their client's rights and interests with the potential societal consequences.

avoid criminal law reflects an attorney's inability to reconcile an advocacy orientation with a broader conception of obligation to society. This provocative research, although based on a small sample of lawyers, suggests that decisions about practice may be related to the compatibility of one's personal values with the idealized advocate's ethical role.

The third objective of this research is to simultaneously examine two hypotheses about specialization: first, that professional marginality leads to higher levels of involvement in criminal defense work and, second, that attitudes and beliefs about criminal defense work and defendants influence lawyers' levels of involvement in criminal practice. Of course these hypotheses are not mutually exclusive, but they carry different implications, both for social scientists' understanding of the professional lives of lawyers and, possibly, for the quality and commitment of the criminal defense bar. In an attempt to further explore these alternative accounts of the process of specialization and to shed some light on the socialization process among lawyers, a final objective of this study is replication of Heinz and Laumann's examination of the homogeneity of attitudes among specialists of different cohorts and reconsideration of the implications of homogeneity and heterogeneity within cohorts for our understanding of socialization.

⚞ Data and Analyses

Our understanding of criminal defense lawyers' choices and motivations is somewhat limited by the fact that most empirical studies have examined only attorneys who engaged in that specialization, in the public or private sector. Such samples cannot reveal much about the ways in which these lawyers are similar to or different from their colleagues in civil practice. Furthermore, most research on lawyers has been conducted in urban areas, where specialization is undoubtedly more prevalent, and perhaps more necessary for professional survival, than is

the case in small towns. The generalizability of such research is therefore limited. Very little is known about the small-town counterparts of urban advocates. However, research on this sector of the bar is important and interesting in its own right. Studies of small-town courts reveal important urban-rural differences in processes and practices (Austin, 1981; Eisenstein, 1982; Myers & Talarico, 1986, 1987), differences that might be attributable in part to differences in the characters of local bars. Moreover, the type of practice that is most typically encountered in small towns, one that is diverse rather than highly specialized, is not extinct in larger communities, although it has seldom been the subject of social scientists' attention. Hence the present study examines the attitudes, values, and practices of a sample of small-town lawyers, lawyers practicing in communities with 30,000 or fewer residents.

Testing hypotheses about lawyers' attitudes and work requires attitudinal and professional data from a large and diverse enough sample of attorneys to justify generalizing about differences in values. Data were collected through a survey of attorneys in Georgia, during the summer of 1986.[6] Georgia is an appropriate site for this study for several reasons. It is demographically diverse, yielding significant variation in community size and structure. The small communities within the state are also politically and economically diverse, including stereotypically traditional, long-settled, predominantly African-American communities in the southern part of the state, politically liberal college towns, very rural villages still reliant on agricultural employment, and mill towns elsewhere in the state. Further, it has been the site of a number of significant studies of criminal court decision making, in part because its court system, which is highly localized, characterized by strong prosecutors, and statutorily reliant on indeterminate sentencing, is quite typical of many other states (Gibson, 1978; Giles & Walker, 1975; Myers & Talarico, 1987).

---

[6]Although an attempt was made to survey public defenders (in those few circuits that provided such an agency), these individuals were not readily identified in either of the sources consulted, and those who were identified were excluded from the following analyses. Indigent defense is organized and funded at the county level in Georgia, and in 1986 two thirds of the 159 counties still retained ad hoc assigned counsel systems, although a few were experimenting with contract systems (Worden & Worden, 1989).

Because the focus of this research is the study of criminal defense attorneys and not the entire profession, and because many (in urban areas, most) lawyers exclude criminal work from their practice, the sampling method was designed to access only those lawyers who actually practiced in criminal court. In order to ensure that rural areas were adequately represented, surveys were sent to a sample of approximately 30 attorneys in each of the state's 45 judicial circuits. Attorneys in private practice were initially identified through the *Georgia Legal Directory,* and their fields of practice were ascertained through cross-checking with telephone book business pages in their communities. Samples were drawn from each circuit by means of a three-tiered strategy. As it turned out, in cities of more than 80,000 there were significant numbers of lawyers who advertised themselves as criminal defense practitioners, so it was logical to conclude (and this was confirmed through informal interviewing) that a lawyer who did much criminal work in that venue would advertise accordingly. Hence samples from communities of this size were randomly drawn from those who advertised criminal work. In cities of 30,000 to 80,000 there were at least 30 lawyers who represented themselves as at least general practitioners (and whose advertisements did not explicitly exclude criminal work from their specialties), so again a random sample of 30 was taken from these communities. Lawyers in communities of fewer than 30,000 seldom identified any specialty at all, although some designated themselves as general practitioners, so random samples of 30 were taken from these as well (although, in very rural circuits, the entire population of practicing lawyers was included to reach that target number).[7]

The focus of this paper is on criminal defense practice in small towns, so the analyses reported below were conducted on the subsample of respondents who practiced in communities with populations of no more than 30,000. The overall response rate on the survey was 41 percent, a rate that compares favorably with those achieved by previous surveys of legal actors (Bernat & Zupan, 1989; Carbon, Holden, & Berkson, 1982; Martin, 1987; Ryan & Alfini, 1979).[8] The survey included items on general attitudes and beliefs regarding the criminal justice system, as well as items dealing with more specific perceptions of local criminal justice systems. Questions were also included on respondents' social and professional backgrounds.

Both the resulting sample of lawyers and the communities were diverse. The lawyers worked in small communities scattered throughout 38 of the state's 45 circuits and 105 of the state's 159 counties. Most of the unrepresented circuits were, of course, those that make up the Atlanta metropolitan area. The average town population was 8,289, although communities ranged in size from 317 to 29,654. The average household income in the counties in which lawyers worked ranged from $9,930 to $22,600, and the percentage of the counties' populations engaged in white-collar occupations ranged from 33 percent to 63 percent. These figures suggest that these communities are not uniformly poor and agricultural, despite their small size and despite popular stereotypes of rural southern poverty. Not surprisingly, 90 percent of the lawyers practiced in county seats.

The bars in these communities appear to be relatively unspecialized, at least insofar as a broad distinction is made between predominantly civil and predominantly criminal practice. On average, attorneys reported that their practices consisted of 21 percent criminal work, but about half the respondents reported figures lower than 10 percent, and fewer than

---

[7]There existed the possibility, of course, that a lawyer might work in a small community that is simply a suburb of a more populous city and hence would draw clients from the larger urban area (and should not, therefore, be considered a "small town" lawyer). This turned out to be the case in one community adjacent to Atlanta. Respondents from that community were excluded.

[8]Of the 1,238 attorneys originally surveyed, 639 returned questionnaires. However, of these 639, 509 completed all items needed for these analyses, for an effective response rate of 41 percent. Of these 509, 360 practiced in small towns; this group comprised the sample reported in the analyses. An examination of the differences, in terms of sex, age, practice type, and community, revealed no significant differences between those who completed all attitudinal items and those who did not.

1 in 10 respondents reported practices of greater than 50 percent criminal work. The lawyers themselves were predominantly male (91 percent) and middle-aged (average age 42, range from 25 to 82).[9] Although 41 percent reported that they practiced alone, the modal firm in which respondents worked had two or three attorneys, and 18 percent of lawyers reported that their firms had at least four partners and associates. One in four respondents had previously worked as a prosecutor.

It is instructive to note that respondents excluded from this study—those practicing in communities of more than 30,000, identified on the basis of their advertised specialization in criminal law—did not differ as dramatically from the small-town sample as might have been expected. In terms of sex, average age, and prosecutorial experience these two subsamples were identical, and although as a result of the sampling strategy lawyers in larger communities were more involved in criminal law (on average, 43 percent of their practices were criminal work) only a few reported practices consisting of greater than 60 percent criminal work. Fewer lawyers in the more urbanized subsample practiced alone (32 percent), but the typical respondent's firm had no more than three partners and associates. The potential significance of these subsample similarities is addressed in the conclusions. They are worth noting at this point because they speak to the generalizability of small-town samples, insofar as they suggest that the bars of small communities may resemble subsets of more urban bars, the subsets that are most likely to appear in criminal court.

Dimensions of Professional Values

In order to explore the dimensions of lawyers' professional values, a factor analysis of 16 attitudinal items was performed. The factor analysis produced four factors with eigenvalues exceeding 1.0, and items loading at .50

or above on each factor were included in an index variable for that dimension. Factor scales correlate with their corresponding indices at .89 or above for all four dimensions. Virtually identical factor results were obtained when the analysis was run on the full state sample.

The four attitudinal dimensions emerging from this analysis are described in Table 3.6. Although at first glance one might observe that each of the included items in some fashion taps respondents' feelings about criminal defendants, in fact the factor analysis suggests that attorneys' attitudes cannot be simplistically characterized as unidimensional. Lawyers vary in their views of the importance of due process and defendant rights, in their views on capital punishment, in their beliefs about the value of deterrence as a punishment philosophy, and in their outlook on the rehabilitative potential of criminal defendants.

Clearly, all these dimensions reflect variation in what could be broadly labeled an advocacy or pro-defendant orientation. Those who highly value due process rights, oppose the death penalty, are skeptical of the efficacy of deterrence policies, and are optimistic about rehabilitation are archetypical advocates, committed to legal principles and correctional philosophies that well serve accused clients in an adversarial arena. Although these dimensions are associated with each other in predictable ways (higher levels of cynicism are associated with greater belief in deterrence, for example), correlations among these four indices do not exceed .30, suggesting that they are in fact independent dimensions of attorneys' professional perspectives.

Importantly, these dimensions reflect themes that have emerged elsewhere in the literature on defense lawyers. The strength of one's commitment to due process, as contrasted with crime control, is not necessarily associated with a rehabilitative outlook toward accused criminals; Jack and Jack (1989) and McIntyre (1987) have documented some lawyers' ability to dissociate their role as protector of individual rights

---

[9]An item about racial identity was excluded from the survey after pretests in two circuits suggested that attorneys were likely to leave it blank. A possible explanation for this emerged from subsequent interviews with court actors, as well as comments made in the margins of surveys, indicating that race remains a sensitive topic in some legal communities and that, despite the fact that the surveys guaranteed anonymity, black (and, in some circuits, female) lawyers were so rare that they felt their anonymity could not be ensured if they revealed their race or sex.

Table 3.6   Dimensions of Lawyers' Professional Values

Due process orientation (range 3–18; mean = 13.82; *SD* = 3.45)

Defendants have so many constitutionally protected rights today that they can usually avoid the penalties they deserve (high values = disagreement with statement).

Self-placement of respondent on a 6-point scale anchored by the values of crime control and due process (What do you see as the most appropriate function of a criminal defense attorney—protecting the rights of clients or protecting society from crime?).

Placement of the court system on a 6-point scale anchored by the values of crime control and due process (What do you see as the most important function of the criminal courts—protecting the rights of defendants or protecting society from crime?).

Opposition to capital punishment (range 0–3; mean = .61; *SD* = .89)

The death penalty is morally wrong (high values = agreement).

Some crimes are so heinous that the death penalty is the only appropriate penalty (high values = disagreement).

If the law allowed for life imprisonment without parole, the death penalty would not be necessary (high values = agreement).

Skepticism about deterrence (range 0–3; mean = 2.13; *SD* = .89)

Deterrence is the most appropriate sentencing philosophy for the courts to adopt (high values = disagreement).

The death penalty deters (high values = disagreement).

The appeals process for the death penalty should be shortened (high values = disagreement).

Rehabilitative outlook (range 0–4, mean = 2.43; *SD* = 1.18)

Individuals are fundamentally good or bad, and there aren't many events or experiences that change their basic characters (high values = disagreement).

Once someone has demonstrated a willingness to commit crime, there's not much to be gained in trying to convince him that crime doesn't pay (high values = disagreement).

Rehabilitation is the most appropriate sentencing philosophy for the courts to adopt (high values = disagreement).

Incapacitation is the most appropriate sentencing philosophy for the courts to adopt (high values = disagreement).

against powerful prosecutors from any conviction that their clients are particularly worthy or redeemable persons. Five items about the death penalty were included in the survey and, although they tap differing moral and policy issues, they emerge as significant on two different factors, the first associated with deterrence and the second with the moral acceptability of the death penalty. This suggests that lawyers, unlike many members of the general public, distinguish between utilitarian and symbolic or moral justifications for capital punishment (Bohm, Flanagan, & Harris, 1990; Finckenauer, 1988). Finally, as the means and standard deviations suggest, lawyers varied a great deal on all of these dimensions, and their overall means, while only somewhat more pro-defendant than those of judges who were included in a parallel survey, were significantly more pro-defendant than the views of prosecutors in the same study (Worden, 1990), a finding that is consistent with others' research on courthouse actors (Church, 1985; Nardulli, Flemming, & Eisenstein, 1984).

 # Correlates of Professional Values

Table 3.7 examines correlations between attorneys' professional values and seven variables that are frequently, if casually, associated with attitudes toward criminal justice, some of them in the general public as well as among court actors: age, sex, prosecutorial experience, three measures of professional status (firm size, hourly fee, and solo practice), and town population (which is included as a control variable in regression analyses that follow). It should be noted that these associations are not necessarily expected to be causal. For instance, professional status variables such as solo practice are examined in order to guard against spurious findings in the subsequent analysis of criminal defense practice. Regression analyses yielded coefficients of similar (small) magnitudes, indicating that these variables apparently do not confound each others' effects on attitudes.

Age was hypothesized to be associated with more conservative views. In the criminal justice context, conservatism is most commonly associated with attitudes that are unsympathetic to the accused. Indeed, these data indicate that older lawyers were less strongly oriented toward due process than their younger colleagues, and they were slightly more likely to believe that deterrence is a viable sentencing philosophy and that rehabilitation is not. Age is associated in the predicted direction with opposition to capital punishment, although the correlation does not reach statistical significance.[10] Consistently with predictions, women were found to be slightly less aligned with the due process ideal than men, and slightly more likely to believe in rehabilitation, although both associations are very modest. Former prosecutors differed from their colleagues only insofar as they were less likely to register opposition to the death penalty—not a surprising finding in a state in which chief prosecutors experience political pressure to seek capital punishment and hence probably seldom hire assistants who do not share that perspective.

Because low status is often ascribed to criminal defense work, its relationship to attitudinal variables is

Table 3.7 Correlations Between Attorney Attributes and Attitudes				
	Due Process Orientation	**Opposition to Death Penalty**	**Skepticism About Deterrence**	**Rehabilitative Outlook**
Age	−.273*	.011	−.088*	−.075*
Sex (female)	−.080*	−.023	.021	.064
Prosecutorial experience	.023	−.170*	.060	−.042
Hourly fee for criminal work	.038	−.035	.012	.001
Firm size: 4 members or larger	.014	−.045	.002	−.010
Solo practitioner	−.009	.014	.014	.057
Town population in 1000s	.082*	−.035	−.028	.022

* Indicates correlation coefficient statistically significant at the .10 level, one-tailed test.

---

[10]Strictly speaking, of course, tests of statistical significance are irrelevant because no argument is made here that the sample is representative of lawyers either in the state or within constituent circuits. Statistical significance guides are included only for those readers who may cautiously employ them in an effort to judge the substantive significance of the observed associations.

examined in order to assess the possibility that empirical relationships between either attitudes or professional status and criminal defense specialization are spurious. Without data on income, size and stability of clientele, and reputation, professional status is difficult to measure. However, data were available on three proxies for success. Hourly fees, membership in a larger firm (four or more partners and associates), and solo practitioner status are variables that are associated with degree of professional success and stability. Respondents were asked how much they charged, at an estimated hourly rate, for criminal defense work. Values ranged from $20 to $300 per hour, with a mean of $75.[11] Membership in a larger firm denotes more professional status and security than two- or three-person partnerships. Solo practice denotes the opposite end of the scale; such individuals often lack the infrastructure, research resources, professional status, and personal connections to attract and retain clients with financially rewarding legal problems, and their practices may serve primarily "one-shotters" seeking counsel in personal crises such as divorce, injury, or arrest rather than individuals and businesses seeking ongoing advice in negotiating legal agreements and preventing legal problems (Galanter, 1975; Sarat & Grossman, 1975). As Table 3.7 indicates, these limited measures of professional success or status exhibit no substantively significant correlations with attitudes toward criminal defense work.

Finally, the size of respondents' towns was included in regression analyses as a control for the opportunity to specialize (larger towns offer a larger and more diverse potential clientele, as well as more competition). Town size is not correlated at meaningful levels with any of the attitudinal variables. In analyses of the full sample of lawyers, which over-samples criminal specialists in larger towns, city respondents appeared to be more strongly oriented toward due process, more likely to oppose capital punishment, less enthusiastic about deterrence, and less cynical about human nature than those in small towns. However, it cannot be conclusively determined that this is an effect or correlate of urbanization rather than of criminal specialization, particularly given the results that are reported in the next section.

To summarize, despite conventional wisdom and widespread perceptions about the relationship between social and individual characteristics and criminal justice attitudes (Finckenauer, 1988; Glick & Pruet, 1985; Miller, Rossi, & Simpson, 1986) it appears that at, least among small-town lawyers, variables such as age, sex, and professional circumstances do not covary with views about the criminal justice system and defendants, at least as measured here. The discovery that the hypotheses tested here, derived from what we know about popular opinion and attitudes, are not supported among lawyers is a significant one, insofar as it corroborates research on other court actors that has found surprisingly few associations between social background characteristics, attitudes, and decision making (Myers, 1988; Spohn, 1990). Based on these null findings, one might very cautiously speculate that, even though lawyers who work in criminal court are by no means attitudinally homogeneous, factors such as self-selection into the career, legal education, and professional socialization tend to dilute or displace the effects of social background that are found among the nonlawyer public.

Criminal Defense Practice: Choice or Necessity?

The preceding section examined bivariate relationships between personal and professional characteristics and attitudes. These data offer little evidence that the available measures of lawyers' personal and professional backgrounds (other than perhaps age) predict their views on criminal defense work. The next step in this study is to examine the alternative explanations for variation in levels of involvement with criminal defense work that were raised at the outset of this paper: Is it the case that lawyers who devote more of their practice to criminal law do so because they hold values compatible with that specialization, or because they occupy the

---

[11]These figures do not include attorneys' estimates of compensation for court appointments in indigent cases.

margins of the profession and have little choice but to accept cases that other attorneys can turn down? The analyses in Tables 3.8 and 3.9 present some suggestive evidence bearing on this question.

Table 3.8 presents two models of the proportion of practice devoted to criminal defense work. Model I, presented in the first columns of Table 3.8, presents regression analyses of the influences of social background characteristics and professional status on criminal practice, measured as the percentage of practice

devoted to criminal work.[12] Not surprisingly, solo practitioners invested a little more of their practice in criminal defense than members of firms, and members of larger firms did somewhat less criminal work than their colleagues in small partnerships. As expected, specialization was more prevalent (in criminal defense and probably in other fields as well) in more populous towns, probably because below a certain population threshold specialization of many kinds is simply not feasible for lack of clients.[13]

Table 3.8 Correlations Between Attorney Attributes and Attitudes

	Model I		Model II	
	B(SEB)	b	B(SEB)	b
Age	−.094 (.096)	−.053	−.000 (.096)	−.000
Sex (female)	−.906 (3.645)	−.013	.357 (3.515)	.004
Prosecutorial experience	−.152 (2.322)	−.003	.801 (2.272)	.018
Hourly fee for criminal work	.025 (.049)	.028	.021 (.047)	.023
Firm of 4 or more attorneys	−6.915 (2.860)	−.140*	−6.335 (2.738)	−.128*
Solo practitioner	4.936 (2.284)	.126*	4.781 (2.189)	.122*
Town population in 1000s	.547 (.165)	.178**	.540 (.156)	.176**
Due process orientation			.838 (.313)	.150**
Opposition to capital punishment			3.715 (1.197)	.171*
Skepticism about deterrence			2.259 (1.179)	.105*
Rehabilitative outlook			.136 (.866)	.008
Constant	17.707 (5.478)		−5.259 (7.765)	
R^2	.063		.155	
$n = 360$				

* Indicates correlation coefficient statistically significant at the .05 level, one-tailed test.

** Indicates correlation coefficient statistically significant at the .01 level, one-tailed test.

---

[12]Because percentage of practice devoted to criminal defense work is an interval level variable, it is appropriate for ordinary least squares regression. There are many other ways of conceptualizing degree of specialization, however. Parallel analyses that employed categorical variables (0% to 24%, 25% to 49%, 50% to 74%, 75% and above) yielded very similar findings, indicating that the results here do not mask curvilinear relationships between attitudes and practice.

[13]It was originally hypothesized that, once other factors were controlled, characteristics of indigent defense programs might influence levels of involvement in criminal work. In particular, it was hypothesized that the generosity with which indigent defense was provided, as well as the presence of a public defender or contract system (which presumably would monopolize a large share of criminal cases), might reduce the market for private practitioners' services. Data on these two variables were acquired at the circuit level, but neither appeared to be associated with an aggregate measure of specialization (the proportion of respondents whose practices consisted of at least 25 percent criminal work). This may be due to the often overlooked fact that criminal lawyers do a great deal of misdemeanor work, and their estimates of time spent on criminal cases reflect that, but they may have relatively few court assignments on misdemeanors.

However, age, sex, prosecutorial experience, and hourly fee were not associated with criminal defense work.

Model II adds to the social and professional background variables the attitudinal measures described above. Although age, sex, prosecutorial experience, and hourly fee continue to exert no significant effects on specialization in criminal work, and although the coefficients for firm size, solo practice, and town population remain the same, three of the four attitudinal measures exert statistically significant effects on criminal practice. Lawyers who expressed higher valuations of due process, greater opposition to capital punishment, and greater skepticism about the value of deterrence were more likely to devote significant shares of their practices to criminal defense work. It should be noted that, although the proportion of variance explained by this equation is modest, the inclusion of these attitude measures increases explained variance by almost 150 percent.[14]

The Attitude-Specialization Correlation: Adoption or Adaptation?

The finding that professional values are associated with greater involvement in criminal defense work when measures of professional success and standing are controlled is significant in that it offers some support for the view that advocacy-oriented lawyers choose to practice criminal law. This finding echoes, albeit with a more precise measure of criminal defense specialization and more focused measures of professional values, Heinz and Laumann's conclusions about the relationships between attitudes and practice in urban Chicago and their inference regarding self-selection into fields of specialization, and it reproduces these general findings in a sample of lawyers in small-town rather than urban settings.

Of course, cross-sectional analysis of this type cannot convincingly demonstrate a process of choice. An alternative interpretation of these relationships is that the causal arrow points the other way—that lawyers

who find themselves immersed in criminal defense work become more advocacy-oriented as their experience with criminal courts and criminal clients accumulates. This might be the case because the actual experience of regularly representing criminal defendants makes one more sympathetic to their needs and interests, or because criminal lawyers adopt a professional perspective that justifies their unpopular role as advocate for accused criminals. Research that directly addresses this question is scarce and conflicting. Although Heumann's study of Connecticut defense lawyers (1981) found that lawyers' allegiance to clients weakened as their understanding of their role in the courthouse work group evolved, McIntyre (1987) has presented some evidence indicating that experience rendered Chicago public defenders more protective of client rights, in part because they became more disillusioned with local prosecutors and judges and in part because they came to see their clients as interesting and likeable people notwithstanding their alleged misdeeds.

Without longitudinal data on lawyers' attitudes and socialization, this alternative hypothesis, that lawyers adapt to the practices that befall them by espousing attitudes consistent with their clients' interests (and consistent with the actions they must take on their clients' behalf), cannot be conclusively tested. However, it can be subjected to cautious inferential investigation, as demonstrated by Heinz and Laumann in their analysis of cohorts and specialization. Heinz and Laumann observed that, although age and experience made lawyers more conservative, the attitudinal gap between specialists in some fields and nonspecialists was most pronounced in older cohorts. They inferred from this pattern that lawyers who find that their values are not compatible with the interests and needs of a particular clientele work harder at finding alternatives and at minimizing their investment in that field of practice. This process of self-selection produces more homogeneous professional values, values compatible with client interests, among older cohorts of lawyers in a field. If lawyers merely adapted

---

[14]It is interesting to note that when the same analyses are run on the full sample the same results obtain (with the exception of a larger coefficient for town population).

their expressed beliefs to comport with practices that evolved out of opportunity, expediency, or financial necessity, one might have expected differences in attitudes among specialists that were relatively consistent across cohorts. Table 3.9 presents results of an attempt to replicate Heinz and Laumann's analysis with the Georgia small-town sample data.

Heinz and Laumann classified as criminal defense specialists lawyers who devoted more than 25 percent of their practice to that subfield. The same threshold was adopted for the categorical analysis in Table 3.9. Although Heinz and Laumann trichotomized age to reflect natural breaks in their distribution, in preliminary analyses a similar approach with the present data suggested that, in contrast with Heinz and Laumann's sample, the middle group (32 to 42 years old) were more advocacy-oriented on some measures than either older or younger cohorts. Therefore an effort was made

to categorize age by generation, on the assumption that the experiences of coming of age in a certain era may have as much effect on one's values as the maturing process or years of experience.

This strategy produced a four-category variable for generation. The first category included respondents born before 1927, who came of age before or during World War II and who were at least of draft age during the end of that war *(n* = 20 nonspecialists, 13 specialists). The second category included respondents born between 1927 and 1946, whose late adolescence and early adulthood occurred in the affluent postwar era *(n* = 105 nonspecialists, 40 specialists). The third category included lawyers born between 1947 and 1956, a category now known as baby boomers, whose common cultural experiences include knowledge of, if not necessarily participation in, Vietnam, the civil rights movement, and the

Table 3.9 Values, Generation, and Criminal Practice

Generation	Due Process Orientation			Opposition to Death Penalty		
	Less Than 25% Crim		At Least 25% Crim	Less Than 25% Crim		At Least 25% Crim
Born prior to 1926	11.43	−.12	11.31	.50	+.19	.69
Born 1927–1946	13.10	+*.140*	14.50	.52	+*.43*	.95
Born 1947–1957	14.11	+*1.34*	15.45	.47	+*.43*	.90
Born after 1958	13.58	+1.10	14.69	.25	+.38	.63
Generation	Skepticism About Deterrence			Rehabilitative Outlook		
	Less Than 25% Crim		At Least 25% Crim	Less Than 25% Crim		At Least 25% Crim
Born prior to 1926	1.90	−.13	1.77	2.15	+.16	2.31
Born 1927–1946	2.17	+.03	2.20	2.38	+.14	2.53
Born 1947–1957	1.96	+*.55*	2.51	2.38	+*.27*	2.64
Born after 1958	1.92	.33	2.25	2.75	−.50	2.25

NOTE. Entries are mean values for subcategories. Columns in bold show the differences between specialists and nonspecialists within each category. Italics indicate that differences are statistically significant at the .05 level.

counterculture of the 1960s (*n* = 103 nonspecialists, 59 specialists), and of growing cynicism about the reforms of the 1960s (*n* = 12 nonspecialists, 8 specialists).[15]

Table 3.9 offers tentative information about three issues in the form of mean values on each of the four attitudinal dimensions, broken down by generation and specialization. These data must be interpreted very cautiously because of the small number of respondents included in the youngest and oldest categories, but they offer some intriguing, if only suggestive, findings. First, as one might have predicted from the foregoing analyses, these data suggest that, across most values and within most generational groupings, specialists were in fact more advocacy-oriented than lawyers who did less than 25 percent of their business with criminal clients. They were more strongly oriented toward due process, were more strongly opposed to the death penalty, were less cynical, and had less confidence in the value of deterrence.

Second, however, this breakdown does not clearly reproduce Heinz and Laumann's finding about the role of cohort as a surrogate for self-selection in widening the attitudinal gap between specialists and nonspecialists on relevant professional values. One could not derive suggestive evidence from these data that time provides increasing opportunity to develop a practice compatible with one's personal values (as Heinz and Laumann did). This leaves open the possibility, although it by no means confirms it, that lawyers in fact adapt to the practices in which they find themselves.

If anything, the oldest cohort exhibits the smallest differences between the two groups of lawyers across two of the four dimensions, and very small differences are exhibited on the other two. It is important to note that these differences are substantively small and do not just fail to reach statistical significance (which might have been predicted from the small *n*s). The youngest lawyers, the most senior of whom in 1986 could not have been practicing for more than four or five years, exhibited overall differences of similar magnitude to those in other categories, with one surprising exception: Young specialists were less favorably inclined toward rehabilitation than all other categories except the oldest nonspecialists. Further, the differences between specialists and nonspecialists across the two middle cohorts, which are represented by larger samples of attorneys, also fail to support the notion that experience increases the gap.

Finally, one unexpected pattern in these data merits notice.[16] Across the cohorts, among both specialists and nonspecialists, on all attitudinal dimensions except rehabilitative outlook, there is a slight curvilinear relationship. The youngest lawyers, those who went to college during the Carter years and who were making key educational and career decisions as the national climate became increasingly conservative, exhibited weaker pro-defendant attitudes than their more seasoned colleagues. Notably, they were more committed to capital punishment than even their most senior fellow lawyers. This pattern may reflect either the generally more conservative, anti-defendant attitudes expressed in public discourse at the time or a shift in the types of young people pursuing careers in law, including criminal law.[17] These

---

[15]It is worth noting that, in terms of their criminal practices at least, this definition of specialist produces remarkably similar distributions of specialists and nonspecialists across cohorts. The mean values for criminal defense work across cohorts of nonspecialists range from 6 percent to 9 percent, and the mean values for such work across cohorts of specialists range from 42 percent to 47 percent.

[16]There is no clear pattern of exceptionally strong pro-defendant attitudes among either specialists or nonspecialists among baby boomers, the group most likely to have been socialized into greater empathy with criminal defendants and stronger commitment to defendants' rights. With the exception of stronger due process views, they were little different from their slightly older colleagues. This may come as something of a surprise to those who believe that law schools in the late 1960s and 1970s turned out liberal advocates (although such a phenomenon, if indeed it occurred at all, may have been particularly subtle in Georgia).

[17]Illustrative evidence of this might be seen in the fact that the greatest divergence between specialists and nonspecialists on the deterrence and rehabilitative dimensions exists among baby boomers. Law schools may attract students with different sorts of values in different eras, and the law may have seemed like a particularly efficacious career choice for reform-minded students during the civil rights campaigns, the antipoverty movement, and the Supreme Court's "due process revolution." Hence a subset of "baby boom" lawyers may have opted into the career with particularly liberal views, while no doubt a significant number of their classmates were more typically oriented towards success in business. The result may have been that this particular generation produced an unusually heterogeneous crop of attorneys, whose disparate views on the legal system led them into different career paths.

data, of course, do not permit empirical examination of these competing possibilities. At the same time, the oldest lawyers were, less surprisingly, more conservative than their younger colleagues. The middle groups were most strongly defendant-oriented among both specialists and nonspecialists.

It must be emphasized that these apparent patterns were generated by small samples, and also that very young lawyers practicing in small towns in a state that offers many metropolitan opportunities may be particularly unrepresentative of their generation. However, subsequent research replicating these patterns would constitute a strong argument for carefully reconsidering the routine inclusion of age as an indicator of a universal maturation process in studies of attitudes and behavior of all court actors, as well as a justification for further exploration of the impact of broad temporal and generational socialization effects on professional attitudes.

Hence, although these results do not support the hypothesis that aging cohorts of attorneys become increasingly polarized as they consolidate their practices in ideologically comfortable fields, and they cannot exclude the possibility that lawyers merely adapt their professional views to minimize dissonance with their professional obligations, these findings are not inconsistent with the initial conclusion that lawyers' beliefs are significant determinants of the choice to practice criminal law, more significant than professional status and success. The divergence between the present findings and those of Heinz and Laumann highlights the value of examining differing populations of lawyers. These differences may be attributable to the pronounced differences in the two samples: Heinz and Laumann's urban sample represents an environment in which some degree of specialization may be almost imperative for competitive practice; in the small-town subsample examined here, lawyers probably make choices not about which specialties will define their practices but rather about which specialties they should eschew altogether and which they should more routinely incorporate into their work. In small towns, one is more likely to be known as a lawyer who takes criminal cases, not as a criminal lawyer.

 Summary

These analyses offer some empirical insight into the dimensions along which lawyers' professional values, or at least their professional values that are associated with criminal adjudication, vary. It appears that lawyers' perspectives on the criminal process and the attorney's role therein are not unidimensional. Instead, they encompass distinguishable attitudes about process, punishment, and defendants themselves. Furthermore, these data offer little support for the expectation that age—conceptualized in a linear fashion, connoting a cumulative maturation process—sex, and prosecutorial experience are related to professional values. Nor is there much evidence that lawyers in different practice settings, or of varying levels of success, differ much in their values. It would be erroneous to dismiss these results as nonfindings, or to characterize the findings as insignificant, merely because they are null findings (or, more accurately, are findings of null relationships). These results do add to growing evidence that, although attitudes about criminal justice issues vary among professionals as well as lay people, the explanations for that variation reside in different sets of variables for these two populations.

Most significantly, these data offer some evidence that, in spite of longstanding stereotypes about the type of person relegated to criminal defense work, lawyers' involvement in criminal defense is not associated with indicators of professional success, and it is only modestly associated with the size of their community; investment in criminal practice does covary, however, with professional values that reflect an advocacy orientation. Although cross-sectional data may shed more shadows than light on the alternative interpretation of these relationships—that expressed attitudes are the consequence rather than the cause of a concentration in criminal defense work—the analyses presented here suggest that the gaps in the perspectives of criminal law specialists and nonspecialists are about as strong among young attorneys as they are among those in their professional prime, and are even stronger than among older lawyers.

⊠ Discussion and Conclusions

Despite a growing literature on the professional lives of lawyers, little is known about the attitudes that they hold toward their clients, their roles, and the public policies that infuse their daily work. Even less is known about the extent to which variations in lawyers' values and beliefs influence the ways in which they carry out their professional responsibilities. Drawing upon the observations and predictions of three decades of qualitative (and, to a much more limited extent, quantitative) studies, this study provides systematic documentation of the complexity of lawyers' professional perspectives, highlights contrasting descriptions of the socialization and specialization processes, and illustrates the value of research in small towns.

Like all efforts to study attitudes and behavior of criminal justice decision makers, this exploratory analysis is subject to many qualifications. Survey designs that elicit attitudinal information are subject to exaggeration and inaccuracy on the part of respondents and, in a field that is well supplied with qualitative and interview-based studies, only more systematic and extensive data collection is likely to permit testing of the many hypotheses generated by earlier work. The generalizability of this study's findings for the issue of lawyers' specialization is limited because, in the area of criminal defense practice—a field that, compared with real estate or tax law, arguably requires more conscious reconciliation of one's role as an advocate with one's role as a citizen, businessperson, or parent (Jack & Jack, 1989; McIntyre, 1987)—one might expect to find that professional values more strongly influence the choice to specialize than would be the case in fields that less explicitly pit the interests of clients against the protection of society. Finally, because lawyers' attitudes, and not their behavior, were subject to study here, this study can offer no observations about whether or not lawyers' orientations influence the way they do their jobs, or even whether or not advocacy-oriented lawyers are more effective than those with less pro-defendant views. It remains for future research to examine those perplexing associations.

One additional caveat is in order. Because this study focused primarily on private practice, these data do not reveal the extent to which lawyers' practices involve court appointments (although presumably lawyers would include such work in their estimates of how much of their practices are devoted to criminal defense work). Two thirds of the respondents reported working in circuits characterized by appointed counsel rather than public defender or contract systems, and of these respondents 85 percent reported accepting at least one criminal court appointment during the preceding five years. Although there is no way of knowing the extent to which some respondents' practices may have consisted of significant numbers of such appointments, the wide distribution of this responsibility suggests that in many if not most jurisdictions these cases are distributed throughout the bar rather than concentrated in the hands of a few lawyers.

Within the limitations imposed by these caveats, however, this study offers some insight into lawyers' views of their work and highlights some directions for future research. First, this analysis suggests that lawyers' professional attitudes toward criminal defense work are not unidimensional. Although this is not a surprising finding, it is one that has not been systematically documented in the literature. Future research might profitably attempt to replicate, and perhaps add to, the dimensions uncovered in these data and to ascertain which among them are most salient in lawyers' professional decisions and behavior.

Second, and most importantly, these data offer evidence that lawyers' values are associated with their choices about criminal defense work. This finding echoes in the criminal court context some of the more generalized results of Heinz and Laumann's research, supporting the view that lawyers are more likely to take on clients whose needs and interests are compatible with their own perceptions of the advocate's role in the court. The question of whether or not this pattern is generalizable to other fields of practice, such as labor law or corporate work, cannot be ascertained from these data, of course.

Third, these data suggest that patterns of professional values and practice that have been documented in urban areas may not altogether accurately characterize small towns, and they invite speculation on whether the lawyers who are most often studied in urban areas, public defenders and private practitioners whose practices consist almost completely of criminal work, do in fact monopolize the criminal courts as much as is popularly supposed. The larger-town lawyers excluded from the analyses presented here, who were identified through explicit efforts to survey self-identified criminal specialists in communities with populations over 30,000, did not differ as dramatically from the small-town sample as might have been expected. Apparently, a large number of lawyers who maintain some involvement in criminal courts, both in large and small towns, do not fit the portrait of the criminal court "regular" reported in early literature. Hence these findings invite further research to better map the demographics and beliefs of defense bars in communities of various sorts.

Further, although the distinction between criminal specialists and other specialists, or between criminal court regulars and occasional, may be meaningful in describing both the professional opportunities and the behavior of some urban attorneys, it is not useful for describing those who practice in small towns. There, the more useful but subtle distinction may be between those who are willing to take in criminal clients and those who rarely or never do so. Given the weak and negligible associations between measures of professional success and criminal practice in the small-town subsample examined here, and the positive associations between pro-defendant values and practice, one is led to cautiously conclude that, in small towns at least, lawyers can and do choose to accept criminal work, not that they are compelled to when they cannot attract enough civil clients to their practices. For two decades scholars have been increasingly sensitive to the impact of community characteristics on judges' and prosecutors' decisions. The present findings further underscore the importance of studying variation in

lawyers' communities and professional contexts as well (see Flemming et al., 1992).

Finally, and on a related note, these findings suggest the possibility that, if lawyers' perspectives vary, and vary with their involvement in criminal defense work, the character of criminal defense bars may vary as well, insofar as the criminal work is concentrated or dispersed to varying degrees in different communities. There is ample evidence that local legal cultures—the shared values and practices of court actors—vary significantly across communities (Church, 1985; Eisenstein, Flemming, & Nardulli, 1988; Eisenstein & Jacob, 1977). Much of this variation has been attributed to prosecutorial power, judges' beliefs and policies, and institutional and resource constraints. Less attention has been paid to the potential role of the local bar. However, it is reasonable to hypothesize that in small jurisdictions, where criminal defense work is shared among a relatively homogeneous group of lawyers, the norms and values of the courthouse will be influenced by those lawyers' perspectives—perspectives that may be only weakly oriented toward defendant interests. A strong advocacy-oriented defense bar (or important subset of the bar, such as the Legal Aid and Defender Association observed by Eisenstein and Jacob in Detroit, 1977) may have a very different impact on local practices than a bar composed of criminal court "occasionals." Future research should address the connections between individual lawyers' views, their roles in criminal defense bars, and the collective contribution of defense lawyers to local legal culture.

 # References

Austin, T. L. (1981). The influence of court location on type of criminal sentence: The rural-urban factor. *Journal of Criminal Justice, 9,* 305–316.

Bernat, F., & Zupan, L. (1989, May). *Prosecutorial discretion: A study of victim characteristics as it impacts the decision to prosecute in sexual assault cases.* Paper presented at the annual meeting of the Law and Society Association, Madison, WI.

Blumberg, A. S. (1967). The practice of law as a confidence game: Organizational cooptation of a profession. *Law and Society Review, I,* 15–39.

Bohm, R. M., Flanagan, T. J., & Harris, P. W. (1990). Current death penalty opinion in New York State, *Albany Law Review, 54*(3/4), 819–844.

Cain, P. A. (1988). Good and bad bias: A comment on feminist theory and judging. *Southern California Law Review, 61,* 1945–1955.

Carbon, S., Holden, P., & Berkson, L. (1982). Women on the state bench: Their characteristics and attitudes about judicial selection. *Judicature, 65,* 294–299.

Casper, J. (1972). *American criminal justice: The defendant's perspective.* Englewood Cliffs, NJ: Prentice-Hall.

Chambers, D. (1989). Accommodation and satisfaction: Women and men lawyers and the balance of work and family. *Law and Social Inquiry, 14,* 251–288.

Church, T., Jr. (1985). Examining local legal culture. *American Bar Foundation Research Journal, 1985,* 449–518.

Curran, B. A. (1986). American lawyers in the 1980's: A profession in transition. *Law and Society Review, 20(1),* 19–52.

DuBois, E. C., Dunlap, M. C., Gilligan, C. J., MacKinnon, C. A., & Menkel-Meadow, C. J. (1985). Feminist discourse, moral values, and the law—A conversation. *Buffalo Law Review, 34,* 11–87.

Eisenstein, J. (1982). Research on rural criminal justice: A summary. In S. D. Cronk (Ed.), *Criminal justice in rural America.* Washington, DC: National Institute of Justice.

Eisenstein, J., Flemming, R. B., & Nardulli, P. (1988). *The contours of justice: Communities and their courts.* Boston, MA: Little-Brown.

Eisenstein, J., & Jacob, H. (1977). *Felony justice.* Boston, MA: Little-Brown.

Epstein, C. F. (1988). *Deceptive distinctions: Sex, gender and the social order.* New Haven, CT: Yale University Press.

Finckenauer, J. O. (1988). Public support for the death penalty: Retribution as just deserts or retribution as revenge? *Justice Quarterly, 5*(1), 81–100.

Flemming, R. B. (1986). Client games: Defense attorney perspectives on their relationships with criminal clients. *American Bar Foundation Research Journal, 1986,* 253–277.

Flemming, R. B., Nardulli, P. F., & Eisenstein, J. (1992). *The craft of justice.* Philadelphia, PA: University of Pennsylvania Press.

Galanter, M. (1975). Afterword: Explaining litigation. *Law and Society Review, 9,* 347–368.

Gibson, J. (1978). Judges' role orientations, attitudes, and decisions: An interactive model. *American Political Science Review, 72,* 911–924.

Giles, M. W., & Walker, T. G. (1975). Judicial policy-making and southern school desegregation. *Journal of Politics, 37,* 917–936.

Gilligan, C. (1982). *In a different voice.* Cambridge, MA: Harvard University Press.

Glick, H. R., & Pruet, G. W., Jr. (1985). Crime, public opinion, and trial courts: An analysis of sentencing policy. *Justice Quarterly, 2*(3), 319–343.

Halliday, T. C. (1986). Six score years and ten: Demographic transitions in the American legal profession 1850–1950. *Law and Society Review, 20*(1), 53–78.

Heinz, J., & Laumann, E. (1982). *Chicago lawyers: The social structure of the bar.* Chicago, IL: University of Chicago Press.

Heumann, M. (1981). *Plea bargaining.* Chicago, IL: University of Chicago Press.

Jack, R., & Jack, D. C. (1989). *Moral vision and professional decisions: The changing values of women and men lawyers.* Cambridge, MA: Harvard University Press.

Levin, M. (1977). *Urban politics and the criminal courts.* Chicago, IL: University of Chicago Press.

Lichtenstein, M. J. (1984). Public defenders: Dimensions of cooperation. *Justice System Journal, 9*(1), 102–110.

Martin, S. (1987). Gender and judicial selection: A comparison of the Reagan and Carter administrations. *Judicature, 71,* 136–142.

Mather, L. M. (1974). The outsider in the courtroom: An alternative role for the defense. In H. Jacob (Ed.), *The potential for reform of criminal justice.* Beverly Hills, CA: Sage.

Maynard, D. A. (1984). The structure of discourse in misdemeanor plea bargaining. *Law and Society Review,18*(1), 75–104.

McIntyre, L. J. (1987). *The public defender: The practice of law in the shadows of repute.* Chicago, IL: University of Chicago Press.

Menkel-Meadow, C. (1989). Exploring a research agenda of the feminization of the legal profession: Theories of gender and social change. *Law and Social Inquiry, 14*(2), 289–319.

Miller, J. L., Rossi, P., & Simpson, J. E. (1986). Perceptions of justice: Race and gender differences in judgements of appropriate prison sentences. *Law and Society Review, 20*(3), 313–334.

Myers, M. A. (1988). Social background factors and the sentencing behavior of judges. *Criminology, 26*(4), 649–675.

Myers, M. A. (1993). Inequality and the punishment of minor offenders in the early 20th century. *Law and Society Review, 27*(2), 313–343.

Myers, M. A., & Talarico, S. M. (1986). The social contexts of racial discrimination in sentencing. *Social Problems, 35*(3), 236–251.

Myers, M. A., & Talarico, S. M. (1987). *The social contexts of criminal sentencing.* New York, NY: Springer Verlag.

Nardulli, P. F. (1986). "Insider justice": Defense attorneys and the handling of felony cases. *Journal of Criminal Law and Criminology, 77,* 379–417.

Nardulli, P. F., Flemming, R. B., & Eisenstein, J. (1984). Unraveling the complexities of decision making in face-to-face groups: A contextual analysis of plea-bargained sentences. *American Political Science Review, 78,* 912–928.

Ryan, J. P., & Alfini, J. J. (1979). Trial judges' participation in plea bargaining: An empirical perspective. *Law and Society Review, 13,* 479–507.

Sarat, A., & Grossman, J. (1975). Courts and conflict resolution: Problems in the mobilization of adjudication. *American Political Science Review, 69,* 1200–1217.

Schulhofer, S. J. (1988). Criminal justice discretion as a regulatory system. *Journal of Legal Studies, 17,* 43–82.

Skolnick, J. (1967). Social control in the adversary system. *Journal of Conflict Resolution, 11,* 52–67.

Spohn, C. (1990). The sentencing decisions of black and white judges: Expected and unexpected similarities. *Law and Society Review, 24*(5), 1997–1216.

Sudnow, D. (1965). Normal crimes: Sociological features of the penal code in a public defender office. *Social Problems, 12,* 255–276.

Worden, A. P. (1990). Policymaking by prosecutors: The uses of discretion in regulating plea bargaining. *Judicature, 73*(6), 335–340.

Worden, A. P., & Worden, R. E. (1989). Local politics and the provision of indigent defense counsel. *Law and Policy, 11*(4), 401–424.

DISCUSSION QUESTIONS

1. What are the "two stereotypes of criminal lawyers"?

2. Worden hypothesized that "older lawyers hold less strongly pro-defendant views and that male lawyers exhibit stronger affinity than female lawyers for some (but not all) elements of criminal defense work." What was the basis for these hypotheses? Were the hypotheses confirmed by Worden's research?

3. According to Worden, why is it important to study small town lawyers?

4. Worden's research revealed "four attitudinal dimensions" that differentiated the lawyers in her study. Why would defense attorneys have varying attitudes on such things as due process, support for capital punishment, a belief in the deterrent value of punishment, and attitudes toward offenders' potential for rehabilitation? Were these variations explained by the respondent's demographic characteristics or professional background?

5. What factors were associated with the amount of time that the respondent devoted to criminal defense work?

6. What do the results of this study tell us about differences between lawyers who practice in small towns and those who practice in large urban areas?

READING

Critics of public defenders contend that indigent defendants are not served well by the lawyers assigned to represent them. Hanson and Ostrom assessed the validity of this criticism. They studied nine trial courts of general jurisdiction located in seven states. They described the indigent defense system found in each jurisdiction, and they compared indigent defenders and private attorneys on a number of indicators of effective representation: length of time from arrest to disposition, conviction rates, charge reductions, and incarceration rates. They concluded that indigent defenders are just as successful as private attorneys in securing positive outcomes for their clients.

SOURCE: Hanson, Roger A., & Ostrom, Brian J. (2004). Indigent defenders get the job done, and done well. In George F. Cole, Marc G. Gertz, & Amy Bunger (Eds.), *The criminal justice system: Politics and policies* (9th ed.). Belmont, CA: Wadsworth. Reprinted by permission of the author.

Indigent Defenders Get the Job Done and Done Well

Roger A. Hanson and Brian J. Ostrom

 ## Introduction

It has been nearly thirty years since the U.S. Supreme Court in the case of *Gideon* v. *Wainwright* required that the states provide counsel for indigent defendants in criminal cases. Since that time the debate over whether indigent defenders are effective advocates or merely functionaries has continued unabated. Do attorneys paid by the state have the same skill, autonomy, and freedom to represent their clients as privately retained attorneys? Serious doubts were expressed shortly after *Gideon* and continue to be echoed today. Moreover, current skeptics do not limit their judgments to backwater areas, as evidenced by the following view of McConville and Mirsky concerning New York City's appointed counsel arrangement:

> Against this background, the creation of an indigent defense system whose object is the mass disposal of criminal cases through guilty pleas, lesser pleas, and other non-trial dispositions should not be viewed as a heroic response to the needs of poor people by public-spirited individuals. Nor should it be viewed as a rational response to modern case pressure, as a product of the individual, or collective behavior of courtroom actors, or as the logical result of procedural and evidential complexity attendant upon a trial. Instead, the routine processing of defendants is exactly what the indigent defense system was designed to accomplish.[1]

The assertions that indigent defenders are inferior in training, limited advocates for their clients, and without sufficient resources accentuate the importance of understanding this area of legal policy. Are the critics correct or incorrect in their generalizations? Unfortunately, the answer is not obvious. There are several reasons for taking another look at this topic due to the inherent limitations in past research.

Prior studies have three deficiencies. First, many of the studies fail to go beyond the boundaries of a single court and thereby lack comparative perspective.[2] Second, cross-court studies tend not to incorporate large-, medium-, and small-sized communities.[3] This omission fails to control for the effects of population size, which generally are regarded as influential in shaping the delivery of public policy services. Third, none of the prior studies compare all of the basic types of defenders (for example, public defender, assigned counsel, and contract attorneys) to privately retained counsel.[4] As a result, available evaluations of indigent defense performance are incomplete.

The objective of this article is to describe the knowledge gained from an examination of felony case processing in nine state general jurisdiction trial courts and the role that indigent defenders play in their respective systems. The research was aimed at addressing a series of interrelated issues that are central to understanding the positive and negative effects that indigent defenders have both on court operations and on defendants. Do indigent defenders frustrate or promote the court's desire to dispose of cases expeditiously? How well do indigent defenders serve their clients? Do indigent defenders rush their clients to guilty pleas? When they go to trial, how frequently do they win?

The answers to these questions are drawn from the examination of felony case processing in the following nine diverse courts: (1) Wayne County (Detroit, Michigan) Circuit Court; (2) King County (Seattle, Washington) Superior Court; (3) Denver County (Colorado) District

Court; (4) Norfolk (Virginia) Circuit Court; (5) Monterey County (Salinas, California) Superior Court; (6) Oxford County (South Paris, Maine) Superior Court; (7) Gila County (Globe, Arizona) Superior Court; (8) Island County (Coupeville, Washington) Superior Court; and (9) San Juan County (Friday Harbor, Washington) Superior Court.[5] These courts were selected in order to gain a mixture of the basic categories of indigent defenders (public defender, assigned counsel, contract attorney) in large-, and small-sized communities located in different parts of the country. They are not necessarily representative of all courts, but they do represent a broad spectrum along which many courts in the country are found.

Information was obtained from an examination of random samples of felony cases disposed of in 1987. As a result, this article provides a description of the courts in 1987 except where explicit references are made to other years. The analysis of case-level data was augmented with interviews with over 125 defense attorneys, prosecutors, judges, and court staff.

 ## What Do the Indigent Defense Systems Look Like?

Legal representation of indigent defendants is viewed commonly as fitting into one of three basic categories: (1) public defender, (2) assigned counsel, and (3) contract attorneys. Each category is assumed to have a particular organizational structure and a particular method of financing, and each is oriented toward achieving one or more of several different goals, such as efficiency, accountability, or effectiveness. Moreover, systems in each category are presumed to be alike (for example, all public defender offices are similar).

One or more of these three basic categories is represented in each of the nine courts. If the courts are classified according to the major provider of services, as shown in Table 3.10, then Seattle, Denver, and Monterey are public defender systems; Detroit, Norfolk, Oxford, and Island are assigned counsel systems; and Globe and San Juan are contract systems.

This configuration corresponds to the expected pattern of public defender offices existing primarily in large-sized communities and rarely, if at all, in small communities. The occurrence of assigned counsel systems in four of the nine courts is consistent with the national pattern of assigned counsel systems being the most frequent type of system. And the two contract systems in Globe and in San Juan fit the national estimate that this type of system exists in a minority of, usually small-sized, courts.[6]

Table 3.11 indicates the percent of felony dispositions in 1987 drawn from random samples of case files involving indigent defendants (represented by public defenders, assigned counsel, contract attorneys) and nonindigent defendants (represented by privately retained counsel) in each of the nine courts. Privately retained counsel represent 20 percent or more in five of the courts (Denver, Norfolk, Oxford, Island, and San Juan), and nearly that many in Globe (18 percent) and in Detroit (17.1 percent). Despite assertions to the contrary by some observers,[7] the evidence from the nine courts indicates that the private bar is not an endangered species, unless privately retained counsel are expected to handle a majority of the cases in order to be deemed viable.[8]

These data also provide a background against which to reconsider the conventional wisdom that indigent defenders fall into three mutually exclusive categories (public defender, assigned counsel, and contract attorney). The experiences of the nine courts suggest that there is considerable flexibility in constructing indigent defense systems. For example, it is neither necessary nor true that the public defender's office must be the major provider of legal services, if it is to be used. Detroit's Legal Aid and Defender Association, which handles 25 percent of the appointments, is a counterexample to that proposition. Additionally, the types of indigent defense structures may be complementary rather than competitive, as commonly supposed. Monterey's use of all three types of indigent defenders illustrates this situation. Finally, the data from the nine courts do not support the inexorable law that says that a particular type of structure must exist in a particular size of community (for example, public

Table 3.10 Defense Representation: Structure and Institutional Issues

	Detroit	Seattle	Denver	Norfolk	Monterey	Globe	Oxford	San Juan and Island
Percent of all felony dispositions handled by indigent defenders	83%	88%	80%	71%	90%	82%	53%	SJ: 61% I: 66%
Type(s) of indigent defense structures	Assigned counsel, public defender	Three public defender firms on contract, assigned counsel	Public defender, assigned counsel, contract attorneys	Assigned counsel	Public defenders, contract attorneys, assigned counsel	Contract attorneys, assigned counsel	Assigned counsel	Contract attorneys, assigned counsel
Level of funding	County	County	State	State	County	County	State	County
Eligibility of attorneys for appointment	Certification by court; judge appoints to case at first appearance	Private assignment rare and handled informally	Pre-1990, no formal requirements and handled informally by judge at first appearance	Attorney requests to be added to list; no formal requirements	No formal requirements on rare occasions when individual attorney	Not applicable	Informal by judge or clerk	SJ: N/A I: Must be approved by defender association
Average attorney tenure	3–6 years (LADA)	3–5 years	6–7 years	Not available	5–8 years	15–18 years	10–12 years	SJ: 3 years (1989) I: 3–8 years

Table 3.11   Percent of Felony Dispositions Handled by the Different Types of Defense Attorneys in the Courts

Types of Defense Attorneys	Detroit	Seattle	Denver	Norfolk	Monterey	Globe	Oxford	Island	San Juan
Public defender	18.4% (84)	86.8% (526)	74.6% (276)	0.0 (0) (297)	72.8% (0)	0.0 (0)	0.0 (0)	0.0 (0)	0.0
Assigned counsel	64.6% (295)	1.2% (7)	5.4% (20)	71.1% (329)	3.7% (15)	0.0 (0)	52.9% (118)	65.6% (82)	0.0 (0)
Contract attorneys	0.0 (0)	0.0 (0)	0.0 (0)	0.0 (0) (55)	13.5% (140)	82.4% (0)	0.0 (0)	0.0 (19)	61.3%
Private counsel	17.1% (78)	12.0% (73)	20.0% (74)	28.9% (134)	10.0% (41)	17.6% (30)	47.1% (105)	34.4% (43)	38.7% (12)
Totals	100.1% (457)	100% (606)	100% (370)	100% (463)	100% (408)	100% (170)	100% (223)	100% (125)	100% (31)

defenders in a large-sized community). Again, Detroit, where the dominant category is assigned counsel, is a strong counterexample to that notion. The only linkage between the categories of indigent defenders and size is the absence of public defenders in the four small-sized communities. But even this remnant of the conventional wisdom unravels on closer examination. As noted below, Island County's system of assigned counsel exhibits several characteristics of a public defender office. A closer examination of the nine systems reveals interesting similarities and differences in the defense structures in greater detail.

Detroit's Indigent Defense System[9]

Detroit uses primarily assigned counsel for indigent defense. The assignments, however, are distributed between two major groups. Approximately 75 percent of the caseload is assigned by judges to individual private attorneys, with the remaining 25 percent going to the Legal Aid and Defender Association (LADA). LADA is essentially a public defender's office but without the usual publicly provided budget and management. It is a private, nonprofit defender organization that was established in 1968. The caseload division is the result of a

1972 Michigan Supreme Court ruling that mandated 25 percent of all criminal cases go to LADA. The director of LADA monitors this allocation very closely and ensures that it is met.

All indigent defenders, both assigned counsel and LADA attorneys, operate under the voucher system. The Wayne County payment system for assigned counsel underwent substantial change in 1988. Prior to July 1, 1988, attorneys were paid on an event-based schedule. They were paid separately for every court event (for example, each hearing, motion, trial day, and so forth) based upon the seriousness of the offense. Now attorney are paid a fixed fee based on the statutory maximum penalty for the offense (ranging from a low of $475 for a twenty-four month maximum case to $1,400 for first-degree murder).

There are currently about 653 individual private attorneys on the assigned counsel list, with about ten new attorneys being added each month and an indeterminate number (less than ten) dropping off the roll or moving to a more occasional status. This total is composed of approximately 200 hard-core "regulars," who depend on the assigned counsel system for a substantial share of their clients and income, and about 450 "irregulars," who use the assigned counsel system to supplement their private (criminal and/or civil) practice.

There are nineteen defense attorneys (in addition to the director and deputy director) who work for the Legal Aid and Defender Association. Although LADA is often referred to as a public defender organization, its structure is closer to an assigned counsel/public defender hybrid. As with a public defender, the operation of LADA is overseen by an independent board, with no formal government connection, that chooses the office head and sets general policy. However, LADA attorneys generate fees in the same way as private assigned counsel (vouchers are submitted to the administrative office of the court and payments are calculated on the same scale), and this accounts for the vast majority of office funding. Finally, LADA attorneys have no overhead to pay and have access to good secretarial support and experienced in-house investigators. The average tenure of attorneys at LADA is three to six years.

Seattle's Indigent Defense System[10]

The provision of indigent defense services is overseen by the King County Office of Public Defense (OPD). The OPD contracts with three nonprofit public defender firms to provide the majority of defense representation for persons charged with felony offenses.[11] Each of the defender firms has its own board of directors and internal management structure. The oldest and largest of the three firms is The Defender Association (TDA). In 1990–1991, TDA was scheduled to handle approximately 41 percent of the felonies, 25 percent of the misdemeanors, 33 percent of the juvenile offender cases, 40 percent of the juvenile dependency cases, 100 percent of the involuntary commitments, and 43 percent of the cases in the Seattle municipal court.[12] The second largest firm is the Associated Counsel for the Accused (ACA), which was assigned 37 percent of the felonies, 50 percent of the misdemeanors, 22 percent of the juvenile offender cases, and 34 percent of the cases in the Seattle municipal court.[13] The third firm, the Society of Counsel Representing Accused Persons (SCRAP), was allocated 22 percent of the felonies, 25 percent of the misdemeanors, 33 percent of the juvenile offender cases, and 60 percent of the juvenile dependency cases.[14]

OPD is a division within the County Department of Human Services that provides management oversight of the indigent defense budget and services, and it assigns all indigent clients to the contracting public defender firms. OPD staff complete a two-page form during a defendant interview. It covers various aspects of the charged offense, whether an interpreter is needed, and the defendant's financial situation. Individuals are determined to be indigent if their total resources are less than 125 percent of the poverty line or if they are on public assistance.

OPD assigns each case to a particular defender firm the same day as indigency is determined. Notice of the case (defendant name, charge, and bail status) is delivered to the defender firm the following day. All payments to each defender firm are specified in the contract, except payments for aggravated homicide and complex fraud cases and conflicts appointments. The payment in these cases is based upon negotiation between OPD and the defender firm. The defense firms are paid monthly through OPD.[15]

Denver's Indigent Defense System[16]

A statewide public defender system has been in place in Colorado since the early 1970s. Organizationally, it is part of the judicial branch. It is responsible for all indigent representation except in conflict cases (in every court, an attorney may decline to accept appointment because it would conflict with the representation of defendants that were already being represented). There are eighteen regional trial offices with attorneys, two regional offices staffed only with support staff (paralegals and investigators), and an appellate division. The system is administered by a state public defender, a chief trial deputy, a chief deputy, and an administrative unit of five (three professionals). The public defender is appointed by an independent public defender commission established by the supreme court.

The Colorado public defender in Denver handles representation for the city and county of Denver. In 1987, the office had twenty-seven staff attorneys and eight contract attorneys. There were twenty-six staff attorneys in 1990. The appointment of counsel in felony cases generally takes place in the Denver County Court. Colorado uses federal guidelines for determining indigency, but the information that defendants give is not verified. Eligibility determination is done by the public defender.

The Denver office is unique in several ways. First, many public defenders begin their employment doing misdemeanor and juvenile casework there and then move to other locations in the state. Denver proper (as opposed to the surrounding counties) is decreasing in caseload, so the office is not expanding. Because it is easy to find private attorneys to do contract work, contract attorneys are used in Denver for county court work on misdemeanors at the rate of $2,025 per month. A similar use of contract attorneys elsewhere in the state is not typical.

The average tenure of public defenders in Denver was six to seven years, with the statewide average estimated at five years. Salaries of public defenders statewide are higher than those of prosecuting attorneys, but in Denver, the salaries start off even, with the public defenders losing ground as they go up. Attorneys who leave tend to go into solo practice, although some have gone to private firms, judgeships, and so forth.

Counsel are appointed by the court when the public defender must decline the representation of an indigent defendant. The assigned counsel attorneys indicate their areas of interest and expertise (for example, misdemeanors, lesser felonies, more serious felonies), and appointments are taken from the appropriate lists. The amount of reimbursement is determined by the judge, but since 1985, the state public defender administers the funds appropriated. Control over the conflict budget by the state public defender has created an incentive to minimize conflicts and to scrutinize requests by assigned counsel for payments. The state public defender is said to earn credit with the state legislature by returning unspent funds at the end of the year.

Norfolk's Indigent Defense System[17]

Representation of indigent defendants in the upper (circuit) court is provided by private attorneys who are appointed to individual cases. Appointments generally are made in lower (district) court; however, the circuit court appoints counsel for indigent defendants when the cases do not originate in the lower court.

Appointment of counsel is made from a list of attorneys that is maintained by the circuit court but is also used by the general district court. The list contains seventy-eight names. There is apparently no formal process for getting on the list: an individual writes to the court and sets forth whatever information is deemed relevant (for example, experience and references).

Compensation is by voucher. At the conclusion of the representation the attorney completes a form indicating the total of in-court (compensated at the rate $60 per hour) and out-of-court ($40 per hour) time.

There were recent changes in how individuals received appointments. At one time, appointments were made from the list at the first appearance in the district court, with the attorney then being notified by mail that he or she had been appointed to a case. The approach had two shortcomings. First, the attorney was not present at the first appearance, thus missing an early opportunity to speak with the client. The attorney then had to arrange to see the client in jail or try to locate the individual in the community. Second, some attorneys contended that appointments were not being equitably made from the list.

To address both issues, the district court now assigns attorneys to specific court days. The designated attorney will be appointed to all new indigent cases that come before the court for first appearance on that day. With seventy-eight people on the list, an attorney will have a "duty day" about once every two and a half months. This system equalizes the number of appointments, or at least eliminates biased use of the list. A disadvantage, however, is that it treats the attorneys as fungible commodities and can result in inappropriate appointments when it is applied inflexibly by the court.

Monterey's Indigent Defense System[18]

Monterey's indigent defense services are provided primarily by the county public defender's office. Conflict cases are farmed out to a "consortium," which consists of six attorneys who contract with the county. Each consortium attorney handles a narrow range of cases and negotiates his own contract to provide those services. When neither the public defender's office nor a consortium attorney can be appointed, the court has a list of local attorneys on whom it can call.

The public defender's office has a staff of thirty-three individuals structured as follows: chief public defender, two assistant public defenders, eighteen deputy public defenders, seven secretaries, and five investigators. The office handles most of the indigent felony defendants. Felony cases are assigned to individual attorneys by the criminal division supervisor, taking work load and experience into account. Most of the new attorneys have worked in another public defender's office, usually in a metropolitan area. There is a low turnover rate, and those who have left have gone on to be judges or defenders in other jurisdictions or have gone into private practice. Training is primarily informal, by interoffice discussion, California Public Defender Association Briefs, bar courses, and communication with the bench.

The county contracts with six attorneys to provide indigent representation in conflict cases. Each attorney submits a monthly claim with a list of her or his active caseload to receive a monthly check from the county. The attorney must cover all expenses out of the contract (with the exception of investigative costs). The consortium attorneys tend to be experienced practitioners. All of them have been in practice for at least fifteen years. They include attorneys with prior experience in the public defender's office, including one of the former heads of the office.

When consortium attorneys are not able to take appointments, private attorneys are assigned. In 1987, there was no clear indication of what attorneys were eligible for these appointments, the process of how attorneys could be placed on the list was unspecified, and attorneys were not graded in a systematic way to handle different types of cases. More recently, the court has taken steps to formalize the assignment system by clarifying the criteria for appointment and what attorneys satisfy the criteria.

Globe's Indigent Defense System[19]

Gila County contracts with private lawyers for indigent services. From 1986 through 1989 three lawyers held contracts. A fourth attorney was added in 1990 to handle lesser felonies and juvenile dependency cases exclusively. Attorneys contract with the County Board of Supervisors, who fund indigent defense services. The system is not merely "low-bid," however, and the court plays a meaningful role in the process of awarding the contracts. Although the County Board of Supervisors issues a request for proposals, bids are returned to the judges of the court. Thereafter, applicants negotiate with the court before contracts are finalized. The system for assigning cases to each of the contract attorneys blends work load and geographic considerations. In theory, each contract attorney receives an equal number of new cases each year. One of the indigent defense attorneys practices almost exclusively in a remote community within the county (Payson-Pine), and the other attorneys occasionally practice there.

All of the attorneys have a private practice in addition to the Gila County contract. One attorney estimates that 60 percent of his work was indigent defense and 40 percent private practice. Another attorney supplements his Gila County practice with additional contract indigent defense work in an adjacent county, which compensates him on an hourly rather than flat-fee basis. All of the attorneys maintain an office in Gila County, except for the recently hired contract attorney, who handles the misdemeanors and less serious felony work.

The three attorneys who handle felony cases are veteran lawyers with more than fifteen years of experience in criminal practice, which includes forty to sixty felony cases each year. In Globe, the superiority of experience by indigent defense counsel over the deputy prosecuting attorneys is apparent and generally acknowledged. They go to trial infrequently, but they usually win when they do go.

Oxford's Indigent Defense System[20]

The state funds indigent defense in Maine, and Oxford County uses an assigned counsel system. Attorneys are appointed to a case by a judge from a list of available attorneys, with the assistance of the superior court clerk (in the instance of a direct indictment) and the chief deputy district court clerk (in the instance of a felony bind over). Attorneys who wish to be considered for assigned criminal cases inform the clerks of the respective courts who maintain the appointment lists. About twelve Oxford County lawyers accepted indigent criminal cases during the study period, with six of them receiving the majority of the appointments.

Although the state office manages the fiscal elements of the program, the local clerk of court processes the vouchers to get them approved by the judge and forwards them to the administrator in Portland. The state office reviews them and forwards them to Augusta for payment. Checks are written from the state capital in Augusta and mailed to the attorneys. Attorneys receive their checks four to ten weeks after submitting a voucher. The judges must approve vouchers submitted by counsel, and they may adjust the approved amount. The fee structure is set by the supreme court. No ceilings have been legislated for permissible attorney's fees, although the judge must approve the voucher. The judges have discretion to pay less than the full hourly rate.

Island's Indigent Defense System[21]

Island delivers indigent defense services through an assigned counsel system. In the 1970s an association of lawyers—Island County Defender's Association—was formed to certify lawyers for the service, to manage referrals and appointments, and to negotiate with the board of commissioners over fee schedules. The association maintained a governing board and employed a secretary to provide administrative services. The same secretary was hired later by the county commissioners as the full-time administrator of the indigent defense system. Through the association, the consortium of attorneys continued to speak to the county as a group, set standards for eligibility, and, in effect, controlled admission to the indigent defense practice. Thus, even though Island is classified as an assigned system, it has important elements characteristic of a public defender system.

The indigent defense administrator for the Island County Defender's Association runs a tight ship with lots of statistics, careful scrutiny of appointment documentation and the fees charged, review of defendant eligibility, and determination of partial ability to pay. She is responsible for quality control of services, fiscal control, and arrangement for promissory notes when clients have some ability to pay. There is an expectation that attorneys will meet with clients within forty-eight hours of admission to jail.

The assigned counsel system matches attorneys to case severity, with the more experienced attorneys getting the more serious cases. There are approximately twelve attorneys on the assigned counsel roster, all of whom have had several years of experience. Judges and other court personnel state that Island County's system appears to represent the values that should be present in a system of criminal defense—access to experienced attorneys who specialize in trial practice and criminal law and the opportunity for a "personal" relationship.

San Juan's Indigent Defense System

San Juan is an island community with no bridges to the mainland. Indigent defense service has been provided there since 1980 through a contract system. Before that time, defense was provided by an assigned counsel system, similar to Oxford County's. Most attorneys accepted appointments reluctantly, however. From 1979 to 1980, some local lawyers lobbied the county to revise the fee schedule upward; instead, a contract system was initiated by the county commissioners. Until recently, the contract was strictly on a low-bid criterion. The contract attorney assumed responsibility for all criminal, juvenile, and mental health cases, including all overhead. The court at the time was passive, under the theory that so long as there was a vehicle for appointment of counsel, the commissioners were free to fund the service in whatever manner they saw fit.

During the first year of the contract program, the contract attorney moved from the island to a mainland community, three hours distant by automobile and ferry. Thereafter, until 1990, a succession of three attorneys who did not live in the county held the contracts. One of these attorneys had previously been the deputy prosecutor responsible for criminal cases. Throughout this period there was general dissatisfaction with the contract service among the bar and criminal justice community, but no organized attempts to intervene with the commissioners were undertaken. Complaints generally had to do with the unavailability of the lawyer at critical times. Not only was the lawyer rarely available to clients immediately following arrest, but he also often would be late for, or entirely miss, scheduled court appearances. These proceedings would have to be rescheduled.

 Comparative Perspective

Indigent defense should be thought of in terms of a flexible system of interrelated elements rather than three mutually exclusive structures. There is no doubt that there are public defenders, assigned counsel, and contract attorneys and that the methods by which they receive appointments tend to be different. Looking at these systems in the nine courts, however, the following three lessons emerge.

First, there is no single organizational model of public defenders, assigned counsel, or contract attorneys. There are important variants within each of these three categories. Second, virtually all possible combinations of public defenders, assigned counsel, and contract attorneys are feasible. Courts have the opportunity to design the arrangements that meet their particular needs and circumstances. Third, indigent defense systems should not be assessed simply in terms of organizational structure and the assumed advantages of the preferred structure. Instead, the performance of a given structure should be measured in terms of how well the indigent defenders actually handle their cases. That topic is the subject of the next two sections.

 Timeliness

The expeditious resolution of criminal cases is both a right guaranteed under the U.S. Constitution and a standard to which courts are held accountable. According to the Sixth Amendment, defendants are entitled to a speedy trial as well as the assistance of counsel. Consequently, indigent defenders have a fiduciary obligation to avoid unnecessary delays.

Timeliness is also a goal that the courts are expected to achieve. Both the American Bar Association (ABA) and the Conference of State Court Administrators (COSCA) have stipulated standards for courts. Specifically, the ABA states, that all felony cases should take no longer than one year from the date of the arrest to be adjudicated. It is expected, moreover, that most cases should take considerably less than one year to reach final disposition. According to the ABA, 90 percent of all felony cases should be adjudicated within 120 days from the date of arrest and 98 percent should be adjudicated within 180 days from the date of arrest.

Length of Time From Arrest to Disposition

The indigent defenders consistently process the typical case in less time than privately retained attorneys, except in Island County. As shown in Table 3.12, the median number of days from the date of arrest to the date of adjudication for indigent defenders is less than it is for privately retained counsel in each of the eight other courts for all types of indigent defenders except for the small group of assigned counsel in Monterey. In Monterey, assigned counsel have a median number of days (115) that is longer than the time associated with privately retained counsel (eighty-nine days). However, both the public defenders (fifty-six days) and the contract attorneys (seventy-eight days), which are the primary and secondary providers of indigent defense in Monterey, are more timely than privately retained counsel (eighty-nine days).

Meeting the ABA Standard

The same pattern of positive performance by indigent defenders emerges when the ABA's standard of resolving 98 percent of felony cases within 180 days of the arrest data is used. Only San Juan meets the standard; in the other eight courts more than 2 percent of the

Table 3.12 Typical Length of Time That Indigent Defenders and Privately Retained Counsel Take to Resolve Cases (Median Number of Days From Date of Arrest to Adjudication,[a] Felony Dispositions)

	Detroit	Seattle[b]	Denver	Norfolk	Monterey	Globe	Oxford	Island	San Juan
Public defender	79	75	151	—	56	—	—	—	—
Contract attorney	—	—	—	—	78	125	—	—	79
Assigned counsel	62	—	162	114	115	—	134	156	—
Privately retained counsel	102	101	167	184	89	141	215	131	88
All cases	71	85	156	126	63	129	161	146	83

a. Adjudication is the entry of a dismissal, guilty plea, deferred adjudication, diversion, or verdict.

b. In Seattle, the indigent defense attorneys represented are from three public defender firms (The Defender Association [TDA]; Associated Counsel for the Accused [ACA]; Society of Counsel Representing Accused Persons [SCRAPI]). The typical case processing time for each firm is as follows: TDA, 89 days; ACA, 77 days; SCRAP, 59 days.

felony cases are still open at 180 days. However, as shown in Table 3.13, the percentages of cases remaining open after 180 days is consistently less for the indigent defenders in all the courts except Globe. In Globe, 28.6 percent of the cases represented by contract attorneys remain open after 180 days, and 27.2 percent of the cases represented by privately retained attorneys remain open after 180 days from the date of arrest. Additionally, in Monterey, relatively more of the cases with privately retained counsel meet the ABA standard than do the cases with assigned counsel. However, the two larger groups of indigent defenders in Monterey (public defender and contract attorneys) approximate the standard more closely than do the privately retained attorneys.

The quantitative results, which indicate that indigent defenders do well in terms of timeliness, have profound implications. One implication is that the expeditious adjudication of cases reduces the demand for additional court appearances and the length of time that defendants spend in jail awaiting disposition of their cases. The assembling of all the participants in the legal process for court proceedings and the pretrial detention of defendants are undeniably costly. Hence, indigent defenders contribute to cost savings by their timeliness.

Second, the closer approximation by indigent defenders to established time standards presents a picture that diverges from the popular image. A common view of indigent defenders is that they are engaging in dilatory tactics in one case in order to meet deadlines in other cases. Simply stated, they are viewed as unable to schedule their work, to satisfy time requirements, and to live within budgetary constraints. That point of view is not supported by the data from the nine courts under study. In terms of approximating time standards, indigent defenders perform better than privately retained attorneys. What other public institutions can make the claim that they perform as well as (or better than) the private sector?

Third, the achievement of timeliness frames the issue of effective representation in a new light. Instead of engaging in a philosophical debate over whether timeliness is inherently good or bad, one can ask the empirical question, Are the gains in efficiency made at the expense of the defendants? Are the rights or interests of defendants sacrificed in some way? The achievement of timeliness needs to be viewed side by side with

Table 3.13   Percent of Felony Cases Unresolved After 180 Days From the Date of Arrest for Indigent Defenders and Privately Retained Counsel (ABA Standards Stipulate That 2 Percent or Less of the Cases Should Be Unresolved)

	Detroit	Seattle[a]	Denver	Norfolk	Monterey	Globe	Oxford	Island	San Juan
Public defender	16.7%	19.0%	43.8%	—	8.3%	—	—	—	—
Contract attorney	—	—	—	—	3.9%	28.6%	—	—	0%
Assigned counsel	11.9%	—	45.5%	20.9%	20.0%	—	42.4%	44.6%	—
Privately retained attorneys	21.8%	26.4%	45.6%	51.1%	11.5%	27.2%	60.0%	47.2%	9.1%
All cases	14.4%	21.1%	44.2%	29.7%	8.0%	28.3%	49.1%	45.6%	3.4%

a. In Seattle, the indigent defense attorneys represented are from three public defender agencies (The Defender Association [TDA]; Associated Counsel for the Accused [ACA]; Society of Counsel Representing Accused Persons [SCRAP]). The percentages of unresolved cases after 180 days for the three firms are as follows: TDA. 23.0%; ACA, 17.6%; SCRAP, 16.3%.

information on the outcomes for defendants. The tasks of presenting and interpreting the necessary information are the subject of the next section.

 ## Performance and Indigent Defense

There are two basic approaches to assessing indigent defenders in the literature. The first approach has what may be called an input orientation. Indigent defenders are expected to represent their clients by being adequately prepared—meeting with clients, contacting witnesses, conducting research, reviewing presentence investigation reports, and so forth. Hence, a body of guidelines has been formulated that identifies how effective representation is to be conducted and the resources required to facilitate advocacy.[22]

The second approach has what may be called an output orientation.[23] Indigent defenders are expected to represent their clients by achieving favorable outcomes, such as acquittals and dismissals, charge reductions, noncustodial sentences, and the shortest possible periods of incarceration in prison. In this approach, the performance of indigent defenders is determined by comparing them with privately retained counsel. Do indigent defenders achieve the same percentage of favorable outcomes for their clients as privately retained counsel? This comparison sets a very high standard of evaluation for indigent defenders. There are several factors that have very little to do with the relative capabilities of attorneys that make it more difficult for indigent than nonindigent defendants to gain favorable outcomes. First, indigent defendants are more likely to be detained than defendants who can afford an attorney. Second, indigent defendants are more likely to have prior records that will be influential at sentencing. Third, indigent defendants are thought to be less assertive of their rights than defendants who can afford to pay for attorneys.[24]

Both of these approaches have their role to play in assessing indigent defense counsel. The first approach is appropriate for examining work that individual attorneys put into specific cases, but it provides no assessment of what the attorney accomplishes. Certainly, an attorney may meet with the client, interview witnesses, research the law, but do none of these activities effectively. Because the second approach draws conclusions concerning the performance of attorneys, it is the preferred orientation.

Conviction Rates

A fundamental concern to criminal defendants is gaining an acquittal or a dismissal. With a conviction comes the imposition of penalties. One basic goal of the defense attorney is to minimize the possibility of criminal penalties. In terms of measuring this goal, the standard is that the lower the conviction rate for a given set of attorneys, the more successful they are in gaining favorable outcomes for their clients.

The data indicate that indigent defenders perform as well as privately retained counsel in meeting this standard under a wide range of conditions. The conviction rates of defendants represented by public defenders, contract attorneys, assigned counsel, and privately retained counsel, when all nine courts are combined, are strikingly similar. Public defenders have a rate of 84.4 percent, contract attorneys have a rate of 83.6 percent, assigned counsel have a rate of 85.3 percent, and privately retained counsel have a rate of 83.4 percent. There is no statistically significant difference (chi-square = 1.26, significance level = .77) among these rates.[25] Defendants are no worse off with one type of defense attorney than another, which means that defendants with privately retained counsel do no better, on average, than do indigent defendants with a publicly appointed attorney.

The similarity in the conviction rates among the different types of defense attorneys extends to cases that go to trial. Public defenders secured acquittal or dismissal in 23.2 percent of cases; contract attorneys, 28.6 percent; assigned counsel, 33.3 percent; and privately retained counsel, 25.6 percent. Thus indigent defenders are no less successful in gaining acquittals or dismissals for their clients than are privately retained counsel. There is no statistically significant relationship (chi-square = 2.74, significance level = .43) between the types of attorneys and the likelihood of conviction at trial.

These results raise an additional question. Are the conviction rates similar for different types of attorneys in both the large- and small-sized courts? This more refined question outstrips the available data to some extent. There are too few contract attorneys in either the large-sized or the small-sized courts to permit valid statistical testing. However, if all the indigent defenders are collapsed into one category, then this question can be addressed in terms of the conviction rates of publicly appointed attorneys versus privately retained counsel.

The data indicate that there is no linkage between the type of attorney and the likelihood of conviction either in the large-sized or in the small-sized courts. The conviction rates for publicly appointed and privately retained attorneys in the large courts (Detroit, Seattle, Denver, Norfolk, and Monterey) are 84.8 percent and 82 percent, respectively. In the small-sized courts (Oxford, Globe, Island, and San Juan), the parallel percentages are 84.1 and 86.3.[26] These are not statistically significant differences. Hence, within the limitations of the available data, the evidence indicates that indigent defenders do as well as privately retained counsel in terms of a fundamental criterion of performance. The likelihood of an indigent defendant being convicted is not influenced significantly by the fact that the defense attorney is publicly appointed.

Charge Reductions

From the perspective of the defendant and the defense attorney, any success is a victory. Given the fact that most defendants are convicted, one of the best outcomes that most defendants can realistically strive for is a reduction in the seriousness of charge. If the offense at conviction is a less serious offense than the offense with which the defendant was initially charged, this outcome is favorable to the defendant. The empirical question is, Do privately retained counsel have significantly different charge reduction rates from those of indigent defenders?

For the four types of defense attorneys, this question can be addressed only for the cases disposed of by guilty pleas, because the number of trials is limited for

some categories of attorneys. The data reveal that there are significant differences in charge reduction rates among the categories of defense attorneys. The charge reduction rates for public defenders, contract attorneys, assigned counsel, and privately retained counsel are 25.7, 50.9, 26.4, and 31.9 percent, respectively. Contract attorneys do considerably better than the privately retained counsel, who do slightly better than the public defenders or the assigned counsel.[27] Hence, for cases involving guilty pleas, there are mixed results concerning the performance of indigent defenders. Some indigent defenders perform quite well whereas others perform less well than privately retained counsel.

If all indigent defenders are combined into one category, then the question of the linkage between type of attorney and charge reductions also can be examined for different-sized courts. From this perspective the size of the court produces opposite effects. In the large courts, privately retained attorneys gain more reductions (32 percent) than do publicly appointed counsel (26.3 percent). In the small-sized courts, privately retained counsel gain fewer reductions (28.7 percent) than do publicly appointed counsel (37.4 percent). Both sets of results are weak, statistically, however.[28] In the large courts the correlation between the type of attorney and the likelihood of a charge reduction is very low (phi-square = .05). For the small-sized courts, the relationship is not statistically significant.[29] Hence, while the type of defense attorney may have some effect on charge reductions, the effect is negligible.

On the basis of these data, the performance of indigent defenders in gaining charge reductions is somewhat mixed. Contract attorneys do better than privately retained counsel, while public defenders and assigned counsel do less well. This connection, however, is weak statistically (Cramer's V = .15). Similarly, publicly appointed counsel gain more charge reductions in small-sized courts and fewer charge reductions in large-sized courts than do privately retained counsel. These connections, while demonstrating opposite effects, are weak. Thus, overall, indigent defenders perform about as well as privately retained counsel in obtaining charge reductions.

Incarceration Rates

The potential advantage that privately retained counsel have over indigent defenders should be the greatest in determining whether a convicted defendant is incarcerated in jail or prison, sentenced to probation, given community service, or fined. The prior record of the defendant is likely to play a major role in this decision. Unfortunately, the collection of data on the defendant's prior record was beyond the scope of this research. If it is true that indigent defendants are more likely to have prior records than nonindigent defendants, this missing information means that the examination of incarceration rates, without controlling for the effects of prior record, is tipped somewhat in favor of privately retained counsel. Yet, despite this potential advantage, privately retained counsel are only slightly more successful in keeping their clients out of jail or prison.

The incarceration rates are lower for cases represented by privately retained counsel. Assigned counsel and privately retained counsel have approximately the same incarceration rates (60.3 versus 57.1). Public defenders (78.2) and contract attorneys (74.6) are less successful in keeping their clients out of penal institutions. However, the association between the four types of defense attorneys and the corresponding incarceration rates is only moderate (Cramer's $V = .20$).[30] This correlation means that privately retained attorneys are more likely to gain favorable outcomes for their clients, but this advantage is limited. A majority of the convicted defendants represented by every type of defense attorney are incarcerated. The size of the majority is greater for indigent defense attorneys, but nearly six of every ten defendants represented by privately retained counsel are incarcerated.

How indigent defenders and privately retained counsel compare is seen more clearly when all indigent defenders are grouped together. Felony defendants with publicly appointed counsel are incarcerated 72.4 percent of the time, while those who privately retain their attorneys end up in prison or jail 58.2 percent of the time. The correlation between these two types of defense attorneys and the in/out decision is a very weak one (phi-square $= .12$).[31] The slightly better performance by privately retained counsel, moreover, appears to be due to the effect of public defenders on the population of all indigent defenders. The use of a public defender appears to influence the higher incarceration rate among publicly appointed attorneys. The question thus arises, If public defenders are excluded from the analysis, then what do the results look like? The absence of public defenders occurs naturally when the courts are separated according to size. Whereas public defenders work in four of the five large courts, they are not present in any of the four small courts. The results of this analysis show that privately retained attorneys perform better than publicly appointed attorneys in both the large courts and the small courts.

In the large courts, privately retained attorneys perform better (50.5 percent of clients incarcerated) than publicly appointed counsel (71.5 percent of clients incarcerated). The difference in incarceration rates is statistically significant, but it is limited, as indicated by a weak correlation coefficient (phi-square $= .17$).[32] The underlying reason why the connection is weak rests on the fact that indigent defenders represented 83 percent of defendants and obtained 74 percent of the sentences involving some penalty other than incarceration. Privately retained counsel represented 17 percent of the defendants and obtained 26 percent of the sentences involving nonincarceration. Given that indigent defenders cannot choose their clients, and privately retained counsel do have some control over whom they represent, these differences are much smaller than expected. Moreover, in the small-sized courts, the differences are in favor of publicly appointed counsel, although the incarceration rates are not statistically different. The incarceration rate is 77.4 percent for privately retained counsel and 75.2 percent for publicly appointed counsel, which is in the opposite direction of the advantage that privately retained counsel are expected to enjoy.[33]

Thus, privately retained counsel perform somewhat better than indigent defenders on the basic in/out dimension. However, the greater likelihood that privately retained counsel keep their clients out of jail or prison is limited both in magnitude and in the scope of the effects. In the small-sized courts, privately retained counsel and publicly appointed attorneys perform at the same level. Given the assumption that indigent defendants are much less likely to win favorable outcomes because of their prior records, limited ties to the community, and other social circumstances, the limited degree of success by privately retained counsel falls short of that expectation. The results suggests that indigent defenders are able to overcome the potential liabilities of their clients to a very great extent.

 ## Conclusion

How frequently do indigent defenders gain favorable outcomes for their clients? Are they more successful than, less successful than, or equally as successful as privately retained counsel in gaining favorable outcomes? The evidence gained from an examination of felony dispositions in the nine courts is that indigent defenders generally are as successful as privately retained counsel. The conviction rates, the charge reduction rates, and the incarceration rates for their clients are similar to the outcomes associated with privately retained counsel. These results raise a couple of issues for future consideration.

First, the results are helpful in identifying what aspects of performance are translatable into management information systems and what aspects warrant further research and development. The measurement of case outcomes seems sufficiently feasible and the results seem sufficiently meaningful to merit inclusion into the monitoring of indigent defense systems. Consequently, judges, policy makers, and others concerned with the quality of indigent defense representation should take the necessary steps to gather information on how well indigent defenders do in gaining favorable outcomes for their clients.

However, the measures of performance in this article do not speak to the issue of lawyer–client relations, especially the time that indigent defenders give to individual defendants. How frequently do they meet with clients? What is the average amount of time spent with clients? Previous research has indicated that the amount of time that indigent defenders spend with their clients makes a difference in client satisfaction.

The more time that is spent, the more defendants are satisfied with their attorneys.

Satisfaction should not be confused with productive work. Indigent defenders know how to husband resources and to gain the most favorable outcomes for their clients expeditiously. However, satisfaction is part of performance and deserves further examination. Future research needs to be conducted on this topic in order to establish more precisely what amount and what kind of time indigent defenders should be expected to devote to meeting with their clients, within the constraints of their caseloads.[34]

Second, the results suggest that judges, policy makers, attorneys, and others are not required to choose between timeliness and performance. Evidence from the nine courts in this study indicate that both goals are possible to achieve. The fact that these goals are not necessarily in conflict means that the task confronting the courts is to organize an indigent defense system responsible to community needs and circumstances that achieves both goals. That task, which is neither easy nor obvious, is possible. However, the lesson to be learned is that courts have the opportunity to design a system where both timeliness and performance are attained.

 ## Notes

1. Michael McConville and Chester L. Mirsky, "Criminal Defense of the Poor in New York City." 15 *New York University Review of Law and Social Change* 881 (1986–1987). An underlying theme to McConville and Mirsky's work is that indigent defenders are coopted by the courthouse community. This theme is a traditional one in the literature. See, for example, David Sudnow, "Normal Crimes: A Sociological Feature of the Penal Code in a Public Defender Office," 12 *Social Problems* 253 (1965); Abraham S. Blumberg, "The Practice of Law Is a Confidence Game: Organizational Cooptation of a Profession," 1 *Law and Society Review* 15 (1967); Dennis R. Eckart and Robert V. Stover, "Public Defenders and Routinized Criminal Defense Processes," 51 *Journal of Urban Law* 665 (May 1974); J. P. Levine, "The Impact of 'Gideon': The Performance of Public and Private Defense Lawyers," 8 *Polity* 215 (1975): Suzanne E. Mounts and Richard Wilson, "Systems for Providing Indigent Defense: An Introduction," 14 *New York University Review of Law and Social Change* 193 (1986).

2. See, for example, Lisa J. McIntyre, *The Public Defender: The Practice of Law in the Shadows of Repute* (Chicago: University of Chicago Press, 1987).

3. Some studies focus on very large communities. See, for example, Robert Hermann, Eric Single, and John Boston's study of New York, Los Angeles, and Washington, D.C., in *Counsel for the Poor: Criminal Defense in Urban America* (Lexington, Mass.: D.C. Heath, 1977). See also James Eisenstein and Herbert Jacob's study of Baltimore, Detroit, and Chicago in *Felony Justice: An Organizational Analysis of Criminal Courts* (Boston: Little, Brown, 1977). On the other hand, Peter Nardulli focuses exclusively on nine medium-sized communities (DuPage, Peoria, and St. Clair counties in Illinois; Kalamazoo, Oakland, and Saginaw counties in Michigan; Dauphin, Erie, and Montgomery counties in Pennsylvania) in "Insider's Justice: Defense Attorneys and the Handling of Felony Cases," 77 *Journal of Criminal Law and Criminology* 379 (1986). Prior research with the broadest scope is a study of eight medium-sized and small-sized communities all located in Virginia by Larry J. Cohen, Patricia P. Semple, and Robert E. Crew, Jr., "Assigned Counsel versus Public Defender Systems in Virginia: A Comparison of Relative Benefits," in *The Defense Counsel,* edited by William F. McDonald (Newbury Park, Calif.: Sage Publications, 1983).

4. Some of the studies, in fact, do not compare indigent defenders with privately retained counsel. See, for example, McConville and Mirsky, "Criminal Defense of the Poor in New York City" (note 1). The lack of a comparison group poses severe methodological problems because evaluations require some form of comparison.

5. Hereafter the courts will be referred to by the names that they commonly are called in order to facilitate exposition. The names are Detroit, Seattle, Denver, Norfolk, Monterey, Oxford, Globe, Island, and San Juan.

6. Robert. L. Spangenberg, Beverly Lee, Michael Badaglia, Patricia Smith, and A. David Davis, *National Criminal Defense System Study: Final Report* (Washington, D.C: U.S. Department of Justice, 1986).

7. Paul B. Wice, *Criminal Lawyers: An Endangered Species* (Newbury Park, Calif.: Sage Publications, 1978).

8. There are minor differences in the caseload composition of defense attorneys. All three basic categories of indigent defenders tend to have the same distribution of felony cases. Most of their cases involve burglary and theft offenses, followed by, in descending order of frequency, crimes against the person, drug sale and possession, and other types of felonies. The only difference between their caseloads and those of privately retained counsel lies in the fact that privately retained counsel have more crimes against the person than burglary and theft cases. However, this difference is not sharp.

9. The population of Wayne County was 2,164,300 in 1986. The city of Detroit accounted for just over one-half of the total county population (1,086,220), making it the sixth-largest city in the United States. The total population living within the city, however, has been in decline since the 1950s. Approximately 39 percent of the

Wayne County population is identified as nonwhite. Per capita income is $10,681, with just over 14 percent of the population living below the poverty level. Wayne County's crime rate was 9,864 serious crimes per 100,000 population.

10. In 1988, the Seattle primary metropolitan area had a population of 1,862,000, with the city of Seattle accounting for just under one-third of the total (502,000). Seattle, the twenty-fourth-largest city in the country, experienced a growth in population of 1.7 percent from 1980 to 1988; just over 12 percent of its population is identified as nonwhite. Of the nine communities under examination, Seattle had the second-highest per capita income ($13,192) and the lowest percentage of individuals living below the poverty line (7.7 percent).

11. Several years ago, the Seattle City Council, members of the bar, and some indigent defendants questioned whether there was insufficient minority representation on the board of directors and in management positions at TDA, ACA, and SCRAP. The response, in addition to increasing the awareness of affirmative action in the three agencies, was to create a fourth firm with management by minority-group members, Northwest Defenders Association (NDA). NDA, which did not represent felony cases in 1990–1991, is not investigated in this study.

12. The Defender Association. an outgrowth of Seattle's Model City Program, was created in 1969 with a staff of five. In 1967, 166 individuals were employed at TDA, seventy-one of whom were attorneys. It was the only agency that provided indigent defense services for all case types: felony, misdemeanor, juvenile offender, juvenile dependency, and municipal court cases.

13. In 1987, ACA employed eighty-three individuals, fifty-five of whom were professional staff. The types of cases handled by ACA are felony, misdemeanor, juvenile offender, and Seattle municipal court cases. The director of ACA values having a core of experienced attorneys (that is, four to six years), but he has reservations about "lifers." About 20 percent of the attorneys have five to seven years of experience, and most attorneys have about three years of experience.

14. In 1987, SCRAP employed 29.5 full-time equivalents, 18 of whom were professionals. Most attorneys are recent law school graduates. New attorneys start in juvenile offender or dependency and may work into felonies if they are interested. Most felony attorneys gain experience within the firm in other divisions, but there are some lateral hires of experienced felony lawyers. Felony attorneys are hired by an ad hoc, two-member hiring committee consisting of the felony supervisor and another felony lawyer. Tenure in the felony division was difficult to assess because the firm had been handling these cases for only about the last five years.

15. The defender firms have no funding in their own budgets for expert witnesses. Funds for experts are found in the superior court budget, and defenders obtain them through an order from the judge. The judge is able to sign off for up to $350. If a higher amount is

requested, it goes to an audit committee for acceptance or rejection. Some of the attorneys who were interviewed were not aware of the procedure for obtaining an amount in excess of $350.

16. Denver is the largest city in the Rocky Mountain region. Its population of 505,000 in 1986 tended to be divided between a relatively affluent majority and a very poor minority. A most striking feature of Denver is its crime rate of 10,557 serious crimes per 100,000 population.

17. Norfolk, Virginia, is a core city declining in population, with limited growth due to the out-migration of both middle-income residents and some poor residents (through the demolition of housing projects). Racial minorities constitute 38.4 percent of the population, and about 21 percent live below the poverty level. Norfolk had a violent crime rate in 1985 of 6,561 per 100.000.

18. The population of Monterey County was 340,000 in 1986. Approximately 15 percent of the county's population is Hispanic. In 1985, the per capita income was $10,420, with 11.4 percent of the population below the poverty level. Monterey County's crime rate was 5,419 serious crimes per 100,000 population.

19. Gila County is a large geographic area (4,752 square miles), approximately half the size of Rhode Island. It is located approximately 90 miles east of Phoenix in the state's copper mining region. It also includes a growing recreational and retirement community (Payson-Pine), although the Miami-Globe community is larger. Demographically, Gila County is a community of 37,000 persons, with 15 percent of the population identified as nonwhite (primarily Hispanic and American Indian, since the county is bordered on the east by two Indian reservations). The per capita income in 1985 was $7,399.

20. The population of Oxford County was 50,200 in 1986, approximately 4 percent of Maine's total population of 1,250,000. Oxford County is located in the southwestern mountain region of Maine. The basic industries in this area center around lumbering and paper production. The per capital income is $8,379, with just under 13 percent of the population living below the poverty level. Less than one-half of 1 percent of Oxford County is identified as nonwhite. The serious crime rate for Oxford was 1,781 index crimes per 100,000 population in 1985.

21. Island and San Juan counties are adjacent counties that consist only of islands. By Western United States standards they are very small in area (212 square miles for Island; 179 square miles for San Juan). Both counties are rural in character; however, a Naval Air Station in Island County gives Island a somewhat different flavor. Both counties have a low to virtually nonexistent minority population and high real estate values. The median value of homes in San Juan county is $87,300—the highest in the state and nearly one-third higher than the state median—and the median real estate value in Island County is nearly identical to the state median of $60,700. Crime rates are 2,278 and 2,843 per 100,000 population for Island and San Juan, respectively.

22. Roberta Rovner-Pieczenik, Alan Rapoport, and Martha Lane, *How Does Your Defender Office Rate? Self-Evaluation Manual for Public Defender Offices* (Washington, D.C.: Government Publications Office, 1977), especially pages 38–43 concerning measures of "attorney competence," American Bar Association Project on Standards for Criminal Justice, *Standards Relating to the Prosecution Function and the Defense Function* (Washington, D.C.: American Bar Association, 1971), especially pages 225–228 concerning the "duty to investigate." William Genego, "Future of Effective Assistance of Counsel: Performance Standards and Complete Representation," 22 *American Criminal Law Review* 181 (Fall 1984). National Study Commission on Defense Services, *Guidelines for Legal Defense System in the United States* (Washington, D.C.: National Legal Aid and Defender Association, 1976), especially pages 428–447 on "ensuring effectiveness."

23. See, for example, Hermann, Single and Boston, *Counsel for the Poor* (note 3); Joyce Sterling, "Retained Counsel Versus the Public Defender," in William F, McDonald, ed., *The Defense Counsel* (Newbury Park, Calif: Sage Publications. 1983), pp. 68–76; David Willison, "The Effects of Counsel on the Severity of Criminal Sentences: A Statistical Assessment," 9 *Justice System Journal* 87 (1984).

24. Some scholars suggest that it is Utopian to expect that indigent defenders will perform as well as privately retained counsel. Willison, "The Effects of the Severity of Criminal Sentences" (note 23), writes that indigent defenders will "fail to perform as successfully as privately retained counsel even if they are adequately funded and have workable caseloads so long as they continue to represent disadvantaged defendants facing serious criminal charges and possessing extensive criminal records" (88).

25. In this section, two basic statistical tests are applied to determine whether there is a connection between the different types of defense attorneys and performance and the strength of the connection. The first test is a test of significance. The test of significance indicates whether there is a systematic connection as opposed to a coincidental connection. The chi-square test is the particular test that is applied. This technique generates a number and a corresponding level of significance. The smaller the significance level, the less likely it is that the observed pattern could have happened by chance alone. In this article, the benchmark of .01 is used to determine when there are statistically significant differences (that is, results could have happened by chance alone only one time out of a hundred). In all of the tables, the chi-square value and the level at which it is significant are reported.

The second test is a test of association. If there is a systematic connection, how close is it? The test of association measures the strength of connection in terms of a correlation coefficient. The coefficient ranges in value from zero to one. Basically, the larger the value of the coefficient, the tighter the connection is between the different types of attorneys and various case outcomes. The phi-square and the Cramer's V correlations are the tests of association that are applied. Phi-square is appropriate for all two-by-two tables, and Cramer's V is appropriate for all the others. Finally, the rule of thumb is that coefficients below .20 are considered to be indications of weak connections between the types of attorneys and case outcomes, those from .21 to .40 are considered to indicate moderate connections, and coefficients from .41 to 1.0 are considered to indicate strong connections.

26. Large courts: chi-square = 1.91, significance level = .17, phi-square = .03. Small courts: chi-square = .46, significance level = .49, phi-square = .46.

27. The relatively high level of success among contract attorneys may be due to the unusually high level of experience, especially among the contract attorneys in Monterey and Globe.

28. Chi-square = 48.12, significance level = .0001, Cramer's V = .15.

29. Large courts: chi-square = 4.43, significance level = .04, phi-square = .05. Small courts: chi-square = .46, significance level = .49, phi-square = .03.

30. Chi-square = 87.79, significance level = .0001. Cramer's V = .20.

31. Chi-square = 36.00, significance level = .0001, phi-square = .12.

32. Chi-square = 55.00, significance level = .0001, phi-square = .17.

33. Chi-square = .261, significance level = .01, phi-square = .03.

34. Jonathan D. Casper, "Did You Have a Lawyer When You Went to Court? No. I Had a Public Defender," *Yale Review of Law and Social Action* 4–9 (Spring 1971). More generally, researchers have found that the felony defendant's degree of satisfaction with the outcome of the case is shaped by the procedural fairness of the process. Procedural fairness includes measures of the defendant's views of the defense attorney's, prosecutor's, and judge's behavior (for example, Did your lawyer listen to you? Did the prosecutor pay careful attention to your case? Did the judge try hard to find out if you were guilty or innocent?). See also Jonathan D. Casper, Tom Tyler, and Bonnie Fisher, "Procedural Justice in Felony Cases," 22 *Law and Society Review* 483 (1988).

DISCUSSION QUESTIONS

1. Why do critics of indigent defense argue that "you get what you pay for"?

2. Hanson and Ostrom examined the indigent defense systems in nine diverse courts. What are the similarities and differences in the systems found in these nine jurisdictions?

3. The authors argued that indigent defense systems should be analyzed in terms of how well the indigent defenders handle their cases. What measures of effectiveness did they use? Are there other, perhaps better, ways to measure effectiveness?

4. How do indigent defenders compare to private attorneys in terms of (1) timeliness of case disposition, (2) conviction rates, (3) charge reductions, and (4) incarceration rates?

5. What are the policy implications of this study?

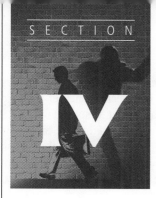

SECTION

IV

Judges and Jurors

Judges and Jurors: Fact Finding and Applying the Law

In the minds of most Americans, the judge, and to a lesser extent the jury, symbolizes justice. This is especially true in criminal cases, where the role of the judge is to ensure that proper procedures are followed and the defendant's rights are protected and where the jury—assuming there is one—is responsible for deciding whether the evidence proves the defendant's guilt. If the defendant waives his or her right to a jury trial and is tried by a judge at a bench trial, the judge plays both roles: The judge determines the facts and applies the law. The judge's role is more circumscribed if the defendant pleads guilty. In this case, the judge, perhaps with input from the prosecuting attorney, determines the appropriate sentence but does not decide whether the prosecutor has proved his or her case beyond a reasonable doubt.

The typical criminal case, then, involves both fact finding and **application of the law**; it involves "determining the facts and then choosing—often crafting, sometimes even creating—the appropriate rules of law to apply to these facts" (Murphy et al., 2006, p. 381). When we say that judges apply the law, we mean that judges decide the legal—as opposed to factual—matters before the court. For example, the defendant's attorney may file a motion requesting that illegally obtained evidence be excluded. Perhaps the attorney believes that the defendant's confession was coerced or that physical evidence was seized during an improper search. The judge, who will consider both appellate court decisions regarding these issues and relevant state and local rules governing the admissibility of evidence, will decide whether the evidence should be excluded or not. His or her decision amounts to applying the law, either as spelled out in statutes or as interpreted by other courts' decisions. Judges also may be asked to decide whether the case should be moved to another jurisdiction as a result of prejudicial pretrial publicity or whether potential jurors should be excused from the jury panel as a result of bias or other factors, and judges ensure that questioning of witnesses at trial comports with the rules of evidence. These complex legal matters are not left in the hands of jurors, the nonexperts in the courtroom drama.

The role that jurors play is that of **fact finding**. In the typical jury trial, jurors listen to the "facts" of the case as laid out by the defense attorney and prosecutor. They then decide based on that information what "happened." Their decisions about what happened ultimately affect whether the defendant will be held accountable for the crime with which he or she is charged. For example, if an expert witness for the defense convinces the jury that the defendant was not of sound mind at the time of the crime, or an alibi witness is able to create reasonable doubt about the defendant's involvement in the crime, the jury may elect to find the defendant not guilty. Alternatively, if the prosecution calls 10 persuasive witnesses to the stand and the defense calls only 1 witness, the jury may be swayed by the prosecution's version of the events that landed the defendant in court. We put the word *facts* in quotes at the beginning of this paragraph for just this reason; they are relative. Because jurors were not present when the crime occurred, they must determine the "facts" as presented to them by the prosecution and defense.

Both the application of the law by judges and fact finding by the jury are imperfect. For example, although most judges are impartial and fair, not all are. Judges' decisions may be motivated by bribes, by fear of electoral defeat, or by prejudice or bias against one side in the case. In 1991, for example, U.S. District Judge Robert Collins was convicted of taking a $100,000 bribe from a drug smuggler in exchange for a lighter sentence, and in 2000, Judge Calvin Hotard of Jefferson, Louisiana 2d Parish Court was forced to retire from the bench after it was revealed that he dismissed cases or imposed lenient sentences in exchange for sexual favors (Cox, 2001). Judges are also human, which means they do not always apply the law correctly. The judge might misinterpret an appellate court ruling on criminal procedure or allow the use of irrelevant evidence.

The jury system also is imperfect. The jury may not hear all of the facts in the case; the prosecutor and the defense may try to conceal facts that work to the other side's advantage. For example, the defendant might decide not to testify, which means that the jury will not hear the defendant's version of events. Although jurors are instructed not to assume anything as a result of the defendant's failure to testify, they will nonetheless wonder why they didn't hear from the defendant. Moreover, jurors usually hear two versions of the facts—one from the defense attorney and another from the prosecutor (see Box 4.1). Even if all of the facts come out at trial, the jurors will not necessarily take all of them into consideration in reaching a verdict. If the jurors believe that the defendant, for whatever reason, should be acquitted, they may ignore or minimize evidence that establishes the defendant's guilt. Finally, jurors, like judges, are also human and therefore fallible.

In this section, then, we focus on judges and jurors. We begin with a discussion of judges. We consider such topics as constraints on the discretion of judges, the methods of selecting judges, and the question of diversity (or the lack thereof) in the courtroom. We also consider the issue of nonlawyer judges. Our discussion of juries focuses on jury selection, jury decision making, and the controversial—though relatively rare—practice of jury nullification.

BOX 4.1

The Adversary Judge

With partisan counsel fighting to win, and with the judge as umpire to ensure the rules of the fight, there might seem *a priori* no reason in the nature of the contest why the judge should himself be, or seem to be, or perceive himself as being drawn into the fray. . . . The adversary trial, however, happens to be a game in which the role of umpire includes unorthodox features. Although it has no instant replays or particular events, its participants have a large stake in increasing the probability that the whole game be replayed. This possibility depends, largely, of course, on whether the judicial umpire himself commits fouls—"errors," as we say—in the regulating of the contest. And this element is liable to cause the detachment of the trial judge to be tested, threatened, and sometimes impaired, if not entirely lost.

—Former U.S. District Judge Marvin Frankel (Frankel, 2006, p. 398)

 Judges

In the eyes of most Americans, the judge is the key player in the courtroom workgroup. The symbolism and ceremony of a criminal trial reinforce this view. The judge is seated on a raised bench, robed in black, and wields a gavel to maintain order in the courtroom. Moreover, the participants and spectators—including the defense attorney and the prosecutor—are commanded to "all rise" when the judge enters or leaves the courtroom. It is no wonder, then, that the judge is seen as the most influential person in court.

This view of the judge, though accurate to some degree, is misleading for at least two reasons. First, although the judge clearly plays an important role—in many cases, the lead role—in state and federal criminal courts, other actors play significant supporting roles. This is particularly the case in the majority of criminal cases that are settled by plea, not trial. In these cases, the key player may be the prosecutor rather than the judge; the prosecutor determines the charges the defendant will face, negotiates a guilty plea to these (or lesser) charges with the defense attorney, and may even recommend a sentence to the judge. A second reason why the traditional view of the judge is misleading is that it is based on an inaccurate assessment of the role of the judge. Judging involves more than presiding at trials. In fact, most of what judges do during a typical day or week is something other than presiding at trials—reading case files, conducting hearings, accepting guilty pleas, pronouncing sentences, and managing court dockets.

The role played by the judge, in other words, is both less influential and more varied than the traditional view would have people believe.

Constraints on Judges

Judges are expected to be impartial and to decide cases fairly; the judge is to be an "impartial arbiter between the parties and faithful guide of the jury toward the truth" (Frankel, 2006, p. 398). There is, however, no constitutional requirement to this effect. The Sixth Amendment, for example, states that "in all criminal prosecutions, the accused shall enjoy the right to a speedy and public trial, by an impartial jury," but it says nothing about the impartiality of the judge. Even so, the Supreme Court has held that the Due Process Clause of the Fourteenth Amendment guarantees criminal defendants the right to trial by an impartial judge. The Court arrived at this decision in *Tumey v. Ohio* (1927), a case involving the judge of a municipal court who received the fines and fees that he levied against those convicted in his courtroom. The Supreme Court concluded that due process is violated when the judge "has a direct, personal, substantial pecuniary interest" in the outcome of the case (*Tumey v. Ohio*, 1927, p. 523).

A related case is *Ward v. Village of Monroeville* (1972). In this case, a mayor/judge collected fines and fees that went to the town's budget, as opposed to him personally. These fines and fees, however, provided a substantial portion of Monroeville's total budget. The Supreme Court concluded, again, that due process was violated. It held that "the mayor's executive responsibilities for village finances may make him partisan to maintain the high level of contribution from the mayor's court" (*Ward v. Village of Monroeville*, 1972, p. 59). Contrast this decision with *Dugan v. Ohio* (1928), a case in which the Supreme Court held that due process was *not* violated because the mayor/judge was one of several members of a city commission and did not have substantial control over the city's funding sources.

Disqualification or Challenges of Judges. What happens if the judge is not neutral and detached and therefore cannot decide the case fairly? Judges, like defense attorneys and prosecutors, are required to abide by codes of conduct that require them to remove (or **recuse**) themselves when conflicts of interest exist or if they are biased or prejudiced toward either party. But what happens if the judge does not voluntarily recuse himself or herself? In most jurisdictions, the prosecution or defense can move to have the judge disqualified or removed for cause; the side seeking to remove the judge files a motion that explains why the judge to whom the case is assigned should be disqualified. The criteria for disqualification vary, but generally they require that judges be disqualified only if they have a "substantial interest" in the outcome of the case. Montana law, for example, provides that a judge cannot sit on any case (1) to which he or she is a party, or in which he or she is interested; (2) if he or she is related to either party; or (3) if he or she previously represented either side or rendered a decision in the case. According to the U.S. Supreme Court,

> Disqualification is required if an objective observer would entertain reasonable questions about the judge's impartiality. If a judge's attitude or state of mind leads a detached observer to conclude that a fair and impartial hearing is unlikely, the judge must be disqualified. (*Liteky v. U.S.,* 1994)

If the judge being challenged does not recuse himself or herself, another judge (in Texas, e.g., it is the presiding judge of the judicial district) decides whether the motion should be granted.

Another method of removing biased judges, at least in the few states in which it is an option, is through a peremptory challenge (King, 1998). Under this system, the judge assigned to the case can be removed or struck by either side, without providing any reason (Miller, 2004). Under Alaska's Criminal Rule 25(d), both the prosecutor and the defense attorney have the right to one change of judge. Generally, each side gets only one challenge, and the challenge must be made soon after the identity of the judge to whom the case is assigned is known. The advantage of this procedure is that it allows either side to exclude a judge without having to prove that the judge is unable to be fair and impartial.

The Appellate Process. Another formal method of constraining judges is through the appellate process. Appellate courts can alter the outcomes of criminal cases by overturning the offender's conviction or sentence.

Although offenders do not have a constitutional right to appeal their convictions, every jurisdiction has created a statutory right to appeal to one higher court. The purpose of this is to ensure that proper procedures were followed by all of the parties to the case, including the judge. A state court defendant who believes that his or her conviction was obtained improperly can appeal a conviction to the intermediate appellate court or, in states that do not have a two-tiered appellate court system, to the state supreme court. Similarly, a defendant who has been tried and convicted in one of the U.S. District Courts can appeal his or her conviction to the U.S. Courts of Appeals. If the appellate court sustains the appeal and rules that procedures were violated, the court will overturn the conviction and send the case back to the trial court. The case then may be retried or dismissed. If the appellate court rules against the offender, he or she can appeal to the next highest court, but that court does not have to hear the appeal.

Although the scope of **appellate review** is limited to final judgments of lower courts on questions of law (and not of fact), many of the decisions judges make are subject to appeal. This might include pretrial decisions regarding bail and provision of counsel, as well as a host of decisions during the trial itself. For instance, a defendant might appeal the judge's decision to refuse to grant a change of **venue**, to allow the prosecutor to use his or her **peremptory challenges** to exclude racial minorities from the jury, to admit evidence that was obtained in violation of the law, or to refuse to exclude hearsay evidence. That judges' decisions are potentially subject to review by an appellate court obviously constrains their behavior in court.

The ability of appellate courts to alter *sentences* imposed by trial court judges is more limited. The United States Supreme Court has ruled that "review by an appellate court of the final judgment in a criminal case . . . is not a necessary element of due process of law, and that the **right of appeal** may be accorded by the state to the accused upon such conditions as the state deems proper" (*Murphy* v. *Com. of Massachusetts*, 1900). Although all states with death penalty statutes provide for appellate review of death sentences, only half of the states permit appellate review of noncapital sentences that fall within statutory limits (U.S. Justice Department, 2000, Table 45). The standards for review vary; in some states, appellate courts are authorized to modify sentences deemed "excessive," while in other states only sentences determined to be "manifestly excessive," "clearly erroneous," or "an abuse of discretion" can be altered (Miller, Dawson, Dix, & Parnas, 1991, p. 1106). A defendant sentenced under the federal sentencing guidelines can appeal a sentence that is more severe than the guidelines permit; federal law also allows the government to appeal a sentence that is more lenient than provided for in the guidelines. If an offender appeals his or her sentence and the appeal is sustained, the sentence must be corrected. An appellate court decision to vacate the sentence does not mean, however, that the offender will escape punishment. As the Supreme Court stated in 1947, "The Constitution does not require that sentencing should be a game in which a wrong move by the judge means immunity for the prisoner" (*Bozza v. United States*, 1947). Thus, the case will be sent back to the trial court for resentencing.

Discipline and Impeachment. The behavior of judges is also regulated by procedures for disciplining or removing unfit judges. The only formal mechanism for removing federal judges is **impeachment**, which involves impeachment (or accusation) by the House of Representatives and trial in the Senate. As discussed in Section I, very few federal judges have been removed from the bench through impeachment. Since 1789 the House has impeached 16 judges, only 8 of whom were convicted by the Senate and removed. These numbers are somewhat misleading, however. The House has investigated about 50 judges; some of these judges were censured and some resigned during the investigation (Murphy et al., 2006, p. 156).

The procedures for removing state court judges are spelled out in each state's constitution. Like federal judges, state judges can be impeached by the state legislature. Most states also provide for recall of state officials, including judges. This requires that a certain percentage of registered voters in the jurisdiction sign a petition requesting a special recall election; for example, a number of states require signatures from 25% or 30% of the voters who voted in the last election for the targeted office. The voters then decide whether the judge should be retained or removed.

Because impeachment and recall are cumbersome and slow procedures for disciplining judges, all of the states have adopted **judicial disciplinary commissions**. These commissions, which usually are made up of sitting or retired judges, lawyers, and laypersons, investigate complaints filed against judges. The investigation, however, is not made public unless the commission finds that there is probable cause to substantiate the complaint. The commission can dismiss the complaint or admonish, censure, or remove the judge. The California Commission on Judicial Performance, for example, issues an advisory letter expressing disapproval of the judge's conduct if the misconduct is minor and issues a private admonishment if the misconduct is more serious. Both of these outcomes are confidential, however; not even the person who lodged the complaint is informed. In cases involving more serious misconduct, the commission can issue a public admonishment or censure or can remove the judge from office. In 2006, the California Commission considered 1,019 complaints against 848 judges; the commission removed two judges, publicly censured four judges, and publicly admonished nine judges (see http://cjp.ca.gov/).

Even though few judges are removed from office through impeachment or other means, the existence of these procedures serves as a check on the behavior of corrupt, inept, unethical, or rude judges. Judicial conduct commissions, in particular, remind judges "of their obligations and the price they will pay for ignoring litigants' and lawyers' legal rights as well as their rights to be treated with dignity and respect" (Murphy et al., 2006, p. 158).

The Politics of Judicial Selection

In the United States today there is no one method of selecting judges. There is uniformity at the federal level, where judges are appointed for life by the president with the advice and consent of the Senate, but the procedures used by the states vary enormously. As one commentator noted, "Almost no two states are alike, and many states employ different methods of selection depending upon the different levels of the judiciary, creating 'hybrid' systems of selection" (Berkson, 2005). Despite these variations, the *primary difference* in selection procedures for state court judges is whether judges are elected, appointed, or chosen using some type of a merit system.

There is considerable controversy surrounding the various methods of selecting state court judges. The controversy largely revolves around the issues of accountability and independence. Proponents of electing judges argue that popular elections are a means of ensuring that judges remain accountable to the people. They are a means of ensuring that judges consider the will of the people in rendering decisions and guaranteeing that unfit or corrupt judges are voted out of office at the next election. Critics of elections, on the other hand, contend that voters typically know very little about the behavior of judges on the bench and thus cannot hold them accountable for their decisions. Critics also charge that electing judges reduces judicial independence and thus makes it less likely that judges will hand down fair and impartial decisions (Blankenship & Janikowski, 1992). Judges who must face election, in other words, may decide cases with one eye toward the upcoming election; they may hand down decisions that reflect, not an impartial interpretation of the law, but an analysis of where the voters stand on the issue. (For more on this, see Reading 10 by Bright and Keenan, below.)

Advocates of appointing judges or using the merit system assert that appointment maximizes judicial independence by removing politics from the process. They also contend that appointment results in the selection of judges based on their experience and scholarship, rather than on the basis of party affiliation or popular appeal. Not everyone agrees, however, that appointment of judges eliminates politics from the selection process. One scholar, for example, has pointed out that appointment of judges by elected governors or state legislators leads to "the logical inference that regardless of the academic merits or professional credentials of the candidate, the person chosen reflects the social, political, and economic views" of the person or persons making the appointment (Alarcon, 1983, p. 10). Politics, in other words, may be an inevitable part of judicial selection.

Methods of Selecting State Judges. Historically, judges were appointed by the governor or the state legislature (American Judicature Society, 2004). As shown in Table 4.1, only five states currently use gubernatorial or legislative appointment for judges in trial courts of general jurisdiction. In three states (Maine, New Jersey,

Table 4.1   Methods of Selecting Judges for State Trial Courts of General Jurisdiction

Merit Selection	Partisan Election	Nonpartisan Election	Appointment by Governor (G) or Legislature (L)	Combined Methods[a]
Alaska	Alabama	Arkansas	Maine (G)	Arizona
Colorado	Illinois	California	New Hampshire (G)	Indiana
Connecticut	Louisiana	Florida	New Jersey (G)	Kansas
Delaware	New York	Georgia	South Carolina (L)	Missouri
District of Columbia	Ohio[b]	Idaho	Virginia (L)	
Hawaii	Pennsylvania	Kentucky		
Iowa	Tennessee	Michigan		
Maryland	Texas	Minnesota		
Massachusetts	West Virginia	Mississippi		
Nebraska		Montana		
Nevada		North Carolina		
New Mexico		North Dakota		
Rhode Island		Oklahoma		
Utah		Oregon		
Vermont		South Dakota		
Wyoming		Washington		
		Wisconsin		

a. In these states, some judges are chosen through merit selection and some are chosen in competitive elections.

b. Candidates appear on the general election ballot without party affiliation but are nominated in partisan primaries.

and New Hampshire), the governor appoints judges; the appointment must be approved by either the state senate or some other elected or appointed body. In Virginia and South Carolina, judges are appointed by the state legislature. As discussed later, many states use a merit system, in which the governor appoints a judge from a list of candidates selected by a nominating commission.

More than half of the states elect at least some of their judges. Partisan elections are found in 11 states; in these states, the candidates are nominated by a political party and their party affiliation is included on the ballot. In an additional 20 states, judges are elected on nonpartisan ballots. In these states, the candidate's party affiliation does not appear on the ballot. Selecting judges by partisan elections is, by definition, political. Historically, in fact, political party bosses used elected judgeships to reward campaign workers and those who contributed large amounts of money to the party coffers. Nonpartisan elections can also involve party politics. The local political parties may endorse judicial candidates and donate money to the candidates they support, and the candidates themselves may publicize their party affiliations.

Regardless of whether they are running in partisan or nonpartisan elections, judicial candidates tend to run low-key campaigns in which few controversial issues are raised; voter turnout for these elections is low, and sitting judges who are running for reelection typically keep their seats. In fact, many judicial candidates run unopposed. In the past two decades, however, judicial elections—and particularly elections for state supreme courts—have become more contentious, more costly, and more politicized (Thomas, Boyer, & Hrebenar, 2005). According to Thomas and his colleagues, "These changes were largely a result of interest groups entering judicial campaigns with tactics and a level of funding more akin to legislative and executive elections" (p. 53). In 1986, for example, death-penalty advocates targeted three California Supreme Court justices who were opposed to the death penalty; all three were defeated (Wold & Culver, 1987). More recently, interest groups spent $8 million on television commercials in an attempt to reelect or defeat an Ohio Supreme Court justice. According to one commentator, "The content of ads bought by interest groups was hard hitting, very direct, and largely unconstrained, which enabled them to get more rhetorical force from their expenditures" (Thomas et al., 2005, p. 56).

The third method of judicial selection is the merit system, which is also called the Missouri Plan (Missouri was the first state to adopt this method of judicial selection). This system combines appointment and election. Three steps take place. First, a judicial nominating commission, which is usually composed of laypersons, lawyers, and judges, screens potential candidates and nominates several individuals (typically three) for the vacant position. Second, the governor appoints one of the individuals nominated by the commission to the bench. Third, after the initial term and at designated times thereafter, the appointee runs in a **retention election** in which the voters are asked whether the judge should be retained or not. Fourteen states use this plan, or some version of it, in selecting judges; other states use a nominating commission to select judicial candidates, but judges do not run in retention elections.

Although the Missouri Plan was designed to achieve both judicial independence and accountability, critics charge that it does not achieve either of these goals. At least some members of the nominating commission, as well as the judge, are appointed by the governor, an elected official, which raises questions about the independence of judges appointed using this process. Moreover, research shows that few of the judges who run for retention are defeated; from 1964 to 1998, only 52 of the 4,588 judges who ran for retention were defeated (Aspin, 2005). Retention elections, then, do not appear to have the capacity to hold judges accountable for their decisions.

Despite the controversy surrounding the various methods of selecting state court judges, there is little empirical evidence that the quality of judges varies depending on the method used (Atkins & Glick, 1974;

Dubois, 1986; Nagel, 1975). Judges selected by one method rather than another have not been found to be more competent, honest, or effective. As we point out in the section that follows, this may reflect the fact that the judicial recruitment process produces a relatively uniform pool of candidates from which judges are chosen.

Diversity on the Bench

Researchers have only recently begun to ask whether judges from different backgrounds decide cases differently. This is not surprising, given the homogeneity of the individuals who don judicial robes in courts throughout the United States. The typical judge—federal and state—is white, male, and middle-aged. Only about 10% of all state court judges, for example, are racial minorities and fewer than 15% are women (Carp & Stidham, 1998, p. 261). Most state court judges also were born and went to law school in the state in which they serve; they typically came to the bench either from the private practice of law or from a lower court judgeship, such as a magistrate's position. As Carp and Stidham noted, "They tend to be home-grown fellows who are moderately conservative and staunchly committed to the status quo . . . [they are] local boys who made good" (p. 261). Stumpf's (1988) conclusion was even more pointed:

> If you are young, female, a member of a racial minority, are of the wrong political party, or presumably have few contacts within the organized legal community in your state, the chances of making it to the trial bench are slight. (p. 184)

Judges appointed to the U.S. District Courts also "come from a very narrow stratum of American society" (Carp & Stidham, 1998, p. 210, Note 30). As shown in Table 4.2, more than three-fourths of the district court judges appointed by Presidents Carter, Bush (George H.), and Reagan; two-thirds of those appointed by President Clinton; and three-fourths of those appointed by President George W. Bush were men. Similarly, at least three-fourths of the judges appointed by these five presidents were white (Goldman, Slotnick, Gryski, Zuk, & Schiavoni, 2005). In fact, a majority of the judges appointed by Presidents Carter, Reagan, Bush (George H.), and Bush (George W.) were white men; in contrast, slightly more than a third of President Clinton's appointees were either women or racial minorities.[1] The typical district court judge was about 48 years old at the time of appointment and came to the bench from either a prior judicial position or a position as a public prosecutor. Not surprisingly, the political party affiliation of judges matches that of the president who appointed them; in fact, about 90% of the judges appointed by each president belonged to that president's political party.

How does the fact that state and federal court judges are "much more alike than they are different" (Carp & Stidham, 1998, p. 218) affect the sentencing process? Does the judicial recruitment process produce "a corps of jurists who agree on how the judicial game is played" (Carp & Stidham, 1998, p. 218)? Would judicial decisions be different if more women and racial minorities were elected or appointed to the bench? If there were more diversity in terms of age, religion, and prior experience?

The answers to questions such as these are varied. Most of the debate centers on whether increasing the number of black and female judges would produce a different type of justice. Those on one side of the debate argue that it would not. They contend that the judicial selection process produces a relatively homogenous

---

[1] A similar pattern is found for appointments to the United States Courts of Appeals. The percentage of appointees who were white men was 60.7% (Carter), 92.3% (Reagan), 70.3% (Bush), and 44.8% (Clinton; see Carp & Stidham, 1998, Note 30, Table 8.2).

Table 4.2   Race and Sex of U.S. District Court Appointees, by Administration

	George W. Bush		Reagan		Carter		George H. Bush		Clinton	
	N	%	N	%	N	%	N	%	N	%
Sex										
Male	66	79.5	218	71.5	119	80.4	266	91.7	173	85.6
Female	17	20.5	87	28.5	29	19.6	24	8.3	29	14.4
Race/Ethnicity										
White	71	85.5	229	75.1	132	89.2	268	92.4	159	78.7
Black	6	7.2	53	17.4	10	6.8	6	2.1	28	13.9
Hispanic	6	7.2	18	5.9	6	4.0	14	4.8	14	6.9
Asian	—	—	4	1.3	—	—	2	0.7	1	0.5
Native American	—	—	1	0.3	—	—	—	—	—	—

bench and that judges of all racial groups—male and female—share similar background characteristics. The judicial recruitment process, according to this view, screens out candidates with unconventional views, with the result that women and racial minorities selected for judgeships "tend to be 'safe' candidates who are generally supportive of the system" (Walker & Barrow, 1985, p. 615). They are judges, in other words, who know how the judicial game is played.

Those who take the "no difference position" argue that the homogeneity of the bench is reinforced by the judicial socialization process, which produces a subculture of justice that encourages judges to adhere to prevailing norms, practices, and precedents (Frazier & Bock, 1982). It also is reinforced by the courtroom workgroup—the judges, prosecutors, and defense attorneys who work together day after day to process cases as efficiently as possible. To expedite sentencing, for example, members of the courtroom workgroup may informally agree on the parameters of acceptable plea negotiations and on the range of penalties appropriate for each type of crime. Although individual judges might deviate from these norms, there is no reason to expect women or racial minorities to deviate more often than men or whites.

Some commentators assert that even unconventional or maverick judges eventually are forced to conform. As Bruce Wright, a black man who sat on the New York Supreme Court from 1982 to 1994, stated in 1973, "No matter how 'liberal' black judges may believe themselves to be, the law remains essentially a conservative doctrine, and those who practice it conform" (p. 22). Twenty years later, Judge Wright made an even more pointed comment, noting that some black judges

> are so white in their imitation of life and in their reactions to black defendants that they are known as 'Afro-Saxons.' As soon as these black judges put on the black robes, they become emotionally white. But it's not surprising. We have Eurocentric educations. We learn white values. (Washington, 1994, p. 251)

Those who champion diversity in the courtroom argue that black judges and women judges can make a difference. They suggest that black judges and women judges bring to the bench beliefs, attitudes, and experiences that differ from those of whites and men. Goldman (1979), for example, maintains that racial minorities and women will bring to the court "a certain sensitivity—indeed, certain qualities of heart and mind—that may be particularly helpful in dealing with [issues of racial and sexual discrimination]" (p. 494).

Advocates of the "difference position," then, contend that women judges and black judges contribute something unique to the judicial process. In support of the argument that women judges "speak in a different voice," some point to the work of Carol Gilligan (1982), who claimed that women's moral reasoning differs from that of men. Whereas men emphasize legal rules and reasoning based on an ethic of justice, women, who are more concerned about preserving relationships and more sensitive to the needs of others, reason using an ethic of care. Others, who counter that "the language of law is explicitly the language of justice rather than care" (Berns, 1999, p. 197), claim that the differences women bring to the bench stem more from their experiences as women than from differences in moral reasoning. They maintain, for example, that women are substantially more likely than men to be victimized by rape, sexual harassment, domestic violence, and other forms of predatory violence and that their experiences as crime victims or their fears about crime shape their attitudes toward and their response to crime and criminals. Noting that "human beings are products of their experiences," Martha Fineman (1994) suggested that "if women collectively have different actual *and* potential experiences from men, they are likely to have different perspectives—different sets of values, beliefs, and concerns as a group" (pp. 239–240).

How might these gender differences influence judges' sentencing decisions? If, in fact, women are more compassionate—more caring—than men, they might sentence offenders more leniently than men do. A female judge, in other words, might be more willing than a male judge to sentence a nonviolent offender struggling to provide for his family to probation rather than prison. Alternatively, that women are more likely to be victims of sexualized violence and are more fearful of crime in general might incline them to impose harsher sentences than men would, particularly for violent crimes, crimes against women, and crimes involving dangerous repeat offenders. Still another possibility is that the life experiences of women judges—and particularly black or Hispanic women judges—will make them more sensitive to the existence of racism or sexism; as a result, they might make more equitable sentencing decisions than would white male judges.

Similar arguments are advanced by those who contend that increasing the number of racial minorities on state and federal courts will alter the character of justice and the outcomes of the criminal justice system. Because the life histories and experiences of blacks differ dramatically from those of whites, in other words, the beliefs and attitudes they bring to the bench also will differ. Justice A. Leon Higginbotham Jr., a black man who retired from the U.S. Court of Appeals for the Third Circuit in 1993, wrote that "the advantage of pluralism is that it brings a multitude of different experiences to the judicial process" (Washington, 1994, p. 11). More to the point, he stated that "someone who has been a victim of racial injustice has greater sensitivity of the court's making sure that racism is not perpetrated, even inadvertently" (p. 11–12). Judge George Crockett's (1984) assessment of the role of the black judge was even more pointed:

> I think a black judge . . . has got to be a reformist—he cannot be a member of the club. The whole purpose of selecting him is that the people are dissatisfied with the status quo and they want him to shake it up, and his role is to shake it up. (p. 393)

Assuming that black judges agree with Judge Crockett's assertion that their role is to "shake it up," how would this affect their behavior on the bench? One possibility is that black judges might attempt to stop—or at least slow—the flow of young black men into state and federal prisons. If, in other words, black judges view the disproportionately high number of young black men incarcerated in state and federal prisons as a symptom of racial discrimination, they might be more willing than white judges to experiment with alternatives to incarceration for offenders convicted of nonviolent drug and property crimes. Welch and her colleagues (Welch, Combs, & Gruhl, 1988) made an analogous argument. Noting that blacks tend to view themselves as liberal rather than conservative, the authors speculated that black judges might be "more sympathetic to criminal defendants than whites judges are, since liberal views are associated with support for the underdog and the poor, which defendants disproportionately are" (p. 127). Others similarly suggest that increasing the number of black judges would reduce racism in the criminal justice system and produce more equitable treatment of black and white defendants (Welch et al., 1988).

Do Members of Racial Minorities or Women Dispense a Different Kind of Justice?

Research investigating the effects of judicial characteristics on sentencing decisions have produced somewhat inconsistent findings. Most researchers find few overall differences in the sentences imposed by black and white judges. For instance, Engle (1971) concluded that there were only minor differences in the sentences imposed by black and white judges; Uhlman (1978) found that although the sentencing patterns of individual black judges varied considerably, their overall sentencing patterns didn't differ from those of white judges; and Spohn (1990b) concluded that there were "remarkable similarities" in the sentencing decisions of black and white judges. One study (Spohn, 1990a) found that black female judges imposed longer sentences on offenders convicted of sexual assault, and another (Spears, 1999) found that black male judges sentenced offenders to prison at a lower rate but imposed longer sentences on those who were incarcerated. Depending on the time period, the jurisdiction, and the types of offenses included in the analysis, black judges sentenced either no differently, more harshly, or more leniently than white judges.

The evidence regarding the degree to which black and Hispanic judges impose more racially equitable sentences is also mixed. Two studies (Spears, 1999; Welch et al., 1988) found that black judges imposed similar sentences on black and white offenders, whereas white judges gave more lenient sentences to white offenders than to black offenders. Another (Holmes et al., 1993) found a similar pattern of results for Hispanic judges and Anglo judges. Both studies concluded that white judges discriminate in favor of white offenders. A third study (Spohn, 1990b), on the other hand, found no race-of-judge differences in the sentences imposed on black and white offenders convicted of violent felonies.

These inconsistencies suggest that we do not know, on the basis of the limited amount of research that has been conducted to date, whether black judges dispense a different kind of justice than white judges. We do not know the extent to which black judges believe that their role is, to use Judge Crockett's words, "to shake it up." The degree to which female judges sentence differently than male judges is somewhat more conclusive. There is no evidence that women dispense a "gentler" form of justice; that is, there is no evidence that women, in contrast to men, are "soft on crime." In fact, the differences that do appear suggest just the opposite. Three studies (Gruhl, Spohn, & Welch, 1981; Spears, 1999; Steffensmeier & Hebert, 1999) found that offenders sentenced by female judges were significantly more likely to be sent to prison than comparable offenders sentenced by male judges. Female judges in Pennsylvania also imposed longer sentences than their male colleagues (Steffensmeier & Hebert, 1999), and black female judges in Detroit imposed substantially longer sentences on offenders convicted of sexual assault than black male judges did (Spohn, 1990a). The evidence regarding the treatment of female and male offenders by female and male judges is less consistent. Two studies (Gruhl et al., 1984; Spears, 1999) found that female judges imposed similar sentences on male and female defendants, whereas male judges sentenced female defendants more leniently than male defendants.

Although these results suggest that female judges are less likely than male judges to see female defendants through a paternalistic or chivalrous lens, Steffensmeier and Hebert's (1999) analysis of sentencing decisions in Pennsylvania found a different pattern of results, which complicates the issue. They found that both women and men judges sentenced blacks more harshly than whites and sentenced females more leniently than males. Moreover, the race and gender of the offender had a more pronounced effect on the sentencing decisions of female judges, who were particularly harsh toward repeat black offenders.

There is some evidence, then, that female judges speak in a different voice from the bench. Perhaps because of their greater fear of crime, they tend to impose somewhat harsher sentences than their male colleagues. There is also some evidence that female judges, like black and Hispanic judges, are more even-handed in their sentencing decisions and that the recruitment of increasing numbers of women and members of racial minorities will promote more equitable sentencing decisions.

Overall, however, the differences between male and female judges and between black or Hispanic judges and white judges are not large. All judges, regardless of their race or gender or the race or gender of the person being sentenced, base their sentencing decisions primarily on the seriousness of the crime and the offender's prior criminal record. The similarities in the sentencing practices of judges suggest that "they are governed more by their legal training and legal socialization than by their socially structured personal experiences" (Steffensmeier & Hebert, 1999, p. 1187).

Nonlawyer Judges: A Dying Breed?

Most judges are lawyers, but nonlawyer, or lay, judges have been common throughout American history. Even today, 34 states use **nonlawyer judges** in some capacity; most of them serve on state courts of limited jurisdiction, but some of them, such as the surrogate judges in New Jersey, serve on courts of general jurisdiction (McFarland, 2004). Lay judges, who are referred to by names such as *magistrate*, *justice of the peace*, and *associate judge*, decide millions of cases each year (Provine, 1986). An example can be found in Arizona Justice of the Peace Courts. There are only four requirements to be a justice of the peace: (1) aged 18 years or older, (2) a resident of the state, (3) an elector of the county or jurisdiction in which the duties are to be performed, and (4) able to read and write English. Those who meet these minimum qualifications can run for the elected position; if elected, they participate in a 19-day training program before taking the bench. Their responsibility is not to adjudicate criminal offenses but rather to settle disputes involving small amounts of money, usually $1,000 or less.

The history of lay judges in this country is one of ebbs and flows. In 17th-century New England, legal matters were handled almost exclusively without lawyers. By the early 1700s, population growth, urban development, and the accumulation of wealth ushered in an era of a more formalized legal profession. As the legal profession began to grow in power and influence, adjudication of legal matters was increasingly delegated to legally trained judges. Eventually, lay judge positions were all but abolished in larger urban areas. Today, they are more likely to be found in thinly populated rural areas where lawyers are in short supply. They also suffer from what Doris Provine (1986), the author of *Judging Credentials: Nonlawyer Judges and the Politics of Professionalism*, referred to as an image problem (Chapter 5). This is not surprising, according to Provine, given that lay judges are "the worst paid, worst housed, worst outfitted, and least supervised judges in the nation" (p. 122). Provine's analysis of lawyer and lay judges on New York's Justice Courts, however, found no major differences in either their attitudes or behavior (other scholars are highly critical of lay judges; see, e.g., Mansfield, 1999).

Jurors and Jury Decision Making

The jury plays a critically important role in the criminal justice system. Indeed, "the jury is the heart of the criminal justice system" (Cole, 2000, p. 101). Although it is true that most cases are settled by plea and not by trial, many of the cases that go to trial involve serious crimes in which defendants are facing long prison terms or even the death penalty. In these serious—and highly publicized—cases, the jury serves as the conscience of the community and, in the words of the United States Supreme Court, as "an inestimable safeguard against the corrupt or overzealous prosecutor and against the compliant, biased, or eccentric judge" (*Duncan v. Louisiana*, 1968). As the Court has repeatedly emphasized, the jury also serves as "the criminal defendant's fundamental 'protection of life and liberty against race or color prejudice'" (*McCleskey v. Kemp*, 1987, quoting *Strauder v. West Virginia*, 1880).

Although the rarity of jury trials limits the jury's overall influence on the criminal process, decisions made by the jury in the cases they do decide are obviously important. The jury decides whether to convict the defendant or not. The jury also may decide whether to convict the defendant for the offense charged or for a lesser included offense. In a murder case, for example, the jury might have the option of finding the defendant guilty of first-degree murder, second-degree murder, or manslaughter. Like the prosecutor's charging decisions, these conviction decisions affect the sentence that will be imposed. A defendant who is charged with first-degree murder but convicted of manslaughter will be sentenced more leniently than if convicted of the more serious charge. The role of the jury in the criminal justice system, though limited to those cases in which the defendant elects a jury trial, is thus both symbolically and substantively important.

Issues in Jury Selection

We noted in Section I that the Supreme Court has interpreted the Sixth Amendment's requirement that the defendant be tried by an **impartial jury** to mean that the jury pool must be a **random cross-section of the community**. Many of the Supreme Court cases regarding jury selection have involved the question of racial discrimination. Black and Hispanic defendants have repeatedly challenged the procedures used to select juries, arguing that the procedures, which often produced all-white juries, violated both the Sixth Amendment and the Equal Protection Clause of the Fourteenth Amendment. Questions also have been raised about the potential for juror dishonesty during voir dire. There is evidence that jurors do not always tell the truth when asked about their backgrounds, their prior experiences with the justice system, and their attitudes and beliefs. We explore these issues in the following sections.

Race and the Jury Selection Process. The Supreme Court first addressed the issue of racial discrimination in jury selection in its 1880 decision in *Strauder v. West Virginia*. The Court ruled that a West Virginia statute limiting jury service to white males violated the Equal Protection Clause of the Fourteenth Amendment and therefore was unconstitutional. The Court stated that the West Virginia statute denied black defendants the right—in fact, even the *chance*—to have people of their own race on their juries. "How can it be maintained," the justices asked, "that compelling a man to submit to trial for his life by a jury drawn from a panel from which the State has expressly excluded every man of his race, because of his color alone, however well qualified in other respects, is not a denial to him of equal legal protection?" (p. 309). The Court added that this was precisely the type of discrimination the equal protection clause was designed to prevent.

After *Strauder v. West Virginia*, it was clear that states could not pass laws excluding blacks from jury service. This ruling, however, did not prevent states from developing techniques designed to preserve the all-white jury. In Delaware, for example, local jurisdictions used lists of taxpayers to select "sober and judicious" persons for jury service. Under this system, black taxpayers were eligible for jury service, but were seldom, if ever, selected for the jury pool. The state explained this result by noting that few of the black people in Delaware were intelligent, experienced, or moral enough to serve as jurors. The Supreme Court refused to accept this explanation. In *Neal v. Delaware* (1880), decided the same year as *Strauder*, the court ruled that the practice had systematically excluded black people from jury service and was therefore a case of purposeful—and unconstitutional—racial discrimination.

Since the mid-1930s, the Supreme Court has made it increasingly difficult for court systems to exclude blacks or Hispanics from the jury pool. It consistently has struck down the techniques used to circumvent the requirement of racial neutrality in the selection of the jury pool. The Court, for example, ruled that it was unconstitutional for a Georgia county to put the names of white potential jurors on white cards, the names of black potential jurors on yellow cards, and then "randomly" draw cards to determine who would be summoned (*Avery v. Georgia*, 1953). Similarly, the Court struck down the "random" selection of jurors from tax books in which the names of white taxpayers were in one section and the names of black taxpayers were in another (*Whitus v. Georgia*, 1967). As the justices stated in *Avery* v. *Georgia*, "the State may not draw up its jury lists pursuant to neutral procedures but then resort to discrimination at other stages in the selection process."

The states' response to the Supreme Court's increasingly vigilant oversight of the jury selection process was not always positive. The response in some Southern jurisdictions "was a new round of tokenism aimed at maintaining as much of the white supremacist status quo as possible while avoiding judicial intervention" (Kennedy, 1997, p. 179). These jurisdictions, in other words, included a token number of racial minorities in the jury pool in an attempt to head off charges of racial discrimination. The Supreme Court addressed this issue as late as 1988 (*Amadeo v. Zant*, 1988). The Court reversed the conviction of Tony Amadeo, who was sentenced to death for murder in Putnam County, Georgia, after it was revealed that the Putnam County district attorney asked the jury commissioner to limit the number of blacks and women on the master lists from which potential jurors were chosen.

The Supreme Court's rulings that the jury must be drawn from a representative cross-section of the community and that race is not a valid qualification for jury service apply only to the selection of the jury pool. They do not apply to the selection of individual jurors for a particular case. In fact, the Court has repeatedly stated that a defendant is *not* entitled to a jury "composed in whole or in part of persons of his own race" (*Batson v. Kentucky*, 1986; *Strauder v. West Virginia*, 1880). This means that prosecutors and defense attorneys can use their peremptory challenges—"challenges without cause, without explanation, and without judicial scrutiny" (*Swain v. Alabama*, 1965)—as they see fit. They can, in essence, use their peremptory challenges in a racially discriminatory manner.

It is clear that lawyers do take the race of the juror into consideration during the jury selection process. Prosecutors assume that racial minorities will side with minority defendants, and defense attorneys assume that racial minorities will be more inclined than whites to convict white defendants. As a result of these assumptions, both prosecutors and defense attorneys have used their peremptory challenges to strike racial minorities from the jury pool. Randall Kennedy, in fact, has characterized the peremptory challenge as "a creature of unbridled discretion that, in the hands of white prosecutors and white defendants, has often been used to sustain racial subordination in the courthouse" (Kennedy, 1997, p. 214, Note 64).

There is compelling evidence that prosecutors use their peremptory challenges to strike racial minorities from the jury pool. As a result, black and Hispanic defendants are frequently tried by all-white juries. In 1964, for example, Robert Swain, a 19-year-old black man, was sentenced to death by an all-white jury for raping a white woman in Alabama. The prosecutor had used his peremptory challenges to strike all six blacks on the jury panel (*Swain v. Alabama*, 1965). In 1990, the state used all of its peremptory challenges to eliminate blacks from the jury that would try Marion Barry, the black mayor of Washington, D.C., on drug charges.

The Supreme Court initially was reluctant to restrict the prosecutor's right to use peremptory challenges to excuse jurors on the basis of race. In 1965, the Court ruled in *Swain v. Alabama* (1965) that the prosecutor's use of peremptory challenges to strike all six black people in the jury pool did not violate the equal protection clause of the Constitution. The Court reasoned,

> The presumption in any particular case must be that the prosecutor is using the State's challenges to obtain a fair and impartial jury. . . . The presumption is not overcome and the prosecutor therefore subjected to examination by allegations that in the case at hand all Negroes were removed from the jury or that they were removed because they were Negroes. (*Swain v. Alabama*, 1965, p. 222)

The Court went on to observe that the Constitution places some limits on the use of the peremptory challenge. The justices stated that a defendant could establish a prima facie case of purposeful racial discrimination by showing that the elimination of black people from a particular jury was part of a pattern of discrimination in that jurisdiction. The problem, of course, was that the defendants in *Swain* (1965), and in the cases that followed, could not meet this stringent test. The ruling, therefore, provided no protection to the individual black or Hispanic defendant deprived of a jury of his or her peers by the prosecutor's use of racially discriminatory strikes.

Despite harsh criticism from legal scholars and civil libertarians ("Rethinking Limitations," 1983; "*Swain v. Alabama*: A constitutional blueprint," 1966), who argued that *Swain* imposed a "crushing burden . . . on defendants alleging racially discriminatory jury selection" (Serr & Maney, 1988, p. 13), the decision stood for 21 years. It was not until 1986 that the Court, in *Batson v. Kentucky*, rejected *Swain*'s systematic exclusion requirement and ruled "that a defendant may establish a *prima facie* case of purposeful discrimination in selection of the petit jury solely on evidence concerning the prosecutor's exercise of peremptory challenges at the defendant's trial" (pp. 93–94, 96). The justices added that once the defendant makes a **prima facie case of racial discrimination**, the burden shifts to the state to provide a racially neutral explanation for excluding black jurors.

Although *Batson* (1986) seemed to offer hope that the goal of a representative jury was attainable, an examination of cases decided since 1986 suggests otherwise. State and federal appellate courts have ruled, for example, that leaving one or two black people on the jury precludes any inference of purposeful racial discrimination on the part of the prosecutor (*United States v. Montgomery*, 1987)[2] and that striking only one or two jurors of the defendant's race does not constitute a "pattern" of strikes (*Fields v. People*, 1987; *United States v. Vaccaro*, 1987). Trial and appellate courts have also been willing to accept virtually any explanation offered by the prosecutor to rebut the defendant's inference of purposeful discrimination

---

[2]The Court of Appeals for the Eleventh Circuit, however, rejected this line of reasoning in *Fleming v. Kemp* (1986).

(Serr & Maney, 1988, pp. 43–47). As Kennedy (1997) noted, "judges tend to give the benefit of the doubt to the prosecutor" (p. 211). Kennedy cited as an example *State v. Jackson*, a case in which the prosecutor used her peremptory challenges to strike four black people in the jury pool. According to Kennedy,

> the prosecutor said that she struck one black prospective juror because she was unemployed and had previously served as a student counselor at a university, a position that bothered the prosecution because it was "too liberal a background." The prosecution said that it struck another black prospective juror because she, too, was unemployed, and, through her demeanor, had displayed hostility or indifference. By contrast, two whites who were unemployed were seated without objection by the prosecution. (p. 213)

Although Kennedy (1997) acknowledged that "one should give due deference to the trial judge who was in a position to see directly the indescribable subtleties," he stated that he "still has difficulty believing that, had these prospective jurors been white, the prosecutor would have struck them just the same" (p. 213). Echoing these concerns, Serr and Maney (1988) concluded that the "cost of forfeiting truly peremptory challenges has yielded little corresponding benefit, as a myriad of 'acceptable' explanations and excuses cloud any hope of detecting racially based motivations" (p. 63).

Critics of *Batson* (1986) and its progeny maintain that until the courts articulate and apply a more meaningful standard or eliminate peremptory challenges altogether, "peremptory strikes will be color-blind in theory only" (Cole, 2000, p. 124).

Juror (Dis)honesty During Voir Dire. During the voir dire, jurors are asked questions designed to determine whether they can decide the case fairly and impartially. They are asked about their background and experiences and about their attitudes regarding issues, such as insanity or testimony by expert witnesses or law enforcement officers, that may come up in the case. In death penalty cases, they are asked questions about their views of capital punishment. There is an assumption—indeed, a legal requirement if the jurors are under oath—that jurors will answer these questions honestly. But do they? One researcher (Bush, 1976) interviewed jurors after a 1976 trial verdict and found that one in three of them had lied under oath. Another researcher (Spaeth, 2001) found that 71% of jurors had a fixed opinion regarding a defendant's guilt, but only 15% admitted this during the voir dire phase. Others have found that the voir dire process itself inhibits full disclosure on the part of prospective jurors, possibly because of the intimidation factor (Suggs & Sales, 1980). According to one author,

> these statistics are striking. If they are representative of juror honesty generally, they suggest that questions put to jurors in certain formats are more likely to elicit a false response. This lack of candor by jurors can have a significant effect in trial strategy and in the verdicts rendered, because juror honesty during open voir dire in the courtroom is now the critical method for exposing juror bias and impartiality. (Spaeth, 2001, p. 39)

The question then becomes, what do we do about juror dishonesty? If prospective jurors are less than forthcoming during voir dire, what is the remedy? One solution would be to advise jurors that lies are subject to perjury charges. Most jurors, though, are aware of the consequences of being untruthful. Another problem with this solution is that prospective jurors are not always "under oath" during voir dire. An alternative solution involves the use of a written questionnaire that jurors can complete in relative anonymity. A number of reformers have called for just this approach, citing research from other fields that shows that people are more truthful in their written responses regarding questions about their drug use, sexual practices, and other sensitive topics (Acree, Ekstrand, Coates, & Stall, 1999; Aquilino, 1990; Rasinski, Willis, Baldwin, Yeh, & Lee, 1999).

If prospective jurors regularly lie during voir dire, then perhaps attorneys should be given all the leverage they need to excuse questionable individuals. Challenges for cause are reserved for cases where prospective jurors have clear conflicts of interest, are biased toward one side or the other, or have already made up their minds in the case. Peremptory challenges, on the other hand, are challenges that the attorneys can use to excuse anyone, without giving a reason. Peremptory challenges are therefore useful for removing jurors whom the attorneys might have nagging doubts about, even if they are unable to convince the judge that these jurors should be removed for cause. Peremptory challenges also can be used to excuse jurors who fit a certain profile, possibly on the advice of a **jury consultant** (see next section).

There is considerable controversy about the peremptory challenge. We already noted that critics of the peremptory challenge charge that it is used in a racially discriminatory way. Defenders of the peremptory challenge, who acknowledge that there is inherent tension between peremptory challenges and the quest for a representative jury, argue that the availability of the challenge ensures an impartial jury. Defenders of the process further argue that restricting the number of peremptory challenges or requiring attorneys to provide reasons for exercising them would make selection of an impartial jury more difficult. Those who advocate elimination of the peremptory challenge, on the other hand, assert that prosecutors and defense attorneys can use the **challenge for cause** to eliminate biased or prejudiced jurors.

Some commentators contend that the system would be fairer without peremptory challenges. As Morris B. Hoffman (1997) put it,

> even assuming the peremptory challenge ever worked in this country as anything other than a tool for racial purity, and even assuming it is working today in its post-*Batson* configuration to eliminate hidden juror biases without being either unconstitutionally discriminating or unconstitutionally irrational, I submit that its institutional costs outweigh any of its most highly-touted benefits. Those costs—in juror distrust, cynicism, and prejudice—simply obliterate any benefits achieved by permitting trial lawyers to test their home-grown theories of human behavior on the most precious commodity we have—impartial citizens. (p. 871)

Jury Consultants

In 2004, a jury composed of six men and six women convicted Scott Peterson of murdering his wife and their unborn child. This high-profile case stands out both because of the publicity it received and the length of the trial—almost 6 months. Even jury selection, which took nearly 3 months and involved interviews with 1,500 prospective jurors, received a wealth of publicity. What did *not* receive much press, though, was the behind-the-scenes process of jury selection, particularly the role of jury consultants during the voir dire phase. Jury consultants Howard Varinksky (for the prosecution) and Jo-Ellan Dimitrus (for the defense) both worked in relative obscurity to ensure that their side would benefit from a jury stacked in their favor. Varinksky, Dimitrus, and others like them perform an interesting function in the jury selection process, particularly for high-profile trials.

Where did jury consultants come from? Researchers who have tracked the evolution of jury consulting look back to the defense of the so-called Harrisburg Seven, a group of Vietnam War protestors who were accused of several acts of civil disobedience (Strier & Shestowsky, 1999). The trial was to take place in the conservative city of Harrisburg, Pennsylvania, and in an effort to combat the resources the government was devoting to the case and the negative views of the defendants, the defense attorneys hired a team of social scientists to help them select a jury that would be favorable to their side. The researchers created a demographic profile of people likely to be sympathetic to the defendants' antiwar views, and this profile was used to select the jurors for the case. The government spent two million dollars on the trial, but the jury acquitted the defendants. The verdict was largely attributed to the jury consultants and, so, the jury consulting profession was born.

Jury consultants use a number of different strategies. Although the most common strategy is to develop a profile of jurors likely to vote in favor of the defense, consultants also may perform background checks on prospective jurors or hire field investigators to gather additional information. Profiling involves surveying a large number of people about their views on the case and the issues surrounding the case and, at the same time, gathering demographic data, such as age, gender, race, education, occupation, political party affiliation, social standing, and marital status. Then the consultants use the data to develop models of juror decisions. These are basically statistical models that indicate the probability that individuals will decide the case a certain way based on their background characteristics and attitudes. The results of the analysis are then used to create a profile of a juror who would be likely to acquit the defendant. The defense team uses this profile during the peremptory challenge phase of the voir dire process; potential jurors who fit the profile are retained, whereas those who don't fit it are excused.

There are arguments for and against professional jury consulting. One argument in consultants' favor is that they take some of the guesswork out of selecting a jury. Prospective jurors are excluded based on what the data show, rather than the attorney's preconceived notions regarding the types of people who will decide in his or her favor. An argument against juror consultants is that because they are expensive, only wealthy defendants and those whose cases attract national attention can afford them (Hartje, 2005). Critics also have challenged jury experts' claims of success, arguing that

> if jury consultants are as effective as they claim, and if the results of a trial can be controlled simply by choosing jurors labeled acceptable by social scientists, then trial by jury would cease to function impartially and would ultimately have to be abandoned. (Hartje, 2005, pp. 501–502)

Whether jury consultants perform a useful service or negatively affect the fairness of a trial remains to be seen. What seems unlikely is that they will disappear any time soon. As long as attorneys—especially defense attorneys—believe that jury consultants increase their odds of winning, they are likely to use them whenever the situation warrants it and the defendant can afford it.

Factors Affecting Juror Decision Making

The role of the jury in the criminal process is to determine what actually happened. After listening to evidence presented by the state and the defense and after being instructed on the law by the judge, the jurors go off by themselves to "deliberate" and to decide whether the defendant is guilty of the crime with which he or she is charged. How do the jurors make this decision? What factors do they consider as they attempt to determine the facts?

Questions such as these have long fascinated researchers, who have conducted hundreds of studies designed to explain how jurors arrive at their decisions. Because jury deliberations are conducted behind closed doors, researchers are unable to observe the actual deliberation process. Instead, they use a **mock jury study** or mock trial that involves hypothetical scenarios. These may be actual mock trials, such as in a university classroom, or simple written scenarios wherein people (often college students) are asked to decide a hypothetical defendant's fate. Then the researchers compare people's demographic characteristics to the decisions they hand down. One problem with this approach is that the hypothetical situations presented are not real and therefore no one's liberty is at stake. In addition, the vignettes are typically short and provide very limited information about the crime, the defendant, and the victim. The decisions that "jurors" make in these situations may or may not be the same as decisions they would make in actual trials.

Research on jury decision making generally has focused on the effects of procedural characteristics, juror characteristics, case characteristics, and deliberation characteristics (Devine, Clayton, Dunford, Seying, & Pryce, 2001). Procedural characteristics refer to such factors as jury size, juror involvement during the trial, and jury instructions. Juror characteristics refer to demographic factors, such as age, race/ethnicity, gender, employment status, and other individual variables. Case characteristics refer to variables associated with specific trials, such as the charges involved or the strength of the evidence. Finally, deliberation characteristics refer to such factors as polling procedures or participation in deliberation.

In an extensive review of the literature, Devine and his colleagues (2001) drew several conclusions regarding juror decision making (pp. 700–701). Not surprisingly, the studies revealed that juror decisions are affected by the quality and the quantity of the evidence; jurors are more likely to convict when the evidence is strong and conclusive. The personal characteristics of the participants (i.e., the mock juror, the victim, the defendant), on the other hand, do not reliably predict juror verdicts. These factors come into play primarily in cases where the evidence is ambiguous and the outcome is therefore less predictable. This has been explained using the **liberation hypothesis** (Kalven & Zeisel, 1966), which suggests that when the evidence is uncertain jurors are "liberated" from the constraints imposed by the law and therefore feel free to take legally irrelevant factors into consideration. Research also reveals that the deliberation process produces a reversal of the verdict preference initially favored by the majority in 1 of every 10 trials. Finally, the studies conducted to date indicate that jurors' decisions reflect their past experiences, their stereotypes about crime and criminals, and their beliefs about what is right, wrong, and fair.

Two studies of jury verdicts in actual cases addressed the issue of the factors that influence verdicts, reaching somewhat contradictory conclusions. Myers (1978–1979) analyzed jury verdicts in 201 felony trials in Marion County, Indiana. Her objective was to determine to extent to which the jury's verdict was affected by various types of evidence, indicators of witness credibility, and legally irrelevant characteristics of the victim and defendant. She found that juries were more likely to convict if a weapon was recovered, if there were several witnesses, if the defendant had a lengthy prior record or was unemployed, if the defendant or an accomplice testified, and if the victim was young. The likelihood of conviction, on the other hand, was not affected by eyewitness identification of the defendant, expert testimony, the relationship between the victim and the defendant, or the race of either the victim or the defendant. In these cases, then, the jury's decision to acquit or convict the defendant was predicted primarily by legally relevant indicators of the strength of evidence in the case, the victim's vulnerability, and the defendant's credibility.

A study of jury verdicts in 38 sexual assault trials in Indianapolis similarly found that the likelihood of a guilty verdict was affected by the strength of evidence in the case: whether a weapon was recovered, whether there was evidence that the victim suffered collateral injuries, other physical evidence, and eyewitness testimony (Reskin & Visher, 1986). However, the juror's perceptions of the victim also played a role. Jurors were less likely to convict the defendant if they believed that the victim had not exercised sufficient caution at the time of the alleged assault or if they had questions about the victim's moral character. Consistent with Kalven and Zeisel's (1966) liberation hypothesis, the study also revealed that these legally irrelevant victim characteristics came into play only in weak cases—that is, in cases with no more than one of the four types of hard evidence. This led the authors to conclude that "the influence of extralegal factors [was] largely confined to weak cases in which the defendant's guilt was ambiguous because the prosecution did not present enough hard evidence" (p. 436).

Jury Decision Making in Capital Cases

In Texas, as in other states that have the death penalty, there is a bifurcated trial. The jury first decides whether the offender is guilty of a capital crime and then, in a separate punishment proceeding, decides whether the offender should be sentenced to death. To impose the death penalty, the jury must answer yes to each of the following questions (Marquart, Ekland-Olson, & Sorensen, 1989, p. 450):

1. Whether the conduct of the defendant that caused the death of the deceased was committed deliberately and with the reasonable expectation that the death of the deceased would result;

2. Whether there is a probability that the defendant would commit additional acts of violence that would constitute a continuing threat to society;

3. If raised by the evidence, whether the conduct of the defendant in killing the deceased was unreasonable in response to the provocation, if any, by the deceased.

Because the first and third questions are almost always answered affirmatively, the imposition of the death penalty in effect rests on the jury's answer to the second question. As Marquart and his colleagues noted, whether the defendant will be sentenced to death or not depends on the jury's prediction of future dangerousness.

The purpose of the Marquart et al. (1989) study was to assess the accuracy of these predictions of future dangerousness. The authors compared the institutional and postrelease behavior of offenders whose death sentences were commuted to life in prison to that of offenders who were convicted of capital murder but were not sentenced to die. In other words, they compared the behavior of offenders whom jurors concluded *would* constitute a continuing threat to society to that of offenders whom jurors predicted *would not* be dangerous in the future.

The authors found very few differences in the prior criminal histories of offenders in the two groups. For example, 60% of the inmates who were released from death row had a prior violent conviction, compared to 69% of the inmates sentenced to life in prison. The types of murders for which offenders were convicted were also very similar: 50% of the former death row inmates and 52% of the offenders who received life sentences were convicted of homicides that involved robbery, and three-fourths of the offenders in each group victimized a stranger. The authors also noted the frequency with which psychiatrists testified about the offender's likelihood of future dangerousness in the cases involving offenders who were originally sentenced to death. One psychiatrist, who was nicknamed "Dr. Death" as a result of his testimony for the prosecution in a large number of potential death penalty cases, expressed especially strong opinions on this. In one case, for instance, he answered the prosecutor's question as to whether the offender would kill again in this way: "Yes, he certainly will; if there is any way at all he was given the opportunity to, he certainly will . . . even in areas of confinement this behavior [killing people] will continue" (Marquart et al., 1989, p. 457).

The authors also found very few differences in the institutional and postrelease behavior of offenders in the two groups. In fact, the former death row inmates had lower rates of assaultive institutional misconduct than did the capital offenders who were given life sentences. Most of the former death row inmates committed no serious rule violations at all during their time in the general prison population. Of the 12 death row inmates who eventually were released, only one was returned to prison for another crime (a brutal murder very similar to the ones for which he was originally sentenced).

The overall conclusion reached by the authors of this study was that these juries' predictions of future dangerousness involved "a large proportion of false positives" (Marquart et al., 1989, p. 465). Jurors, in other words, did not accurately predict offenders' future dangerousness. This led the authors to call for future research "to assess whether jurors, consciously or unconsciously, decide that an offender deserves to die and then tailor their responses to the questions accordingly" (p. 466).

Requirement of Unanimity

In most jurisdictions, the jury verdict must be unanimous. This reflects the fact that the jury's role is to determine the truth, and there can be but one "true" version of the facts. It also reflects an assumption that a verdict rendered by a jury that speaks with a single voice will be more likely to be accepted as authoritative and final (Jonakait, 2003). These arguments notwithstanding, in 1972 the U.S. Supreme Court ruled that the Sixth Amendment to the Constitution did not require unanimous verdicts in criminal cases. In doing so, the court upheld an Oregon law that permitted criminal defendants to be convicted by a 10 to 2 vote (*Apodaca v. Oregon*, 1972) and a Louisiana law that allowed conviction by a 9 to 3 vote (*Johnson v. Louisiana*, 1972). The Court stated that unanimity was not required for the jury to exercise its "commonsense judgment."

Seven years later, the Court returned to this issue, ruling in *Burch v. Louisiana* (1979) that a Louisiana law permitting conviction by a vote of 5 to 1 in felony cases tried with six-person juries did violate the Sixth Amendment. In his opinion for the Court, Justice Rehnquist stated that "lines must be drawn somewhere if the substance of the jury trial right is to be preserved," adding that "conviction for a nonpetty offense by only five members of a six-person jury presents a threat to preservation of the substance of the jury trial guarantee and justifies requiring verdicts rendered by such juries to be unanimous."

The Court's decisions allowing non-unanimous verdicts notwithstanding, today only two states—Oregon and Louisiana—allow a defendant to be convicted of a felony by a non-unanimous verdict. Unanimity also is required in all federal criminal cases.

Jury Nullification

Most jury trials result in convictions. In 2002, for example, 85% of all defendants tried by juries in the 75 largest counties in the United States were convicted (U.S. Justice Department, 2006, p. 26). A jury's decision to acquit the defendant usually means that the state has failed to prove its case beyond a reasonable doubt. Sometimes, however, the jury votes to acquit despite overwhelming evidence that the defendant is guilty. In this case, the jury ignores, or nullifies, the law.

Jury nullification, which has its roots in English common law, occurs when a juror believes that the evidence presented at trial establishes the defendant's guilt, but nonetheless the juror votes to acquit. The juror's decision may be motivated either by a belief that the law under which the defendant is being prosecuted is unfair or by an objection to the application of the law in a particular case. In the first instance, a juror might refuse to convict a defendant charged in U.S. District Court with possession of more than five grams of crack cocaine, based on his or her belief that the long prison sentence mandated by the law is unfair. In the second instance, a juror might vote to acquit a defendant charged with petty theft but also charged as a habitual criminal and facing a mandatory life sentence, not because the juror believes the law is unfair but because he or she believes that this particular defendant does not deserve life in prison (Dodge & Harris, 2000).

Although nullification enables the jury to be merciful when it believes that either the punishment or a criminal conviction is undeserved, it also enables the jury to make arbitrary or discriminatory decisions. For example, there is evidence that Southern juries have—and, some would say, still do—refused to convict white defendants charged with offenses against black victims, even in the face of convincing evidence of their guilt (Hodes, 1996). Nullification can also be used to make a political statement, such as to express dissatisfaction with a policy. Some have alleged that O. J. Simpson's acquittal on murder charges reflected, in part, the jurors' beliefs that the Los Angeles Police Department was racist (Rosen, 1996). An even darker form of jury nullification has been called jury vilification (Horowitz, Kerr, & Niedermeier, 2001). "Juries may return verdicts that reflect prejudiced or bigoted community standards and convict when the evidence does not warrant a conviction" (Horowitz et al., 2001, p. 1210).

Jurors clearly have the power to nullify the law and vote their conscience (Scheflin & Van Dyke, 1980). If the jury votes to acquit, the Double Jeopardy Clause of the Fifth Amendment prohibits reversal of the jury's decision. The jury's decision to acquit, even in the face of overwhelming evidence of guilt, is final and cannot be reversed by the trial judge or an appellate court. In most jurisdictions, however, jurors do not have to be told that they have the right to nullify the law (see, e.g., *United States v. Dougherty*, 1972).

There is no way to know with any certainty how often jury nullification occurs. However, researchers have sought to identify the circumstances under which jurors will disregard the law. Some experimental evidence shows that as penalties become more severe, jurors are less likely to convict and in fact apply higher standards of proof (Kerr, 1978). Niedermeier, Horowitz, and Kerr (1999), for example, reported on an experiment they conducted wherein a physician was accused of knowingly transfusing a patient with blood he knew hadn't been screened for HIV. Holding everything else constant (e.g., the evidence), the authors found that mock jurors were less likely to declare the physician guilty when the penalty was severe (25 years in prison relative to a $100 fine). The findings from these studies show that jurors are influenced by something other than the facts of the case as laid out by the prosecution and defense.

Hung Juries

If the jury cannot reach a unanimous verdict (or a 9 to 3 verdict in Louisiana or a 10 to 2 verdict in Oregon), the jury is said to be deadlocked, or hung. This ends the trial, and the prosecutor has to decide whether to dismiss the charges, offer the defendant a plea bargain, or try the defendant again before a new jury.

There are limited data on the frequency of hung juries. One study of jury trials in the 10 largest counties in California in the early 1970s found that 12.2% of the trials resulted in hung juries (Planning and Management Consulting Corporation, 1975). This study also found that 26% of the cases involving deadlocked juries were dismissed, 41% were resolved with a plea agreement, and 33% resulted in a new trial. A more recent study by the National Center for State Courts (2002) found that many states did not compile data on interim dispositions such as hung juries. The rate in the 30 jurisdictions that did compile such data was 6.2%. Like the earlier research in California, this study also found that only a third of the cases that resulted in a deadlocked jury were retried before a new jury.

According to the research conducted by the National Center for State Courts (2002), three factors were significant predictors of the likelihood of a hung jury: (1) the complexity of the case and the ambiguity of the evidence; (2) the group dynamics of the jury deliberation process, including the level of conflict among the jurors, the extent to which the deliberations were dominated by one or two individuals, whether the jury took an early vote, and whether the members of the jury had previously served on a jury (juries with jurors with previous experience were more likely to deadlock); and (3) jurors' concerns about the fairness of the process that brought the defendant to court to face criminal charges. In contrast, the study found no relationship between the likelihood of a deadlock and the racial, ethnic, gender, or socioeconomic composition of the jury. Although the authors of the report stated that eliminating the unanimity requirement would reduce the number of hung juries, doing so "would address the symptoms of disagreement among jurors without necessarily addressing the actual causes—namely, weak evidence, poor interpersonal dynamics during deliberations, and jurors' concerns about the appropriateness of legal enforcement in particular cases" (p. 86).

Summary: Judges and Jurors in the Courtroom

The judge, whose job it is to interpret the law and to ensure that proper procedures are followed at every step in the process, plays a key role in the criminal court system. The powers that judges wield are not, however, unlimited; their powers are constrained by rules that require them to be fair and unbiased, by procedures to disqualify or remove them if they are not impartial, and by appellate court rulings on questions of law and procedure. Jurors, whose job it is to determine the facts in a case and to decide whether the state has proved the defendant's guilt beyond a reasonable doubt, also play an important role. Even though jury trials are rare, the cases that do go to trial typically involve serious crimes in which defendants are facing long prison sentences. In these serious cases, the jury serves as the conscience of the community and as a safeguard against the improper use of the criminal law.

In this section, we provided an introduction to some of the controversies surrounding judges and juries. Questions have been raised about the methods of selecting judges, the effects of recruiting more women and racial minorities to the bench, and the consequences of using nonlawyer judges. Issues related to juries include the use of peremptory challenges, the role of jury consultants, the factors that jurors take into consideration during deliberations, the unanimity requirement, and the practice of jury nullification. The edited readings included in this section explore a number of these issues in greater detail.

KEY TERMS

Appellate review

Challenge for cause

Fact finding

Impeachment

Judicial disciplinary commission

Jury consultant

Jury nullification

Liberation hypothesis

Mock jury study

Peremptory challenge

Random cross-section of the community

Recuse

Retention election

Right of appeal

Venue

DISCUSSION QUESTIONS

1. In a criminal case, who determines the facts? Who applies or interprets the law? Why are both of these processes imperfect?

2. What is the traditional view of the judge, and why is it misleading?

3. Under what circumstances should a judge recuse (remove) himself or herself from a case?

4. When can a defendant challenge his or her sentence? What are the standards that might be applied in reviewing the challenge?

5. How are federal judges removed from office? What procedures can be used to remove state court judges? What would justify removing a federal or state court judge?

6. What are the advantages and disadvantages of electing judges? Of appointing judges?

7. In your opinion, why is the typical judge white, male, and middle-aged? At least in theory, how might electing or appointing more women and racial minorities change the quality of justice meted out by the courts?

8. Why is the role of the jury in the criminal justice system "both symbolically and substantively important"?

9. What has the U.S. Supreme Court said regarding race and the jury selection process? Why are the standards different for selection of the jury pool and selection of the jurors for a particular case?

10. What are the problems inherent in the use of the peremptory challenge? Should the peremptory challenge by eliminated? Why or why not?

11. Should either side in a criminal trial be prohibited from using jury consultants? Why or why not?

12. Why do you think so few states allow defendants charged with felonies to be convicted by non-unanimous juries?

13. Why do jurors have the right to nullify the law? Should they have this right? Should they be told that they have this right?

WEB RESOURCES

American Judicature Society: http://www.ajs.org

Biographical Directory of Federal Judges, Federal Judicial Center: http://www.fjc.gov/history/home.nsf

Decision Quest (jury consultants): http://www.decisionquest.com/

California Commission on Judicial Performance: http://cjp.ca.gov/

Federal Habeas Corpus Review: Challenging State Court Criminal Convictions: http://bjs.ojp.usdoj.gov/index.cfm?ty=pbdetail&iid=861

Federal Judges Association: http://www.federaljudgesassoc.org/

Jury Selection, Cook County, Illinois: http://www.cookcountycourt.org/jury/faq-selection.html

National Conference of State Trial Judges, American Bar Association: http://www.abanet.org/jd/ncstj/

National Consortium on Racial and Ethnic Fairness in the Courts: http://www.consortiumonline.net/index.html

Outline of the U.S. Legal System, U.S. Department of State: http://usinfo.state.gov/products/pubs/legalotln/judges.htm

READING

Although research generally reveals that the competence of judges does not vary dramatically depending on their method of selection, concerns have been raised about judicial impartiality in capital cases. Stephen Bright and Patrick Keenan argue that elected judges are influenced by politics in cases involving the death penalty. According to these authors, elected judges face "overwhelming pressure ... to heed, and perhaps even to lead, the popular cries for the death of criminal defendants" (see also Wold & Culver, 1987). These authors discuss a number of problems inherent in electing judges who adjudicate capital cases. They also present several possible solutions to these problems.

Judges and the Politics of Death

Deciding Between the Bill of Rights and the Next Election in Capital Cases

Stephen B. Bright and Patrick J. Keenan

The "higher authority" to whom present-day capital judges may be "too responsive" is a political climate in which judges who covet higher office—or who merely wish to remain judges—must constantly profess their fealty to the death penalty. ... The danger that they will bend to political pressures when pronouncing sentence in highly publicized capital cases is the same danger confronted by judges beholden to King George III.

—Justice John Paul Stevens, dissenting in *Harris v. Alabama*[1]

The thunderous voice of the present-day "higher authority" that Justice Stevens described is heard today with unmistakable clarity in the courts throughout the United States. Those judges who do not listen and bend to political pressures may lose their positions on the bench.

Decisions in capital cases have increasingly become campaign fodder in both judicial and nonjudicial elections. The focus in these campaigns has been almost entirely on the gruesome facts of particular murders, not the reason for the judicial decisions. Judges have come under attack and have been removed from the

SOURCE: "Judges and the Politics of Death: Deciding Between the Bill of Rights and the Next Election in Capital Cases." Stephen B. Bright and Patrick J. Keenan, Volume 73 *Boston University Law Review*. Page 759 (May 1995).

bench for their decisions in capital cases—with perhaps the most notable examples in states with some of the largest death rows and where the death penalty has been a dominant political issue. Recent challenges to state court judges in both direct and retention elections have made it clear that unpopular decisions in capital cases, even when clearly compelled by law, may cost a judge her seat on the bench, or promotion to a higher court. This raises serious questions about the independence and integrity of the judiciary and the ability of judges to enforce the Bill of Rights and otherwise be fair and impartial in capital cases.

California has the largest death row of any state in the nation. In 1986, Governor George Deukmejian publicly warned two justices of the state's supreme court that he would oppose them in their retention elections unless they voted to uphold more death sentences. He had already announced his opposition to Chief Justice Rose Bird because of her votes in capital cases. Apparently unsatisfied with the subsequent votes of the other two justices, the governor carried out his threat. He opposed the retention of all three justices and all lost their seats after a campaign dominated by the death penalty. Deukmejian appointed their replacements in 1987.

The removal and replacement of the three justices has affected every capital case the court has subsequently reviewed, resulting in a dramatic change. In the last five years, the Court has affirmed nearly 97% of the capital cases it has reviewed, one of the highest rates in the nation.[2] A law professor who watches the court observed, "One thing it shows is that when the voters speak loudly enough, even the judiciary listens."[3] The once highly regarded court now distinguishes itself primarily by its readiness to find trial court error harmless in capital cases. The new court has "reversed every premise underlying the Bird Court's harmless error analysis," displaying an eagerness that reflects "jurisprudential theory" less than a "desire to carry out the death penalty."[4]

The voice of "higher authority" has also been heard and felt in Texas, which has the nation's second largest death row. After a decision by the state's highest criminal court, the Court of Criminal Appeals, reversing the conviction in a particularly notorious capital case, a former chairman of the state Republican Party called for Republicans to take over the court in the 1994 election. The voters responded to the call. Republicans won every position they sought on the court.

One of the Republicans elected to the court was Stephen W. Mansfield, who had been a member of the Texas bar only two years, but campaigned for the court on promises of the death penalty for killers, greater use of harmless-error doctrine, and sanctions for attorneys who file "frivolous appeals especially in death penalty cases." Even before the election it came to light that Mansfield had misrepresented his prior background, experience, and record; that he had been fined for practicing law without a license in Florida; and that—contrary to his assertions that he had experience in criminal cases and had "written extensively on criminal and civil justice issues"—he had virtually no experience in criminal law and his writing in the area of criminal law consisted of a guest column in a local newspaper criticizing the same decision that prompted the former Republican chairman to call for a takeover of the court. Nevertheless, Mansfield defeated the incumbent judge, a conservative former prosecutor who had served twelve years on the court and was supported by both sides of the criminal bar. Mansfield was sworn in to serve for a six-year term in January 1995. Among his responsibilities will be the review of every capital case coming before the court on direct appeal and in postconviction review.

The single county in America responsible for the most death sentences and executions is Harris County, Texas, which includes Houston. Judge Norman E. Lanford, a Republican, was voted off the state district court in Houston in 1992 after he recommended in postconviction proceedings that a death sentence be set aside due to prosecutorial misconduct, and directed an acquittal in another murder case due to constitutional violations. A prosecutor who specialized in death cases, Caprice Cosper, defeated Judge Lanford in the Republican primary. Lanford accused District Attorney John B. Holmes of causing congestion of Lanford's docket to help bring about his defeat. In the November election, Cosper was elected after a campaign in which radio advertisements on her behalf attacked her Democratic opponent for having once opposed the death penalty.

Judges in other states have had similar campaigns waged against them. Justice James Robertson was voted off the Mississippi Supreme Court in 1992. His opponent in the Democratic primary ran as a "law and order candidate" with the support of the Mississippi Prosecutors Association. Among the decisions for which Robertson's opponent attacked him was a concurring opinion expressing the view that the Constitution did not permit the death penalty for rape where there was no loss of life. Robertson's opponent exploited the opinion even though the U.S. Supreme Court had held ten years earlier that the Eighth Amendment did not permit the death penalty in such cases.[5] Opponents also attacked Robertson for his dissenting opinions in two cases that the U.S. Supreme Court later reversed.

The voice of "higher authority" can also be heard in less direct, but equally compelling ways. As Justice Stevens observed in his dissent in *Harris v Alabama,* some members of the United States Senate have "made the death penalty a litmus test in judicial confirmation hearings for nominees to the federal bench."[6] Several challengers for Senate seats in the 1994 elections "routinely savaged their incumbent opponents for supporting federal judicial nominees perceived to be 'soft' on capital punishment."

It is becoming increasingly apparent that these political pressures have a significant impact on the fairness and integrity of capital trials When presiding over a highly publicized capital case, a judge who declines to hand down a sentence of death, or who insists on upholding the Bill of Rights, may thereby sign his own political death warrant. In such circumstances, state court judges who desire to remain in office are no more able to protect the rights of an accused in a criminal case than elected judges have been to protect the civil rights of racial minorities against majority sentiment. In the three states that permit elected judges to override jury sentences in capital cases, judges override jury sentences of life imprisonment and impose death far more often than they override death sentences and impose life imprisonment. Judges have also failed to enforce constitutional guarantees of fairness. It has been

observed that "[t]he more susceptible judges are to political challenge, the less likely they are to reverse a death penalty judgment."[7] Affirmance rates over a ten-year period suggest that "[n]ationally there is a close correlation between the method of selection of a state supreme court and that court's affirmance rate in death penalty appeals."[8] Even greater pressure exists at the local level. Elected trial judges are under considerable pressure not to suppress evidence, grant a change of venue, or protect other constitutional rights of the accused. An indigent defendant may face the death penalty at trial without one of the most fundamental protections of the Constitution, a competent lawyer, because judges frequently appoint inexperienced, uncaring, incompetent, or inadequately compensated attorneys.[9] State trial court judges in many states routinely dispose of complex legal and factual issues in capital postconviction proceedings by adopting "orders" ghostwritten by state attorneys general—orders that make no pretense of fairly resolving the issues before the court.

This article examines the influence of the politics of crime on judicial behavior in capital cases. A fair and impartial judge is essential in any proceeding, but perhaps nowhere more so than in capital cases, where race, poverty, inadequate court-appointed counsel, and popular passions can influence the extermination of a human life. The legal system indulges the presumption that judges are impartial. The Supreme Court has steadily reduced the availability of habeas corpus review of capital convictions, placing its confidence in the notion that state judges, who take the same oath as federal judges to uphold the Constitution, can be trusted to enforce it. This confidence, however, is frequently misplaced, given the overwhelming pressure on elected state judges to heed, and perhaps even to lead, the popular cries for the death of criminal defendants.

Part I of this article briefly summarizes the increasing use of the crime issue in local and national politics and the extraordinary prominence of the death penalty as a litmus test for politicians, including politicians who serve as judges, purporting to be "tough" on crime. Part II examines the politics of becoming and remaining a judge in such a climate. Part III assesses the effect of this political climate on a judge's ability to preside impartially over highly publicized capital cases. Part IV proposes some modest steps that might limit the influence of politics and the passions of the moment on judicial behavior.

Crime in Politics and the Death Penalty in the Politics of Crime

During the Cold War, many politicians, seeking to avoid more controversial and difficult issues, professed their opposition to Communism. Because almost everyone aspiring to public office was against Communism, politicians sought in various ways—such as support for loyalty oaths and investigation of un-American activities— to demonstrate just how strongly they were opposed to Communism. Those who questioned the wisdom of such measures were accused of not being sufficiently strident—"soft" on Communism.

Since the collapse of the Soviet Union and other Soviet-bloc governments, crime has emerged as an issue that appears equally one-sided. No one is in favor of violent crime. Politicians demonstrate their toughness by supporting the death penalty, longer prison sentences, and measures to make prison life even harsher than it is already. Those who question the wisdom, cost, and effectiveness of such measures are branded "soft on crime." Whether sound public policy emerges from such a discussion of crime is a question to be addressed elsewhere. The emergence of crime as a dominant political issue is, however, not only having an impact on the behavior of politicians seeking positions in the legislative and executive branches of government, but also on the behavior of judges who are sworn to uphold the Constitution, a document that protects the rights of those accused of even the most serious crimes.

Even before the end of the Cold War, Richard Nixon demonstrated the potency of the crime issue by promising, in campaign speeches and in his acceptance of the Republican nomination for President in 1968, to replace Democrat Ramsey Clark as Attorney General. Clark's defense of civil liberties and procedural safeguards had led some, including Nixon, to denounce him as "soft on crime." In 1988, Lee Atwater urged Republicans to concentrate on the crime issue because "[a]lmost every candidate running out there as a Democrat is opposed to the death penalty."[10] George Bush was elected President that year with the help of advertisements criticizing his opponent for allowing the furlough of Willie Horton, who committed a rape in Maryland while on a weekend furlough from a Massachusetts prison.

As crime has become a more prominent issue in political campaigns, the death penalty has become the ultimate vehicle for politicians to demonstrate just how tough they are on crime. During California's 1990 gubernatorial primary, an aide to one Democratic candidate observed wistfully that the carrying out of an execution would be a "coup" for her opponent, the state attorney general. Candidates for governor of Texas in 1990 argued about which of them was responsible for the most executions and who could do the best job in executing more people. One candidate ran television advertisements in which he walked in front of photographs of the men executed during his tenure as governor and boasted that he had "made sure they received the ultimate penalty: death." Another candidate ran advertisements taking credit for thirty-two executions.[11] In Florida, the incumbent gubernatorial candidate ran television advertisements in 1990 showing the face of serial killer Ted Bundy, who was executed during his tenure as governor. The governor stated that he had signed over ninety death warrants in his four years in office.

Presidential candidate Bill Clinton demonstrated that he was tough on crime in his 1992 campaign by scheduling the execution of a brain-damaged man shortly before the New Hampshire primary. Clinton had embraced the death penalty in 1982 after his defeat in a bid for reelection as governor of Arkansas in 1980. In his presidential campaign ten years later, Clinton returned from New Hampshire to preside over the execution of Rickey Ray Rector, an African-American who had been sentenced to death by an all-white jury. Rector had destroyed part of his brain when he turned his gun on himself after killing the police officer for whose murder he received the death sentence. Logs at the prison show that in the days leading up to his execution, Rector was howling and barking like a dog, dancing, singing, laughing inappropriately, and saying that he was going to vote for Clinton. Clinton denied clemency and allowed the execution to proceed, thereby protecting himself from being labeled as "soft on crime" and helping the Democrats to take back the crime issue. Clinton's first three television advertisements in his bid for reelection—already begun a year and a half before the 1996 presidential election—all focused on crime and Clinton's support to expand the death penalty.

By 1994, crime had so eclipsed other issues that an official of the National Governor's Association commented that the "top three issues in gubernatorial campaigns this year are crime, crime, and crime."[12] Stark images of violence, flashing police lights, and shackled prisoners dominated the campaign, and candidates went to considerable lengths to emphasize their enthusiasm for the death penalty and attack their opponents for any perceived hesitancy to carry out executions swiftly. Even after Texas carried out forty-five executions during Democrat Ann Richards's four years as governor, George W. Bush attacked Governor Richards during his successful 1994 campaign against her, complaining that Texas should execute even more people, even more quickly. Bush's younger brother Jeb ran a television advertisement in his 1994 campaign for governor of Florida in which the mother of a murder victim blamed incumbent Governor Lawton Chiles for allowing the convicted killer to remain on death row for thirteen years. Jeb Bush knew, and acknowledged when asked, that there was nothing Chiles could have done to speed up the execution because the case was pending in federal court. Jeb Bush also argued that Florida's eight executions since Chiles's election in 1990 were not enough.

In her quest to win the 1994 California gubernatorial race, Kathleen Brown found that her personal opposition to the death penalty was widely viewed as a major liability even though she promised to carry out executions as governor. She had to defend herself against Governor Pete Wilson's charges that, because of her personal moral convictions, she would appoint judges like Rose Bird. Governor Wilson, whose approval ratings had been "abysmal," recovered by following the advice of the old master, Richard Nixon, who told him to hit his opponent hard on crime. Candidate Brown responded to the charges by producing an advertisement proclaiming her willingness to enforce the death penalty. Nevertheless, she lost to Wilson. Both Illinois Governor Jim Edgar and Iowa Governor Terry E. Branstad similarly attacked their opponents' personal opposition to the death penalty. Both were reelected. New York Governor Mario Cuomo faced heated attacks for his vetoes of death-penalty legislation during twelve years in office and his refusal to return a New York prisoner to Oklahoma for execution. Cuomo defended himself by proposing a referendum on the death penalty, but still lost his office to a candidate who promised to reinstate capital punishment and to send the prisoner back to Oklahoma for execution.

As the public debate on crime and its solutions has become increasingly one-sided and vacuous, the death penalty has become the ultimate litmus test for demonstrating that one is not "soft on crime." The impact of this development has been felt not only in the executive and legislative branches of government, where popular sentiment is expected to play a major role in the development of policy, but also in the judiciary, where judges are expected to follow the law, not the election returns.

The Politics of Becoming and Staying a Judge

Judges in most states that have capital punishment are subject to election or retention. Although all judges take oaths to uphold the Constitution, including its provisions guaranteeing certain protections for persons accused of crimes, judges who must stand for election or retention depend on the continued approval of the voters for their jobs and concomitant salaries and retirement benefits. A common route to the bench is through a prosecutor's office, where trying high-profile capital cases can result in publicity and name recognition for a prosecutor with judicial ambitions. A judge who has used capital cases to advance to the bench finds that presiding over capital cases results in continued public attention. Regardless of how one becomes a judge, rulings in capital cases may significantly affect whether a judge remains in office or moves to a higher court.

Judges Face Election in Most States That Employ the Death Penalty

Almost all judicial selection systems fall into one of four categories. First, judges in eleven states and the District of Columbia are never subjected to election at any time in their judicial careers. Second, the judges of three states are elected by vote of the state legislature. Third, the judges of twenty-nine states are subjected to contested elections, either partisan or nonpartisan, at some point in their careers, whether during initial selection for the bench or after appointment by the governor. The fourth category of judicial selection systems includes those systems in which the judge or justice is at some time subjected to a retention election but never faces an opponent. Thirteen states employ such a system.

There are currently thirty-eight states that have capital punishment statutes. Thirty-two states both elect their judges and sentence people to death.

In nine states—including Alabama and Texas—judges run under party affiliations. The success of the party in national or state elections may have a significant impact on the judiciary. For example, Texas Republicans swept into state judicial offices as part of the party's general success in the 1994 elections. Republicans won every elected position they sought on the Texas Court of Criminal Appeals and the Texas Supreme Court. Republican straight-ticket voting contributed to the defeat of nineteen Democratic judges and a Republican sweep of all but one of the forty-two contested races for countywide judgeships in Harris County, Texas, which includes Houston. Such straight-ticket voting, which comprised one-quarter of all votes cast in Harris County, also resulted in the removal of the only three black judges and left only one Hispanic on the bench.

The lack of racial diversity now found in Houston is consistent with the exclusion of minorities from the bench throughout the country. One reason for the lack of minority judges is that in many states—particularly those in the "death belt" states such as Florida and Texas—judges have long been elected from judicial districts in which the voting strength of racial minorities is diluted.

Prosecuting Capital Cases as a Stepping Stone to the Bench

One of the most frequently traveled routes to the state trial bench is through prosecutors' offices. A capital case provides a prosecutor with a particularly rich opportunity for media exposure and name recognition that can later be helpful in a judicial campaign. Calling a press conference to announce that the police have captured a suspect and the prosecutor will seek the death penalty provides an opportunity for a prosecutor to obtain news coverage and ride popular sentiments that almost any politician would welcome. The prosecutor can then sustain prominent media coverage by announcing various developments in the case as they occur. A capital trial provides one of the greatest opportunities for sustained coverage on the nightly newscasts and in the newspapers. A noncapital trial or resolution with a guilty plea does not produce such coverage.

The relationship between prosecuting capital cases and moving to the bench is evident in Georgia's Chattahoochee Judicial Circuit, which sends more people to death row than any other judicial circuit in the state. Two of the four superior court judges in the circuit obtained their seats on the bench after trying high-profile capital cases. Mullins Whisnant, who now serves as chief superior court judge in the circuit, became a judge in 1978 after serving as the elected district attorney. He personally tried many of the ten capital cases the office prosecuted in 1976 and 1977, five of which involved African-Americans tried before all-white juries for homicides of white victims. His last capital trial as prosecutor involved a highly publicized rape, robbery, kidnapping, and murder of a white Methodist Church organist by an African-American. The extensive news coverage of the case included electronic and photographic coverage of the trial. Whisnant made a highly emotional plea to jurors to join a "war on crime" and "send a message" by sentencing the defendant to death.

Once Whisnant became a judge, his chief assistant, William Smith, took over as the district attorney. Smith personally tried many of the fourteen capital cases that took place during his tenure before he joined his former boss on the bench in 1988. One of those cases involved the highly publicized trial of an African-American accused of being the "Silk Stocking Strangler" responsible for the murders of several elderly white women in the community.

And benefits other than publicity came to Smith's eventual campaign for judge as a result of his use of the death penalty as a district attorney. In a case involving the murder of the daughter of a local contractor, Smith contacted the victim's father and asked him if he wanted the death penalty. When he replied in the affirmative, Smith said that was all he needed to know, and subsequently obtained the death penalty at trial. The victim's father rewarded Smith with a contribution of $5000 during Smith's successful run for judge in the next election. The contribution was the largest Smith received. Smith's chief assistant succeeded him as district attorney and, after prosecuting eight capital cases, has announced an interest in the next opening on the Superior Court bench. So close is the relationship between the judiciary and the prosecutor's office in the circuit that the prosecutor's office has made the assignments of criminal cases to judges for the last six years, assigning the more serious drug and homicide cases to former prosecutors Whisnant and Smith.

These prosecutors in the Chattahoochee Judicial Circuit have demonstrated that capital cases produce good publicity even when a guilty verdict is reversed for prosecutorial misconduct. After the United States Court of Appeals set aside a death sentence because of a lynch-mob-type appeal for the death penalty by then-District Attorney Smith, which the court characterized as a "dramatic appeal to gut emotion" that "has no place in a courtroom,"[13] Smith called a press conference, insisted he had done nothing wrong, and announced that he would seek the death penalty again in the case. When a federal court set aside a second death sentence due to similar misconduct, Smith called another press conference and expressed his "anger" at the decision, accused the reviewing court of "sensationalism" and "emotionalism," suggested that the "judges of this court

have personal feelings against the death penalty," and vowed to seek the death penalty again.[14]

Attempts to exploit capital cases for political purposes may backfire, however, particularly if the prosecution is not ultimately successful in obtaining the death penalty. For example, a verdict of voluntary manslaughter instead of first degree murder transformed the case of Bruce R. Morris in St. Charles County, Missouri, from one in which a defendant's life was at stake to one in which a political career was at stake. "[C]ourthouse observers, including [the prosecutor's] former employees" criticized the prosecutor, who was a candidate for circuit court judge, and stated that the trial was the prosecutor's first jury trial in memory. They also accused him of taking the case to trial just because he was running for judge.

Prosecutors may be criticized for failure to seek the death penalty, even when the law does not permit it. For example, a California prosecutor criticized a Colorado prosecutor for not seeking the death penalty against a defendant who had committed crimes in both states even though the Colorado prosecutor explained that there were no statutory aggravating circumstances that would permit him to seek the death penalty.

Although it may be unethical and improper for prosecutors to campaign on promises to seek the death penalty or on their success in obtaining it, there is no effective remedy to prevent the practice. Moreover, capital cases produce so much publicity and name recognition that explicit promises to seek death are hardly necessary. As a result, prosecuting capital cases remains a way of obtaining a judgeship. As will be discussed later, some persons who reach the bench in this manner have difficulty relinquishing the prosecutorial role. But even when a prosecutor is not seeking a judicial post, or is unsuccessful in obtaining one, the political use of the death penalty in the discharge of prosecutorial responsibilities may spill over into elections for judicial office and influence the exercise of judicial discretion. The political consequences of decisions by both prosecutor and judge become apparent for all to see.

The Death Penalty's Prominence in the Election, Retention, and Promotion of Judges

With campaigning for the death penalty and against judges who overturn capital cases an effective tactic in the quest for other offices, it is not surprising that the death penalty has become increasingly prominent in contested and retention elections for judges. Not only the judge, but her political supporters as well, may suffer the consequences of an unpopular ruling in a capital case.

In the 1994 primary election for the Texas Court of Criminal Appeals, the incumbent presiding judge accused another member of the court of voting to grant relief for convicted defendants more often than other judges. Although a Republican candidate for the second seat on the court lamented what he called the "lynch mentality" of the campaign, two other candidates for the Republican nomination, both former prosecutors, indicated their willingness to treat defendants severely. One stated that the role of the court is to ensure justice, not to reverse conviction because of "technicalities" or "honest mistakes," while the other called the Court of Criminal Appeals a "citadel of technicality" that neglected the interests of crime victims and citizens at large. Two candidates for the third position on the court criticized the incumbent for granting a new trial to a man convicted of homicide. One challenger promised to bring a "common sense" approach to such cases.

A judge's votes in capital cases can threaten his or her elevation to a higher court. No matter how well qualified a judge may be, perceived "softness" on crime or on the death penalty may have consequences not only for the judge, but also for those who would nominate or vote to confirm the judge for another court. For example, in 1992 groups campaigned against the retention of Florida Chief Justice Rosemary Barkett for the Florida Supreme Court because of her votes in capital cases. Then in 1994 Barkett's nomination to the U.S. Court of Appeals for the Eleventh Circuit came under fire because of her record on capital punishment during nine years on the Florida Supreme Court. After a long delay, the Senate finally confirmed Barkett by a vote of sixty-one to thirty-seven.

Despite Barkett's confirmation to the Eleventh Circuit, campaigns against her and other judges tagged as "soft on crime" continued. Bill Frist, in his successful campaign to unseat Tennessee Senator Jim Sasser, attacked Sasser for voting for Barkett and for having recommended the nomination of a federal district judge who, two months before the election, granted habeas corpus relief to a death-sentenced man. Frist appeared at a news conference with the sister of the victim in the case in which habeas relief had been granted. After the victim's sister criticized Sasser for recommending U.S. District Judge John Nixon for the federal bench, Frist said that Sasser's vote to confirm Judge Barkett showed that he "still hasn't learned his lesson."

Although pro-death-penalty campaigns are not always successful in defeating judges, even the threat of such a campaign may intimidate a judge. Challenges also make retaining a judgeship more expensive than it would otherwise be, thereby forcing a candidate to raise more money and contributing to the perception that those who contribute to judicial campaigns can get more justice than others. One of the saddest and most recent examples is the bitter campaign waged for chief justice of Alabama's supreme court in 1994. The challenger accused the incumbent of shaking down attorneys who had cases before the court for contributions, while the incumbent ran advertisements in which the father of a murder victim accused the challenger of being an accomplice to the murder.

Whether the "hydraulic pressure" of public opinion that Justice Holmes once described and the political incentives accompanying it are appropriate considerations for publicly elected prosecutors is doubtful, but clearly such considerations have no place in the exercise of the judicial function. Yet in jurisdictions where judges stand for election—often with the prosecution in a position tantamount to that of a running mate—judges are subject to the same pressures. As a result of the increasing prominence of the death penalty in judicial elections as well as other campaigns for public office, judges are well aware of the conse- quences to their careers of unpopular decisions in capital cases.

 # The Impact on the Impartiality of Judges

The political liability facing judges who enforce the Bill of Rights in capital cases undermines the independence, integrity, and impartiality of the state judiciary. Judicial candidates who promise to base their rulings on "common sense," unencumbered by technicalities, essentially promise to ignore constitutional limits on the process by which society may extinguish the life of one of its members. Justice Byron White once observed, "If [for example,] a judge's ruling for the defendant . . . may determine his fate at the next election, even though his ruling was affirmed and is unquestionably right, constitutional protections would be subject to serious erosion." Justice William Brennan noted that the risk of a biased judge is "particularly acute" in capital cases:

> Passions, as we all know, can run to extreme when the State tries one accused of a bar- baric act against society, or one accused of a crime that—for whatever reason—inflames the community. Pressures on the govern- ment to secure a conviction, to "do some- thing," can overwhelm even those of good conscience. When prosecutors and judges are elected, or when they harbor political ambitions, such pressures are particularly dangerous.[15]

Rulings in a publicized case can have major political effects, such as loss of one's position or any hope of promotion, and judges are aware of this as they make controversial decisions, particularly in capital cases.

The American Bar Association's Commission on Professionalism found that "judges are far less likely to . . . take . . . tough action if they must run for reelection or retention every few years."[16] In no other area of American law are so many tough decisions presented as in a capital case. And no other cases demonstrate so clearly the validity of the ABA Commission's finding.

A judge who faces election is more likely to sen- tence a defendant to death than a jury that heard the same evidence. In some instances, political consider- ations make it virtually impossible for judges to enforce the constitutional protections to a fair trial for the accused, such as granting a change of venue or continu- ance, or suppressing evidence. Judges have failed mis- erably to enforce the most fundamental right of all, the Sixth Amendment right to counsel, in capital cases. And many judges routinely abdicate their judicial responsibility and allow the lawyers for the state to write their orders resolving disputed factual and legal issues in capital cases.

Overrides of Jury Sentences

Four states—Alabama, Florida, Indiana, and Delaware— permit a judge to override a jury's sentence of life imprisonment and impose the death penalty. Alabama judges, who face partisan elections every six years, have overridden jury sentences of life without parole and imposed the death penalty forty-seven times, but have vetoed only five jury recommendations of death. Between 1972 and early 1992, Florida trial judges, who face contested elections every six years, imposed death sentences over 134 jury recommendations of life imprisonment, but overrode only fifty-one death recommendations. Between 1980 and early 1994, Indiana judges, who face retention elections every six years, imposed death sentences over eight jury recom- mendations of life imprisonment, but overrode only four death recommendations to impose sentences of life imprisonment. Delaware did not adopt the over- ride until 1991, and that state's judges do not stand for election; the first seven times judges used it, they overrode jury recommendations of death and imposed life sentences.

Indeed, the sentencing decisions of some judges are a foregone conclusion. Members of the U.S. Supreme Court have noticed the tendency of Jacksonville, Florida judge Hudson Olliff to override jury sentences of life imprisonment and impose death. An override could also be anticipated from another Florida circuit judge, William Lamar Rose, who protested the U.S. Supreme Court's decision in 1972 finding the death penalty unconstitutional by slinging a noose over a tree limb on the courthouse lawn. In Alabama, three judges account for fifteen of the forty-seven instances in which jury sentences of life imprisonment were overridden and death imposed.

Failure to Protect the Constitutional Rights of the Accused

The Bill of Rights guarantees an accused certain procedural safeguards, regardless of whether those safeguards are supported by popular sentiment at the time of the trial, in order to protect the accused from the passions of the moment. But nothing protects an elected judge who enforces the Constitution from an angry constituency that is concerned only about the end result of a ruling and may have little understanding of what the law requires. Judges who must keep one eye on the next election often cannot resist the temptation to wink at the Constitution.

As previously discussed, some judges have scheduled capital cases for before an election or have refused to continue a case until after an election in order to gain the publicity and other political benefits that accompany presiding over such a trial. In these situations, the judge is under immense pressure to make rulings that favor the prosecution because an unpopular decision will quickly turn the anticipated benefits of association with the case into a major liability that could result in defeat in the election.

But even in less politically charged circumstances, judges face conflicts between personal political considerations and their duty to enforce the law in making decisions on a wide range of issues. For example, among the many decisions by trial judges to which

reviewing courts defer are determinations under *Batson* v. *Kentucky*[17] of whether the use of peremptory jury strikes was racially motivated. As previously discussed, many judges are former prosecutors. Before going to the bench, a judge may have hired the prosecutor appearing before him as an assistant. Even if the judge is not personally close to the prosecutor, she may be dependent upon the prosecutor's support in the next election to remain in office. Therefore, it may be personally difficult or politically impossible for a judge to reject the prosecutor's proffered reason for striking a minority juror.

Judges may find it difficult to make other decisions required by law and remain popular with the voters. The Mississippi Supreme Court has acknowledged that the discretion to grant a change of venue places a burden on the trial judge because "the judge serves at the will of the citizenry of the district ... [and] might be perceived as implying that a fair trial cannot be had among his or her constituents and neighbors."[18]

Even when a judge grants a change of venue, the objective may not be to protect the right of the accused to a fair trial. The clerk of a circuit court in Florida revealed several years after the death sentence was entered against Raleigh Porter that the presiding judge, Richard M. Stanley, had told the clerk that he was changing the venue to another county that had "good, fair minded people here who would listen and consider the evidence and then convict the son-of-a-bitch. Then, Judge Stanley said he would send Porter to the chair." The jury returned the expected verdict and Judge Stanley, wearing brass knuckles and a gun at the sentencing hearing, sentenced Porter to death.

In *Coleman* v. *Kemp*,[19] a Georgia trial judge denied a change of venue from a small rural community inundated with media coverage of six murders committed by Maryland prison escapees. The media coverage included strong anti-defendant sentiments, such as those of the local sheriff who publicly expressed his desire to "pre-cook [the defendants] several days, just keep them alive and let them punish," and of an editorial writer who compared the defendants to rattlesnakes and rabid dogs. A local citizen who served as a juror in one of the cases testified that news of the murders spread in the small community "like fire in a broom sage," that "everybody was so excited and upset over it," and that the sentiment of "everybody" prior to trial was "fry 'em, electrocute 'em." The elected trial judge, faced with a choice between his community's urge for a quick and violent response to the crime and the defendants' constitutional rights, refused to grant a change of venue. The local jury convicted the defendants and the elected Georgia Supreme Court upheld the convictions.

The difficult job of setting aside the convictions obtained at three trials that lacked any semblance of fairness was left to the judges serving life tenure on the United States Court of Appeals for the Eleventh Circuit. The political consequences of protecting the rights of the accused became even more apparent after the grant of habeas corpus relief. Citizens throughout Georgia presented petitions containing over 100,000 signatures to U.S. House of Representatives Judiciary Committee's Subcommittee on Courts, urging it to impeach the three members of the Court of Appeals panel who voted unanimously for the new trials.

The price paid for an elected judiciary in Alabama, California, Georgia, Texas, and other states has been the corruption of the judges and the courts of those states. Once a judge makes a decision influenced by political considerations, in violation of the oath he or she has taken to uphold the law, both the judge and the judicial system are diminished, not only in that case, but in all cases. The realization that a ruling in a case was made with more of an eye toward the next election than the requirements of the law can irreparably damage a judge's self-perception and commitment to justice. After the first such breach of one's judicial responsibility, it is more easily repeated in future cases. Once the public understands that courts are basing their rulings on political considerations—even when the courts are giving the voters the results they want, as the California Supreme Court is now doing—it undermines the legitimacy and the moral authority of courts as enforcers of the Constitution and law.

Appointment and Tolerance of Incompetent Counsel for Indigent Persons

Judges often fail to enforce the most fundamental protection of an accused, the Sixth Amendment right to counsel, by assigning an inexperienced or incompetent lawyer to represent the accused. As a result of appointments by state court judges, defendants in capital cases have been represented by lawyers—and in at least one instance a third-year law student—trying their cases or with little or no experience in trying serious cases, lawyers who were senile or intoxicated or under the influence of drugs while trying the cases, lawyers who were completely ignorant of the law and procedures governing a capital trial, lawyers who used racial slurs to refer to their clients, lawyers who handled cases without any investigative or expert assistance, lawyers who slept or were absent during crucial parts of the trial, lawyers who lacked even the most minimal skills, lawyers who filed one-page to ten-page briefs on direct appeal, and other equally incompetent lawyers who were deficient in a number of other respects.

When the community that elects the judge is demanding an execution, the judge has no political incentive to appoint an experienced lawyer who will devote large amounts of time to the case and file applications for expert and investigative assistance, all of which will only increase the cost of the case for the community. As a result, judges frequently assign lawyers who are not willing or able to provide a vigorous defense.

For example, judges in Houston, Texas have repeatedly appointed an attorney who occasionally falls asleep in court, and is known primarily for hurrying through capital trials like "greased lightning" without much questioning or making objections. Ten of his clients have received death sentences. Similarly, judges in Long Beach, California, assigned the representation of numerous indigent defendants to a lawyer who tried cases in very little time, not even obtaining discovery in some of them. The attorney has the distinction of having more of his clients sentenced to death, eight, than any other attorney in California.

Local elected judges in Georgia have repeatedly refused to appoint for retrials of capital cases the lawyers who had successfully represented the defendants in postconviction proceedings, even after the Georgia Supreme Court made it abundantly clear that counsel familiar with the case should be appointed.

Local elected judges may base their assignment of counsel to indigent defendants on political ties or other considerations than the ability of the lawyer to provide competent representation. A defense attorney in Cleveland contributes thousands of dollars toward the reelection campaigns of judges and is "notorious for picking up the judges' dinner and drink tabs. They, in turn, send [the attorney] as much business as he can handle in the form of case assignments."[20] A study of capital cases in Philadelphia found that "Philadelphia's poor defendants often find themselves being represented by ward leaders, ward committeemen, failed politicians, the sons of judges and party leaders, and contributors to the judge's election campaign."[21] The lawyer who received the most appointments one year to homicide cases in Philadelphia was a former judge whom the state's supreme court removed from the bench for receiving union money. He handled thirty-four murder cases in that year and submitted bills for $84,650 for fees and expenses.

As might be expected, treating the assignment of criminal cases as part of a judicial patronage system does not always result in the best legal representation. The study of capital cases in Philadelphia found that "even officials in charge of the system say they wouldn't want to be represented in Traffic Court by some of the people appointed to defend poor people accused of murder."

Regardless of the basis for selection, assignment of cases to lawyers by judges undermines the fairness and integrity of the adversary system in other ways. Lawyers who owe their livelihood to judicial appointments may be unwilling to provide zealous representation out of fear that it will cost them future appointments. So long as this system continues, neither the judges nor the lawyers are truly independent and able to play their proper role in the adversary system.

Judges Acting as Prosecutors

The prosecution of high-profile capital cases is often a stepping stone to a judgeship, as has been described. Unfortunately, more than a few prosecutors who become judges continue to prosecute from the bench. Although they fail to discharge their responsibility to be neutral, disinterested judges, they may continue to reap the same political benefits from capital cases that they received as prosecutors.

In a recent Georgia capital trial, a sitting superior court judge took the witness stand to tell the jury why, while serving as district attorney, he had sought the death penalty and had refused to agree to a plea disposition in the case. After testifying that the governor appointed him to the bench after having "serve[d] the citizens of Hall and Dawson count[ies] as their district attorney" for six years, the judge summarized the factors he had considered in making the decision as prosecutor to seek the death penalty for Stephen Anthony Mobley:

> [The defendant's] lack of remorse and a personality of "pure unadulterated meanness";
>
> The financial cost of death cases to taxpayers;
>
> Discussion with the victim's family and their support for a death sentence as the appropriate penalty;
>
> Consideration of whether the "last minutes of [the victims'] lives were more horrible to them than in other cases";
>
> [The judge's] feeling that Mobley's description of the murder to [one victim] was "unmerciful";
>
> The strength of the State's evidence.[22]

The judge summarized his decision by stating that "I've handled many cases with heinous facts of a killing, but I have never, never seen a defendant like Mr. Mobley." Remarkably, the Georgia Supreme Court upheld Mobley's death sentence over the dissent of only a single member.

Edward D. Webster, a former prosecutor in Riverside, California, publicly criticized a federal court of appeals for its decision in a capital case, even though he is now the presiding superior court judge in Riverside. Judge Webster, speaking "as a former prosecutor," expressed his "outrage" at a decision by the United States Court of Appeals for the Ninth Circuit remanding a capital habeas corpus case on grounds that the federal district court had failed to provide funds for expert assistance in support of the habeas petition. Judge Webster accused the federal court of anti-death-penalty bias and called upon Congress to prevent all federal courts except the Supreme Court from reviewing death-penalty cases.

A former prosecutor who now presides as a judge over capital cases in Houston, Texas, William Harmon, stated to a defendant during a 1991 capital trial that he was doing "God's work" to see that the defendant was executed. In the same case, Judge Harmon taped a photograph of the "hanging saloon" of Texas Judge Roy Bean on the front of the bench with his own name superimposed over Judge Bean's, and referred to the judges of the Texas Court of Criminal Appeals as "liberal bastards" and "idiots." In another capital case, Judge Harmon, upon a witness's suggestion that some death row inmates should be transported to court, stated, "Could we arrange for a van to blow up the bus on the way down here?"[23] In another capital trial in 1994, Judge Harmon allowed the victim's father to yell obscenities at the defendant in the presence of jurors and the press.

These are among the more pronounced examples of judges who have continued the prosecutorial role upon assuming the bench. Other judges may be more sophisticated in understanding their role and more subtle in their approach to capital cases. A judge does far more to undermine the fairness of a trial and hasten the imposition of a death sentence by appointing deficient counsel and in making discretionary rulings, as previously described, than by engaging in conduct such as Judge Harmon's.

It is not surprising that such judges are produced by a system that rewards prosecutors for obtaining the death penalty by giving them the public recognition and support needed to be elected judges. But this system often does not produce judges who will be fair and impartial in capital cases. It is most difficult for a

prosecutor who has made his name prosecuting capital cases to refrain as a judge from further exploitation of capital cases upon assuming the bench.

 ## Remedies for the Resulting Lack of Impartiality

Elected judges are expected to "remain faithful to the values and sentiments of the people who elected them, and to render decisions using common sense rather than newfangled legalisms." But remaining faithful to popular sentiment is sometimes inconsistent with a judge's duty to mete out equal justice and to enforce the Bill of Rights. As Justice Jackson wrote:

> The very purpose of a Bill of Rights was to withdraw certain subjects from the vicissitudes of political controversy, to place them beyond the reach of majorities and officials and to establish them as legal principles to be applied by the courts. One's right to life, liberty, and property, to free speech, a free press, freedom of worship and assembly, and other fundamental rights may not be submitted to vote; they depend on the outcome of no elections.[24]

In contrast, federal judges have life tenure and are appointed by the President with the advice and consent of the Senate in order to ensure the independence of the judiciary and to guarantee that the courts will perform their roles as protectors of "the rights of individuals." Recognizing that "a steady, upright, and impartial administration of the laws" was essential because "no man can be sure that he may not be tomorrow the victim of a spirit of injustice, by which he may be the gainer today," Alexander Hamilton wrote in *The Federalist* No. 78: "That inflexible and uniform adherence to the rights of the Constitution, and of individuals, which we perceive to be indispensable in the courts of justice, can certainly not be expected from judges who hold their offices by temporary commission."[25]

The state bench also differs from the federal bench in that it is more likely to be a stepping stone to a higher political office. In comparing the state and federal judiciary, Chief Justice William Rehnquist has pointed out that the life tenure of federal judges makes for a "different kind of judge" than someone "looking out of one corner of his eye for the next political opportunity that comes along."[26] However, the politics of crime have increasingly had an impact on nominations to the federal judiciary and even the Supreme Court has seemed responsive to the political potency of the crime issue.

Nevertheless, although some appointees may take a political agenda with them to the federal bench, life tenure still insulates judges from the threat of being voted out of office for an unpopular decision. Every new election reminds state judges of their vulnerability to popular sentiment. Such constant reminders make it politically and practically impossible for many judges to enforce the Constitution when doing so would be unpopular.

If courts are to have integrity and credibility, judges must be selected, evaluated, and assigned cases in a way that makes it possible for them to uphold the law without imperiling their jobs. Political considerations will always be a factor in the selection and promotion of judges in both the state and federal courts, and some who become judges will allow their personal prejudices to interfere with the faithful discharge of their duties, regardless of how they are selected. But the selection and promotion process should not allow a judge's ruling in a particular case to dominate his or her prospects for remaining on the bench. If this is not the case, judges will continue to work under unreasonable pressures and the public will not view their decisions as fair, impartial, and legitimate. The judiciary and bar should exercise leadership in bringing about the replacement of judicial elections—both retention and contested—with merit selection and periodic performance review. Although such systems are desirable and may be more likely after elections that have significantly diminished the standing of the courts in Alabama, California, Mississippi, Texas, and other states, one can expect that elections will remain in many jurisdictions.

As long as judges are selected at the ballot box, several less effective measures, small and large, should be taken to reduce the influence of political considerations on judicial rulings. Judges must recognize their constitutional and ethical responsibility to disqualify themselves in cases in which one might reasonably question their impartiality due to political pressures. Capital cases should be assigned to judges who do not face the voters from the locality of the crime. The discretion of trial judges in areas where they are under political pressures should be limited and reviewing courts should give more careful scrutiny to rulings that are susceptible to influence by political considerations. Regardless of how judges are selected, they should not appoint counsel for indigent defendants. Removal of appointment responsibility from judges is necessary to ensure the independence of the judiciary and the zealous defense of the accused.

Using Diffuse and Indirect Citizen Input in Appointment and Evaluation Systems

The elimination of direct and retention elections is a necessary step to improve the fairness and impartiality of the judiciary. Eleven states and the District of Columbia already employ systems in which judges never face election. The systems in those states provide for removal of judges only for misbehavior or other ethical improprieties, avoiding the opportunity to turn a judicial election into a popular referendum on a judge's rulings in controversial cases.

Although judicial elections appear to be immensely popular in the United States, judges were not always selected and retained this way. The American colonial governments utilized executive selection of judges and service during good behavior in an effort to depoliticize the judiciary. Resentment toward the Crown's control of the judiciary resulted in a shift from judges serving in the pleasure of the executive to judges serving during good behavior.

Dissatisfaction with the appointed judiciary during the period of populist Jacksonian democracy led to the election of judges. The public viewed judges as too protective of the interests of property owners. States began to adopt systems of electing judges in an effort to divorce the judiciary from property owners. However, it became apparent that popular election resulted in a highly politicized judiciary, with political machines often controlling judges. States again began to tinker with judicial selection methods, with some eventually adopting a selection plan that included gubernatorial appointment from a list compiled by a judicial selection committee, with a subsequent retention election after a certain period of time. This reform sought to depoliticize the judiciary and allow judges to make decisions unswayed by political considerations while still allowing for some form of input from citizens. But, as has been the case in California, Florida, and other places, even a retention election can degenerate into a referendum on a judge's rulings in capital or other controversial cases. Indeed, a strong argument can be made that retention elections are even worse than direct elections where the incumbent is challenged. In retention elections, there is no comparison to be made among candidates. The judge standing for retention may be a target for negative votes from various groups dissatisfied with decisions on issues ranging from crime to abortion. Voters may want to express their disapproval of the judge with no consideration of whether the replacement judge will be any better.

The independence of the judiciary can be best preserved by a merit selection system in which a bipartisan judicial qualifications commission nominates a slate of qualified candidates to the executive, who then nominates a judge subject to confirmation by at least one branch of the state legislature. Meaningful citizen input can come by ensuring that a substantial number of persons on the judicial qualifications commission are not lawyers, but people who represent various segments of the public. Such a system should provide for terms for judges of substantial length, such as ten to fifteen years. Retention in office for additional terms should depend upon an evaluation of the judge's performance by the commission, not a retention election.

One state that employs such a system is Hawaii, where the governor selects judges with the consent of the senate, from a list of nominees that a judicial selection commission compiles. The judicial selection commission's list must contain not less than six nominees.

If a judge indicates at least six months before the end of his term that he wishes reappointment, the commission determines whether the judge should be retained. The primary purpose of the retention process is to "exclude or, at least, reduce partisan political action."

There are many positive aspects to Hawaii's selection and retention process. First, it provides for diffuse and indirect input in the judicial selection and retention process by allowing the governor, the president of the senate, and the speaker of the house of representatives, all of whom are elected, to appoint a total of five members of the commission. Thus, there is public accountability in a selection process that provides a layer of protection for judges who may make unpopular decisions.

Second, a judge serves a term of ten years, after which time the judicial selection commission again evaluates and either retains or rejects the judge. Commission review allows an informed body to evaluate a judge's entire ten-year record. The commission sees any unpopular or controversial decisions in the context of a broader record. In addition, the commission can review the legal reasons for the judge's decision, not just the result.

Third, commission review avoids judicial electoral campaigns, some of which can be demagogic, undignified, and unsophisticated. Judges create complicated records of rulings on a variety of issues, and an informed body representing the public can examine a judge's entire record rather than merely focus on a judge's rulings in the most notorious or highly publicized cases. Because a judge knows that an informed body will review her performance, she will be less susceptible to community pressures and will be more likely to enforce constitutional and statutory law. Such a method of selection would also result in better judges. Many capable and highly qualified individuals are unwilling to seek judgeships where they must stand for election, knowing that the responsible discharge of their duties in a controversial case could cost them their positions. Such individuals may also be unwilling to solicit campaign contributions to finance a judicial campaign, knowing that it creates an appearance of impropriety, engage in campaign tactics that are inconsistent with the Model Code of Judicial Conduct but may be necessary to obtain office, or assume the bench knowing that they will be unable to defend themselves when attacked politically for a single ruling or decision.

Fourth, the public may have more confidence in and respect for the judiciary because it knows that judges who do not have to worry about offending a particular segment of the population in order to raise campaign funds or stay in office are more likely to be impartial. At the same time, periodic review of judicial behavior protects the public from those who are unfit for judicial service.

Finally, and most importantly, such a system ensures that when an individual takes the bench, he or she is independent in the sense that former United States Supreme Court Justice Owen Roberts described:

> When a man goes on the Court he ought not to have to depend upon the strength . . . of his own character to resist the temptation to shade a sentence in an opinion or shade a view. [He should not have] to put an umbrella up in case it should rain. He ought to be free to say his say, knowing as the founding fathers meant he should know, that nothing could reach him and his conscience was as free as could be.[27]

To be independent, a judge must be free to disregard public sentiment when required by the law, and to take unpopular, but constitutionally mandated, action.

Until recently judicial elections, whether direct or retention, attracted little public attention. Judges seldom encountered opposition either from opponents or from interest groups opposing their retention. However, this is no longer the case. The judiciary in states all across the nation is becoming increasingly politicized. The success in defeating incumbent judges in some states is leading to new efforts in others. No judge can risk alienating a powerful special interest group or being viewed as "soft on crime." The elimination of both direct and retention elections is essential if courts are to be responsive to the commands of the law and Constitution instead of the will of the majority.

Judicial Disqualification When Rulings Could Imperil Election

In jurisdictions in which judges stand for election or retention, judges should be disqualified from presiding over cases in which there is the appearance that political considerations could tempt judges in their ruling. The law of judicial disqualification and due process currently provides for this, but courts fail to apply this law properly, relying on fictions of impartiality while ignoring political realities.

In *Tumey v. Ohio*,[28] the Supreme Court held as violative of due process a judicial system in which a mayor sat in judgment of alleged violators of a Prohibition ordinance, and was not paid unless he convicted and fined at least some of those brought before him. The Court concluded such a system deprives the accused of due process in several ways. First, it "subjects [a defendant's] liberty or property to the judgment of a court the judge of which has a direct, personal, substantial, pecuniary interest in reaching a conclusion against him in his case." Second, "It is certainly not fair to each defendant, brought before the Mayor for the careful and judicial consideration of his guilt or innocence, that the prospect of such a loss by the Mayor should weigh against his acquittal." Third, any system that "offer[s] a possible temptation to the average man as a judge to forget the burden of proof required to convict the defendant, or [that] might lead him not to hold the balance nice, clear and true between the State and the accused, denies the latter due process." Fourth, given the mayor's position, "might not a defendant with reason say that he feared he could not get a fair trial or a fair sentence from one who would have so strong a motive to help his village by conviction and a heavy fine?"

In *Ward v. Village of Monroeville*, the Court extended the *Tumey* principle to prohibit a mayor from acting as a judge in a case in which his financial interest was not personal, but in which his general mayoral responsibilities included revenue production. The Court rejected the village's argument that this system does not deprive defendants of due process because the mayor's decisions were correctable on appeal and trial de novo in the

County Court of Common Pleas. Justice Brennan wrote that "there is nothing to suggest that the incentive to convict would be diminished by the possibility of reversal on appeal. . . . [The defendant] is entitled to a neutral and detached judge in the first instance."

The impartiality of judges who promise to be "tough on crime" is also called into question by the Model Code of Judicial Conduct. Canon 3 provides that a judge "should not be swayed by partisan interests, public clamor or fear of criticism."[29] Canon 5 provides that a judge "shall not (i) make pledges or promises of conduct in office other than the faithful and impartial performance of the duties of the office; [or] (ii) make statements that commit or appear to commit the candidate with respect to cases, controversies, or issues that are likely to come before the court."[30]

The *Tumey* situation is analogous to a typical capital case tried, appealed, or brought for postconviction review before an elected judge. The justices of the Supreme Courts of California and Mississippi, the judges of the Texas Court of Criminal Appeals, and trial judges in Houston and other jurisdictions certainly know that their future on the courts and their judicial salaries and pensions are closely related to their decisions in capital cases. At the very least, these pressures create the appearance of partiality.

The legitimacy of judicial decisions depends on the appearance of fairness, and elected judges hearing capital cases too often make rulings that appear to be patently unfair. It is apparent not only to Justice Stevens but also to those who observe the courts that judges are frequently responding to a "higher authority" than the Constitution. In some instances, that voice sounds too much like the cries of a lynch mob. *Tumey* commands judges not have an improper temptation to rule in one way or the other. A judge who will lose his position by ruling against the prosecution in a single case is under far greater pressure not to "hold the balance nice, clear and true between the state and the accused" than is a judge whose salary comes from fines that may be imposed in some of the many cases that come before him. It is possible to construct fictions of impartiality and impute them to every judge, but the reality is that capital punishment is popular

and judicial elections can become referenda on the death penalty.

One step in the right direction would be to permit disqualification of at least one judge without attempting to assess the question of impartiality. For example, in Maryland, a party who believes that a fair and impartial trial cannot be had before the assigned judge may file a suggestion that the judge is incapable of affording him or her an impartial trial and the case must be removed to another court. A judge in a capital case may not refuse to grant the motion. This at least allows the defendant to decide if the judge originally assigned to his case may not be in a position to put aside political considerations, such as a judge facing a tough election. This system is attractive because it does not operate on the presumption that judges become somehow immune to influences that would weigh strongly on non-judges. This system does not attempt to discern a judge's actual biases, but recognizes that the appearance of bias may make it appropriate for another judge to hear the case. On the other hand, when there is no concern about improper influences, the judge will remain on the case. There is no assurance, however, that the new judge assigned to a case will not also be facing a tough reelection campaign and be subject to the same pressures.

It may be that practical considerations prevent courts from acknowledging the appearance of partiality of elected judges due to political pressures. If an entire state supreme court is disqualified, how is the case decided? If a judge is disqualified from all criminal cases because he promised to be "too tough on criminals," how is the criminal docket to be managed? The answer to these practical problems, however, is not to substitute legal fictions for political reality.

The popular frustration regarding crime is making it increasingly difficult for courts to discharge their constitutional obligation of fairness. Judges who realize they cannot hold the balance nice, clear, and true between the state and the accused in particular cases because of political considerations have a duty to recuse themselves. Lawyers have a duty to move for the disqualification of judges who are subject to the temptation to give in to political pressures in the cases before them. In reviewing disqualification issues, trial and appellate courts should face the reality of the political pressures that are present instead of hiding behind legal fictions. If disqualification in cases in which one might reasonably question judges' partiality due to political pressures begins to burden dockets, the legislature and the bar will be forced to devise different selection systems that will minimize the influence of political pressures on judges.

Altering Judicial Assignment Systems

One way to reduce the political pressures on elected judges is to prohibit those judges from presiding over capital cases in the districts that elect them. This could be accomplished through the judicial assignment system.

For example, in both North and South Carolina judges rotate among judicial districts within the state. When out of his county of residence, the judge is relieved from the political pressure of having to portray himself as the protector of his community; a judge would not necessarily stand for election in the very place in which he had made controversial rulings.

This system would help to diminish the role of political pressure on judicial decision making, but would not eliminate it. A judge could still seek to impress the voters at home with his toughness in the case before him in another district. In a highly publicized case, a controversial ruling would still be well known and, even if it were not, an opponent could still seize upon an unpopular but correct ruling and use it in opposing the judge. Additionally, in any system a judge who intends to run for higher office may want to use his or her position for visibility.

Limiting the Deference Reviewing Courts Give to Judges Influenced by Political Pressures

So long as judges are subject to election or retention, the discretion of trial judges on crucial matters should be limited by objective standards that are carefully reviewed on appeal and in postconviction proceedings.

Reviewing courts should acknowledge the reality of the political pressures on trial judges, and, where the potential for such influence is present, they should carefully scrutinize rulings without the normal deference accorded to trial judges.

Appellate courts routinely defer to findings of fact of state trial judges, and review decisions of trial judges under the highly deferential abuse-of-discretion and clearly-erroneous standards on critical issues such as granting of a change of venue, allowing a continuance, the extent and scope of voir dire, whether there has been racial discrimination in the exercise of jury strikes, the impartiality of prospective jurors, and the admission of certain types of evidence. Federal courts, when reviewing state court judgments in habeas corpus proceedings, are required to give a presumption of correctness to findings of fact by the state courts. The notion that the trial judge, having observed the demeanor of the witnesses and heard all of the evidence first hand, is in a better position to make determination of credibility forms much of the basis for the deference accorded the trial judge. This deference also rests upon the prevailing legal fiction that assumes the impartiality of judges.

In reality, however, political considerations may be more important than legal principles or the demeanor of witnesses. As previously discussed, judges are under immense political pressure in making discretionary rulings in high-profile capital cases. A classic example is the case of *Sheppard v. Maxwell*. The murder trial of Dr. Samuel H. Sheppard started, after extensive pretrial publicity, just two weeks before a November election in which the chief prosecutor was a candidate for judge and the trial judge was a candidate for reelection. The Supreme Court held that Sheppard was entitled to habeas corpus relief because the trial court had failed to protect his right to a fair trial by taking measures such as continuing the case until after the election, changing venue, and controlling the trial participants' release of prejudicial information to the press.

Unfortunately, since *Sheppard*, the Supreme Court has not mandated procedures to minimize the risk of prejudice in such volatile situations or required careful scrutiny based on objective standards of similar discretionary decisions by trial judges. The Court has also retreated from its earlier pronouncements that because of the exceptional and irrevocable nature of the death penalty, capital cases require a heightened degree of procedural protection.

A few state supreme courts have recognized the political pressures on trial judges and have fashioned more objective standards and mandatory procedures to reduce the discretion of trial judges in making rulings that may be politically unpopular. For example, the Mississippi Supreme Court, after acknowledging the political pressures that may influence a judge's decision on whether to grant a change of venue, decided that "some objective standards should be available to shield the [trial] court from even the appearance of such subtle coercion."[31]

The Mississippi Supreme Court described the political reality for elected trial judges in considering a motion to change venue:

[B]y perennially holding that a change of venue is granted solely at the discretion of the court, we perpetuate a burden on the trial judge. On the one hand, the judge is to act impartially, dispassionately and with scrupulous objectivity. On the other hand, in reality, the judge serves at the will of the citizenry of the district; the judge is, after all, a public official who must occasionally, perhaps even subconsciously, respond to public sentiment when making the decision to refuse a change of venue. It must be observed that, in granting a change, the trial judge might be perceived as implying that a fair trial cannot be had among his or her constituents and neighbors.

To keep such sentiment from influencing the judge, the court held that

the accused has a right to a change of venue when it is doubtful that an impartial jury can be obtained; such doubt is implicit when there is present strong public sentiment against the

defendant; upon proper application, there arises a presumption that such sentiment exists; and, the state then bears the burden of rebutting that presumption.

The court also emphasized the importance of fairness in capital cases:

A heightened standard of review is employed on appeal where the defendant's life is at stake.... It follows then that the trial court should, likewise, be particularly sensitive to the need for a change of venue in capital cases.

The Georgia Supreme Court also modified its standard of review of denials of motions for a change to venue and directed trial judges in Georgia to grant changes of venue when a capital defendant makes "a substantive showing of the likelihood of prejudice by reason of publicity."[32] The Court rejected the argument of the dissent that the determination of the trial judge was subject to "special deference" and should not be overturned unless it was "manifestly erroneous."

Venue decisions are but one example of potential for the influence of improper political considerations on judicial rulings and the need for reviewing courts to remedy politically influenced decisions by adopting and applying objective standards. Where a particularly notorious crime produces volumes of publicity, that publicity often creates pressure on the judge to score political points. The more objective standards that the Supreme Courts of Mississippi and Georgia have adopted lessen the discretion allowed the trial judge, and allow courts a greater distance from the political influences to review trial decisions. A reviewing court can examine the testimony, the newspaper articles, and the tapes of broadcasts and make its own determination of whether there is a "likelihood of prejudice" or the prosecution has rebutted a defendant's showing that public sentiment makes the likelihood of an impartial jury doubtful.

Although these decisions of the Supreme Courts of Georgia and Mississippi providing for greater protection of the rights of the accused than the decisions of the U.S. Supreme Court may appear encouraging they say more about the retreat of the U.S. Supreme Court from protecting the rights of the accused than it does about the willingness—or political practicality—of the state courts upholding the Constitution in these situations. Most courts have shown little inclination to face reality with regard to many other discretionary decisions of trial judges that political considerations may influence. Decisions recognizing the political pressures on elected judges and adopting and applying more objective standards to limit discretion are the rare exceptions to thousands of decisions routinely deferring to decisions by trial judges on a wide range of issues. The deference in federal habeas corpus actions to state court fact finding, as well as other increasingly severe restrictions on habeas review, insulate many decisions by state courts from federal review.

Nevertheless, a reexamination of the deference given to elected judges on discretionary matters is urgently needed. The outcomes of the judicial elections in California, Texas, Mississippi, and other states discussed in this article are exposing for all to see the political pressures that influence the decisions of judges who face election or retention. It is of course impossible to know the number of judges who simply give in, either consciously or subconsciously, to their political pressures or the number of judicial rulings and opinions that political considerations influence. But the political realities are apparent to anyone who practices in the courts and observes these pressures at work. In many of the jurisdictions where the death penalty is frequently imposed, the political reality is that the elected state court judge cannot even consider granting relief to one facing the death penalty.

If judges continue to be voted off trial and appellate courts for their decisions in capital cases and are replaced with judges who are little more that conductors on railroads to the execution chambers, it will be impossible for courts to maintain the fiction that judges who face election are impartial without risking public ridicule and immense damage to the perception of the legitimacy and credibility of the courts. Until more fundamental reform of judicial selection is feasible, courts must acknowledge and deal with the political pressures on judges. In addition, full federal habeas corpus review of state court convictions should be restored. The once Great Writ of habeas corpus barely survives the blows that have rained upon it from the efforts of the Supreme Court and the Congress to expedite executions, achieve finality, and reduce friction between the state and federal courts. Yet as numerous examples set out in this article make clear, only federal judges have the independence and job security that enable them to enforce the protections of the Constitution when doing so would be vastly unpopular. If the Constitution is to serve its purpose as fundamental law that protects us from "our baser selves" when there is "a demand for vengeance on the part of many persons in the community against one who is convicted of a particularly offensive act,"[33] its enforcers must be judges who cannot be swept from office for making a controversial decision.

Appointment of Counsel Independent of Judges

Regardless of how judges are selected, they should not be responsible for the appointment of counsel for poor persons accused of crimes. An independent judiciary should be independent not only of political influences and the prosecution, but also of the defense. Judges have a different role to play in the adversary system than the management of the defense. In addition, defense counsel should be independent of the judge in order to fulfill the obligation of providing zealous representation to the accused.

The American Bar Association recommends that there be a defender office or a special appointments committee to select counsel for indigent defendants. Removing the responsibility for the representation of defendants from judges and placing it with a program charged with protecting only the best interests of the defendants will not completely depoliticize the process or always ensure adequate counsel, but it would be an important step toward a properly working adversary system and effective representation of indigent defendants.

 ## Conclusion

Justice Hugo Black once observed that "[u]nder our constitutional system, courts stand against any winds that blow as havens of refuge for those who might otherwise suffer because they are helpless, weak, outnumbered, or because they are . . . victims of prejudice and public excitement."[34] This role is of particular importance in capital cases, where the winds of public excitement blow especially hard against the poor, members of racial minorities, and the despised who stand accused of heinous crimes. Judges are not legislators; they have a different role than simply carrying out the wishes of their constituents to impose the death penalty.

Capital cases put extraordinary pressures on all participants in the legal system. Even the most conscientious and independent judge faces an enormous challenge of reining in the emotions that accompany a brutal crime and the loss of innocent life. If decisions about guilt and punishment are to be made fairly, objectively, and reliably, it is critical that judges be guided by the Constitution, not personal political considerations.

Yet in high-visibility capital cases in which public opinion is overwhelmingly one-sided though often ill-informed, the political pressures may be so great that a judge who has an interest in remaining on the bench cannot ignore them. In today's political climate, a commitment to fairness is too often perceived as "softness" on crime—a political liability for a judge who must run for office. The lack of electoral clout of those facing the death penalty makes the political equation easy; however, the cost to justice and the rule of law is significant.

Nevertheless, it appears unlikely that even the most modest proposals discussed in this article will be implemented in many jurisdictions—particularly those where they are most urgently needed—in the near future. In part, this is because there are many people who prefer judges who follow the election returns to judges who follow the law. It is also partly because the judiciary and the bar persist in hiding behind the legal fiction that judges are impartial instead of acknowledging the reality that in many instances they are not. The U.S. Supreme Court indulges in wishful thinking about what the state courts should be, instead of facing what they are, including the political pressures on those judges.

It is, however, time for open and honest discussion of the political pressures on judges who must stand for election and retention. The integrity, credibility, and legitimacy of the courts are at stake. Judges themselves should lead the discussion by disqualifying themselves *sua sponte* from cases in which they recognize that political considerations may keep them from holding the balance "nice, clear and true." But it may be necessary for lawyers to prompt the discussion by filing motions for recusal in cases in which such pressures are present. The judiciary and the bar have a duty to explain to the public the difference between the representative function of legislative bodies and the adjudicatory function of courts. These steps are urgently needed to bring about reforms that will increase the likelihood that the only "higher authority" to which judges are responsive is the Constitution and laws of the United States.

 ## Notes

1. 115 S. Ct. 1031, 1039 (1995) (Stevens, J., dissenting) (quoting Duncan v. Louisiana, 391 U.S. 145, 156 (1968)).

2. Maura Dolan, *State High Court Is Strong Enforcer of Death Penalty,* L.A. Times, Apr. 9, 1995, at A1.

3. Dolan, *State High Court Is Strong Enforcer of Death Penalty, supra* note 7, at A1 (quoting Professor Clark Kelso).

4. Elliot C. Kessler, *Death and Harmlessness: Application of the Harmless Error Rule by the Bird and Lucas Courts in Death Penalty Cases—A Comparison & Critique,* 26 U.S.F.L. REV. 41, 85, 89 (1991).

5. Coker v. Georgia, 433 U.S. 584 (1977).

6. Harris v. Alabama, 115 S. Ct. 1031, 1039 n.5 (1995) (dissenting opinion).

7. Lisa Stansky, Elected Judges Favor Death Penalty, *Fulton County Daily Rep.* (GA), Nov. 24, 1989, at 11 (quoting Dean Gerald Uelmen of Santa Clara University Law School, who has studied the relation between methods of selection and judicial behavior).

8. Gerald Uelmen, Elected Judiciary, in *Encyclopedia of the American Constitution* 170–71 (Leonard W. Levy et al. eds., Supp. 1 1992).

9. See Stephen B. Bright, *Counsel for the Poor: The Death Sentence Not for the Crime but for the Worst Lawyer,* 103 Yale L.J. 1835 (1994).

10. John Harwood, Approving Atwater: GOP Committee Backs Its Chairman, *St. Petersburg Times,* June 17, 1989, at 1A.

11. Richard Cohen, Playing Politics with the Death Penalty, *Wash. Post,* Mar. 20, 1990, at A19.

12. Leslie Phillips, Crime Pays as a Political Issue, *USA Today,* Oct. 10, 1994, at 1A.

13. Hance v. Zant, 696 F.2nd 940, 952–53 (11th Cir.).

14. Phil Gast, District Attorney Criticizes Court for Rejecting Sentence, *Columbus Enquirer* (Ga.), Sept. 17, 1983, at A-1, A-2.

15. Wainwright v. Witt, 469 U.S. 412, 459 (1984) (Brennan, J., dissenting) (citations omitted).

16. American Bar Ass'n, Report of Commission on Professionalism, 112 F.R.D. 243, 293 (1986).

17. 476 U.S. 79 (1986).

18. Johnson v. state, 476 So. 2d 1195, 1209 (Miss. 1985).

19. 778 F.2d 1487 (11th Cir. 1985).

20. James F. McCarty, Law and Disorder with Rumpled Suits and Befuddled Ways, Thomas Shaughnessy Has Managed to Become the Matlock of Cuyahoga County, *Plain Dealer* (Cleveland), Oct. 23, 1994, at 8, 13.

21. See Fredric N. Tulsky, Big-time Trials, Small Time Defenses, *Phila Inquirer,* Sept. 14, 1992, at A1, A8.

22. Mobley v. State, 455 S.E.2d 61, 69–70 (Ga. 1995).

23. Nichols v. Collins, 802 F. Supp. 66, 78–79 (S.D. Tex. 1992) (granting writ of habeas corpus).

24. West Virginia State Bd. Of Educ. v. Barnette, 319 U.S. 624, 638 (1943).

25. *The Federalist* No. 78, (Alexander Hamilton) (Clinton Rossiter ed., 1961).

26. Chief Justice William Rehnquist, Press Conferences 5 (Mar. 15, 1989) (unofficial transcript, on file with *Boston University Law Review*).

27. Robert W. Raven, Does the Bar Have an Obligation to Help Ensure the Independence of the Judiciary? 69 *Judicature* 66, 67 (1985) (quoting Justice Roberts).

28. 273 U.S. 510 (1927).

29. *Model Code of Judicial Conduct* Canon 311(2) (1990). For further discussion of the Model Code of Judicial Conduct and elected judges, see Ross, *supra* note 120, at 128–30 (applying the 1972 Model Code to the problem of elected judiciaries).

30. *Model Code of Judicial Conduct* Canon 5A(3)(d)(i), (ii) (1990).

31. Johnson v. State, 476 So. 2d 1195, 1209 (Miss. 1985).

32. Jones v. State, 409 S.E. 2d 642, 643 (Ga. 1991).

33. Furman v. Georgia, 408 U.S. 238, 344–45 (1972) (Marshall, J., concurring).

34. Chambers v. Florida, 309 U.S. 227, 241 (1940).

DISCUSSION QUESTIONS

1. Why do Bright and Keenan argue that a judge who opposes the death penalty "may thereby sign his own political death warrant"? What evidence do they provide in support of this?

2. What types of judicial selection systems are found in the states with the death penalty? According to Bright and Keenan, why is it problematic that more than half of the states elect judges and sentence people to death?

3. What are the effects of electing judges who must render decisions in capital cases? How does election affect the impartiality of judges in these types?

4. What are the remedies advocated by Bright and Keenan? In your opinion, which of these would be the most effective? The most politically palatable?

READING

Because jury deliberations are conducted behind closed doors, we know very little about the dynamics of the jury deliberation process. However, the author of this article was selected as a juror for a rape trial that took place in 1999 and therefore is able to provide a first-hand account of the jury decision making process. The author discusses the circumstances of the case, the evidence and arguments of the prosecution and defense, the deliberations among jurors during the first trial, and the outcome of each trial. She also raises questions about the treatment of sexual assault victims in the courts, the effect of jury selection on the outcomes of trials, and the persistence of myths regarding women and sexual assault in American society.

Reflections on a Rape Trial

The Role of Rape Myths and Jury Selection in the Outcome of a Trial

Judy Shepherd

Sexual assault continues to be the most underreported violent crime in the United States. According to a report by the Bureau of Justice Statistics (Rennison, 1998), only 31.6% of all rapes and sexual assaults were reported to law enforcement officials in 1998 compared to 62% of all robberies, 57.6% of all aggravated assaults, and 40.3% of all simple assaults. Even with such underreporting, 330,000 women aged 12 and older were the victims of rape, attempted rape, or sexual assault in the United States in 1998, a 7.1% increase from 1997 (Rennison, 1998).

The common rationale for such underreporting of this serious crime is the treatment that victims receive from societal institutions, especially the legal system. The difficulty of bringing a rape case to trial and of obtaining a conviction for this crime has been well documented. For example, in 1984, Russell found that "less than 1% of rapes and attempted rapes result in

convictions in the U.S." (as cited in Ward, 1995, p. 196). Furthermore, a 3-year investigation of state rape prosecutions by the Committee on the Judiciary, U.S. Senate (1993) revealed:

> Ninety-eight percent of rape victims will never see their attacker apprehended, convicted and incarcerated;
>
> Over half (54 percent) of all rape prosecutions result in either a dismissal or an acquittal;
>
> A rape prosecution is more than twice as likely as a murder prosecution to be dismissed and 30 percent more likely to be dismissed than a robbery prosecution;
>
> Approximately 1 in 10 rapes reported to the police result in time served in prison;

SOURCE: Shepherd, J. (2002). Reflections on a rape trial: The role of rape myths and jury selection in the outcome of a trial. *Affilia, 17,* 69–92.

Almost one-quarter of convicted rapists are not sentenced to prison, but instead, are released on probation;

Nearly one-quarter of convicted rapists receives a sentence to a local jail—for only 11 months (according to national estimates);

Adding together the convicted rapists sentenced to probation and those sentenced to local jails, almost half of all convicted rapists are sentenced to less than 1 year behind bars. (p. 1)

This article presents an in-depth case study of a rape trial that occurred in Alaska in the spring and fall of 1999, with particular attention to the jury selection process and the reliance on rape-myth arguments throughout the deliberations. It also points to areas for further research and advocacy regarding attitudes toward rape and the treatment of rape victims in this society.

Review of the Literature

The acceptance of the myths about rape, which are commonly held beliefs that shift the blame for a sexual assault from the assailant to the victim and serve to minimize the prevalence and seriousness of rape (Stout & McPhail, 1998), has been the focus of many studies. Common myths include the beliefs that "victims are lying, victims are malicious, sex was consensual, and rape is not damaging. . . . The underlying assumptions about rape suggest that women are essentially responsible for male sexual behavior" (Ward, 1995, p. 25). Ward (1995), who studied attitudes toward rape on college campuses, found in 1980 that only 36% of those surveyed disagreed with the statement that rape is provoked by women's appearance and behavior, and 60% maintained that women who go out alone put themselves in a position to be raped. In a 1991 attitude survey by Halcomb and others (as cited in Ward, 1995),

24% of the respondents agreed with the statement, "women frequently cry rape falsely"

and 22% agreed that rape is often provoked by the victim, 22% agreed a woman could prevent a rape if she really wanted to, 32% agreed that some women ask to be raped and may enjoy it, and 29% agreed that if a woman says no to having sex, she means maybe or even yes. (p. 45)

Several studies have demonstrated that gender is correlated with the acceptance of rape myths. According to Ward's (1995) review of the literature on rape attitudes, "Studies show men are more accepting of rape myths than women (Margolin et al., 1989), more tolerant of rape (Hall et al., 1986), and have less empathy towards victims (Bradley et al., 1991)" (p. 45). Ward also cited Giacopassi and Dull's 1986 study that found that men were more likely to agree that normal men do not commit rape and that women were more likely to disagree with the statements that "women who ask men out are probably looking for sex, that women say no but mean yes, and that date rape should not be considered as serious as stranger rape" (p. 46). After reviewing studies on attitudes toward rape, Ward concluded, "The sensitive issue of coercive sex between people who know each other, the most common form of sexual violence, appears to be trivialized more frequently by men" (p. 46).

It is also important to note that

the danger of false rape complaints has been vastly overrated. The police find the number of false rape charges to be comparable to the level of false charges brought in other types of crimes. There are rare occasions when individuals falsely accuse others of crimes, but evidence suggests that the episodes are no more frequent in rape cases than in other serious cases. (Hans & Vidmar, 1986, p. 206)

And as Stout and McPhail (1998) noted,

Although false charges of rape are often widely publicized, FBI statistics (as cited in Lonsway & Fitzgerald, 1994) suggest that only 2% of rape charges are false; this rate is lower than or comparable to the rate for other felonies. (p. 261)

Educational level has also been correlated with the acceptance of rape myths, as noted in Ward's (1995) review of studies of rape. Burt (as cited in Ward, 1995), who sampled approximately 600 adults in Minnesota, found that "education exerted a direct effect on the rejection of stereotyped, prejudicial views of rape. Better educated respondents were less willing to endorse such statements as, 'in the majority of rapes, the victim is promiscuous or has a bad reputation'" (p. 47). Other studies on educational level found similar results. Jeffords and Dull (as cited in Ward, 1995) found that supporters of marital rape legislation in Texas were more likely to be female, single, young, and well educated, and Williams (as cited in Ward, 1995), in a survey of 1,000 San Antonio residents, found education to be the most powerful predictor of attitudes toward rape.

A review of the literature on jurors' attitudes, based on mock juries or posttrial interviews, demonstrated that jurors are influenced by the prior relationship of the victim and assailant as well as the victim's character. In reviewing Kalvin and Zeisel's studies on jury trials, Epstein and Langenbahn (1994) noted "not only that juries are prejudiced against the prosecution in rape cases, but also that they were extremely lenient with defendants if there was any suggestion of 'contributory behavior' on the part of the victim" (p. 66). One contributing behavior that clearly affects perceptions of rape is the consumption of alcohol. According to a study by Richardson and Campbell (as cited in Ward, 1995), "People are more likely to see intoxication as contributing to the woman's responsibility in sexual assault" (p. 76). A study by Lafree (as cited in Hans & Vidmar, 1986), which included posttrial interviews with 331 jurors who heard cases of forcible sexual assault, found that none of the measures of evidence, including eyewitnesses, the number of prosecution witnesses and exhibits, the use of a weapon, or injury to the victim, affected jurors' beliefs about the defendant's guilt or innocence prior to deliberations. However, jurors were affected by the characteristics of the victim

and defendant. When the victim held a blue-collar job, when she reportedly had sexual intercourse outside marriage, or when she drank or used drugs, jurors were more likely to believe the defendant was innocent. Jurors who had conservative attitudes about sex roles were especially likely to believe the defendant was not guilty of rape when they learned that the victim used drugs or alcohol. Thus, in cases where the victim's word was a primary issue, jurors were influenced more by the character of the victim than by hard evidence, even corroborative evidence.

Another factor that has been found to contribute to the outcomes of rape trials is whether physical force was used. Deitz (as cited in Ward, 1995) found in jury simulation studies that guilty verdicts are less likely to be rendered in rape cases when there is no evidence that the victim resisted, and Wyler (as cited in Ward, 1995) noted that "women who resist attempted rape are perceived as less responsible and less to blame for their assault than those who do not resist" (p. 77). Also, Williams (as cited in Ward, 1995) found that "when the victim is acquainted with the rapist, the latter is less likely to be charged or convicted" (p. 110).

In light of these studies, Hans and Vidmar (1986), who extensively studied the jury system, noted:

> The results of these studies on jury decisions in rape cases, taken together, are troubling in some respects. Widespread adherence to rape stereotypes and myths make it difficult not only for victims who fail to match the pristine picture of the ideal victim, but also for [the defendant] whose courtroom appearance and lifestyle make him seem like a rapist. (p. 214)

All the studies on jurors' attitudes just reviewed were either with mock juries made up of university students, in which no challenges and dismissals were involved, or posttrial interviews with jurors. The case study reported in this article is unique in that I served as a juror and thus had the opportunity to participate in and note (immediately after the deliberations) the jurors' arguments and the dynamics of the jury, which were not recorded or open to the public.

Method

In spring 1999, I was chosen to serve as a juror on a rape and burglary (forcible entry) trial. Because I teach in both the Social Work Department and the Women's Studies Program at the University of Alaska, the lack of challenges to my serving as a juror was a surprise. My service as a juror gave me a unique opportunity to learn firsthand about the court system, to become knowledgeable about court proceedings in a rape trial, to become aware of the treatment of jurors and the dynamics of juries, and to be a participant in a jury's deliberations. This trial lasted 6 days, with jury deliberations covering 2 days.

At the end of each day of jury deliberations, I went directly to my office and recorded as precisely as I could information on arguments and proceedings of the trial and discussions that took place during the deliberations. I recorded only arguments and comments presented during the deliberations but no information about specific jurors, and I did not link comments made during the deliberations to any particular juror.

When this case was retried 7 months later, I attended almost every day of the 9-day trial, including the jury selection proceedings. Doing so afforded me the opportunity to ascertain how the makeup of juries is affected by peremptory challenges and to check the accuracy of details in my notes from the first trial regarding the presentations of the defense's and prosecution's cases as well as to record any differences in evidence presented during the two trials. All this information gave me the opportunity to check the validity of my impressions as a participant observer during the first rape trial and to gain a fuller picture of the case, the court proceedings, and the outcome of the trial. Because I could not take down verbatim quotes during the first trial, I used statements made by the attorneys for the defense and prosecution during the jury selection proceedings and opening and closing statements at the second trial to present exact quotations. The arguments presented by the defense and prosecution were consistent in the two trials. The only significant difference between the cases in the two trials was the amount of expert testimony and evidence presented on DNA in the second trial.

The Case

Description

The alleged rape and burglary (forced entry) that was the focus of this trial took place in fall 1998 in a primarily Athabascan Indian village in Alaska. The village is not on the road system and has a population of 150 to 200 people. It is a wet village, meaning that alcohol can be purchased and consumed within the village boundaries. In this remote village, the only law enforcement presence is one village public safety officer (VPSO), whose job is to keep order in the community. The VPSO does not carry a gun and does not make arrests or investigate felony crimes. In the case of an allegation of a serious crime, such as a rape, the VPSO would take the victim's statement and then call state troopers, who would fly into the village to investigate the crime. In this village, routine health care is provided by a health aide, a local resident who is trained in basic first-aid techniques. The health aides in the villages are instructed in procedures to follow in cases of alleged rape and are given rape kits to use during their examinations of victims. The kits include swabs for collecting evidence and procedures to follow so that evidence is not contaminated.

The incident that was the focus of this trial took place on a weekend of celebrations in the village that included a softball tournament and a wedding and brought many out-of-town visitors to the village. The alleged crime was the rape of a 66-year-old Alaska Native woman from the village where the incident occurred. The alleged victim had lived her entire life in the village, had never received any formal schooling, was the mother of 12 children and a grandmother, and recently had back surgery and walked with a slight limp.

The alleged assailant was a 55-year-old Alaska Native man from a neighboring village who had known the alleged victim since childhood and who occasionally hunted and fished with her husband and brother. He stated that he was in the village where the attack took place to visit his brother who lived in the village and to partake in the celebrations.

The Prosecution's Case

According to the alleged victim, she had been visiting the homes of friends and relatives on the evening before the assault and had consumed some alcoholic beverages along with her friends. In the evening, she returned to her home alone (her husband was out of town fishing) and locked the door to her house and went to bed. At around 5:00 a.m., someone knocked on her door. Thinking it was her brother who had planned to come over for coffee, she opened the door. According to the alleged victim, the alleged assailant pushed her into the house and into the bedroom, pulled off her pants, raped her, and then left her house. The alleged victim stated that she felt dirty and showered and burned the clothes she had been wearing along with the trash. When her grandson came over to do laundry later in the day, he found her lying on the couch looking depressed. He asked her what was wrong, and she told him that she had been raped and asked him to get the VPSO.

The VPSO took the alleged victim's statement in which she identified the alleged assailant and then drove her to the village health clinic, where she was given a pelvic examination. A swab from her vaginal area was taken and subsequently sent to the crime lab in Anchorage as possible evidence. The alleged victim was later sent by plane to the hospital in the nearest urban center for an examination with a culpascope, a machine that takes pictures of the inside of the vagina to see if internal bruising, which may be consistent with forced sexual intercourse, is present. The alleged victim underwent a second culpascope examination 9 days after the first examination. The second examination, a standard procedure in the case of a sexual assault, is used to determine whether any bruising that was present in the first examination is also present 9 days later. If the bruising is not present in the second examination, it is assumed that a trauma, such as a sexual assault, caused the bruising, which has subsequently healed. If the bruising or anomaly in the vaginal area is still present in the second examination, it is assumed that this is a normal condition for the woman examined and was not the result of trauma to the vaginal area.

In the courtroom, the alleged victim identified the alleged assailant as the man who had entered her home and raped her. This was the same man she identified to the VPSO, the village health aide, and the hospital nurse.

The evidence presented by the prosecuting attorney included a chart showing the match between the accused assailant's DNA and the semen that was on the swab taken during the initial examination of the alleged victim. The DNA analysis was done by the crime lab in Anchorage using a six-marker test. The alleged assailant accused another man, who he said had sexual intercourse with the alleged victim, but the DNA profile precluded this possibility. The prosecuting attorney explained that an Athabascan database establishing the statistical probability of another DNA match in the Athabascan population had not been established; however, research on neighboring Alaska Native populations showed that the likelihood of a similar DNA profile using the six-marker test would be in the range of 3,000 to 1.

The prosecuting attorney also showed full-color photographs and a television-screen image of the alleged victim's vaginal area taken from the culpascope examination, which showed severe internal bruising. The nurse who examined the alleged victim testified that the bruising evident in the pictures was consistent with a sexual assault. The bruising in the vaginal area was not evident 9 days later, demonstrating that such bruises were not normal for this woman.

The Defense's Case

The accused assailant maintained that he "never touched that woman," and the defense attorney claimed this was a case of mistaken identity and an inadequate targeted investigation by the VPSO and state troopers. The defense attorney discredited the alleged victim's identification of the alleged assailant, stating that she had been drinking and thus would have difficulty identifying anyone. The questions that the defense attorney asked the alleged victim included, "Weren't you drunk? Weren't you obnoxious? Did you drink this much or this much? Is 'My back hurt' all you said to the assailant?"

The defense attorney also discounted the utility of DNA evidence, noting that it gave information only on a DNA match, but there was always a possibility that there were other matches. He also focused on the lack of established DNA probability ratios for Athabascan Indians and challenged the statistical background of the state's DNA expert and her credibility as an expert witness. He further argued that the culpascope examination provided no useful information because there was a strong possibility that a 66-year-old woman would not lubricate during sexual intercourse, and thus the bruising apparent in the culpascope pictures could have been the result of vigorous consensual sex. He also questioned the credibility of the nurse who explained the culpascope pictures because of the length of training she had received on the culpascope.

Witnesses who were called by the defense included a woman (who appeared to be intoxicated on the stand) who stated that the alleged assailant had slept on her living room floor on the night of the attack and the VPSO's wife, who testified that she saw the alleged assailant knock on the alleged victim's door the morning of the attack. The defense asked her what the man was wearing to determine if it was the same man the alleged victim identified. The VPSO's wife stated emphatically that the man she saw knocking on the alleged victim's door was the same man she saw the next day at the softball field and was the alleged assailant who was present in the courtroom, only he was wearing a different jacket on the morning she saw him at the alleged victim's house.

In his concluding remarks, the defense attorney maintained there were too many unanswered questions in this case. He stated:

> We're not here to say [alleged victim] didn't have sex with someone. What she did and who she did it with is her business. Maybe she doesn't want to reveal that. We're saying this man didn't do it. He had no reason to hurt that lady. He didn't break in to physically assault her or hurt her. This wasn't like breaking in to jimmy a door. No one forced their way into this house. Her husband was away. She partied. One way she partied was she got drunk. She got pretty good and drunk. She was so drunk she said it happened on Friday morning but didn't report it 'till 15 hours later. She may have had sex with somebody when she was passed out, and she may think it was [defendant], but she is wrong.

According to Epstein and Langenbahn (1994), defense attorneys use the following three basic strategies in rape cases: consent, identification, and denying that the crime occurred. In the consent defense, the attorney acknowledges that the defendant engaged in sexual relations with the complainant but argues that the complainant consented. In the identification defense, the attorney neither denies nor acknowledges that rape occurred but claims that the accused was not the attacker. In the third defense, the attorney argues either that the alleged acts do not constitute rape or that no such acts occurred.

In this case, the defense used the identification strategy by claiming that this was a case of mistaken identity. He attempted to establish that the alleged assailant had on different clothes than the man who had been seen by the VPSO and his wife knocking on the alleged victim's door. He noted that DNA testing is not an accurate test and that there was a likelihood of a similar DNA profile. He called a witness who stated that the alleged assailant was asleep on her floor along with several others the morning of the attack, and he claimed that the state trooper had too quickly arrested the alleged assailant without looking for other possible suspects. The defense attorney also noted that the alleged victim was drunk and that the bruising evidenced in her vaginal area could be the result of "vigorous sex," not necessarily sexual assault. Thus, in accordance with the literature on public perceptions of good rapes versus bad rapes, the defense attorney attempted to present this case as a dubious or bad rape, an acquaintance rape in the alleged victim's home where there was no sign of a physical struggle and where the alleged victim had consumed alcohol.

⚔ Outcome of the First Trial

The jury deliberated on this case for approximately 12 hours over the course of 2 days. The outcome was a deadlocked jury, meaning that no consensus was reached. Deadlocked juries occur in about 1 in 20 cases (Hans & Vidmar, 1986). With a deadlocked or hung jury, the alleged assailant would go free unless the prosecution thought that there was a strong enough case to go forward with a retrial and the alleged victim agreed to undergo a second trial.

Jury Selection

To understand this trial's outcome, one must first consider the jury selection process and resultant makeup of the jury. The jury selection process for the first trial lasted a day and a half. In this process, the names of 14 jurors (12 jurors and 2 alternates) were chosen at random out of a pool of approximately 40 people. Each of the 14 potential jurors gave information on his or her place of residence, occupation, spouse's occupation, number of children and ages, birthplace, interests, involvement in prior lawsuits, previous experience as a juror, and whether he or she knew anyone associated with the trial. The potential jurors were each interviewed by the prosecution and defense attorneys.

Potential jurors can be dismissed in two ways. They can be released for cause, meaning that because of prior knowledge of the case, a relationship with someone associated with the trial, or previous experiences that may prejudice them, they could be deemed unable to be objective and thus would be dismissed. They can also be dismissed from a case through peremptory challenges. In criminal cases in Alaska, each lawyer is allowed 10 peremptory challenges (and an additional challenge for each alternate on a case) in which potential jurors can be dismissed from the case without stating a cause. In this case, the defense attorney first asked questions of all potential jurors as a group. The following examples of the questions he asked illustrate the criteria that the defense used to select jurors who were favorable to his case and his attempt to build his case during the jury selection process: Do you feel when police investigate

crimes they have an obligation to be thorough and investigate both sides? How many know enough about fingerprint evidence to know it might be useful in an investigation? Raise your hand if you feel fibers and hair are useful to an investigation. Raise your hand if you have ever had mistaken identity happen to you. Do any of you personally know of anyone who when they are real drunk has made a claim that is fantastic or unbelievable? Do you feel police investigators have a duty to produce evidence they know exists? Raise your hand if you know what the letters *DNA* stand for. Have any of you had special courses in the fields of biology? Any particular courses in DNA? Any particular training in statistics? Is there anybody that cannot accept the proposition that the accused does not have the burden of proving anything? Have you ever had to rely on lab tests and later found out the lab test was wrong? Anybody here ever heard the phrase "There are lies, damn lies, and statistics?"

The prosecuting attorney's questions focused on whether anyone had been on a jury and if so, whether the jury had reached a verdict. He also asked the potential jurors about their views on drinking.

In the first trial, those who were dismissed by the defense attorney included a woman who had written a master's thesis on DNA, an individual related to a police officer, a lawyer and relative of a lawyer, and a middle-aged Alaska Native woman. The prosecuting attorney dismissed anyone who had a prior negative experience with the courts; the prosecution's other reasons for dismissals were not clear to me. The jury that remained was made up of 8 men and 4 women. All the jurors were non-Native and Caucasian and currently resided in the urban center where the trial was held; 2 of the jurors (both female) had college degrees.

Because I was a potential juror, I did not have the opportunity to take notes on all who were selected and dismissed during this trial. However, during the retrial of this case, I kept notes on all the potential jurors and compared the initial and final juror seatings. From this analysis, I found that in the retrial, the defense dismissed significantly more women (6) than men (3) and that of the 8 individuals who were dismissed, 7 were in occupations that required a college degree. Thus, in keeping with the literature on the believability of rape myths (that level of education and gender are the best predictors of acceptance of rape myths), the final jury seated after the defense and prosecution challenges would be expected to be more likely to believe rape myths than the initial jurors who were randomly selected.

Jury Deliberations

In the first deadlocked jury, 5 jurors voted for a guilty verdict (3 women and 2 men), and 7 voted for acquittal (1 woman and 6 men). However, during most of the jury deliberations, 2 female jurors held out for a guilty verdict while others argued either for an acquittal or were undecided. Throughout the deliberations, 7 of the 8 male jurors sat at one end of the table, and all 4 female jurors and 1 male juror sat together at the other end. At the final vote, the 3 female and 1 male jurors who sat together voted guilty, and 6 of the 7 male jurors who sat together voted for acquittal.

The jurors who voted for acquittal agreed with the defense attorney's arguments. Many thought that the alleged victim was not credible because she had consumed alcoholic beverages and suspected that she was lying to cover up consensual sex. Most of the jurors agreed with the defense attorney that both the DNA evidence and the pictures taken from the culpascope examination should not be considered in this case because DNA tests show only a probable match and the severe bruising evident in the alleged victim's vaginal area could have been the result of vigorous consensual sex. Also, many jurors believed that the state did a sloppy job of investigation and that a targeted investigation had occurred. The sentiment among some jurors was that the VPSO's wife started spreading the word around the village that the man she saw knocking at the alleged victim's door that morning committed the rape because "she wanted to be a big cheese" and was "the perfect police officer's wife." Some jurors believed that she told her husband her feelings, which he then told the state trooper, and that the trooper immediately arrested the alleged assailant upon entering the village.

Examples of statements made during jury deliberations in the first trial are presented next, organized in relation to some of the commonly held rape myths presented in Stout and McPhail (1998). The jurors' comments demonstrate arguments that were used in and affected the outcome of the trial. It is important to remember that in this case, the alleged victim identified the alleged assailant consistently, and the alleged assailant maintained that he never touched the woman. Also, no one other than the alleged assailant made any claims that the alleged victim had slept with anyone else, and the man that the alleged assailant claimed had sex with the alleged victim had a DNA profile that excluded him as a sexual partner.

1. Women routinely lie about rape for their purposes: "She had sex with someone else and said it was him to cover it up." "She claimed rape so her husband wouldn't get mad." "It wasn't [the defendant] but someone with close DNA."

2. Only bad women are raped: "She was drunk." "How could she recognize who it was?"

3. You can't rape an unwilling woman: "When asked what she said to him, she said 'My back is hurting.' Why didn't she just say no?" "She didn't fight him off."

4. Women who are raped must have provoked the rape by leading men on or dressing provocatively: "She had consensual sex with him and wanted to cover it up so her husband wouldn't get mad." "She encouraged him at [name's] house and later he came over and it went too far." "'Don't, stop' can mean two different things."

5. Most rape is committed by African American men against European women: This myth was not evident in this trial, but racism was apparent as can be seen in such comments as, "They were all soused and lying." "They were all soused; it just depends which drunk you want to believe." "Want to know my personal experience with Natives and sex? They all cover up for one another." "I lived in a village; I know how they party."

6. Most women secretly desire rape and enjoy it: "He was on top of her, and then she started feeling guilty and worried her husband would find out."

7. It can be called rape only if the assailant is a stranger who has a weapon and causes great physical injury: "She had no bruises."

8. Our society abhors rape and gives rapists long and harsh sentences: "We could ruin a guy's life." "If there is a reasonable doubt, we are required to give a verdict of not guilty." "I think he's guilty, but I don't feel comfortable passing a guilty verdict and knowing he's going to prison."

 ## Discussion of the Outcome of the First Trial

The outcome of this trial was a shock to me because I found the alleged victim to be believable (she was a 66-year-old grandmother who consistently identified the alleged assailant, who was reported to be extremely distraught by all who came in contact with her after the assault, and who broke down in tears on the stand when discussing the sexual assault). I also thought that the state had provided sound scientific data that a sexual assault had occurred and that the alleged assailant was linked in several ways to the crime. During the trial, I thought that without scientific tests, the prosecution would have had great difficulty getting a conviction in this case but that with DNA evidence linking the alleged assailant to the crime and with pictures taken during the culpascope examination showing severe bruising of the victim's vaginal area, a conviction would be the outcome. The fact that both the DNA evidence and the results of the culpascope examination were disregarded was surprising. In regard to the pictures showing serious vaginal bruising being disregarded because of the alleged victim's age and lack of lubrication, I asked the other jurors, "Why would a woman who just had recent back surgery and who bruised so severely have consensual sex?" Their response was that she was too drunk to care or feel any pain. Thus, this

jury's verdict was consistent with Lafree's (as cited in Hans & Vidmar, 1986) findings that jurors may disregard even corroborative evidence if they believe that the alleged victim's character is questionable.

The jurors' fascination with a targeted investigation and the idea of mistaken identity was also surprising. Throughout the jury deliberations, I thought that sexism was evident because many jurors discredited both the crime lab expert ("Who does she think she is strolling in here with a suit and briefcase?") and the female nurse who did the culpascope examination ("Why did the state bring a nurse; a doctor would have had instant credibility?"). Similarly, many jurors thought that the VPSO's wife, who stated she saw the alleged assailant knock on the alleged victim's door, contributed to a targeted investigation although neither attorney implied or even mentioned this possibility. Most of the jurors did not consider the alleged victim to be believable, believing that she was lying to cover up other sexual escapades or consensual sex with the alleged assailant. Most of the jurors thought that the state did not prove its case because fingerprints were not taken, clothing and bedclothes were not tested for semen, and other suspects were not considered, although a DNA specimen was taken during the vaginal examination and the alleged victim consistently identified the alleged assailant.

In conclusion, one could say that in this sexual assault case, most jurors thought there was reasonable doubt that the alleged victim had been sexually assaulted. Rather, they believed that the alleged victim either had consensual sex with the alleged assailant or consensual sex with someone else but was not raped and did not suffer harm. When statements made during the jury deliberations were considered in regard to common rape myths, it became apparent that almost every myth was validated by some jurors and used as an argument for acquittal. Many male jurors could identify on some level with the alleged assailant, as was evidenced by comments such as these: "Mistaken identity happened to me once"; "'Don't, stop' can mean two different things, and it's hard to know which"; and "Would you want to ruin a man's life?" The lack of gravity about this sexual assault trial was apparent in such jurors' comments as the following: "Why don't they have *Playboy* magazines here to read?" in reference to reading materials supplied in the jurors' quarters. Other comments that trivialized the case included "They were all soused; it just depends which drunk you want to believe" and "They all cover up for one another." At the end of the deliberations, when the final vote had been taken, a male juror stated, "Seven to five, we still kicked ass."

The outcome of this trial raises some serious questions regarding our judicial system in general and sexual assault trials in particular. The first concern is with the jury selection process. If this jury were indeed a representative sample of the community and a true jury by peers, the outcome would be disturbing in terms of prevalent attitudes toward women and sexual assault. As I mentioned earlier, throughout the jury deliberations, it was apparent that the majority of jurors strongly held many rape myths. Unfortunately, it is obvious that this jury was neither a randomly selected cross-section of the community nor a jury of peers. Potential jurors were excluded if they knew anything about DNA or were familiar with the law or law enforcement officers, more women than men were excused, and the only Native woman who was selected as a potential juror was excused. The result was a jury consisting of twice as many men as women, with only two jurors in occupations requiring college degrees and no Alaska Natives or residents of rural villages.

In 1999, Supreme Court Justice Sandra Day O'Connor called for a review of lawyers' rights to exclude possible jurors without giving a reason or for cause because they heard about the case from the media. She said that these practices give the impression of "unrepresentative juries." O'Connor warned that

> the use of unlimited "cause" challenges to prospective jurors, coupled with extensive media coverage of some cases, leaves some courts to search out the most ignorant and poorly informed citizens to serve as jurors in high-profile cases, because only those citizens are likely to have avoided forming any opinion. ("O'Connor Urges Examination," 1999, p. A-8)

Furthermore, in this case, both the alleged assailant and the alleged victim were from small rural villages, but the jurors were all non-Natives living in an urban area. Such a jury allows for stereotypes and suppositions that would probably not enter into the deliberations of a true jury of one's peers. Blatantly racist comments, including suppositions about Natives' alcohol consumption and sexual practices, were made, as were comments about small villages and the way people gossip and stick together. It is important to note that felony trials in interior Alaska are routinely scheduled in the urban center, although the defense can request that a trial be moved to a regional center closer to the village. In a regional center, however, it would probably be difficult to select jurors who had no prior knowledge of the case or anyone involved in it.

Another issue of concern in this trial was the treatment of the alleged victim, who was asked grilling questions about her alcohol consumption. In addition, although the defense attorney said in his concluding statement that he would not go into the sex life of a 66-year-old woman, he implied that the jurors should consider it (which they clearly did), asking such questions in the retrial as, "Can you tell this jury that absolutely you did not have sex with anyone there?" Full-color pictures of the alleged victim's genital area taken during the culpascope examination were passed around to the jurors and displayed on two television screens with the caption, "Genital Area of [alleged victim]." If a 66-year-old grandmother is treated this way and suspected of lying to cover up sexual escapades, one wonders what would be included in the court proceedings and jury deliberations of a date rape trial of a young woman.

 ## The Retrial

Seven months after the original trial, a retrial was held, conducted by the same judge with the same prosecuting and defense attorneys. The jury was different in its gender makeup (7 men and 7 women), and one of the jurors was married to an Alaska Native woman. At the retrial, I took detailed notes on all the potential jurors who were called and questioned by the prosecuting and defense attorneys to ascertain how peremptory challenges changed the makeup of the jury.

Of the initial randomly selected pool of 14 jurors in the second trial, 9 were women and 5 were men, and in terms of educational background related to current occupation, there were 2 undergraduate college students, 1 doctoral student, 1 accountant, and 3 school teachers. No Alaska Natives were included in this initial pool. Both the defense and prosecution dismissed 9 jurors each, which meant that 32 potential jurors were reviewed for this case.

The nine potential jurors who were dismissed by the defense in the second trial were six Caucasian women and three Caucasian men, eight of whom were either college students or in careers that required college degrees. Of the nine jurors who were dismissed by the defense, eight were in occupations that require college degrees: three college students, one high school math teacher, two accountants, one social worker, and one engineer. Thus, there was a high level of educational attainment in that seven potential jurors were seeking or had completed postsecondary degrees. The defense also dismissed an Alaska Native woman. The nine who were dismissed by the prosecution included six men and three women. Occupational status did not seem to matter in the prosecution's dismissals as much as attitudes toward drinking (two persons were dismissed who believed that drinking was wrong) and prior experience with the courts either for driving while intoxicated, child custody, or past service as a juror on a criminal trial. After peremptory challenges, the final jurors included 7 men and 7 women. Two of the men were school teachers, but no other jurors were in occupations in which an educational degree beyond the secondary level was required. Thus, peremptory challenges in this case changed the juror pool in terms of its gender makeup and educational level as determined by current occupational status. As one female observer during the jury selection process stated, "They sure don't want any smart women on that jury, do they?"

Additional evidence presented by the state in the second trial included a database for the probability of a DNA match in the Athabascan population, a more sophisticated DNA analysis done by a Seattle laboratory with results presented by its director (a man with a Ph.D.), a local respected (male) physician's corroboration of the nurse's culpascope conclusions, and a young girl who said the assailant made lewd comments to her on the morning of the alleged rape. The defense again used the mistaken identity argument and attempted to discredit the alleged victim because she was drunk and had not fought off her assailant. The prosecution meticulously presented the DNA evidence showing the probability of another matching DNA profile in the Athabascan population to be in the range of 1 to 2.5 million.

After fewer than 3 hours, the jury in the second trial found the alleged assailant guilty of both first-degree rape and first-degree burglary. Jurors' comments to the judge on returning to the jurors' room after the verdict had been given indicated that the DNA evidence convinced them because this was argued as a case of mistaken identity. However, in both trials, some jurors questioned why the defense did not use the argument that this was a case of consensual sex. In both trials, some jurors stated that there would not have been a case if the defense had argued consensual sex (i.e., the alleged victim's testimony and evidence of bruising from the culpascope examination would not have mattered).

 Conclusion

Participation as a juror in this 1999 sexual assault trial was a disconcerting and eye-opening experience both in terms of the jury selection process and the sexist, racist remarks that were evident in the jury's deliberations, which are not open to the public or recorded. Because this was a review of only one trial in one location, it is possible that the deliberations and outcome of the trial can be attributed merely to the poor job of jury selection and case presentation by the prosecuting attorney or to the uniqueness of the region where the trial took place. This would be a comforting thought and might be the case. On the other hand, in light of the previously mentioned findings that (a) almost all rape victims never see their attackers caught, tried, and imprisoned; (b) about 25% of convicted rapists never go to prison; and (c) another 25% receive sentences in local jails, where the average sentence is 11 months, the outcome of this trial does not appear to be an aberration. Rather, it seems consistent with the outcomes of other sexual assault trials, and thus an examination of jury selection and deliberations in this trial can perhaps contribute to an understanding of why the rates for reporting of and conviction for rape are so low in the United States.

Involvement as a juror in the first trial led me to conclude that there are several areas that people who are concerned about violence against women must focus. First, the court system needs to be monitored in regard to the treatment of rape victims and the representativeness of jurors. Gender, educational background, and racial and class representation are important considerations for a true trial by peers. Ten peremptory juror challenges coupled with challenges for cause can dramatically alter the composition of juries and affect the outcomes of trials. As Ward (1995) noted, "Legal analysts frequently argue that on many occasions the evidence presented at a rape case does not reliably predict a verdict as trial outcome is based more on jurors' attitudes about rape" (p. 111).

Second, more research is necessary in relation to factors that affect the outcomes of sexual assault trials and the sentencing of assailants, and this research should be widely publicized. Third, rape victims still need to know clearly what they will face in court in terms of the continued prevalence of rape myths, peremptory challenges, and the state's need to prove the case beyond a "reasonable doubt."

Finally, and of utmost importance, there is a need for more education about sexual respect and sexual assault in the American educational system and workplace. Rape myths are still persistent in our society in spite of the efforts of women's groups and feminist researchers. As Stout and McPhail (1998) stated, "Changes in laws have made it somewhat easier for rapists to be prosecuted and for rape victims to be protected, yet if the jury still believes in rape acceptance myths, all is lost" (p. 283). Rape myths serve "to blame

women for the rape and shift the blame from the perpetrators to the victim and allow men to justify their sexual aggression. Accepting rape myths also serves to minimize the seriousness and prevalence of rape" (Stout & McPhail, 1998, p. 260). Educational programs in schools, workplaces, and universities must strive to reach a broad audience, which includes those who are the most likely to hold rape myths. From a more societal perspective,

> Rape is not an isolated symptom to be plucked out of society. It is an act that is often supported, condoned, tolerated, encouraged, and regulated by a patriarchal society that gives men a sense of entitlement and privilege. The conditions in society that allow rape to flourish must be confronted. (Stout & McPhail, 1998, p. 284)

This case demonstrated that DNA evidence, culpascope pictures of bruising consistent with sexual assault, and the victim's identification of the assailant can all be readily disregarded by jurors who believe common rape myths that blame the victim and minimize the seriousness of the crime. As I noted previously, members of both juries stated that in this case, a defense argument of consensual sex would have been readily believed. Only through careful monitoring of legal procedures that include the selection of a jury for representativeness from one's community and one's peers and through widespread educational efforts regarding sexual assault can we expect to see a change in both the rate of reporting and prosecution for rape.

 References

Committee on the Judiciary, U.S. Senate. (1993). *The response to rape: Detours on the road to equal justice.* Washington, DC: Government Printing Office.

Epstein, J., & Langenbahn, S. (1994). *The criminal justice and community response to rape.* Washington, DC: Department of Justice, National Institute of Justice.

Hans, C., & Vidmar, N. (1986). *Judging the jury.* New York: Plenum.

O'Connor urges examination of jury challenges. (1999, May 16). *Fairbanks Daily News-Miner,* p. A-8.

Rennison, M. (1998). *Criminal victimization 1998, changes 1997–98 with trends 1993–98: Bureau of Labor Statistics, National Victimization Survey.* Retrieved October 9, 2001, from http://www.ojp.usdoj.gov/bjs/pub/pdf/cv98/pdf

Stout, K., & McPhail, B. (1998). *Confronting sexism and violence against women: A challenge for social work.* New York: Longman.

Ward, C. (1995). *Attitudes toward rape: Feminist and social psychological perspectives.* Thousand Oaks, CA: Sage.

DISCUSSION QUESTIONS

1. What are the rape myths discussed in the introduction to this article and how do they affect juror decision making in rape trials?

2. How did the defense attorney challenge the evidence presented by the prosecution? What type of defense did he present?

3. What types of questions did the two attorneys ask during voir dire? Based on the questions they asked, do you think they were attempting to secure a fair and unbiased jury?

4. What issues came up during jury deliberations?

5. Why was the outcome of the first trial "a shock" to the author?

6. The author concludes that the outcome of the trial "raises some serious questions regarding our judicial system in general and sexual assault trials in particular." Discuss this statement and the evidence the author provides to support it.

7. How did the second trial of this case differ from the first trial? Why, in your opinion, was the outcome of the second trial different from that of the first trial?

READING

In a provocative essay published in the *Yale Law Journal* shortly after O. J. Simpson's acquittal, Paul Butler, a black law professor at George Washington University Law School, argued for "racially based jury nullification." That is, he urged black jurors to refuse to convict black defendants accused of nonviolent crimes, regardless of the strength of the evidence mounted against them. Butler's position on jury nullification was that the "black community is better off when some nonviolent lawbreakers remain in the community rather than go to prison." Arguing that there are far too many black men in prison, Butler suggested that there should be a presumption in favor of nullification in cases involving black defendants charged with *nonviolent, victimless* crimes, such as possession of drugs.

SOURCE: Butler, Paul (1995). Racially Based Jury Nullification: Black Power in the Criminal Justice System. *Yale Law Journal, 105,* 677–725. Reprinted by permission of the author.

Racially Based Jury Nullification

Black Power in the Criminal Justice System

Paul Butler

 ## Introduction

I was a Special Assistant United States Attorney in the District of Columbia in 1990. I prosecuted people accused of misdemeanor crimes, mainly the drug and gun cases that overwhelm the local courts of most American cities. As a federal prosecutor, I represented the United States of America and used that power to put people, mainly African-American men, in prison. I am also an African-American man. While at the U.S. Attorney's office, I made two discoveries that profoundly changed the way I viewed my work as a prosecutor and my responsibilities as a black person.

The first discovery occurred during a training session for new Assistants conducted by experienced prosecutors. We rookies were informed that we would lose many of our cases, despite having persuaded a jury beyond a reasonable doubt that the defendant was guilty. We would lose because some black jurors would refuse to convict black defendants who they knew were guilty.

The second discovery was related to the first, but was even more unsettling. It occurred during the trial of Marion Barry, then the second-term mayor of the District of Columbia. Barry was being prosecuted by my office for drug possession and perjury. I learned, to my surprise, that some of my fellow African-American prosecutors hoped that the mayor would be acquitted, despite the fact that he was obviously guilty of at least one of the charges—he had smoked cocaine on FBI videotape. These black prosecutors wanted their office to lose its case because they believed that the prosecution of Barry was racist.

Federal prosecutors in the nation's capital hear many rumors about prominent officials engaging in illegal conduct, including drug use. Some African-American prosecutors wondered why, of all those people, the government chose to "set up" the most famous black politician in Washington, D.C. They also asked themselves why, if crack is so dangerous, the FBI had allowed the mayor to smoke it. Some members of the predominantly black jury must have had similar concerns: They convicted the mayor of only one count of a fourteen-count indictment, despite the trial judge's assessment that he had "never seen a stronger government case."[1] Some African-American prosecutors thought that the jury, in rendering its verdict, jabbed its black thumb in the face of a racist prosecution, and that idea made those prosecutors glad.

As such reactions suggest, lawyers and judges increasingly perceive that some African-American jurors vote to acquit black defendants for racial reasons, a decision sometimes expressed as the juror's desire not to send yet another black man to jail. This essay examines the question of what role race should play in black jurors' decisions to acquit defendants in criminal cases. Specifically, I consider trials that include both African-American defendants and African-American jurors. I argue that the race of a black defendant is sometimes a legally and morally appropriate factor for jurors to consider in reaching a verdict of not guilty or for an individual juror to consider in refusing to vote for conviction.

My thesis is that, for pragmatic and political reasons, the black community is better off when some nonviolent lawbreakers remain in the community rather than go to prison. The decision as to what kind of conduct by African-Americans ought to be punished is better made by African-Americans themselves, based on the costs and benefits to their community, than by the traditional criminal justice process, which is controlled by white lawmakers and white law enforcers. Legally, the doctrine of jury nullification gives the power to make this decision to African-American jurors who sit in judgment of African-American defendants. Considering the costs of law enforcement to the black community and the failure of white lawmakers to devise significant nonincarcerative responses to black antisocial conduct, it is the moral responsibility of black jurors to emancipate some guilty black outlaws.

Part I of this essay describes two criminal cases in the District of Columbia in which judges feared that defendants or their lawyers were sending race-conscious, "forbidden" messages to black jurors and attempted to regulate those messages. I suggest that the judicial and public responses to those cases signal a dangerous reluctance among many Americans to engage in meaningful discourse about the relationship between race and crime. In Part II, I describe racial critiques of the criminal justice system. I then examine the evolution of the doctrine of jury nullification and suggest, in light of this doctrine, that racial considerations by African-American jurors are legally and morally right. Part III proposes a framework for analysis of the kind of criminal cases involving black defendants in which jury nullification is appropriate, and considers some of the concerns that implementation of the proposal raises.

My goal is the subversion of American criminal justice, at least as it now exists. Through jury nullification, I want to dismantle the master's house with the master's tools. My intent, however, is not purely destructive; this project is also constructive, because I hope that the destruction of the status quo will not lead to anarchy, but rather to the implementation of certain noncriminal ways of addressing antisocial conduct. Criminal conduct among African-Americans is often a predictable reaction to oppression. Sometimes black crime is a symptom of internalized white supremacy; other times it is a reasonable response to the racial and economic subordination every African-American faces every day. Punishing black people for the fruits of racism is wrong if that punishment is premised on the idea that it is the black criminal's "just deserts." Hence, the new paradigm of justice that I suggest in Part III rejects punishment for the sake of retribution and endorses it, with qualifications, for the ends of deterrence and incapacitation.

In a sense, this essay simply may argue for the return of rehabilitation as the purpose of American criminal justice, but a rehabilitation that begins with the white-supremacist beliefs that poison the minds of us all—you, me, and the black criminal. I wish that black people had the power to end racial oppression right now. African-Americans can prevent the application of one particularly destructive instrument of white supremacy—American criminal justice—to some African-American people, and this they can do immediately. I hope that this essay makes the case for why and how they should.

I. Secret Messages Everyone Hears

Americans seem reluctant to have an open conversation about the relationship between race and crime. Lawmakers ignore the issue, judges run from it, and crafty defense lawyers exploit it. It is not surprising, then, that some African-American jurors are forced to sneak through the back door what is not allowed to come in through the front: the idea that "race matters" in criminal justice. In this part, I tell two stories about attempts by defense attorneys to encourage black jurors' sympathy for their clients, and then I examine how these attempts provoked many people to act as though the idea of racial identification with black defendants was ridiculous or insulting to black people. In fact, the defense attorneys may well have been attempting to encourage black jurors' sympathy as part of their trial strategies. The lesson of the stories is that the failure of the law to address openly the relationship between race and crime fosters a willful and unhelpful blindness in many who really ought to see and allows jury nullification to go on without a principled framework. This essay offers such a framework and encourages nullification for the purpose of black self-help.

A. United States v. Marion Barry

The time is January 1990. The mayor of the District of Columbia is an African-American man named Marion Barry. African-Americans make up approximately sixty-six percent of the population of the city. The mayor is so popular in the black community that one local newspaper columnist has dubbed him "Mayor for Life." Barry is hounded, however, by rumors of his using drugs and "'chasing women.'" Barry denies the rumors and claims that they are racist.

On January 18, 1990, the mayor is contacted by an old friend, Rasheeda Moore, who tells him that she is visiting for a short time, and staying at a local hotel.[2] The mayor stops by later that afternoon and telephones Ms. Moore's room from the lobby of the hotel. He wants her to come downstairs to the lobby for a drink, but she requests that he come up to her room. The mayor assents, joins Ms. Moore in the room, and the two converse. At some point, Ms. Moore produces crack cocaine and a pipe, and invites the mayor to smoke it. He first demurs, then consents, and after he inhales smoke from the pipe, agents of the FBI and the Metropolitan Police Department storm the room. It turns out that Ms. Moore is a government informant, and the police have observed and videotaped the entire proceeding in the hotel room. The mayor is arrested and subsequently charged with one count of conspiracy to possess cocaine, ten counts of possession of cocaine, and three counts of perjury for allegedly lying to the grand jury that had investigated him. The mayor publicly asserts that he is the victim of a racist prosecution.

It is the last week in June 1990. The mayor is on trial in federal court.[3] The judge is white. Of the twelve jurors, ten are African-American. Rasheeda Moore, the government's star witness, is expected to testify. The mayor has four passes to give to guests he would like to attend his trial. On this day, he has given one pass to Minister Louis Farrakhan, the controversial leader of the Nation of Islam. Farrakhan has publicly supported Barry since his arrest, in part by suggesting that the sting operation and the prosecution were racist. When Farrakhan attempts to walk into the courtroom, a U.S. deputy marshal bars his entry. When Barry's attorney protests, the judge states, outside of the jury's hearing, that Farrakhan's "presence would be potentially disruptive, very likely intimidating, and he is a persona non grata for the [rest] of this case."[4] Rasheeda Moore then takes the stand.

The next day, the Reverend George Stallings appears at the trial with one of Barry's guest passes in hand. Stallings is a black Roman Catholic priest who, the previous year, received extensive publicity when he accused the Catholic Church of being hopelessly racist, left it, and founded his own church. When Stallings reaches the courtroom, the deputy marshal, following the instructions of the judge, does not let him enter. The judge explains, again outside of the jury's hearing, that Stallings is "in my judgment, not an ordinary member of the public and his presence would very likely have the same effect as Mr. Farrakhan's." The judge also indicates that there are "others who fit the same category." Barry's attorney asks for a list of those persons. The judge replies, "I think you will know them when you see them."

In the wake of these two episodes, the American Civil Liberties Union, representing Barry, Farrakhan, and Stallings, files an emergency appeal of the trial judge's decision. It argues that the judge's refusal to allow Barry's guests to attend the trial violated Barry's Sixth Amendment right to a fair trial and the First Amendment rights of the guests. In response, the judge's attorneys state that the judge excluded Farrakhan and Stallings because their presence in the courtroom would send an "impermissible message" of "intimidation" and "racial animosity" to jurors and witnesses. The judge's attorneys argue that the excluded persons' views of the prosecution had been highly publicized and that their appearance at the trial was consistent with Barry's "publicly avowed strategies of seeking a hung jury and jury nullification." The judge's attorneys argue that Farrakhan and Stallings attended the trial "not to view the proceeding or to show generalized concern, but instead to send a forbidden message to the jury and witness."

The U.S. Court of Appeals for the District of Columbia Circuit rules that Farrakhan and Stallings should have presented their constitutional claims to the trial judge prior to seeking relief in the appellate court.[5] Accordingly, it remands the case back to the trial judge. Because the trial has been halted pending appeal, however, the D.C. Circuit, in light of the "exigent circumstances," lists several "pertinent considerations" for the trial judge on remand. The considerations mainly concern the judge's power to regulate the attendance of those who threaten physically to disrupt a courtroom. The court does note, though, that:

> No individual can be wholly excluded from the courtroom merely because he advocates a particular political, legal or religious point of view—even a point of view that the district court or we may regard as antithetical to the fair administration, of justice. Nor can an individual be wholly excluded from the courtroom because his presence is thought to send an undesirable message to the jurors except that of physical intimidation.

The trial judge hears the message of the court of appeals. In lieu of resolving Farrakhan and Stallings's constitutional claims, he instead seeks assurances from their attorneys that their clients know how to conduct themselves in a courtroom. Indeed, the judge provides the attorneys with his own "special rules" of decorum regarding the trial, stating that "any attempt to communicate with a juror may be punished as criminal contempt of court." Farrakhan and Stallings's attorneys assure the court that their clients will act with decorum in the courtroom. The trial continues. The mayor is eventually convicted of one of the indictment's fourteen counts (for perjury), but not of the count in which he smoked the cocaine on videotape.

B. The Attorney Who Wore *Kente* Cloth

It is now June 11, 1992. John T. Harvey, III is an African-American criminal defense attorney who practices in the District of Columbia. Harvey represents a black man who is charged with assault with intent to murder. The case is scheduled for arraignment before a white judge. At the arraignment, Harvey wears a business suit and tie, and his jacket is accessorized by a colorful stole made of *kente* cloth. *Kente* cloth is a multihued woven fabric originally worn by ancient African royalty, and many African-Americans have adopted it as a fashion statement and a symbol of racial pride.

In pretrial proceedings, the judge had warned Harvey that he would not be permitted to wear *kente* cloth before a jury. According to Harvey, the judge told him that wearing the fabric during a jury trial "was sending a hidden message to jurors."[6] The judge had informed Harvey that he had three options: He could refrain from wearing the *kente* cloth; he could withdraw from the case; or he could agree to try the case before the judge, without a jury. Harvey's client decided to plead guilty. At the June 11 hearing, however, Harvey refuses to enter his client's plea before the judge because he doubts that the judge will be impartial. The judge then removes Harvey from the case, "not on the basis of [the] kente cloth, but on the basis that [Harvey] will not enter a plea which [his] client wishes to enter."

The same day, another client of Harvey's is scheduled to go to trial, also for assault with intent to kill, before another white judge. During the voir dire, the judge asks if any of the jurors are familiar with Harvey, whose battle with the other judge was well publicized. Four of the potential jurors know of the controversy. "[T]he concern we think we have here," the judge says, is "that we won't influence a juror improperly." He also informs them of case law in another jurisdiction suggesting that a court may prevent a Catholic priest from wearing a clerical collar in court. When Harvey asks the judge to inform the potential jurors of contrary cases, the judge refuses.

Ultimately, the judge allows Harvey to wear the cloth, but he suggests that when Harvey submits an attorney fee voucher to him for approval, he might not allow Harvey to be paid for the time the *kente* cloth issue has consumed. Harvey's client is tried before an all-black jury and is acquitted.

C. The Judicial and Popular Response: Willful Blindness

As described above, the trial judge's attempt to exclude Farrakhan and Stallings from Barry's trial met with disapproval from the D.C. Circuit. In the case of John Harvey, no higher court had occasion to review the judge's prohibition against the *kente* cloth but, as discussed below, much of the public reaction to the judge's prohibition was critical. These responses scorned the trial judge's fears that black jurors might acquit on the basis of racial identification rather than the "evidence." The D.C. Circuit and many observers, however, failed to acknowledge the significance of the "forbidden" message. I believe that this failure was deliberate. It reflected an intention to avoid serious consideration of the issue of black jurors acquitting black defendants on the basis of racial identification. Simply put, the D.C. Circuit and some of the public did not want to face the reality that race matters, in general and in jury adjudications of guilt and innocence.

1. The D.C. Circuit: We Hate Fights

The D.C. Circuit's per curiam opinion discussed the issue before it as though the judge's concern was that Barry's invitees would cause some type of physical disruption. The court listed a series of live "pertinent considerations,"[7] four of which actually were not pertinent because they involved the physical disruption of courtrooms or physical threats to witnesses. The only *relevant* consideration was so vague that it was nearly useless: The trial judge must exercise his discretion to exclude people from attending criminal matters "consistently with the First and Fifth Amendment rights of individuals to attend criminal trials." The court's discussion of this consideration is even more ambivalent: No one can be "*wholly*" excluded from a trial, even if he advocates a point of view that "we *may* regard as antithetical to the fair administration of justice" or if his presence sends an "undesirable message" to jurors. Because the appellate court did not suggest a procedure for *partial* exclusion of courtroom spectators, the trial judge's response was to pretend as though he had been concerned all along about physical disruption and subsequently to insist that Farrakhan and Stallings act in accordance with his rules of decorum. In the view of the D.C. Circuit, trial guests should keep their hands and their feet to themselves, but their messages may run amuck. In reality, Farrakhan's and Stallings's manners in the courtroom were an issue created by the appellate court. Ironically, the trial judge's response—the patronizing insistence that Farrakhan and Stallings agree to behave themselves—smacks of

racism more than does his initial decision to exclude them from the courtroom.

United States v. Barry suggests that no trial spectator can be barred from a courtroom unless she threatens physically to disrupt the trial. In this respect, the court established a severe restriction on the discretion of judges to control public access to trials. Not all courts have taken this position, however. Two of the few other federal appellate courts that have considered symbolic communication by trial spectators have found it appropriate to regulate this type of communication. In one case, the Ninth Circuit stated that "[w]hen fair trial rights are at significant risk . . . the first amendment rights of trial attendees can and must be curtailed at the courthouse door."[8] In another case, the Eleventh Circuit ordered the retrial of a man convicted of the murder of a prison guard, partly because of the presence, at the first trial, of numerous uniformed prison guards.[9] The court was concerned that the guards' presence posed an unacceptable risk of prejudicing the jurors.

Significantly, the decisions from the Ninth and Eleventh Circuits involved cases in which the presence of the spectators was not thought to implicate race. The D.C. Circuit is the first appellate court to consider a "forbidden" racial message. My intention in noting this distinction is not to criticize the restrictive standard the D.C. Circuit established; indeed, there are potentially troubling implications of standards that allow trial judges more discretion in terms of which "secret" messages to regulate. I suggest, however, that the D.C. Circuit's holding was not mandated by clear constitutional dictates and was not supported by precedent from other federal jurisdictions. Indeed, other appellate courts have considered and regulated the contents of the messages that trial spectators were thought to be sending. Those cases suggest that the D.C. Circuit could have talked about race, and yet it did not.

2. The Skeptics: What's Race Got to Do With It?

The response of a number of commentators to the controversy over John Harvey's *kente* cloth was disdainful of the trial judge's apprehension about race-based appeals to black jurors. For example, the *Washington Times* characterized one of the judge's concerns as "[s]heer, unadulterated goofiness."[12] The editorial continued:

> [The judge] apparently believes that the [kente] cloth is no innocent fabric but rather possesses hypnotic powers of seduction, powers that will turn the judicial system on its head and hold jurors in its sway. . . .
>
> . . . [W]hile most of us common folk are puzzled by this kind of judicial behavior, lawyers are widely inured to the fact that judges are free to act like fools with impunity—even when it is an abuse of discretion, an abuse of power, a waste of time and an injustice to someone who has come before the court seeking justice.

The National Bar Association, an African-American lawyers' group, expressed a similar concern, and one black attorney called the judge's actions "almost unbelievable" and wondered why the judge "injected race" into the trial proceedings by making an issue of the *kente* cloth. Even the prosecutors in the *kente* cloth case "remained conspicuously silent" and refrained from endorsing the judge's concerns about the cloth.

D. The Forbidden Message Revealed

I am fascinated by the refusal of these actors to take seriously the possibility and legal implications of black jurors' sympathy with black defendants. The criminal justice system would be better served if there were less reluctance to consider the significance of race in black jurors' adjudications of guilt or innocence. The remainder of this essay argues that race matters when a black person violates American criminal law and when a black juror decides how she should exercise her power to put another black man in prison.

The idea that race matters in criminal justice is hardly shocking; it surely does not surprise most

African-Americans. In the Barry and Harvey stories, I believe that it was known by all of the key players: judges, jurors, attorneys, defendants and spectators. The trial judges in those cases were correct: Somebody—the controversial black demagogue, the radical black priest, the *kente*-cloth-wearing lawyer—was trying to send the black jurors a message. The message, in my view, was that the black jurors should consider the evidence presented at trial in light of the idea that the American criminal justice system discriminates against blacks. The message was that the jurors should not send another black man to prison.

There is no way to "prove" what Farrakhan's and Stallings's purposes were in attending Barry's trial—nor can I "prove" the intent of the *kente*-cloth-wearing lawyer. I believe that my theory that they were encouraging black jurors' sympathy is reasonable, based on the relevant players' statements, the trial judge's observations, and common sense and experience. Even if one is unwilling to ascribe to those players the same racially based motivations that I do, acknowledgement and concern that some black jurors acquit black defendants on the basis of race are increasing, as my experience at the U.S. Attorney's Office showed. For the remainder of this essay, I focus on the legal and social implications of this conduct by black jurors.

 ## II. "Justice Outside the Formal Rules of Law"

Why would a black juror vote to let a guilty person go free? Assuming that the juror is a rational actor, she must believe that she and her community are, in some way, better off with the defendant out of prison than in prison. But how could any rational person believe that about a criminal? The following section describes racial critiques of the American criminal justice system. I then examine the evolution of the doctrine of jury nullification and argue that its practice by African-Americans is, in many cases, consistent with the Anglo-American tradition and, moreover, is legally and morally right.

A. The Criminal Law and African-Americans: Justice or "Just us"?

Imagine a country in which more than half of the young male citizens are under the supervision of the criminal justice system, either awaiting trial, in prison, or on probation or parole. Imagine a country in which two-thirds of the men can anticipate being arrested before they reach age thirty. Imagine a country in which there are more young men in prison than in college. Now give the citizens of the country the key to the prison. Should they use it?

Such a country bears some resemblance to a police state. When we criticize a police state, we think that the problem lies not with the citizens of the state, but rather with the form of government or law, or with the powerful elites and petty bureaucrats whose interests the state serves. Similarly, racial critics of American criminal justice locate the problem not so much with the black prisoners as with the state and its actors and beneficiaries. As evidence, they cite their own experiences and other people's stories, African-American history, understanding gained from social science research on the power and pervasiveness of white supremacy, and ugly statistics like those in the preceding paragraph.

For analytical purposes, I will create a false dichotomy among racial critics by dividing them into two camps: liberal critics and radical critics. Those are not names that the critics have given themselves or that they would necessarily accept, and there would undoubtedly be disagreement within each camp and theoretical overlap between the camps. Nonetheless, for the purposes of a brief explication of racial critiques, my oversimplification may be useful.

1. The Liberal Critique

According to this critique, American criminal justice is racist because it is controlled primarily by white people, who are unable to escape the culture's dominant message of white supremacy, and who are therefore inevitably, even if unintentionally, prejudiced. These white actors include legislators, police, prosecutors, judges, and jurors. They exercise their discretion to make and enforce the criminal law in a discriminatory fashion. Sometimes the discrimination is overt, as in the case of Mark Fuhrman, the police officer in the O. J. Simpson case who, in interviews, used racist language and boasted of his own brutality, and sometimes it is unintentional, as with a hypothetical white juror who invariably credits the testimony of a white witness over that of a black witness.

The problem with the liberal critique is that it does not adequately explain the extent of the difference between the incidence of black and white crime, especially violent crime. For example, in 1991, blacks constituted about fifty-five percent of the 18,096 people arrested for murder and non-negligent manslaughter in the United States (9924 people). One explanation the liberal critique offers for this unfortunate statistic is that the police pursue black murder suspects more aggressively than they do white murder suspects. In other words, but for discrimination, the percentage of blacks arrested for murder would be closer to their percentage of the population, roughly twelve percent. The liberal critique would attribute some portion of the additional forty-three percent of non-negligent homicide arrestees (in 1991, approximately 7781 people) to race prejudice. Ultimately, however, those assumptions strain credulity, not because many police officers are not racist, but because there is no evidence that there is a crisis of that magnitude in criminal justice. In fact, for all the faults of American law enforcement, catching the bad guys seems to be something it does rather well. The liberal critique fails to account convincingly for the incidence of black crime.

2. The Radical Critique

The radical critique does not discount the role of discrimination in accounting for some of the racial disparity in crime rates, but it also does not, in contrast to the liberal critique, attribute all or even most of the differential to police and prosecutor prejudice. The radical critique offers a more fundamental, structural explanation.

It suggests that criminal law is racist because, like other American law, it is an instrument of white supremacy. Law is made by white elites to protect their interests and, especially, to preserve the economic status quo, which benefits those elites at the expense of blacks, among others. Due to discrimination and segregation, the majority of African-Americans receive few meaningful educational and employment opportunities and, accordingly, are unable to succeed, at least in the terms of the capitalist ideal. Some property crimes committed by blacks may be understood as an inevitable result of the tension between the dominant societal message equating possession of material resources with success and happiness and the power of white supremacy to prevent most African-Americans from acquiring "enough" of those resources in a legal manner. "Black-on-black" violent crime, and even "victimless" crime like drug offenses, can be attributed to internalized racism, which causes some African-Americans to devalue black lives—either those of others or their own. The political process does not allow for the creation or implementation of effective "legal" solutions to this plight, and the criminal law punishes predictable reactions to it.

I am persuaded by the radical critique when I wonder about the roots of the ugly truth that blacks commit many crimes at substantially higher rates than whites. Most white Americans, especially liberals, would publicly offer an environmental, as opposed to genetic, explanation for this fact. They would probably concede that racism, historical and current, plays a major role in creating an environment that breeds criminal conduct. From this premise, the radical critic deduces that but for the (racist) environment, the African-American criminal would not be a criminal. In other words, racism creates and sustains the criminal breeding ground, which produces the black criminal. Thus, when many African-Americans are locked up, it is because of a situation that white supremacy created.

Obviously, most blacks are not criminals, even if every black is exposed to racism. To the radical critics, however, the law-abiding conduct of the majority of African-Americans does not mean that racism does not create black criminals. Not everyone exposed to a virus will become sick, but that does not mean that the virus does not cause the illness of the people who do.

The radical racial critique of criminal justice is premised as much on the criminal law's *effect* as on its intent. The system is discriminatory, in part, because of the disparate impact law enforcement has on the black community. This unjust effect is measured in terms of the costs to the black community of having so many African-Americans, particularly males, incarcerated or otherwise involved in the criminal justice system. These costs are social and economic, and include the perceived dearth of men "eligible" for marriage, the large percentage of black children who live in female-headed households, the lack of male "role models" for black children, especially boys, the absence of wealth in the black community, and the large unemployment rate among black men.

3. Examples of Racism in Criminal Justice

Examples commonly cited by both liberal and radical critics as evidence of racism in criminal justice include: the Scottsboro case; the history of the criminalization of drug use; past and contemporary administration of the death penalty; the use of imagery linking crime to race in the 1988 presidential campaign and other political campaigns; the beating of Rodney King and the acquittal of his police assailants; disparities between punishments for white-collar crimes and punishments for other crimes; more severe penalties for crack cocaine users than for powder cocaine users; the Charles Murray and Susan Smith cases; police corruption scandals in minority neighborhoods in New York and Philadelphia; the O. J. Simpson case, including the extraordinary public and media fascination with it, the racist police officer who was the prosecution's star witness, and the response of many white people to the jury's verdict of acquittal; and, cited most frequently, the extraordinary rate of incarceration of African-American men.

4. Law Enforcement Enthusiasts

Of course, the idea that the criminal justice system is racist and oppressive is not without dissent, and among the dissenters are some African-Americans. Randall Kennedy succinctly poses the counterargument:

Although the administration of criminal justice has, at times, been used as an instrument of racial oppression, the principal problem facing African-Americans in the context of criminal justice today is not over-enforcement but *under* enforcement of the laws. The most lethal danger facing African-Americans in their day-to-day lives is not white, racist officials of the state, but private, violent criminals (typically black) who attack those most vulnerable to them without regard to racial identity.[13]

According to these theorists, whom I will call law enforcement enthusiasts, the criminal law may have a disproportionate impact on the black community, but this is not a moral or racial issue because the disproportionate impact is the law's effect, not its intent. For law enforcement enthusiasts, intent is the most appropriate barometer of governmental racism. Because law enforcement is a public good, it is in the best interest of the black community to have more, rather than less, of it. Allowing criminals to live unfettered in the community would harm, in particular, the black poor, who are disproportionately the victims of violent crime. Indeed, the logical conclusion of the enthusiasts' argument is that African-Americans would be better off with more, not fewer, black criminals behind bars.

To my mind, the enthusiasts embrace law enforcement too uncritically: They are blind to its opportunity costs. I agree that criminal law enforcement constitutes a public good for African-Americans when it serves the social protection goals that Professor Kennedy highlights. In other words, when locking up black men means that "violent criminals ... who attack those most vulnerable" are off the streets, most people— including most law enforcement critics—would endorse the incarceration. But what about when locking up a black man has no or little net effect on public safety, when, for example, the crime with which he was charged is victimless? Putting aside for a moment the legal implications, couldn't an analysis of the costs and benefits to the African-American community present an argument against incarceration? I argue "yes" in

light of the substantial costs to the community of law enforcement. I accept that other reasonable people may disagree. But the law enforcement enthusiasts seldom acknowledge that racial critics even weigh the costs and benefits; their assumption seems to be that the racial critics are foolish or blinded by history or motivated by their own ethnocentrism.

5. The Body Politic and the Racial Critiques

I suspect that many white people would agree with the racial critics' analysis, even if most whites would not support a solution involving the emancipation of black criminals. I write this essay, however, out of concern for African-Americans and how they can use the power they have now to create change. The important practicability question is how many African-Americans embrace racial critiques of the criminal justice system and how many are law enforcement enthusiasts?

According to a recent *USA Today*/CNN/Gallup poll, sixty-six percent of blacks believe that the criminal justice system is racist and only thirty-two percent believe it is not racist. Interestingly, other polls suggest that blacks also tend to be more worried about crime than whites; this seems logical when one considers that blacks are more likely to be the victims of crime. This enhanced concern, however, does not appear to translate into endorsement of tougher enforcement of traditional criminal law. For example, substantially fewer blacks than whites support the death penalty, and many more blacks than whites were concerned with the potential racial consequences of the strict provisions of the Crime Bill of 1994. While polls are not, perhaps, the most reliable means of measuring sentiment in the African-American community, the polls, along with significant evidence from popular culture, suggest that a substantial portion of the African-American community sympathizes with racial critiques of the criminal justice system.

African-American jurors who endorse these critiques are in a unique position to act on their beliefs when they sit in judgment of a black defendant. As jurors, they have the power to convict the defendant or to set him free. May the responsible exercise of that power include voting to free a black defendant who the juror believes is guilty? The next section suggests that, based on legal doctrine concerning the role of juries in general, and the role of black jurors in particular, the answer to this question is "yes."

B. Jury Nullification

When a jury disregards evidence presented at trial and acquits an otherwise guilty defendant, because the jury objects to the law that the defendant violated or to the application of the law to that defendant, it has practiced jury nullification. In this section, I describe the evolution of this doctrine and consider its applicability to African-Americans. I then examine Supreme Court cases that discuss the role of black people on juries. In light of judicial rulings in these areas, I argue that it is both lawful and morally right that black jurors consider race in reaching verdicts in criminal cases

1. What Is Jury Nullification?

Jury nullification occurs when a jury acquits a defendant who it believes is guilty of the crime with which he is charged. In finding the defendant not guilty, the jury refuses to be bound by the facts of the case or the judge's instructions regarding the law. Instead, the jury votes its conscience.

In the United States, the doctrine of jury nullification originally was based on the common law idea that the function of a jury was, broadly, to decide justice, which included judging the law as well as the facts. If jurors believed that applying a law would lead to an unjust conviction, they were not compelled to convict someone who had broken that law. Although most American courts now disapprove of a jury's deciding anything other than the "facts," the Double Jeopardy Clause of the Fifth Amendment prohibits appellate reversal of a jury's decision to acquit, regardless of the reason for the acquittal. Thus, even when a trial judge thinks that a jury's acquittal directly contradicts the evidence, the jury's verdict must be accepted as final. The jurors, in judging the law, function as an important and necessary check on government power.

2. A Brief History

The prerogative of juries to nullify has been part of English and American law for centuries. In 1670, the landmark decision in *Bushell's Case*[14] established the right of juries under English common law to nullify on the basis of an objection to the law the defendant had violated. Two members of an unpopular minority group—the Quakers—were prosecuted for unlawful assembly and disturbance of the peace. At trial, the defendants, William Penn and William Mead, admitted that they had assembled a large crowd on the streets of London. Upon that admission, the judge asked the men if they wished to plead guilty. Penn replied that the issue was not "'whether I am guilty of this Indictment but whether this Indictment be legal,'" and argued that the jurors should go "behind" the law and use their consciences to decide whether he was guilty. The judge disagreed, and he instructed the jurors that the defendants' admissions compelled a guilty verdict. After extended deliberation, however, the jurors found both defendants not guilty. The judge then fined the jurors for rendering a decision contrary to the evidence and to his instructions. When one juror, Bushell, refused to pay his fine, the issue reached the Court of Common Pleas, which held that jurors in criminal cases could not be punished for voting to acquit, even when the trial judge believed that the verdict contradicted the evidence. The reason was stated by the Chief Justice of the Court of Common Pleas:

> A man cannot see by another's eye, nor hear by another's ear, no more can a man conclude or infer the thing to be resolved by another's understanding or reasoning; and though the verdict be right the jury give, yet they being not assured it is so from their own understanding, are forsworn, at least in foro conscientiae.[15]

This decision "changed the course of jury history." It is unclear why the jurors acquitted Penn and Mead, but their act has been viewed in near mythological terms. Bushell and his fellow jurors have come to be seen as representing the best ideals of democracy because they "rebuffed the tyranny of the judiciary and vindicated their own true historical and moral purpose."[16]

American colonial law incorporated the common law prerogative of jurors to vote according to their consciences after the British government began prosecuting American revolutionaries for political crimes. The best known of these cases involved John Peter Zenger, who was accused of seditious libel for publishing statements critical of British colonial rule in North America. In seditious libel cases, English law required that the judge determine whether the statements made by the defendant were libelous; the jury was not supposed to question the judge's finding on this issue. At trial, Zenger's attorney told the jury that it should ignore the judge's instructions that Zenger's remarks were libelous because the jury "ha[d] the right beyond all dispute to determine both the law and the facts." The lawyer then echoed the language of *Bushell's Case*, arguing that the jurors had "to see with their eyes, to hear with their own ears, and to make use of their own consciences and understandings, in judging of the lives, liberties or estates of their fellow subjects."[17] Famously, the jury acquitted Zenger, and another case entered the canon as a shining example of the benefits of the jury system.

After Zenger's trial, the notion that juries should decide "justice," as opposed to simply applying the law to the facts, became relatively settled in American jurisprudence. In addition to pointing to political prosecutions of white American revolutionaries like Zenger, modern courts and legal historians often cite with approval nullification in trials of defendants "guilty" of helping to free black slaves. In these cases, Northern jurors with abolitionist sentiments used their power as jurors to subvert federal law that supported slavery. In *United States v. Morris*,[18] for example, three defendants were accused of aiding and abetting a runaway slave's escape to Canada. The defense attorney told the jury that, because it was hearing a criminal case, it had the right to judge the law, and if it believed that the Fugitive Slave Act was unconstitutional, it was bound to disregard any contrary instructions given by the judge. The defendants were acquitted, and the government dropped the charges against five other people accused of the same crime. Another success story entered the canon.

3. Sparf and Other Critiques

In the mid-nineteenth century, as memories of the tyranny of British rule faded, some American courts began to criticize the idea of jurors deciding justice. A number of the state decisions that allowed this practice were overruled, and in the 1895 case of *Sparf v. United States*,[19] the Supreme Court spoke regarding jury nullification in federal courts.

In *Sparf*, two men on trial for murder requested that the judge instruct the jury that it had the option of convicting them of manslaughter, a lesser-included offense. The trial court refused this request and instead instructed the jurors that if they convicted the defendants of any crime less than murder, or if they acquitted them, the jurors would be in violation of their legal oath and duties. The Supreme Court held that this instruction was not contrary to law and affirmed the defendants' murder convictions. The Court acknowledged that juries have the "physical power" to disregard the law, but stated that they have no "moral right" to do so. Indeed, the Court observed, "If the jury were at liberty to settle the law for themselves, the effect would be . . . that the law itself would be most uncertain, from the different views, which different juries might take of it." Despite this criticism, *Sparf* conceded that, as a matter of law, a judge could not prevent jury nullification, because in criminal cases "[a] verdict of acquittal cannot be set aside." An anomaly was thus created, and has been a feature of American criminal law ever since: Jurors have the power to nullify, but, in most jurisdictions, they have no right to be informed of this power.

Since *Sparf*, most of the appellate courts that have considered jury nullification have addressed that anomaly and have endorsed it. Some of these courts, however, have not been as critical of the concept of jury nullification as the *Sparf* Court. The D.C. Circuit's opinion in *United States v. Dougherty*[20] is illustrative. In *Dougherty*, the court noted that the ability of juries to nullify was widely recognized and even approved "as a 'necessary counter to case-hardened judges and arbitrary prosecutors.'" This necessity, however, did not establish "as an imperative" that a jury be informed by the judge of its power to nullify. The D.C. Circuit was concerned that "[w]hat makes for health as an occasional medicine would be disastrous as a daily diet." Specifically:

> Rules of law or justice involve choice of values and ordering of objectives for which unanimity is unlikely in any society, or group representing the society, especially a society as diverse in cultures and interests as ours. To seek unity out of diversity, under the national motto, there must be a procedure for decision by vote of a majority or prescribed plurality—in accordance with democratic philosophy. To assign the role of mini-legislature to the various petit juries, who must hang if not unanimous, exposes criminal law and administration to paralysis, and to a deadlock that betrays rather than furthers the assumptions of viable democracy.

The idea that jury nullification undermines the rule of law is the most common criticism of the doctrine. The concern is that the meaning of self-government is threatened when twelve individuals on a jury in essence remake the criminal law after it has already been made in accordance with traditional democratic principles. Another critique of African-American jurors engaging in racially based jury nullification is that the practice by black jurors is distinct from the historically approved cases because the black jurors are not so much "judging" the law as preventing its application to members of their own race. The reader should recognize that these are moral, not legal, critiques because, as discussed above, the legal prerogative of any juror to acquit is well established. In the next section, I respond to these moral critiques.

C. The Moral Case for Jury Nullification by African-Americans

Any juror legally may vote for nullification in any case, but, certainly, jurors should not do so without some principled basis. The reason that some historical examples of nullification are viewed approvingly is that most of us now believe that the jurors in those cases did the morally right thing; it would have been unconscionable, for example, to punish those slaves who committed the crime of escaping to the North for their freedom. It is true that nullification later would be used as a means of racial subordination by some Southern jurors, but that does not mean that nullification in the approved cases was wrong. It only means that those Southern jurors erred in their calculus of justice. I distinguish racially based nullification by African-Americans from recent right-wing proposals for jury nullification on the ground that the former is sometimes morally right and the latter is not.

The question of how to assign the power of moral choice is a difficult one. Yet we should not allow that difficulty to obscure the fact that legal resolutions involve moral decisions, judgments of right and wrong. The fullness of time permits us to judge the fugitive slave case differently than the Southern pro-white-violence case. One day we will be able to distinguish between racially based nullification and that proposed by certain right-wing activist groups. We should remember that the morality of the historically approved cases was not so clear when those brave jurors acted. After all, the fugitive slave law was enacted through the democratic process, and those jurors who disregarded it subverted the rule of law. Presumably, they were harshly criticized by those whose interests the slave law protected. Then, as now, it is difficult to see the picture when you are inside the frame.

In this section, I explain why African-Americans have the moral right to practice nullification in particular cases. I do so by responding to the traditional moral critiques of jury nullification.

1. African-Americans and the "Betrayal" of Democracy

There is no question that jury nullification is subversive of the rule of law. It appears to be the antithesis of the view that courts apply settled, standing laws and do not "dispense justice in some ad hoc, case-by-case basis."[22] To borrow a phrase from the D.C. Circuit, jury nullification "betrays rather than furthers the assumptions of viable democracy." Because the Double Jeopardy Clause makes this power part-and-parcel of the jury system, the issue becomes whether black jurors have any moral right to "betray democracy" in this sense. I believe that they do for two reasons that I borrow from the jurisprudence of legal realism and critical race theory: First, the idea of "the rule of law" is more mythological than real, and second, "democracy," as practiced in the United States, has betrayed African-Americans far more than they could ever betray it. Explication of these theories has consumed legal scholars for years, and is well beyond the scope of this essay. I describe the theories below not to persuade the reader of their rightness, but rather to make the case that a reasonable juror might hold such beliefs, and thus be morally justified in subverting democracy through nullification.

2. The Rule of Law as Myth

The idea that "any result can be derived from the preexisting legal doctrine" either in every case or many cases, is a fundamental principle of legal realism (and, now, critical legal theory). The argument, in brief, is that law is indeterminate and incapable of neutral interpretation. When judges "decide" cases, they "choose" legal principles to determine particular outcomes. Even if a judge wants to be neutral, she cannot, because, ultimately, she is vulnerable to an array of personal and cultural biases and influences; she is only human. In an implicit endorsement of the doctrine of jury nullification, legal realists also suggest that, even if neutrality were possible, it would not be desirable, because no general principle of law can lead to justice in every case.

It is difficult for an African-American knowledgeable of the history of her people in the United States not to profess, at minimum, sympathy for legal realism. Most blacks are aware of countless historical examples in which African-Americans were not afforded the benefit of the rule of law: Think, for example, of the existence of slavery in a republic purportedly dedicated to the proposition that all men are created equal, or the law's support of state-sponsored segregation even after the Fourteenth Amendment guaranteed blacks equal

protection. That the rule of law ultimately corrected some of the large holes in the American fabric is evidence more of its malleability than of its virtue; the rule of law had, in the first instance, justified the holes.

The Supreme Court's decisions in the major "race" cases of the last term underscore the continuing failure of the rule of law to protect African-Americans through consistent application. Dissenting in a school desegregation case,[23] four Justices stated that "[t]he Court's process of orderly adjudication has broken down in this case." The dissent noted that the majority opinion "effectively . . . overrule[d] a unanimous constitutional precedent of 20 years standing, which was not even addressed in argument, was mentioned merely in passing by one of the parties, and discussed by another of them only in a misleading way." Similarly, in a voting rights case, Justice Stevens, in dissent, described the majority opinion as a "law-changing decision." And in an affirmative action case,[24] Justice Stevens began his dissent by declaring that, "[i]nstead of deciding this case in accordance with controlling precedent, the Court today delivers a disconcerting lecture about the evils of governmental racial classifications." At the end of his dissent, Stevens argued that "the majority's concept of stare decisis ignores the force of binding precedent."

If the rule of law is a myth, or at least is not applicable to African-Americans, the criticism that jury nullification undermines it loses force. The black juror is simply another actor in the system, using her power to fashion a particular outcome; the juror's act of nullification—like the act of the citizen who dials 911 to report Ricky but not Bob, or the police officer who arrests Lisa but not Mary, or the prosecutor who charges Kwame but not Brad, or the judge who finds that Nancy was illegally entrapped but Verna was not—exposes the indeterminacy of law, but does not create it.

3. The Moral Obligation to Disobey Unjust Laws

For the reader who is unwilling to concede the mythology of the rule of law, I offer another response to the concern about violating it. Assuming, for the purposes of argument, that the rule of law exists, there still is no moral obligation to follow an unjust law. This principle is familiar to many African-Americans who practiced civil disobedience during the civil rights protests of the 1950s and 1960s. Indeed, Martin Luther King suggested that morality requires that unjust laws not be obeyed. As I state above, the difficulty of determining which laws are unjust should not obscure the need to make that determination.

Radical critics believe that the criminal law is unjust when applied to some antisocial conduct by African-American: The law uses punishment to treat social problems that are the result of racism and that should be addressed by other means such as medical care or the redistribution of wealth. Later, I suggest a utilitarian justification for why African-Americans should obey most criminal law: It protects them. I concede, however, that this limitation is not morally required if one accepts the radical critique, which applies to all criminal law.

4. Democratic Domination

Related to the "undermining the law" critique is the charge that jury nullification is antidemocratic. The trial judge in the Barry case, for example, in remarks made after the conclusion of the trial, expressed this criticism of the jury's verdict: "'The jury is not a mini-democracy, or a mini-legislature. . . . They are not to go back and do right as they see fit. That's anarchy. They are supposed to follow the law.'" A jury that nullifies "betrays rather than furthers the assumptions of viable democracy." In a sense, the argument suggests that the jurors are not playing fair: The citizenry made the rules, so the jurors, as citizens, ought to follow them.

What does "viable democracy" assume about the power of an unpopular minority group to make the laws that affect them? It assumes that the group has the power to influence legislation. The American majority-rule electoral system is premised on the hope that the majority will not tyrannize the minority, but rather represent the minority's interests. Indeed, in creating the Constitution, the Framers attempted to guard against the oppression of the minority by the majority. Unfortunately, these attempts were expressed more in theory than in actual constitutional guarantees,

a point made by some legal scholars, particularly critical race theorists.

The implication of the failure to protect blacks from the tyrannical majority is that the majority rule of whites over African-Americans is, morally speaking, illegitimate. Lani Guinier suggests that the moral legitimacy of majority rule hinges on two assumptions: (1) that majorities are not fixed; and (2) that minorities will be able to become members of some majorities. Racial prejudice "to such a degree that the majority consistently excludes the minority, or refuses to inform itself about the relative merit of the minority's preferences," defeats both assumptions. Similarly, Owen Fiss has given three reasons for the failure of blacks to prosper through American democracy: They are a numerical minority, they have low economic status, and, "as a 'discrete and insular' minority, they are the object of 'prejudice'"—that is, the subject of fear, hatred, and distaste that make it particularly difficult for them to form coalitions with others (such as the white poor).

According to both theories, blacks are unable to achieve substantial progress through regular electoral politics. Their only "democratic" route to success—coalition building with similarly situated groups—is blocked because other groups resist the stigma of the association. The stigma is powerful enough to prevent alignment with African-Americans even when a group—like low income whites—has similar interests.

In addition to individual white citizens, legislative bodies experience the Negrophobia described above. Professor Guinier defines such legislative racism as

> a pattern of actions [that] persistently disadvantag[es] a fixed, legislative minority and encompasses conscious exclusion as well as marginalization that results from "a lack of interracial empathy." It means that where a prejudiced majority rules, its representatives are not compelled to identify its interests with those of the African-American minority.

Such racism excludes blacks from the governing legislative coalitions. A permanent, homogeneous majority emerges, which effectively marginalizes minority interests and "transform[s] majority rule into majority tyranny." Derrick Bell calls this condition "democratic domination."

Democratic domination undermines the basis of political stability, which depends on the inducement of "losers to continue to play the political game, to continue to work within the system rather than to try to overthrow it." Resistance by minorities to the operation of majority rule may take several forms, including "overt compliance and secret rejection of the legitimacy of the political order." I suggest that another form of this resistance is racially based jury nullification.

If African-Americans believe that democratic domination exists (and the 1994 congressional elections seem to provide compelling recent support for such a belief), they should not back away from lawful self-help measures, like jury nullification, on the ground that the self-help is antidemocratic. African-Americans are not a numerical majority in any of the fifty states, which are the primary sources of criminal law. In addition, they are not even proportionally represented in the U.S. House of Representatives or in the Senate. As a result, African-Americans wield little influence over criminal law, state or federal. African-Americans should embrace the antidemocratic nature of jury nullification because it provides them with the power to determine justice in a way that majority rule does not.

D. "Justice Must Satisfy the Appearance of Justice": The Symbolic Function of Black Jurors

A second distinction one might draw between the traditionally approved examples of jury nullification and its practice by contemporary African-Americans is that, in the case of the former, jurors refused to apply a particular law, e.g., a fugitive slave law, on the grounds that it was unfair, while in the case of the latter, jurors are not so much judging discrete statutes as they are refusing to apply those statutes to members of their own race. This application of race consciousness by jurors may appear to be antithetical to the American ideal of equality under the law.

This critique, however, like the "betraying democracy" critique, begs the question of whether the ideal actually applies to African-Americans. As stated above, racial critics answer this question in the negative. They, especially the liberal critics, argue that the criminal law is applied in a discriminatory fashion. Furthermore, on several occasions, the Supreme Court has referred to the usefulness of black jurors to the rule of law in the United States. In essence, black jurors symbolize the fairness and impartiality of the law. Here I examine this rhetoric and suggest that, if the presence of black jurors sends a political message, it is right that these jurors use their power to control or negate the meaning of that message.

As a result of the ugly history of discrimination against African-Americans in the criminal justice system, the Supreme Court has had numerous opportunities to consider the significance of black jurors. In so doing, the Court has suggested that these jurors perform a symbolic function, especially when they sit on cases involving African-American defendants, and the Court has typically made these suggestions in the form of rhetoric about the social harm caused by the exclusion of blacks from jury service. I will refer to this role of black jurors as the "legitimization function."

The legitimization function stems from every jury's political function of providing American citizens with "the security . . . that they, as jurors actual or possible, being part of the judicial system of the country can prevent its arbitrary use or abuse." In addition to, and perhaps more important than, seeking the truth, the purpose of the jury system is "to impress upon the criminal defendant and the community as a whole that a verdict of conviction or acquittal is given in accordance with the law by persons who are fair." This purpose is consistent with the original purpose of the constitutional right to a jury trial, which was "to prevent oppression by the Government."

When blacks are excluded from juries, beyond any harm done to the juror who suffers the discrimination or to the defendant, the social injury of the exclusion is that it "undermine[s] . . . public confidence—as well [it] should." Because the United States is both a democracy and a pluralist society, it is important that diverse groups appear to have a voice in the laws that govern them. Allowing black people to serve on juries strengthens "public respect for our criminal justice system and the rule of law."

The Supreme Court has found that the legitimization function is particularly valuable in cases involving "race-related" crimes. According to the Court, in these cases, "emotions in the affected community [are] inevitably . . . heated and volatile." The potential presence of black people on the jury in a "race related" case calms the natives, which is especially important in this type of case because "[p]ublic confidence in the integrity of the criminal justice system is essential for preserving community peace." The very fact that a black person can be on a jury is evidence that the criminal justice system is one in which black people should have confidence and one that they should respect.

But what of the black juror who endorses racial critiques of American criminal justice? Such a person holds no "confidence in the integrity of the criminal justice system." If she is cognizant of the implicit message that the Supreme Court believes her presence sends, she might not want her presence to be the vehicle for that message. Let us assume that there is a black defendant who the evidence suggests is guilty of the crime with which he has been charged and a black juror who thinks that there are too many black men in prison. The black juror has two choices: She can vote for conviction, thus sending another black man to prison and implicitly allowing her presence to support public confidence in the system that puts him there, or she can vote "not guilty," thereby acquitting the defendant or at least causing a mistrial. In choosing the latter, the juror makes a decision not to be a passive symbol of support for a system for which she has no respect: Rather than signaling her displeasure with the system by breaching "community peace," the black juror invokes the political nature of her role in the criminal justice system and votes "no." In a sense the black juror engages in an act of civil disobedience, except that her choice is better than civil disobedience because it is lawful. Is the black juror's race-conscious act moral? Absolutely. It would be farcical for her to be

the sole color-blind actor in the criminal process, especially when it is her blackness that advertises the system's fairness.

At this point every African-American should ask herself whether the operation of the criminal law in the United States advances the interests of black people. If it does not, the doctrine of jury nullification affords African-American jurors the opportunity to control the authority of the law over some African-American criminal defendants. In essence black people can "opt out" of American criminal law.

How far should they go? Completely to anarchy? Or is there some place between here and there, safer than both? The next part describes such a place, and how to get there.

 # III. A Proposal for Racially Based Jury Nullification

To allow African-American jurors to exercise their responsibility in a principled way, I make the following proposal: African-American jurors should approach their work cognizant of its political nature and their prerogative to exercise their power in the best interests of the black community. In every case, the juror should be guided by her view of what is "just." For the reasons stated in the preceding parts of this essay, I have more faith in the average black juror's idea of justice than I do in the idea that is embodied in the "rule of law."

A. A Framework for Criminal Justice in the Black Community

In cases involving violent *malum in se* crimes like murder, rape, and assault jurors should consider the case strictly on the evidence presented, and, if they have no reasonable doubt that the defendant is guilty, they should convict. For nonviolent *malum in se* crimes such as theft or perjury, nullification is an option that the juror should consider, although there should be no presumption in favor of it. A juror might vote for acquittal for example, when a poor woman steals from Tiffany's, but not when the same woman steals from her next-door neighbor. Finally in cases involving nonviolent, *malum prohibitum* offenses, including "victimless" crimes like narcotics offenses, there should be a presumption in favor of nullification.

This approach seeks to incorporate the most persuasive arguments of both the racial critics and the law enforcement enthusiasts. If my model is faithfully executed, the result would be that fewer black people would go to prison; to that extent, the proposal ameliorates one of the most severe consequences of law enforcement in the African-American community. At the same time, the proposal, by punishing violent offenses and certain others, preserves any protection against harmful conduct that the law may offer potential victims. If the experienced prosecutors at the U.S. Attorney's Office are correct some violent offenders currently receive the benefit of jury nullification, doubtless from a misguided if well-intentioned attempt by racial critics to make a political point. Under my proposal violent lawbreakers would go to prison.

In the language of criminal law, the proposal adopts utilitarian justifications for punishment: deterrence and isolation. To that extent, it accepts the law enforcement enthusiasts' faith in the possibility that law can prevent crime. The proposal does not however judge the lawbreakers as harshly as the enthusiasts would judge them. Rather, the proposal assumes that regardless of the reasons for their antisocial conduct people who are violent should be separated from the community for the sake of the nonviolent. The proposal's justifications for the separation are that the community is protected from the offender for the duration of the sentence and that the threat of punishment may discourage future offenses and offenders. I am confident that balancing the social costs and benefits of incarceration would not lead black jurors to release violent criminals simply because of race. While I confess agnosticism about whether the law can deter antisocial conduct, I am unwilling to experiment by abandoning any punishment premised on deterrence.

Of the remaining traditional justifications for punishment, the proposal eschews the retributive or "just deserts" theory for two reasons. First, I am persuaded by racial and other critiques of the unfairness of punishing people for "negative" reactions to racist oppressive conditions. In fact, I sympathize with people who react "negatively" to the countless manifestations of white supremacy that black people experience daily. While my proposal does not "excuse" all antisocial conduct, it will not punish such conduct on the premise that the intent to engage in it is "evil." The antisocial conduct is no more evil than the conditions that cause it, and, accordingly, the "just deserts" of a black offender are impossible to know. And even if just deserts were susceptible to accurate measure, I would reject the idea of punishment for retribution's sake.

My argument here is that the consequences are too severe: African-Americans cannot afford to lock up other African-Americans simply on account of anger. There is too little bang for the buck. Black people have a community that needs building and children who need rescuing and as long as a person will not hurt anyone, the community needs him there to help. Assuming that he actually will help is a gamble, but not a reckless one, for the "just" African-American community will not leave the lawbreaker be: It will for example, encourage his education and provide his health care (including narcotics dependency treatment) and, if necessary, sue him for child support. In other words the proposal demands of African-Americans responsible self-help outside of the criminal courtroom as well as inside it. When the community is richer, perhaps then it can afford anger.

The final traditional justification for punishment rehabilitation can be dealt with summarily. If rehabilitation were a meaningful option in American criminal justice, I would not endorse nullification in any case. It would be counterproductive for utilitarian reasons: The community is better off with the antisocial person cured than sick. Unfortunately, however, rehabilitation is no longer an objective of criminal law in the United States and prison appears to have an antirehabilitative effect. For this reason, unless a juror is provided with a specific compelling reason to believe that a conviction would result in some useful treatment for an offender, she should not use her vote to achieve this end, because almost certainly it will not occur.

B. Hypothetical Cases

How would a juror decide individual cases under any proposal? For the purposes of the following hypothesis let us assume criminal prosecutions in state or federal court and technically guilty African-American defendants. Easy cases under my proposal include a defendant who possessed crack cocaine and a defendant who killed another person. The former should be acquitted and the latter should go to prison.

The crack cocaine case is simple: Because the crime is victimless the proposal presumes nullification. According to racial critiques, acquittal is just, due in part to the longer sentences given for crack offenses than for powder cocaine offenses. This case should be particularly compelling to the liberal racial critic, given the extreme disparity between crack and powder in both enforcement of the law and in actual sentencing. According to a recent study, African-Americans make up 13% of the nation's regular drug users but they account for 35% of narcotics arrests, 55% of drug convictions, and 74% of those receiving prison sentences. Most of the people who are arrested for crack cocaine offenses are black: most arrested for powder cocaine are white. Under federal law if someone possesses fifty grams of crack cocaine the mandatory-minimum sentence is ten years; in order to receive the same sentence for powder cocaine, the defendant must possess 5000 grams. Given the racial consequences of this disparity, I hope that many racial critics will nullify without hesitation in these cases.

The case of the murderer is "easy" solely for the utilitarian reasons I discussed above. Although I do not believe that prison will serve any rehabilitative function for the murderer, there is a possibility that a guilty verdict will prevent another person from becoming a victim and the juror should err on the side of that possibility. In effect, I "write off" the black person who takes a life not for retributive reasons but because the black community cannot afford the risks of leaving this person in its midst. Accordingly, for the sake of potential victims (given the possibility that the criminal law deters homicide), nullification is not morally justifiable here.

Difficult hypothetical cases include the ghetto drug dealer and the thief who burglarizes the home of a rich family. Under the proposal nullification is presumed in the first case because drug distribution is a nonviolent, *malum prohibitum* offense. Is nullification morally justifiable here? It depends. There is no question that encouraging people to engage in self-destructive behavior is evil; the question the juror should ask herself is whether the remedy is less evil. I suspect that the usual answer would be "yes," premised on deterrence and isolation theories of punishment. Accordingly, the drug dealer would be convicted. The answer might change, however, depending on the particular facts of the case: the type of narcotic sold, the ages of the buyers, whether the dealer "marketed" the drugs to customers or whether they sought him out, whether it is a first offense, whether there is reason to believe that the drug dealer would cease this conduct if given another chance, and whether, as in the crack case, there are racial disparities in sentencing for this kind of crime. I recognize that, in this hypothetical nullification carries some societal risk. The risk however is less consequential than with violent crimes. Furthermore the cost to the community of imprisoning all drug dealers is great. I would allow the juror in this case more discretion.

The juror should also remember that many ghetto "drug" dealers are not African-American and that the state does not punish these dealers—instead, it licenses them. Liquor stores are ubiquitous on the ghetto streets of America. By almost every measure, alcoholism causes great injury to society, and yet the state does not use the criminal law to address this severe social problem. When the government tried to treat the problem of alcohol use with criminal law during Prohibition a violent "black" market formed. Even if the juror does not believe that drug dealing is a "victimless" crime, she might question why it is that of all drug dealers, many of the black capitalists are imprisoned, and many of the non-black capitalists are legally enriched. When the juror remembers that the cost to the community of having so many young men in jail means that law enforcement also is not "victimless," the juror's calculus of justice might lead her to vote for acquittal.

As for the burglar who steals from the rich family the case is troubling, first of all because the conduct is so clearly "wrong." As a nonviolent *malum in se* crime, there is no presumption in favor of nullification though it remains an option. Here, again, the facts of the case are relevant to the juror's decision of what outcome is fair. For example if the offense was committed to support a drug habit, I think there is a moral case to be made for nullification, at least until drug rehabilitation services are available to all.

If the burglary victim is a rich white person, the hypothetical is troubling for the additional reason that it demonstrates how a black juror's sense of justice might, in some cases, lead her to treat defendants differently based on the class and race of their victims. I expect that this distinction would occur most often in property offenses because, under the proposal, no violent offenders would be excused. In an ideal world, whether the victim is rich or poor or black or white would be irrelevant to adjudication of the defendant's culpability. In the United States, my sense is that some black jurors will believe that these factors are relevant to the calculus of justice. The rationale is implicitly premised on a critique of the legitimacy of property rights in a society marked by gross economic inequities. While I endorse this critique, I would encourage nullification here only in extreme cases (i.e., nonviolent theft from the very wealthy) and mainly for political reasons: If the rich cannot rely on criminal law for the protection of their property and the law prevents more direct self-help measures, perhaps they will focus on correcting the conditions that make others want to steal from them. This view may be naive, but arguably no more so than that of the black people who thought that if they refused to ride the bus, they could end legally enforced segregation in the South.

C. Some Political and Procedural Concerns

1. What If White People Start Nullifying Too?

One concern is that whites will nullify in cases of white-on-black crime. The best response to this concern is that often white people do nullify in those cases. The white jurors who acquitted the police officers who beat up Rodney King are a good example. There is no reason why my proposal should cause white jurors to acquit white defendants who are guilty of violence against blacks any more frequently. My model assumes that black violence against whites would be punished by black jurors: I hope that white jurors would do the same in cases involving white defendants.

If white jurors were to begin applying my proposal to cases with white defendants, then they, like the black jurors, would be choosing to opt out of the criminal justice system. For pragmatic political purposes, that would be excellent. Attention would then be focused on alternative methods of correcting antisocial conduct much sooner than it would if only African-Americans raised the issue.

2. How Do You Control Anarchy?

Why would a juror who is willing to ignore a law created through the democratic process be inclined to follow my proposal? There is no guarantee that she would. But when we consider that black jurors are already nullifying on the basis of race because they do not want to send another black man to prison, we recognize that these jurors are willing to use their power in a politically conscious manner. Many black people have concerns about their participation in the criminal justice system as jurors and might be willing to engage in some organized political conduct, not unlike the civil disobedience that African-Americans practiced in the South in the 1950s and 1960s. It appears that some black jurors now excuse some conduct—like murder—that they should not excuse. My proposal, however, provides a principled structure for the exercise of the black juror's vote. I am not encouraging anarchy. Instead I am reminding black jurors of their privilege to serve a higher calling than law: justice. I am suggesting a framework for what justice means in the African-American community.

3. How Do You Implement the Proposal?

Because *Sparf*, as well as the law of many states, prohibits jurors from being instructed about jury nullification in criminal cases, information about this privilege would have to be communicated to black jurors before they heard such cases. In addition jurors would need to be familiar with my proposal's framework for analyzing whether nullification is appropriate in a particular case. Disseminating this information should not be difficult. African-American culture—through mediums such as church, music (particularly rap songs), black newspapers and magazines, literature, storytelling, film (including music videos), soapbox speeches, and convention gatherings—facilitates intraracial communication. At African-American cultural events, such as concerts or theatrical productions, the audience could be instructed on the proposal, either verbally or through the dissemination of written material; this type of political expression at a cultural event would hardly be unique—voter registration campaigns are often conducted at such events. The proposal could be the subject of rap songs, which are already popular vehicles for racial critiques, or of ministers' sermons.

One can also imagine more direct approaches. For example, advocates of this proposal might stand outside a courthouse and distribute flyers explaining the proposal to prospective jurors. During deliberations, those jurors could then explain to other jurors their prerogative—their power—to decide justice rather than simply the facts. *Sparf* is one Supreme Court decision whose holding is rather easy to circumvent: If the defense attorneys cannot inform the people of their power, the people can inform themselves. And once informed, the people would have a formula for what justice means in the African-American community, rather than having to decide it on an ad hoc basis.

I hope that all African-American jurors will follow my proposal, and I am encouraged by the success of other grass-roots campaigns, like the famous Montgomery bus boycott, aimed at eliminating racial oppression. I note, however, that even with limited participation by African-Americans my proposal could have a significant impact. In most American jurisdictions, jury verdicts in criminal cases must be unanimous. One juror could prevent the conviction of a defendant. The prosecution would then have to retry the case and risk facing another African-American juror with emancipation tendencies. I hope that there are enough of us out there, fed up with prison as the answer to black desperation and white supremacy, to cause retrial after retrial until finally the United States "retries" its idea of justice.

 Conclusion

This essay's proposal raises other concerns such as the problem of providing jurors with information relevant to their decision within the restrictive evidentiary confines of a trial. Some of these issues can be resolved through creative lawyering. Other policy questions are not as easily answered, including the issue of how long (years, decades, centuries?) black jurors would need to pursue racially based jury nullification. I think this concern is related to the issue of the appropriate time span of other race-conscious remedies, including affirmative action. Perhaps when policymakers acknowledge that race matters in criminal justice, the criminal law can benefit from the successes and failures of race consciousness in other areas of the law. I fear, however, that this day of acknowledgement will be long in coming. Until then, I expect that many black jurors will perceive the necessity of employing the self-help measures prescribed here.

I concede that the justice my proposal achieves is rough because it is as susceptible to human foibles as the jury system. I am sufficiently optimistic to hope that my proposal will be only an intermediate plan, a stopping point between the status quo and real justice. I hope that this essay will encourage

African-Americans to use responsibly the power they already have to get criminal justice past the middle point. I hope that the essay will facilitate a dialogue among all Americans in which the significance of race will not be dismissed or feared but addressed. The most dangerous "forbidden" message is that it is better to ignore the truth than to face it.

 ## Notes

1. Christopher B. Daly. Hurry Judge Castigates Four Jurors: Evidence of Guilt was "Overwhelming." Jurkson Tells Forum. *Wash. Post*, Oct. 31. 1990, at Al (quoting U.S. District Judge Thomas Penfield Jackson). The trial judge's comments were made after the verdict.

2. The following account is drawn from Michael York, Excerpts from Videotape of Barry's Arrest at the Vista Hotel, *Wash. Post*, June 29, 1990, at A22.

3. The trial decision can be found at United States v. Barry, No. 90-0068, 1990 WL 174907 (D.D.C. Oct. 26, 1990), *aff'd*, 938 F.2d 1327 (D.C. Cir. 1991).

4. Saundra Torry, Stallings Excluded From Barry Trial: ACLU to Appeal Judge's Actions Barring Bishop, Farrakhan, *Wash. Post*, June 30, 1990, at A13.

5. United States v. Barry. Nos. 90-3150, 90-3149, & 90-3151, 1990 WI. 104925 (D.C. Cir. July 5, 1990).

6. Black D.C. Atty. Is At Odds with Judge Over Kente Cloth. *Jet*, June 22, 1992, at 35.

7. United States v. Barry, Nos. 90-3149, & 90-3151, 1990 WL 104925, at 1–2 (D.C. Cir. July 5, 1990).

8. Norris v. Risley, 918 F.2d 828, 832 (9th Cir. 1990).

9. Woods v. Dugger, 923 F.2d 1454 (11th Cir.), *cert. denied*, 502 U.S. 953 (1991). In this case, the hidden message was pro-conviction, see *id.* at 1459–60, unlike the pro-acquittal messages in the cases involving Barry and Harvey.

10. Norris v. Risley, 918 F.2d 828, 832 (9th Cir., 1990).

11. Woods v. Dugger, 923 F.2d 1454 (11th Cir.), cert. denied, 502 U.S. 953 (1991). In this case, the hidden message was proconviction, unlike the proacquittal messages in the cases involving Barry and Harvey.

12. Kente Cloth in the Dock, *Wash. Times*, June 13, 1992, at D2.

13. Randall Kennedy, "The State, Criminal Law, and Racial Discrimination: A Comment," 107 Harvard Law Review (1994), at 1259.

14. 124 Eng Rep 1006 (C.P. 1670).

15. *Bushell's Case*, 124 Eng. Rep. at 1013.

16. Philip B. Scott, Jury Nullification: An Historical Perspective on a Modern Debate, 91 W. VA. 1 Rev. 389, 414 (1989), quoted in M. Kristine Creagan, *Jury Nullification: Assessing Recent Legislative Developments*, 43 CASE W. RES. L. REV. 1101, 1109 (1993).

17. James Alexander, A Brief Narrative of the Case and Trial of John Peter Zenger, Printer of *The New York Weekly Journal* 93 (Stanley N. Katz, ed., 1963) (1736).

18. 26 F. Cas. 1323 (C.C.D. Mass. 1851) (No. 15.815).

19. 156 U.S. 51 (1895).

20. 473 F.2d 1113 (D.C. Cir. 1972).

21. Michael S. Moore, *A Natural Law Theory of Interpretation*, 58 S. (AL. L.REV. 277, 313 (1985).

22. Michael S. Moore, A Natural Law Theory of Interpretation, 58 S. (AL. L. REV. 277, 313 (1985).

23. United States v. Dougherty, 473 F.2d 1113, 1136 (D.C. Cir. 1972)

24. Missouri v. Jenkins, 115 S. Ct. 2038 (1995) (holding that district court order to attract nonminority students to school district in furtherance of interdistrict goal was beyond scope of court's authority).

25. Miller v. Johnson, 115 S. Ct. 2475 (1995) (affirming holding, in case brought by white constituents claiming vote dilution, that Georgia's congressional redistricting plan violated Equal Protection Clause, in part because of its allegedly racial rationale).

26. Adarand Constructors v. Pena, 115 S. Ct. 2097 (1995) (holding that racial classifications imposed by government actors must withstand strict scrutiny).

DISCUSSION QUESTIONS

1. Why does Butler contend that "the black community would be better off when some nonviolent lawbreakers remain in the community rather than go to prison"? Do you agree or disagree with his analysis?

2. What are the "secret messages everyone hears" in the two cases Butler discusses (i.e., Marion Barry and the attorney who wore kente cloth)?

3. Why does Butler advocate racially based jury nullification? What justifies this course of action, in his view?

4. Butler argued that nullification should be confined to nonviolent crimes and that defendants charged with violent crimes, such as murder, rape, and armed robbery, should be convicted if there is proof beyond a reasonable doubt of guilt. Why is nullification not morally justifiable (in Butler's opinion) in cases of offenders charged with violent crimes?

5. The more difficult cases, according to Butler, involve defendants charged with nonviolent property offenses or with more serious drug trafficking offenses. How does he answer the question, "Is nullification morally justifiable" in these types of cases?

6. Randall Kennedy, a black law professor, critiqued Butler's proposal in his book, *Race, Crime, and the Law* (Kennedy, 1997, pp. 305–307). He objected to Butler's expression of more sympathy for nonviolent black offenders than for "the law-abiding people compelled by circumstances to live in close proximity to the criminals for whom he is willing to urge subversion of the legal system." He asserted that law-abiding black people "desire *more* rather than *less* prosecution and punishment for *all* types of criminals." How might Butler answer Kennedy's criticisms?

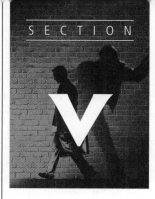

SECTION

V

Pretrial Proceedings

Introduction

In this chapter, we provide an overview of the pretrial process, from arrest to trial. There are a number of stages in this process, each of which serves a different purpose. The goal of the pretrial process is to screen cases and dispose of, through dismissal or a plea agreement, those that are either too weak to pursue or so strong that the defendant seeks to avoid going to trial.

At many of these points in the process, the defendant has the opportunity to examine the prosecution's case against him or her, through a variety of procedures generally known as discovery. During the pretrial period, the defendant may also seek to have evidence the prosecution wishes to use against him or her suppressed, or excluded from evidence, via the exclusionary rule.

Although the defendant has the opportunity to challenge the sufficiency of the evidence prior to trial, the prosecution is not required to demonstrate proof of the defendant's guilt beyond a reasonable doubt—that standard applies only at the trial. Typically, the court will continue the proceedings if the prosecution can provide evidence demonstrating "probable cause" to believe that the defendant committed the crime.

Once the pretrial maneuvering is complete, the last task before the trial starts is the selection of the jury. Although this process varies from jurisdiction to jurisdiction, in general both the prosecutor and defense attorney participate in selecting which individuals will (and will not) serve on the jury.

 ## Arrest

The criminal process begins either with the filing of a complaint or an arrest. A **complaint** may be filled out by a police officer, a prosecutor, or a private citizen. If an arrest is made first, a complaint will be sworn out afterward, usually by the arresting officer. The complaint serves as the charging document for the preliminary hearing.

The criminal process usually begins with an **arrest**. Virtually all arrests are made by a police officer, although a private citizen can, in limited circumstances, make a "citizen's arrest." For an arrest to be made, a police officer must have probable cause to believe a crime has been committed and that the person being arrested committed the crime or was in some way involved in the criminal activity. An arrest may be made by an officer with or without an arrest warrant, depending on the circumstances.

Search and arrest warrants are obtained by police officers, who first must fill out an **affidavit** stating the facts relied upon to create probable cause. There must be probable cause to either arrest or search. **Probable cause** is a legal concept referring to the amount of proof a police officer must have in order to search or arrest someone.

 ## Booking

The arrestee will be booked at the arresting officer's station. **Booking** consists of filling out paperwork that records who is arrested, the time of the alleged offense, the facts involved, and so on. Fingerprints and photographs will be taken. Then the arrestee may be placed in a holding cell and allowed to contact family and/or an attorney. Many arrestees are promptly released, especially if the offense in question is minor and there is no concern that he or she won't show up for court proceedings.

 ## Information

The information is prepared and signed by the prosecutor. It is adequate if it informs the defendant of the facts and the elements of the offense charged. It is a substitute for a grand jury indictment and is a more efficient way to proceed because it eliminates the need to organize a grand jury and present evidence.

Indictment

The Fifth Amendment requires the federal government to proceed via an indictment handed down by a grand jury. This clause of the Fifth Amendment is one of the few that has not been applied to the states, however, so states may use an information instead. A little less than half the states require an indictment. Twelve states require indictment by a grand jury only for felonies, while three states require indictment by a grand jury only for capital offenses. Four states require indictment by a grand jury for all felonies and misdemeanors.

Grand Jury

The typical grand jury is composed of 23 people, and proceedings are not open to the public. Some states follow the federal model and seat grand juries of 23 members; other states seat anywhere from 6 to 23 members. Few states require grand juries in all felony cases, and in some states, a grand jury is formed at the discretion of the prosecutor. The only persons present aside from the members of the grand jury are the district attorney and any witnesses he or she calls.

The rationale behind requiring indictment by a grand jury is that this body can act as check on an overzealous prosecutor, preventing him from prosecuting cases for which there is not sufficient evidence. In reality the grand jury today is unlikely to refuse to indict anyone. This does not necessarily mean it is not achieving its purpose of preventing improper prosecutions, however, as its very existence may prevent prosecutors from taking shaky cases to the grand jury. In this way, the grand jury does check the prosecutor's power. If the grand jury returns an indictment, it is referred to as a **true bill**. If the grand jury refuses to indict the defendant, it is referred to as a **no bill**.

Initial Appearance

If a suspect is arrested, booked, and placed in confinement, he or she will then be brought before a lower court judge for an initial appearance. Once a person is arrested, he or she must be brought before a magistrate "without unnecessary delay." The **initial appearance**, which is usually held within a few hours or, at most, a few days of arrest, serves to advise the accused why he or she is being detained and to explain his or her rights. The judge will read the charges filed against the defendant (suspects become defendants once officially indicted) and will explain the penalties for each charge. The judge also will inform the defendant of the right to a trial by jury and the right to counsel, including the right to have an attorney appointed if the defendant is indigent.

Persons charged with misdemeanors typically enter a plea at this stage in the process. If the defendant pleads guilty, the judge either imposes a sentence immediately (typically, a fine, probation, or a jail term) or sets a date for sentencing; if the defendant enters a "not guilty" plea, the judge sets a date for trial. Felony defendants, on the other hand, do not enter a plea at the initial appearance; judges in courts of limited jurisdiction generally are not authorized to accept pleas in felony cases. The judge informs the defendant of the right to a preliminary hearing, explains the purpose of the preliminary hearing, and sets a date for the hearing.

Bail

Decisions regarding bail may be made at the initial appearance or at a bail hearing that will be scheduled soon after the initial appearance. The judge must decide whether to release the defendant on bail and the type and amount of bail to impose. When a judge concludes that a defendant poses a significant risk of flight or of harm to others, bail will not be granted. But if the defendant's failure to appear at trial is not a concern and he or she is not seen as dangerous, the defendant may either be released on his or her own recognizance (i.e., without paying bail) or be required to pay monetary bail. Interestingly, there is no constitutional right to bail. The Eighth Amendment only provides that "excessive bail shall not be required." This means that bail should be an amount that is not unreasonable but that will guarantee the defendant's appearance at trial. In many jurisdictions, judges follow bail schedules, except in cases of serious or unusual offenses.

When a defendant does not have the money to post bail, he or she may pay a bail bondsman a fee (usually 10% of the bail bond) to post bail for him or her. If a defendant cannot raise the money to post bail or even hire a bondsman, then he or she will remain in jail until trial. This is a common fate for many indigent criminal defendants.

◩ Arraignment

After the judge at the initial appearance or the grand jury has decided that there is sufficient evidence to proceed with the case, the defendant will be arraigned. The purpose of **arraignment** is to formally notify the defendant of the charge(s) and to ask the defendant to enter a plea. Possible pleas include "guilty," "not guilty," "no contest," and "standing mute." *Standing mute* means refusing to plead—in these instances, the court enters a "not guilty" plea for the defendant, thus preserving the defendant's constitutional right to trial. A "no contest" plea, also referred to as a **nolo contendere plea**, means "I do not desire to contest the action." This plea resembles a guilty plea, but it is different in one important respect: It cannot be used against the defendant in any later civil litigation arising from the acts that led to the initial criminal charge. Also, a plea of nolo contendere means that the defendant does not admit to the crime. A guilty plea, by contrast, requires that the defendant admit and *explain* (known as allocution) what happened.

A fourth possible plea, not accepted as a valid option in all states and only conservatively allowed in the federal system, is the Alford plea. An **Alford plea** is one in which the defendant enters a guilty plea but denies having committed the crime to which he or she is pleading. The reason that the Alford plea is not recognized in some states and only reluctantly accepted in special circumstances in others is that when a defendant enters a plea of guilty, he or she is expected to so state on the record. Judges do not take it lightly when defendants say they are guilty on the one hand and then assert their innocence on the other.

◩ Discovery

Discovery is the process by which both parties to the case learn of the evidence the opposing side will use. Rule 16 of the Federal Rules of Evidence provides, for example, that the defendant may, upon request, discover from the prosecution "any written statements or transcriptions of oral statements made by the defendant that are in the prosecution's possession; (2) the defendant's prior criminal record; and (3) documents, photographs, tangible items, results from physical and mental evaluations, as well as other forms of real evidence considered material to the prosecution's case."

There is considerable variation among the states in the types of information that are discoverable by the defense and the prosecution. In some states only the defendant's statements and physical evidence need be disclosed to the defense; in other states there is a presumption that the prosecutor, with only narrow exceptions, will disclose most of the evidence against the defendant.

The defendant has a constitutional right to any exculpatory evidence. According to the Supreme Court's decision in *Brady v. Maryland*,[1] prosecutors are not allowed to conceal **exculpatory evidence**, which is evidence tending to show that the defendant is innocent. Some states also require reciprocal discovery—that is, the defense is required to turn over certain types of evidence to the prosecutor. Generally, the defense is required to notify the prosecutor if the defendant is going to enter an insanity plea or use an alibi defense; in the latter situation, the defense may have to provide a list of witnesses who will support the alibi defense so that the state can be prepared to cross-examine them.

Pretrial Motions

Before the trial commences, each side may file one or more pretrial motions, which are then ruled on by the judge hearing the case. The party filing the motion must state in writing the grounds on which the motion is based and the type of relief requested. For example, the prosecuting attorney might file a motion asking the judge to rule that one of the key witnesses for the defense—a homeless woman who has a history of mental illness—is not competent to testify and therefore should be excluded as a witness at trial. If there has been substantial pretrial publicity about the case, the defense attorney might file a motion for a **change of venue**; in the motion, the defense would argue that it will be difficult to obtain an impartial jury, and therefore the trial should be moved to a jurisdiction where there has been less publicity. If the defense attorney believes that the police did not have probable cause to arrest the defendant or that there is insufficient evidence to justify the charges filed by the state, the attorney can move for a dismissal of the charges.

Pretrial motions—or, more accurately, the judge's rulings on pretrial motions—set the boundaries of the case and may play an important role in determining whether the case goes to trial at all and, if so, what the outcome will be. If the defense attorney's case rests entirely on the testimony of a witness who will provide an alibi for the defendant and the prosecutor's motion to exclude that witness is successful, the defense attorney may have little recourse but to try to convince the defendant to plead guilty. Similarly, if the state's case against a drug dealer hinges on the introduction of drugs and drug paraphernalia seized from the defendant at the time of his arrest and the judge grants the defense attorney's motion to exclude that evidence on the grounds that it was illegally obtained, the prosecutor may not want to take the case to trial and may instead offer the defendant a plea bargain. If the defendant in the first case insists on going to trial, the judge's ruling that the alibi witness cannot testify will make it difficult for him to win his case. And if the defendant in the second case refuses the plea bargain, the prosecutor may decide to dismiss the charges rather than risk losing at trial.

A variety of pretrial motions can be filed in a criminal case. Some of the more common motions are the following:

- *Motion for dismissal of charges:* Motion to dismiss the charges against the defendant on the grounds that there was not probable cause for the police to make an arrest or there is insufficient evidence to support the charges filed by the state.
- *Motion for a change of venue:* Motion to move the case to another jurisdiction because of prejudicial pretrial publicity about the case. Only the defendant, and not the prosecution, may file a motion for a change of venue. This is because the Sixth Amendment provides that the accused in a criminal

---

[1]*Brady v. Maryland*, 397 U.S. 742 (1970).

trial has the right to be tried "by an impartial jury of the State and district wherein the crime shall have been committed." By filing a motion for a change of venue, the defendant waives this right.

- *Motion for discovery:* Motion filed by the defense attorney requesting that the prosecution provide the documents and evidence that will be used against the defendant at trial, as well as a list of witnesses who will be called to testify. In many states, there is reciprocal discovery, which means that the prosecution can request certain types of evidence from the defense. Although the evidence that must be disclosed by the defense varies from state to state, most states require the defense to notify the prosecution if the defendant plans to plead not guilty by reason of insanity or to enter an alibi defense. Other types of evidence that fall under the reciprocal discovery rule include results of physical and mental examinations of the defendant, the names and addresses of witnesses the defense intends to call, and any witness statements.

- *Motion to suppress evidence:* Motion to exclude evidence obtained illegally—that is, evidence obtained as a result of an illegal search or interrogation. The so-called exclusionary rule prohibits the introduction at trial of evidence obtained illegally; such evidence, which is referred to as the "fruit of the poisonous tree," is inadmissible because it is tainted and therefore is not credible or trustworthy.

- *Motion for severance of defendants:* Typically, co-defendants in a case are tried together. This saves the court time and money and prevents witnesses having to testify about the same matter multiple times. However, there may be situations in which it is not in a defendant's best interest to be tried with his or her co-defendants. For example, there may be evidence against one defendant that is not applicable to the other defendants in the case, or the testimony of one defendant may incriminate the others. In this case, the defense attorney may file a motion for separate trials of co-defendants.

- *Motion for a determination of competency:* Motion to determine whether the defendant is competent to stand trial. According to the United States Code, the motion is to be granted "if there is reasonable cause to believe that the defendant may presently be suffering from a mental disease or defect rendering him mentally incompetent to the extent that he is unable to understand the nature and consequences of the proceedings against him or to assist properly in his defense" (U.S. Code, Title 18 §4241). If the motion is granted, the defendant's competency is evaluated by a psychiatrist or a clinical psychologist.

Plea Bargaining

The predominance of jury trials in television dramas such as *Law and Order* and *The Practice* notwithstanding, most convictions in the U.S. result from guilty pleas. In 2002, for instance, 95% of all felony convictions in state courts were the result of a guilty plea;[2] the rate was even higher—96%—for defendants convicted of felonies in federal courts in 2004.[3] Although the actual number of guilty pleas that result from plea bargains is unknown, most experts would argue that some type of negotiation between the prosecutor and the defendant (or his attorney) occurs prior to the entry of the guilty plea. The importance of the plea bargain cannot be overstated; because of its importance, we devote an entire section to it (Section VI).

---

[2]U.S. Department of Justice, Bureau of Justice Statistics, *State Court Sentences of Convicted Felons, 2002.* Washington, DC: Author (2005), Table 4.2.

[3]U.S. Department of Justice, Bureau of Justice Statistics, *Federal Criminal Case Processing, 2004.* Washington, DC (2005), Table 4.

Jury Selection

When defendants plead not guilty, the next step in the process is the trial. Once a trial date is set, jury selection begins. The jury is selected from the eligible members of the community, who are selected at random, usually from voting records or automobile registration records. These records are used to obtain as complete a list as possible of all the residents of a community.

The legal term for the order to summon jurors is the *venire,* which is Latin for "to cause" or to "make come" (to the courthouse). Prospective jurors are examined by the judge and/or the attorneys for the prosecution and defense to determine whether they have any bias, prejudice, or interest that would prevent the potential juror from being impartial. This process of questioning the jurors is referred to as the *voir dire,* which literally means "to speak the truth."

It should be noted that although the purpose of the voir dire is to obtain an unbiased jury, in reality each side seeks not only to excuse potential jurors who are biased against their side, but also to keep on the jury those individuals who are biased toward their side. Attorneys sometimes employ the services of professional jury consultants to help them determine what type of person is more likely to favor the prosecution or defense.

Challenges to the Jury

Jurors may be challenged for cause or removed through the use of a peremptory challenge. A peremptory challenge is one for which no reason need be given. Although both sides are allowed an unlimited number of challenges for cause, the number of peremptory challenges is usually limited. The Supreme Court has recently held that peremptory challenges may not be used to exclude potential jurors on the basis of race (*Batson v. Kentucky*, 1986) or gender (*J. E. B. v. Alabama*, 1994).

The Supreme Court has also held that the jury need not be composed of the traditional 12 members. Juries as small as six have been approved for both civil and criminal trials (*Williams v. Florida*, 1970). Furthermore, there is no constitutional requirement that the jury verdict be unanimous, even in criminal cases. The Supreme Court has approved both 9–3 and 10–2 verdicts (*Johnson v. Louisiana*, 1972; *Apodaca v. Oregon*, 1972). However, a six-person jury must be unanimous.

Finally, the requirement of a "jury of one's peers" has been interpreted simply to require a jury selected from the community where the crime took place. It does not mean the jury must share any other similarities with the defendant. To require otherwise would make jury selection next to impossible. A perfect example is the O. J. Simpson case. If the jury should have been composed of people with similar attributes, how would we have defined them? As black men, rich people, ex-football players, or bad actors? Instead, they simply had to be Los Angeles county residents.

Summary: Pretrial Proceedings

The idealized adversarial model of the criminal courts suggests that prosecutors and defense attorneys are in constant battle with one another. In reality, criminal case processing is characterized more by cooperation and consensus than by conflict. This reflects, in large part, the fact that trials are rare, and thus the opportunities for conflict are limited. It also can be attributed to the fact that both prosecutors and defense attorneys are part of a courtroom workgroup with common goals (i.e., efficient and expeditious case processing) and agreed-upon procedures for attaining those goals.

Researchers interested in the roles played by prosecutors and defense attorneys have focused on two questions: What factors influence charging decisions by prosecutors? and Do defendants with private attorneys receive more effective representation than those represented by public defenders? Studies of prosecutors' charging decisions reveal that these highly discretionary and largely invisible decisions reflect a mix of (1) legally relevant measures of case seriousness and evidence strength and (2) legally irrelevant characteristics of the victim and suspect. Studies comparing public and private attorneys reveal that there are few differences in case outcomes.

The American criminal justice system is dominated by guilty pleas, not trials. The members of the courtroom workgroup develop case processing routines designed to ensure that cases are handled as efficiently and expeditiously as possible. Plea negotiations—which may involve a reduction in the severity of the charge, a reduction in the number of counts, or some type of sentence agreement—produce high numbers of guilty pleas and limit the number of cases that go to trial. Supporters of plea bargaining argue that the system benefits both defendants and members of the courtroom workgroup; critics counter that plea bargains pervert justice, undercut the protections afforded to defendants, and coerce innocent defendants to plead guilty. Although a number of jurisdictions have attempted to eliminate or restrict plea bargaining, the effects of these reforms are symbolic rather than instrumental. It thus seems likely that for the foreseeable future, courts in the United States will continue to process most criminal cases using negotiated guilty pleas.

KEY TERMS

Affidavit	Change of venue	Nolo contendere plea
Alford plea	Complaint	Probable cause
Arraignment	Exculpatory evidence	True bill
Arrest	Initial appearance	
Booking	No bill	

DISCUSSION QUESTIONS

1. What is the meaning of probable cause?

2. What are the types of pleas, and how do they differ?

3. What is the purpose of bail?

4. What is the purpose of discovery?

WEB RESOURCES

Federal Grand Juries: http://www.udayton.edu/~grandjur/

National Center for State Courts: http://www.ncsc.org/

United States Courts: http://www.uscourts.gov/

Voir Dire: Creating the Jury: http://www.crfc.org/americanjury/voir_dire.html

READING

This article examines the difference that type of attorney (court-appointed or privately retained) has on the bail set for Hispanic defendants. The authors hypothesized that Hispanic defendants who retain the assistance of private counsel will receive lower bail amounts than defendants assigned a court-appointed attorney. The analyses show that although Hispanic defendants utilizing private counsel receive lower bail amounts than defendants assigned a court-appointed attorney, only the variables *age, residency,* and *offense seriousness* significantly affect bail amount set.

The Relationship Between Type of Attorney and Bail Amount Set for Hispanic Defendants

K. B. Turner and James B. Johnson

Competent legal representation for all criminal proceedings is crucial for defendants facing the possibility of the loss of liberty. It can be argued that one of the reasons the "Founding Fathers" included the Sixth Amendment in the Bill of Rights is to address this issue. The Sixth Amendment holds that "In all criminal prosecutions, the accused shall enjoy the right to have the assistance of counsel for his defense."

The Sixth Amendment right to counsel ostensibly serves two distinct purposes. First, the right to counsel helps prevent the conviction of innocent people. This notion is premised on the recognition that the criminal justice system is a complicated process that is foreign to many lay citizens. Therefore, defendants need to have competent guidance through the legal maze to ensure that they are not wrongfully convicted.

A second purpose for the Sixth Amendment right to counsel is to serve as a safety net to ensure that the defendant's constitutionally protected rights are not infringed on; that is, it ensures that the various procedural rules are followed and protect the defendant's constitutional rights, including the right to privacy; suppression of the fruits of an illegal arrest, search, or seizure; and the right to remain silent in custodial interrogations and at trial (Klotter, Kanovitz, & Kanovitz, 1999). This is of paramount importance because a criminal defendant may be unaware of how constitutionally protected rights can be infringed on during the criminal court proceedings.

Historically, the Sixth Amendment right to assistance of counsel was viewed as applying only at trial (Klotter et al., 1999). However, the Supreme Court has correctly asserted that decisions at earlier crucial stages in judicial proceedings could substantially prejudice the rights of an accused at a later time in the criminal justice process. In response, the Court has handed down several key rulings (*Coleman v. Alabama,* 1970; *Gideon v. Wainwright,* 1963; *Powell v. Alabama,* 1932: *Strickland v. Washington,* 1984) to ensure that those accused of crimes are afforded the right to counsel during the many stages of the criminal justice process.

SOURCE: Turner, K. B., & Johnson, James B. (2007). The relationship between type of attorney and bail amount set for Hispanic defendants. *Hispanic Journal of Behavioral Sciences, 29*(3), 384–400.

For the accused to receive the benefits of the constitutionally guaranteed right to counsel, the criminal justice system must afford the accused this right at critical stages of the legal proceedings. Through case law, the Supreme Court has determined that this right to counsel is not absolute in every phase of the criminal process. In fact, the Court has determined defendants are not constitutionally entitled to the assistance of counsel during (a) preindictment lineups, (b) booking procedures, (c) grand jury investigations, (d) appeals beyond the first review, (e) disciplinary proceedings in correctional institutions, and (f) postrelease revocation hearings (Senna & Siegal, 1996). Missing from this list is the bail hearing phase of criminal court proceedings. Consequently, bail, security provided to the court to ensure the appearance of the defendant at every subsequent stage of the criminal justice process (Senna & Siegel, 1996), is one of those critical stages wherein the Court has determined that the accused has a fundamental right to the assistance of counsel (*Coleman v. Alabama,* 1970). Regarding bail, the Eighth Amendment to the U.S. Constitution states that "Excessive bail shall not be required, nor excessive fines imposed, nor cruel and unusual punishments inflicted."

The simple guarantee of counsel secured by the Sixth Amendment, however, may not provide equal justice. Those who can afford it are able to hire their own attorney; those who cannot must rely on a lawyer paid from public funds, either a court-appointed attorney or a public defender, depending on the jurisdiction. The question remains, does it matter whether one is defended by a privately hired or publicly paid lawyer? This article seeks a partial answer to that question in regard to the amount of bail set for felony defendants. More specifically, this research focuses on Hispanic defendants charged with felony offenses to determine if privately retained or court-appointed attorneys produce a more favorable bail outcome for Hispanic defendants. To answer this question, the following were explored: (a) the necessity for criminological research on Hispanics, (b) the importance of bail in criminal justice processing, (c) prior bail research, (d) right to counsel in criminal proceedings,

(e) the type of attorneys that handle criminal cases, and (f) empirical analyses of bail decisions on Hispanic defendants in a midwestern jurisdiction.

 ## The Necessity for Criminological Research on Hispanics

It is a gross understatement that most of the criminological research examining racial differences in criminal justice processing has focused primarily on African Americans (Mann, 1993; Walker, Spohn, & DeLong, 2000). Although researchers have vigorously investigated the impact of criminal justice decision making on African Americans, other racial or ethnic groups, including American Indians (Nielsen, 1996), Asian Americans (Ho, 1998; National Minority Advisory Council on Criminal Justice, 1982), and Hispanics (Mirande, 1987) have largely been neglected as a single unit of analysis. A rather common practice on the part of social scientists is to engage in the "racial lumping" (see, e.g., Espiritu, 1992; Turner & Johnson, 2005) of these groups (typically African Americans and Hispanics) into one category and refer to them as "minority" or "non-White." When this occurs, according to Walker et al. (2000), "we do not know whether Hispanic Americans are treated worse, better, or about the same as African Americans" (p. 3).

Flowers (1990) contended that one reason for the scant research on Hispanics stems from the narrowsightedness of researchers who believe that essentially there are very few differences between Hispanics and African Americans because they are a "mirror image" of each other. It that is the case, it stands to reason that Hispanics are not deserving of individual attention when it comes to examining the impact of criminal justice processing. However, whether Hispanics simply "mirror" African Americans is an empirical question and should not be simply assumed. Indeed, research reported below suggests that this assumption is incorrect.

A compelling reason that it is critical to increase the research focus on Hispanics comes from the 2000 Census that revealed Hispanics to be the fastest-growing racial or ethnic group in the United States, surpassing African Americans as the largest minority group. The Hispanic proportion of the population had increased from 6.4% in 1980 to 12.5% in 2000 and is estimated to reach 24.3% by the year 2050 (U.S. Bureau of the Census, 2001). Given the growth of the Hispanic population, it is incumbent on researchers to more deliberately make the effort to examine how criminal justice decision making affects this group. Farnworth, Teske, and Thurman (1991) asserted over a decade ago that "the sheer number of Hispanics in our society and our courts suggests a need for researchers to extend their conceptualization of minority status to consider both ethnic and racial disparity during processing" (p. 55).

As alluded to earlier, much of the criminological research examining the treatment of Hispanics by the criminal justice system has analyzed them together with other groups, most often African Americans, under the heading "minorities." It has been documented that Hispanics and African Americans have had similar American experiences. For instance, both groups have experienced mistreatment and indifference by members of the dominant society, high rates of unemployment and poverty, low rates of education attainment and female-headed households, and [are] overrepresented in essentially every criminal justice statistical category, from arrest to incarceration (Healey, 1995; Moore & Pinderhughes, 1993). Although it may be convenient to discuss these two groups as being monocultural, it is insensitive and inaccurate to do so as there are numerous unique historical and cultural differences between them.

 # Bail and Criminal Justice Processing

It has been established that the pretrial stage of the criminal justice process is a very important point in criminal court proceedings. Perhaps no pretrial proceeding is more crucial than the decision regarding whether or not to grant the defendant bail. Within this context, numerous means for pretrial release for the defendant exist.

Although the cash bond system tends to dominate the way bail is administered, many other options are used by a number of states and the federal government. These alternatives include (a) release on recognizance, (b) property bond, (c) deposit bail, (d) conditional release, (e) third-party custody, (f) unsecured or signature bond, and (g) attorney affidavit (Schmalleger, 2001, pp. 308–311). However, the use of money bail became widespread as more and more individuals were less known in the community and money was determined to be the most forceful mechanism to ensure appearance (Ozzane, Wilson, & Gedney, 1980).

Most criminal offenses are bailable; therefore, accused persons have the right to be released on reasonable bail to assist in their defense and lead an otherwise "normal" life while awaiting trial. Not all defendants, however, enjoy the benefits of the Eighth Amendment. Those unable to make bail can face substantial negative consequences. Thus, nothing may be more crucial than the decision regarding whether or not to grant the defendant bail and, if granted, the amount at which bail is set.

The bail decision has significance because ability to make bail affects whether a defendant is detained prior to trial. Defendants who cannot make bail are placed in detention while awaiting trial. This effectively hinders their ability to assist in their defense by limiting access to counsel and preventing them from locating evidence and witnesses (Inciardi, 1984). In addition, detained defendants may be stereotyped as dangerous (Katz & Spohn, 1995). This may affect the treatment of the defendant at trial. For example, research has shown that defendants who are detained prior to trial are more likely to be convicted than defendants who are not detained (Albonetti, 1991; Rankin, 1964). As well, it has been observed that convicted defendants who had been unable to make money bail tend to get longer prison sentences (Goldkamp, 1985; Rhodes, 1985). Thus, the amount at which bail is set has significant consequences and outcomes that can adversely affect the accused at later stages of the process.

If ethnicity and effective assistance of counsel are factors in these crucial decisions, it is paramount that the legal representation provided to Hispanic defendants is adequate to avoid differential treatment and possible harmful consequences in later stages of the criminal court process (Mann, 1993). Certainly, the relationship between ethnicity, legal representation, and bail decisions is worthy of research.

 ## Prior Bail Research

Although prior research has explored the effect of race and ethnicity on various aspects of criminal and juvenile justice processing, the bail decision has not received much attention. The fact that racial differences in bail decisions have not been the primary focus of researchers does not detract from its importance. As noted earlier, this decision may have serious consequences later in the process.

A search for literature on race and ethnicity in regard to bail suggests that few studies have investigated the assignment of bail (Albonetti, 1989; Frazier, Bock, & Henretta, 1980; Goldkamp & Gottfredson, 1979; Mann, 1993; Nagel, 1983; National Minority Advisory Council on Criminal Justice, 1980; Turner & Johnson, 2005; Turner, Secret, & Johnson, 2003). Free (2002) examined the literature investigating pretrial release, a decision that may be affected by the bail decision, [and] observed that non-Whites were less likely than Whites to receive bail amounts below the guidelines. Moreover, Free found in several of the reviewed studies that African Americans and Hispanics were required more often than Whites to post cash or surety bonds. Previously Bynum (1982) examined judges' decisions to grant the defendant release without monetary bail. In particular, Bynum concluded that African Americans and American Indians are less likely than are Whites to be released on their own recognizance. Furthermore, regarding pretrial release, some research has found disparate treatment by race, with non-Whites (which includes non-White Hispanics and African Americans) faring worse than Whites (Albonetti, 1989; Katz & Spohn, 1995; Patterson & Lynch, 1991; Petee, 1994; Reeves & Perez, 1994).

Although there is a scarcity of research focusing on Hispanics and bail, there is some recent scholarship. For instance, Demuth and Steffensmeier (2004) included in their analyses 75 of the most populous counties in the United States and found that Hispanic and African American males were less likely than White males to be granted pretrial release. In fact, the researchers found that Hispanics received the least favorable pretrial decisions.

Ayres and Waldfogel (1994), analyzing data from Connecticut, concluded that courts systematically set bail for Hispanic male and female defendants at unjustifiably high amounts. They further observed that, after controlling for the severity of the alleged offense, bail amounts set for Hispanic male defendants were 19% higher than those set for their White male counterparts, but lower than those set for African American males. In drug cases, the study found that in several Connecticut cities the average bond for Hispanics and African Americans was 4 times higher than the bond for Whites. For women with no prior record, the average bond for Hispanics was 197% higher than for White women. Essentially, judges were punishing Hispanics and African Americans who had not been convicted of a crime, an unintended consequence of bail and defendants' exercise of their Eighth Amendment rights. Finally, Turner and Johnson (2005) found in their analyses that bail amounts given to Hispanics are excessive when compared to similarly situated White and African American defendants.

In sum, a review of the limited literature concludes that Hispanics are treated differently in bail decisions; that is, Hispanics are likely to have higher bail amounts assigned to them. Is this practice related to the type of attorney representing this group or some other reason(s)? The next section of this article discusses the literature regarding defendants' use of legal counsel.

 ## Right to Counsel in Criminal Proceedings

Private Versus Public Defender

Because the literature on the bail decision is rare, literature focusing specifically on the effectiveness of legal representation in relation to bail amounts is even rarer. To date, few studies have been published. However, a majority of these few studies on type of attorney and bail suggest that defendants fare better when utilizing the services of a privately retained attorney. An early study of murder charges over two decades found that privately retained attorneys are more successful than court-appointed attorneys in securing bail for their clients, even when controlling for legal factors such as defendant's prior record (Swigert & Farell, 1991). Moreover, other researchers have found that bail status and representation by a court-appointed attorney led to a greater probability of receiving a prison sentence even when severity of offense and prior record were controlled (Clarke & Koch, 1976). In addition, some researchers found that defendants who used private attorneys were also more likely to be released prior to trial (Holmes, Hosch, Daudistel, Perez, & Graves, 1996; Turner & Johnson, 2003).

The small amount of research focusing specifically on bail and types of attorney is alarming. As outlined above, this decision point is of great significance as it can have monumental adverse effects on the defendant at subsequent stages of the criminal justice process. Accordingly, the current study is a response to the need for additional research on the relationship between ethnicity, type of attorney, and the amount of bail set by the judge.

In sum, the few studies examining the effectiveness of assistance of counsel in relation to bail suggest that there is a difference in effectiveness between a privately retained attorney and a court-appointed attorney; that is, in connection with bail, defendants fare better when utilizing the services of a privately retained attorney.

Current Study

The current study extends the literature on ethnicity and bail setting by determining if the judicial decision of the amount of bail set is independently affected by the ethnicity of the defendant. Moreover, this current research adds to the literature by investigating how critical judicial decisions affect a rarely studied group: Hispanics, the largest single minority group in the United States. This is valuable because, as indicated above, most of the research focusing on minorities and criminal justice processing that includes Hispanics in

the data lumps them together with other racial and ethnic groups, effectively hiding any differences that might arise between Hispanics, Whites, and other minorities. Research on Hispanics as a single ethnic category will contribute to our understanding and increase our knowledge on the effect of ethnicity on bail decisions. It is against this backdrop that this article seeks to add to our knowledge regarding the difference type of attorney makes on bail amount. Specifically, it examines the following hypothesis:

> *Hypothesis 1.* After controlling for the effect of several available legal and extralegal factors, Hispanic defendants who retain the assistance of private counsel will receive lower bail amounts than defendants assigned a court-appointed attorney.

Method

Data

The data for the current study comes from the Nebraska District Court files of Lancaster County, Nebraska, which includes Lincoln, the state capital and second largest city in Nebraska. We viewed the Court's data files on persons processed by the District Court in 1996 that were available for public access. The data set contains information on all persons accused of felony offenses who were eligible for bail in 1996, excluding defendants with nonbailable offenses ($N = 921$). The official court record, filed by the Clerk of the Court, indicates the defendant's racial and/or ethnic self-identification as either White, Black, Hispanic, Asian, or Native American. In those rare occasions where the defendant's race or ethnicity was left blank, we assigned the defendant to the Other category. The sample included 560 Whites, 233 African Americans, 55 Hispanics, 33 Asians, 24 Native Americans, and 16 Other. For purposes of the current research, only the subsample of Hispanics ($n = 55$) was utilized. Only those cases for which information on all relevant variables was available are included in the analyses. Table 5.1 presents summary statistics on the variables used in the analyses.

Table 5.1   Sample Means and Percentages

Variables	M	SD	n	%
Dependent variable				
Bail amount set	24404.55	32610.96	55	
Independent variables				
Age	27.84	8.39	55	
Prior arrests	4.78	3.65	55	
Felony			55	
Type 4 (least serious)			20	36.4
Type 3			16	29.1
Type 2			14	25.5
Type 1 (most serious)			5	9.1
Sex			55	
Female			4	7.3
Male			51	92.7
Counsel			55	
Private			21	38.2
Public			34	61.8
Jurisdiction			55	
Lancaster County			39	70.9
Nebraska (not Lancaster County)			3	5.5
Other state			7	12.7
Transient			6	10.9

Measures

Dependent variable. The dependent variable is the dollar amount of bail set by the judge to insure the appearance of the accused at trial. This continuous variable ranges from U.S. $1,000 to $150,000 for these defendants and averages $24,404.

Extralegal independent variables. The major extralegal independent variable, and the major test variable of this research, is type of attorney (*private* = 0, *public* = 1).[1] Almost 62% of these defendants were represented by public defenders. The other extralegal variables are age

(a continuous variable), sex (*female* = 0, *male* = 1), and place of residence. Place of residence is a dummy variable consisting of four elements: those living in Lancaster County; those living in Nebraska, but not Lancaster County; those with an address in a state other than Nebraska; and transients, those with no address.

Legal independent variables. Two legal variables are controlled: offense seriousness and prior record. Previous research has demonstrated that seriousness of the offense and prior record are important predictors of outcomes at various stages of the criminal justice system, specifically judges' bail decisions (Albonetti, 1989; Frazier et al., 1980; Goldkamp & Gottfredson, 1979; Nagel, 1983). Offense seriousness is treated as a dummy variable based on a 4-point index of seriousness of the felony (Type IV= *least serious,* Type I = *most serious*) as defined in Nebraska statutes (Revised Statutes of Nebraska, 1995).[2] Prior criminal record is a continuous variable measured by the total number of felony and misdemeanor arrests preceding the instant offense.

The extralegal variables we control for are consistent with prior research: sex (Crew, 1991; Goldkamp & Gottfredson, 1979; Katz & Spohn, 1995; Nagel, 1983), age (Bynum & Paternoster, 1994), and area of residence (Freed & Wald, 1964; Ozanne et al., 1980; Patterson & Lynch, 1991; Turner et al., 2003; Turner & Johnson, 2003, 2005). Of these, residency is less commonly employed. We control for it because one might expect judges to see nonresidents as having a greater risk of nonappearance than those with ties to the community. Indeed, in the research cited above, the residency of defendants was found to affect bail decisions.

Statistical Methods

The analysis proceeds in two steps. A test is used to ascertain if there is a statistically significant difference in mean bail amount set for Hispanic defendants relating to whether the counsel for the accused is a public defender or is privately retained. The second stage of analysis uses multiple regressions to assess the independent effect of type of counsel on bail amounts after controlling for the combined effects of the live independent variables available for the current study. To estimate the amount of variance explained, we employ the R^2 derived from the recession equation analysis.

 # Results

Bivariate Analysis

A test was used to determine if Hispanic defendants represented by public defenders were given bail amounts significantly different than the amount given to those represented by private counsel. The average bail set for the 21 defendants who used private counsel was $30,352, higher (by $9,622) than the average bail ($20,730) set for those 34 defendants who were represented by public defenders. This difference, however, was within sampling error ($t = 1,064, df = 53, p = .29$).

Multivariate Analysis

The second level of analysis is an additive OLS regression that controls for variables that might cause a difference

in outcome for the two groups (see Table 5.2). For example, if seriousness of offense affects bail amounts, and those accused of more serious offenses are more likely to use one type of attorney than the other, differences shown in the t test may actually be the result of offense seriousness rather than type of counsel. In this model, for the dummy variable of residence, Lancaster County residence is the comparison variable, and Type 4 felony (the least serious offenses) is the omitted category for the seriousness of offense dummy variable.

The model for these Hispanic defendants explains 39.8% of the variation in the amount set for their bails. However, as can be seen, though those represented by a public defender do receive higher bail amounts on average ($b = \$7830.98$), type of attorney does not significantly explain bail amounts when other variables are controlled ($p = .388$).

Rather than type of counsel, it is age, offense seriousness, and residence that significantly affect these bails. Those charged with the most serious crimes (Felony I) receive bail amounts on average $34,304.23 more than those charged with the least serious offenses

Table 5.2 Ordinary Least Squares Regression of Bail Amounts for Hispanic Defendants

	Unstandardized Coefficients	Significance	Tolerance
(Constant)	−1773.891	.941	
Age	1173.811	.021	.860
Sex (1 = *Male*)	−21428.465	.185	.835
Prior arrests	540.386	.654	.765
Felony 3	−13920.986	.170	.696
Felony 2	13658.900	.192	709
Felony 1	34304.228	.053	.580
Nebraska	−20133.561	.337	.644
Other state	38109.057	.010	.638
Transient	−3197.639	.800	.933
Type of counsel (1 = *Public Defender*)	7830.981 $R^2 = .398$	.388	.749

($p = .053$). Each year of age adds \$1,173.81 to the average bail. Finally, the average bail set for those from states other than Nebraska is \$38,109.06 higher than those given to defendants who reside in Lancaster County ($p = .010$); defendants residing in other residence categories were not significantly different in their bail amounts.

✎ Discussion

In a study completed by Harlow (2000), the researcher reported that minority inmates were more likely than Whites to have appointed counsel. Specifically, the study observed that though 69% of White inmates reported they had lawyers appointed by the court, 77% of Blacks and 73% of Hispanics had public defenders or assigned counsel (Harlow, 2000). This analysis shows that there is a difference in bail amount set for Hispanic defendants based on the type of legal counsel employed, privately retained or public defender. In the bivariate analysis, the results showed that the average bail set for those with private counsel was actually higher by \$9,622.00 than the average bail amount set for those represented by public defenders.

In the second stage of our analysis we employed an additive OLS regression controlling for several variables (age, sex, residence, offense, and prior arrests). With these variables controlled, Hispanic defendants utilizing the services of a public defender received higher bail amount (\$7830.98) as predicted. However, in the bivariate and multivariate analyses, type of attorney failed to reach statistical significance. The lack of significance finding could be because of the small sample size. In light of the small sample size and lack of statistical significance, it is plausible that, in fact, type of counsel makes no real difference when other variables are controlled, and that judges are not biased against Hispanic defendants using public defenders.

The OLS regression found that other variables, especially *age, residence,* and *offense seriousness,* did achieve statistical significance. Why the variables *age, residence,* and *offense seriousness* are significant is an interesting question. With respect

to the age variable, the analysis suggests that as defendants get 1 year older they on average pay \$1,173.81. Is it plausible that judges consider age, albeit an extralegal variable, important in the setting of bail (Bynum & Paternoster, 1994)? The rarely employed variable *residence* is worthy of comment. As alluded to earlier, judges may consider defendants living beyond the court's jurisdiction, particularly outside the state, a greater flight risk and therefore set higher bail amounts for this group. The belief by some judges that Hispanics present a greater flight risk has been examined by other researchers. For instance, Reaves and Perez (1994) investigated pretrial release and found failure to appear rates to be higher for Hispanics. Specifically, the researchers found the failure to appear rates to be 21% for White defendants, 27% for Black defendants, and 30% for Hispanic defendants. Therefore, judges set higher bail amounts for Hispanic defendants compared to other defendants. In the current research, this assumption has support as Hispanic defendants residing in states other than Nebraska, on average, have bail amounts set \$38,109.06 higher than Lancaster residents.

The final statistically significant variable, *offense seriousness,* according to Cohen and Klugel (1978, p. 149) and Liska and Tausig (1979, p. 200) is a "legal characteristic" and refers to offense-related attributes of the accused that have an official legal status in decision making. It is generally accepted that all else being equal, legal characteristics should have a causal connection to criminal justice outcomes such as the bail decision. The analysis revealed that Hispanic defendants charged with the most serious crimes (Felony I) received bail amounts that were on average \$34,304.23 more than those charged with the least serious offenses.

As the Hispanic population continues to grow in Nebraska and elsewhere, criminal justice experts and policy makers should be concerned about what will happen to the largest "minority" group as they increasingly become clients of the criminal justice system. The Census Bureau, as alluded to earlier, has predicted that Hispanics will be the largest minority group in the United States. It is plausible to believe that some members of this group will come into contact with the criminal justice system. It behooves officials associated with the criminal justice system to prepare for this eventuality.

It is hoped that the current study will generate interest among other researchers to conduct future research focusing on Hispanics as clients in the criminal justice system. Any future inquiries into differences in bail amount set for Hispanic defendants should utilize larger contemporary data sets. Nebraska's Hispanic population has increased such that there undoubtedly is a larger sample of Hispanic defendants in Lancaster County. Moreover, the inclusion of additional jurisdictions with varying proportions of Hispanic residents is strongly encouraged. Future researchers should also add to the control variables information concerning the defendant's demeanor, an assessment (albeit subjective) that is pertinent to the bail decision (Petee, 1994). Despite these limitations, we feel that the current study does add to the limited knowledge concerning Hispanics and criminal justice processing in general, and in particular the difference type of attorney makes on the judicial decision bail amount set for Hispanic defendants.

Notes

1. Lancaster County utilizes the public defender system for representation of indigent defendants.

2. Nebraska felony classifications and concomitant punishments for each: Class I: death; Class IA: life imprisonment; Class IB: maximum—life imprisonment, minimum—20 years imprisonment; Class IC: maximum—50 years imprisonment, mandatory minimum—5 years imprisonment; Class ID: maximum—50 years imprisonment, mandatory minimum—3 years imprisonment; Class II: maximum—50 years imprisonment, minimum—1 year imprisonment; Class III: maximum—20 years imprisonment, or U.S. $25,000 fine, or both, minimum—none; Class IV: maximum—5 years imprisonment, or $ 1,000 fine, or both, minimum—none (Revised Statutes of Nebraska Annotated, 1995).

References

Albonetti, C. (1989). An integration of theories to explain judicial discretion. *Social Problems, 38,* 247–266.

Ayres, I., & Waldfogel, J. (1994). A market test for race discrimination in bail setting. *Stanford Law Review, 46,* 987–1047.

Bynum, T. S. (1982). Release on recognizance: Substantive or superficial? *Criminology, 20,* 67–82.

Bynum, T. S., & Paternoster, R. (1994). Discrimination revisited: An exploration of frontstage and backstage criminal justice decision making. *Sociology and Research, 69,* 90–108.

Clarke, S. H., & Koch, G. G. (1976). The influence of income and other factors on whether criminal defendants go to prison. *Law and Society Review, 11,* 57–92.

Cohen, L. E., & Klugel, J. R. (1978). Determinants of juvenile court dispositions: Ascriptive and achievement factors in two metropolitan courts. *American Sociological Review, 43,* 162–176.

Coleman v Alabama, 399 U.S. I (1970).

Crew, K. B. (1991). Sex differences in criminal sentencing: Chivalry or patriarchy? *Justice Quarterly, 8,* 59–83.

Demuth, S., & Steffensmeier, D. (2004). The impact of gender and race-ethnicity in the pretrial release process. *Social Problems, 51,* 222–242.

Espiritu, Y. L. (1992). Panethnicity and U.S. racial politics: The Asian American case. In C. Calhoun & G. Ritzer (Eds.), *Racial politics: Introduction to social problems* (pp. 21–38). New York: McGraw-Hill.

Farnworth, M., Teske, R. H. C. Jr., & Thurman, G. (1991). Ethnic, racial, and minority disparity in felony court processing. In M. J. Lynch & E. B. Patterson (Eds.), *Race and criminal justice* (pp. 54–70). New York: Harrow and Heston.

Flowers, R. B. (1990). *Minorities and criminality.* Westport, CT: Greenwood.

Frazier, C. E., Bock, W., & Henretta, J. C. (1980). Pretrial release and bail decisions. *Criminology, 18,* 162–181.

Free, M. D. (2002). Racial bias and the American criminal justice system: Race and presentencing revisited. *Critical Criminology, 10,* 195–223.

Freed, D., & Wald, P. (1964) *Bail in the United States.* Washington, DC: U.S. Department of Justice and Vera Foundation.

Gideon v. Wainwright, 372 U S. 335 (1963).

Goldkamp, J. S. (1985). Danger and detention: A second generation of bail reform. *Journal of Criminal Law and Criminology, 76,* 1–74.

Goldkamp, J. S., & Gottfredson, M. (1979). Bail decision making and pretrial detention: Surfacing policy. *Law and Human Behavior, 3,* 227–249.

Hamilton, L. C. (1992). *Regression with graphics: A second course in applied statistics.* Pacific Grove, CA: Brooks/Cole.

Harlow, C. W. (2000). *Defense counsel in criminal cases* (Bureau of Justice Statistics bulletin special report). Washington, DC: Government Printing Office.

Healey, J. (1995). *Race, ethnicity, and class.* Thousand Oaks, CA: Pine Forge Press.

Ho, T. (1998). Images of crime and punishment: Vice crime and Asian Americans. In C. R. Mann & M. S. Zatz (Eds.), *Images of color; images of crime* (pp. 195–204). Los Angeles: Roxbury.

Holmes, M. D., Hosch, H. M., Daudistel, H. C., Perez, D. A., & Graves, J. B. (1996). Ethnicity, legal resources, and felony dispositions in two southwestern jurisdictions. *Justice Quarterly, 13,* 11–30.

Inciardi, J. A. (1984). *Criminal justice.* Orlando: Academic Press.

Katz, C., & Spohn, C. (1995). The effect of race and gender on bail outcomes: A test of an interactive model. *American Journal of Criminal Justice, 19,* 161–184.

Klotter, J. C., Kanovitz, J. R., & Kanovitz, M. I. (1999). *Constitutional law.* Cincinnati, OH: Anderson.

Liska, E. M., & Tausig, M. (1979). Theoretical interpretations of social class and racial differences in legal decision-making for juveniles. *Sociological Quarterly, 20,* 197–207.

Mann, C. R. (1993). *Unequal justice: A question of color.* Bloomington: Indiana University Press.

Mirande, A. (1987). *Gringo justice.* Notre Dame, IN: Notre Dame University Press.

Moore, J., & Pinderhughes, R. (1993). *In the barrios: Latinos and the underclass debate.* New York: Russell Sage Foundation.

Nagel, I. H. (1983). The legal/extralegal controversy: Judicial decisions in pretrial release. *Law and Society Review, 17,* 481–515.

National Minority Advisory Council on Criminal Justice. (1982). *The inequality of justice: A report on crime and the administration of justice in the minority community.* Washington, DC: U.S. Government Printing Office.

Nielsen, M. O. (1996). Contextualization for Native American crime and criminal justice involvement. In M. O. Nielsen & R. A. Silverman (Eds.), *Native Americans, crime, and justice* (pp. 10–19). Boulder, CO: Westview.

Ozzane, M. Q., Wilson, R. A., & Gedney, D. L. (1980). Toward a theory of bail risk. *Criminology, 18,* 147–161.

Patterson, E. B., & Lynch, M. J. (1991). Bias in formalized bail procedures. In M. J. Lynch & E. B. Patterson (Eds.), *Race and criminal justice* (pp. 36–53). New York: Harrow and Heston.

Petee, T. (1994). Recommended for release on recognizance: Factors affecting pretrial release recommendations. *Journal of Social Psychology, 134,* 327–335.

Powell v. Alabama. 287 US 45 (1932).

Rankin. A. (1964). The effect of pretrial detention. *New York University Law Review, 39,* 641–655.

Reeves, B., & Perez, J. (1994). *Pretrial release of felony defendants, 1992: National pretrial reporting program.* Retrieved February 6, 2006, from http://www.ojp.usjoj.gov/bjs/puh/ascii/nprp9

Revised Statutes of Nebraska Annotated. Chapter 28. Section 105 (1995).

Rhodes, W. (1985). *Pretrial release and misconduct.* Washington, DC: Bureau of Justice Statistics.

Rodriguez, C. E., & Cordero Guzman, H. (1992). Placing race in context. *Ethnic and Racial Studies, 15*(4), 523–542.

Schmalleger, F. (2001). *Criminal justice today: An introductory text for the 21st century.* Upper Saddle River, NJ: Prentice Hall.

Senna, J. J., & Siegal, L. (1996). *Introduction to criminal justice.* Minneapolis/St. Paul: West.

Strickland v. Washington, 466 U.S. 668 (1984).

Swigen, V., & Farell, R. A. (1991). Normal homicides and the law. *American Sociological Review, 42,* 24–25.

Turner, K. B., & Johnson, J. B. (2003). The effect of legal representation on bail decisions. *Criminal Law Bulletin, 39*(4), 426–444.

Turner, K. B., & Johnson, J. B. (2005). A comparison of bail amounts for Hispanics, Whites, and African Americans: A single county analysis. *American Journal of Criminal Justice, 30*(1), 35–53.

Turner, K. B., Secret, P. E., & Johnson, J. B. (2003). Race as a factor in the judicial decision of bail amount in a midwestern jurisdiction. *Journal of Ethnicity in Criminal Justice, 1*(3/4), 21–39.

Walker, S., Spohn, C., & DeLong, M. (2000). *The color of justice: Race, ethnicity, and crime in America.* Belmont, CA: Wadsworth.

U.S. Bureau of the Census. (2001). *Statistical abstract of the United States.* Washington, DC: Government Printing Office.

READING

This article examines an understudied aspect of judicial decision making: the pretrial release decision. Pretrial release is important because it has been strongly correlated with a final sentence of incarceration and deprives defendants of their freedom. This study examined whether race, gender, and age influence judges' decisions to detain or release a defendant prior to trial. The results indicate that females and younger defendants were less likely to be detained. When examining males and females separately, race was significant for females, with black females being the least likely to be detained. Younger and older white females were not significantly more likely to be detained than their black female counterparts.

SOURCE: Freiburger, T. L., & Hilinski, C. M. (2010). The impact of race, gender, and age on the pretrial decision. *Criminal Justice Review, 35*(3), 318–334.

The Impact of Race, Gender, and Age on the Pretrial Decision

Tina L. Freiburger and Carly M. Hilinski

The majority of sentencing literature has examined the final sentencing decision (i.e., the in/out decision) and the sentence length. Few studies have examined earlier decision-making points in the judicial system, such as the pretrial release outcome. Because of this, advancements in final sentencing literature have not extended to pretrial release research. Most notably, the examination of race, gender, and age interactions has not been examined in the pretrial release research. Using the focal concerns perspective, the current research addresses this gap by examining how race, gender, and age affect defendants' odds of pretrial detention.

Instead of focusing solely on race or gender, current sentencing research has carefully examined how courtroom experiences vary across different race and gender combinations. The development of the focal concerns perspective by Steffensmeier et al. (Steffensmeier, 1980; Steffensmeier, Kramer, & Streifel, 1993; Steffensmeier, Ulmer, & Kramer, 1998) has greatly contributed to this line of sentencing research. The focal concerns perspective is comprised of the three focal concerns of blameworthiness, dangerousness, and practical constraints. Blameworthiness is largely determined by the legal factors of offense severity and prior record. Dangerousness is determined by variables such as offense type (e.g., personal, property, or drug), use of a weapon, and education and employment status of the defendant. Practical constraints consist of factors that influence a defendant's ability to serve a period of incarceration, including organizational factors such as jail space and case flow as well as individual factors such as familial responsibilities (e.g., child care duties and marital status).

According to focal concerns theory, it is through these three focal concerns that judges make their sentencing decisions. However, when judges make sentencing decisions, they must often do so with limited information and with limited time and do not have access to all of the information included in each of the three focal concerns. Thus, the demographic characteristics of an offender are often used to shape the three focal concerns. Certain demographic combinations, specifically age, gender, and race, are especially influential, as judges tend to view younger minority males as more dangerous and more blameworthy leading to harsher sentences for these individuals (e.g., Spohn & Beichner, 2000; Steffensmeier & Demuth, 2006; Steffensmeier, Kramer, et al., 1993; Steffensmeier, Ulmer, et al., 1998). Current research examining these interactions has supported the focal concerns perspective. Specifically, this research has found that both Black and White females are treated more leniently than males (e.g., Freiburger & Hilinski, 2009; Steffensmeier & Demuth, 2006) and that Black males are sentenced more harshly than White males (e.g., Albonetti, 1997; Steffensmeier & Demuth, 2006; Steffensmeier, Ulmer, et al., 1998). Research specifically focusing on the treatment of females, however, has been more mixed, with some studies finding that Black females are treated more leniently than White females (e.g., Bickle & Peterson, 1991; Spohn & Beichner, 2000; Steffensmeier & Demuth, 2006) whereas others have found the opposite (Crawford, 2000; Steffensmeier, Ulmer, et al., 1998).

Prior sentencing studies also have found that age has varying impacts on the sentences of males and females and Black and White defendants (Steffensmeier, Ulmer, et al., 1998). The results here also are mixed, with several studies finding that young Black men are treated most harshly (Spohn & Holleran, 2000; Steffensmeier, Ulmer, et al., 1998) and others finding that middle-aged Black men are treated most harshly (Freiburger & Hilinski, 2009; Harrington & Spohn, 2007). Despite the numerous studies examining the impact of race, gender, and age on sentencing decisions, no studies have been conducted that examined the impact of gender, race, and age interactions on early court decisions. The current research fills this gap by examining how these three factors interact to affect the pretrial release decision.

Literature Review

The pretrial release decision is a crucial point in the judicial system. A common finding in the final sentencing research is that the pretrial release status of a defendant is significantly correlated with their likelihood of incarceration; offenders who are detained have a greater chance of receiving a sentence of incarceration (see Freiburger & Hilinski, 2009; Spohn & Beichner, 2000; Steffensmeier & Demuth, 2006). There is also less scrutiny on the pretrial release decision, which allows judges a great deal of discretion. This has led some researchers to argue that it might actually be subject to more bias in judicial decision making (Hagan, 1974; Steffensmeier, 1980). Pretrial detention can further negatively affect defendants' final sentences by hindering their ability to participate in the preparation of their defense (Foote, 1954). Despite these findings illustrating the importance and significance of the pretrial decision, few studies have been conducted to examine the factors that affect this decision.

Race and Pretrial Release

The majority of research examining the effects of race on pretrial release decisions has found that White defendants receive greater leniency at this stage than Black defendants (Demuth, 2003; Katz & Spohn, 1995). Demuth (2003) and Katz and Spohn (1995) found that Black defendants were less likely to be released than White defendants. Although these studies failed to find a significant relationship between race and bail amount for both White and Black defendants, Demuth found that Black defendants were less likely to make bail. Furthermore, Demuth also found that Black defendants were significantly more likely to be ordered to detention (denied bail). No race difference was found, however, for Black and White defendants' odds of receiving a nonfinancial release (release on recognizance [ROR]) rather than bail.

Other studies examining slightly different outcome measures also have produced evidence to suggest White defendants are granted greater leniency in pretrial release. Patterson and Lynch (1991) found that non-White defendants were less likely than White defendants to receive bail amounts that were lower than the amount recommended by bail guidelines. However, they also found that White and non-White defendants were equally likely to receive bail amounts that were more than the amount recommended by bail guidelines. Albonetti (1989) did not find a direct race effect, though she did find that White defendants were less likely to be detained if they had higher levels of educational attainment and a higher income. White defendants' outcomes, however, were more negatively affected by increases in the severity of the offense.

Gender and Pretrial Release

Few studies have been conducted that examine the effect of gender on pretrial release and outcome. Overall, the studies that have examined this relationship have found that females were treated more leniently than male defendants. Daly (1987b) and Kruttschnitt and Green (1984) found that females were less likely to be detained prior to trial. Additional studies have found that females were more likely to be granted a nonfinancial release (Nagel, 1983) and be assigned lower bail amounts (Kruttschnitt, 1984). Unfortunately, no recent studies were located that focused solely on the effect of gender on pretrial release.

Race-Gender-Age Effects and Pretrial Release

Only one study has examined the interactions of race/ ethnicity and gender. Demuth and Steffensmeier (2004) analyzed data from felony defendants in 75 of the most populous counties in state courts for the years 1990, 1992, 1994, and 1996. Their results indicated that race and gender significantly affected whether defendants were released prior to trial. More specifically, females were more likely to be released than males and White defendants were more likely to be released than Black and Hispanic defendants. Although females experienced leniency at every decision point (they were less likely to be detained due to failure to make bail or ordered to detention, more likely to secure nonfinancial release, and received lower bail), the findings for race were more mixed across the different decision points. Blacks were more likely to be detained than White defendants, but Black and White defendants were equally likely to be ordered to detention (not granted bail) and be given a nonfinancial release. Demuth and Steffensmeier (2004) also found that there was no difference in the amount of bail assigned to Black and White offenders. It appeared, therefore, that the race effect was due to Black defendants' failure to post bail.

When race and gender interactions were examined, female defendants were less likely to be detained than their male counterparts across all racial and ethnic groups. The gender gap, however, was the smallest for White defendants (followed by Black defendants and Hispanic defendants).

Using categorical gender/race variables, the results further indicated that White women were the least likely to be detained, followed by Black women, Hispanic women, White men, Black men, and Hispanic men.

We were not able to locate any studies that examined the interactions of race, gender, and age on pretrial release; however, prior sentencing studies have examined the interacting effects of these factors on the final sentencing decisions. The findings of these studies are mixed. Steffensmeier et al. (1998) found that young offenders were more likely to be sentenced to incarceration, with young Black males being treated the harshest. In their examination of sentencing decisions in Chicago, Miami, and Kansas City, Spohn and Holleran (2000) found that offenders aged 20–29 received the harshest sentences. When age and race were examined, they found that young and middle-aged Black males were more likely to be incarcerated than middle-aged White defendants. In Kansas City, young Black and White males had higher odds of incarceration than middle-aged White males.

Harrington and Spohn (2007) found that Black males in the middle age (30–39) category were less likely than White males of all age groups to be sentenced to probation versus jail. When the decision to sentence an offender to prison instead of jail was examined, however, the opposite was found. White males of all ages were more likely than middle-aged Black men to receive a prison sentence. Freiburger and Hilinski (2009) found that being young benefited White males but resulted in harsher sentences for Black males. Older Black males were only granted leniency in the decision to incarcerate in jail rather than prison. For Black females, age was not a significant predictor of sentencing. Young White women, however, were treated more leniently in the decision to sentence to probation or jail.

Previous studies that have examined the influence of race and gender on pretrial release decisions have failed to consider factors that are likely to influence release decisions. When judges make pretrial release decisions, they are typically concerned with the level of risk the offender poses to the community and the likelihood that the offender will return to court for future appearances (Goldkamp & Gottfredson, 1979). Although prior record and offense severity are important factors that judges consider in this stage, other factors such as marital status, education, community ties, and employment also are used to assess these concerns (Goldkamp & Gottfredson, 1979; Nagel, 1983; Petee, 1994; Walker, 1993). In addition, the focal concerns perspective notes these factors as influential to the focal concern of dangerousness (Steffensmeier, Ulmer, et al., 1998). The only previous study that examined race and gender interactions (Demuth & Steffensmeier, 2004) did not assess the impact of these important factors. Additionally, no studies have examined the interactions of race, gender, and age on the pretrial release decision despite the fact that judges are differently influenced by these various combinations. Thus, the current study builds on the previous research by examining the effect of race, gender, and age interactions on pretrial release outcomes while considering other factors (e.g. income, education, and marital status) that have been linked to the pretrial release decision and the focal concerns perspective.

Methods

The current study examined the effects of race, gender, and age on the pretrial detention outcomes of felony offenders in an urban county in Michigan. The data analyzed contains information collected from presentence investigation reports completed for all offenders convicted of a personal, drug, property, or public order offense in the county during 2006. The original data set contained 3,316 offenders. We removed defendants who were Hispanic or of another ethnicity *(N = 73)* from the data set because a meaningful analysis was not possible with such a small number of cases; cases that were missing important information pertaining to offense severity level and prior record level *(N = 608)* also were removed from

the data set because it is necessary to include these variables in sentencing research.[1] Thus, the final data set contained 2,635 cases.

Dependent Variable

The dependent variable in the current study was a dichotomized measure of the actual pretrial outcome, with 0 representing defendants released prior to sentencing and 1 representing those detained prior to sentencing. Coding for this variable, and all independent variables, is included in Table 5.3. Although we agree with prior research that argues that the pretrial release is best assessed through the examination of both the judicial decision and the actual outcome (see arguments by Demuth, 2003 and Demuth & Steffensmeier,

Table 5.3 Description of Variables

Independent Variable	Description
Individual characteristics	
Age	Separate dummy variables for ages 15–29, 30–39, and 40+; age 30–39 is the reference category
Race	Black =1, White = 0
Gender	Male =1, Female = 0
Marital status	Married = 1, Female = 0
High school (HS)	HS diploma/GED = 1, No HS diploma/GED = 0
Income over $75/ month	Income over $75/month = 1, income less than $75/month = 0
Assets over $ 1,500	Assets over $1,500 = 1, assets < $1,500 = 0
Case characteristics	
Prior record variable (PRV)	7-category scale (1 = least serious, 7 = most serious[a])
Offense variable (OV)	6-category scale (1 = least serious, 6 = most serious)
Type of conviction charge	Separate dummy variables for property offense, public order offense, personal offense, and drug offense, personal offense is the reference category
CJS supervision	CJS supervision (probation, parole incarceration) = 1, no CJS supervision = 0
Dependent variable	
Pretrial detention	Detention = 1, Release = 0

NOTE: CJS = Criminal Justice System supervision.

a. None of the cases in the current data set had a prior record score of 7.

2004), the current data only allows for the assessment of the actual pretrial outcome (whether the defendant was detained or released). This is considered a limitation of the current study; however, the pretrial outcome is the most telling of the decision points. It signifies the actual experience of the defendant by considering the consequences of pretrial detention (e.g., reduced ability to prepare defense and severed social ties due to incarceration). Despite this limitation, the ability to assess race, gender, and age interactions while including other facts relevant to pretrial release contributes substantially to the current literature.

Independent Variables

Several legal variables shown to be relevant in sentencing decisions were included in the analysis. The Michigan Statutory Sentencing Guideline's 6-point offense severity measure was used to control for the seriousness of the crime.[2] The state guideline 7-point measure of prior record also was used.[3] The analysis also controlled for offense type through four separate dummy variables (property, drug, personal, and public order offense), with personal crimes left out as the reference category. A dummy variable also was included for current criminal justice supervision. Those who were on probation, parole, or incarcerated at the time of the bail decision were considered under criminal justice supervision and were coded as 1.[4]

The main extralegal variables of interest (gender, race, and age) also were included in the analysis. Gender was included and coded as 0 for female and 1 for male and race was coded as 0 for White and 1 for Black. Because age was found to have a curvilinear effect on pretrial detention, it was entered into the models as three categorical variables. Similar to prior research (Freiburger & Hilinski, 2009; Harrington & Spohn, 2007), the three age categories created were 15–29, 30–39, and 40+ years, with 30–39 being left out of the analysis as the reference variable. Several other variables that measured defendants' stability in the community also were included in the models. These variables also were important in assessing the focal concerns perspective as these factors have been theorized by Steffensmeier and colleagues (Steffensmeier, 1980; Steffensmeier, Kramer, et al., 1993; Steffensmeier, Ulmer, et al., 1998) to affect judges' perceptions of dangerousness. None of the defendants in the sample had a college education; therefore, education was entered as a dichotomous variable of high school education or General Education Diploma (GED) coded as 1 or no high school education coded 0. Marital status also was included as a dummy variable; those who were not married were coded as 0 and those who were married were coded as 1. A direct employment measure was not available; however, two income variables were recorded in the presentence investigation (PSI) reports and were included in the analysis. The first assessed whether the defendant had an income of $75 or more a month (0 = no income above $75 and 1 = income above $75). The second variable indicated whether the defendant had assets of $1,500 or more (0 = no assets totaling $1,500 and 1 = assets totaling $1,500 or more).

Results

The individual and case characteristics of the offenders included in the current research are presented in Table 5.4. The majority of both male and female offenders were 15–29 years of age. Both male and female offenders were more likely to be White, unmarried, and without a high school diploma. Further examination of the descriptive statistics reveals that over half of the females had a monthly income over $75 but less than 40% of the males earned more than $75 per month. Across both males and females, only about 15% had assets that were worth $1,500 or more. Case characteristics reveal that male offenders were charged most often with a personal offense, but female offenders were most often charged with a property offense. Males were also more likely to be under some form of criminal justice supervision at the time of the current offense. Finally, both men and women were more likely to be released prior to trial.

We estimated the effect of race, gender, and age on pretrial release using logistic regression models. First the effects of race, gender, and age were examined separately. The models were then split by gender and race;

Table 5.4 Descriptive Statistics

	Total (n = 2635)		Males (n = 2187)		Females (n = 448)	
	n	Percentage	n	Percentage	n	Percentage
Individual characteristics						
Age 15–29	1,397	53.0	1,184	54.1	213	47.5
Age 30–39	597	22.7	480	21.9	117	26.1
Age 40+	641	24.3	523	23.9	118	26.3
Race						
White	1,421	53.9	1,139	52.1	282	62.9
Black	1,214	46.1	1,048	47.9	166	37.1
Gender						
Male	2,187	83.0	—	—	—	—
Female	448	17.0	—	—	—	—
Marital status						
Married	289	11.0	237	10.8	52	11.6
Not married	2,346	89.0	1,950	89.2	396	88.4
High school (HS)						
HS diploma/GED	1,277	48.5	1,070	48.8	207	46.2
No HS diploma/GED	1,358	51.5	1,117	51.1	241	53.8
Income over $75/month						
Yes	1,081	41.0	835	38.2	246	54.9
No	1,554	59.0	1,352	61.8	202	45.1
Assets over $1500						
Yes	382	14.5	314	14.4	68	15.2
No	2,253	85.5	1,873	85.6	360	84.8
Case characteristics						
Prior record						
1	431	16.4	322	14.7	109	24.3
2	369	14.0	278	12.7	91	20.3
3	571	21.7	469	21.4	102	22.8
4	613	23.3	525	24.0	88	19.6
5	370	14.0	323	14.8	47	10.5
6	281	10.7	270	12.3	11	2.5
Offense severity						
1	1.323	50.2	1,081	49.4	242	54.0
2	812	30.8	672	30.7	140	31.3

	Total (n = 2635)		Males (n = 2187)		Females (n = 448)	
	n	Percentage	n	Percentage	n	Percentage
3	298	11.3	245	11.2	53	11.8
4	98	3.7	88	4.0	10	2.2
5	70	2.7	69	3.2	1	0.2
6	34	1.3	32	1.5	2	0.4
Conviction charge						
Property offense	805	30.6	580	26.5	225	50.2
Public order offense	190	7.2	140	6.4	50	11.2
Personal offense	963	36.5	871	39.8	92	20.5
Drug offense	677	25.7	596	27.3	81	18.1
CJS supervision						
Supervision	912	34.6	774	64.6	138	30.8
No supervision	1,723	65.4	1,413	35.4	310	69.2
Pretrial detention						
Detained	960	36.4	866	39.6	94	21.0
Not detained	1,675	63.6	1,321	60.4	354	79.0

z scores also were calculated to determine whether the independent variables had a significantly different effect on the pretrial outcome for male and female and Black and White defendants. The final models contain categorical variables for gender and race and categorical variables for race, gender, and age combinations.

The logistic regression coefficients for pretrial detention are presented in Table 5.5. Four models are presented. The first model presented displays the effects of age, race, and gender without the inclusion of any other independent variables. In this model, gender, race, and both age variables are significant. The variable for gender indicates males have a significantly greater likelihood of being detained than females $(b = .909, p < .01)$. Black defendants had a significantly greater likelihood of detention than White defendants $(b = .253, p < .01)$. The age variables show that young defendants $(b = -.467, p < .01)$ and older defendants $(b = .371, p < .01)$ were less likely to be detained than offenders 30–39. Model 2 shows the coefficients after the income variables are controlled. Although the gender $(b = .832, p < .01)$ and age (15–29, $b = -.664, p < .01$; 40–above, $b = -.254, p < .05$)

variables remain significant, race is no longer significant $(b = .010, p = .910)$. When the legal variables are added in Model 3, the gender, age, and income variables remain significant. Race, however, is not significant. Therefore, it appears that the initial effect of race was due in part to differences in the financial capabilities of Black and White defendants.

The full model also is presented in Table 5.5 and contains all of the independent variables. As shown in the table, males were significantly more likely to remain detained than females $(b = .565, p < .01)$; however, the coefficient for race was not significant. Young defendants $(b = -.422, p < .01)$ and older defendants $(b = -.253, p < .01)$ were less likely to be detained than defendants in the middle age category. Completing high school or obtaining a GED further resulted in a lower likelihood of being detained $(b = -.287, p < .01)$. Both income variables also were significant, indicating that defendants with an income over $75 a month $(b = -1.072, p < 01)$ and assets exceeding $1,500 $(b = -.970, p < .01)$ were less likely to be detained.

In an attempt to garner a better understanding of the differences in the detention status of male and

Table 5.5 Logistic Regression Estimates

Variable	Model 1 B	Model 1 SE	Model 1 Exp(B)	Model 2 B	Model 2 SE	Model 2 Exp(B)	Model 3 B	Model 3 SE	Model 3 Exp(B)	Full Model B	Full Model SE	Full Model Exp(B)
Offender characteristics												
Age 15–29	−.467**	.102	.627	−.664**	.110	.515	−.341**	.122	.711	−.422**	.125	.656
Age 40+	−.371**	.119	.690	−.254*	.128	.776	−.259*	.139	.772	−.253**	.139	.776
Race (Black = 1)	.253**	.083	1.288	.010	.089	1.010	−.172	.102	.842	−.184	.102	.832
Gender (male = 1)	.909**	-.125	2.482	.832**	.132	2.297	.533**	.146	1.705	.565**	.147	1.760
Marital status										−.270	.175	.764
High school										−.287**	.099	.750
Income over $75				−1.292**	.097	.275	−1.087**	.104	.337	−1.072**	.104	.342
Assets over $1,500				−1.255**	.164	.285	−1.056**	.176	.348	−.970**	.179	.379
Case characteristics												
Prior record							.456**	.039	1.578	.461**	.039	1.585
Offense severity							.194**	.048	1.214	.202**	.049	1.224
Property offense							−.542**	.126	.582	−.531**	.126	.588
Public order offense							−.276	.201	.758	−.266	.202	.588
Drug offense							−.530**	.134	.589	−.527**	.135	.590
CJS supervision							.733**	.103	2.082	.745**	.104	2.107
Constant	−1.116***	.138	.328	−.258*	.151	.773	−2.127***	.246	.119	-2.007**	.249	.134
Nagelkerke R^2	.046						.344			.348		
Cox and Snell R^2	.034						.251			.254		

Significance: $*p < .05$; $**p < .01$.

female defendants, we estimated split models to determine whether the same factors influenced the pretrial status of both groups. The z scores also were calculated (using the formula[5] by Paternoster, Brame, Mazerolle, & Piquero, 1998) to determine whether the coefficients had significantly different impacts on pretrial detention for males and females. The results of this analysis are presented in Table 5.6. Examination of the female model shows that race was significant in the pretrial status for females with Black female defendants having a reduced odds of being detained compared to White females ($b = -.979, p < .01$). Race did not, however, significantly affect the pretrial release status of males. The z score for race also was significant, indicating that the effect of race was significantly stronger for females than males. The coefficients for age indicate that young males were significantly less likely to be detained than males aged 30–39. Neither the age coefficient for females nor the z score for females was significant. Thus, the impact of age was not significantly different for males and females.

Table 5.6   Female and Male Split Models

Variable	Females			Males			Z score
	B	**SE**	**Exp(B)**	**B**	**SE**	**Exp(B)**	
Offender characteristics							
Age 15–29	−.072	.358	.931	−.461**	.135	.631	1.02
Age 40+	−.198	.377	.820	−.243	.151	.784	0.11
Race (Black = 1)	−.979**	.331	.376	−.090	.110	.913	2.55*
Marital status	−.854	.576	.426	−.191	.187	..826	1.09
High school	.137	.302	1.146	−.310**	.106	.733	1.40
Income over $75	−.898**	.296	.407	−1.072**	.112	.342	0.55
Assets over $1500	−.737	.589	.479	−.981**	.190	.375	0.39
Case characteristics							
Prior record	.716**	.139	2.047	.435**	.041	1.545	1.94
Offense severity	−.234	.206	.791	.234**	.051	1.264	2.21*
Property offense	−1.531**	.392	.216	−.379	.135	.685	2.78*
Public order offense	−.223	.4485	.800	−.553*	.237	.576	0.61
Drug offense	−1.556**	.512	.211	−.452**	.140	.636	2.08*
CJS supervision	.955	.313	2.598	.723**	.111	2.061	0.70
Constant	−1.811*	.728	.163	−1.465	.241	.231	
Nagelkerke R^2	.423			.308			
Cox and Snell R^2	.272			.229			

$*p < .05; **p < .01.$

Further examination of the split models indicates that males ($b = .435, p < .01$) and females ($b = .716, p < .01$) had an increased odds of detention with each increase in prior record severity. The z score reveals that prior record did not have a significantly greater impact on the pretrial release of males than females; however, it came very close to reaching significance ($z = 1.94$). Severity of offense, conversely, was significant for males ($b = .234, p < .01$) but not for females. The z score reveals that the difference was significant for males and females, with offense severity more strongly affecting males' pretrial detention status. Committing a property crime (compared to committing a personal crime) resulted in a decreased likelihood of being detained for females ($b = 1.531, p < .01$) but not for males. The z score was significant, indicating that the differing effect was significant. The coefficient for drug offense was significant for both males ($b = −.452, p < .01$) and females ($b = −1.556, p < .01$). The z score also was significant, suggesting that committing a drug offense had a stronger impact for females than for males.

In the race split models, presented in Table 5.7, the z scores indicate that gender and criminal justice supervision were the only factors that had a significantly different impact for Black and White defendants. The z score was significant for gender showing a stronger

Table 5.7   Black and White Split Models

Variable	Black			White			Z score
	B	SE	Exp(B)	B	SE	Exp(B)	
Offender characteristics							
Age 15–29	−.442*	.188	.643	−.445**	.172	.641	0.01
Age 40+	−.240	.201	.787	−.237	.195	.789	0.01
Gender (Male = 1)	.971**	.256	2.640	.307	.183	1.359	2.11*
Marital status	−.350	.267	.705	−.166	.234	.847	0.52
High school	−.297*	.144	.743	−.294	.138	.745	0.02
Income over $75	−.873**	.152	.418	−1.257**	.145	.284	1.83
Assets over $1500	−.960**	.361	.383	−.924**	.210	.397	0.09
Case characteristics							
Prior record	.417**	.058	1.264	.520**	.054	1.683	1.30
Offense severity	−.234	.075	.533	.180**	.065	1.198	0.54
Property offense	−.628**	.197	.623	−.474**	.167	.623	0.60
Public order offense	−.473	.178	.523	−.762*	.222	.467	1.02
Drug offense	.647	.350	2.675	−.086	.252	.918	1.30
CJS supervision	.984**	.147	1.517	.454**	.149	1.575	2.53*
Constant	−2.558**	.396	.077	−1.781**	.328	.169	
Nagelkerke R^2	.334			.366			
Cox and Snell R^2	.247			.264			

$*p < .05; **p < .01.$

effect for Black defendants ($b = .971, p < .01$) than for White defendants. Criminal justice supervision also had a stronger effect on pretrial detention for Black defendants ($b = .984, p < .01$) than for White defendants ($b = .454, p < .01$). The effects of age did not vary significantly by race; both young Black ($b = −.442, p < .05$) and young White defendants ($b = −.445, p < .01$) had equally significant decreased odds of incarceration.

We also created race and gender categorical variables to compare the treatment of Black females, White females, Black males, and White males, presented in Table 5.8. With Black males left out as the reference

group, the results indicate that Black females were significantly less likely to be detained ($b = −1.004, p < .01$) compared to Black males. The coefficients for White males and White females, however, did not reach statistical significance. When Black females were left out as the reference variable (coefficients not shown but available from the first author upon request), all coefficients were significant (White female, $b = .780, p < .01$; Black male $b = 1.004, p < .01$; White male $b = 1.105, p < .01$). Therefore, it appears that Black females were the least likely to be detained, followed by White females, Black males, and White males. When comparing defendants

Table 5.8 **Table 5.8**   Logistic Regression Estimates Using Race × Gender and Race × Gender × Age Interaction Terms

Variables	B	SE	Exp(B)
Race × gender			
Black male[a]			
White male	.101	.109	1.107
Black female	−1.004**	.253	.098
White female	−.224	.184	.799
Race × gender × age			
Black male 30–39[a]			
Black female 15–29	−1.096**	.409	.334
Black female 30–39	−1.432**	.444	.239
Black female 40+	−1.281**	.471	.278
White female 15–29	−.764**	.295	.466
White female 30–39	−.091**	.334	.913
White female 40+	−.570	.364	.566
Black male 15–29	−.455*	.187	.635
Black male 40+	−.342	.213	.710
White male 15–29	−.377*	.192	.686
White male 30–39	.044	.223	1.045
White male 40+	−.124	.219	.883

a. Reference variable.

*$p < .05$; **$p < .01$.

in the other groups to each other (leaving out White females and White males), none of the groups had significantly different odds of detention.

When categorical variables for gender, race, and age were examined with 30–39-year-old Black males left out as the reference variable (coefficients presented in Table 5.8), the results indicate that Black females in all age categories (15–29, $b = -1.096$, $p < .01$; 30–39, $b = 1.432, p < .01$; 40 and over, $b = -1.281, p < .01$) were less likely to be detained. For White females, only those in the young ($b = -.764$, $p < .01$) and middle-aged group ($b = .091, p < .01$) were significantly less likely to

be detained compared to middle-aged Black men. For male offenders, only young Black ($b = -.455, p < .05$) and young White males ($b = -.377, p < .05$) were significantly less likely to be incarcerated than middle-aged Black men.

The coefficients were reanalyzed in several different models with a different age/gender/race group left out each time, allowing for comprehensive comparisons of all groups (coefficients not shown but are available from the first author upon request). The results suggested that those in the 30–39-year age category were significantly more likely to be detained than their younger counterparts (15–29) for all groups except Black females. In fact, Black females in the middle age category were the least likely to be detained, followed by older Black females and young Black females (none of the differences between these groups were significant). White females 30–39 also were less likely to be detained than Black males 30–39; however, no difference was found for White males and females of the same age group. The only other significant difference found between the age/race gender categories was that White males in the middle age category were more likely to be detained than older White females.

Discussion

The current study attempted to further the understanding of the effects of race, gender, and age on pretrial release outcomes. Given the logic of the focal concerns perspective (Steffensmeier, 1980; Steffensmeier, Kramer, et al., 1993; Steffensmeier, Ulmer, et al., 1998), it is not surprising that gender and age directly affect pretrial outcomes as females and young defendants are often viewed as less blameworthy and dangerous. The findings for race, however, were more complex. A strong race effect was found prior to entering the economic variables into the model, with Black defendants less likely to be released pretrial than Whites. Once these variables were included, however, race was no longer significant. In fact, the sign of the coefficient changed, suggesting Whites were actually more likely to be detained. Therefore, it appears that Black defendants are more likely to be detained because they do not have the financial means necessary to secure release. This indicates that Black disadvantage in the court system may not be as simple as racial bias, but instead stems from inequality and general disadvantage in society. This is especially noteworthy because prior studies on pretrial release have not included these variables (e.g., Demuth & Steffensmeier, 2004).

The effect of race was significant, however, when examining the sentences of men and women separately. Consistent with prior research conducted by Demuth and Steffensmeier (2004), the results also indicated that the gender gap was the smallest for White defendants. Unlike Demuth and Steffensmeier, however, White females were not most likely to be released pretrial. Instead, Black females were the least likely to be detained. This finding held across Black females of every age group. The odds of release for White women, however, were not significantly different than that of White and Black males. Although Black females were less likely to be detained than White females, the age/race/gender analysis showed that this finding was only applicable to White females aged 30–39. Younger and older White females were not significantly more likely to be detained than their Black female counterparts. When compared to males (both Black and White), however, Black females of all age groups were the least likely to be detained.

Although these findings seem inconsistent with the focal concerns perspective, it is possible that this inconsistency is actually due to the absence of practical constraint factors. Steffensmeier and colleagues (Steffensmeier, 1980; Steffensmeier, Kramer, et al., 1993; Steffensmeier, Ulmer, et al., 1998) suggest that defendants whose incarceration poses a greater practical constraint (e.g., leaving behind dependent children that will require care, need correctional facilities that are not available) will be granted leniency. It is possible, therefore, that the inclusion of family responsibility variables might account for the increased odds of Black females being released. Daly (1987a) suggests that judges are concerned with the social costs of incarcerating defendants who perform vital familial responsibilities. This is especially pertinent, given that more Black women in the criminal justice system are often single parents to dependent children (U.S. Bureau of the Census, 2000). Furthermore, prior research on the effect of gender on pretrial release has shown that the inclusion of these controls reduces the gender gap (Daly, 1987b; Kruttschnitt & Green, 1984). Unfortunately, the data used for the current study had a great deal of missing data for the measure of dependent children, making it impossible to assess this possibility.

The gender split models also show that judges give less consideration to legal factors for females than for men. This might indicate that judges find males with more serious offenses as posing a greater risk to society. Therefore, it is possible that legal factors play less of a role in shaping the focal concerns associated with early court decisions for women than they do for men. This finding indicates a need for additional studies that closely examine the different factors that affect males' and females' sentencing decisions. It is possible that judges' focal concerns for males and females are influenced by different factors. The inconsistencies across research studies also question the ability to generalize these findings and signify a need for future research that examines the impact of race, gender, and age on sentencing decisions in other jurisdictions.

Overall, the current study has made an important contribution to the literature examining the factors affecting the pretrial decision. Most notably, it is the only study to date that has examined the effect of race, gender, and age interactions on the pretrial release outcome of defendants while also considering extralegal factors, including income, educational attainment, and marital status. The current study is limited, however, in its examination of only one jurisdiction. Although this is not uncommon in the sentencing literature, it does pose as a limitation as findings may vary across location. This study also is limited in its ability to measure the focal concern of practical constraint. It is likely that individual practical constraints (e.g., familial responsibility) as well as organization constraints (e.g., available jail space) could have an effect on pretrial detention. Additionally, these constraints may have varying effects by race, gender, and age of the defendant.

Future research should assess the impacts of race after controlling for economic factors on a more comprehensive set of dependent variables (e.g., ROR or bail, bail amount, ability to make bail). This is especially important given the finding that the race effect was eliminated once economic variables were included in the analysis. In addition, Demuth (2003) found that Black defendants were less likely to post bail than White defendants. If a more comprehensive dependent variable is assessed, it can be determined whether the Black disadvantage is due to a difference in bail amounts. In other words, are Black defendants receiving higher bail amounts or are Blacks simply more often than Whites in situations where they cannot afford to pay bail? The ability to examine a dependent variable of this nature would greatly contribute to the understanding of the effect of race on the pretrial release.

Independent Variable	Pearson Chi-Square
Age 15–29	15.357**
Age 30–39	1.333
Age 40+	12.249**
Race	4.437**
Gender	.156
Marital status	1.105
High school	20.071**
Income	11.720**
Assets	25.536**
Property offense	.909
Public order offense	.558
Personal offense	.130
Drug offense	1.128
CJS supervision	113.839**

$*p < .05; **p < .01.$

Notes

1. Significance tests performed to determine whether any differences existed between the cases excluded from the data set due to missing data and the cases included in the final analysis indicated that there were some significant differences between the two groups (presented in the table here). Two age groups, ages 15–29 and 40+, were significantly different across the two groups: race also was significantly different across the two groups. An examination of the remaining independent variables reveals that cases excluded due to missing information were less likely to have a high school diploma or GED, less likely to have a monthly income of $75 or more, and less likely to have assets of more than $1,500. They were also less likely to be under criminal justice system supervision at the time of their arrest and more likely to be detained prior to trial. Although the missing data poses a limitation to the research, it is not unique to this study; most sentencing literature is limited in the amount of usable data. For instance, Harrington and Spohn (2007) were only able to use 59% of the cases in their original data set and Freiburger and Hilinski (2009) were only able to use 62.4% of the cases in their original data set. In the current study, nearly 80% of the cases in the original data set were able to be included in the final analysis.

2. The Michigan Statutory Sentencing Guidelines assigns an offense variable (OV) to each offense. There are 19 possible offense variables that can be scored, including aggravated use of a weapon, physical or psychological injury to the victim, victim asportation or captivity, and criminal sexual penetration; the sentencing guidelines stipulate which variables will be scored based on the crime group of the current offense (e.g., crimes against a person, crimes against property, and crimes involving a controlled substance). Based on the crime group, each relevant variable is scored and then combined to create a total offense variable that ranges from 1 (least serious) to 6 (most serious) (Michigan Judicial Institute, 2007). This offense variable (coded 1–6) was included in each model to control for the severity of the offense.

3. The prior record variable is a composite score based on factors such as prior adult felony and misdemeanor convictions, prior juvenile felony and misdemeanor adjudications, and the offender's relationship with the criminal justice system at the time of the current offense (i.e., whether the offender is a probationer or parolee). For each of the seven prior record variables, a numerical score is assigned. The sum of these seven scores determines the offender's prior record level, which ranges from A (least serious) to F (most serious; Michigan Judicial Institute, 2007).

This variable was recoded and included in the models (coded 1–6) to control for prior record.

4. Although it is likely that those who are incarcerated are more likely to be detained pretrial than those on probation or parole, only seven offenders in the sample were actually incarcerated in jail or in prison. Due to the small number, it was impossible to meaningfully assess this difference; therefore, they were combined with those on probation and parole.

5. $$\frac{b_1 - b_2}{\sqrt{(se_1)^2 + (se_2)^2}}$$

 # References

Albonetti, C. A. (1989). Bail and judicial discretion in the District of Columbia. *Sociology and Social Research, 74,* 40–47.

Albonetti, C. A. (1997). Sentencing under the federal sentencing guidelines: Effects of defendant characteristics, guilty pleas and departures on sentencing outcomes for drug offenses, 1991–1992. *Law and Society Review, 31,* 789–822.

Bickle, G. S., & Peterson, R. D. (1991). The impact of gender-based family roles on criminal sentencing. *Social Problems, 38,* 372–394.

Crawford, C. (2000). Gender, race, and habitual offender sentencing in Florida. *Criminology, 38,* 263–280.

Daly, K. (1987a). Structure and practice of familial-based justice in a criminal court. *Law & Society Review, 21,* 267–290.

Daly, K. (1987b). Discrimination in the criminal courts: Family, gender, and the problem of equal treatment. *Social Forces, 66,* 152–175.

Demuth, S. (2003). Racial and ethnic differences in pretrial release decisions and outcomes: A comparison of Hispanic, Black and White felony arrestees. *Criminology, 41,* 873–907.

Demuth, S., & Steffensmeier, D. (2004). The impact of gender and race-ethnicity in the pretrial release process. *Social Problems, 51,* 222–242.

Foote, C. (1954). *Compelling appearance in court: Administration of bail in Philadelphia.* Philadelphia: Temple University Press.

Freiburger, T. L., & Hilinski, C. M. (24 February, 2009). An examination of the interactions of race and gender on sentencing decisions using a trichotomous dependent variable. *Crime & Delinquency,* DOI: 10.1177/ 0011128708330178.

Goldkamp, J. S., & Gottfredson, M. R. (1979). Bail decision making and pretrial detention: Surfacing judicial policy. *Law and Human Behavior, 3,* 227–249.

Hagan, J. (1974). Extra-legal attributes and criminal sentencing: An assessment of a sociological viewpoint. *Law and Society Review, 8,* 337–383.

Harrington, M. P., & Spohn, C. (2007). Defining sentence type: Further evidence against use of the total incarceration variable. *Journal of Research in Crime and Delinquency, 44,* 36–63.

Katz, C., & Spohn, C. (1995). The effect of race and gender on bail outcomes: Test of an interactive model. *American Journal of Criminal Justice, 19,* 161–184.

Kruttschnitt, C. (1984). Sex and criminal court dispositions: An unresolved controversy. *Journal of Research in Crime and Delinquency, 12*(3), 213–232.

Kruttschnitt, C., & Green, D. E. (1984). The sex-sanctioning issue: Is it history? *American Sociology Review, 49,* 541–551.

Mertler, C., & Vannata, R. (2002). *Advanced and multivariate statistical methods* (2nd ed.). Los Angeles: Pyrezak.

Michigan Judicial Institute. (2007). *Sentencing guidelines manual.* Retrieved from http://courts.michigan.gov/mji/resources/sentencing-guidelines/sg.htm#srdanaly

Nagel, I. (1983). The legal/extra-legal controversy: Judicial decision in pretrial release. *Law and Society Review, 17,* 481–515.

Paternoster, R., Brame, R., Mazerolle, P., & Piquero, A. (1998). Using the correct statistical test for the quality of regression coefficients. *Criminology, 36,* 859–866.

Patterson, E., & Lynch, M. (1991). The biases of bail: Race effects on bail decisions. In M. J. Lynch & E. Brill Patterson (Eds.), *Race and criminal justice.* New York: Harrow and Heston.

Petee, T. A. (1994). Recommended for release on recognizance. Factors affecting pretrial release recommendations. *Journal of Social Psychology, 134,* 375–382.

Spohn, C., & Beichner, D. (2000). Is preferential treatment of felony offenders a thing of the past? A multisite study of gender, race, and imprisonment. *Criminal Justice Policy Review, 11,* 149–184.

Spohn, C., & Holleran, D. (2000). The imprisonment penalty paid by young unemployed black and Hispanic male offenders. *Criminology, 38,* 281–306.

Steffensmeier, D. (1980). Assessing the impact of the women's movement on sex-based differences in the handling of adult criminal defendants. *Crime & Delinquency, 26,* 344–358.

Steffensmeier, D., & Demuth, S. (2006). Does gender modify the effects of race-ethnicity on criminal sanctions? Sentences for male and female, White, Black, and Hispanic defendants. *Journal of Quantitative Criminology, 22,* 241–261.

Steffensmeier, D., Kramer, J., & Streifel, C. (1993). Gender and imprisonment decisions. *Criminology, 31,* 411–446.

Steffensmeier, D., Ulmer, J., & Kramer, J. (1998). The interaction of race, gender, and age in criminal sentencing: The punishment cost of being young, black, and male. *Criminology, 36,* 763–797.

U.S. Bureau of the Census. (2003). *2000 census of the population.* Washington, DC: U.S. Government Printing Office. Available from http://www.factfinder.census.gov

Walker, S. (1993). *Taming the system: The control of discretion in criminal justice, 1950–1990.* New York: Oxford University Press.

READING

Relatively few studies have examined the legal and extralegal factors that influence prosecutorial and judicial decision making in cases of domestic violence. Among the few studies available in the extant literature, none have looked at the full range of decisions made during the adjudication process (i.e., pretrial release, prosecution, disposition, and sentencing). Similarly, few of the available studies have included female defendants, despite recent increases in the number of women charged with this offense. This article identifies the suspect and offense characteristics that have the greatest effect on court decisions. Explanations for the resulting findings and recommendations for further research are discussed.

Criminal Prosecution of Domestic Violence Offenses

An Investigation of Factors Predictive of Court Outcomes

Kris Henning and Lynette Feder

During the past two decades, mandatory arrest (i.e., arrest based on the presumption of guilt) has become the preferred law enforcement response to domestic violence (Fagan, 1996). Most of the research on this policy shows that it has increased the number of cases brought into the criminal justice system (Mignon & Holmes, 1995; Victim Services Agency, 1989). More debatable is whether these arrests lead to a decreased likelihood that offenders will engage in subsequent domestic violence incidents (Maxwell, Garner, & Fagan, 2001). To be fair, arrest is but one decision point in the criminal justice system. A coordinated criminal justice system whereby offenders are arrested, prosecuted, and upon conviction, sentenced would provide a better test of the law's ability to deter domestic violence (Tolman & Weisz, 1995). Comparatively few studies are available, however, to

describe what happens to domestic violence cases once they enter the courts. In addition, there is limited information on how specific characteristics of the offense and offender influence court outcomes (Hirschel & Hutchison, 2001). This research seeks to fill this gap in understanding by examining court outcomes for a large sample of individuals arrested for domestic violence in one large midsouthern city. The study's intent is to provide initial information on variables affecting decision making at four separate points in the court process. Of particular importance is the effect of the defendant's gender on court outcomes, as significant increases have been reported in female arrests for this offense during the past decade (Martin, 1997).

In 1984, Sherman and Berk conducted the first empirical test on the effectiveness of arrest for domestic violence offenses. Prior to the mid-1980s, police in

SOURCE: Henning, K., & Feder, L. (2005). Criminal prosecution of domestic violence offenses. *Criminal Justice and Behavior, 32*(6), 612–642.

most communities used informal responses to domestic violence including mediating or temporarily separating the partners during a dispute. These practices were widely criticized by victim advocacy and feminist groups as being inequitable and ineffective (Buzawa & Buzawa, 1996). Sherman and Berk (1984) randomly assigned Minneapolis, Minnesota police officers answering domestic violence calls for service to one of three responses (separation, mediation, or arrest). Results from their study indicated that an arrest response led to significantly lower rates of recidivism in comparison to separating or mediating the partners.

Subsequent replications of Sherman and Berk's (1984) study, commonly referred to as the Spousal Assault Replication Projects (SARPs), produced inconsistent findings. In some of the study locations, arrest deterred offenders whereas in others, there was evidence that it led to an increase in risk for the victim (Schmidt & Sherman, 1993). Analyses of the combined SARP datasets also have provided contradictory findings with regard to the deterrent benefits of arrest. Berk, Campbell, Klap, and Western (1992) found that arrest increased recidivism among offenders with a low stake in conformity (i.e., unemployed, unmarried), whereas Maxwell et al. (2001) reported a small but significant reduction in recidivism among male aggressors in heterosexual intimate relationships. Despite early questions about the efficacy of this policy, mandatory arrest laws quickly became the norm across the country through the 1990s (Sherman & Cohn, 1989).

Even though mandatory arrest laws are present in most jurisdictions, this does not mean that all domestic incidents result in the arrest of the perpetrator (Feder, 1999). Researchers have sought to identify those factors predictive of an arrest response. In general, this body of research has found that legal variables now predominate in police officers' decisions to arrest. In terms of offender characteristics, researchers have usually found that a suspect's prior criminal record and use of drugs or alcohol are positively correlated with the likelihood of arrest (Smith & Klein, 1984). Similarly, various indicators of offense severity increase the odds that officers will make an arrest,

including the presence of a weapon (Eigenberg, Scarborough, & Kappeler, 1996; Smith, 1987) and victim injuries (Ferraro, 1989). It should be noted that research conducted prior to mandatory arrest laws often yielded very different findings. Specifically, extralegal factors like the victim-offender relationship and the victim's demeanor toward officers appeared to exert a greater influence on the arrest decision than legal factors (Black, 1976).

Compared to the research available on police response to domestic violence calls, there has been significantly less attention paid to the handling of these cases once they have been handed over to the courts. Prosecutors, like the police, have in the past been reluctant to proceed with cases involving domestic violence (Buzawa & Buzawa, 1996). The reasons given for disinterest in prosecuting domestic assault cases often echoed the arguments previously used by police for their failure to arrest. These included that victims were likely to recant and were therefore unreliable witnesses, that domestic violence was a private matter that should not come under the purview of the state, and the view that incarcerating the batterer removed the breadwinner and therefore might be more harmful to the family (Elliott, 1989; Ford, 1993). Given these attitudes, it was not surprising that prosecution rates rarely exceeded 10% of those who were arrested (Dillon, 1988; Fagan, 1989; Ford, 1993; Schmidt & Steury, 1989).

The low rate of prosecution seen historically with domestic violence very likely had a reciprocal effect on police behavior; officers reported that they were less inclined to arrest suspects given that the district attorney's (DA) office usually declined to prosecute (Belknap, 1996). Recognizing this link between police and court behavior, some working in the system began to advocate for a coordinated community response to domestic violence (Tolman & Weisz, 1995; Zorza, 1992). Proponents of this strategy view arrest as a necessary ingredient in the community's response to domestic violence. Just as critical, they argue, are prosecution and sanctions so as to communicate a clear and consistent message to the batterer that this behavior is not going to be tolerated. Thus, novel court procedures were developed to aggressively adjudicate domestic violence cases, including vertical prosecution, specialized DA units, no-drop policies, and victimless prosecution (Buzawa & Buzawa, 1996; Cahn, 1992; Corsilles, 1994; Fagan, 1996).

These aggressive prosecution strategies, coupled with the new mandatory arrest laws, have led to dramatic increases in the number of domestic violence cases entering the courts (Mignon & Holmes, 1995; Victim Services Agency, 1989). Whereas the police previously acted us gatekeepers in selecting cases to enter the system, mandatory arrest laws have severely limited their discretion and transferred most of this responsibility to the courts. Therefore, it has become more critical than ever that researchers investigate factors affecting decision making in the courts. As with previous research on police officers' decisions to arrest (e.g., Black, 1976), it cannot be assumed that court personnel are wisely or fairly using the discretion they have been granted when making decisions.

A review of the literature identified nine empirical studies that examined factors affecting court decision making with domestic violence cases (see Table 5.9 for study details). Seven of these studies addressed prosecutorial discretion (i.e., the DA's decision to accept or reject a case) and two studies looked at the verdicts resulting from prosecution. Three of the nine studies also presented analyses on the sentencing of domestic violence offenders. The various predictor variables considered in these studies can be grouped into four categories: (a) victim characteristics, (b) suspect characteristics, (c) the nature of the offense, and (d) evidence availability/case processing factors. The results of the nine studies within each of these four categories of predictor variables have been summarized in Table 5.9. In some cases, the authors presented data on multiple decision points in the adjudication process and these findings are presented in sequential order in the table (e.g., case reviewed by DA, charges filed by DA; Rauma, 1984).

One of the more apparent conclusions that can be drawn from a review of Table 5.9 is that there is significant variability in the associations between the predictor and criterion variables, both across and within studies. Several factors may account for this variability. First, the data for these studies were collected at different time periods, ranging from the early 1980s to the late 1990s. Significant changes have likely occurred during this time frame in the nature of cases coming into the courts, the availability of evidence, and the policies governing prosecutors and judges. A second source of inconsistency may be the different criterion variables used in these studies (e.g., case reviewed by DA, preliminary charge filed, case fully prosecuted by DA). Moreover, two studies (Kingsnorth, Macintosh, Berdahl, Blades, & Rossi, 2001; Rauma, 1984) suggest that the factors influencing prosecutorial decisions vary at different stages of the charging process. Finally, some of the variability in the results may be attributable to a lack of uniformity in measuring the predictor variables (e.g., race of the couple vs. suspect's race).

A review of Table 5.9 also reveals several areas where the studies have produced largely consistent results. None of the studies found that prosecution efforts, court dispositions, or sentencing is influenced by the victim's age or race. Court decisions do appear to be influenced by the victim's gender, behavior during the incident, and level of cooperation with prosecution. With regard to suspect characteristics, the findings suggest that a defendant's age has no bearing on decisions made within the courts, and with but two exceptions (Belknap & Graham, 2000; Cramer, 1999), the race of the defendant also appears to be unrelated to court outcomes. Defendants under the influence of alcohol or drugs at the time of their offense and defendants with prior criminal histories are subject to greater prosecution and receive more severe sentences. The offense characteristic most commonly associated with active prosecution is victim injury, with prosecution being more likely in cases involving physical harm.

Although the studies reviewed above provide a good foundation on which to build, their usefulness for more fully understanding the factors that influence court decisions with domestic violence offenders remains somewhat limited. For one thing, the sample sizes employed in some of these studies were

Table 5.9 Summary of Research Studies Examining Predictors of Court Decisions With Domestic Violence (DV) Cases

Study	Sample and Year Data Collected	Case Decision (Criterion %)	Predictor Variables and Relationship to Decision With Defendant				
			Victim Characteristics	Defendant Characteristics	Offense	Evidence/Case Characteristics
Prosecutorial decisions						
Rauma (1984)[a]	199 men cited by police for domestic incident involving a female intimate partner (years not reported)	Case reviewed by DA (48%)	• Married to suspect (–); under the influence and/or aggressive (–); race of couple (ns) • Married to suspect (ns); under the influence and/or aggressive (ns); race of couple	• Race of couple (ns) • Prior criminal charges (+); race of couple (ns)	• Victim injured (+) restraining order present, weapon used, and/or suspect abusive with police (+); suspect arrested at scene (+); suspect injured (–) • Victim injured (–) suspect injured (+); restraining order present, weapon used and/or suspect abusive with police (ns); suspect arrested for battery (ns)	• Number of cases set for review that week (–) • Number of pieces of evidence (ns); victim cooperative (ns)
Schmidt & Steury (1989)[a]	409 men cited for a misdemeanor assault of a current/former female intimate partner (1983–1984)	Charged by DA (9%)	Active intimate relationship at time of incident (ns); living with suspect at time of incident (ns)	Unemployed (+); under the influence (+); prior convictions (+); on probation/parole (ns); prior abuse vs. victim (ns)	Victim injured (+); fist or weapon used (+); victim medical Tx (ns);	Suspect absent at hearing (+); witness availability (ns)
Hirschel & Hutchison (2001)[a]	424 men cited or arrested for misdemeanor assault of a female intimate partner (1987–1989)	Prosecuted by DA (36%)	Race (ns); age (ns); married (ns); employed (ns); under the influence (ns)	Race (ns); age (ns); employed (ns); under the influence (ns); prior arrest (ns); # prior arrests (ns)	Victim injured (+); physical assault (ns); property damage (ns); arrest vs. citation (ns); drinking cause of incident (ns)	Victim argued vs. arrest (–); victim argued vs. citation (ns); officer observed incident (ns); other witnesses (ns); suspect represented by attorney (ns)

				Predictor Variables and Relationship to Decision With Defendant		
Study	Sample and Year Data Collected	Case Decision (Criterion %)	Victim Characteristics	Defendant Characteristics	Offense	Evidence/Case Characteristics
Kingsnorth, Macintosh, Berdahl, Blades, & Rossi (2001)	383 men and 73 women arrested for misdemeanor or felony DV involving intimate partner (1995–1996)	• Preliminary charge filed by DA (81%) • Fully prosecuted by DA (72% of 455)	• Victim arrested (−); married & cohabitating (ns); race of couple (ns); intoxicated (ns) • Victim arrested (ns); married & cohabitating (ns); race of couple (ns); intoxicated (ns)	• Under the influence (+); prior DV arrest (ns?); prior prison term (ns); race of couple (ns) • Under the influence (+); prior DV arrest (ns); prior prison term (ns); race of couple (ns)	• Hospital Tx for victim (+); severity of attack (ns); victim injury (ns) • Victim injury (+); hospital Tx for victim (ns); severity of attack (ns)	• Witnesses (+); photos available (ns); victim cooperative (ns) • Victim cooperative (+); witnesses (ns); photos available (ns)
Dawson & Dinovitzer (2001)[a]	441 men and 33 women arrested for DV involving intimate partner (1997–1998)	Prosecuted by DA (83%)	Female (+); dating suspect (−); age (ns)	Female (−); age (ns); prior DV (ns); prior non-DV violence (ns); prior nonviolent crime (ns)	Minor victim injuries (ns); major victim injuries (ns); weapon used (ns); children present (ns)	Victim cooperative (+); victim met with advocates (+); victim video testimony (+); victim met prosecutors (ns); victim statement (ns); photos available (ns); witnesses (ns); 911 tapes (ns);medical reports (ns)
Kingsnorth, Macintosh, & Sutherland (2002)[a]	1,427 men and women arrested for misdemeanor or felony DV involving intimate partner (1999)	Prosecuted by DA or VOP charges filed (82%)	Married & noncohabitating (−); victim arrested (−); race (ns)	Prior non-DV arrest (+); prior DV arrest (ns); gender (ns)	Victim injured (+)	Witness (+); victim wanted arrest (+)
Davis, Smith, & Taylor (2003)	692 men and 52 women arrested for DV involving intimate partner or blood relative (1994–1995)	Charged by DA (% not provided)	Intoxicated (−); married to suspect (ns)	Female (−); prior arrest for battery (+); prior felony convictions (ns); prior misdemeanor convictions (ns)	Weapon used (ns); victim injured (ns); active restraining order (ns); physical assault (ns)	Victim attended charging (+); victim cooperative (ns)

(Continued)

Table 5.9 (Continued)

			Predictor Variables and Relationship to Decision With Defendant			
Study	Sample and Year Data Collected	Case Decision (Criterion %)	Victim Characteristics	Defendant Characteristics	Offense	Evidence/Case Characteristics
Case dispositions						
Belknap & Graham (2000)	2,284 men and 370 women arrested for misdemeanor DV involving current or former intimate partner 1997	Guilty verdict (44%)	Active intimate relationship at time of incident (+)	Gender (ns); age (ns); race (ns); prior violent offense (ns)	Severity of charges (ns); kicked/hit victim (ns); weapon used (ns); strangled victim (ns)	Victim statement (+); # meetings between prosecutor & victim (+); victim changed story (–); prosecutor caseload (–); victim subpoenaed (ns); photos available (ns); witnesses (ns); 911 tapes (ns); medical reports (ns); officer testified (ns)
Cramer (1999)[e]	110 men and 30 women arrested for domestic offense involving intimate partner (1997)	Guilty verdict (25%)	Married to or living with suspect (+)	Female (–); Caucasian (+); prior criminal history (+)		Photos available (+)
Sentencing						
Kingsnorth, Macintosh, Berdahl, Blades, & Rossi (2001)	(see above)	Sentence length	Married & cohabitating (ns); race of couple (ns); intoxicated (ns)	Prior DV arrest (+); prior prison term (+); under the influence (ns); race of couple (ns)	Victim injury (ns); hospital Tx for victim (ns); severity of attack (ns)	Felony conviction on current charge (+); photos available (ns)

Predictor Variables and Relationship to Decision With Defendant

Study	Sample and Year Data Collected	Case Decision (Criterion %)	Victim Characteristics	Defendant Characteristics	Offense	Evidence/Case Characteristics
Belknap & Graham (2000)	(see above)	Sentence length	Active intimate relationship at time of incident (+)	Female (–); African American (–); prior violent offense (+); age (ns)	Severity of charges (+); kicked/hit victim (ns); weapon used (ns); strangled victim (ns)	Number of meetings between prosecutor & victim (+); photos available (+); medical reports (+); victim changed story (–); prosecutor caseload (–); victim statement (ns); victim subpoenaed (ns); witnesses (ns); 911 tapes (ns); officer testified (ns)
Kingsnorth, Macintosh, & Sutherland (2002)c	(see above)	Sentence length	Relationship (ns); race (ns)	Prior DV convictions (+); current DV probation (–); gender (ns); non-DV prior arrests (ns)	Victim medical Tx (+); gun used (+)	Felony conviction on current charge (+); jury trial (+)

NOTE: Relationships were coded as positive (+), negative (–) or nonsignificant (ns) using $p < .05$. DA = district attorney; Tx = treatment; VOP = violation of probation.

a. Bivariate analyses presented in table.

b. Includes all cases charged by DA ($n = 209$) and random sample ($n = 200$) from 2003 where charges were not filed.

c. Multivariate analyses presented in table (may not include all variables in model).

d. Includes cases drawn from two distinct periods during which case screening processes changed; results presented are for main effect independent of time.

e. Results based on a stepwise discriminant function analysis with three-level outcome. Unclear whether other variables were examined not related to outcome.

333

relatively small; six of the nine studies had fewer than 500 cases. In addition, only two of the studies clearly included felony cases (Kingsnorth et al., 2001; Kingsnorth, Macintosh, & Sutherland, 2002). The lack of variation in this factor (i.e., severity of present offense) may restrict these studies' value in understanding the full use of prosecutorial and judicial discretion.

Another major limitation with some of the studies is either their exclusive use of cases involving male offenders and female victims (Hirschel & Hutchison, 2001; Rauma, 1984; Schmidt & Steury, 1989) or the use of very small samples of female defendants (Cramer, 1999; Davis, Smith, & Taylor, 2003; Dawson & Dinovitzer, 2001; Kingsnorth et al., 2001). This is especially problematic given recent trends. Following the implementation of mandatory arrest laws, there has been a rise in both the overall number of women arrested and the proportion of arrests involving female defendants (Henning & Feder, 2004; Martin, 1997; Saunders, 1995; Swan & Snow, 2002). In California, for example, the proportion of domestic violence arrests involving a female offender increased from 6% in 1988 to 17% by 1998 (State of California, 1999). Cases involving nonintimate partners (e.g., siblings, parent-child) are also deserving of attention as they account for a sizable proportion of domestic violence arrests in most communities (11% in this study). Further research, therefore, on these factors and their effect on court outcomes is essential.

A defendant's gender may also be important to the extent that this variable correlates with another recent phenomenon—the use of dual arrests when police respond to domestic assault calls. Researchers have found that women are significantly more likely to be dually arrested for domestic violence compared to men (Henning & Feder, 2004). Only two studies (Kingsnorth et al., 2001; Kingsnorth et al., 2002) have addressed the relationship between dual arrest and court decisions, both finding that it decreased the likelihood of prosecution.

One final point distinguishes this study from those reviewed in Table 5.9. Four out of the nine studies looked at a single point in the processing of these court cases (Davis et al., 2003; Dawson & Dinovitzer, 2001; Hirschel & Hutchison, 2001; Schmidt & Steury, 1989), and one (Cramer, 1999) combined aspects of prosecutorial discretion and case dispositions into a single variable. Of the remaining studies that looked at multiple decision points (Belknap & Graham, 2000; Kingsnorth et al., 2001; Kingsnorth et al., 2002; Rauma, 1984), none examined the full range of major decisions that are made during the adjudication process. The data used in this study allow for analyses across the full continuum of decisions within the court system from pretrial release to final sentencing.

In summary, there is a need for continued research on the handling of domestic violence offenders beyond the decision to arrest. This study provides information on prosecutorial and judicial decision making with male and female defendants who have been arrested for a domestic assault. Various legal and extralegal factors are examined to determine their association with decisions at four points in the court process—pretrial release, active prosecution, final case disposition, and sentencing. With regard to the hypotheses, the researchers expected findings that mirrored Rauma's (1984) conclusion that "good cases have good victims and bad offenders" (p. 384). Specifically, the researchers believed that defendants with a prior criminal history, unemployed defendants, and those using substances at the time of the offense would receive greater attention at all stages of the adjudication process. Similarly, arrestees who injured their victim, those using weapons, and those charged with a felony as opposed to a misdemeanor also would be treated more seriously (i.e., higher bond, active prosecution, guilty verdict, longer sentence). In contrast, cases involving dual arrest were expected to result in reduced prosecution efforts because the behavior of the victim might be called into question. Based on the results of prior studies within domestic violence (Cramer, 1999; Davis et al., 2003; Dawson & Dinovitzer, 2001; Kingsnorth et al., 2001) and general offender populations (Spohn & Beichner, 2000), it is also expected that female defendants would be treated more leniently than their male counterparts. Finally, the researchers believed that cases involving intimate partners would be treated more seriously than nonintimate cases, given the significantly greater attention paid to the former during the past decade.

 Method

Data Source and Procedures

Court records for a 12-month period starting in August, 2000 were obtained on all criminal defendants arrested for a domestic offense in Shelby County, Tennessee. Shelby County has a population of roughly 800,000 and the county's court system has jurisdiction over the city of Memphis and the surrounding unincorporated areas. Unlike some jurisdictions where prosecutors make charging decisions, in Shelby County, law enforcement officers file criminal charges at the time of an arrest. The DA's office then reviews each case and decides whether to pursue prosecution or decline the charges (nolle prosequi).

In Tennessee, offenses classified as domestic violence include a wide variety of charges (e.g., assault, stalking, harassment, vandalism, burglary, or violation of a restraining order). The central feature is that the offense must involve intimates or family members. Once a defendant is booked into the local jail, a counselor working for the county's Pretrial Release division conducts a brief interview with the individual. The pretrial counselor also reviews the defendant's local criminal history and the arrest report filed by the responding officers. The information obtained during this evaluation is forwarded to a judicial magistrate who determines the bond and release conditions for the defendant.

All domestic violence cases entering the Shelby County court system during the given study period were assigned to a specialized Domestic Violence Court presided over by a single judge. A rotating team of four prosecutors and a continuing lead prosecutor handled these cases for the DA's office. The lead prosecutor maintained a computerized database with disposition information on all cases closed in the Domestic Violence Court. Data from Pretrial Release and the DA's database were transferred to the first author. A unique ID contained in both databases allowed for the records to be merged into a single file, thus creating a database that contained information on every domestic violence arrest during the 12-month study period.

A total of 5,461 domestic violence cases leading to arrest were recorded during this 1-year period. The lead prosecutor reported having reached a final disposition in the Domestic Violence Court for 4,873 (89.2%) of these cases by April, 2002. Of these 4,873 cases, 692 (14.2%) were transferred to another court, usually at the request of the defense attorney. It is interesting that male defendants were more likely ($p < .05$) than female defendants to have their cases transferred out of the Domestic Violence Court (15.0% vs. 10.9%). Similarly, defendants charged with felonies were more likely to have their cases transferred to another docket (41.8% vs. 7.2%, $p < .01$). Because final dispositions on transfer cases were not available to the researchers, all transfer cases were excluded from further analyses. Three additional cases were eliminated from the sample due to the death of the defendant. This left 4,178 domestic violence cases with disposition information from the local Domestic Violence Court.

Predictor Variables

Jail release counselors working in Pretrial Services and the lead prosecutor in the Domestic Violence Court recorded defendants' gender, age, race, and employment status. Race was dichotomized into minority versus Caucasian; however, it should be noted that 82.1% of the sample were African American and only 2.0% were of another minority racial group. Defendants' SES was estimated by geographically mapping the defendant's home address. Each defendant was assigned the median household income from his or her respective 1990 census block. Although aggregate proxies for income contain some bias as compared to individual-level income, this bias is reduced by using smaller geographic units for estimation such as in this study (Soobader, LeClere, Hadden, & Maury, 2001). Mean substitutions were used for defendants lacking address information (26.8%) to prevent the loss of cases in multivariate analyses.

Finally, defendants' employment status was defined as employment outside the house.

Three dichotomous variables were available from the dataset to detail the defendants' local adult criminal record: (a) whether the defendant was previously arrested for a violent offense against a nonfamily member, (b) whether he or she had a prior domestic violence arrest, and (c) whether he or she had an arrest for a nonviolent offense. Pretrial release counselors recorded several characteristics of the arrest offense after reviewing the affidavits, interviewing the defendant, and talking with the victim when available. Information obtained included the nature of the arrest (single defendant vs. dual arrest), the criminal assault charge (misdemeanor vs. felony), use of a weapon such as a gun or knife by the defendant (yes/no), victim injury requiring medical attention (yes/no), and whether the offender had been using alcohol or drugs at the time of the offense (yes/no). Last, the victim/offender relationship was dichotomized as either an intimate partner or some other form of familial relation (e.g., brother-sister, parent-child, cousins).

Criterion Variables

Four dependent variables were available in the dataset to characterize the court outcomes at various points in the decision-making process. Bond amount was considered as one of the dependent variables under investigation, with defendants either being released on their own recognizance (ROR) or having to post a cash bond to secure release while awaiting trial. With the exception of capital murder cases, all defendants in this jurisdiction are issued a bond or ROR. A second variable indicated whether the DA's office accepted or declined to prosecute the case. For those cases prosecuted within the Domestic Violence Court, the researchers coded the final disposition into a dichotomous variable (dismissed/not guilty vs. pled guilty/found guilty/diversion[1]). Last, the length of sentence reflects the actual number of days that the defendant was ordered to serve in jail or prison after taking into account the proportion of the sentence suspended by the judge, usually for probation purposes.

Results

Table 5.10 provides descriptive information on the defendants in this study and the characteristics of the offenses resulting in their arrest (i.e., predictor variables). Table 5.10 also provides descriptive statistics on the four court outcomes addressed in this study. Seventy-seven percent ($n = 2,338$) of the defendants were required to post a cash bond, with a mean cash bond of $5,323 and a median bond amount of $2,000. Prosecutors in the Domestic Violence Court declined to proceed with the charges in 20.6% ($n = 861$) of the cases. With regard to the final dispositions obtained for cases prosecuted by the DA's office, more than two thirds (70.5%; $n = 2,340$) of the defendants were found guilty, pled guilty, or were placed on diversion. Among defendants pleading guilty or found guilty at trial, the number of days they were ordered to serve in jail/prison ranged from 0 to 1,800, with a mean sentence of 35 days and a median sentence of 2 days.

Table 5.11 provides the results of bivariate analyses examining the relationship between defendant characteristics, the characteristics of the offense, and the four court outcome variables. In these and all subsequent analyses, pretrial release bond and length of sentence imposed were dichotomized to address skewed distributions with the original variables. Pretrial release was coded to reflect whether any cash bond was required as opposed to the defendant being released ROR. Length of sentence imposed was recoded into no jail or prison sentence versus a jail or prison sentence of 1 or more days.

As shown in Table 5.11, bivariate analyses indicate that many of the factors associated with the offender correlated in the expected direction with court outcomes. However, of particular note are findings that minority defendants were less likely to be granted a ROR release and were less likely to have their cases declined by prosecutors in comparison to White defendants. Also interesting was the finding that gender was significantly associated with pretrial release, prosecution, and sentencing decisions. That is, female defendants were more likely to be released ROR, to have their charges dropped by prosecutors, and to receive no

Table 5.10	Descriptive Information on Defendants Charged With Domestic Violence (DV; $N = 4,178$)

	M or %
Defendant characteristics	
Mean age (SD)	32.3 (9.5)
Race (minority)	84.0
Gender (female)	20.5
Estimated income in thousands (SD)	22.6 (12.9)
Unemployed (% yes)	38.1
Prior arrest for nonfamily violence (% yes)	24.8
Prior arrest for DV (% yes)	32.5
Prior arrest for nonviolent offense (% yes)	71.3
Offense characteristics	
Relationship to victim (% intimate)	83.4
Felony charge (% yes)	13.8
Dual arrest (% yes)	12.2
Weapon used (% yes)	18.9
Victim injured (% yes)	8.3
Defendant using substances (% yes)	20.0
Prosecution outcomes	
Average cash bond in thousands (SD)[a]	5.3 (9.2)
Released ROR (% yes)	23.5
Prosecutor accepted case	
Yes	79.4
No	20.6
Disposition of cases prosecuted in DV court	
Pled guilty, found guilty, or diversion	70.5
Found not guilty or dismissed	29.5
Average number of days to serve in prison (SD)	34.6 (82.8)
Any days to serve in prison (% yes)	51.5

a. Excludes cases where defendant was released on own recognizance (ROR).

prison time when found guilty in comparison to their male counterparts.

With regard to the influence of factors associated with the offense, felony offenders, as compared to misdemeanants, were less likely to be given a ROR release and were more likely to have their case proceed through prosecution; no significant differences appeared between these groups in their likelihood of being found guilty or the length of sentence they received upon being adjudicated. Weapon usage and victim injury showed a similar pattern, influencing ROR and the prosecutor's decision to accept a case. Finally, Table 5.11 also indicates that defendants who were part of a dual arrest were more likely to be released ROR, were more likely to have their cases declined by prosecutors, and when convicted, were less likely to receive jail or prison time in comparison to singly arrested defendants. It is interesting that dually arrested defendants were more likely than singly arrested defendants to plead or be found guilty.

Results from bivariate analyses may be misleading to the extent that there is high multicollinearity among these variables. Logistic regressions were used to address this concern, thereby identifying factors that independently predicted each of the four court decisions considered. Starting with the defendant characteristics, the researchers found that gender was independently associated with all four decisions (see Table 5.12). Compared to males, female defendants were more likely to be released ROR, were less likely to be prosecuted, were less likely to plead or be found guilty, and when found guilty, were less likely to be incarcerated. Having a prior arrest for domestic violence also was associated with decision making at all four points in the process; those with a prior arrest compared to those without were more likely to have a cash bond and were more likely to be prosecuted, convicted, and sent to prison. A defendant's history of criminal involvement outside the family also was independently associated with most decisions made in the case, as was true for the defendant's employment status. Finally, prosecutors were more likely to drop a case if the defendant was Caucasian, older, and from a higher SES.

The results of the four logistic regression analyses suggest that few of the offense characteristics were

Table 5.11 Bivariate Analyses Examining Relationship Between Defendant Characteristics, Characteristics of the Instant Offense, and Case Outcome Variable

	Case Outcome Variables (% yes)			
	ROR	Prosecutor Took Case	Guilty or Diversion[a]	Served 1+ Days[b]
Defendant characteristics				
Age[c]				
Younger than 32	24.8*	80.2	68.0**	51.7
32 or older	21.7	79.8	72.9	51.8
Race				
Minority	21.9***	82.4***	70.4	52.7
Caucasian	32.4	66.1	70.4	46.6
Gender				
Male	18.3***	84.4***	70.8	53.1***
Female	44.6	60.0	69.1	40.7
Estimated income				
< $20,694	16.5***	84.4***	73.6**	55.6**
$20,694+	31.0	74.0	70.1	49.3
Unemployed				
Yes	18.0***	84.4***	73.6**	55.6**
No	27.8	77.1	68.6	49.3
Prior arrest for nonfamily violence				
Yes	5.8***	93.2***	70.6	61.0***
No	29.9	75.7	70.5	47.4
Prior arrest for DV				
Yes	5.5***	91.3***	74.3**	63.1***
No	32.8	74.4	68.7	42.9
Prior arrest for nonviolent offense				
Yes	15.0***	86.8***	71.8*	54.8***
No	46.4	62.9	67.3	35.1
Offense characteristics				
Victim-offender relation (intimate)				

	Case Outcome Variables (% yes)			
	ROR	**Prosecutor Took Case**	**Guilty or Diversion**[a]	**Served 1+ Days**[b]
Yes	22.9	79.5	69.2**	51.8
No	25.8	78.6	75.9	49.1
Type of charge				
Felony	14.4***	89.8***	72.4	50.3
Misdemeanor	24.8	77.8	70.3	52.0
Dual arrest				
Yes	38.6***	34.3***	82.8***	35.5***
No	21.7	85.7	69.9	52.5
Weapon used				
Yes	16.2***	64.9***	73.5	52.3
No	25.5	78.9	69.9	52.2
Victim injured				
Yes	10.2***	88.0***	71.0	55.9
No	25.1	79.2	70.7	52.0
Defendant using substances				
Yes	17.9***	81.9*	78.0***	51.6
No	27.8	77.5	68.9	50.9

NOTE: Sample sizes vary by comparison due to missing data. ROR = released on own recognizance.

a. Only includes cases where prosecutors took case.

b. Only includes cases where defendant was found/pled guilty (excludes diversion).

c. Based on median split.

$*p < .05; **p < .01; ***p < .001.$

consistently associated with decisions made during the adjudication process. Dual arrest was the only factor independently related to three of the four decision points considered. Compared to singly arrested defendants, those who were dually arrested were less likely to be prosecuted and less likely to be sentenced to prison when convicted. Consistent with the bivariate analyses, dually arrested defendants were more likely to be found guilty or plead guilty once the case was accepted for prosecution. Defendants charged with felonies were less likely to be granted a ROR release

than misdemeanants and the DA was more likely to prosecute cases involving felony offenses. Similarly, defendants who injured their victim as opposed to those with an uninjured victim were more commonly denied ROR and such cases were more likely to be targeted for prosecution. Defendants using substances at the time of the offense and those who used a weapon were less likely to be given a ROR. Finally, it is interesting to note that the victim-offender relationship was not independently associated with adjudication decisions.

Table 5.12 Simultaneous Logistic Regressions Predicting Case Outcomes by Characteristics of the Defendant and the Instant Offense

	Case Outcome Variables							
	ROR		**Prosecutor Took Case**		**Guilty or Diversion**[a]		**Served 1+ Days**[b]	
Model								
N	2,071		2,521		1,975		1,167	
−2 log likelihood	1,839.1		1,894.5		2,328.4		1,522.5	
χ^2	550.1***		740.2***		55.9***		94.5***	
df	14		14		14		14	
	B	**Odds**	**B**	**Odds**	**B**	**Odds**	**B**	**Odds**
Defendant characteristics								
Age	0.01	1.01	−0.02***	0.98	0.00	1.00	−0.01*	0.99
Race (minority)	0.07	1.07	0.67***	1.96	−0.07	0.93	0.08	1.08
Gender (male)	−1.13***	0.32	0.91***	2.48	0.42***	1.52	0.57**	1.78
Estimated income in thousands	0.02***	1.02	−0.03	0.97	0.00	1.00	0.00	1.00
Unemployed	−0.63***	0.53	0.47***	1.60	0.23*	1.26	0.21	1.24
Prior arrest for nonfamily violence	−0.94**	0.39	0.59**	1.81	−0.21	0.81	0.42**	1.51
Prior arrest for DV	−1.59***	0.20	0.64***	1.90	0.32**	1.38	0.66***	1.94
Prior arrest for nonviolent offense	−0.79***	0.45	0.70***	2.01	0.07	1.07	0.51**	1.67
Offense characteristics								
Victim-offender relation (intimate)	−0.03	0.97	−0.09	.92	−0.22	0.81	0.04	1.04
Type of charge (felony)	−0.99***	0.37	1.33***	3.79	0.30	1.35	0.07	1.07
Dual arrest	0.20	1.22	−2.52***	0.08	0.74**	2.11	−0.72**	0.49
Weapon used	−0.38*	0.68	0.23	1.26	0.09	1.09	0.03	1.03
Victim injured	−0.56*	0.57	0.68*	1.97	−0.24	0.78	0.15	0.10
Defendant using substances	−0.43**	0.65	0.29	1.34	0.43**	1.54	0.10	1.10

NOTE: ROR = released on own recognizance.

a. Only includes cases where prosecutors took case.

b. Only includes cases where defendant was found/pled guilty (excludes diversion).

*$p < .05$; **$p < .01$; ***$p < .001$.

✕ Discussion

This study addressed a continuing gap in the extant research on the processing of domestic violence offenders within the criminal justice system. Specifically, few studies have examined factors associated with the use of prosecutorial and judicial discretion (i.e., active prosecution vs. dropping charges) and fewer still have identified variables that influence the outcomes of court cases involving domestic violence. This study used a large cohort of cases ($N = 4{,}178$) assigned to a single specialized domestic violence court to address these issues. The cases in the cohort included all domestic violence arrests in the given county for an entire year. As such, it included male and female defendants, arrestees charged with intimate partner violence, those who offended against nonintimate family members, as well as those facing misdemeanor and felony prosecution. A variety of legal and extralegal variables was collected on each case, including characteristics of the offender (e.g., age, race, gender, SES, employment status, and prior criminal record) and the offense (e.g., victim/offender relationship, charge type, dual arrest, weapon usage, victim injury, and defendant's use of substances).

With regard to the factors associated with prosecutorial and judicial decisions, like most of the prior studies (see Table 5.9), results indicated that a mixture of legal and extralegal factors was predictive of the various outcomes considered. Logistic regression analyses revealed that the pretrial release decisions (i.e., cash bond vs. ROR) were heavily influenced by legal factors such as the prior criminal history of the defendant, the type of charge, and the severity of the offense (i.e., weapon use, victim injury). Nevertheless, extralegal variables like the defendant's gender and income independently predicted the use of cash bonds as opposed to offenders being released on their own recognizance (ROR).

A greater balance was observed between legal and extralegal factors predicting the DA's decision to either accept or reject cases. Of greatest importance were the nature of the charge (felony vs. misdemeanor), the type of arrest (dual vs. single), and the gender of the defendant. Fewer of the predictor variables considered were independently associated with the dispositions

reached in cases brought forward by prosecutors, but again it was a mixture of legal and extralegal factors that were important. Finally, the sentence imposed by the judge appeared to have been more heavily influenced by legal factors like the defendant's prior criminal history. When the researchers compared the characteristics associated with police decision making with those found to be predictive of court outcomes with domestic violence cases, the results indicated what might be a subtle but important difference. More recent studies have shown that characteristics associated with the offense (i.e., legal factors) have the largest and most consistent effect on police likelihood to arrest (Jones & Belknap, 1999). However, court decisions in this study's jurisdiction and others seemed as likely to be influenced by extralegal variables as they were to involve legal factors. A few points are worth noting with regard to this comparison. It is critical to understand factors that are now found to be predictive of an arrest response did not always enter into police decision making. Earlier research on police likelihood to arrest indicated that officers often misused their discretionary powers by largely overlooking legal variables when responding to domestic violence calls for service (Black, 1976). Later research showed a gradual but steady shift among police to giving greater consideration to legal variables (Feder, 1999; Jones & Belknap, 1999).

It is likely that this change in police behavior was due, in part, to the external pressures placed on law enforcement to change their response to domestic violence. New laws and policies mandated or presumed an arrest response. It probably also helped that courts began holding police departments liable for their officers' failure to comply with the new laws (e.g., McFarlane, 1991). Finally, to the extent that researchers followed up with studies investigating police behavior in this arena, law enforcement received continual feedback on their performance. In all, oversight of police response to domestic violence from concerned community and citizen groups, courts, and researchers doubtlessly helped to keep the police motivated to change both their response to domestic violence as well as the public's perception of their response.

Similar mechanisms for oversight have yet to be applied to prosecutorial and judicial decision making.

There are many possible reasons for this difference. A comparison of the vast number of studies done on law enforcement versus the few studies conducted on court procedures may be indicative of the greater difficulty researchers have in gaining access to the courts and their records. In addition, advocacy groups and concerned citizens have been far less vocal about any dissatisfaction they may feel concerning the court's handling of domestic violence cases. The immediacy of most domestic assaults may also lead victims to be more critical of law enforcement's response compared to the response of the courts.

Whether additional research and attention to prosecutorial and judicial decision making results in a reduced attention to extralegal factors, the pattern observed with police arrests remains a question for further study. Moreover, additional studies are needed to understand prosecutors' and judges' reasons for considering extralegal factors in their decision making. The apparent influence of age and work status, for example, may be based on a rational assessment of the greater risks posed by younger and unemployed defendants. As such, the prioritization of cases based on certain extralegal variables may be appropriate in situations where resource limitations prevent the adjudication of all cases (Nagel, 1983; Rauma, 1984). Other extralegal factors associated with prosecutors' decisions in this study certainly warrant further attention by researchers.

For example, the researchers found that the DA's decision to pursue a case was associated with the defendant's race, even after controlling for other demographic factors and offense characteristics. Does this finding indicate that prosecutors are biased in their treatment of minorities (primarily African Americans in this study), or might there be another explanation for this result (e.g., representation by public vs. private defense attorney, racial differences in victim cooperation)? As noted by a previous review of this article, the apparently differential treatment by prosecutors also raises the question of whether systematic biases might account for the over representation of minorities in this arrest sample. African Americans accounted for 82% of those arrested for domestic violence in the given study year, whereas 2000 census data indicate that 49% of the county's residents are African American. It should also be noted, however, that these results contradict those of other studies looking at prosecutorial discretion (Hirschel & Hutchison, 2001; Kingsnorth et al., 2001; Kingsnorth et al., 2002; Rauma, 1984) and police arrest decisions (Berk & Loseke, 1980–1981; Smith & Klein, 1984), where race was unrelated or inconsistently related to outcomes. Thus, additional research is needed to determine whether this finding is replicable in other jurisdictions.

Gender was another extralegal factor considered in this study that is deserving of further discussion. Female defendants made up 21% of all arrested and charged domestic violence offenders in our cohort. Although there are few published reports documenting the prevalence of women arrested for domestic violence, the little information available indicates a moderate degree of comparability with other studies (16.5%; State of California, 1999, 20%–35%; Swan & Snow, 2002). This study is one of the few to examine whether a defendant's gender influences prosecution outcomes. The results suggest that gender is a significant predictor of the decisions made throughout the adjudication process. Compared to males, females were more likely to be released ROR and have their charges dropped by prosecutors. They were also less likely to be convicted, and where convicted, they received lighter sentences. These differences persisted even once other legal and extralegal variables were controlled.

The apparent lenient treatment of female defendants in this study and prior research (Belknap & Graham, 2000; Cramer, 1999; Davis et al., 2003; Dawson & Dinovitzer, 2001) may be the result of the domestic violence field's historical emphasis on cases involving male offenders and female victims. Most of the available research on domestic violence, the theories used to explain this behavior, and the resulting interventions have focused on aggression perpetrated by males. The fact that men account for a disproportionate number of domestic assaults, injuries, and intimate partner homicides (e.g., Greenfeld et al., 1998; Tjaden & Thoennes, 2000) certainly explains much of this emphasis on their use of aggression. Consequently, prosecutors and judges may be more sensitized to the factors involved in male-perpetrated domestic abuse.

Prior research would also suggest that many of the women in the sample were victims of abuse who were arrested after they used physical means to defend themselves (Hamberger & Potente, 1994; Saunders, 1995). As such, the more lenient treatment observed with the female defendants may be justified based on the merits of these cases. Finally, the leniency encountered by female domestic violence offenders in the courts may be part of a larger pattern of moderate treatment of all female criminal defendants, based in part on the consideration of women's familial responsibilities, blameworthiness, and perceived likelihood of reoffending (e.g., Spohn & Beichner, 2000).

These analyses also highlight the importance of a dual arrest versus single arrest in predicting court dispositions. Although this factor did not predict pretrial release, it was significantly related to prosecution efforts, court dispositions, and the sentences imposed. That is, where defendants were part of a dual arrest, they were more likely to have their cases dropped by prosecutors and were less likely to be sentenced to jail or prison time. It is interesting that dually arrested defendants were more likely than singly arrested defendants to be convicted once the decision to prosecute had been made. This latter finding may be the result of the heavy screening done by prosecutors at the outset of the adjudication process. Only 34% of dually arrested defendants were prosecuted compared to 86% of those singly arrested. As research consistently indicates, prosecutors view victims in terms of their ability to serve as credible witnesses (Dawson & Dinovitzer, 2001). Where an individual is both a victim and defendant, it cannot help but make the prosecutor's job more difficult. The dual arrest cases that remain after this initial screening by prosecutors are likely to be incidents with clear evidence supporting mutual aggression; thus, conviction rates are likely to be higher. Last, it is also worth noting that a significantly higher percentage of women were involved in a dual arrest than were men (29% versus 8%, respectively).

Finally, the researchers wish to comment on the rate of prosecution observed in this sample. Whereas older studies noted low rates of prosecution for domestic violence (Ford, 1993; Rauma, 1984; Schmidt & Steury, 1989; Sherman, 1992), this study found that prosecution was the norm rather than the exception. The DA's office proceeded with charges against 79% of the 4,178 defendants booked into the jail during the 1-year period. Of the 3,317 cases where the DA's office proceeded with charges, only 30% of them were later dismissed by the judge or found not guilty. Put differently, of all the domestic violence arrestees whose cases were disposed in this specialized court, 56% entered a plea of guilty, were found guilty, or were placed on diversion.

Several factors might account for this comparatively high rate of successful prosecutions. First, all of the cases were assigned to a specialized court overseen by a single judge. The use of specialized courts may lead to increased consistency in handling cases and a greater understanding of the dynamics of domestic violence (Tsai, 2000). Second, with the advent of the domestic violence court, the local DA created a specialized prosecution unit to aggressively pursue cases. Prosecutors in this unit received additional training in domestic violence and were likely selected for the positions based on an interest in family violence. Moreover, a full-time investigator was assigned to the unit to facilitate the collection of evidence and assist in interviewing victims. Finally, the federal grant supporting the court provided for several advocates to do victim outreach, both within the courtroom and by phone. These services may have led to greater cooperation between victims and prosecutors, a factor previously linked to prosecution efforts (e.g., Belknap & Graham, 2000; Dawson & Dinovitzer, 2001; Kingsnorth et al., 2001).

Alternatively, some might choose to look at the 56% prosecution figure cited above as a failure of the local system because 44% of the victims from these cases were not afforded full protection or justice under the law. As discussed previously, some of the declined cases involved female defendants who may have been arrested in error whereas others involved dual arrest, an obvious challenge to prosecutors. There are other cases, however, where neither of these two conditions applied and prosecutors still declined to charge the defendant. Factors accounting for such decisions might include uncooperative victims, limited evidence gathering by police, and technical difficulties with the arrest. All of these factors could make it more difficult for the DA to successfully prosecute a case, thereby increasing the odds that they decline the charges and pursue more fruitful quarry. With prosecutors in this jurisdiction each averaging more than 90 cases per month, it seems reasonable to expect that resource limitations play a role in their charging decisions. Nevertheless, additional studies are clearly needed to more explicitly detail the decision-making processes engaged in by prosecutors and to accurately determine the proportion of justified charges that are being dropped.

With regard to the limitations of this study, it must be emphasized that all of the cases were drawn from a single jurisdiction. As such, the specific policies and procedures governing the local court personnel may have influenced the associations observed between the predictor and criterion variables. This may reduce the generalizability of the findings to other localities. The fact that the researchers did not include measures of victim cooperation and evidence availability undoubtedly represents an important omission given that prior studies have shown that such factors may influence court decisions. Although the intent was to include both felony and misdemeanor cases in the final sample, many of the felony cases initially assigned to the Domestic Violence Court were transferred to other judges and the outcomes of these cases were unknown. Finally, many of the predictor variables examined were collected by pretrial release counselors working in the jail. The extent to which prosecutors and judges were actually aware of these factors prior to making their decisions is unclear.

In all, this study points to the need for additional attention to several issues. Research is needed in other jurisdictions to verify the high rates of prosecution and successful dispositions observed in this sample. In addition, subsequent studies need to address whether extralegal variables are consistently entering into the decision-making process within the courtroom, and the reasons for considering such factors. This latter point is especially pertinent in light of the fact that police have recently been required to forego using their discretion and work under mandatory or presumption in favor of arrest statutes when responding to domestic violence calls for service. To the extent that courts must now serve as gatekeepers into the system, it is incumbent on researchers to investigate how these decisions are being made.

Last, additional research is needed to understand police decisions concerning female and dual arrest, the nature of these cases, and their effect on court outcomes. Again, this becomes even more critical in light of the growing concerns surrounding the increased numbers of women who are now being arrested for domestic violence.

Note

1. Diversion in this county is essentially the same as a guilty plea and probation, but the defendant has the right to have his or her record expunged after 1 year if all court ordered conditions are met.

References

Belknap, J. (1996). *The invisible woman: Gender, crime and justice.* Cincinnati, OH: Wadsworth.

Belknap, J., & Graham, D. (2000). *Factors related to domestic violence court dispositions in a large urban area: The role of victim/witness reluctance and other variables—final report.* Washington, DC: National Institute of Justice.

Berk, R., Campbell, A., Klap, R., & Western, B. (1992). The deterrent effect of arrest in incidents of domestic violence: A Bayesian analysis of four field experiments. *American Sociological Review, 57,* 698–708.

Berk, S., & Loseke, D. (1980–1981). "Handling" family violence: Situational determinants of police arrest in domestic disturbances. *Law and Society Review, 15*(2), 317–346.

Black, D. (1976). *The behavior of law.* New York: Academic Press.

Buzawa, E., & Buzawa, C. (1996). *Domestic violence: The criminal justice response* (2nd ed.). Thousand Oaks, CA: Sage.

Cahn, N. (1992). Innovative approaches to the prosecution of domestic violence crimes: An overview. In E. S. Buzawa & C. G. Buzawa (Eds.), *Domestic violence: The changing criminal justice response* (pp. 161–180). Westwood CT: Auburn House.

Corsilles, A. (1994). No-drop policies in the prosecution of domestic violence cases: Guarantee to action or dangerous solution? *Fordham Law Review, 63*(3), 853–881.

Cramer, E. (1999). Variables that predict verdicts in domestic violence cases. *Journal of Interpersonal Violence, 14*(11), 1137–1150.

Davis, R., Smith, B., & Taylor, B. (2003). Increasing the proportion of domestic violence arrests that are prosecuted: A natural experiment in Milwaukee. *Criminology & Public Policy, 2*(2), 263–282.

Dawson, M., & Dinovitzer, R. (2001). Victim cooperation and the prosecution of domestic violence in a specialized court. *Justice Quarterly, 18*(3), 593–622.

Dutton, D. (1988). *The domestic assault of women: Psychological and criminal justice perspectives.* Boston: Allyn & Bacon.

Eigenberg, H., Scarborough, K., & Kappeler, V. (1996). Contributory factors affecting arrest in domestic and non-domestic assaults. *American Journal of Police, 15*(4), 27–54.

Elliott, D. (1989). Criminal justice procedures in family violence crimes. In L. Ohlin & M. Tonry (Eds.), *Family violence* (pp. 427–480). Chicago: University of Chicago Press.

Fagan, J. (1989). Cessation from family violence: Deterrence and discussion. In L. Ohlin & M. Tonry (Eds.), *Family violence* (pp. 357–426). Chicago: University of Chicago Press.

Fagan, J. (1996). *The criminalization of domestic violence: Promises and limits* (NCJ 157641). Washington, DC: Office of Justice Programs.

Feder, L. (1999). Police handling of domestic violence calls: An overview and further investigation. *Women & Criminal Justice, 10*(2), 49–68.

Ferraro, K. (1989). Policing woman battering. *Social Problems, 36*(1), 61–74.

Ford, D. A. (1993). *The Indianapolis domestic violence prosecution experiment—final report.* Washington, DC: National Institute of Justice.

Greenfeld, L., Rand, M., Craven, D., Klaus, P., Perkins, C., Ringel, C., et al. (1998). *Violence by intimates: Analysis of data on crimes by current or former spouses, boyfriends and girlfriends* (NCJ 167237). Washington, DC: U.S. Department of Justice, Bureau of Justice Statistics.

Hamberger, L. K., & Potente, T. (1994). Counseling heterosexual women arrested for domestic violence: Implications for theory and practice. *Violence & Victims, 9*(2), 125–137.

Henning, K., & Feder, L. (2004). A comparison of men and women arrested for domestic violence: Who presents the greater threat? *Journal of Family Violence, 19*(2), 69–80.

Hirschel, D., & Hutchison, I. W. (2001). The relative effects of offense, offender, and victim variables on the decision to prosecute domestic violence cases. *Violence Against Women, 7*(1), 46–59.

Jones, D., & Belknap, J. (1999). Police responses to battering in a progressive pro-arrest jurisdiction. *Justice Quarterly, 16*(2), 249–273.

Kingsnorth, R., MacIntosh, R., Berdahl, T., Blades, C., & Rossi, S. (2001). Domestic violence: The role of interracial/ethnic dyads in criminal court processing. *Journal of Contemporary Criminal Justice, 17*(2), 123–141.

Kingsnorth, R., MacIntosh, R., & Sutherland, S. (2002). Criminal charge or probation violation? Prosecutorial discretion and implications for research in criminal court processing. *Criminology: An Interdisciplinary Journal, 40*(3), 553–578.

Martin, M. (1997). Double your trouble: Dual arrest in family violence. *Journal of Family Violence, 12*(2), 139–157.

Maxwell, C., Garner, J. A., Fagan, J. (2001). *The effects of arrest on intimate partner violence: New evidence from the Spouse Assault Replication Program* (NCJ 188199). Washington, DC: U.S. Department of Justice.

McFarlane, L. (1991). Domestic violence victims v. municipalities: Who pays when the police will not respond? *Case Western Reserve Law Review, 4*(3), 929–968.

Mignon, S., & Holmes, W. (1995). Police response to mandatory arrest laws. *Crime & Delinquency, 41*(4), 430–443.

Nagel, I. (1981). The legal/extra legal controversy: Judicial decisions in pretrial release. *Law and Society Review, 17*(3), 481–515.

Rauma, D. (1984). Going for the gold: Prosecutorial decision making in cases of wife assault. *Social Science Research, 13,* 321–351.

Saunders, D. (1995). The tendency to arrest victims of domestic violence. *Journal of Interpersonal Violence, 10*(2), 147–158.

Schmidt, J., & Sherman, L. (1993). Does arrest deter domestic violence? *American Behavioral Scientist, 36*(5), 601–610.

Schmidt, J., & Steury, E. (1989). Prosecutorial discretion in filing charges in domestic violence cases. *Criminology, 27*(3), 487–510.

Sherman, L. (1992). *Policing domestic violence: Experiments and dilemmas.* New York: Free Press.

Sherman, L., & Berk, R. (1984). The specific deterrent effects of arrest for domestic assault. *American Sociological Review, 49,* 261–272.

Sherman, L., & Cohn, E. (1989). The impact of research on legal policy. The Minneapolis domestic violence experiment. *Law & Society Review, 23*(1), 117–144.

Smith, D. (1987). Police response to interpersonal violence: Defining the parameters of legal control. *Social Forces, 65*(3), 767–782.

Smith, D., & Klein, J. (1984). Police control of interpersonal disputes. *Social Problems, 31*(4), 468–481.

Soobader, M., LeClere, F. B., Hadden, W., & Maury, B. (2001). Using aggregate geographic data to proxy individual socioeconomic status: Does size matter? *American Journal of Public Health, 91,* 632–636.

Spohn, C., & Beichner, D. (2000). Is preferential treatment of female offenders a thing of the past? A multisite study of gender, race, and imprisonment. *Criminal Justice Policy Review, 11*(2), 149–184.

State of California. (1999). Report on arrest for domestic violence in California, 1998 (Office of the Attorney General). *Criminal Justice Statistics Center Report Series, 1*(3), 1–21.

Swan, S., & Snow, D. (2002). A typology of women's use of violence in intimate relationships. *Violence Against Women, 8*(3), 286–319.

Tjaden, P., & Thoennes, N. (2000). Prevalence and consequences of male-to-female and female-to-male intimate partner violence as measured by the National Violence Against Women Survey. *Violence Against Women, 6*(2), 142–161.

Tolman, R. M., & Weisz, A. (1995). Coordinated community intervention for domestic violence: The effects of arrest and prosecution on recidivism of woman abuse perpetrators. *Crime and Delinquency, 41*(4), 481–495.

Tsai, B. (2000). The trend toward specialized domestic violence courts: Improvements on an effective innovation. *Fordham Law Review, 68,* 1285–1327.

Victim Services Agency. (1989). State legislation providing for law enforcement response to family violence. *Response, 12*(3), 6–9.

Zorza, J. (1992). The criminal law of misdemeanor domestic violence, 1970–1990. *Journal of Criminal Law and Criminology, 83,* 46–72.

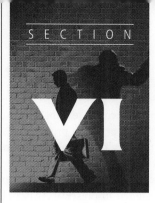

VI

Plea Bargaining and Trial Dynamics

Section Highlights

- The Court Process
- Plea Bargaining
- The Courtroom Workgroup: Cooperation Rather Than Conflict
- Media Influence in Criminal Trials
- Edited Readings

 ## The Court Process

The predominance of jury trials in television dramas such as *Law and Order* and *The Good Wife* notwith-standing, most convictions result from guilty pleas. In 2002, for instance, 95% of all felony convictions in state courts were the result of a guilty plea (Bureau of Justice Statistics, 2005b, Table 4.2); in 2004, the rate was even higher, 96%, for defendants convicted of felonies in federal courts (Bureau of Justice Statistics, 2005a, Table 4). Although the actual number of guilty pleas that result from plea bargains is unknown, most experts would argue that some type of negotiation between the prosecutor and the defendant (or his attorney) occurs prior to the entry of the guilty plea.

In the introduction to this section, we focus on plea bargaining and trial dynamics. We begin with a discussion of the history and current status of plea bargaining in the United States. We also present the arguments for and against plea bargaining and discuss attempts to restrict or ban plea bargaining in several jurisdictions. We then cover a diverse range of court-related topics, including the courtroom workgroup, courtroom legal culture, and media influence in criminal trials.

Plea Bargaining

Article II, Section 2, of the U.S. Constitution provides that "the trial of all Crimes, except in Cases of Impeachment, shall be by Jury." The Sixth Amendment also declares that "in all criminal prosecutions, the accused shall enjoy the right to a speedy and public trial, by an impartial jury." Although the Founding Fathers may have expected that "all crimes" would be tried by juries, in the United States today very few criminal cases are settled by jury trials. As one commentator noted, "our system of criminal dispute resolution differs enormously from the one that the Sixth Amendment was designed to preserve" (Alschuler & Deiss, 1994, p. 867).

Historically, jury trials were the norm, not the exception, in the United States. In fact, courts initially were reluctant to accept guilty pleas from persons charged with serious crimes. An example is the 1804 case of *Commonwealth v. Battis*, which involved a 20-year-old black man who was accused of raping and murdering a 13-year-old white girl. When the defendant notified a Massachusetts court that he wanted to plead guilty as charged, the court "informed him of the consequence of his plea" and explained that "he was under no legal or moral obligation to plead guilty" (*Commonwealth v. Battis*, 1804, p. 95). When the defendant refused to withdraw his plea, the court sent the defendant back to prison to think about the effects of pleading guilty. When the defendant returned to court, he again pled guilty, which prompted the court to examine

> under oath, the sheriff, the jailer, and the justice [who had conducted the preliminary examination of the defendant] as to the sanity of the prisoner; and whether there had been tampering with him, either by promises, persuasions, or hopes of pardon if he would plead guilty. (p. 96)

In this case, then, the Massachusetts court made an oblique reference to the practice of plea bargaining; the court wanted to be assured that the defendant had not been promised anything in exchange for his guilty plea.

Following the Civil War, plea bargaining became increasingly common. By the beginning of the 20th century, it was the dominant method of resolving criminal cases, especially in large urban jurisdictions. As can be seen in the language of an 1878 Michigan court decision, most of the early commentary on the practice of plea bargaining was negative. In *Edwards v. People* (1878), the court discussed a Michigan statute that set forth various plea bargaining requirements. The court observed that Michigan passed the statute "for the protection of prisoners and of the public" in response "to serious abuses caused by [prosecutors] procuring prisoners to plead guilty when a fair trial might show they were not guilty, or might show other facts important to be known" (p. 761). The court also pointed out that it was

> easy to see that the Legislature thought there was danger that prosecuting attorneys . . . would procure prisoners to plead guilty by assurances they have no power to make, of influence in lowering the sentence, or by bringing some other unjust influence to bear on them. (p. 762)

As plea bargaining proliferated and concerns about its fairness increased, many states impaneled crime commissions to study the operation of the criminal justice system. Nearly every report published by these commissions reported an increase in the practice of plea bargaining. For example, the Georgia Department of Public Welfare (1924) reported that guilty plea rates increased 70% from 1916 to 1921. A report from New York (Moley, 1929) revealed that between 1839 and 1920 the guilty plea rate rose to 90% of all cases. These commissions also stated that plea bargains were too common and recommended that more cases should go to trial. One early critic of the practice called plea bargaining an "incompetent, inefficient, and lazy method of administering justice" (Alschuler, 1968, p. 211, quoting *Chicago Tribune*, April 27, 1928, p. 1).

Why did plea bargaining increase so dramatically during the 1800s and early 1900s? One school of thought is that plea bargaining emerged during the mid-19th century as a result of the increasing professionalism of the criminal court system (Langbein, 1979). That is, trials became more complex and adversarial, and defendants were more likely to have competent attorneys to represent them; as a result, prosecutors turned to plea bargaining as a way of reducing the uncertainty of case outcomes. According to this view, "plea bargaining should be viewed as a natural outgrowth of a progressively adversarial criminal justice system" (Guidorizzi, 1998, p. 756). Another explanation holds that the growth of plea bargaining as a means of resolving criminal cases can be attributed to case pressure. This explanation suggests that plea bargaining was a natural response to increasing caseloads and limited resources to deal with them (Fisher, 2003). In a recent book on the origins of plea bargaining, McConville and Mirsky (2005) refuted both of these arguments. They argued that the political context in which criminal courts were operating, rather than professionalism or case pressure, explains the increase in plea bargaining that began in 1850. According to these authors, the advent of the elected district attorney, coupled with the influx of large numbers of immigrants, led district attorneys to search for effective and politically palatable ways of controlling the immigrant population. As the authors noted, district attorneys allowed defendants to plead guilty to less serious charges "to avoid the discontent that harsh terms of punishment would engender among the immigrant underclass, who, under the movement for universal suffrage, had become part of the newly formed electorate" (McConville & Mirsky, 2005, p. 197).

Regardless of whether the growth of plea bargaining is explained as a result of an increasingly professional criminal court system, caseload pressure, or the political context in which elected district attorneys were operating, it is clear that it has become a key feature of the American criminal justice system. In the words of the United States Supreme Court, plea bargaining is "an essential component of the administration of justice" (*Santobello v. New York*, 1971).

Defining Plea Bargaining

It is important to understand that although all plea bargains involve guilty pleas, not all guilty pleas result from plea bargains. A guilty plea occurs when a defendant admits committing a crime. When a guilty plea is entered, the defendant usually will be required to explain what happened to the judge. This process is known as allocution. A guilty plea can be entered without any type of plea bargaining; that is, the defendant can plead guilty to the original charge without any concessions or promises from the prosecutor. A defendant who believes that the state's evidence is overwhelming or who is plagued by guilt might simply decide to admit involvement in the crime. These types of guilty pleas are the exception, however. Most guilty pleas are preceded by plea bargaining.

What exactly is plea bargaining? *Black's Law Dictionary* defines it as follows:

> The process whereby the accused and the prosecutor in a criminal case work out a mutually satisfactory disposition of the case subject to court approval. It usually involves the defendant pleading guilty to a lesser offense or to only some of the counts of a multi-count indictment in return for a lighter sentence than the sentence possible for the graver charge. (p. 1152)

The problem with this definition is that it fails to capture the range of concessions prosecutors may offer. They can offer more than just reductions in charges and counts or favorable sentencing recommendations. We consider some of these in the section about ad hoc plea bargaining. A better, more all-encompassing definition of plea bargaining is "the defendant's agreement to plead guilty to a criminal charge with the reasonable expectation of receiving some consideration from the state" (Miller, McDonald, & Cramer, 1978, pp. 1–2).

There are several different forms of plea bargaining and they can be used alone or in combination with one another. Consider the following scenario: A 19-year-old man holds a gun to the head of a convenience store clerk, demands money, and escapes on foot with a bag containing more than $1,000. Thirty minutes later he is spotted and arrested by the police. The prosecutor reviewing the case charges the defendant with one count of aggravated robbery, which is punishable by 3 to 10 years in prison, and one count of use of a weapon during the commission of a felony, which adds an additional 2 years to the sentence. The plea negotiations in this case might center on the charges that were filed. If the defendant agrees to plead guilty, the prosecutor might reduce the aggravated robbery charge to a less serious charge of robbery or might dismiss the weapons charge. Both types of **charge reductions** would reduce the potential sentence that the defendant is facing.

The plea negotiations also might revolve around the sentence. In exchange for a guilty plea, the prosecutor might agree to recommend a sentence of 3 years on the aggravated robbery and 2 years on the weapons charge, with the sentences to be served concurrently rather than consecutively. Alternatively, the prosecutor might agree to *stand mute at sentencing* or might agree to a *sentence lid.* In the first instance, the prosecutor would not recommend any particular sentence or challenge the defense attorney's presentation of mitigating evidence and recommendation for leniency; he would, in other words, say nothing about the sentence the defendant should receive. In the second instance, the prosecutor would recommend that the judge impose a sentence that does not exceed the **sentence lid**; in this case, for example, the prosecutor might state that the sentence should be no greater than 3 years in prison.

Both charge reductions and sentence agreements limit the judge's options at sentencing. Judges have little, if any, recourse if the prosecutor decides to reduce the number or the severity of the charges in exchange for a guilty plea. Because the charging decision "generally rests entirely in [the prosecutor's] discretion" (*Bordenkircher v. Hayes*, 1978), the judge ordinarily cannot refuse to accept the plea to a reduced charge and force the defendant to go to trial. In *United States v. Ammidown* (1973), for example, the United States Court of Appeals ruled that a judge who rejected a plea agreement because he believed that the "public interest" required that the defendant be tried on a more serious charge "had exceeded his discretion." Although the justices stated that the trial court should not "serve merely as a rubber stamp for the prosecutor's decision," they ruled that the judge cannot reject the agreement reached between the prosecution and defense unless the judge determines that the prosecutor abused his or her discretion. Moreover, the Court said that the

> question is not what the judge would do if he were the prosecuting attorney, but whether he can say that the action of the prosecuting attorney is such a departure from sound prosecutorial principle as to mark it an abuse of prosecutorial discretion. (*Ammidown*, 1973)[1]

Sentence agreements also reduce the judge's discretion, even though the prosecutor does not have any official authority to impose sentence. If, for example, the prosecution and the defense negotiate an agreement whereby the defendant agrees to plead guilty and the state agrees that a probation sentence is the appropriate disposition, the judge must either accept the plea agreement and place the defendant on probation

---

[1]However, it should be noted that other appellate courts have adopted a less restrictive standard. In *United States v. Bean* (1977), the Court of Appeals for the 5th Circuit ruled that a "decision that a plea bargain will result in the defendant's receiving too light a sentence under the circumstances of the case is a sound reason for the judge's refusing to accept the agreement."

or reject the agreement and allow the defendant to withdraw his guilty plea.[2] As the Supreme Court stated in the case of *Santobello v. New York* (1971), "when a plea rests in any significant degree on a promise or agreement of the prosecutor, so that it can be said to be part of the inducement or consideration, such promise must be fulfilled." Moreover, judges face organizational pressure to approve plea agreements. Like other members of the courtroom workgroup, they view guilty pleas as an efficient and effective method of case disposition. As a result, they are unlikely to reject the sentence agreements that make a high rate of guilty pleas possible.

Ad Hoc Plea Bargaining

Although plea negotiations usually produce charge or sentence reductions, there are other practices that fall within the definition of plea bargaining. Joe Colquitt (2001) recently used the term **ad hoc plea bargaining** to refer to the unusual concessions defendants agree to make during the plea negotiation process. Colquitt stated:

> Ad hoc bargains exist in at least five forms: (1) the court may impose an extraordinary condition of probation following a guilty plea, (2) the defendant may offer or be required to perform some act as a quid pro quo for a dismissal or more lenient sentence, (3) the court may impose an unauthorized form of punishment as a substitute for a statutorily established method of punishment, (4) the State may offer some unauthorized benefit in return for a plea of guilty, or (5) the defendant may be permitted to plead guilty to an unauthorized offense, such as a "hypothetical" or nonexistent charge, a nonapplicable lesser-included offense, or a nonrelated charge. (p. 712)

There are numerous examples of these five forms of ad hoc plea bargaining. Defendants have been given the option of providing charitable contributions in lieu of fines or jail terms (see, e.g., *State v. Stellato*, 1987, p. 1349; *Ratliff v. State*, 1992, p. 243) and have agreed to relinquish property ownership in exchange for leniency (see, e.g., *United States v. Thao Dinh Lee*, 1999, p. 1278). Other defendants have agreed to not work in particular professions or to surrender professional licenses (see, e.g., *United States v. Hoffer*, 1997, p. 1199). One defendant consented to undergo voluntary sterilization (*State v. Pasicznyk*, 1997), and another agreed to enlist in the U.S. Army (*State v. Hamrick*, 1999, p. 494). Defendants have also consented to perform shaming punishments, such as affixing a bumper sticker labeling the driver of a car as a convicted DUI offender (see, e.g., *Ballenger v. State*, 1993, p. 794). Defendants have even agreed to surrender profits, such as from books written about their crimes (*Rolling v. State ex rel. Butterworth*, 1999) or to be banished to another location (see, e.g., *State v. Culp*, 1976, p. 842; *Phillips v. State*, 1999, p. 33).

Arguments for and Against Plea Bargaining

Arguments in favor of plea bargaining are really arguments about the *benefits* of plea bargaining. Most people would agree that the primary benefit of plea bargaining is that it enables courts to dispose of large

---

[2]Rule 11 of the Federal Rules of Criminal Procedure, which applies to cases adjudicated in federal court, states: "If the court accepts the plea agreement, the court shall inform the defendant that it will embody in the judgment and sentence the disposition provided for in the plea agreement. . . . If the court rejects the plea agreement, the court shall, on the record, inform the parties of this fact, advise the defendant personally in open court . . . that the court is not bound by the plea agreement, afford the defendant the opportunity to then withdraw his plea, and advise the defendant that if he persists in this guilty plea . . . the disposition of the case may be less favorable to the defendant than that contemplated by the plea agreement."

numbers of criminal cases quickly. As we have already discussed, the crime control model contends that a high rate of guilty pleas—which implies a high rate of plea bargaining—is necessary if the system is to operate with maximal efficiency. The Supreme Court, which recognized the legitimacy of plea bargaining more than 40 years ago, has also emphasized the economic benefits of plea bargaining. The Court noted that "if every criminal charge were subject to a full scale trial, the states and the Federal Government would need to multiply by many times the number of judges and court facilities" (*Santobello v. New York,* 1971).

Plea bargaining clearly benefits prosecutors, who are concerned about securing convictions and avoiding acquittals at trial. Like other public officials, prosecutors are faced with limited resources. They cannot prosecute every criminal case, and they certainly cannot take all of the cases they prosecute to trial before juries. The cases that go to trial are likely to be high-profile cases or those in which defendants are facing harsh potential sentences. Less serious cases, or cases with evidentiary or witness problems, are prime candidates for plea bargains. Giving the defendant in a less serious or weaker case some type of concession in exchange for a guilty plea allows the prosecutor to secure a conviction and sentence without risking an acquittal at trial. Plea bargaining, in other words, may be favored by the prosecution because it allows the courtroom workgroup to further its "mutual interest in avoiding conflict, reducing uncertainty, and maintaining group cohesion" (Weninger, 1987, pp. 265, 267).

Other actors in the criminal court system also benefit from plea bargaining. Defense attorneys, including public defenders, have high caseloads and limited resources and, like prosecutors, are concerned about disposing of cases quickly and efficiently. In addition, plea bargaining allows the defense attorney to mitigate the harshness of the sentence the defendant would face following conviction at trial. In this sense, plea bargaining also benefits defendants, who receive more lenient sentences by pleading guilty to less serious charges or to fewer counts. As the Supreme Court itself noted, plea bargaining affords the defendant the opportunity of "avoiding the anxieties and uncertainties of trial" (*Blackledge v. Allison*, 1977, p. 71). Finally, victims may benefit from plea bargaining; if the defendant pleads guilty, the victim will not have to testify at the trial or face the possibility that the prosecution will not succeed in obtaining a conviction (Demarest, 1994).

There are many arguments against plea bargaining. One is that plea bargaining effectively allows prosecutors and defense attorneys to decide matters of guilt; no judge and no jury are involved. Another criticism is that, in an effort to secure a guilty plea, the prosecutor may start with the most serious charge and work down from there; the prosecutor may "overcharge" as a first step in the bargaining process. If, for example, the prosecutor believes that the appropriate charge in a case is simple assault, he or she may initially file a charge of aggravated assault and then offer to reduce the charge to simple assault if the defendant agrees to plead guilty. In this situation, the effect of the charge reduction is symbolic rather than substantive.

Critics also charge that plea bargaining is inefficient. This criticism rests on two assumptions. The first is that defense attorneys draw out the negotiations in an attempt to get prosecutors to offer better deals. As one researcher observed, "defense attorneys commonly devise strategies whose only utility lies in the threat they pose to the court's and prosecutor's time" (Alschuler, 1968, p. 56). The second assumption is that plea bargaining is unnecessary to induce guilty pleas. That is, critics of plea bargaining contend that most defendants will plead guilty without any concessions or promises of leniency if they think it is likely that they will be found guilty at trial (Arenella, 1983).

One of the most pervasive criticisms of plea bargaining is that it undermines the integrity of the criminal justice system. Plea bargaining, which amounts to deciding guilt without trial, circumvents the "rigorous standards of due process and proof imposed during trials" (Worden, 1990, p. 338). The prosecutor is not required to prove the defendant's guilt beyond a reasonable doubt, and the defendant does not have an opportunity to cross-examine the witnesses against him or her or otherwise test the prosecutor's case.

Plea bargaining also may result in convictions and sentences that do not accurately reflect the seriousness of the crime committed by the defendant. A defendant who commits a robbery with a gun, but whose charge is reduced from armed robbery to robbery during plea negotiations, may receive a more lenient sentence than he or she deserves. Finally, critics of plea bargaining claim that innocent individuals may be coerced to plead guilty. As one of the staunchest critics of plea bargaining stated, plea bargaining "darkens the prospect of going to trial as it brightens the prospect of pleading guilty" (Kipnis, 1976, p. 94).

An example of the type of pressure to plead guilty that defendants face can be found in the case of *North Carolina v. Alford* (1970). In its opinion in this case, the Supreme Court reprinted a statement made by the defendant, who pled guilty to second-degree murder to avoid the death penalty:

> I pleaded guilty on second degree murder because they said there is too much evidence, but I ain't shot no man. . . . We never had an argument in our life and I just pleaded guilty because they said if I didn't they would gas me for it, and that is all. (p. 28)

In this case, the Court ruled that it was not a violation of due process to accept the plea despite Alford's insistence that he was innocent because there was a strong factual basis for his guilt. The Constitution, according to the Court, does not preclude "imposition of a prison sentence upon an accused who is unwilling expressly to admit his guilt but who, faced with grim alternatives, is willing to waive his trial and accept the sentence" (*North Carolina v. Alford*, 1970, p. 28). Justice Brennan, one of the dissenting justices in the case, disagreed with the Court's assessment regarding the voluntariness of the plea. He wrote that the facts in the case demonstrated that "Alford was 'so gripped by fear of the death penalty' that his decision to plead guilty was not voluntary but was the product of duress."

In summary, plea bargaining is an issue that continues to evoke controversy and spark debate. Advocates, many of whom see plea bargaining as a necessary evil, argue that it is an essential element of an overburdened court system and that it benefits most, if not all, of the participants in the court process. Opponents counter that it perverts justice, undercuts the protections afforded to criminal defendants, and coerces innocent defendants to plead guilty, and should therefore be restricted or eliminated.

Attempts to Restrict or Ban Plea Bargaining

Given the controversy surrounding plea bargaining, it is not surprising that a number of jurisdictions have attempted to restrict, or even to eliminate, it. In 1975, for example, the Alaska attorney general issued an order that banned all forms of plea bargaining. Under this policy, prosecutors could not reduce charges or dismiss counts in exchange for guilty pleas; they also were not supposed to ask the court to impose a particular sentence if the defendant agreed to plead guilty. The attorney general imposed the ban on plea bargaining in an effort to increase convictions and restore public confidence in the justice system (Carns & Kruse, 1992). An evaluation of the impact of the ban found that explicit sentence bargaining disappeared and that charge bargaining continued for a few months and then "dried up" (Rubinstein & White, 1979). The evaluation also revealed that, contrary to predictions that defendants would refuse to plead guilty and that the Alaska criminal justice system would therefore grind to a halt, guilty pleas did not decrease and trials did not increase dramatically. Although the authors of the study concluded that the Alaska experience showed that "the incidence of plea bargaining *can* be substantially reduced without wrecking a criminal justice system," they also cautioned that the results of the Alaska reform could not necessarily be generalized to other, larger jurisdictions (Rubinstein & White, 1979, p. 382).

A number of other jurisdictions have taken a more modest approach with respect to limiting the practice of plea bargaining. One such method is to impose cutoff dates that prohibit plea bargaining after a case has been underway for a certain amount of time. As an example of this, the Brooklyn district attorney adopted a cutoff date of 74 days after indictment (Mirsky, 1994). Prior to the deadline, plea bargaining is acceptable, but after the deadline plea negotiation is prohibited. If the case goes to trial before the cutoff period, plea bargaining can even take place during trial or during jury deliberations. Some jurisdictions have also experimented with banning plea bargaining for certain offenses. For example, the Bronx County district attorney enacted a ban on plea bargaining whenever a grand jury returned a felony indictment. This was a controversial move on the district attorney's part, but he justified it by stating that plea bargaining "means that society has ceded control to those it has accused of violating its laws; and it means that our system is running us, instead of the other way around" (Johnson, 1992).

Another approach to restricting plea bargaining is the Philadelphia jury waiver. The jury waiver gives defendants the opportunity to engage in plea negotiations in exchange for giving up their right to a jury trial. This is something of a hybrid approach, with elements of plea bargaining and trial. Defendants get their day in court, but to receive concessions from the prosecutor, they cannot demand a jury trial. This practice is known as the **slow plea of guilty**, which reflects the fact that it does not result in the disposition of a case prior to trial. According to Levin (1977),

> slow pleas are informal and abbreviated, and consist largely of the defense's presentation of statements concerning the defendant's allegedly favorable personal characteristics.... The defense presentation is not concerned with guilt or innocence since it usually is implicitly assumed by all parties involved in the process that the defendant is guilty of at least some wrongdoing. (p. 80)

Other states have used the initiative process to restrict plea bargaining. In 1982, for example, California voters passed a referendum (now codified as Cal. Penal Code 1192.7) that imposed the following restrictions: no plea bargaining in any case involving a serious felony, a felony where a firearm was used, or the offense of driving under the influence. Plea bargaining is permissible, however, if the prosecution's evidence is weak, witnesses are unavailable, or a plea agreement does not result in a significantly reduced sentence (*People v. Brown*, 1986).

El Paso, Texas, also experimented with plea bargaining restrictions. There, two state district judges adopted a policy of prohibiting all plea negotiations in their courts as a method of ensuring equal treatment for similarly situated defendants (Weninger, 1987). Maricopa County (Phoenix, Arizona) Superior Court judges adopted a policy that prohibited plea agreements based on stipulated (i.e., agreed-upon) sentences. In other words, the judges refused to accept plea agreements that included a negotiated sentence. They felt that sentencing should be a decision left to the trial courts. These and other efforts to restrict plea bargaining have become fairly common, but it is difficult to argue that they are much more than symbolic gestures.

The Predictors of Plea Bargaining Decisions: Does Race Matter?

There is relatively little research on the factors that affect prosecutors' plea bargaining decisions. In part, this reflects the fact that plea negotiations typically take place "behind closed doors." Generally, there are no written records that document the concessions that were offered or the promises made. Although it may be possible to measure count or charge reductions, sentence agreements and the types of ad hoc plea agreements mentioned earlier are more difficult to document.

The research that does exist reveals that prosecutors' plea bargaining decisions are determined by the strength of evidence against the defendant, the defendant's prior criminal record, and the seriousness of the offense (Mather, 1979). Prosecutors are more willing to offer concessions to defendants who commit less serious crimes and have less serious prior records. They also are more willing to alter charges when the evidence against the defendant is weak or inconsistent. These findings are not surprising, given the prosecutor's desire to avoid uncertainty and secure convictions.

There also is some evidence that examines the impact of the defendant's race or ethnicity on plea bargaining outcomes. A number of studies conclude that white defendants are offered plea bargains more frequently and get better deals than do racial minorities. A study of the charging process in New York, for example, found that race did not affect charge reductions if the case was disposed of at the first presentation. Among defendants who did not plead guilty at the first opportunity, on the other hand, blacks received less substantial sentence reductions than did whites (Bernstein, Kick, Leung, & Schultz, 1977). An analysis of 683,513 criminal cases in California concluded that "Whites were more successful in getting charges reduced or dropped, in avoiding 'enhancements' or extra charges, and in getting diversion, probation, or fines instead of incarceration" (Weitzer, 1996, p. 313).

An analysis of plea bargaining under the federal **sentencing guidelines** also concluded that whites receive better deals than do racial minorities (Maxfield & Kramer, 1998). This study, which was conducted by the United States Sentencing Commission, examined sentence reductions for offenders who provided "substantial assistance" to the government. According to §5K1.1 of the *Guidelines Manual* (U.S. Sentencing Commission, n.d.), if an offender assists in the investigation and prosecution of another person who has committed a crime, the prosecutor can ask the court to reduce the offender's sentence. Because the guidelines do not specify either the types of cooperation that "count" as substantial assistance or the magnitude of the sentence reduction that is to be given, this is a highly discretionary decision.

The Sentencing Commission estimated the effect of race and ethnicity on both the probability of receiving a **substantial assistance departure** and the magnitude of the sentence reduction. The researchers controlled for other variables, such as the seriousness of the offense, use of a weapon, the offender's prior criminal record, and other factors deemed relevant under the sentencing guidelines. They found that blacks and Hispanics were less likely than whites to receive a substantial assistance departure; among offenders who did receive a departure, whites received a larger sentence reduction than either blacks or Hispanics (Maxfield & Kramer, 1998, pp. 14–19). According to the commission's report, "the evidence consistently indicated that factors that were associated with either the making of a §5K1.1 motion and/or the magnitude of the departure were not consistent with principles of equity" (p. 21).

Two studies found that race did not affect plea bargaining decisions in the predicted way. An examination of the guilty plea process in nine counties in Illinois, Michigan, and Pennsylvania revealed that defendant race had no effect on four measures of charge reduction (Nardulli et al., 1988). The authors of this study concluded that "the allocation of charge concessions did not seem to be dictated by blatantly discriminatory criteria or punitive motives" (p. 238). A study of charge reductions in two jurisdictions found that racial minorities received more *favorable* treatment than whites. In one county, black defendants received more favorable charge reductions than did white defendants; in the other county, Hispanics were treated more favorably than were whites (Holmes, Daudistel, & Farrell, 1987). The authors of this study speculated that these results might reflect devaluation of minority victims. As they noted, "if minority victims are devalued because of racist beliefs, such sentiments could, paradoxically, produce more favorable legal outcomes for minority defendants." The authors also suggested that the results might reflect overcharging of minority defendants by the police; prosecutors may have been forced "to accept pleas to lesser charges from black defendants because of the initial overcharging" (pp. 248–249).

In sum, the evidence concerning the factors that affect prosecutors' plea bargaining decisions is both scanty and inconsistent, especially regarding the effects of the defendant's race or ethnicity. Given the importance of these decisions, these contradictory findings "call for the kind of scrutiny in the pretrial stages that has been so rightly given to the convicting and sentencing stages" (Spohn et al., 1987, p. 189).

The Courtroom Workgroup: Cooperation Rather Than Conflict

Criminal courts are complex political and social institutions. They are bureaucratic organizations composed of members who play clearly defined roles and whose values, beliefs, and perceptions shape the way they operate and the outcomes they produce. Although the procedures that individual court systems use to process cases and sentence defendants vary depending on the size of the jurisdiction, caseload pressure, and the types of cases that dominate the court's docket, there are a number of features that are common to all courts. One of these is the courtroom workgroup (Eisenstein & Jacob, 1977).

The key players in the courtroom workgroup are the judges, prosecutors, and defense attorneys, who work together every day to process criminal cases. The members of the courtroom workgroup—or courthouse community (Eisenstein et al., 1988)—have a common goal (i.e., expeditious and efficient case processing) and shared expectations about how cases should be handled and the types of sentences that should be imposed. The members of the courtroom workgroup may believe, for example, that efficiency demands a high rate of guilty pleas; consequently, plea bargaining will be encouraged and defendants who cooperate by pleading guilty will be rewarded. The members of the courthouse community may also believe that there are "normal penalties" (Sudnow, 1965) or "going rates" (Eisenstein et al., 1988, pp. 30–31) for particular types of crimes and particular types of defendants. They may agree on the appropriate disposition and sentence for the run-of-the-mill burglary or for the offender who repeatedly appears in court on drug charges. Because the members of the courtroom workgroup are concerned about maintaining cordial relationships with other members of the community and ensuring the smooth flow of cases through the criminal justice system, case processing will be characterized by consensus and cooperation, rather than conflict (Walker, 2001, p. 53).

Courtroom Workgroups and Local Legal Culture

Although all court systems have courtroom workgroups, not all workgroups process cases or assign punishments in the same way. The case processing routines and the going rates are not necessarily the same in all jurisdictions. Certain categories of crimes are viewed as more serious, and certain types of offenders are perceived as more dangerous in some jurisdictions than in others. What accounts for these variations?

A number of scholars assert that differences in the way courts work can be attributed to variations in **local legal culture**. According to Eisenstein and his colleagues (1988), local legal culture "consists of the values and perceptions of the principal members of the court community about how they ought to behave and their beliefs about how they actually do behave in performing their duties" (p. 28). A similar definition was offered by Church (1982), who stated that local legal culture "consists of practitioners' attitudes and norms governing case handling and participant behavior in a criminal court" (p. 7). Another view of local legal culture is that it reflects the courtroom workgroup's notions of "how we do things here" (see Kritzer & Zemans, 1993).

Eisenstein et al.'s (1988) study of nine medium-sized courts in three states uncovered five elements of local legal culture. The first was the degree to which the members of the courtroom workgroup thought of themselves as a community; in some of the counties studied, there was a strong sense of community, but in others conflicts between prosecutors and the defense led to the formation of several smaller subcommunities or cliques. The second element was shared beliefs regarding interpersonal relations and how members of the community were expected to treat one another (e.g., don't rock the boat, keep your word, cooperate), and the third element was shared attitudes about case-processing routines, plea bargains, and going rates. The fourth element of the local legal culture was a "shared special language and commonly understood nonverbal communication" (p. 32). The authors found, for example, that certain types of cases were referred to as "dogs" in one county, that everyone in another county referred to a certain proceeding as the "cattle call," and that court sessions to handle pleas and minor offenses were referred to as "junk court." The final aspect of the local legal culture was a sense of tradition; the members of the courtroom workgroup in each county "had in varying degrees a sense of history that they call upon to explain and to evaluate current patterns" (p. 33).

Each county's local legal culture, then, affects the way the county's courts operate. If there is widespread agreement about "the way things should work and they way they do work," cooperation and consensus will be more common than conflict. If, on the other hand, the members of the courthouse community do not think of themselves as a unified community with a sense of tradition and shared expectations about interpersonal relations and case-processing routines, conflict will emerge more frequently.

Workgroup Circumvention of Policy Changes

There are a number of studies examining the effects of policy changes on the courtroom workgroup (Feeley & Kamin, 1996; McCoy, 1990). Many of these studies focus on attempts to limit the discretion of prosecutors and judges by, for example, restricting plea bargaining or requiring the imposition of **mandatory minimum sentences**. A common finding is that the members of the courtroom workgroup are able to devise ways of circumventing the policy changes. This is not surprising: Laws designed to dramatically change charging, plea bargaining, and sentencing practices will be resisted by judges and prosecutors if they believe that the changes will interfere with the efficient processing of cases or will result in outcomes that members of the workgroup view as inappropriately harsh or lenient.

Critics of state and federal sentencing guidelines predicted that members of the courtroom workgroup would find ways to circumvent or sabotage the guidelines. Skeptics, for example, predicted that discretion simply would shift from the judge to the prosecutor, who would manipulate the charges so that the defendant's sentence would approximate the going rate for the offense in the preguidelines era (Miethe, 1987). If, in other words, the going rate for a first offender convicted of armed robbery in the preguideline period was 7 years but the guidelines call for 10 years, the prosecutor could reduce the defendant's sentence liability by downgrading the charge to unarmed robbery. Because the prosecutor's discretion is essentially unregulated, the courtroom workgroup could effectively undermine the guidelines in this way.

Evidence regarding the so-called "**hydraulic displacement of discretion**" (Miethe, 1987, p. 156) from the judge at sentencing to the prosecutor at charging can be found in studies of offenders sentenced before and after the guidelines were implemented in Minnesota and before and after amendments to the guidelines in Washington State. Researchers in Minnesota found that prosecutors manipulated charges for property offenders, who faced a lower likelihood of imprisonment under the guidelines than in the preguideline era, and for sex offenders, who faced substantially more serious penalties under the guidelines (Knapp, 1987). In the postguideline period, prosecutors required property offenders to plead guilty to multiple counts, which enhanced their odds of imprisonment. Conversely, prosecutors would agree to a downward departure from the guidelines for offenders convicted of sex offenses. Engen and Steen (2000) found a similar pattern of charge manipulation in Washington State, where amendments to the guidelines toughened the penalties for first offenders convicted of delivery of heroin or cocaine and a court decision made conspiracy to deliver illegal drugs an unranked offense with a presumptive sentencing range of 0 to 12 months. Consistent with the hydraulic displacement argument, Engen and Steen found that the proportion of drug offenders convicted of simple possession increased, the proportion convicted of delivery decreased, and the proportion convicted of conspiracy to deliver drugs increased five-fold. Prosecutors in Washington, in other words, were using their charging and plea bargaining discretion to minimize the effect of the sentencing guideline amendments. As Engen and Steen concluded, the "severity of charges at conviction changed significantly following each change in the law, which suggests the manipulation of charges (and subsequent sentences) rather than a strict application of charges to the crimes committed" (p. 1384).

Evaluations of mandatory minimum sentences in New York, Massachusetts, and Michigan also revealed high rates of noncompliance and circumvention. An examination of the impact of New York's Rockefeller Drug Laws (Joint Committee on New York Drug Law Evaluation, 1978), touted as the nation's toughest drug laws, found that the proportion of felony arrests that resulted in indictment declined, as did the percentage of indictments that led to conviction. Although the likelihood of incarceration and the average sentence imposed on offenders convicted of drug felonies increased, the lower rates of indictment and conviction meant that the overall likelihood that someone arrested for a drug felony would be sentenced to prison remained about the same. A similar pattern was observed in Massachusetts (Beha, 1977; Rossman, Floyd, Pierce, McDevitt, & Bowers, 1979) and Michigan (Loftin & McDowall, 1981), which adopted mandatory sentencing provisions for carrying or using a firearm. For offenses targeted by these gun laws, the rate at which charges were dismissed increased and the conviction rate decreased. In all three states, prosecutors and judges devised ways to avoid application of the mandatory penalties.

Media Influence in Criminal Trials

The media in the United States are obsessed with celebrities, as are the citizens of this country. The media are also fascinated by crime, especially violent crime. The reporter's mantra, "if it bleeds, it leads," is manifested by what is shown on the evening news each night. When celebrities are accused of crime, media interest intensifies: Consider the media circuses surrounding the trials of O. J. Simpson, Winona Ryder, Michael Jackson, and Martha Stewart. The media also play up stories of otherwise anonymous individuals who are accused of particularly disturbing and heinous crimes. Prominent examples include the case of Scott Peterson, who was charged with killing his pregnant wife and unborn child, Andrea Yates, who was accused of drowning her five young children, and Casey Anthony, who was accused of murdering her two-year-old daughter.

All of this is important not just from an entertainment standpoint but because, according to one researcher, it is altering the American judicial process. In Johnson's (2003) view, the "possible detriments to the judicial system that arise from allowing cameras in the courtroom include prejudice to the defendant and his or her right to a fair trial, distraction from the court's need to 'maintain decorum,' and frustration to the public's interest in a fair justice system" (p. 147). Prejudicial media coverage is not confined to the courtroom. Pretrial coverage, for instance, can corrupt the jury pool by ensuring that all of those called for jury duty are familiar with the case.

The potential for a criminal trial to turn into a media circus (*Sheppard v. Maxwell*, 1966) stems from the Sixth Amendment, which states that the accused is entitled to a "speedy and public trial." The requirement of a public trial was designed to ensure that the defendant's rights are protected and that neither the judge nor the prosecutor abuses his or her power during the trial. The Supreme Court called attention to this in *In re Oliver* (1948):

> the knowledge that every criminal trial is subject to contemporaneous review in the forum of public opinion is an effective restraint on possible abuse of power.... Without publicity, all other checks are insufficient; in comparison of publicity, all other checks are of small account. [Furthermore,] the presence of interested spectators may keep [the defendant's] triers keenly alive to a sense of their responsibility and to the importance of their functions. (p. 271)

A public trial does not necessarily mean a trial with full participation by the media, however. In many cases, judges ban cameras from the courtroom because they believe that cameras are a distraction. The Supreme Court, in fact, has ruled that freedom of the press, which is protected by the First Amendment, "does not confer the right to use equipment in the courtroom which might jeopardize a fair trial, the atmosphere for which must be preserved at all costs" (*Estes v. Texas*, 1965, pp. 539–540). What judges cannot do without violating the First Amendment, at least in most cases and most types of court proceedings, is close the doors of their courtrooms to the media. The Supreme Court has stated that a judge cannot close the courtroom unless there are

> specific findings ... demonstrating that first, there is a substantial probability that the defendant's right to a fair trial will be prejudiced by publicity that closure would prevent, and second, reasonable alternatives to closure cannot adequately protect the defendant's fair trial rights. (*Press-Enterprise Co. v. Superior Court*, 1986)

According to the Court, judges should pursue other methods of dealing with trial publicity, including granting a continuance until pretrial publicity dies down, granting a motion for a change of venue, conducting the voir dire with special attention to potential jurors' familiarity with the case, sequestering jurors for the duration of the trial, and issuing gag orders, which prohibit the attorneys and other participants from talking about the case until it is over.

Summary: Plea Bargaining and Trial Dynamics

The American criminal justice system is dominated by guilty pleas, not trials. The members of the courtroom workgroup develop case-processing routines designed to ensure that cases are handled as efficiently and expeditiously as possible. Plea negotiations—which may involve a reduction in the severity of the charge, a reduction in the number of counts, or some type of sentence agreement—produce high rates of guilty pleas and limit the number of cases that go to trial. Supporters of plea bargaining argue that the system benefits both defendants and members of the courtroom workgroup; critics counter that plea bargains pervert justice, undercut the protections afforded to defendants, and coerce innocent defendants to plead guilty. Although a number of jurisdictions have attempted to eliminate or restrict plea bargaining, the effects of these reforms are symbolic rather than instrumental. It thus seems likely that for the foreseeable future, courts in the United States will continue to process most criminal cases using negotiated guilty pleas.

KEY TERMS

Ad hoc plea bargaining

Charge reduction

Hydraulic displacement of discretion

Local legal culture

Mandatory minimum sentences

Sentence agreement

Sentence lid

Sentencing guidelines

Slow plea of guilty

Substantial assistance departure

DISCUSSION QUESTIONS

1. Why were the U.S. courts initially reluctant to accept guilty pleas?

2. What do you believe is the most convincing explanation for the dramatic increase in guilty pleas during the 1800s and early 1900s?

3. Should judges be allowed to reject plea bargains involving charge reductions? Why or why not?

4. What are the advantages and disadvantages of plea bargaining? In your opinion, do the advantages outweigh the disadvantages?

5. Why do critics of plea bargaining claim that it is inefficient?

6. Why would it be difficult to ban or severely restrict plea bargaining? What are the various means that jurisdictions have used to reduce plea bargaining?

7. Summarize the results of the U.S. Sentencing Commission's study of the effect of race on substantial assistance departures from the sentencing guidelines.

8. Why did critics of sentencing guidelines predict that members of the courtroom workgroup would find ways to circumvent the guidelines? Were their predictions accurate?

9. The Sixth Amendment states that the accused is entitled to a "speedy and public trial." What does this mean? How does the First Amendment limit judges' ability to limit media access to trials?

WEB RESOURCES

The Case Against Plea Bargaining, Thomas Lynch (Cato Institute): http://www.cato.org/pubs/regulation/regv26n3/v26n3-7.pdf

Felony Defendants in Large Urban Counties, Bureau of Justice Statistics: http://bjs.ojp.usdoj.gov/index.cfm?ty=pbdetail&iid=2193

Frontline TV series: "The Plea" (available on video): http://www.pbs.org/wgbh/pages/frontline/shows/plea/

United States Sentencing Commission: http://www.ussc.gov

READING

Critics of plea bargaining have long argued that American reformers should turn their attention to the case-processing procedures used in European courts. As Ma notes in this article, plea bargaining, though not unknown in continental Europe, is much less ubiquitous in countries other than the United States. In this article, Ma compares prosecutorial practices in the United States with those in France, Germany, and Italy.

Prosecutorial Discretion and Plea Bargaining in the United States, France, Germany, and Italy

A Comparative Perspective

Yue Ma

Prosecutorial discretion has long been a point of controversy in the United States. Prosecutors, as the central figure in the administration of American criminal justice, make perhaps the most crucial decisions in the daily administration of justice. Prosecutors face the task of choosing, from a mass of overlapping criminal statutes, which of them best fits the facts presented by the police. The responsibility of prosecutors, however, is not limited to demonstrating their legal expertise in fitting charges to different fact situations. In making charging decisions, they are expected to take into consideration a broad range of factors, including evidentiary sufficiency, the extent of the harm caused by the offense, the disproportion of the authorized punishment in relation to the particular offense or the offender, cooperation of the accused in the apprehension or conviction of others, and the cost of prosecution to the criminal justice system (American Bar Association, 1986).

Given the complex nature of prosecutorial decision making, it is well recognized that prosecutors must be afforded a certain degree of discretion. Even commentators who are most critical of American prosecutorial discretion agree that discretionary power when properly exercised facilitates rather than hinders the cause of justice (Davis, 1969; Vorenberg, 1981). What concerns the critics is prosecutors' overly broad and essentially unchecked discretion. More than 60 years ago, then Attorney General and later U.S. Supreme Court Justice Robert Jackson described the prosecutor as having "more control over life, liberty, and reputation than any other person in America" (R. H. Jackson, 1940, p. 18). Jackson warned that, because the prosecutor stands a fair chance of finding at least a technical violation of some act on the part of almost anyone, the prosecuting power, if not properly exercised, is susceptible to the greatest danger of abuse. Another early commentator, Thurman Arnold, also cautioned about the great potential of prosecutorial abuse. Arnold opined that "the idea that a prosecuting attorney should be permitted to use his discretion concerning the laws which he will enforce and those which

SOURCE: Ma, Yue. (2002). Prosecutorial Discretion and Plea Bargaining in the United States, France, Germany, and Italy. *International Criminal Justice Review*, 12. © 2002 College of Health and Human Sciences, Georgia State University.

he will disregard appears to the ordinary citizens to border on anarchy" (Arnold, 1932, p. 7).

Despite the concerns raised by the early commentators, in the ensuing years neither legislatures nor courts have taken serious steps to restrain prosecutorial discretion. The past 30 years have actually witnessed a dramatic expansion of the power and prestige of prosecutors (Currie, 1998; Gershman, 1992; Walker, 1993). With the transition from a due process–oriented criminal justice model to a model that attaches overriding emphasis on crime control, and with the rise of the mentality of winning the "war on crime" at all costs, instead of restraining prosecutorial discretion, legislatures have granted even more power to prosecutors (Gordon, 1994). As legislatures have armed prosecutors with broad new weapons such as RICO, sentencing guidelines, the Violent Crime Control and Law Enforcement Act, three-strikes laws, and truth-in-sentencing laws, the courts have cooperated in the efforts by taking an increasingly passive stance in providing supervision over prosecutors. The expanded power of the prosecutor, coupled with the relaxed judicial supervision, has made the prosecutor truly the most preeminent figure in the administration of criminal justice in America. Commentators who are critical of the continuing expansion of prosecutorial power argue that the current scope of discretion is unjustifiably broad in terms of the principles of fairness, equity, and accountability on which the American criminal justice system is based, and it creates a potential for prosecutorial abuse greater than ever before (Ely, 1980; Gershman, 1992; Ohlin & Remington, 1993; Uviller, 1999; Vorenberg, 1981).

In debating whether and how prosecutorial discretion should be restrained, reform-minded commentators have time and again turned their attention to continental European countries' practices and experience, believing that the continental law models may offer cures for several troublesome aspects of the American system of justice (Davis, 1969; Langbein, 1974, 1977, 1979, 1981; Schlesinger, 1977; Weigend, 1980). In the 1970s, as the American system turned increasingly to plea bargaining as the way of resolving criminal cases, advocates of American law reform spoke with great admiration of the lack of plea bargaining

in continental law countries and suggested that the American system be reformed on the model of "the land without plea bargaining" (Langbein, 1979, p. 224). Other commentators, skeptical of the claim that continental countries had succeeded in running a smooth system without resource to bargaining justice, argued that the nonexistence of plea bargaining in Europe was more a myth than a reality. They maintained that plea bargaining was by no means an American phenomenon and that analogues of plea bargaining existed in continental countries as well. In their view, continental systems in substance operated not much differently from the way the American system operated; there was therefore little to gain in attempting reforms on continental models (B. L. Goldstein & Marcus, 1977). The debate in the 1970s produced few conclusions and virtually no reform efforts.

Since the early 1990s, there seems to be a rekindled interest in referring to foreign experience as a source of ideas and inspiration for American law reform (Dubber, 1997; Frase, 1990; Frase & Weigend, 1995; Van Kessel, 1992). However, continental law systems in the past 30 years have undergone significant changes. In the context of prosecutorial practice, nothing illustrates the extent of the changes better than the emergence of plea bargaining and the gradual expansion of prosecutors' autonomy. Nevertheless, a careful analysis of continental and American prosecutorial systems reveals that—the recent expansion of prosecutorial autonomy in continental law countries notwithstanding—American prosecutors still stand virtually alone in their overly broad and largely unchecked discretion. Though plea bargaining has emerged in continental law countries, it remains a unique American feature that prosecutors are allowed to gain such an overwhelming dominance in the bargaining process that they can exact highly pressurized pleas from defendants. It is in this context that continental models may still offer valuable lessons in fashioning reforms of the American system.

This article seeks to provide readers with a comparative analysis of the prosecutorial practices in the United States and in three continental European countries. The three European countries included in the study, France, Germany, and Italy, are traditionally regarded as preeminent continental law countries (Merryman, 1985; Zweigert & Kötz, 1987). The selection of the three countries is further justified on the ground that comparative legal scholars in most instances include criminal procedures of the three countries in their exploration of the possibilities of American law reform on continental models (Davis, 1969; B. L. Goldstein & Marcus, 1977; Langbein, 1974, 1977, 1979, 1981; Weigend, 1980). Discussion of the prosecutorial practices in these three countries therefore offers a better reference point for American readers. The article introduces to readers the recent developments in both the United States and the three continental countries, such as the vast accretion of prosecutorial power in the United States and the various forms of plea bargaining in the three continental countries. Attention will be given especially to the differences between the American and continental prosecutorial practices and to those aspects that the American system may borrow from the continental systems.

 ## Prosecutorial Discretion and Plea Bargaining in the United States

Charging and plea bargaining are at the core of prosecutors' power. A prosecutor's first formal duty is to determine whether a defendant should be charged with a crime and, if so, what charge should be brought. But what makes American prosecutors such powerful figures in the administration of justice is not their power to charge but rather their power *not* to prosecute further even in the face of sufficient evidence. Prosecutors' absolute power to dismiss a case can be traced to the old common law doctrine *nolle prosequi*. Although the power of *nolle prosequi* is commonly justified on the ground that prosecutors' discretion not to act is a form of leniency, commentators have long warned that the power to be lenient is the power to discriminate. Through decisions about whether and what to charge, prosecutors hold the power to decide who will undergo the expense, anxiety, and embarrassment of criminal proceedings

and who will face society's most fundamental sanctions. Injustice may easily result from the improper exercise of the discretion to be or not to be lenient (Davis, 1969; Vorenberg, 1981).

While prosecutors' discretion to engage in selective enforcement has been heavily criticized, their power to do so has been repeatedly upheld by appellate courts. The judicial reluctance to interfere with prosecutors' charging authority is perhaps best explained by then Judge of the U.S. Court of Appeals for the District of Columbia and later Chief Justice of the U.S. Supreme Court Warren Burger. Burger stated that "few subjects are less adapted to judicial review than the exercise by the Executive of his discretion in deciding when and whether to institute criminal proceedings, or what precise charge should be made, or whether to dismiss a proceeding once brought" (*Newman v. United States*, 1967, p. 480). Today, with more than 90 percent of criminal cases in the American system being disposed of by way of guilty pleas, the full display of American prosecutors' discretionary power probably can be best seen in the process of plea bargaining.

Thirty years ago, when the U.S. Supreme Court recognized the legality of plea bargaining, it justified the acceptance of the bargaining of justice largely on economic grounds. The Court reasoned that "if every criminal charge were subject to a full scale trial, the states and the Federal Government would need to multiply by many times the number of judges and court facilities." Based on this concern, the Court described plea bargaining as "an essential component of the administration of justice" and held that "properly administered, it is to be encouraged" (*Santobello v. New York*, 1971, p. 261). Although the Court justified plea bargaining on economic grounds, it assumed at the same time that the bargaining process would be a fair give-and-take process. The Court assumed that the defendant, represented by counsel and protected by procedural safeguards, would be capable of "intelligent choice in response to prosecutorial persuasion" (*Bordenkircher v. Hayes*, 1978, p. 363). Commentators, however, are quick to note the radically skewed balance of advantage in the bargaining process. They point out that plea bargaining is far from a process in which defendants enter into consensual agreements with prosecutors after adversarial negotiations. Defendants in many cases must simply choose between pleading guilty and getting mercy, on the one hand, or proceeding to trial and facing the risk of receiving a much more severe penalty, on the other. Commentators therefore characterize plea bargaining as prosecutors' unilateral determination of the level of defendants' criminal culpability and the appropriate punishment for defendants (Alschuler, 1983; Gifford, 1983).

If the playing field was tilted in favor of prosecutors when the Court first sanctioned the practice three decades ago, today, with the vastly expanded prosecutorial power, the inherent inequality in the bargaining process has only intensified, making the idea of adversarial negotiation between the defense and the prosecution almost obsolete (Gershman, 1992; Uviller, 1999). Though plea bargaining has now become the most prevalent form of resolving criminal cases, the U.S. Supreme Court, relative to its case law on trial adjudication, has not developed clear constitutional limitations on the guilty plea process. The Court in principle maintains the basic voluntariness standard for accepting guilty pleas. It has held that a guilty plea that is compelled by the government is unconstitutional because it violates the Fifth Amendment protection against self-incrimination (*Brady v. United States*, 1970). It has further held that punishing a defendant for his exercise of his legal rights is "a due process violation of the most basic sort" (*Bordenkircher v. Hayes*, 1978, p. 363). In the context of plea bargaining, however, the Court has placed very few limitations on the types of inducements that prosecutors may use to obtain guilty pleas. Prosecutors today, with their vastly expanded power, have greater leverage than ever to compel plea bargaining and to force cooperation. A fundamental issue raised by the current bargaining practice is that, with prosecutors having the power to coerce defendants into pleading guilty by threatening draconian penalties for noncooperation, it becomes highly questionable whether the guilty pleas agreed upon by defendants can be considered to truly rest on voluntariness.

The coercive nature of American plea bargaining is well illustrated in various tactics that prosecutors may use in the bargaining process. "Overcharging" is a tactic often employed by prosecutors to augment leverage in bargaining. Overcharging is an ambiguous term and may include both unlawful and lawful but ethically inappropriate prosecutorial decision making. The basic legal criterion that prosecutors meet in making a charging decision is that charges filed must be supported by probable cause (*Bordenkircher v. Hayes*, 1978). However, prosecutors may deliberately file charges that are not supported by probable cause as a bargaining strategy. The strategy, though it is unlawful, can be a successful one. Because American law does not require prosecutors to open their entire file for inspection by the defense, the defense may well be kept in the dark as to the true strength of the prosecutor's case against the defendant.

Charging defendants with offenses without the support of probable cause is clearly unlawful, but a more difficult issue is whether all charging decisions that are supported by probable cause should be considered appropriate. Legally speaking, prosecutors' charging decisions are not in violation of law so long as the charges are supported by probable cause. In reality, however, if the goal of filing the charges is to secure convictions at trial, no cautious and responsible prosecutor would charge a defendant with crimes that are supported only by probable cause. The prosecutor must be confident that evidence is strong enough to meet the trial standard of proof beyond a reasonable doubt. But prosecutors may well decide to file charges that are only supported by probable cause in order to gain bargaining leverage. Because American prosecutors enjoy literally unlimited power to drop charges at later stages, they never have to suffer the embarrassment that the charges cannot be proven at trial. They can drop the weak charges and go to trial with only charges that are supported by stronger evidence. Considering that prosecutors bear an ethical duty to "seek justice, not merely to convict" (American Bar Association, 1986, p. 3.6), filing multiple charges with the intent to compel plea bargaining, though not unlawful, is arguably in violation of prosecutors' ethical duty not to be mere partisan advocates.

Apart from filing multiple charges, another powerful weapon available to prosecutors is charging defendants under penalty-enhancing statutes. Penalty-enhancing statutes authorize enhanced punishments for offenders who have a certain number of prior convictions or who have committed offenses with certain aggravating circumstances. If a defendant is convicted under these statutes, the defendant cannot escape the minimum mandatory sentences stipulated in the statutes. Prosecutors, however, maintain the discretion to charge a defendant with offenses that would trigger the enhancement. Prosecutors' freedom to charge or not to charge under penalty-enhancing statutes therefore provides a powerful leverage to pressure defendants to accept deals desired by prosecutors.

Prosecutors' ability to influence the penalty of defendants is further strengthened by the adoption of federal and state sentencing guidelines. Sentencing guidelines are adopted in the name of curtailing sentencing judges' discretion in order to avoid sentencing disparity. The guidelines, however, have hardly solved the problem of sentencing disparity. Although they have greatly reduced sentencing judges' discretion, the guidelines have made no attempt to restrict prosecutors' charging decisions. Prosecutors' decision making on whether and what to charge has therefore become the most crucial factor in determining the length of defendants' sentences.

One of the most disturbing aspects of sentencing guidelines is the granting of prosecutorial power to request that defendants be punished for crimes of which they were not convicted. Under most sentencing guidelines, prosecutors are allowed to introduce at the sentencing phase far more serious but unproven crimes in order to enhance defendants' punishment. Because at the sentencing stage courts follow a more lenient standard in determining whether unproven crimes should be admitted as a factor in determining defendants' sentences, a tactic that prosecutors may use is to charge defendants with crimes of which they are confident of conviction and to save the weaker but possibly more serious charges to be introduced at the sentencing hearings as aggravating factors to enhance defendants' penalty. Using this tactic, prosecutors in many cases have succeeded in imposing on defendants sentences that are far more severe than the sentences that are stipulated for the crimes of which the defendants were convicted.

The accretion of prosecutorial power is also seen in the effect of the "federalization" of crime. In the past several decades the federal government has become increasingly involved in regulating criminal conduct that was traditionally regarded as matters for states. The federal expansion into the criminal law arena has created a vast area of concurrent federal and state jurisdiction. This dual jurisdiction is best illustrated in the area of illegal drugs. Because of generally more severe penalties provided in federal statutes for similar offenses, the mere prospect of being prosecuted in the federal system, rather than in the state system, constitutes a potent threat to defendants.

To be fair to prosecutors, as legislatures have created new crimes without providing the resources for trial and punishment of all those who could be convicted, prosecutors have increasingly been forced to allocate resources by exercising discretion to decide whether to charge and whether to offer leniency in exchange for guilty pleas. Plea bargaining undoubtedly plays an important role in conserving the limited criminal justice resources. Nevertheless, considering that what prosecutors try to persuade defendants to give up is defendants' constitutionally protected right to trial, it is quite reasonable to insist that everything be done to ensure that the bargaining process is a fair and just one. The current practice of providing prosecutors with such great power to compel guilty pleas and to force cooperation can hardly be said to have met this fairness standard. To allow prosecutors to threaten defendants with such enormous sentencing differential between pleading guilty and proceeding to trial serves only to underscore the discrepancy between promise and performance in the American criminal justice system and its hypocrisy vis-à-vis the constitutionally guaranteed right to a jury trial.

Prosecutors' power, though broad, is not totally unconstrained. The U.S. Supreme Court has long held that the exercise of prosecutorial discretion is subject to constitutional constraints. The Supreme Court first addressed the issue of selective prosecution in the seminal decision *Yick Wo v. Hopkins* (1886). In that case, the Court overturned Yick Wo's conviction on the grounds of improper exercise of prosecutorial discretion. A San Francisco ordinance prohibited operating a laundry in a wooden building without the consent of the Board of Supervisors. The Board routinely granted permits to Caucasian but not to Chinese applicants.

In invalidating the prosecutor's decision, the Court stated that even though the law is fair and impartial on its face, if it is "applied and administered by public authority with an evil eye and an unequal hand, so as practically to make unjust and illegal discriminations between persons in similar circumstances, material to their rights, the denial of equal justice is still within the prohibition of the Constitution" (*Yick Wo v. Hopkins*, 1886, pp. 373–374). The Court in later cases, however, made it clear that not all forms of arbitrary prosecution are prohibited by the Constitution. The Constitution prohibits selective prosecution on such grounds as race, gender, religion, and the exercise of First Amendment rights (*Oyler v. Boles*, 1962; *Wayte v. United States*, 1985).

Although the modern Court still upholds the position that prosecutors are prohibited from filing prosecution on constitutionally impermissible grounds, it has set a high evidentiary threshold for proving such improper exercise of prosecutorial discretion. The modern Court takes the position that mere discriminatory effect does not suffice to show a constitutional violation. To prevail in a claim on equal protection grounds, a party must provide evidence to show discriminatory purpose (*Washington v. Davis*, 1976). In challenging improper exercise of prosecutorial discretion, defendants therefore must show impermissible motive on the part of prosecutors. The problems involved in showing such motive are enormous. A prosecutor would rarely admit that the charging decision was based on constitutionally impermissible grounds. The Court meanwhile is reluctant to make other means available for defendants to prove prosecutors' motive. The Court's recent decision in *United States v. Armstrong* (1996) provides the best example to illustrate the difficulty that the Court has created for defendants in such an attempt.

The *Armstrong* case involves a challenge to a prosecuting decision based on race. The respondents in *Armstrong* were all blacks and they were indicted on crack cocaine and federal firearms charges. The respondents filed a motion for discovery, alleging that they were improperly selected for prosecution in the federal court in the crack cases. Based on statistical evidence showing that nonblacks were disproportionately being prosecuted in state courts, thus facing less severe penalties, the respondents sought a court order to compel the U.S. Attorney's Office to disclose relevant information regarding the selective prosecution of crack cases. The district court issued the order, but the U.S. Supreme Court reversed.

In reversing the discovery order, the Court stated the need to establish a "substantial barrier" to proving selective prosecution claims. The Court held that, before prosecutors can be required to comply with a discovery request regarding selective prosecution, defendants must meet the threshold requirement of a credible showing that there is a different treatment of similarly situated persons. The Court justified its ruling on the grounds of respect for the separation of powers between judicial and executive branches and the interests in facilitating effective law enforcement. The Court reasoned that judicial deference to prosecutorial discretion would serve the purposes of avoiding unnecessary delay in criminal proceedings and protecting the prosecution from being compelled to reveal prosecutorial strategies.

The *Armstrong* case poses hurdles for defendants to overcome. If defendants want to request discovery from the prosecution, they must first demonstrate with credible evidence that similarly situated persons are not prosecuted, but such evidence is usually available only to prosecutors. Without access to such evidence, defendants may never succeed in seeking a discovery order or prevail in a claim challenging the constitutionality of a prosecutorial decision. Given the modern Court's prosecution-oriented approach, one should not be surprised to learn that *Yick Wo* was the first and the last time the Supreme Court struck down a prosecution on the grounds of improper selection of the target by prosecutors.

Setting formidable evidentiary thresholds for defendants seeking discovery is not the only step that the Court has taken to insulate prosecutors from judicial supervision. The Court has also strengthened prosecutors' discretionary power by relaxing the constitutional protections embodied in the exclusionary rule and due process (*New York v. Quarles*, 1984; *Nix v. Williams*, 1984; *United States v. Leon*, 1984) and by interpreting statutory and evidentiary rules in favor of the prosecution (*United States v. Mezzanatto*, 1995).

The passive stance taken by the Court with respect to judicial supervision over prosecutorial behavior has undoubtedly stimulated a law enforcement mentality that the "end justifies the means." The approach of extreme deference to prosecutorial decision making has created a great incentive on the part of prosecutors to enact bold and aggressive prosecutorial initiatives and to test judicial tolerance for highly offensive law enforcement methods.

 ## Prosecutorial Discretion in Continental Law Countries

Despite the common perception that all continental law systems operate in more or less the same fashion, there are marked differences in criminal justice practices between continental law systems. In the context of prosecutorial practice, the principle of compulsory prosecution is far from universally accepted. Prosecutorial discretion in filing charges differs among continental law countries, depending on whether a country follows the "expediency principle" or the "legality principle." In countries that follow the expediency principle, prosecutors are allowed a high degree of autonomy in making charging decisions; prosecutors have discretion to consider various public interest factors in deciding whether charges should be filed in a particular case. In countries that follow the legality principle, by contrast, prosecutors are required to file charges whenever sufficient evidence exists to support the guilt of the accused; public interest considerations are irrelevant in prosecutors' decision making (Fionda, 1995).

Few countries follow either principle strictly. However, based on the extent to which a country follows one principle or the other, commentators are still able to determine whether a country follows the expediency principle or the legality principle. For instance, the prosecutorial systems in France and the Netherlands are classified as following the expediency principle, whereas the systems in Germany and Italy are categorized as following the legality principle (Fionda, 1995; Grande, 2000; Verrest, 2000).

A noticeable development in recent years is that even in countries that follow the legality principle there are signs of moving away from strict adherence to compulsory prosecution. This trend is probably best seen in the emergence of plea bargaining in Germany and Italy. What is equally noticeable, however, is that, despite the emergence of plea bargaining in continental law countries, no country has allowed prosecutors to gain such bargaining advantage over the accused that they are in a position to exact highly pressurized pleas from the accused. This point is amply illustrated in the following discussion of plea bargaining analogues in France, Germany, and Italy.

France

France follows the expediency principle. The enforcement of the law does not oblige prosecutors to file charges in all cases with a view to obtaining the severest sentences possible. On the contrary, a long-established principle in France is that prosecutors, as members of the judiciary, are not entrusted with the task of securing convictions in all cases. Prosecutors' obligation is rather to determine a just solution to the case and present it to the judge (Sheehan, 1975; Vouin, 1970). This principle is embodied in the French Code of Penal Procedure. The provision in the Code that defines the responsibility of prosecutors simply provides that "the prosecutor receives complaints and denunciations and decides what to do with them" (Code of Penal Procedure, Art. 40). This language is interpreted to permit prosecutors not to prosecute even when sufficient evidence exists to prove the guilt of an accused. Available statistics indicate that in France, as in the United States, the majority of cases reported to prosecutors do not end with a criminal trial. It is estimated that between 50 percent and 80 percent of cases brought to the attention of prosecutors in France are disposed of by no-further-proceeding (Frase, 1990; Verrest, 2000; West, Desdevises, Fenet, Gaurier, & Heussaff, 1993).

French law classifies criminal offenses into three categories: *contraventions* (minor offenses), *délits* (intermediate offenses), and *crimes* (serious offenses). Corresponding to the three types of offenses, there are three first-instance trial courts. *Contraventions* are tried in the Police Court; *délits* are tried in the Correctional Court; and *crimes* are tried in the Assize Court (Terrill, 1999).

The pretrial screening process differs depending on the type of offense involved and the court in which the prosecution is to be instituted. The law mandates a stringent pretrial screening for cases to be tried as *crimes* in the Assize Court. Once a decision is made that a case is to be tried in the Assize Court, the prosecutor must send the case to the examining magistrate for a judicial investigation. If the magistrate finds sufficient evidence to bind the case over for trial, the case must be sent to the indicting chamber for further screening. The role of prosecutors is quite limited in cases that involve a judicial investigation. Prosecutors have the discretion to make the initial decision whether to refer the case to the examining magistrate, but once the case is sent to the magistrate prosecutors lose control over the case. At the completion of the magistrate's investigation, prosecutors must follow the magistrate's recommendation for disposition (Frase, 1990; Tomlinson, 1983; West et al., 1993).

In contrast to the stringent pretrial screening for cases to be tried in the Assize Court, French law requires no pretrial screening of any kind for cases to be tried in the Correctional Court or the Police Court. Prosecutors have the sole authority to decide whether a case should be prosecuted or dismissed. Because of the cumbersome procedures involved in prosecuting a case in the Assize Court, prosecutors understandably view with distaste the prospect of trying all *crimes* in the Assize Court. Although the law requires that all *crimes* be tried in the Assize Court, prosecutors may circumvent this limitation by charging an offender who has committed a *crime* with only a *délit* or a *contravention*. The prosecutors' power to reduce charges is known as *correctionalization*. It is this power of correctionalization that is referred to by American commentators as the French analogue of plea bargaining (Frase, 1990; B. L. Goldstein & Marcus, 1977; Tomlinson, 1983).

The correctionalization of a *crime* to a *délit* or a *contravention* is undoubtedly similar to the charge reduction used by American prosecutors. The varied reasons cited by French prosecutors for correctionalizing a *crime* are also similar to those given by American prosecutors for reducing charges. French prosecutors may correctionalize a *crime* to avoid subjecting defendants to the possibility of more severe penalties imposed by the Assize Court. There are times that,

though an offense is technically a *crime*, the prosecutor may feel that under the particular circumstances it is not appropriate to subject the defendant to the harsh punishment that is spelled out for the offense. The prosecutor may then charge the defendant with a less serious offense to avoid the harsh penalty. Prosecutors may also use correctionalization as a means to alleviate the congested calendar in the Assize Court (Frase, 1990; Leigh & Zedner, 1992; Tomlinson, 1983).

The similarities between American plea bargaining and French correctionalization, however, end here. In France, there is no evidence indicating that the reduction of charges or the decision to correctionalize a *crime* is a result of bargains and negotiations between prosecutors and the defense. The decision to correctionalize a case is the unilateral decision of prosecutors. The only role that defendants play is their right to reject a prosecutor's decision to correctionalize a *crime* to a *délit* or a *contravention*. Because defendants enjoy more elaborate procedural protections if their cases are tried in the Assize Court, if defendants are willing to risk more severe penalties in case of conviction, they have the right to insist that their cases be tried in the Assize Court. In reality, however, few defendants choose to challenge prosecutors' decisions to correctionalize a *crime* to a *délit* or a *contravention* (Frase, 1990; Tomlinson, 1983).

In the American system, a prosecutor's promise to reduce charges is usually made on the condition that the defendant makes a full and irrevocable confession of guilt. By contrast, a French prosecutor's decision to correctionalize a *crime* is not dependent on whether a confession is made by the accused. Relative to the procedural protections granted to suspects by American law, French law grants suspects very limited protections at the police investigative stage. Under French law, the accused has the right to remain silent, but police bear no obligation to inform. A limited right to counsel at the police inquiry was not introduced into the French criminal procedure until 1993. Under the amended law, suspects have the right to seek legal consultation only after the first 20 hours of detention have expired (Field & West, 1995; Hatchard, Huber, & Volger, 1996). During the first 20 hours, police are therefore given the opportunity to interrogate suspects without informing them of their right to remain silent or providing them with legal representation. Because suspects at this stage are not represented by counsel, it is unlikely that their confessions are made with the expectation that the confessions will lead to prosecutors deciding to reduce their offenses to less serious ones.

Furthermore, under French law a defendant's admission of guilt does not replace trial, and a confession is never irrevocable. Even after an admission of guilt, a defendant still has to go through a trial. A defendant's decision not to contest his guilt, however, will make the trial shorter. A defendant may retract the confession at any time, either before or during the trial. The defendant's retraction, however, would not prevent the confession from being introduced at trial. The defendant's confession, retracted or not, will be introduced to court for consideration. The only effect of a retraction is that the prosecutor in such a case will introduce to court both the defendant's confession and the fact that it was retracted (West et al., 1993).

Unlike American prosecutors, who have unlimited power to drop charges before and after they are filed with the court, French prosecutors' broad charging authority is confined to the initial decision whether to file a charge with the court. Once prosecutors file charges with the examining magistrate or the court, they cannot drop the charges without the approval of the magistrate or the court (Frase, 1990; Tomlinson, 1983). French prosecutors' inability to drop charges at post-filing makes it impossible for them to use overcharging as a means to coerce cooperation from the accused. Because prosecutors cannot drop charges once they are filed, if the charges are not supported by sufficient evidence they can only be rejected by the magistrate or the court (Frase, 1990; West et al., 1993). From the prosecutor's point of view, to file charges that would be rejected by the court or the magistrate as inadequately supported by the evidence could serve no purpose and would negatively reflect on the prosecutor's professional ability. It is hard to imagine that cautious prosecutors would be willing to risk their professional reputation for the doubtful advantage of using overcharging as a means to induce cooperation from the accused.

Charging defendants with multiple offenses is another powerful weapon available to American prosecutors. What makes multiple-offense charges a potent threat is the likelihood that defendants may be subject to multiple consecutive sentences if convicted. French prosecutors, with their broad charging discretion, can certainly decide to charge an accused with multiple offenses. Under the French sentencing law, however, it is unlikely that such a move would provide prosecutors with powerful leverage to induce cooperation from the accused. French law prohibits the imposition of multiple consecutive sentences in multiple-offense cases. This means that, even though an accused is convicted of multiple offenses, only one sentence for the most serious offense can be pronounced. The maximum sentence for the most serious offense cannot be enhanced on the ground that the accused was also convicted of collateral offenses (Frase, 1990; West et al., 1993).

Prosecutorial discretion in France can also be constrained by victims. French law provides several means for victims to challenge prosecutors' decision not to prosecute. French law also recognizes the right of victims to seek compensation by joining the criminal proceedings as a civil party. The law stipulates two ways in which victims may do this. Victims may make a request to be joined as a party to criminal proceedings already instituted by prosecutors. However, if prosecutors decline to prosecute a case, victims may open the proceedings for compensation in a criminal court by themselves. If a victim chooses to open the proceedings for compensation in a criminal court, the prosecutor is then obligated to prosecute the case, even though prosecution was initially declined (Terrill, 1999; West et al., 1993).

Victims also have the power to prevent prosecutors from correctionalizing a *crime* to a *délit* or a *contravention*. If victims wish to seek a more severe penalty than the Correctional Court or Police Court can impose, they may file a complaint directly with the examining magistrate and request that the magistrate commence a judicial inquiry into the case. The reference of a case to the magistrate by a victim has the same effect as the reference of a case by prosecutors. Once the case is referred to the magistrate, prosecutors are no longer in control of the case. The magistrate, upon finding sufficient evidence, may order prosecutors to prosecute the case in the Assize Court (Tomlinson, 1983; West et al., 1993; Zauberman, 1991).

It should be noted that correctionalization is not the only means available to French prosecutors to avoid lengthy trials in the Assize Court. Since the early 1980s, there has been a steady increase in the number of criminal offenses in France. To allow prosecutors to dispose of the dramatically increased number of cases in a timely fashion, French law makes available to them several options of settling cases. In minor offense cases, instead of prosecuting, the prosecutor may give an order to the police to issue an official warning to the offender. In cases of vandalism and petty theft, the prosecutor may ask the offender to repair the damage or compensate the loss suffered by the victim as a condition to dismiss the case. The prosecutor can also settle a case through mediation. If a mediation agreement can be reached by the victim and the offender, the prosecutor may decide to dismiss the case on the condition that the offender follow through on the terms of the agreement (e.g., pay damages to the victim) (Verrest, 2000).

For offenses that are punishable by no more than seven years imprisonment, the law also permits prosecutors, with the consent of the accused, to process the case through speeded up trial proceedings (*comparution immédiate*). These proceedings are most commonly used in cases where offenders are caught red-handed. In the speeded up trial proceedings, suspects, after a brief meeting with their lawyers, are brought to trial immediately. Prosecutors, however, do not have the sole control over the proceedings. The court has the final authority to decide whether the speeded up proceedings are appropriate. The court can decide to postpone dealing with the case and refer it back to the prosecutor if it feels that the case was insufficiently investigated (Verrest, 2000).

Germany

The appeal of the German prosecutorial system to American law reformers lies largely in the principle of compulsory prosecution. Many American readers believe that, under the rule of compulsory prosecution, prosecutors are allowed no discretion and are required to prosecute all cases that are supported by the evidence.

This view, however, does not represent a correct understanding of the rule. The rule of compulsory prosecution was incorporated into the German Code of Criminal Procedure in 1877 when the Code was first drawn up (Fionda, 1995). The aim of incorporating the rule into the Code was to achieve an equal application of law and to prevent the possibility that prosecutors would use law enforcement power to persecute political opponents (Schramm, 1970). Since 1877, a variety of new provisions aimed at widening prosecutors' discretion have been incorporated into the Code. These new provisions have led to a gradual erosion of the principle of mandatory prosecution.

The celebrated rule of compulsory prosecution is prescribed in Section 152 (II) of the Code of Criminal Procedure. The Section provides that prosecutors must "take action against all prosecutable offenses, to the extent that there is sufficient factual basis." The Code, however, contains several exceptions to the rule. A major exception is provided in Section 153a. This section, which was added to the Code in 1975, authorizes prosecutors to refrain from prosecuting any minor offenses on the condition that the accused agrees to pay a sum of money to a charitable organization or to the state. The section, when it was enacted, was designed to limit prosecutorial discretion to misdemeanor cases only. It was further expected that prosecutors, guided by the rule of compulsory prosecution, would exercise the power of dismissal only in trivial misdemeanor cases (Langbein, 1979). Implementation since the section's enactment, however, shows that prosecutors have used the section to dismiss both petty and serious crimes. The exceptions to the rule of compulsory prosecution have provided opportunities for the development of plea bargaining in Germany.

The origin of plea bargaining in Germany can be traced back to the early 1970s. Initially, the bargaining practice was limited in scope and restricted to minor offenses. By the mid-1970s, with the increase in prosecutions against white-collar crimes and drug offenses, plea bargaining became more prevalent. Since the 1990s, the rise in popularity of plea bargaining is attributable directly to the sharp increase in white-collar crimes, economic crimes, drug offenses, and the increased caseload brought about by German reunification. Plea bargaining, as noted by the commentators, occurs most frequently in cases involving white-collar crimes, tax evasion, drug offenses, and crimes against the environment (Dubber, 1997; Frase & Weigend, 1995; Herrmann, 1992; Swenson, 1995).

Plea bargaining in Germany takes different forms. The most commonly identified forms are (a) diversion bargains under Section 153a, (b) bargains over penal orders, and (c) bargains over confessions. Section 153a permits the prosecutor to conditionally dismiss cases when the crime is minor and the public interest does not require prosecution. Under the section, prosecutors may refrain from prosecuting on condition that the offender either provides some form of compensation to the victim or makes payment to a charity or to the Treasury. Since its enactment in 1975, Section 153a has opened up the possibility for the prosecutor and the defense to negotiate as to whether a case should be settled.

In complicated cases, if prosecutors believe that further investigation may occupy too much time, they may offer to settle the case under the section. To induce defendants to settle, prosecutors may make it clear to the defense counsel that the offer is a one-time offer and if it is refused there will be no further chance for negotiation. Defense counsel may also influence prosecutorial decision making on whether to settle a case. Under German law, defense counsel at trial has the right to make motions to request that the judge consider additional evidence favorable to the accused. To induce prosecutors to settle the case before the case goes to trial, defense counsel may threaten to make numerous motions requesting the court to examine additional evidence. Concerned that such moves may delay the trial, prosecutors may agree to settle the case under Section 153a (Albrecht, 2000; Frase & Weigend, 1995; Herrmann, 1992).

The second form of plea bargaining originates from the penal order procedure. The penal order is a document prepared by the prosecutor, which contains the accused's offense and the punishment for the offense. Punishments in the penal order include day fines, a suspended prison sentence of up to one year,

suspension of a driving license, and forfeiture of the profits of the crime. The prosecutor must obtain the consent from a judge to make the order legally binding. Once judicial authorization is obtained, the prosecutor dispatches the order to the accused. The accused has 14 days to decide whether to accept the order or to request a trial in court.

The attractiveness of the penal order for the accused lies in less severe penalties contained in the order compared to the potential sentences that could be imposed if the accused were convicted at trial. In the vast majority of cases, the penalty contained in the penal order is a monetary fine. By paying the fine, the accused avoids embarrassment, publicity, and the costs of trial. Under the penal order procedure, though there is a possibility that the accused may receive more severe penalties by choosing to go to trial, a higher sentence is not an automatic consequence of the accused's rejection of the penal order. If the court were to increase the severity of the accused's penalty after a trial, the judge must indicate the reasons for such a decision. Rejection of the penal order alone is not sufficient grounds to increase the severity of the penalty to be imposed on the accused. There is therefore no evidence showing that prosecutors use the possible higher sentences to pressure the accused to accept a penal order (Frase & Weigend, 1995; Herrmann, 1992).

The third form of plea bargaining is bargaining over confessions. In Germany, as in France, an accused's confession and guilty plea do not replace the trial. The advantage for the prosecutor in obtaining a confession is that an accused's admission of guilt could shorten the length of the trial. A noticeable distinction between German bargaining over confessions and American plea bargaining is the role of the judge in the bargaining process. Plea bargaining in the United States is typically a negotiation between prosecutor and defense counsel. The judge is not an active participant in the bargaining. In Germany, before a formal charge is filed with the court, the prosecutor plays a major part in negotiating with defense counsel regarding the prospect of an accused's confession; the prosecutor may offer to charge the accused with fewer offenses than the accused is alleged to have committed or to move for a lenient sentence at trial. Once the charge is filed with the court, however, the judge may become an active participant in the plea negotiation.

A judge who is faced with a backlog on the docket may contact defense counsel and inquire whether the accused would be willing to make a confession at the beginning of the trial. To encourage the accused to confess, the judge may indicate an upper sentencing limit that might be imposed. Under German law, the judge cannot make a definite settlement of the case until after the trial. The understanding reached between judge and defense counsel is therefore *de jure* nonbinding. In most cases, however, if the accused agrees to make a confession, the sentence that the accused eventually receives will be below the upper limit indicated by the judge. Negotiations could also occur during the trial. For instance, defense counsel may agree not to call additional evidence or promise not to bring an appeal in exchange for sentencing concessions from the judge (Dubber, 1997; Herrmann, 1992; Swenson, 1995).

The increased popularity of plea bargaining in Germany, a country once praised as a land without plea bargaining, unquestionably represents one of the most significant developments in prosecutorial practices in continental law countries. German plea bargaining, however, differs in several aspects from the bargaining practice in the United States. In Germany, defendants' decisions to plead guilty after negotiating with prosecutors are usually well informed. In the German system, defense counsel at the pretrial stage has the right to inspect the prosecutor's file in its entirety. In negotiations with the prosecutor, the defense attorney would have the full knowledge of the strength of the prosecutor's evidence. This broad pretrial discovery right not only makes it easier for defense attorneys to provide well informed advice to defendants; it also makes it difficult for prosecutors to resort to tactics such as overcharging or charging the accused with offenses that are not supported by evidence (Frase & Weigend, 1995; Swenson, 1995).

German prosecutors may indeed use the tactic of dropping collateral charges as leverage to encourage the accused to admit guilt. This charge bargain nevertheless is not conducted in a highly pressurized fashion.

In Germany, although prosecutors' offer to drop collateral charges may provide incentives on the part of the accused to co-operate, prosecutors are not in a position to drastically increase the severity of the penalty to be imposed on the accused in multiple-offense cases. German law does not permit the imposition of multiple consecutive sentences. Prosecutors therefore cannot expect that a threat to charge the accused with multiple crimes would create pressure on the accused to plead guilty or cooperate with the government (Frase & Weigend, 1995; Swenson, 1995).

In Germany, the prosecutor's discretionary power is also constrained by victims. In contrast to victims' powerless position in the American system, victims in Germany may take several courses of action to influence prosecutors' charging decisions. If a victim is not satisfied with the prosecutor's decision not to prosecute, the victim may file a formal complaint with a chief prosecutor. The chief prosecutor must internally review the dismissal decision and decide whether a prosecution should be ordered. If the chief prosecutor upholds the decision to dismiss, the victim has the right to request an appellate court judge to review the case. The victim's right to request judicial review, however, is limited to cases in which the prosecutor's decision to dismiss is made on evidentiary grounds. In those cases, if the judge finds evidence to be sufficient for prosecution, the prosecutor can be ordered to prosecute. The victim has no right to ask the court to review the prosecutor's decision of non-prosecution if the prosecutor's decision rests on policy grounds (for instance, the prosecutor's belief that the public interest does not require prosecution; Albrecht, 2000; Fionda, 1995).

The German system imposes more restrictions on the exercise of prosecutorial discretion, but the system is by no means perfect. The German prosecutorial service is organized at the state level instead of nationally. This fragmented organizational structure makes it difficult to maintain consistent prosecutorial decision making throughout the system. There are usually guidelines in local prosecutors' offices to aid individual prosecutors in their decision making. These guidelines, however, differ from office to office. The statutory criteria for non-prosecution, such as lack of public interest and the seriousness of the offense, are often subject to different interpretations. To reduce these discrepancies, some states have attempted to impose statewide rules. These rules, nevertheless, tend to be short and lacking in detail, making them unlikely to harness the use of prosecutorial discretion effectively (Fionda, 1995). The weaknesses notwithstanding, one aspect of the German system that may have made German prosecutors more accountable than their American counterparts is the requirement that prosecutors provide written reasons for their disposal of cases. Such requirements undoubtedly encourage prosecutors to consider their decisions more carefully and to rest them on defensible grounds.

Italy

Comparative legal scholars in the past several decades have noted the trend of convergence between civil and common law systems (Frase & Weigend, 1995; Glendon, 1984; Zweigert & Kötz, 1987). Recent changes in the Italian criminal justice system probably offer the best example of trends in the convergence between the two systems. Italy's adoption of the new Criminal Procedure Code in 1989 has attracted wide attention from the world legal community. One of the most noticeable features of the new code is its introduction of adversarial elements into Italy's deep-rooted inquisitorial trial proceedings (Fassler, 1991; Pizzi & Marafioti, 1992). In the context of prosecutorial practice, what is equally noticeable is the new code's introduction of plea bargaining analogues into the Italian criminal justice system.

Before the adoption of the new code, Italy was one of the few countries that followed the legality principle in its strictest sense. The strict adherence to the principle had resulted in a tremendous judicial backlog. Because no trial avoidance mechanisms were available in the Italian procedure, the system relied principally on regularly granted amnesties as a way to alleviate overcrowded courts. The amnesties, however, were far from a solution to the problem. Finding ways to solve the problem of congested courts thus became a primary task of the drafters of the new code. The new code does not use language of plea bargaining, but it

contains two trial avoidance procedures that allow imposition of sentences on the accused without a full trial. These special procedures have become known as Italy's plea bargaining analogues (Boari, 1997; Grande, 2000; Mack, 1996; J. J. Miller, 1990; Van Cleave, 1997).

The two trial avoidance procedures are (a) party-agreed sentences and (b) abbreviated or summary trials. The procedure of party-agreed sentences means that the prosecutor and the defense may enter into an agreement as to the appropriate sentence to be imposed on the defendant without going through a trial. The statutory requirement for the two parties to enter into such an agreement is that the final punishment cannot exceed two years of imprisonment. This statutory requirement does not prohibit the procedure from being used in crimes that are punishable by more than two years of imprisonment. It simply means that, after considering all the circumstances surrounding the case, if the prosecutor and the defense attorney agree that the final sentence would not exceed two years of imprisonment, the procedure can then be applied (Grande, 2000; Van Cleave, 1997).

The agreement entered into by the prosecutor and the defense attorney is subject to judicial review. The Code of Criminal Procedure contains the specific standards by which the judge is to evaluate the party-agreed sentences. The judge is required to evaluate whether the parties have correctly determined the nature of the offense and whether the sentence agreed upon by the parties is appropriate in light of the evidence. The judge may reject the agreement if he or she believes that the agreement was inappropriately reached (Code of Penal Procedure, Art. 444).

In Italy it is a constitutional requirement that judges give written reasons for all dispositive judicial actions (Italian Constitution, Article 102[1]). A controversy that arose after the adoption of the new Criminal Procedure Code was whether judges should give reasons when they are performing the function of evaluating party-agreed sentences. Some argued that the constitutional requirement should not apply to cases where a judge is simply performing the function of accepting party-agreed sentences (Van Cleave, 1997). The Italian Constitutional Court, however, rejected this argument, holding that even when judges are imposing party-agreed sentences they must still issue written reasons for the sentences (*Decision of March 29, 1993*). The ruling of the Italian Constitutional Court strongly indicates that the Court does not want judges to simply perform a rubber-stamp function and endorse all agreements reached by the parties. Under the ruling of the Court, judges must faithfully execute their judicial duties to ensure that agreements reached by the parties are truly in compliance with the law.

In the United States, in order for a deal to be presented to a judge for approval, there must be an agreed upon deal between prosecution and defense. Prosecutors have total freedom to refuse to offer a deal to a defendant or to stop dealing with the defendant at any time after the initiation of the negotiation. The Italian procedure by contrast has not granted prosecutors the absolute power to deny defendants the opportunity to enter into a deal with the government. In party-agreed sentences, prosecutors' consent is required; there is nevertheless a requirement that prosecutors not withhold consent unreasonably (Code of Penal Procedure, Art. 448[1]). Prosecutors must justify their decision to reject a defendant's request for party-agreed sentences in writing, and the justifications given by prosecutors are subject to judicial evaluation. A prosecutorial rejection to a defendant's request to cut a deal technically will force the case to trial. However, if the judge at trial determines that the prosecutor unreasonably withheld consent to the defendant's request to settle the case, the judge may grant the defendant the reduced sentence that the defendant originally requested (Boari, 1997; Grande, 2000; Van Cleave, 1997).

Abbreviated trial is another procedure designed to unclog the courts by quickly disposing of cases. In contrast to party-agreed sentences, which can be initiated by either the prosecutor or the defense, abbreviated trial procedure can only be requested by the defendant. At the preliminary hearing, the defendant may request that the court dispose of the case on the basis of the evidence thus far accumulated. Although this procedure cannot be initiated by the prosecutor, the prosecutor's consent is required. If the prosecutor gives consent

to the defendant's request, the judge will determine whether it is possible to dispose of the case by using the abbreviated trial. If the judge determines that the case can be so disposed, the judge will issue a sentence of conviction (Code of Penal Procedure, Arts. 438, 440[1], 442). The incentive given to defendants for availing themselves of this special procedure is that, after being convicted under this special procedure, they will receive a statutorily mandated one-third reduction of the sentence that would have been imposed on them should they have been convicted after a full trial (Code of Penal Procedure, Art. 442[2]).

An interesting point, once again, is the role of the prosecutor. The prosecutor's consent is required before a case can be settled under the abbreviated trial procedure. But there is a similar requirement that the prosecutor not withhold consent unreasonably (Code of Penal Procedure, Art. 440[1]). The prosecutor's dissent to a defendant's request to settle the case under the abbreviated trial procedure will have the effect of forcing the case to go to a full trial. If the judge, however, determines that the prosecutor's dissent is unreasonable, the judge may grant the defendant the one-third sentence reduction in disregard of the prosecutor's dissent (Grande, 2000; Van Cleave, 1997).

There are no explicit provisions in the Italian Code of Criminal Procedure that require prosecutors to provide reasons for their dissent to a defendant's request to settle a case under the abbreviated trial procedure. However, the Italian Constitutional Court has held that it is a constitutional requirement that prosecutors give reasons for not granting consent. The basic reason for the Court to impose such an obligation is to ensure that the courts may evaluate the appropriateness of prosecutors' decisions (*Decision of February 8, 1990; Decision of April 18, 1990; Decision of February 15, 1991*). The Court rested its decisions to subject the prosecutor's dissent to judicial scrutiny on two grounds. The first is the principle of equality between prosecutor and defense. The Court reasoned that, because the prosecutor's dissent would affect the ultimate choice of sentences, the principle of equality calls for a judicial review of the prosecutor's decision. The second reason for the Court's insistence on judicial review is based on the concern that giving prosecutors the unreviewable power to decide who may avail themselves of the abbreviated trial may result in a situation that similarly situated defendants may receive different sentences.

Comparison and Observations

Three decades have passed since the great debate in the 1970s on the merits of reforming the American system based on the continental models. The past 30 years have seen dramatic changes in continental law systems. The emergence of plea bargaining represents one of the most significant changes that have taken place in continental law systems. Today, none of the major continental law countries can still be described as a land without plea bargaining. The recent expansion of prosecutorial autonomy in continental law countries notwithstanding, it remains true that continental prosecutors' discretion is subject to much stricter control and supervision than that enjoyed by their American counterparts. Furthermore, despite the emergence of plea bargaining, no continental law countries have allowed plea bargaining to be conducted in a highly pressurized fashion. If the goal is to narrow the scope of prosecutorial discretion and to subject prosecutorial discretion to more meaningful control and supervision, the American system can still benefit from the experience of continental law countries.

When comparing the inquisitorial and the adversarial systems, it is generally recognized that the inquisitorial system places more emphasis on the search for the substantive truth, whereas the adversarial system focuses more on ensuring procedural fairness for the adversaries (Ehrmann, 1976; Merryman, 1985; Van Kessel, 1992; Zweigert & Kötz, 1987). Philosophical differences regarding the criminal justice process are apparent in the structural differences between the two systems. In the inquisitorial system, the procedures, from investigation to trial, are designed with the aim of facilitating the ascertainment of the substantive truth. Investigators are under the legal obligation to conduct an objective investigation by following all leads that may shed light on the case, regardless of whether they are against or in favor of the accused. At trial, the judge, in the interest of searching for the truth, is obligated to examine all evidence with the same vigor, regardless of whether it points to the accused's guilt or innocence (Frase, 1990; Sheehan, 1975; Tomlinson, 1983; Van Kessel, 1992).

Tension may develop, however, between the zeal of searching for the truth and the interest of efficient administration of justice. As illustrated by what happened in Germany and Italy, the growing number of cases may make it difficult for the criminal justice system to handle all cases through formal trials. Continental law countries therefore have also turned to plea bargaining as a way to alleviate the burdened system of justice. An examination of various forms of plea bargaining in continental law countries, however, suggests that the bargaining proceedings are designed to allow prosecutors only to encourage the accused to admit guilt. Prosecutors in none of the continental law countries are given the power to threaten the accused with sentencing differentials as a way to compel plea bargaining and force cooperation. In other words, even with their embrace of the bargaining justice, continental law countries have not allowed the interest of efficient administration of criminal justice to unduly outweigh the interest of ascertaining the truth.

Scholars have long criticized the distortive effect of American plea bargaining on the roles of the prosecutor, judge, and defense counsel (Alschuler, 1983; Gifford, 1983; Misner, 1996). The players in the bargaining process in many cases are more interested in working out deals for their respective interests than in searching for the substantive truth. A perplexing aspect of American plea bargaining is that defendants in many jurisdictions are allowed to plead guilty to offenses that do not represent the facts of the cases. Some jurisdictions require the judge who reviews the plea agreement to examine whether there is a factual basis for the plea. Rule 11 of the Federal Rule of Criminal Procedures prohibits the court from accepting a plea without inquiry into whether there is a factual basis for the plea. Not all jurisdictions, however, require the judge to conduct such an inquiry. In many jurisdictions, defendants are allowed to plead guilty to offenses that include elements that their conduct does not satisfy. In those cases, the truth is apparently allowed to be distorted for the convenience of cutting deals between prosecution and defense.

Truth seeking is also an important concern in the adversarial system. In the United States, prosecutors in particular have an obligation to seek the truth. Both the law and professional ethics demand that prosecutors be "something more than a partisan advocate intent on winning cases." Prosecutors bear a special duty "to protect the innocent and to safeguard the rights guaranteed to all, including those who may be guilty" (American Bar Association, 1986, p. 20). In the adversarial system, however, the goal of truth seeking centers on the trial. At trial, detailed rules are developed with the aim of providing the prosecutor and the defense attorney with the fair opportunities to present and debate the evidence that they have each discovered. It is expected that from the clash of the adversaries the truth will emerge. But the problem with current American criminal justice administration is that trial procedures—so painstakingly developed in practice—contribute little to the cause of truth seeking when the vast majority of cases are settled not through trials but through guilty pleas. Despite the overwhelming dominance of plea bargaining in the American system, neither legislatures nor courts have shown any interest in developing mechanisms that would ensure that the truth will emerge from the bargaining process.

Although American plea bargaining is criticized, few advocate its abolition. It seems that plea bargaining, as reasoned by the U.S. Supreme Court over 30 years ago, has indeed become "an essential component of the administration of justice" (*Santobello v. New York*, 1971, p. 261). Commentators, however, do believe that there is an urgent need to reform the way in which plea bargaining is currently conducted (Davis, 1969; Dubber, 1997; Frase, 1990; Frase & Weigend, 1995; Uviller, 1999; Vorenberg, 1981). It is in this context that the experience of continental law countries may provide important insights into how the American prosecutorial system may be reformed.

Lower Penalties

A look at continental systems suggests several reforms to reduce coercion within the American system of plea bargaining. In comparison with the sentencing laws of continental law countries, American law imposes far more severe penalties on convicted offenders. The availability of long prison terms for a large number of crimes has provided prosecutors with the power to subject defendants to extremely severe penalties by charging multiple offenses or by seeking consecutive sentences. Prosecutors' discretion to decide whether to subject a defendant to the most severe sanction authorized by the penal law provides powerful leverage to coerce defendants to accept deals desired by prosecutors.

American scholars have long engaged in a debate on the relationship between harshness of criminal sanctions and prosecutorial discretion. It is commonly agreed that a desirable aspect of prosecutorial discretion is that it allows the prosecutor to mitigate the severity of the criminal law and to individualize justice (A. S. Goldstein, 1981). Some commentators further suggest that an important reason for the legislature's tendency to pass harsh laws is the legislature's belief that prosecutors will play the role of softening the harshness of criminal penalties by fitting them to the circumstances of individual offenders (Pizzi, 1993).

There is no evidence indicating whether the harshness of criminal penalties is a cause of broad prosecutorial discretion or an effect of it. Commentators who are critical of broad prosecutorial discretion, however, are against the notion that prosecutors should be allowed to play the role of mitigating the harshness of the penal law. They argue that prosecutors should not be put in a position to overrule the legislature's judgment by dispensing mercy in the face of harsh sentences (Vorenberg, 1981). Moreover, arming prosecutors with the power to choose from a wide range of sentences creates a great potential for prosecutors to misuse the power as leverage in coercing deals from defendants.

Broader Pretrial Discovery Rights

A great disadvantage that an American defendant suffers in the bargaining process is a lack of complete knowledge about the prosecutor's case. In the continental criminal justice process, there is usually only one official criminal investigation. The investigation is carried out by either an examining magistrate or a prosecutor, with the assistance of the police. The officer responsible for the investigation is obligated to conduct an objective inquiry into the case, examining both evidence in favor of and against the accused. At the end of the investigation, a dossier is prepared, which contains all of the information gathered during the investigation. The defense has the unlimited right to examine the dossier. The advantage of this open process is that, because the defense is fully aware of the strength of the evidence held by the prosecution, it is unlikely that the prosecutor would use the tactics of overcharging or charging the defendant with unprovable offenses to gain bargaining advantages.

Most defendants in the American system, by contrast, do not know the true strength of the prosecution's case against them. Under present discovery rules, the prosecution has no obligation to reveal all evidence amassed against the defendant. Although the U.S. Supreme Court has held that prosecutors bear a constitutional duty to disclose exculpatory information that is material to the defense (*Brady v. Maryland*, 1963), the scope of this prosecutorial duty is quite narrow because of the Court's conservative interpretation of the materiality rule (*Kyles v. Whitley*, 1995; *United States v. Agurs*, 1976; *United States v. Bagley*, 1985). Because defendants have no right to have full access to the prosecutor's file, they are likely to be kept in the dark, during the plea negotiation, as to the strength of the evidence in the charges that prosecutors have filed. Limited pretrial defense discovery rights provide the opportunity and the incentive for prosecutors to overcharge or to charge defendants with

unprovable offenses as a bargaining strategy. The introduction of broader discovery rules therefore would reduce prosecutors' incentive to overcharge and would prevent prosecutors from threatening defendants with unprovable charges.

Judicial Supervision

Despite the recognized judicial power to constrain prosecutorial excesses, the American judiciary has traditionally played a passive role in providing supervision over the exercise of prosecutorial discretion (A. S. Goldstein, 1981). It is for this reason that comparative legal scholars long ago observed that prosecutorial discretion in continental law countries is consistently controlled, whereas prosecutorial discretion in the United States is consistently uncontrolled (Davis, 1969; Langbein, 1979). Today, even with the emergence of plea bargaining and the expansion of prosecutorial discretion in continental law systems, the observation remains true that continental prosecutors are subject to far greater judicial control and supervision than their American counterparts.

Judges play an active role in various bargaining analogues in France, Germany, and Italy. In France, although the prosecutor has the power to correctionalize a *crime* to a *délit* or a *contravention,* a correctionalized case still goes to a regular trial. At trial, the judge must examine whether there is a factual basis for the charge and whether the charge is supported by sufficient evidence. Similarly, in Germany, after a confession agreement is reached between the prosecutor and the defendant, the case must still go to trial and be examined in open court by the judge. Commentators believe that the requirements that the defendant make a public confession and that the judge inquire into the case in open court can serve as a deterrent to prosecutorial overreaching, which in turn would reduce the likelihood of false convictions (Dubber, 1997; Herrmann, 1992).

In Italy, in both party-agreed sentences and abbreviated trial procedures, the judge is required to vigorously scrutinize the appropriateness of prosecutorial discretion. To ensure that prosecutors would not withhold consent to an accused's request to employ the special procedures, the law provides the judge—rather than the prosecutor—with the final authority to determine whether the benefit provided under the special procedure should be granted to the accused. The strict judicial supervision is designed to ensure that prosecutors exercise their discretion in conformity with the law (Grande, 2000; Van Cleave, 1997).

The United States boasts of a constitutionalized code of criminal procedure. Because improper exercise of prosecutorial discretion in many cases may implicate citizens' constitutionally protected rights, it seems logical that the courts should be more vigilant on the likelihood of prosecutorial abuse. But the American judiciary plays a much less vigorous role than courts in continental law countries in providing supervision over the exercise of prosecutorial discretion. The U.S. Supreme Court seems to have justified its reluctance to encourage more vigorous judicial supervision over prosecutors on three grounds: the separation of powers, the faith in prosecutors to discharge their duties properly, and the concern that vigorous judicial supervision over prosecutors may produce a chilling effect on law enforcement. Though each of these grounds has its merits, none of them provides sufficient justification for complete judicial deference to prosecutorial discretion.

Separation of powers provides a primary justification for the American judiciary's passive stance in supervising the prosecutorial function. It is reasoned that law enforcement is a function of the executive branch and that the judiciary therefore should show deference to prosecutorial decision making. The courts, however, routinely review the appropriateness of the decision making of other executive agencies and they seldom decline review by citing the separation of powers. Judicial review of police action since the 1960s has imposed numerous new restrictions on law enforcement. The U.S. Supreme Court regularly reviews the appropriateness of police decision making. The issues covered by the Court in its decisions range from the circumstances under which police may establish probable cause and reasonable suspicion (*Florida v. J. L.,* 2000; *Illinois v. Gates,* 1983; *Illinois v. Wardlow,* 2000; *Terry v. Ohio,* 1968) to the appropriateness of various

law enforcement tactics (*Atwater v. City of Logo Vista,* 2001; *Indianapolis v. Edmond,* 2001; *Michigan Department of State Police v. Sitz,* 1990) and the circumstances that may give rise to police civil liability (*Anderson v. Creighton, 1987; Monroe v. Pape,* 1961). Beyond the review of police actions, the Court has similarly determined issues such as school integration (*Alexander v. Holmes County Board of Education,* 1969; *Swann v. Charlotte-Mecklenburg Board of Education,* 1971) and the adequacy of prisons (*Rhodes v. Chapman,* 1981; *Whitley v. Albers,* 1986) and mental hospitals (*Connecticut Dept. of Income Maint. v. Heckler,* 1985; *Zinermon v. Burch,* 1990).

Because judicial review of executive decision making is commonplace, Davis observed more than 30 years ago that "if separation of powers prevents review of discretion of executive officers, then more than a hundred Supreme Court decisions spread over a century and three quarters will have to be found contrary to the Constitution!" (Davis, 1969, p. 210). It is certainly true that the doctrine of separation of powers prohibits courts from usurping the prosecutor's power to execute the law. But there is a difference between the judiciary stepping into prosecutors' shoes to discharge the duties that should be performed by prosecutors and the judiciary providing necessary supervision to prevent arbitrary and unjustifiable prosecutorial decision making. Separation of powers therefore should not be a justification for the judiciary to withdraw from its obligation to control the abuse or misuse of prosecutorial power (Davis, 1969; A. S. Goldstein, 1981; Vorenberg, 1981).

A fundamentally important principle that has repeatedly been upheld by the U.S. Supreme Court is that effective law enforcement cannot be accomplished at the expense of citizens' constitutional rights (*Mapp v. Ohio,* 1961; *Miranda v. Arizona,* 1966; *Payton v. New York,* 1980). If effective law enforcement were the only goal of criminal justice, the Court might well relax judicial scrutiny of law enforcement actions. The Court, however, has never felt comfortable leaving freewheeling powers in the hands of police. Appreciating the special status that the Court has granted to prosecutors requires an examination of the Court's long-held presumption that prosecutors will discharge their duties properly.

The Supreme Court has held, in case after case, that judicial deference to prosecutorial decision making is justified on the presumption that prosecutors, as members of a respected profession, are able to discharge their official duties properly (*United States v. Ash*, 1973; *United States v. Bagley*, 1985; *United States v. Chemical Foundation Inc.*, 1926; *Wayte v. United States*, 1985). Although no one should doubt that prosecutors in most cases properly discharge their official duties, there is no reason to disregard the possibility that prosecutorial irregularities may occur. In the American system, the political process has played a significant part in the shaping of the role of the prosecutor, and there is a real possibility that political influence may enter into the prosecutor's decision-making process (Dubber, 1997; Gershman, 1992; Heller, 1997; Vorenberg, 1981). Prosecutors may deal with particular individuals harshly or gently for political reasons. It is also possible that race may play a role in prosecutorial decision making. It is for these reasons that Justice Stevens in his dissent in *Armstrong* said, "The possibility that political or racial animosity may infect a decision to institute criminal proceedings cannot be ignored" (*United States v. Armstrong*, 1996, p. 476). This possibility, however, is mostly overlooked by the Court's current approach of insulating prosecutors from judicial review and supervision.

The American judiciary could play a more active role in supervising the exercise of prosecutorial discretion without American judges assuming the roles of continental judges. Prosecutorial accountability can be enhanced without drastically changing the traditional role played by judges in the American system. A modest step toward enhancing prosecutorial accountability through judicial supervision would be to require prosecutors to provide written reasons for prosecutorial decisions. Continental law countries seem to be quite aware of the importance of requiring prosecutors to provide justifications for their decisions. In Germany, prosecutors are required to provide written reasons for their disposition of cases, including their decisions in various forms of plea bargaining. In Italy, prosecutors are similarly required to justify their prosecutorial decisions in writing. Moreover, to ensure that judicial

supervision over the newly introduced trial avoidance procedures would not be turned into a mere formality, the law further requires judges to give reasons for their acceptance of bargained agreements reached by prosecutors and defendants.

American prosecutors in general are not required to give reasons for their decisions. Courts are willing to accept prosecutors' decisions as constitutionally and legally appropriate without independent inquiry. In *Singer v. United States* (1965), the U.S. Supreme Court ruled that the prosecutor need not articulate reasons for withholding consent to a defendant's waiver of a jury trial. The Court rested its decision on familiar ground, i.e., its "confidence in the integrity of the federal prosecutor" (*Singer v. United States*, 1965, p. 34). The willingness of the Court to tolerate a degree of secrecy in the decision making of one of the most crucial criminal justice agencies is quite inconsistent with the ideal of an open and decent system of justice.

There are multiple advantages to requiring prosecutors to provide justifications for their decisions. Prosecutors' obligation to justify their decisions would certainly compel individual prosecutors to be more careful in their decision making. The requirement would also make it easier for prosecutors' offices to exercise internal supervision. But the most significant advantage of such a requirement is that the written record left by prosecutors would allow courts to better evaluate the appropriateness of prosecutorial decision making. When the appropriateness of a prosecutor's decision is challenged, if the judge finds that the prosecutor's decision making is consistent with fairness and established procedures, the judge would concur with the propriety of the decision. If the prosecutor's decision grossly deviates from general patterns of fairness and law, the prosecutor must be required to furnish a rational basis for the deviation and to convince the court that the deviation is not based on constitutionally or legally impermissible grounds.

In making prosecutorial decisions, prosecutors consider a full range of factors. In addition to evidentiary sufficiency, prosecutors consider the attitude of the victim, the cost of prosecution to the criminal justice system, the avoidance of undue harm to the suspect, the availability of alternative procedures, the use of civil sanctions, and the willingness of the suspect to cooperate with law enforcement authorities (F. W. Miller, 1970; Wallace, 1995). No one should question the legitimacy of prosecutors' consideration of these factors. Courts under the doctrine of separation of powers indeed should not interfere with prosecutors' decisions as to which factors to consider and how much weight to give to each factor, but courts do have a duty to supervise prosecutors' decision making to ensure that discretion is applied consistently and evenhandedly. Due process demands no less.

Conclusion

American prosecutors' overly broad and essentially unchecked discretion remains one of the most distinctive features of American criminal justice. In the past 30 years, courts and legislatures, in the name of enhancing the fairness of American criminal justice and protecting relevant parties' due process rights, have imposed restrictions on the discretionary power of the police, sentencing judges, parole boards, and correctional authorities. Prosecutors, however, have been spared this shrinking of discretionary power. Indeed, as the discretionary authority of other criminal justice officials has contracted, that of prosecutors has expanded. Prosecutors now are truly the most central figures in the administration of justice. They are entrusted with the power to determine on whom penal resources will be spent and against whom society's harshest sanctions will be dispensed, but their decision-making process is for most part insulated from judicial review and supervision. The uncontrolled prosecutorial discretion has created a great potential for abuse.

In contrast to American prosecutors' essentially unchecked power, continental prosecutors' discretion is subject to much stricter control and supervision. Faced with the pressure of handling a growing number of cases with limited resources, continental law countries have also turned to plea bargaining as a means to streamline criminal justice and alleviate overcrowded

courts. But they have so far avoided turning plea bargaining into a prosecutor-dominated unilateral process. Their experience seems to indicate that, even though plea bargaining needs to be recognized as a component of the administration of justice, it is possible to have plea bargaining without it being coercive.

Comparative legal scholars have long argued for utilizing comparative criminal justice as a guide to American law reform. Despite the misgivings about the suitability of reforming one nation's legal system on the experience of another, the evolution of the world legal systems shows that there have been frequent migrations of legal institutions from one culture to another. Legal transplants are not only feasible but desirable (Ehrmann, 1976; Jackson & Tushnet, 1999; Schlesinger, Baade, Herzog, & Wise, 1998; Zweigert & Kötz, 1987). Today, as the world enters a new era of globalization, people who hold the view that the American system, because of its unique features, can never be reformed on foreign models seem to still be looking at problems from a parochial and self-centered perspective. In today's rapidly shrinking world, to effect meaningful law reforms American reformers must be willing to look outward to other countries' experience and open up to the possibility that others may have developed approaches and procedures that can serve as a guide to American law reform.

References

Albrecht, H. J. (2000). Criminal prosecution: Developments, trends and open questions in the Federal Republic of Germany. *European Journal of Crime, Criminal Law, and Criminal Justice, 8*(3), 245–256.

Alexander v. Holmes County Board of Education, 396 U.S. 19 (1969).

Alschuler, A. (1983). Implementing the criminal defendant's right to trial: Alternatives to the plea bargaining system. *University of Chicago Law Review, 50,* 931–1050.

American Bar Association. (1986). *Standards for criminal justice: The prosecution function.* Boston: Little, Brown, and Company.

Anderson v. Creighton, 483 U.S. 635 (1987).

Arnold, T. (1932). Law enforcement: An attempt at social discretion. *Yale Law Journal, 42,* 1–24.

Atwater v. City of Lago Vista, 533 US. 924 (2001).

Boari, N. (1997). On the efficiency of penal systems: Several lessons from the Italian experience. *International Review of Law and Economics, 17,* 115–125.

Bordenkircher v. Hayes, 434 U.S. 357 (1978).

Brady v. Maryland, 373 U.S. 83 (1963).

Brady v. United States, 397 U.S. 742 (1970).

Connecticut Dept. of Income Maint. v. Heckler, 471 U.S. 524 (1985).

Currie, E. (1998). *Crime and punishment in America.* New York: Metropolitan Books.

Davis, K. C. (1969). *Discretionary justice.* Baton Rouge: Louisiana State University Press.

Decision of February 8, 1990, Italian Constitutional Court.

Decision of April 18, 1990, Italian Constitutional Court

Decision of February 15, 1991, Italian Constitutional Court.

Decision of March 29, 1993, Italian Constitutional Court.

Dubber, M. D. (1997). American plea bargaining, German lay judges, and the crisis of criminal procedure. *Stanford Law Review, 49,* 547–605.

Ehrmann, H. W. (1976). *Comparative legal cultures.* Englewood Cliffs, NJ: Prentice-Hall.

Ely, J. (1980). *Democracy and distrust.* Cambridge, MA: Harvard University Press.

Fassler, L. J. (1991). The Italian Penal Procedure Code: An adversarial system of criminal procedure in continental Europe. *Columbia Journal of Transnational Law, 29,* 245–278.

Field, S., & West, A. (1995). A tale of two reforms: French defense rights and police powers in transition. *Criminal Law Forum, 6,* 473–506.

Fionda, J. (1995). *Public prosecutors and discretion: A comparative study.* Oxford, NY: Clarendon Press.

Florida v. J. L., 529 U.S. 266 (2000).

Frase, R. S. (1990). Comparative criminal justice as a guide to American law reform: How do the French do it, how can we find out, and why should we care? *California Law Review, 78,* 539–683.

Frase, R. S., & Weigend, T. (1995). German criminal justice as a guide to American law reform: Similar problems, better solutions? *Boston College International and Comparative Law Review, 18,* 317–360.

Gershman, B. L. (1992). The new prosecutors. *University of Pittsburgh Law Review, 53,* 393–458.

Gifford, D. G. (1983). Meaningful reform of plea bargaining: The control of prosecutorial discretion. *University of Illinois Law Review, 1983,* 37–98.

Glendon, M. A. (1984). The sources of law in a changing legal order. *Creighton Law Review, 17,* 663–698.

Goldstein, A. S. (1981). *The passive judiciary: Prosecutorial discretion and the guilty plea.* Baton Rouge: Louisiana State University Press.

Goldstein, B. L., & Marcus, M. (1977). The myth of judicial supervision in three "inquisitorial" systems: France, Italy, and Germany. *Yale Law Journal, 87,* 240–283.

Gordon, D. R. (1994). *The return of the dangerous classes.* New York: Norton.

Grande, E. (2000). Italian criminal justice: Borrowing and resistance. *American Journal of Comparative Law, 48,* 227–260.

Hatchard, J., Huber, B., & Vogler, R. (1996). *Comparative criminal procedure.* London: British Institute of International and Comparative Law.

Heller, R. (1997). Selective prosecution and the federalization of criminal law: The need for meaningful judicial review of prosecutorial discretion. *University of Pennsylvania Law Review, 145,* 1039–1358.

Herrmann, J. (1992). Bargaining justice: A bargain for German criminal justice? *University of Pittsburgh Law Review, 53,* 755–776.

Illinois v. Gates, 462 U.S. 213 (1983).

Illinois v. Wardlow, 528 U.S. 119 (2000).

Indianapolis v. Edmond, 531 U.S. 32 (2001).

Jackson, R. H. (1940). The federal prosecutor. *Journal of American Judicature Society, 24,* 18–19.

Jackson, V. C., & Tushnet, M. (1999). *Comparative constitutional law.* New York: Foundation Press.

Kyles v. Whitley, 514 U.S. 419 (1995).

Langbein, J. H. (1974). Controlling prosecutorial discretion in Germany. *University of Chicago Law Review, 41,* 439–467.

Langbein, J. H. (1977). *Comparative criminal procedure: Germany.* St. Paul: West.

Langbein, J. H. (1979). Land without plea bargaining: How the Germans do it. *Michigan Law Review, 78,* 204–225.

Langbein, J. H. (1981). Mixed court and jury court: Could the continental alternative fill the American need? *American Bar Foundation Research Journal, 1981,* 195–219.

Leigh, L. H., & Zedner, L. (1992). *The Royal Commission on Criminal Justice: A report on the administration of criminal justice in the pretrial phase in France and Germany.* London: HMSO.

Mack, R. L. (1996). It's broken so let's fix it: Using a quasi-inquisitorial approach to limit the impact of bias in the American criminal justice system. *Indiana International & Comparative Law Review, 7,* 63–93.

Mapp v. Ohio, 367 U.S. 643 (1961).

Merryman, J. H. (1985). *The civil law tradition.* Stanford, CA: Stanford University Press.

Michigan Department of State Police v. Sitz, 496 U.S. 444 (1990).

Miller, F. W. (1970). *Prosecution: The decision to charge a suspect with a crime.* Boston: Little Brown.

Miller, J. J. (1990). Plea bargaining and its analogues under the new Italian Criminal Procedure Code and in the United States: Towards a new understanding of comparative criminal procedure. *New York University Journal of International Law & Politics, 22,* 215–251.

Miranda v. Arizona, 384 U.S. 436 (1966).

Misner, R. (1996). Recasting prosecutorial discretion. *Journal of Criminal Law & Criminology, 56,* 717–777.

Monroe v. Pape, 365 U.S. 167 (1961).

New York v. Quarles, 467 U.S. 649 (1984).

Newman v. United States, 382 F.2d 479 (D.C. Cir. 1967).

Nix v. Williams, 467 U.S. 431 (1984).

Ohlin, L. E., & Remington, F. J. (Eds.). (1993). *Discretion in criminal justice: The tension between individualization and uniformity.* Albany: SUNY Press.

Oyler v. Boles, 368 U.S. 448 (1962).

Payton v. New York, 445 U.S. 537 (1980).

Pizzi, W. T. (1993). Understanding prosecutorial discretion in the United States: Limits of comparative criminal procedure as an instrument of reform. *Ohio State Law Journal, 54,* 1325–1373.

Pizzi, W. T., & Marafioti, L. (1992). The new Italian Code of Criminal Procedure: The difficulties of building an adversarial system on a civil law foundation. *Yale Journal of International Law, 17,* 1–40.

Rhodes v. Chapman, 452 U.S. 337 (1981).

Santobello v. New York, 404 U.S. 257 (1971).

Schlesinger, R. (1977). Comparative criminal procedure: A plea for utilizing foreign experience. *Buffalo Law Review, 26,* 361–385.

Schlesinger, R., Baade, H. W., Herzog, P. E., & Wise, E. M. (1998). *Comparative law.* New York: Foundation Press.

Schramm, G. (1970). The obligation to prosecute in West Germany. *American Journal of Comparative Law, 18,* 627–632.

Sheehan, A. V. (1975). *Criminal procedure in Scotland and France.* Edinburgh, Scotland: HMSO.

Singer v. United States, 380 U.S. 24 (1965).

Swann v. Charlotte-Mecklenburg Board of Education, 402 U.S. 1 (1971).

Swenson, T. (1995). The German plea bargaining debate. *Pace International Law Review, 7,* 373–429.

Terrill, R. J. (1999). *World criminal justice systems.* Cincinnati: Anderson.

Terry v. Ohio, 392 U.S. 1 (1968).

Tomlinson, E. (1983). Nonadversarial justice: The French experience. *Maryland Law Review, 42,* 131–195.

United States v. Agurs, 427 U.S. 97 (1976).

United States v. Armstrong, 517 U.S. 456 (1996).

United States v. Ash, 413 U.S. 300 (1973).

United States v. Bagley, 473 U.S. 667 (1985).

United States v. Chemical Foundation Inc., 272 U.S. 1 (1926).

United States v. Leon, 468 U.S. 897 (1984).

United States v. Mezzanatto, 513 U.S. 196 (1995).

Uviller, H. R. (1999). *The tilted playing field.* New Haven, CT: Yale University Press.

Van Cleave, R. A. (1997). An offer you can't refuse? Punishment without trial in Italy and the United States: The search for truth and an efficient criminal justice system. *Emory International Law Review, 11,* 419–469.

Van Kessel, G. (1992). Adversarial excesses in the American criminal trial. *Notre Dame Law Review, 67,* 403–551.

Verrest, P. (2000). The French Public Prosecution Service. *European Journal of Crime, Criminal Law, and Criminal Justice, 8*(3), 210–244.

Vorenberg, J. (1981). Decent restraint of prosecutorial power. *Harvard Law Review, 94,* 1521–1573.

Vouin, R. (1970). The role of the prosecutor in French criminal trial. *American Journal of Comparative Law, 18,* 483–497.

Walker, S. (1993). *Taming the system: The control of discretion in criminal justice, 1950–1990.* New York: Oxford University Press.

Wallace, H. (1995). A prosecutor's guide to stalking. *The Prosecutor, 29,* 26–30.

Washington v. Davis, 426 U.S. 229 (1976).

Wayte v. United States, 470 U.S. 598 (1985).

Weigend, T. (1980). Continental cures for American ailments: European criminal procedure as a model for law reform. *Crime and Justice: An Annual Review of Research, 2,* 381–428.

West, A., Desdevises, Y., Fenet, A., Gaurier, D., & Heussaff, M. C. (1993). *The French legal system.* London: Format Publishing.

Whitley v. Albers, 475 U.S. 312 (1986).

Yick Wo v. Hopkins, 118 U.S. 356 (1886).

Zauberman, R. (1991). Victims en France: Des positions, intérêts et stratégies diverses. *Déviance et Société, 15*(1), 27–49.

Zinermon v. Burch, 494 U.S. 113 (1990).

Zweigert, K., & Kötz, H. (1987). *Introduction to comparative law.* Oxford, NY: Clarendon Press.

DISCUSSION QUESTIONS

1. How has the power and prestige of prosecutors in the United States been expanded during the past 30 years?

2. Discuss the Supreme Court cases that have shaped prosecutorial discretion in the United States.

3. Ma contended that "compulsory prosecution" depends on whether a country follows the expediency principle or the legality principle. Discuss these two principles and explain how they affect prosecution in France, Germany, and Italy.

4. What are the key differences between an inquisitorial system and an adversarial system?

5. How do prosecutorial practices differ in France, Germany, and Italy?

6. Ma concluded that "the experience of continental law countries may provide important insights into how the American prosecutorial system may be reformed" (p. 376). What are these reforms? Which would have the greatest likelihood of significantly changing the American prosecutorial system?

READING

One explanation for the prevalence of plea bargaining is that it is a response to high caseloads and limited resources for handling these caseloads. The authors of this study examine the impact of a statutory change in California that had the potential to reduce caseloads for Superior Courts; they focus on the impact of the change on felony complaints, type of disposition (plea or trial), and sentence. The results of their analysis reveal that the statutory change did affect case processing, but not always in the expected way.

Court Caseloads, Plea Bargains, and Criminal Sanctions

The Effects of Section 17 P.C. in California

James W. Meeker and Henry N. Pontell

Social scientists have long had an interest in the functioning of criminal courts. The "crime surveys" of the 1920s and 1930s represented the first attempts at empirically examining the processes by which American courts operate. Since then, there have been numerous theoretical and empirical studies concerned with both describing and explaining criminal adjudication. Such research concerns not only fundamental theoretical issues in the sociology of law, but bears directly on central policy questions as well. No attempt will be made here to summarize the entire literature because competent reviews exist elsewhere (Eisenstein and Jacob, 1977; Heumann, 1978; Nardulli, 1978). This paper focuses on the important aspect of research on court processes which Nardulli (1979) has labelled "the caseload controversy." Basically, the "controversy" revolves around the salience of court caseloads in affecting criminal adjudication and, more specifically, the quasi-official practice of plea bargaining.

Recent empirical research on court caseloads has been conducted by political scientists whose analyses have concentrated on the relationship between caseloads and adversariness in disposing of cases. That is, as caseloads increase, so might the use of plea bargains in order to process large numbers of defendants. Of central concern is the phenomenon of plea bargaining, or the negotiations between prosecutor and defense attorney which set reduced charges and/or punishment conditions in return for a plea of guilty by the accused. Plea bargaining is not a recent development in American criminal justice; it dates back over one hundred years in criminal proceedings (Heumann, 1975). In a recent study which examines this phenomenon, Heumann found that comments from court officials tend to support a case pressure-plea bargaining relationship,

SOURCE: "Court Caseloads, Plea Bargains, and Criminal Sanctions: The Effects of Section 17 P.C. in California," by James W. Meeker and Henry N. Pontell in *Criminology*, vol. 23, issue 1, pp. 119-143, February 1985. Reprinted by permission of the American Society of Criminology.

although the scientific literature has yet to specify the exact nature of the connection between the two.

> Heavy caseloads in the criminal courts coupled with the prevalence of plea bargaining suggest to many that plea bargaining is the expedient developed to manage these caseloads. The impression conveyed by this theory is that plea bargaining results from increases in case pressure, although quantitative analysis of the relationship has not been undertaken. The literature does not posit direct variation between plea bargaining and case pressure; for the most part it is silent on the precise nature of the relationship and is content to observe that case pressure and plea bargaining "go together." (1978: 25)

A similar assessment is made by Nardulli, who states:

> Up until recently, plea bargaining was viewed mainly as a result of officials being "forced" to plea bargain, either because of their heavy caseloads or because of their desire to individualize justice. (1978: 52)

Studies of the relationship between caseloads and plea bargaining have thus far failed to show a strong link between the two (Feeley, 1975, 1979a; Heumann, 1975, 1978; Nardulli, 1978, 1979). Researchers tend to favor an explanation of plea bargaining which centers on the common interests of official actors to dispose of cases expeditiously rather than the caseload hypothesis. For example, Mileski (1971) finds that shortcuts and rapid processing tend to occur even where caseloads are less pronounced. Both Skolnick's (1967) and Cole's (1970) analyses indicate that such patterns of cooperation may not be due only to caseloads, but are a consequence of long relationships and acquaintances among court personnel as well as other administrative concerns of which moving cases is only part. While not entirely discounting the importance of caseloads, Mather (1973: 187)

notes: "While caseload pressures are doubtlessly important, they may be overemphasized in the current literature." It seems apparent that while researchers acknowledge the presence of court caseloads as a factor influencing organizational processes, its significance in the disposition of defendants remains unclear in the scientific literature

While such research has added to our knowledge of court processes and the possible effects of caseload on criminal dispositions, many questions remain unanswered. First, the precise nature of the effects of caseloads on plea bargains remains uncertain. One reason for this has to do with the measures which studies employ to examine "adversariness," or the conflict present in the adjudication of criminal cases. Most research has compared rates of plea bargaining to trial rates in assessing the effects of caseloads. This conceptualization may, in fact, cloud the possible influence of caseloads in several ways. As mentioned earlier, a much broader view has only recently begun to appear which suggests that plea bargaining, rather than being a new form of processing tied to increasing workloads and bureaucratization, has deep roots in the history of American courts (Heumann, 1978; Feeley, 1979b; Friedman, 1979). Feeley (1979b), for example, favors an explanation for plea bargaining which centers around the ideas of specialization and professionalism. That is, better trained court personnel and the availability of defense counsel have made many trials unnecessary. Prosecution and defense can now reach decisions earlier in the process regarding charges and sentencing. However, during bargaining sessions both parties negotiate from positions which remain formally structured as adversarial, and many "deals" are not struck the first time around. That is, irrespective of its prevalence, there is a qualitative difference between bargaining in which the adversaries agree immediately ("original" or "fast" guilty pleas) and cases that are fought over for weeks or months ("changed" or "slow" guilty pleas). If, as the current research literature suggests, plea bargaining has long been the "normal state of affairs" in criminal courts, the speed at which it takes place may provide a finer measure for assessing caseload effects. Since the vast majority of convictions are obtained through guilty pleas, the use of fast and slow pleas as *relative* indicators of adversariness seems reasonable. Original or fast pleas represent less adversarial proceedings than changed or slow pleas. This distinction between type of plea also has implications for studying the linkages among caseloads, plea bargains, and sentencing, which are discussed below.

Another major difficulty in research on plea bargaining and caseloads has been the nondelineation between the *quality* of plea bargaining, or the content of deals made, and the rate of plea bargains. This distinction is necessary not only for assessing possible caseload effects, but for examining plea bargaining in relation to criminal sentencing. "Going rates" used to bargain cases reflect the system's sanctioning capacity, which is dependent in part on the availability of organizational resources and the number of cases to be processed (Pontell, 1982). Where resources are low relative to the number of cases to be processed, the going rate used to bargain cases should also be low. Conversely, where resources are high compared to the volume of cases, the going rate should be high. In other words, court caseloads might influence the going rates used to bargain cases as well as the overall rate of guilty pleas. Thus, caseloads may affect the *qualitative* as well as the *quantitative* aspects of plea bargains. This point is important in assessing the possible effects of caseloads, as it indicates how they may: (1) influence plea bargaining without affecting its overall frequency; and (2) affect the generation and administration of punishment by influencing the going rate used to bargain cases. The latter point is important for understanding how criminal justice workloads serve to diminish organizational capacity for meting out criminal punishments (Green and Allen, 1982; Pepinsky, 1980; Pontell, 1982, 1984).

The aim of this paper is to further examine the caseload controversy. Using an interrupted time-series design, we will document the effects of a change in the California Penal Code (Section 17) which was intended to reduce caseloads at the superior court level by allowing lesser felonies to be prosecuted in the lower courts. This legislative action provides a "natural experiment" for assessing the effects of a reduction in caseloads on criminal adjudications and plea bargaining.

Background of Change in Section 17

During the 1969 regular session of the California Legislature, a bill amending Section 17 of the Penal Code was introduced by Senator Robert J. Lagomarsino (Senate Bill 1032). Its purpose was to relieve the overburdened superior courts of the state of California by allowing lesser felonies carrying alternative sentences of jail or prison ("wobblers") to be adjudicated in the municipal courts at the discretion of the prosecuting attorney. The individual convicted of such a crime would be considered guilty of a misdemeanor. The bill passed through the legislature fairly rapidly and went into effect November 19, 1969.

Prior to 1969 in California, felony cases could be adjudicated only in superior courts. Concern arose that, because of limited resources, these courts could not adequately handle all of the cases brought before them. As a result, Senate Bill 1032 was introduced in an effort to divert less serious cases from the superior courts.

There is no written record of events which led to the formulation of Senate Bill 1032. However, there have been numerous court decisions which describe this change in Section 17 as an attempt to provide relief to the overcrowded superior courts (*Malone vs. Superior Court for Sacramento County*, 120 Cal Rptr. 851; *Nechochea vs. Superior Court for Los Angeles County*, 100 Cal. Rptr. 693). One comment, in particular, makes clear the intentions of this change in law.

> Enactment of statute, subsection, providing that case shall proceed as if defendant had been arraigned on a misdemeanor complaint when magistrate determines that offense is a felony, had in view the unburdening of superior courts from cases which were likely to result in no more than misdemeanor penalties, the consequent more expeditious handling of such cases, the encouragement of guilty pleas by defendants who could know in

advance that no penalty could be imposed more severe than jail sentence or fine and the consequent saving of time to municipal courts by elimination of some preliminary hearings. (*Henry vs. Department of Motor Vehicles,* 102 Cal. Rptr. 36, 37)

The version of Senate Bill 1032 eventually codified into law reads in part as follows:

(b) When a crime is punishable, in the discretion of the court, by imprisonment in the state prison or by fine or imprisonment in the county jail, it is a misdemeanor for all purposes under the following circumstances . . . :

(4) When the prosecuting attorney files in a court having jurisdiction over misdemeanor offenses a complaint specifying that the offense is a misdemeanor, unless the defendant at the time of his arraignment or plea objects to the offense being made a misdemeanor, in which event the complaint shall be amended to charge the felony and the case shall proceed on the felony complaint.

(5) When, at or before the preliminary examination and with the consent of the prosecuting attorney and the defendant, the magistrate determines that the offense is a misdemeanor, in which event the case shall proceed as if the defendant had been arraigned on a misdemeanor complaint [Cal. Penal Code § 17(b) (4), (5) (west 1970)].

In 1971, the section requiring consent of the prosecuting attorney before a magistrate could determine that a charged offense was to be treated as a misdemeanor was found to violate the constitutional doctrine of separation of powers (*Esteybar vs. Municipal Court for Long Beach Judicial District,* 95 Cal. Rptr. 524). The current version of Penal Code Section 17 reflects this judicial decision:

(5) When, at or before the preliminary examination or prior to filing an order pursuant to Section 872, the magistrate determines that the offense is a misdemeanor, in which event the case shall proceed as if the defendant had been arraigned on a misdemeanor complaint [Cal. Penal Code § 17(b)(5) (West 1971)].

In summary, the change to Section 17 granted district attorneys and magistrates further discretion in managing their caseloads by allowing them to file and charge as misdemeanors any offenses that were punishable either as felonies or misdemeanors. If the defendant objected to the offense being filed as a misdemeanor, it had to be prosecuted as a felony. The bill also provided that the court could order an offense filed as a felony to be prosecuted as a misdemeanor if the order was made at or prior to the preliminary hearing. The bill was enacted to provide more expeditious handling of lesser felonies in superior courts by allowing them to be shifted to municipal courts where they would be prosecuted as misdemeanors.

We will examine the impact of this change in law on the processing activities in superior courts. First, we will assess the magnitude of its effects on superior court caseloads. We will then compare patterns of defendant processing both before and after the change in Section 17 in order to examine its possible effects on plea bargaining practices and sanctioning activities.

 ## Data

Data on superior courts were obtained from published reports of the California Bureau of Criminal Statistics of 1966 to 1974. The analysis was restricted to these years because earlier data were not available and changes in reporting and collection procedures produced comparability problems with data subsequent to 1974. This time span may appear somewhat short given that procedures like plea bargaining tend to be deeply embedded in the ways in which courtroom participants carry out their work. The data indicate, however, that there was a major impact on the system almost immediately. The change in Section 17 went into effect late in 1969 (November 10); consequently 1970 is the first year in which meaningful effects can be seen. For the years 1970 through 1972 respectively, 14,758; 22,234; and 32,168 cases were shifted to municipal courts due to the change in Section 17. If these cases had been handled by superior courts, dispositions for the same three years would have been increased by 25%, 34%, and 41% respectively.

Determining whether or not this shift in cases had produced a corresponding impact on caseloads and sentencing patterns is the focus of this research. Specifically, felony complaints, actual dispositions (cases), superior court personnel (judges and related personnel, excluding prosecutors), means of conviction (original or fast guilty plea, later pleas of guilty, and trials resulting in a guilty verdict), and sentence (prison, jail, probation with jail and "straight" probation) are analyzed to determine the impact of the change in Section 17.

 ## Methodology

The data are analyzed through the use of an interrupted time-series methodology. The interrupted time-series quasi-experimental design was originally proposed by Campbell (1963; Campbell and Stanley, 1966; see also McDowell, McCleary, Meidinger, and Hay, 1980) as a method for determining the impact of a discrete intervention on a social process. In its simplest form, it is represented by the one-group pretest-posttest design (Campbell, 1971). This particular design is extremely vulnerable to external threats to its validity, rendering the analysis of such designs problematic. It can be vastly improved by including a series of both preintervention and postintervention observations.

This type of design is uniquely suited to the study of legal interventions. Many laws are enacted to create a specific change in the behavior of the people or organizations which are the target of the particular legislation. Indeed, the widest use of interrupted time-series designs has been in the area of legal impact assessment (McDowell et al., 1980: 11). This design has been used to test and measure the impacts of new traffic laws (Campbell and Ross, 1968; Glass, 1968; Ross, Campbell, and Glass, 1970; Ross, McCleary, and Epperlein, 1982); the impacts of decriminalization (Aaronson, Dienes, and Musheno, 1978; McCleary and Musheno, 1980); the impact of gun control laws (Deutsch and Alt, 1977; Hay

and McCleary, 1979; Zimring, 1975); the impact of air pollution control laws (Box and Tiao, 1975); and the impact of organizational structure on the uniform crime reports (McCleary, Nienstedt, and Gruen, 1982).

This analytic strategy is employed in the present study to determine if the shift in cases created by Section 17 produced a corresponding impact on caseloads and sentencing patterns. First, as suggested by Cook and Campbell (1979), the graphs for the observed values will be visually inspected for trends. In addition, constant-rate and preintervention-postintervention two-rate models will be fitted to the data. These models will be compared to determine whether the two-rate model provides a significant improvement of fit over the constant-rate model.

 ## Results

Figure 6.1 presents the trends for superior court filings, dispositions, and number of convictions from 1966 to 1974. Several trends are worth noting. First, both dispositions and convictions parallel each other almost perfectly, indicating that the relationship between convictions and dispositions has remained stable over this time period. Second, for all three variables there is a rapid and consistent increase from 1966 to 1969. The trends after 1969, however, are not as consistent. For superior court filings, there is a leveling off in 1970 and 1971 with a fairly steady decline afterwards. Dispositions and convictions, on the other hand, level off in 1970, peak in 1971, and decline steadily thereafter. These data offer only partial support for a Section 17 effect. Clearly the rate of increase diminishes between 1969 and 1970. If one were only considering the years 1966 through 1970, one could conclude that the implementation of Section 17 coincides with a dramatic leveling off of the rate of increase in these variables over the prior years. The patterns after 1970, however, make such a simple interpretation problematic.

It was asserted previously that one of the expected effects of a statute designed to take large numbers of cases off of the superior court docket would be to decrease its caseload. Ideally, we would talk in terms of prosecutors' caseloads, since prosecutors play a pivotal role in processing cases. As Reiss notes, "by legal authority

Figure 6.1   Court Filings, Dispositions, and Convictions: California Superior Court, 1966 to 1974

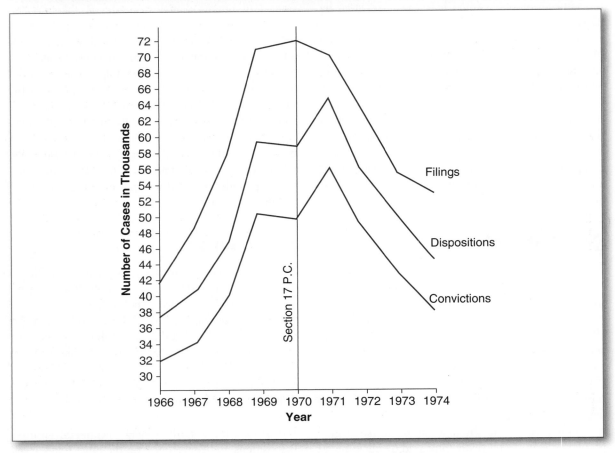

SOURCE: Criminal Justice Profile—1976 and 1979, California Bureau of Criminal Statistics and Special Services.

and by practice, prosecutors have the greatest discretion in the formally organized criminal justice network" (1974: 690). Previously, others have used case volume as a surrogate indicator for caseload (Feeley, 1975; Heumann, 1975, 1978). Unless one is willing to assume a constant prosecutorial staff size, such an indicator is problematic. Data concerning prosecutorial staff were not available for this study, but data are available for superior court personnel. The ratio of case dispositions to court personnel is a better indicator of caseload pressure than volume of cases for several reasons. First, given the increase in superior court personnel over the years (see Table 6.1), it is highly unlikely that prosecutorial staffs have remained constant. Indeed, while the number of court personnel has increased over time, dispositions have increased then decreased, casting doubt on the simple assumption that the size of prosecutorial staff is monotonically related to case volume. In addition, dispositions are used instead of convictions to measure caseloads because we are unwilling to assume that Section 17 felonies have the same outcome distribution as other felonies (for a similar argument on the use of dispositions, see Nardulli, 1978: 51).

Table 6.1   Dispositions, Caseloads, Court Personnel, and Means of Convictions: California Superior Courts, 1966 to 1974

Measure	Year								
	1966	**1967**	**1968**	**1969**	**1970**	**1971**	**1972**	**1973**	**1974**
Dispositions	37584	41027	47277	59497	59257	65236	56586	49827	44263
Court Personnel Caseloads	N/A	N/A	462	487	503	534	564	573	573
(Disposition/Court Personnel)	—	—	102.33	122.17	117.81	122.16	100.33	86.96	77.25
%	—	—	—	19.39	−3.57	3.69	−17.87	−13.33	−11.17
Total Guilty Pleas	27136	29047	28123	37502	36114	44454	40444	36000	33146
Guilty Pleas/Disposition	.7220	.7080	.5949	.6303	.6094	.6814	.7147	.7225	.7488
%	—	−1.94	−15.97	5.95	−3.32	11.81	4.89	1.09	3.64
Fast Guilty Pleas	13681	13416	12069	15073	11836	15419	12613	9222	8565
Fast Pleas/Disposition	.3640	.3270	.2553	.2533	.1997	.2364	.2229	.1851	.1935
%	—	6.42	−10.87	11.01	8.67	8.64	10.49	9.27	3.33
Slow Guilty Pleas	13455	15631	16054	22429	24278	29035	27831	26778	24581
Slow Pleas/Disposition	.3580	.3810	.3396	.3770	.4097	.4451	.4918	.5374	.5553
%	—	−8.39	−7.08	−6.36	−18.46	5.86	−10.09	−17.86	86
Fast Pleas/Total Pleas	.5042	.4619	.4292	.4019	.3277	.3469	.3119	.2562	.2584
%	—	−8.39	−7.08	6.36	−18.46	.86	−10.09	−17.86	.86
Trial Convictions	10448	11980	12354	13066	13836	11564	8580	6672	4861
Trial Convictions/ Disposition	.2780	.2920	.2613	.2196	.235	.1773	.1516	.1339	.1098
%	—	5.04	−10.51	−15.96	6.33	−24.07	−14.50	−11.68	−18.00

SOURCE: Criminal Justice Profile—1976 and 1979, California Bureau of Criminal Statistics and Special Services.

Table 6.1 presents the data for dispositions and court personnel, while Figure 6.2 presents the disposition/court personnel ratio over time. Dispositions per personnel increase in 1968 to 1969, level off from 1969 to 1971, and show a steady decline thereafter. Table 6.2 presents the chi square tests for both the constant- and two-rate models for these data. The constant-rate model does not fit the disposition/court personnel ratio over time. The two-rate model does have a higher disposition/court personnel ratio of 112.51 for the preintervention period compared to 100.17 for the postintervention period which is consistent with a Section 17 effect. While the two-rate model does provide a significant improvement of fit, and reduces the error in fit for the constant-rate model by 10%, it too does not fit the data according to the traditional log-linear criteria of a nonsignificant chi square value. Because significance levels for the chi square distribution are strongly influenced by the total frequency for a given rank table, it is highly unlikely that one will find a model that will fit when dealing with frequencies that total over 380,000 for only seven categories. Consequently, for the remainder of the analysis, we focus our attention on the relative reduction in error produced by the two-rate model over the constant-rate model, coupled with visual inspection of the trends in the data.

Returning to the examination of caseloads, it is clear that the rate of increase during the preintervention period stops and the trend reverses during the postintervention period (see Table 6.1). Given that there are only two observations before the change in Section 17 and that the trend changes during the post period, we cannot conclude that the statutory intervention was totally responsible for the resulting pattern. Even so, caseloads did level off after the change in Section 17 and declined in subsequent years.

Figure 6.2 Proportions of Means of Convictions to Dispositions

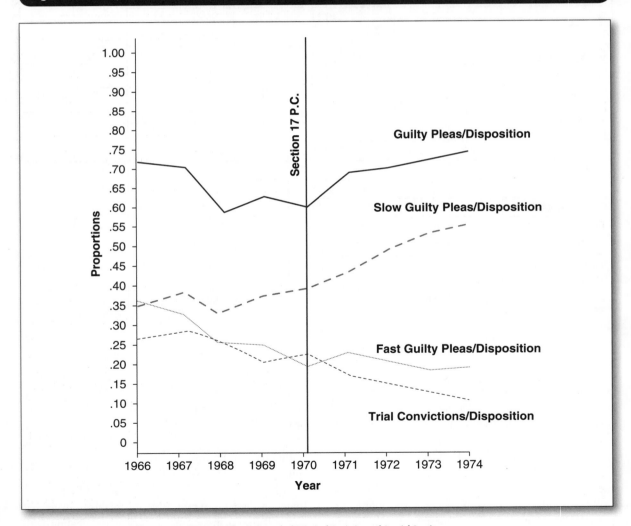

SOURCE: Criminal Justice Profile—1976 and 1979, California Bureau of Criminal Statistics and Special Services.

Table 6.2 Chi Square Summary Table

Measure	Constant Rate Model			Two Rate Model				Percentage Reduction[b] in Error
	Rate	L[2a]	df	Prerate	Postrate	L²	df	
Disposition/Court Personnel	103.34	10049.39	6	112.51	100.17	9037.00	5	10.07
Guilty Pleas/Disposition	.6774	1835.69	8	.6571	.6911	1632.99	7	1.04
Fast Guilty Pleas/Disposition	.2430	4873.88	8	.2926	.2095	1829.44	7	62.45
Slow Guilty Pleas/Disposition	.4344	5378.59	8	.3645	.4815	1807.24	7	66.40
Fast Pleas/Total Pleas	.3587	5326.52	8	.4453	.3032	1249.77	7	76.84
Trial Convictions/Dispositions	.2027	8055.23	8	.2581	.1654	3444.22	7	57.24
Jail/Disposition	.0919	3388.89	8	.1155	.0760	1545.23	7	54.40
Jail and Probation/Disposition	.2712	5330.05	8	.2232	.3035	2654.39	7	50.20
Probation/Disposition	.2927	2789.61	8	.2911	.2938	2774.65	7	0.54
Prison/Disposition	.1121	3569.05	8	.1301	.1000	2673.36	7	25.10

a. Log likelihood ratio chi square statistic $L^2 = 2 \sum f1 \log\left(\dfrac{f_i}{F_i}\right)$ where f_i = observed frequencies and F_i = expected frequencies.

b. Percentage reduction in error = $\left(\dfrac{L^2 \text{ constant-rate} - L^2 \text{ two-rate}}{L^2 \text{ constant-rate}}\right)(100)$.

Others have speculated that caseload pressures are related to court outcomes (Blumberg, 1967). As caseloads pressures increase, there may be an increase in the use of guilty pleas to reduce docket congestion. This relationship, if it exists, may not be so straightforward when a statutory intervention is utilized to decrease congestion. One of the purposes of Section 17 was to reduce congestion, but it did so by removing relatively minor felonies to the municipal courts. Reducing the caseload in this fashion may or may not influence court outcomes depending upon whether the outcome distribution for minor felonies is the same as for other felonies. With this in mind, we will examine court outcome measures.

Total guilty pleas, as well as guilty pleas per disposition, are presented in Table 6.1 and Figure 6.2. There is a

general decline during the preintervention period that first levels off, and then increases during the postintervention period. Table 6.2 reveals that the two-rate model has a preintervention rate of .6571 that increases slightly to .6911 for the postintervention period. While the two-rate model does provide a significant improvement of fit, the reduction of error is relatively small at one percent. The guilty-plea trend does not follow the relative decline in caseload pressure.

All guilty pleas are not the same. Some defendants enter pleas of guilty immediately (original or "fast" guilty pleas), while others originally plead not guilty and later changed their plea to guilty (changed or "slow" guilty pleas). Looking at original or fast guilty pleas (Table 6.1 and Figure 6.2), there is a decline during the preintervention period with a large drop after

Section 17 and a slight leveling off followed by a further decline during the postintervention period. Table 6.2 reveals that the two-rate model produces a decline in the proportion of fast pleas to dispositions that is consistent with an intervention effect. The two-rate model provides a significant improvement in fit coupled with a large 62% reduction in error over the constant-rate model.

Analysis of changed, or slow guilty pleas, reveals a similar pattern, but, as would be expected, in the opposite direction. The two-rate model has pre- and postintervention proportions of .3645 and .4815 respectively. The improvement of fit is significant with a large reduction of error equal to 66%.

Similarly, the ratio of fast to total pleas follows the same pattern as the proportion of fast pleas to dispositions. The two-rate model has proportions of .4453 and .3032 for the pre- and postintervention periods, producing a 76% reduction in error.

These results are consistent with a major impact produced by Section 17. Assuming that slow pleas are relatively more adversarial in nature than fast pleas, this pattern supports the argument that decreased caseloads increase adversariness. Alternatively, if it is assumed that minor felonies are more likely to be processed by fast pleas, then the decline of fast pleas during the postintervention period along with the corresponding rise in slow pleas suggest that Section 17 produced a noticeable impact on plea bargaining rates.

The interpretation of the ratios of trial convictions to dispositions is more complicated. The proportion of trial convictions steadily declines with one of the largest drops occurring *before* the intervention in 1969. The two-rate model indicates a decline in the proportion of trial convictions with pre- and postintervention proportions of .2581 and .1654. While this is a significant improvement of fit with a large reduction of error equal to 57%, we are hesitant to attribute this solely to an intervention effect because of the steady nature of the decline both before and after the enactment of changes in Section 17.

Table 6.3 and Figure 6.3 present the data on sentencing. The caseload argument suggests that with declining caseloads, sanctioning capacity would increase and sentencing would become more severe. Given that Section 17 is directed at relatively minor felonies, a major impact would suggest a decline in the proportion of jail sentences and a corresponding increase in the proportion of prison sentences. The proportion of jail sentences to dispositions appear to be relatively stable during the preintervention period with a steady decline during the postintervention period. The two-rate model has pre- and postintervention proportions of .1155 and .0760, producing a significant improvement with a 54% reduction in error. Thus, the pattern of jail sentences is consistent with both a Section 17 impact and the caseload argument.

Sentences of jail with probation, like the conviction by trial data, also have a constant trend over time, but in this case the proportion increases. The two-rate model has pre- and postintervention proportions of .2232 and .3035. While this is a significant improvement of fit (a 50% reduction in error), Figure 6.3 indicates that the trend is gradual over time, with little indication of an intervention effect or relationship with caseloads.

The probation sentencing data show little indication of an impact at all. Indeed, for this variable the two-rate model provides only a 0.5 percent reduction in error.

Finally, there is the prison sentencing data. We would expect the proportion of prison sentences to increase with the change in Section 17 for two reasons: lowered caseloads would increase the "going rate" used to bargain cases and the case mix would become more serious as lesser felonies are switched to lower courts. While prison sentences decline at first, the major drop is in 1969, before the intervention. During the postintervention years the proportion levels off and then begins to rise after 1972. The two-rate model has proportions of .1301 and .1000 for the pre- and postintervention periods. This is a significant improvement with a 25% reduction in error. Visual inspection of the trend in Figure 6.3 provides additional support for the caseload explanation. Remembering that caseloads decreased from 1971 to 1974, the increase in prison sentences from 1971 onward does follow the caseload argument. Additionally, caseloads increased from

Table 6.3   Dispositions and Sentencing Data: California Superior Courts, 1966 to 1974

Measures	Year								
	1966	**1967**	**1968**	**1969**	**1970**	**1971**	**1972**	**1973**	**1974**
Dispositions	37584	41027	47277	59497	59257	65236	56586	49827	44263
Jail	4777	4335	5283	7020	6118	5771	4062	2849	2114
Jail/Disposition	.1271	.1057	.1117	.1180	.1032	.0885	.0718	.0572	.0478
%	—	−20.25	5.37	5.34	−14.34	−16.61	−23.26	−25.52	−19.67
Jail and Probation	6871	9265	11524	13718	14564	17703	17318	16196	17736
Jail and Probation/ Disposition	.1828	.2258	.2438	.2306	.2458	.2714	.3060	.3250	.4007
%	—	19.04	7.38	−5.72	6.18	9.43	11.31	5.85	18.89
Probation	9883	11070	13536	19470	19249	21738	17606	13682	8566
Probation/Disposition	.2630	.2698	.2863	.3272	.3248	.3332	.3111	.2746	.1935
%	—	2.52	5.76	12.50	−0.74	2.52	−7.10	−13.29	−41.91
Prison	6731	5990	6473	4931	5006	5386	5660	5826	5628
Prison/Disposition	.1791	.1460	.1369	.0829	.0845	.0826	.1000	.1169	.1271
%	—	−22.67	−6.65	−65.14	1.89	−2.30	17.40	14.46	8.03

SOURCE: Criminal Justice Profile—1976 and 1979, California Bureau of Criminal Statistics and Special Series.

1968 to 1969, and there was a corresponding decrease in prison sentences in 1968 to 1969. Similar to the situation with the fast-and-slow-guilty-plea analysis, the prison data cannot differentiate between the caseload and case-mix explanations because of the unavailability of specific felony data.

Both the data for fast and slow guilty pleas as well as prison sentences support the decreased caseload-increased adversariness arguments. However, the results are confounded by the alternative explanation of changes in case mix produced through the elimination of lesser felonies. A detailed analysis of felony homicide cases with the limited available data provides a test of the caseload argument that is free of this confounding effect. Felony homicides are studied because these cases are least likely to be directly affected by Section 17 and tried in lower courts. As the most serious of felony

offenses, homicide cases offer the best test of specific caseload effects. For the years in which data are available, 1970 to 1973, less than one percent of the felony homicide cases were tried in municipal court through the use of Section 17. Although the data at the specific felony level is limited, there is information on how homicide cases were disposed of in terms of trial acquittals, trial convictions, and convictions by guilty pleas. We will examine these measures to test whether the caseload argument is supported.

The decreased caseload–increased adversariness argument would be supported by trial-to-guilty-plea ratios for homicide cases that increased after the implementation of Section 17. From 1968 to 1973 these ratios are as follows: 1.02, .96, .97, 1.01, 1.15, and 1.21. The constant-rate model has a trial-to-guilty-plea ratio of 1.07, and a L^2 equal to 22.88 with 5 degrees of freedom.

Figure 6.3 Proportion of Sentencing to Dispositions: California Superior Court, 1966 to 1974

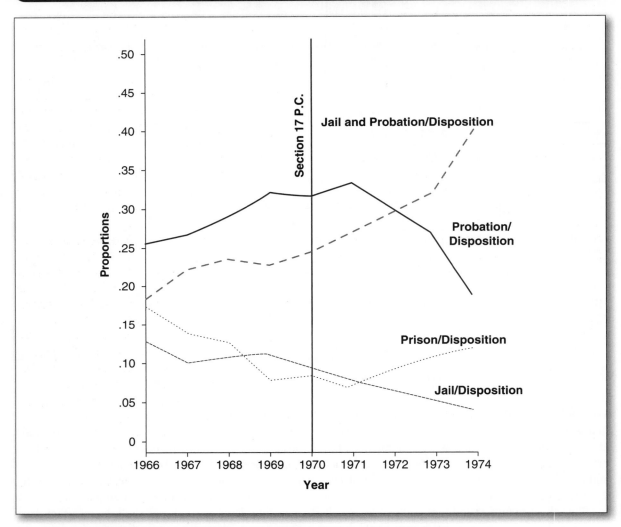

SOURCE: Criminal Justice Profile—1976 and 1979, California Bureau of Criminal Statistics and Special Services.

The two-rate model has a preintervention rate of .99 and a postintervention rate of 1.09 and a L^2 equal to 17.54 with 4 degrees of freedom. This is a significant improvement in fit at the .05 level with a 23% reduction in error over the constant-rate model. This analysis clearly supports the caseload argument. Not only are homicide cases more likely to be disposed of by trials than guilty pleas after the implementation of Section 17, but the postintervention trend is opposite that of the preintervention trend, indicating a steady increase in the likelihood of trial disposition in the years following the statutory intervention.

Like most interrupted time-series quasi-experimental designs, this analysis is subject to internal threats to validity, such as history, that the design cannot control for. There may have been other major legislative interventions in 1970 that could explain the changes that have been observed. Alternatively, the police could have radically changed their arrest patterns for felonies and misdemeanors starting in 1970, which would have influenced the type of defendants being tried at the superior court level.

Berk, Brackman, and Lesser (1977), have conducted an exhaustive study of changes in the California Penal Code from 1955 to 1971. Their analysis of legislation favorable to defendants reveals that defendants did better before 1965 than after, and that 1963 was their best year (1977:136–145). The analysis does not reveal any major legislative changes in addition to Section 17, implemented in 1970, that benefited defendants in such a way as to suggest the patterns observed here.

Examination of arrest data also fails to indicate any major changes in 1970 that would account for the patterns observed. According to data issued by the California Department of Justice, total felony arrests and the felony arrest rate per 100,000 population continually increased from 1966 to 1974 without any dramatic changes occurring in 1970. Total adult misdemeanor arrests and the misdemeanor arrest rate per 100,000 population also continually increased during this period with a slight decrease between 1970 and 1971.

We are aware that this does not exhaust all possible threats to the external validity of this analysis. However, we know of no other major influences that could have produced the changes observed.

Summary

The change in Section 17 was designed to reduce California superior court caseloads by shifting lesser felonies to lower courts. The analysis indicates that there was, in fact, a reduction in superior court caseloads. This reduction was accompanied by a change in rates of plea bargaining. While the overall rate of plea bargaining remained relatively constant, there were substantial changes in types of plea bargains. The proportion of original or fast guilty pleas, representing the least adversarial proceedings, declined, while the proportion of changed or slow guilty pleas increased. This finding indicates that there may well be a relationship between caseloads and plea bargaining. While these

results are undoubtedly influenced by the change in case mix that reduced the number of lesser felonies in superior courts, the analysis of homicide cases indicates that there is an independent caseload effect on adversariness in terms of increased trial dispositions compared to guilty pleas.

Noticeable changes in rates of sentencing also occurred following the change in Section 17. The proportion of jail sentencing, which would be used primarily for lesser felonies, was reduced. On the other band, the proportion of prison sentencing appeared to be best understood in terms of changing caseload patterns. The proportion of prison sentences increased when caseloads decreased. This finding is consistent with the notion that "going rates" used to bargain cases are influenced by court caseloads.

This analysis of a statutory change represents a further exploration into the "caseload controversy." While our conclusions must be tentative given the limitations of available official data and the analytical design used, the study has added to research on court caseloads in several ways. First, to perhaps belabor the obvious, how caseloads are operationalized strongly influences one's results. Reliance on volume of cases alone is not sufficient, and some measure of court resources must be included. Second, finer measures of adversariness may lead to different findings concerning the relationship between caseloads and plea bargaining. This is particularly important not only for testing theories on how court cases are adjudicated, but also for the analysis of policy changes which may affect the case mix in criminal courts.

This study also indicates that future research on the effects of caseloads should address the issue of criminal sanctioning, as well as adversarial issues in the disposition of cases. Sentencing rates, including both the certainty and severity of punishment, are likely to be influenced by the sanctioning capacity of courts. Capacity is at least partially determined by organizational caseloads. As demonstrated by the change in law examined here, caseloads can in fact be manipulated through legislation, resulting in changes in the adjudication of cases. The fact that the case mix will usually change simultaneously with caseloads necessitates extensive data on single offense dispositions for a more conclusive research study. While such data are generally rare, available data for the single crime of homicide did show an independent caseload effect in this study.

Finally, this research has touched on important topics related to criminal justice policy. Caseloads did indeed respond to a change in law. However, other changes in processing occurred that were not anticipated by the original legislation. Reduced caseloads did not lessen plea bargaining although it may have affected how it occurred. The fragmented and hydraulic nature of courts assures that sweeping changes in policy will produce a chain reaction of adjustments that may not have been originally anticipated (Feeley, 1983). Further research on such organizational processes will go far in informing social policies aimed at improving the performance of courts.

References

Aaronson, David, C. Thomas Dienes, and Michael C. Musheno. 1978. Changing the public drunkenness laws: The impact of decriminalization. *Law and Society Review* 12: 405–436.

Berk, Richard A., Harold Brackman, and Selma Lesser. 1977. *A Measure of Justice*. New York: Academic Press.

Blumberg, Abraham S. 1967. *Criminal Justice*. Chicago: Quadrangle Books.

Bock, Richard D. 1963. Multivariate analysis of variance of repeated measures. In Chester W. Harris (ed.), *Problems in Measuring Change*. Madison: University of Wisconsin Press.

Bock, Richard D. 1975. *Multivariate Statistical Methods in Behavioral Research*. New York: McGraw-Hill.

Box, George E. P. and Gwilym M. Jenkins. 1976. *Time Series and Analysis: Forecasting and Control*. San Francisco: Holden-Day.

Box, George E. P. and George C. Tiao. 1975. Intervention analysis with applications to economic and environmental problems. *Journal of the American Statistical Association* 70: 70–79.

California Department of Justice. 1976. *Criminal Justice Profile–1976*. Sacramento: Bureau of Criminal Statistics.

California Department of Justice. 1979. *Criminal Justice Profile–1979*. Sacramento: Bureau of Criminal Statistics.

Campbell, Donald T. 1963. From description to experimentation: Interpreting trends as quasi-experiments. In Cheater W. Harris (ed.), *Problems of Measuring Change*. Madison: University of Wisconsin Press.

Campbell, Donald T. 1971. Legal reforms as experiments. *Journal of Legal Education* 23: 217–239.

Campbell, Donald T. and H. Laurence Ross. 1968. The Connecticut crackdown on speeding: Time series data in quasi-experimental analysis. *Law and Society Review* 3: 33–53.

Campbell, Donald T. and Julian C. Stanley. 1966. *Experimental and Quasi-Experimental Designs for Research*. Skokie, IL: Rand-McNally.

Cole, George F. 1970. The decision to prosecute. *Law and Society Review* 4: 331–343.

Cook, Thomas D. and Donald T. Campbell. 1979. *Quasi-Experimentation: Design and Analysis Issues for Field Studies*. Chicago: Rand-McNally.

Deutsch, Stuart J. and Francis B. Alt. 1977. The effect of Massachusetts' gun control law on gun-related crimes in the city of Boston. *Evaluation Quarterly* 1: 543–568.

Eisenstein, James and Herbert Jacob. 1977. *Felony Justice: An Organizational Analysis of Criminal Courts*. Boston: Little, Brown.

Feeley, Malcolm M. 1975. *The effects of heavy caseloads*. Presented at the annual meeting of the American Political Science Association.

Feeley, Malcolm M. 1979a. *The Process is the Punishment*. New York: Russell Sage Foundation.

Feeley, Malcolm M. 1979b. Perspectives on plea bargaining. *Law and Society Review* 13: 199–209.

Feeley, Malcolm M. 1983. *Court Reform on Trial: Why Simple Solutions Fail*. New York: Basic Books.

Friedman, Lawrence M. 1979. Plea bargaining in historical perspective. *Law and Society Review* 13: 247–259.

Geisser, Seymour and Samuel W. Greenhouse. 1958. An extension of Box's results on the use of F-distribution in multivariate analysis. *Annals of Mathematical Statistics* 29: 885–891.

Glass, Gene V. 1968. Analysis of data on the Connecticut speeding crackdown as a time series quasi-experiment. *Law and Society Review* 3: 55–76.

Green, Penny A. and H. David Allen. 1982. Severity of societal response to crime: A synthesis of models. *Law and Society Review* 16: 181–205.

Greenhouse, Samuel W. and Seymour Geisser. 1959. On methods in the analysis of profile data *Psychometrika* 24: 95–112.

Haberman, Shelby. 1978. *Analysis of Qualitative Data: Volume I Introductory Topics*. New York: Academic Press.

Hay, Richard A., Jr., and Richard McCleary. 1979. Box-Tiao time series models for impact assessment: A comment on the recent work of Deutsch and Alt. *Evaluation Quarterly* 3: 277–314.

Heumann, Milton. 1975. A note on plea bargaining and caseload pressure. *Law and Society Review* 9: 515–528.

Heumann, Milton. 1978. *Plea Bargaining: The Experiences of Prosecutors, Judges and Defense Attorneys*. Chicago: University of Chicago Press.

McCain, Leslie J. and Richard McCleary. 1979. The statistical analysis of the simple interrupted time series quasi-experiment. In Thomas D. Cook and Donald T. Campbell (eds.), *Quasi-Experimentation: Design and Analysis Issues for Field Settings*. Chicago: Rand McNally.

McCleary, Richard and Michael C. Musheno. 1981. Floor effects in the time series quasi-experiment. *Political Methodology* 7: 181–204.

McCleary, Richard, Barbara C. Nienstedt, and James M. Erven. 1982. Uniform crime reports as organizational outcomes: Three time series experiments. *Social Problems* 29: 361–372.

McDowell, David, Richard McCleary, Erroll E. Meidinger, and Richard A. Hay, Jr. 1980. *Interrupted Time Series Analysis*. Beverly Hills: Sage.

Magidson, Jay and Greg Kennington. 1981. *Analysis of data from interrupted time series designs*. Paper presented to Conference on Experimental Research in the Social Sciences, University of Florida.

Mather, Lynn M. 1973. Some determinants of the method of case disposition: Decision-making by public defenders in Los Angeles. *Law and Society Review* 8: 187–216.

Mileski, Maureen. 1971. Courtroom Encounters: An observation study of a lower criminal court. *Law and Society Review* 3: 473–538.

Nardulli, Peter F. 1978. *The Courtroom Elite: An Organizational Perspective on Criminal Justice.* Cambridge, MA: Ballinger.

Nardulli, Peter F. 1979. The caseload controversy and the study of criminal courts. *Journal of Criminal Law and Criminology* 70: 89–101.

Pepinsky, Harold E. 1980. *Crime Control Strategies: An Introduction to the Study of Crime.* New York: Oxford University Press.

Pontell, Henry N. 1982. System capacity and criminal justice: Theoretical and substantive considerations. In Harold E. Pepinsky (ed.), *Rethinking Criminology.* Beverly Hills: Sage.

Pontell, Henry N. 1984. *A Capacity to Punish: The Ecology of Crime and Punishment.* Bloomington: Indiana University Press.

Pothoff, Richard R. and S. N. Roy. 1964. A generalized multivariate analysis of variance models useful especially for growth curve problems. *Biometrika* 51: 313–326.

Reiss, Albert J., Jr. 1974. Discretionary justice. In Daniel Glaser (ed.), *Handbook of Criminology.* Chicago: Rand-McNally.

Ross, H. Laurence, Donald T. Campbell, and Gene V. Glass. 1970. Determining the effects of a legal reform: The British 'breathalyzer' crackdown of 1967. *American Behavioral Scientist* 13: 493–509.

Ross, H. Laurence, Richard McCleary, and Thomas Epperlein. 1981. Deterrence of drinking and driving in France: An evaluation of the law of July 12, 1978. *Law and Society Review* 16: 345–374.

Skonick, Jerome H. 1967. Social control in the adversary system. *Journal of Conflict Resolution* 11: 52–70.

Zimring, Franklin E. 1975. Firearms and federal law: The gun control act of 1968. *Journal of Legal Studies* 4: 133–198.

DISCUSSION QUESTIONS

1. What is the "caseload controversy" and how does it relate to the practice of plea bargaining? What are the alternative explanations for the prevalence of plea bargaining?

2. What was Section 17 of the California Penal Code and how did it provide a "natural experiment" for assessing the effects of caseload on plea bargaining?

3. What is interrupted time series analysis and why is it appropriate for addressing the impact of Section 17?

4. The authors of this study conclude that implementation of Section 17 "produced a noticeable impact on plea bargaining rates." What evidence do they present that supports this conclusion? (See Figure 6.2.)

5. What were the expected effects of Section 17 on sentences? Do the authors' findings support these expectations? Why or why not?

6. How do the results of this study add to knowledge regarding the caseload controversy?

READING

The Sixth Amendment to the U.S. Constitution guarantees that a person accused of a crime has the right to be tried by a jury. However, there is evidence that those who invoke that right and are tried by a jury receive harsher sentences than those who plead guilty. This so-called "trial penalty" is the subject of the article by Ulmer and Bradley. Using data on offenders convicted of serious violent offenses in Pennsylvania, the authors test a number of hypotheses about the sentences imposed on offenders who plead guilty, elect a bench trial, or

SOURCE: "Variation in Trial Penalties Among Serious Violent Offenses," by Jeffery T. Ulmer and Mindy S. Bradley in *Criminology*, vol. 44, issue 3, pp. 631-670, August 2006. Reprinted by permission of the American Society of Criminology.

ask for a jury trial. The results of their analyses reveal that the odds of incarceration are higher and the length of the sentence is longer for offenders who are tried (either by a judge or jury) than for offenders who enter guilty pleas. They also find that the size of the trial penalty varies by offense characteristics, the offender's criminal history, and the characteristics of the court and the county in which the case is adjudicated. They conclude that "defendants accused of serious violent offenses are substantially penalized if they exercise [their right to a trial by jury] and then lose."

Variation in Trial Penalties Among Serious Violent Offenses

Jeffery T. Ulmer and Mindy S. Bradley

The right to a jury trial is fundamental to the American legal system. Thus the practice of punishing those convicted by trial more severely than similar offenders who plead guilty constitutes an important potential form of sentencing disparity (King et al., 2005; LaFree, 1985; Uhlman and Walker, 1979, 1980), one that presents a tension between legally recognized rights and organizational realities of courts. Compared to the amount of research on racial, ethnic, or gender disparity in sentencing, or on sentencing guidelines issues, relatively few studies examine plea and trial sentencing differences per se, and try to unpack their variation and meaning. More typically, in most studies the mode of conviction (type of plea or trial) is included as a control variable while focusing on the effects of other variables such as defendant characteristics (for example, race, gender). Our goal in this study is to investigate whether such "trial penalties" exist among serious violent offense cases and how they might vary according to offense types, defendant characteristics, and court contextual features.

We focus on serious violent offenses because of the relatively larger number of jury trials present among them (7 percent of these serious violent offenses were convicted in jury trials, versus 3 percent among Pennsylvania sentencing cases overall). We

also focus on such offenses because of the substantial sentencing stakes involved for defendants and other court actors, and because of the seriousness with which they are taken by the public. In addition, as we discuss, serious violent offenses present the possibility of multiple and perhaps competing focal concerns and interests in criminal justice decision making (for example, blameworthiness and community protection versus the practical constraints of organizational efficiency or public scrutiny). We do this using sentencing data on a sample of serious violent offenses (third degree murder, aggravated assault, rape, involuntary deviant sexual intercourse, and robbery) from Pennsylvania from 1997 to 2000.

Research

The literature is mixed as to whether significant trial penalties exist, and only a handful of studies examine how they might vary. Numerous studies focused on the sentencing effects of different modes of conviction show that those convicted by trial, especially jury trials, receive more severe sentences (for example, Brereton and Casper, 1982; Johnson, 2003; Ulmer, 1997; Uhlman and Walker, 1979,1980; Zatz and Hagan, 1985). In one recent analysis, King and colleagues (2005) even found significant "process discounts," or plea-trial sentencing differences in five sentencing guidelines states. Numerous other studies not focused on the plea-trial sentencing issue found that trials are sentenced more severely than guilty pleas when mode of conviction is treated as a control variable (see, as a few among many examples, Albonetti, 1991, 1998; Dixon, 1995; Engen and Gainey, 2000; Kurlychek and Johnson, 2004; Peterson and Hagan, 1984; Spohn and Holleran, 2000; Spohn, Gruhl, and Welch, 1982; Steffensmeier, Ulmer, and Kramer. 1998; Steffensmeier and Demuth, 2000, 2001; Steffensmeier and Hebert, 1999; Steffensmeier, Kramer, and Streifel, 1993; Ulmer and Kramer, 1996; Zatz, 1984).

Many studies suggest that the size of any plea-trial sentencing differences likely varies by jurisdiction (Brereton and Casper, 1982; Eisenstein and Jacob, 1977; King et al., 2005; Nardulli, Eisenstein, and Hemming, 1988; Ulmer, 1997). Specifically, scholars have debated the relationship between trial penalties-plea rewards and court caseloads, with some arguing that heavy caseloads drive mode of conviction differences, and others that such differences are independent of caseload pressure (for reviews, see Brereton and Casper, 1982; Dixon, 1995; Farr, 1984; Holmes, Daudistel, and Taggart, 1992; Meeker and Pontell, 1985; Nardulli, Eisenstein, and Hemming, 1988; Wooldredge, 1989). Furthermore, trial penalties have been found to be stronger for defendants with more substantial criminal histories (for example, Smith, 1986; Ulmer, 1997), and to be stronger for blacks (Ulmer, 1997). In addition, Johnson (2003) also found that racial disparity varied by mode of conviction—blacks were least likely to obtain downward guideline departures following trials, especially jury trials.

Other studies fail to find significant plea rewards or trial penalties (Eisenstein and Jacob, 1977; Hagan, 1975; Smith, 1986). Rhodes (1979) finds that the size of plea-trial sentencing differences varies by offense type, with meaningful differences in robbery cases but not assault, burglary, or larceny. Rhodes (1979), Smith (1986), and LaFree (1985) argue that the chances of acquittal may offset the potential for a

greater penalty after losing at trial, and may also offset the potential for a more lenient sentence through plea bargaining (leniency that Rhodes [1979] argues is largely illusory).

Smith (1986) and Rhodes (1979) in particular hinge the assessment of trial penalties on the comparison of sentences defendants received after pleading guilty with those they would have gotten had they gone to trial, adjusted for the probability of conviction at trial (in other words, the chance of being acquitted, which defendants forgo if they plead guilty). Using this approach, both Smith (1986) and Rhodes (1979) find limited evidence for trial penalties. On the other hand, Zatz and Hagan (1985) find the opposite—significant plea-trial sentencing differences appeared only after they controlled for the likelihood of conviction versus acquittal or charge dismissal.

Relatedly, Eisenstein and Jacob (1977) and Brereton and Casper (1982) note that trial penalties need not be significant in the aggregate to meaningfully shape what court participants believe about the punishment costs of going to trial and losing. Rather, penalizing losing trials may not need to be done often to be effective, and may occur only in unusually visible cases to "send a message" to the court community.

Overall, then, the literature shows mixed findings on (and approaches to studying) trial penalties—most studies find them, yet some important ones do not. The literature also suggests that plea-trial differences may vary by jurisdiction, with caseload being especially important in conditioning such differences. Finally, a few studies suggest that trial penalties may vary by offense type, prior record, or race-ethnicity.

We view the issue of trial penalties and their possible variation from an integrated focal concerns and court community-social worlds perspective to make theoretical sense of jury trial penalties. We first test for the existence and size of trial penalties. Then, in a sense, we treat the effect of jury trial conviction on incarceration and its length as a dependent variable and investigate how factors suggested by the focal concerns-court community perspective condition variation in trial penalties.

Focal Concerns of Sentencing and Their Embeddedness in Court Communities

The focal concerns perspective emphasizes particular kinds of substantive rationalities (Savelsberg, 1992) at work as court actors make sentencing decisions. Its roots were articulated by Steffensmeier (1980) and then expanded by Steffensmeier and colleagues (1993), Ulmer (1997), Steffensmeier, Ulmer, and Kramer (1998), Steffensmeier and DeMuth (2000, 2001), and Kramer and Ulmer (2002). Focal concerns theory also is somewhat congruent with and partially incorporates Albonetti's (1986) uncertainty avoidance theory of criminal case processing and her causal attribution theory of judicial discretion (1991).

According to Albonetti (1991), sentencing reflects the use of bounded rationality (March and Simon, 1958), in which court actors make highly consequential decisions with insufficient information, which produces uncertainty. Sometimes, there is little information on the background and moral character of the defendant (though this lack of information is often alleviated by presentence reports or information brought out at trial). Beyond that, even when more extensive information is available, the risk and seriousness of recidivism is never fully predictable, a defendant's moral character is never fully knowable, and human decision-making processes have built-in limitations to the amount and complexity of information that can be considered.

In this context, judges and other court community actors make situational imputations about defendants' characters and expected future behaviors (Steffensmeier, 1980), and assess the implications of these imputed characteristics in terms of three focal concerns: defendant blameworthiness, defendant dangerousness–community protection, and practical constraints and consequences connected to the punishment decision. These situational definitions of defendants vis-à-vis the focal concerns determine sentencing decisions Our study focuses on two questions. Does going to trial and losing, especially losing at jury trial, result

in more severe sentences for convicted defendants? If so, which focal concerns, if any, might be related to variation in such trial penalties, as evidenced by particular interaction effects?

A practical constraint highly relevant to the issue of plea rewards and trial penalties is organizational efficiency. Most commonly, researchers explain guilty plea versus trial sentencing differences as the product of courts rewarding those who plead guilty for behavior or attitudes that courts organizationally value. Most researchers argue that rewarding those who plead guilty and penalizing those who lose at trial reflects the need for efficiency in case processing. This organizational efficiency model (see Dixon, 1995; Engen and Steen, 2000; Holmes, Daudistel, and Taggert, 1992; Uhlman and Walker, 1980) views rewarding people who plead guilty and avoiding time- and resource-intensive trials as an effort by courts to keep cases moving smoothly and avoid docket backlogs. Relatedly, those who focus on interorganizational and interpersonal relations between court actors, such as adherents of the court community perspective, suggest that court actors often view trials as unpleasant, conflictive, and disruptive of court community working relations, and thus seek to discourage them (Flemming, Nardulli, and Eisenstein, 1992; Ulmer, 1997).

However, it is unlikely that these kinds of organizational factors are the dominant concern in the sentencing of serious violent offenders. The stakes are higher for all parties in serious violent cases, which are relatively more visible to the news media and public. In serious violent offense cases, judges and prosecutors tend to take blameworthiness, protection of the community, and public perceptions of criminal punishment very seriously (Kramer and Ulmer, 2002).

Pleading guilty as opposed to losing at trial might also be associated with differences in perceived blameworthiness. Rewarding those who plead guilty with lighter sentences is widely seen as necessary to encourage defendants' "remorse," "acceptance of responsibility" for crimes, and perhaps cooperation with law enforcement. In fact, these kinds of guilty plea rewards are explicitly built into the U.S. Sentencing Guidelines, where federal defendants get guideline-based sentencing discounts or departures for "acceptance of responsibility" and "substantial assistance to law enforcement" (U.S. Sentencing Commission, 2001). A Pennsylvania judge illustrates how going to trial and losing may signal a defendant's lack of remorse, and therefore greater blameworthiness, to judges:

> People who plead guilty always argue that remorse is a mitigating factor, and one cannot deny that. They are saying 'I am sorry, I did it.' I consider that a mitigating factor. If you don't plead guilty and go to trial, then there is the absence of a mitigating factor. Sure enough after a trial at the time of sentencing he will be remorseful. He might have taken the stand and said he didn't do it, now he is remorseful. I ask what he is remorseful about. He will say that he hates to be in this situation. I say that I am sure you do, and maybe I don't want to be in this position either. You could look at it as a penalty but there is no other way of doing it. You have to give people credit for pleading guilty and expressing remorse. It is that simple. I choose not to call it a sentencing penalty. (Ulmer, 1997:88)

Finally, trials may bring out "bad facts," or facts about crimes or defendants that increase perceived blameworthiness. Such facts could be covered up, or at least not have as much visceral impact, in a guilty plea agreement (see Brereton and Casper, 1982; Flemming, Nardulli, and Eisenstein, 1992; Ulmer, 1997). As Brereton and Casper (1982) note:

> In addition, the trial is likely to produce more publicity and attendant public scrutiny, *as well as providing the sentencer with much more detail about the nature of the harm done by the defendant.* Both of these may militate against the leniency that often attends the privacy and flexibility of the plea bargain. (68, emphasis added)

A Pennsylvania defense attorney interview from Ulmer (1997) provides another example of this reasoning:

> Sure, there is a plea discount, but the trial penalty you have to worry about is that the judge is going to learn too much when you go to trial that he wouldn't otherwise, *because you can present a much better sentencing case if the judge doesn't learn all the ugly facts.* (99, emphasis added)

Garfinkel (1956) explicitly identifies criminal trials (at least those where the defendants lose) as a special type of "status degradation ceremony" in modern societies, and in fact argues that these degradation practices are professional role expectations for court officials. In the course of such degradation ceremonies, unsuccessful trials may mobilize more negative attributions about blameworthiness toward convicted defendants than guilty pleas, and this may then influence subsequent sentencing decisions.

Thus, one would expect significant plea-trial sentencing differences based on both notions of organizational efficiency and differential constructions of blameworthiness of those who plead guilty and those who go to trial. We would anticipate this effect to be especially pronounced for jury trials, which are typically longer, more elaborate, more visible, and entail disclosing more information than bench trials (Brereton and Casper, 1982; Eisenstein and Jacob, 1977; Mather, 1979; Nardulli, Eisenstein, and Flemming, 1988; Ulmer, 1997). Bench trials typically tend to resemble "slow guilty pleas," are relatively short, and entail less information disclosure (Eisenstein and Jacob, 1977; Ulmer, 1997).

Hypothesis 1: Among convicted defendants, those convicted by jury trial will be sentenced more severely than those convicted by guilty plea.

Our interest in plea-trial sentencing differences only begins here, however. The other interesting, and seldom examined questions are: How might trial penalties vary between individual cases or between jurisdictions? What might such variation suggest about which of the focal concerns are most related to trial penalties? Are trial penalties primarily driven by practical constraints like caseload pressure? Or are there variations produced by factors plausibly linked to social identities and person constructions relevant to blameworthiness and dangerousness? What jurisdictional characteristics besides caseloads might be associated with variation in trial penalties?

"The Caseload Controversy"

Trial penalties and plea rewards have most frequently been discussed in relation to court caseload pressure. Scholars debated throughout the 1980s and early 1990s about whether the pressure to keep cases moving and avoid docket backlogs was the major reason for the existence and variation in plea-trial sentencing differences (see discussions by Dixon, 1995; Engen and Steen, 2000; Holmes, Daudistel and Taggart, 1992; Meeker and Pontell, 1985; Nardulli, Eisenstein, and Hemming, 1988). An organizational efficiency perspective would suggest that differentially punishing pleas and trials is an organizationally rational response to the need to keep cases moving efficiently. Trials consume scarce prosecutorial and judicial time and resources. Presenting incentives to plead guilty or imposing costs on going to trial and losing would seem to be a rational organizational strategy for prosecutors and judges alike. The greater the caseload pressure, the more a court would rely on such costs and incentives. On the other hand, several have argued that plea bargaining and its potential for plea-trial sentencing differences persist despite variations in caseload pressure because they are sustained by other courtroom incentives and cultural practices (Church, 1979; Eisenstein and Jacobs, 1977; Meeker and Pontell, 1985; Nardulli, Eisenstein, and Flemming, 1988).

Smith (1986) argues that plea bargaining is a rational rather than a coercive process. He argues that from the perspective of defendants, plea-trial sentencing differences must be weighed against the possibility of acquittal that a trial affords. He found little difference on average in the sentences of people who

pled guilty and those who went to trial. Even though plea bargaining is neutral in its sentencing consequences. Smith argues, guilty pleas arc rational for prosecutors to pursue: "Perhaps the primary advantage of a system of negotiated pleas is that it allows prosecutors to pursue more cases than otherwise would be possible" (1966).

Smith's (1986) logic is at least congruent with the idea that caseloads might produce variation in plea-trial sentencing differences, as the organizational efficiency hypothesis suggests. In fact, this study found that plea-trial sentencing differences varied substantially between jurisdictions, and that "we need to know more about the factors which may contribute to this inter-jurisdictional variation" (967). Variations in caseload might be just such a factor, and a key one at that.

A strong version of the organizational efficiency hypothesis would be that trial penalties are primarily driven by caseloads. Thus caseload should be the only factor that conditions variation in trial penalties. A weaker version would suggest that caseload would be one of several factors that might significantly interact with trial penalties. To make clear comparisons with regard to the caseload controversy, we state the strong version as hypothesis 2.

> **Hypothesis 2:** Among convicted defendants, trial penalties will increase as court caseloads increase.

Pleas, Trials, and Differential Constructions of Blameworthiness

If, as Garfinkel says, unsuccessful trials are a type of status degradation ceremony (and sentencing hearings are another status degradation ceremony following the first one), the effects of such ceremonies on sentences may be more severe for those with more extensive criminal histories (1956). Garfinkel maintains that status degradation ceremonies are occasions where the past (and prospective future) behavior of the accused is reinterpreted by authorities in light of his or her present degradation. Goffman (1963) describes a similar process, in which the biography of the stigmatized is reinterpreted retrospectively, and past negative events or behaviors intensify the "spoiled identity" of the deviant.

A record of criminality then, especially an extensive one, might be a resource to be used by the prosecution after a trial conviction to dramatize the criminality, and thus the blameworthiness, of the defendant. Trials, and the sentencing hearings before the judge that follow them would likely provide an opportunity for prosecutors to "dirty up" the defendant (to use a phrase common among defense lawyers). In fact, Smith (1986) found that defendants with no prior felony or drug arrests reduced their odds of incarceration by pleading guilty, whereas those with more extensive criminal records did not. Further, Ulmer (1997) found that plea-trial sentencing differences increased as criminal histories increased. Thus we suspect that those with more extensive criminal records will experience a greater trial penalty.

Hypothesis 3: The jury trial penalty noted in hypothesis 1 will be significantly greater among those with more extensive prior criminal records.

In addition, it is likely that trial penalties vary among types of serious violent offenses, given the particular nature and relative severity of different offense types. Rhodes (1979), for example, found that plea-trial sentencing differences varied by offense, with only robbery offenses displaying significant plea rewards and trial penalties. In our analysis, the trial penalty for homicide, for example, might be significantly greater than that for robbery or aggravated assault. Furthermore, the serious violent offenses we examine here can all vary in degree of severity within offense categories as well as between them. In general, we expect that the more serious the offense, the greater the trial penalty, given that the more serious the offense, the greater the potential for portraying the defendant as especially blameworthy.

Hypothesis 4: Jury trial penalties will be significantly greater among those convicted of relatively more serious offenses than among those convicted of relatively less serious offenses.

Hypothesis 5: Among those convicted of serious violent offenses, the jury trial penalty will vary by offense type.

Race, Ethnicity, and Gender

Bonilla-Silva (1997) argues that in racialized social systems such as that of the United States, racial ideologies and asymmetrical power relations between races are pervasive and deeply rooted in social structure. Obviously, as a central mechanism of formal social control, the criminal justice system is also an important arena of racialized interaction. In the United States today, blacks and Hispanics tend to be objects of crime-related fear and are seen as particularly threatening (Britt, 2000; Spohn, 2000; Spohn and Holleran, 2000; Steffensmeier and Demuth, 2001). In fact, recent U.S. survey evidence shows that whites are concerned with black violence in particular, and whites with antiblack prejudices especially focus on black violence, and support punitive criminal justice responses to deal with it (Barkan and Conn, 2005).

Therefore, court actors' interpretations and assessments of focal concerns such as perceived dangerousness or blameworthiness, as well as the salience of relevant practical constraints and consequences, might be influenced by race, ethnicity, and gender (Peterson and Hagan, 1984; Spohn and Holleran, 2000; Steffensmeier, Ulmer, and Kramer, 1998). Marginalized racial or ethnic identities might mobilize more negative emotional responses—especially fear (which implicates perceived dangerousness, or the focal concern of community protection)—after jury trials than whites, and their trial penalties might then be correspondingly greater than whites. In fact, in two studies of broad samples of offenses in Pennsylvania, Ulmer (1997) found that trial penalties were greater for blacks, and Johnson (2003) found that blacks convicted by jury trial were especially less likely to receive sentencing leniency in the form of downward guideline departures.

In contrast, female defendants tend to arouse less fear, are often seen as less crime-prone and less morally blameworthy, and tend to be the objects of more sympathy (see Koons-Witt, 2002; Steffensmeier, Kramer, and Streifel, 1993). Therefore, trials involving women defendants might arouse more sympathy and fewer negative feelings toward the defendant, and their trial penalties would be correspondingly lighter. Thus

> **Hypothesis 6:** Among convicted offenders, the jury trial penalty will be greater for blacks than for whites.
>
> **Hypothesis 7:** Among convicted offenders, the jury trial penalty will be greater for Hispanics than for whites.
>
> **Hypothesis 8:** Among convicted offenders, the jury trial penalty will be greater for men than for women.

We also note that our hypothesis about offense severity and trial penalties are relevant to the influential "liberation hypothesis" of sentencing discretion (Kalven and Zeisel, 1966; Spohn and Cederblom, 1991). As Smith and Dampbousse (1998) characterize a basic premise of the liberation hypothesis: "As seriousness of offense increases, the level of variance explained by legal variables increases, while the level of variance explained by extralegal variables either remains moderately low or is further diminished" (71).

In the case of trial penalties, however, we argue the opposite. The liberation hypothesis predicts that as offense severity increases, the effects of extralegal variables will decrease. Instead, we predict that among a set of serious violent offenses, an arguably extralegal effect, the trial penalty, will be substantial, and will actually increase with offense severity. Furthermore, we predict that this trial penalty will also interact with other extralegal variables—race, ethnicity, and gender among serious violent offenders. Thus, not only will jury trial penalties be substantial among serious violent offenses and be relatively greater for more severe offenses, but these trial penalties in serious cases will also occasion the differential influence of defendant status characteristics.

Court Community Features

The interpretation and prioritization of the three focal concerns are said to be embedded in court communities (Kautt, 2002; Ulmer and Johnson, 2004). The court community perspective (Eisenstein, Flemming, and Nardulli, 1988) views courts as communities based on participants' shared workplace and interdependent working relations between key sponsoring agencies (prosecutor's office, bench, defense bar). Court communities are distinct, localized social worlds with their own relationship networks, organizational culture, political arrangements, and the like (Eisenstein, Flemming, and Nardulli, 1988; Ulmer, 2005, 1997). These localized social worlds, with their organizational cultures and political realities, shape formal and informal case processing and sentencing norms (see Eisenstein, Flemming, and Nardulli, 1988; Ulmer, 1997). The jury trial penalty is a sentencing practice that is particularly likely to vary between court communities.

We thus expect trial penalties to vary according to certain contextual characteristics. We have already mentioned court caseload pressure as a practical constraint we include as a hypothesized interaction with jury trial effects. Beyond that, the literature provides little guidance; we know of no published studies that have investigated contextual variation in trial penalties with multilevel statistical methods. However, it is reasonable to suspect that court size, violent crime rate, and percentage black would be associated with variation in trial penalties. Eisenstein and colleagues (1988) paid particular attention to court community size, and argued that large urban courts are typically more lenient than smaller courts, and that their routine case processing (that is to say, their guilty plea process) is relatively invisible to the public. However, such courts have more media scrutiny and large media markets (perhaps even newspapers and television stations with national visibility), and serious violent offense jury trials might get relatively more public attention. Due to this atypical scrutiny, judges and prosecutors might feel more pressure to sentence defendants more severely after such trials (compared with more routine and less visible guilty pleas) to politically demonstrate their seriousness and toughness regarding violent crime. This would be especially true in jurisdictions where judges and prosecutors are elected by partisan vote, as they are in Pennsylvania. However, to our knowledge, this proposition has never been empirically tested.

Hypothesis 9: Large court communities will exhibit greater jury trial penalties than smaller court communities.

Relatedly, a community's violent crime problem might condition variation in trial penalties. Again, if trials are relatively more publicly visible than guilty pleas, regardless of county size, and a county has a more serious violent crime problem, prosecutors face more political pressure to push for more substantial sentences in serious violent trial cases, and judges face more pressure to mete out those sentences to visibly demonstrate their concern for public safety and retribution.

Hypothesis 10: Jury trial penalties will increase with county violent crime rates.

Finally, percentage black has been found to be an important factor in previous multilevel analyses of sentencing (Britt, 2000; Ulmer and Johnson, 2004). Given these arguments regarding racial threat and trial penalties, it is reasonable to expect that trial penalties will be greater in counties with larger black populations, again because of the opportunity that the visibility of serious violent crime trials present for "sending a message" to the local (majority white) electorate that violent crime, which prejudiced whites tend to equate with black crime (Barkan and Conn, 2005), will be dealt with severely.

Hypothesis 11: Jury trial penalties will increase with county percentage black.

 Data

We test these expectations using aggregate and individual-level sentencing data from county criminal trial court in Pennsylvania. The criminal sentencing data we use span 3 recent years (1997 to 2000) and come from the Pennsylvania Commission on Sentencing (PCS). By law, the PCS is required to collect information on all misdemeanors and felonies sentenced in the state, except for first and second degree homicide (which are outside the scope of the sentencing guidelines, because they are punishable by life imprisonment or death). Cases in this analysis were limited to the most serious offense per transaction and to those cases sentenced under the 1997 guidelines.

Dependent Variables

The sentencing of criminal defendants can be broken down into a two-stage decision-making process (Wheeler, Weisburd, and Bode, 1982): the decision whether to incarcerate, and if incarceration is selected, the decision about its length. We therefore separately model these two distinct sentencing decisions, first examining the probability of offenders receiving incarceration, and then examining how long incarceration sentences are. *Incarceration* was coded 1 if the offender was sentenced to any length of confinement in a county jail or state prison and coded 0 if they were sentenced to any combination of non-incarceration options (for example, probation, restitution, intermediate sanctions, and the like).

Sentence length is the minimum number of months of incarceration the offender was sentenced to serve. In our subsequent models, we logged the sentence length for two reasons. First, the distribution of sentence lengths in our sample of violent offenses is quite skewed, and logging the dependent variable is a commonly used technique for addressing this kind of violation of OLS assumptions (Hanushek and Jackson, 1977). Second and more important, the offenses in our sample differ in the lengths of sentences courts can give, because they each have different sentencing guidelines and statutory maximums. This means that the offenses differ in the absolute size of effects that trial conviction could possibly have. In other words, a bigger trial penalty in terms of absolute size is possible for third degree homicide than for robbery, because the statutorily defined maximum sentence (as well as the guideline recommendation) is higher for third degree homicide. Logging the sentence length (and interpreting the antilog of predictors' coefficients) therefore allows us to examine the proportional rather than absolute differences in sentence lengths associated with our variables of interest, and thus allows us to avoid findings that are merely an artifact of differences between offenses in the sentences that are legally possible (for a similar use of logged sentence length, see Kurlychek and Johnson, 2004).

The number of cases used in our incarceration models is 8,585. In our sentence length models, which are restricted to those who received incarceration, the number is 7,643. Because 275 cases were missing data for race-ethnicity, 101 were missing data on gender, and 912 were missing data on mode of conviction, we included dummy variables for whether these variables were missing in our models. This allowed us to retain cases with missing data for these variables in our models, and control for whether these missing cases were systematically different in their sentencing outcomes (they were not—their effects were not statistically significant). These three dummy variables for missing data are included in the models, but are not shown, for table clarity (results available on request).

Independent Variables

We use several individual case and contextual level factors as independent variables. The legally relevant sentencing variables that we include in the analyses are the severity of the current offense, the offense type, the prior criminality of the offender, and the presumptive guideline sentence recommendation. The Pennsylvania sentencing guidelines provide direct measures of both the severity of the offense and the prior criminality of the offender. *Offense severity* is measured by the offense gravity score (OGS). The OGS itself ranges from 1 to 14 (where 14 is the most serious), but in our sample of serious violent offenses, OGS varies from 8 to 14. The OGS rankings by the PCS incorporate such considerations of harm and loss to victims and society, as well as the state's judgment about criminal wrongfulness and culpability. The offender's *prior record* is measured by the prior record score (PRS), an eight-category scale ranging from 0 to 8, with the last two categories (6 and 8, there is no category 7) reserved for repeat felons and repeat violent offenders. This scale represents an offender's past convictions for misdemeanors and felonies, as well as certain juvenile adjudications.

The offense type is measured with dummy variables, coded 1 if the offender was convicted of a particular offense, and 0 otherwise. The serious violent offenses we focus on are homicide, rape and involuntary deviant sexual intercourse (IDSI), aggravated assault, and robbery. It is important to note that offense severity can vary within these offense categories as well as between them, so offense type and severity are not redundant variables. We combined rape and involuntary deviant sexual intercourse into one category because there were relatively few IDSI cases, and because their guideline severity rankings are the same (12 points). These five offenses are identified by the sentencing guidelines and state statute as particularly serious violent offenses. They are among those offenses singled out to count as "strikes" under Pennsylvania's Three Strikes law, which counts only prior violent felonies (for details, see Kramer and Ulmer, 2002). We also removed cases that were subject to mandatory minimum sentences from our analyses, since these cases leave no room for post conviction sentencing discretion.

The presumptive guideline sentence recommendation variable provides a measure of what the sentencing guidelines indicate is an appropriate sentence. For the incarceration models, this variable was coded 1 if the guidelines recommended incarceration and 0 otherwise. For the sentence length models, this variable was coded to equal the minimum number of months of incarceration recommended by the guidelines. We use the minimum of the guideline range, because this is intended to be the most presumptive recommendation in Pennsylvania's guidelines (Kramer and Scirica, 1986). Albonetti (1998) and Engen and Gainey (2000) argue for the importance of including the presumptive guideline sentence recommendation as a further control when examining extralegal effects. Therefore, we include it here as well (but see Bushway and Piehl, 2001).

We also included the race-ethnicity, gender, and age of the offender. We created dummy variables for our racial-ethnic and gender distinctions. "Black" was coded 1 if the offender was African American and 0 otherwise. Similarly, "Hispanic" was coded 1 if the offender was Hispanic and 0 otherwise. "Female" was coded 1 if the offender was a woman and 0 otherwise. Finally, age was coded as the age of the offender at the time of sentencing.

The key variable of interest in our analysis is mode of conviction, or whether the defendant was convicted by guilty plea, bench trial (trial by judge), or jury trial. We measure mode of conviction with two dummy variables, coded 1 if the offender was convicted by a bench or a jury trial, and coded 0 if the offender pled guilty.

Another key variable of interest is court caseload. We measure this as the mean of the annual number of cases processed by a given court from 1997 to 2000. Other contextual variables include: court size, coded small, medium, and large based on the number of judgeships per county court and the proportion of the state's caseload the size categories accounted for (see Ulmer, 1997, for details); county violent crime rate for 1998 (from the Uniform Crime Reports); and percentage black (coded from the 1998 Current Population Survey).

Some limitations of these data are that they lack measures of defendants' socioeconomic status, type of attorney, pretrial release status (bail), or most consequential for this analysis, the identity or characteristics of victims (a point we return to in the conclusion). Unfortunately, these are limitations shared with the majority of sentencing studies (see review by Zatz, 2000). These variables are not collected by the PCS. Another important limitation of our analysis is that because the PCS does not collect preconviction data, we cannot control for the likelihood of conviction or acquittal at trial as the studies by Rhodes (1979), Smith (1986), and LaFree (1985) do. Thus our analysis is limited to convicted offenders, and we cannot generalize our findings to all individuals charged with crimes.

Analytical Techniques

The logic of our second hypothesis requires examining the conditioning effects of a county court characteristic, mean annual caseload, on the size of jury trial effects. We also hypothesize three other cross-level interaction effects. The importance of intercourt variation in sentencing outcomes and the factors that affect them, and the desirability of using HLM for analyses of sentencing outcomes has by now been well established (see Britt, 2000; Fearn, 2005; Kautt, 2002; Ulmer and Johnson, 2004; Wooldredge and Thistlethwaite, 2004). For our analyses, we used HLM 6 software (Raudenbush

et al., 2004). We used hierarchical logistic regression for incarceration decisions and hierarchical linear regression for logged sentence length (for similar applications, see Britt, 2000; Kautt, 2002; Ulmer and Johnson, 2004; Wooldredge and Thistlethwaite, 2004).

Before turning to our main models, we estimated unconditional models (available on request) for incarceration and logged length. These showed modest but significant intercounty variation in both dependent variables, indicating that HLM was appropriate. For logged sentence length, the intraclass correlation was .048, indicating that about 5 percent of the variance in sentence length was between courts, a small but statistically significant ($p < .001$) amount.

Findings

Table 6.4 summarizes the descriptive statistics for the variables included in our analyses.

Approximately 88 percent of the sample received incarceration sentences, with an average minimum length of confinement of about 28 months. (The mean for logged length is about 2.9, with a standard deviation of about 1.1; logging sentence length thus considerably normalizes its distribution.) The large percentage of incarceration is not surprising, considering that the data consist of only serious violent offenses. In addition, this table shows that trials are relatively rare; bench trials and jury trials constitute roughly 9 percent and 7 percent of convictions, respectively.

Table 6.5 presents HLM fixed effects models for incarceration decisions (logistic regression) and logged incarceration length (linear regression).

Turning first to the incarceration decision, we see that the legally prescribed factors—offense severity, prior record, and presumptive guideline sentence recommendations—are positively related to incarceration likelihood and are the strongest variables in the model. Note that the effect of both variables is cumulative—each increase in prior record score, increases incarceration odds by .40, for example. Also, robbery is significantly more likely to result in incarceration than the reference category of aggravated assault, and, implicitly, the other serious violent offenses in the model. Additionally, females are roughly

Table 6.4   Descriptive Statistics: Homicide, Aggravated Assault, Robbery, Rape, and Involuntary Deviant Sexual Intercourse Cases in Pennsylvania, 1997 to 2000 (N = 8,685)

Variables	Frequency	%	Mean	SD
Incarceration (1 = yes)	7,643	88.1		
Logged sentence length (incarceration cases)			2.9	1.1
Sentence length (incarceration cases only)			27.6	35.4
Level 1 predictors				
Homicide	521	6.2		
Aggravated assault	3,648	42.1		
Rape and IDSI	434	5.2		
Robbery	3,995	46.1		
Bench trial	781	9.0		
Jury trial	608	7.0		
Black	4,256	49.0		
Hispanic	608	7.0		
Female	869	10.0		
Age			28.9	9.9
Offense gravity score (OGS)			8.4	2.3
Prior record score (PRS)			1.6	2.0
Presumptive disposition (1 = incarceration)	8,250	95.1		
Presumptive guideline minimum sentence			24.7	25.5
Level 2 predictors				
Mean annual court caseload			2271.0	3031.0
Large courts	2	2.9		
Medium courts	14	20.9		
Small courts	51	76.1		
Violent crime rate			693.7	557.1
Percentage black			18.8	17.9

Table 6.5 Hierarchical Logistic and Linear Models of Sentencing Outcomes—Fixed Effects[a]

Models	In/Out Odds Ratio	Logged Length b	Logged Length Antilog of b
Intercept (B_0, G_{00})	31.7 (logit, 3.45)***	3.01***	
Level 1 Predictors			
Bench trial	2.22***	.20	1.22***
Jury trial	2.65**	.45	1.57***
Homicide	.98	.51	1.66***
Rape or IDSI	1.13	.25	1.28***
Robbery	1.88***	.23	1.24***
Offense gravity score	1.26***	.35	1.42***
Prior record score	1.40***	.20	1.22***
Presumptive disposition guideline minimum	2.12***	.003	.997***
Black	1.30***	.11	1.12***
Hispanic	1.80***	.14	1.15*
Female	.44***	.27	.76***
Age	.99*	.003	.997**
Level 2 Predictors			
Mean annual court caseload	.999*	.0001	.999*
Percentage black	.95	.02	.98*
Violent crime rate	1.002	.001	1.001*
Large court	8.9	.79	2.18*
Small court	.54	.11	.90
Level 2 R^2		.43	
Level 1 R^2		.57	
N	8,685	7,643	

a. Aggravated assault is the reference category for offense type, guilty pleas are the reference category for mode of conviction, medium courts are the reference category for court size. The models also include dummy variables for missing data on race-ethnicity and gender.

$*p < .05$; $** p < .01$; $***p < .001$.

half as likely to be incarcerated as males, and Hispanics are more likely to be incarcerated than whites or (indirectly) blacks. Blacks are also more likely to be incarcerated than whites. These effects are not unusual, and are consistent with much of the sentencing literature, as well as recent studies of sentencing in Pennsylvania (Johnson, 2003; Holleran and Spohn, 2004; Steffensmeier and Demuth, 2001; Ulmer and Johnson, 2004). Furthermore, court caseload, our level 2 predictor, has a significant negative direct effect on incarceration. The coefficient seems small, but it produces meaningful cumulative differences—each one unit increase in caseload is associated with a .001 decrease in the odds of incarceration. Thus, a between-court difference of

1000 cases would be associated with a .37 decrease in the odds of incarceration ($.999^{1000}$). None of the other county-level variables display any significant direct effects on incarceration. The effect of being sentenced in a large urban court on incarceration is substantively large, but is probably not statistically significant due to the small number of such courts.

Our focus, however, is on the effect of jury trials, and how this effect is conditioned by other factors. Hypothesis 1 predicted a differential penalty for those convicted by jury trial. That is, those who are convicted by jury trial should be more likely to be incarcerated and receive longer sentences, controlling for other factors. Consistent with hypothesis 1, the odds of incarceration following a bench trial are roughly 2.2 times the odds for a guilty plea, while a jury trial conviction has roughly 2.7 times the incarceration odds of a guilty plea. In fact, jury or bench trial convictions have the fourth and fifth strongest effects on the odds of incarceration, respectively, after offense severity, prior record, and presumptive sentence recommendations. Overall, then, conviction by trial, especially jury trial, carries a meaningful additional sentencing penalty for the serious violent offenses examined here. The size of the plea-trial differences in incarceration here are larger than those found by Ulmer and Johnson (2004). They found incarceration odds of 1.77 associated with overall trial conviction, but their analysis combined both bench and jury trials, and included a broad sample of violent, property, and drug offenses. Our incarceration trial penalty is also slightly larger than that found by Zatz and Hagan (1985) in their convicted offenders sample. They found incarceration odds of 2.16 associated with jury trial conviction. Of course, our findings are quite different from those of Smith (1986), who found no significant overall difference between pleas and trials in the probabilities of offenders being sentenced to at least a year in prison, after accounting for the likelihood of being convicted.

In the model of logged sentence length in Table 6.5, we find that the model explains 57 percent of the level 1 variance, and 43 percent of the level 2 variance. The antilog of the predictors' coefficients allows a proportional interpretation of the effects on sentence length, which, as we explained earlier, is the appropriate interpretation here because different sentences are legally possible for the different offenses in the sample. The strongest influences are again legally prescribed ones—offense severity and type, prior record, and presumptive guideline recommendations. Interestingly, the presumptive guideline minimum has a significant negative effect on sentence lengths. That is, for every month the guidelines recommended minimum sentence increases, actual sentence lengths decrease by .003 percent. This supports Kramer and Ulmer's (2002) argument that judges and other court actors tend to perceive the guidelines' penalties for serious violent offenses as too severe in many cases, and tend to find ways to sentence below the guidelines. Each of the offense categories exhibited longer sentences than the reference category, aggravated assault. Sentences were longest for third degree homicide, followed by robbery, rape, and involuntary deviant sexual intercourse.

Blacks and Hispanics both receive moderately longer sentences than whites for these serious violent offenses (12 percent and 15 percent respectively). Gender also negatively relates to sentence length among these serious violent offenses. Females receive incarceration sentences that are on average about 24 percent shorter than males. Age was also significantly and negatively related to sentence lengths.

Relevant to hypothesis 1, jury trials result in significantly longer sentences than guilty pleas, controlling for court caseloads. On average, those who were found guilty by bench trials received roughly 22 percent longer incarceration sentences than those who plead guilty. Being convicted by jury trial increases sentence lengths by roughly 57 percent. Thus, trial convictions for serious violent offenses apparently carry considerable sentence length costs as well as incarceration costs.

In addition to caseload, other direct effects for county court characteristics on sentence length appear. County percentage black has a negative direct effect on sentence lengths; a 1 percent increase in percent black is associated with a 2 percent decrease in mean sentence lengths. On the other hand, violent crime rate and especially large court size exhibit more severe sentences for serious violent offenses. A one unit increase in county violent crime rate is associated with a .1 percent increase in mean sentence length, so a county with a violent crime rate that was 300 points higher than another county would have a 30 percent greater mean sentence length. Furthermore, sentence lengths for serious violent crimes in large urban counties are 118 percent greater than in medium-sized courts.

Hypothesis 3 expects that the jury trial penalty will be greater for those with more extensive criminal records. Contrary to our prediction, these terms were significant and negative for both incarceration and length, indicating that the jury trial penalty decreases as the prior record score of the defendant increases. Each increase in prior record score decreases the size of incarceration trial penalty by 32, and each increase in prior record decreases the sentence length trial penalty by 3 percent.

Based on these findings, we ran separate models (not shown) to compare the jury trial penalties for those with high criminal record scores (prior record scores of 4 or higher) and low criminal record scores (prior record scores of 3 or lower). These models found substantial differences in jury trial effects, particularly with respect to incarceration. Those with more extensive criminal histories who are found guilty at jury trial have 1.19 times the odds of incarceration, an effect that is not statistically significant. By contrast, low PRS jury trial cases have 3.5 times the odds of incarceration compared to guilty pleas. Thus, contrary to our expectations, jury trials hurt those with more serious criminal histories less than those with less serious and extensive criminal histories.

Hypothesis 4 expects jury trial penalties to increase as offense severity increases. This term was not significant in the length model but was in the incarceration model, indicating that the jury trial penalty in terms of incarceration increases substantially as offense severity increases. The effect of the offense severity × jury trial interaction term on the odds of incarceration was 136. In other words, for each one-point increase in offense severity, the odds of incarceration following a jury trial conviction go up by .36. This provides support for hypothesis 4, at least in terms of incarceration decisions.

Next, we assessed variations in the jury trial penalty across types of offenses as directed by hypothesis 5. We found that the jury trial penalty for homicide did not differ significantly for either incarceration or length. In contrast, the significant robbery × jury interaction term for incarceration indicates that the jury trial penalty for robbery is .68 less than that for aggravated assault (the reference category).

To further explore these findings, we ran separate models comparing jury trial effects within specific offenses. Among robbery cases, the jury trial effect on incarceration is 1.30, which is not significant. The incarceration trial penalty for robbery is thus much less than the 2.7 incarceration odds for jury trial in the full model. The effect of jury trial convictions on length among robberies is also smaller than in the full model, but the interaction is not statistically significant. Thus, jury trial convictions seem to hurt robbery defendants' sentencing outcomes less than for those convicted of other serious violent offenses, at least in terms of incarceration.

Insufficient variation in incarceration outcomes prevented assessing an interaction term for rape-IDSI; all jury trial convictions for such offenses resulted in incarceration. However, we find that those convicted of rape-IDSI at jury trial received 19 percent shorter sentences compared to those convicted of aggravated assault.

Separate analyses of rape and IDSI offenses find a significant jury trial effect on logged length (.35). This estimate is significantly lower than the jury trial length penalty of .45 in the full model. In other words, those with rape or IDSI convictions face moderately smaller sentence length penalties for going to jury trial, compared with those convicted by jury trial of aggravated assault (and implicitly, the other offenses). Overall, these findings lend considerable support for hypothesis 5—we do in fact find significant variation in jury trial penalties for different serious violent offenses.

Hypotheses 6 and 7 predicted that the jury trial penalty would be greater for blacks and Hispanics. Interaction terms for Hispanic × jury trial were not significant for incarceration or sentence length. Thus, the size of the jury trial penalty did not differ significantly between Hispanics and whites. The interaction of black × jury trial presents a more complicated picture.

In a model that excludes the cross-level interaction effects of caseload × jury trial, the interaction of black × jury trial is significant at $p < .05$, and indicates that the length trial penalty for blacks is 15 percent greater than for whites. Thus, it would first appear that among these serious violent offenses, the effect of jury trial is conditioned by race. However, when we control for the conditioning effect of court caseload on trial penalty (not shown in Table 6.5), the black × jury trial interaction drops to a nonsignificant .06 (antilog = 1.06). The same thing happens when controlling for any of the other cross-level interaction effects in Table 6.5. Thus, it appears that the modest black × jury trial interaction is explained away by between-county differences in trial penalties. Most plausibly, the individual-level black × jury trial interaction is spurious in the face of the percentage black × jury trial interaction, as we explain below.

We found no evidence to support hypothesis 8. Although gender has a direct effect on odds of incarceration and sentence length, we found no significant gender × jury trial interaction effect. That is, the jury trial penalties for women did not differ significantly from those of men with regard to either outcome. In supplemental analyses, we also found no evidence that gender significantly interacted with offense type to condition trial penalties. Apparently, then, gender does not condition the size of trial penalties, at least in these data.

Finally, we hypothesized three additional cross-level interaction effects. First, note that none of the cross-level interaction effects alter the level one interaction effects of prior record × jury trial and rape-ISDI × jury trial. As mentioned, though, each one washes out the black × jury trial effect.

Hypothesis 9 predicted that serious violent offenses in large urban courts would result in greater jury trial penalties than in other courts, and this hypothesis is strongly supported for sentence length. The length trial penalty for such offenses in the large counties is 28 percent greater than in other-sized courts. Hypothesis 10 predicted that counties with more violent crime would have greater trial penalties for serious violent offenses, and this idea receives support in our models of sentence length as well. Each unit increase in violent crime rate increases the trial penalty by .02 percent, a seemingly small effect, but one that would add up to meaningful cumulative differences between counties with substantially different crime rates. A county with a violent crime rate of 800 would have a 12 percent greater length trial penalty than a county with a violent crime rate of 200.

In hypothesis 11, we reasoned that counties with larger black populations would have greater trial penalties for serious violent offenses, and the sentence length analysis also supports this idea. A one unit increase in percentage black increases the trial penalty by 1 percent. Thus, the trial penalty for a county with a 30 percent black population would be 20 percent greater than that for a county with a 10 percentage black population. This cross-level interaction effect may explain why the black × jury trial effect is significant in the absence of cross-level interaction effects, but disappears when they are added to the model. To the extent that percentage black is correlated with defendant's race (the county percentage black-black defendant correlation is 36), and to the extent that percentage black, court size, caseload, and violent crime are intercorrelated (and they are all correlated at the $p < .0001$ level), interacting any of these contextual variables with jury trial would eliminate the black × trial interaction effect.

Discussion

This study has some consequential limitations. First, although the PCS offense gravity score incorporates elements of victim harm, loss, and impact, we have no direct information beyond this about victims in our data which is a potentially important omission. It is quite likely that the identities, social statuses, and characteristics of victims condition the assessment of focal concerns and the type of interpretive work that goes on in trials and guilty pleas (see Black, 1976; Loseke, 1993). Assessing the role of victim characteristics on trial penalties must await future research.

Also, our analysis hinges on the premise that guilty pleas, bench trials, and jury trials are comparable and can be modeled together. The large majority of sentencing studies in the past two decades have taken a similar approach and included these different modes of conviction in the same models. However, at least one important piece (Kiepper, Nagin, and Tierney, 1983) has argued against this practice. Kiepper and his colleagues (1983) argue that guilty pleas and trials are qualitatively different and are generated by inherently different processes. This, they contend, makes it inappropriate to lump modes of conviction together in the same models and compare the way they are sentenced. On the other hand, we argue that any criminal case can potentially end up as a guilty plea or a trial at any point in the preconviction process—people plead guilty the night before a trial is set to begin, and people withdraw their guilty pleas at colloquy hearings and insist on trials. In principle, at least, one should be able to compare the ensuing sentences following the different modes of conviction. Furthermore, American legal ideology holds that every defendant has the right to a trial, that guilty pleas should not be coercive. Some commentators argue that the practice of punishing those who lose at trial more severely than those who plead guilty constitutes just such coercion (Rosett and Cressey, 1976; Uhlman and Walker, 1979). To us, the importance of presenting evidence, imperfect as it is, on plea-trial sentencing differences and their variation outweighs Kiepper and colleagues' (1983) methodological caution. We realize, however, that others might take the opposite position.

Most seriously, this analysis was limited to data on convicted offenders. We cannot control for potential selection bias stemming from conviction or acquittal. Because we cannot control for the likelihood of conviction, we cannot rule out the possibility that our findings might reflect differences in conviction rates by offense severity and type, prior record, or court contexts. Smith (1986), LaFree (1985), and Rhodes (1979) show that this limitation is potentially important—these studies showed that trial penalties were not substantial once balanced against the chances of acquittal at trial. On the other hand, Zatz and Hagan (1985) found that trial penalties appeared only after they controlled for the likelihood of conviction. Similarly, we lack a measure of evidence strength, which some prior literature suggests is important in the decision to go to trial, and in

influencing the attractiveness of prosecutors' plea bargain offers for defendants (Albonetti, 1986; Farr, 1984; Reinming, Nardulli, and Eisenstein, 1992; Mather, 1973).

What we can say is that once convicted, those who plead guilty and those who lose at trial tend to face very different sentencing outcomes, and that the size of plea-trial conviction sentencing differences varies by offense characteristics, criminal history, and court- and county-level factors. In this way, our findings closely parallel those of LaFree (1985), who found that while those who pled guilty lost out on the chance of an acquittal, those who went to trial and lost received more severe sentences. Also, the failure to control for the likelihood of conviction may not be as serious a limitation in this study of serious violent offenses as it would be with a sample of less serious offenses. One reason is that serious violent offenses tend to have higher conviction rates due to the amount of time and resources police and prosecutors devote to investigating them (Cole and Smith, 2005). Second, we would argue that the size of the trial penalties we have found here are so substantial that it is unlikely that they would be completely offset by the chances of acquittal. Nevertheless, future research of guilty plea-trial sentencing differences should strive to incorporate preconviction data and determine whether such differences are meaningful even when accounting for the chances of avoiding conviction at trial.

That said, we argue that our findings are consistent with the notion that differential attributions of blameworthiness and dangerousness—along with differences in perceived group threats and in practical political constraints and incentives between court community contexts—are key reasons behind the patterns in jury trial penalties we have found among serious violent offenses. On one hand, we find partial support for hypothesis 2, in that trial penalties tend to increase as court caseload increases. This finding supports the notion of organizational efficiency as a factor behind plea-trial differences, at least for length, and thus informs the "caseload controversy" regarding trial penalties. However, if sentencing differences between jury trials and other modes of conviction were simply due to courts' desire for organizational efficiency, the court caseload × jury trial cross-level interaction would have rendered the other interaction effects we tested spurious.

In fact, under an organizational efficiency explanation, by far the most common in the sentencing literature, one might even expect greater trial penalties among the relatively less serious cases here like robbery, because these might be seen as wasting the courts' time with unsuccessful trials when stakes (potential sentence severity) are lower compared to more severe cases. We find the opposite pattern—trial penalties increase with offense severity, at least for incarceration. An organizational efficiency explanation cannot, by itself, account for this pattern. It is unlikely that efficiency would be a more important concern in processing offenses like homicide, of which there are relatively few, than in processing offenses such as robbery, which take up a much bigger share of courts' caseloads.

Instead, increased offense severity seems to provide occasions for constructing offenders in the trial courtroom as particularly more morally repugnant, blameworthy, or dangerous, and these "types of person constructions" (Loseke, 1993) may then affect judges' sentences. That is, trials, particularly the trials in our data in which the defendants are always the losers, can be seen as status degradation ceremonies (Garfinkel, 1956). Judges, who witnessed in detail all the evidence, characteristics of the crime, and depictions of the defendant that were presented to the jury, may assess defendants as more blameworthy or more of a danger to the community, and administer a much harsher sentence than he or she would if the case was a guilty plea. Recall the judge who told us earlier how his directly seeing and experiencing the human consequences of a violent crime during a trial affected the subsequent sentences he gave. As the defense attorney said, a guilty plea lets one hide the "ugly facts" of a case, whereas a losing jury trial (or even a bench trial) puts the ugly facts right out in the open, where they can influence judges' constructions of the blameworthiness or dangerousness of defendants (see Ulmer, 1997). Furthermore, judges (and prosecutors) often take pleading guilty as an indicator of remorse, and trials as an indicator of a lack of remorse (Kramer and

Ulmer, 2002; Ulmer, 1997). Perhaps the more severe the violent offense, the more salient such remorse or lack thereof could be to judges.

Relatedly, our finding that trial penalties increased slightly but significantly with violent crime rates suggests that trial sentencing may be a vehicle by which prosecutors and judges communicate their seriousness about violent crime to the larger community. As we hypothesized, if trials are relatively visible, and a county has a more substantial violent crime problem, this may create political pressure on prosecutors to push for more substantial sentences in serious violent trial cases, and on judges to mete out those sentences.

Our findings about court size and trial penalties seem counterintuitive, given that research typically finds large urban courts to be more lenient. However, though such courts might be more lenient overall, our data show that large courts treat serious violent crimes more severely and sentence jury trial defendants to substantially longer sentences than other counties. We interpret this as support for Eisenstein and colleagues' (1988) description of how court community politics differ according to court size. Large courts have more media scrutiny and large media markets, and serious violent offense trials might get significant public attention. Due to this public attention, judges and prosecutors might feel more pressure to sentence defendants more severely after such trials. Severe sentencing may be a tool to politically demonstrate their seriousness and toughness regarding violent crime, at least in jurisdictions where judges and prosecutors are elected, as they are in Pennsylvania.

Our data also point to the possibility that such a process may not be racially neutral, at least in contextual terms. The jury trial penalty for the serious violent offenses we examined here was moderately larger in counties with relatively greater numbers of black residents. Given the strong positive link between anti-black stereotypes and concern about black violence demonstrated by Barkan and Conn (2005), jury trial penalties for serious violent crimes may present a new twist for racial threat theories of criminal justice. Barkan and Conn's (2005) research implies that when prejudiced whites hear about violent crime, they see black faces in their minds. Because serious violent crime trials are relatively visible to the public through heightened media coverage, the stiffer punishment of trial defendants in such cases might be a way that judges and prosecutors signal their toughness in dealing with violence, and this process could be exacerbated by racial threat and white fear. However, we find it puzzling that increases in percentage black increase trial penalties for all defendants, not just blacks (as a racial threat argument would predict), and that the effect of percentage black washes out the individual-level interaction effect of race and jury trial. The causal processes by which the racial context of a county might condition trial penalties for serious violence among both blacks and whites are certainly intriguing and deserve further research.

On the other hand, and contrary to our expectations, certain circumstances seem to mitigate the trial penalty. Those with extensive prior records, those convicted of robbery, and those convicted of rape-IDSI all face significantly reduced trial penalties in terms of either incarceration or sentence length. In these situations, perhaps trials provide a context in which the defense might be effective in presenting the defendant in a better light, bringing out extenuating circumstances, or telling the defendant's story in a way that mobilizes judicial sympathy.

We expected prior record to condition greater trial penalties as prosecutors took the opportunity to dirty up defendants, and convincingly dramatize the repeated criminality of defendants to judges. Instead, trials, and sentencing hearings following trials, may provide defense attorneys whose clients have extensive prior records with an opportunity to argue that defendants' prior convictions were actually less serious than they appeared (an argument supported by some ethnographic research, see Kramer and Ulmer, 2002; Ulmer, 1997). Such trial and posttrial circumstances might provide defense attorneys with the opportunity to tell a story of the defendant's biography and circumstances. This information may counterbalance his or her prior record score and blunt more negative attributions from judges. Alternately, it could be that prosecutors offer smaller plea discounts to those with extensive prior

records (Ulmer, 1997; see also Smith, 1986). That is, prosecutors might be less willing to offer attractive sentence bargaining terms to those with more serious criminal histories, and who might therefore be seen as more blameworthy or dangerous. Rather than this finding being explained by a pattern in which jury trial defendants with high prior records receive more lenient sentences, it might be explained by their counterparts who plead guilty getting less leniency. In other words, it might not benefit high prior record defendants to go to trial so much as it fails to benefit them to plead guilty.

In addition, the finding of lesser trial penalties for those with more extensive prior records could be explained by a pattern in which those with extensive prior records are more likely to be convicted. That is, high prior record defendants might exhibit smaller sentence differences between guilty pleas and trial convictions if they have greater likelihoods of conviction, and if this likelihood offsets potential plea discounts they might receive. We cannot rule this possibility out, but qualitative interview data show that the greater exposure to more severe and certain punishment that an extensive criminal history carries can actually dampen defendants enthusiasm for pleading guilty (Ulmer, 1997: 96). Significant criminal records also tend to reduce the willingness of prosecutors to offer attractive plea concessions (Ulmer, 1997: 94–96). A criminal history thus raises the punishment stakes higher, and such defendants might think they are better off "taking their chances at trial." If so, it may be that those with higher prior record scores might go to trial more often, not less, with the possibility for acquittal that trial entails.

One additional possible explanation for our findings regarding rape and IDSI may lie in differences in blame attributions during rape or IDSI trials. Rape trials may be more likely to involve disputes over consent, and thus over believability, than other trials (for example, if both sides acknowledge sex occurred, but are trying to establish if consent was present). Also, it is well known that the character of the victim may be subjected to more intense scrutiny in rape trials than in other kinds of trials. The defense has the opportunity to construct the victim in a negative light (for example, she is promiscuous, spurned, intoxicated, manipulative, irresponsible, or negligent) as well as to evoke sympathetic feelings toward the offender so as to downplay his responsibility (for example, he was intoxicated, there was a misunderstanding, he is being humiliated by false charges). Future qualitative research is necessary to explicitly capture the construction of defendants and victims during trials, and connecting these constructions to sentencing consequences.

 ## Conclusion

First, we seem to have identified a key exception to the liberation hypothesis of sentencing discretion (Kalven and Zeisel, 1966; Smith and Damphousse, 1998; Spohn and Cederblom, 1991). The liberation hypothesis predicts that as offense severity increases, the effects of extralegal variables will decrease. Instead, we find that a key extralegal effect, the jury trial penalty, is substantial among a set of serious violent offenses; other extralegal contextual variables condition variation in trial penalties among these serious violent offenses; and the incarceration trial penalty actually increases, not decreases, with offense severity. Thus jury trial penalties may be greater for more severe offenses, and these severe offenses may condition the differential influence of other extra legal variables. Perhaps, then, trial penalties are an important exception to the notion that extralegal sentencing differences decline with the severity of offenses.

Second, our findings also have important implications for legal ethics. The U.S. legal system guarantees every criminal defendant the right to a jury trial, yet we find that defendants accused of serious violent offenses are substantially penalized if they exercise this right and then lose. Furthermore, this jury trial penalty is not evenly assessed, but depends on the seriousness and type of offense, the offender's prior record, and several court contextual characteristics. It is also worth pointing out that Pennsylvania is a "truth in sentencing" state, meaning that offenders cannot be released before they have served at least their minimum sentence lengths. In fact, the average Pennsylvania state prisoner serves 127 percent of his or her minimum sentence

(personal communication from the Pennsylvania Department of Corrections). These sentence length trial penalties and their variations therefore represent very real and meaningful differences in the amount of punishment and loss of liberty experienced by offenders. Such realities may seem inconsistent with the American notion of "equal justice under law." More research that improves on the limitations of this study is certainly warranted. In particular, research should assess trial penalties while accounting for possible selection bias stemming from the likelihood of conviction, and balancing plea-trial sentencing differences against the odds of acquittal.

Finally, we believe that this study points the way to an underresearched role of emotion in a vital social institution—courts and their punishment decisions. As Lawrence Sherman recently stated, the study of criminal justice should better understand the role of emotion, and "emotional 'hot spots' of criminal justice activity could be mapped and studied, including arrests, high speed chases, *sentencing decisions,* the first day's release from prison" (2003: 26, emphasis added). Certainly, many scholars have discussed the role of emotions, especially fear, in communities and collective discourse about crime and punishment (for example, Reiman, 1995). However, there has been very little explicit attention to the potential role of emotion in actual criminal punishment decisions, such as sentencing.

The focal concerns perspective has not explicitly addressed the role of emotion in sentencing, but such a role is quite compatible with it, and is arguably implicit within the notion of focal concerns. That is, types of cases and defendants could mobilize negative emotional responses toward defendants among sentencing decision makers, and this could color the assessment of defendants and appropriate punishments with relation to focal concerns, especially perceived blameworthiness or perceived dangerousness-community protection. The criminal justice process exemplifies the formalized process of constructing and judging moral character, and constructing and assessing levels of criminal threat to the community. This process requires both the rational-legal work of establishing guilt (whether the defendant's actions caused the accused harm to the victim) and the emotion work (Hochschild, 1979, 1983) of establishing moral blameworthiness (feelings that the offender is morally culpable and deserves punishment) or dangerousness to the community (fear of the offender).

Our findings suggest that sentencing processes for serious violent offenses involving guilty pleas may involve less emotion work and are less emotionally evocative than sentencing processes that follow an unsuccessful trial, especially a full jury trial. Thus, research on criminal punishment could incorporate insights from the sociology of emotions to achieve a more accurate understanding of sentencing, including sentencing differences between modes of conviction and how those differences might vary between types of cases, defendants, and contexts.

References

Albonetti, Celesta. 1986. Criminality, prosecutorial screening, and uncertainty: Toward a theory of discretionary decision-making in felony case processing. *Criminology* 24:623–44.

Albonetti, Celesta. 1991. An integration of theories to explain judicial discretion. *Social Problems* 38:247–66.

Albonetti, Celesta. 1998. The role of gender and departures in the sentencing of defendants convicted of a white collar offense under the federal sentencing guidelines. In *Sociology of Crime, Law, and Deviance*, vol. 1, ed. Jeffery T. Ulmer. Greenwich. CT: JAI.

Barkan, Steven, and Steven Cohn. 2005. Why whites favor spending more money to fight crime: The role of racial prejudice. *Social Problems* 52:300–14.

Berk, Richard. 1983. An introduction to sample selection bias in sociological data. *American Sociological Review* 48:386–98.

Black, Donald. 1976. *The Behavior of Law.* New York: Academic Press.

Bonilla-Silva, Eduardo. 1997. Rethinking racism: Toward a structural interpretation. *American Sociological Review* 62:465–80.

Brereton, David, and Jonathan Casper. 1982. Does it pay to plead guilty? Differential sentencing and the functioning of criminal courts. *Law and Society Review* 16:45–70.

Britt, Chester. 2000. Social context and racial disparities in punishment decisions. *Justice Quarterly* 17:707–32.

Bushway, Shawn, and Anne Morrison Piehl. 2001. Judging judicial discretion: Legal factors and racial discrimination in sentencing. *Law and Society Review* 35:733–64.

Engen, Rodney, and Randy Gainey. 2000. Modeling the effects of legally-relevant and extralegal factors under sentencing guidelines: The rules have changed. *Criminology* 38:1207–230.

Engen, Rodney, and Sara Steen. 2000. The power to punish: Discretion and sentencing reform in the war on drugs. *American Journal of Sociology* 105:1357–395.

Eisenstein, James, and Herbert Jacob. 1977. *Felony Justice: An Organizational Analysis of Criminal Courts.* Boston, MA: Little, Brown.

Eisenstein, James, Roy Flemming, and Peter Nardulli. 1988. *The Contours of Justice: Communities and Their Courts.* Boston, MA: Little, Brown.

Fair, Kathryn A. 1984. Maintaining balance through an institutionalized plea negotiation process. *Criminology* 22:291–319.

Fearn, Noelle. 2005. A multilevel analysis of community effects on criminal sentencing. *Justice Quarterly* 22:452–87.

Flemming, Roy B., Peter F. Nardulli, and James Eisenstein. 1992. *The Craft of Justice: Politics and Work in Criminal Court Communities.* Philadelphia: University of Pennsylvania Press.

Garfinkel, Harold. 1956. Conditions of successful status degradation ceremonies. *American Journal of Sociology* 61:420–24.

Goffman, Erving. 1963. *Stigma: Notes on the Management of Spoiled Identity.* Englewood Cliffs, NJ: Prentice Hall.

Hagan, John. 1975. The social and legal construction of criminal justice: A study of the presentence process. *Social Problems* 22:620–37.

Hanushek, Eric A., and John Jackson. 1977. *Statistical Methods for Social Scientists.* New York: Academic Press.

Hochschild, Arlie Russell. 1979. Emotion work, feeling rules, and social structure. *American Journal of Sociology* 85:551–75.

Hochschild, Arlie Russell. 1983. *The Managed Heart: The Commercialization of Human Feeling.* Berkeley: University of California Press.

Holleran, David, and Cassia Spohn. 2004. On the use of the total incarceration variable in sentencing research. *Criminology* 42:211–40.

Holmes, Malcolm, Howard Daudistel, and William Taggart. 1992. Plea bargaining policy and state district court caseloads: An interrupted time series analysis. *Law and Society Review* 26:139–59.

Johnson, Brian. 2003. Racial and ethnic disparities in sentencing departures across modes of conviction. *Criminology* 41:449–88.

Kalberg, Stephen. 1980. Max Weber's types of rationality: Cornerstones for the analysis of rationalization processes in history. *American Journal of Sociology* 85:1145–179.

Kalven, Harry, and Hans Zeisel. 1966. *The American Jury.* Boston, MA: Little, Brown.

Kautt, Paula. 2002. Location, location, location: Interdistrict and inter-circuit variation in sentencing outcomes for federal drug-trafficking offenses. *Justice Quarterly* 19:633–71.

King, Nancy, David Soule, Sara Steen, and Robert Weidner. 2005. When process affects punishment: Differences in sentences after guilty plea, bench trial, and jury trial in five guideline states. *Columbia Law Review* 105:960–1009.

Klepper, Steven, Daniel Nagin, and Luke-John Tierney. 1983. Discrimination in the criminal justice system: A critical appraisal of the literature. In *Research on Sentencing: The Search for Reform*, eds. Alfred Blumstein, Jacqueline Cohen, Susan E. Martin, and Michael H. Tonry. Washington, DC: National Academy Press.

Koons-Witt, Barbara. 2002. The effect of gender on the decision to incarcerate before and after the introduction of sentencing guidelines. *Criminology* 40:297–328.

Kramer, John H., and Anthony Scirica. 1986. Complex policy choices: The Pennsylvania Commission on Sentencing. *Federal Probation* L: 15 23.

Kramer, John H., and Jeffery T. Ulmer. 2002. Downward departures for serious violent offenders: Local court "corrections" to Pennsylvania's sentencing guidelines. *Criminology* 40:601–36.

Kurlychek, Megan, and Brian Johnson. 2004. The juvenile penalty. A comparison of juvenile and young adult sentencing outcomes in criminal court. *Criminology* 42:485–515.

LaFree, Gary. 1985. Adversarial and nonadversarial justice: A comparison of guilty pleas and trials. *Criminology* 23:289–312.

Loseke, Donileen. 1993. Constructing conditions, people, morality, and emotion: Expanding the agenda of constructionism. In *Constructionist Controversies: Issues in Social Problems Theory*, eds. Gale Miller and James A. Holstein. New York: Aldine de Gruyter.

Maines, David. 2001. *The Faultline of Consciousness: A View of Interactionism in Sociology*. New York: Aldine de Gruyter.

March, James, and Herbert Simon. 1958. *Organizations*. New York: John Wiley & Sons.

Mather, Lyon. 1973. Some determinants of the method of case disposition: Decision-making by public defenders in Los Angeles. *Law and Society Review* 7:187–216.

Mather, Lynn. 1979. Comments on the history of plea bargaining. *Law and Society Review* 13:281–85.

Meeker, James, and Henry Pontell. 1985. Court caseloads, plea bargains, and criminal sanctions: The effects of section 17 P.C. in California. *Criminology* 23:119–43.

Nardulli, Peter F., James Eisenstein, and Roy B. Flemming. 1988. *The Tenor of Justice' Criminal Courts and the Guilty Plea Process*. Urbana: University of Illinois Press.

Peterson, Ruth D., and John Hagan. 1984. Changing conceptions of race: Towards an account of anomalous findings of sentencing research. *American Sociological Review* 49:56–70.

Raudenbush, Stephen, Anthony Bryk, Yuk Fai Cheong, and Richard Congdon. 2004. *HLM 6: Hierarchical Linear and Non-Linear Modeling*. Lincolnwood, IL: Scientific Software International.

Reiman, Jeffrey. 1995. *The Rich Get Richer and the Poor Get Prison*. Boston, MA: Allyn and Bacon.

Rhodes, William. 1979. Plea bargaining: Its effect on sentencing and convictions in the District of Columbia. *Journal of Criminal Law and Criminology* 70, 360–75.

Rosett, Arthur, and Donald Cressey. 1976. *Justice by Consent: Plea Bargaining in the American Courthouse*. Philadelphia: Lippincott.

Savelsberg, Joachim. 1992. Law that does not fit society. Sentencing guidelines as a neoclassical reaction to the dilemmas of substantivized law. *American Journal of Sociology* 97:1346–381.

Sherman, Lawrence. 2003. Reason for emotion: Reinventing justice with theories, innovations, and research. *Criminology* 41(1): 1–38.

Smith, Brent, and Kelly Dampbousse. 1998. Terrorism, politics, and punishment: A test of structural-contextual theory and the "liberation hypothesis." *Criminology* 36:67–92.

Smith, Douglas A 1986. The plea bargaining controversy. *Journal of Criminal Law and Criminology* 77:949–68.

Spohn, Cassia. 2000. Thirty years of sentencing reform: The quest for a racially neutral sentencing process. *Criminal Justice: The National Institute of Justice Journal* 3:427–501.

Spohn, Cassia, and Jerry Cederblom. 1991. Race and disparities in sentencing: A test of the liberation hypothesis. *Justice Quarterly* 8:305–27.

Spohn, Cassia, John Gruhl, and Susan Welch. 1982. The effect of race on sentencing: A reexamination of an unsettled question. *Law and Society Review* 16:71–88.

Spohn, Cassia, and David Holleran. 2000. The imprisonment penalty paid by young unemployed black and Hispanic male offenders. *Criminology* 38:281–306.

Steffensmeier, Darrell. 1980. Assessing the impact of the women's movement on sex-based differences in the handling of adult criminal defendants. *Crime & Delinquency* 26:344–57.

Steffensmeier, Darrell, and Stephen DeMuth. 2000. Ethnicity and sentencing outcomes in U.S. federal courts: Who is punished more harshly? *American Sociological Review* 65:705–29.

Steffensmeier, Darrell, and Stephen DeMuth. 2001. Ethnicity and judges' sentencing decisions: Hispanic-black-white comparisons. *Criminology* 39:145–78.

Steffensmeier, Darrell, and Chris Hebert 1999. Women and men policymakers: Does the judge's gender affect the sentencing of criminal defendants? *Social Forces* 77:1163–196.

Steffensmeier, Darrell, John H. Kramer, and Cathy Streifel. 1993. Gender and imprisonment decisions. *Criminology* 31:411–46.

Steffensmeier, Darrell, Jeffery T. Ulmer, and John Kramer. 1998. The interaction of race, gender, and age in criminal sentencing: The punishment cost of being young, black, and male. *Criminology* 36:763–98.

Stolzenberg, Ross, and Daniel Relies. 1997. Tools for intuition about sample selection bias and its correction. *American Sociological Review* 62:494–507.

Uhlman, Thomas, and N. Darlene Walker. 1979. A plea is no bargain: The impact of case disposition on sentence. *Social Science Quarterly* 60:218–34.

Uhlman, Thomas, and N. Darlene Walker. 1980. "He takes some of my time, I take some of his": An analysis of judicial sentencing patterns in jury cases. *Law and Society Review* 14:323–41.

Ulmer, Jeffery T. 1997. *Social Worlds of Sentencing: Court Communities Under Sentencing Guidelines*. Albany: State University of New York Press.

Ulmer, Jeffery T. 2005. The localized uses of federal sentencing guidelines in four U.S. District Courts: Evidence of processual order. *Symbolic Interaction* 28:255–79.

Ulmer, Jeffery T., and Brian D. Johnson. 2004. Sentencing in context: A multilevel analysis. *Criminology* 42:137–77.

Ulmer, Jeffery T., and John Kramer. 1996. Court communities under sentencing guidelines: Dilemmas of formal rationality and sentencing disparity. *Criminology* 3:306–32.

U.S. Sentencing Commission. 2001. *Office of Policy Analysis Variable Codebook*. Washington, DC: U.S. Sentencing Commission.

Wheeler, Stanton, David Weisburd, and Nancy Bode. 1982. Sentencing the white collar offender: Rhetoric and reality. *American Sociological Review* 47:641–59.

Winship, Christopher, and Robert Mare. 1992. Models for sample selection bias. *Annual Review of Sociology* 18:327–50.

Wooldredge, John. 1989. An aggregate level examination of the caseload pressure hypothesis. *Journal of Quantitative Criminology* 5:259–70.

Wooldredge, John, and Amy Thistlethwaite. 2004. Bilevel disparities in court dispositions for intimate assault. *Criminology* 42:417–56.

Zatz, Marjorie. 1984. Race, ethnicity, and determinate sentencing: A new dimension to an old controversy. *Criminology* 22:147–71.

Zatz, Marjorie. 2000. The convergence of race, ethnicity, gender, and class on court decision making: Looking toward the 21st century. *Criminal Justice: The National Institute of Justice Journal* 3:503–52.

Zatz, Marjorie, and John Hagan. 1985. Crime, time, and punishment: An exploration of selection bias in sentencing research. *Journal of Quantitative Criminology* 1(1):103–26.

DISCUSSION QUESTIONS

1. The authors of this study focus on trial penalties for offenders convicted of serious violent offenses. Why are these offenses the focus of their study?

2. How do researchers "explain" harsher sentences for those who exercise their right to trial by jury? How do these explanations fit with the focal concerns perspective on sentencing?

3. Why might higher court caseload pressure produce larger trial penalties? Do the authors' findings support their hypothesis about this relationship?

4. Why might those with more extensive criminal histories receive larger trial penalties than those with less extensive prior records? Do the authors' findings support their hypothesis about this relationship?

5. What are the most important findings of this study?

6. How do the authors explain their "counterintuitive" finding that trial penalties are larger in larger court communities?

7. What is the "liberation hypothesis" and how do the authors' findings represent a "key exception" to this hypothesis?

READING

The role of the media—and, in particular, the presence of cameras in the courtroom—is a subject that sparks controversy and generates debate. Those on one side of the debate argue that the First Amendment gives the media a right to access criminal proceedings, whereas those on the other side contend that the media's role is limited by the defendant's Sixth Amendment right to a fair trial. Johnson explored these issues, focusing on Supreme Court cases regarding media presence in the courtroom. He also examined how various jurisdictions approach the issue and explored the costs and benefits of allowing cameras in the courtroom.

SOURCE: "The Entertainment Value of a Trial: How Media Access to the Courtroom Is Changing the American Judicial Process," by Jeffrey S. Johnson in *Villanova Sports and Entertainment Law Journal*, vol. 10, pp. 131, 2003. Reprinted with permission.

The Entertainment Value of a Trial

How Media Access to the Courtroom Is Changing the American Judicial Process

Jeffrey S. Johnson

 ## I. Introduction

Recent interest by the American public in high profile court cases has led to an increased media presence in the courtroom. At the time of the O. J. Simpson trial, every American had the power to turn on their televisions and witness the unfolding of a real-life courtroom drama at any time of day. More recently in 2000 and 2001, the "hockey dad" trial dominated headlines across the country. In that case, two fathers engaged in a physical altercation stemming from rough play at their children's hockey practice, resulting in one of the fathers beating the other to death. These are only two examples of the media's presence in the courtroom. Such high profile trials have left courts and scholars debating the role and significance of television cameras in the courtroom. Does the media presence taint the jury or influence how a lawyer may address the jury? Are jurors distracted by the way they appear on camera, instead of focusing on the matter at hand? Does the media have a constitutional right to videotape in-court proceedings? All of these are questions that must be answered when examining the proper role of television cameras in the courtroom.

Gone are the days when reporters observed a trial and then published a story about it in the next edition of the paper. Today, in addition to regular media coverage, homes have access to Court TV, an independent cable network devoted entirely to broadcasting courtroom trials and related commentary.

Court TV was founded by Steven Brill in 1991. Since its first broadcast, the network has televised over seven hundred trials. Though Court TV's popularity may have peaked with the O. J. Simpson verdict when its TV ratings were at their highest, the network claims that interest in televised trials remains constant. While critics may blast Court TV for being a cheap take on the popular television program *L.A. Law,* the network has its avid followers and supporters, who laud the educational value of the programming.

Court TV is experiencing steadily increasing ratings, as Americans' appetite for original reality television continues to grow. The popularity of programs such as *The People's Court, Judge Judy,* and *Divorce Court* cannot be disputed. Yet, such popularity causes concern for how far public access to real-life trials will go. For example, in a recent California case, the media was granted access to an execution. Also, the media has desired television access to jurors post-trial to observe their deliberations.

Today, forty-seven states permit television coverage of trials and their respective proceedings. In the federal court system, however, television cameras are not permitted in courtrooms at the trial level.

This Comment analyzes the distinction between courts that allow television coverage and those that do not. It further examines the logic behind both positions and reviews several important cases. This Comment also discusses the effects of television cameras on the judge, jury, counsel, and key witnesses, and whether such effects support allowing or banning television cameras in the courtroom.

 ## II. History of Television Cameras in the Courtroom

Members of the media have pitted themselves against the courts consistently on the issue of televised trials by claiming a First Amendment right of access to judicial proceedings. The courts find against media presence in the courtroom by holding that defendants have a Sixth Amendment right to a fair trial and a Fourteenth Amendment right to due process.

Several significant cases have guided state and federal courts' perceptions of television cameras in their courtrooms. Many state courts that allow media presence in courtrooms believe it is an exercise of the media and public's constitutional right to access public information. Other courts view media presence as a violation of a party's Sixth Amendment right to a fair trial. In response to these arguments, federal courts have banned cameras at the trial level. At the appellate level, however, cameras are often permitted.

This controversy first gained national attention in *Estes v. Texas*. The opinion was issued in 1965, when media access to the courtroom surfaced in America. Because of the significance of this issue, the Supreme Court granted certiorari. The main issue for the Court was whether the defendant was prejudiced by the presence of cameras during his trial. The Court responded in the affirmative, holding that the defendant was prejudiced and was denied due process under the Fourteenth Amendment due to the chaotic nature of his trial. The State argued that there was no showing of actual prejudice as a result of the cameras, but the Court reasoned that a showing of actual prejudice was not necessary. The high probability of prejudice in such an atmosphere was sufficient to persuade the Court that the defendant's Fourteenth Amendment right was violated.

In its analysis, the Supreme Court examined several factors that contributed to the defendant's being prejudiced by cameras in the courtroom. These factors included the impact on the jury, the impact on the quality of the testimony from witnesses, the additional responsibilities placed on the judge, and the impact of cameras on the defendant. Interestingly, the Court did not examine the possible effects of cameras on counsel. Subsequent courts, however, found the Court's decision unclear as to whether *Estes* represented a ban on all cameras at all trials. While in fact it did not, the Supreme Court did not answer this question until 1981.

In *Chandler v. Florida,* the Supreme Court again addressed the issue of allowing cameras in the courtroom. The *Chandler* case arose out of Florida's experimentation with allowing cameras in the courtroom. In *Chandler,* the State of Florida had taken precautions to ensure that the defendant's constitutional rights were protected in the event that cameras were used in a courtroom. These precautions included protecting the identities of certain witnesses, protecting a defendant's right to a fair trial, and letting the defendant's objections to media coverage be heard and considered by the court.

The Court in *Chandler* found for the State of Florida, holding that the *Estes* decision did not require a ban on all cameras in courtrooms. The Court further held that the defendants were not prejudiced by the presence of television cameras in the courtroom. The Court explained that when claiming prejudice because of the presence of television cameras, one must show actual prejudice in order to establish a violation of Sixth or Fourteenth Amendment rights. Showing the mere possibility of prejudice is not enough.

After the *Estes* and *Chandler* decisions, scholars concluded that "the Constitution neither prohibited or mandated televised coverage of trial proceedings where there were safeguards in place to ensure the court could honor the defendant's right to a fair trial and there was no showing of specific prejudice."[1] Scholars also note that every case is unique, requiring fact-specific precautions in order to protect the defendant from prejudice.

In *Richmond Newspapers, Inc. v. Virginia,* the Supreme Court confronted the issue of public access to trials. The Court interpreted the Constitution broadly and held that public access to trials, while not an absolute right, could be implied from the First and Fourteenth Amendments. "Closure," the closing of a trial to public access, can only be justified by extenuating circumstances, such as where the defendant is prejudiced or where there is need to protect witnesses. Therefore, as a rule, there are no mandatory closures of trials. A trial can be closed only upon a significant showing of need. This standard is very strict, but is satisfied by showing a substantial probability of prejudice.

In light of these decisions, several core concepts emerge regarding public access to courtroom proceedings. First, "courtrooms are closed to the public in extreme circumstances" where closure is necessary to carry out a fair trial. Second, all proceedings are open to the public if they meet the standards created by the Supreme Court. Third, if claiming prejudice, a defendant must prove actual prejudice and not merely the possibility of prejudice. Fourth, *Estes* banned cameras when a trial becomes "circus-like" and the presence of cameras is very likely to prejudice the defendant, while *Chandler* found no prejudice because the State of Florida had taken significant safeguards. Therefore, cameras are permitted in certain circumstances where the risk of prejudice is low and safeguards are in place. When the risk of prejudice is high, making it substantially probable that prejudice will result, cameras should not be permitted.

In most cases, the media's argument is based on the First Amendment right of access to all trials and proceedings. Specifically, the media in *Estes* argued, "to refuse to honor this privilege is to discriminate between the newspapers and television." Justice Clark reasoned differently, labeling this argument "a misconception of the rights of the press."

Several federal court cases have followed the Supreme Court's lead by not allowing televised trials despite the media's analogy of such action to the right of a person to attend a trial. An example of this can be seen in *Westmoreland v. Columbia Broadcasting System, Inc.* The Second Circuit reasoned that there was a huge difference "between a public right under the First Amendment to attend trials and a public right under the First Amendment to see a given trial televised." The same reasoning was applied in *United States v. Hastings.* In *Hastings,* the court ruled that the media misconceived that the First Amendment right to attend trials extended to televising the trial.

In addition to the First Amendment, the media has argued for access to proceedings based on the due process clause of the Fourteenth Amendment and the Sixth Amendment's guarantee of a "public trial." Both of these arguments have merit, but must be considered in light of the concerns of the court involving prejudice to a defendant. Defendants to the litigation counter that media presence during trial creates prejudice against the integrity of the trial and infringes upon the Sixth Amendment right to a fair trial.

The Supreme Court has stated that a proceeding should be closed only if there is a "substantial probability" that the right to a fair trial will be prejudiced, if closure would prevent the prejudice, and if reasonable alternatives to closure cannot adequately protect the right. Moreover, some defendants argue that the cameras violate their Fourteenth Amendment rights to due process because of the prejudice they cause.

III. Analysis

A. State Experimentation

Subsequent to the decisions above, many states experimented with the idea of television cameras in the courtroom. Some states viewed this as a great addition to the trial process, while other states viewed it as detrimental to both the defendant and the judicial process.

Florida is one state that viewed cameras as a valuable addition to the trial process. Florida conducted a two-year experiment beginning in 1975 and found "no indication of any of the adverse effects predicated by the proponents of the ban on cameras and concluded that more was gained than was lost by the admission of cameras." This experiment eventually led to the *Chandler* decision because the defendant claimed he was prejudiced by the presence of cameras while on trial in Florida for burglary and grand larceny.

Other states soon followed Florida's example and found that cameras provided no harm to defendants. Many states noted the importance of public access to the judicial process and the benefits of an informed and involved citizenry. Also, many states have adopted or incorporated into their court rules Canon 3 of the ABA *Code of Judicial Conduct,* which allows a judge in his or her discretion to permit the broadcast of a courtroom proceeding. The amount of discretion permitted by a presiding judge varies for each state, as do the restrictions that each state court employs. Some state courts allow a participant to object to the presence of the camera at the proceeding, but reserve the ultimate decision regarding access to the judge's discretion. A minority of state courts find that any objection to the camera by the defendant is sufficient cause for its exclusion. Other state courts, conversely, impose a high evidentiary burden on a defendant, requiring a demonstration of actual harm before barring the broadcast media from the proceeding. Demonstration of actual harm by a defendant is rarely successful, however, because of the typical absence of tangible evidence of prejudice or bias.[2]

Thus, numerous states deem in-court cameras to be a valuable tool, while at the same time acknowledging the potential for prejudice.

B. Viewpoints From Around the Nation

This section examines how other jurisdictions are approaching the issue of television cameras in the courtroom and discusses past methods for dealing with the issue. California and New York are at the forefront of state experimentation of television cameras in courtrooms. A recent New York case, *People v. Boss,* held that New York's statute banning cameras in state courtrooms was unconstitutional. The case was highly publicized and involved New York police officers who shot an unarmed West-African immigrant, Amadou Diallo, nineteen times on his front porch after firing forty-one rounds. Presiding Judge Teresi reasoned that allowing cameras in the courtroom would "further the interest of justice, enhance public understanding of the judicial system and maintain a high level of public confidence in the judiciary."

The statute at issue in *Boss* states: "no person, firm, association, or corporation shall televise, broadcast, take motion pictures . . . within this state of proceedings, in which the testimony of witnesses by subpoena or other compulsory process is or may be taken, conducted by a court, commission, committee, administrative agency or other tribunal in this state." New York had recently ended a ten-year experiment with cameras in the courtroom, and despite positive results, it was not renewed. Therefore, as of 1997, New York was one of only three states to ban televised trials, even though cameras have been permitted at other proceedings, such as state appellate proceedings.

California, another leading state on this issue, conducted experiments in 1980 and 1981 that yielded positive results showing that in-court cameras had no effect on judicial proceedings. Following these experiments, California permitted televised trials at both the criminal and civil divisions. Today, Hollywood benefits from this twenty-year-old study, providing America with much of its legal drama. At the same time, Hollywood provides Court TV with much of its business.

California continues to push the limits of televised trials, demonstrated in a recent case where a reporter desired access to an actual execution. While the access was granted, there is still no live coverage of such an event and no plans for pay-per-view screenings in the near future. Also, California has an open court statute, opening all civil proceedings to the press and public "unless notice of intent to close is given, there is [an] overriding interest that may be prejudiced absent narrowly tailored closure order, and there are no less restrictive means of achieving that interest."

Ultimately, two of the most populous, most highly regarded, and most watched jurisdictions have reached differing views on the topic of in-court cameras. California praises the benefits of televised trials, while New York decries their liabilities.

C. Cost/Benefit Analysis of the Presence of Television Cameras

1. The Benefits

According to supporters of televised trials, the potential benefits of television cameras in the courtroom are numerous. One of the supporters' arguments is that cameras bring out the truth. This is because witnesses are less likely to lie, and judges and the jury may pay more attention to the facts of the case if a camera and thousands of viewers are watching them. These advocates of in-court cameras also believe that televised trials "enhance public scrutiny of the judicial system."

Cameras in the courtroom play a positive role for judges as well because they are more likely to take precautions to ensure a fair trial for defendants if they know the entire public is watching. Judges will not be inclined to nod off while cameras are taping, thus ensuring their full attention. Judges may also use cameras to elicit truth because the in-court scrutiny represents a constant reminder to witnesses that they are under oath. Moreover, the presence of cameras may affect witnesses positively because they will be compelled to tell the truth under the pressure of a camera peering at them. This helps to ensure that the defendant receives a fair trial and that justice is served. In addition, many studies show that witnesses do not become overly nervous at the presence of cameras in the courtroom.

On the whole, the effect on jurors is minimal because they are not the focus of the cameras. Yet, jurors may be less likely to acquit a defendant because they fear being chastised by their community. Further, jurors will focus more on the trial, resisting the urge to daydream.

As for the effect on counsel, cameras may compel attorneys to be more prepared when they know countless watchful eyes are upon them. Counsel may exert more effort knowing that the world is watching, including potential clients. These factors play a role in the defendant's receiving a fair trial and in ensuring a just result. Such are the goals of the judicial system; nonetheless, there are strong arguments for banning such approaches to courtroom decorum.

2. The Costs

The possible detriments to the judicial system that arise from allowing cameras in the courtroom include prejudice to the defendant and his or her right to a fair trial, distraction from the court's need to "maintain decorum," and frustration to the public's interest in a fair system. Another downfall is the possibility of lawyers' grandstanding for the jury to the detriment of their client, witnesses, and jurors.

Witnesses may seem nervous in the presence of cameras and appear unreliable to the jury. Some witnesses may appear arrogant, seeming to strive for the limelight, such as Kato Kaelin in the O. J. Simpson trial. Also, witnesses may not be inclined to testify, fearing national coverage of their testimony. Further, witnesses

may be encouraged to lie to protect themselves or loved ones from media ridicule.

Cameras may have a negative effect on juries because jurors might focus on the cameras and not the trial. Jurors may view witnesses as not credible by the way they react to the cameras, thereby thwarting their ability to assess the evidence properly. In addition, an overall feeling of uneasiness that can lead to distraction may overcome members of the jury, thereby negatively affecting the trial process. "The camera may also impact jurors indirectly, by affecting the duration of a trial, the length of which directly affects jurors' attitude, or [by] motivating attorney 'grandstanding,' behavior that may influence jurors as well." Jurors may make a decision that the public wants, and not what the law mandates.[3]

Regarding the effect on judges, cameras may have a negative impact on a judge who, if elected or seeking political office, could use television as a means to promote his or her candidacy. Many courts give judges discretion as to how cameras may be used in their courtrooms, which may amount to an additional burden on the judge during the trial. These factors can distract a judge from conducting a fair trial for the defendant.

Counsel for both parties may also be affected negatively by the presence of television cameras. Specifically, lawyers may not expend their best efforts in representing their clients because they are more concerned with being presented favorably by the media. Lawyers may use the publicity to further their own interests, whether political or personal. Some lawyers may avoid settlement so that the case will proceed to trial and their faces will be seen on television, thus raising ethical concerns.

3. The Result

Ultimately, those harmed most by cameras in the courtroom are the parties to the litigation themselves. Those whom the justice system is designed to protect must deal with the consequences. The parties to the litigation are the real victims who are directly affected by the above-mentioned possibilities, including prejudice. Further, these people may have very little power to fight the issue.

Although there is some concrete evidence on the effect of television cameras on certain parties, much of the commentary is mere speculation based on hypothetical situations. Even so, if any of these situations were to become reality, the judicial system would be vulnerable to constant ridicule due to its degeneration from justice to entertainment. Cameras affect people in different ways; some love the limelight, while others shun it. Some people perform well under the pressure of a gazing public eye, while others fare much worse. Should we risk a judge's failure to reach a just result simply because of his or her response to being on camera?

The reality of the above concerns cannot be denied. When a defendant is sentenced to prison or even death, the issue of cameras in the courtroom should not be undervalued. More worrisome is that some of the scenarios mentioned above are currently occurring, but they may go unrecognized until a defendant's rights have already been violated. Therefore, it is imperative that more studies be conducted. The result depends on how certain people, whether a witness, attorney, juror, or judge respond to certain situations. Inevitably, results will vary because studies involve different people and circumstances, but that should not hinder development in this area.

Fundamentally, cameras present too great a risk of prejudice to the defendant and should therefore be banned from all courts at all times. Access to proceedings is already available through other sources such as transcripts, or one can simply attend the trial in person. If Americans are so interested in the judicial system, and Judge Judy is inadequate, they can exercise their constitutional rights to observe a trial as it unfolds, using one of the traditional methods of public access.

IV. Conclusion

The debate over cameras in the courtroom is ongoing and may not be resolved in the near future. Federal courts may someday allow cameras, and more experiments are certain to be performed. State courts are volatile and may change their rules based on public opinion at any time. In September of 1989, the Judicial Conference Ad Hoc Committee on Cameras in the Courtroom made recommendations and findings on this issue. The Committee found that the monitoring of state court experiments should continue to gather more information. The Committee also thought current rules should be relaxed to allow access to non-trial hearings. Furthermore, the Committee believed access should be allowed to maintain the record, provide security, present evidence, and uphold other purposes of judicial administration.

The Supreme Court tends to remain silent about its thoughts on television cameras in the courtroom. The Supreme Court justices rarely speak of cameras in the courtroom or expressly state their opinions. Most commentators and observers believe that no action can be taken without the approval of the Chief Justice of the Supreme Court. Former Chief Justice Warren E. Burger "was openly hostile to [cameras in the courtroom], although the Supreme Court as an institution has never taken a formal position on the subject outside of its decisions." Thus, the current views of the Supreme Court justices are difficult to decipher due to their silence on the issue.

In the meantime, judges can invoke remedies such as gag orders or other limits on the press, exercising their discretion to disallow prejudicial information. Ultimately, this issue is wholly indefinite. It is highly doubtful the Supreme Court will ever issue a total ban on television cameras, or allow for total access to trials and proceedings. The question, however, should be decided on a case-sensitive basis. This would protect certain trials and the participants of those trials who are significantly vulnerable to prejudice as a result of the nature of the proceeding.

Foreseeably, television will remain prevalent in our society forever, thereby making it likely that cameras will infiltrate courtrooms in some form for years to come. As technology improves and the physical burdens of carrying and installing cameras in the courtroom diminish, the day may come when television cameras enter even the Supreme Court. Until technology becomes that pervasive, Court TV and Judge Judy will have to suffice.

Legal Topics

For related research and practice materials, see the following legal topics:

- Civil Procedure
- Judicial Officers
- Judges
- General Overview
- Communications Law
- Cable Systems
- Public Access
- Constitutional Law
- Bill of Rights
- Fundamental Freedoms
- Freedom of Speech
- Free Press
- Public Access

 Notes

1. Lassiter, supra Christo Lassiter, The Appearance of Justice: TV or Note TV—That Is the Question, 86 J. Crim. L. & Criminology (1996) at 942 (discussing Supreme Court's logic in regard to matters of televised courtroom proceedings).

2. Corbett, supra Melissa A. Corbett, Comment, Lights, Camera, Trial: Pursuit of Justice or the Emmy? 27 Seton Hall L. Rev. (1997) at 1555–57 (discussing differing approaches among states) (footnotes omitted). Canon 3A (7) of the ABA Code of Judicial Conduct states:

> A judge should prohibit broadcasting, televising, recording or photographing in courtrooms and areas immediately adjacent thereto during sessions of court, or recesses between sessions, except that under rules prescribed by a supervising appellate court or other appropriate authority, a judge may authorize broadcasting, television, recording or photographing of judicial proceedings in courtrooms and areas immediately adjacent thereto consistent with the right of the parties to a fair trial and subject to express conditions, limitations, and guidelines which allow such coverage in a manner that will be unobtrusive, will not distract the trial participants, and will not otherwise interfere with the administration of justice.

3. Corbett, supra note 1, at 1562–65 (citing Christo Lassiter, Put the Lens Cap Back on Cameras in the Courtroom: A Fair Trial Is at Stake, N.Y. St. B.J., Jan. 1995, at 8); see also Betsy Streisand, And Justice for All, U.S. News & World Rep., Oct. 9, 1995, at 50. These indirect effects may be the ones not noticeable on a survey or in an experiment. See id. Americans need to be wary of these subtle effects. See id.

DISCUSSION QUESTIONS

1. Which constitutional rights clash in cases involving media presence in the courtroom? How have the Supreme Court and other federal courts ruled in these cases?

2. What are the pros and cons of allowing cameras in the courtroom?

3. How do states handle the issue of cameras in the courtroom? Who decides whether the proceedings will be televised?

4. Are there any types of cases in which cameras would be particularly useful? In which cameras would be especially harmful?

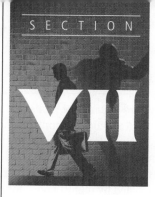

SECTION

VII

Sentencing

Seated on a raised bench, clothed in black robes, and wielding a gavel that he uses to maintain order in the courtroom, the judge pronounces sentence on the defendant, who has been found guilty of robbery and sexual assault. "After considering all of the facts and circumstances in the case," he states, "I have decided to impose the maximum sentence—15 years in prison. I believe that this is the appropriate sentence, given the heinousness of the crime and the fact that the defendant has a prior conviction for aggravated assault."

Scenes like this are played out every day in courtrooms throughout the United States. Judges must decide the appropriate punishment for offenders convicted of crimes, some of which are serious and merit imprisonment and others of which are minor and deserve fines or other alternatives to incarceration. In determining the sentence, judges attempt to tailor sentences to fit both the crimes and the offenders convicted of them. Judges also attempt to fashion sentences that are designed to meet one or more of the goals of punishment.

In this chapter, we focus on judges' sentencing decisions. We begin by discussing the philosophical justifications for punishment. We then discuss the judge's options at sentencing and follow with a discussion of the factors that affect judges' sentencing decisions. We conclude the chapter with an overview of current issues and controversies in sentencing.

⊠ The Goals of Sentencing

What should be done with a person found guilty of a crime? Should a convicted offender be punished? If so, what is the purpose of the punishment? And if punishment is justified, what should the punishment be? Should the offender be required to pay a fine or provide restitution to the victim? How much should he or she pay? Should the offender be placed on probation? For how long and under what conditions? Should the offender be incarcerated in jail or prison? If so, for how long? Or should the offender receive the "ultimate punishment"—death? Questions such as these have been pondered and debated by philosophers and legal scholars for thousands of years.

Why do we punish those who violate the law? Although answers to this question vary widely, they can be classified into two distinct categories: retributive (desert-based) justifications and utilitarian (result-based) justifications. According to retributive theory, an offender is punished because he has done something wrong—something blameworthy—and therefore deserves to be punished (Hospers, 1977; Moore, 1968; von Hirsch, 1976). Retributive justifications of punishment, in other words, "rest on the idea that it is right for the wicked to be punished; because man is responsible for his actions, he ought to receive his just deserts" (Packer, 1968, p. 37). In contrast, utilitarian justifications of punishment emphasize the prevention of future crimes. Punishment prevents future crime by deterring the offender from reoffending or by discouraging others from following the offender's example (deterrence), by locking him or her up (incapacitation), or by reforming the offender (rehabilitation). Whereas retributivists equate punishment with desert, then, utilitarians justify punishment by the results it is designed to achieve. We discuss these justifications for punishment in more detail in the following sections.

Retribution: The "Just Deserts" Theory of Punishment

Why punish? The retributivist's answer to this question is straightforward: People who violate the law are punished because they have done something wrong—justice demands that the person be punished. Stated another way, "we are justified in punishing because and only because offenders deserve it" (Moore, 1992, p. 188). The basis for this principle—that is, the answer to the question, "Why do the guilty deserve to be punished?"—is more complex. One school of thought simply holds that there is "intrinsic good in the guilty suffering" (Braithwaite & Pettit, 1990, p. 157). Just as those who believe in an afterlife think that it is morally justified that those who lead good lives will be rewarded while those who lead wicked lives will suffer, advocates of this position believe that punishment of those who violate the law is inherently right (Kant, 1887; Moore, 1992, note 3). Man, in other words, "is a responsible moral agent to whom rewards are due when he makes right moral choices and to whom punishment is due when he makes wrong ones" (Packer, 1968, p. 9).

Another school of thought holds that all members of a civilized society agree—either explicitly or implicitly—to follow the rules that govern the society (Finnis, 1980; Moore, 1992, note 1; Murphy, 1979; Sadurski, 1985). Those who hold this philosophy agree that they will not attack or kill one another, steal one another's property, or behave in other ways that cause harm. This agreement benefits all members of the society. Therefore, someone who violates the rules—by killing or stealing, for example—gains an unfair advantage over law-abiding members of society. Punishment, by penalizing the offender, rectifies this unfair advantage; it restores the equilibrium. As Nigel Walker (1991) noted, "Penalties put matters right, either by removing what the offender has gained or by imposing a disadvantage" (p. 25).

In summary, the **retributive justification for punishment** focuses on what the offender "deserves" as a result of his or her criminal behavior. It is a backward-looking approach that focuses exclusively on the offender's wrongdoing as the reason for punishment.

Utilitarian Justifications for Punishment

In contrast to desert theory, which, as noted previously, is a backward-looking approach, the **utilitarian justifications for punishment**—deterrence, incapacitation, rehabilitation, and restoration—are forward looking. Rather than looking back to the crime that has been committed, these justifications focus on the future behavior of both the person being punished and other members of society. Punishment, thus, does not occur because a crime has been committed and the offender deserves to be punished; rather, "the punishment is *in order to* promote good (and/or prevent evil) in the future" (Hospers, 1977, p. 25). According to the utilitarian theorist, if punishment cannot achieve this, "it is immoral; merely the adding of one evil (punishing) to another (the crime)" (p. 25). Strictly speaking, then, if no "good consequences" will result from punishing an individual, no punishment is justified.

One of the utilitarian justifications for punishment is **deterrence**. As developed by 18th-century utilitarian philosophers such as Jeremy Bentham (1970) and Cesare Beccaria (1974/1986), deterrence theory suggests that crime results from a rational calculation of the costs and benefits of criminal activity. Individuals commit crimes, in other words, when the benefits outweigh the costs. Because an important "cost" of crime is apprehension and punishment, deterrence theorists suggest that potential offenders will refrain from committing a crime if they believe that the odds of getting caught and being severely punished are high and are not outweighed by any anticipated gain from the crime. Deterrence can be either specific or general. **Specific deterrence** occurs when someone who has been legally punished ceases offending because of a fear of future punishment. **General deterrence** occurs when potential offenders "learn of the consequences of criminal involvement [for actual offenders] and decide not to risk subjecting themselves to such punishment" (Durham, 1994, p. 134). If, for example, a young woman is sentenced to 30 days in jail for drunk driving and, as a result of being punished, never again gets behind the wheel of a car after she has been drinking, we would say that specific deterrence has occurred. If those who learn of her sentence similarly resolve to refrain from drinking and driving, we would conclude that general deterrence has occurred.

A second forward-looking utilitarian justification of punishment is **incapacitation**, which is sometimes referred to as isolation, neutralization, or predictive restraint. Incapacitation involves locking up—or otherwise physically disabling—dangerous or high-risk offenders to prevent them from committing crimes in the future. The justification for punishment can rest on two related, but conceptually distinct, views of incapacitation. The first is **collective incapacitation**, which refers to the incapacitation of all offenders found guilty of a particular type of crime, without regard to their prior record or other personal characteristics. Offenders convicted of certain types of crimes—armed robberies, aggravated rapes, or drug sales involving large amounts of cocaine or methamphetamine, for example—are deemed dangerous and are locked up to protect society. **Selective incapacitation** focuses on the *offender* as well as the crime. Whereas collective incapacitation means incarcerating those whose crimes are deemed dangerous, selective incapacitation involves incarcerating primarily "those who, when free, commit the most crimes" (Wilson, 1992, p. 152). It involves predicting that an individual offender, or offenders with certain characteristics, will commit additional crimes if not locked up.

Rehabilitation is the third utilitarian justification for punishment. Sometimes referred to simply as treatment, rehabilitation refers to "any measure taken to change an offender's character, habits, or behavior patterns so as to diminish his criminal propensities" (von Hirsch, 1976, p. 11). Like deterrence and incapacitation, the goal of rehabilitation is crime prevention. Rehabilitation achieves this goal not by making offenders fearful of additional punishment (deterrence) or by isolating offenders so that their opportunities for crime are limited (incapacitation), but by reforming offenders. The techniques used to reform or rehabilitate offenders include such things as individual or group counseling, education, job training, substance abuse treatment, and behavior modification programs. The advocate of rehabilitation, then, justifies punishment on the grounds that it will "'cure' an offender of his or her criminal tendencies" (von Hirsch & Ashworth, 1992, p. 1).

The final utilitarian justification for punishment is restoration or **restorative justice**. Unlike the other three utilitarian perspectives, all of which emphasize punishment for crime prevention and focus almost exclusively on the offender, restorative justice views punishment as a means to repair the harm and injury caused by the crime and focuses on the victim and the community as well as the offender (see, e.g., Bazemore, 1998; Braithwaite, 1998; Carey, 1996; Hahn, 1997; Kurki, 2000). The goal of restorative justice "is to restore the victim and the community and to rebuild ruptured relationships in a process that allows all three parties to participate" (Kurki, 2000, p. 236). Restorative justice achieves its goals through a variety of practices. These practices include victim-offender mediation, family group conferencing, sentencing circles, and citizen supervision of probation. What typically occurs is a face-to-face meeting involving the victim, the offender, the victim's and offender's families, and other members of the community (a thorough discussion of these techniques can be found in Kurki, 2000, pp. 268–284). Participants in the process discuss the effects of the crime on the victim, the offender, and the community and attempt to reach a collective agreement regarding the most appropriate sanction.

In summary, punishment, which involves the intentional infliction of harm or suffering, must be morally justified. It does not suffice to say that punishment is justified because it is prescribed by law—this is a legal justification for punishment, not a moral justification. A moral justification for punishment rests on ethical principles, not legal rules. Punishment is justified either because of the offender's guilt and blameworthiness (retribution) or to achieve good results (**utilitarianism**). The retributivist looks backward to the crime and the criminal, arguing that punishment is justified because it is deserved. Punishment is deserved either because it is inherently right that the guilty suffer for their wrongdoing or because those who violate the rules gain an unfair advantage over those who abide by the rules. The utilitarian, on the other hand, looks forward to future consequences or results, arguing that punishment is justified because it leads to good results: It prevents future crime, reforms the offender, or helps the victim and the community heal. The harm done to the offender in the name of punishment, in other words, is outweighed by the good consequences that result from punishment.

BOX 7.1.   WHY DO WE PUNISH THOSE WHO VIOLATE THE LAW?

The Case of "The Brothel Boy"

In "The Brothel Boy," Norval Morris (1992) tells the story of District Officer Eric Blair, a young and inexperienced Burmese magistrate who must decide the fate of a young man who has been charged with the rape and murder of a 12-year-old girl. The "brothel boy," perhaps mimicking the behavior of adults in the brothel where he worked, offered the girl money to have sex with him. She refused, they struggled, and she fell, hitting her head on a sharp rock. Several days later, she died. District Officer Blair wonders whether this unfortunate young man—who is described as "illiterate," "stupid," and "quite retarded"—should be punished at all and, if so, what his punishment should be. While acknowledging that the brothel boy should be blamed for what he did, he questions whether he is guilty of the crimes with which he is charged. "[T]he boy meant no harm, no evil," he states. "The more I thought about him and his crime, the less wicked it seemed, though the injury to the girl and her family was obviously extreme; but it was a tragedy, not a sin" (p. 16).

As he attempts to understand the accused and his crime, Officer Blair discusses the case with Dr. Veraswami, a Burmese physician. Unlike Blair, Veraswami has no doubts about "what should be done with him." "He will be hanged, of course," Veraswami tells Blair. Officer Blair argues that the brothel boy "meant no harm insofar as he understood what was happening" and therefore, is "less worthy of being hanged than most murderers" (p. 16). Dr. Veraswami disagrees:

> He was conscious of what he was doing. And being conscious, backward and confused though he iss, mistreated and bewildered though he wass, he must be held responsible. You must convict him, punish him, hang him.... you must treat him ass a responsible adult and punish him. (p. 19)

When Officer Blair asks the doctor if there was no room under the law for mercy, for clemency, the doctor replies, "Justice, Mr. Blair, iss your job. Justice, not mercy" (p. 21). Eventually, of course, the brothel boy is hanged.

According to Dr. Veraswami, justice requires that the brothel boy be punished. But why is this so? Why is punishment, rather than forgiveness or revenge, the appropriate response to his offense? What purpose does punishment serve in this case?

The Judge's Options at Sentencing

An individual who has been convicted of a crime faces a number of different sentence alternatives, depending on the seriousness of the crime and the willingness of the judge to experiment with alternative sentences. The judge has more discretion, and thus more opportunities to tailor the sentence to fit the individual offender, if the crime is a misdemeanor or a less serious felony. In this type of case, the judge might impose a fine, order the offender to perform community service, place the offender on probation, or impose some other alternative to incarceration. The judge's options are more limited if the crime is serious or if the offender has a lengthy prior criminal record. In this situation, a jail or prison sentence is likely; the only question is how long the offender will serve.

In this section, we discuss the options available to the judge at sentencing. We begin with the death penalty, which is the ultimate sanction that society can impose on the guilty. We then discuss incarceration and the various alternatives to incarceration.

The Death Penalty

In the United States, 35 states and the federal government have statutes that authorize the death penalty.[1] Once imposed for a variety of offenses including armed robbery and rape,[2] the death penalty today is imposed almost exclusively for first-degree murder. It is, however, a penalty that is rarely applied. In 2006, more than 13,000 persons were arrested for murder and nonnegligent manslaughter (Federal Bureau of Investigation, 2007), but only 115 persons were sentenced to death (U.S. Justice Department, 2007, p. 8).

A sentence of death does not necessarily mean that the offender will be executed. The offender's conviction or sentence might be overturned by a higher court, the sentence might be commuted to life in prison by the governor, or the offender might die in prison. Of the 7,433 prisoners under sentence of death from 1977 to 2006, 1,057 (14.2%) were executed and 3,148 (42.4%) received some other type of disposition; the remaining 3,228 inmates were still incarcerated in 2006. The average amount of time these offenders had been on death row was 11 years and 3 months (U.S. Justice Department, 2007, pp. 11–12).

From September, 2007 through April, 2008, there was an unofficial moratorium on executions as the states awaited the U.S. Supreme Court's decision regarding the constitutionality of the use of lethal injection. This moratorium ended when the Supreme Court ruled that lethal injection was not cruel and unusual punishment in violation of the Eighth Amendment (*Baze v. Rees*, 2008).

Current death penalty statutes have a number of common features.[3] Most are what is referred to as **guided discretion statutes**, which allow the death penalty to be imposed only if at least one statutorily defined aggravating circumstance is present. Although the aggravating circumstances vary among jurisdictions, the list typically includes such things as murder for hire, murder of more than one person, murder of a police officer, murder that involves torture, or murder during the commission of another crime, such as armed robbery or sexual assault. Most jurisdictions also require a bifurcated trial in capital cases. The first stage involves the determination of the defendant's guilt or innocence. If the defendant is convicted of a capital crime—that is, a crime for which the death penalty is an option—a separate sentencing proceeding is held. At this stage, evidence regarding the aggravating and mitigating circumstances of the case is presented. The jury or the judge, or both, weigh the evidence and decide whether the defendant should be sentenced to death or should receive a lesser sentence of life without parole, life, or a specified term of years. Finally, most death penalty statutes also provide for automatic review of the conviction and death sentence by the state's highest court. If either the conviction or the sentence is overturned, the case can be sent back to the trial court for retrial or resentencing (U.S. Justice Department, 2007, pp. 2–4).

---

[1]The following states do not have capital punishment statutes: Alaska, Hawaii, Iowa, Maine, Massachusetts, Michigan, Minnesota, New Jersey, North Dakota, New Mexico, New York, Rhode Island, Vermont, West Virginia, and Wisconsin.

[2]In 1977, the Supreme Court ruled that the death penalty was a disproportionately severe penalty for the rape of an adult woman (*Coker v. Georgia*, 433 U.S. 584 [1977]).

[3]In 1972 the Supreme Court struck down federal and state laws that permitted wide discretion in the imposition of the death penalty. In the case of *Furman v. Georgia* (1972), the Court characterized death penalty decisions under these laws as "arbitrary and capricious" and ruled that they constituted cruel and unusual punishment in violation of the Eighth Amendment. In the wake of this decision, most states enacted new death penalty statutes. These statutes were of two types: those that required the death penalty for all offenders convicted of specified crimes and those that allowed the death penalty to be imposed depending on the presence of certain aggravating circumstances. In 1976, the Court struck down the mandatory death sentence statutes (*Roberts v. Louisiana*, 1976; *Woodson v. North Carolina*, 1976) but upheld the guided discretion statutes (*Gregg v. Georgia*, 1972; *Jurek v. Texas*, 1976; *Proffitt v. Florida*, 1976).

Incarceration

Unlike the death penalty, which can be imposed only for first-degree murder and a handful of other offenses, a jail or prison sentence is an option in most criminal cases. This includes misdemeanors as well as felonies. The Texas Penal Code, for example, categorizes misdemeanors as Class A, Class B, or Class C; Class A misdemeanors are the most serious, Class C the least serious. Although offenders convicted of Class C misdemeanors cannot be sentenced to jail, those convicted of Class B offenses can be confined in jail for up to 180 days, and those found guilty of Class A offenses can be sentenced to jail for as long as one year (Texas Statutes, 2000). In most jurisdictions, sentences of less than one year are served in a local jail, whereas those of one year or more are served in a state prison. All offenders who are tried in U.S. District Courts and who receive a prison sentence are incarcerated in a federal prison; there are no federal jails.

For some offenses, a prison sentence is not simply an option; it is required. All jurisdictions in the United States now have laws that prescribe mandatory minimum terms of incarceration for selected crimes. Almost all states have **mandatory sentences** for repeat or habitual offenders and for crimes involving possession of a deadly weapon. Most states also require minimum prison sentences for certain types of drug offenses: trafficking, selling drugs to minors, or selling drugs within 1,000 feet of a school (Bureau of Justice Assistance, 2000; see also Tonry, 1996). At the federal level, more than 100 crimes are subject to laws requiring from 2- to 20-year minimum sentences. Although mandatory minimum provisions can be circumvented by prosecutors who refuse to charge an offense that triggers a minimum sentence (see, e.g., Shichor & Sechrest, 1996; U.S. Sentencing Commission, 1991) or by judges who either refuse to convict or who ignore the statute and impose something less than the mandatory minimum sentence (Heumann & Loftin, 1979), these "tough on crime" laws limit the options available to the judge at sentencing. They generally require the judge to sentence the offender to prison for a specified period of time.

BOX 7.2. SENTENCING SYSTEMS IN STATE AND FEDERAL JURISDICTIONS

- **Indeterminate sentence:** The legislature specifies a minimum and maximum sentence for each offense or class of offenses. The judge imposes either a minimum and a maximum term of years or the maximum term only. The parole board decides when the offender will be released from prison.
- **Determinate sentence:** The legislature provides a presumptive range of confinement for each offense or class of offenses. The judge imposes a fixed term of years within this range. The offender serves this sentence, minus time off for good behavior.
- **Mandatory sentence:** The legislature requires a mandatory minimum prison sentence for habitual offenders or for offenders convicted of certain crimes. Examples of such crimes include the use of a weapon during the commission of a crime, drug trafficking, and the sale of drugs to minors.
- **Sentencing guidelines:** A legislatively authorized sentencing commission establishes presumptive sentencing guidelines. The guidelines typically are based on the seriousness of the offense and the offender's prior record. Judges are required to follow the guidelines or explain in writing why they did not.

Judges' options also are limited by the type of sentencing system used in the jurisdiction (see Box 7.2). Some state laws require judges to impose **indeterminate sentences.**[4] In these states, the legislature specifies a minimum and a maximum sentence for a particular offense or category of offenses. In sentencing an offender, the judge either imposes a minimum and maximum sentence from within this range or, alternatively, determines only the maximum sentence that the offender can serve. Assume, for example, that the sentence range for armed robbery is 5 to 20 years. In the first scenario, the judge determines both the minimum and the maximum sentence, sentencing the offender to 5 to 10 years, 10 to 15 years, 5 to 20 years, or any other range of years within the statutory minimums and maximums. In the second scenario, the judge determines only the maximum penalty; the minimum penalty would be automatically applied. Regardless of whether the maximum penalty was 10 years, 15 years, or 20 years, in other words, the minimum would always be 5 years. In either case, the actual amount of time the offender will serve is determined by the parole board, based on its judgment of whether the offender has been rehabilitated or has simply served enough time. An armed robber sentenced to an indeterminate sentence of 5 to 10 years, then, will serve at least 5 years but no more than 10 years, depending on the parole board's assessment of offender's case.

In other states, judges impose **determinate sentences,** which are fixed-term sentences that may be reduced if the offender behaves while incarcerated (i.e., through so-called "good time credits"; Bureau of Justice Assistance, 2000).[5] The offender's date of release is based on the sentence imposed minus any good time credits. The parole board may supervise offenders who have been released from prison, but it does not determine when offenders will be released. In states that have adopted this type of system, the legislature provides a presumptive range of confinement for various categories of offenses. Although some offenses are nonprobationable, for most crimes the judge has discretion to determine whether the offender will be incarcerated and, if so, for how long. If, for example, the presumptive range of confinement for robbery is 4 to 15 years and the statute does not specify that offenders convicted of robbery must be sentenced to prison, the judge could impose either a probation sentence or a prison sentence of anywhere from 4 to 15 years. If the sentence were 10 years in prison, the offender would serve that time, minus credit for good behavior.

In still other states and at the federal level, judges' incarceration options are limited by presumptive sentencing guidelines (Bureau of Justice Assistance, 2000).[6] In jurisdictions that use this model, a sentencing commission develops guidelines—based on the seriousness of the offense and the offender's prior criminal record—that judges are required to use in determining the appropriate sentence. Judges are allowed to depart from the guidelines and impose a more or less severe sentence than the guidelines require, but they must provide a written justification for doing so. The judge's decision to depart either upward or downward can be appealed, generally to a state or federal appellate court. (See Box 7.3 for a discussion of recent Supreme Court cases that have reshaped the sentencing process.)

---

[4]The Bureau of Justice Assistance (2000) conducted a national survey of sentencing practices in the United States in 1993 and 1994. They classified 29 states and the District of Columbia as having "primarily" indeterminate sentencing. (A few states use indeterminate sentences for some classes of offenses and determinate sentences for others.)

[5]The Bureau of Justice Assistance survey revealed that five states—Arizona, California, Illinois, Indiana, and Maine—used determinate sentencing.

[6]The Bureau of Justice Assistance (2000) categorized 16 states as having sentencing guidelines. Of these, 10 states had presumptive guidelines and 6 had advisory or voluntary guidelines.

BOX 7.3. THE SUPREME COURT'S OVERSIGHT OF THE SENTENCING PROCESS

Since 2000, a series of important decisions by the United States Supreme Court have reshaped the sentencing process, particularly in jurisdictions with determinate sentencing or sentencing guidelines. More to the point, these decisions, which rest on the Sixth Amendment right to trial by jury and the Due Process Clause of the Fifth and Fourteenth Amendments, have constrained the role of the judge and enhanced the role played by the jury.

The first ruling handed down by the Supreme Court was *Apprendi v. New Jersey* (530 U.S. 466 [2000]). This case involved an offender, Charles Apprendi, Jr., who fired several shots into the home of a black family. At the time of his arrest, Apprendi made a number of statements, which he later retracted, suggesting that he had fired into the home because he did not want the family living in his neighborhood. Apprendi pled guilty to possession of a weapon for an unlawful purpose, which carried a term of imprisonment of 5 to 10 years. The prosecutor then filed a motion for an enhanced sentence under the New Jersey hate crime statute. The judge in the case found by a preponderance of the evidence that the shooting was racially motivated and sentenced Apprendi to 12 years in prison. Apprendi appealed, claiming that the Due Process Clause of the Constitution required the state to prove the allegation of bias to the jury beyond a reasonable doubt. The Supreme Court ruled in Apprendi's favor, stating that any fact that increases the penalty for a crime beyond the prescribed statutory maximum, other than the fact of a prior conviction, must be submitted to a jury and proved beyond a reasonable doubt. In 2002 the Justices similarly ruled that a jury—not a judge—must find the aggravating circumstances necessary for imposition of the death penalty (*Ring v. Arizona*, 536 U.S. 584 [2002]).

The Court reiterated this position in subsequent decisions involving defendants who were challenging sentences imposed under state and federal sentencing guidelines. In 2004, for example, the court ruled in *Blakely v. Washington* (542 U.S. 296 [2004]) that the judge's decision to impose a sentence more severe than the statutory maximum allowed under the Washington sentencing guidelines violated the defendant's Sixth Amendment right to trial by jury.

The Court revisited this issue six months later. This time the issue was the power of federal judges to impose sentences more severe than called for under the United States sentencing guidelines. In *United States v. Booker* (543 U.S. 220 [2005]), the Court ruled, consistent with its decisions in *Apprendi* and *Blakely*, that the jury must determine beyond a reasonable doubt any fact that increases the defendant's sentence beyond the maximum sentence allowed under the sentencing guidelines. The facts in this case were similar to those in *Blakely*. Booker was found guilty of a drug offense that, under the guidelines, carried a sentence of 210 to 262 months. At the sentencing hearing, however, the judge found additional

(Continued)

(Continued)

facts that justified a harsher sentence; he sentenced Booker to 360 months in prison. The court held that the 30-year sentence imposed by the judge violated the Sixth Amendment right to a jury trial and ordered the District Court either to sentence Booker within the sentencing range supported by the jury's findings or to hold a separate sentencing hearing before a jury. The Court also ruled that the federal sentencing guidelines were advisory, not mandatory.

The final decision handed down by the Supreme Court (at least as of early 2011) was *Cunningham v. California* (549 U.S. 270 [2007]), which addressed sentences imposed under California's determinate sentencing law. The California law at issue allowed judges to choose one of three specified sentences for people convicted of particular offenses. The judge was supposed to choose the middle term unless there were aggravating or mitigating circumstances that justified imposing the higher or lower terms. In this case, the judge sentenced John Cunningham to the higher term, based on six aggravating circumstances that the judge found by a preponderance of the evidence during a posttrial sentencing hearing. In striking down Cunningham's sentence, the Court stated that it had "repeatedly held that, under the Sixth Amendment, any fact that exposes a defendant to a greater potential sentence must be found by a jury, not a judge, and established beyond a reasonable doubt, not merely by a preponderance of the evidence."

In the *Cunningham* case, the Supreme Court also explained how states with structured sentencing procedures could comply with the Court's rulings. One way is to require the prosecutor to include facts which increase the defendant's sentence exposure in the charging document and then requiring the jury—either at trial or in a post-conviction sentencing hearing—to find these facts beyond a reasonable doubt. This is the approach taken by most jurisdictions with legally binding guidelines (Frase, 2007, p. 426). Another remedy is to permit judges to exercise broad discretion within a statutory sentencing range; in this situation, the judge does not need to show that there are aggravating factors that justify a sentence at the top of the range. This is the approach taken by California; under SB 40, which Governor Arnold Schwarzenegger signed into law in April of 2007, the judge in each case can choose between the lower, middle, or upper term provided by the law for the particular crime.

The Supreme Court's decisions in these sentencing cases enhance the role played by the jury in both capital and non-capital cases. The decisions emphasize that the jury, not the judge, is to determine the facts in the case; that juries must determine the existence of aggravating factors that justify the imposition of the death penalty; and that sentences cannot exceed the maximum sentence based on the facts that were admitted in a guilty plea or found by the jury.

Recent data on the types of sentences imposed on felony offenders reveal that most of these offenders are incarcerated; fewer than one third receive straight probation (i.e., probation only, not jail or prison followed by probation; Bureau of Justice Statistics, 2009b). In 2006, 41% of all offenders convicted of felonies in state courts were sentenced to prison, 28% were sentenced to jail, and 31% were placed on probation or given some other alternative to incarceration. The proportion of federal offenders sentenced to prison was even higher (Bureau of Justice Statistics, 2009a). In 2008, 78% of all federal offenders were sentenced to prison, 12% were placed on probation, and 3% were ordered to pay a fine. Incarceration, then, is a widely prescribed and frequently imposed sentencing option. In the United States, in fact, it is now the option of choice for offenders convicted of felonies in both state and federal courts.

Probation

The primary alternative to incarceration is **probation**. A straight probation sentence does not entail confinement in jail or prison.[7] Rather, the judge releases the offender into the community and imposes a set of conditions that the offender agrees to abide by. The conditions of probation typically include regular meetings with a probation officer and a requirement that the offender obey all laws; other conditions might include drug testing, substance abuse treatment, and enrollment in educational programs. The court retains control over the offender while he or she is on probation; if the offender violates the conditions of probation, the judge can modify the conditions or revoke the offender's probation and sentence the offender to jail or prison. Revocation of probation is more likely if the offender is arrested for a new offense, particularly a felony offense, than if the offender is cited for violating the conditions of probation.

Although the proliferation of statutes requiring mandatory minimum prison sentences has reduced the number of offenses for which probation is an option, judges retain wide discretion in deciding between prison and probation for offenses that are not subject to mandatory minimums. Most state statutes allow the judge to impose probation unless he or she believes that (1) the offender is likely to commit additional crimes if released, (2) the offender is in need of treatment that can be provided more effectively in jail or prison, or (3) probation would be inappropriate given the seriousness of the offender's crime. Probation was developed primarily as a means of diverting juvenile offenders and adults convicted of misdemeanors and nonviolent felonies from jail or prison, but it is not reserved for these minor crimes. In 2006, in fact, 23% of all offenders convicted of violent offenses in state courts were sentenced to probation (Bureau of Justice Statistics, 2009b).

Intermediate Sanctions

Although incarceration—in jail or in prison—and probation are the principal sentences imposed on criminal offenders in the United States, they are not the only sentencing options. Indeed, a variety of **intermediate sanctions** are available: boot camps, house arrest and electronic monitoring, day reporting centers, community service, restitution, and fines. These alternative punishments are intended to fill the void between routine probation and protracted imprisonment. They are designed to free up prison beds and "to provide a continuum of sanctions that satisfies the just deserts concern for proportionality in punishment" (Bureau of Justice Statistics, 2004, note 34). A detailed discussion of each of these alternatives is beyond the scope of this chapter. Instead, we provide a brief introduction to four intermediate sanctions: boot camps, house arrest and electronic monitoring, community service, and monetary penalties.

Correctional **boot camp**, or shock incarceration, programs target young, nonviolent felony offenders who do not have extensive prior criminal records (for a detailed description of correctional boot camps, see MacKenzie & Hebert, 1996). Modeled on the military boot camp, the correctional boot camp emphasizes strict discipline, military drill and ceremony, and hard labor and physical training. Most also provide substance

---

[7]This is in contrast to a mixed or a split sentence, which involves a term of incarceration followed by period of probation.

abuse counseling and educational and vocational training. Offenders selected for these programs, which typically last from three to six months, are separated from the general prison population. They live in barracks-style housing, address the guards by military titles, and are required to stand at attention and obey all orders.

Prison boot camps began in Georgia and Oklahoma in 1983. Today, these programs are found in more than half of the states. Most serve young adult males, but programs that target women and juvenile offenders are becoming increasingly popular (U.S. Justice Department, 2000). Most programs limit eligibility to offenders who are younger than 30 years of age, but some have a higher upper age limit. Georgia, which has one of the largest programs, admits offenders ages 17 to 35 years, and Massachusetts takes offenders as old as 40 years. About a third of the programs restrict eligibility to first offenders; the others admit first-time felony offenders or those without a prior prison sentence. Although the structure and focus of the programs vary widely, their primary goal is to divert young offenders from "a life outside the law using the same tactics successfully employed by the military to turn civilians into soldiers" (U.S. Justice Department, 2000, p. vii).

House arrest, with or without electronic monitoring, is an alternative sanction used primarily for nonviolent offenders. Offenders placed on house arrest, which is also referred to as home confinement, are ordered to remain at home for a designated period of time. They are allowed to leave only at specified times and for specific purposes—to obtain food or medical services, to meet with a probation officer, and, sometimes, to go to school or work. Both back-end and front-end programs exist. In some jurisdictions, such as Oklahoma, offenders are released early from jail or prison sentences if they agree to participate in a home confinement program. In other jurisdictions, such as Florida, house arrest is a front-end program in which offenders who otherwise would be sentenced to jail or prison are confined to their homes instead. Both types of programs "aim simultaneously to offer a community sentence that is seen as burdensome and intrusive . . . and to reduce pressure on overcrowded prisons and jails" (Morris & Tonry, 1990, p. 213).

Offenders who are placed on house arrest often are also subject to **electronic monitoring**, which is a means of ensuring that offenders are at home when they are supposed to be. The most popular system today is one in which the offender is fitted with a wrist or ankle bracelet that he or she wears 24 hours a day. The bracelet serves as a transmitter; it emits a constant radio signal to a home monitoring unit, which is attached to the offender's home phone. The monitoring unit informs the monitoring center when the offender enters and leaves the home; it also sends a message if the offender tampers with or attempts to remove the bracelet. The monitoring officer is informed if the offender deviates from the preapproved schedule—if, for example, the offender returns from school at 9 p.m. when he or she is expected at 4 p.m. Ideally, the officer responds immediately to a violation notice. The offender can be terminated from the program for tampering with the device, for repeated unauthorized absences from home, and for a variety of other violations.

An underused, but potentially important, intermediate sanction is the **community service** order. Rather than being sentenced to jail or placed on routine probation, offenders are ordered to perform a certain number of hours of unpaid work at schools, hospitals, parks, and other public and private nonprofit agencies. Thus, an accountant convicted of fraud might be sentenced to provide advice to poor taxpayers, a baseball player convicted of a drug offense might be required to lecture to junior high school students on the dangers of using drugs, and traffic offenders might be required to pick up trash along highways or in public parks.

Community service is not widely used as an alternative punishment in the United States. Here, the primary use of community service is as a condition of probation or as a punishment for minor traffic offenses. Judges' reluctance to use this alternative as a stand-alone sanction for misdemeanors and less serious felonies may reflect a belief that requiring an offender to perform community service is not adequate punishment for most crimes. Judges may believe, in other words, that removing graffiti or cleaning up parks for 200 hours is not as onerous as even a short stint in jail. Those who advocate wider use of intermediate sanctions disagree. They contend that community service should not be regarded as merely a slap on the wrist. Rather, it is a constructive and burdensome penalty "that is inexpensive to administer, that produces public value, and that can to a degree be scaled to the seriousness of crimes" (Tonry, 1996, p. 121).

Monetary penalties—fines, fees, and restitution to the victim—are frequently imposed on offenders convicted of misdemeanors and felonies in American courts. Every year, millions of offenders convicted of traffic offenses and less serious misdemeanors are ordered to pay fines that are to some degree calibrated to the seriousness of the crime. Offenders placed on probation are required to pay fees for probation supervision, for substance abuse treatment, for urinalysis, and for use of electronic monitoring equipment. And offenders who steal or damage someone else's property or cause physical or emotional injuries are ordered to pay restitution to the victim, often as a condition of probation.

Although these types of monetary penalties are common, their use as a stand-alone sentence is not. Fines, for example, are seldom used as an alternative to incarceration for offenders convicted of less serious felonies and are often used only in conjunction with probation for more serious misdemeanors. Although the fine is "unambiguously punitive" (McDonald, Greene, & Worzella, 1992, p. 1), studies reveal that judges do not regard it as a meaningful alternative to incarceration or probation (Cole, Mahoney, Thornton, & Hanson, 1987). Use of fines also poses dilemmas for the courts. If the amount of the fine is commensurate with the seriousness of the offense, with no consideration given to the ability of the offender to pay the fine, then fines will be relatively more burdensome to the poor than the rich. To avoid this potential problem, a number of jurisdictions use what is referred to as a **day fine**. Imported from Europe and Latin America, the day fine is calibrated both to the seriousness of the offense and to the offender's ability to pay. Rather than requiring all offenders convicted of shoplifting to pay $1,000, for example, judges determine how many punishment units each offender deserves. Typically, each punishment unit is equal to one day's pay or some fraction of one day's pay. Two offenders convicted of shoplifting might each be ordered to pay five punishment units, equal to five days' pay. If one offender earns $50 per day and the other earns $500 per day, the fines paid by the two offenders will differ; the first would pay $250, the second $2,500.

The day fine has obvious advantages over the traditional fine. Because it can be tailored more precisely to an offender's ability to pay, the day fine is more equitable. It also is more likely to be paid in full, which means that offenders are less likely to be called back to court or sentenced to jail for nonpayment. But there are disadvantages as well. Courts that use the day fine must define a unit of punishment other than time in jail or dollars to be paid, establish the range of units to be imposed on offenders convicted of various offenses, and devise a means of translating these units into dollars. Implementing a system of day fines, in other words, involves "changing—or, at least accommodating—existing habits, customs, and laws" (McDonald et al., 1992, p. 5).

The Future of Intermediate Sanctions

As we enter the second decade of the 21st century, prison, jail, and probation sentences remain the dominant form of punishment imposed on criminal offenders—especially those convicted of felonies. In fact, state and federal prison statistics suggest that the trend over time has been one of increasing reliance on imprisonment. In the United States, the rate of incarceration was relatively stable from 1925 through 1975, but it skyrocketed from 1980 to 2000. Despite stable or falling crime rates, the number of offenders incarcerated in state and federal prisons ballooned from 329,821 in 1980 to 1,381,892 in 2000—an increase of nearly 400%. At the turn of the century, 6.3 million people—3.1% of all adult residents—were on probation, in jail or prison, or on parole in the United States (U.S. Justice Department, 2001). Rather than replacing incarceration and probation with "a portfolio of intermediate punishments," the United States "has been engaged in an unprecedented imprisonment binge" during the past two decades (Austin & Irwin, 2001, p. 1).

The question, of course, is why this is so. Some scholars suggest that it can be attributed in large part to the public's fear of drugs and crime, which led to a movement for more punitive sentences for felony offenders in general and for drug offenders in particular (Austin & Irwin, 2001, pp. 4–7). Others contend that the **imprisonment binge** reflects a view on the part of judges and policy makers that only imprisonment counts as punishment. Michael Tonry (1996), for example, suggested that this emphasis on absolute severity "frustrates efforts to devise intermediate sanctions for the psychological (not to mention political) reason that few other sanctions seem commensurable with a multiyear prison sentence" (p. 128). If, in other words, the philosophy of just deserts demands that felony offenders be punished harshly, and only incarceration is regarded as harsh punishment, then nonincarceration sentences will be viewed as inappropriately lenient. Unless these attitudes change, it seems unlikely that intermediate sanctions will play anything more than a supporting role in sentencing policies and practices in the United States.

How Do Judges Decide? Modeling the Sentencing Process

Every day, in state and federal courts throughout the United States, judges must determine the appropriate punishment for offenders convicted of crimes. They must fashion sentences that fit offenders and their crimes. But how do judges arrive at these decisions? What factors do they consider as they attempt to decide whether an offender should be sentenced to prison and, if so, the length of time that he or she should be incarcerated? Do sentences depend on the nature of the crime or the characteristics of the offender and victim? If so, which are most important? In this section, we address these questions. Our goal is to explain how judges decide—that is, how judges arrive at the appropriate sentence for a particular offender.

Modeling the Sentencing Process

Researchers have conducted dozens of studies designed to enhance people's understanding of judges' sentencing decisions and to identify the factors that predict sentence outcomes. These studies generally use one of two different approaches. Some researchers present judges with a set of hypothetical cases and ask each judge to indicate the sentence that he or she would impose (see, e.g., Cook, 1973; Clancy, Bartolomeo, Richardson, & Wellford, 1981; Ewart & Pennington, 1997; Forst & Wellford, 1981; Kapardis & Farrington, 1982; Spohn & Horney, 1991). The judge also might be asked to explain why he or she imposed a certain sentence. The advantage of this approach is that each judge is making decisions about identical cases; the researcher can determine whether sentences are consistent from one judge to another and can isolate the characteristics of cases (and judges) that affect sentence severity. The main disadvantage of this approach is that the researcher can include only a limited amount of information about each hypothetical case and cannot ask each judge to respond to hundreds, or even dozens, of cases. The hypothetical cases, therefore, may not reflect the reality of the sentencing process. Related to this, the decision-making context is artificial; judges are making sentencing decisions about hypothetical—not real—defendants.

A second, and more common, approach is to collect data on actual cases decided by judges in a particular jurisdiction (examples of this approach include Albonetti, 1997; Britt, 2000; Spohn & Holleran, 2000; Steffensmeier, Kramer, & Ulmer, 1995; Steffensmeier et al., 1998; Ulmer, 1997). Researchers collect information about the crime, the offender, and the case from court files or electronic databases. They analyze the data using statistical techniques that allow them to isolate the effect of one factor—the offender's prior criminal record, for example—while controlling for other factors that influence sentence severity—crime seriousness, the offender's background characteristics, whether the offender pled guilty or went to trial, whether the offender was free on bond or detained in jail prior to trial, whether the offender had a private attorney or a public defender, and so on. Researchers typically separately analyze the decision to incarcerate or not and the length of sentence imposed on those who are incarcerated. They assert that sentencing is, in fact, a two-stage process: Judges first decide whether the offender should be incarcerated and then decide how long the sentence should be. They also argue that different case attributes may affect each decision.[8]

In studying the sentencing process, researchers typically differentiate between legally relevant and legally irrelevant factors. Legally relevant factors are case characteristics and offender attributes that judges are legally authorized to take into consideration. Included would be such things as the statutory seriousness of the charge(s); the number of charges; use of a weapon; the age of the victim; the extent of injury to the victim; and the offender's prior criminal record and current legal status. Legally irrelevant factors are case characteristics and offender attributes that judges either are legally prohibited from taking into consideration or that bear no rational relationship to the purposes of sentencing. Race or ethnicity, gender, and social class obviously are legally irrelevant. Both the Equal Protection Clause of the Fourteenth Amendment and state and federal civil rights laws prohibit racial, gender, and class discrimination. Thus, judges are not supposed to consider the offender's (or the victim's) race or ethnicity, gender, or social class.

The categorization of other offender characteristics is more problematic. Is employment status legally relevant? What about age or education? Marital status and responsibility for dependent children? Some jurisdictions allow judges to consider these offender characteristics; other jurisdictions explicitly prohibit judges from considering them. The Illinois Criminal Code (730 ILSC 5/5-5-3.1, Illinois Compiled Statutes Annotated), for example, states that judges, in deciding whether to sentence the offender to prison or not, should consider a number of mitigating factors, including whether imprisonment would entail excessive hardship to the offender's dependents. In contrast, the Minnesota sentencing guidelines explicitly prohibit consideration of the offender's employment status, and the federal sentencing guidelines state that the offender's age, education, mental and emotional conditions, history of alcohol or drug abuse, employment history, family ties and responsibilities, and community ties are "not ordinarily relevant in determining whether a sentence should be outside the applicable guideline range" (U.S. Sentencing Commission, n.d., Part H, §§5H1.1-5H1.6). Offender characteristics other than race and ethnicity, gender, and social class, then, may be legally relevant or irrelevant, depending on the laws in the jurisdiction.

Offense Seriousness and Prior Record

Studies of judges' sentencing decisions reveal that these decisions are based, first and most important, on the seriousness of the offense and the offender's prior criminal record (Albonetti, 1997; Spohn & DeLone, 2000; Steffensmeier et al., 1998; Ulmer, 1997). Offenders who commit more serious crimes are sentenced more harshly than those who commit less serious crimes. Offenders with more extensive criminal histories receive more severe sentences than those with shorter criminal histories. As the National Academy of Sciences Panel on Sentencing Research concluded in 1983, offense seriousness and prior criminal record are the "key determinants of sentences" (Blumstein et al., 1983, p. 83).

---

[8]Research has shown, for example, that prior criminal record is a better predictor of the decision to incarcerate or not than of sentence length (see Spohn et al., 1981) and that offender characteristics have a stronger effect on the decision to incarcerate than on length of sentence (see Chiricos & Crawford, 1995; Spohn, 2000).

This is not surprising. Legislators devise penal codes or sentencing guidelines based explicitly on these two factors. Offenders who commit more serious crimes or who repeat their crimes are legally eligible for more punishment than are first offenders or those who commit less serious crimes. Moreover, judges who see retribution as the primary purpose of punishment believe that sentences should be proportionate to the seriousness of the crime and the culpability of the offender. Even utilitarian judges would not contend that these two factors are irrelevant to the sentence that should be imposed. Judges, in other words, are legally and morally justified in taking crime seriousness and prior record into account in making sentencing decisions.

There are a number of ways to measure crime seriousness and criminal history. Crime seriousness, for example, might be defined by the type of crime (e.g., armed robbery or drug trafficking); the statutory classification of the crime (e.g., first-degree felony, second-degree misdemeanor); whether the offender used a gun; the degree of injury to the victim; the amount of property stolen; whether the offender victimized a stranger or a nonstranger; and so on. Similarly, there are a number of indicators of the offender's criminal history that judges might take into consideration: whether the offender had previously been convicted of a misdemeanor or felony, whether the offender had ever been convicted of a violent crime, whether the offender was on probation or parole at the time of arrest for the current crime, or whether the offender's crimes were increasing in frequency or seriousness. Researchers often include multiple indicators of these legally relevant variables in their models of the sentencing process.

Regardless of the way in which they are measured, there is compelling evidence that crime seriousness and prior criminal record are important determinants of sentence severity. Research consistently reveals that judges impose harsher sentences on offenders who commit more serious crimes and who have more serious prior criminal records.

Offender Characteristics

Prior criminal record is not the only offender characteristic that affects judges' sentencing decisions. Studies have shown that the sentences offenders receive may depend on their demographic characteristics (gender, age, and race or ethnicity), their socioeconomic status (education and income), and their social stability (employment history, marital status, responsibility for dependent children, history of drug or alcohol abuse). There is evidence, for example, that men are sentenced more harshly than women (Daly & Bordt, 1995; Daly & Tonry, 1997; Steffensmeier, Kramer, & Streifel, 1993), that young adults are sentenced more harshly than either teenagers or older adults (Spohn & Holleran 2000; Steffensmeier et al., 1995; Steffensmeier et al., 1998), and that blacks and Hispanics are sentenced more harshly than whites (Chiricos & Crawford, 1995; Spohn, Gruhl, & Welch, 1981). In fact, two studies concluded that the harshest sentences are imposed on young black and Hispanic males (Spohn & Holleran, 2001; Steffensmeier et al., 1998). There also is evidence that the offender's education (Albonetti, 1997), income (Smith, 1991), and employment status (Nobiling, Spohn, & DeLone, 1998) affect sentence severity: Harsher sentences are imposed on the less educated, the poor, and the unemployed.

There are relatively few studies that test for the effects of offender characteristics such as marital status, responsibility for dependent children, or a history of drug or alcohol abuse. Kathleen Daly's (1987, 1989) research on gender bias in sentencing suggests that judges take offenders' family circumstances into consideration in making pretrial release and sentencing decisions. Daly found that defendants who were living with a spouse, living with parents or other relatives, or caring for young children were treated more leniently than "non-familied" defendants. According to Daly (1989), this more lenient treatment of familied defendants reflects judges' beliefs that these offenders have more informal social controls in their lives, as well as judges' concerns about maintaining families and protecting innocent children, which she labels the "social costs of punishment" (p. 138).

In summary, judges appear to take offenders' background characteristics into consideration when determining the appropriate sentence. Race and ethnicity, gender, and social class clearly are illegitimate considerations; judges are legally precluded from using these "suspect classifications" in sentencing. Indicators of the offender's social stability or measures of the degree to which the offender has informal social control in his or her life, on the other hand, may be legally or practically relevant. Judges who believe that punishment serves purposes other than retribution and who therefore attempt to individualize sentences may believe that the offender's social and economic circumstances are not irrelevant. Michael Tonry (1995) contended that judges ought to consider offenders' social and economic disadvantages at sentencing. He argued that allowing judges to use "social adversity" as a mitigating consideration is not incompatible with a "just sentencing system." In fact, he called for the repeal of all sentencing policies "that forbid mitigation of sentences on grounds of the offenders' personal characteristics or special circumstances" (pp. 154, 195). He argued that these policies "damage disadvantaged and minority offenders, especially those who have to some degree overcome dismal life chances" (p. 195).

Characteristics of the Victim

In attempting to determine the appropriate sentence, do judges consider the characteristics of the victim or the behavior of the victim at the time of the crime? Are offenders who victimize whites, especially white women, treated differently than those who victimize blacks? Are offenders who victimize strangers sentenced differently than those who victimize relatives, friends, or intimate partners? Do judges mitigate the sentence if the victim "provoked" or "precipitated" the crime?

Evidence regarding the effect of victim characteristics on sentence severity comes primarily from research regarding the imposition of the death penalty and from research examining sexual assault case outcomes. There is a substantial body of research demonstrating that blacks who murder whites are much more likely to be sentenced to death than blacks who murder blacks or whites who murder blacks or whites (Baldus, Woodworth, & Pulaski, 1990; Gross & Mauro, 1989; Paternoster, 1984). The most widely cited of these studies found that defendants convicted of killing whites in Georgia were over four times as likely to receive a death sentence as defendants convicted of killing blacks (Baldus et al., 1990). Baldus and his colleagues also found that blacks who killed whites had the greatest likelihood of receiving the death penalty. There also are a number of studies that found that black men convicted of sexually assaulting white women are sentenced more harshly than other race-of-offender/race-of-victim pairs (LaFree, 1989; Spohn, 1994; Walsh, 1987).

Other evidence of the role played by victim characteristics is found in research examining the legal processing of sexual assault cases. This research provides evidence that supports the claims of feminist theorists, who assert that outcomes of rape cases reflect decision makers' beliefs about acceptable and unacceptable behavior by women or their stereotypes of sexual assault. Although sentences in sexual assault cases, like those in other types of cases, are strongly influenced by legally relevant factors such as the seriousness of the crime and the offender's prior criminal record, victim characteristics also come into play. A number of studies, for example, revealed that sexual assault case-processing decisions—including decisions regarding sentence severity—are affected by the victim's age, occupation, and education (Kingsnorth, MacIntosh, & Wentworth, 1999; McCahill, Meyer, & Fischman, 1979); by "risk-taking" behavior, such as hitchhiking, drinking, or using drugs (Kingsnorth et al., 1999; Spohn & Spears, 1996); and by the reputation of the victim (McCahill et al., 1979). Sexual assault case outcomes also are affected by the relationship between the victim and the offender: Men convicted of sexually assaulting women who are strangers to them are sentenced more harshly than men convicted of sexually assaulting women who are relatives or friends (Kingsnorth et al., 1999; Spohn & Spears, 1996).

In summary, victim characteristics affect the sentences that judges impose. Offenders who murder or sexually assault whites—particularly blacks who murder or sexually assault whites—are sentenced more harshly than offenders who murder or sexually assault blacks. The sentences imposed on offenders convicted of sexual assault are less severe if the victim's character, reputation, or behavior suggest that he or she is not a "genuine victim."

Case Processing Factors

Three case-processing attributes have been linked to sentence severity: the type of disposition (plea vs. trial), the defendant's pretrial status (released or in custody prior to trial), and the type of attorney representing the defendant (private attorney vs. public defender). Critics of the sentencing process charge that defendants who plead guilty are treated more leniently than those who are tried by a judge or jury, that defendants who are released pending trial are sentenced more leniently than those who are detained in jail prior to trial, and that defendants represented by a private attorney receive more lenient sentences than those represented by a public defender. Some critics (Holmes, Hosch, Daudistel, Perez, & Graves, 1996) suggest that these findings reflect discrimination against the poor. That is, indigent defendants who are unable to make bail or hire an attorney to defend them are sentenced more harshly than nonindigent defendants.

Although there is little evidence that defendants represented by public defenders receive harsher sentences than those represented by private attorneys, studies of sentencing outcomes reveal that both the type of disposition in the case and the defendant's pretrial status affect sentence severity. Evidence of a **trial penalty** or **jury tax** comes from studies conducted in both federal and state courts. Two studies of sentences imposed on drug offenders in U.S. District Courts, for example, found that pleading guilty reduced both the likelihood of a prison sentence and the length of sentence imposed on offenders who were incarcerated (Albonetti, 1997; Kautt & Spohn, 2002). Research in Pennsylvania also uncovered a substantial trial penalty (Steffensmeier & Hebert, 1999). Defendants tried by a jury were 25% more likely than those who pled guilty to be sentenced to prison; they also received prison sentences that averaged 19 months longer than those imposed on defendants who pled guilty.

A number of studies also demonstrated that offenders held in jail prior to trial get harsher sentences than those who are released pending trial. A study of sentencing decisions in two Florida counties, for example, found that defendants who were held in jail prior to trial were significantly more likely to be incarcerated following conviction, even after controlling for other predictors of sentence severity (Chiricos & Bales, 1991). Moreover, pretrial detention increased the odds of incarceration for offenders convicted of drug offenses, property crimes, and violent crimes. A study of sentencing decisions in Chicago, Miami, and Kansas City reached a similar conclusion (Spohn & DeLone, 2000). In each city, offenders who were released prior to trial faced substantially lower odds of imprisonment than those who were detained. In Chicago, the probability of incarceration for offenders who were released was 41.7% less than the probability for offenders who were in custody. The difference in the probability of imprisonment was 32.0% in Kansas City and 10.2% in Miami. The harsher sentences imposed on offenders detained prior to trial may reflect that defendants held in jail in the months prior to trial are less able to assist in their own defense or that judges and jurors assume that defendants locked up prior to trial are more dangerous and pose greater risks than those who are free.

⊠ Summary: Sentencing—An Inexact Science

The sentencing decision results from a process of gathering and interpreting information about the offense and the offender. Judges use this information to evaluate the harm done by the crime and to paint a portrait of the offender. As John Hogarth (1971) wrote more than 30 years ago, sentencing "is a cognitive process in which information concerning the offender, the offense, and the surrounding circumstances is read, organized in relation to other information and integrated into an overall assessment of the case" (p. 279).

As they attempt to fashion sentences that fit individual offenders and struggle to impose just punishments, judges consider the harm done by the crime, the blameworthiness and culpability of the offender, and the offender's potential for reform and rehabilitation. Their assessment of harm rests squarely on the nature and seriousness of the crime. It rests on both the statutory seriousness of the offense and the gravity and consequences of the crime. Thus, armed robbers will be sentenced more harshly than those who steal cars or write bad checks, and offenders who use deadly weapons or inflict serious injuries on their victims will receive more severe punishment than those who do not. Similarly, offenders who play a primary role in a crime will be punished more harshly than accomplices or those who play secondary roles. The punishment imposed by the judge, in other words, will be proportionate to the harm done by the crime; the punishment will "fit the crime."

Judges also attempt to fashion sentences that fit the offender. Judges' evaluation of the offender rests primarily, but not exclusively, on the offender's prior criminal record. In attempting to understand the offender, assess the offender's blameworthiness, and predict his or her future dangerousness, the judge examines not only the offender's past criminal behavior, but also the offender's life history and current circumstances. The judge considers the offender's educational history, family and work situation, community ties, and conduct since the arrest. The judge also attempts to determine the offender's motivation for the crime, the extent to which the offender feels remorse for his or her behavior, and the degree to which the offender cooperated in the prosecution of his or her (or another's) case. Assessing the offender in this way "allows judges to make substantial and refined distinctions between offenders who might appear quite similar if one looked only at the legal wrong committed and the harm it caused" (Wheeler, Mann, & Sarat, 1988, p. 120).

To tailor sentences to the facts and circumstances of each case, the judge needs detailed information about the crime and the offender. Although cases tried before a jury may provide the judge with this needed information, most convictions result from guilty pleas, not trials. Thus, the judge may know little more about the case than the facts necessary to support a guilty plea. A presentence investigation might fill in some of the details about the crime and offender, but the offender might waive the investigation or the probation department might conduct a cursory review. And if the prosecutor and the defense attorney have negotiated a deal that affects the sentence, the judge may believe that gathering additional information about the case would be a waste of the court's resources. Consequently, the judge may have incomplete information about the crime and the offender.

That the information judges have is typically incomplete and the predictions they are required to make are uncertain helps explain why offender characteristics—including the legally irrelevant characteristics of race, gender, and social class—influence sentencing decisions. Because they don't have all the information they need to fashion sentences to fit crimes and offenders, judges may resort to stereotypes of dangerousness and threat that are linked to offender characteristics (Hawkins, 1981). Thus, men may be perceived as more dangerous than women, younger offenders may be regarded as more crime prone than older offenders, gang members may be viewed as more threatening than people not in gangs, the unemployed may be seen as more likely to recidivate than the employed, and those who abuse drugs or alcohol may be viewed as less amenable to rehabilitation that those who abstain from drugs or alcohol. Similarly, racial minorities—particularly those who are also male, young, members of gangs, and unemployed—may be seen as more dangerous and threatening than whites. Judges use these perceptions to simplify and routinize the decision-making process and to reduce the uncertainty inherent in sentencing. As a result, men may be sentenced more harshly than women, blacks and Hispanics may be sentenced more harshly than whites, the unemployed may be sentenced more harshly than the employed, and so on.

The sentences judges impose also may reflect their part in the courtroom workgroup (Eisenstein & Jacob, 1977) or courthouse community (Eisenstein et al., 1988), with common goals and shared expectations about how cases should be handled and the types of sentences that should be imposed. The members of the courtroom workgroup, for example, may believe that efficiency demands a high rate of guilty pleas; consequently, plea bargaining is encouraged, and defendants who cooperate by pleading guilty are rewarded. The members of the courthouse community also may believe that there are "**normal penalties**" (Sudnow, 1965) or "**going rates**" (Eisenstein et al., 1988, pp. 30–31) for particular types of crimes or particular types of offenders. They may agree on the appropriate penalty for the run-of-the-mill burglary or for the offender who repeatedly appears in court on drug charges. Because judges are concerned about maintaining relationships with other members of the courtroom workgroup and ensuring the smooth flow of cases through the criminal justice system, these expectations will constrain their discretion and affect the sentences they impose.

The ambiguity and uncertainty inherent in the sentencing process, coupled with judges' considerable discretion in deciding what a sentence will be, means that one cannot conclusively determine how a judge arrived at a particular sentence in a particular case. Judges' sentencing decisions rest to a considerable degree on their assessments of harm and blameworthiness and their predictions of dangerousness, but one doesn't know with certainty how these assessments and predictions are made. Sentencing, in other words, is an inexact science.

KEY TERMS

Boot camp	Going rate/normal penalty	Rehabilitation
Collective incapacitation	Guided discretion statute	Restorative justice
Community service	House arrest	Retributive justification for punishment
Day fine	Incapacitation	
Determinate sentence	Indeterminate sentence	Selective incapacitation
Deterrence	Intermediate sanction	Specific deterrence
Electronic monitoring	Mandatory sentence	Trial penalty/jury tax
General deterrence	Probation	Utilitarian justifications for punishment

DISCUSSION QUESTIONS

1. How would a judge using a retributive justification for punishment answer the following question: Why do we punish those who violate the law? How would a judge using a utilitarian justification answer the question?

2. According to retributive theory, why do those who violate the law deserve to be punished?

3. What are the most common types of sentences imposed by judges in state and federal courts in the United States? Why are intermediate sanctions used so infrequently?

4. How do researchers model the sentencing process?

5. What are the key determinants of judges' sentencing decisions? Why are these two factors so important?

6. Should judges take the characteristics of the victim or the relationship between the victim and the offender into consideration when determining the appropriate punishment? Why or why not? According to research on the death penalty and on sentencing decisions in sexual assault cases, do judges take these factors into account?

7. Is it legitimate for judges to impose a trial penalty or jury tax on defendants who refuse to plead guilty? What are the arguments in favor of the trial penalty? Against the trial penalty?

8. Why is sentencing referred to as an inexact science? Could it be made more exact? Should it be?

WEB RESOURCES

Publications and Reports from the National Criminal Justice Reference: http://www.ncjrs.gov/App/Publications/alphaList.aspx?alpha=S

Sentencing and Corrections in the 21st Century, National Criminal Justice Reference Service: http://www.ncjrs.gov/pdffiles1/nij/grants/189089.pdf

READING

During the past two decades, the number of women incarcerated in state and federal prisons has increased dramatically: 107,518 women were under the jurisdiction of state and federal authorities in 2005, compared to only 12,331 in 1980 (Bureau of Justice Statistics, 2006a, p. 4). Much of this growth in women's imprisonment is attributed not to an increase in the seriousness of crimes women commit but to the crime control policies pursued during the past three decades. Some scholars suggest that these policies had a particularly pronounced effect on women. Meda Chesney-Lind (1997), for example, contended that public calls to get tough on crime, "coupled with a legal system that now espouses 'equality' for women with a vengeance when it comes to the punishment of crime, has resulted in a much greater use of imprisonment in response to women's crime" (p. 251).

A number of authors suggest that recent increases in the number of women incarcerated in state and federal prisons can be traced directly to the War on Drugs and the resultant emphasis on increasing the penalties for possession and sale of drugs (Chesney-Lind, 1995). Data on incarcerated offenders support this assertion. Surveys of state prison inmates, for example, revealed that the number of women incarcerated for drug offenses increased from 2,400 in 1986 to 12,600 in 1991, an increase of 432%. Among offenders committed to state prisons in 2002, 37.1% of the women, but only 29.7% of the men, were convicted of drug offenses (Bureau of Justice Statistics, 2003, Table 4). Among offenders incarcerated in federal prisons in 2003, 63.3% of the black women and 65.5% of the white women were committed for a drug offense (U.S. Justice Department, 2004, p. 519).

Citing evidence such as this, Chesney-Lind (1997) concluded that the "'war on drugs' has translated into a war on women" (p. 111). Other scholars have made analogous arguments. Noting that the increase of women in prison has been fueled by the war on drugs, Durham (1994) suggested that "women who had previously been the beneficiary of more lenient sentencing . . . are now being treated like their male counterparts, or even more harshly" (p. 111). Daly and Tonry (1997) similarly contended that reformers' attempts to enhance gender equality in sentencing, "coupled with the War on Drugs and the law-and-order campaigns of the 1980s, has yielded dramatically increasing incarceration rates" (p. 241).

These statements imply that chivalrous or paternalistic treatment of women offenders is a thing of the past. More to the point, they imply that equal treatment of men and women offenders, particularly for drug offenses, has resulted in spectacular increases in the female prison population. The article by Spohn and Beichner assesses the validity of these arguments. They also addressed another important issue—whether preferential treatment of women offenders is reserved for white women.

AUTHORS' NOTE: This article is based on work supported by the National Science Foundation under Grant SBR-93321852. Points of view are those of the authors and do not necessarily represent the position of the National Science Foundation.

SOURCE: Spohn, C., & Beichner, D. (2000). Is preferential treatment of female offenders a thing of the past? A multisite study of gender, race, and imprisonment. *Criminal Justice Policy Review, 11*(2), 149–184.

Is Preferential Treatment of Female Offenders a Thing of the Past?

A Multisite Study of Gender, Race, and Imprisonment

Cassia Spohn and Dawn Beichner

During the past decade, the number of women incarcerated in state and federal prisons has increased dramatically: 79,624 women were under the jurisdiction of state and federal authorities in 1997 compared to only 23,115 in 1985 (Bureau of Justice Statistics, 1998). Much of this growth in women's imprisonment is attributed not to an increase in the seriousness of crimes women commit but to the crime control policies pursued during the past 20 years. A number of authors suggest that these policies, which produced an "unprecedented imprisonment binge" (Irwin & Austin, 1997, p. 1), had a particularly pronounced effect on women. Chesney-Lind (1997), for example, contends that public calls to get tough on crime, "coupled with a legal system that now espouses 'equality' for women with a vengeance when it comes to the punishment of crime, has resulted in a much greater use of imprisonment in response to women's crime" (p. 151). Durham (1994) similarly asserts that "women who had previously been the beneficiary of more lenient sentencing...are now being treated like their male counterparts, or even more harshly" (p. 111).

Assertions such as these imply that chivalry is a thing of the past. They suggest that contemporary case-processing decisions are gender neutral and that female offenders are treated no differently than similarly situated male offenders. This study uses data on offenders convicted of felonies in Chicago, Miami, and Kansas City to address this issue. We test the hypothesis that female and male offenders will face similar odds of incarceration once controls for crime seriousness, prior record, and other legal factors are taken into consideration.

The purpose of this study, however, is not simply to add another voice to the debate over the existence of preferential treatment of female offenders in the criminal justice system. Although we do attempt to determine whether female offenders are treated more leniently than are male offenders, we believe that this is a theoretically unsophisticated and incomplete approach to a complex phenomenon. Similar to Wonders (1996), we believe that the more interesting question is, "When does the particular social characteristic matter—under what circumstances, for whom, and in interaction with what other factors?" (p. 617). Similar to Steffensmeier, Kramer, and Streifel (1993) and Steffensmeier, Ulmer, and Kramer (1998), we believe that it is particularly important to explore the possibility of interaction between the offender's race and gender. As explained in more detail below, there is a growing body of literature suggesting that judges' sentencing decisions reflect attributions of blameworthiness, dangerousness, and threat, and that these attributions themselves reflect the intersections among defendant characteristics such as gender, race, age, employment status, and family situation. We therefore test for interaction between offender gender and offender race/ethnicity. We also explore the possibility that the effects of the legal and extralegal predictors of incarceration depend on or are conditioned by gender.

 ## Previous Research on Gender and Case-Processing Decisions

Research investigating the effect of gender on criminal justice case-processing decisions has produced inconsistent findings (for reviews of this literature, see Daly & Bordt, 1995; Daly & Tonry, 1997; Steffensmeier et al., 1993).

Some studies find that female defendants are treated more leniently than are male defendants, a result that often is attributed to paternalism or chivalry on the part of criminal justice officials (Albonetti, 1997; Curran, 1983; Daly, 1987, 1994; Frazier, Bock, & Henretta, 1980; Gruhl, Welch, & Spohn, 1984; Johnston, Kennedy, & Shuman, 1987; Miethe & Moore, 1986; Myers & Talarico, 1986; Nagel & Hagan, 1982; Spohn, Gruhl, & Welch, 1987; Spohn & Spears, 1997; Steffensmeier et al., 1993, 1998; Zingraff & Thomsen, 1984). Other studies, in accord with the so-called evil woman thesis, conclude that women, particularly those who commit the more "masculine" violent crimes, are treated either no differently or more harshly than are men who commit these crimes (Bernstein, Kelly, & Doyle, 1977; Farnworth & Horan, 1980; Nagel & Hagan, 1983; Rasche, 1975). These contradictory findings have led to conclusions that "evidence on the role of sex in sentencing is only preliminary" (Blumstein, Cohen, Martin, & Tonry, 1983, p. 17) and to suggestions that findings of leniency in the treatment of female defendants may be "misleading" (Daly & Tonry, 1997, p. 230) because of theoretical and/ or methodological shortcomings in the existing research.

Recent reviews of research on gender and sentencing decisions (Daly & Bordt, 1995; Daly & Tonry, 1997; Steffensmeier et al., 1993, 1998) highlight these conceptual and methodological limitations. The extant research has been criticized for its reliance on vague and inadequately articulated explanations of differential treatment of men and women. As Daly and Tonry (1997) note, concepts such as chivalry, paternalism, and evil women "lack an empirical referent and analytical bite" (p. 234). Similar to Steffensmeier and his colleagues (1993), they assert that judges who sentence female offenders more leniently than similarly situated male offenders may be motivated more by beliefs regarding blameworthiness and by concerns about the social costs of incarcerating women than by paternalism or stereotypes of sex-appropriate behavior. Daly and Tonry (1997) further suggest that researchers consider whether "gender-linked criteria" such as responsibility for dependent children and reform potential "are embedded in decisions and whether such criteria are warranted or not" (p. 232).

Methodological limitations of the existing research also have been noted. Steffensmeier et al. (1993), for example, challenge the oft-cited conclusion that female defendants receive preferential treatment, noting that methodological problems, coupled with "the ambiguity in the findings reported, cloud the issue" (p. 439). Studies have been faulted for their failure to control adequately for important legal variables such as crime seriousness and prior record, failure to control for "gender-linked criteria" (Daly & Tonry, 1997, p. 232) such as family status or pregnancy, and poor conceptualization and operationalization of the dependent variables (especially the sentencing decision). They also have been criticized for their use of bivariate rather than multivariate statistical techniques, reliance on data sets from the 1960s and 1970s, and failure to test for interaction between offender race and gender.

The findings of recent studies (Daly, 1987, 1989, 1994; Spohn & Spears, 1997; Steffensmeier et al., 1993, 1998) comparing case outcomes for male and female defendants, each of which attempted to address at least some of the limitations outlined above, confirm that the issue of gender discrimination in the criminal justice system is far from settled. Each of these more methodologically sophisticated studies used different research designs and analytical approaches and each reached somewhat different conclusions.

Spohn and Spears (1997) used data on defendants charged with violent felonies in Detroit to examine the effect of gender and race on a series of charging, convicting, and sentencing decisions. Building on research suggesting that chivalry is denied to women who violate sex-role stereotypes and commit violent crimes, they hypothesized that men and women charged with these crimes would be treated similarly. They found that women were more likely than men to have all of the charges against them dismissed; women also were less likely to be incarcerated and received shorter prison sentences than did their male counterparts. Further analysis revealed an interaction between race and gender: White women, but not Black women, were more likely than men of either race to have their charges dismissed, and Black women were sentenced less harshly than either Black men or White men. The authors conclude (Spohn & Spears, 1997) that their results "highlight the importance of testing an interactive model that incorporates the effects of both gender and race" (p. 52).

The importance of testing for interaction effects also is illustrated by two recent studies of sentencing in Pennsylvania (Steffensmeier et al., 1993, 1998). Steffensmeier et al. (1993) used guideline sentencing data to assess the effect of gender on the decision to incarcerate and the length of the prison sentence; they also examined departures from the guidelines and judges' reasons for these departures. They found that female offenders faced somewhat lower odds of incarceration than did male offenders (a difference of 12 percentage points) but that gender did not affect the length of the prison sentence. When they estimated separate models of sentence length for men and women, however, they found that gender interacted with both race and the type of offense (Steffensmeier et al., 1993, p. 430). There were no racial differences in the sentences imposed on men, but Black women received sentences that averaged 3 months longer than the sentences imposed on White women. Women received slightly shorter sentences when convicted of a serious felony and slightly longer sentences when convicted of a less serious felony or a misdemeanor.

Somewhat different results surfaced in a later study that also examined sentencing decisions in Pennsylvania (Steffensmeier et al., 1998). Although the authors of this study found that female offenders faced both lower odds of incarceration and shorter sentences than did male offenders and that Black offenders were sentenced more harshly than were White offenders, they also found that the effects of race and age were conditioned by gender. Younger male offenders were sentenced more harshly than older male offenders, but age had a negligible effect on sentence severity among female offenders. Among men, race affected sentence severity for younger offenders but not for older offenders. Among women, on the other hand, the effect of race did not vary by age; Black women, regardless of age, were sentenced more harshly than White women. The authors also found that the harshest sentences were imposed on young, Black men. These findings led them to conclude that "the main effects of race and gender

are relatively modest compared to the interactive effects of race, gender, and age" (p. 785).

Steffensmeier and his colleagues (1993, 1998) advanced two complementary explanations for the patterns of findings revealed by their research. They based these explanations on two types of qualitative data: the reasons given by judges for dispositional departures from the Pennsylvania sentencing guidelines and comments made by judges whom they interviewed. Regarding the more lenient treatment of female offenders, they noted that judges viewed female offenders as less dangerous, less culpable, and more repentant than male offenders. Pennsylvania judges also believed that differential treatment of women was justified and sensible. It was justified because of differences in blameworthiness and sensible because women were more likely than men to have child care responsibilities and mental or health problems that could not be treated in a jail or prison setting.

A similar explanation is offered for the gender, race, and age interactions uncovered in the later study. Steffensmeier et al. (1998) assert that their findings are consistent with what they refer to as the "focal concerns framework of criminal sentencing" (p. 766). Building on sociological theories of organizational decision making and attribution, the authors suggest that judges' determinations of the appropriate sentence reflect their beliefs about offenders' blameworthiness, dangerousness, and recidivism risk, as well as their assessments of the organizational constraints on and the practical consequences of their decisions. They state that judges, who are expected to make rational sentencing decisions in the face of uncertainty and incomplete information, develop a "perceptual shorthand" (p. 767) that incorporates attributions based simultaneously on race, gender, and age. Male offenders—particularly young, Black male offenders—are perceived as more blameworthy, more dangerous, and more threatening than female offenders. According to Steffensmeier et al. (1998),

> Younger offenders and male defendants appear to be seen as more of a threat to the community or not as reformable, and so also are black offenders, particularly those who are young and male. Likewise, concerns such as

"ability to do time" and the costs of incarceration appear linked to race-, gender-, and age-based perceptions and stereotypes. (p. 787)

Similar conclusions are found in Daly's (1987, 1989, 1994) influential work. Daly contends that whereas statistical studies of sentencing "may reveal more lenient outcomes for women, they tell us little about how court officials arrive at these decisions" (Daly, 1987, p. 268). Daly's own research (1987, 1989) suggests that judges' pretrial release and sentencing decisions are affected by defendants' family circumstances; "familied" defendants (i.e., those who are married and living with a spouse, living with parents or other relatives, or caring for young children) are treated more leniently than are nonfamilied defendants. According to Daly, this more lenient treatment of familied defendants reflects judges' beliefs that these offenders have greater informal social control in their lives, as well as judges' concerns about maintaining families and protecting innocent children, which she labels the "social costs of punishment" (Daly, 1989, p. 138).

Daly's work also reveals that family circumstances have a more pronounced mitigating effect on outcomes for female defendants (particularly Black women) (see Daly, 1989) than for male defendants, a result that she attributes to the combined effect of the fact that "court officials see more 'good' mothers than 'good' fathers" (Daly, 1987, p. 279) and the fact that judges view child care (which is typically provided by women) as more essential to the maintenance of families than economic support (which is more typically provided by men). She also suggests that judges make "gender-based character judgments" (Daly, 1994, p. 227). Women are viewed as better candidates for reform than men because of their greater conventionality and less serious prior records; they are perceived as less blameworthy than men because of "blurred boundaries" (p. 260) between their past victimization and their current criminality. Daly concludes that judges' sentencing decisions are motivated not by a desire to protect women but by an intent to protect families, a motivation that she refers to as "familial paternalism" (Daly, 1987, p. 268; see Bickle & Peterson, 1991; Crew, 1991).

Considered together, the findings of these recent studies highlight the importance not only of testing for interaction between gender and factors such as race, family status/family ties, and type of crime but also of attempting to uncover the underlying motivations for differential treatment of men and women. Daly (1994) suggests that the paternalism and evil woman theses "be laid to rest" (p. 197), and Daly and Bordt (1995) urge researchers to document and understand both "the circumstances that bring women to felony court" and the ways in which "gender-linked determinations enter into court decisions" (p. 163). Our study responds to these suggestions.

⊠ Objectives and Hypotheses

The primary objective of this study is to provide an empirical test of assertions suggesting that contemporary case-processing decisions are gender neutral. We test the hypothesis that female and male offenders will face similar odds of incarceration once crime seriousness, prior criminal record, and other legally relevant factors are taken into consideration.

Our second objective is to test for interaction between offender gender, offender race/ethnicity, and incarceration decisions. As noted above, researchers have suggested that failure to consider the interaction between gender and race may lead to misleading conclusions about the effects of these extralegal variables (Crew, 1991; Steffensmeier et al., 1993, 1998). Several studies have found that discriminatory treatment of criminal defendants is restricted primarily to Black men, whereas preferential treatment generally is reserved for White women (Kruttschnitt, 1980–1981; Patterson & Lynch, 1991; Spohn & Spears, 1997; Spohn, Welch, & Gruhl, 1985; regarding the intersections among race, gender, and age, see Spohn & Holleran, 2000; Steffensmeier et al., 1998). Other studies have shown that female offenders, regardless of race/ethnicity, are treated more leniently than their male counterparts (Spohn et al., 1987). To explore these issues, we compare the likelihood of incarceration for Black women and Black men and for White women and White men. We suggest that if chivalry is, in fact, a thing of the past, there should be no significant differences in the odds of incarceration for female and male offenders of either race.

The third objective of this study is to explore the possibility that the effects of the legal and extralegal predictors of incarceration are conditioned by gender. A number of scholars have questioned the adequacy of additive models that estimate only the main effects of variables such as gender and race. Zatz (1987), for example, contends that models of the relationship between race and sentencing that exclude indirect or interactive effects "may erroneously conclude that discrimination does not exist when, in fact, it does" (p. 83) Miethe and Moore (1986) also argue that an interactive model is more appropriate than an additive model in assessing racial discrimination in criminal justice decision making. They suggest that use of an additive model, which "presumes that no systematic variation exists within racial groups *and* that between-race differences are constant across levels of other social, case, and legal attributes" (p. 230), minimizes racial differences in case processing, whereas use of an interactive (or race-specific) model allows the researcher to discern differential treatment between racial groups.

A similar argument can be made regarding the effect of gender. A finding that female offenders are, net of controls for other legal and extralegal predictors of incarceration, treated no differently than male offenders does not necessarily mean that the decision-making process is gender neutral. Although the other variables included in the models may have similar effects on incarceration decisions for men and women, it also is possible that the effects of these variables depend on or are conditioned by the offender's gender. The presence of young children in the home, for example, may benefit women but not men, whereas being unemployed or having a serious prior criminal record may disadvantage men more than women. Preferential treatment of female offenders may be concentrated among the less serious offenses, where criminal justice officials have more discretion and thus more opportunities to consider extralegal characteristics such as gender. The effects of other variables may similarly vary between men and women.

 # Research Design and Methods

The Context of Sentencing

The three jurisdictions included in this study are Cook County (Chicago), Illinois; Dade County (Miami), Florida; and Jackson County (Kansas City), Missouri. Chicago and Miami were chosen to represent northern and southern jurisdictions with large Black and Hispanic populations and with crime rates significantly higher than the national average. Kansas City was chosen to represent a medium-size, Midwestern jurisdiction with a relatively small minority population. Chicago also was chosen because it is one of only a few jurisdictions in the United States with more than a handful of Black judges.

There are important differences in the statutory sentencing provisions found in each jurisdiction. These differences are summarized below.

Illinois. Judges in Illinois impose determinate sentences. Felonies are classified as either first-degree murder, Class X, Class 1, Class 2, Class 3, or Class 4 felonies. The minimum and maximum terms of imprisonment for the six categories of felonies are as follows:

First-degree murder: 20–60 years, life or death

Class X: 6–30 years

Class 1: 4–15 years

Class 2: 3–7 years

Class 3: 2–5 years

Class 4: 1–3 years

The judge cannot impose a sentence that exceeds the maximum term of imprisonment unless he or she finds that at least one of the aggravating factors specified in the statute (e.g., the defendant received compensation for committing the crime or committed a crime against a person 60 years of age or older) was present.

Missouri. Missouri also has a determinate sentencing structure. Felonies are classified into four categories:

Class A, Class B, Class C, or Class D. The terms of imprisonment associated with each category are as follows:

Class A: 10–30 years or life

Class B: 5–15 years

Class C: a maximum of 7 years

Class D: a maximum of 5 years

For Class C and Class D felonies, the court can sentence the offender to 1 year or less in the county jail. The maximum terms for each category are increased if the offender is proved to be either a persistent offender or a dangerous offender. In this case, for example, the maximum term for Class B felonies is 30 years, the maximum term for Class C felonies is 20 years, and the maximum term for Class D felonies is 10 years.

If the offender is tried and found guilty by a jury, then the jury determines the sentence unless the defendant requests in writing prior to voir dire that the court assess the punishment or the state pleads and proves the defendant as a prior offender, persistent offender, or dangerous offender. If the jury sentences the offender to prison, then the judge cannot impose a harsher sentence (unless the term of years is less than the authorized lowest term for the offense); the judge can, on the other hand, impose a shorter sentence.

Florida. The state of Florida has had sentencing guidelines since 1983. The purpose of the guidelines is "to establish a uniform set of standards to guide the sentencing judge" and "to eliminate unwarranted variation in the sentencing process by reducing the subjectivity in interpreting specific offense-related and offender-related criteria" (see Florida Statute §921.001 [4]). To meet these objectives, each offender is assigned a "sentence score" based on the seriousness of the offense(s) and his or her prior criminal record. This score determines the recommended sentence.

Judges retain some discretion under the guidelines. For example, if the total sentence points for a particular offender are less than 40, the presumptive sentence is a nonstate prison sentence. In this situation, the judge has discretion to sentence the offender to county jail for a maximum term of 364 days or to impose probation or some other alternative to incarceration; the judge also has discretion to withhold adjudication. If the total points are greater than 40 but less than or equal to 52, the judge has discretion to sentence the offender to state prison. If the points total more than 52, the sentence must be a prison sentence, with the months in state prison calculated by subtracting 28 from the total sentence points; the judge can, however, increase or decrease the sentence length by 25% (without providing a written statement delineating the reasons for the departure) or more (with a written statement of the reasons for the departure).

Data Collection Procedures

We analyzed data on 7,070 offenders convicted of felonies in the three jurisdictions. This includes 2,905 offenders in Chicago, 2,700 offenders in Miami, and 1,465 offenders in Kansas City. The data collection procedures varied somewhat in each jurisdiction. In Chicago, we selected a random sample of all offenders convicted of felonies in 1993 from a list prepared by the Clerk of the Cook County Circuit Court. Data collectors read through the court file for each case included in the sample and recorded information about the offender and the case on an optical-scan form designed for the project. In Miami, we selected a random sample of all offenders convicted of felonies in 1993 and 1994; information concerning the case and the offender was provided by the Administrative Office of the Courts. In Kansas City, we obtained data on all offenders convicted of felonies in 1993. The Department of Computer Services provided a printout listing the charges filed, the disposition of each charge, and other information about the case; information concerning the offender's background and prior criminal record was obtained from court files.

We also interviewed a purposive sample of judges, prosecutors, and public defenders in each jurisdiction. All of the interviews were conducted by the first author and the coprincipal investigator for the project; we took detailed notes during the interviews and later entered the responses in a text data file. The interviews were conducted during the second year of the project while the data were being collected, entered, and analyzed. Respondents were asked a series of standardized, open-ended questions. They were asked to discuss their sentencing philosophies, to identify the factors that influenced their determination of the appropriate sentence, to describe the charging and plea bargaining process in their particular jurisdiction, and to identify areas in need of reform. Information gleaned from the interviews enabled us to pinpoint contextual differences in criminal justice policies and practices. We also gained a fuller understanding of the sentencing process and of the role played by judges, prosecutors, and defense attorneys in each jurisdiction.

Dependent and Independent Variables

The dependent and independent variables, their codes, and their frequencies are displayed in Table 7.1. We present separate data for each of the three jurisdictions.

The dependent variable is a dichotomous variable that measures whether the offender was incarcerated (coded 1) or not (coded 0). Because of the small number of female offenders who were sentenced to prison, we cannot analyze the length of the prison sentence. In Miami, we analyze the decision to incarcerate (in jail or prison) rather than the prison/no prison variable. We use this measure of incarceration because of the large number of offenders ($n = 1,167$) who were sentenced to the Dade County Jail and the small number of female offenders ($n = 54$) who were sentenced to prison. Under the Florida sentencing guidelines in effect in 1993 and 1994, many offenders convicted of property offenses and drug offenses did not qualify for a state prison sentence; instead, such offenders were sentenced to the Dade County Jail.

The independent variables included in the analysis are offender and case characteristics that have been shown to affect judges' sentencing decisions. In addition to gender, we control for the offender's race, age, and prior criminal record. In Chicago and Miami, offender race is measured by three dummy variables—Black, Hispanic, and White. Because there were only 47 Hispanic offenders (and only 13 Hispanic women) in Kansas City, we could not analyze Hispanics

separately; therefore, we eliminated Hispanics from the Kansas City data file and created two dummy variables (Black offender, White offender) measuring offender race. White offenders are the reference category in all of the multivariate analyses.

The data collected for this project included a number of measures of prior criminal record: number of prior arrests, number of prior felony arrests, number of prior felony convictions, number of prior prison terms of more than 1 year, whether the offender previously had been convicted of a drug offense, and whether the offender previously had been convicted of a violent offense. Some of these measures were highly correlated with one another; they also differed in terms of their relationship to sentence severity. The variable we use— the number of times the offender previously had been sentenced to prison for more than 1 year—is the measure of prior record that had the most consistently strong (and statistically significant) relationship to the dependent variables.

We control for three measures of offense seriousness— the most serious conviction charge, the statutory classification of the most serious conviction charge, and the number of charges on which the offender was convicted.

We also control for characteristics of the offender's case that might influence decisions concerning sentence severity. We take into account whether the offender was on probation at the time of his or her arrest for the current offense, whether the offender was represented by a private attorney, whether the offender was released pending trial, and whether the offender pled guilty.

Previous research has shown that the offender's employment status (Chiricos & Bales, 1991; Nobiling, Spohn, & DeLone, 1998; Spohn & Holleran, 2000) and family circumstances (Daly, 1987, 1989; Steffensmeier et al., 1993) may affect case-processing decisions. More important, this research has shown that the preferential treatment of female offenders may reflect judges' concerns about their child care responsibilities. Although we were able to obtain data on the offender's employment status and whether the offender had dependent children for more than three quarters of the offenders in Chicago and Kansas City, there is some missing data

Table 7.1 Dependent and Independent Variables: Codes and Frequencies for Offenders in Chicago, Miami, and Kansas City

Variable	Code	Chicago (N = 2,905)		Miami (N = 2,700)		Kansas City (N = 1,465)	
		n	%	n	%	n	%
Dependent variables[a]							
Sentenced to jail (Chicago and Kansas City) or prison (Miami)	1 = yes 0 = no	1,779 1,126	61.2 38.8	1,846 854	68.4 31.6	615 850	42.0 58.0
Independent variables							
Offender's gender	1 = male 0 = female	2,642 263	90.9 9.1	2,452 248	90.8 9.2	1,242 223	84.8 15.2
Offender's race[b]							
Black		2,341	80.6	1,608	59.6	970	66.2
Hispanic		298	9.2	565	20.9	NA	NA
White		266	10.3	527	19.5	495	33.8
Offender's age	Mean	27.8		31.18		28.65	
Most serious conviction charge							
Violent crime		523	18.2	495	18.3	306	20.9
Property crime		828	28.5	1,021	37.8	733	50.0
Drug offense		1,554	53.5	1,184	43.9	426	29.1
Class of most serious conviction charge							
Chicago							
Class X		281	9.7				
Class 1		474	16.3				
Class 2		973	33.5				
Class 3		412	14.2				
Class 4		765	26.3				
Miami							
Life or first-degree				269	10.0		
Second-degree				823	30.5		
Third-degree				1,608	59.6		
Kansas City							
Class A						143	9.8
Class B						369	25.2
Class C						808	55.2
Class D						145	9.9
Mean number of current felony convictions		1.14		1.44		1.45	
Mean number of prior prison terms of > 1 year		0.52		0.65		0.63	

Variable	Code	Chicago (N = 2,905)		Miami (N = 2,700)		Kansas City (N = 1,465)	
		n	**%**	**n**	**%**	**n**	**%**
Offender on probation at time of offense	1 = yes	275	9.5	331	12.3	229	15.6
	0 = no	2,630	90.5	2,369	87.7	1,236	84.4
Private attorney	1 = yes	259	8.9	712	26.4	427	29.1
	0 = no	2,646	91.1	1,988	73.6	1,038	70.9
Offender released prior to trial	1 = yes	1,071	36.9	1,172	43.4	576	39.3
	0 = no	1,834	63.1	1,527	56.6	889	60.7
Offender pled guilty	1 = yes	2,630	90.5	2,655	98.3	1,392	95.0
	0 = no	275	9.5	45	1.7	73	5.0
Offender unemployed	1 = yes	1,793	61.7	NA^c	NA	943	64.4
	0 = no	681	23.4	NA	NA	394	26.9
	8 = missing	431	14.8	NA	NA	128	8.7
Offender has dependent children	1 = yes	422	14.5	NA^c	NA	392	26.8
	0 = no	2,122	73.0	NA	NA	796	54.3
	8 = missing	361	12.4	NA	NA	277	18.9

NOTE: NA = not applicable.

a. In Miami, we analyze the decision to incarcerate (in jail or prison) rather than the decision to imprison because of the large number of offenders who were sentenced to the Dade County jail and the small number of female offenders who were sentenced to prison.

b. There were only 47 Hispanic offenders in Kansas City; therefore, we eliminated Hispanics from the data file.

c. Information on the offender's employment status and on whether the offender had dependent children was not included in the Miami data file.

on each variable (see Table 7.1). Moreover, we were not able to obtain this information for offenders in Miami. Because we believe it is important to use the same controls in each jurisdiction, we first model the sentencing decisions without these variables; we then add variables measuring whether the offender was unemployed and whether the offender had dependent children to the models for Chicago and Kansas City. We present the results from the initial analyses in the tables and discuss the results of the analyses including controls for unemployment and dependent children in the text. Because previous research has suggested that child care responsibilities may have a greater effect on case outcomes for women than for men (Daly, 1987), whereas unemployment may have a more pronounced effect for men than for women (Chiricos & Bales, 1991; Nobiling et al., 1998; Spohn & Holleran, 2000), we include these variables when we estimate separate models for women and for men (in Chicago and Kansas City).

 Findings

The results of our analysis of the decision to incarcerate are contrary to the gender neutrality hypothesis. In all three jurisdictions, men faced significantly greater odds of incarceration than did women; men were about 1½ times more likely than women to be incarcerated in Miami and more than 2½ times more likely than women to be incarcerated in Chicago and Kansas City. The offender's race/ethnicity also affected the likelihood of incarceration in Chicago and Miami but not in Kansas City. In Chicago, both Blacks and Hispanics were imprisoned more frequently than Whites, whereas in Miami, Blacks (but not Hispanics) were incarcerated more often than Whites. Adding the offender's employment status and family situation to the models for Chicago and Kansas City did not alter these results. In fact, neither of these variables had a significant effect on the likelihood of incarceration in either jurisdiction.

As expected, the seriousness of the offense and the offender's prior criminal record significantly influenced the sentencing decision in all three jurisdictions. It is important to note, however, that the odds of incarceration were affected by two extralegal variables in addition to the gender and race/ethnicity of the offender. In Miami and Kansas City, offenders who pled guilty were significantly less likely than those who went through a trial to be incarcerated. And in all three cities, offenders who were detained in jail prior to trial faced significantly greater odds of incarceration than did those who were released pending trial.

The Interaction of Gender and Race

The findings discussed thus far reveal that both gender and race/ethnicity affect the likelihood of incarceration. Women faced significantly lower odds of incarceration than men in all three jurisdictions, and Black offenders faced higher odds of incarceration than White offenders in Chicago and Miami. These results suggest the potential for interaction between gender and race. Although it is certainly possible that female offenders, regardless of race, are treated more leniently than male offenders and that Black offenders, regardless of gender, are treated more harshly than White offenders, other results also are possible. As noted earlier, previous research has suggested that preferential treatment may be reserved for White women, whereas harsher treatment may be reserved for Black men.

To explore these possibilities, we created four gender of offender/race of offender dummy variables: Black female, White female, Black male, and White male. (Because there were no Hispanic offenders in Kansas City and very few Hispanic women in the other two jurisdictions, we eliminated Hispanic offenders from this part of the analysis.) We then reestimated the models using these variables rather than the individual gender and race variables. To test for significant differences between Black men and Black women, and to test for the possibility that Black men are treated more

harshly than all other offenders, we ran the analysis with Black men as the omitted category. To test for significant differences between White women and White men, and to test for the possibility that White women are treated more leniently than all other offenders, we ran the analysis with White women as the omitted category.

We use the results of the multivariate analyses to answer three questions concerning the interaction of gender and race. The first question is whether female offenders, regardless of race, are treated more leniently than male offenders. The answer to this question depends on the jurisdiction being examined. In Chicago and Kansas City, both Black and White women are significantly less likely than their male counterparts to be sentenced to prison. In Miami, on the other hand, preferential treatment at sentencing is found for Black women but not for White women.

The second question addressed is whether Black men are treated more harshly than all other offenders. The answer to this question is no. Our analysis of the decision to incarcerate revealed an inconsistent pattern of results. Black men were sentenced to prison more often than Black women and White women (but not White men) in Chicago and Kansas City; in Miami, on the other hand, Black men were incarcerated more often than Black women and White men (but not White women).

The final question is whether White women are treated more leniently than all other offenders. The answer to this question, without exception, is no. In Miami, there were no significant differences between White women and any of the three other groups of offenders. In Chicago and Kansas City, White women faced lower odds of imprisonment than White men and Black men but not Black women.

These results are illustrated more clearly by the data presented in Table 7.2. We used the results of the logistic regression analyses to calculate the probability of incarceration for "typical" male and female offenders in each racial group (Hanuschek & Jackson, 1977; Lichter, 1989). All of the other independent variables were set at their mean. Thus, we calculate probabilities for offenders with the following characteristics:

- 29 years old;
- convicted of 1.4 counts of a drug offense classified as a Class 2 felony (Chicago), a third-degree felony (Miami), or a Class C felony (Kansas City);
- one prior prison term of more than 1 year;
- not on probation at time of arrest for current offense;
- represented by a public defender;
- released prior to trial; and
- pled guilty.

We noted earlier that there were statistically significant gender differences in the odds of incarceration in all three jurisdictions. The data presented in Table 7.2

Table 7.2   Predicted Probabilities of Incarceration for Typical Offenders

	Chicago	Miami	Kansas City
Sentenced to prison			
Black women	.32	NA	.10
Black men	.55*		.20*
White women	.18		.07
White men	.48*		.20*
Sentenced to jail or prison			
Black women	NA	.61	NA
Black men		.75*	
White women		.75	
White men		.67	

NOTE: We used the results of the logistic regression analyses to calculate probabilities for offenders with the following characteristics: age = 29 years; convicted of 1.4 counts of a drug offense; class of the conviction charge = Class 2 felony (Chicago), third-degree felony (Miami), Class C felony (Kansas City); one prior prison term of more than 1 year; not on probation; represented by a public defender; released prior to trial; pled guilty. NA = not applicable.

*$p < .05$ for differences between men and women in each racial group.

illustrate that these are not trivial differences. The discrepancies are particularly pronounced in Chicago. In that jurisdiction, in fact, there is a 30-percentage-point difference in the probabilities of imprisonment for Whites (48% for men vs. 18% for women); there is a 23-percentage-point difference for Blacks (55% for men vs. 32% for women). In Kansas City, where the odds of imprisonment are, regardless of gender, considerably lower than in Chicago, the probabilities are 20% for White men, 7% for White women, 20% for Black men, and 10% for Black women. In Miami, on the other hand, gender has a significant effect only among Blacks; there is a 14-percentage-point difference in the probabilities of incarceration for Black men (75%) and Black women (61%).

A Further Test for Interaction

The third objective of this study is to explore the possibility that the effects of the legal and extralegal predictors of imprisonment decisions depend on or are conditioned by gender. To test this, we estimate separate models for men and for women in each of the three jurisdictions.

The results of the gender-specific models of the decision to incarcerate indicate that although some of the legally relevant variables produce the predicted effects on incarceration regardless of gender, overall, these variables more consistently affect the likelihood of incarceration for men than for women. The seriousness of the offense, as measured by the statutory classification of the conviction charge, and the offender's prior criminal record affect the decision to incarcerate among both male and female offenders in all three jurisdictions, and the number of charges and the offender's probation status predict incarceration for male and female offenders in Kansas City. On the other hand, the likelihood that a female offender will be sentenced to prison is not affected by the type of conviction charge in any jurisdiction or by her probation status in Chicago.

Although, as noted above, the statutory classification of the offense had a significant effect on incarceration among both male and female offenders in all three jurisdictions, in Kansas City, the magnitude of the effects for Class C offenses varied by gender. In this jurisdiction, in other words, female offenders convicted of Class C offenses faced significantly lower odds of incarceration than male offenders, convicted of these lesser offenses. Also in Kansas City, being on probation at the time of arrest produced a significantly greater increase in the likelihood of incarceration for women than for men. In Chicago, on the other hand, prior record, as measured by a prior prison term of more than 1 year, increased the odds of incarceration more for men than for women.

The effects of some of the extralegal variables also were conditioned by gender. In Chicago and Miami, Black and Hispanic men faced significantly greater odds of incarceration than did White men, but race did not affect the likelihood of incarceration among women; the gender differences in the effect of race on incarceration were significant in Miami but not in Chicago. In Chicago and Kansas City, older female offenders were more likely than younger female offenders to be sentenced to prison, but age had no effect on incarceration decisions involving male offenders. With only one exception, neither employment status nor the presence of dependent children affected the likelihood of incarceration for either male or female offenders in Chicago or Kansas City. In Kansas City, female offenders with dependent children were sentenced to prison less often than were female offenders without children. Also in Kansas City, representation by a private attorney reduced the odds of incarceration for female, but not for male, offenders.

To summarize, the effects of the legal and extralegal variables included in our gender-specific models of postconviction incarceration are not invariant. The type of offense and the seriousness of the offense are more consistent predictors of incarceration for men than for women. Similarly, the effect of race/ethnicity on posttrial incarceration is confined to male offenders in Chicago and Miami, whereas the effect of dependent children is confined to female offenders in Kansas City.

Discussion

The results of this study contradict assertions that "differential treatment of women in sentencing . . . is a thing of the past" (Chesney-Lind, 1997, p. 163). In fact, our results provide compelling evidence that female offenders are treated more leniently than male offenders. In all

three jurisdictions, women faced significantly lower odds of incarceration than men. Moreover, preferential treatment was not reserved for White women. In Chicago and Kansas City, both White and Black women were considerably less likely than their male counterparts to be sentenced to prison following conviction; in Miami, Black women faced lower odds of incarceration than Black men. In addition, in all three jurisdictions the effects of other legal and extralegal variables were conditioned by gender.

These results call into question claims that "previous findings on the effect of gender on sentencing decisions are *time bounded*" or are artifacts of inadequate controls for legally relevant variables (Steffensmeier et al., 1993, p. 436). We examined data on offenders convicted of felonies in three large urban jurisdictions in the mid-1990s and included controls for offense seriousness, prior criminal record, and other offender and case characteristics. The fact that we found a consistent pattern of preferential treatment of female offenders, coupled with the fact that the differences uncovered were both statistically and substantively significant, suggests that contemporary judges evaluate female offenders differently than male offenders.

Our findings also suggest that judges evaluate Black and Hispanic male offenders differently than White male offenders but view Black female offenders no differently than White female offenders. In fact, one of the most interesting findings of this study is that the effect of race was conditioned by gender but the effect of gender was, with only one exception, not conditioned by race. Our initial analysis revealed that gender was a significant predictor of the decision to incarcerate the offender in all three jurisdictions. It also revealed that race/ethnicity had a significant effect on incarceration in Miami and Chicago. Further analysis, however, revealed that the effect of race/ethnicity was confined to men. Black and Hispanic men were more likely than White men to be incarcerated in Miami and Chicago; there were no racial differences among women. The effect of gender, on the other hand, did not depend on race in either Chicago or Kansas City; in these two jurisdictions, both Black and White women were treated more leniently than their male counterparts. And in Miami, Black (but not White) women were less likely than Black men to be sentenced to jail or prison. Thus, harsher treatment of racial minorities was confined to men but more lenient treatment of women was found for both racial minorities and Whites.

The question, of course, is why judges treat women differently than men, Black and Hispanic men differently than White men, but Black women no differently than White women. Daly (1987) contends that statistical studies revealing more lenient treatment of female offenders or harsher treatment of racial minorities "tell us little about how court officials arrive at these decisions" (p. 268). Bridges and Steen (1998) similarly assert that studies exploring the effect of race on sentencing often fail to "identify the mechanisms by which the accused's race influences official assessments" (p. 554) of offenders and their cases.

The results of our quantitative analysis, coupled with qualitative data obtained from interviews with criminal justice officials in each city, provide clues to the "mechanisms" by which gender- and race-linked criteria lead to harsher or more lenient treatment. Collectively, our findings lend credence to assertions that court officials attempt to simplify and routinize the sentencing process by relying on stereotypes that link defendant characteristics such as race/ethnicity and gender to perceptions of blameworthiness, dangerousness, and risk of recidivism (Albonetti, 1997; Bridges & Steen, 1998; Steffensmeier et al., 1998). In these three jurisdictions, court officials apparently stereotype Black and Hispanic male defendants as particularly blameworthy, violent, and threatening. Conversely, they appear to view all female defendants as less culpable, less likely to recidivate, and more amenable to rehabilitation. Paraphrasing Steffensmeier et al. (1998, p. 767), our findings suggest that judges in Chicago, Kansas City, and Miami have developed a "perceptual shorthand" that incorporates gender- and race-linked attributions and that leads to harsher treatment of Black and Hispanic male defendants and more lenient treatment of female defendants.

The results of our analysis of case outcomes in Chicago and Kansas City provide further evidence of the mechanisms by which gender influences the decision-making process. These results suggest that judges' perceptions of male and female offenders rest not only on attributions of blameworthiness and dangerousness but also on concerns about the social costs (Daly, 1987) of incarcerating female offenders with child care responsibilities. They also highlight the importance of testing for interaction between gender and other variables of interest. When we included the offender's family situation, as measured by his or her responsibility for the care of young children, in the additive models, we found that this variable did not affect the decision to incarcerate in either jurisdiction. Based on these results, we might have concluded that the offender's family situation had no effect on case outcomes in Chicago or Kansas City. This conclusion, although accurate for all offenders in the aggregate, would have been misleading. When we estimated gender-specific models, we found effects that had been masked in the additive analysis. We also found that the effect of the offender's family situation was confined to female offenders. Female offenders with young children were significantly less likely than women without young children to be sentenced to prison in Kansas City. In deciding whether to incarcerate female offenders, in other words, judges in Kansas City took the offender's child care responsibilities into account.

Interviews conducted with judges, prosecutors, and public defenders in each jurisdiction support our conclusions concerning the factors that motivate judges to treat female offenders more leniently than male offenders. We asked court officials if they thought it was appropriate to consider the offender's social and economic circumstances in determining the sentence; we also asked a more direct question about the effect of gender on sentencing decisions. These questions elicited comments about the less serious nature of female offenders and their crimes. A Kansas City prosecutor, who asserted that "judges give special treatment to females across the board," attributed the more lenient treatment of female offenders to "a little bit of paternalism and a little bit of concern for kids at home" and to the fact that judges realize that "it's unlikely that the typical female offender is going to graduate to violent crime." A Chicago prosecutor, who admitted that "there are male judges in this building who are reluctant to convict female defendants or to sentence females to prison," qualified his comments in the following manner:

> To be fair, however, the women who come into court don't carry the same baggage in terms of seriousness of charge and prior criminal record. If you took these factors into account, I don't think you'd find a huge difference.

A judge in Chicago candidly admitted that he viewed female offenders differently than male offenders and that, as a result, "they get off easier." He also stated that he believed that "the forces that motivate female offenders are different—it's a lack of self-esteem rather than machismo." A judge in Miami similarly acknowledged that his "one big fault" was that he was "more attuned to women" and that he usually "took the time to find out why they're in court." He added that "there's almost always a story there."

A number of respondents commented on the legitimacy of considering the fact that the offender was responsible for the care of young children. A judge in Kansas City, for example, who prefaced his remarks by stating, "I won't give you the socially desirable answer and tell you that gender is irrelevant in my courtroom," said,

> We still hold the somewhat outdated belief that women are the primary caretakers of children. It may not be irrational to sentence them less harshly than men—we all know that females are not as likely to commit violent crimes, not as likely to recidivate, more likely to be the sole caretakers of young children.

A female judge in Kansas City stated that she was "very sensitive to women who are trying to raise their kids alone." She also noted that in these situations she asked herself, "Is it worth it to take this person away from her family?" A Kansas City public defender echoed these comments, noting that he was "in favor of giving mothers a break." He also stated that "it's important to help them get their lives in order and ensure that their children don't follow the same path.

Some might say it's sexist but I think that it's pragmatic and prudent."

Court officials in Chicago and Miami made similar comments. A Cook County judge, who emphasized that the seriousness of the crime and the offender's prior criminal record were the most important considerations, also stated,

> If the offender is employed or is caring for young children, the defense attorney may have a pretty good argument that if you send this person away you're going to be putting four people on welfare. It may be true that the defendant is getting a break but society is getting a break as well.

A judge in Miami observed that although he gave "very little weight to gender or marital status," he had "given breaks to women who were supporting young children." A Dade County prosecutor, who asserted that "the offender's social and economic circumstances should have no effect on the sentence," qualified his remarks by noting, "If the offender is a female with kids at home to take care of, and she's charged with a drug offense, I may be looking for drug treatment rather than jail or prison."

Comments made during the interviews also shed light on the reasons why the presence of dependent children affects pretrial detention and sentencing decisions for female, but not for male, offenders. Respondents in each jurisdiction emphasized that the defendant's social and economic circumstances, including child care responsibilities, only come into play if the offense is not serious and if the offender does not have an extensive prior criminal record. When asked if it was appropriate to consider social and economic factors, a Kansas City judge, for example, stated,

> Yes, but it depends upon the crime. All of those things factor in differently depending on the crime. If it's a nonserious, nonviolent crime, those things might generate a sympathetic reaction to the defendant's situation. This would be a rational response. In a vicious,

predatory crime, the offender's family situation or employment history play virtually no role; if it's a drug offense or a drug-related crime, they carry more weight.

A Dade County prosecutor made a similar comment:

If it's a nonserious property offense or a drug offense involving someone without a previous violent felony conviction, I might give an offender from a disadvantaged background a break. Especially if he or she has a job or kids to support. There is nothing to be gained by recommending that such a person go to jail or prison, and the costs are enormous.

Several respondents also stressed that the mere presence of young children in the household was not sufficient to mitigate the sentence—rather, the key factor was whether the offender was supporting the children emotionally and financially. They also indicated that the men they saw in court often had not assumed responsibility for their children. A Cook County public defender stated explicitly that he attempted to use dependent children to mitigate the punishment only if the offender was a woman.

If I'm representing a woman I'll bring it up because judges don't want to send women who are the sole support of young children to prison. Most judges, on the other hand, don't view it favorably if a male offender has several kids with different mothers and is not supporting any of them.

Judges in Chicago and Kansas City made very similar comments. A Chicago judge stated that "if the offender has been contributing to the support of his family, I might give the minimum sentence so that he can be restored to his family." A judge in Kansas City similarly remarked,

I don't think that one's social and economic situation should be an excuse, so to that extent it's not relevant. But a defendant who has a job and a family that he is supporting is at least attempting to make a contribution to society and that may influence my decision if the crime is nonviolent.

These comments suggest that family responsibilities affect case outcomes for female offenders but not for male offenders because criminal justice officials are only willing to take child care responsibilities into consideration if the crime is not serious (and women typically are charged with less serious crimes than are men) and because male offenders with children often are not viewed as providing adequate support for them. As Daly (1987) has noted, "Court officials see more 'good' mothers than 'good' fathers" (p. 277).

Conclusion

This research adds to a growing body of literature suggesting that judicial decision making reflects the interplay of legally relevant case characteristics and of attributional stereotypes that portray certain types of offenders as more blameworthy, more dangerous, and more threatening than other offenders. Our findings take us one step closer toward understanding the complex ways in which judges' assessments of offense seriousness and offender culpability interact with their concerns about protecting society from crime and about the practical effects of incarceration to produce more severe treatment of Black and Hispanic male offenders and more lenient treatment of female offenders. Judges have fairly detailed records of offenders' crimes and criminal histories but relatively little information that can be used to assess their blameworthiness, risk of future violence, or risk of recidivism. This uncertainty may lead judges to stereotype Black and Hispanic male offenders as "particularly predatory" and "disposed to chronic criminal offending" (Bridges & Steen, 1998, p. 555) and to view female offenders—particularly those with child care responsibilities—in the opposite terms. In attempting to make rational decisions about the appropriate treatment of criminal offenders, in other words, judges may be influenced not only by the seriousness of the offense and the offender's criminal record but also by these race- and gender-linked stereotypes.

Our conclusions concerning the mechanisms by which race and gender influence case outcomes are obviously speculative. Based on the quantitative and qualitative data analyzed for this study, we cannot be certain that the more lenient treatment of female offenders or the harsher treatment of Black and Hispanic men reflects judges' race- and gender-linked beliefs about the types of offenders who are dangerous or who pose a threat to society and thus should be incarcerated. Future research should attempt to validate these linkages by, for example, analyzing the transcripts of sentence hearings or by presenting judges with sentencing scenarios and asking them to explain their decisions. Future research also should continue to probe for interactions among case characteristics and defendant characteristics. As we stated at the outset, the more interesting question regarding gender and case outcomes is not whether female offenders are treated differently than male offenders but under what conditions or in what contexts the treatment of women differs from that of men.

 References

Albonetti, C. A. (1997). Sentencing under the Federal Sentencing Guidelines: Effects of defendant characteristics, guilty pleas, and departures on sentence outcomes for drug offenses, 1991–1992. *Law & Society Review, 31*, 789–822.

Bernstein, I. N., Kelly, W. R., & Doyle, P. A. (1977). Societal reaction to deviants: The case of criminal defendants. *American Sociological Review, 42*, 743–755.

Bickle, G. S., & Peterson, R. D. (1991). The impact of gender-based family roles on criminal sentencing. *Social Problems, 38*, 372–394.

Blumstein, A., Cohen, J., Martin, S. E., & Tonry, M. H. (1983). *Research on sentencing: The search for reform* (Vol. 1). Washington, DC: National Academy Press.

Bridges, G. S., & Steen, S. (1998). Racial disparities in official assessments of juvenile offenders: Attributional stereotypes as mediating, mechanisms. *American Sociological Review, 63*, 554–570.

Bureau of Justice Statistics. (1998). *Prisoners in 1997*. Washington, DC: U.S. Department of Justice.

Chesney-Lind, M. (1997). *The female offender: Girls, women, and crime.* Thousand Oaks, CA: Sage.

Chiricos, T. G., & Bales, W. D. (1991). Unemployment and punishment: An empirical assessment. *Criminology, 29*, 701–724.

Crew, K. B. (1991). Sex differences in criminal sentencing: Chivalry or patriarchy? *Justice Quarterly, 8*, 59–84.

Curran, D. (1983). Judicial discretion and defendant's sex. *Criminology, 21*, 41–58.

Daly, K. (1987). Structure and practice of familial-based justice in a criminal court. *Law & Society Review, 21*, 267–290.

Daly, K. (1989). Neither conflict nor labeling nor paternalism will suffice: Intersections of race, ethnicity, gender, and family in criminal court decisions. *Crime & Delinquency, 35*, 136–168.

Daly, K. (1994). *Gender, crime, and punishment.* New Haven, CT: Yale University Press.

Daly, K., & Bordt, R. (1995). Sex effects and sentencing: A review of the statistical literature. *Justice Quarterly, 12*, 143–177.

Daly, K., & Tonry, M. (1997). Gender, race and sentencing. In M. Tonry (Ed.), *Crime and justice: A review of research* (Vol. 22). Chicago: University of Chicago Press.

Durham, A. M., III. (1994). *Crisis and reform: Current issues in American punishment.* Boston: Little, Brown.

Farnworth, M., & Horan, P. (1980). Separate justice: An analysis of race differences in court processes. *Social Science Research, 9*, 381–399.

Frazier, C. E., Bock, W. E., & Henretta, J. C. (1980). Pretrial release and bail decisions: The effects of legal, community, and personal variables. *Criminology, 18*, 162–181.

Gruhl, J., Welch, S., & Spohn, C. (1984). Women as criminal defendants: A test for paternalism. *Western Political Quarterly, 37*, 456–467.

Hanuschek, E. A., & Jackson, J. E. (1977). *Statistical methods for social scientists.* New York: Academic Press.

Irwin, J., & Austin, J. (1997). *It's about time: America's imprisonment binge.* Belmont, CA: Wadsworth.

Johnston, J. B., Kennedy, T. D., & Shuman, I. G. (1987). Gender differences in the sentencing of felony offenders. *Federal Probation, 51*, 49–55.

Kruttschnitt, C. (1980–1981). Social status and sentences of female offenders. *Law & Society Review, 15*, 247–265.

Lichter, D. T. (1989). Race, employment hardship, and inequality in the American nonmetropolitan South. *American Sociological Review, 54*, 436–446.

Menard, S. (1995). *Applied logistic regression analysis.* Thousand Oaks, CA: Sage.

Miethe, T. D., & Moore, C. A. (1986). Racial differences in criminal processing: The consequences of model selection on conclusions about differential treatment. *Sociological Quarterly, 27*, 217–237.

Myers, M. A., & Talarico, S. M. (1986). Urban justice, rural injustice? Urbanization and its effect on sentencing. *Criminology, 24*, 367–390.

Nagel, I. H., & Hagan, J. (1982). The sentencing of white-collar criminals in federal courts: A socio-legal exploration of disparity. *Michigan Law Review, 80*, 427–465.

Nagel, I. H., & Hagan, J. (1983). Gender and crime: Offense patterns and criminal court sanctions. In M. Tonry (Ed.), *Crime and justice: A review of research* (Vol. 4). Chicago: University of Chicago Press.

Nobiling, T., Spohn, C., & DeLone, M. (1998). A tale of two counties: Unemployment and sentence severity. *Justice Quarterly, 15,* 459–485.

Paternoster, R., Brame, R., Mazerolle, P., & Piquero, A. (1998). Using the correct statistical test for the equality of regression coefficients. *Criminology, 36,* 859–866.

Patterson, E. B., & Lynch, M. J. (1991). Biases in formalized bail procedures. In M. J. Lynch & E. B. Patterson (Eds.), *Race and criminal justice.* New York: Harrow and Heston.

Rasche, C. (1975). The female offender as an object of criminological research. In A. Brodsky (Ed.), *The female offender.* Beverly Hills, CA: Sage.

Spohn, C., DeLone, M., & Spears, J. (1998). Race/ethnicity, gender, and sentence severity in Dade County, Florida: An examination of the decision to withhold adjudication. *Journal of Crime & Justice, 21,* 111–138.

Spohn, C., Gruhl, J., & Welch, S. (1987). The impact of the ethnicity and gender of defendants on the decision to reject or dismiss felony charges. *Criminology, 25,* 171–195.

Spohn, C., & Holleran, D. (2000). The imprisonment penalty paid by young, unemployed Black and Hispanic male offenders. *Criminology, 38,* 281–306.

Spohn, C. C., & Spears, J. W. (1997). Gender and case-processing decisions: A comparison of case outcomes for male and female defendants charged with violent felonies. *Women & Criminal Justice, 8,* 29–59.

Spohn, C., Welch, S., & Gruhl, J. (1985). Women defendants in court: The interaction between sex and race in convicting and sentencing. *Social Science Quarterly, 66,* 178–185.

Steffensmeier, D., Kramer, J., & Streifel, C. (1993). Gender and imprisonment decisions. *Criminology, 31,* 411–446.

Steffensmeier, D., Ulmer, J., & Kramer, J. (1998). The interaction of race, gender, and age in criminal sentencing: The punishment cost of being young, Black, and male. *Criminology, 36,* 763–797.

Studenmund, A. H. (1992) *Using econometrics: A practical guide.* New York: HarperCollins.

Wonders, N. A. (1996). Determinate sentencing: a feminist and postmodern story. *Justice Quarterly, 13,* 611–648.

Zatz, M. (1987). The changing forms of racial/ethnic biases in sentencing. *Journal of Research in Crime and Delinquency, 24,* 69–92.

Zingraff, M., & Thomsen, R. (1984). Differential sentencing of women and men in the U.S.A. *International Journal of the Sociology of Law, 12,* 401–413.

DISCUSSION QUESTIONS

1. What are the possible explanations for the "sex effect" in sentencing? How might judges justify imposing more lenient sentences on female offenders than on male offenders? Do these sex-linked factors justify differential treatment?

2. Spohn and Beichner tested for the direct effect of the offender's sex on sentencing, for interaction between offender sex and offender race, and for the possibility that the effects of other predictors of sentencing are conditioned by the sex of the offender. Discuss each of their study's objectives.

3. How does the context of sentencing differ in the three jurisdictions included in this study?

4. The authors compared the likelihood of incarceration for male and female offenders in the three jurisdictions. What did they find (see Table 7.1)? Did the differences disappear when they controlled for crime seriousness, prior record, and other offender and case characteristics?

5. The authors asked three questions regarding the interaction of the offenders' sex and race: Are female offenders, regardless of race, treated more leniently than male offenders? Are black men treated more harshly than all other offenders? Are white women treated more leniently than all other offenders? How did they answer these questions?

6. According to the authors, what are the mechanisms by which gender- and race-linked criteria lead to harsher or more lenient treatment?

READING

One of the most consistent findings of research on the capital sentencing process is that those who kill whites are substantially more likely to be sentenced to death than those who kill blacks. A report by the United States General Accounting Office (1990), which reviewed 28 studies conducted since 1972, noted that the race of the victim had a significant effect in all but five studies. Those who murdered whites were more likely than those who murdered blacks to be charged with capital murder and sentenced to death. Moreover, these differences could not be attributed to differences in the defendant's criminal record, the seriousness of the crime, or other legally relevant factors. The General Accounting Office noted that although the evidence regarding the race of the defendant was "equivocal," about half of the studies found that blacks were more likely than whites to be charged with capital crimes and sentenced to death. The overall conclusion proffered by the General Accounting Office was that there was "a pattern of evidence indicating racial disparity in the charging, sentencing, and imposition of the death penalty" (p. 5).

The article by Williams and Holcomb examines the capital sentencing processing, with a focus on the interactive effects of the victim's race and gender. The authors note that studies of capital sentencing decisions typically find not only that those who kill whites are more likely to receive a death sentence but also that those who kill women are more likely to be sentenced to death. The authors therefore hypothesize that "a White female victim effect will be observed in death penalty cases . . . those who kill White females are more likely to receive a death sentence than those who kill other victim race-gender combinations, even after controlling for other legally relevant factors." The results of their provocative study highlight the importance of considering the joint effects of race and gender in sentencing research.

The Interactive Effects of Victim Race and Gender on Death Sentence Disparity Findings

Marian R. Williams and Jefferson E. Holcomb

Research on factors associated with particular sentencing outcomes is common in the social science literature. There has long been an interest in determining whether there is equitable distribution of punishment for similarly situated offenders. This research has varied from the consideration of different offenses, defendant characteristics, victim characteristics, and combinations of these factors (for reviews, see Daly & Tonry, 1997; Kleck, 1981; Nagel & Hagan, 1983; Sampson & Lauritsen, 1997; Steffensmeier & Demuth, 2000;

AUTHORS' NOTE: The authors wish to acknowledge the helpful input of Stephen Demuth and the anonymous reviewers from *Homicide Studies* for their suggestions and comments on an earlier draft of this work.

SOURCE: Williams, M. R., & Holcomb, J. E. (2004). The interactive effects of victim race and gender on death sentence disparity findings. *Homicide Studies*, 8(4), 350–376.

Zatz, 1984). Generally, research seeks to evaluate the quality of justice and determine whether extralegal or impermissible factors such as race or gender of defendants are associated with more severe punishments and to what extent this may be an indication of unequal treatment under the law. Increasingly, research identifies the potential interactive impact of defendant characteristics such as defendant race and gender on sentencing outcomes (e.g., Spohn & Holleran, 2000; Steffensmeier, Ulmer, & Kramer, 1998). We extend this approach to examine whether the joint effect of victim characteristics, in particular victim race and gender, are associated with death sentences in Ohio.

Recent research on the death penalty demonstrates that defendant race is related only marginally to whether a homicide results in a death sentence (for a notable exception, see Baldus, Woodworth, Zuckerman, Weiner, & Broffitt, 1998). Despite this, the race of a homicide victim does appear to be a significant predictor of whether a homicide results in a death sentence. Death penalty research finds that even controlling for legally relevant factors, homicides involving White victims are more likely to result in a death sentence than homicides with Black victims (e.g., Baldus, Woodworth, & Pulaski, 1990; Radelet & Pierce, 1991; Sorensen & Wallace, 1995; Williams & Holcomb, 2001). This is particularly interesting given the fact that Blacks have a considerably higher rate of victimization than Whites and make up the majority of homicide victims in many states (see Marvell & Moody, 1999). These and other studies also find that a victim's gender is associated with different sentencing outcomes. Specifically, homicides with female victims are more likely to result in a death sentence than those with male victims. Little research, however, has been conducted on the interaction between victim race and victim gender and its association with the imposition of death sentences.

Current Study

The present study explores the interaction of victim gender-race characteristics and its impact on the likelihood of a homicide resulting in a death sentence. We contend that the specification of victim characteristics

may affect the previously noted independent relationships between victim race and victim gender and homicide case outcomes. After reviewing the prior research on victim characteristics and sentencing outcomes, we consider why future research should consider a more complete picture of victim characteristics when examining decision making in criminal cases. We specifically identify White female victims as theoretically important to the examination of victim race and gender disparities in death sentencing outcomes. An initial test of the proposed impact of victim characteristics on disparity research is then reported.

Caveats and Limitations

The authors wish to note at the outset several limitations and caveats to the present study. There is no claim that the present analyses are conclusive or that we have considered every substantive issue that affects decision making in capital cases. Although we have considerable confidence in the conceptual and theoretical premise of this work, we are certainly more modest about the following test of those ideas. We would prefer to consider this study as a preliminary examination of a methodologically complex relationship.

In particular, the use of Supplementary Homicide Reports (SHR) data for analyzing homicides and sentencing outcomes, as we have done, has been criticized in the scholarly literature (Maxfield, 1989). Unlike recent research on sentencing outcomes in other jurisdictions, Ohio does not have a centralized sentencing guideline system that allows for accessible and standardized data for all cases (e.g., Mustard, 2001; Steffensmeier & Demuth, 2000; Steffensmeier, Kramer, & Streifel, 1993). The tracking of all homicides during more than a decade would require resources that simply were not available (see Baldus et al., 1990, 1998, for exceptions). The present study was unable, therefore, to distinguish decision making at various stages of the legal process and could not determine if any observed disparities were the result of prosecutorial discretion (e.g., Paternoster, 1984; Stanko, 1981–1982) or occurred at later decision-making points in the legal process (e.g., Baldus et al., 1990, 1998). In addition, the researchers did not have access to the case files of each homicide. This limited the ability to control for several potentially relevant factors, especially the more "qualitative" aspects of a particular homicide (e.g., see Daly, 1994; Daly & Tonry, 1997) that may affect case outcomes. Therefore, the present analysis should be considered instructive but certainly not conclusive.

Victim Characteristics and Sentencing Outcomes

Research on sentencing outcomes has historically been interested in identifying those factors and variables closely associated with criminal justice decision making. Several recent studies emphasize the importance of three "focal concerns" that appear to influence decision making (e.g., Steffensmeier & Demuth, 2000; Steffensmeier et al., 1998). These include the perceived blameworthiness of the defendant, concerns about the protection of the community, and the practical implications of the sentencing decision (Steffensmeier & Demuth, 2000; Steffensmeier et al., 1998; see also Daly, 1994). For the most part, however, these have been incorporated into understanding the relationship between defendant behavior and characteristics and sentencing outcomes.

Recently, Baumer, Messner, and Felson (2000) applied the logic of these focal concerns in examining how victim characteristics may affect decision making in homicide cases. In particular, they distinguished victim conduct from victim demographic characteristics. Victim conduct refers to actions that may have directly or indirectly contributed to victimization as well as behaviors that may affect the perceptions of the moral character of the victim. As such, victim conduct may affect perceptions of the blameworthiness of the offender. If the victim's behavior is perceived to be a contributing factor in his or her victimization, decision makers are likely to view the offender as less blameworthy and adjust decision making accordingly. Victim conduct may also affect the considerations of the amount of harm done and the perceived threat to the community (Baumer et al., 2000). Finally, victim conduct has practical implications because of questions of credibility of the victim as a witness or in the perceived role as victim (Stanko, 1981–1982).

A distinct, though perhaps not unrelated, concern is whether victim demographic characteristics are associated with decision making (Baumer et al., 2000; Farrell & Swigert, 1986; Myers, 1979). As Baumer et al. (2000) noted, the race, class, and gender of the victim may contribute to sentencing outcomes, especially if the perceived status of the victim influences the attribution of blameworthiness or the perceived harm and threat that such victimizations represent (Kleck, 1981; see also Friedman, 1993). The race of the victim is often linked to sentencing disparity in two ways. First, homicides with Black victims may be perceived as less harmful to society relative to crimes against Whites (Baumer et al., 2000; Kleck, 1981). Given the historical marginalization and oppression of Blacks in American society, Black victim crimes may be considered unworthy of the most severe criminal justice response (Friedman, 1993). A second and perhaps related explanation relates to stereotypes about Black conduct. As noted above, if decision makers perceive victim conduct as contributing to their victimization, then they typically assign less blame to the defendant. Stereotypes about the behavior of Blacks that suggest they are more likely to engage in illegal or morally questionable behavior may affect the perceived blameworthiness of the defendant, the amount of harm done, and the credibility of the victim as a victim (Baumer et al., 2000; Myers, 1979).

Although the gender and sentencing literature tends to focus on the gender of the defendant (e.g., Daly, 1989; Daly & Bordt, 1995; Daly & Tonry, 1997; Kruttschnitt, 1981; Steffensmeier et al., 1993), the gender of the victim has also been considered as a factor in sentencing outcomes (e.g., Farrell & Swigert, 1986; Myers, 1979). To date, explanations of victim gender effects resemble explanations of defendant-based gender effects. One view of the impact of victim gender suggests that crimes with female victims are likely to be treated less severely than those with male victims. A gender conflict perspective maintains that the devalued role of women in American society marginalizes their status as victim and the perceived harm that has been done to the community (Baumer et al., 2000; Daly & Tonry, 1997). A contradictory perspective suggests that crime, and in particular violence against females, is viewed as more harmful than crimes against male victims (Baumer et al., 2000; Kleck, 1981). This may be mitigated or aggravated by decision makers' perceptions of the victim's familial role and responsibilities (see Daly, 1989, 1994). Furthermore, females are thought to engage in fewer behaviors that contribute to their victimization (Baumer et al., 2000; Hill & Crawford, 1990; Nagel & Hagan, 1983) or are perceived to be more threatening to their victims (Gross & Mauro, 1989). As a consequence, female victims may be perceived as less blameworthy for their own victimization and decision makers will respond to such acts more severely. The resulting argument maintains that in general, cases with female victims will receive more punitive response from decision makers than those with male victims.

The Victim in Prior Research

Studies examining the relationship of race and/or gender on sentencing decisions primarily focus on the defendant's characteristics rather than the victim's (Crawford, 2000; Crawford, Chiricos, & Kleck, 1998; Mustard, 2001; Spohn & Holleran, 2000; Steffensmeier et al., 1993, 1998). The relationship between victim characteristics and sentence outcome has not been researched as thoroughly. This is understandable considering that for many crimes, such as drug law violations, there is no readily identifiable victim. The limited harm to or involvement of the victim makes identification for several types of crime, such as property offenses, difficult with existing data. Furthermore, the conceptual links between property crime victim characteristics and their impact on sentence outcome is not as clear as with violent crime. This is not to concede that victim characteristics do not play a significant role in these sentencing decisions, merely that research on this question is extremely limited.

Research on the impact of victim characteristics on sentencing is predominantly found in research on homicide case outcomes and death penalty research (for notable exceptions, see LaFree, 1989; Spohn & Spears, 1996; Walsh, 1987). Although recent death penalty research does not find a significant race-of-defendant bias (but see Baldus et al., 1998), both victim race and victim gender continue to be associated with differential sentencing outcomes (Baldus et al., 1990; Baumer et al., 2000; Farrell

& Swigert, 1986; Gross & Mauro, 1989; Keil & Vito, 1992; Paternoster, 1984; Radelet & Pierce, 1991; Thomson, 1997; Williams & Holcomb, 2001). Numerous studies find that those who kill Whites are more likely to receive death sentences than those who kill Blacks (for reviews, see Baldus et al., 1998; General Accounting Office, 1990). Furthermore, this same body of research generally reports that cases with female victims receive more severe sanctions than those with male victims (Baldus et al., 1990; Baumer et al., 2000; Farrell & Swigert, 1986). For example, Williams and Holcomb (2001) found that homicides with White victims and homicides with female victims were significantly more likely to result in a death sentence than those with Black or male victims. Similar to other studies, however, the authors failed to specify victim gender-race combinations in their analyses. The Baldus et al. (1990) study, thought by many to be the most comprehensive examination of racial disparity and death sentencing practices, does not examine the potential interactive effects of victim race and gender on case outcomes, even though both victim race and victim gender were significantly associated with sentencing outcomes. More recently, Baumer et al. (2000) examined the role of victim conduct and demographics on several decision-making points in the disposition of homicide cases. In particular, the authors examined if victim conduct and victim demographics were associated with sentencing outcomes and how the interaction of these affected these relationships. Consistent with prior research, Baumer et al. found that even controlling for victim conduct, cases involving White victims and female victims were generally treated more severely than those with Black victims and male victims. If the prior research has consistently found a race-of-victim effect and a gender-of-victim effect, a relevant question is whether the joint effect of these characters could affect such findings and if so, why.

 Interaction Effects of Victim Race and Gender

Research is increasingly emphasizing the importance of potential interactive effects of race and gender on sentencing (e.g., Daly, 1994; Spohn, Gruhl, & Welch, 1987;

Steffensmeier et al., 1998). As Daly and Tonry (1997) noted, "the most interesting analytical and political questions center on the *intersections* of race and gender, not merely the separate categories of 'black', 'white', 'male', and 'female'" (p. 208). However, all of the above-mentioned research focuses exclusively on the intersection of a defendant's race and gender, not on the characteristics of the victim. As the previous discussion indicates, victim characteristics can have both a direct and indirect impact on criminal justice decision making and sentencing outcomes. If defendant characteristics are best thought of as intersecting and not independent, then it seems reasonable that victim characteristics should be examined with a similar perspective.

Similar to comments on the intersection of defendant characteristics, it is unlikely that decision makers consider the race or gender of a victim independent of one another. If, as previous research suggests, perceptions of a victim's status and personal characteristics affect decision making, then researchers should more comprehensively consider the characteristics that may affect such attributions (see also LaFree, 1989). By considering victim race and gender independently, research likely overlooks meaningful differences among victims within these categories. The suggestion that White victim and female victim cases are treated more severely because of an elevated status of those victims may be premature.

Consistent with the view that attributions of victim status affect decision making, we posit that a White female victim effect will be observed in death penalty cases that may alter previous findings of general White and female victim disparity. There is considerable historical evidence of a heightened concern with the victimization of White females in the United States. The cultural and symbolic power of White females as a protected class has resulted in numerous social changes and legal responses when that group has been perceived as threatened. For example, the passage of anti-opium laws in California in the 19th century was accomplished, in part, by the portrayal of opium as making White women susceptible to immoral behavior and victimization (Morgan, 1978). The White Slavery Act (also known as the Mann Act), passed in the early 20th century, was partially a response to the perceived moral temptations of the urban areas and the victimization of innocent White females through forced and consensual prostitution (Langum, 1994). Finally, the imposition of capital punishment for rape, especially in the South, provides additional evidence of the differential response to White female victimization (Friedman, 1993; Wolfgang, 1974). Historically, the killing of persons suspected of rape was reserved primarily for the rape of White females. The lynching of rapists was almost exclusively for Blacks suspected of raping Whites in the South (Friedman, 1993). Legal death sentences were rarely imposed in rape cases with non-White female victims and were disproportionately given in cases involving Black male offenders and White female victims (Kleck, 1981; Wolfgang, 1974).

Research demonstrates that legal decision making is strongly related to particular focal concerns of criminal justice actors (Daly, 1994; Steffensmeier et al., 1998). Furthermore, research on victims notes that the perceived status of the victim affects decision making through the attribution of blame, the perceived threat to the community that a particular crime represents, and the practical concerns of those decision makers (e.g., Baumer et al., 2000; Farrell & Swigert, 1986; LaFree, 1989; Stanko, 1981–1982). In relation to these focal concerns, considerable research suggests that the victimization of Whites and females is responded to differently than the victimization of Blacks and males, respectively. In individual cases, however, decision makers must consider the intersection of various victim characteristics rather than viewing them as independent. Thus, the aggravating effect of one characteristic may be offset by the mitigating effect of another characteristic. Consistent with this more complex understanding of victim attributes, the previous discussion provides some evidence of a general cultural bias that considers the victimization of White females particularly problematic. As the discussion of the impact of victim demographics indicates, male victims are likely to be perceived as more responsible for their own victimization. The victimization of White males, therefore, may not represent the same threat or harm to the community as the victimization of females, who are perceived as less able to defend themselves

(Gross & Mauro, 1989). Drawing on these findings, we hypothesize that those who kill White females are more likely to receive a death sentence than those who kill other victim race-gender combinations, even after controlling for other legally relevant factors. Furthermore, the independent effects of White and female victims may partially be a function of the severity with which White female victim cases are handled.

Research on Victim Interaction Effects

The prior research on the interactive effects of victim characteristics on sentencing outcomes is quite limited. In fact, the available research on this topic comes from studies that report such joint effects as secondary to their primary analyses. For example, Paternoster's (1984) examination of prosecutorial decision making in South Carolina found that prosecutors were significantly more likely to seek the death penalty in cases with White victims. Although the focus of this study was race-of-victim disparities, in several analyses the author distinguished victims by race-gender combinations (Paternoster, 1984, Tables 5–8). Paternoster found that prosecutors were generally more likely to seek the death penalty in homicides with either male or female White victims compared to those with Black victims, with White female victim cases having the greatest likelihood and Black male cases having the least. Radelet and Pierce (1991) found that Florida homicides with White victims and female victims were more likely to result in a death sentence. Furthermore, cases with White female victims were most likely to result in a death sentence and cases with Black male victims were the least likely to result in a death sentence.

There are, however, some limitations to these studies. Radelet and Pierce (1991) distinguished victim race and gender only for cross-tabulation and did not include a joint interaction variable in their regression model. Conclusions from that unadjusted model are therefore merely suggestive (Baldus et al., 1998). The data from the Paternoster (1984) study were gathered during a smaller time period (1977–1981), and data from both the Paternoster and the Radelet and Pierce studies were from a Southern jurisdiction.

Therefore, it is unclear whether those findings can be generalized to current sentencing practices, especially in non-Southern jurisdictions (Gross & Mauro, 1989; Peterson & Hagan, 1984). Despite these limitations, the general pattern appears to be that homicides with White female victims tend to be treated the most severely and homicides with Black male victims tend to be treated the least severely, even when controlling for legally relevant factors. This indicates that the interaction between victim race and victim gender may be an important factor in examining sentencing outcomes in homicide cases.

Method

Data Source

The current study is an examination of the relationship between victim race-gender and death sentences in Ohio. The methods used were adapted from Gross and Mauro (1989) and from Radelet and Pierce (1991). Data on homicides in Ohio were taken from the SHR, compiled by the FBI. Although some researchers (e.g., Maxfield, 1989) have indicated potential problems with SHR data, a number of studies use the SHR in death penalty research, including those investigating issues of deterrence (e.g., Bailey, 1998; Cochran, Chamlin, & Seth, 1994; Peterson & Bailey, 1991) and racial disparities in sentencing (e.g., Radelet & Pierce, 1991; Sorensen & Wallace, 1995; Thomson, 1997).

The SHR data used for the current study were for the years 1981 (the year Ohio reintroduced the death penalty into law) through 1994. SHR data included information on several variables for each homicide: offender's age, gender, race; victim's age, gender, race; circumstances surrounding the offense; weapon used; relationship between offender and victim; and county where the crime took place.

Data about homicides resulting in a death sentence were gathered from the Office of the Ohio Public Defender, the Office of the Ohio Attorney General, and the Ohio Department of Rehabilitation and Correction. Death sentence data included the same information as that found in the SHR.

Sample

Information was coded regarding the number of death sentences imposed, not the number of individuals who received a death sentence. For instance, although only 185 individual death row inmates were used in this study, the number of death sentences imposed was 271, reflecting those inmates who killed multiple victims and those homicides with multiple offenders. All death sentences were considered, including those that were eventually overturned and acquitted, overturned and resentenced to a lesser sentence, and overturned and resentenced to death. For the purpose of this study, a case refers to a single homicide victim. This allows us to compare differences across victim characteristics.

The SHR data contain information regarding incidents of murder and negligent and nonnegligent manslaughter. The SHR data are coded in such a way to distinguish between murder and nonnegligent manslaughter and negligent manslaughter. Cases of negligent manslaughter were omitted from the analyses because the criminal nature of such acts is often in dispute and penalties are considerably less than those for other homicides. The SHR–death sentence database used in the analysis (1981–1994) consisted of 6,443 cases. However, the usable sample was reduced by two factors. First, those cases in which there was no known information about the suspect were excluded from the analysis. Second, cases in which the offender was younger than the age of 18 at the time of the offense were not included in the analysis because under Ohio law, individuals younger than the age of 18 are not eligible for the death penalty (Ohio Revised Code 2929.023, 1999). A sample of 5,320 cases was used in the final analyses. This includes 271 homicides for which a death sentence was imposed and excludes those cases in which missing data were found.

Variables

The variables used in the study consisted of one dependent variable, whether a death sentence was imposed, and multiple independent variables. Because Ohio has executed only eight persons (at the time of the study)

since 1981, death sentence data rather than execution data were used. Many SHR variables contained multiple values and therefore, some of these variables were collapsed for the purpose of the current study. These variables are listed in Table 7.3. To determine whether victim race and gender, played a role in determining who received a death sentence, the variables identified in Table 7.3 are included as control variables that could be associated with sentencing outcomes.

Prior Record

Before addressing the results, the authors believe it is important to discuss the omission of prior record as a control variable. Although commentaries have been made about the importance of including information on prior record in research on the imposition of death sentences and executions (e.g., Kleck, 1981), the authors feel that there are three arguments that mitigate such criticism. The first issue is a pragmatic one. Although researchers should always seek the most complete, reliable, and valid data available, the data on the prior record for more than 5,000 cases were simply not available to the researchers. This left the authors in the position of choosing between continuing on an important topic in a jurisdiction where little research had been conducted or abandoning the project in fear of the obvious criticism. Believing that the methodology had at least facial validity, the former was chosen.

Second, it was clear from prior research that race of the defendant was unlikely to be an independent predictor of whether a homicide resulted in a death sentence. Critics could contend that prior record has a significant role in who receives a death sentence in those jurisdictions where it is an aggravating factor, as in Ohio. Theoretically, this could mitigate disparities noted among the imposition of death sentences. However, if this were so, homicides with Black victims, who are most likely to be killed by Black offenders, should result in a substantial number of death sentences because Black offenders are more likely to have serious prior arrests than are White offenders (Donziger, 1996). The present study finds just the opposite. Homicides with Black victims were less likely to result in a death

Table 7.3   Variables in the Analysis

Variable (N)	0 = No % (n)	1 = Yes % (n)
Was a death sentence imposed? (6,443)	96 (6,172)	4 (271)
Was victim female? (6,442)	73 (4,691)	27 (1,751)
Was victim White?[a] (6,434)	55 (3,521)	45 (2,913)
Was offender male? (6,437)	15 (973)	85 (5,464)
Was offender White?[a] (6,432)	60 (3,860)	40 (2,572)
Was a gun used?[b] (6,313)	37 (2,329)	63 (3,984)
Was it a stranger homicide?[c] (6,228)	77 (4,786)	23 (1,442)
Did homicide involve other felony?[d] (5,589)	82 (4,595)	18 (994)
Was offense a multiple homicide? (6,443)	91 (5,859)	9 (584)
Did homicide occur in urban area? (6,443)	8 (484)	92 (5,959)
Was victim 12 or younger? (6,422)	94 (6,011)	6 (411)
Was offender younger than 25? (6,443)	64 (4,121)	36 (2,322)
Was victim a White male?		30 (1,925)
Was victim a Black female?		12 (762)
Was victim a Black male?		44 (2,759)

a. Supplementary Homicide Reports (SHR) data coded race as White, Black, Native American, Asian and Islander, and Other. For the current study, the race variable was collapsed, reflecting White (White, Native American, Asian, and Islander) and non-White (Black). This did not affect the results of the analysis, because few Native Americans, Asians, and Islanders appeared as offenders or victims. It should be noted that Hispanics are coded as White in the SHR.

b. SHR data coded weapon as 1 of 17 possible choices, ranging from 5 different types of guns to poisoning, asphyxiation, and so forth. The current study combined all guns into one value and all nonguns into another.

c. SHR data coded relationship as 1 of 29 possible choices, ranging from various nonstranger categories such as family members, friends, acquaintances, coworkers, and so on to a separate category of stranger. The nonstranger categories were collapsed into one value and the stranger category was left as is. This is consistent with previous death penalty research such as Bailey (1998) and Sorensen and Wallace (1995).

d. SHR data coded circumstances as one of 33 possible choices, ranging from various crimes committed during the course of the homicide to gang killing to lovers' triangle, and so forth. All SHR values that involved a felony incident were collapsed into one value and all other values were treated as nonfelony homicides.

sentence than those homicides with White victims. In particular, Blacks killed by other Blacks were consistently the racial combination least likely to result in a death sentence.

Third and most important, previous research actually shows that prior record has little impact on the race-of-victim disparity (Gross & Mauro, 1989, p. 102).

As Gross and Mauro (1989) pointed out, the Baldus et al. (1990) study was perhaps the most comprehensive analysis ever conducted on racial disparity and the death penalty. Baldus et al. (1990) included more than 200 variables in their analysis, including serious prior record; their finding that homicides in Georgia with White victims were 4.3 times more likely to result in a death sentence was not mitigated when prior record was controlled. Furthermore, the findings of the Baldus et al. (1990) study in Georgia reflect a pattern of racial disparity similar to that found in Gross and Mauro's examination of the same jurisdiction for roughly the same time period. This study replicated the methods used in Gross and Mauro, and the authors are encouraged by the degree of reliability those studies suggest for the current research.

 Results

Table 7.4 provides the descriptive statistics for the data under analysis. The majority of homicide victims are males, with Black males outnumbering White males. Blacks compose about 55% of homicide victims, whereas Whites compose about 45% of homicide victims. Females compose 27% of homicide victims, with White female victims slightly outnumbering Black female victim homicides.

Although cases involving male victims compose a slight majority of death sentences, female victim homicides are disproportionately represented in death sentences. Furthermore, although Blacks compose the majority of homicide victims, they are underrepresented in death penalty cases relative to their percentage in all homicide cases. When examining victim gender-race interaction and death sentences, further disparity exists. Although White females compose only 15% of homicide victims, they compose 35% of all death sentences. These initial results indicate that White victims, and in particular White female victims, are disproportionately represented when it comes to the imposition of death sentences. This is consistent with findings reported in previous studies (e.g., Gross & Mauro, 1989; Radelet & Pierce, 1991). Another important finding is that homicide in Ohio is predominantly an intraracial phenomenon (89%), and that the death sentences generally reflect this distribution (77%), although interracial homicides are overrepresented among death sentences.

To test the hypothesized relationship that those who kill Whites and those who kill females are more likely to receive a death sentence, logistic regression analysis was employed using the control variables found in Table 7.3. Findings from this analysis indicate that race and gender of the victim are significantly related to the imposition of a death sentence. In particular, homicides with female victims are more likely to result in a death sentence and those with White victims are more likely to receive a death sentence.

There was no observed relationship between the race of the defendant and sentence outcome, and gender of defendant (male) was significant only at a weaker alpha level (.05). These results are similar to findings in previous research on the imposition of death sentences (e.g., Baldus et al., 1990; Gross & Mauro, 1989; Radelet & Pierce, 1991).

To test the primary research hypothesis, dummy variables were created using different victim gender-race combinations and were analyzed as single predictors of death sentences (Black female, White male, Black male victims). Note that White female was omitted from the analysis as it was used as the reference variable in the analysis. This method of testing the interactive effects of race and gender of the victim was based on previous research by Steffensmeier et al. (1998) and by Spohn and Holleran (2000). Similar to the present study, these authors suspected that analyses of main (or direct) effects of independent race and gender variables masked significant differences that could be revealed by examining the interactive effects of race and gender.

Findings of the logistic model incorporating a victim race-gender interaction variable reveal that homicides with victim race-gender combinations other than White female were significantly less likely to result in a death sentence compared to homicides with White female victims. Homicides with Black female victims were significantly less likely to receive death sentences than homicides involving White female victims. This suggests that the general female victim disparity is primarily a function of White female victim homicides. Furthermore, we also found that homicides with White male victims were significantly less likely to result in a death sentence compared to those with White female victims. These findings suggest that the initial White

Table 7.4 Characteristics of Ohio Homicides by Gender and Race of Offender and Victim

Offender-Victim	All Homicides % (n)	No Death Sentence % (n)	Death Sentence % (n)
WM-WM	20 (1,310)	20 (1,254)	21 (56)
WM-WF	12 (788)	12 (715)	28 (73)
WM-BM	2 (146)	2 (140)	2 (6)
WM-BF	<1 (14)	<1 (12)	<1 (2)
BM-BM	32 (2,067)	33 (2,026)	15 (41)
BM-BF	10 (637)	10 (605)	12 (32)
BM-WM	6 (361)	5 (326)	13 (35)
BM-WF	2 (130)	2 (110)	8 (20)
WF-WF	1 (58)	1 (58)	—
WF-WM	4 (231)	4 (230)	<1 (1)
WF-BM	<1 (20)	<1 (20)	—
WF-BF	<1 (4)	<1 (4)	—
BF-BF	2 (107)	2 (106)	<1 (1)
BF-BM	8 (526)	8 (522)	1 (4)
BF-WM	<1 (16)	<1 (16)	—
BF-WF	<1 (10)	<1 (10)	—
N	6,425	6,154	271

NOTE: W = White; B = Black; M = male; F = female.

victim and female victim disparity found is the product of a specific victim gender-race combination (White female) rather than race or gender alone.

Additional Analyses

The authors conducted two additional analyses of the data to increase confidence in the above findings. As previously noted, the SHR does not distinguish between murder and nonnegligent manslaughter; therefore, cases of nonnegligent manslaughter (which are not death eligible) were likely included in the present analysis. To account for this, a separate logistic analysis was conducted on a subsample limited to those cases with felony circumstances, which is an aggravating circumstance under Ohio law. Felony circumstances were strongly correlated with a death sentence, and the analysis of the felony circumstance–only subsample was viewed as a way of increasing the likelihood of obtaining a more death-eligible sample of cases. This could be used to determine if there were differences between the sample as a whole and those cases with a greater likelihood of receiving a death sentence. Limiting the sample to homicides with felony circumstances reduced the sample to 994 homicides and 236 death sentences (thus omitting 35 death sentences).

The model included the same variables used in the original model on the entire sample. The only substantive change is that gender of offender (male) is no longer significant and stranger homicides are only significant at the lower alpha level (.05). Most important, results indicate that the primary variable of interest (victim race-gender interaction) remained significant. In effect, significantly reducing the sample to a population that is more likely to be death eligible did not alter our original findings. Homicides with White female victims continue to be more likely to result in a death sentence than other victim race gender combinations.

Second, there is the possibility that in addition to a victim interaction effect, the interaction of offender characteristics will be related to sentencing outcomes in particular cases. As previously noted, research has established that Blacks who kill Whites are disproportionately represented among death sentences. In particular, Black males who kill White females may partially explain the female, White, and/or White female victim effect noted in prior research and the current study. As a preliminary test of such an interaction, the authors created an interracial variable to control for interracial homicides. This could provide some initial insight into the impact interracial homicides have on present findings. The interracial variable was included in a separate logistic regression model including the original variables of interest. Interracial homicides were not found to be significant even at a lower (.05) level and did not alter substantive findings from previous analyses. Even after controlling for interracial homicides, the victim interaction variables remained significant.

Implications and Future Research

This study examines the relationship between victim gender and race on the imposition of death sentences in Ohio. Initially, it appeared that homicides with female victims and those with White victims were more likely to receive a death sentence than those with male or Black victims. However, by examining the combined effect of the victim's gender and race, it was discovered that homicides with White females are significantly more likely to result in a death sentence than homicides with other victim gender-race combinations.

Similar to previous studies (e.g., Paternoster, 1984; Radelet & Pierce, 1991), the present study finds that homicides with White female victims had the highest likelihood of resulting in a death sentence, whereas homicides with Black male victims had the lowest probability. However, results indicate that the correlation between White female victim homicides and death sentences was strong enough to create the appearance of a relationship between general White victim homicides and death sentences and general female victim homicides and death sentences. The present study suggests that the central factor in understanding existing racial disparity in death sentences may be the severity with which those who kill White females are treated relative to other gender-race victim combinations. This finding is consistent with the view that Black female victims do not have the same status as White female victims (see Belknap, 1996; Zack, 1998) but challenges the argument that an elevated status extends to all White victims. It appears that potential gender-of-victim and race-of-victim effects on sentencing may be more specific than previously thought.

Numerous authors have argued that prior record is an essential control variable for sentencing research (Klein, Petersilia, & Turner, 1990; Steffensmeier et al., 1993). We have argued that although such data could strengthen confidence in the present findings, there is little logical basis to expect that prior record would affect an observed relationship between sentences and victim characteristics. The methods used in the present study are a replication of Gross and Mauro's (1989) analysis of racial disparity in Georgia and other states. Their research examines the same jurisdiction during an overlapping time frame as the Baldus et al. (1990) study. The fact that Gross and Mauro found similar results as the more rigorous Baldus et al. (1998)

project adds to the validity of the methodology used by Gross and Mauro and by the present study.

Given the preliminary nature of this study, it would be prudent to identify several unresolved questions and suggestions for future research. First, it is possible that homicides involving White female victims are more heinous or aggravated than homicides involving other victims (see Baldus et al., 1990). To account for this, mitigating and aggravating circumstances were included in the analyses. Most important, felony circumstance was included as a control variable and an analysis of a subsample of cases involving only felony circumstances was conducted. These steps likely reduced, but did not eliminate, the possibility that there is something unique about White female victim homicides that could explain the present findings. Future research should attempt to control for all potential aggravating circumstances and mitigating factors. Prior research finds that disparity is most likely to occur in less aggravated circumstances (Baldus et al., 1990, 1998; Baumer, 2000; see also Spohn & Cederblom, 1991), suggesting that sentencing disparity may be the strongest for those cases that tend to draw the least public attention and in which decision makers are "freed" from statutory constraints (see Kalven & Zeisel, 1966). The consideration of interactive victim characteristics in models with more complete case information would help determine whether homicides with White females are more aggravated and thus, would partially explain the proposed relationship.

Future research should also consider whether homicides involving White females are different from those involving other victim race-gender categories in a manner that has not been quantitatively captured by the present study. As researchers have noted, the context and qualitative aspects of particular cases and settings can greatly alter decision making yet escape the attention of quantitative studies (Daly, 1994). Such questions, however, are more appropriately addressed with detailed analyses of case files and naturalistic observations during a considerable time period (e.g., Daly, 1994).

A significant limitation of the present study was its inability to analyze the data at different decision-making points. This would have allowed researchers to examine when the observed disparities were produced. The consideration of the tremendous role prosecutorial discretion has on sentencing outcomes seems particularly important. Previous research has indicated that prosecutorial decision making can result in considerable disparities (Baldus et al., 1990; Paternoster, 1984). Such research would complement our emphasis on the effect that victim characteristics have on the focal concerns of decision makers. The practical implications of decisions, especially the concern about outcome uncertainty, appear to dramatically shape prosecutorial decision making (Albonetti, 1987; Albonetti & Hepburn, 1996; Stanko, 1981–1982). A more complete understanding of how perceptions of victim status affect these decisions would provide additional insight into the validity of the ideas presented here.

Though unique in the literature, the present study suffers from the obvious limitations of available data. We call on interested scholars with access to more complete data to test our hypotheses and challenge our findings. A major question is whether previous research findings of a general victim race disparity are similarly explained by a White female victim effect. The authors suggest that researchers consider reexamining existing data and previously published research to determine if findings of a White victim or female victim effect are partially explained by a specific victim race-gender combination. It is clear, however, that in addition to continuing inquiries into defendant-based disparities, future researchers should consider examining the relationship between the intersections of victim race and victim gender on disparity in capital and noncapital sentencing outcomes.

References

Albonetti, C. A. (1987). Prosecutorial discretion: The effects of uncertainty. *Law & Society Review*, 21, 291–313.

Albonetti, C. A., & Hepburn, J. R. (1996). Prosecutorial discretion to defer criminalization: The effects of defendant's ascribed and achieved status characteristics. *Journal of Quantitative Criminology*, 12, 63–81.

Bailey, W. (1998). Deterrence, brutalization and the death penalty: Another examination of Oklahoma's return to capital punishment. *Criminology*, 36, 711–734.

Baldus, D., Woodworth, G., & Pulaski, C. (1990). *Equal justice and the death penalty: A legal and empirical analysis.* Boston: Northeastern University Press.

Baldus, D., Woodworth, G., Zuckerman, D., Weiner, N. A., & Broffitt, B. (1998). Racial discrimination and the death penalty in the post-Furman era: An empirical and legal overview, with recent findings from Philadelphia. *Cornell Law Review, 83,* 1638–1770.

Baumer, E. P., Messner, S. F., & Felson, R. B. (2000). The role of victim characteristics in the disposition of murder cases. *Justice Quarterly, 17,* 281–307.

Belknap, J. (1996). *The invisible woman: Gender, crime, and justice.* Belmont, CA: Wadsworth.

Cochran, J., Chamlin, M., & Seth, M. (1994). Deterrence or brutalization? An impact assessment of Oklahoma's return to capital punishment. *Criminology, 32,* 107–134.

Crawford, C. (2000). Gender, race, and habitual offender sentencing in Florida. *Criminology, 38,* 263–280.

Crawford, C., Chiricos, T., & Kleck, G. (1998). Race, racial threat, and sentencing of habited offenders. *Criminology, 36,* 481–512.

Daly, K. (1989). Neither conflict nor labeling nor paternalism will suffice: Intersections of race, ethnicity, gender, and family in criminal justice decisions. *Crime & Delinquency, 3,* 136–168.

Daly, K. (1994). *Gender, crime, and punishment.* New Haven, CT: Yale University Press.

Daly, K., & Bordt, R. L. (1995). Sex effects and sentencing: An analysis of the statistical literature. *Justice Quarterly, 12,* 141–175.

Daly, K. A., & Tonry, M. (1997). Gender, race, and sentencing. In M. Tonry (Ed.), *Crime and justice: A review of research* (pp. 201–252). Chicago: University of Chicago Press.

Donziger, S. (Ed.). (1996). *The real war on crime: The report of the National Criminal Justice Commission.* New York: Harper Perennial.

Farrell, R. A., & Swigert, V. L. (1986). Adjudication in homicide: An interpretive analysis the effects of defendant and victim social characteristics. *Journal of Research in Crime and Delinquency, 23,* 349–369.

Friedman, L. (1993). *Crime and punishment in American history.* New York: Basic Books.

General Accounting Office. (1990). *Death penalty sentencing research indicates pattern of racial disparities.* Washington, DC: Author.

Gross, S., & Mauro, R. (1989). *Death and discrimination: Racial disparities in capital sentencing.* Boston: Northeastern University Press.

Hill, G. D., & Crawford, E. M. (1990). Women, race, and crime. *Criminology, 28,* 601–623.

Kalven, H., & Zeisel, H. (1966). *The American jury.* Boston: Little, Brown.

Keil, T., & Vito, G. (1992). The effects of the Furman and Gregg decisions on Black-White execution ratios in the South. *Journal of Criminal Justice, 20,* 217–226.

Kleck, G. (1981). Racial discrimination in criminal sentencing: A critical evaluation of the evidence with additional evidence on the death penalty. *American Sociological Review, 46,* 783–805.

Klein, S., Petersilia, J., & Turner, S. (1990). Race and imprisonment decisions in California. *Science, 247,* 812–816.

Kruttschnitt, C. (1981). Social status and sentences of female offenders. *Law & Society Review, 15,* 247–265.

LaFree, G. D. (1989). *Rape and criminal justice.* Belmont, CA: Wadsworth.

Langum, D. J. (1994). *Crossing over the line: Legislating morality and the Mann Act.* Chicago: University of Chicago Press.

Marvell, T., & Moody, C. (1999). Female and male homicide victimization rates: Comparing trends and aggressors. *Criminology, 37,* 879–902.

Maxfield, M. G. (1989). Circumstances in supplemental homicide reports: Variety and validity. *Criminology, 27,* 671–695.

Morgan, P. A. (1978). The legislation of drug law: Economic crisis and social control. *Journal of Drug Issues, 8,* 53–62.

Mustard, D. (2001). Racial, ethnic, and gender disparities in sentencing: Evidence from the U.S. federal courts. *Journal of Law and Economics, 44,* 285–314.

Myers, M. A. (1979). Offended parties and official reactions: Victims and the sentencing of criminal defendants. *The Sociological Quarterly, 20,* 529–540.

Nagel, I., & Hagan, J. (1983). Gender and crime: Offense patterns and criminal court sanctions. In M. Tonry & N. Morris (Eds.), *Crime and justice: A review of research* (pp. 91–144). Chicago: University of Chicago Press.

Ohio Revised Code. (1999). In L. Katz & P. Giannelli (Eds.), *Ohio criminal justice* (p. 469). Cleveland: WestGroup.

Paternoster, R. (1984). Prosecutorial discretion in requesting the death penalty: A case of victim-based racial discrimination. *Law & Society Review, 18,* 437–478.

Peterson, R., & Bailey, W. (1991). Felony murder and capital punishment: An examination of the deterrence question. *Criminology, 29,* 367–395.

Peterson, R., & Hagan, J. (1984). Changing conceptions of race: Towards an account of anomalous findings of sentencing research. *American Sociological Review, 49,* 56–70.

Radelet, M., & Pierce, G. (1991). Choosing who will die: Race and the death penalty in Florida. *Florida Law Review, 43,* 1–34.

Riedel, M., & Rinehart, T. (1996). Murder clearances and missing data. *Journal of Crime and Justice, 19,* 83–102.

Sampson, R., & Lauritsen, J. (1997). Racial and ethnic disparities in crime and criminal justice in the United States. In M. Tonry (Ed.), *Ethnicity, crime, and immigration: Comparative and cross-national perspectives* (pp. 311–374). Chicago: University of Chicago Press.

Sorensen, J., & Wallace, D. (1995). Capital punishment in Missouri: Examining the issues of racial disparity. *Behavioral Sciences and the Law, 13,* 61–80.

Spohn, C., & Cederblom, J. (1991). Race and disparities in sentencing: A test of the liberation hypothesis. *Justice Quarterly, 8,* 305–325.

Spohn, C., Gruhl, J., & Welch, S. (1987). The impact of the ethnicity and gender of defendants on the decision to reject or dismiss felony charges. *Criminology, 25,* 175–191.

Spohn, C., & Holleran, D. (2000). The imprisonment penalty paid by young, unemployed, Black, and Hispanic male offenders. *Criminology, 38,* 281–306,

Spohn, C., & Spears, J. (1996). The effect of offender and victim characteristics on sexual assault case processing decisions. *Justice Quarterly, 13,* 649–679.

Stanko, E. A. (1981–1982). The impact of victim assessment on prosecutors' screening decisions: The case of the New York County District Attorney's Office. *Law & Society Review, 16,* 225–239.

Steffensmeier, D., & Demuth, S. (2000). Ethnicity and sentencing outcomes in U.S. federal courts: Who is punished more harshly—White, Black, White-Hispanic, or Black-Hispanic defendants? *American Sociological Review, 65,* 705–729.

Steffensmeier, D., Kramer, J., & Streifel, C. (1993). Gender and imprisonment decisions. *Criminology, 31,* 411–446.

Steffensmeier, D., Ulmer, J., & Kramer, J. (1998). The interaction of race, gender, and age in criminal sentencing: The punishment cost of being young, Black, and male. *Criminology, 36,* 763–798.

Thomson, E. (1997). Discrimination and the death penalty in Arizona. *Criminal Justice Review, 22,* 65–76.

Walsh, A. (1987). The sexual stratification hypothesis and sexual assault in light of the changing conceptions of race. *Criminology, 25,* 153–173.

Williams, M., & Holcomb, J. (2001). Racial disparity and death sentences in Ohio. *Journal of Criminal Justice, 29,* 207–218.

Wolfgang, M. E. (1974), Racial discrimination in the death sentence for rape. In W. J. Bowers (Ed.), *Executions in America* (pp. 109–120). Lexington, MA: Lexington Books.

Zack, N. (1998). *Thinking about race.* Belmont, CA: Wadsworth.

Zatz, M. (1984). Race, ethnicity, and determinate sentencing: A new dimension to an old controversy. *Criminology, 22,* 147–171.

DISCUSSION QUESTIONS

1. What does the research reviewed by Williams and Holcomb reveal about the effects of the race of the offender, the race of the victim, and the gender of the victim on death penalty decisions?

2. Why do the researchers argue that "the most interesting analytical and political questions center on the *intersections* of race and gender, not merely the separate categories of 'black,' 'white,' 'male,' and 'female'"?

3. Williams and Holcomb contended that there is considerable historical evidence of preferential treatment of white females. What evidence did they cite to support this statement?

4. The authors hypothesized that those who kill white females are more likely than other offenders to receive a death sentence. Does their analysis support or refute this hypothesis?

5. What are the implications of the results of this study for research and policy?

READING

In June of 2001, Lionel Tate, a black boy who was 12 years old when he killed a 6-year-old family friend while demonstrating a wrestling move he had seen on television, was sentenced to life in prison without the possibility of parole. Tate, who claimed that the death was an accident, was tried as an adult in Broward County, Florida; he was convicted of first-degree murder. One month later, Nathaniel Brazill, a 14-year-old black boy, was sentenced by a Florida judge to 28 years in prison without the possibility of parole. Brazill was 13 years old

AUTHORS' NOTE: An earlier version of this paper was presented at the 2002 American Society of Criminology meetings in Chicago, Illinois and received the American Sociological Association's student paper award for Crime, Law and Deviance and the American Society of Criminology Gene Carte Award. The authors would like to acknowledge the many helpful comments they received on earlier versions of this paper from D. Wayne Osgood, Thomas Bernard, John Kramer, and Darrell Steffensmeier.

SOURCE: "The Juvenile Penalty: A Comparison of Juvenile and Young Adult Sentencing Outcomes in Criminal Court," by Megan C. Kurlychek and Brian D. Johnson in *Criminology*, vol. 42, no. 2, pp. 485–517, November, 2004. Reprinted by permission of the American Society of Criminology.

when he shot and killed Barry Grunow, a popular 30-year-old seventh-grade teacher at a middle school in Lake Worth, Florida. Although Brazill did not deny that he fired the shot that killed his teacher, he claimed that he had only meant to scare Grunow and that the shooting was an accident. Like Tate, Brazill was tried as an adult; he was convicted of second-degree murder.

These two cases raised a storm of controversy regarding the prosecution of children as adults. Those on one side argue that children who commit adult crimes, such as murder, should be treated as adults; they should be prosecuted as adults and sentenced to adult correctional institutions. As Marc Shiner, the prosecutor in Brazill's case, put it, "This was a heinous crime committed by a young man with a difficult personality who should be behind bars. Let us not forget a man's life has been taken away" (Randall, 2001). Those on the other side contend that prosecuting children as adults is "unwarranted and misguided." They assert that children who commit crimes of violence typically suffer from severe mental and emotional problems and that locking kids up in adult jails does not deter crime or rehabilitate juvenile offenders. Although they acknowledge that juvenile offenders should be punished for their actions, they claim that incarcerating them in adult prisons for the rest of their lives "is an outrage" ("Juvenile Justice," n.d.). According to Vincent Schiraldi, president of the Justice Policy Institute, "In adult prisons, Brazill will never receive the treatment he needs to reform himself. Instead, he will spend his time trying to avoid being beaten, assaulted, or raped in a world where adults prey on, rather than protect, the young" ("Juvenile Justice," n.d.).

The increase in juvenile crime during the 1980s and early 1990s, coupled with highly publicized cases of very young children accused of murder and other violent crimes, prompted a number of states to alter procedures for handling certain types of juvenile offenders (Torbet & Szymanski, 1998). Some states lowered the age at which youth could be admitted to adult prisons. Other states responded by lowering the age when children can be transferred from juvenile court to criminal court or by expanding the list of offenses for which juveniles can be waived to criminal court. All states specify the age at which the jurisdiction of the juvenile court ends. In Connecticut, North Carolina, and New York, for example, the jurisdiction of the juvenile court ends after age 15. Offenders who are 16 years of age or older are processed by the adult courts. Ten other states (Georgia, Illinois, Louisiana, Massachusetts, Michigan, Mississippi, New Hampshire, South Carolina, Texas, and Wisconsin) extend the jurisdiction of the juvenile court through a youth's 17th birthday. In all other states the jurisdiction of the juvenile court ends at the 18th birthday (Griffin, Torbet, & Szymanski, 1998). Juvenile waiver laws ignore some of these cutoffs altogether. For example, Colorado legislators enacted a statute that provides for 14- to 17-year-olds charged with violent felonies to be tried as adults. California voters recently enacted Proposition 21, an initiative that, among other things, reduced the waiver age from 16 to 14 years of age. These changes signal an increasing desire to treat juvenile offenders more harshly than in the past. Despite the emergence of waiver laws, though, the vast majority of juvenile cases are still processed in the traditional fashion (Sickmund, Stahl, Finnegan, Snyder, & Butts, 1998). Whereas one study from the mid-1990s showed that 12,000 juveniles were waived to adult court in the space of 1 year (Bureau of Justice Statistics, 1998), another more recent study showed a reduction throughout the latter part of the 1990s in the number of juvenile waivers to adult court (Puzzanchera, 2003). Researchers have also looked at the effects of juvenile waivers on sentences, and there does not appear to be clear evidence that the former affects the latter (Fagan, 1995).

The article by Megan Kurlychek and Brian Johnson compares the sentences imposed on juvenile offenders transferred to adult court with the sentences imposed on similarly situated young adult offenders. The results of their study show that juveniles processed in adult courts in Pennsylvania were sentenced more harshly than young adults. According to these authors, juvenile status exerts "a significant influence on courtroom decision making, resulting in a substantial juvenile penalty."

The Juvenile Penalty

A Comparison of Juvenile and Young Adult Sentencing Outcomes in Criminal Court

Megan C. Kurlychek and Brian D. Johnson

"If you're old enough to do the crime, you're old enough to do the time." Slogans such as this graced media headlines and dominated political campaigns across the nation during the 1990s (Zimring, 1998). Sparked by an increase in juvenile violent crime during a period when other forms of crime were decreasing, legislatures in nearly every state took action to "get tough" on juvenile crime (Torbet, Gable, Hurst, Montgomery, Szymanski and Thomas, 1996). While these changes affected various aspects of the juvenile justice system, such as judicial sentencing authority and the confidentiality of juvenile proceedings, by far the most common and controversial change was to remove increasing numbers of juveniles from the jurisdiction of the juvenile court and to process them as adults (Torbet et al., 1996; Griffin, Torbet and Szymanski, 1998). This study investigates the adult court processing of these transferred juveniles, focusing on the impact that "juvenile status" exerts on judicial sentencing decisions in adult criminal court.

While relying on the adult court to sentence certain juvenile offenders is not a new concept, 49 states and the District of Columbia expanded the provisions by which juveniles could reach adult court during the 1990s (Sickmund, 2003). Incorporating such provisions as statutory exclusion and prosecutorial direct file, these new laws allow for the transfer of broad classes of juveniles based on consideration of their current offense and prior criminal histories, with limited concern for individual characteristics or circumstances (Torbet et al., 1996; Bishop, 2000; Zatz, 2000). The result of these provisions has been a dramatic increase in the population of juveniles being processed and sentenced in adult court. Indeed, early reports found the use of expanded statutory exclusion provisions alone to have accounted for an additional 218,000 juveniles being tried in adult courts between 1996 and 1999 (Snyder and Sickmund, 1999).

With this increase of juveniles in the adult criminal justice system, it has become increasingly important to better understand the criminal processing and sentencing outcomes associated with this unique population. To date, most research on juveniles transferred to adult court has focused on describing the population of transferred juveniles (for example, Fagan, Forst and Vivona, 1987; Poulos and Orchowsky, 1994; Clement, 1997; Klein, 1998; Snyder, Sickmund and Poe-Yamagata, 2000), or comparing the sentencing decisions of adult and juvenile court judges for similar offenders (for example Hamparian, Estep, Muntean, Priestine, Swisher, Wallace and White, 1982; Rudman, Hartstone, Fagan and Moore, 1986; Champion, 1989; Fagan, 1991; Lemmon, 1991). Combined, this research provides a wealth of information regarding the population characteristics of juvenile offenders reaching adult court as well as the potential differences between juvenile and adult court dispositions.

However, an equally important question has received considerably less attention in the literature. It is: "How do the criminal justice outcomes of transferred juveniles compare to those of other young adult offenders?" If the purpose of the transfer policy is to redefine these juveniles as "adults," then an equally important measure of its effectiveness is to determine if transferred juveniles are indeed receiving similar sentences to other adult offenders. In addition to furthering current knowledge on juvenile sentencing outcomes, such a comparison has the added advantage of ensuring equality of the dispositional options available to the judge at the time of sentencing, which better isolates the influence that "juvenile status" exerts on judicial sentencing decisions in criminal court.

To address this question, the current research systematically compares the sentencing of juvenile offenders in adult court to other young adult offenders (ages 18 to 24). By using this alternative comparison group, this study provides an important first look at the potential influence of juvenile status on adult court sentencing outcomes. Because our study focuses on adult court sentencing practices, we frame our analysis using the focal concerns theoretical perspective on adult court sentencing. Before outlining our theoretical framework, though, we first incorporate relevant research on the historical influence juvenile status has held in legal proceedings. We then review previous literature on juvenile transfer to adult court.

 ## The Juvenile Court and Transfer Proceedings

In considering the processing of juveniles in adult court, it is useful to first understand the historical role juvenile status has played in society and how it has influenced the legal processing of young offenders. The idea that children are in some way different from adults and therefore worthy of differential treatment before the law, can be traced over 4,000 years to the earliest legal writing in the Hammurabi Code. These laws set forth the legal precedent that children were to be given more lenient treatment than adults—a distinction that has remained prevalent in legal and religious codes (Bernard, 1992). In general, the laws set an age below which all acts are exempt from punishment and a second age below which acts have reduced or "mitigated" consequences (Bernard, 1992).

In the United States, these ideas crystallized in 1899 in Cook County, Illinois with the nation's first juvenile court. Resting on the notion that "children are more innocent and less guilty of criminal intent" than adults (Empey, Stafford and Hay, 1999), this legislation created an entirely separate system of justice for youths in which the role of the state was to rehabilitate and care for delinquent children rather than to punish them for illegal acts (Platt, 1969; Gettis, 2000).

Given this rationale for a separate system of justice for youths, how are juvenile transfers to adult court justified? Zimring's (1998) account of youth violence in America provides one plausible explanation, suggesting that an act itself can imply maturity. According to Zimring (1998), children are thought capable of minor transgressions, but when they engage in particularly violent acts, they cross into the domain of adult responsibility. Their juvenile status is revoked and the criminal justice system becomes justified in treating them as adults. Snyder and Sickmund (1999) suggest an alternate explanation, focusing instead on scrutiny of the juvenile court's ability to deal with serious offenders. As juvenile violence continued to increase during a time when other types of crime and violence were decreasing, blame for the phenomenon was largely placed on the lenient practices of the juvenile court. The retributive focus of the adult criminal justice system was thus seen as a more appropriate alternative.

Whether the focus is on offender culpability or system response, the outcome is the same: A select group of offenders is targeted for transfer to adult court. As such, the majority of research on juvenile transfer policies has been designed to determine if those juveniles reaching adult court are indeed the targeted offenders (Bishop et al., 1989; Bishop and Frazier, 1991; Feld, 1987; Lemon, Sontheimer and Saylor, 1991; Poulos and Orchowsky, 1994; Clement, 1997; Bishop, 2000). Research addressing this question has consistently found that those most likely to reach adult court are not necessarily violent offenders, but instead older juveniles with accumulated extensive court histories, primarily for repeat drug and property offenses (Feld, 1987; Bishop, 1989; Champion, 1989; Howell, 1996). Because the frenzy of legislative activity in the 1990s changed transfer provisions to specifically target violent offenders, one could logically assume that the proportion of violent offenses in this population might be increasing (Bishop, 2000; Zatz, 2000). Surprisingly, though, reviews of the consequences of these new transfer provisions are mixed with some studies suggesting that the new laws provide for the explicit transfer of less-serious property and drug offenders (Klein, 1998) and others showing an increasing proportion of violent offenders reaching adult court (Sickmund, 2003).

The traditional question addressed in the literature has been whether juveniles processed in adult court receive more severe treatment than those in juvenile court. Evidence is mixed. Most research suggests that even in adult court, the historical tendency to treat youths with compassion and clemency might linger (Hamparian et al., 1982; Bortner, 1986; Rudman et al., 1986; Champion, 1989; Fagan, 1991; McNulty, 1996; Clement, 1997). Other findings suggest that the adult system is harder on juvenile offenders than the juvenile system, especially for those juveniles fitting the "targeted" offender profile (Fagan, Forst and Vivona, 1987; Barnes and Franze, 1989; Lemon, 1991; Fagan, 1996).

It is important to note, however, that these studies rely on comparisons of sentences across judicial systems. Inherent in such a comparison is the assumption that judges have before them similar alternatives from which to choose. For example, in the studies cited above it is assumed that a 6-month term in a residential juvenile facility is as severe as the same term in state prison. We suggest that one must consider that the sentences themselves may mean something different, both symbolically and in reality, across systems.

If the purpose of transfer to adult court is to mete out adult punishment, then it is instructive to compare the sentencing outcomes of these juveniles to those of other adult offenders. Such a comparison ensures equivalence of the outcome measures for the two samples and allows for a more direct measurement of the influence that juvenile status exerts on adult court sentencing outcomes.

The limited research addressing this issue offers preliminary evidence that juveniles receive more severe sentencing outcomes than their adult counterparts. A 1996 report released by the U.S. Department of Justice finds that juveniles transferred to adult court are more likely than other adults to be sentenced to prison—particularly for burglary and larceny (Levin, Langan and Brown, 1996). Findings were mixed, though, regarding sentence length, with juveniles receiving longer sentences for weapon-related offenses and shorter sentences for most drug and property offenses (Levin, Langan and Brown, 1996). More recently, Rainville and Smith (2003) reported on juvenile felony defendants from 39 urban counties in 19 states and found that

juveniles were as likely as adult offenders to be convicted (about 66 percent) and that once convicted, they were more likely to receive sentences of incarceration (63.6 percent of juveniles versus 59.6 percent of adults), and to be confined in state prisons (60 percent of juveniles versus 43 percent of adults).

While these studies provided a first look at how juvenile criminal court outcomes compare to those of other adult offenders, they offered no theoretical rationale for the disparities. Furthermore, their analyses relied solely on bivariate descriptive statistics. This is particularly problematic because both studies reported that the juveniles examined differed significantly from the adults on a number of important legal and extralegal characteristics previously found to influence adult court sentencing outcomes. Specifically, juveniles were more likely to be male, minority (black or Hispanic) and convicted of a violent offense. This study therefore advances previous research by conducting the first systematic, multivariate analysis of the impact of juvenile status in adult court, controlling for a multitude of factors associated with adult court criminal sentencing outcomes. The analysis is largely descriptive and is guided by the focal concerns perspective on criminal sentencing, which offers a useful theoretical framework for interpreting the potential effects that juvenile status exerts on adult court sentencing outcomes.

Juvenile Status in Adult Court: A Focal Concerns Perspective

The focal concerns theoretical perspective on sentencing offers a valuable framework to guide our investigation because it recognizes sentencing as a multifaceted and complex process (see Hogarth, 1971) in which judges must simultaneously consider numerous relevant factors and diverse sentencing goals (see Steffensmeier, 1980; Steffensmeier et al., 1998; Steffensmeier and Demuth, 2001 for elaborations). While extant literature on adult court sentencing outcomes generally acknowledges that legal factors, such as the seriousness of the offense and criminal history of the offender, account for the most variation in sentencing outcomes (for example, Kramer and Steffensmeier, 1993), the substantive interest is often on extralegal considerations such as race, gender and age. The focal concerns perspective incorporates many of the diverse and seemingly divergent findings regarding the role of extralegal factors into a coherent framework. In the following section we draw on this perspective to demonstrate various ways that "juvenile status" may be incorporated as an additional extralegal consideration affecting the criminal court decision making process.

According to the focal concerns perspective, judges (and other courtroom actors) assess three primary considerations before making sentencing decisions: offender blameworthiness, protection of the community and the practical constraints and consequences of their decision.

The first, blameworthiness, is based on the concept of retribution as punishment and emphasizes both offender culpability for the offense committed and the degree of injury caused to any victims. Concerns over blameworthiness are generally tied to the seriousness of the offense and the prior criminality of the offender, and to additional factors such as criminal intent and the offender's role in the crime. More serious crimes and more experienced criminals are perceived as more blameworthy, resulting in increased severity at sentencing.

Courtroom actor concerns with blameworthiness may also be related to specific offender characteristics. To the extent that juvenile status is associated with perceived blameworthiness and culpability, it may then be an important determinant of sentencing outcomes in adult court. Indeed, the very premise of the juvenile justice system is that juvenile offenders are less culpable for their behavior and have more potential for reform (Bernard, 1992; Platt, 1969; Gettis, 2000). Recent research on adult court sentencing appears to support this premise, finding a curvilinear relationship between age and sentencing with leniency being given to very young (age 18–19) and older (over 30) offenders (Steffensmeier, Kramer and Ulmer, 1995). Juvenile status may therefore further serve to mitigate perceived blameworthiness, particularly in adult court

where the contrast between juveniles and other, older offenders is most stark.

The second focal concern, protection of the community, is grounded in philosophies of punishment associated with incapacitation and deterrence. It is closely related to the work of Albonetti (1991), who offered an uncertainty avoidance/causal attribution perspective on judicial sentencing emphasizing that judges seldom have complete information about the future behavior of offenders. In this state of "bounded rationality," they must rely on patterned responses tied to causal attributions about the likelihood of future crime. These attributions are the product of various considerations, including the nature of the offense, case information and the offender's criminal history. A long criminal history, for instance, may serve as an indicator of an internal criminal propensity and result in increased concern over community protection and more severe sentences.

In contrast to blameworthiness, courtroom actor concerns with community protection, may suggest harsher sentencing outcomes for juveniles processed in adult court. First, as noted, the majority of juveniles processed in adult court have already accumulated long prior records in the juvenile system, thus demonstrating the propensity to recidivate. Second, prior research suggests that judicial sentencing outcomes are influenced by prior decision making stages in the criminal justice system. For example, numerous studies have found that pretrial detention increases sentencing severity (for example, Lizotte, 1978; Zatz, 1985). Similarly, we suggest that judges may use the decision to process a juvenile in adult court as an independent and important indicator of increased community risk.

The third focal concern, practical constraints and consequences, has two components. The first is organizational and includes the impact of workgroup relations, caseload concerns and availability of criminal justice resources. It addresses the ways in which sentencing decisions are influenced by practical limitations within the criminal justice system. The second pertains to the individual offender. It emphasizes judicial constraints tied to specific offenders, such as the offender's ability to do time, his or her physical and/or health needs, family responsibilities, and other special needs. It also incorporates the impact of an individual offender on the criminal justice system and practical concerns related to the reputation of the court in the community.

For juveniles being sentenced in adult court, this third focal concern may be especially salient. Issues such as appropriate facilities for confining juvenile offenders and public perception of undue leniency or severity toward this population may be especially important. On the one hand, judges may be reluctant to sentence juveniles to serve time with older, more hardened criminals because research shows that juveniles are perceived as especially vulnerable targets in the adult criminal justice system (Forst, Fagan and Vivona, 1989; Reddington and Sapp, 1997). Juveniles are also traditionally seen as having special psychological or rehabilitative needs that may not be adequately addressed in an adult correctional setting (Redding, 1999). When sentencing a juvenile to an adult facility, judges may therefore consider such practical concerns as the increased potential for victimization and the need for specialized schooling and programming. However, the court's reputation in the community may also be an important practical consideration. That is, if the judge sentences leniently and the individual re-offends, the court's standing in the community suffers. To the degree that the juvenile justice reforms of the 1990s reflect a heightened concern with juvenile violence and crime, judges may be reluctant to show leniency towards transferred juveniles regardless of the availability of appropriate facilities.

As these various focal concerns demonstrate, the impact of juvenile status on adult court decision making is not straightforward. As judges and other courtroom actors balance multiple considerations, an offender's "juvenile status" may introduce new and complex dynamics into their deliberations. Some focal concerns suggest leniency toward juveniles and others suggest severity. We therefore use the framework to suggest several competitive research hypotheses about the influence of juvenile status in adult court:

Null Hypothesis: Juvenile offenders in the adult system will receive sentences similar to young adult offenders (ages 18 to 24). The American criminal justice system is premised on strong ideals of impartiality and equality under the law. Therefore, it is possible that few differences will exist between juvenile and young adults sentenced within the criminal justice system.

Hypothesis 1: Juvenile offenders in the adult system will be sentenced more leniently than young adult offenders (ages 18 to 24). The historical treatment of juveniles in the legal system suggests that youth below a certain age are generally viewed as less blameworthy for their behavior than adults. Courtroom actors may also focus on the potential for rehabilitation and consider the detrimental impact of adult incarceration on a juvenile rather than on punishment for the offense committed.

Hypothesis 2: Juvenile offenders in the adult system will be sentenced more severely than young adult offenders (ages 18 to 24). Alternatively, juvenile status in adult court may be interpreted as an aggravating factor if courtroom actors are swayed by the fact that juvenile offenders were so hopelessly incorrigible that they required transfer to the adult system. The judges may thus use the transfer decision itself as an indicator of the increased dangerousness to the community and reduced potential for rehabilitation.

Hypothesis 3: Juvenile offenders in the adult system convicted of personal (for example, violent) crimes will be sentenced more severely. Recent juvenile justice reforms have emphasized increasing concern over young, violent offenders (Torbet et al., 1996; Griffin et al., 1998). Zimring (1998) argued that society has created an image of these offenders as different from other juveniles. The focal concerns perspective suggests that courtroom actors are aware of, and responsive to, community perceptions. Court room actors may therefore symbolically separate these youths from other juveniles and attribute increased blameworthiness and/or dangerousness to this class of offender.

Methods

Data

To test these hypotheses, we examine the sentencing outcomes of juveniles and young adults processed in Pennsylvania's adult criminal justice system over a 3-year period (1997–1999). Pennsylvania was selected for both substantive and practical purposes. Recent legislative changes have expanded the scope and number of juveniles prosecuted in adult court in that state, making it a useful and appropriate research site. Also, Pennsylvania's Sentencing Commission systematically collects detailed information regarding criminal sentencing outcomes. Since the implementation of sentencing guidelines in 1982, judges have been statutorily required to report information on every sentencing proceeding to the Pennsylvania Commission on Sentencing (PCS).

This data collection process has led to the accumulation of a rich data set that, in addition to information on guideline conformity, includes offender demographics (age, race/ethnicity and gender), current offense severity, prior criminal history and details of the conviction mechanism and final sentences.

Because legislation took effect in mid-1996 that altered the mechanisms through which juveniles can be processed in adult court in Pennsylvania, 1997 was selected as the base year for the study. Data were then collected through 1999, the most recent year for which the PCS data were available. From this data set, the sample was further restricted to only the most serious offense per judicial transaction and to all cases that fell under the auspices of the 1997 revised sentencing guidelines.

Because our primary research question focuses on the influence of juvenile status on adult court sentencing outcomes, we selected all cases involving offenders under the age of 18 at the time of their offense. We also selected a group of adult offenders, composed of their most direct counterparts—young adults ages 18 to 24. The study was limited to these age groups to make the adult sample as comparable to the juvenile as possible.

The adult sample was further constrained by selecting only those cases for which offenses were similar to those represented within the juvenile sample (for example, some offenses such as corruption of minors do not apply to juveniles and many broad classes of offenses such as theft by extortion and the sale of large amounts of illegal drugs were not represented in the juvenile sample). The final sample consists of 1,042 juvenile offenders (ages 14 to 17 at the time of the offense) and 33,962 adult offenders (age 18 to 24 at the time of the offense).

Measures

The dependent variable, severity of sentence, reflects the length of incarceration ordered ranging from 0 (for no incarceration) to 240 months.

The primary independent variable of interest is "juvenile status." For this study juvenile status is defined as an individual being under the age of 18 at the time of the offense. We determined this by subtracting the offender's date of birth from the date of offense.

Several other important control variables are also included in our models of sentence severity. These include legally relevant variables and extralegal offender characteristics. The first are the severity of the current offense, the prior criminality of the offender, the type of offense and the application of mandatory sentences.

Offense severity is measured according to the offense gravity score (OGS) defined by Pennsylvania's sentencing guidelines. This is a 14-point scale ranging from 1, least serious, to 14, most serious. It is particularly useful because it offers a detailed breakdown of offenses into subcategories that reflect the actual impact and harm from the crime. For example, the score for an "aggravated assault" can range from 6 to 11 based on the specific conditions of the offense including the age of the victim, the location of the offense, the use of a weapon and the amount of bodily harm inflicted.

The prior criminality of the offender is measured by the prior record score (PRS), and is determined by all prior adult convictions for felonies and misdemeanors as well as juvenile adjudications for felony offenses and certain misdemeanors. It takes into account both the number and severity of prior convictions, and consists of eight categories, ranging from 0, least serious, to 7, most serious. Together, the offense gravity score and prior record score control for the most important legally relevant variables and capture the presumptive sentence recommendations of Pennsylvania's sentencing guidelines.

We also include measures for the legally relevant factors of offense type and legislatively required mandatory sentences (a dichotomous variable coded 1 for cases involving a mandatory sentence and 0 for cases not involving a mandatory sentence).

The extralegal offender characteristics examined include the race/ethnicity and gender of the offender. Race/ethnicity is measured by two dummy variables, black and Hispanic, with white offenders serving as the reference category. Because "other" racial/ethnic groups constituted only about 3 percent of our total sample, and because their sentencing outcomes were not significantly different from white offenders, they are also included in the reference category. The gender of the offender is measured with a dichotomous variable, coded 1 for male offenders and 0 for female offenders.

Finally, we include a measure of court case processing indicating the mode of conviction for each offender. Research consistently finds strong effects for mode of conviction such that offenders convicted through trials receive increased severity at sentencing (LaFree, 1985; Engen and Steen, 2000; Johnson, 2003). We control for this effect with four dummy variables—nonnegotiated pleas, negotiated pleas, bench trials and jury trials. The first represents open guilty pleas and the third those cases tried in front of a sentencing judge. The second and fourth are self defined. This four-category distinction offers an advantage over many previous studies that combine types of pleas and trials (Johnson, 2003). Collectively, these control variables provide for a wide range of potentially important sentencing factors, allowing us to effectively isolate the impact of juvenile status in the adult criminal justice system.

 ## Results

The Main Effect of Juvenile Status

There are statistically significant differences in the mean sentence length for young adult and juvenile offenders sentenced in adult court (see Table 7.5). Specifically, juveniles receive an average sentence of 18 months while young adults receive an average incarceration sentence of only 6 months. Further investigation of the results in Table 7.5, however, demonstrates important sample differences on other key legal and extralegal characteristics associated with sentencing severity. For instance, the juvenile sample has significantly higher mean scores than the young adult sample for both offense gravity and prior record scores—the primary factors determining recommended sentence lengths under Pennsylvania's sentencing guidelines. In addition, juveniles are more likely to have committed an offense against the person, be convicted at jury trial, have a mandatory sentence applied, and be black and male. In sum, the juvenile sample significantly differs from the adult sample on several key variables. It is therefore necessary to control for these differences in the multivariate analyses to further investigate the relationship between juvenile status and adult court criminal sentencing outcomes.

The results of our multivariate analyses, consistent with prior research, indicate that being male, Hispanic and going to jury trial significantly increase sentence severity (Steffensmeier et al., 1993; Steffensmeier and Demuth, 2001; Johnson, 2003). Although many of the extralegal offender characteristics were significantly related to sentence severity, their being included did not reduce the effect of juvenile status. Juvenile offenders received longer sentences than young adult offenders.

Overall, our analysis offers preliminary evidence that juvenile status is an important determinant of sentencing outcomes in adult courts, allowing us to reject our null hypothesis. Furthermore, the findings appear to contradict the expectation that juveniles receive more lenient sentencing treatment (hypothesis 1) and support the expectation that they are sentenced more severely than comparable young adult offenders (hypothesis 2). Even after controlling for a host of legal and extralegal sentencing factors, transferred juveniles appear to receive sentences that are 83 percent more severe. While these results are largely descriptive, they may suggest that courtroom actors are influenced more strongly by concern about increased dangerousness and reduced rehabilitative potential than they are by decreased blameworthiness or

Table 7.5 Sample Descriptive Statistics for Juveniles and Adults Sentenced in Adult Court

Variables	Adults (N = 33,962)		Juveniles (N = 1,042)	
	Mean	**Std.Dev.**	**Mean**	**Std.Dev.**
Independent Variables				
Offense Severity*	4.05	2.37	6.15	3.05
Prior Criminality*	0.94	1.55	1.25	1.79
Age*	20.37	1.94	16.62	0.66
	Frequency	**Percent**	**Frequency**	**Percent**
Mandatory	592	1.7	62	6.0
No Mandatory*	33,370	98.3	980	94.0
Offense Type[a]				
Property*	13,079	38.5	306	29.4
Personal*	6,659	19.6	479	46.0
Drug*	9,736	28.7	168	16.1
Other*	4,488	13.2	89	8.5
Race[b]				
White*	19,325	56.9	498	47.8
Black*	11,768	34.7	447	42.9
Hispanic*	2,869	8.4	97	9.3
Gender				
Male*	30,814	88.8	982	94.2
Female*	3,814	11.2	60	5.8
Conviction Mode[c]				
Non-negotiated Plea	5,461	16.1	154	14.8
Negotiated Plea	22,556	66.4	681	65.4
Bench Trial	1,193	3.5	45	4.3
Jury Trial*	427	1.3	41	3.0
	Mean	**Std.Dev.**	**Mean**	**Std.Dev.**
Dependent Variable				
Sentence Length[d]*	5.71	14.4	18.42	30.96

* Indicates statistically significant differences between adults and juvenile samples ($p < .001$)

a. Other crimes = reference category

b. White offenders = reference category; includes "other" races which accounts for less than 3% of total.

c. Negotiated pleas = reference category

d. Means and standard deviations reported for total sample. Removing censored values results in the following adjustments: Juveniles (mean = 25.52; SD = 33.87) Adults (Mn = 12.41; SD = 19.17).

practical constraints associated with incarcerating juveniles in the adult system.

 To further our understanding of these findings, we examined differences between juvenile and young adult offenders on both the probability and length of incarceration. We found that for the average offender in our sample, "being juvenile" results in a 10-percent greater likelihood of incarceration and a 29-percent increase in sentence length, from 1.69 months for an adult to 2.18 months for a juvenile. Additional examination indicates that at lower levels of offense severity and prior record, juveniles are particularly more likely to receive incarceration than adults, while at higher levels of offense severity and prior record, they tend to receive increasingly longer sentence lengths. Overall, juveniles appear to be more likely than young adults to be incarcerated for lesser offenses and they tend to receive considerably longer sentence lengths for more serious offenses.

⊠ The Interaction of Juvenile Status With Other Sentencing Factors

In addition to testing the main effect of juvenile status in adult court, we also explored the possibility that juvenile status would interact with other legal and extralegal factors. In particular, we were interested in whether the type of offense exerted unique effects for juveniles and adults. As specified by hypothesis 3, our expectation was that juveniles sentenced for personal (that is, violent) crimes would be more severely sentenced. Results of these analyses strongly support this. Although the effect of personal crimes is negligible for adults (decreasing sentence length by about 2 percent), it is substantial for juveniles, increasing their sentence length by 97 percent. Being convicted of a personal offense appears to significantly disadvantage juveniles sentenced in adult court. This finding is consistent with recent legislation targeting a "new breed" of violent juvenile offender (Zimring, 1998).

Despite the fact that most youths are transferred to adult court for nonviolent, property and drug crimes (Feld, 1987; Bishop, 1989; Champion 1989;

Howell, 1996), our findings suggest that those convicted of violent crimes receive especially harsh sentences. Courtroom actor concerns over serious juvenile violence seem evident in the sentencing of juvenile offenders in adult court. If judges and other courtroom actors are influenced by focal concerns regarding both dangerousness and community protection, then the intersection of these two may be most prominent for juveniles transferred for violent crimes. For example, the transfer process may indicate a lack of rehabilitative potential whereas conviction for a crime of violence indicates increased dangerousness and blameworthiness.

⊠ Discussion

Juvenile transfer policies are designed to target specific offenders for processing in the adult criminal justice system and to subject them to adult penalties. Although research suggests that juveniles receive shorter sentences in adult court, little is known about how juvenile status affects sentencing decisions in adult court or how juvenile outcomes in criminal court compare to those of young adults. This study explicitly addressed this question by comparing the sentencing outcomes of transferred juveniles to similar young adults processed in criminal court.

Contrary to the null hypothesis, which stressed the American criminal justice system's valued ideals of equality before the law, we find strong evidence that juveniles and adults are sentenced differently. These findings contradict the first hypothesis, that juveniles will be treated with leniency, and support the second, that they are sentenced more harshly than their adult counterparts. This is particularly interesting given common expectations that juveniles in adult court will be sentenced more leniently (Bernard, 1992; Hamparian et al., 1982; Bortner, 1986; Rudman et al., 1986).

In the context of the focal concerns perspective, these findings may indicate that concerns about decreased blameworthiness and culpability of juveniles (Empey, Stafford and Hay, 1999) and practical constraints regarding victimization and the special needs

Table 7.6   Tobit Coefficients for Individual Models of Juvenile and Adult Sentence Severity

	Adults				Juveniles				Z-Tests	
	b	S.E	Exp		b	S.E	Exp			
Constant	−9.84	1.88	.00	***	−6.32	29.18	.00		.12	
Independent Variables										
Age	.41	.18	1.51	*	.32	3.65	1.38		−.02	
Age Squared	−.01	.00	.99	*	−.01	.11	.99		.02	
Legal Factors										
OGS	.73	.01	2.07	***	.42	.03	1.52	***	−11.04	***
PRS	.54	.01	1.71	***	.26	.04	1.30	***	−7.64	***
Mandatory Applied	.89	.10	2.44	***	.94	.28	2.55	***	.15	
Property Offense	.83	.05	2.29		.17	.26	1.18		−2.48	***
Personal Offense	−.02	.06	.98	*	.68	.27	1.97	**	2.54	***
Drug Offense	−.03	.05	.97	**	.07	.28	1.07		.34	
Extralegal Factors										
Gender										
Male	.86	.05	2.37	***	.86	.29	2.36	**	−.01	
Race										
Black	.06	.03	1.07		.20	.15	1.22		.88	
Hispanic	.32	.05	1.37	****	.21	.23	1.23		−.48	
Conviction Mode										
Negotiated Plea	−.04	.04	.96		−.16	.19	.85		−.64	
Bench Trial	.11	.08	1.11		.68	.32	1.97	*	1.76	*
Jury Trial	.53	.12	1.70	***	.43	.37	1.53		−.26	
R-Squared	.34				.33					
N	33,692				1042					
Sigma	2.33				1.96					

NOTE: Z-scores calculated using $Z = (b_1 - b_2)/(SEb_1^2 + SEb_2^3)$ (see Paternoster et al., 1998). Z-scores reported with statistical significance determined by 2-tailed tests.

$*p < .05$ ** $p < .01$ *** $p < .001$

of incarcerated juveniles (Forst, Fagan and Vivona, 1989; Reddington and Sapp, 1997; Redding, 1999) are outweighed by other sentencing concerns. The findings suggest that judges may assign greater levels of culpability and dangerousness to transferred juveniles than to young adult offenders. If judges are aware of and influenced by decision making points in the criminal justice system (for example, Lizotte, 1978; Zatz, 1985), it may be that the transfer decision itself is used as an indicator of incorrigibility, threat to the community, and/or lack of potential for rehabilitation, resulting in a considerable "juvenile penalty."

The focal concerns perspective also suggests that courtroom decision making may be influenced by public perceptions. Negative judicial attributions related to transferred juveniles may be related to recent publicity depicting a coming storm of "juvenile super-predators" (Zimring, 1998). The interaction between juvenile status and violent offending offers some preliminary support for this notion. Furthermore, certain types of offending may be viewed as outside the realm of juvenile capability. Thus any perception of reduced blameworthiness that may have historically been attached to juvenile status may be negated. Indeed, our research suggests that a juvenile who crosses this boundary is then viewed as a more serious offender, relative to other juveniles and young adults.

Interestingly, our findings also provide some preliminary evidence that judges may attribute less importance to traditional legal variables when sentencing juveniles in adult court. Our results indicate that the impact of both offense severity and prior record are significantly less for juvenile offenders than for young adult offenders. While this finding may suggest that juvenile status overshadows other traditional sentencing considerations typically found to impact sentencing in adult court, future research is needed to substantiate this claim. We suggest this decreased reliance on legal criteria may be related to the overt salience of juvenile status in adult court. That is, while all other legal and extra legal factors included in this analysis are typical considerations before the adult court judge, juvenile status is a unique identifier for this category of offender that is not present in the majority of sentencing decisions. As such, courtroom actors may afford it more weight relative to other sentencing considerations.

⊠ Conclusions

As the legislative trends of the 1990s continue to influence the present and future by relying more heavily on juvenile transfer, it is imperative that we understand the implications of transfer policies, for both the individual youths affected and society. This study begins to address the issue in asking a neglected question: "Are juveniles processed in adult court sentenced as other adults are or does their juvenile status in some way mitigate or aggravate the outcome?" Our results from comparing sentencing outcomes indicate that juvenile status does exert a significant influence on courtroom decision making, resulting in a substantial juvenile penalty.

Courtroom actors are willing not only to apply adult punishments to these transferred juveniles, but also to do so more severely than to adult offenders. This tendency appears to override general age effects and provides an influence above and beyond traditional legal and extralegal sentencing considerations. Moreover, our findings suggest that juvenile status may interact with other crucial variables to determine sentencing outcomes for transferred juveniles. In particular, we find that juvenile offenders convicted of personal crimes in adult court receive an additional violent juvenile penalty.

The considerable weight exerted by juvenile status in adult court has several important implications for the ongoing debate on juvenile transfer policies. First is the dimension of unwarranted disparity. Although the intended purpose of juvenile transfer policies is to apply adult punishments to certain juvenile offenders, few would argue that transferred juveniles deserve more severe treatment than comparable adult offenders. Yet our findings suggest that being a juvenile in adult court holds a penalty all its own.

While all unwarranted sentencing disparities are cause for alarm, evidence of disparities disadvantaging juvenile offenders may be especially troubling given their historical status. The implications are especially noteworthy given that the juvenile court, and the protections provided by it, were premised on the notion that those under a certain age are still developing and warrant different treatment. Indeed, early findings suggest that transferred youths are more likely to recidivate compared to those within the juvenile system (Fagan, 1996; Winner et al., 1997; Bishop et al., 1997). Future discussions on juvenile transfer policies must therefore be expanded to consider the symbolic stigma associated with transfer, its immediate impact on adult court processing and sentencing decisions, and its potential for long-term detrimental effects experienced by transferred offenders.

Second, we believe that our findings, given prior research that juveniles in juvenile courts are sentenced more severely than those in adult courts, suggest that comparing sentencing outcomes across systems may be more problematic than previously believed. We therefore suggest that more research is needed before conclusions can be drawn regarding the relative leniency or severity of either system.

It is important to emphasize that few prior studies have compared juvenile and young adult sentencing outcomes in adult court. Before our "juvenile penalty" can be generalized, then, future research is needed to replicate these findings. In particular, it is critical that future research implement additional controls for legal variables so that any observed disparities between juveniles and adults can be attributed solely to juvenile status. Similarly, future work should attempt to incorporate additional offender information, such as socioeconomic status, which is absent from the majority of research on state-level sentencing outcomes (Zatz, 2000). Another productive avenue would be to further delineate juvenile effects in different types of sentencing outcomes. While the present study suggests juvenile disparities in incarceration and sentence length decisions, little is known about potential disparities in other sentencing decisions, such as departure and probation sentences or intermediate sanctions.

Our study was also unable to capture pre-sentencing processes such as the mode of transfer itself and pre-trial decision making. For example, our data do not offer information on the specific type of transfer to adult court. It is possible that different types of juvenile transfer processes (for example, judicial waiver, statutory exclusion, prosecutorial direct file) may result in greater or lesser "juvenile penalties." This too should be studied. In addition, because our data pertain explicitly to juveniles sentenced in adult court, we cannot offer information on those transferred juveniles who are not convicted or otherwise have their charges dismissed before conviction. Our findings of increased severity for juveniles are therefore specific to the sentencing phase of adult court processing and may miss leniency—such as the decisions to grant bail, reduce charges, or dismiss cases altogether—applied earlier in the process. Finally, because we examine data for a single state over a specific time period, it is important for future research to attempt to replicate our results across time and place.

Despite these limitations, this study fills an important void in the literature and is a useful foundation for future work. If transfer of juveniles to adult court does result in increased sentencing disparities, and the nation is relying increasingly on juvenile transfer policies to address juvenile offending, the implications for society are far reaching and problematic. Future research should therefore continue to investigate the impact of juvenile transfer on adult court processes to better inform the policy debate surrounding the potentially unhealthy marriage of juvenile offending and adult criminal sanctions.

 References

Albonetti, Celesta 1991 "An integration of theories to explain judicial discretion." *Social Problems,* 38(2): 247–266.

Albonetti, Celesta 1997 "Sentencing under the federal sentencing guidelines: Effects of defendant characteristics, guilty pleas and departures on sentence outcomes for drug offenses, 1991–1992." *Law and Society Review,* 31(4): 789–822.

Barnes, Carole and Randal S. Franze 1989 "Questionably Adult: Determinants and Effects of the Juveniles Waiver Decision." *Justice Quarterly,* 6: 117–135.

Bernard, Thomas J. 1992 *The Cycle of Juvenile Justice.* New York: Oxford University Press.

Bishop, Donna M. 2000 "Juvenile offenders in the adult criminal justice system." in *Crime and Justice: A Review of Research* (edited by M. Tonry.). Chicago: University of Chicago Press, 81–167.

Bishop, Donna M., and Charles E. Frazier 1991 "Transfer of Juveniles to Criminal Courts: A Case Study and Analysis of Prosecutorial Waiver." *Notre Dame Journal of Law, Ethics and Public Policy,* 5:281–302.

Bishop, Donna M., Charles E. Frazier and John C. Henretta 1989 "Prosecutorial Waiver: Case Study of a Questionable Reform." *Crime and Delinquency,* 35:179–201.

Bishop, Donna M., Charles E. Frazier, Lonn Lanza-Kaduce and Lawrence Winner 1996 "The transfer of juveniles to criminal court: Does it make a difference?" *Crime and Delinquency,* 42(2): 171–191.

Breen, Richard 1996 *Regression Models: Censored, Sample Selected, or Truncated Data.* Thousand Oaks, CA: Sage.

Bridges, G. S. and Sara Steen 1998 "Racial disparities in official assessments of juvenile offenders: Attributional stereotypes as mediating mechanisms." *American Sociological Review,* 63:554–570.

Bortner, M. A. 1986 "Traditional rhetoric, organizational realities: Remand of juveniles to adult court." *Crime and Delinquency,* 32(1): 53–73.

Bushway, Shawn and Anne Piehl 2001. "Judging judicial discretion: Legal factors and racial discrimination in sentencing" *Law and Society Review,* 35(4): 733–67.

Champion, Dean J. 1989 "Teenage felons and waiver hearings: some recent trends, 1980–1988." *Crime and Delinquency,* 35(4): 577–585.

Clement, Mary J. 1997 "A Five-Year Study of Juvenile Waiver and Adult Sentences: Implications for Policy." *Criminal Justice Policy Review,* 8(2–3): 201–219.

Dixon, Joe 1995 "The organizational context of criminal sentencing." *American Journal of Sociology,* 100(5): 1157–1198.

Engen, Rodney and R. Gainey 2000 "Modeling the Effects of Legally Relevant and Extralegal Factors Under Sentencing Guidelines: The Rules Have Changed." *Criminology,* 38(4).

Engen, Rodney and Sara Steen 2000 "The Power to Punish: Discretion and Sentencing Reform in the War on Drugs." *American Journal of Sociology,* 105:1357–1395.

Empey, Lamar, M. Stafford and C. Hay 1999 *American Delinquency.* Fourth Edition. Belmont, CA: Wadsworth Publishing Company.

Fagan, Jeffrey 1991 *The Comparative Impacts of Juvenile and Criminal Court Sanctions on Adolescent Offenders. Report.* Washington, DC: U.S. Department of Justice, Office of Justice Programs, National Institute of Justice.

Fagan, Jeffrey 1996 "The Comparative Advantage of Juvenile Versus Criminal Court Sanctions on Recidivism among Adolescent Felony Offenders." *Law and Policy,* 18: 77–114.

Fagan, Jeffrey, Martin Forst and T. Scott Vivona 1987 "Racial determinants of the judicial transfer decision: prosecuting violent youth in criminal court." *Crime and Delinquency,* 33: 259–286.

Feld, Barry 1987 "The juvenile court meets the principle of the offense: Legislative changes in juvenile waiver statutes." *Journal of Criminal Law and Criminology,* 78(3): 471–533.

Forst, Martin, Jeffrey Fagan and T. Scott Vivona 1989 "Youth in prisons and training schools: perceptions and consequences of the treatment-custody dichotomy." *Juvenile and Family Court Journal,* 40: 1–14.

Gettis, Victoria 2000 *Juvenile Court and the Progressives.* Chicago: University of Chicago Press.

Griffin, Patrick, Patricia McCall Torbet and Linda Szymanski 1998 *Trying Juveniles as Adults in Criminal Court: An Analysis of State Transfer Provisions.* Washington, DC: U.S. Department of Justice, Office of Justice Programs, Office of Juvenile Justice and Delinquency Prevention.

Hamparian, Donna M., Linda K. Estep, Susan Muntean, Ramon R. Priestine, Robert G. Swisher, Paul L. Wallace and Joseph L. White 1982 *Major Issues in Juvenile Justice Information and Training: Youth in Adult Courts—Between Two Worlds.* Washington, DC: U.S. Department of Justice, Office of Justice Programs, Office of Juvenile Justice and Delinquency Prevention.

Harris, Paul 1988 "Juvenile sentence reform and its evaluation: A demonstration of the need for more precise measures of offense seriousness in juvenile justice research." *Evaluation Review,* 12(6): 655–666.

Helms, Ronald and David Jacobs 2002 "The political context of sentencing: An analysis of community and individual determinants." *Social Forces,* 81(2): 577–604.

Hogarth, J. 1971 *Sentencing as a Human Process.* Toronto: University of Toronto Press in Association with the Centre of Criminology.

Howell, James 1996 "Juvenile transfers to the criminal justice system: State of the art." *Law and Policy,* 18: 17–60.

Johnson, Brian D. 2003 "Racial and Ethnic Disparities in Judicial Departures Across Modes of Conviction." *Criminology,* 41(2): 449–490.

Kleck, Gary 1981 "Racial Discrimination in Criminal Sentencing: A Critical Evaluation of the Evidence with Additional Evidence on the Death Penalty." *American Sociological Review,* 46(6): 783–805.

Klein, E. K. 1998 "Dennis the Menace or Billy the Kid: An analysis of the role of transfer to criminal court in juvenile justice." *The American Criminal Law Review,* 371–410.

Kramer, John and Darrell Steffensmeier 1993 "Race and imprisonment decisions." *The Sociological Quarterly,* 34(2); 357–376.

LaFree, Gary 1985 "Adversarial and nonadversarial justice: A comparison of guilty pleas and trials." *Criminology,* 23: 289–312.

Lemmon, John, Henry Sontheimer and Keith Saylor 1991 *A Study of Pennsylvania Juveniles Transferred to Criminal Court in 1986.* Unpublished manuscript prepared for the Pennsylvania Juvenile Court Judges' Commission. Harrisburg, Pennsylvania.

Levin, David J., Patrick A. Langan and Jodi M. Brown 1996 *State Court Sentencing of Convicted Felons, 1996.* Washington, DC: Bureau of Justice Statistics, Office of Justice Programs, U.S. Department of Justice.

Lizotte, A. 1978 "Extralegal factors in Chicago's criminal courts: Testing the conflict model of criminal justice." *Social Problems,* 25: 564–580.

Long, John 1997 *Regression Models for Categorical and Limited Dependent Variables.* Thousand Oaks, CA: Sage.

McDonald J. F. and Moffit R. F. 1980 "The uses of Tobit Analysis." *Review of Economics and Statistics,* 62: 318–321.

Mustard, David 2001 "Racial, ethnic, and gender disparities in sentencing: Evidence from the U.S. federal courts." *Journal of Law and Economics,* 44(1): 285–315.

Osgood, Wayne and David Rowe 1994 "Bridging criminal careers, theory, and policy through latent variable models of individual offending." *Criminology,* 32(4): 517–538.

Osgood, D. Wayne, Laura L. Finken and Barbara J. McMorris 2002 "Analyzing Multiple-Item Measures of Crime and Deviance II: Tobit Regression Analysis of Transformed Scores." *Journal of Quantitative Criminology,* 18(4): 319–347.

Paternoster, Raymond, Robert Brame and Alex Piquero 1998 "Using the Correct Statistical Test for the Equality of Regression Coefficients." *Criminology,* 36(4): 859–866.

Platt, Anthony 1969 *The Childsavers: The Invention of Delinquency.* Chicago: The University of Chicago Press.

Podkopacz, M. R. and Barry Feld 1995 "Judicial wavier policy and practice: Persistence, seriousness and race." *Law and Inequality: A Journal of Theory and Practice,* 14:73–178.

Poulos, Tammy M. and Stan Orchowsky 1994 "Serious juvenile offenders: Predicting the probability of transfer to criminal court." *Crime and Delinquency,* 40(1): 3–17.

Rainville, G. A. and Steven K. Smith 2003 *Juvenile Felony Defendants in Criminal Courts.* Washington, DC: Bureau of Justice Statistics, Office of Justice Programs, U.S. Department of Justice.

Redding, Richard 1999 "Examining legal issues: Juvenile offenders in criminal court and adult prison." *Corrections Today,* 92–124.

Reddington, F. P. and A. D. Sapp 1997 "Juveniles in adult prisons: problems and prospects." *Journal of Crime and Justice,* 20:139–152.

Rudman, Cary, Elliot Hartston, Jeffrey Fagan and Melinda Moore 1986 "Violent youth in adult court: processes and punishment." *Crime and Delinquency,* 32:75–96.

Sellin, J. and Marvin Wolfgang 1964 *The Measurements of Delinquency.* Wiley: New York.

Sickmund, Melissa 2003 *Juveniles in Court.* Washington, DC: U.S. Department of Justice, Office of Justice Programs, Office of Juvenile Justice and Delinquency Prevention.

Snyder, Howard, Melissa Sickmund and Eileen Poe-Yamagata 2000 *Juvenile Transfers to Criminal Court in the 1990s: Lessons Learned from Four Studies.* Washington, DC: U.S. Department of Justice, Office of Justice Programs, Office of Juvenile Justice and Delinquency Prevention.

Snyder, Howard and Melissa Sickmund 1999 *Juvenile Offenders and Victims: A National Report.* Washington, DC: U.S. Department of Justice, Office of Justice Programs, Office of Juvenile Justice and Delinquency Prevention.

Spohn, Cassia and D. Holleran 2000 "The imprisonment penalty paid by young, unemployed, black and Hispanic male offenders." *Criminology,* 38(1): 281–306.

Steffensmeier, Darrell and Steven Demuth 2001 "Ethnicity and judges' sentencing decisions: Hispanic-black-white comparisons." *Criminology,* 39:145–178.

Steffensmeier, Darrel, John Kramer and J. Striefel 1993 "Gender and imprisonment decisions." *Criminology,* 31:411–46.

Steffensmeier, Darrell, Jeffrey Ulmer, and John Kramer. 1998 "The interaction of race, gender, and age in criminal sentencing: The punishment cost of being young, black and male." *Criminology,* 36(4):763–797.

Steffensmeier, Darrell, John Kramer and Jeffery Ulmer 1995 "Age differences in sentencing." *Justice Quarterly,* 12(3):583–602.

Steffensmeier, Darrell 1980 "Assessing the Impact of the Women's Movement on Sex-Based Differences in the Handling of Adult Criminal Defendants." *Crime and Delinquency,* 26:344–357.

Tobin, J. 1958 "Estimation of relationships for limited dependent variables." *Econometrica,* 26:24–36.

Tonry, Michael 1996 *Sentencing Matters.* New York: Oxford University Press.

Torbet, Patricia, Richard Gable, Hunter Hurst, Imogene Montgomery, Linda Szymanski and Doug Thomas 1996 *State Responses to Serious and Violent Juvenile Crime.* Washington, DC: U.S. Department of Justice, Office of Justice Programs, Office of Juvenile Justice and Delinquency Prevention.

Ulmer, Jeffery 1997 *Social Worlds of Sentencing: Court Communities Under Sentencing Guidelines.* Albany, NY: SUNY Press.

Von Hirsch, Andrew, Michael Tonry and Kay Knapp 1987. *The Sentencing Commission and its Guidelines.* Boston: Northeastern University Press.

Wheeler, Stanton, David Weisburd and Nancy Bode 1982 "Sentencing the White Collar Offender: Rhetoric and Reality." *American Sociological Review,* 47(5): 641–659.

Winner, Lawrence, Lonn Lanza-Kaduce, Donna M. Bishop and Charles E. Frazier 1997 "The transfer of juveniles to criminal court: Reexamining recidivism over the long term." *Crime and Delinquency,* 43(4): 548–563.

Zatz, M. 1985 "Los Cholos: Legal processing of Chicano gang members." *Social Problems,* 33:13–30.

Zatz, M. 2000 "The Convergence of Race, Ethnicity, Gender, and Class on Court Decision making: Looking Toward the 21st Century." From Policies, Processes, and Decisions of the Criminal Justice System; *Criminal Justice 2000,* 3:503–552, 2000, Julie Homey, ed.

Zimring, Franklin E. 1998 *American Youth Violence.* New York: Oxford University Press.

DISCUSSION QUESTIONS

1. What are the theoretical justifications for treating juvenile offenders differently than adult offenders?

2. Who are the juvenile offenders most likely to reach adult court?

3. The theoretical perspective that Kurlychek and Johnson used to frame their research is the "focal concerns perspective." What is the focal concerns perspective and how can it be applied to juveniles sentenced in adult court?

4. Why did the authors conduct their study using data from the Pennsylvania adult criminal justice system?

5. The authors compared the sentences imposed on offenders who were younger than 18 of age at the time of their offense and offenders who were 18 to 24 years old when the offense was committed. Do the juvenile offenders get significantly different sentences than the adults (Table 7.5)? What might account for these differences? Did these differences disappear when the authors controlled for crime seriousness, prior record, and other case and offender characteristics?

6. What are the policy implications of the authors' finding that there is a "substantial juvenile penalty" in the sentencing of juveniles in adult court?

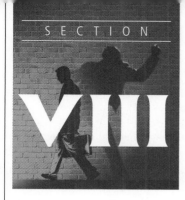

SECTION

VIII

Beyond Conviction and Sentencing

Section Highlights

- What Happens Next?
- Underlying Concepts
- Appeals
- Habeas Corpus
- Considering Clemency
- Edited Readings

 What Happens Next?

If a defendant is convicted, he or she may elect to challenge the conviction. This can be accomplished in two ways. The defendant (now convict) can appeal. Alternatively, the convicted criminal can file a habeas corpus petition. In practice, however, appeals almost always precede habeas corpus petitions. The purpose of this section is to discuss appeals and habeas corpus, with attention to the purpose and scope of the appeals process and current issues, such as recently imposed limitations placed on appeals. We conclude with a brief look at clemency, which is gubernatorial or presidential pardons of certain convicted criminals.

Underlying Concepts

Direct and Indirect Appeals

Once a person is convicted and sentenced, there are two ways to challenge the trial outcome. A defendant may file either a direct appeal or an indirect appeal, also known as a writ of habeas corpus. *Habeas corpus* translates as "you have the body," and the writ requires the person to whom it is directed to either produce the person named in the writ or release that person from custody. A direct appeal is essentially a request made by the now-convicted defendant to a higher court (the appeals court) to review the trial to determine whether it was fair. There is no federal constitutional right to an appeal, but every state allows a direct appeal, either by statute or state constitutional provision.

The writ of habeas corpus is considered an indirect appeal because it does not directly challenge the defendant's conviction but instead challenges the authority of the state to incarcerate the defendant. The state defense to a habeas writ is based on the conviction, however—that is why the defendant has been incarcerated. Habeas corpus is an ancient legal remedy, dating back at least to the Magna Carta. It is often referred to as the Great Writ.

There is no time limit for filing a habeas petition, unlike direct appeals, which in most jurisdictions must be filed within a set period, usually several months. However, Congress recently restricted the use of habeas corpus by imposing time limits on federal habeas petitions if there is evidence of intentional delay by the defendant that injures the prosecution's case. Additionally, Congress and the Supreme Court have restricted habeas corpus by imposing limits on how such appeals are filed and pursued.

Precedent and *Stare Decisis*

After an appeals court considers either a direct or an indirect appeal, typically it issues a written opinion explaining its decision. These opinions serve to explain to both the current litigants and future litigants why the appeals court decided the appeal the way it did. Under the common law system, a final decision by an appeals court creates a precedent. This precedent governs the court issuing the decision as well as any lower, or "inferior" courts—primarily the trial courts. The common law system, developed in England, was brought to America by the early colonists. Many of the principles of the common law, including precedent and a belief in stare decisis, remain in force today in American courts. Thus, all courts in a state are bound to follow the decisions of the highest court in the state, usually known as the state supreme court. All courts in the federal court system are bound to follow the decisions of the United States Supreme Court.

Precedent is binding only on those courts within the jurisdiction of the court issuing the opinion. Thus, a decision of the Idaho Supreme Court is not binding on a court in Arizona. Arizona courts are not subject to the jurisdiction or control of Idaho courts and thus are free to interpret the law differently from Idaho courts, if they see fit to do so. Decisions from courts in other jurisdictions, though not binding, may be persuasive, however. This simply means that another court may give consideration and weight to the opinion of other courts. Thus, an Arizona court may consider, if it chooses, the judgment of an Idaho court, or an American court can consider the judgment of a British, Australian, New Zealand, or any other common law court. Courts may do this when faced with an issue that they have not dealt with but that other courts have examined.

Stare decisis means "let the decision stand." Under the principle of stare decisis, if there is a prior decision on a legal issue that applies to a current case, the court will be guided by that prior decision and apply the same legal principles in the current case. Stare decisis, then, is the principle behind establishing the value of prior decisions, or precedent. It is a principle that ensures that issues that have been decided one way will continue to be decided that way in future cases. As a result of the reliance on precedent and the principle of stare decisis, common law courts are able to provide litigants with some degree of predictability regarding the courts' decisions.

Precedent establishes a legal principle, but not every pronouncement that a court makes in a ruling establishes precedent. Pronouncements that establish precedent are known as **ratio decidendi**, meaning "the reason for the decision." Ratio decidendi is the legal principle or rationale used by the courts to arrive at their decisions. Additional supporting statements are called **obiter dicta** (meaning "things said by the way"), or simply dicta. These statements are other legal or nonlegal arguments used to support the ratio decidendi and do not set a precedent.

Precedent is not necessarily unchangeable. Judge-made law may be set aside, or overruled, by an act of the legislature if the constitution permits the legislature to do so. Additionally, the court that issued the precedent may overrule it, or a higher court may reverse the decision of a lower court. If an intermediate-level appeals court decides an issue one way and the losing party appeals to a higher appeals court (such as a state supreme court), the higher court may reverse the decision of the lower court. Higher level courts are not bound by the judgments of lower courts. They are bound only by the decisions of courts above them in the court structure.

Stare decisis, then, involves a respect for and belief in the validity of precedent. Precedent is simply the influence of prior cases on current cases. Understandably, courts are reluctant to reverse decisions they made previously, as this is a tacit admission of error. Courts do so, however, when presented with a compelling justification. Thus, stare decisis is not an inflexible doctrine but merely the general rule. There are always exceptions, as with most areas of the law.

Alternatively, rather than expressly overrule a prior decision, a court may instead seek to distinguish the prior case from the present case on grounds that the facts are slightly different. By doing so, the court can avoid overruling a prior decision while coming to what it considers the proper result in the present case. Until a decision is expressly overruled, it stands as an accurate statement of legal principles, or "good law."

Judicial Review

Given the varied sources of law, and the ambiguous language of many statutes and constitutional provisions, it is inevitable that laws will conflict or interpretations of statutes will differ. When this happens, who decides which law is paramount? In the United States, the answer to that question is the courts, through the power of judicial review.

Judicial review simply means the power of the court to examine a law and determine whether it is constitutional. To make this determination, judges must examine the law and compare it with the Constitution. This requires them to interpret the language of both the statute and the Constitution. If the judge determines the law is constitutional, he or she upholds the law; if not, the judge declares it unconstitutional and therefore void. For example, the Fourth Amendment prohibits "unreasonable" searches. Suppose a state legislature passes a law allowing police officers to search anyone they encounter on a public street. Is this law constitutional? Or does it violate the prohibition on unreasonable searches? To answer this question, judges must examine the history and meaning of "unreasonable" as contained in the Fourth Amendment. They do this by examining precedent.

Judicial review is not specifically provided for in the Constitution. Rather, judicial review is judge-made law. *Marbury v. Madison* (1803) established the authority of the United States Supreme Court to engage in judicial review of the acts of the other branches of government. The Supreme Court stated in *Marbury* that it was the duty of the judiciary to interpret the Constitution and to apply it to particular fact situations. The

Court also said that it was the job of the courts to decide when other laws (acts of Congress or state laws) were in violation of the Constitution and to declare these laws null and void if they were. This is the doctrine of judicial review.

Appeals

When convicted criminals appeal their conviction, they ask a higher court to examine the trial court's decision to determine whether the proper procedure was followed. In other words, the convicted argue that the trial court made a legal error that prevented them from receiving a fair trial. The United States Constitution requires a criminal defendant receive due process. This term is obviously vague, but it has consistently been interpreted by courts and legislatures as requiring that a criminal defendant receive a fair trial. The appeals process helps ensure that trial courts apply the law correctly. Appeals can also be filed at a higher level. For example, if an intermediate appellate court rules against a party, that party may be able to appeal to the next highest court, such as a state supreme court or one of the U.S. circuit courts of appeals.

Appeals are quite common in the American criminal justice system, but the Supreme Court has never held that they are constitutionally required; the Constitution does not specify the granting of a certain number of appeals to each convicted criminal. In *McKane v. Durston* (1894), the Supreme Court stated that a "review by an appellate court of the final judgment in a criminal case, however grave the offense of which the accused is convicted, was not at common law, and is not now, a necessary element of due process of law." Even in the face of this decision, every state and the federal government has rules providing a certain number of appeals.

When an appeal is heard, the appellate court can reach a number of decisions. Most often it will either affirm or reverse the lower court's decision. As an alternative, it may remand the case for further proceedings consistent with its opinion. This is akin to asking the lower court to "do it again the right way." Importantly, if an appeal is successful, that does not mean that the defendant will be released from confinement. Consider this example: If an appellate court reverses a lower court's decision to exclude evidence, this simply means the evidence should have been excluded, not that the defendant should be acquitted and released. Instead, the defendant is merely entitled to a new trial. Many students are familiar with the famous *Miranda* case (*Miranda v. Arizona*, 1966), in which the Supreme Court laid down rules for advising criminal suspects of their Fifth Amendment privilege against compelled self-incrimination. Though the Court agreed with Ernesto Miranda's argument, it only granted him a new trial, whereupon he was convicted and sentenced to more than 20 years in prison.

The Appellate Process

The appellate process has evolved to the point that the U.S. Supreme Court has granted a number of protections to appellants. These protections are intended to ensure access to trial transcripts, the right to counsel, and the right to be free from government retaliation for successful appeals. Our concern is more with those protections than with the rules for appeals one finds in one jurisdiction to the next.

In *Griffin v. Illinois* (1956), the Supreme Court decided that indigent defendants *must* be given access to trial transcripts. The Court held that the government cannot act "in a way that discriminates against some convicted defendants on account of their poverty" (p. 18). Why is access to the transcripts important? They form the basis for an appeal. When a court reporter documents the trial, a record of the trial is produced. If, say, the defense attorney objects to the introduction of some testimony or a piece of physical evidence, the objection is noted in the record. Such objections often provide the basis for an appeal.

The Supreme Court has also required that counsel be provided to indigent defendants on appeal, as a matter of either equal protection or due process. This decision was reached in the case of *Douglas v. California* (1963), where the Court concluded that the government must provide indigent defendants with counsel to assist in their appeals of right. It stated that "where the merits of the *one and only* appeal an indigent has as of right are decided without benefit of counsel . . . an unconstitutional line has been drawn between rich and poor" (p. 357). The Court also held that more than just counsel is necessary—the counsel needs to be effective (*Evitts v. Lucey*, 1985).

The Court has not been so sympathetic when it comes to discretionary appeals:

> A defendant in respondent's circumstances is not denied meaningful access to the State Supreme Court simply because the State does not appoint counsel to aid him in seeking review in that court, since at that stage, under North Carolina's multitiered appellate system, he will have, at the very least, a transcript or other record of the trial proceedings, a brief in the Court of Appeals setting forth his claims of error, and frequently an opinion by that court disposing of his case, materials which, when supplemented by any pro se submission that might be made, would provide the Supreme Court with an adequate basis for its decision to grant or deny review under its standards of whether the case has "significant public interest," involves "legal principles of major significance," or likely conflicts with a previous Supreme Court decision. (*Ross v. Moffitt*, 1974, pp. 614–615)

It is also important that the government not retaliate following successful appeals. This was the decision reached in *North Carolina v. Pierce* (1969), a case in which a defendant was not only reconvicted after a successful appeal but punished more harshly the second time around. The Court concluded that due process required that the "defendant be freed of apprehension of such a retaliatory motivation on the part of the sentencing judge" (p. 725). A similar decision was reached in *Blackledge v. Perry* (1974), in which the Supreme Court held that a prosecutor's decision to increase the charge against a defendant who was convicted but appealed was unconstitutional.

Timing Issues

A convicted criminal can appeal at one of two stages during the adjudication process. An appeal first can be filed prior to the reading of the verdict. Appeals also can be filed following adjudication. Appeals filed prior to adjudication are known as **interlocutory appeals**. The only interlocutory appeals likely to succeed are those addressing critical constitutional questions and those that have no bearing on the defendant's guilt (or lack thereof). If either of these conditions is not met, defendants face what is known as the **final judgment rule.** This rule limits appeals until the court hands down its final judgment as to the defendant's guilt.

In *Cohen v. Beneficial Industrial Loan Corp.* (1949), the Supreme Court held that only a few interlocutory appeals are likely to succeed, namely, those that involve the following:

> a small class [of pre-adjudication decisions] which finally determine claims of right separable from, and collateral to, rights asserted in the action, too important to be denied review and too independent of the cause itself to require that appellate consideration be deferred until the whole case is adjudicated. (p. 546)

Some additional examples shed light on the Court's observation. In *Stack v. Boyle* (1951), the Court held that the defendant could appeal a judge's decision rejecting the defendant's argument that bail was excessive, in apparent violation of the Eighth Amendment. In another case (*Abney v. United States*, 1977), the Court held that a defendant's appeal of a preadjudication order denying dismissal of the indictment on double jeopardy grounds was permissible. Both of these appeals dealt with critical constitutional questions, which is why they were granted.

Appeals filed after adjudication, in contrast, are subject to few restrictions. Such appeals can raise a number of issues, perhaps challenging the following actions:

1. An involuntary guilty plea,

2. The use of a coerced confession,

3. The use of evidence gained pursuant to an unconstitutional search or seizure,

4. The use of evidence obtained pursuant to an unlawful arrest,

5. A violation of the privilege against self-incrimination,

6. The unconstitutional failure of the prosecution to disclose to the defendant evidence favorable to him or her,

7. A violation of the Fifth Amendment's double jeopardy clause,

8. A conviction based on a jury that was unconstitutionally selected and impaneled,

9. The denial of effective assistance of counsel, or

10. The denial of the rights to speedy trial and appeal.

The typical appeal is by someone convicted of a crime. Surprisingly, though, the prosecution can also appeal some trial court decisions prior to the entry of a final judgment by the trial court. Such appeals are permitted only as authorized by law. For example, a federal statute found in 18 U.S.C.A. Section 3731 provides for interlocutory prosecution appeals of a district court's decision to suppress or exclude evidence from trial. In other words, if a trial judge excludes evidence, which then makes it difficult for the prosecution to present its case, then the prosecution is allowed to file an interlocutory appeal.

Harmless Errors

Sometimes an appellate court agrees to hear an appeal, and it may even agree with the appellant's argument, but nonetheless rule that the lower court's error was harmless. In other words, lower courts' **harmless errors** may not lead to the reversal of a conviction.

For example, in *Chapman v. California* (1967), the Supreme Court considered whether a trial court made a harmless error by permitting the prosecutor, during closing arguments, to repeatedly refer to the defendant's refusal to take the stand and testify. The Court reversed the defendant's conviction, claiming that "though the case in which this occurred presented a reasonably strong 'circumstantial web of evidence' against petitioners, it was also a case in which, absent the constitutionally forbidden comments, honest fair-minded jurors might very well have brought in not-guilty verdicts" (pp. 25–26).

Similarly, in *Connecticut v. Johnson* (1983), the Court concluded that a judge's flawed instructions to the jury could not be considered harmless. The judge told the jury that it could infer the defendant's guilt when the defendant was charged with a specific intent crime (actually, the prosecutor is supposed to present evidence of intent for such offenses). The Court said that the judge "permitted the jury to convict respondent without ever examining the evidence concerning an element of the crime charged" (p. 88).

⬚ Habeas Corpus

Habeas corpus is not unlike the appellate process in the sense that it affords the convicted an opportunity to challenge convictions. But, unlike an appeal, habeas corpus is something of an indirect method of challenging a conviction, as we show later in the text. Also unlike an appeal, habeas corpus is a constitutional right, which is spelled out in Article I, Section 9, Clause 2 of the United States Constitution.

How does habeas corpus work? Only incarcerated people can seek a writ of habeas corpus. If the prisoner chooses to do so, he or she petitions a federal court, most often a district court, and asks it to issue a writ of habeas corpus. If the court decides to issue the writ, then the prisoner (called the petitioner) is brought before the court so the constitutionality of his or her confinement can be reviewed. Importantly, the Constitution only provides the right to petition for habeas review, not the right to a hearing. The court decides whether it wants to grant a hearing.

The writ is also different from an appeal in its purpose. Whereas an appeal is intended to challenge a lower court's legal decision, habeas corpus challenges the constitutionality of one's confinement. It is an option only after one has been convicted and sentenced to a term of confinement. The Supreme Court emphasized the importance of habeas corpus in a number of decisions. For example, it pointed out that "conventional notions of finality of litigation have no place where life or liberty is at stake and infringement of constitutional rights is alleged" (*Sanders v. United States*, 1963). Likewise, in *Kaufman v. United States* (1969), the Court held that the writ is necessary to provide "adequate protection of constitutional rights."

More recently, though, the Supreme Court argued that the writ should be restricted. To illustrate, in one decision (*Stone v. Powell*, 1976), the Court held that writs should not be liberally issued for claims arising from state courts:

> Despite differences in institutional environment and the unsympathetic attitude to federal constitutional claims of some state judges in years past, we are unwilling to assume that there now exists a general lack of appropriate sensitivity to constitutional rights in the trial and appellate courts of the several States.

The recently enacted Antiterrorism and Effective Death Penalty Act (AEDPA), which we touch on later, is also illustrative of sentiments that habeas corpus should be restricted, to some extent.

Origins of the Writ

Why did the framers make habeas corpus a constitutional right? As we explained earlier, the U.S. Supreme Court has not held that appeals are constitutionally granted, but habeas corpus is. Why? Robert Pursley, whose article on the habeas corpus process we included in this volume, showed that the writ has origins in four centuries of English common law. As early as the 13th century, courts were given the power to summon individuals held by the executive. The purpose of this practice, though, was not to challenge convictions but rather to challenge unwarranted confinement of citizens by the executive. Only later was the opportunity afforded to higher courts to review lower court convictions. This came to be known as the writ of *habeas corpus cum causa*.

Pursley also described how the writ became a "pawn in the struggle for judicial primacy." It gave the Crown courts an opportunity to free individuals wrongfully convicted in lower courts, such as the ecclesiastical courts. Parliament then adopted the Habeas Corpus Act of 1679. Given the framers' English heritage and concern over the prospect of an intrusive executive, it is no mystery why the writ was incorporated into the U.S. Constitution. Pursley did a fine job of explaining the rest of the history of the writ, as well as the habeas corpus process. We can, however, offer a short overview here.

Process Concerns

The habeas corpus process is much more restrictive than the appellate process, for several reasons. First, several types of writs will not be issued. For example, in *Stone v. Powell* (1976), the Court held that "where the State has provided an opportunity for full and fair litigation of a Fourth Amendment claim" a federal court should not issue a writ of habeas corpus. Also, if a claim is "dictated by precedent" it cannot be heard on habeas review (*Teague v. Lane*, 1989). There are exceptions to this rule, but habeas courts generally steer clear of creating new rules of criminal procedure.

Habeas corpus petitions also must raise constitutional questions. In one relevant case, the petitioner claimed that his death sentence should be vacated because new evidence pointed to his innocence. The Supreme Court did not grant review, explaining that "in light of the historical availability of new trials . . . and the contemporary practice in the States, we cannot say that Texas' refusal to entertain petitioner's newly discovered evidence eight years after his convictions transgresses a principle of fundamental fairness" (*Herrera v. Collins*, 1993). Harmless errors by lower courts also cannot form the basis of a habeas petition.

There are also timing restrictions for habeas corpus petitions. Usually, there are strict timing guidelines that must be followed (this is especially true in regard to the recent legislation we touch on in the next section). Only if the petitioner can show evidence of "actual innocence" can a habeas corpus petition filed after the cutoff date be considered. To do this, the Supreme Court held that

> the prisoner must show a fair probability that, in light of all the evidence, including that alleged to have been illegally admitted (but with due regard to any unreliability of it) and evidence tenably claimed to have been wrongly excluded or to have become available only after the trial, the trier of the facts would have entertained a reasonable doubt of his guilt. (*Kuhlmann v. Wilson*, 1986, note 17)

In other words, when a prisoner has failed to file a habeas petition in a timely manner, he or she may still succeed in doing so provided that the petition sets forth sufficient facts as to the prisoner's "actual innocence."

Before habeas corpus becomes an option for a prisoner, he or she must usually exhaust all available state-level appeals. As the Supreme Court stated, "ordinarily an application for habeas corpus by one detained under a state court judgment of conviction will be entertained . . . only after all state remedies available, including all appellate remedies in the state courts and in this Court by appeal or writ of certiorari have been exhausted" (*Ex parte Hawk*, 1944). Next, there are restrictions, especially recently, on filing multiple petitions, especially those that repeatedly raise the same claims.

Finally, habeas corpus is difficult because there is no right to counsel. Because habeas corpus is purely discretionary, the Supreme Court held that no right to counsel exists (*Ross v. Moffitt*, 1974). Of course, if the petitioner can hire an attorney, then one can most certainly draft a petition and represent the petitioner. The Court held, however, that federal prisoners have a "constitutional right of access to the courts (*Bounds v. Smith*, 1977)" and decided that states cannot prohibit prisoners from helping each other prepare and submit habeas corpus petitions (*Johnson v. Avery*, 1969). Finally, the Supreme Court held that indigent habeas corpus petitioners are entitled to a free transcript of their trial to assist in preparing the appropriate paperwork (*Griffin v. Illinois*, 1956). Taking all these process restrictions into account, it is easy to see how habeas corpus petitions do not succeed in record numbers. They are most definitely the exception.

The Antiterrorism and Effective Death Penalty Act

The 1995 Oklahoma City bombing was certainly overshadowed by the September 11, 2001, attacks in New York City, but the Oklahoma bombing was America's first major encounter with terrorism. No sooner did attention turn to radical fringe militia groups throughout the United States than Congress started debating various legislative proposals to combat the new problem. The result was passage of the Antiterrorism and Effective Death Penalty Act of 1996 (AEDPA).

AEDPA supporters heralded it as a significant bipartisan achievement that would help root out terrorism. Critics claimed that its very name, with emphasis on the death penalty, was evidence that it would do little, if anything, to combat domestic terrorism. It is difficult to disagree with the critics in this regard because one of the most significant components of AEDPA places restrictions on habeas corpus petitions for death row inmates. You can draw your conclusion as to the relationship between habeas corpus and domestic terrorism, but the end result was legislation that basically restricted federal habeas corpus petitions by death row inmates—in the name of terrorism prevention. The portion of the AEDPA dealing with habeas corpus is what concerns us here.

The AEDPA significantly altered habeas corpus procedure in the United States. For example, it permits habeas review only when the state-level decision (1) "resulted in a decision that was contrary to, or involved an unreasonable application of, clearly established federal law, as determined by the Supreme Court of the United States" or (2) "resulted in a decision that was based on an unreasonable determination of the facts in light of the evidence presented in the state court proceeding" (28 U.S.C.A. Section 2254[d]).

Second, the AEDPA alters habeas review in capital cases by providing that prisoners who "default" and fail to submit a petition in a timely fashion will only be granted review when the prisoner's failure to file a petition is (1) "the result of State action in violation of the Constitution or laws of the United States"; (2) "the result of the Supreme Court's recognition of a new federal right that is made retroactively applicable"; or (3) "based on a factual predicate that could not have been discovered through the exercise of due diligence in time to present the claim for state or federal post-conviction review" (28 U.S.C.S. Section 2264[a]).

The legislation also restricts successive habeas corpus petitions. It states that a "claim presented in a second or successive habeas corpus application shall be dismissed" (28 U.S.C.A. Section 2244[b][1]). Moreover, it restricts a prisoner's successive and different petition to one that (1) "relies on a new rule of constitutional law, made retroactive to cases on collateral review by the Supreme Court, that was previously unavailable" or (2) a claim "the factual predicate [for which] could not have been discovered previously through the exercise of due diligence" and which "would be sufficient to establish by clear and convincing evidence that, but for constitutional error, no reasonable fact-finder would have found the applicant guilty of the underlying offense" (28 U.S.C.A. Section 2244[b][2]).

Strict habeas corpus filing petitions have also been put into effect as a result of the legislation. The AEDPA requires, for instance, that most habeas corpus petitions be filed within one year of the date of the final state-level appellate judgment. For death penalty cases, the legislation is even more restrictive, requiring that death row petitions be filed within six months of the "final state court affirmance of the conviction and sentence on direct review or the expiration of the time for seeking review" (28 U.S.C.S. Sections 2244[d][1][A] & 2263).

⧗ Considering Clemency

Often lost in discussions over appeals and habeas corpus is the concept of **clemency**, also known as a pardon. The power to grant a pardon or clemency (both terms are synonymous for our purposes) rests with the chief executive—the president at the federal level, the governor at the state level. Pardons can be (and have been) issued for all manner of crimes. One of the most well-known pardons was that given by President Gerald Ford to Richard Nixon on September 8, 1974. Others include President Jimmy Carter's grant of amnesty to draft evaders following the Vietnam war, President George H. W. Bush's pardon of various Reagan-era officials involved in the Iran Contra scandal, and President Clinton's pardon of 16 members of FALN, a violent Puerto Rican group that set off more than 100 bombs in the United States. Perhaps no pardons are more controversial, though, than those granted to death row inmates. The American Bar Association has put it this way:

> Perhaps no decision in the course of a governor's term has a more direct or immediate effect on the welfare of an individual and his or her family than executive clemency. Yet, it is a prickly issue in that it concerns a readily identifiable individual who the state has successfully prosecuted, and who may be perceived to have committed a crime (which may or may not be true). The act of clemency is not like other executive powers that are easily generalized as matters of policy, the ultimate fate of an individual who is easily identified and known to the public—and perhaps even despised—is in question. (Ortiz, 2002, p. 121)

According to the Death Penalty Information Center, since 1976, 229 death row inmates have been granted clemency, largely for humanitarian reasons (see http://www.deathpenaltyinfo.org). These have included three broad grants of clemency by governors in New Mexico, Ohio, and Illinois to all death row inmates in those states.

◤ Summary: Beyond Conviction and Sentencing

The appeal is perhaps the most complicated part of the entire criminal adjudication process. Criminal defendants have, at the time of their conviction, several ways to challenge that conviction. They may challenge the conviction through a direct appeal. If convicted in a state court, the defendant can receive a review of the trial by an intermediate appellate court and, possibly, the state supreme court. If the defendant claims a violation of a federal constitutional right, then the appeal may go to the United States Supreme Court, although the likelihood of this is very slight, as the Supreme Court has almost total discretion over which cases to accept on appeal.

The criminal defendant may also challenge his or her conviction indirectly, through the use of the writ of habeas corpus. This writ, which is of ancient origin and is enshrined in the United States Constitution and the various state constitutions, allows an incarcerated person to go to court to challenge the legality of his or her confinement. The state typically justifies this confinement on the basis of the defendant's conviction and sentence to prison. Habeas corpus is considered an indirect appeal because, though the writ is intended to challenge the person's incarceration, the incarceration is based on a conviction, so the defendant/inmate will argue that the incarceration is illegal because his or conviction was illegal. Habeas corpus may be pursued in both state and federal courts.

The result is an appeal process that, combined with overburdened and understaffed courts (particularly at the federal level), may take many years to play out. For those inmates serving the longest and harshest sentences (i.e., life in prison, death sentence), this means they have many years to fight their conviction. Appellate courts have developed a number of procedural rules that govern the appeals process and generally serve to make it very difficult for convicted people to have their conviction or sentence overturned. Procedural bars such as filing deadlines, exhaustion requirements, choice of venue rules, and the harmless error standard all serve to make the process both difficult and confusing. Added to these procedural bars in recent years are legislative acts such as the AEDPA, which imposes significant limits on the ability of federal courts to entertain writs of habeas corpus arising from state proceedings.

KEY TERMS

Clemency

Final judgment rule

Harmless errors

Interlocutory appeal

Judicial review

Obiter dicta

Ratio decidendi

DISCUSSION QUESTIONS

1. Why does the court system provide defendants with the opportunity for both a direct appeal and an indirect appeal? What purpose does each appeal serve?

2. Why are precedent and stare decisis such important concepts? How do appellate courts use them to guide their decision making?

3. What is the difference between a "harmless error" and an error that requires an appellate court to reverse the decision of a lower court? How do appellate courts determine when an error is harmless?

4. Why does the writ of habeas corpus exist? How is it used today in ways that early common law courts would not recognize?

5. Is the Antiterrorism and Effective Death Penalty Act (AEDPA) an appropriate response to the increase in inmate litigation? Why or why not? What other means can courts use to deal with the flood of inmate lawsuits?

WEB RESOURCES

American Bar Association: http://www.abanet.org/

American Judicature Society: http://www.ajs.org/

Death Penalty Information Center: http://www.deathpenaltyinfo.org/

Federal Judiciary Center: http://www.fjc.gov/

National Center for State Courts: http://www.ncsconline.org/

OYEZ (discusses current and recent Supreme Court decisions): http://www.oyez.org/oyez/frontpage

The Sentencing Project (information on the appeals process and habeas corpus): http://www.sentencingproject.org/

State Attorneys General Association: http://www.naag.org/

State Bar Associations: http://www.vtbar.org/Links/StateBarAssociations.htm

Supreme Court homepage: http://www.supremecourtus.gov/

READING

The use of habeas corpus, particularly in death penalty cases, has created a great deal of controversy and led to a number of judicial and legislative efforts to curtail its use by the federal judiciary. In this article, the author explores the historical origins of the writ of habeas corpus, its evolution, recent efforts to limit its use in federal courts, and the major issues that it presents in courts today.

The Federal Habeas Corpus Process

Unraveling the Issues

Robert D. Pursley

The writ of habeas corpus has become a much-maligned legal principle, one that has been widely vilified by the general public. Yet, like the insanity defense, many have an opinion on the subject, but few, including even members of the criminal justice and legal communities, really understand this arcane area of the law. What understanding exists is relegated to a few lawyers and judges, and even then, only to those who have occasion to entertain and explore its complexities. The article is not meant to be a legal exposition on the subject as found in law reviews, legal journals or treatises. The subject of habeas corpus is framed in the context of an issue of public policy—especially the issue of the writ's use in the so-called federal habeas process. By providing an oversight of this area of the law without the complex technicalities of the ever-evolving and tortuous case law holdings in this area, it is hoped that it will make the subject and its surrounding debate more understandable to the criminal justice professional.

The History of Habeas Corpus

The writ of habeas corpus was referred to by Chief Justice John Marshall as "the Great Writ" (*Ex Parte Bollma*, 1807). Others have been far less complimentary. The origins of the writ can be traced to an English common law creation that was four centuries in evolving. Legal historians have traced its beginnings to the thirteenth century. The English Crown courts of the time, faced with the widespread reluctance of the executive authority to surrender prisoners to the courts for review, were empowered to use a summonsing process to produce the prisoner. In its origin, the writ was not designed to challenge judgments of conviction rendered after trial, but only to challenge unlawful detention of citizens by the executive. Later, in an effort to correct any injustices of an initial trial court in reviewing the petitioner's plea for relief, the summons was accompanied by a central court issued order giving such a court the authority to

SOURCE: Pursley, R. D. (1995). The federal habeas corpus process: Unraveling the issues. *Criminal Justice Policy Review, 7*(2), 115–141.

question the cause of imprisonment. Together, the summons process and the order eventually united to form what became the writ of *habeas corpus cum causa* (Mells and Duffey, 1991).

But this tells only part of the story. Beyond any concern to merely protect the prisoner from injustices inflicted by the executive authority, the writ had a more practical application in English jurisprudence: It became a pawn in the struggle for judicial primacy. During the 15th and 16th centuries, the English courts verged on the chaotic. The Crown courts had evolved into the superior common law courts and these courts found themselves involved in a struggle for supremacy. The encroaching jurisdictional reach of the equity and ecclesiastical courts and various quasi-legal councils were developing threats. In that environment the writ became a tool in this struggle. It provided the means by which common law courts in their role as a rival tribunal could release a subject convicted by these other courts. How often this occurred history fails to reveal, but it seems likely that under such circumstances, habeas corpus was nothing if not a disruption to a well-functioning system of English jurisprudence.

Recognizing the need for reform, Parliament adopted the Habeas Corpus Act of 1679. While not supplanting its common law origins, the Act supplemented the common law foundation by creating a coexisting statutory authority for the writ and its method of issuance. Although not removing all common law features, the Act managed to remedy some existing abuses and clarified what courts could issue the writ and under what circumstances. It also spelled out certain procedural conditions such as requirements for jailers to return the writ within a specified time.

Given their English heritage, the framers of the Constitution were aware of the writ and it was incorporated in Article I, Sec. 9 of the Constitution. The importance of the writ can be seen from the fact that it was incorporated into the Constitution itself, and not as an amendment in the later adopted Bill of Rights. As originally constituted—and following the English model—it too, was solely for protecting citizens from arbitrary imprisonment by the executive authority. It

would remain so for many years. Interestingly, in spite of the arguments of Jefferson and others, the Constitutional delegates declined to incorporate an affirmative guarantee, instead opting to include a provision that in seemingly simple and straightforward language merely barred suspension of the writ.[1] With the passage of the Judiciary Act of 1789 came the first grant of federal court jurisdiction, and with it, following early Constitutional principle, authority for the federal courts to issue the writ where federal prisoners were held under provisions of federal law.

During the early years of our nation's history there existed so few federal prisoners that the writ proved to be of little legal consequence simply because so few federal prisoners actually existed, and because the federal courts of the time were generally unwilling to employ it. As for relief for state prisoners detained by executive authority, in 1845 the Supreme Court went as far as to hold that the federal common law writ of habeas corpus did not extend to such individuals (*Ex Parte Dor,* 1845). The Civil War focused attention on the writ. Many Americans are familiar with the fact that Lincoln suspended the habeas corpus writ during the Civil War and imprisoned several thousand putative southern sympathizers. The public are less aware that when murmuring from the Supreme Court about this action reached his ears, Lincoln considered an even more drastic and Constitutionally thought-provoking step: abolishing the Court's habeas review power itself.[2]

An important step—and one that would prove to be of major consequence—was taken in expanding the doctrine in the immediate post Civil War period. Fearing that southern states might vengefully incarcerate postwar northern reconstructionists, Congress sought a means to provide the federal courts with a mechanism for the oversight of state court convictions. Responding to this fear, the right to federal court habeas review by state prisoners was granted by Congressional enactment in 1867.[3] With this legislative step, the "federalizing" protection of the writ had been accomplished. The 1867 Congressional action is an extremely important feature of habeas corpus and it has become a current focus of today's raging debate over the use and reform of the writ. It was also the point at which the machinery was set in place for the writ to evolve into what it has primarily become today: A postconviction remedy to challenge trial judgement.[4]

Since the provisions for the writ and the legal process itself is primarily statutory in nature, in theory at least, it is Congress who holds the power to be the major player in at least defining federal habeas procedure. But, as in other areas of public policymaking, it has been the federal courts that have stepped in to assume an important role. And not unlike other areas of legal policymaking by the federal judiciary, the Courts' major role has been a relatively recent phenomenon. In 1953 an important Supreme Court decision interpreted the 1867 statute as providing the federal courts with broad review of federal habeas petitions (*Brown v. Allen,* 1953). This proved to be only the prologue. An important expansion of the rights of state prisoners to have their cases reviewed under federal habeas corpus was part of the so-called due process revolution during the Warren era of the Supreme Court in the 1960s (Bureau of Justice Statistics, 1989).

In hindsight it seems that the Supreme Court of the time meant to develop habeas corpus as the enforcement machinery not only for carving-out new principles of constitutional law, but, perhaps even more importantly, to serve as a cachet for charting a new era in federal-state judicial relations. The writ of habeas corpus provided an important mechanism whereby the federal courts could review state court determinations. The civil rights/due process expansionists on the Court understood the obvious: Through the vehicle of habeas corpus, the Court had within their power an important tool to further extend the supervisory constitutional review authority of the federal judiciary.

1963 seems to have been the watershed year. The Supreme Court in three separate cases expanded the rights of state prisoners to seek federal habeas relief.[5] As a result of these specific Supreme Court decisions, together with the simultaneous expanding doctrine of due process and the broad extension of prisoners' rights doctrines, the filing of federal habeas petitions by state prisoners began to grow. Whereas the number of habeas petitions filed with the federal courts

remained, on average, uniformly low with less than a thousand such filings a year from 1941–61, since then the number of habeas filings has generally been going up with an all-time high of nearly 12,000 filed with the federal courts in 1992.[6] Although a significant portion of this increase can be accounted for by the simple fact that state inmate populations have increased so drastically, even factoring in the increase in number of state prison inmates over this period cannot alone account for such a proportional increase.

However, the long-term analysis of federal habeas corpus filings by state inmates shows some interesting facts and changes. First, the last several years shows a general decline in number of federal filings. Given the increases in numbers of state prisoners, this figures out to a large relative decline. When plotting increases in state inmate populations against state prisoner initiated habeas corpus filings in the lower federal courts since 1961, the peak years for filing reached an all-time high in the early 1970s. As a percentage of state prisoner population, it hit its peak in 1970. In that year, as a percentage of the overall state prisoner population, state prisoner filings stood at over 5 percent. Today, as a percentage of state inmates it hovers around 1 percent (Flango, 1994). It might be inferred from this that changes in procedural requirements instituted by the Supreme Court, are having an effect.[7] But this is highly conjectural in the absence of specific empirical evidence that the two are related.[8]

It is also interesting to compare the size of the state's inmate population with the number of federal habeas corpus filings by prisoners in that state. Although there is some relationship, it is a weak one. Several larger states such as New York, Illinois and Ohio, who have large inmate populations, have fewer habeas corpus petitions filed in federal court than would be expected based upon this fact alone. Conversely, states such as Alabama, Louisiana, Nebraska, Tennessee and West Virginia have a higher percentage of their prison populations filing for federal habeas corpus relief. In research done by the National Center for State Courts it was found in 1990 that more than half of all federal habeas filings in that year came from only nine states (Flango, 1994: 18–20).[9]

General Characteristics

Habeas corpus petitions constitute what is called in the law *collateral* attacks upon state criminal judgments: separate civil legal filings that call into question the validity of those judgments as a basis for incarceration. These collateral attacks are supplemental to and occur after *direct* attacks. Direct attacks (or postconviction appeals) are ones in which the appellate court considers whether the conviction should be affirmed. Convicted defendants have the right to file direct appeals based upon their conviction. Over the course of state proceedings, criminal defendants usually have an opportunity to raise federal complaints about their treatment and the state courts adjudicate such issues routinely.[10] These are filed through the various state appellate courts and certiorari appeal to the U.S. Supreme Court. Upon conclusion of these direct appeals, the defendant then can attack the judgment of the trial court by means of a collateral attack on the issues.

Both state and federal courts have jurisdiction to entertain habeas corpus petitions from state prisoners claiming they are held in custody in violation of the Constitution. In federal courts this is extended to federal laws and treaties.[11] This usually takes the form of some kind of Constitutional issue that the habeas petitioner contends has violated his or her rights. A common claim, for example, is that the petitioner was denied effective assistance of counsel in violation of the Sixth Amendment. The fact that he or she is incarcerated together with this violation of federal law becomes the co-joining basis for the federal habeas petition. In the case of a habeas petition before the federal court, the federal court is asked to determine whether the petitioner's rights may have been violated in the state process that resulted in "custody."

The Issues in Federal Habeas Corpus Today

In recent years, habeas corpus—really, more correctly, federal habeas corpus—has become a very heated and widely debated legal principle. The debate regarding

habeas corpus seems to focus on a number of issues. These can be placed into four broad categories: Crime control and its political underpinnings; jurisprudential, constitutional, and workload issues; federal-state considerations; and recent attempts by the Supreme Court to curtail the right of state prisoners to seek federal review.

The Debate Over Habeas Corpus and the "Politics" of Crime Control

Federal habeas corpus of state prisoner petitions has been injected into the "politics" of crime control. It is argued that habeas corpus has a deleterious effect on anti-crime efforts and the overall administration of justice. It is, for example, said that habeas corpus procedures defeat the goal of deterring crime by undermining the certainty that sanctions will be applied where criminal laws are violated. The writ also comes under attack by those claiming that the lengthy time delays and uncertainties that may result from federal review of habeas corpus actions frustrate the interests of victims. Its widely publicized delay-inducing nature is also criticized for bringing disrepute to the administrative machinery of justice and it is also said it encourages ridicule of the system and fosters lack of witness cooperation and public respect. It is also argued that the length of time that elapses prior to federal habeas corpus review (and subsequent relitigation at the state level) limits the availability and reliability of evidence and witnesses. Finally, there are those who suggest that changes in the scope of habeas corpus review might have an impact on prisoners' conduct by increasing prisoners' frustrations (Bureau of Justice Statistics, 1984:1).

In the area of crime control it is especially in the ongoing debate over the death penalty that the federal habeas process has assumed a centerpiece role. Although the right to habeas review extends to the conviction (and incarceration) for any offense, it has become an issue most closely identified with those convicted and sentenced to death. More than anything, federal habeas has become singularly associated with inordinate delays in the carrying out of the death penalty.[12] This has led to a widespread denunciation of the writ.

Still, these death-penalty habeas filings are only the tip of the iceberg as the bulk of state prisoner habeas petitions emanate from non-capital convictions. Just as death sentences constitute only a small number of felony-level sentences imposed by our courts, so, too, are habeas corpus appeals from such sentences only a small portion of all such habeas filings. The vast majority of habeas petitions directed at both state and federal courts come from prisoners in state prisons who have been convicted of more conventional violent and property crimes. For the state prisoner filing a petition in a non-capital sentence, the federal courts have been much more reluctant to entertain the writ and to grant relief to the petitioner.[13] However, unlike the "non-capital" state prisoner federal habeas corpus case, the federal courts, including the U.S. Supreme Court, have granted relief to a more significant proportion of prisoners under sentence of death.[14]

Part of the reason for the denunciation of the federal habeas process is the chaotic situation habeas appeals have become in death penalty cases. Several years ago, a scholar in the field placed the issue into perspective when he said: "As the process operates, a state court and jury can sentence an offender to death and, through a series of appeals usually culminating in habeas corpus petition(s) to the federal courts, the convicted offender is able to stave off legal execution for years. As things stand, the least complicated case in which relief is denied at every stage can be presented to the U.S. Supreme Court a minimum of three times, and to the federal district and appellate courts at least twice each."[15] Whether this is still the case today given the "tightening up" of the appeals procedure by recent actions of the Court is, at present, an unanswered question. The effects of the Court's newly imposed guidelines on the lower federal courts have yet to be studied, or at least reported.[16] Such a circumstance has permeated the consciousness of the American public. Given the publicity surrounding execution delays, this

difficult to understand legal remedy is seen (but certainly not fully understood by even the knowledgeable public) as a cause for this delay.

The delay problem is abetted by the fact that in capital cases there is no incentive to speed up the exhaustion of direct state and federal appeals in order to be eligible for federal collateral review. Nor is there an inherent statute of limitations. In conventional felony convictions, someone who is convicted and sentenced to prison for a term of years in state court, and wishes to challenge that conviction and sentence in a federal habeas proceeding, has every incentive to move promptly to make that challenge. He must continue to serve his sentence while his federal claims are being adjudicated in the federal courts. The sooner a decision can be reached, the more quickly he receives any benefits. On the other hand, the offender sentenced to death knowing that all federal review must take place before the sentence is actually carried out, has no incentive to apply until the death warrant is issued by the state.

Adding to the controversy is the ideological struggle over the death penalty: Anti-capital punishment groups have made the habeas writ a tool of their determined efforts to at least frustrate the states in their imposition of the ultimate sanction. Citing one controversial study—one that claims that since 1900, 350 persons have been wrongfully convicted of capital or "potentially capital" crimes and twenty-three innocent persons have in fact been executed—has become a rallying cry for those opposed at efforts to restrict federal court review (Swafford, 1995).[17] Abolitionists might hope that federal habeas relief in association with other available postconviction appeal remedies, will weary state legislative bodies. Given the drawn out delay inherent in court challenges, lawmakers might just abolish capital punishment rather than continue the lengthy and costly court battles that anti-capital punishment groups have effectively waged.

This strategy has had obvious consequences. In a resolution passed in 1990, the Conference of State Chief Justices noted that the abuse of the writ existing at that time and encouraged by existing practices, "has effectively negated the law of the 37 states that impose the death penalty."[18] Federal habeas procedures have pitted as antagonists the anti-capital punishment and the pro-death penalty punishment groups. It has certainly singled out federal habeas as a major flash point in this ideological battle. It is no mere accident that pro-death penalty interests are strongly in favor of the Court's recently imposed restrictions on federal review and those opposed to the death penalty are howling about the Court's efforts.

In the crime control area, the federal habeas process has also taken a centerpiece position in the Congressional and administration debates that ultimately led to a new federal crime bill. Over the years that Congress haggled over a comprehensive crime bill, it provided the trappings of a highly charged political issue. Both the Reagan and Bush administrations sought to have Congress introduce legislation to cut back on the availability of the federal provisions of the writ to state prisoners. It was in fact, one of two cornerstones—the other being the "war on drugs"—of the Bush administration's anti-crime efforts.

In 1991, the Senate approved significant restrictions on habeas corpus as proposed by the Bush administration. A less restrictive proposal that emerged from the House as part of the crime bill that nearly passed the Congress, included watered-down limits on convict appeals. But in the end it could not survive a wave of attacks. Republicans and conservatives felt that the proposed curbs did not go far enough; liberal Democrats argued that anything more restrictive would permit executions of innocent persons who would not have an adequate chance to make their cases in the trial and appellate courts. In the end, Republican objections to the language, together with the objections of many state prosecutors, the National District Attorneys Association, and state attorneys general—all of whom wanted greater restrictions imposed on its availability to state prisoners—enabled opponents of the proposal to marshal their efforts and capture the necessary Congressional support to defeat the bill.

The issues of crime control and the effect of the federal habeas process on crime control measures have also been important to Chief Justice Rehnquist and other conservative members of the Supreme Court. Although these members of the Court have not addressed directly the issue of their feelings about the role of habeas in anti-crime efforts, their concerns over the delays caused by the use of the tactic and, implicitly then, the deterrent effect of the law, especially in capital cases, can be inferred from both their public comments on the issue and their case decisions.[19]

There have also been two prestigious groups that have joined the fray. In 1989, the Ad Hoc Committee on Federal Habeas Corpus in Capital Cases (called the Powell Committee after its chair, retired Justice Lewis F. Powell, Jr., of the United States Supreme Court) produced a report suggesting alterations to the habeas statutes (Bureau of National Affairs, 1989). The committee found that the existing system of multi-layered state and federal appeal and collateral review resulted in piecemeal and repetitious litigation. This resulted in years of delay between sentencing and a judicial resolution as to whether the sentence was permissible under the law. The report listed several major recommendations: to limit the period within which a federal habeas petition must be filed to 180 days after exhaustion of direct appeal and certiorari petition to the U.S. Supreme Court; to establish an automatic stay of execution until federal habeas proceedings are completed to avoid the last minute time pressures caused by impending execution; and to prevent prisoners from filing repetitive claims for habeas corpus in federal court (unless it is a claim of actual innocence) after they have had one full course of judicial review.

At about the time of the Powell Committee report, a voluminous report was issued by the American Bar Association Task Force on Death Penalty Habeas Corpus (1989). In its report, it set forth the findings and recommendations of its year-long study of the entire system of postconviction review of state capital convictions and sentences. Like the Powell Committee, the ABA Committee came out in favor of expediting the process (although the time frames were longer than the Powell Committee recommendations).[20]

The ABA Task Force was particularly unequivocal in its feelings that streamlining the postconviction death penalty review must include assurances that qualified counsel as determined by explicitly imposed ABA standards be provided at every step in capital proceedings—all stages in all courts. On the other hand, it was the Powell Committee's recommendation that such assurances for counsel be provided in state postconviction relief, but the states were to be free to determine the establishment of qualifications of counsel.

The outcome was inevitable: Conservatives embraced the Powell Committee report while more liberal law scholars and the defense bar inveighed against it (for example, Berger, 1990; Mello and Duffey, 1990–1; Goldstein, 1990–1). Liberals, on the other hand, sought some measure of solace in the ABA recommendations. Much of the criticism of the Powell report was focused on the fact that it was formed by Chief Justice Rehnquist who is no darling of the liberal legal establishment. The querulous liberal law factions were quick to accuse the committee of being composed of parochial, Rehnquist mirror-imaged southern judges. The inference was that the Courts of Appeals judges selected from the southern Circuits to serve on the committee (ostensibly because these were the Circuits with the largest number of habeas filings) were biased pro-death penalty and anti-habeas advocates.[21] It was this kind of tone that established the legal (and ideological-laden) disquisition in the law review articles that were to follow.

Adding to the issue was the so-called Biden proposal named after Senator Joseph Biden, chair of the Senate Judiciary Committee, who promptly introduced legislation, the "Habeas Corpus Reform Act" containing some Powell Committee Report's recommendations and altering others to fit the ABA report (S.1441, Sec. 2., 1993). In response, Senator Strom Thurmond, supported by the Bush administration, proposed to make the Powell Committee's recommendations law.[22] Vigorous debate on these proposals ensued. The habeas controversy has been one of the reasons, along with such controversial topics added to the mix as gun control and increasing the number of federal death penalty crimes, that Congress found itself stymied from 1988 until 1994

in adopting a new comprehensive federal crime bill. Finally, after prolonged haggling the Violent Crime Control and Law Enforcement Act of 1994 was passed.

This new Act is absent any reference to federal habeas corpus appeal. This is an interesting omission. It can only be inferred that Congressional conferees in their concern to enact a crime bill under scathing media attack over political partisanship and legislative ineptitude chose purposely to exclude such a flash-point issue. After six unsuccessful years of trying to get a comprehensive federal crime bill passed, they were not ready to jeopardize the tenuous thread of adoption by prolonging the debate over yet another controversial feature.

Hidden in all the controversy over the new crime bill is a little known fact. Although President Clinton as candidate made no direct reference to his position on habeas corpus, in 1993, when the Clinton administration sent to Congress its proposed provisions for consideration in the crime bill, it contained specific habeas-related recommendations.[23] The administration, aware of what had happened in earlier attempts at reaching accord on a federal crime bill, and perhaps sensing the need to mollify the nation's district attorneys, state judges, and attorneys general, proposed an adoption of the Biden and Powell Committee recommendation—one that will set a six-month time limit on inmates to file a single, federal habeas corpus appeal. As conceived, this time limit would generally operate from the exhaustion of all direct appeal rights. In this respect, the proposal, in terms of language and intent, interestingly paralleled the efforts of the Reagan and Bush administrations who, too, sought Congressional action that would limit the number of times a petitioner can use the process as a vehicle of review before the federal courts.

However, there was one important difference in the Biden and Clinton administration proposals and it may have been a good one. The major complaint of state inmates on habeas appeal is that they did not have competent counsel at their trial. This is especially true among those inmates sentenced to death. Since a large majority of criminal defendants are represented by indigent defense schemes, there may be some merit in such claims. The bill as proposed by the administration, and in line with the ABA Task Force recommendations, would have required that in all states that have the death penalty, a state counsel authority be established.

The state counsel authority as conceived by the administration would have been an agency partially supported by federal funds that would be responsible for seeing that defense counsel in capital cases meet certain standards. This includes required defense experience in capital cases, including trial, appellate and postconviction evidentiary hearing experience. It would also be required to establish application, training and certification procedures for attorneys defending such cases. Such composed qualified defense teams would then be made available to a defendant in a capital case as well as for direct and collateral (including habeas corpus) appeals upon conviction. Such a sweeping proposal is not incorporated in the 1994 crime bill; instead, Congress chose to ignore the thrust of the administration's major recommendation. The new crime bill merely requires that in federal death penalty cases, two defense counsels be assigned, one of whom at least "shall be learned in the law applicable to capital cases" (See: Sec. 60026, Violent Crime Control and Law Enforcement Act of 1994).

In the final analysis it is questionable whether habeas corpus has managed to foil our nation's anti-crime efforts as some detractors suggest. Any such cause and effect pronouncements on an issue as complex as the nation's crime problem rests on very shaky common sense, let alone empirical grounds. Although it is true that its complexities and awkward procedures have lengthened delay, the problems of crime in the United States cannot be laid at the doorstep of a single legal process, especially a procedure that involves only a very small percentage of all convicted offenders. This is especially true when one considers that for those who are successful in obtaining its application to overturn a conviction, the number of such successes is ridiculously small. What it does seem to do, however, is serve as a convenient jeremiad for the nation's frustration with crime.

Where it may have an impact, however, is on the public's perception. This should not be ruled out as unimportant. Habeas corpus litigation has created among wide segments of the American public another way to criticize and hold in disrepute the administration of justice, our legal system, and our nation's legal culture itself. The idea, for example, that it has and continues to lead to delays in death penalty cases has caused extensive public criticism—especially when the public perceives that its basis is generally frivolous and turns on the mockery of construed legal technicalities rather than on the issue of substantive innocence. Such attitudes are no doubt abetted by the publicity given official pronouncements. One such widely-publicized denunciation was by former Attorney General Edwin Meese who reportedly said, "most habeas cases are frivolous" (Chicago Daily Law Bulletin, 1986).

Jurisprudential, Constitutional and Workload Issues

It is also argued that habeas corpus affects both proper notions of legal jurisprudence and Constitutional safeguards. For example, some common arguments are that the current likelihood that issues may be relitigated at the federal level affects the incentives for a comprehensive analysis of cases in the state courts. This could be construed to be then affecting the rights of those individuals who do not pursue federal review actions.

There are also those who say that habeas corpus claims are often determined to be without merit, and yet, result in an undue workload at both the state and federal court levels. State officials, for example, often complain of the additional workload imposed upon them to defend the actions of state courts and juries as unwarranted, costly and burdensome—that in periods of limited financial resources, the drain of time and cost is becoming prohibitive. Such criticism has become more strident in recent years as state courts struggle to maintain some control of growing civil and criminal case dockets.

Yet, the limited four-state study of state and federal habeas corpus filings by the National Center for State

Courts contradicts some of these assumptions and pronouncements. They found among other things that few of the petitions are successful in either state or federal courts. The vast majority are dismissed summarily without hearing. This alone limits the time-consuming nature of the process. While the researchers found overlap and duplication of effort between the two levels of courts, this comes as no surprising revelation given the inherent nature of the process. They concluded that in both the state and federal courts that they studied, habeas corpus petitions were found to be a very small part of the overall judicial workload (Flango, 1994:23).[24]

In spite of such findings, this workload issue has become one of concern among at least some members of the federal judiciary. For example, Chief Justice Rehnquist in a 1990 speech delivered to the American Law Institute did voice open criticism of the imposed workload. He pointed out that "the members of the federal appellate judiciary were often faced with having pending appeals within a matter of days of not merely one application for a stay of execution but two from the same person; one seeking review of collateral state proceedings and the other seeking review of federal habeas proceedings, both brought in the court of first instance within a matter of days before the execution is set to take place." He referred to the situation as "[verging] on the chaotic" (Rehnquist, 1991).

Along this line, although no one would argue that constitutional issues are ever to be superseded by resource requirements and associated costs, there is still the question and the contention that practical factors (such as manpower and fiscal matters) should be reasonably considered in evaluating procedures designed to protect alleged constitutional violations.[25] The Supreme Court has been moving in this direction by emphasizing that mere constitutional error should not be solely determinative; it is the effect of any such error on trial court disposition that should be the issue.

There is no doubt that some of these claims have a basis. Still, one must consider the obvious: the protection and uniform enforcement of federally established constitutional rights through habeas corpus review represents overriding considerations in the American

system of jurisprudence. It is often said, for example, that rights without remedies are rights denied. There is a significant risk factor here. Any limitation on habeas corpus review poses the threat of undermining the constitutional rights of individuals. Under such circumstances, it is an area that must be approached with extreme caution.

Federal and State Relations: Federalism

Unknown to most citizens and even many members of the legal and criminal justice communities is the bitterness that has developed over the federal courts' willingness to use the habeas process and over the unwillingness of Congress to entertain a number of proposals that would provide more deference to state court determinations. The subject of habeas corpus relief has evolved to a point where it has managed to assume the trappings of a federal-state issue, even the issue of federalism itself—the fundamental question of what is the proper balance between the lawful authority of the states and the role of federal courts in protecting constitutional rights (Lungren, 1991). The Federal Courts Study Committee has said: "the scope of federal habeas corpus is one of the most politically divisive questions of federal jurisdiction."

At stake in the habeas corpus process are decisions made by two sovereign court systems. It begins with the state court process that produced a conviction and a sentence of imprisonment which have been upheld on direct appeal by the court of last resort in the convicting and sentencing state. It is also a conviction and sentence that have at least passed the implied muster of refusal by the U.S. Supreme Court to hear the appeal by means of a certiorari filing.

This is the cusp of the issue: arguments of state court finality and comity balanced with the concern for the rights of convicted defendants and the fundamental concept of federalism—that state courts be given every opportunity to manage their own criminal dockets before federal review (Lay, 1993:1048). It is in this context that many legal historians see habeas corpus as one of the penultimate questions of legal federalism—the sharing of powers and responsibilities between the federal and state governments. As Robbins, a noted legal scholar in this area, has said, "It echoes the debates of more than 200 years ago: the sovereignty of the states in preserving domestic order versus the preeminence of the federal government in vouchsafing national interests—in this case, constitutional criminal law" (Robbins, 1990:215).

State courts along with state prosecutors and attorneys general have grown increasing restive over the federal courts' preemptive willingness to entertain, and in some cases overturn, by means of prisoner habeas filings, state court decisions, judgments that have been fully reviewed by the full-range of state courts at the trial and appellate levels and not found wanting.[26] Such bodies as the Conference of State Chief Justices in a series of resolutions in 1989, came out strongly for efforts at identifying ways to relieve the existing tensions between state and federal courts resulting from the writ of habeas corpus.[27] An unprecedented step was taken in 1994 when 26 state attorneys general went on record severely criticizing the federal courts in capital appeals cases for "undermining slate judicial processes" and [for] "ignoring the constitutional precepts of federalism and the traditional authority of the state court determinations in the criminal process" (Roberts, 1994).

To state prosecutors and Attorneys General the issues are clear: Current federal procedures reduce or eliminate the finality of criminal cases by allowing federal collateral review of decisions that have been fully appealed on the state level. It is said that potential federal re-analysis of issues and facts that have been fully adjudicated at the highest level in the state judicial system exacerbates existing federal-state judicial relations (Bureau of Justice Statistics, 1984:1–2). States have complained, for example, that under federal habeas corpus, their post-conviction remedies are "out of control" (Lay, 1993:1025). One of the results of this continuing controversy has been found in the attempts by some states to limit their collateral procedures.

One cannot separate the arguments over habeas corpus use today without also dealing with these issues. The federalism issue does not center on the filing of these petitions in state courts by state inmates.

The real issue has become the right of convicted state prisoners to attack state court determinations by the use of a writ of habeas corpus *filed with the federal courts*. This continuing controversy is being fueled in an era when Congress is showing increasing deference to the states and the Supreme Court seems to be increasingly restive with its (and the federal government's) supervisory intrusiveness over the states.

In the final analysis, it is proving to have all the characteristics of a defining example of inherent federal-state tensions. After all, the 1867 Act was specifically brought about because the federal government felt that the states could not be trusted. Not only did it extend federal habeas corpus to state prisoners, it also furnished an additional collateral method independent of direct Supreme Court review of state court decisions for the vindication of new Constitutional guarantees (Jochmer, 1993:251). This legislation profoundly altered the balance of federalism. One must be struck by the irony that this legislation came at a time in our nation's history when Americans had just concluded their most sanguinary war—a momentous struggle that in itself was in large part precipitated by the issue of federal-state powers.

 ## Attempts by the Court to Limit Review

Any discussion of federal habeas corpus would be incomplete without some brief attention to recent attempts by the Supreme Court to limit, or at least change, the procedures governing the availability of this remedy to state inmates. Civil libertarians and anti-capital punishment groups are very disturbed by the efforts of the existing Supreme Court to reintegrate the use of this tactic in the federal courts (for example, see Frank, 1991; Patchell, 1991; Weisberg, 1990; Ledewitz, 1990–1; Tabak and Lane, 1991). This opposition, first begun during the Burger Court, such efforts have picked up momentum in recent years. Like liberal members of Congress, opponent groups argue that this will have disastrous consequences. Liberal anti-revisionist legal scholars and groups such as the American Civil Liberties Union (ACLU), and anti-capital punishment interests argue that the Court's case decisions in the area of habeas corpus in recent years have dangerously and improperly foreclosed the federal courts to state prisoners (for example, see Koosed, 1993; Hallisey, 1993; Rice, 1991). At least one of these groups contends that federal appellate courts have found constitutional flaws in as many as 73 percent of state death penalty cases reviewed on the merits.[28] While this is an exaggeration not supported by the facts, still it has become a gravamen of concern. The issues and the arguments have been further abetted among legal scholars and the defense and prosecution bars by the recommendations of those committees that have studied the subject and the issues.

Those who favor full federal habeas review argue that it is justified by the liberty interest at stake in habeas proceedings, by the importance of vindicating constitutional rights, by the structural superiority of federal courts in considering issues of federal constitutional law, and by the importance of federal court appellate style review of constitutional questions given the impracticality of Supreme Court review (Woolhandler, 1993:578–579).

There is no doubt that a majority of the Supreme Court has shown in recent years a willingness to limit this recourse to state petitioners. An examination of recent court decisions indicates that a majority of the Court by a series of case decisions seems bent on charting out still another page in federal-state judicial relations. In an effort to return to state review finality, the Court has, by a series of decisions, managed to begin to restrict habeas review by the federal courts.

Some major decisions are illustrative of this trend. In the past few years, the Court's majority has among other things: held that "new rules" of criminal procedure did not apply retroactively to cases that had become final on direct review at the time the new rule was decided (*Teague v. Lane*, 1989); federal courts may not hear successive habeas claims raising new issues unless the petitioner has cause for failure to bring the claim earlier, such as constitutionally ineffective assistance of counsel or interference by state officials (*McClesky v. Zant*, 1991); and barred the habeas appeal of a death-row inmate because his lawyers had filed notice that they would appeal a state habeas decision three days late (*Coleman v. Thompson*, 1991).

The last two sessions of the Court have generally seen a continued trend toward greater restriction on federal habeas appeal. The Court made it harder for persons to obtain habeas relief based on constitutional errors during the trial by holding such error harmless if it did not have a substantial and injurious effect or influence on the verdict (*Brecht v. Abrahamson*, 1993); ruled that habeas petitioners are entitled to a federal evidentiary hearing on their petition only if they can show cause for their failure to develop the facts in state court proceedings and actual prejudice resulted from that failure (*Keeney v. Tamayo-Reyes*, 1992); and pronounced perhaps its most controversial recent ruling, that a death row inmate who offers new evidence suggesting that he is innocent is not ordinarily entitled to a federal habeas corpus hearing, unless he can show a Constitutional violation in the underlying state court procedure (*Herrera v. Collins*, 1993).

What is happening is noteworthy. For example, Chief Justice Rehnquist, writing for the majority in the recent case barring a hearing on the petitioner's contention that he is innocent, expressed clearly the conviction of the Court's majority members: that the state's interest in the finality of the conviction must be considered and that state courts have equal ability, and perhaps are in a superior position, to evaluate the effect of trial error.

Yet, the Court has also zigzagged a bit. Its decisions have not always been following the path of closing off habeas review by a state prisoner. In 1993, a 5–4 majority held that Miranda errors must be continued to be entertained in federal habeas proceedings. In this case the state argued that the Court should invoke in Miranda cases a doctrine applied in a 1976 case that forbids federal courts to grant habeas relief to state prisoners on the basis of Fourth Amendment claims that have been fully and fairly adjudicated in state courts (*Stone v. Powell*, 1976). In 1994 thru early 1995, it established more lenient guidelines for successive claims if a successive claim bears on the innocence of the accused in death penalty cases (*Schlup v. Deb*, 1995). In another case, the Court ruled that the lower courts if they find Constitutional error and are in doubt about its "substantial and injurious effect" on the jury's verdict, must side with the petitioner (*O'Neal v. McAninch*, 1995).

◤ Conclusion

What will come out of all the controversy that surrounds the federal habeas corpus process is anybody's guess. It promises to remain an open question that will not suddenly disappear. While the present majority composition of the Supreme Court seems clearly inclined to limit the use of habeas corpus tactic to obtain federal review. But the Court's inclination can change with a change in the composition of the Court's membership. And it could be an abrupt change. During each session of the Court in recent years, at least several habeas corpus cases have come before it for decision. There is ample opportunity then, for a new ideological majority of the court to have a significant impact.

As for Congress, it may be poised to become the prominent player in addressing the many issues that federal habeas corpus presents. It seems to be moving in that direction. While the 1994 Crime Bill stands as an excellent example of Congressional paralysis to address the issues of federal court oversight in this area, this may now be changing with the heightened Republican presence in Congress. Congress under Democratic control was obviously reluctant to enter the fray. While under Democratic leadership, the 1994 Crime Bill managed to increase substantially the number of federal capital crimes while sidestepping the issue of habeas corpus reform. It even found itself embroiled in other controversial features of the death penalty such as the efforts by the Congressional Black Caucus for the inclusion of a "Racial Justice Act" provision that would have extended rather than curtail federal appeal jurisdiction; one that would allow appeals to review statistical disproportionality of the death penalty meted out to minority defendants.

In the final analysis, the 1994 Crime Bill was an expedient political compromise to shore-up the flagging fortunes of the Democrats in both Congress and the administration. It was also recognized as an expedient political necessity: A need to address the widespread concern among Americans that something was being done to combat crime. Congress now seems to be returning to this issue of federal oversight of habeas corpus for state prisoners. Anti-terrorism legislation just passed by the Senate has major provisions to overhaul federal habeas corpus law. Not surprisingly, the habeas corpus part of the new Senate anti-terrorism law again proved to be the most partisan and heatedly debated part of the proposed legislation. Democrats led by Senator Biden (D-Del.) tried to limit the habeas corpus measures in the bill to federal prisoners, arguing that because the bill as a whole concerned the federal response to terrorism, provisions changing habeas as it applies to state prisoners were not germane. But Senator Hatch (R-UT) among others, spoke against a "piecemeal approach" to habeas reform and said the amendment proposed by Biden would "gut" the bill's habeas provisions. Hatch's view prevailed, and the bill as passed addresses habeas petitions by federal and state prisoners in both capital and non-capital cases (Criminal Law Reporter, 1995).[29] The proposal now goes to the House. Proponents contend these proposed reforms would shorten delay in state imposed death penalty cases from an average of eight years to five (Washington Post, 1995). Congress, it seems, cannot continue to sidestep the problem. It is likely, that now a full Congress will be forced to address it.

In the end, the whole may be greater than the sum of the parts. After all there are two primary actors involved: Congress itself and its statutory role in habeas corpus, and the Supreme Court in its existing interpretive role (and subsequent interpretation should Congress act), which could be affected by a changing mix of Supreme Court members. There are, of course, other considerations, not the least of which are special interest groups and the tugs and pulls of an American public and its feverish concern over crime and our nation's crime control policies, two factors that seem to have carved-out a stake in the future of habeas corpus.

One thing about "the Great Writ" is obvious: its use and even its symbolism far transcend mere concern over its effect as an appellate remedy—or its argued practical effect as a means to delay justice. Hidden within habeas corpus are some broad and fundamental issues of governmental sovereignty, the administration of criminal justice, constitutional review, rights of the convicted, political partisanship and issues of race, the public's perception of our legal system, and our nation's crime control anxieties.

✎ Notes

1. "The privilege of the writ of habeas corpus shall not be suspended unless when in cases of rebellion or invasion the public safety may require it."

2. Although criticized for his suspension of the writ and the imprisonment of thousands of suspected southern sympathizers, Lincoln had no compunctions about his action. In a letter to Eustus Corning and others, dated June 12, 1863 he states: "Ours is a case of rebellion. . . . [The Suspension Clause] plainly attests the understanding of those who made the Constitution that ordinary courts of justice are inadequate to cases of rebellion—attests their purpose that, in such cases, men may be held in custody whom the courts, acting on ordinary rules, would discharge. Habeas corpus does not discharge men who are proved to be guilty of defined crime; and its suspension is allowed by the Constitution on the purpose that men may be arrested and held who cannot be proved to be guilty of defined crimes." Lincoln's actions were unanimously overturned by the Supreme Court in 1866, a year after his death and the conclusion of the Civil War in *Ex Parte Milligan*, 1866.

3. Actually, the 1867 act did not specifically mention states. This amendment by Congress to the federal habeas corpus statutes authorized federal courts to issue writs of habeas corpus on behalf of any person in custody "in violation of the Constitution." This implicitly extended this review authority of prisoners held by state action.

4. Author's note: This system in unique to the United States. No such collateral attack is allowed on a conviction in England, where the writ of habeas corpus originated.

5. The specific cases expanding habeas corpus were *Fay v. Noia*, 1963; *Townsend v. Sain*, 1963; and *Sanders v. U.S.*, 1963.

6. Information supplied by Statistical Analysis Section, Administrative Office, United States Supreme Court, 1994.

7. Of course, more than merely "tightening up" the availability of this remedy may be playing a role in this decline. It may reflect this fact coupled with the changes in inmate characteristics. For example, a growing segment of state inmates are imprisoned on drug charges. The filing of federal habeas corpus petitions are more likely to be filed by those serving long-term sentences. Perhaps many state drug sentencing patterns and parole policies do not trigger the long periods of incarceration that are necessary to exhaust all state and federal direct post-conviction remedies that are first required before the federal courts will entertain a habeas corpus petition. There is also the fact that drug-related charges are most likely to be contested on the grounds of illegal search and seizure. Such Fourth Amendment challenges as a basis for federal habeas have been generally foreclosed by the Supreme Court. It would be interesting to see if the new "three strike" laws being adopted by states which mandate life imprisonment proves to increase federal habeas filings by those so sentenced.

8. Still, it may reflect the fact that the Supreme Court in recent years has limited the opportunity for inmates to file successive petitions, requiring that they be "bundled" for consideration. The fact that inmates except in certain circumstances cannot file successive petitions, but must lump them together into one, would decrease the number of petitions filed as counted against an ever-growing number of state prisoners. A report by the Federal Courts Study Committee, *Working Papers and Subcommittee Reports* (July 1, 1990, at 468), speculates that the decline in filings are attributable to the lack of prisoner success in obtaining habeas review combined with the liberalizing for prisoners of Title 42, Section 1983 (civil rights violation). The report suggests that this has "deflected" many habeas cases to filings under Section 1983.

9. The states were California, Texas, New York, Florida, Pennsylvania, Alabama, Missouri, Louisiana and Michigan. What accounts for this is anybody's guess. It could be any number of factors: More "jailhouse lawyering," personal characteristics of the inmates, state sentencing schemes, and policies and views of state and federal courts in certain geographical areas. One possible explanation is pointed out by the National Center for State Courts in its recent examination of federal habeas filings by state inmates. They suggest that procedural differences among the states in how they handle state post-conviction relief seems to be associated with the number of inmates filing federal habeas corpus (Flango, 1994:18–20).

10. Defendants may raise federal defenses to state trial courts before, during, and after trial-level proceedings. They may ask state appellate courts to review trial courts determinations for error, and they may seek state postconviction relief in both trial-level and appellate courts.

11. See: 28 U.S.C. 2241(c)(3), 2254(a) 1988. Technically, habeas corpus is available only to *state* prisoners because actions under these statutes by federal prisoners are "motions" that are part of an ongoing federal action.

12. This opinion is strongly held by Chief Justice Rehnquist who, in his 1989 remarks to the ABA mid-year meeting, remarked: "[T]o my mind the flaw in the present system is not that capital sentences are set aside by federal courts, but the litigation ultimately resolved in favor of the state takes literally years and years and years."

13. This was also obvious from some recent research conducted by the author as part of a habeas corpus project conducted by the National Center for State Courts into habeas filings and actions in four selected states.

14. According to one source, federal appellate courts have found constitutional flaws in as many as 73 percent of state death penalty cases reviewed on the merits. See Brief Amicus Curiae for the NAACP Legal Defense and Education Fund at 1-b *Barefoot v. Estelle,* 1983. Still, as one noted expert points out, this figure may be misleading as virtually every death penalty state had to amend its laws after 1976 (Robbins, 1990). Other sources have put the figure at 40–60 percent.

15. Robbins (1990) has pointed out, the first petition for certiorari to the U.S. Supreme Court will typically follow affirmance of conviction by the state's court of last resort. Following state post-conviction proceedings (including appeals within the state judicial system of lower state court denials of post-conviction relief, and perhaps including as well another petition for certiorari to the Supreme Court), a first federal habeas petition will be filed in federal district court, where a full-scale hearing will often be held. An appeal will follow, in which the appeal will also be given full—not expedited—attention. Another petition for certiorari will be filed in the Supreme Court. Following Supreme Court review, if any, the case will become the subject of state executive branch clemency proceedings. If clemency is denied, emergency post-conviction proceedings will be filed in both state and federal trial courts, with expedited appeals to the state and federal intermediate and ultimate appellate courts.

16. The Federal Court Study Committee, Working Papers And Subcommittee Reports (July 1, 1990) suggested that the falling numbers of federal habeas petitions in recent years as a percentage of inmate populations may be a combination of lack of prisoner success with this remedy combined with a "deflection" by inmates to 42 U.S. Sec. 1983 (civil rights) filings in its place.

17. What they are referring to is Radelet, Bedau and Putnam (1992). Also see Bedau and Radelet (1987). Their methodology and conclusions have come under sharp attack; for an example see Markman and Cassell (1988).

18. Resolution XVIII, Habeas Corpus in Capital Cases, adopted as proposed by the State-Federal Relations Committee of the Conference of Chief Justices (February 1, 1990).

19. For example, Chief Justice Rehnquist in *Coleman v. Balkcom* (1981) in dissent wrote "[the current system] has made it virtually impossible for States to enforce with reasonable promptness their constitutionally valid capital punishment statutes."

20. The ABA committee recommended a required time period to file federal habeas relief of a full year after exhaustion of direct appeals and certiorari to the U.S. Supreme Court. It also recommended the possibility of a 90 day extension for cause and an overall exception to any time limit for a colorable claim, not previously presented, either of factual innocence or the petitioner's ineligibility for the death penalty.

21. It should be pointed out that even some of the chief judges of the U.S. Court of Appeals in an unprecedented move attacked the Powell Committee report and Chief Justice Rehnquist's behavior in directly submitting the Committee's report to Congress (Reinhardt, 1989).

22. Senator Strom Thurmond (R-SC) introduced the "Reform of Federal Intervention in State Proceedings Act" beginning with the 97th Congress, which would bar federal habeas corpus litigation of a claim if the issue was "fully and fairly" litigated in state court.

23. The Clinton bill had three major provisions. In addition to the federal habeas corpus feature, the other two major prongs of the administration's crime bill was the so-called Brady Bill and its five-day waiting period for purchase of handguns, and a $3.5 billion scheme to put more police officers on the street.

24. However, it should be noted that this is only part of the issue. Most non-death row prisoners' claims are filed pro se. This requires staff time to screen for constitutional violations and determine if counsel should be appointed. U.S. District Courts have pro se clerks who have this responsibility. In death penalty cases a great deal of "tracking" of such petitions by court staff occurs. Keeping up with both non-capital and capital case filings can be time-consuming and tedious.

25. The Chief Judge of the Court of Appeals (Eighth Circuit) argues that if states eliminated the death penalty, a large amount of litigation would disappear and the savings to state government would be enormous (Lay, 1993). The cost of reviewing cases in state and federal courts has been estimated to be between $3.5 and $4.5 million dollars per death row inmate (Linder, 1993). There are those, however, who argue that death penalty abolitionists purposely exaggerate death penalty costs while understating the cost of life imprisonment.

26. For example see, *Schneckloth v. Bustamonte,* 1973, quoting Massachusetts Supreme Court Justice Paul C. Reardon on the "humiliation of review from the full bench of the highest state appellate court to a single, United States District Court judge." Yet, at least one state judge has testified to the necessity of federal oversight. Justice Garter, a former state judge noted that state court improvements were encouraged by such oversight (*Withrow v. Williams,* 1993).

27. Specifically, Resolution XI as adopted August 31, 1989 as proposed by the State-Federal Relations Committee. It mentions that "the Conference of Chief Justices has repeatedly expressed the view that duplicative and overlapping reviews of state criminal convictions by federal courts unduly prolong and conflict with state criminal proceedings." It also expressed the need to reduce resulting tensions between state and federal courts.

28. See Amicus Curiae brief by the NAACP Legal Defense and Education Fund in *Barefoot v. Estelle,* 1983. However, noted legal authority on the subject Robbins (1990) feels this may be misleading as virtually every death penalty state had to amend its laws after 1976. He appears to be more inclined to agree with those who put the figure at 40–60 percent. For example, the ABA studied published

habeas decisions by federal appeals courts in capital cases from July 1976 to May 1991. It found that in 40 percent of the cases, the state conviction or death sentence was reversed because of constitutional violations or errors (Moss, 1992).

29. Among some of the main features of the proposed bill are the following: State prisoners in non-capital cases would have just one year to apply for habeas relief; in capital cases it would add to Title 28, a new chapter titled, "Special Habeas Corpus Procedures in Capital Cases." In brief, it would establish timetables and limit the issues available on habeas, but these provisions would apply only if the state established a system for appointing and compensating competent counsel for post-conviction proceedings brought by condemned prisoners. If such a system is in place, then a prisoner would have 180 days to file for federal habeas. The period would run from the final state court affirmance of the conviction and sentence on direct review, but would be tolled while the U.S. Supreme Court review or state postconviction relief is sought. It bars second or successive application of claims. The language of the proposal pays a much greater deference to state court determinations that have been litigated in state courts. Federal review would be limited to claims raised and decided on the merits in state courts, unless the failure to raise the claim is the result of such things as state action in violation of the federal Constitution or laws; the recognition of a new federal right recognized and applied retroactively by the Supreme Court; or based on a factual predicate (e.g., the facts underlying the claim would be sufficiently established by clear and convincing evidence that but for constitutional error, no reasonable fact finder would have found the applicant guilty of the offense).

 ## Cases Cited

Barefoot v. Estelle 463 U.S. 880 (1983)
Brecht v. Abrahamson 113 S. Ct. 1710 (1993)
Brown v. Allen 344 U.S. 443 (1953)
Coleman v. Thompson 111 S. Ct. 2546 (1991)
Ex Parte Bollman 8 U.S. (4 Cranch) 75, 95 (1807)
Ex Parte Dorr 44 U.S. (3 How.) 103. (1845)
Ex Parte Milligan 71 U.S. (4 Wall.) (1866)
Fay v. Noia 83 S. Ct. 822 (1963)
Herrera v. Collins 113 S. Ct. 853 (1993)
Keeney v. Tamayo-Reyes 112 S. Ct. 1715 (1992)
McClesky v. Zant 111 S. Ct. 1454 (1991)
O'Neal v. McAninch 93–7407 (decided February 21, 1995)
Sanders v. U.S. 83 S. Ct. 822 (1963)
Schlup v. Deb 93–7901 (decided January 23, 1995)
Schneckloth v. Bustamonte 412 U.S. 218 (1973)
Stone v. Powell 428 U.S. 465 (1976)
Teague v. Lane 109 S. Ct. 1060 (1989)
Townsend v. Sain 83 S. Ct. 745 (1963)
Withrow v. Williams 113 S. Ct. 1745 (1993)

 ## References

American Bar Association Task Force on Death Penalty Habeas Corpus. 1989. *Toward a more just and effective system of review in state death penalty cases, recommendations and report of the ABA Task Force On Death Penalty Habeas Corpus.* Chicago: ABA.

Bedau, H. A. and M. L. Radelet. 1987. Miscarriages of justice in potentially capital cases. *Stanford University Law Review,* 40:21–179.

Berger, V. 1990. Comment on recent proposal to reform death penalty habeas corpus. *Columbia Law Review,* 90: 1665–1714.

Bureau of Justice Statistics. 1989. *Correctional populations in the United States* (series). Washington, D.C.: U.S. Department of Justice.

Bureau of Justice Statistics. 1984. *Habeas corpus - Federal review of state prisoner petitions.* Special Report. Washington, D.C.: U.S. Department of Justice.

Bureau of National Affairs. 1989. Ad hoc committee on federal habeas corpus in capital cases. *Criminal Law Reporter,* 45.

Bureau of National Affairs. 1995. Senate passes anti-terrorism bill with limits on federal habeas corpus. *Criminal Law Reporter,* 57, 11: 1260–1263.

Chicago Daily Law Bulletin. 1986 Volume 132, May 20, p. 1, col 1.

Flango, V. E. 1994. *Habeas corpus in state and federal courts.* Williamsburg, VA: National Center for State Courts.

Frank, J. P. 1991. The new court forgetting old values. *Legal Times,* July: 25.

Goldstein, S. M. 1990–1. Chipping away at the great writ: Will death sentenced federal habeas corpus petitioners be able to seek and utilize changes in the law? *New York University Review of Law and Social Change,* 18, 2: 357–414.

Hallisey, M. 1993. To habe or not to habe: Curtailing the writ of habeas corpus. *New England Journal on Criminal and Civil Confinement.* Summer.

Jochner, M. M. 1993. Til habeas do us part: Recent Supreme Court habeas corpus rulings. *Illinois Bar Journal,* 81:251.

Koosed, M. M. 1993. Habeas corpus: Where have all the remedies gone? *Trial,* 29, 7: 70–79.

Lay, D. P. 1993. The writ of habeas corpus: A complex procedure for a simple process. *Minnesota Law Review,* 77: 1015–1016.

Ledewitz, B. 1990–1. Habeas corpus as a safety valve for innocence. *New York University Review Of Law and Social Change,* 18: 415–449.

Linder, C. 1993. Cost of death: A billion dollars and counting. *Los Angeles Times,* August 29, p. 1.

Lungren, D. E. 1991. Federal state relations in the habeas corpus process. *Intergovernmental Perspective,* 16: 18–20.

Markman, S. J. and P. G. Cassell. 1988. Protecting the innocent: A response to Bedau-Radelet study. *Stanford University Law Review,* 41:121–160.

Mello, M. and D. Duffey. 1990–1. Suspending justice: The unconstitutionality of the proposed time limit on the filing of habeas corpus petitions by state death row inmates. *Review of Law and Social Change,* 18:451–498.

Moss, D.C. 1992. Death, habeas and good lawyers—Balancing fairness and finality. *ABA Journal,* December: 82–86.

Patchell, K. 1991. The new habeas. *The Hastings Law Journal*, 42: 939–1066.

Radelet, M. L., H. A. Bedau and C. E. Putnam. 1992. *In Spite of Innocence.* Boston: Northeastern University Press.

Rehnquist, W. H. 1991. Limitless appeals make the death penalty ineffective. In *The Death Penalty: Opposing Viewpoints,* D. L. Bender and B. Leone (Eds.). San Diego, California: Greenhaven Press.

Reinhardt, St. 1989. Must we rush the executioner? *Los Angeles Times,* November 7, p. 1, col. 4.

Rice, S. D. 1991. ACLU fights habeas corpus changes. *The Los Angeles Daily Journal,* August 22, p. 7.

Robbins, I. P. 1990. Death penalty habeas corpus: Defining the issues. *Judicature,* 73:215–219.

Roberts, C. 1994. Attorneys general blast capital appeals. *Los Angeles Daily Journal,* April 18, p. 5, col. 1.

Swafford, T. L. 1995. Responding to Herrera v. Collins: Ensuring the innocent are not executed. *Case Western Reserve Law Review,* 45:603–639.

Tabak, R. and J. M. Lane. 1991. Judicial activism and legislative reform of federal habeas corpus: A critical analysis of recent developments and current proposals. *Albany Law Review,* 55.

Washington Post. 1995. *Oklahoma bombing spurs anti-terrorism laws.* July 25, 1, 4.

Weisberg, R. 1990. A great writ while it lasted. *The Journal of Criminal Law and Criminology,* 81: 9–36.

Woodhandler, A. 1993. Demodeling habeas. *Stanford Law Review,* 45: 578–579.

DISCUSSION QUESTIONS

1. What makes the writ of habeas corpus so controversial? And, if it is so controversial, why has it survived for so long?

2. How has the use of habeas corpus changed in the past 50 years? How has this change affected public perception of the writ?

3. Do you believe the writ of habeas corpus is necessary in today's modern criminal justice system, or has it outlived its usefulness?

READING

Criminal Justice System Reform and Wrongful Conviction

A Research Agenda

Marvin Zalman

The exoneration of hundreds of prisoners since 1989, and the plausible belief that thousands of wrongful convictions occur each year, underlie the importance of wrongful conviction as a policy issue (Gross, Jacoby, Matheson, Montgomery, & Patil, 2005). "Wrongful conviction" is not only the conviction of a factually or "actually" innocent person.[1] It also describes an emerging movement and an evolving multidisciplinary academic subject. Paradoxically, although wrongful conviction has generated extensive legal,

SOURCE: Zalman, M. (2006). Criminal justice system reform and wrongful conviction: A research agenda. *Criminal Justice Policy Review, 17*(4), 468–492.

psychological, and forensic science research, the subject has not been significantly addressed by criminal justice scholars (Leo, 2005). This article highlights the issue's policy significance and suggests avenues for research by criminal justice scholars.

 # Wrongful Conviction as a Policy Issue

This section describes the policy salience of wrongful conviction, the nature of the emerging innocence movement, the movement's reform and research agenda and the limited nature of innocence research by criminologists and criminal justice scholars. This discussion sets the stage for discussing potential avenues of criminal justice innocence research.

Wrongful Conviction on the Public and Policy Agendas

Fear of convicting the innocent is intrinsic to justice systems and predates the wrongful conviction (or innocence) movement (Blackstone, 1769/1979, p. 352; Volokh, 1997). Several 20th-century books and films identified wrongful convictions but had little influence on criminal justice thinking or practices prior to the mid-1980s (Borchard, 1932; Frank & Frank, 1957/1971; Leo, 2005).[2] Earle Stanley Gardner (1952), creator of the fictional defense attorney Perry Mason, failed in the late 1940s to institutionalize a short-lived "Court of Last Resort" created to correct miscarriages of justice. In political science terms, wrongful conviction was not on the public or governmental agendas.

The innocence movement that now exists is based in part on research that significantly undermined faith in the accuracy of the criminal justice process, especially DNA testing, first used to exonerate a defendant in 1989 (Leo, 2005, pp. 205–206; Medwed, 2005, p. 1117). Its ability to prove with astronomically high probability that likely perpetrators deposited biological evidence, and its power to absolutely rule out DNA donors among convicted defendants, shattered social and professional disinterest in miscarriages of justice and created traction

for wrongful conviction as a public issue (Connors, Lundregan, Miller, & McEwun, 1996; Leo, 2005, p. 205). In addition to DNA testing, the cumulative work of psychologists since the 1970s has cast doubt on the unerring accuracy of eyewitness identification (Doyle, 2005, pp. 129–132; Wells et al., 1998). The "DNA revolution" forced a reevaluation of the criminal justice system's capacity to function according to Packer's (1968, pp. 160–161) crime control model, in which factual errors are thought to be minuscule.

Two factors were especially salient in putting wrongful conviction on the public and policy agendas. First, Attorney General Janet Reno authorized an influential Justice Department study that highlighted the ability of DNA testing to undermine convictions, especially those based on eyewitness identification (Connors et al., 1996; Doyle, 2005, pp. 127–130, 165–167). The Justice Department followed up with a report on improved methods of interviewing witnesses and conducting lineups (Doyle, 2005, pp. 169–187; Technical Working Group for Eyewitness Evidence, 1999). Second, *Actual Innocence* was published (Scheck, Neufeld, & Dwyer, 2000). To their great credit, the lawyer and journalist authors of this popular book went beyond empathetic storytelling about the innocent people they helped free. They conceptualized the wrongful conviction project in terms of specific kinds of errors and organized the chapters of *Actual Innocence* around them. These were drawn together in an appendix—a "Short List of Reforms to Protect the Innocent" which was slightly expanded in the 2003 edition (Scheck et al., 2000; Scheck, Neufeld, & Dwyer, 2003, pp. 351–362). The book's lack of academic refinement is an advantage in reaching a mass audience. The inclusion of sources, however, acknowledges the debt owed by the innocence movement to varied and expanding fields of knowledge outside the law. To a significant degree, the innocence movement's policy and research agenda is set out in *Actual Innocence* and has been shaped by Scheck and Neufeld's leadership in opening new arenas, including programs to assist exonerees.[3]

Wrongful conviction is now an issue on the public agenda. The news media, long supportive of prosecutors, are now sensitized to miscarriages of justice, and their continuing reports of exonerations keeps the issue in the public eye (Tulsky, 2006; Warden, 2003). A stream of popular books and documentaries attest to a market for true accounts (Blakeslee, 2005; Edds, 2003; Holden, 2005; Humes, 1999; Johnson, 2003; Junkin, 2004). Novels and dramas portray wrongful convictions (Barnes, 2005; Feige, 2006a; Patterson, 2005). *The Exonerated* (Blank & Jensen, 2004) not only played off Broadway and on tour but was made into a television production and shown on Court TV. This publicity is not entirely happenstance, as innocence projects (described in the next section) have promoted some of it (Scheck et al., 2000; Vollen & Eygers, 2005). The movement's leaders appear to understand that innocence reforms require public opinion support.

Innocence movement reforms are on the governmental agenda (see Zalman, 2005). The Innocence Protection Act, passed after four years in the congressional hopper, was a most significant movement victory (Leahy, 2004a, 2004b). This watered-down part of the 2004 Justice For All Act provides, inter alia, standards and funding for DNA testing of potential exonerees (Weich, 2005). At least 38 states and the District of Columbia have passed innocence statutes allowing appeals by prisoners with claims based on DNA evidence but who have exhausted appellate remedies (C. E. Jones, 2005, p. 1249; Zacharias, 2005, pp. 193–195). The videotaping of police interrogations is spreading (Sullivan, 2005). Several states and a number of police departments have begun to adopt lineup reforms (Lindo, 2000). The Justice for All Act "increased the amount of compensation for those wrongfully convicted of federal crimes to up to $100,000 a year for death row exonerees, and $50,000 a year for non-death row exonerees" (Innocence Project, n.d.), and bills to compensate exonerees have been introduced in several state legislatures, including those of Georgia, Michigan, and Utah (Hunt, 2006; "State Should Offer," 2006; C. Tucker, 2005).

The most notable item on the innocence reform agenda is capital punishment. In what is arguably the best known wrongful conviction story, by 2000, 13 men on death row in Illinois had been exonerated, prompting then-Governor George Ryan to impose a moratorium on executions, appoint a commission to study the death penalty, and, before leaving office in 2002, commute the death sentences of all Illinois death row inmates. The 207-page report of the Illinois Governor's Commission on Capital Punishment (2002) made 85 recommendations that have become blueprints for reform. Other states have considered or imposed death penalty moratoria, and the American Bar Association (ABA) established a Death Penalty Moratorium Implementation Project. Widespread knowledge of death row exonerations is credited with reenergizing the anti-death penalty movement and with a decline in capital sentences and executions since 2000 (Kirchmeier, 2002; Steiker & Steiker, 2005; Warden, 2005).

The Innocence Movement

Unlike Gardner's (1952) abortive efforts to create a court of last resort, an institutional response has emerged to do the legal work needed to exonerate prisoners and the policy work designed to promote the issue. It began with a law school-based clinical program in 1992 led by Barry Scheck and Peter Neufeld (Scheck et al., 2000, 2003), which has grown into a multipurpose nonprofit organization—the Innocence Project (n.d.). About 40 law school clinical programs or other legal organizations (e.g., public defenders' offices), half of them established after 2000, now screen and litigate cases for prisoners claiming innocence (Medwed, 2003; Stiglitz, Brooks, & Shulman, 2002). These projects reflect an American penchant for grassroots solutions to contentious issues that involve governmental impropriety (Zalman, 2005, pp. 187–189).

Two innocence projects, the Innocence Project (n.d.) at Cardozo Law School and the Center for Wrongful Conviction (n.d.) at Northwestern University, have expanded into multifunction organizations designed to promote systemic reforms.[4] The Center for Wrongful Conviction has three stated functions: legal representation, research into the systemic problems that cause wrongful convictions, and community service to raise awareness of the causes and costs of wrongful conviction. The latter goal includes assisting exonerees to reintegrate into the community after years in prison (Center for Wrongful Conviction, n.d.).

Beginning in 2001, Scheck and Neufeld and other innocence project leaders met annually to consider their collective interests. The National Innocence Network was formalized in 2005 with membership limited to innocence projects. Its three goals are to represent potential exonerees in court, to provide assistance for exonerees on release, and to work for policy reforms designed to reduce wrongful convictions. To advance the latter goal, the Innocence Project hired a policy director to manage legislative and policy reform and to train local innocence projects' personnel in lobbying skills (National Innocence Network Conference, 2005). In one policy area for example—improving the accuracy and integrity of forensic laboratories—the Innocence Project has worked to create audit oversight committees in a number of states to ensure laboratory quality, to suggest improvements, "and possibly to evaluate wrongful convictions and assist in determining what went wrong" (Cromett & Thurston Myster, 2005).

The innocence movement is not limited to innocence projects. It includes cognitive psychologists who have tested new lineup methods in thousands of experiments (Wells et al., 1998) and innocence commissions established to investigate the wrongful conviction issue (Mumma, 2004). It includes nonprofit organizations designed to promote the goals of criminal justice reform (Justice Project, n.d.). to investigate cases (Centurion Ministries, n.d.), or to report wrongful conviction news (Justice Denied, n.d.). It includes authors who write about miscarriages of justice, documentary filmmakers, lawyers who take appeals on behalf of potentially innocent appellants, therapists who help exonerees and scholars who research wrongful conviction issues. Exonerees such as Kirk Bloodsworth have become part of the movement by working for innocence reform or by participating in publicity events. The innocence movement has some attributes of a reformist social movement, a point of departure for potential research initiatives discussed below.

The Innocence Movement's Reform and Research Agenda

If wrongful conviction is viewed as a multidisciplinary academic subject, its backbone of knowledge is contained in a list of topics that are deemed to be causes of wrongful conviction. This perspective makes the innocence movement's reform agenda coterminous with the wrongful conviction research agenda. Leo (2005) notes that the "standard list" of causes began with Borchard's (1932) tally of factors associated with wrongful convictions. A version is found in the chapter outline and appendices of Scheck et al. (2003, pp. 205, 212–213), and it may have achieved canonical status with its adoption by an ABA committee (Gianelli & Raeder, 2006). The ABA report includes separate chapters with analyses and recommendations on six causes of wrongful conviction: false confessions, eyewitness identification procedures, forensic evidence, jailhouse informants, defense counsel practices, investigative policies and personnel, and prosecution practices. It concludes with a chapter on compensation for the wrongly convicted. Similar lists and parallel analyses are found in many sources, including the Illinois Governor's Commission on Capital Punishment (2002), the Innocence Commission for Virginia (2005), and a scholarly anthology (Westervelt & Humphrey, 2001). The basic list of causes and remedies can be expanded. Scheck et al. (2003, pp. 358–362), for example, include creating statewide innocence commissions and the creation of an innocence network, reflecting the Innocence Project's goals.

A point worth noting is that some rhetoric of innocence advocates is radically transformative. Neufeld asserted that the larger goals of innocence projects "is 'nothing less than the complete overhaul of the criminal justice system with a new awareness of how to make it more reliable'" (Vollen & Eggers, 2005, p. 256). A lawyer who litigated cases for exonerees believes that large judgments in civil lawsuits for exonerees might bring "diverse actors together to collaborate on systemic change in our criminal justice system," leading to "widening ripple effects throughout the policing Industry . . . [having] a great impact on law enforcement" and "the most far-reaching and effective criminal justice system reform that our country has experienced since the Warren Court's criminal procedure revolution" (Garrett, 2005, pp. 45, 7–8, 111).[5] Although not all rhetoric by the movement's leaders is so transformative,[6] it suggests that emotions among innocence activists are akin to those of participants in reformist social movements. Transformative rhetoric may be driven by a belief that urgent action is needed because widespread DNA testing in criminal cases will eliminate easily observable miscarriages; this may cause publicized exonerations to decline and so undermine popular support for innocence reforms before the problems that cause wrongful convictions are corrected (Scheck et al., 2003, p. 323: Steiker & Steiker, 2005, p. 622).[7] This fear is belied by the high proportion of exonerations not based on DNA testing and by the plausibility that thousands of miscarriages of justice occur every year (Gross et al., 2005).

Each component of the standard list of innocence reform is itself a major area of research, whose scholars and scientists command daunting bodies of recondite knowledge and research. This poses potential tensions between activists eager to implement reforms based on existing knowledge and scholars who argue for continuing research. A legal scholar eager for implementation, for example, has incautiously suggested that "the scholarly work on false confessions, faulty eyewitness identifications, and other predictable problems of proof is largely complete" (Siegel, 2005, p. 1222). Few doubt that imposing best-practices laboratory standards, videotaping interrogations, improving lineup procedures, or the like will reduce errors and improve criminal justice practices, but it seems risky to shut the door on continuing research in these areas. In addition, further research may qualify or enrich earlier findings, necessitating updating and modification. Conflicting research findings or challenges to the quality of innocence research can be expected to generate controversy.[8]

The wrongful conviction research agenda is curiously incomplete. It fails to acknowledge the adversary system itself as a source of error despite recent innovative scholarship on comparative trial and justice systems and on evidence law theory and practice (Burns, 1999; Damaska, 1996, 1997; Lerner, 2001). Perhaps such studies are so theoretical and so unlikely to change constitutionally embedded practices as to be irrelevant to the innocence movement. But more practical jury research exists on issues such as the comprehensibility of jury instructions, juror note taking and witness questioning, and jurors discussing cases before formal deliberations begin (Dann & Hans, 2004). Jury research has been underway for decades and has generated proposals adopted in several jurisdictions, so it is unlikely that innocence movement leaders are unaware of it. These practical jury reforms might plausibly reduce wrongful convictions and yet are not found on the standard list of wrongful conviction issues.

Speculation as to why the innocence movement has largely overlooked the adversary trial includes the fact that the innocence narratives did not make a connection between trial procedures and erroneous verdicts. Such connections are not as easily observed as the effects of mistaken eyewitness identification and the like. Trial errors are embedded in trial transcripts (which are expensive and not automatically provided), and it requires painstaking legal analysis to sift through them to identify errors, as was done by pro bono lawyers for the Innocence Commission of Virginia (2005). In addition, the innocence movement's leaders are litigators who are not conditioned to see a properly operating trial as a problem, even while documenting such failures as a prosecutor, acting within the bounds of professional propriety, befuddling an honest witness on cross-examination (Scheck et al., 2003, pp. 25–27).

Trial issues were not entirely ignored by legal scholars concerned with wrongful convictions. An early and insightful article explored but did not completely answer the questions of whether the adversary jury trial, when working properly, can be a source of error and why trials often fail to filter out errors occurring earlier in the criminal justice process (Givelber, 1997). More recently, an evidence law theorist has generated an intriguing potential solution to trial-generated error by proposing two kinds of adversary system jury trial procedures (Risinger, 2004). The usual criminal trial would be reserved for cases involving "polyvalent facts" (e.g., intent in a homicide or rape case) where the criminal act is stipulated and a jury is well-suited to explore issues of motive and intent. For "who done-it" cases, where a jury is called on to determine what happened ("binary facts"), Risinger (2004) sketches a stipulated procedure in which the adversaries agree to forego the rich storytelling tradition of adversary advocacy and instead focus on the facts (pp. 1307–1311). He also suggests adopting an "unsafe verdict" standard of guilt under such a procedure that has been adopted for appeals in England (pp. 1313–1333). Additional recent analyses by legal scholars have explored trial issues and wrongful conviction including acquittals (Givelber, 2005), the pretrial process (Leipold, 2005), an archaic and arguably unconstitutional South Carolina procedure that allows prosecutors to control criminal trial dockets (Sieget, 2005), and the preservation of evidence (C. E. Jones, 2005).

A final point about the wrongful conviction policy agenda, related to its partial locus, is the practicality of the standard list of reforms. The list was derived from counting factors associated with miscarriages of justice in the wrongful conviction narratives, beginning with Borchard (1932; see Harmon, 2001; Leo, 2005). Given the terrible consequences of wrongful convictions, there is an urgency to establish policies to correct such deficiencies as inadequate defense counsel, poorly equipped and operated forensic laboratories, and the like. There is little premium on conducting theoretical or basic research into the items on the innocence agenda, although some exists (e.g., Cole, 2005). Many items on the agenda are the special preserve of lawyers (e.g., prosecution and defense counsel issues), and most of the law review writing on innocence-related subjects is aimed at generating policy rather than legal theory. Issues concerning forensic science require major input from forensic scientists, laboratory directors, and forensic examiners, and innocence activists are not competent to generate innovation but only to lobby to ensure that proper procedures are followed. Police investigation intersects with important matters on the innocence agenda, but the study of the investigative process had its heyday in the 1970s, and there has been little research focusing on investigation by criminal justice scholars in recent years. In sum, much of the research on wrongful conviction is fragmented into various specialties, is mostly applied research, and is not within the competence of most criminal justice scholars.

The Paucity of Criminal Justice Innocence Research

Richard Leo (2003, pp. 208–211), noting that most wrongful conviction research has been conducted by lawyers and psychologists, identified three specialized areas of empirical research: eyewitness identification, child suggestibility, and false confessions. Significantly, this work has led to proposed reforms. Leading research psychologists, for example, made their findings about eyewitness identification accessible to policy makers and have assisted in policy reform efforts (Doyle, 2005; Wells, 2001; Wells et al., 1998). Research by child witness experts has led to substantial improvements in how police and courts treat child witnesses (ABA Task Force on Child Witnesses, 2002; Ceci & Bruck, 1995; Gilstrap, Fritz, Torres, & Melinder, 2005). Leo, a leading authority on confessions, has helped to make the study of false confessions an area of sociolegal and criminal justice scholarship (Drizin & Leo, 2004; Leo & Ofshe, 1998) and a concern of psychologists (Gudjonsson, 2003; Wrightsman & Kassin, 1993). As a result, many police departments have begun to videotape interrogations (Sullivan, 2005).

In contrast, Leo (2005, p. 214) identified only two or three studies by criminologists that have explored the causes of wrongful conviction (Harmon, 2001; Huff, Rattner, & Sagarin, 1986; Lofquist, 2001).[9] Although a few others can be located (Denov & Campbell, 2005; Poveda, 2001; Schehr, 2005; Schoenfeld, 2005), this is remarkable when considering that Wells et al. (1998) estimated that more than 2,000 psychological research articles on eyewitness identification were in print almost a decade ago. I estimate that several hundred law review articles have been published on wrongful conviction topics in recent years, with a few based on empirical analysis (e.g., Campbell & Denov, 2004; Gross et al., 2005).[10] Leo does not ask why so few criminologists have studied wrongful conviction but seeks to stimulate empirical research by urging criminologists to eschew research into the "legal causes" and instead study the "actual root causes" of wrongful convictions. In this perspective, it is a simplistic or unexamined assumption that once the causes of wrongful conviction are identified "we will know how and why the problem of wrongful conviction occurs" (Leo, 2005, p. 213). Deeper causal and theory-generating research is needed to determine why the causes of wrongful conviction occur in the first place. Criminologists, for example, should ask, "What are the causes of eyewitness misidentification?" and the like (Leo, 2005, p. 213). Leo cites Lofquist (2001) as an exemplary study. Lofquist explored the structural dynamics within a police department that led to the identification of an innocent suspect as the perpetrator. Note that Leo's conclusion that the deeper "criminological" research called for relies on organizational methods and theory.

Leo (2005) concludes by urging criminologists to move beyond legal categories and to draw on "existing social science frameworks" to build theories of miscarriages of justice. He specifically references psychological, sociological, and organizational frameworks for research. For example, psychological research could "study how the process of memory and perception formation" and the like "underlie a variety of psychological errors, and how those errors then lead to wrongful prosecution and conviction" (p. 215). "Sociologically, [criminologists] . . . need to study how the institutions of criminal justice . . . are structured and how the decision making, actions, and ideologies of these social actors are patterned in the production of both accurate and inaccurate outcomes" (p. 215). As for an organizational perspective, Leo recommends that "criminologists need to look at the microlevel and macrolevel forces, contexts, and structures that underlie the normal processes and production of perception, belief, and error in American criminal justice" (p. 216). He ends by tempering enthusiasm of potential wrongful conviction scholars by specifying the huge obstacles to this research: the lack of a database, the unlikelihood of police and prosecution support, and the inherent difficulties of determining whether wrongful convictions occurred from assembled case files (pp. 217–218).

 ## A Criminal Justice Wrongful Conviction Research Agenda

Leo's (2005) insightful depiction of the state of wrongful conviction research misspecifies the target audience by directing his remarks to criminologists and suggests too narrow a model of empirical innocence research, oriented mainly toward generating theories of the causal dynamics of wrongful convictions. He then suggests that this worthy goal is virtually unattainable because no database exists, primary case materials are very difficult to assemble, and it is inherently difficult to prove that a conviction was erroneous (pp. 216–217). Curiously, by holding up Lofquist (2001) as a model of wrongful conviction research, Leo glosses over the fact that it is more aptly categorized as organizational rather than criminological research. Analysts in business schools and in departments of public administration, organizational psychology, sociology, and criminal justice are better equipped to pursue such studies. Leo may be using criminology as shorthand for criminology and criminal justice, a reasonable assumption as these disciplines are coming to be housed in the same departments and as their research foci overlap to a greater extent than heretofore. If so, Leo takes a narrow view of criminological research. Kraska (2006), by contrast, posits criminal justice as a multifaceted discipline that, like criminology, has generated a variety of theoretical constructs. The theories generated by the subdisciplines within criminal justice may be macro theories of the entire criminal justice system (e.g., systems theory, late modernity), micro theories of system components (e.g., a theory of police management, of investigator behavior), or normative theories (e.g., democracy and policing, criminal jurisprudence).

Building on this broader foundation, I propose a number of innocence research strategies that could be pursued by "justician" scholars, whether their academic roots are in criminology, criminal justice, or allied disciplines. This perspective diverges from Leo's (2005) hint that undervalues existing lines of innocence research because of the "simplistic assumption" that the standard list of causes provides a theoretically robust explanation

of wrongful convictions. I agree that the kind of empirical and theory-building research conducted by Harmon
(2001) and Lofquist (2001) ought to be pursued. In
addition, however, criminal justice scholars capable of
conducting eyewitness identification experiments, for
example, or adept at the legal analysis of recent bills
designed to strip federal courts of habeas corpus jurisdiction (Bergman, 2005) ought to attend to these and
other areas where research questions need to be refined
and resolved. Likewise, American scholars of police and
prosecution need to explore the construction of the
truth in criminal cases, an understudied area, in the
light of recent knowledge of miscarriages of justice
(Fisher, 1993; Martin, 2001; McConville, Sanders, &
Leng, 1991; Schoenfeld, 2005). That said, much of the
research agenda proposed in this article is aimed not
only at understanding wrongful convictions but also at
understanding the reform process (i.e., the innocence
movement and its research agenda).

The Context of Reform

The DNA revolution is used as a shorthand explanation
for the emergence of the innocence movement. This
kernel of truth masks other likely reasons for why the
movement emerged when it did. Edwin Borchard
(1932), Jerome Frank (Frank & Frank, 1957/1971), and
Gardner (1952) understood the deep problems of criminal justice, but their failure to establish lasting reforms
such as widespread exoneree compensation or prisoner
review tribunals suggests that structural factors
impeded progress on the wrongful conviction issue.

A social history of wrongful conviction that goes
beyond a description of the 20th century wrongful conviction literature is needed (Leo, 2005, pp. 203–205).
The current innocence reform movement presupposes
a criminal justice system with national prosecutorial
standards, criminalistics labs in every jurisdiction,
managerial-style police departments, and the like. The
criminal justice system of the early 21st century is a
product of major changes that began in the 1960s.
Police are far more professional today, as measured
by increased education, less corruption, a manage-
rial mentality among ranking officers, a legacy of
constitutional reform that makes policing relatively

law abiding, and a growing commitment to community policing (Silverman, 1999; S. Walker, 2005).
Another structural change critical to the existence and
operation of innocence projects is the rise of law
school clinical education in the 1970s (Panel Discussion,
1987). A research question amenable to social historical inquiry is whether the 2006 innocence research
agenda (Gianelli & Raeder, 2006) was feasible, or even
conceivable, in the middle of the 20th century. A study
of these kinds of institutional innovations would have
to be placed in the context of evolving social expectations such as Lawrence Friedman's (1985) sociolegal
theory of total justice

Understanding the Innocence Movement

Study of the innocence movement itself can shed light on
the capacity of the criminal justice system to change.
Several large, well-developed, and partially overlapping
subfields of sociology and political science—social
movements, interest groups, policy analysis—provide
models of inquiry (Burstein, 1999; Burstem & Linton,
2002; Heinz & Manikas, 1992; Mack, 1997, pp. 18–24;
Weed, 1995; Zalman, 2005). Characterizing the innocence movement as a social movement may be odd as
the latter category typically applies to the collective
behavior of masses of people with common grievances
who are typically excluded from political decision making and who coalesce to protest policies and to promote
various interests (Eyerman & Jamison, 1991; Green &
Bigelow, 2005; Morris & Mueller, 1992). It may be more
accurate to describe the Innocence Network (n.d.) as an
association type of interest group because of its organizational membership (31 innocence projects; Lowery &
Brasher, 2004, p. 5). The lawyer leaders of the innocence
movement seem to fit the model of interest group participants in that they are highly educated and well positioned to get results in various policy venues. They can
marshal arguments before legislative committees, newspaper editorial boards, and a host of places where public
opinion is shaped and policy decisions made. They are
adept at working with scientists and experts and in
mobilizing recondite information and techniques to gain
attainable ends. The innocence movement, however,

promotes a highly generalized interest—justice—and is marked by the kind of fervor encountered in reformist social movements. This is seen in the prodigious efforts of pro bono litigators on behalf of truly innocent (Blakeslee, 2005) and ultimately guilty defendants (Dao, 2006; J. C. Tucker, 1997). This zeal also motivates movement participants toward criminal justice system reform efforts.

Research strategies and themes from sociology and political science can produce useful insights about the movement. Methodological modifications may be necessary as the innocence movement can be viewed as a species of social movement organization (SMO) without a mass social movement as a foundation (McCarthy & Zald, 1977). The sociology of social movements, which prior to the 1960s emphasized the social psychology of collective behavior, has been eclipsed by newer theoretical models. The resource mobilization model, although perhaps not the focus of recent sociological analyses, provides useful research themes. Researchers could explore, among other themes, the constellation of innocence SMOs as organizations, studying their mobilization patterns, the confederated structure of the movement, modes of cooperation and competition, alliances with congruent groups (e.g., NAACP-Legal Defense Fund, ACLU: Death Penalty Information Center, n.d.), strategies for survival and growth, and the division of labor among innocence projects in regard to different areas of policy innovation (McCarthy & Zald, 1977; pp. 1226–1227; Minkoff, 2002). These kinds of organizational studies can be categorized under Kraska's (2004, pp. 177–213) theoretical orientation of criminal justice as a "growth complex." This list is meant to be suggestive of the wide variety of issues that could be explored through the resource mobilization lens.

Successful social movements often generate countermovements (Marx, 1979; Meyer & Staggenborg, 1996). Recent writings indicate some outright prosecutorial opposition to the innocence movement's policy goals (Marquis, 2005) and potential rifts among those supportive of the innocence movement's aims (Steiker & Steiker, 2005).[11] Although prominent conservatives have strongly supported and even led innocence reforms (Mumma, 2004; Sevsions, 2003), the dogged opposition by many prosecutors to postconviction DNA testing (Medwed, 2004) suggests an ideological component among prosecutors at the core of a countermovement. Defense lawyers and prosecutors are natural enemies. However much they may cooperate in plea negotiations, they are combatants in an adversary system, reflexively wary and initially antagonistic to any proposal coming from the "other side" (Doyle, 2005, pp. 169–187).

Research at this point can explore whether the oppositional themes sounded by Marquis (2005) are widespread among prosecutors, what threats are perceived by potential opponents that could mobilize a countermovement, whether the innocence movement has framed its agenda in a way to avoid opposition, and the elite sponsorship of both the movement and any countermovement that arises (Loge, 2005). Given the relatively high status of innocence movement leaders, they may be able to win the allegiance of political elites.

More recent social movement research has focused theory-building energies on individuals within social movements, examining the social psychology of recruitment patterns into SMOs and the influence of social movements on individuals' political activities (Eyerman & Jamison, 1991; Morris & Mueller, 1992). This is linked to the emergence of "new social movements," such as the environmental movement, that are largely postindustrial, middle-class movements that focus on contemporary quality of life issues (Pichardo, 1997). Such approaches may yield useful insights as innocence movement participants for the most part are middle class. More recent attention to broader theoretical themes in social movement research, including mobilizing political opportunity structures and cultural dynamics and emphases on tactical solutions, movement leadership, and the impact of transformative events, readily suggests applications to the study of the innocence movement (Morris, 2000).

Studies of SMOs can also be approached from the political science interest group perspective. Some studies examine the mobilization of individuals and institutions through the lenses of niche theory and exchange theory to explain organizational maintenance (Lowery & Brasher, 2004, pp. 29–69). Given the newness of the innocence movement, it may be premature to study its environment (a parallel concept to that of a social movement "industry"). The logic of studying the innocence movement's organizations as interest groups is that they seek policy changes in government agencies and from legislatures and courts. Although the study of interest groups has waxed and waned within political science, there is no doubt that interest groups are a large and important sector in the public policy universe (Baumgartner & Leech, 1998). A variety of issues are open to innocence movement researchers. One is the way in which the news and popular media have promoted the movement's interests or how the movement has utilized the media (i.e., "lobbied the public"; Browne, 1998, pp. 84–108; Kingdon, 1984, pp. 61–64; Molotch, 1979); this parallels the sociological category of frame analysis. Given the salience of legal issues, attention can be paid to legal strategies used by innocence groups to influence judicial bureaucracies and to use litigation as a policy lever (Smith, 1997; Wasby, 1983). As a small movement consisting mostly of tiny organizations, it is worth examining the nature of the lobbying or influence strategies employed (e.g., inside vs. outside strategies; Green & Bigelow, 2005; Kingdon, 1984; Strate & Zalman, 2003). These approaches could be applied to a case study of the passage of the Innocence Protection Act or to studies of other policy advances.

Network analysis, described as "a powerful new approach to the study of social structure" (Emirbayer & Goodwin, 1994, p. 1411), is used by interest group and social movement researchers. Network analysis examines relationship patterns to overcome the limits of explaining human behavior "solely in terms of the categorical attributes of actors." Its central insight is that networks of social relations ("nodes" or behavioral networks), which can be precisely described, constrain and enable "patterned relationships among social actors within systems" (Emirbayer & Goodwin, 1994, pp. 1414–1418). Two "conceptual strategies" used to explain patterned relationships are (a) a social cohesion approach "that focuses on the direct and indirect connections among actors" (Emirbayer & Goodwin, 1994, pp. 1419–1422) and (b) a "positional" strategy that explores "actors' ties not to one another, but to third parties," so as to define an actor's position relative to other actors in a social system (Emirbayer & Goodwin, 1994, pp. 1422–1424).

A number of methods used in conjunction with network analysis could help describe and explain the behavior of innocence movement participants when acting as policy entrepreneurs (Diani, 2002; D. Friedman & McAdam, 1992). Scheck, one of the most prominent figures in the innocence movement, has, for example, placed himself in existing policy networks as past president of the National Association of Criminal Defense Lawyers and as a commissioner on the New York Forensic Science Review Board. By deliberately pursuing a networking strategy, Scheck has almost perfectly followed the script of a policy entrepreneur who creates opportunities to "persuade others to support their policy ideas" (Mintrom, 1997) and thus stimulate the diffusion of innovation (discussed below; Kingdon, 1984, pp. 188–193; Ward, 1998).[12] The quantity and intensity of network ties could, when combined with substantive knowledge of policy events, produce the kind of rich understanding that has illuminated elite criminal justice networks in one jurisdiction (Heinz & Manikas, 1992).

Studying the Innocence Reform Agenda

In addition to studying the innocence movement itself, criminal justice scholarly analysis and research can improve the understanding of the innocence reform agenda and its prospects for success. The focus of such research can include studies of established reforms and evaluations of claims about the innocence research agenda.

Diffusion of Innocence Innovations

The diffusion of innovation is an autonomous research tradition employed in many disciplines and is reported in more than 5,000 publications in the social and behavioral sciences and in other disciplines (Rogers, 2003, pp. 43–45, 477). "*Diffusion* is the process in which an innovation is communicated through certain channels over time among the members of a social system" (p. 5). The four elements of innovation, communication, time, and social system have been the focus of much diffusion research (pp. 11–38), and much research has also been devoted to the process of making innovations decisions, focusing on the elements of knowledge, persuasion, decision, implementation, and confirmation (pp. 168–2181).

The unit of analysis in most diffusion research has been individuals, but in recent years diffusion research has focused more on organizations (pp. 402–435) and can include states of the union in political diffusion studies (Mintrom, 1997; J. Walker, 1969).

An opportunity exists to capture the recent spread of innovations such as videotaping interrogations and lineup reforms because the ability to "gather data at several points during the diffusion process" (Rogers, 2003, p. 129) can be helpful in resolving causality issues. Of special importance to innocence reform studies are the existence of diffusion networks. This can allow criminal justice scholars to move away from the study of the innocence movement and to focus on more familiar venues such as police agencies. Political and policy analysis among criminal justice scholars could examine the spread of state innocence laws (C. E. Jones, 2005), perhaps analyzing the role of policy entrepreneurs (Kingdon, 1984, pp. 188–193; Mintrom, 1997). An important concept of diffusion research is the critical mass, akin to the idea of a "tipping point," which is "the point after which further diffusion becomes self-sustaining" (Rogers, 2003, p. 343). This concept, interestingly, was borrowed from social movement research. Given the tendency of pro-innovation bias in innovation research, innocence movement scholars should be cautious in finding that a critical mass has occurred and should be sensitive to the existence of reinvention of innovations, which is common (Rogers, 2003, pp. 106, 180–189).

Diffusion methods could be applied to the spread of state innocence commissions (Mumma, 2004; Scheck & Neufeld, 2002) or to a group of specific issues on the standard list of reforms. Correcting errors caused by lying jailhouse informants, for example, requires not one but a variety of solutions. Diffusion research could measure the spread of (a) jail procedures regarding the placement and control of prisoners, (b) police and prosecutors' policies on screening panels and evaluative techniques for properly evaluating the use of informants' testimonies, (c) judicial precedents allowing or requiring cautionary instructions to juries concerning the weighing of informants' testimonies, (d) prosecutorial policies requiring prosecutors to divulge any inducements to informants and procedures to ensure compliance, and (e) rules requiring extensive discovery when informants' testimonies are used (Gianelli & Raeder, 2006, pp. 63–78). One can imagine a legal analysis of appellate-judicial precedents concerning jury instructions that sheds light on that rule. Such a study, however, would not fully cover the more important question of whether policies have been adopted that in combination may reduce wrongful combination caused by jailhouse snitches. Awareness of diffusions research could stimulate such broader studies.

Criminal justice researchers should be aware of political fragmentation in the United States as an impediment to the diffusion of innovations within criminal justice agencies. Consider, for example, the videotaping of interrogations. Sullivan (2005, p. 1128) reported that all police departments in Alaska and Minnesota and more than 300 additional departments have adopted the innovation. As of this writing, seven states and the District of Columbia have required electronic recording by statute or judicial decision, with a variety of conditions and limitations.[13] Sullivan (2005) noted that although many police departments have voluntarily adopted a recording requirement, "they represent only a small percentage of all law enforcement departments in the country" (p. 1136). A recent study indicates that 40% of big city police department administrators oppose videotaping, suggesting considerable potential resistance (Zalman & Smith, 2005). This finding, in light of the existence of 3,070 sheriff's offices, 12,666 local police departments, and 49 state police agencies in the United States, suggests at least that the diffusion of recording interrogations will be a major undertaking (Hickman & Reeves, 2003, p. 1). The fragmentation of the American polity refers not only to the large number of jurisdictions but to the relative autonomy of local units of government. With no centralized authority over local police departments or sheriffs, the adoption of an innovation such as the recording of interrogation will be made on a department-by-department basis.

Case Studies of Innocence Legislation

A few law review articles have described the federal Innocence Protection Act of 2004, which was a watered-down version of its original proposal and was passed as part of the comprehensive Justice For All Act that included support for law enforcement. In addition, almost 40 states have passed laws that authorize postconviction appeals on the grounds of innocence, typically where DNA evidence can be found. Legal writing tends to be instrumental and practical, and legislative surveys published in law journals are useful to innocence policy advocates in understanding the strengths and limitations of the legislation (C. E. Jones, 2005; Kleinert, 2006). A retrospective case study of the efforts needed to pass the Innocence Protection Act, perhaps utilizing network analysis, ought to lead to a more theoretically robust understanding of the innocence movement and shed more light on the nature of the movement's policy goals. Indeed, Sen. Patrick Leahy's statement on passage of the act names the Justice Project (n.d.) and a number of individuals and legislators who were instrumental in the passage of the act (Leahy, 2004b). The discrepancy between the act's initial goals and the act as passed could be analyzed in terms of the incrementalism that is characteristic of American politics and policy making (Haller, 2001; Kingdon, 1984, pp. 83–88).

Critiquing the Innocence Reform Agenda

As noted above, some of the descriptive, legal, or policy-oriented innocence movement rhetoric is often transformative. Criminal justice scholars can analyze the innocence reform agenda, applying what is known about change in criminal justice, to suggest the possible shape and limits of reform. However sympathetic researchers may be to the aims of innocence reforms, deep knowledge of the nature of justice bureaucracies suggests that claims of imminent criminal justice transformation may be premature.

The limits of litigated reform. Garrett (2005), for example, asserted that criminal justice can be transformed through civil litigation on behalf of exonerees. Because defendants' constitutional rights are viewed negatively as "truth-defeating" in criminal cases by a conservative judiciary, few defendants win retrials based on police or prosecution error. Federal civil rights actions by exonerees against the police under 42 U.S.C. §1983, however, reverse the "guilt

paradigm." In civil cases, "fair trial rights vindicate the truth, while government misconduct is revealed as having concealed evidence of a person's innocence, leading to a gross miscarriage of justice" (Garrett, 2005, p. 38). Many such cases have resulted in large monetary awards. Garrett's legal tour de force, proposing that the cost of civil lawsuits will force wholesale criminal justice reforms and even restore the Warren Court-era respect for defendant's rights, is a rationalistic idea that needs to be subjected to empirical testing.

Sociolegal and political science research offers at best a tempered view of the ability of court cases to effect social change. Some political scientists have written well-researched books positing that Supreme Court cases have had limited or no effect on important areas of social life (Horowitz, 1977; Rosenberg, 1991). Other authors counter that litigation strategies have a place in social action as, for example, catalyzing correctional reform (Epstein & Kobylka, 1992; Feeley & Rubin, 1998; Zalman, 1991, 1998). Even if a view that the law has no effect is too extreme, empirical evaluations of the law's impact simply do not find that litigation itself can institute radical institutional change. A program of sustained litigation can initiate and highlight problems, but without other levers of change, it is unlikely that deep policy modifications will occur (Feeley & Rubin, 1998). Cross-sectional research could compare innocence reforms in police departments that have been hit with large awards (and perhaps in close-by departments) to a matched set of police departments that have not been subjected to such suits to find whether the suits have had a policy effect.

Implementing reforms. Most legal writing on innocence reforms is conceptual and descriptive and tends to equate reform with rule creation. The formal adoption of a policy by legislation, court decision, or administrative rule, however, is only the beginning of reform; to be effective, a policy must be implemented. Implementation is only one step in the policy process, which extends conceptually from problem perception and agenda building, to policy formulation, legitimation, adoption, and budgeting, and to implementation, evaluation, and termination or redesign (C. O. Jones, 1984).[14] Every step of the policy process may be the subject of policy analysis, and this author has previously called for a public policy approach to understanding the innocence movement's agenda (Zalman, 2005). Criminal justice researchers, with their knowledge of criminal justice system functioning, are well positioned to engage in implementation research at a time when a number of agencies are formally adopting innocence reforms.

Implementation is a well-developed area of policy analysis that provides a variety of methodological and conceptual tools. Criminal justice scholars contemplating the study of agency adoption of lineup procedural changes or the like should be aware of the consensus among policy scholars that implementation is itself a political process that is intimately connected to earlier policy design stages. In other words, implementation is not a mechanical process but a continuation of policy making. The inevitable gap between early policy designs and the programs that emerge led early policy researchers to view the entire policy process in harshly negative terms. On mature reflection, they have come to accept such gaps not as policy failures per se but as evidence of a dynamic policy process that endures through the implementation phase (Hill & Hupe, 2002; C. O. Jones, 1984, pp. 164–195; Palumbo & Calista, 1990).

Again using the electronic recording of interrogation as an example, case studies of implementation could apply qualitative and quantitative methods. Researchers would have to define what is meant by implementation (the dependent variable). For example, if a state law mandated recording, the statutory elements can provide measures of compliance. Independent variables could include such organizational features as the strength of the chief's policy support, officer training and monitoring, the means interrogating detectives might have to evade recording, and internal sanctions for rules violations. Such research potentially transcends the innocence issue and provides the foundation for theory-oriented research about police agencies.

Conclusion

Wrongful conviction narratives have exposed serious flaws in the investigation, prosecution, and adjudication of felony cases. As a result of the DNA revolution, it is now thought that wrongful convictions are so numerous

as to constitute a major policy concern that poses a serious challenge to the fairness and accuracy of the criminal justice process. Most innocence research has been conducted by psychologists and lawyers and has focused on specific subprocesses such as lineups. This research has been oriented toward understanding the ways in which these processes have failed and have caused wrongful convictions. Innocence research that goes beyond these specific areas can potentially provide a better understanding of the way in which the criminal justice system systemically generates errors. Unfortunately, the difficulties in collecting and evaluating case materials and unresolved issues in defining a wrongful conviction limits this kind of research at the present time.

This article has proposed a broad research agenda addressing the new innocence movement that works to exonerate wrongly convicted inmates and to generate and publicize policy changes that logically should reduce miscarriages of justice. The innocence research agenda sketched here is primarily useful for understanding the innocence movement, itself a worthy object of research. Beyond this, the proposed kinds of research into the innocence movement and its reform agenda will possibly illuminate the capacity of the criminal justice system to reflect on its own shortcomings and to correct them. This wider goal should be of interest to the community of criminal justice policy scholars.

 ## Notes

1. A strict legalist differs:

   I count myself among those who use the term "wrongful conviction" to refer not only to the conviction of the [factually] innocent but also to any conviction achieved in part through the violation of constitutional rights or through the use of systems and procedures that render the proceedings fundamentally unfair. (Siegel, 2005, p. 1219)

   Factual innocence can include a "wrong person" error (i.e., the person had no involvement with the facts of a criminal event) and legal innocence under substantive criminal law:

   An acquittal is historically accurate whenever the jury correctly determines that the defendant either did not engage in the prohibited conduct or, if he did so engage, he either lacked the state of mind required to make the conduct criminal or his action was the product of appropriate beliefs that justify it. (Givelber, 2005, p. 1175)

Forst (2004) describes two broad kinds of errors of justice: errors of due process, which can range from violations of a defendant's rights to the conviction of a factually innocent person, and errors of impunity, which range from the failure to apprehend a criminal to the acquittal of a factually guilty defendant. The latter kinds of cases have caused dismay in recent decades (Fletcher, 1995). Nevertheless, it seems improper to speak of "wrongful acquittals," however logical the term. This reflects the common law balance that accepts such acquittals as a necessary price to be paid, however grudgingly, for a fair trial.

Take the following hypotheticals. (a) A defendant whom the police investigator thinks is guilty is acquitted. Depending on the crime's heinousness, different reactions are deemed acceptable. In a drug case, for example, the chagrined officer can expect the defendant to recidivate and get caught in the future, thinking, "We will put together a stronger case and get a conviction." Another reaction to a vicious crime, say the rape and murder of a child, is to have the acquitted defendant closely monitored as a means of individualized crime prevention. A third approach, arguably improper but facially lawful, is to monitor the defendant to catch him or her in any criminal act for which some punishment can be imposed. This may have happened to Oreste Fulminante *(Arizona v Fulminante,* 1991*).* This is the strategy of organized crime enforcement. In contrast to these acceptable reactions, it is beyond the pale, even after acquittal for a vicious crime, for the officer to engage in private retribution. (b) After a conviction the investigating officer is left with a belief that the wrong man was convicted. Although not obliged to do so, the officer investigates the case on her own time. This results in an exoneration. Such action is deemed noble. The different societal reactions to private retribution in (a) and private investigation in (b) bring out the essential difference between social acceptance of an acquittal of the factually guilty and the moral imperative to free the factually innocent. Incidentally, the error of wrongful conviction can be compounded if police in hypothetical (a) wrongly believe that an innocent defendant has been acquitted and add the person to a list of usual suspects in later criminal investigations. This can lead to a wrongful conviction (Johnson, 2003).

2. Films based on actual cases include *The Wrong Man* (1956), directed by Alfred Hitchcock, starring Henry Fonda and *Call Northside 777* (1948), starring James Stewart (see Mnookin & West, 2001). "From the time Borchard published his book . . . until the early 1990s, there was typically one big-picture book or major article published every decade or so on the subject of miscarriages of justice" (Leo, 2005, p. 203).

3. They learned to their surprise that exonerees face many adjustment problems and helped to establish a framework for action—the establishment of the Life After Exoneration Program (n.d.), an organization that provides assistance for exonerees (Vollen & Eggers, 2005).

4. A comparable organization in Canada is AIDWYC, Association in Defence of the Wrongly Convicted (http://www.aidwyc.org).

5. Brandon Gurrett practiced with law firms headed by innocence movement leaders (Cochran Neufeld & Scheck, LLP) and with Beldock Levine & Hoffman LLP, one of whose partners, Myron Beldock, represented Rubin "Hurricane" Carter (Hirsch, 2001). The acknowledgments in Garreti (2005, p. 35) include many leaders in the wrongful conviction movement.

6. Scheck (2005), in a more restrained vein as president of a national defense lawyer's association, expressed "cautious optimism" for reforms emanating for the innocence movement.

7. The "policy window" for innocence reforms can be the subject of more sustained discussion or analysis (Kingdon, 1984, pp. 173–204).

8. News accounts discuss a rare 2006 field experiment of lineup methods in Chicago that purportedly finds more error using sequential compared to simultaneous lineups, contrary to the general findings of lab experiments. Some claim that this undermines reform efforts; others claim that the study was flawed (Feige, 2006b; Paulson & Liana, 2006; Zernike, 2006).

9. A number of studies can be bundled into a frequency-of-wrongful-conviction category: Bedau and Radelet (1987); Huff, Rattner, and Sagarin (1986, 1996); Rattner (1988); Poveda (2001); Ramsey and Frank (in press); and Zalman, Smith, and Kazaleh (2006).

10. A Lexis search for the terms *wrongful conviction* or *innocence* in the files of U.S. and Canadian law journals produced 226 articles, and a search for the term *wrongful conviction* anywhere in the article produced 1,455 articles (June 7, 2006). The author's personal bibliography on the subject is extremely long.

11. Some defense lawyers worry that an emphasis on actual innocence will make jurors and appellate courts even more hostile to procedural claims of defendants who are or appear to be "factually guilty" (Siegel, 2005, p. 1221).

12. The practice of networking is not the focus of network analysis; network analysis assumes that networks arise naturally from contacts between individuals and organizations and studies the nature and intensity of those contacts and their influence on behavior.

13. Alaska: *Stephen v. State* (1985); District of Columbia: D.C. Code (2006); Illinois: 20 ILCS (2006); Maine: 25 M.R.S. (2005); Massachusetts: *Commonwealth v. DiGiambattista* (2004); Minnesota: *State v. Scales* (1994); New Mexico: Michie's Ann. Stat. (n d.); Texas: Tex. Crim. P. Code Ann. (2005).

14. Diffusion of innovation research has also examined implementation by individuals and organizations and has generated

findings about the "re-invention" of innovations as implementers modify the innovation or how it is used in a number of ways (Rogers, 2003, pp. 179–180, 424–433).

References

ABA Task force on Child Witnesses. (2002). *The child witness in criminal cases.* Chicago: American Bar Association.

Arizona v. Fulminante, 499 U S 279 (1991).

Barnes, J. (2006). *Arthur & George.* New York: Knopf.

Baumgartner, F. R., & Leech, B. L. (1998). *Basic interests: The importance of groups in politics and in political science.* Princeton, NJ: Princeton University Press.

Bedau, H. A., & Radelet, M. L. (1987). Miscarriages of justice in potentially capital cases. *Stanford Law Review, 40,* 21–120.

Bergman, B. E. (2005, September/October). From the president: Great writ endangered. *Champion, 29*(4), 68.

Blackstone, W. (1979). *Commentaries on the laws of England, Volume IV. Of public wrongs.* Chicago: University of Chicago Press. (Original work published 1769)

Blakeslee, N. (2005). *Tulia: Race, cocaine, and corruption in a small Texas town.* New York: Public Affairs.

Blank, J., & Jensen, E. (2004). *The exonerated: A play.* New York: Faber & Faber.

Borehard, E. M. (1932). *Convicting the innocent: Sixty-five actual errors of criminal justice.* Garden City, NY: Garden City Publishing.

Browne, W. P. (1998). *Groups, interests, and U.S. public policy.* Washington, DC: Georgetown University Press.

Burns, R. (1999). *A theory of the trial.* Princeton, NJ: Princeton University Press.

Burstein, P. (1999). Social movements and public policy. In M. G. Giugni, D. McAdam, & C. Tilly (Eds.), *How social movements matter* (Vol. 10, pp. 3–21). Minneapolis: University of Minnesota Press.

Burstein, P., & Union, A. (2002). The impact of political panics, interest groups, and social movement organizations on public policy: Some recent evidence and theoretical concerns. *Social Forces, 81,* 381–408.

Campbell, K., & Denov, M. (2004). The burden of innocence: Coping with a wrongful imprisonment. *Canadian Journal of Criminology and Criminal Justice, 46*(2), 139–163.

Ceci, S. J., & Bruck, M. (1995). *Jeopardy in the courtroom: A scientific analysis of children's testimony.* Washington, DC: American Psychological Association.

Center for Wrongful Conviction. (n.d.). Retrieved February 23, 2006, from http://www.law.northwestern.edu/wrongfulconvictions/

Centurion Ministries. (n.d.). Retrieved June 19, 2006, from http://www.centurionministries.org/

Cole, S. A. (2005). More than zero: Accounting for error in latent fingerprint identification. *Journal of Criminal Law & Criminology, 95*(3), 985–1078.

Commonwealth v. DiGiambattista, 813 N.E. 2d 516. 533 (Mass. 2004).

Connors, E., Lundregan, T., Miller, N., & McEwan, T. (1996). *Convicted by juries, exonerated by science: Case studies in the use of DNA evidence to establish innocence after trial* (NCJ 161258). Washington, DC: National Institute of Justice.

Cromett, M. F. & Thurston Myster, S. M. (2005, October/November). The work of an innocence project. *Forensic Magazine.* Retrieved February 23, 2006, from http://www.forensicmag.com/articles .asp?pid = 60

Damaska, M. (1986). *The facts of justice and state authority: A comparative approach to the legal process.* New Haven, CT: Yale University Press.

Damaska, M. (1997). *Evidence law adrift.* New Haven, CT: Yale University Press.

Dann, B. M., & Hans, V. P. (2004). Recent evaluative research on jury trial innovations. *Court Review, 41,* 12–19.

Dao, J. (2006, January 13). DNA ties man executed in '92 to the murder he denied. *New York Times,* p. AI4.

D.C. Code §5-116.01-.03 (2006).

Death Penalty Information Center. (n.d.). Retrieved January 15, 2006, from http://www.deathpenaltyinfo.org

Denov, M. S., & Campbell, K. M. (2005). Criminal injustice: Understanding the causes, effects, and responses to wrongful conviction in Canada. *Journal of Contemporary Criminal Justice, 21,* 224–249.

Diani, M. (2002). Network analysis. In B. Klandermans & S. Staggenborg (Eds.), *Methods of social movement research* (pp. 173–200). Minneapolis: University of Minnesota Press.

Doyle, J. M. (2005). *True witness: Cops, courts, science, and the battle against misidentification.* New York: Palgrave Macmillan.

Drizin, S. A., & Leo, R. A. (2004). The problem of false confessions in the post-DNA world. *North Carolina Law Review, 82,* 891–1007.

Edds, M. (2003). *An expendable man: The near execution of Earl Washington, Jr.* New York: New York University Press.

Emirbayer, M., & Goodwin, J. (1994). Network analysis, culture, and the problem of agency. *American Journal of Sociology, 99,* 1411–1454.

Epstein, L., & Kohylka, J. F. (1992). *The Supreme Court & legal change: Abortion and the death penalty.* Chapel Hill: University of North Carolina Press.

Eyerman, R., & Jamison, A. (1991). *Social movements: A cognitive approach.* Cambridge, UK: Polity.

Feeley, M. M., & Rubin, E. L. (1998). *Judicial policy and the modern state: How the courts reformed America's prisons.* Cambridge, UK: Cambridge University Press.

Feige, D. (2006a, January 1). We find the defendant not guilty (if that's O.K. with everyone). *New York Times,* p. 23.

Feige, D. (2006b, June 6). Witnessing guilt, ignoring innocence? *New York Times,* p. A1.

Fisher, S. Z. (1993). "Just the facts, ma'am": Lying and the omission of exculpatory evidence in police reports. *New England Law Review, 28,* I–62.

Fletcher, G. (1995). *With justice for some: Victims' rights in criminal trials.* Reading, MA: Addison Wesley.

Forst, B. (2004). *Errors of justice: Nature, sources, and remedies.* Cambridge, UK: Cambridge University Press.

Frank, J., & Frank, B. (1971). *Not guilty.* New York: DaCapo Press. (Original work published 1957)

Friedman, D., & McAdam, D. (1992). Collective identity and activism: Networks, choices, and the life of a social movement. In A. D. Morris & C. M. Mueller (Eds.), *Frontiers in social movement theory* (pp. 156–173). New Haven, CT: Yale University Press.

Friedman, L. M. (1985). *Total justice.* New York: Russell Sage.

Gardner, E. S. (1952). *The court of last resort.* New York: W. Sloane.

Garrett, B. L. (2005). Innocence, harmless error, and federal wrongful conviction law. *Wisconsin Law Review, 2005,* 35–114.

Gianelli, P., & Raeder, M. (Eds.). (2006). *Achieving justice: Freeing the innocent, convicting the guilty: Report of the ABA Criminal Justice Section's Ad Hoc Committee to Ensure the Integrity of the Criminal Process.* Washington, DC: American Bar Association.

Gilstrap, L. L., Fritz, K., Torres, A., & Melinder, A. (2005). Child witnesses: Common ground and controversies in the scientific community. *William Michell Law Review, 32,* 59–79.

Givelber, D. (1997). Meaningless acquittals, meaningful convictions: Do we reliably acquit the innocent? *Rutgers Law Review, 49,* 1317–1396.

Givelber, D. (2005). Lost innocence: Speculation and data about the acquitted. *American Criminal Law Review, 42,* 1167–1199.

Green, J. C., & Bigelow, N. S. (2005). The Christian right goes to Washington: Social movements resources and the legislative process. In P. S. Herrnson, R. G Shaiko, & C. Wilcox (Eds.), *The interest group connection: Electioneering, lobbying, and policymaking in Washington* (pp. 189–211). Washington, DC: CQ Press.

Gross, S. R., Jacoby, K., Matheson, D. J., Montgomery, N., & Patil, S. (2005). Exonerations in the United States, 1989 through 2003. *Journal of Criminal Law & Criminology, 95,* 523–60.

Gudjonsson, G. (2003). The *psychology of interrogation and confessions: A handbook.* Chichester, UK: Wiley.

Haller, R. L. (2001). Notes & comments: The Innocence Protection Act: Why federal measures requiring post-conviction DNA testing and preservation of evidence are needed in order to reduce the risk of wrongful executions. *New York Law School Journal of Human Rights, 18,* 101–132.

Harmon, T. R. (2001). Predictors of miscarriages of justice in capital cases. *Justice Quarterly, 18,* 949–968.

Heinz, J. P., & Manikas, P. M. (1992). Networks among elites in a local criminal justice system. *Law and Society Review, 26,* 831–861.

Hickman, M. J., & Reaves, B. A. (2003). *Local police departments 2000* (NCJ 196002). Washington, DC: Bureau of Justice Statistics.

Hill, M., & Hupe, P. (2002). *Implementing public policy: Governance in theory and in practice.* London, UK: Sage.

Hirsch, J. S. (2001). *Hurricane: The miraculous journey of Rubin Carter.* New York: Houghton Mifflin.

Holden, S. (2005, October 21). Highlighting a tragic chink in the criminal justice system (movie review, *After Innocence*). *New York Times,* p. E1.

Horowitz, D. L. (1977). *The courts and social policy.* Washington, DC: Brookings Institution.

Huff, C. R., Rattner, A., & Sagarin, E. (1986). Guilty until proved innocent. *Crime & Delinquency, 32,* 518.

Huff, C. R., Rattner, A., & Sagarin, E. (1996). *Convicted but innocent: Wrongful conviction and public policy.* Thousand Oaks, CA: Sage.

Humes, E. (1999). *Mean justice.* New York: Simon & Schuster.

Hunt, S. (2006, January 15). Bill seeks to pay for wrongful conviction. *Salt Lake Tribune,* p. B1.

Illinois Governor's Commission on Capital Punishment. (2002, April). *Report.* Retrieved February 23, 2006, from http://www.idoc.state .il.us/ccp/ccp/reports/commission report/index html

Innocence Commission for Virginia. (2005, March). *A vision for justice: Report and recommendation regarding wrongful convictions in the Commonwealth of Virginia.* Retrieved February 23, 2006, from http://www.icva.us

The Innocence Network. (n.d.). Retrieved June 12, 2006, from http:// www.innocenetwork.org/

The Innocence Project. (n.d.). Retrieved February 23, 2006, from http:// www.innocenceproject.org/

Johnson, C. C., Jr. (with Hampikian, G.). (2003). *Exit to freedom.* Athens: University of Georgia Press.

Jones, C. O. (1984). *An introduction to the study of public policy* (3rd ed.). Monterey, CA: Brooks/Cole.

Jones, C. E. (2005). Evidence destroyed, innocence lost: The preservation of biological evidence under innocence protection statutes. *American Criminal Law Review, 42,* 1239–1270.

Junkin, T. (2004). *Bloodsworth: The true story of the first death row inmate exonerated by DNA.* Chapel Hill, NC: Algonquin Books.

Justice Denied. (n.d.). *Justice denied: The magazine for the wrongly convicted.* Retrieved June 19, 2006, from http//www.justicedenied.org/ index.htm

The Justice Project. (n.d.). Retrieved June 19, 2006, from http://ccjr .policy.net/

Kingdon, J. W. (1984). *Agendas, alternatives and public policies.* New York: HarperCollins.

Kirchmeier, J. L. (2002). Another place beyond here: The death penalty moratorium movement in the United States. *University of Colorado Law Review, 73,* 1–116.

Kleinert, M. E. (2006). Note: Improving the quality of justice: The Innocence Protection Act of 2004 ensures post-conviction DNA testing, better legal representation, and increased compensation for the wrongfully imprisoned. *Brandeis Law Journal, 44,* 491–508.

Kraska, P. (2004). *Theorizing criminal justice: Eight essential orientations.* Prospect Heights, IL: Waveland Press.

Kraska, P. (2006). Criminal justice theory: Toward legitimacy and an infrastructure. *Justice Quarterly, 23*(2), 167–185.

Leahy, P. (2004a). *Justice for All Act of 2004: Section-by-section analysis.* Retrieved February 23, 2006, from http://leahy.senate.gov/ press/200410/100904E.html

Leahy, P. (2004b). *Statement of Senator Patrick Leahy—The Justice For All Act Of 2004.* Retrieved February 23, 2006, from http://leahy .senate.gov/press/200410/100904B.html

Leipold, A. D. (2005). How the pretrial process contributes to wrongful convictions. *American Criminal Law Review, 42,* 1123–1165.

Leo, R. A. (2005). Rethinking the study of miscarriages of justice: Developing a criminology of wrongful conviction. *Journal of Contemporary Criminal Justice, 2*(3), 201–223.

Leo, R. A., & Ofshe, R. J. (1998). The consequences of false confessions: Deprivations of liberty and miscarriages of justice in the age of psychological interrogation. *Journal of Criminal Law & Criminology, 88,* 429–496.

Lerner, R. L. (2001). The intersection of two systems: An American on trial for an American murder in the French cour d'assises. *University of Illinois Law Review, 2001,* 791–856.

Life After Exoneration Program. (n.d.). Retrieved February 23, 2006, from http//www exonerated org/

Lindo, J. L. (2000). Note: New Jersey jurors are no longer color-blind regarding eyewitness identification. *Seton Hall Law Review, 30,* 1224–1254.

Loge, P. (2005). How to talk crimey and influence people; language and the politics of criminal justice policy. *Drake Law Review, 53,* 693–709.

Lolquist, W. S. (2001). Whodunit? An examination of the production of wrongful convictions. In S. D. Westervelt & J. A. Humphrey (Eds.), *Wrongly convicted: Perspective on failed justice* (pp. 174–196). New Brunswick, NJ: Rutgers University Press.

Lowery, D., & Brasher, H. (2004). *Organized interests and American government.* Boston: McGraw-Hill.

Mack, C. S. (1997). *Business, politics, and the practice of governmental relations.* Westport, CT: Quorum.

Marquis, J. (2005). The myth of innocence. *Journal of Criminal Law & Criminology, 95*(2), 501–521.

Martin, D. L. (2001). The police role in wrongful convictions: An international and comparative study. In S. D. Westervelt & J. A. Humphrey (Eds.), *Wrongly convicted: Perspectives on failed justice* (pp. 77–93). New Brunswick, NJ: Rutgers University Press.

Mars, G. (1979). External efforts to damage or facilitate social movements: Some patterns, explanations, outcomes, and complications. In M. N. Zald & J. D. McCarthy (Eds.), *The dynamics of social movements* (pp. 94–125). Cambridge, MA: Winthrop.

McCarthy, J. D., & Zald, M. N. (1977). Resource mobilization and social movements: A partial theory. *American Journal of Sociology, 82,* 1212–1241.

McConville, M., Sanders, A., & Leng, R. (1991). *The case for the prosecution: Police suspects and the construction of criminality.* London: Routledge.

Medwed, D. S. (2003). Actual innocents: Considerations in selecting cases for a new innocence project. *Nebraska Law Review, 81,* 1097–1151.

Medwed, D. S. (2004). The zeal deal? Prosecutorial resistance to post-conviction claims of innocence. *Boston University Law Review, 84,* 125–183.

Medwed, D. S. (2005). Looking foreword: Wrongful convictions and systemic reform. *American Criminal Law Review, 42,* 1117–1121.

Meyer, D. S., & Staggenborg, S. (1996). Movements, countermovements, and the structure of political opportunity. *American Journal of Sociology, 101,* 1628–1660.

Michies Ann. Stat. N. M. 29–1–16.

Minkol, T. D. (2002). Micro-organizational analysis. In B. Klandermans & S. Staggenborg (Eds.), *Methods of social movement research* (pp. 260–285). Minneapolis: University of Minnesota Press.

Mintrom, M. (1997). Policy entrepreneurs and the diffusion of innovation. *American Journal of Political Science, 41,* 738–770.

Mnookin, J. L., & West, N. (2001). Theaters of proof: Visual evidence and the law in *Call Northside 777. Yale Journal of Law & the Humanities, 13,* 329–390.

Molotch, H. (1979). Media and movements. In M. N. Zald & J. D McCarthy (Eds.), *The dynamics of social movements* (pp. 71–93). Cambridge, MA: Winthrop.

Morris, A. D. (2000). Reflections on social movement theory: Criticisms and proposals. *Contemporary Sociology, 29,* 445–454.

Morris, A. D., & Mueller, C. M. (Eds.). (1992). *Frontiers in social movement theory.* New Haven, CT: Yale University Press.

Mumma, C. C. (2004). The North Carolina actual innocence commission. Uncommon perspectives joined by a common cause. *Drake Law Review, 52,* 647.

National Innocence Network Conference. (2005). *Conference information packet.* Retrieved November 9, 2005, from http://www.regonline.com/Checkin.asp?Event Id = 20222

Packer, H. (1968). *The limits of the criminal sanction.* Stanford, CA: Stanford University Press.

Palumbo, D. J., & Calista, D. J. (Eds.). (1990). *Implementation and the policy process: Opening up the black box.* Westport, CT: Greenwood.

Panel Discussion. (1987). Panel discussion, symposium on clinical legal education. Clinical legal education: Reflections on the past fifteen years and aspirations for the future. *Catholic University Law Review, 36,* 337–365.

Patterson, R. N. (2005). *Conviction.* New York: Random House.

Paulson, A., & Llana, S. M. (2006, April 24). In police lineups, is the method the suspect? *Christian Science Monitor,* p. 1.

Pichardo, N. A. (1997). New social movements: A critical review. *Annual Review of Sociology, 23,* 411–430.

Poveda, T. G. (2001). Research note: Estimating wrongful convictions. *Justice Quarterly, 18,* 689–708.

Ramsey, R. J., & Frank, J. (in press). Wrongful conviction: Perspectives of criminal justice professionals regarding the frequency of wrongful conviction and the extent of system errors. *Crime & Delinquency.*

Rattner, A. (1988). Convicted but innocent: Wrongful conviction and the criminal justice system. *Law and Human Behavior, 12,* 283–293.

Risinger, D. M. (2004). Unsafe verdicts: The need for reformed standards for the trial and review of factual innocence claims. *Houston Law Review, 41,* 1281–1336.

Rogers, E. M. (2003). *Diffusion of innovations* (5th ed.). New York: Free Press.

Rosenberg, G. N. (1991). *The hollow hope: Can courts bring about social change?* Chicago: University of Chicago Press.

Scheck, B. (2005, April). A time for cautious optimism. *The Champion, 29,* 4.

Scheck, B. G., & Neufeld, P. J. (2002, September/October). Toward the formation of "innocence commissions" in America. *Judicature, 86*(2), 98–105.

Scheck, B., Neufeld, P., & Dwyer, J. (2000). *Actual innocence and other dispatches from the wrongly convicted.* New York: Doubleday.

Scheck, B., Neufeld, P., & Dwyer, J. (2003). *Actual innocence: When justice goes wrong and how to make it right.* New York: Penguin/New American Library.

Schehr, R. C. (2005). The Criminal Cases Review Commission as a state strategic selection mechanism. *American Criminal Law Review, 42,* 1289–1302.

Schoenfeld, H. (2005). Violated trust: Conceptualizing prosecutorial misconduct. *Journal of Contemporary Criminal Justice, 21,* 250–271.

Sessions, W. S. (2003, September 21). DNA tests can free the innocent. How can we ignore that? *Washington Post,* p. B2.

Siegel, A. M. (2005). Moving down the wedge of injustice: A proposal for a third generation of wrongful convictions scholarship and advocacy. *American Criminal Law Review, 42,* 1219–1237.

Silverman, E. (1999). *NYPD battles crime. Innovative strategies in policing.* Boston: Northeastern University Press.

Smith, C. (1997). The capacity of courts as policy-making forums. In H. S. Hancock & P. M. Sharp (Eds.), *Public policy: Crime and criminal justice* (pp. 232–248). Upper Saddle River, NJ: Prentice Hall.

State should offer compensation to the exonerated. (2006, February 8). *Detroit Free Press,* p. 10A.

State v Scales, 518 NW 2d 587 (Minn. 1994).

Steiker, C. S., & Steiker, J. M. (2005). The seduction of innocence: The attraction and limitations of the focus on innocence in capital punishment law and advocacy. *Journal of Criminal Law & Criminology, 95,* 587–624.

Stephen v. State, 7 11 P 2d I 156 (Alaska 1985).

Stiglitz, J., Brooks, J., & Shulman, T. (2002). The hurricane meets the paper chase: Innocence projects new emerging role in clinical legal education. *California Western Law Review, 38,* 413–430.

Strate, J., & Zalman, M. (2003). Interest group lobbying on a morality policy issue: The case of physician assisted suicide. *American Review of Politics, 24,* 321–342.

Sullivan, T. P. (2005). Recent developments: Electronic recording of custodial interrogations: Everybody wins. *Journal of Criminal Law & Criminology, 95,* 1127–1140.

Technical Working Group for Eyewitness Evidence. (1999). *Eyewitness evidence: A guide for law enforcement* (NCJ 178204). Washington, DC: National Institute of Justice.

Tex. Crim. P. Code Ann. 38.22(3)(4) (West 2005).

Tucker, J. C. (1997). *May God have mercy: A true story of crime and punishment.* New York: Norton.

Tucker, C. (2005, December 14). Let's arrest wrongful convictions. *Atlanta Journal-Constitution,* p. 15A.

Tulsky, F. (2006, January 21–26). Tainted trials, stolen justice. *San Jose Mercury News.* Retrieved January 28, 2006, from http://www.mercurynews.com/mid/mercurynews/news/special_packages/stolenjustice/

20 ILCS 3930/7.2 (2006).

25 M.R.S. § 2803-B (1) (K) (2005).

Vollen, L., & Eggers, D. (Eds.). (2005). *Surviving justice: America's wrongfully convicted and exonerated.* San Francisco: McSweeny's.

Volokh, A. (1997). Aside: n guilty men. *University of Pennsylvania Law Review, 146,* 173–216.

Walker, J. (1969). The diffusion of innovations among the American states. *American Political Science Review, 63,* 880–899.

Walker, S. (2005). *The new world of police accountability.* Thousand Oaks, CA: Sage.

Ward, J. D. (1998). Public policy entrepreneur. In J. M. Shafritz (Ed.), *The international encyclopedia of public policy and administration* (Vol. 3, pp. 1850–1851). Boulder, CO: Westview.

Warden, R. (2003). The revolutionary role of journalism in identifying and rectifying wrongful convictions. *UMKC Law Review, 70,* 803.

Warden, R. (2005). Illinois death penalty reform: How it happened, what it promises. *Journal of Criminal Law & Criminology, 95,* 381–426.

Wasby, S. L. (1983). Interest groups in court: Race relations litigation. In A. J. Cigler & B. A. Loomis (Eds.), *Interest group politics* (pp. 251–274). Washington, DC: CQ Press.

Weed, F. (1995). *Certainty of justice: Reform in the crime victim movement.* New York: Aldine de Gruyter.

Weich, R. (2005, March). The Innocence Protection Act of 2004: A small step forward and a framework for larger reforms. *The Champion, 29,* 28–31.

Wells, G. L. (2001). Police lineups: Data, theory and policy. *Psychology, Public Policy and Law, 7,* 791–801.

Wells, G. L., Small, M., Penrod, S., Malpass, R. S., Fulero, S. M., & Brimcomb, C. A. E. (1998). Eyewitness identification procedures: Recommendations for lineups. *Law & Human Behavior, 22,* 603–647.

Westervelt, S. D., & Humphrey, J. A. (Eds.). (2001). *Wrongly convicted: Perspectives on failed justice.* New Brunswick, NJ: Rutgers University Press.

Wrightsman, L., & Kassin, S. (1993). *Confessions in the courtroom.* Newbury Park, CA: Sage.

Zacharias, F. C. (2005). The rule of prosecutors in serving justice after convictions. *Vanderbilt Law Review, 58,* 171–239.

Zalman, M. (1991). *Wayne County Jail inmates v. Wayne County Sheriff: The anatomy of a lawsuit. The Prison Journal, 71*(1), 4–23.

Zalman, M. (1998). Juricide. In D. A. Schultz (Ed.), *Leveraging the law: Using the courts to achieve social change* (pp. 293–318). New York: Peter Lang.

Zalman, M. (2005). Cautionary notes on commission recommendations: A public policy approach to wrongful convictions. *Criminal Law Bulletin, 41*(2), 169–194.

Zalman, M., & Smith, B. (2005). *The attitudes of police executives toward* Miranda *and interrogation policies.* Unpublished manuscript.

Zalman, M., Smith, B., & Kazaleh, A. (2006, March). *Officials' estimates of the prevalence of wrongful convictions.* Paper presented at the annual meeting of the Academy of Criminal Justice Sciences, Baltimore.

Zeinike, K. (2006, April 19). Questions raised over new trend in police lineups. *New York Times,* p. Al.

IX

Specialized Courts and Other Trends in Adjudication

Section Highlights

- The Specialized Court Movement
- Restorative Justice
- Edited Readings

During the 1980s, the number of drug offenders locked up in state and federal prisons skyrocketed. In fact, the rate at which drug offenders were sent to prison went from 19 per 1,000 adult arrests for drug offenses in 1980 to 104 per 1,000 arrests in 1992 (Bureau of Justice Statistics, 1998). The staggering costs of incarcerating increasing numbers of drug offenders, coupled with mounting evidence that imprisonment was not an effective approach to dealing with drug abuse, led policymakers to search for alternative solutions that would be cost-effective, politically palatable, and successful in reducing drug abuse and drug-related crime.

This search for a more effective strategy led to the development of the **drug treatment court.** The movement started in 1989, when then-State Attorney General Janet Reno joined forces with Florida judges and the Dade County (Miami) public defender to establish the nation's first treatment-based drug diversion court. Unlike a traditional court, which operates according to an adversarial model and emphasizes punishment, the Miami Drug Court stressed collaboration among criminal justice officials, ongoing judicial supervision of offenders, mandatory drug treatment, and a rehabilitation program providing vocational, education, family, and medical services. The drug court movement spread rapidly. By 2010 there were more than 2,400 programs for adult and juvenile offenders operating in state and federal courts throughout the United States (Office of National Drug Control Policy, n.d.).

As evidence mounted that drug treatment courts were both more cost-effective and more successful in reducing drug use and drug-related crime, states began to experiment with other specialized courts: domestic violence courts, mental health courts, reentry courts, community courts, and homeless courts. These courts, which generally are referred to as "problem-solving" courts, are distinguished by several unique characteristics: a focus on solving offenders' underlying problems; a nonadversarial approach to decision making that involves social service providers as well as criminal justice officials; ongoing judicial supervision and monitoring of offenders in the program; and sanctions for noncompliance with program requirements (Farole, Puffett, Rempel, & Byrne, 2005, p. 57). All of these courts, in other words, are designed to address the problems that landed the offender in court and not just respond to the offender's criminal behavior, while at the same time holding the offender accountable and protecting the safety of the community.

In this section, we focus on specialized, or problem-solving, courts. We emphasize the two types of courts that have spread most rapidly and have generated the most research: drug treatment courts and domestic violence courts. We also discuss restorative justice and its application in specialized courts.

The Specialized Court Movement

Specialized courts are the recently developed limited jurisdiction courts specializing in certain crime problems, such as drugs, guns, and domestic violence. These courts are similar to traffic courts in that they address a specific problem, but, as we explain later, several factors set them apart. Specialized courts go by a number of names. Sometimes they are called problem-solving courts. Other times they are called boutique courts. They are also sometimes called limited jurisdiction courts. We use the terms *specialized* or *problem-solving* courts throughout the discussion that follows.

Origins

Where did **problem-solving courts** originate? The answer lies in the problem-solving movement that has been seen elsewhere in criminal justice, particularly in the policing arena. Changes in policing were sparked by influential scholarship, such as Goldstein's 1979 problem-oriented policing article (see also Goldstein, 1990) and Wilson and Kelling's 1982 "broken windows" article in the *Atlantic Monthly*. These scholars argued, in essence, that targeting minor crimes, such as drug use, vandalism, or loitering, would eventually lead to reductions in more serious crimes. Other developments in and outside the criminal justice system also encouraged the development of problem-oriented approaches, according to Center for Court Innovation researchers:

> (1) breakdowns among the kinds of social and community institutions (including families and churches) that have traditionally addressed problems like addiction, mental illness, quality-of-life crime and domestic violence; (2) the struggles of other government efforts, whether legislative or executive, to address these problems . . . (3) a surge in the nation's incarcerated population and the resulting prison overcrowding . . . (4) trends emphasizing the accountability of public institutions . . . (5) advances in the quality and availability of therapeutic interventions, which have given many within the criminal justice system greater confidence in using certain forms of treatment . . . and (6) shifts in public policies and priorities—for example, the way the "broken windows" theory has alerted perceptions of the importance of low-level crime. (Berman & Feinblatt, 2001, pp. 5–6)

Not long after *problem oriented* and *broken windows* became familiar terms in criminal justice circles, Philadelphia implemented a court for protection from abuse. There, a judge oversaw all of the civil protection orders in one courtroom. Next, Cook County, Illinois, established a domestic violence calendar in one of its criminal courts. These two projects were somewhat obscure, though, compared to Dade County, Florida's drug court, which opened to much fanfare in 1989. This court was the first in the United States to sentence drug offenders to judicially supervised drug treatment. Shortly thereafter, Dade County started a specialized **domestic violence court** and, in 1993, the first **community court**, the Midtown Community Court, opened in Times Square, New York City. This court was among the first to combine punishment and assistance to offenders and victims. It also focused exclusively on minor quality-of-life offenses.

The movement to establish problem-solving courts also was affected by passage of the Violent Crime Control and Law Enforcement Act of 1994. This legislation authorized the U.S. Attorney General to fund drug courts across the country. By the end of 1994, more than 40 drug courts were operating in jurisdictions throughout the United States. The Violence Against Women Act, which provided funding to states and local communities in an effort to combat domestic violence, sexual assault, and other crimes of violence targeting women, was also passed in 1994. Enactment of this law prompted a number of jurisdictions to establish domestic violence courts.

Other jurisdictions experimented with courts designed to target problems such as mental illness, homelessness, and reentry. In 1996, Marion County, Indiana started its Psychiatric Assertive Identification Referral/Response (PAIR) Program; this was the nation's first **mental health court**. Brooklyn, New York then started the first domestic violence court that processed felony cases. In 1989, San Diego, California implemented the first **homeless court**. Its focus has been on assistance to those who are homeless rather than just traditional adjudication of criminal offenses. In fact, the court does not adjudicate new offenses. Rather, prosecutors, defense attorneys, and a judge work together to help clear the criminal histories of homeless individuals who are interested in getting their lives back on track. Also in 1999, the Office of Justice Programs in the U.S. Department of Justice funded nine reentry courts, which are specialized courts that help reintegrate parolees into the community.

Specialized courts continue to proliferate in jurisdictions throughout the United States. Three such courts—drug courts, domestic violence courts, and mental health courts—are essentially staples of the criminal justice system. The less prominent courts, such as homeless courts, are also beginning to gain a foothold. Community courts, such as the one found in Brooklyn's Red Hook Community Justice Center, are also becoming more common. Even **teen courts**, in which teens assume the roles of various court officials (with adult supervision) and adjudicate minor juvenile offenses, are beginning to emerge.

Distinguishing Features

The New York-based Center for Court Innovation (CCI) identified six principles and practices that make problem-solving courts different from traditional courts (Berman & Feinblatt, 2001). The first is a focus on case outcomes, rather than case processing. One judge summarized this principle as follows: "Outcomes—not just process and precedents—matter. Protecting the rights of an addicted mother is important. So is protecting her children and getting her off drugs" (Kaye, 1999, p. 13).

Judicial monitoring also sets specialized courts apart from traditional courts. Under the traditional approach, the judge's involvement typically ends when the sentence is imposed. Contrast this with the problem-solving-court approach, in which judges may stay involved in the case from beginning to end. Drug court judges, for example, closely supervise offenders, who are required to participate in substance abuse treatment. The judge receives regular updates on offenders' progress, and offenders return to court frequently so that the judge can congratulate them on staying drug and crime free or admonish them for failing to follow the prescribed treatment program.

This leads to the third principle, which is informed decision making. Judges attempt to gather as much information as possible concerning the offender's predicament before rendering a decision. To do this, they rely on innovative technologies and on-site staff to help them stay informed about what is happening with offenders. In some community courts, for example, on-site case workers even evaluate defendants' needs (e.g., determine whether they need drug treatment) so that the judge can hand down an appropriate sentence.

The next three distinguishing features of problem-solving courts are collaboration, nontraditional roles, and systemic change. Collaboration refers to officials from various public and private agencies working together to determine appropriate sanctions and to monitor offenders' progress. Next, there are many nontraditional practices that take place in problem-solving courts. One example is the weakening of the adversarial approach to justice. Many problem-solving courts see prosecutors and defense attorneys working together to ensure that the needs of offenders can be met. Lastly, systemic change refers to applying problem-solving-court lessons to the administration of justice in general.

Another way to think of problem-solving courts is in terms of collaboration, judicial participation, and citizen involvement:

> Instead of adversarial sparring, prosecutors and defenders in some problem-solving courts work together to encourage defendants to succeed in drug treatment. Instead of embracing the tradition of judicial isolation, judges in problem-solving courts become actively involved in their communities, meeting with residents and brokering relationships with local service providers. Perhaps most importantly, instead of being passive observers, citizens are welcomed into the process, participating in advisory boards, organizing community service projects and meeting face to face with offenders to explain the impact of crimes on neighborhoods. (Center for Court Innovation, n.d.)

Drug Courts

Increases in the number of drug offenders appearing in state and federal courts, coupled with mounting evidence of both the link between drug use and crime and the efficacy of drug treatment programs, led a number of jurisdictions "to rethink their approach to handling defendants charged with drug and drug-related offenses" (Drug Court Clearinghouse and Technical Assistance Project, 1999, p. 3). Some jurisdictions, such as Cook County (Chicago), Illinois, established specialized dockets designed to manage the drug caseload more efficiently and to alleviate stress on the felony court system (Inciardi, McBride, & Rivers, 1996). Other jurisdictions, such as Dade County (Miami), Florida, created drug treatment courts that incorporate intensive judicial supervision of drug offenders; mandatory drug treatment; and a rehabilitation program providing vocational, education, family, and medical services.

Although the nature and characteristics of drug courts throughout the United States vary widely, they share several key elements:

- Integration of substance abuse treatment with justice system case processing;
- Use of a nonadversarial approach;
- Early identification and prompt placement of eligible participants;

- Access to a continuum of treatment, rehabilitation, and related services;
- Frequent testing for alcohol and illicit drugs;
- A coordinated strategy among judge, prosecutor, defense, and treatment providers to govern offender compliance; and
- Ongoing judicial interaction with each participant. (National Association of Drug Court Professionals, 1997, pp. 9–38)

In the typical preadjudication drug court (Drug Court Clearinghouse and Technical Assistance Project, 1999, p. 3), drug offenders who meet the eligibility criteria for the program are given a choice between participation in the drug court and traditional adjudication. Although the eligibility criteria vary, most programs exclude offenders who have prior convictions for violent offenses or whose current offense involved violence or use of a weapon. These programs target offenders whose involvement with the criminal justice system is due primarily to their substance abuse. Offenders who are accepted into the program—which may last 12 months, 18 months, or longer—and who agree to abide by the requirements of the program are immediately referred to a substance abuse treatment program for counseling, therapy, and education. They also are subject to random urinalysis and are required to appear frequently before the drug court judge. Offenders who do not show up for treatment sessions or drug court or who fail drug tests are subject to sanctions; repeated violations may result in termination from the program and adjudication and sentencing on the original charges. If the offender completes the program, the charges against him or her are dismissed.

Domestic Violence Courts

Domestic violence courts are not as common as drug courts, but their numbers are growing (Little, 2003; Weber, 2000). Like other specialized courts, domestic violence courts focus on tailoring interventions to the needs of victims; they also closely monitor offenders. Like drug courts, domestic violence courts enlist community participation and draw on the services of various public agencies:

> Domestic violence courts seek to coordinate with medical, social service, and treatment providers and establish special procedures and alternative sentencing options to promote effective outcomes. Success necessitates system-wide collaboration and the ongoing commitment of judges, health care professionals, the police, prosecution, and citizens who witness violent acts. (Ostrom, 2003, p. 105)

According to a survey conducted by the National Center for State Courts, there were approximately 200 domestic violence courts in 1998 (Karan, Keilitz, & Denaro, 1999). More recent estimates suggest that more than 300 courts nationwide are giving specialized attention to domestic violence cases (Keilitz, 2000). Not all of these are stand-alone domestic violence courts, however. Some simply reserve time for specialized processing of such cases (Levey, Steketee, & Keilitz, 2001). An example of a domestic violence court can be found in the state of Rhode Island. According to the court's website,

> The mission of the Domestic Violence Court is to effectively manage a specialized domestic abuse docket within the overall framework of affording protective orders and services to victims and their families while at the same time ensuring batterer accountability and encouraging behavior changes. (see http://www.courts.state.ri.us/family/domesticviolence.htm)

To accomplish its mission, the court assesses family needs and holds abusers accountable. It also has routine compliance reviews, just like drug courts. As stated on the court's website, the court has the following goals:

1. To promote the cessation of the violence.

2. To protect the abused party, the children of the parties and other family members.

3. To protect the general public.

4. To hold perpetrators accountable for their violent behavior and for stopping the behavior.

5. To rehabilitate the perpetrator through appropriate interventions.

6. To convey the message that domestic violence will *not* be tolerated.

Another domestic violence court is found in Lexington County, South Carolina. In that court, all non-felony domestic violence cases are processed by a single court. The court relies on the collaboration of sheriff's office investigators, a victim advocate, and a full-time prosecutor. Mental health officials also work with the court to diagnose offenders' needs and assign them to the proper treatment program. The court even draws on the services of a legal advocate from a local domestic violence shelter. Most of the offenders who come before the court participate in a 26-week group-based cognitive therapy program in exchange for a suspended jail sentence.

Other Specialized Courts

Another type of specialized court is the community court. The CCI describes the typical community court in this way:

> It can take many forms, but at its core, a community court is about partnership and problem solving. It's about creating new relationships, both within the justice system and with outside stakeholders such as residents, merchants, churches and schools. And it's about testing new and aggressive approaches to public safety rather than merely responding to crime after it has occurred. (see http://www.communityjustice.org)

Perhaps the best known community court is the Midtown Community Court, which opened in October of 1993 in New York City's Times Square. The court was implemented following a two-year collaborative planning effort between the New York State Unified Court System, the City of New York, and the Fund for the City of New York. The purpose of this neighborhood-based court is to provide "accessible justice" for **quality-of-life crimes** occurring in and around Times Square. The Midtown Community Court focuses on devising innovative responses to less serious crimes, such as vandalism, shoplifting, prostitution, and minor drug offenses. Offenders convicted of these crimes are required to perform community service or make other types of restitution to the community. Social workers and other social service agency personnel work with court officials to address offenders' underlying problems, such as homelessness, unemployment, and substance abuse. The goal is to give offenders the structure and support they need to avoid reoffending.

Homeless courts—such as the one found in San Diego—represent another example of specialized courts. California's Administrative Office of the Courts (2004) described the need for homeless courts in this way:

Resolution of outstanding warrants not only meets a fundamental need of homeless people but also eases court case-processing backlogs and reduces vagrancy. Homeless people tend to be fearful of attending court, yet their outstanding warrants limit their reintegration into society, deterring them from using social services and impeding their access to employment. They are effectively blocked from obtaining driver's licenses, job applications, and rental agreements.

To address these needs, homeless courts—which in San Diego and other cities hold sessions at local homeless shelters—help homeless individuals pay fines and resolve outstanding infractions and misdemeanor offenses.

Mental health courts are also becoming more common. Traditionally, the criminal justice system and mental health agencies have not been close collaborators (Denckla & Berman, 2001). The purpose of mental health courts is to bring these entities together to provide needed services to mentally ill offenders. Mental health courts are important and necessary because there are many mentally ill offenders who historically have not received the services they need (Watson, Luchins, Hanrahan, Heyrman, & Lurigio, 2000). By some estimates, there are more than a quarter-million mentally ill offenders in America's prisons and jails (Ditton, 1999).

The four original mental health courts are located in Broward County, Florida; Anchorage, Alaska; King County, Washington; and San Bernardino, California. Participation in the courts is voluntary and is usually reserved for low-level offenders. In the King County Mental Health Court, a court liaison to the treatment community is present at all hearings and is responsible for linking defendants with appropriate services. Defendants participate in court-ordered treatment programs and often have their charges dropped after successful completion of treatment. They are supervised by probation officers who have small caseloads and a background in the mental health field.

Another interesting specialized court is the so-called **reentry court**. One such court, the Harlem Parole Reentry Court, began its operations in June of 2001. Its purpose is to "test the feasibility and effectiveness of a collaborative, community-based approach to managing offender reentry, with the ultimate goal of reducing recidivism and prison return rates" (Farole, 2003, p. 1). The court was funded by the U.S. Justice Department's Reentry Court Initiative and was a partnership between the New York State Division of Parole, the Center for Court Innovation, and the New York State Divisions of Criminal Justice Services. The court does not adjudicate new offenses but instead provides oversight and support services to offenders reentering the community. Parolees who violate the terms of their supervision, however, are dealt with in a fairly traditional fashion.

Do Specialized Courts Work?

Have specialized courts achieved their objectives? Have they helped people address the underlying problems that landed them in court? Have they reduced recidivism? In short, do they work? Researchers interested in specialized courts have sought to answer these questions. Most of the available literature concerns the courts that have been around the longest: drug courts.

There is mounting evidence that drug courts reduce offender recidivism and prevent drug relapse. A report by the U.S. General Accounting Office (GAO; 1997) summarized the results of 20 evaluations of 16 drug courts that were completed by early 1997. The GAO report indicated that these early evaluations generally concluded that drug courts were effective in reducing drug use and criminal behavior. A later review by Belenko (1998) summarized the results of 30 evaluations of 24 drug courts that were completed by

May of 1998. Belenko observed that most of these evaluations concluded "that drug use and criminal behavior are substantially reduced while clients are participating in drug court" (p. 21). For example, an evaluation of a Ventura County, California drug court, which tracked recidivism over an eight-month period, found that only 12% of the drug court participants were rearrested, compared with 32% of those in a comparison group. A Jackson County, Missouri evaluation similarly revealed six-month rearrest rates of 4% for program participants and 13% for nonparticipants. Belenko's review also included studies that assessed the impact of drug court participation on postprogram recidivism. Eight of the nine evaluations reported lower recidivism rates for the drug court group compared with a comparison group of similarly situated offenders who did not participate in the drug court program. An evaluation of the Multnomah County, Oregon drug court, for example, found statistically significant differences between drug court participants (0.59 new arrests) and drug court-eligible nonparticipants (1.53 new arrests) over a 24-month tracking period.

Belenko (1998) came to the following conclusion:

> Although the evaluations vary considerably in scope, methodology and quality, the results are consistent in finding that . . . drug courts provide more comprehensive and closer supervision of the drug-using offender than other forms of community supervision, drug use and criminal behavior are substantially reduced while clients are participating in drug court, [and] criminal behavior is lower after program participation. (pp. 17–18)

Belenko's (1998) concerns about the studies' research designs and methodologies were echoed by another team of researchers who analyzed the results of 42 separate drug court evaluations. Their conclusion was that "drug offenders participating in drug court are less likely to reoffend than similar offenders sentenced to traditional correctional options, such as probation" (Wilson, Ojmarrh, & MacKenzie, 2002, p. 20). Their main criticism of the available literature was that many of the research designs "made no attempt to statistically control for differences between drug court and comparison participants, and a common comparison group, drug court drop-outs, has a bias favoring the drug court condition" (p. 20).

A number of drug court researchers have compared the records of those who complete treatment with those who were sent to treatment but did not complete it. This is a less than ideal approach because, as the authors of one study pointed out, it amounts to saying that the "successes succeed and failures fail" (Goldkamp, White, & Robinson, 2001, p. 32). What is needed are comparisons of those who participated in the drug court with those who would have been eligible for drug court but did not participate. Fortunately, a number of drug court evaluations have done this (Finigan, 1998; Goldkamp & Weiland, 1993; Gottfredson, Coblentz, & Harmon, 1997; Harrell, Mitchell, Hirst, Marlowe, & Merrill, 2002; Peters & Murrin, 1998; Sechrest, Shichor, Artist, & Briceno, 1998). Other researchers, including the authors of a study we reprint in this section, have randomly assigned subjects to treatment and control conditions, finding less recidivism among drug court participants (Gottfredson & Exum, 2002).

⊠ Restorative Justice

Restorative justice fits well with the emergence of problem-solving courts. According to Braithwaite (1999), "restorative justice is a process whereby all the parties with a stake in a particular offence come together to resolve collectively how to deal with the aftermath of the offence and its implications for the future" (p. 5).

Restorative justice has also been described as "every action that is primarily oriented toward doing justice by repairing the harm that has been caused by a crime" (Bazemore & Walgrave, 1999, p. 48). Others have argued that restorative justice represents a "return to tribal justice and a rejection of retributive Western legal practice. For others, it is a response to the needs of crime victims, who typically are ignored in current practice" (Karp, 2001, p. 728).

Restorative justice is concerned with two key concepts: harm and repair. First, it is clear that crime causes several types of harm (Karp, 2001, p. 729). For example, there is the material harm, especially the damage to property and lost wages associated with crime. There is also personal and relationship harm. This can include everything from physical injury to emotional damage. Restorative justice also identifies public and private harms. Private harms are borne by individual victims of crime, and public harm amounts to damaged community cohesiveness. The concern with harm is what distinguishes restorative justice from the practices discussed thus far.

Restorative justice is not just about harm, however. Repair is critical. That is, restorative justice advocates favor repairing the harm that crime causes and thereby restoring a sense of community. Repair can be manifested in a number of ways, such as by having the perpetrator fix damaged property. Or, as Karp (2001) put it, repair "may involve restoring offenders by creating social support, integrative opportunities, and competencies" (p. 730). Repair may also

> involve rebuilding communities by renewing respect for and commitment to the criminal justice system; by fostering new social ties among community members; by enriching the deliberative democratic process; and by focusing attention on community problems so that broader institutional weaknesses, such as in schools or families, can be addressed. (p. 730)

Restorative justice looks good on paper, but it faces serious obstacles depending on where it is attempted. For example, it has almost no chance of succeeding in areas where there is no defined sense of community. The whole practice is premised on the idea of community and of welcoming offenders "back into the fold." It is also unlikely that victims of serious crimes would opt for the restorative justice approach because it requires that victims and offenders work together to repair harm. Some have therefore argued that restorative justice is most likely to succeed in tightly knit rural communities or with offenders (especially young ones) who are accused of committing relatively minor offenses (for other criticisms of restorative justice, see Levrant, Cullen, & Fulton, 1999). Others, though, have argued that restorative justice can be effective for dealing with crimes as serious as homicide (Eschholz, Reed, & Beck, 2003; Umbreit & Vos, 2000).

Restorative Justice in Action

Restorative justice achieves its goals through a variety of practices. These practices include victim-offender mediation, family group conferencing, sentencing circles, and citizen supervision of probation. What typically occurs is a face-to-face meeting involving the victim, the offender, the victim's and offender's families, and other members of the community (a thorough discussion of these techniques can be found in Kurki, 2000). Participants in the process discuss the effects of the crime on the victim, the offender, and the community and attempt to reach a collective agreement regarding the most appropriate sanction. Although this process differs significantly from the traditional criminal justice process, the outcomes are often similar to those imposed by judges and other criminal justice officials: apologies, restitution, fines, community service, alcohol or drug abuse treatment, anger management programs, intensive supervision probation, or short jail terms. Advocates of restorative justice contend that the use of these traditional methods does not conflict with "the belief that communities must be more heavily involved and given much greater responsibility in the quest for justice" (Hahn, 1997).

Combining Restorative Justice With Shaming

John Braithwaite's (1989) idea of **reintegrative shaming** merges restorative justice with shaming. Historically, shaming involved such things as the stocks and pillory. More recently, judges have sentenced offenders to a number of shaming penalties. Drunk drivers, for instance, have been required to put warning stickers on their cars alerting other drivers of their past transgressions. In Arizona, individuals convicted of driving under the influence may have their pictures posted on a website. Countless more innocuous shaming penalties can be identified. All have the common goal of singling out criminal activity and scorning it publicly.

Braithwaite (1989) is not a fan of public humiliation and debasement penalties. He is concerned that such penalties may ostracize criminals and cause them to either band together and form delinquent subcultures or remain isolated from society. In that vein, he argued that shaming can put a lot of distance between the offender and the community, a rift that needs to be repaired. Braithwaite did not totally dismiss shaming, however. Instead, he argued that offenders must first be shamed, which sends a message that crime will not be tolerated, and then they must be reintegrated into society:

> Reintegrative shaming means that expressions of community disapproval, which may range from mild rebuke to degradation ceremonies, are followed by gestures of reacceptance into the community of law-abiding citizens. These gestures of reacceptance will vary from a simple smile expressing forgiveness and love to quite formal ceremonies to decertify the offender as deviant. Disintegrative shaming (stigmatization), in contrast, divides the community by creating a class of outcasts. (p. 55)

There is very little research that attempts to test the predictions of reintegrative shaming theory—that is, that reintegrative shaming will lead to reductions in delinquency and criminality. One exception is a study by Carter Hay (2001), who examined the relationship between adolescents' perceptions of their parents' methods of sanctioning them for wrongdoing and their self-reported involvement in delinquency. He found that sanctioning methods that involved shaming (i.e., the parents emphasized that the act was immoral or unfair, attempted to make the youth feel guilty or ashamed, or insisted that the youth make up for what had been done) had a significant negative effect on youths' assessments that they would engage in future delinquency. Hay concluded that these results "clearly suggest the potential importance of shaming" (p. 148).

⊠ Summary: Specialized Courts

Frustration with conventional criminal courts and traditional adjudication procedures led state and local jurisdictions throughout the United States to establish problem-solving courts. These courts—drug courts, domestic violence courts, homeless courts, teen courts, and reentry courts—take a broader and more comprehensive approach to delinquency and criminality. Rather than focusing solely on the crime for which the defendant has been arrested, problem-solving courts attempt to address the underlying social and economic factors that contributed to the defendant's involvement in crime. Specialized courts also involve collaboration among criminal justice and social service agencies and are more likely than traditional courts to incorporate the principles of restorative justice. Although most of these courts have not yet been subjected to extensive evaluation, there is evidence that drug courts are effective in reducing recidivism and preventing drug relapse.

KEY TERMS

Community court	Mental health court	Specialized court
Domestic violence court	Problem-solving courts	Teen court
Drug treatment court	Reentry court	
Homeless court	Reintegrative shaming	

DISCUSSION QUESTIONS

1. How do specialized courts, such as drug treatment courts, differ from traditional courts?

2. What are the advantages of adjudicating cases—for example, domestic violence cases or cases involving defendants with mental health problems—in a specialized court?

3. Assume that you have been asked to evaluate a specialized court. You are to determine whether defendants processed through the specialized court are less likely to recidivate than defendants adjudicated in a traditional court. How would you determine this?

4. How does the concept of reintegrative shaming differ from public humiliation? What types of crimes would be appropriately punished using reintegrative shaming?

WEB RESOURCES

Bridging the Gap: Researchers, Practitioners and the Future of Drug Courts: http://www.courtinnovation.org/_uploads/documents/bridgingthegap.pdf

Center for Court Innovation: http://www.courtinnovation.org

National Association of Drug Court Professionals: http://www.nadcp.org

National Association of Youth Courts: http://www.youthcourt.net

National Drug Court Institute: http://www.ndci.org

Office on Violence Against Women: http://www.ovw.usdoj.gov

Restorative Justice Online: http://www.restorativejustice.org

READING

The Baltimore City Drug Treatment Court, which targets nonviolent, drug-involved adult offenders, was established in 1994. An evaluation of the court was conducted by Gottfredson and Exum in 1997. For this study, eligible offenders were randomly assigned either to the drug court or to traditional adjudication. The results of the evaluation revealed that offenders assigned to the drug court were less likely than offenders who were placed in the traditional adjudication group to be rearrested during the 12-month follow-up period.

The Baltimore City Drug Treatment Court

One-Year Results From a Randomized Study

Denise C. Gottfredson and M. Lyn Exum

During the 1980s, a dramatic increase in drug-related arrests and prosecutions clogged the criminal justice system. Court dockets became inundated with drug cases, and prisons were filled to overcrowding with drug offenders (The National Center on Addiction and Substance Abuse at Columbia University [CASA] 1998; U.S. General Accounting Office [GAO] 1997). Today, drug-involved offenders continue to tax the criminal justice system. According to the 1999 Arrestee Drug Abuse Monitoring Program (formerly the Drug Use Forecasting Program), at least one half of all adult men arrested in the participating jurisdictions tested positive for one or more drugs (National Institute of Justice 2000). Similarly, CASA (1998) reported that of the 1.7 million adults behind bars in 1996, 80 percent had been "seriously involved" in alcohol or other drug abuse.

These offenders place a great financial burden on the criminal justice system. In 1996, the nation spent approximately $30 billion incarcerating drug-involved offenders (The National Center on Addiction and Substance Abuse at Columbia University 1998). Compounding this cost is the estimated 45 percent of offenders who are expected to recidivate (OJP Drug Court Clearinghouse and Technical Assistance Program 1998). Given this cycle of drugs and crime and the current levels of drug use, CASA (1998) projected that the cost of incarcerating drug-involved offenders would exceed $100 million per day by 2000.

 The Drug Court Concept

Realizing that incarceration per se does not break the cycle of drugs and crime and that drug treatment has the potential to reduce drug usage and associated criminal activity, many jurisdictions have developed drug treatment courts (drug courts, for short) to process offenders with drug and alcohol addictions (OJP Drug Court Clearinghouse and Technical Assistance

AUTHORS' NOTE: Support for this research was provided by the Maryland Department of Public Safety and Correctional Services.

SOURCE: Gottfredson, D. C., & Exum, M. L. (2002). The Baltimore City Drug Treatment Court: One-year results from a randomized study. *Journal of Research in Crime and Delinquency*, *39*(3), 337–356.

Program 1998). Drug courts are specialized courts that provide judicially monitored treatment, drug testing, and other services to drug-involved offenders. Drug courts typically process offenders through either a diversion program or postadjudication treatment. Diversionary drug courts typically enroll offenders into treatment shortly after arrest and dismiss charges on their graduation from the program. Postadjudication drug courts intervene after defendants have been tried and convicted, offering deferred or suspended sentences to those who complete treatment programs. Some drug courts employ a combination of these approaches.

Drug courts can differ greatly with respect to their target populations, treatment methods, and monitoring processes. Despite this variability, most exclusively target nonviolent, drug-abusing offenders. Treatment programs are typically one year in length and are provided largely on an outpatient basis. Inpatient services are reserved for those with special treatment needs. Treatment regimens are designed with three primary goals. First, an offender's physical dependence on drugs is to be eliminated through a period of detoxification. Second, the psychological "craving for drugs" is to be treated through medication, individual and group counseling, or drug education programs. Third, drug courts seek to increase offenders' educational levels and employment status. General education, vocational training, and job placement services are generally offered during this final phase of treatment (U.S. General Accounting Office 1997).

Throughout all phases of the program, a drug court judge monitors a defendant's progress through regularly scheduled status hearings. At these hearings, the judge reviews reports from the parole and probation agent (hereafter referred to simply as the probation agent) regarding the defendant's compliance with the program and the results of scheduled drug tests. On the basis of these reports, the judge prescribes graduated sanctions as needed. For example, a defendant's "dirty" urine sample or failure to attend treatment sessions may result in jail time, more frequent drug tests, treatment meetings, and/or status hearings. Whatever the penalty, drug courts prescribe sanctions designed to augment or enforce treatment regimens, not simply to punish offenders (U.S. General Accounting Office 1997).

The Appeal and Growth of Drug Courts

The first drug court was established in Dade County, Florida, in 1989. Since that time, the number of drug courts has grown, in part because of their intuitive practicality and multifaceted appeal. Because traditional incarceration did not appear to break the cycle of drugs and crime, mandatory treatment emerged as a plausible and commonsense alternative. Drug courts appeal to the public and to policymakers on a variety of levels: (1) They offer more intensive community supervision than standard probation; (2) they treat drug cases more seriously than before, adding greater credibility to the criminal justice system; (3) they hold offenders to a higher degree of accountability for noncompliance with conditions of probation; (4) they may increase coordination between community providers, thereby reducing the duplication of services and taxpayer expense; and (5) they are intended to free other courts from processing drug cases, thereby allowing them to handle more serious felony charges (OJP Drug Court Clearinghouse and Technical Assistance Program 1998).

Because of these apparent advantages, drug courts have been embraced as an effective and efficient solution to the problems that drug-involved offenders pose for the criminal justice system. As of June 2001, drug court activity was under way in all 50 states as well as in the District of Columbia, Puerto Rico, Guam, a number of Native American tribal courts, and two federal districts. Since the first drug court appeared in 1989, approximately 697 programs have been established, with an additional 427 under development (OJP Drug Court Clearinghouse and Technical Assistance Project 2001). In addition to their growth in number, drug courts have also increased in scope. For example, drug courts have been developed in recent years to process drug-involved juveniles as well as drug-involved parents (Cooper and Bartlett 1998).

The Success of Drug Courts

Recent reviews of drug court programs have reported several positive outcomes. For example, despite the attrition typical of drug treatment, drug courts have maintained a high rate of participation in treatment. Belenko (1998) noted that one year after their enrollment into programs, approximately 60 percent of offenders continued to receive treatment.[1] The GAO (1997) reported that approximately one third of all offenders enrolled in drug courts since 1989 have "graduated," with an additional 40 percent currently receiving treatment. Among drug courts that are currently active, completion rates vary from 8 percent to 95 percent, with approximately one half of all participants graduating.

Nevertheless, effects on the outcomes of greatest interest, recidivism and drug use, are the least well documented. Many evaluations of drug courts have been conducted, but few allow confident conclusions to be drawn about their effects. The GAO (1997) found that two thirds of all drug court programs did not collect follow-up measures on drug relapse, and about half did not collect recidivism data. Among the handful of evaluations that have considered relapse and recidivism, nonequivalent comparison groups and short follow-up periods weaken the studies, and methodological differences across studies (e.g., differences in measurement, follow-up periods, etc.) make comparisons and generalizations to other programs difficult.

Despite these problems, research has demonstrated that drug use, as determined by urine tests, appears to be reduced while defendants are enrolled in drug court programs. Comparisons with groups not receiving services are also generally favorable: During programs, recidivism rates for participants are generally found to be lower than for comparison groups (Belenko 2001). Postprogram drug use and crime outcomes are less well understood. Most studies have found that recidivism rates for drug treatment clients are often lower than for nonparticipants, but the differences are usually small (OJP Drug Court Clearinghouse and Technical Assistance Program 1998). In a review of recent evaluations of adult drug courts, Belenko (2001) reported that of six studies that examined one-year postprogram recidivism, four found a reduction for drug treatment clients relative to controls. None of these studies reported postprogram drug use, and they all employed nonrandomized designs, which did not rule out selection artifacts. Belenko (2001) concluded that there is a continuing need for more rigorous and detailed studies of drug courts. A recent National Research Council report on drug policy (Committee on Data and Research for Policy on Illegal Drugs 2001) similarly concluded that the effects of drug treatment courts are largely unknown and raised questions about the complex trade-offs involved in any intervention that imposes legal sanctions for drug use.

Despite the high likelihood that drug treatment courts do help solve the problem of overcrowding due to high rates of incarceration of drug abusers, there are many gaps in our understanding of the extent of their effectiveness. Belenko (1998) concluded that evaluations would be enhanced by (1) longer follow-up periods, (2) follow-up data on outcomes other than rearrest, (3) studies of mechanisms affecting outcomes, (4) studies of more "mature" drug treatment courts, (5) cost-benefit analyses, and (6) baseline measures that describe how drug offenders have historically been processed. The study of the Baltimore City Drug Treatment Court (BDTC) addresses the first four of these needs.

The BDTC

In 1994, Baltimore, Maryland, established a drug court program for nonviolent adult offenders. The BDTC is a program for district and circuit court cases supervised by the Baltimore City Division of Parole and Probation.[2] A technical report (Gottfredson and Exum 2000) describes the eligibility criteria, screening and intake process, and major components of the program. It concludes that the BDTC is similar to the "typical" drug court in terms of its components. According to recent self-reports of operating drug courts (OJP Drug Court Clearinghouse and Technical Assistance Project 2001), 60 percent of adult drug courts involve participants both after conviction and at some other point (e.g., before trial, probation violators), as did the BDTC during the period covered by this study. The BDTC initially involved a preconviction ("diversion") track as well as a postconviction track but dropped the diversion track in December 1999. The results of an earlier survey of drug courts (Cooper 1997) showed that the typical drug court screens clients for substance use; assigns clients to treatment provided by community-based organizations; and requires at least three contacts per week with treatment providers, two urine tests per week, and weekly or biweekly contact with drug court judges in the initial phases. The typical drug court uses increased frequency of court status hearings, urinalysis, and treatment as sanctions for relapse, and 60 percent use short periods of incarceration. Finally, the typical drug court imposes incarceration sentences on defendants who are unsuccessfully terminated from the program. The BDTC is like the typical drug court on these dimensions. It is atypical in the type of population it serves (primarily African American, male heroin addicts) and the active involvement of the Division of Parole and Probation in the operation of the program. For example, the initial screening for substance use problems is conducted by this division in Baltimore, but in only 16 percent of drug courts nationwide. Also, intensive probation supervision is an element of the BDTC but is not generally found elsewhere. Other unusual aspects of the BDTC include its large size (as of spring 2001, 1,218 clients had either graduated or were currently enrolled) and the extensive screening conducted prior to program participation (e.g., the Psychopathy Checklist is used to screen out offenders who are likely to be unsuitable for the program).

Initial evaluation. In 1995, researchers at the University of Maryland's Department of Criminology and Criminal Justice, in conjunction with the Division of Parole and Probation, began an evaluation of the BDTC program (Gottfredson, Coblentz, and Harmon 1997). In all, 145 offenders assigned to the BDTC from district court, circuit court, and violation of probation hearings were compared to a control group of more than 500 offenders receiving traditional parole and probation services.

Although control group members were selected to match the BDTC treatment group as closely as possible, preexisting differences across groups were found. In general, the pretreatment offenses committed by the BDTC group were more serious than those of the comparison group.

The findings of this short-term (six-month), quasi-experimental evaluation were promising. It found that the BDTC program was successfully targeting nonviolent, drug-involved offenders and that after controlling for the preexisting differences across the treatment and control groups, participation in the BDTC program was associated with a 50 percent decrease in the odds of rearrest for a new offense. However, the researchers concluded that a more rigorous evaluation was needed to yield conclusive results. The study's authors recommended repeating the evaluation with a longer follow-up period, a larger number of study participants, and random assignment of BDTC-eligible study participants to treatment and control conditions. The results of this second study are reported here.

✄ Methods

The second study of the BDTC began in February 1997, when the University of Maryland research personnel began to randomly assign clients who were eligible for drug treatment court to be placed in the drug treatment court or in "treatment as usual." Clients came from three distinct sources: circuit court cases supervised by the Division of Parole and Probation, district court cases supervised by the Division of Parole and Probation, and less serious district court cases to be processed by the Alternative Sentencing Unit. The randomization of study participants to treatment and control conditions was added as a final step in the process of identifying drug treatment court clients. Once potential study participants were identified according to normal procedures as eligible, they were given "conditional" drug court offers. That is, they were told that they would have a 50 percent (circuit court) or 67 percent (district court)[3] chance of being assigned to the drug treatment court if they accepted the conditional offers. Those who accepted these conditions were randomly assigned to treatment and control conditions. The randomization results were given to the judge as a recommendation and were followed in most cases (because the judges had agreed to participate in the study). Randomization continued through August 1998, by which time 235 clients had been assigned randomly to one of the two conditions.

Data were collected on prior offense history, the offense that resulted in inclusion in the study, recidivism through 12 months following entry into the program, and several intake measures. These included demographic characteristics, educational and employment status, and drug use history. Data are also being collected on the nature and duration of the drug treatment experiences, interactions with the criminal justice system (e.g., meetings with parole officers, hearings, warrants, technical violations), and recidivism (arrests, dispositions, sentences, and time incarcerated) through 36 months following entry into the program. All of the data for this study are from the official records of the Maryland Department of Public Safety and Correctional Services and Baltimore Substance Abuse Services, an organization that coordinates drug treatment services in Baltimore.

This report summarizes the results of an analysis of intake data, prior criminal history records, and 12-month treatment and recidivism data for the study participants. In all analyses, participants were treated as assigned. That is, participants randomly assigned to the drug court were analyzed as members of the treatment group regardless of their actual treatment, and participants randomly assigned to the control group were analyzed as members of the control group regardless of their actual treatment. This conservative strategy was adopted to preserve the comparability of the study groups. When treatment and control participants were compared, t tests or chi-square tests were used. Because the randomization procedure blocked on the originating court and used different selection ratios for cases from the district and circuit courts, analyses were conducted to control for the originating court. One set of analyses weighted the data according to the originating court. All participants originating in the circuit court were given a weight of 1 because these participants were randomly assigned to the drug court and control conditions using a one-to-one ratio. District court cases were weighted so that control and treatment participants received weights of 1.5 and 0.75, respectively. These weight values were used (as opposed to 2 and 1) because they produced a weighted sample size equal to the unweighted sample size ($N = 235$) while creating roughly equal numbers in the drug court ($n = 118$) and control ($n = 117$) samples. A second set of analyses used an ANOVA to explicitly control for the originating court and test for interaction effects between the experimental condition (drug court or control) and the originating court (district or circuit). The results of these two sets of analyses were similar to the unweighted and uncontrolled analyses presented in the text. Instances in which the different analyses produced different results are noted.

Study Participants

The participants in this study included the 235 arrestees who were assigned randomly to receive either BDTC services or treatment as usual in the criminal justice system. The numbers of participants randomly assigned, by condition and source, were as follows: Of the 54 district court cases supervised by the Division of Parole and Probation, 32 participants were assigned to the treatment condition and 22 to the control condition. Of the 72 district court cases supervised by the Alternative Sentencing Unit, 52 participants were assigned to the treatment condition and 20 to the control condition. Of the 109 circuit court cases supervised by the Division of Parole and Probation, 55 participants were assigned to the treatment condition and 54 to the control condition. Across all sources, 139 participants were assigned to the treatment condition and 96 to the control condition. Table 9.1 shows the demographic characteristics of the study sample. These study participants were all adults with an average age of 35. Seventy-four percent were male, and 89 percent were African American.

Table 9.1   Demographic Characteristics by Experimental Status

Demographic Characteristic	Experimental Status	
	Treatment ($n = 139$)	Control ($n = 96$)
Percentage African American	89.2	89.6
Percentage male	74.1	74.0
Age as of February 1, 1997		
M	34.8	34.7
SD	7.5	7.9

NOTE: No differences between treatment and control groups were statistically significant at $p < .05$.

Table 9.2 shows information about the criminal histories of the study participants. The drug court clients had considerable criminal histories, with an average of 12 prior arrests and 5 prior convictions. For 71 percent, the arrest that made the participant eligible for inclusion in the study (henceforth called the initial arrest) involved a drug charge. Only 1 percent were charged with violent crimes in their initial arrests.

No significant differences and no meaningful differences between the experimental and control groups were found on the following variables: percentage African American; percentage male; age at initial arrest; number of prior arrests; number of prior convictions; or percentage whose initial arrests included violent, property, drug, sex, violation of probation, or "other" charges. Therefore, the groups appear similar.

Table 9.2   Offense History and Current Offense Characteristics by Experimental Status

Offense History and Current Offense Characteristic	Experimental Status	
	Treatment ($n = 139$)	Control ($n = 96$)
Prior arrests		
M	12.0 (139)	11.3 (95)
SD	8.8	7.1
Prior convictions		
M	5.3 (137)	4.6 (95)
SD	4.3	3.4
Current offense: percentage of participants with at least one		
Violence or sex charge	1.4 (138)	4.2 (96)
Property charge	21.0 (138)	18.8 (96)
Drug charge	71.0 (138)	71.9 (96)
Prostitution or solicitation charge	5.8 (138)	4.2 (96)
Violation of probation charge	2.2 (138)	4.2 (96)
Weapons charge	.7 (138)	3.1 (96)
Public order charge	10.9 (138)	4.2 (96)

NOTE: No differences between treatment and control groups were statistically significant at $p < .05$. Numbers in parentheses are the numbers of cases for which valid data were available.

Information from the initial assessment prior to drug treatment court participation for the treatment cases[4] showed that the study participants had several problems that usually accompany chronic substance abuse: Only 23 percent were employed, 47 percent had at least a high school education, and only 16 percent were married. Data from the Addiction Severity Index based on interviews conducted by assessment staff members prior to randomization and available for only 49 participants, showed that 69 percent had severe drug problems and 18 percent had severe alcohol problems. Most (87 percent) named heroin as their primary or secondary drug of choice, although 58 percent also used cocaine and 29 percent used alcohol. Seventy-two percent reported daily use of crack, cocaine, or heroin, and the majority (55 percent) had already experienced some form of drug treatment. Clearly, the population being served in the BDTC is at high risk for continued substance use and criminal behavior.

Generalizability of the study participants to the BDTC population. As noted above, the random assignment of defendants occurred between February 1997 and August 1998. It did not, however, occur continuously during that period. Randomization was halted periodically, mostly as a result of staff turnover in the central booking office or in one of the many offices that participated in the process (e.g., the Office of the Public Defender, the State's Attorney's Office, the Division of Parole and Probation). During these periods, study participants were assigned to the drug treatment court according to the procedures that existed prior to the randomization and were not included in the study. To check on the possibility that these lapses in randomization might have affected the generalizability of the results of the study sample to the population of drug treatment court clients, we obtained demographic information for all participants supervised by the Division of Parole and Probation who were assigned to the drug treatment court between the first and last randomization date but who were not randomly assigned and included in our study. These 574 participants did not differ in terms of race, gender, or age from the sample of 87 participants supervised by the Division of Parole and Probation who were included in our study.

Integrity of treatment. The randomization was upheld by the judges in most cases. Of the 139 participants randomly assigned to the treatment, we found records to indicate that 93 percent were actually assigned to the drug treatment court. Only 4 percent of the participants randomly assigned to the control condition were dealt with in the drug treatment court. Graduation records as of February 2001 indicated that 31 percent of the treatment participants and 5 percent of the control participants had graduated from the program.

Data on the level of implementation of the various drug court components suggest that the BDTC is implemented unevenly across participants. During the first year following entry into the study, 77.9 percent of treatment participants and only 14.0 percent of control participants were tested for drugs ($p < .01$). Although a similar percentage of treatment and control participants received probation supervision during the study period (68.9 percent vs. 63.5 percent, *ns*), the average number of days under probation supervision for those supervised at all was 248.7 for treatment participants and 218.7 for control participants ($p < .10$), a difference of about one month. Drug treatment court clients were far more likely to receive judicial monitoring (78.4 percent vs. 7.3 percent, $p < .01$), but the number of status hearings attended with judges was only 7.6 for those treatment participants attending at least one hearing. Table 9.3 shows the percentage of participants receiving drug treatment. In the Baltimore program, a jail-based acupuncture program is used as a sanction for relapsing participants. This program, although considered a treatment, is not a certified drug treatment program. Therefore, it is separated in the table from the other certified drug treatments. The table shows that 66.2 percent of the group randomly assigned to treatment received some form of treatment, as compared with 15.6 percent of the control group ($p < .01$). When only certified drug treatment is considered, the figures are 48.2 percent and 13.5 percent ($p < .01$). After jail-based acupuncture, the most common types of treatment were outpatient (23.7 percent) and intensive outpatient (19.4 percent). Differences between these types of treatment were statistically significant ($p < .01$). Among individuals who received treatment, the number of days in treatment and the number of treatment

Table 9.3   Drug Treatment Experiences 12 Months after Entry Into Study

Treatment Variable	Experimental Status	
	Treatment	Control
All participants		
Percentage receiving		
Any treatment	66.2*** (139)	15.6 (96)
Certified drug treatment	48.2*** (139)	13.5 (96)
Methadone maintenance	5.0 (139)	7.3 (96)
Outpatient	23.7*** (139)	3.1 (96)
Residential	7.2 (139)	4.2 (96)
Correctional	1.4 (139)	0.0 (96)
Detoxification	2.2 (139)	0.0 (96)
Intensive outpatient	19.4*** (139)	2.1 (96)
Other treatment	1.4 (139)	0.0 (96)
Jail-based acupuncture	39.6*** (139)	4.2 (96)
Participants receiving treatment		
Duration of treatment		
M	125.5 (92)	98.9 (15)
SD	101.7 (92)	97.7 (15)
Number of treatment episodes	1.7 (92)	1.3 (15)

NOTE: Numbers in parentheses are the numbers of cases for which valid data were available.

*** Difference between treatment and control groups was significant at $p < .01$.

episodes were higher for drug treatment court cases, but not significantly so. The program therefore sharply increased the drug testing, judicial monitoring, and drug treatment of drug court clients relative to controls, but the amount of these services received by the typical client was not as high as intended.

 Criminal Justice System Response to the Initial Arrest

An important motivating factor built into postconviction drug court programs is the threat of the reimposition of an initial incarceration sentence that was suspended in exchange for participation in the program. Evidence that this aspect of the court is being implemented as planned can be found in Table 9.4,

which shows data related to the handling of the initial arrest (i.e., the arrest that led to participation in the study). The table shows that drug treatment court participants were more often found guilty of at least one of the charges included in the initial arrest, with 92 percent of BDTC and 80 percent of control group study participants being found guilty.[5] This tendency for drug court participants to receive harsher verdicts is as expected. As part of their case preparation, drug court clients agree to plead guilty and accept harsher sentences with the understanding that much of this sentence will be suspended.

Table 9.4 also shows that study participants found guilty were often sentenced to some jail time. Most often, the study participants received split sentences (e.g., some combination of jail and probation). Among sentenced study participants, those assigned to the

Table 9.4   Participant Dispositions and Sentences Resulting from Initial Arrest by Source and Experimental Status

	Source							
	Parole and Probation				Alternative Sentencing Unit		Total	
	District Court		Circuit Court					
Disposition or Sentence	Treatment	Control	Treatment	Control	Treatment	Control	Treatment	Control
Disposition received, all participants[a]	$n = 29$	$n = 21$	$n = 53$	$n = 54$	$n = 41$	$n = 20$	$n = 123$	$n = 95$
Percentage of participants found guilty[b]	86.2**	57.1	100.0**	92.6	85.4	70.0	91.9**	80.0
Sentence received, guilty participants only[b]	$n = 24$	$n = 12$	$n = 53$	$n = 50$	$n = 35$	$n = 14$	$n = 112$	$n = 76$
% no incarceration and no probation	4.2	0.0	0.0	0.0	5.7	7.1	2.7	1.3
% no incarceration but some probation	12.5	0.0	0.0	2.0	20.0	0.0	8.9	1.3
% incarceration without probation	16.7	58.3	5.7	14.0	14.3	50.0	10.7	27.6
% incarceration with probation	66.7	41.7	94.3	84.0	60.0	42.9	77.7	69.7
Chi-square	7.4*		3.2		8.6**		12.6***	

a. Numbers of cases for which valid data were available.

b. Also includes participants with dispositions of probation before judgment.

* Difference between treatment and control groups was significant at $p < .10$.

** Difference between treatment and control groups was significant at $p < .05$.

*** Difference between treatment and control groups was significant at $p < .01$.

BDTC were more likely than controls to receive either no incarceration or a combination of probation and incarceration, and control study participants were more likely than those in the BDTC to receive stand-alone incarceration sentences. One surprising finding was that nearly 11 percent of the offenders randomly assigned to drug treatment court received incarceration-only sentences, given that the aims of the program are to keep offenders out of prison and provide intensive probation supervision. Closer examination revealed that more than half of these sentences were for treatment participants who had not actually been assigned to the drug court.

Table 9.5 shows the average number of days in the incarceration and probation sentences for all study participants.[6] The figures indicate that these sentences were much harsher in the circuit court than in the district court and that in both courts, most of the incarceration days were usually suspended. Because the longer sentences levied in the circuit court dominate the totals in these data, it is important to look at each source separately. In each source, BDTC study participants received harsher sentences than control study participants, both in terms of incarceration and probation sentences. But consistent with expectations, a greater proportion of the incarceration

Table 9.5   Sentence Lengths Resulting From Initial Arrest by Source and Experimental Status, All Participants

	Source							
	Parole and Probation				Alternative Sentencing Unit		Total	
	District Court		Circuit Court					
Sentence Length	Treatment (*n* = 28)	Control (*n* = 21)	Treatment (*n* = 52)	Control (*n* = 54)	Treatment (*n* = 41)	Control (*n* = 20)	Treatment (*n* = 121)	Control (*n* =95)
Assigned days	436*	221	2,564*	2,163	359	233	1,324	1,327
Suspended days	397**	178	2,431***	1,742	340	184	1,252	1,068
Assigned minus suspended days	39	43	133***	421	19	49	72***	259
Credited days	8	14	79***	140	6	7	38***	84
Remaining days to serve	31	29	54**	281	13	42	35**	175
Probation days[a]	483***	190	1,102*	927	472***	210	745*	613

NOTE: Numbers in parentheses are the numbers of cases for which valid data were available.

a. Includes probation days resulting from probation before judgment dispositions.

* Difference between treatment and control groups was significant at *p* < .10.

**Difference between treatment and control groups was significant at *p* < .05.

***Difference between treatment and control groups was significant at *p* < .01.

days were suspended for BDTC study participants. This provides evidence that the judges were acting in accord with the drug court model insofar as the handling of the initial offenses was concerned. Also, for BDTC participants more so than for controls, the portion of the incarceration sentence that was not suspended was for days that had already been served prior to the disposition date. The table shows that the actual incarceration sentences (e.g., assigned days minus suspended days) and the remaining days to be served after preadjudication days had been credited were also considerably shorter for BDTC participants than for controls. This savings in potential days behind bars was especially evident among circuit court cases, for which the typical control participant received 421 days and the typical BDTC participant received 133 days, a difference of more than nine months. These results suggest that the BDTC is

intended as an alternative to incarceration. Whether or not this intention results in fewer days actually incarcerated will be examined in a subsequent report.

 One-Year Recidivism Comparisons

Table 9.6 shows the comparisons between treatment and control participants on recidivism outcomes, including the 12-month period beginning with the date of randomization into the study. BDTC study participants were significantly (*p* < .05) less likely than control study participants to be rearrested: Forty-eight percent of BDTC participants and 64 percent of control study participants were rearrested. The BDTC resulted in an absolute reduction of 16 percent in the rate of rearrest during the year following assignment into the program.

Table 9.6   One-Year Recidivism Outcomes by Experimental Status

Recidivism Measure	Experimental Status			
	Treatment (n = 139)		Control (n = 96)	
Percentage rearrested	48.2**a	(39.8 to 56.6)	63.5	(53.7 to 73.4)
Percentage reconvicted	30.6	(22.7 to 38.5)	35.4	(25.7 to 45.2)
Average number of new arrests	.9**a	(.7 to 1.1)	1.3	(1.0 to 1.5)
Average number of new charges	1.6**	(1.2 to 2.1)	2.4	(1.7 to 3.2)
Average number of new convictions	.5	(.3 to .7)	.5	(.4 to .7)
Percentage of participants with at least one new				
Violent or sex charge	2.9***	(.1 to 5.7)	11.5	(5.0 to 18.0)
Property charge	19.6	(12.9 to 26.3)	24.0	(15.3 to 32.7)
Drug charge	28.3	(20.7 to 35.9)	37.5	(27.6 to 47.4)
Prostitution or solicitation charge	3.6	(.5 to 6.8)	3.1	(−.4 to 6.7)
Public order charge	21.6	(14.7 to 28.5)	27.1	(18.0 to 36.1)
Weapons charge	0.0a	(—)	2.1	(−.8 to 5.0)
Other charge	0.0	(—)	1.0	(−1.0 to 3.1)

NOTE: Values in parentheses are 95 percent confidence intervals. N values range from 133 to 139 for treatment participants and 95 to 96 for control participants.

a. Difference between treatment and control groups was slightly larger and significant at the $p < .01$ level when data were weighted according to originating court. In these analyses, the percentages rearrested are 46.6 and 65.0, and the numbers of arrests are 0.8 and 1.4, respectively.

** Difference between treatment and control groups was significant at $p < .05$.

*** Difference between treatment and control groups was significant at $p < .01$.

The numbers of new arrests (1.3 vs. 0.9) and charges (2.4 vs. 1.6) were also lower for treatment members than for control group members, and these differences were also statistically significant ($p < .05$). The most common type of offense for which study participants were rearrested was a drug offense, followed by public order and property offenses. Relatively few study participants were rearrested for violent offenses, but nearly four times as many control study participants as treatment study participants were arrested for violent offenses (12 percent vs. 3 percent, $p < .01$).

A breakdown of these recidivism outcomes by court shows that the overall difference in recidivism rates between the treatment and control groups was due primarily to cases heard in the circuit court: the felony cases. Among these participants, 57 percent of the controls and 32 percent of the treatment participants were

rearrested in the first year. This difference was statistically significant ($p < .01$).

The recidivism comparisons are conservative because they do not control for the opportunity to reoffend. Significantly more controls than treatment study participants were assigned to additional days behind bars following the dispositions for the offenses that got them into the study, and control study participants were given longer incarceration sentences. The disposition data suggest, then, that a higher percentage of drug treatment court participants than controls were "on the street" and hence had greater opportunities to reoffend. Data on actual days served are not yet available, but when the number of days sentenced to incarceration is taken into consideration, the number of arrests per day free in the community during the 12 months following randomization (e.g., 365–Days

Sentenced to Incarceration–Suspended Days) is nearly three times greater for controls than for treatment participants.[7] This difference was statistically significant ($p < .05$).

 Limitations

Many of the limitations of the study are related to the preliminary nature of the findings. This report covers the first year of a three-year study. Data on additional outcomes and intervening mechanisms that will eventually be available to provide a more detailed analysis of the BDTC are not yet available. Currently under way is an extension of the original study that tracks and interviews the 235 study participants to obtain client perceptions of how the drug treatment court experience affected their lives. This extension will (1) augment the existing official records on criminal activity, substance abuse treatment experiences, and criminal justice involvement with self-reports of the same; (2) assess the effectiveness of the BDTC in improving the following outcomes: criminal activity and substance use (according to client self-reports), welfare status, employment status, educational level, mental health, physical health, and family and social relationships; and (3) measure the relative importance of the different mechanisms through which drug treatment courts might work. These include increased supervision and monitoring (e.g., through intensive supervision, frequent hearings, and drug testing), increased personal accountability for behavior and empowerment (e.g., through graduated sanctions), drug treatment and other services (employment, legal, medical, psychological), and perceptions of procedural justice. Subsequent reports will also extend the follow-up period to cover the three-year period following sentencing.

A limitation not related to the preliminary nature of the study is that the results reported here pertain to BDTC clients assigned to the program between February 1997 and August 1998. During this time, program administrators were concerned about keeping the drug treatment court slots filled to capacity. This is in stark contrast to the current situation, which according to newspaper accounts (Francke and Dresser 2000) is one of overcrowding, waiting lists, and closing down the intake of newly referred cases because the program cannot effectively handle all of the cases currently assigned to it. The positive results obtained during the period examined in this study may not be achieved in a program that has higher caseloads and fewer treatment slots available.

 Conclusion and Discussion

The BDTC set out to provide drug treatment to drug-involved, nonviolent offenders; increase the swiftness and certainty of punishment for continued offending behavior; and improve perceptions of procedural justice. The program was intended also to provide these services in the community as opposed to a secure setting, therefore saving criminal justice dollars. The results of the first year following random assignment to the program show that the program succeeded at targeting high-rate, drug-involved offenders at high risk for continued offending. The study also shows that the mean nonsuspended incarceration sentence for control study participants is 187 days longer than for drug court participants. This overall difference in days sentenced behind bars is statistically significant and practically meaningful. The overall difference masks an even larger difference among the more serious cases processed in the circuit court. In this court, the difference in sentenced days that are not suspended is 288, more than nine months. Clearly, the program is used as an alternative to incarceration, particularly for the most serious cases. Data on actual time served are currently being analyzed and will be included in a subsequent report.

Other aspects of program implementation suggest that the program was implemented unevenly across the intended population. Sixty-six percent of the group randomly assigned to treatment received some form of treatment, 48 percent received certified drug treatment, 84 percent judicial monitoring, 78 percent drug testing, and 69 percent intensive supervision. The level of services received was not as high as anticipated, however. Among clients receiving any judicial monitoring in the form of status hearings, the typical client attended only eight hearings. Among those who received drug treatment, the typical participant received 125 days.

BDTC study participants received harsher sentences than control study participants, but a greater proportion of the incarceration days were suspended for BDTC study participants. This suggests that the judges are manipulating the severity of the punishment for potential subsequent offenses, because this suspended sentence can be reimposed when a client recidivates. Whether or not swiftness and certainty are also manipulated remains to be examined. Although less than ideal implementation of the critical elements undoubtedly dilutes the effects of the drug court intervention, it also creates heterogeneity that might be useful for understanding the relative influence of the different intervening mechanisms hypothesized to alter drug use and crime. Examination of these mechanisms—treatment, deterrence, and perceptions of procedural justice—are the subject of a subsequent report on the BDTC.

Research on drug treatment courts is still in its early stages. Beyond the obvious value of the information provided by this study to the Maryland criminal justice community, this study will add one additional data point for future studies that seek to learn about the critical components of drug treatment courts. The Baltimore experience is in some ways similar to and in other ways dissimilar from the typical drug treatment court in the nation. It is not possible in the current study to determine which of the many contextual factors surrounding the Baltimore experience contribute to its success. The task of future reviews and meta-analyses is to use this and other local studies to generalize knowledge about drug treatment courts.

Notes

1. The remainder of study participants were either terminated from programs or withdrew voluntarily, or their status was "unknown."

2. District court cases supervised by the city's Alternative Sentencing Unit (which presides over less serious cases) were also eligible for the program during the first several years of program operation, but this unit was disbanded in December 1999.

3. Study participants were randomly assigned at ratios of one treatment to one control for circuit court cases and two treatment to one control for district court cases. This was done at the

request of the district court judge, who was concerned that all drug treatment court slots might not be filled if we kept a one-to-one ratio.

4. Intake data were not available for the study participants who entered the BDTC though the Alternative Sentencing Unit, and records could not be located for most of the control cases. Only the 87 treatment cases supervised by the Division of Parole and Probation (31 from district court and 56 from circuit court) are included in this discussion.

5. Note that the disposition of the initial arrest could not be located for 25 percent of the drug treatment court participants supervised by the Alternative Sentencing Unit. This is consistent with the diversionary nature of the program: The Alternative Sentencing Unit participants were diverted from normal processing and had their charges dropped on successful completion of the program.

6. These figures were also examined for only guilty participants. The pattern of results was similar.

7. This analysis excludes 15 controls and 3 treatment participants who were incarcerated for the entire year.

References

Belenko, S. 1998. "Research on Drug Courts: A Critical Review." *National Drug Court Institute Review* 1:1–42.

——. 2001. *Research on Drug Courts: A Critical Review 2001 Update.* New York: The National Center on Addiction and Substance Abuse at Columbia University.

Committee on Data and Research for Policy on Illegal Drugs. 2001. *Informing America's Policy on Illegal Drugs: What We Don't Know Keeps Hurting Us.* Washington, DC: National Academy Press.

Cooper, Caroline S. 1997. *1997 Drug Court Survey Report: Executive Summary.* Retrieved from http://www.american.edu/academic.depts/spa/justice/publications/execl.htm

Cooper, Caroline S. and Shanie Bartlett. 1998. *Juvenile and Family Drug Courts: Profile of Program Characteristics and Implementation Issues* (NCJ 171142). Washington, DC: U.S. Department of Justice, Office of Justice Programs, Drug Courts Program Office.

Francke, Caitlin and Michael Dresser. 2000. "Drug Court Turns Away Admissions." *The Baltimore Sun,* January 20, p. 1B.

Gottfredson, D. C., K. Coblentz, and M. A. Harmon. 1997. "A Short-Term Outcome Evaluation of the Baltimore City Drug Treatment Court Program." *Perspectives,* Winter: 33–38.

Gottfredson, D. C. and M. L. Exum. 2001. "The Baltimore City Drug Treatment Court: One-Year Results from a Randomized Study." Unpublished technical report.

The National Center on Addiction and Substance Abuse at Columbia University. 1998. *Behind Bars: Substance Abuse and America's Prison Population.* New York: The National Center on Addiction and Substance Abuse at Columbia University.

National Institute of Justice. 2000.*1999 Annual Report on Adult and Juvenile Arrestees* (NCJ 181426). Washington, DC: U.S. Department of Justice, Office of Justice Programs, National Institute of Justice.

OJP Drug Court Clearinghouse and Technical Assistance Project. 1998. *Looking at a Decade of Drug Courts* (NCJ 171140). Washington, DC: U.S. Department of Justice, Office of Justice Programs, Drug Courts Program Office.

———. 2001. *Drug Court Activity Update: Summary Information on All Programs and Detailed Information on Adult Drug Courts.* Retrieved from http://www.american.edu/acadernic.depts/spa/justice/publications/allcourtactivity.pdf

U.S. General Accounting Office. 1997. *Drug Courts: An Overview of Growth, Characteristics, and Results* (GGD-97-106). Washington, DC: U.S. General Accounting Office.

DISCUSSION QUESTIONS

1. What are the primary differences in drug courts?

2. What are the goals of the Baltimore City Drug Treatment Court (BCDTC)? How does this drug court differ from the typical drug treatment court? How do its clients differ from those found in the typical drug court?

3. Why did the research design used in this study call for random assignment of eligible defendants to either the drug treatment court or traditional adjudication?

4. What did the authors find when they compared recidivism rates for the two groups of defendants (see Table 9.6)?

5. Based on the results reported by the authors, is the BCDTC a success?

READING

The implementation of domestic violence courts has proceeded with little, if any, evidence regarding their effectiveness in holding offenders accountable and reducing recidivism. Moreover, most of the research that does exist focuses on courts in urban areas. The authors of this study focus on a domestic violence court in a rural county: Lexington County, South Carolina. All nonfelony battery cases of domestic violence in Lexington County are referred to the Criminal Domestic Violence Court; the goals of the court, according to Gover and her coauthors, are "to improve investigations and prosecution of domestic violence cases through increased resources, improved collaboration, and a progressive new court approach . . . [and] to improve victim safety by holding defendants accountable for their actions and reducing recidivism." The purpose of this study was to evaluate the effectiveness of the court in meeting these goals.

AUTHORS' NOTE: Support for this research was provided by the National Institute of Justice, Office of Justice Programs, U.S. Department of Justice, to the University of South Carolina (Project #2000-WT-VX-0015). Points of view in this document are those of the authors and do not necessarily represent the official position of the Department of Justice.

SOURCE: "Combating Domestic Violence: Findings from an Evaluation of a Local Domestic Violence Court," by Angela R. Gover, John M. MacDonald and Geoffrey P. Alpert in *Criminology and Public Policy*, vol. 3, pp. 109-132, 2003. Reprinted by permission of the American Society of Criminology.

Combating Domestic Violence

Findings From an Evaluation of a Local Domestic Violence Court

Angela R. Gover, John M. MacDonald, and Geoffrey P. Alpert

Over the past decade, there has been a growing awareness that domestic violence is a serious social problem. Much of this attention can be credited to increased efforts to collect empirical data on this issue. According to the National Violence Against Women (NVAW) Survey, for example, approximately 4.5 million women in the United States were physically assaulted by their intimate partners during the 12 months preceding the survey (Tjaden and Thoennes, 2000). In addition, over a half million women in the United States were stalked by an intimate partner and 322,230 women were raped by an intimate partner (Tjaden and Thoennes, 2000).

In addition to the increased awareness of domestic violence, during the past decade, there have been significant changes in the criminal justice system's response to domestic violence (Buzawa and Buzawa, 1996; Clark et al., 1996; Dobash and Dobash, 1992; Epstein, 1999; Ptacek, 1999). Although most attention has been placed on law enforcement's response to domestic violence (e.g., mandatory arrest laws; Sherman, 1992), the criminal court has also experienced an increase in processing domestic violence cases over the past decade (Bell and Goodman, 2001). Between 1989 and 1998, for example, domestic relations cases in state courts across the United States grew by 178% (Ostrom and Kauder, 1999). In response to the growing awareness of domestic violence as a serious social problem and rising caseloads, judicial systems have been searching for innovative methods to deal with domestic violence cases. Traditionally, domestic violence cases have been handled in various criminal and civil courts. Recently, specialized domestic violence courts have emerged as a more effective means to combat intimate partner violence (Belknap and Graham, 2000; Dawson and Dinovitzer, 2001; Fritzler and Simon, 2000; Goldkamp et al., 1996; Karan et al., 1999; Levey et al., 2001; Weber, 2000). Domestic violence courts attempt to

improve the judiciary's response to this issue by increasing coordination among criminal justice and social service agencies, holding defendants accountable, and to address properly the needs of victims. This type of specialized court adopts a therapeutic jurisprudence approach to courtroom justice (Fritzler and Simon, 2000; Rottman and Casey, 1999). In essence, the therapeutic jurisprudence approach focuses on offender accountability and victim safety, and it requires those who are making decisions to consider the potential benefits and consequences of their decisions on those involved (Fritzler and Simon, 2000). Most experts agree that a multi-agency approach to domestic violence is the most appropriate strategy (Hofford, 1991).

Domestic Violence Courts

Domestic violence courts, similar to other specialized courts (i.e., drug courts, juvenile courts, family courts), emphasize the need for treating domestic violence with special attention and separating and distinguishing the process from the traditional criminal court process (Karan et al., 1999; Keilitz, 2000). According to a survey conducted by the National Center for State Courts in 1998, more than 200 courts throughout the United States were providing specialized processing practices for domestic violence cases, such as specialized intake centers, separate court calendars. and specific domestic violence units (Karan et al., 1999). More recent estimates indicate that over 300 courts have recognized the need for special attention to domestic violence cases by incorporating specialized processing and structure within existing judicial systems (Keilitz, 2000; Levey et al., 2001).

Little empirical evidence, however, has been collected to evaluate the effectiveness of specific domestic violence courts and their processes (Buzawa et al., 1998). Despite the lack of empirical studies, numbers of specialized domestic violence courts have been increasing (Karan et al., 1999). Although many jurisdictions have implemented domestic violence courts, there is no standardized definition that directs judicial practices within these courts (Weber, 2000). There are only a few published process or outcome evaluation studies of domestic violence courts that can serve as guides for local jurisdictions interested in implementing this type of specialized court (see Goldkamp et al., 1996).

One of the few published studies of domestic violence courts involves a court established in 1993 in Miami, Florida (Karan et al., 1999). This court sought to improve judicial response through the establishment of specialized intake units, dedicated calendars, specialized judges, and a fully integrated domestic violence court. According to a process evaluation of the domestic violence court, misdemeanor cases had a 37% lower dismissal rate compared with common practices prior to the implementation of the court (Goldkamp et al., 1996). In addition, this study found 40% to 50% of the offenders who were processed by the domestic violence court were under the influence of alcohol or drugs at the time of the domestic violence incident. The integrated batterer substance abuse treatment program was found to be successful in enrolling offenders in the treatment and retaining participants in the program compared with the control group. Further, offenders who participated in the integrated treatment program reoffended against the same victims at a lower rate compared with control offenders (6% versus 14%; Goldkamp et al., 1996).

Other research has been published on specialized domestic violence courts developed in Washington, D.C.; Clark County; Vancouver, Canada; and Leeds, England that also incorporated a multi-agency approach with input from law enforcement, social services, victim support services, and probation services (Fritzler and Simon, 2000; Levey et al., 2001; Walsh, 2001). The intention of these courts was to structure offenders' sentences toward a rehabilitative approach, as opposed to a custodial sentence, so that offenders would be able to attend community-based treatment programs focused on the cause and the control of their violent behavior. All of these courts focused on increasing collaboration from several agencies working together to deliver a more effective response to issues of family violence.

In addition, treatment-focused domestic violence courts anticipate that victims will have a higher likelihood of reporting domestic violence incidences given the rehabilitative philosophy (Walsh, 2001).

A limited amount of research suggests that increased collaborative efforts between agencies that increase victim participation and hold offenders accountable can lead to reductions in domestic violence recidivism (Gamache et al., 1988; Harrell, 1991; Tolman and Weiz, 1995). According to a recidivism analysis of offenders who were convicted of misdemeanor domestic violence in Hamilton County, Ohio, offenders who received more severe sentences were less likely to recidivate compared with offenders who received less severe sentences one year after sentencing (Thistlewaite et al., 1998). The findings from this study indicated that recidivism reduction was significantly related to sentence severity in misdemeanor domestic violence cases (Thistlewaite et al., 1998). Few other studies, however, exist that explicitly examine the impact of specialized domestic violence courts in holding offenders accountable and reducing recidivism. As a result, it is unclear whether designing specialized domestic violence courts provides any improvement over traditional methods of adjudicating domestic violence cases.

Most research on this topic examines specialized domestic violence courts located in urban settings. In general, less research is devoted to the issues of domestic violence in rural settings and appropriate programs for addressing the needs of battered women. Yet research indicates that there are not dramatic differences in the rates of domestic violence between urban and rural settings (Rennison, 2000). Domestic violence receives less attention in rural areas compared with urban areas because there is a lack of accessible social and health care services, the population is more dispersed and isolated, law enforcement has to service large geographic areas with limited resources, and cultural beliefs regarding gender roles and family violence inhibit victims from seeking services (Orchowsky, 1998). As a result of the lack of attention to issues of domestic violence in rural settings, less evidence is available from which criminal justice agencies located in rural areas can use to design appropriate interventions for combating domestic violence.

Domestic Violence in Lexington County

Lexington County, South Carolina is a rural county located in the midlands region of the state. The population of Lexington County is approximately 220,000, and 84% of the residents are white. Most of the county is geographically dispersed in small rural communities. The county is predominately working class, and the per capita income is approximately $22,000 a year (Bureau of Census, 2000). Throughout the state of South Carolina, there has been a growing concern with issues related to domestic violence. In 1996, 54,602 domestic violence reports were filed in South Carolina, a 34.8% increase from 1992 (Uniform Crime Reports, 1998). During this same year in South Carolina, 76% of female homicide victims (who knew their assailants) were murdered by their husbands, common-law husbands, ex-husbands, or boyfriends, compared with 56% nationally (Violence Policy Center, 2000), Domestic violence is of particular concern to the Lexington County Sheriff's Department, because this county has seen a recent insurgence of domestic violence abuse incidents. Their records indicated a dramatic growth in domestic violence between 1997 and 1998. However, using their current staffing resources, the Lexington County Sheriff's Department had to assign all of the criminal domestic violence cases to the same three investigators who were responsible for robbery, aggravated assault and battery, homicide, and criminal sexual conduct investigations. Not surprisingly, because of the shortage of resources, many domestic violence cases were not getting the attention for a complete investigation and eventual prosecution.

In addition, once a domestic violence case was processed to court, it was historically assigned to one of the eight Lexington County magistrate's courts. Magistrate courts in the state of South Carolina handle all non-felony-related cases (such as traffic cases) and can assign a maximum penalty of 30 days in jail or a $1,000 fine. Because the magistrate courts process all misdemeanor cases, individual domestic violence cases typically did not get the proper amount of attention they needed. The eight magistrate's courts also do not maintain a centralized database for tracking domestic violence defendants throughout the county. In other words, as a result of a lack of resources within the magistrate courts, many domestic violence cases were either dismissed or assigned minor fines. It was believed that the lack of resources and attention was perpetuating a continued trend of inattention to domestic violence in Lexington County.

 ## The Lexington County Specialized Domestic Violence Court

To address shortcomings in both the investigation and prosecution of criminal domestic violence cases, the Lexington County Sheriff's Department applied for and received a Violence Against Women Act (VAWA) grant to establish a separate Criminal Domestic Violence Court within the Lexington County magistrate court system. All non-felony battery cases of domestic violence in Lexington County are referred to this specialized court. The separate domestic violence court was designed to hold perpetrators of domestic violence accountable through increasing fines and time spent in jail, as well as placing a strong emphasis on mandatory batterer treatment.

The Domestic Violence Court in Lexington County was established in November 1999. Since the inception of the court, all non-felony battery cases of domestic violence cases in Lexington County have been processed by the Criminal Domestic Violence Court. To improve the criminal justice system's response to this social problem, the Lexington County Sheriff's Office established a multi-agency collaborative approach to preceding domestic violence cases. For example, the Sheriff's Office appointed two full-time investigators and a full-time prosecutor to work as a team on domestic violence cases. In addition, the Sheriff's Office hired a full-time victims advocate to assist domestic violence victims referred to the court. Also, a court administrator was hired to handle the administrative tasks involved in running a separate court docket for domestic violence cases. The Lexington County Department of Mental Health also dedicated two mental health counselors to diagnose and assign proper treatment programs for perpetrators of domestic violence. In addition, a legal advocate from a local domestic violence shelter was also dedicated to the court and was present in each court session. Together, the Lexington County Criminal Domestic Violence Court has been operating as a multi-agency collaborative effort involving Sheriff's investigators, a full-time prosecutor, court officials, local domestic violence shelter services, and the Department of Mental Health. The basic court intervention is displayed in Figure 9.1. Overall, the broad goal of the Lexington County Criminal Domestic Violence Court is to improve investigations and prosecution of domestic violence cases through increased resources, improved collaboration, and a progressive new court approach. Additionally, the goal of this specialized court is to improve victim safety by holding defendants accountable for their actions and reducing recidivism.

The court attempted to achieve these goals by focusing its efforts of coordination and cooperation among agencies responding to domestic violence. This was accomplished by having all key representatives from agencies dealing with the problem of domestic violence present during the court proceedings, including law enforcement, prosecution, mental health, victims' services, and shelter services. Through the increased knowledge and skills of domestic violence associated with a dedicated full-time prosecutor and investigators who only handle domestic violence cases, the court attempted to improve the investigation and prosecution of domestic violence cases. The focus of the court was a therapeutic model of jurisprudence to processing domestic violence cases. Specifically, the prosecutor, investigators, judges, advocates, and mental health officials worked together in a coordinated approach that placed the primary emphasis on treatment options for defendants convicted of domestic violence offenses.

Typically, this was accomplished through suspending jail sentences in lieu of the successful completion of a 26-week group-based cognitive therapy program for domestic violence batterers. These referrals were accompanied by a strict weekly follow-up on defendants' progress in the treatment program. If defendants failed to comply with their treatment conditions, then a bench warrant would be issued by a judge for their arrest and

Figure 9.1   The CDV Court Intervention Strategy

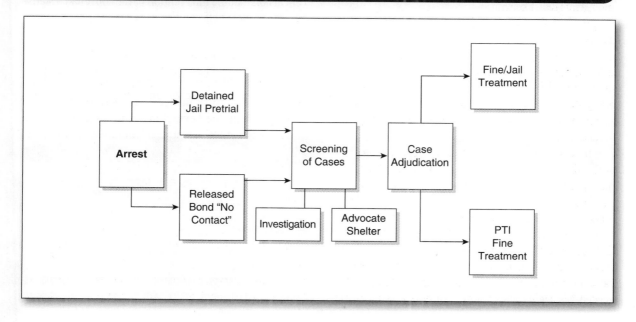

their suspended jail sentence would be imposed. The Lexington County Criminal Domestic Violence Court emphasized the idea that criminal justice mental health professionals must work together to attack the social problem of domestic violence. Since the domestic violence court began operating, over 2,500 court cases have been processed. The federal funding for court expired in June 2002. Since the expiration of the federal grant, the Lexington County government has absorbed the operational costs of the court.

Methodology

The current study evaluates the effectiveness of the misdemeanor criminal domestic violence court in Lexington County, South Carolina. Two methods of quantitative analysis were used to examine the overall impact of the court on case outcomes and community safety. First, to examine the general impact of the Criminal Domestic Violence Court (CDVC) on domestic violence in Lexington County, a time series intervention analysis was used. Second, a recidivism analysis was conducted that examined the impact of the domestic violence court on individual case outcomes. A sample of cases processed in the CDVC were compared with a historical sample of cases processed in the traditional magistrate court setting.

Time Series Analysis

The time series intervention analysis examined the monthly frequency of criminal domestic violence for the years 1997 through 2001 (60 months). Criminal domestic

violence cases were compared for the 34 months before the establishment of the CDVC (January 1997 to October 1999) to the first 26 months after the courts implementation (November 1999 to December 2001). Prior to conducting the intervention analysis, a simple before-after comparison of the average monthly number of arrests was conducted. The trends in arrests for domestic violence were compared with the trends in simple assault and aggravated assault. The results displayed in Table 9.7 indicate a significantly higher number of average monthly domestic violence arrests after the establishment of the CDVC. Specifically, the average monthly number of arrests for domestic violence was approximately 55 in the pre-court period compared with 61 in the post-court period ($t = -2.55$; $p < 0.05$). In contrast, there were no changes in simple assault. The average monthly number of arrests for simple assault was roughly 21 before and after the court was established. Aggravated assaults did, however, decrease in the post-court period. The average monthly number of aggravated assaults pre-court was approximately 14 compared with 12 in the post-court period ($t = 1.89$; $p < 0.05$—one tailed). A simple comparison of the average arrest numbers between time periods, however, cannot determine if a true causal relationship exists. It is possible, for example. that a positive trend in domestic violence arrests (autocorrelation) would lead to the conclusion that the intervention of the court had a statistically significant effect when in fact it had not.

ARIMA Intervention

To obtain a more rigorous estimate of the effects of the CDVC on domestic violence in Lexington County,

Table 9.7   Comparison of Monthly Arrests Before and After CDVC ($N = 384$)

Average Monthly Arrests	Pre-CDVC ($n = 34$)	Post-CDVC ($n = 26$)	t-test
Domestic Violence	55.35	60.92	−2.55*
Simple Assault	21.58	21.84	−.15
Aggravated Assault	14.14	11.76	1.89

*Statistically significant change ($p < .05$).

the data were analyzed as a set of interrupted time-series experiments. The time series analysis involved a quasi-experimental design that rules out a number of rival hypotheses (Cook and Campbell, 1979). This method of analysis has been used in many other areas of policy research, such as drunk-driving crackdowns and changes in firearms policies (Loftin and McDowall, 1984; McDowall et al., 1992), and it is one of the strongest quasi-experimental methods for examining the impact of policy interventions (Campbell and Stanley, 1966).

To reduce the chance of historical threats, such as law enforcement officers reclassifying simple assault and aggravated assaults between intimates as criminal domestic violence cases, a control series was included in the Analysis. Domestic violence arrests were compared with simple and aggravated assault arrests. If the experimental series of domestic violence arrests increased or decreased in the post-court period while the control series remained stable, it would be possible to conclude that the establishment of the court had an effect. If all three series increased or decreased, this would lead to the conclusion that the introduction of the court was confounded with history. Although this method is less superior to a no-treatment comparison group for ruling out alternative explanations, it does provide a defensible method for analyzing the impact of the domestic violence court (see Loftin and McDowall, 1984). Because Lexington County is different from other neighboring counties in terms of its demographic make-up and crime rates, it was not possible to find a no-treatment comparison group. The time series for domestic violence, simple assault, and aggravated assault arrests are displayed in Figure 9.2.

Figure 9.2   Monthly Arrest Numbers

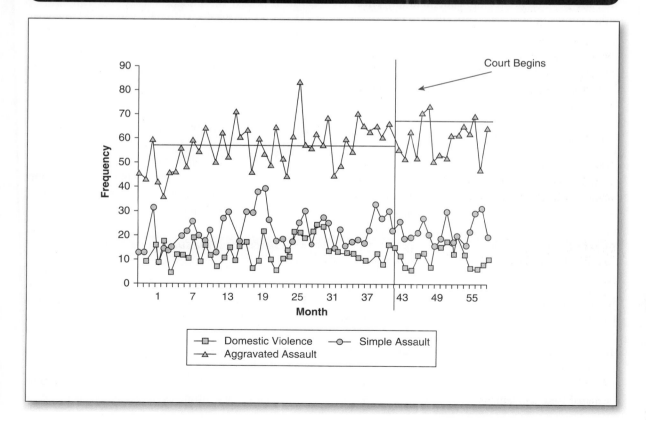

Findings

Now that the time series process for all three series have been properly identified, the effects of the CDVC on domestic violence, simple assault, and aggravated assault were estimated by adding the intervention effect. A change in the level of the series (domestic violence, simple assault, aggravated assault) after the inception of the CDVC should show up in the estimates of the ARIMA intervention model if the court had an effect.

The main conclusion from the analysis is that the introduction of the criminal domestic violence court in Lexington County had a statistically significant positive effect on the number of domestic violence arrests. The coefficient interpretation suggests that on average, the court increased domestic violence arrests by 5.57 arrests per month. This translates into a 10% increase in the average monthly number of domestic violence arrests. In contrast, there is little evidence that the introduction of the court had any effect on either simple or aggravated assault arrests.

These results indicate that the establishment of the domestic violence court had a significant effect on the increase in the number of domestic violence arrests in Lexington County over time. These findings lead to the conclusion that the establishment of a centralized court for processing domestic violence cases increased the responsiveness of law enforcement to this crime. The fact that the series for simple assault and aggravated assault did not significantly change for the establishment of the court suggests that the increase in domestic violence arrests was not an artifact of charge displacement. Therefore, there is clear and convincing evidence that the court increased the response to domestic violence in Lexington County.

Recidivism

In an effort to examine the impact of the Lexington County CDVC on individual case outcomes, a recidivism analysis was performed on a random sample of 400 criminal domestic violence cases. A simple random sample of 200 cases was drawn from the Lexington County Sheriff's Department's arrest database that occurred between January 1997 and June 1999. This sample represented the historical comparison group of cases that were processed through traditional magistrate courts in Lexington County prior to the establishment of the CDVC. This sample period was chosen to provide the closest time comparison and to ensure that cases were disposed of before the inception of the CDVC. The experimental group comprised a simple random sample of 200 domestic violence arrest cases that occurred between December 1999 and December 2000 and were processed through the CDVC. The overall recidivism analysis, therefore, included a final sample of 400 cases (200 control and 200 treatment).

Correlates

From the hard copies of the case files, research staff coded information on each domestic violence case. The following is a list of information that was included: (1) offender's race, (2) offender's age, (3) offender's gender, (4) offender's employment status, (5) time spent in jail by the offender after arrest, (6) the offender's domestic violence criminal history, (7) number of charges pending at the time of the arrest, and (8) diversion or court disposition. Race of the offender was dummy coded "1" if the suspect was Black. Gender of the offender was dummy coded "1" if the offender was female. Employment status was dummy coded "1" if the offender was unemployed. Domestic violence criminal history represented the number of prior arrests for domestic violence. Number of charges pending represented the defendant's number of charges on the given domestic violence case. Diversion or court disposition was dummy coded "1" if the defendant was diverted from court into a pretrial intervention program.

Outcome Measure

Each case was followed for 18 months after their initial domestic violence arrest. Each case was censored at exactly 551 days post-arrest. This procedure ensured that each case had exactly the same exposure time (Schmidt and Witte, 1988). Post-disposition rearrest data for domestic violence offenses were then collected through the examination of arrest records. Rearrests for domestic violence, simple assaults, or aggravated assaults involving intimates were included as failures.

Table 9.8   Sample Comparison of Baseline Data (N = 386)

Characteristic	Pre-CDVC (*n* = 189)	SD	CDVC (*n* = 197)	SD	*t*-test
African-American	26.9%		25.3%		
Female defendant	12.7%		13.2%		
Mean days in jail pretrial	4.14	11.19	5.00	20.33	
Mean age of offender	33.5	8.89	33.62	9.91	
Employed	82.5%		80.8%		
Pretrial Diversion	57.1%		56.3%		
Mean number of charges	1.19	.53	1.20	.73	
Mean prior domestic	.34	.79	.48	.97	
Recidivism	19.0%		11.6%		2.00

* Statistically significant difference ($p < .05$).

Sample Characteristics

Table 9.8 presents descriptive-level data for the historical control group and the domestic violence court sample. Fourteen cases were dropped from the analysis because they involved domestic violence against a minor and were therefore processed by the county's family court. The final sample resulted in 386 cases. In general, the two samples resembled each other. No differences were found between the pre-CDVC and the CDVC samples on age, race, gender, employment status, number of days in jail pretrial, number of charges, number of prior domestic violence arrests, and pretrial intervention. In both samples, the average age of an offender was approximately 34 years old and roughly 20% of the offenders were unemployed. Few offenders had prior domestic violence arrests. Together these descriptive data indicate that the control and treatment groups closely resembled each other in terms of personal background factors. The only statistically significant difference between the two samples was for domestic violence recidivism rates. In terms of recidivism, 19% of the pre-CDVC sample were rearrested for a domestic violence offense during the follow-up period compared with only 11.6% of the CDVC sample ($r = 2.00$; $p < .05$). Although the recidivism

rate for both groups was relatively low, the CDVC sample had a significantly lower rate of recidivism than did the pre-CDVC sample.

To more accurately isolate the effects of the domestic violence court on recidivism for domestic violence offenses, a logistic regression model was used. This model estimates the impact of the court, controlling for prior domestic violence arrests, number of charges, pretrial diversion, employment status, race, gender, and the number of days in jail pre-trial. The findings indicate that only three variables are significant predictors of recidivism. Defendants with a greater number of prior domestic violence arrests are significantly more likely to recidivate, holding all other factors constant. The findings indicate that an additional prior domestic violence arrest increased the odds of recidivism by 46%. Those with a greater number of charges filed were also significantly more likely to recidivate. Specifically, an additional charge increased the odds of recidivism by 77%. In contrast defendants who were processed by the domestic violence court were significantly less likely to recidivate. Being processed through the domestic violence court decreased the odds of recidivism by 50%. Overall, the results from the logistic regression model provide additional strong evidence for the effectiveness of the court in reducing recidivism for domestic violence.

To provide a more meaningful interpretation of these results the estimates were converted into predicted probabilities. This method allows one to examine the effects of isolated factors, which holds other variables constant at their mean values (Long, 1997). These probabilities provide a profile of the effect of the specialized domestic violence court on recidivism, whereas all other characteristics of an offender are held constant at their average levels. In other words, the predicted probabilities of a hypothetical offender who was processed through the domestic violence court were compared with those of a hypothetical offender from the historical control group who was average on all other factors. The results from a series of predicted probabilities are displayed in Figures 9.3 to 9.5. The predicted probability of being rearrested for domestic violence was 18% for the comparison group and 10% for the CDVC group. Additionally, the predicted probability of recidivism for the CDVC sample and the comparison group were examined for varying levels of prior domestic violence arrests and a number of charges. The predicted probability for recidivism was, for instance, 16% for those with no prior arrests for domestic violence in the comparison group and 9% for those in the CDVC group. For those with one prior arrest for domestic violence, there was a 22% chance of recidivism for the comparison group versus only 12% in the CDVC group. In terms of number of charges, the predicted probability of recidivism for those with two pending charges was 26% for the comparison group and only 15% for the CDVC group.

In addition to the probability of being rearrested during the 18-month follow-up period, the predictors of the time (number of days) until rearrest were analyzed. The model shows a significant reduction in the

Figure 9.3   Predicted Difference Between Samples on Recidivism, All Other Variables Held at Mean Values

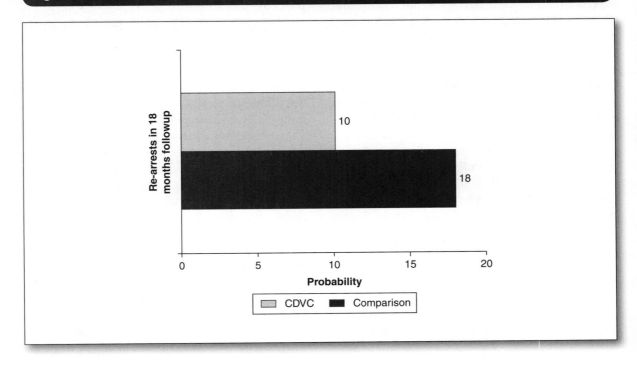

Figure 9.4   Predicted Difference Between Samples by Number of Prior Domestic Violence Arrests, All Other Variables Held at Mean Values

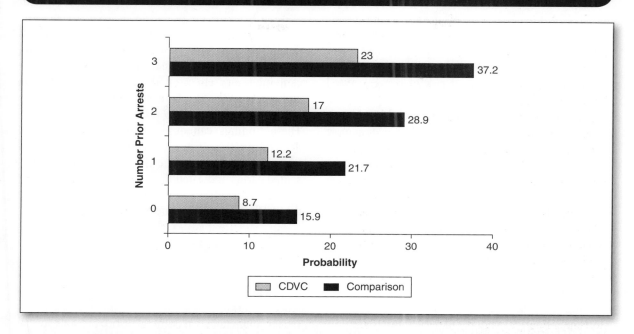

Figure 9.5   Predicted Difference Between Samples by Number of Charges, All Other Variables Held at Mean Values

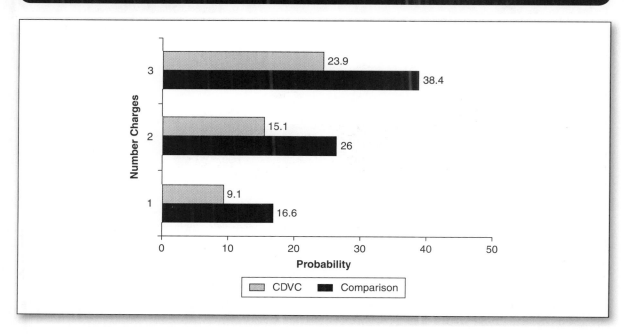

time to rearrest for domestic violence for the CDVC sample compared with the historical comparison group. Specifically, these findings indicate that those in the CDVC group have 53% risk for time to failure compared with those in the historical comparison group. The findings also indicate that offenders with prior domestic violence arrests and a greater number of charges were at an increased risk of being arrested earlier over time.

To provide a graphical depiction of this relationship, the probability of survival for the CDVC sample and the comparison group are plotted in Figure 9.6. It is evident from this graph that the probability of staying arrest free over time is greater for those processed in the CDVC. These findings suggest that in addition to lowering the overall likelihood that domestic violence offenders will be rearrested in the 18-month follow-up period, a longer period of time passed before defendants in the CDVC group were rearrested for domestic violence compared with offenders in the control group.

Together, the findings from the logistic regression model and the predicted probabilities indicate that being processed through the CDVC significantly reduced the likelihood that an individual would be rearrested for a domestic violence offense over an 18-month follow-up period. This effect is not the result of different types of offenders being processed during the two time periods. Therefore, it appears from the available data that the CDVC has a significant inhibitory effect on the likelihood of rearrest compared with the traditional magistrate court approach to processing domestic violence cases. These findings cannot be explained by a general decrease in the stringency of enforcement between the two time periods. The time series analysis presented earlier indicated that the general enforcement of criminal domestic violence increased significantly during the post-CDVC time period.

 ## Discussion

Most domestic violence court evaluations have been conducted in urban settings, although domestic violence is certainly not limited to these areas. Policy makers often note that criminal justice presents special

Figure 9.6 Days Until Re-arrest for Domestic Violence

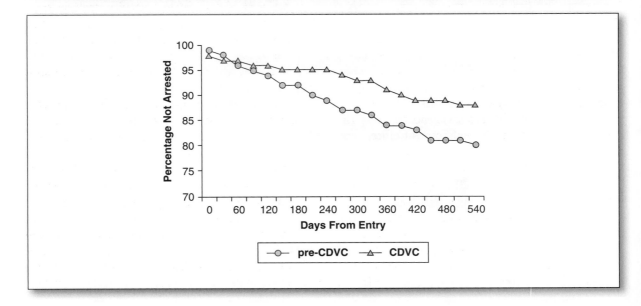

difficulties in rural settings because the infrastructure for dealing with such problems is often more limited. For example, there tends to be fewer domestic violence shelters and programs for victims in general in rural areas compared with urban environments. The results from this study provide an in-depth evaluation of a domestic violence court located in a rural environment. Therefore, this study provides a unique contribution to the literature. The findings indicate that a coordinated response among local law enforcement, mental health, and the courts can be effective in combating domestic violence in local settings. Importantly, this court model did not involve a significant amount of infrastructure or resources.

The quantitative results suggest that domestic violence can be affected by increased attention from representatives of the criminal justice system and coordination with service providers. Specifically, recidivism for domestic violence offenders was significantly reduced during a period when the overall number of domestic violence arrests increased. The findings suggest that evaluations of criminal justice interventions need to examine systemic effects at multiple levels. A focus at only the aggregate level would have suggested this specialized court was increasing domestic violence, when in fact the probability of reoffending was decreasing. This dual methodological approach emphasizes the importance of understanding the nature of the research and making sure all measures of change are explored.

Results from this study show the effectiveness of a specialized domestic violence court in increasing law enforcement responsiveness to domestic violence and reducing recidivism of domestic violence batterers. The results suggest that the law enforcement officers and investigators responded to the actions of the court by making more arrests of domestic violence abusers. This likely occurred because officers realized the court was taking the charges and offenders seriously.

The success of this domestic violence court had a lot to do with the centralized structure of the court and the extensive coordination among key agencies dealing with the problem of domestic violence. Having all domestic violence cases processed through one specialized domestic violence court with trained and dedicated personnel permitted the coordination of resources, supervision of defendants, and consistency in case processing that was not available when cases were assigned to one of eight geographically dispersed magistrate's courts. Maintaining a full-time dedicated prosecutor was especially beneficial for maintaining consistency in case processing and holding defendants accountable for their sanctions. An additional ingredient to the success of this court was the fact that mental health and the victim and defendant service providers were present in every court session. As a result, defendants and victims could immediately receive assistance from these service providers. Given that victims and defendants often lived in rural outlying communities and had difficulty making travel arrangements to get to court, it was key that all services be available to them in the same court so that the burdens of travel could be minimized. Additionally, the court placed an emphasis on holding convicted defendants accountable for the treatment programs they were assigned to by maintaining weekly follow-ups on their progress. The judges made it clear to defendants that if they failed to comply with their treatment conditions, they would spend time in jail. The results from this research, therefore, suggest that policy makers interested in combating domestic violence should seriously consider a centralized therapeutic court approach that permits a greater level of coordination between the diversity of agencies that are needed to handle domestic violence situations and holds defendants accountable for their actions.

Indeed, these findings underscore the benefits of a coordinated response to domestic violence and the ability of local communities to act in a proactive manner toward the crime of domestic violence. Although traditional approaches to dealing with domestic abuse and violence have shown little hope, the specialized court system provides evidence for positive change. A serious and coordinated criminal justice response to domestic violence that focuses on a therapeutic jurisprudence philosophy of justice appears to be an effective method of reducing domestic violence recidivism. The court has the ability to determine treatment needs for offenders and to provide accountability of the sanctioned treatment. These actions need to be taken by the court because victims can be endangered by any breakdown in the system. With these types of assistance, there is a chance to reduce the incidence of domestic violence. Jurisdictions that undertake such efforts need to plan these efforts in advance and identify the resources and roles that each stakeholder will adopt so that a collaborative interagency strategy toward combating domestic violence can be successfully implemented. Such efforts have proved fruitful in Lexington County, South Carolina and should be replicated in other settings.

 References

Belknap, Joanne and Dee L. R. Graham 2000 *Factors Related to Domestic Violence Court Dispositions In a Large Urban Area: The Role of Victim/Witness Reluctance and Other Variables, Final Report.* Washington, DC: National Institute of Justice, U.S. Department of Justice.

Bell, Margaret E. and Lisa A. Goodman 2001 Supporting battered women involved with the court system: An evaluation of a law school-based advocacy program. *Violence Against Women,* 7:1377–1404.

Burawa, Eve S. and Carl G. Buzawa 1996 *Domestic Violence: The Criminal Justice Response.* 2d ed. Thousand Oaks, CA: Sage.

Buzawa, Eve S., Gerald T. Hotaling, and Andrew Klein 1998 The response to domestic violence in a modeled court: Some initial findings, and implications. *Behavioral Sciences and the Law,* 16:185–206.

Campbell Donald T. and Julian C. Stanley 1966 *Experimental and Quasi-Experimental Designs for Research.* Skokie, IL: Rand McNally.

Clark, Sandra J. Martha R. Burt, Margaret M. Schulte, and Karen Maguire 1996 *Coordinated Community Responses to Domestic Violence; in Six Communities: Beyond the Justice System.* Washington, DC: The Urban Institute.

Cook, Thomas D. and Donald T. Campbell 1979 *Quasi-Experimentation: Design and Analysis Issues for Field Settings.* Chicago, IL: Rand McNally.

Dawson, Myrna and Ronit Dinovitzer 2001 Victim cooperation and the prosecution of domestic violence in a specialized court. *Justice Quarterly,* 18:593–622.

Dobash, R. Emerson and Russell P. Dobash 1992 *Women, Violence, and Social Change.* New York: Routledge.

Emders, Walter 1995 *Applied Econometric Time Series.* New York: Wiley.

Epstein, Deborah 1999 Effective intervention in domestic violence cases: Rethinking the roles of prosecutors, judges, and the court system. *Yale Journal of Law and Feminism,* 11:3–50.

Fritzler, Randall B. and Lenore M. J. Simon 2000 Principles of an effective domestic violence court. *American Judges Association Court Review,* 37:1–2.

Gamache, Denise, Jeffry Edleson, and M. Schock 1988 Coordinated police, judicial and social service response to women battering: A multi-baseline evaluation across three communities. In Gerald T. Hotaling, David Finkelhor, John T. Kirkpatrick, and Murray A. Straus (eds.), *Coping with Family Violence. Research and Policy Perspectives.* Thousand Oaks, CA: Sage.

Goldkamp, John S., Doris Weiland, Mark Collins, and Michael D. White 1996 *The Role of Drug and Alcohol Abuse in Domestic Violence and its Treatment: Dade County's Domestic Violence Court Experiment. Report to the National Institute of Justice.* Philadelphia, PA: Crime and Justice Research Institute.

Harrell Adel 1991 *Evaluation of Court-Ordered Treatment for Domestic Violence Offenders: Final Report.* Washington, DC: The Urban Institute.

Hofford, Meredith 1991 Family violence: Challenging cases for probation officers. *Federal Probation,* 55:12–17.

Karan, Amy, Susan L. Keilitz, and Sharon Denaro 1999 Domestic violence courts: What are they and how should we manage them? *Juvenile and Family Court Journal,* 50:75–86.

Keilitz, Susan L. 2000 *Specialization of Domestic Violence Case Management in the Courts: A National Survey.* Washington, DC: National Center for State Courts.

Levey, Lynn S., Martha Wade Steketee, and Susan L. Keilitz 2001 *Lessons Learned in Implementing an Integrated Domestic Violence Court: The District of Columbia Experience.* Williamsburg, VA: National Center for State Courts.

Loftin, Colin and David McDowall 1984 The deterrent effects of the Florida felony firearm law. *The Journal of Criminal Law and Criminology,* 75:250–259.

Long, J. Scott 1997 *Regression Models for Categorical and Limited Dependent Variables.* Thousand Oaks, CA: Sage.

McDowell, David, Colin Loftin, and Brian Wiersema 1992 A comparative study of the preventive effects of mandatory sentencing laws for gun crimes. *The Journal of Criminal Law and Criminology,* 83:378–394.

McDowall David, Richard McCleary, Errol E. Meidinger, and Richard A. Hay 1980 *Interrupted Time Series Analysis.* Thousand Oaks, CA: Sage.

Orchowsky, Stan 1998 Unique nature of domestic violence in rural areas. *Forum,* 16:1–9.

Ostrom, Brian and Neal Kauder 1999 *Examining the Work of State Courts, 1998: A National Perspective From the Court Statistics Project.* Williamsburg, VA: National Center for State Courts.

Ptacek, James 1999 *Battered Women in the Courtroom: The Power of Judicial Responses.* Boston, MA: Northeastern University Press.

Rennison, Callie M. 2000 *Intimate Partner Violence. Special Report: Bureau of Justice Statistics.* Washington, DC: U.S. Department of Justice.

Rottman, David and Pamela Casey 1999 *Therapeutic jurisprudence and the emergence of problem-solving courts. National Institute of Justice Journal 2–19.* Washington, DC: U.S. Department of Justice.

Schmidt, Peter and Ann D. Witte 1988 *Predicting Recidivism Using Survival Models.* New York: Springer-Verlag.

Sherman, Lawrence W. 1992 *Policing Domestic Violence: Experiments and Dilemmas.* New York: Free Press.

Thistlewaite, Amy, John Wooldredge, and David Gibbs 1998 Severity of dispositions and domestic violence recidivism. *Crime & Delinquency,* 44:388–398.

Tjaden Patricia and Nancy Thoennes 2000 *Extent Nature, and Consequences of Intimate Partner Violence: Findings from the National Violence Against Women Survey. Research Report.* Washington, DC: National Institute of Justice, U.S. Department of Justice.

Tolman, Richard and Arlene N. Weiz 1995 Coordinated community intervention for domestic violence: The effects of arrest and prosecution on recidivism of woman abuse perpetrators. *Crime and Delinquency,* 41:481–495.

Uniform Crime Reports 1998 *Crime in the United States 1997.* Washington, DC: Federal Bureau of Investigation, U.S. Department of Justice.

U.S. Census Bureau 2000 *State and County Quick Facts.* Available at http://quick facts.census.gov/gld/index.html

Violence Policy Center 2000 *When Men Murder Women: An Analysis of 1998 Homicide Data.* Washington, DC: Violence Policy Center.

Walsh, Charlotte 2001 The trend towards specialization: West Yorkshire innovations in drugs and domestic violence courts. *The Howard Journal,* 40:26–38.

Weber, Julia F. 2000 Domestic violence courts: Components and considerations. *Journal of the Center for Families, Children, & the Courts,* 2:23–6.

DISCUSSION QUESTIONS

1. How has the criminal justice system response to domestic violence changed since the early 1990s?

2. How does the Lexington County Criminal Domestic Violence Court (CDVC) differ from a typical court of limited jurisdiction? How does its approach to domestic violence cases differ?

3. The authors began by analyzing monthly arrests for domestic violence before and after the implementation of the CDVC. What were the results of their time-series analysis? Is this evidence of success or failure?

4. The authors also examined the impact of the CDVC on offender recidivism. How did they measure recidivism? Did participation in the CDVC reduce domestic violence recidivism? Did it reduce time to rearrest?

5. Based on the findings reported in this study, would you characterize the CDVC as a success or a failure?

READING

Like other specialized or problem-solving courts, teen courts—courts in which youths, under adult supervision, adjudicate cases involving other teens—have become increasingly popular. As Rasmussen points out, however, these courts have not been subject to rigorous evaluation. Therefore, the purpose of his study is to evaluate a teen court operating in a rural county in Illinois.

AUTHOR'S NOTE: This research was supported in part by a National Institute of Mental Health National Research Service Award (MH14257) to the University of Illinois.

SOURCE: Rasmussen, A. (2004). Teen court referral, sentencing, and subsequent recidivism: Two proportional hazards models and a little speculation. *Crime & Delinquency,* 50(4), 615–635.

Teen Court Referral, Sentencing, and Subsequent Recidivism

Two Proportional Hazards Models and a Little Speculation

Andrew Rasmussen

T een court is becoming an increasingly popular dispositional strategy for young offenders throughout the United States. Where there were an estimated 50 teen court programs in a few states in 1991, about 900 in 46 states and the District of Columbia existed in 2002 (Nolan, 2002). Butts, Buck, and Coggeshall (2002) estimated that teen courts handle 100,000 cases a year, accounting for more than one eighth of all cases not processed by traditional courts. The recent explosion of these programs parallels legislative changes in many states' juvenile justice codes, and these programs are seen as a partial solution to the juvenile justice system's failure to give anything more than a "slap on the wrist" to first-time offenders (Godwin, 1997). Teen court's popularity, however, has yet to be justified by research. There have been recent efforts describing demographic and sentencing correlates of recidivism after teen court (e.g., Harrison, Maupin, & Mays, 2001; Minor, Wells, Soderstrom, Bingham, & Williamson, 1999), and some theoretical groundwork situating teen court within the larger system of juvenile justice (Singer, 1998). As of yet there has been no investigation of systems-level variables in teen court. It may be that systemic problems that plague many diversion programs—for example, iatrogenic labeling, net widening—are present in teen courts as well. The current study is an attempt to investigate these issues by integrating referral source and sentencing data into a study of the correlates of recidivism after teen court.

Teen court consists of a courtroom in which youths fill most roles. Offenses addressed by these youths are a mixture of status offenses and misdemeanors, with an occasional low-level felony. These include theft, minor assault, disorderly conduct, alcohol and marijuana possession, vandalism, school disciplinary problems, traffic violations, truancy, and weapons possession (Butts & Buck, 2000). No teen court accepts referrals older than age 18 (Harrison et al., 2001), and offenders usually have no prior charges (Butts & Buck, 2000). Most teen courts require that the offender admit guilt before entering the courtroom (Butts & Buck, 2000; Minor et al., 1999). Hearings thus focus on mitigating and aggravating circumstances that might affect sentencing (King, 1990), including whether he or she is remorseful, his or her behavior at home, and even scholastic achievement. Sentences are thus indicative of the jury's judgment of the offender's character (Williamson, Chalk, & Knepper, 1993), and not just the offense itself.

Sentences imposed by teen court juries are purportedly designed to hold offenders accountable for their actions and repair the relationships between offenders and those affected through restorative justice (Godwin, 2002). Community service has been proposed as the central factor in restorative sentencing (Bazemore & Maloney, 1994), and it is the most common sanction given by teen courts (Butts & Buck, 2000). Other restorative sanctions include teen court jury duty, writing essays on the consequences of offending, making apologies to victims and family members, and monetary restitution. Teen court offenders usually have a period of 3 or 6 months to complete their sentences. Minor et al. (1999) and Harrison et al. (2001) report rates above 70% for completing teen court sentences.

As sentencing involves public judgment of offenders, there may be a risk of inadvertently labeling these youths delinquent when such a label is inappropriate. Labeling is well documented in juvenile diversion (Davidson, Redner, Blakely, & Mitchell, 1987; Klein, 1986), and there is no inherent reason why teen court should be different from other diversion programs in this regard. Labeling theory posits that negative sanctions reinforce deviant behavior, leading to negative outcomes that might not have otherwise occurred (Thomas & Bishop, 1984). This has been found associated with lower self-concept among adolescents (Al-Talib & Griffin, 1994), and an increase in interaction with delinquent peers (Kaplan & Johnson, 1991).

Recidivism After Teen Court

Teen court advocates point to low rates of recidivism as one of the key assets of their programs (e.g., Rothstein, 1985). Reoffense rates in the research literature, however, are varied. Rates of recidivism after teen court have been reported as 25% over 4 years (Harrison et al., 2001), 10% over 18 months (Seyfrit, Reichel, & Stutts, 1987), 32% (Minor et al., 1999) and 13% over 12 months (Weisz, Lott, & Thai, 2002), 20% over 7 months (North Carolina Administrative Office of the Courts, 1995), and 6% to 9% over 6 months (Butts et al., 2002). Inconsistency among these figures may relate to referral structures surrounding the teen court in question. The 32% figure, for instance, comes from a study of Kentucky's state-wide teen court program, which receives one third of its youths from juvenile court after youths have been adjudicated delinquent (Minor et al., 1999).

Results of studies employing comparison groups to study recidivism are similarly equivocal. Two studies reported no differences between teen court youths and comparisons (Butts et al., 2002; Seyfrit et al., 1987), one reported higher recidivism rates among teen court youths (North Carolina Administrative Office of the Courts, 1995), and three reported lower recidivism rates among comparison youths (Butts et al., 2002; Hissong, 1991; Weisz et al., 2002). Questions about teen courts preventing recidivism are likely to persist until studies using random assignment are done. Although preventing recidivism is a stated goal of many teen court programs (Knepper, 1994), it should be noted that it may not be the most important measure of success. For example, it may be that the value of teaching local youths about the law supersedes unimpressive recidivism findings (for an example of research measuring success of a teen court with measures other than recidivism, see Weisz et al., 2002).

Recidivism has been found to be more likely among teen court defendants who are younger, male, sentenced to more community service hours and more jury duty nights (Harrison et al., 2001; Minor et al., 1999). In other words, younger boys who are sentenced to more demanding sentences are more likely to recidivate. This may be a function of a positive association between sentence severity and more severe delinquency in general. Recidivism has also been associated with not completing teen court sentences (Harrison et al., 2001; North Carolina Administrative Office of the Courts, 1995), having a prior referral (Harrison et al., 2001; Minor et al., 1999), and being more alienated from institutional authority (Weisz et al., 2002). These findings taken together evince a familiar pattern: Youths who have exhibited more serious problem behavior before the program are more likely to exhibit problem behavior afterward.

Referral to Teen Court

Teen courts constitute a "loosely coupled" subsystem of juvenile justice, "another legal avenue to administer the kind of juvenile justice that was once handled in the juvenile court" (Singer, 1998, p. 524). Referral has been identified as a critical point in case processing in the multitiered context of today's juvenile justice system (Butts & Harrell, 1998), and yet there has been little discussion of referral agents in the teen court literature. The one study to interview referral agents (Harrison et al., 2001), found that although one of the goals of teen court was diversion, several adults admitted that if teen court had not existed youths would have been sent home with only a stern lecture. As diversion implies that youths would be processed in the traditional juvenile justice system if there existed no diversionary alternative (Davidson & Basta, 1989), this observation sheds doubt on claims that teen court is diversionary. Harrison et al. (2001) also found that nothing was done to those youths sent back to referral agents for not completing their teen court sentences. These findings may suggest iatrogenic effects. From referral agents' reports it seems that net widening was taking place. Net widening can result in unnecessarily labeling many youths who would not otherwise come into contact with the justice system, thus increasing the likelihood of subsequent arrests in the population of juveniles as a whole (Davidson, Redner, Amdur, & Mitchell, 1990; Lemert, 1981). In addition, the lack of accountability noted for noncompliant youths may suggest that some youths are learning that they can reoffend without consequence.

After a referral is made, youths are informed of the teen court program by a staff member who sets a date for a hearing in the near future. Advocates claim that quick processing time gives the offender a sense that justice is immediate, and that this should contribute to accountability (Godwin, 1998). Although a number of coordinators have described benefits of teen court processes (e.g., Zehner, 1997), there has been no investigation of whether quick processing might relate to outcomes.

The Current Study

The current study uses proportional hazards (or Cox) regression to explore patterns of covariates of juvenile and criminal court petitions filed on teen court defendants after teen court. Proportional hazards modeling allows for estimates of relative risk-type ratios (hazard ratios) for selected explanatory variables using censored data (Hosmer & Lemeshow, 1999). This design is supplemented with information from interviews with referral agents and teen court staff. Two models of recidivism are explored, one focusing on sentence content, and another on referral source.

Method

Setting

The participating teen court was situated in an Illinois community of 33,904, centrally located in a rural county of 83,919 (U.S. Census, 2002). The town featured county government offices and courts, a federal district court, a large federal hospital, and a few small businesses. Racial composition in 2000 was 70% White, 25% Black, 2% mixed race, 2% others, 1% Asian, and 0.2% American Indian. Those identifying Latino ethnicity made up 5% of the population (most of Mexican origin; U.S. Census, 2002). The county as a whole was more heavily White (85%).

At the time of data collection, this teen court had operated as the only teen court in the area for nine years. It ran according to the adult judge model (Godwin, 1998), in which an adult judge instructs the youths in the courtroom (jurors, lawyers, court officers) on procedural matters, and a youth jury determines sentences for offenders. Two coordinators administered the program, recruiting jurors and judges, arranging training sessions and hearings, and monitoring sentences. Relations between the teen court staff and local police and court workers were good, and the state teen court association recognized the program as a model for other teen courts in the region (Langacker, 2001).

Sample

Archival records for all 648 youths processed between 1993 and 2001 were provided by the teen court in the course of a program evaluation. This group was 63% male, with a mean age of 13.71 years (SD=1.99, range = 6 to 18). Racially/ethnically this group was identified as 74% White, 21% Black, 4% Hispanic, 1% mixed race, and 0.2% Asian.[1] Three fourths were referred to teen court by law enforcement directly, 16% by municipal attorneys' offices, and 9% by the state's attorney.

All client records had complete information for age, sex, race/ethnicity, referral agent, offense, sentence content, and whether a petition was filed in juvenile or criminal court after teen court. Twenty-nine youths (4%) were missing information on sentence completion, one case was missing offense and intake dates, and another, a hearing date. Access to court records was solicited by researchers and teen court personnel and approved by the presiding judge of the county. Researchers searched for each teen court offender by name, matched with date of birth. For all 168 (26%) offenders appearing in court records, dates of offenses were recorded.

Referral agents and teen court personnel interviewed included six police officers, a municipal attorney, an assistant state's attorney, and two teen court administrators. These key informants were identified through collaboration with teen court staff as people who were involved in the teen court referral process. The police officers were all men, the municipal attorney was a man, the assistant state's attorney a woman, and the teen court staff were women. All were White. Police officers included two police chiefs and four juvenile officers who ranged in experience in their current positions from 2 to 30 years. Teen court staff had been working in their current positions for 6 and 5 years; the municipal attorney, 4 years; and the assistant state's attorney, 2 years. These participants were contacted by the author, met at their places of work, given informed consent forms, and interviewed for approximately 20 minutes. After their interviews, referral agents and teen court staff completed an offense severity rating (OSR).

Transformation of Variables and Measures

While examining the teen court records, it became apparent that some sentencing options were assigned more frequently than others, resulting in skewed distributions of sentence content variables. The number of essays and amount of restitution were thus recoded into yes-no variables for essay assignment and restitution, and the number of apologies assigned greater than three were collapsed into a single category. The number of community service hours and jury duty assignments were recoded to better reflect teen court sentencing practices. The recoding of these was complicated by a change in sentencing guidelines in 1996, when 10 hours of community service and one jury duty assignment became minimum sentences for every offender (a common practice in teen courts; Butts & Buck, 2000). The number of hours was thus transformed into a three-level categorical variable, with 0 to 10 hours representing a minimum sentence, 11 to 29 representing a medium sentence, and 30 to 50 hours, the maximum. The number of jury duty assignments was transformed into a dichotomous variable, with 0 to 1 assignments representing the minimum, and 2 or more (heavily skewed toward 2), the maximum.

To be able to investigate the effect of teen court processing, the number of days between offense and referral, referral and hearing, and hearing and completion

were calculated. These three time periods were kept separate because they involve different primary actors: The time between offense and referral is primarily under control of the referral agent; the time between referral and hearing is jointly controlled by the teen court coordinators and the offender's family (in that they respond to the invitation to appear in teen court); and the time between hearing and completion, by the offender himself or herself. Those youths who did not complete their sentences were assigned the average number of days for completion for the year of their hearing.

In county court records, juvenile and criminal court petitions were taken as evidence of recidivism. To use survival analytic techniques, the number of days between completing the teen court sentence and the county record's offense date or the follow-up date (August 1, 2002) were calculated. In calculating this variable, it was noted that for 26 youths (4% of the sample), this variable was negative. These youths had reoffended before completing their teen court sentence. As survival analysis does not account for nonpositive times to failure, these cases were assigned 1 day for completion time.

The OSR scale was given to referral agents and teen court staff to classify offenses in archival data. It consisted of 35 offenses representing a wide range of severity. Participants were asked to rate each on a scale from 1 to 10, where 1 indicated *not serious* and 10 indicated *very serious*.

 Results

Offenses

The majority of offenses in teen court records were low-level infractions: Shoplifting (43%), criminal damage to property (9%), disorderly conduct (9%), battery (8%), theft of value less than U.S. $300 (6%), curfew violation (6%), possession of alcohol (6%), possession of cannabis (3%), possession of other controlled items (e.g., a gun; 2%), possession of tobacco (1%), burglary (1%), theft of value over $300 (1%), and other offenses (8%) including illegal use of an air rifle, forgery, and using a fictitious license.

Hierarchical clustering (Ward, 1963) followed by K-means clustering (using an iterative random start method; Steinley, 2003) was then used to explore three-, four-, and five-cluster solutions of OSR data. The five-cluster solution was chosen because it differentiated among offenses processed in teen court (as well as between these offenses and others). This included a cluster of status offenses ($M = 3.53, SD = .64$), misdemeanors ($M = 5.38, SD = .44$), low-level felonies (e.g., possession of marijuana of more than 25 grams; $M = 7.57, SD = .48$), medium felonies (e.g., arson; $M = 8.30, SD = .50$), and violence-related felonies (e.g., armed robbery; $M = 9.61, SD = .39$). Teen court offenses were then coded using this typology, with the following results: 183 status offenses (28%), 394 misdemeanors (61%), and 71 low-level felonies (11%). None were coded as medium or violence-related felonies.

Inspection of county records revealed a low (3%, $n = 23$) rate of prior referral to juvenile court among teen court offenders. One case had two prior charges. These priors included criminal damage ($n = 4$), battery ($n = 5$), burglary ($n = 4$), theft ($n = 3$), trespassing ($n = 3$), consumption of alcohol, ($n = 1$) and disorderly conduct ($n = 1$).

Sentence Content and Processing

A summary of sentence content and processing variables is presented in Table 9.9. The average sentence consisted of 11 to 29 hours of community service, two or more times on the jury, an essay, an apology, and no restitution or classes. Mean processing time between offense and referral was about 2½ weeks; between referral and hearing, 3½ weeks; and the average time to complete a sentence was about 4 months. Of youths, 92% ($n = 572$) completed their sentences. Although sentences were supposed to be completed within 90 days, more than three fifths (62%) were given extra time to complete sentences.

Survival Analysis

Proportional hazards regression was used to predict being charged with a crime between the date of sentence completion (or, for those youths not completing,

Table 9.9 Sentence Content and Processing Variables

Categorical Variables	N	%
Community service		
0 to 10 hours	241	37
11 to 29 hours	311	48
30 to 50 hours	96	15
Jury duty		
0 or 1 times on the jury	162	25
2 or more times on the jury	486	75
Restitution		
Yes	50	8
No	598	92
Essay		
Yes	310	48
No	338	52
Apology		
None	176	27
1	222	35
2	164	25
3 or more	86	13
Continuous Variables	**M**	**SD**
Days between		
Offense and referral	18.28	42.17
Referral and hearing	25.60	16.65
Hearing and completion	122.10	67.77

the date corresponding to the average number of days for completion in that year) and the follow-up date. Recidivism was defined as any petition filed in juvenile or criminal court after completing a teen court sentence.

The survival curve for the full sample is presented in Figure 9.7. After 1 year, the survival rate was about .88, implying that 12% of the sample was expected to recidivate within the first year after their teen court sentence. As stated above, 4% committed this crime before their teen court sentence was complete. Within 2 years, the survival rate had decreased to .81, a 19%

Figure 9.7   Cumulative Survival Curve

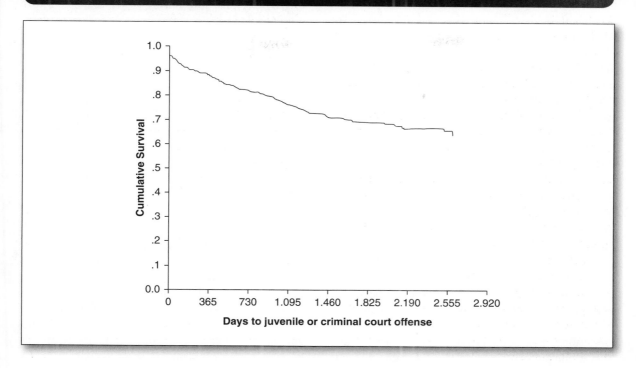

projected recidivism rate. Projected recidivism rates remained at about 7% per year after teen court until 4 years, when the survival curve begins to level.

Given dependency in the data, it was not possible to test all sentencing and processing variables simultaneously in a proportional hazards regression model.[2] Two variable selection approaches were used: The first focused on key sentencing identified by adult participants and the teen court literature, and the second, on key case-processing variables. Using the sentencing model for illustrative purposes, the relative risk for Black youths to be charged with a crime was almost 2½ times that of White youths, and for other non-White youths the risk was 1½ times that of White youths. For Black youths assigned fewer than 30 hours, the risk of later being charged with a crime were about one half that of Black youths assigned more than 30 hours.

Given that the purpose of the current study was to identify patterns of covariates and not to fit a "best model"

comparing referral and sentencing models involved noting what variables were included in each and their patterns of effects. Age was only relevant in the sentencing model. Although magnitudes were not as extreme, the pattern of results for Black and White youths were similar across models. However, unlike the sentencing model, youths in the Other race category were less likely than Whites to recidivate in the referral model.[3] The effect of the number of days between referral and hearing was identical to the effect in the sentencing model.

Referral Agent Interviews

Interviews from referral agents and teen court staff were recorded, transcribed, and their content analyzed by the author and five assistant researchers. Most police described cases they referred as "marginal," "anything that wouldn't be classified as a felony," and first-time offenses. Officers cited informal station adjustment as the primary alternative to teen court: "Most of the cases they get would have probably been handled as a station adjustment. We would not have sent that particular juvenile through the municipal or juvenile court." The state's attorney and municipal attorney reported that they referred ordinance violations, misdemeanors, and low-level felonies. Teen court staff reported that all these would be appropriate and added, "The chief criterion would be that there was no prior," and very violent or "particularly disturbing behavior in younger children would not be appropriate."

Teen court staff justified the deadline extensions evident in lengthy completion times for many youths by explaining that there was a general lack of follow-up by referral agents for those youths who did not complete by the deadline. "If we send them back, you know, probably nothing's going to happen." This was confirmed by police, who explained that any youth sent to teen court who did not complete would only have that noncompletion on his or her contact sheet. Noncompliance was used for subsequent decision making: "That's documented right on his card. And the next time if that kid comes through, he's not going to be a candidate for peer court." The municipal and state's attorneys said they would prosecute a case if they knew that the youth had not completed his or her sentence.

Police explicitly linked the lack of serious offenses referred to teen court to a prediction that recidivism would be minimal: "I think you're probably going to find that the incidence of recidivism is low, but that's primarily because of the way they're designed. And that may not necessarily be reflective of the community." The municipal attorney contrasted the youths he referred to teen court to those that he had contact with regularly, adding that for teen court youths, "At least 99–95 percent I don't see again." Teen court staff, however, thought that recidivism after teen court would be high—one member gave a 40% estimate—and gave examples of offenders who were later arrested as adults and whose names had appeared in the local newspaper.

In general, referral agents and teen court staff were positive about teen court. Police reported that they appreciated having another tier in juvenile justice, a "good alternative" for offending youths. It was also seen as an education program ("It shows the kid what can happen in court"), and in this manner, preventive. One

advantage over traditional processing repeatedly cited by referral agents was quick case processing. A police officer explained:

> One of the things with these kids, their memories aren't very long. They remember talking to you a few months ago, but they thought it was all over. . . . [Teen court] has an immediate impact on that kid, and it's still fresh in the mind: why he's there, what he's done, what's going to happen to him.

 ## Discussion

The current study expands on previous teen court research methodologically by estimating the relative risk of explanatory factors using proportional hazards regression, and theoretically by exploring case processing in addition to sentencing covariates. The recidivism rates found here—12% after 1 year, 19% after 2 years, and increasing steadily until 4 years after sentence completion—are comparable to those found in the literature (Seyfrit et al., 1987; Weisz et al., 2002). Models based on sentence content and case-processing variables were found to be viable frameworks for investigating the covariates of recidivism. The current study found support for previous findings identifying younger age and more community service (Harrison et al., 2001; Minor et al., 1999) and suggests that Black race, slower processing, and referral from the state's attorney's office are also associated with increased risk.

These results suggest that the youth jury's and referral agents' judgments of offenders are central to understanding recidivism after teen court. The general finding that the more of one type of obligation a youth was sentenced to the more likely he or she was to be sentenced to another type of obligation indicates an exponential pattern in teen court sentencing. Given that proceedings in teen courts generally focus on a youth's character and not just the offense itself (Williamson et al., 1993), one can interpret this pattern as a judgment of the offender made by the peer jury. The variable with the most association with other sentence content was community service hours, and thus it is an appropriate index of judgment severity by the peer jury. Descriptions by referral agents suggest that referral source is also an indirect measure of judgment. Police and the municipal attorney reported that they referred low-risk youths that they would probably never see again anyway. The state's attorney, however, referred cases that police had seen fit to refer to her and not to teen court, implying a more severe judgment, and, by extension, a more serious label.

Continuing in this line of interpretation, the finding in the sentencing model that youths assigned 0 to 10 hours of community service had a lower risk of reoffending than others suggests that the peer jury has an accurate impression of most offenders. They assign the minimum sentence to the offenders who are least problematic. For some cases, this may also suggest that jury members do not believe that the youth needs punishing. To apply this to recidivism, even the minimum might not be necessary to keep the youth in question from reoffending. Although many teen courts mandate community service hours (Butts & Buck, 2000), this interpretation suggests that chances of recidivism would not increase if mandatory sentencing guidelines were done away with, and that elimination of sentencing guidelines may facilitate sentencing that is more in line with the judgment of offenders' peers.

Judgment implied by community service hours may also be associated with labeling and offenders' subsequent self-concept. Inasmuch as teen court is an airing of a youth's delinquent activities and family life in front of peers, it may be more stigmatizing than programs administered by adults. In a study of credibility among labelers, youths arrested for misdemeanors rated peers as most credible when a negative label was assigned to them (Morash, 1982). These findings are particularly relevant to teen court in their target population. Future research should explicitly investigate the role of labeling in teen court.

Making judgment central to the referral model is based on the assumption that an assessment of low risk is important in deciding to refer youths to teen court. That the lower risk of recidivism for police referrals thus reflects a lower average assessed risk of this group of offenders does not mean, however, that all these youths are best served by teen court. Post hoc findings that police referrals assigned the minimum sentence (i.e., judged

lowest risk by the jury) are rearrested at disproportionate rates relative to those given the minimum referred by municipal and state's attorneys may point to net widening. These youths are referred as low risk, judged low risk by their peers, but reoffend at relatively high rates. Police in the current study reported that the records that went along with referring juveniles were used as justification for increasing the consequences for future contacts. Such qualitative data suggest that teen court is not strictly a diversion program. Although more research needs to be done to determine the extent of net widening by teen courts, the well-founded negative consequences of net widening (Davidson et al., 1990) should give pause to teen courts that get many of their cases from police. One solution would be to accept referrals only from court officials—that is, accept only those youths who have been judged appropriate for significant juvenile justice intervention—as is done in several jurisdictions already. This would also "tighten up" the relation between the juvenile court and teen court, thus countering the expansion of the system of subsystems with little coordinated accountability that has become juvenile justice today (Singer, 1998).

That younger age at entry into juvenile justice systems is a risk factor has been noted for some time in the delinquency literature (Ganzer & Sarason, 1973; Lueger & Cadman, 1982; Traynelis-Yurek & Giacobbe, 1988), however the implications of this finding are unclear. It may suggest that younger offenders simply have a greater window of opportunity to reoffend because of their age, are identified by police earlier and thus are under surveillance for more time, or it may point to more serious pathology indicated by younger offending (e.g., Moffitt, 1993). Comments from police suggesting increasing consequences for contacts subsequent to teen court processing support the surveillance hypothesis in the current study. Surveillance may be directly related to labeling of teen court youths as well: Referring an offender to teen court may have more potential for labeling that youth as delinquent (and thus "keeping an eye on him") than processing with a station adjustment. The pathology hypothesis seems less likely, as teen court coordinators reported that younger children exhibiting "particularly disturbing behavior" were not eligible for teen court. More interesting, younger age was not a risk factor in the referral model. Why it should be present in one model and not in the other is not clear.

In both models, Black youths' risk of recidivism was higher than Whites'. Although there is little evidence that they offend at higher rates, it is a common finding that Black youths are arrested at higher rates than their White peers (Elliott & Ageton, 1980; Joseph, 2000; Lieber & Jamieson, 1995). It is unlikely that teen court would change racial patterns in arrests, and so it seems feasible that these account for higher risk of recidivism among Black teen court youths. The interaction between race and community service hours provides some nuance to this story. Although the effects of community service hours were exacerbated for Black youths—those assigned 30 to 50 hours had a risk 2½ times that of others—it was not the case that Black youths assigned 11 to 29 hours were as likely to recidivate as those assigned 30 to 50 hours, as it was for the full sample. This suggests bias in judgment among jury members. Those Black youths sentenced to 11 to 29 hours may have been judged more harshly than they would have been had they been White and therefore should be considered "minimum" offenders—comparable to White offenders in the 0 to 10 hours category. Judging Black defendants more severe than Whites is a common phenomenon in the United States (e.g., Sommers & Ellsworth, 2001; Sweeny & Haney, 1992), and there have been advocates who have argued that teen courts should be aware of disproportionate minority confinement issues and labeling Black youth more delinquent in general (Olezene, Cotton, & Hernandez, 2002). Although there were also main effects for the other non-White youths, the small size and heterogeneity of this group makes any interpretation of these findings suspect at best.

In both models, the risk of recidivism was lower for those who waited a shorter time between referral and their teen court hearing, corroborating reports by police and teen court staff and claims by teen court advocates (e.g., Zehner, 1997) that quicker processing is associated with positive outcomes. Longer processing time may make the impact of punishment less salient for the offender, leading to increased chances of reoffending. Adolescents' limited future-time perspective has been proposed as a key element of their decision making in legally relevant contexts (Scott, Reppucci, & Woolard,

1995; Steinberg & Cauffman, 1996). How a future-time perspective hypothesis would fit with the specific nature of processing time in the current study is unclear. The number of days between referral and hearing may indicate an inability on the part of the offender's family to respond quickly to the offer to participate in teen court, reluctance on the part of teen court coordinators to accept the youth, or perhaps inefficiency on the part of staff that the offender interprets as a measure of his or her worth. More research should be done to investigate the psychological sequelae of lengthy processing and to establish the particular connection between length of processing and reoffending. This would have implications well beyond teen courts: Traditional juvenile justice processing is lengthy (Edwards, Roundtree, & Parker, 1982; Humes, 1996), and it may be that this is partially responsible for high rates of recidivism.

Contrary to previous findings (Harrison et al., 2001; Minor et al., 1999), neither model identified prior offense, offense severity, or completion of the teen court sentence as predictors of recidivism. That prior arrest was not associated may be accounted for by a low base rate of priors among teen court youths. Although offense severity ratings made by referral agents were consistent with legal categories, it may be that they did not capture the implications of the offenses for youths' general behavior. That sentence completion was not associated with recidivism might not be surprising given that two thirds of those completing did so after being given at least one extension. This liberal extension policy resulted in a diverse pool of youths who completed, making the difference between whether youths completed or not less pronounced than it might have been in another setting.

There was general agreement among referral agents and teen court staff that teen court was an asset to juvenile justice in the area, giving referral agents another resource in their efforts against youth offending and giving local youths a valuable lesson in law. At times, this approval was expressed in the same breath as comments indicating that many youths were not really in need of preventive intervention. The assumption that teen court is necessarily positive is reflected throughout advocacy literature, although what little research there is provides equivocal support at best. Findings of the current study suggest that teen court is subject to the judgment and labeling involved in other diversion programs, and that these may have similar iatrogenic effects. These findings do not necessarily damn teen court as public policy—it may be that other aspects of teen court such as instilling civic responsibility in local youth who volunteer on the jury counteract, at the community level, the iatrogenic effects of labeling offenders—but do seem to indicate that the current blind enthusiasm for these programs as they are is unwarranted. As teen courts continue to grow in popularity research is needed to point to practices that improve the provision of juvenile justice, and to make sure juvenile justice is not "overserved."

⊠ Notes

1. Race and ethnic labels in teen court data did not match 2000 U.S. Census labels.

2. One exception to excluding dependent variables was investigated further because of the desire to include race in the model. While there was dependency noted between community service hours and race, subsequent analysis of the independent effects of each indicated that hazard ratios (HRs) did not change substantially (0.1 to 0.2) when either variable was absent. The decision was made to keep both in this model.

3. To investigate the effect of the Other racial group on the models, each model was run after deleting these youth from the data. The patterns of effects for Black and White youth were the same.

⊠ References

Al-Talib, N. I., & Griffin, C. (1994). Labelling effect on adolescents' self-concept. *International Journal of Offender Therapy and Comparative Criminology, 38*(1), 47–57.

Bazemore, G., & Maloney, D. (1994). Rehabilitating community service: Toward restorative service sanctions in a balanced justice system. *Federal Probation, 58,* 24–34.

Butts, J. A., & Buck, J. (2000). Teen court: A focus on research. *OJJDP Juvenile Justice Bulletin,* pp. 1–15.

Butts, J. A., Buck, J., & Coggeshall, M. (2002, April). *Effects of youth court: Results of the OJJDP evaluation.* Paper presented at the National Youth Court Conference, Arlington, VA.

Butts, J. A., & Harrell, A. V. (1998). *Delinquents or criminals? Policy options for young offenders.* Washington, DC: Urban Institute.

Cohen, J. (1988). *Statistical power analysis for the behavioral sciences* (2nd ed.). Hillsdale, NJ: Lawrence Erlbaum.

Davidson, W. S., Redner, R., Amdur, R. L., & Mitchell, C. M. (1990). *Alternative treatments for troubled youth: The case of diversion from the justice system.* New York: Plenum Press.

Davidson, W. S., Redner, R., Blakely, C. H., & Mitchell, C. M. (1987). Diversion of juvenile offenders: An experimental comparison. *Journal of Consulting and Clinical Psychology, 55*(1), 68–75.

Davidson, W. S. I., & Basta, J. (1989). Diversion from the juvenile justice system: Research evidence and a discussion of issues. In B. B. Lahey & A. E. Kazdin (Eds.), *Advances in clinical child psychology* (Vol. 12, pp. 85–111). New York: Plenum Press.

Edwards, D. W., Roundtree, G. A., & Parker, J. B. (1982). An investigation of juvenile offenders exposed to a family court before and after implementation of the Juvenile Delinquency Prevention Act of 1974. *Journal of Offender Counseling, Services, and Rehabilitation, 7*(2), 27–43.

Elliott, D. S., & Ageton, S. S. (1980). Reconciling race and class differences on self-reported and official estimates of delinquency. *American Sociological Review, 45,* 95–110.

Ganzer, V. J., & Sarason, I. G. (1973). Variables associated with recidivism among juvenile delinquents. *Journal of Consulting and Clinical Psychology, 40*(1), 1–5.

Godwin, T. M. (1997). The LRE of teen court. *LRE Report, 18*(2), 1–2.

Godwin, T. M. (1998). *Peer justice and youth empowerment: An implementation guide for teen court programs.* Washington, DC: American Probation and Parole Association.

Godwin, T. (2002). *The role of restorative justice in teen courts: A preliminary look.* Lexington, KY: National Youth Court Center.

Harrison, P., Maupin, J. R., & Mays, G. L. (2001). Teen court: An examination of processes and outcomes. *Crime & Delinquency, 47*(2), 243–264.

Hissong, R. (1991). Teen court—Is it an effective alternative to traditional sanctions? *Journal for Juvenile Justice and Detention Services, 6,* 14–23.

Hosmer, D. W., & Lemeshow, S. (1999). *Applied survival analysis: Regression modeling of time to event data.* New York: Wiley.

Humes, E. (1996). *No matter how loud I shout.* New York: Simon & Schuster.

Joseph, J. (2000). Overrepresentation of minority youth in the juvenile justice system: Discrimination or disproportionality of delinquent acts. In M. W. Markowitz & D. D. Jones-Brown (Eds.), *The system in black and white: Exploring the connections between race, crime, and justice* (pp. 227–239). Westport, CT: Praeger.

Kaplan, H. B., & Johnson, R. J. (1991). Negative social sanctions and juvenile delinquency: Effects of labeling in a model of deviant behavior. *Social Science Quarterly, 72*(1), 98–122.

King, S. (1990). LaPorte teen court: Diversionary juvenile rehabilitation and more. *Res Gestae, 34*(1), 10–14.

Klein, M. W. (1986). Labeling theory and delinquency policy: An experimental test. *Criminal Justice and Behavior, 13*(1), 47–79.

Knepper, P. (1994). Kentucky's "teen court" initiative: An assessment. *Kentucky LRE, 2*(3), 1–9.

Langaeker, W. (2001). Peer Court, Inc. background. *Jury Journal, 2*(1), 2.

Lemert, E. M. (1981). Diversion in juvenile justice: What hath been wrought? *Journal of Research in Crime and Delinquency, 18,* 34–46.

Lieber, M. J., & Jamieson, K. M. (1995). Race and decision making within juvenile justice: The importance of context. *Journal of Quantitative Criminology, 11*(4), 363–388.

Lueger, R. J., & Cadman, W. (1982). Variables associated with recidivism and program-termination of delinquent adolescents. *Journal of Clinical Psychology, 38*(4), 861–863.

Minor, K. I., Wells, J. B., Soderstrom, I. R., Bingham, R., & Williamson, D. (1999). Sentence completion and recidivism among juveniles referred to teen courts. *Crime & Delinquency, 45*(4), 467–480.

Moffitt, T. E. (1993). Adolescence-limited and life course persistent antisocial behavior: A developmental taxonomy. *Psychological Review, 100*, 674–701.

Morash, M. (1982). Juvenile reaction to labels: An experiment and an exploratory study. *Sociology & Social Research, 67*(1), 76–88.

Nolan, C. (2002, April). *Youth courts: America's youth justice system.* Paper presented at the National Youth Court Conference, Arlington, VA.

North Carolina Administrative Office of the Courts. (1995). *Report on the teen court programs in North Carolina.* Raleigh, NC: Author.

Olezene, G., Cotton, M., & Hernandez, C. (2002, April). *Overrepresentation of minority youth in the juvenile justice system: "What you can do about it."* Paper presented at the National Youth Court Conferences, Arlington, VA.

Rothstein, N. (1985, February). Teen court. *Corrections Today*, 18–22.

SAS Institute Inc. (1999). *Introduction to survival analysis procedures.* Retrieved November 12, 2002, from http://www.sas.com/rnd/app/da/new/802ce/stat/chap6

Scott, E. S., Reppucci, N. D., & Woolard, J. L. (1995). Evaluating adolescent decision-making in legal contexts. *Law and Human Behavior, 19*(3), 221–244.

Seyfrit, C. L., Reichel, P. L., & Stutts, B. L. (1987). Peer juries as a juvenile justice diversion technique. *Youth & Society, 18*(3), 302–316.

Sommers, S. R., & Ellsworth, P. C. (2001). White juror bias: An investigation of prejudice against Black defendants in the American courtroom. *Psychology, Public Policy, and Law, 7*(1), 201–229.

Singer, S. I. (1998). Criminal and teen courts as loosely coupled systems of juvenile justice. *Wake Forest Law Review, 33*, 509–532.

Steinberg, L., & Cauffman, E. (1996). Maturity of judgment in adolescence: Psychosocial factors in adolescent decision-making. *Law and Human Behavior, 20*(3), 249–272.

Steinley, D. (2003). Local optima in K-means clustering: What you don't know may hurt you. *Psychological Methods, 8*(3), 294–304.

Sweeny, L. T., & Haney, C. (1992). The influence of race on sentencing: A meta-analytic review of experimental studies. *Behavioral Sciences and the Law, 10*(2), 175–179.

Thomas, C. W., & Bishop, D. M. (1984). The effect of formal and informal sanctions on delinquency: A longitudinal comparison of labeling and deterrence theories. *Journal of Criminal Law and Criminology, 75*(4), 1222–1245.

Traynelis-Yurek, E., & Giacobbe, G. A. (1988). Length of stay and age affect recidivism after a quality treatment program. *International Journal of Adolescence and Youth, 1*(3), 257–267.

U.S. Census. (2002). *Quick facts for Vermilion County, Illinois.* Retrieved October 14, 2002, from http://quickfacts.census.gov/qfd/sutes/17/17183.html

Ward, J. H. (1963). Hierarchical grouping to optimize an objective function. *Journal of the American Statistical Association, 58*, 236–244.

Weisz, V., Lott, R. C., & Thai, N. D. (2002). A teen court evaluation with a therapeutic jurisprudence perspective. *Behavioral Sciences and the Law, 20*, 381–392.

Williamson, D., Chalk, M., & Knepper, P. (1993). Teen court: Juvenile justice for the 21st century? *Federal Probation, 57*, 54–58.

Zehner, S. J. (1997). Teen court. *FBI Law Enforcement Bulletin, 66*(3), 1–7.

DISCUSSION QUESTIONS

1. How do teen courts differ from traditional juvenile courts? What are they designed to do?

2. Who were the typical offenders processed in this teen court? For what types of offenses were they referred to the court? What types of sentences did they receive?

3. Rasmussen's evaluation focused on recidivism. How did he measure recidivism? What percentage of offenders recidivated during the first year? During the first two years?

4. What were the predictors of recidivism?

5. How did Rasmussen interpret the finding that youth given 0 to 10 hours of community service had lower recidivism rates than those assigned more hours?

6. How did the author interpret the finding that quicker processing was associated with lower recidivism rates?

7. Assume that you are a decision maker in a jurisdiction that is considering a teen court. Would you vote for or against establishment of this type of specialized court? Why?

Glossary

Ad hoc plea bargaining: Term used to refer to unusual concessions defendants agree to make during the plea negotiation process.

Adjudication: To hear and settle a case by judicial procedure.

Adversarial system: Anglo-American system of criminal justice in which the prosecutor and defense attorney fight it out in a process designed to ensure that truth will emerge. The prosecutor has the burden of proof and must demonstrate beyond a reasonable doubt that the defendant committed the crime. The defense attorney's role is to argue for his client's innocence and to insist that his rights be protected at every stage in the process. The judge serves as a neutral arbitrator, largely to ensure that proper law and procedures are followed, and a jury made of citizens determines issues of fact.

Affidavit: A sworn document stating the facts relied upon to create probable cause. See also **Probable cause.**

Alford plea: A plea in which the defendant enters a guilty plea but denies having committed the crime to which he or she is pleading.

Appellate review: Process of reviewing final judgments of lower courts on questions of law, with the goal of determining whether proper procedures were followed.

Arraignment: The stage in the pretrial process when the defendant enters a plea.

Arrest: An arrest occurs when a reasonable person would conclude that the police in some way had restrained his or her liberty so that he or she was not free to leave.

Assigned counsel system: A method of providing counsel for indigent defendants. Private attorneys are appointed on a case-by-case basis.

Bench trial: A trial in which a judge, rather than a jury, renders a decision.

Binding arbitration: A means of settling disputes that requires the parties to the dispute to agree to abide by a neutral third party's decision, which cannot be appealed.

Booking: An administrative procedure involving the entry into the police blotter of the suspect's name, arrest time, offense charged, and the taking of fingerprints and photographs.

Boot camp: Program that targets young, nonviolent felony offenders who do not have extensive prior criminal records. Modeled on the military boot camp, the correctional boot camp emphasizes strict discipline, military drill and ceremony, and hard labor and physical training. Most also provide substance abuse counseling and educational and vocational training. Offenders selected for these programs live in barracks-style housing, address the guards by military titles, and are required to stand at attention and obey all orders.

Broken windows theory: The notion that communities that allow "broken windows"—which is a metaphor for litter, decay, vandalism, graffiti, and similar types of social disorganization—to proliferate will have higher levels of crime than will communities that attend to these problems and clean up their streets and neighborhoods.

Challenge for cause: During the jury selection process, the method used by the prosecutor or the defense attorney to remove impartial prospective jurors from the jury pool. Jurors can be removed, for example, if there is evidence that they are biased against one side or the other or if they have made up their minds about the defendant's guilt or innocence prior to hearing the evidence in the case. See also **Peremptory challenge**.

Change of venue: A request by the defendant to have his or her trial take place in a different location.

Charge reduction: A type of plea bargaining in which the prosecutor reduces the severity of the charge or the number of counts the defendant is facing in exchange for a guilty plea.

Charging decision: The decision by the prosecuting attorney whether to charge an individual with a crime and, if so, what charges to file.

Clemency: The power of the president (in federal criminal cases) or the governor (in state criminal cases) to pardon a person convicted of a crime, commute (i.e., shorten) the sentence, or reduce it from death to another lesser sentence.

Code of Hammurabi: The first known written legal code. Dating back to 1760 BC in ancient Mesopotamia, the Code delineated crimes and their punishments and also enumerated settlements for common disputes.

Collective incapacitation: The punishment philosophy that holds that all offenders found guilty of a particular type of crime should be incapacitated by imprisonment, without regard to their prior record or other personal characteristics. See also **Selective incapacitation.**

Common law: Laws that developed through court decisions rather than statutes; judge-made law.

Community court: A neighborhood-based court in which criminal justice officials collaborate with other governmental officials, social service agencies, and private agencies to focus on quality of life crimes, such as vandalism, prostitution, and minor drug offenses.

Community prosecution: A style of prosecution, modeled on community policing, in which prosecutors collaborate with other government officials, social service agencies, business leaders, and community stakeholders to respond to specific crime problems, such as misdemeanors and quality of life crimes.

Community service: A type of alternative punishment or intermediate sanction in which offenders are ordered to perform a certain number of hours of unpaid work at schools, hospitals, parks, and other public and private nonprofit agencies.

Complaint: The charging document that begins the criminal process. It may be filled out by a police officer, a prosecutor, or a private citizen.

Contract system: A method of providing counsel for indigent defendants. A group of private attorneys or a law firm enters into a contract with a jurisdiction and agrees to represent indigent defendants brought before the courts in that jurisdiction.

Court of Appeals Act of 1891: Act of Congress that created the circuit courts of appeal, a new layer of intermediate appellate courts that would hear appeals from the district courts, and gave the Supreme Court more discretion in deciding which cases to hear.

Courtroom workgroup: The officials—judge, prosecutor, defense attorney, and courtroom support staff—who work together day after day to process the criminal and civil cases that come before the court.

Courts Christian: See **Ecclesiastical courts.**

Crime control model: A model that views the suppression of criminal conduct—that is, controlling crime—as the most important function of the criminal justice system. Under this model, the primary function of the system is to control crime by apprehending, convicting, and punishing those who violate the law; the model emphasizes efficiency and finality, which is achieved through informal, non-adjudicatory procedures. See also **Presumption of guilt.**

Day fine: A type of fine imported from Europe and Latin America. The fine that the offender is ordered to pay is calibrated both to the seriousness of the offense and to the offender's ability to pay.

Defendant rehabilitation policy: A charging policy based on the notion that the majority of defendants—and particularly first offenders accused of nonviolent crimes—should not be processed through the criminal justice system; the focus of this policy is on early diversion of defendants and the use of noncriminal justice alternatives.

Determinate sentence: Sentencing system in which the legislature provides a presumptive range of confinement for each offense or class of offenses. The judge imposes a fixed term of years within this range. The offender serves this sentence, minus time off for good behavior.

Deterrence: Utilitarian justification of punishment in which punishment is seen as a means of preventing the offender from reoffending or discouraging others from following his example. Deterrence theorists suggest that potential offenders will refrain from committing a crime if they believe that the odds of getting caught and being severely punished are high and are not outweighed by any anticipated gain from the crime.

Discovery: The process by which both parties to a case learn of the evidence the opposing side will use at trial.

Domestic violence court: A problem-solving court with a specialized docket of domestic violence cases. A multidisciplinary team of criminal justice and social service agency officials attempt to craft interventions that will ensure both victim safety and batterer accountability.

Downstream orientation: The notion that prosecutors' charging decisions in criminal cases reflect their predictions about the likelihood of conviction as the case moves toward trial. Prosecutors attempt to predict how the judge and jury will evaluate the defendant, the victim, and the crime.

Drug treatment court: A problem-solving court with a specialized docket of drug offenses. It incorporates intensive judicial supervision of drug offenders, mandatory drug treatment, and a rehabilitation program providing vocational, education, family, and medical services.

Dual court system: The type of court system found in the United States, where there are 50 separate state court systems, which differ from one another on a number of important dimensions, and the federal court system.

Due process model: A model that views protecting the rights of individuals as the most important function of the criminal justice system; the model emphasizes reliability, which is achieved through formal, adversarial procedures. See also **Presumption of innocence.**

Ecclesiastical courts: Courts found in many parts of Europe during the Middle Ages. These courts exercised jurisdiction over both religious and secular matters and dealt with matters of "canon law," or the religious laws put forth by the dominant church, most notably the Roman Catholic Church.

Effective assistance of counsel: According to the code of ethics promulgated by the American Bar Association, defendants are entitled to effective assistance of counsel. The U.S. Supreme Court ruled in *Strickland v. Washington* (1984) that a defendant's attorney is ineffective if he or she makes serious errors and if these errors prejudice the defense and therefore deprive the defendant of a fair trial.

Electronic monitoring: A type of punishment often used in conjunction with house arrest and designed to ensure that offenders are at home when they are supposed to be. The offender is fitted with a wrist or ankle bracelet that is worn 24 hours a day. The bracelet emits a constant radio signal to a home monitoring unit, which is attached to the offender's home phone. The monitoring unit informs the monitoring center when the offender enters and leaves her home; it also sends a message if the offender tampers with or attempts to remove the bracelet. See also **House arrest**.

En banc: A decision by the full court of all the appeals court justices in a jurisdiction. Justices may sit en banc in order to clear up any conflicting decisions in the same circuit court involving the same legal issue.

Exclusionary rule: The rule that states that evidence that is wrongfully obtained, such as through an unconstitutional search, is not admissible at trial. It was developed by the U.S. Supreme Court in *Weeks v. United States* (federal courts) and *Mapp v. Ohio* (state courts).

Exculpatory evidence: Evidence that tends to suggest the defendant is innocent.

Fact finding: The role of the jury in a criminal case; the jury decides whether the evidence proves that the defendant is guilty of the crime of which he or she is charged.

Factual guilt: The evidence shows that there is a high probability that the defendant committed the crime of which he or she is accused.

Final judgment rule: Limits the timing of an appeal until after the court hands down its final judgment as to the defendant's guilt.

General deterrence: Use of punishment to dissuade potential offenders. Potential offenders learn of the consequences of criminal involvement and decide not to risk subjecting themselves to such punishment.

Going rate: The usual sentence for offenders with certain characteristics who are convicted of a certain type of crime. The notion that members of the courtroom workgroup generally agree on the sentences that should be imposed, based on the characteristics of offenders and their crimes.

Guided discretion statute: A statute that allows the death penalty to be imposed only if the crime involves at least one statutorily defined aggravating circumstance.

Harmless error rule: A rule that states that an error that would not have altered the outcome of the case (i.e., a harmless error) does not require the appellate court to overrule the offender's conviction or sentence.

Homeless court: A specialized court that focuses on legal problems common to those who are homeless. For example, the court may help homeless individuals pay fines and resolve outstanding infractions and misdemeanor offenses.

House arrest: A type of punishment in which offenders are ordered to remain at home for a designated period of time. They are allowed to leave only at specified times and for specific purposes—to obtain food or medical services, to meet with a probation officer, and, sometimes, to go to school or work. See also **Electronic monitoring**.

Hydraulic displacement of discretion: The term used to describe the shifting of discretion from one part of the criminal justice system to another. Constraining judges' discretion at sentencing, for example, results in an increase of discretion in charging and plea bargaining decisions made by the prosecutor.

Impeachment: The formal process for removing judges. At the federal level, it involves impeachment (or accusation) of a federal judge in the House of Representatives and trial in the U.S. Senate. Most states also provide for impeachment of state court judges.

Incapacitation: A utilitarian justification of punishment that involves locking up—or otherwise physically disabling—dangerous or high-risk offenders to prevent them from committing crimes.

Indeterminate sentence: A sentencing system in which the legislature specifies a minimum and maximum sentence for each offense or class of offenses. The judge imposes either a minimum and a maximum term of years or the maximum term only. The parole board decides when the offender will be released from prison.

Initial appearance: The first court appearance, at which bail is set. Once a person is arrested, he or she must be brought before a magistrate "without unnecessary delay."

Inquisitorial system: System of justice found in most European countries. The parties to the case provide all of the relevant evidence to the court, and the judge, not the attorneys for the state or the defense, calls and examines witnesses.

Interlocutory appeal: An appeal filed prior to adjudication of a criminal case. This type of appeal focuses on critical constitutional questions that have no bearing on the defendant's guilt or innocence.

Intermediate sanction: A sanction that is more severe than probation but less severe than a prison sentence. Examples include intensive supervision probation, boot camps, house arrest and electronic monitoring, community service, and monetary fines.

Judge: A referee responsible for enforcing court rules, instructing the jury on the law, determining the law, and sentencing offenders.

Judicial disciplinary commission: A state-level commission, which is usually made up of sitting or retired judges, lawyers, and laypersons, that investigates complaints filed against judges. The commission can dismiss the complaint or admonish, censure, or remove the judge.

Judicial review: The power of the court to examine a law and determine whether it is constitutional. To make this determination, judges examine the law and compare it with the constitution. This requires them to interpret the language of both the statute and the constitution. If the judge determines the law is constitutional, he or she upholds the law; if not, he or she declares it unconstitutional and therefore void.

Judiciary Act of 1789: Article III of the U.S. Constitution provides that "the judicial power of the United States shall be vested in one supreme court, and in such inferior courts as the Congress may from time to time ordain and establish." The Judiciary Act created a federal judicial system composed of the Supreme Court; three Circuit Courts, each made of up two Supreme Court Justices and a district court judge; and 13 district courts.

Jurisdiction: The authority of a court to hear a case and render a decision.

Jury consultant: An individual hired by the defense (or, perhaps, by the state) to determine how individuals with certain background characteristics and attitudes will view the case and the parties involved in the case. These results are then used to create a profile of a juror who would be likely to acquit (or convict) the defendant. The lawyers use this profile to guide decisions during the jury selection process.

Jury nullification: A jury's decision to acquit the defendant in spite of overwhelming evidence that the defendant is guilty. The jury's decision is motivated either by a belief that the law under which the defendant is being prosecuted is unfair or by an objection to the application of the law in a particular case.

Jury panel: Individuals selected from the jury pool for a particular case.

Jury pool: The list of names from which actual jurors will be chosen. See also **Venire.**

Jury tax: See **Trial penalty.**

Legal guilt: Refers to the process by which determinations of guilt are made. Defendants are not to be deemed guilty unless all of the mandated procedures and rules designed to protect the rights of the accused have been followed.

Legal sufficiency policy: A charging policy under which prosecutors file charges in all cases in which the legal elements of the crime are present. Because prosecutors operating under this policy do not necessarily "screen out" cases with weak evidence, there is both a high proportion of cases that are accepted for prosecution and a large percentage of cases that are dismissed at preliminary hearings and trials.

Liberation hypothesis: An explanation for research findings suggesting that legally irrelevant factors (e.g., the race or gender of the defendant and victim, the behavior of the victim at the time of the crime) come into play primarily in cases in which the evidence is ambiguous and the outcome is therefore less predictable. The liberation hypothesis suggests that when the evidence is uncertain, jurors will be "liberated" from the constraints imposed by the law and will therefore feel free to take legally irrelevant factors into consideration during decision making.

Local legal culture: Values and beliefs of members of the courtroom workgroup regarding case processing routines and appropriate behavior of participants in adjudicating cases.

Magistrate judges: Lower-level judges who conduct preliminary proceedings in cases before the district court and issue warrants.

Mandatory minimum sentence: The minimum jail or prison sentence that must be imposed on an offender convicted of a particular type of crime; it is especially common for drug offenses and for offenses involving use of a weapon.

Mandatory sentence: A specified term of incarceration for offenders convicted of certain types of crimes or for repeat or habitual offenders.

Mediation: A process of settling disputes that involves bringing in a neutral third party to help the parties to the dispute resolve the matter (e.g., to work out a child custody agreement for a couple seeking a divorce). The mediator works with the parties to the dispute to reach a mutually agreeable solution but does not have any authority to render a decision.

Mental health court: A specialized court that involves collaboration between the criminal justice system and mental health agencies, with the goal of providing needed services to mentally ill offenders. Defendants participate in court-ordered treatment programs and may have their charges dropped upon successful completion of treatment.

Merit system (Missouri Bar Plan): A hybrid method of judicial selection that combines appointment and election. A judicial nominating commission, which is usually composed of laypersons, lawyers, and judges, screens potential candidates and nominates several individuals (typically three) for the vacant position. The governor then appoints one of the individuals nominated by the commission to the bench. After the initial term, and at designated times thereafter, the appointee runs in a retention election in which the voters are asked whether the judge should be retained or not.

Mock jury study: A method of studying jury deliberations. Researchers use mock juries or mock trials that involve hypothetical scenarios. These may be actual mock trials, such as in a university classroom, or simple written scenarios wherein people (often college students) are asked to decide some hypothetical defendant's fate. Then the researchers compare people's demographic characteristics to the decisions they hand down.

No bill: A document reflecting the decision by the grand jury not to vote for an indictment.

Nolo contendere plea: A plea in which the defendant accepts whatever punishment the court would impose on a guilty defendant, but refuses to admit liability. This plea is frequently used by defendants who fear being exposed to civil liability for their criminal misdeeds. Also known as a "no contest" plea.

Normal penalty: see **Going rate.**

Obiter dicta: Latin for "things said by the way." Supporting statements made by the courts in making their decisions. These statements are legal or non-legal arguments used to support the reasons for the decision and do not constitute precedent. See also **Ratio decidendi.**

Oversight: An important function of courts, particularly appellate courts. The process of reviewing the decisions of lower courts and of criminal justice officials to ensure that proper procedures were followed and that neither laws nor constitutional provisions were violated.

Pardon: see **Clemency.**

Parens patriae: The original guiding principle of the juvenile justice system. Literally translated as "the father of the country," the phrase refers to the government's right and obligation to act on behalf of the child—that is, to do what is in the best interest of the child.

Peremptory challenge: During the jury selection process, the prosecutor and the defense attorney will each have a limited number of peremptory challenges, which they can use to excuse prospective jurors from the jury pool without giving reasons for removing them. See also **Challenge for cause.**

Plea bargaining: The process of negotiating a guilty plea. Typically involves either charge bargaining, where the prosecutor will offer to reduce the severity of the charges or the number of counts in exchange for a guilty plea, or sentence bargaining, where the prosecutor will agree to recommend leniency at the sentencing stage.

Precedent: A prior court decision or ruling.

Preliminary hearing: The stage in the pretrial process when the judge determines whether there is probable cause to believe that an offense was committed and it was the defendant who committed it. If probable cause is established, the defendant is "bound over" for trial. The preliminary hearing is a formal adversarial proceeding conducted in open court.

Presumption of guilt: The view, prominent in the crime control model of the criminal process, which holds that defendants who are not screened out early in the process by police and prosecutors are probably guilty and therefore can be passed quickly through the remaining stages in the process. A prediction of outcome: those not screened out early in the process are probably guilty and more than likely will plead guilty or be found guilty at trial. See also **Crime control model.**

Presumption of innocence: The view, prominent in the due process model of the criminal process, which holds that defendants are to be treated as though their guilt is an open question until they have been adjudicated guilty. See also **Due process model.**

Privately retained counsel: Attorneys selected and paid by the defendant.

Probable cause: A legal concept referring to the amount of proof a police officer must have to search or arrest someone.

Probation: A sanction involving community supervision of an offender by a probation officer. May also include other conditions, such as substance abuse treatment or drug testing.

Problem-solving courts: Specialized courts that take a broader and more comprehensive approach to delinquency and criminality. Rather than focusing solely on the crime for which the defendant has been arrested, these courts attempt to address the underlying social and economic factors that contributed to the defendant's involvement in crime. They also involve collaboration among criminal justice and social service agencies and are more likely than traditional courts to incorporate the principles of restorative justice. Examples include drug courts, domestic violence courts, homeless courts, teen courts, and re-entry courts.

Prosecutors: Attorney responsible for prosecuting cases on behalf of the state.

Public defenders: Attorneys hired by the state to work for defendants who cannot afford to hire their own lawyer.

Public defender system: A method of providing counsel for indigent defendants. Lawyers who are employed by the jurisdiction (typically, the county or the state) represent the indigent defendants who are charged with crimes.

Random cross-section of the community: The Supreme Court has interpreted the Sixth Amendment's requirement that the defendant be tried by an "impartial jury" to mean that the jury pool must be a "random cross-section of the community." This means that all members of the community must have an equal chance of being included in the jury pool.

Ratio decidendi: Latin for "the reason for the decision." The legal principle or rationale used by the courts to arrive at their decisions. See also **Obiter dicta.**

Recuse: The act by which judges excuse themselves from a case because they do not believe that they can be fair or impartial.

Reentry court: A specialized court that does not adjudicate new offenses but instead provides oversight and support services to offenders reentering the community, with the goal of reducing recidivism and prison return rates.

Rehabilitation: A utilitarian justification of punishment that involves preventing crime by reforming, or treating, offenders. The techniques used to reform or rehabilitate offenders include such things as individual or group counseling, education, job training, substance abuse treatment, and behavior modification programs.

Reintegrative shaming: The notion that community disapproval of criminal behavior (i.e., shaming) should be followed by reintegration into the community of law-abiding citizens.

Restorative justice: Utilitarian justification of punishment that views punishment as a means to repair the harm and injury caused by the crime and focuses on the victim and the community as well as the offender. Participants in the process discuss the effects of the crime on the victim, the offender, and the community and attempt to reach a collective agreement regarding the most appropriate sanction.

Retention election: A judicial election in which voters are asked whether the judge should be retained or not. See also **Merit system.**

Retributive justification for punishment: Backward-looking justification of punishment which holds that an offender is punished because he has done something wrong—something blameworthy—and therefore deserves to be punished.

Right of appeal: Although offenders do not have a constitutional right to appeal their convictions, every jurisdiction has created a statutory right to appeal to one higher court. The purpose of this is to ensure that proper procedures were followed by all of the parties to the case, including the judge.

Right to counsel: The right to be represented by a lawyer at all of the critical stages of the criminal justice process. Indigent defendants have the right to a lawyer provided by the state.

Rule of four: Rule that U.S. Supreme Court Justices follow in deciding whether to review a lower court decision. The case will be heard and the writ issued if four of the nine justices agree to hear the appeal.

Selective incapacitation: Punishment philosophy that holds that offenders who are dangerous and likely to commit additional crimes should be incapacitated through a jail or prison sentence. Involves predicting that an individual offender, or offenders with certain characteristics, will commit additional crimes if not locked up. See also **Collective incapacitation.**

Sentence agreement: Agreement for sentencing leniency negotiated during the plea bargaining process. The prosecutor might agree to recommend a particular sentence, recommend that sentences be served concurrently rather than consecutively, or agree to recommend that the sentence not exceed some threshold. See also **Sentence lid.**

Sentence lid: A type of plea bargain in which the prosecutor recommends that the sentence not exceed a specific term of years.

Sentencing guidelines: Structured sentencing system implemented by the federal government and some states. Typically, sentence ranges are determined by the intersection of a crime seriousness score and the defendant's criminal history score, and judges cannot depart from the guidelines without providing reasons for doing so.

Slow plea of guilty: A hybrid approach to case adjudication, with elements of both plea bargaining and trial. In order to receive concessions from the prosecutor, the defendant waives the right to a jury trial, and the case is adjudicated by a judge at a bench trial.

Specialized court: See **Problem-solving courts.**

Specific deterrence: Use of punishment to dissuade offenders from re-offending. An offender who has been legally punished ceases offending because of a fear of future punishment.

Stare decisis: A Latin term that means "let the decision stand." It refers to the judicial practice of looking to the past for pertinent decisions (i.e., for precedent) and deferring to them. Thus, a court will not overturn a past decision on an important legal issue unless there is a good reason for doing so.

Substantial assistance departure: A type of downward departure authorized by the federal sentencing guidelines. The judge can impose a more lenient sentence than required by the guidelines if the defendant provides information that leads to the arrest and prosecution of another offender.

System efficiency policy: A charging policy that emphasizes case screening as a way of decreasing office workload. This policy results in high levels of referrals to diversionary programs and in overcharging (for the purpose of enhancing the prosecutor's power in plea negotiations).

Teen court: Specialized court in which youths, under adult supervision, adjudicate cases involving other teens and fashion appropriate punishments.

Trial penalty: Penalty or "tax" imposed on defendants who do not plead guilty but who insist on a jury trial. Notion that defendants who go to trial will get harsher sentences than those who plead guilty.

Trial sufficiency policy: A charging policy under which prosecutors evaluate cases in terms of their likelihood of conviction at trial; they file charges only if the odds of conviction at trial are good. This policy produces both a high rate of rejection at initial screening and a high trial rate for the cases that are not screened out.

True bill: A document reflecting the grand jury's decision to indict.

Utilitarian justifications for punishment: Forward-looking justifications of punishment that focus on the future criminal behavior of both the person being punished and other members of society. The goal is to prevent crime through deterrence, incapacitation, or rehabilitation.

Venire: (a) The list of names from which actual jurors will be chosen. See also **Jury pool.** (b) The judge's order to assemble a pool of prospective jurors.

Venue: The same as geographic jurisdiction.

Voir dire: Old French for "to speak the truth." The process of questioning potential jurors to determine whether they are unbiased and can decide the case fairly and impartially.

Waiver of juveniles to adult court: The process of transferring a juvenile from juvenile court to adult court. Most states give juvenile court judges the power to waive jurisdiction over juvenile cases that meet certain criteria—generally, a minimum age, a specified type or level of offense, and/or a sufficiently serious record of prior delinquency. Some states have direct file waiver provisions, which allow the prosecutor to file certain types of juvenile cases directly in criminal court.

Wedding cake metaphor: A metaphor used to describe the variations in the treatment of criminal offenders and their cases. The big bottom layer of the wedding cake is composed of misdemeanors; the middle, smaller layer includes routine felony cases; and the top layer consists of a much smaller number of especially serious crimes and/or crimes committed by highly visible people. Whereas crimes in the bottom two layers are disposed of quickly and efficiently using routine procedures, the highly publicized and celebrated cases that make up the top layer of the wedding cake are handled in a way that resembles more closely the adversarial ideal.

Writ of certiorari: An order from an appellate court, such as the U.S. Supreme Court, to a lower court requesting that the lower court send the record in the case forward for review. It means that the appellate court will review the lower court's decision for procedural mistakes or legal errors.

Writ of habeas corpus: An order requesting that a prisoner be brought before the court so that the constitutionality of his or her confinement can be reviewed. In the United States, the process begins when an individual who is incarcerated petitions a U.S. District Court or the United States Supreme Court for a writ of habeas corpus. If the court grants the petition and issues the writ, the individual's case will be reviewed.

References

Abadinsky, H. (1988). *Law and justice.* Chicago: Nelson-Hall.

Abney v. United States, 431 U.S. 651 (1977).

Acree, M., Ekstrand, M., Coates, T., & Stall, R. (1999). Mode effects in surveys of gay men: A within-individual comparison of responses by mail and by telephone. *Journal of Sex Research, 36,* 65–75.

Administrative Office of the United States Courts. (n.d.). *Understanding the federal courts.* Retrieved May 7, 2008, from http://www.uscourts.gov/understand02

Administrative Office of the United States Courts. (2010). *Judicial business of the United States Courts: Annual report of the director.* Washington, DC: Author.

Alarcon, A. S. (1983). Political appointments and judicial independence—An unreasonable expectation. *Loyola of Los Angeles Law Review, 16,* 9–15.

Albonetti, C. (1986). Criminality, prosecutorial screening, and uncertainty: Toward a theory of discretionary decision making in felony case processing. *Criminology, 24,* 623–644.

Albonetti, C. (1987). Prosecutorial discretion: The effects of uncertainty. *Law and Society Review, 21,* 291–313.

Albonetti, C. A. (1997). Sentencing under the federal sentencing guidelines: Effects of defendant characteristics, guilty pleas, and departures on sentence outcomes for drug offenses, 1991–1992. *Law and Society Review, 31,* 789–822.

Alschuler, A. (1968). The prosecutor's role in plea bargaining. *Chicago Law Review, 36,* 50–112.

Alschuler, A. W. (1979). Plea bargaining and its history. *Law and Society Review, 13,* 211.

Alschuler, A. W., & Deiss, A. G. (1994). A brief history of the criminal jury in the United States. *University of Chicago Law Review, 61,* 921–928.

Amadeo v. Zant, 486 U.S. 214 (1988).

American Bar Association. (1993). *Standards for criminal justice: The prosecution function.* Retrieved May 11, 2008, from http://www.abanet.org/crimjust/standards/pfunc_toc.html

American Judicature Society. (2004). *Judicial selection in the states: Appellate and general jurisdiction courts.* Des Moines, IA: Author.

Apodaca v. Oregon, 406 U.S. 404 (1972).

Aquilino, W. (1990). Interviewer mode effects in surveys of drug and alcohol use. *Public Opinion Quarterly, 54,* 362–395.

Arenella, P. (1983). Rethinking the functions of criminal procedure: The Warren and Burger Courts' competing ideologies. *Georgetown Law Journal, 72,* 185, 216–219.

Argersinger v. Hamlin, 407 U.S. 25 (1972).

Aspin, A. (2005). Trends in judicial retention elections, 1964–1998. In E. E. Slotnick (Ed.), *Judicial politics: Readings from judicature* (3rd ed., pp. 65–68). Washington, DC: CQ Press.

Atkins, B. M., & Glick, H. R. (1974). Formal judicial recruitment and state supreme court decisions. *American Politics Quarterly, 2,* 427–449.

Austin, J., & Irwin, J. (2001). *It's about time: America's imprisonment binge* (3rd ed.). Belmont, CA: Wadsworth.

Avery v. Georgia, 345 U.S. 559, 562 (1953).

Baldus, D. C., Woodworth, G. G., & Pulaski, C. A. (1990). *Equal justice and the death penalty: A legal and empirical analysis.* Boston: Northeastern University Press.

Baldwin v. New York, 399 U.S. 66 (1970).

Ballenger v. State, 436 S.E.2d 793 (Ga. Ct. App. 1993).

Batson v. Kentucky, 476 U.S. 79 (1986).

Baum, L. (1985). *The Supreme Court.* Washington, DC: Congressional Quarterly.

Baze v. Rees, 128 S.Ct. 1520 (2008).

Bazemore, G. (1998). Restorative justice and earned redemptions: Communities, victims, and offender reintegration. *American Behavioral Scientist, 41,* 768–813.

Bazemore, G., & Walgrave, L. (1999). Restorative juvenile justice: In search of fundamentals and an outline for systematic reform. In G. Bazemore & L. Walgrave (Eds.), *Restorative juvenile justice* (pp. 45–74). Monsey, NY: Criminal Justice Press.

Beard, A. (2007, April 11). Prosecutors drop charges in Duke case. *Boston Globe.* Retrieved May 14, 2008, from http://www.boston.com/news/nation/articles/2007/04/11/prosecutors_drop_charges_in_duke_case/

Beccaria, C. (1986). *On crimes and punishments* (D. Young, Trans.). Indianapolis, IN: Hackett. (Original work published 1974)

Beha, J. A., II. (1977). And nobody can get you out: The impact of a mandatory prison sentence for the illegal carrying of a firearm on the use of firearms and on the administration of criminal justice in Boston. *Boston University Law Review, 57,* 97–146, 289–333.

Belenko, S. (1998). Research on drug courts: A critical review. *National Drug Courts Institute Review, 1,* 3–43.

Bentham, J. (1970). *Introduction to the principles of morals and legislation.* London: Athlone Press.

Berkson, L. C. (2005). Judicial selection in the United States: A special report. In E. E. Slotnick (Ed.), *Judicial politics: Readings from judicature* (3rd ed., pp. 50–52). Washington, DC: CQ Press.

Berman, G., & Feinblatt, J. (2001). *Problem-solving courts: A brief primer.* New York: Center for Court Innovation.

Berns, S. (1999). *To speak as a judge: Difference, voice, and power.* Aldershot, UK: Ashgate.

Bernstein, I. N., Kick, E., Leung, J. T., & Schultz, B. (1977). Charge reduction: An intermediary state in the process of labeling criminal defendants. *Social Forces, 56,* 362–384.

Blackledge v. Allison, 431 U.S. 63 (1977).

Blackledge v. Perry, 417 U.S. 21 (1974).

Blankenship, M. B., & Janikowski, W. R. (1992). Accountability v. independence: Myths of judicial selection. *Criminal Justice Policy Review, 6,* 69–79.

Blumberg, A. (1967). The practice of law as a confidence game: Organizational cooptation of a profession. *Law and Society Review, 1,* 15–39.

Blumberg, A. (1970). *The scales of justice.* Chicago: Aldine.

Blumstein, A., Cohen, J., Martin, S. E., & Tonry, M. H. (Eds.). (1983). *Research on sentencing: The search for reform* (Vol. I). Washington, DC: National Academy Press.

Boland, B. (1996, August). What is community prosecution? *National Institute of Justice Journal,* 35–40.

Bordenkircher v. Hayes, 434 U.S. 357, 364 (1978).

Bounds v. Smith, 430 U.S. 817 (1977).

Bozza v. United States, 330 U.S. 160 (1947).

Brady v. Maryland, 397 U.S. 742 (1970).

Braithwaite, J. (1989). *Crime, shame, and reintegration.* Cambridge, UK: Cambridge University Press.

Braithwaite, J. (1998). Restorative justice: Assessing optimistic and pessimistic accounts. In M. Tonry (Ed.), *The handbook of crime and punishment* (pp. 1–127). New York: Oxford University Press.

Braithwaite, J. (1999). Restorative justice: Assessing optimistic and pessimistic accounts. In M. Tonry (Ed.), *Crime and justice: Review of research.* Chicago: University of Chicago Press.

Braithwaite, J., & Pettit, P. (1990). *Not just deserts: A Republican theory of criminal justice.* New York: Oxford University Press.

Bright, S. B., & Keenan, P. J. (1995). Judges and the politics of death: Deciding between the Bill of Rights and the next election in capital cases. *Boston University Law Review, 75,* 558–835.

Britt, C. L. (2000). Social context and racial disparities in punishment decisions. *Justice Quarterly, 17,* 707–732.

Burch v. Louisiana, 441 U.S. 130 (1979).

Bureau of Justice Assistance. (2000). *National assessment of structured sentencing.* Washington, DC: Author.

Bureau of Justice Statistics. (n.d. a). *Criminal case processing statistics.* Retrieved May 5, 2008, from http://www.ojp.usdoj.gov/bjs/cases.htm

Bureau of Justice Statistics. (n.d. b). *Federal justice statistics.* Retrieved May 5, 2008, from http://www.ojp.usdoj.gov/bjs/fed.htm#Adjudication

Bureau of Justice Statistics. (1998). *State court sentencing of convicted felons.* Washington, DC: Author.

Bureau of Justice Statistics. (2000). *Defense counsel in criminal cases.* Washington, DC: U.S. Department of Justice.

Bureau of Justice Statistics. (2003). *New court commitments to state prison, 2002.* Washington, DC: Author.

Bureau of Justice Statistics. (2004). *Felony sentences in state courts, 2002.* Washington, DC: Author.

Bureau of Justice Statistics. (2005a). *Federal criminal case processing, 2004.* Washington, DC: Author.

Bureau of Justice Statistics. (2005b). *State court sentences of convicted felons, 2002.* Washington, DC: Author.

Bureau of Justice Statistics. (2006a). *Prisoners in 2005.* Washington, DC: Author.

Bureau of Justice Statistics. (2006b). *State court organization 2004.* Washington, DC: Author.

Bureau of Justice Statistics. (2009a). *Federal criminal case processing, 2008.* Washington, DC: Author.

Bureau of Justice Statistics. (2009b). *Felony sentences in state courts, 2006.* Washington, DC: Author.

Bureau of Justice Statistics. (2010). *Felony defendants in large urban counties.* Washington, DC: Author.

Bush, N. (1976). The case for expansive voir dire. *Law and Psychology Review, 2,* 9–25.

California Administrative Office of the Courts. (2004). *Homeless courts.* Sacramento, CA: Author.

Cardozo, B. N. (2005). The nature of the judicial process. In W. F. Murphy, C. H. Pritchett, L. Epstein, & J. Knight (Eds.), *Courts, judges, and politics* (pp. 30–33). New York: McGraw-Hill.

Carey, M. (1996). Restorative justice in community corrections. *Corrections Today, 58,* 152–155.

Carns, T. W., & Kruse, J. A. (1992). Alaska's ban on plea bargaining reevaluated. *Judicature, 75,* 310–317.

Carp, R. A., & Stidham, R. (1998). *Judicial process in America* (4th ed.). Washington, DC: Congressional Quarterly.

Casper, J. D. (1971). Did you have a lawyer when you went to court? No, I had a public defender. *Yale Review of Law and Social Action, 1,* 4–9.

Casper, J. D. (1978). *Criminal courts: The defendant's perspective.* Englewood Cliffs, NJ: Prentice-Hall.

Center for Court Innovation. (n.d.). *Problem-solving courts.* New York: Author.

Chapman v. California, 386 U.S. 18 (1967).

Chesney-Lind, M. (1995). Rethinking women's imprisonment. In B. R. Price & N. J. Sokoloff (Eds.), *The criminal justice system and women: Offenders, victims, and workers* (pp. 105–117). New York: McGraw-Hill.

Chesney-Lind, M. (1997). *The female offender: Girls, women, and crime.* Thousand Oaks, CA: Sage.

Chicago boy, 12, will be youngest in U.S. prison. (1996, January 31). *Omaha World Herald.*

Chiricos, C., & Crawford, C. (1995). Race and imprisonment decisions: A contextual assessment of the evidence. In D. Hawkins (Ed.), *Ethnicity, race, and crime* (pp. 281–309). Albany: State University of New York Press.

Chiricos, T. G., & Bales, W. D. (1991). Unemployment and punishment: An empirical assessment. *Criminology, 29,* 701–724.

Church, T. (1982). *Examining local legal culture: Practitioner attitudes in four criminal courts.* Toronto: Little, Brown.

Clancy, J., Bartolomeo, J., Richardson, D., & Wellford, C. (1981). Sentence decision making: The logic of sentence decisions and the extent and sources of sentence disparity. *The Journal of Criminal Law and Criminology, 72,* 524–554.

Cohen v. Beneficial Industrial Loan Corp., 337 U.S. 541 (1949).

Coker v. Georgia, 433 U.S. 584 (1977).

Cole, D. (2000). *No equal justice: Race and class in the American criminal justice system.* New York: New Press.

Cole, G. F., Mahoney, B., Thornton, M., & Hanson, R. A. (1987). *The practices and attitudes of trial court judges regarding fines as a criminal sanction.* Washington, DC: U.S. Department of Justice.

Coles, C. M., & Kelling, G. L. (1998). *Prosecution in the community: A study of emergent strategies: A cross site analysis.* Cambridge, MA: Harvard University.

Colquitt, J. A. (2001). Ad hoc plea bargaining. *Tulane Law Review, 75,* 695–776.

Commonwealth v. Battis, 1 Mass. 95 (1804).

Connecticut v. Johnson, 460 U.S. 73 (1983).

Cook, B. B. (1973). Sentencing behavior of federal judges: Draft cases, 1972. *University of Cincinnati Law Review, 42,* 597.

Cox, G. D. (2001). Judges behaving badly. *The National Law Journal.* Retrieved May 19, 2008, from http://www.truthinjustice.org/bad-judge.htm

Crockett, G. (1984). The role of the black judge. In E. Georges-Abeyie (Ed.), *The criminal justice system and blacks.* New York: Clark Boardman.

Daly, K. (1987). Structure and practice of familial-based justice in a criminal court. *Law and Society Review, 21,* 267–290.

Daly, K. (1989). Neither conflict nor labeling nor paternalism will suffice: Intersections of race, ethnicity, gender, and family in criminal court decisions. *Crime and Delinquency, 35,* 136–168.

Daly, K., & Bordt, R. (1995). Sex effects and sentencing: A review of the statistical literature. *Justice Quarterly, 12,* 143–177.

Daly, K., & Tonry, M. (1997). Gender, race and sentencing. In M. Tonry (Ed.), *Crime and justice: A review of research* (Vol. 22, pp. 201–252). Chicago: University of Chicago Press.

Davis, K. C. (1969). *Discretionary justice.* Baton Rouge: Louisiana State University Press.

Demarest, C. E. (1994, April 15). Plea bargaining can often protect the victim. *New York Times,* p. A30.

Denckla, D., & Berman, G. (2001). *Rethinking the revolving door: A look at mental illness in the courts.* New York: Center for Court Innovation.

Devine, D. J., Clayton, L. D., Dunford, B. B., Seying, R., & Pryce, J. (2001). Jury decision making: 45 years of empirical research on deliberating groups. *Psychology, Public Policy, and the Law, 7,* 622–725.

Ditton, P. M. (1999). *Mental health and treatment of inmates and probationers.* Washington, DC: Bureau of Justice Statistics.

Dodge, M., & Harris, J. C. (2000). Calling a strike a ball: Jury nullification and "three strikes" cases. In G. L. Mays & P. R. Gregware (Eds.), *Courts and justice: A reader* (2nd ed.). Prospect Heights, IL: Waveland Press.

Douglas v. California, 372 U.S. 353 (1963).

Douglas, W. O. (1974). Stare decisis. In W. F. Murphy & C. H. Pritchett (Eds.), *Courts, judges, and politics* (2nd ed., pp. 401–405). New York: Random House.

Downie, L. (1971). *Justice denied: The case for reform of the courts.* Baltimore, MD: Penguin Books.

Drug Court Clearinghouse and Technical Assistance Project. (1999). *Looking at a decade of drug courts.* Washington, DC: U.S. Department of Justice.

Dubois, P. L. (1986). Accountability, independence, and the selection of state judges: The role of popular judicial elections. *Southwestern Law Journal, 40,* 31–52.

Dugan v. Ohio, 277 U.S. 61 (1928).

Duke DA answers critics: Denies unethical conduct, wants some charges dropped. (2007, February 28). *ABC News online.* Retrieved May 14, 2008, from http://abcnews.go.com/US/Legal Center/story?id=2912209&page=1

Duke rape suspects speak out [Television series episode]. (2006). *60 minutes.*

Duke suspends lacrosse team from play amid rape allegations. (2006, March 28). *USA Today.* Retrieved May 30, 2008, from http://www .usatoday.com/sports/college/lacrosse/2006-03-28-duke-team-suspension_x.htm

Duncan v. Louisiana, 391 U.S. 145 (1968).

Durham, A. L., III. (1994). *Crisis and reform: Current issues in American punishment.* Boston: Little, Brown.

Edwards v. People, 39 Mich. 760 (1878).

Eisenstein, J., Flemming, R. B., & Nardulli, P. F. (1988). *The contours of justice: Communities and their courts.* Boston: Little, Brown.

Eisenstein, J., & Jacob, H. (1977). *Felony justice: Organizational approach to criminal courts.* Boston: Little, Brown.

Elkins v. United States, 364 U.S. 206 (1960).

Engen, R. L., & Steen, S. (2000). The power to punish: Discretion and sentencing reform in the war on drugs. *American Journal of Sociology, 105,* 1357–1395.

Engle, C. D. (1971). *Criminal justice in the city: A study of sentence severity and variation in the Philadelphia court system.* PhD dissertation, Temple University, Philadelphia, PA.

Eschholz, S., Reed, M. D., & Beck, E. (2003). Offenders' family members' responses to capital crimes: The need for restorative justice initiatives. *Homicide Studies, 7,* 154–181.

Estes v. Texas, 381 U.S. 532 (1965).

Evitts v. Lucey, 469 U.S. 387 (1985).

Ewart, D. W., & Pennington, D. C. (1997). Reasons for sentence: An empirical investigation. In M. Wasik (Ed.), *The sentencing process* (pp. 117–134). Aldershot, UK: Dartmouth.

Ex parte Hawk, 321 U.S. 114, 116–117 (1944).

Fagan, J. (1991). *The comparative impacts of juvenile and criminal court sanctions on adolescent offenders.* Washington, DC: Office of Justice Programs, National Institute of Justice.

Fagan, J. (1995). Separating the men from the boys: The comparative advantage of juvenile versus criminal court sanctions on recidivism among adolescent felony offenders. In J. C. Howell, B. Krisberg, J. D. Hawkins, & J. J. Wilson (Eds.), *A sourcebook: Serious, violent and chronic juvenile offenders* (pp. 238–260). Thousand Oaks, CA: Sage.

Farole, D. J. (2003). *The Harlem Parole Reentry Court evaluation: Implementation and preliminary impacts.* New York: Center for Court Innovation.

Farole, D. J., Jr., Puffett, N., Rempel, M., & Byrne, F. (2005). Applying problem-solving principles in mainstream courts: Lessons for state courts. *Justice System Journal, 26,* 57–76.

Federal Bureau of Investigation. (2007). *Uniform crime reports, crime in the United States—2005.* Washington, DC: Author.

Federal Judicial Center. (n.d.). *Federal courts and what they do.* Retrieved May 7, 2008, from http://www.fjc.gov/public/pdf.nsf/lookup/FCtsWhat.pdf/$file/FCtsWhat.pdf

Feeley, M. M., & Kamin, S. (1996). The effect of "three strikes and you're out" on the courts: Looking back to the future. In D. Shichor & D. K. Sechrest (Eds.), *Three strikes and you're out: Vengeance as public policy* (pp. 135–154). Thousand Oaks, CA: Sage.

Fields v. People, 732 P.2d 1145, 1158 n.20 (Colo. 1987).

Fineman, M. (1994). Feminist legal scholarship and women's gendered lives. In C. M. Harrington & C. B. Harrington (Eds.), *Lawyers in a postmodern world: Translation and transgression* (pp. 239–240). New York: New York University Press.

Finigan, M. W. (1998). *An outcome program evaluation of the Multnomah County S.T.O.P. Drug Diversion Program.* Portland, OR: NPC Research.

Finnis, J. (1980). *Natural law and natural rights.* Oxford, UK: Clarendon.

Fisher, G. (2003). *Plea bargaining's triumph: A history of plea bargaining in America.* Stanford, CA: Stanford University Press.

Fleming v. Kemp, 475 U.S. 1058 (1986).

Ford, D. A., & Burke, M. J. (1987, July). *Victim-initiated criminal complaints for wife-battery: An assessment of motives.* Paper presented at the third annual Conference for Family Violence, Durham, NC.

Forst, B., & Wellford, C. (1981). Punishment and sentencing: Developing sentencing guidelines empirically from principles of punishment. *Rutgers Law Review, 33,* 799–837.

Frank, J. (1949). *Courts on trial: Myth and reality in American Justice.* Princeton, NJ: Princeton University Press.

Frankel, M. E. (2006). The adversary judge: The experience of the trial judge. In W. F. Murphy, C. H. Pritchett, L. Epstein, & J. Knight (Eds.), *Courts, judges and politics* (6th ed., pp. 398–401). New York: McGraw-Hill.

Frase, R. S. (2007). The Apprendi-Blakely Cases: Sentencing Reform Counter Revolution? *Criminology and Public Policy, 6,* 403–431.

Frazier, C. E., & Bock, E. W. (1982). Effects of court officials on sentence severity: Do judges make a difference? *Criminology, 20,* 257–278.

Frazier, P. A., & Haney, B. (1996). Sexual assault cases in the legal system: Police, prosecutor, and victim perspectives. *Law and Human Behavior, 20,* 607–628.

Friedman, L. M., & Percival, R. V. (1981). *The roots of justice: Crime and punishment in Alameda County, California, 1870-1910.* Chapel Hill: University of North Carolina Press.

Frohmann, L. (1991). Discrediting victims' allegations of sexual assault: Prosecutorial accounts of case rejections. *Social Problems, 38,* 213–226.

Frohmann, L. (1997). Convictability and discordant locales: Reproducing race, class, and gender ideologies in prosecutorial decision making. *Law and Society Review, 31,* 531–555.

Furman v. Georgia, 408 U.S. 153 (1972).

Georgia Department of Public Welfare. (1924). Crime and the Georgia courts. *Journal of the American Institute of Criminal Law and Criminology, 16,* 169–180.

Gideon v. Wainwright, 372 U.S. 335 (1963).

Gilligan, C. (1982). *In a different voice: Psychological theory and women's development.* Cambridge, MA: Harvard University Press.

Glazer, E. (1999). Thinking strategically: How federal prosecutors can reduce violent crime. *Fordham Urban Law Journal, 26,* 573–606.

Goldberg, N. A., & Hartman, M. J. (1983). The public defender in America. In W. F. McDonald (Ed.), *The defense counsel* (pp. 67–102). Beverly Hills, CA: Sage.

Goldkamp, J. S., & Weiland, D. (1993). *Assessing the impact of Dade County's felony drug court: Research in brief.* Washington, DC: U.S. Department of Justice, National Institute of Justice.

Goldkamp, J. S., White, M. D., & Robinson, J. B. (2001). Do drug courts work? Getting inside the drug court black box. *Journal of Drug Issues, 31,* 27–72.

Goldman, S. (1979). Should there be affirmative action for the judiciary? *Judicature, 62,* 488–494.

Goldman, S., Slotnick, E. Gryski, G., Zuk, G., & Schiavoni, S. (2005). W. Bush remaking the judiciary: Like father like son? In E. E. Slotnick (Ed.), *Judicial politics: Readings from judicature* (3rd ed., pp. 86–111). Washington, DC: CQ Press.

Goldstein, H. (1979). Improving policing: A problem-oriented approach. *Crime and Delinquency, 25,* 236–258.

Goldstein, H. (1990). *Problem oriented policing.* New York: McGraw-Hill.

Gottfredson, D.C., Coblentz, K., & Harmon, M. A. (1997, Winter). A short-term outcome evaluation of the Baltimore City Drug Treatment Court Program. *Perspectives, 33–38.*

Gottfredson, D. C., & Exum, M. L. (2002). The Baltimore City Drug Court: One-year results from a randomized study. *Journal of Research in Crime and Delinquency, 39,* 337–356.

Gottfredson, M. R., & Gottfredson, D. M. (1988). *Decision making in criminal justice: Toward the rational exercise of discretion* (2nd ed.). New York: Plenum.

Greenwood, P. W. (2002). Juvenile crime and juvenile justice. In J. Q. Wilson & J. Petersilia (Eds.), *Crime: Public policies for crime control* (pp. 75–108). Oakland, CA: Institute for Contemporary Studies.

Gregg v. Georgia, 428 U.S. 153 (1972).

Griffin, P., Torbet, P. M., & Szymanski, L. (1998). *Trying juveniles as adults in criminal court: An analysis of state transfer provisions.* Washington, DC: U.S. Department of Justice, Office of Justice Programs, Office of Juvenile Justice and Delinquency Prevention.

Griffin v. Illinois, 351 U.S. 12 (1956).

Gross, S. R., & Mauro, R. (1989). *Death and discrimination: Racial disparities in capital sentencing.* Boston: Northeastern University Press.

Gruhl, J., Spohn, C., & Welch, S. (1981). Women as policymakers: The case of trial judges. *American Journal of Political Science, 25,* 308–322.

Guidorizzi, D. D. (1998). Should we really "ban" plea bargaining? The core concerns of plea bargaining critics. *Emory Law Journal, 47,* 753–760.

Hahn, P. H. (1997). *Emerging criminal justice: Three pillars for a proactive justice system.* Thousand Oaks. CA: Sage.

Harrell, A., Mitchell, O., Hirst, A., Marlowe, D. & Merrill, J. (2002). Breaking the cycle of drugs and crime: Findings from the Birmingham BTC demonstration. *Criminology and Public Policy, 1,* 189–216.

Hartje, R. (2005). A jury of your peers? How jury consulting may actually help trial lawyers resolve constitutional limitations imposed on the selection of juries. *California Western Law Review, 41,* 479–506.

Hartley, R. D. (2005). *Type of counsel and its effects on criminal court outcomes in a large Midwestern jurisdiction: Do you get what you pay for?* Unpublished dissertation, University of Nebraska at Omaha.

Hawkins, D. (1981). Causal attribution and punishment for crime. *Deviant Behavior, 1,* 207–230.

Hay, C. (2001). An exploratory test of Braithwaite's reintegrative shaming theory. *Journal of Research in Crime and Delinquency, 38,* 132–153.

Hepperle, W. (1985). Women victims in the criminal justice system. In I. Moyer (Ed.), *The changing role of women in the criminal justice system* (pp. 165–179). Prospect Heights, IL: Waveland Press.

Herrera v. Collins, 506 U.S. 390, 411 (1993).

Heumann, M., & Loftin, C. (1979). Mandatory sentencing and the abolition of plea bargaining: The Michigan Felony Firearms Statute. *Law and Society Review, 13,* 393–430.

Hodes, W. W. (1996). Lord Brougham, the dream team, and jury nullification of the third kind. *University of Colorado Law Review, 67,* 1075–1108.

Hoffman, M. B. (1997). Peremptory challenges should be abolished: A trial judge's perspective. *University of Chicago Law Review, 64,* 809–871.

Hogarth, J. (1971). *Sentencing as a human process.* Toronto, Canada: University of Toronto Press.

Holmes, M. D., Daudistel, H. C., & Farrell, R. A. (1987). Determinants of charge reductions and final dispositions in cases of burglary and robbery. *Journal of Research in Crime and Delinquency, 24,* 233–254.

Holmes, M. E., Hosch, H. M., Daudistel, H. C., Perez, D. A., & Graves, J. B. (1993). Judges' ethnicity and minority sentencing: Evidence concerning Hispanics. *Social Science Quarterly, 74,* 496–506.

Holmes, M. D., Hosch, H. M., Daudistel, H. C., Perez, D. A., & Graves, J. B. (1996). Ethnicity, legal resources, and felony dispositions in two southwestern jurisdictions. *Justice Quarterly, 13,* 11–30.

Horowitz, I. A., Kerr, N. L., & Niedermeier, K. E. (2001). Jury nullification: Legal and psychological perspectives. *Brooklyn Law Review, 66,* 1207–1249.

Hospers, J. (1977). Punishment, protection, and rehabilitation. In J. Cederblom & W. L. Blizek (Eds.), *Justice and punishment* (pp. 21–50). Cambridge, MA: Ballinger.

Hoyt v. Florida, 368 U.S. 57 (1961).

In re Oliver, 333 U.S. 257 (1948).

Inciardi, J. A., McBride, D. C., & Rivers, J. E. (1996). *Drug control and the courts.* Thousand Oaks, CA: Sage.

Iyengar, R. (2006, May). *Not getting their due process: An evaluation of federal indigent defense counsel.* Paper presented at the American Law and Economics Annual Meetings. Retrieved May 15, 2008, from http://law.bepress.com/alea/16th/art5

Jacoby, J. E. (1980). *The American prosecutor: A search for identity.* Lexington, MA: Lexington Books.

Jason, P. D. (1997). The Courts Christian in Medieval England. *The Catholic Lawyer, 37,* 339–353.

J. E. B. v. Alabama ex rel T. B., 511 U.S. 127 (1994).

Johnson v. Avery, 393 U.S. 483 (1969).

Johnson, J. S. (2003). The entertainment value of a trial: How media access to the courtroom is changing the American judicial process. *Villanova Sports and Entertainment Law Journal, 10,* 131–152.

Johnson, R. T. (1992, November 24). *Office of the District Attorney of Bronx County press release.* New York: Author.

Johnson v. Louisiana, 406 U.S. 356 (1972).

Johnson v. Zerbst, 304 U.S. 458 (1938).

Joint Committee on New York Drug Law Evaluation. (1978). *The nation's toughest drug law: Evaluating the New York experience* (Final report of the Joint Committee on New York Drug Law Evaluation). Washington, DC: U.S. Government Printing Office.

Jonakait, R. N. (2003). *The American jury system.* New Haven, CT: Yale University Press.

Jurek v. Texas, 428 U.S. 262 (1976).

Juvenile justice experts decry severity of life in adult prison for Nathaniel Brazill. (n.d.). Retrieved May 30, 2008, from http://www.cjcj.org/press/life_sentence.html

Kagan, R. A. (2001). *Adversarial legalism: The American way of law.* Cambridge, MA: Harvard University Press.

Kalven, H., & Zeisel, H. (1966). *The American jury.* Chicago: University of Chicago Press.

Kant, I. (1887). *The philosophy of law* (W. Hastie, Trans.). Edinburgh, Scotland: T. T. Clark.

Kapardis, A., & Farrington, D. P. (1982). An experimental study of sentencing by magistrates. *Law and Human Behavior, 5,* 107–121.

Kaplan, J. (1973). *Criminal justice: Introductory cases and materials.* Mineola, NY: Foundation Press.

Karan, A., Keilitz, S. L., & Denaro, S. (1999). Domestic violence courts: What are they and how should we manage them? *Juvenile and Family Court Journal, 50,* 75–86.

Karp, D. R. (2001). Harm and repair: Observing restorative justice in Vermont. *Justice Quarterly, 18,* 727–757.

Kaufman v. United States, 394 U.S. 217, 226 (1969).

Kautt, P., & Spohn, C. (2002). *Crack*-ing down on black drug offenders? Testing for interactions between offender race, drug type, and sentencing strategy in federal drug sentences. *Justice Quarterly, 19,* 1–35.

Kaye, J. (1999, October 11). Making the case for hands-on courts. *Newsweek,* p. 13.

Keil, T., & Vito, G. (1989). Race, homicide severity, and application of the death penalty: A consideration of the Barnett Scale. *Criminology, 27,* 511–533.

Keilitz, S. L. (2000). *Specialization of domestic violence case management in the courts: A National Survey.* Washington, DC: National Center for State Courts.

Kennedy, R. (1997). *Race, crime, and the law.* New York: Vintage Books.

Kerr, N. L. (1978). Severity of penalty and mock jurors' verdicts. *Journal of Personality and Social Psychology, 36,* 1431–1442.

Kerstetter, W. (1990). Gateway to justice: Police and prosecutorial response to sexual assaults against women. *Criminology, 81,* 267–313.

King, N. J. (1998). Batson for the bench? Regulating the peremptory challenges of judges. *Chicago-Kent Law Review, 73,* 509–532.

Kingsnorth, R. F., MacIntosh, R. C., & Wentworth, J. (1999). Sexual assault: The role of prior relationship and victim characteristics in case processing. *Justice Quarterly, 16,* 275–302.

Kipnis, K. (1976). Criminal justice and the negotiated plea. *Ethics, 86,* 93–106.

Knapp, K. A. (1987). Implementation of the Minnesota guidelines: Can the innovative spirit be preserved? In A. von Hirsch, K. A. Knapp, & M. Tonry (Eds.), *The sentencing commission and its guidelines* (pp. 127–140). Boston: Northeastern University Press.

Kritzer, H. M., & Zemans, F. K. (1993). Local legal culture and the control of litigation. *Law and Society Review, 27,* 535–557.

Kuhlmann v. Wilson, 477 U.S. 436, 454, n. 17 (1986).

Kurki, L. (2000). Restorative and community justice. In M. Tonry (Ed.), *Crime and justice: A review of research* (Vol. 27, pp. 235–304). Chicago: University of Chicago Press.

LaFountain, R., Schauffler, R., Strickland, S., Bromage, C., Gibson, C., & Mason, A. (2010). *Examining the work of state courts: An analysis of 2008 state court caseloads.* Williamsburg, VA: National Center for State Courts.

LaFree, G. (1989). *Rape and criminal justice: The social construction of sexual assault.* Belmont, CA: Wadsworth.

Landsman, S. (1984). *The adversary system. A description and defense.* Washington, DC: American Enterprise Institute Studies in Legal Policy.

Langbein, J. (1979). Understanding the short history of plea bargaining. *Law and Society Review, 13,* 261–272.

Legal Information Institute, Cornell Law School. (2007). *Federal rules of criminal procedure.* Retrieved June 1, 2008, from http://www.law.cornell.edu/rules/frcrmp/Rule16.htm

Levey, L. S., Steketee, M. W., & Keilitz, S. L. (2001). *Lessons learned in implementing an integrated domestic violence court: The District of Columbia experience.* Washington, DC: National Center for State Courts.

Levin, M. A. (1977). *Urban politics and the criminal courts.* Chicago: University of Chicago Press.

Levrant, S., Cullen, F. T., & Fulton, B. (1999). Reconsidering restorative justice: The corruption of benevolence revisited? *Crime and Delinquency, 45,* 3–27.

Lewis, A. (1964). *Gideon's trumpet.* New York: Vintage Books.

Liteky v. U.S., 114 S.Ct. 1147, 1162 (1994).

Little, K. (2003). Specialized courts and domestic violence. *Issues of Democracy: The Changing Face of U.S. Courts, 8,* 26–31.

Loftin, C., & McDowall, D. (1981). One with a gun gets you two: Mandatory sentencing and firearms violence in Detroit. *The Annals of the Academy of Political and Social Science, 455,* 150–181.

MacKenzie, D. L., & Hebert, E. E. (Eds.). (1996). *Correctional boot camps: A tough intermediate sanction.* Washington, DC: U.S. Department of Justice.

Mansfield, C. L. (1999). Disorder in the people's court: Rethinking the role of non-lawyer judges in limited jurisdiction court civil cases. *New Mexico Law Review, 29,* 119–120.

Mapp v. Ohio, 367 U.S. 643 (1961).

Marbury v. Madison, 1 Cranch 137 (1803).

Marquart, J. W., Ekland-Olson, S., & Sorensen, J. R. (1989). Gazing into the crystal ball: Can jurors accurately predict dangerousness in capital cases? *Law & Society Review, 23,* 449–468.

Mather, L. (1979). *Plea bargaining or trial? The process of criminal case disposition.* Lexington, MA: Lexington Books.

Maxfield, L. D., & Kramer, J. H. (1998). *Substantial assistance: An empirical yardstick gauging equity in current federal policy and practice.* Washington, DC: United States Sentencing Commission.

McCahill, T. W., Meyer, L. C., & Fischman, A. M. (1979). *The aftermath of rape.* Lexington, MA: Lexington Books.

McCleskey v. Kemp, 481 U.S. 279 (1987).

McConville, M., & Mirsky, C. L. (2005). *Jury trials and plea bargaining: A true history.* Oxford, UK: Hart.

McCoy, C. (1990). *Politics and plea bargaining: Victims' rights in California.* Philadelphia: University of Pennsylvania Press.

McDonald, D. C., Greene, J., & Worzella, C. (1992). *Day fines in American courts: The Staten Island and Milwaukee experiments.* Washington, DC: U.S. Department of Justice.

McFarland, M. C. (2004). The role of quasi-judicial officers in today's changing courts. *Court Manager, 19.* Retrieved May 19, 2008, from http://www.ncsconline.org/wc/courtopics/ResourceGuide.asp?topic=QuaJud

McIntyre, L. J. (1987). *The public defender: The practice of law in the shadows of repute.* Chicago: University of Chicago Press.

McKane v. Durston, 153 U.S. 684, 687 (1894).

McMann v. Richardson, 397 U.S. 759 (1970).

Mempa v. Rhay, 389 U.S. 128 (1967).

Miethe, T. D. (1987). Charging and bargaining under determinate sentencing: An investigation of the hydraulic displacement of discretion. *Journal of Criminal Law and Criminology, 78,* 155–176.

Miller, F., Dawson, R. O., Dix, G. E., & Parnas, R. I. (1991). *Prosecution and adjudication.* Westbury, NY: Foundation Press.

Miller, G. P. (2004). Bad judges. *Berkeley Electronic Press.* Retrieved May 19, 2008, from http://law.bepress.com/cgi/viewcontent.cgi?article=1440&context=expresso

Miller, H. S., McDonald, W. F., & Cramer, J. A. (1978). *Plea bargaining in the United States.* Washington, DC: Government Printing Office.

Miranda v. Arizona, 384 U.S. 436 (1966).

Mirsky, C. (1994, March 4). Plea reform is no bargain. *New York Newsday,* p. 70.

Moley, R. (1929). The vanishing jury. *Southern California Law Review, 2,* 97–107.

Moore, H. (1968). Persons and punishment. *The Monist, 52,* 476–479.

Moore, H. (1992). The moral worth of retribution. In A. von Hirsch & A. Ashworth (Eds.), *Principled sentencing* (pp. 188–194). Boston: Northeastern University Press.

Morris, N. (1992). *The brothel boy and other parables of the law.* Oxford, England: Oxford University Press.

Morris, N., & Tonry, M. (1990). *Between prison and probation: Intermediate punishments in a rational sentencing system.* New York: Oxford University Press.

Murphy v. Com. of Massachusetts, 177 U.S. 155 (1900).

Murphy, J. G. (1979). *Retribution, justice and therapy.* Boston: Reidel.

Murphy, W. F., Pritchett, C. H., Epstein, L., & Knight, J. (Eds.). (2006). *Courts, judges, and politics* (6th ed.). New York: Random House.

Myers, M. A. (1978–1979). Rule departures and making law: Juries and their verdicts. *Law & Society Review, 13,* 781–797.

NAACP v. Levi, 418 F. Supp. 1109 (D.D.C. 1976).

Nagel, S. (1975). *Improving the legal process.* Lexington, MA: Lexington Books.

Nardulli, P. F., Eisenstein, J., & Flemming, R. B. (1988). *The tenor of justice: Criminal courts and the guilty plea process.* Urbana: University of Illinois Press.

National Association of Drug Court Professionals. (1997). *Defining drug courts: The key components.* Washington, DC: U.S. Department of Justice, Drug Courts Program Office.

National Center for Juvenile Justice. (2004a). *Juvenile court statistics 2000.* Pittsburgh, PA: Author.

National Center for Juvenile Justice. (2004b). *Which states waive juveniles to criminal court?* Pittsburgh, PA: Author.

National Center for State Courts. (2002). Are hung juries a problem? Retrieved from http://www.ncsconline.org/WC/Publications/Res_Juries_HungJuriesProblemPub.pdf

National Center for State Courts. (2006). *Examining the work of state courts, 2005.* Williamsburg, VA: Author.

National Center for State Courts. (2010). *State court caseload statistics: An analysis of 2008 state court caseloads.* Williamsburg, VA: National Center for State Courts.

National Symposium on Indigent Defense. (1999). *Improving criminal justice systems through expanded strategies and innovative collaborations.* Washington, DC: Bureau of Justice Assistance.

Neal v. Delaware, 103 U.S. 370 (1880).

Neubauer, D. W. (2002). *America's courts and the criminal justice system* (7th ed.). Belmont, CA: Wadsworth.

Neubauer, D. W. (2005). *America's courts and the criminal justice system* (9th ed.). Belmont, CA: Wadsworth.

Niedermeier, K. E., Horowitz, I. A., & Kerr, N. L. (1999). Informing jurors of their nullification power: A route to a just verdict or judicial chaos. *Law and Human Behavior, 23,* 331–351.

Nix v. Williams, 467 U.S. 431 (1984).

Nobiling, T., Spohn, C., & DeLone, M. (1998). A tale of two counties: Unemployment and sentencing decisions. *Justice Quarterly, 15,* 401–427.

North Carolina v. Alford, 400 U.S. 25 (1970).

North Carolina v. Pierce, 395 U.S. 711 (1969).

Notes: Gideon's promise unfulfilled: The need for litigated reform of indigent defense. (2000). *Harvard Law Review, 113,* 2062–2079.

Oaks, D. H., & Lehman, W. (1970). Lawyers for the poor. In A. S. Blumberg (Ed.), *The scales of justice* (pp. 159–172). Chicago: Aldine.

Office of Juvenile Justice and Delinquency Prevention. (1982). *Major issues in juvenile justice information and training youth in adult courts—Between two worlds.* Washington, DC: Author.

Office of National Drug Control Policy. (n.d.). *Drug courts: A smart approach to criminal justice.* Washington, DC: Author.

Ortiz, A. (2002). *Clemency and consequences: State governors and the impact of granting clemency to death row inmates.* Washington, DC: American Bar Association.

Ostrom, B. J. (2003). Domestic violence courts: Editorial introduction. *Criminology and Public Policy, 3,* 105–108.

Packer, H. L. (1968). *The limits of the criminal sanction.* Stanford, CA: Stanford University Press.

Paternoster, R. (1984). Prosecutorial discretion in requesting the death penalty: A case of victim-based racial discrimination. *Law and Society Review, 18,* 437–478.

People v. Brown, 223 Cal. Rptr. 66 (Ct. App. 1986).

Peters, R. H., & Murrin, M. R. (1998). *Evaluation of treatment-based drug courts in Florida's First Judicial Circuit.* Tampa, FL: Department of Mental Health, Law and Policy, Louis de la Parte Florida Mental Health Institute, University of South Florida.

Phillips v. State, 512 S.E.2d 32 (Ga. Ct. App. 1999).

Planning and Management Consulting Corporation. (1975). *Empirical study of frequency of occurrence, causes, effects, and amount of time consumed by hung juries.* NCJ 019026.

Powell v. Alabama (287 U.S. 45 (1932).

Press-Enterprise Co. v. Superior Court, 478 U.S. 1 (1986).

Proffitt v. Florida, 428 U.S. 242 (1976).

Provine, D. M. (1986). *Judging credentials: Nonlawyer judges and the politics of professionalism.* Chicago: University of Chicago Press.

Puzzanchera, C. M. (2003). *Delinquency cases waived to criminal court, 1990–1999.* Washington, DC: U.S. Department of Justice, Office of Juvenile Justice and Delinquency Prevention.

Radelet, M., & Pierce, G. (1985). Race and prosecutorial discretion in homicide cases. *Law and Society Review, 19,* 587–621.

Rainville, G., & Nugent, M. E. (2002). Community prosecution tenets and practices: The relative mix of "community and prosecution." *American Journal of Criminal Justice, 26,* 149–64.

Randall, K. (2001, August). Another Florida teenager receives harsh adult prison sentence. Retrieved from http://www.wsws.org/articles/2001/aug2001.

Rasinski, K., Willis, G., Baldwin, A., Yeh, W., & Lee, L. (1999). Methods of data collection, perceptions of risks and losses, and motivation to give truthful answers to sensitive survey questions. *Applied Cognitive Psychology, 13,* 465–484.

Ratliff v. State, 596 N.E.2d 241 (Ind. Ct. App. 1992).

Republican Party of Minnesota v. White, 536 U.S. 765 (2002).

Reskin, B. S., & Visher, C. A. (1986). The impacts of evidence and extralegal factors in jurors' decisions. *Law & Society Review, 20,* 423–438.

Rethinking limitations on the peremptory challenge. (1983). *Columbia Law Review, 85,* 1357.

Roberts v. Louisiana, 428 U.S. 325 (1976).

Rolling v. State ex rel. Butterworth, 741 So. 2d 627 (Fla. Dist. Ct. App. 1999).

Rosen, J. (1996). The Bloods and the Crips: O. J. Simpson, critical race theory, and the law and the triumph of color in America. *New Republic,* 27–42.

Ross v. Moffitt, 417 U.S. 600, 614–615 (1974).

Rossett, A., & Cressy, D. (1976). *Justice by consent: Plea bargains in the American courthouse.* Philadelphia: Lippincott.

Rossman, D., Floyd, P., Pierce, G. L., McDevitt, J., & Bowers, W. J. (1979). Massachusetts' mandatory minimum sentence gun law: Enforcement, prosecution, and defense impact. *Criminal Law Bulletin, 16,* 150–163.

Rottman, D., Bromage, C., Zose, M., & Thompson, B. (2006). *Judicial selection 101: What varies and what matters.* Williamsburg, VA: National Center for State Courts.

Rottman, D., Flango, C., Cantrell, M., Hansen, R., & LaFountain, N. (2000). *State court organization, 1998.* Washington, DC: Bureau of Justice Statistics.

Rubinstein, M. L., & White, T. J. (1979). Alaska's ban on plea bargaining. *Law and Society Review, 13,* 367–383.

Sadurski, W. (1985). *Giving desert its due.* Dordrecht, Netherlands: Reidel.

Sanders v. United States, 373 U.S. 1, 8 (1963).

Santobello v. New York, 404 U.S. 257 (1971).

Scheflin, A., & Van Dyke, J. (1980). Merciful juries: The resilience of jury nullification. *Law and Contemporary Problems, 43,* 51–115.

Schmidt, J., & Steury, E. (1989). Prosecutorial discretion in filing charges in domestic violence cases. *Criminology, 27,* 487–510.

Scott v. Illinois, 440 U.S. 367 (1979).

Sechrest, D. K., Shichor, D., Artist, K., & Briceno, G. (1998). *The Riverside County Drug Court: Final research report for the Riverside County Probation Department.* San Bernardino: California State University.

Serr, B. J., & Maney, M. (1988). Racism, peremptory challenges, and the democratic jury: The jurisprudence of a delicate balance. *Journal of Criminal Law and Criminology, 79,* 1–65.

Shapiro, M. (1981). *Courts: A comparative and political analysis.* Chicago: University of Chicago Press.

Sheppard v. Maxwell, 381 U.S. 333 (1966).

Shichor, D., & Sechrest, D. K. (1996). *Three strikes and you're out: Vengeance as public policy.* Thousand Oaks, CA: Sage.

Sickmund, M., Stahl, A. L., Finnegan, T. A., Snyder, N., & Butts, J. A. (1998). *Juvenile court statistics 1995.* Washington, DC: U.S. Department of Justice, Office of Juvenile Justice and Delinquency Prevention.

Silverstein, L. (1965). *Defense of the poor.* Chicago: American Bar Foundation.

Skolnick, J. (1967). Social control in the adversary system. *Journal of Conflict Resolution, 11,* 67.

Smith, C. E. (1991). *Courts and the poor.* Chicago: Nelson-Hall.

Smith v. State, 140 Arizona 355 (1984).

Sorensen, J., & Wallace, D. H. (1996). Prosecutorial discretion in seeking death: An analysis of racial disparity in the pretrial stages of case processing in a Midwestern county. *Justice Quarterly, 16,* 559–578.

Spaeth, J. M. (2001). Swearing with crossed fingers: Juror honesty during voir dire. *Arizona Attorney, 37,* 38–41.

Spears, J. W. (1999). *Diversity in the courtroom: A comparison of the sentencing decisions of black and white judges and male and female judges in Cook County Circuit Court.* PhD dissertation, University of Nebraska at Omaha, Omaha, NE.

Spears, J. W., & Spohn, C. (1997). The effect of evidence factors and victim characteristics on prosecutors' charging decisions in sexual assault cases. *Justice Quarterly, 14,* 501–524.

Spohn, C. (1990a). Decision making in sexual assault cases: Do black and female judges make a difference? *Women & Criminal Justice, 2,* 83–105.

Spohn, C. (1990b). The sentencing decisions of black and white judges: Expected and unexpected similarities. *Law & Society Review, 24,* 1197–1216.

Spohn, C. (1994). Crime and the social control of blacks. In G. S. Bridges & M. A. Myers (Eds.), *Inequality, crime, and social control* (pp. 249–268). Boulder, CO: Westview.

Spohn, C. (2000). Thirty years of sentencing reform: The quest for a racially neutral sentencing process. In J. Horney (Vol. Ed.), *Criminal justice 2000: Vol. 3. Policies, processes, and decisions of the criminal justice system* (pp. 427–501). Washington, DC: U.S. Department of Justice, Office of Justice Program, National Institute of Justice.

Spohn, C., Beichner, D., & Davis-Frenzel, E. (2001). Prosecutorial justifications for sexual assault case rejection: Guarding the "gateway to justice." *Social Problems, 48,* 206–235.

Spohn, C., & DeLone, M. (2000). When does race matter? An analysis of the conditions under which race affects sentence severity. *Sociology of Crime, Law, and Deviance, 2,* 3–37.

Spohn, C. J., Gruhl, J., & Welch, S. (1981). The effect of race on sentencing: A re-examination of an unsettled question. *Law and Society Review, 16,* 71–88.

Spohn, C., Gruhl, J., & Welch, S. (1987). The impact of the ethnicity and gender of defendants on the decision to reject or dismiss felony charges. *Criminology, 25,* 175–191.

Spohn, C., & Holleran, D. (2000). The imprisonment penalty paid by young, unemployed, black and Hispanic offenders. *Criminology, 38,* 281–306.

Spohn, C., & Holleran, D. (2001). Prosecuting sexual assault: A comparison of charging decisions in sexual assault cases involving stranger, acquaintances, and intimate partners. *Justice Quarterly, 18,* 651–688.

Spohn, C., & Horney, J. (1991). "The law's the law, but fair is fair": Rape shield laws and officials' assessment of sexual history evidence. *Criminology, 29,* 137–160.

Spohn, C., & Spears, J. (1996). The effect of offender and victim characteristics on sexual assault case processing decisions. *Justice Quarterly, 13,* 649–679.

Stack v. Boyle, 342 U.S. 1 (1951).

Stahl, A. (2003). *Delinquency cases in juvenile courts, 1999.* Washington, DC: U.S. Department of Justice, Office of Juvenile Justice and Delinquency Prevention.

Stanko, E. (1988). The impact of victim assessment on prosecutor's screening decisions: The case of the New York County District Attorney's Office. In G. Cole (Ed.), *Criminal justice: Law and politics* (pp. 169–180). Pacific Grove, CA: Brooks/Cole.

State v. Culp, 226 S.E.2d 841 (N.C. Ct. App. 1976).

State v. Hamrick, 595 N.W. 2d 492 (Iowa 1999).

State v. Jackson, 368 S.E.2d 838 (N.C. Sup. Ct. 1988).

State v. Pasicznyk, 1997 WL 79501 (Wash. Ct. App. Feb. 25, 1997).

State v. Stellato, 523 A.2d 1345 (Conn. App. Ct. 1987).

Steffensmeier, D., & Hebert, C. (1999). Women and men policymakers: Does the judge's gender affect the sentencing of criminal defendants? *Social Forces, 77,* 1163–1196.

Steffensmeier, D., Kramer, J., & Streifel, C. (1993). Gender and imprisonment decisions. *Criminology, 31,* 411–446.

Steffensmeier, D., Kramer, J., & Ulmer, J. (1995). Age differences in sentencing. *Justice Quarterly, 12,* 701–719.

Steffensmeier, D., Ulmer, J., & Kramer, J. (1998). The interaction of race, gender, and age in criminal sentencing: The punishment cost of being young, black, and male. *Criminology, 36,* 763–798.

Stone v. Powell, 428 U.S. 465, 494, n. 35 (1976).

Strauder v. West Virginia, 100 U.S. 303 (1880).

Strickland v. Washington, 466 U.S. 668, 687 (1984).

Strier, F., & Shestowsky, D. (1999). Profiling the profilers: A study of the trial consulting profession, its impact on trial justice and what, if anything, to do about it. *Wisconsin Law Review, 441,* 441–499.

Stumpf, H. P. (1988). *American judicial politics.* San Diego, CA: Harcourt Brace Jovanovich.

Sudnow, D. (1965). Normal crimes: Sociological features of the penal code in the public defender's office. *Social Problems, 12,* 255–277.

Suggs, D., & Sales, B. D. (1980). Juror self-selection in the voir dire: A social science analysis. *Indiana Law Review, 2,* 245–271.

Swain v. Alabama, 380 U.S. 202, 212 (1965).

Swain v. Alabama: A constitutional blueprint for the perpetuation of the all-white jury. (1966). *Virginia Law Review, 52,* 1157.

Taylor v. Louisiana, 419 U.S. 522 (1975).

Teague v. Lane, 489 U.S. 288 (1989).

Tennessee v. Garner, 471 U.S. 1 (1985).

Texas Statutes, Revised 2000, Title 3, § 12.03 to 12.23.

Thiel v. Southern Pacific Co., 328 U.S. 217 (1946).

Thies v. State, 178 Wis. 98 (1922).

Thomas, C. S., Boyer, M. L., & Hrebenar, R. J. (2005). Interest groups and state court elections: A new era and its challenges. In E. E. Slotnick (Ed.), *Judicial politics: Readings from judicature* (3rd ed., pp. 53–64). Washington, DC: CQ Press.

Tonry, M. (1995). *Malign neglect: Race, crime and punishment in America.* New York: Oxford University Press.

Tonry, M. (1996). *Sentencing matters.* New York: Oxford University Press.

Torbet, P., & Szymanski, L. (1998). *State legislative responses to violent juvenile crime: 1996-97 update.* Washington, DC: U.S. Department of Justice, Office of Juvenile Justice and Delinquency Prevention.

Tumey v. Ohio, 273 U.S. 510 (1927).

Uhlman, T. M. (1978). Black elite decision making: The case of trial judges. *American Journal of Political Science, 22,* 884–895.

Ulmer, J. (1997). *Social worlds of sentencing: Court communities under sentencing guidelines.* Albany: State University of New York Press.

Umbreit, M. S., & Vos, B. (2000). Homicide survivors meet the offender prior to execution: Restorative justice through dialogue. *Homicide Studies, 4,* 63–87.

United States v. Ammidown, 162 U.S. App.D.C. 28, 497 F.2d 615 (1973).

United States v. Batchelder, 442 U.S. 114 (1979).

United States v. Bean, 564 F.2d 700 (1977).

United States v. Dougherty, 473 F.2d 1113 (D.C. Cir., 1972).

United States v. Goodwin, 457 U.S. 368 (1982).

United States v. Hoffer, 129 F.3d 1196 (11th Cir. 1997).

United States v. Montgomery, 819 F.2d at 851 (1987).

United States v. Thao Dinh Lee, 173 F.3d 1258 (10th Cir. 1999).

United States v. Vaccaro, 816 F.2d 443, 457 (9th Cir. 1987).

U.S. General Accounting Office. (1995). *Juvenile justice: Juveniles processed in criminal court and case dispositions.* Washington, DC: Author.

U.S. General Accounting Office. (1997). *Drug courts: Overview of growth, characteristics, and results.* Washington, DC: Author.

U.S. Justice Department. (2000). *State court organization 1998.* Washington, DC: Author.

U.S. Justice Department. (2001). *Prisoners in 2000.* Washington, DC: Author.

U.S. Justice Department. (2004). *Sourcebook of criminal justice statistics, 2003.* Washington, DC: Author.

U.S. Justice Department. (2006). *Felony defendants in large urban counties, 2002.* Washington, DC: U.S. Department of Justice.

U.S. Justice Department. (2007). *Capital punishment 2006.* Washington, DC: Author.

U.S. Sentencing Commission. (n.d.). *Sentencing Commission guidelines manual.* Washington, DC: Author.

U.S. Sentencing Commission. (1991). *Special report to Congress: Mandatory minimum penalties in the federal criminal justice system.* Washington, DC: Author.

U.S. Sentencing Commission. (2007). *Sourcebook of federal sentencing statistics, 2006.* Washington, DC: Author.

Vera Institute of Justice. (1977). *Felony arrests: Their prosecution and disposition in New York City's courts.* New York: Longman.

von Hirsch, A. (1976). *Doing justice: The choice of punishments.* New York: Hill and Wang.

von Hirsch A., & Ashworth, A. (1992). *Principled sentencing.* Boston: Northeastern University Press.

Walker, N. (1991). *Why punish?* Oxford, UK: Oxford University Press.

Walker, S. (2001). *Sense and nonsense about crime and drugs* (5th ed.). Belmont, CA: Wadsworth.

Walker, T. J., & Barrow, D. J. (1985). The diversification of the federal bench: Policy and process ramifications. *Journal of Politics, 47,* 596–617.

Walsh, A. (1987). The sexual stratification hypothesis and sexual assault in light of the changing conceptions of race. *Criminology, 25,* 153–173.

Ward v. Village of Monroeville, 409 U.S. 57 (1972).

Washington, L. (1994). *Black judges on justice: Perspectives from the bench.* New York: The New Press.

Watson, A., Luchins, D., Hanrahan, P., Heyrman, M. J., & Lurigio, A. (2000). Mental health court: Promises and limitations. *Journal of the American Academy of Psychiatry and the Law, 28,* 476–482.

Wayte v. United States, 470 U.S. 598 (1985).

Weber, J. (2000). Domestic violence courts: Components and considerations. *Journal of the Center for Families, Children, and the Courts*, 2, 23–36.

Weeks v. United States, 232 U.S. 383 (1914).

Weitzer, R. (1996). Racial discrimination in the criminal justice system: Findings and problems in the literature. *Journal of Criminal Justice*, 24, 309–322.

Welch, S., Combs, M., & Gruhl, J. (1988). Do black judges make a difference? *American Journal of Political Science*, 32, 126–136.

Weninger, R. A. (1987). The abolition of plea bargaining: A case study of El Paso County, Texas. *UCLA Law Review*, 35, 265, 267.

Wheeler, G. R., & Wheeler, C. L. (1980). Reflections on legal representation of the economically disadvantaged: Beyond assembly line justice. *Crime and Delinquency*, 26, 319–332.

Wheeler, R. R., & Harrison, C. (1994). *Creating the federal judicial system* (2nd ed.). Washington, DC: Federal Judicial Center.

Wheeler, S., Mann, K., & Sarat, A. (1988). *Sitting in judgment: The sentencing of white-collar criminals.* New Haven, CT: Yale University Press.

Whitus v. Georgia, 385 U.S. 545 (1967).

Wice, P. B. (1985). *Chaos in the courthouse: The inner workings of the urban municipal courts.* New York: Praeger.

Williams v. Florida, 399 U.S. 78 (1970).

Williams v. Taylor, 529 U.S. 420 (2000).

Wilson, D. B., Ojmarrh, M., & MacKenzie, D. L. (2002, November). *A systematic review of drug court effects on recidivism.* Paper presented at the annual meeting of the American Society of Criminology, Chicago.

Wilson, J. Q. (1992). Selective incapacitation. In A. von Hirsch & A. Ashworth (Eds.), *Principled sentencing* (pp. 148–163). Boston: Northeastern University Press.

Wilson, J. Q., & Kelling, G. L. (1982). Broken windows: The police and neighborhood safety. *Atlantic Monthly*, 249, 29–38.

Wold, J. T., & Culver, J. H. (1987). The defeat of the California justices: The campaign, the electorate and the issue of judicial accountability. *Judicature*, 6, 348–355.

Woodson v. North Carolina, 428 U.S. 280 (1976).

Worden, A. P. (1990). Policymaking by prosecutors: The uses of discretion in regulating plea bargaining. *Judicature*, 73, 335–336.

Worrall, J. L. (2006). Does targeting minor offenses reduce serious crime? A provisional, affirmative answer based on an analysis of county-level data. *Police Quarterly*, 9, 47–72.

Worrall, J. L., & Hemmens, C. (2005). *Criminal evidence: An introduction.* Los Angeles: Roxbury.

Credits and Sources

Section I. Introduction: Courts and Case Processing

Photo 1.1: Wikimedia Commons, http://commons.wikimedia.org/wiki/File:Supreme_Court_of_the_United_States.jpg

Figure 1.2: Administrative Office of the U.S. Courts on behalf of the Federal Judiciary. Retrieved from the United States Courts website: http://www.uscourts.gov/court_locator.aspx

Photo 1.2: Tim Sloan/AFP/Getty Images

Figure 1.4: Model Rules of Professional Conduct. (2002). Retrieved from the American Bar Association website: http://www.americanbar.org/groups/professional_responsibility/publications/model_rules_of_professional_conduct/model_rules_of_professional_conduct_table_of_contents.html

Section IV. Judges and Jurors

Table 4.2: Goldman, S., Slotnick, E., Gryski, G., Zuk, G., & Schiavoni, S. (2005). W. Bush remaking the judiciary: Like father like son? In E. Slotnick (Ed.), *Judicial politics: Readings from judicature* (pp. 86–111, Table 5). Washington, DC: Congressional Quarterly Press.

Index